THE CHRONOLOGY OF
American Literature

THE CHRONOLOGY OF

AMERICAN
LITERATURE

America's Literary Achievements from
the Colonial Era to Modern Times

Edited by Daniel S. Burt

HOUGHTON MIFFLIN COMPANY
BOSTON   NEW YORK
2004

LIBRARY OF CONGRESS CATALOGING-IN-PUBLICATION
The chronology of American literature : America's
literary achievements from the colonial era to modern
times / edited by Daniel S. Burt.
p.   cm.
Includes index.
ISBN 0-618-16821-4
1. American literature – Chronology. I. Burt, Daniel S.
PS94.C48 2004
810.9 – dc21 2003051142

PRINTED IN THE UNITED STATES OF AMERICA

Book design by Robert Overholtzer

VB 10 9 8 7 6 5 4 3 2 1

For information about this and other Houghton Mifflin
trade and reference books and multimedia products,
visit our Web site: www.houghtonmifflinbooks.com.

CONTENTS

INTRODUCTION

THE CHRONOLOGY OF American Literature is a record of America's literary achievements from the beginning of European exploration and settlement through the end of the twentieth century. It describes more than eighty-four hundred works by some five thousand writers, in a broad survey of American writing wide enough to include authors and works that contemporaries have esteemed as well as those that later literary opinion has rescued from obscurity. Works popular in their day, which may have disappeared from modern view or been relegated to the cabinet of historical curiosities, are noted, as well as important rediscovered figures who were unread or undervalued by their contemporaries, such as Emily Dickinson and Herman Melville. Our goal is to include a wide range of works providing the fullest sense of America's rich and complex literary history — not just the standard canon of "serious" literature but also key popular or representative minor works as well. Their inclusion helps define each era's culture and sets the literary context from which major works emerged.

Proceeding year by year (rather than by author, era, region, or theme — the more traditional formats for examining the literary record), this book allows the entire sequence of America's literary history to become clear. A chronology enhances the reader's ability to evaluate American literary achievement comparatively. By examining American literature as it unfolded over time, the reader can correlate literary expression with historical and social developments that affected literature — war and peace, boom and bust, social change and reaction to change. Unlike a focus on the "great authors" (which, like the "great man" theory of history, elevates some and diminishes others, resulting in a loss of context), a wide-angle perspective offers a greater sampling of significant documents and, we hope, promotes a better grasp of the myriad forces that have helped shape the literary culture of America.

The *Chronology* is divided into five sections, corresponding to major stages in American literary history. Each work is briefly described to indicate what it is about and why it is included. Key birth and death dates and literary prizes are listed in sidebars, along with annual best-seller lists beginning in 1895. The result is intended as a convenient and useful single-volume guide to American literature, helpful to the student and researcher, stimulating for the general reader, and entertaining for the browser.

Section I covers the colonial and Revolutionary periods up to George Washington's inauguration as the first president of the United States in 1789. Within each year, entries in this section are arranged by six category headings: Diaries, Journals, and Letters; Essays and Philosophy; Nonfiction; Poetry, Fiction, and Drama; Publications and Events; and Sermons and Religious Writing. The American literature of this period begins with letters home — the attempt by early explorers and settlers to make sense of a new continent and its challenge to conventional European ways of thinking. The impact of the American landscape on the European sensibility established a difficult though fruitful tension in the development of indigenous American literature. This combination of immigrant cultural influences and a landscape that fostered a sense of starting afresh — a New World defined not by the past but by future possibilities — makes America and its literature a unique hybrid. Various transplanted cultural traditions have over time contributed to this distinctive amalgam, shaped also by the environment, history, and individual genius.

Most early American literature was written by the Puritan settlers of New England, who came to America to create a new social order that centered on expressing and practicing their religious beliefs. This section of the *Chronology* includes many significant firsts derived from their religious practices, such as the first book published in America (*The Bay Psalm Book*, 1640), the first book of poetry by a colonist (Anne Bradstreet's *The Tenth Muse Lately Sprung Up in America*, 1650), the first American bestseller (Michael Wigglesworth's *The Day of Doom*, 1662), and the first complete Bible printed in America (John Eliot's Indian-language translation, 1663). Among the key initial literary figures were clergymen such as John Cotton, Roger Williams, and Increase and Cotton Mather. The most noteworthy nonreligious writings in seventeenth-century America were the records of the New England colonists: William Bradford's *History of Plimmoth Plantation* (completed in 1651) and John Winthrop's *Journal* (published as *The History of New England* in 1825–1826). The writing was overwhelmingly utilitarian and religious in nature, suggesting that the initial literary response to America was determined by issues of physical and spiritual survival. One intriguing question to ponder in reviewing the Puritan literary record is how such an orthodox community, a theocracy that showed little tolerance for dissent, could unite with other regions marked by differing beliefs and together evolve into a democratic nation and one of the most open societies in history.

In the literary record of eighteenth-century America, we see the gradual emergence of a secular society and a shift of emphasis from religious to political themes. Perhaps no figure more typifies this transition than Benjamin Franklin. Born in Puritan Boston, influenced by the moral writings of Cotton Mather, Franklin made his way to the Quaker city of Philadelphia. There the Quakers' tradition of tolerance and esteem of the individual's conscience produced the ideal intellectual climate for Franklin's remarkable career as printer, inventor, scientist, and writer. Franklin, like others in his generation, Americanized European Enlightenment thinking, translating issues of personal liberty and equality into a philosophy and political stance that eventually justified breaking with the British crown.

The magazines and newspapers that Franklin and others created helped shape a consensus of opinion in favor of colonial unity and revolt. Two writers in particular — Thomas Paine and Thomas Jefferson — were decisive in the seismic shift from colony to nationhood. Paine's *Common Sense* (1776) forcefully made the case for independence, and Jefferson's Declaration of Independence synthesized Paine's central ideas into one of the most important political documents ever created (certainly the most eloquent document that ever came out of a committee). During the Revolutionary period, writers such as Francis Hopkinson, John Trumbull, Hugh Henry Brackenridge, Philip Freneau, and Mercy

Otis Warren supported the patriot cause with some of the earliest examples of American nonreligious poetry and drama. The descendants of the early colonists — Europeans in America — had evolved toward a new identity as Americans, and American writing played a key role in making both the nation and its identity a reality.

Section II spans the first seventy years of the national history of the United States. Entries here and through the remainder of the *Chronology* are categorized under the headings Drama and Theater, Fiction, Literary Criticism and Scholarship, Nonfiction, Poetry, and Publication and Events. As America expanded beyond the eastern seaboard of the original colonies and struggled ever more intently over the question of slavery, a national literature gradually emerged. Its earliest attempts were primitive and imitative. At first American writers were still clearly dependent on English and European literary ideas and practices. The plays of the period were adaptations of European models; the poetry echoed the concerns and styles of the English neoclassical and Romantic writers, while America's first novels reworked English picaresque, sentimental, and gothic sources. There is little in the literary record between 1790 and 1820 that stands out today as more than second rate and inferior attempts to replicate European culture in America.

Washington Irving was the first American writer to achieve an international reputation, the first to gain widespread European respect and consequently validation in America. For the first time, an American writer proved that he could be favorably compared to the best European writers. By doing so, Irving helped establish a market for American writing at home and abroad while demonstrating that important subjects and themes could be mined from America's history and landscape. James Fenimore Cooper likewise achieved international distinction by following Irving's lead and adapting Walter Scott's brand of historical novel to an American setting. Cooper, particularly in his Leatherstocking Tales, helped define enduring American myths by delving into the poetic possibilities of the American wilderness, the prototypical American in the frontiersman, and the tragic fate of the American Indian. Cooper also identified a primary and persistent American theme in the tension between the individual and society, between personal freedom and the restraints of civilization. In Cooper's vision, America was the last Eden, steadily being destroyed by progress, expansion, and settlement. This contrast between an ideal America, full of promise and transcendent possibility, and its reality — between America's reach and ts grasp — has been a persistent theme in American writing ever since.

If Irving and Cooper helped establish a market for American writing and its core subjects and themes, the catalyst for the first great fulfillment of American literary promise was Ralph Waldo Emerson. Secularizing Puritan idealism, modifying and applying European Romanticism to American imperatives, Emerson and the New England intellectuals who came to be known as the Transcendentalists lit the fuse for an explosion of creative energy that produced in the 1850s one of the greatest literary decades in U.S. history. Emerson viewed the writer as the literary equivalent of the American frontiersman and pioneer, who abandoned convention and tradition for a direct and original apprehension of a new world. Urging American writers and intellectuals to break with the past and with imitation in favor of what was uniquely American, Emerson wrote in *The Poet* (1842): "Our logrolling, our stumps and their politics, our fisheries, our Negroes, and Indians, our boasts, and our repudiations, the wrath of rogues, and the pusillanimity of honest men, the northern trade, the southern planting, the western clearing, Oregon, and Texas, are yet unsung. Yet America is a poem in our eyes, its ample geography dazzles the imagination, and it will not wait long for metres." Emerson's prophecy was answered in Nathaniel Hawthorne's turning the romance and prose tale into original meditations on the psychology of sin and guilt derived from America's Puritan past; in Herman Melville's radically experimental novel *Moby-Dick*, which converted a whaling adventure into a darkly existential tragedy; in Henry David Thoreau's iconoclastic moral explorations stimulated by the American landscape and social and political scene; in Walt Whitman's grandiloquent attempt to write the first truly American epic poem memorializing every aspect of native experience. By 1860 American writers had begun to make a unique national literary culture independent of European models. Its further development depended on interpreting the impact of the first great tragedy in American history — the Civil War.

Section III covers the Civil War and its aftermath up to the beginning of World War I, a remarkable period of accelerating technological, economic, and social change, which transformed the nation from a predominantly rural, agrarian, and isolated society into an urbanized, industrialized world power. The war that triggered that transformation is the most written-about event in American history. In many ways the first modern war and a defining test of American democracy, the Civil War continues to exert its hold on the American psyche, a watershed between contrasting eras. American writers began to record the changes wrought by the war by documenting America's regional characteristics. For the first time substantial literary contributions were made by writers west of the established cultural centers along America's east coast.

If the prewar American Romantic writers began to delineate the American soul and conscience, the postwar regionalists recorded the nation's outward appearances while developing a realistic aesthetic to complement an inwardly directed literary imagination. The key figures in the development of American realism were Mark Twain, William Dean Howells, and Henry James, as well as writers influenced by naturalism: Stephen Crane, Frank Norris, Jack London, and Theodore Dreiser. Together the realistic writers of the period helped direct American writing toward a truthful, non-idealized depiction of American life, using it as an instrument to expose the dislocations and inequities caused by rapid technological and social change and the evolving conceptions of American identity and destiny as it entered the twentieth century.

Section IV deals with the two world wars of the twentieth century and the dynamic period in between. America's entry into the Great War in 1917 marked a symbolic passage from innocence to experience and another symbolic divide between eras. The war forced a radical reassessment of virtually every measure — political, social, religious, and artistic — formerly used to order and comprehend the human situation. Out of this breakdown of absolutes and crisis of belief emerged American literature's second great explosion of creativity during the 1920s, ignited by such writers as Willa Cather, F. Scott Fitzgerald, Edna St. Vincent Millay, Robert Frost, Ernest Hemingway, T. S. Eliot, Ezra Pound, and William Faulkner. For the first time, American writers played a significant role in the direction of world literature. In poetry, Eliot's *The Waste Land* defined the modern poetic epic; in fiction Hemingway evolved a prose style and stance that was imitated worldwide. Faulkner produced the first great American modernist works, rivaling the achievements of the European modernist masters such as James Joyce, Marcel Proust, and Thomas Mann; in drama America gained its greatest playwright in Eugene O'Neill, who played a significant role in reshaping modern drama.

Like the Great War, the Great Depression forced a similar radical reassessment of the role of the artist in American society and the response of writers to its social challenge. World War II added to the horrors of the Great War, with genocide taking place on an unprecedented scale and the ultimate extension of modern technology in the atomic bomb. American isolation from global issues ended, and the nation entered one of the most contradictory periods in its history.

Section V reviews the last five decades of the twentieth century, the period of America's preeminence as a global superpower and one of the most disruptive and dynamic eras in American history, particularly during the tumultuous 1960s. American writers of the period reflected on the escalating tensions with the Soviet Union, which included the constant threat of nuclear annihilation. Writers also helped provoke and then record racial, gender, and sexual liberations, which shifted what was formerly on the margins of American norms to its center. Writers of color, women, homosexuals and lesbians, along with writers of diverse ethnic backgrounds, altered accepted standards of American identity and experience. The Asian American playwright David Henry Hwang, commenting on recent trends in drama, has observed that "American theater is beginning to discover Americans. Black theater, women's theater, gay theater, Asian American theater, Hispanic theater." His observation could be equally applied to American poetry, fiction, and nonfiction in the last half of the twentieth century. Pluralism and diversity dominated literary expression in the decades leading up to the new millennium.

If American literature began with the discovery of America, it has been sustained by its continuing discovery of Americans. If consensus is lacking about what precisely America has become and where it is headed, American perspectives on those questions have never been as wide-ranging or as challenging as they are today.

I

The Colonial Period

1582–1789

OVER THE COURSE of the more than two centuries of colonial America, a seemingly limitless and unmapped wilderness was transformed into a nation with its own literary traditions. These were the seminal years in the formation of the American character and identity as a diverse collection of displaced Europeans metamorphosed into Americans. The persistent, defining American myths took shape, embodied in the concepts of material success, spiritual rebirth, and unlimited opportunity for all — unfettered by precedent, tradition, or hierarchy. F. Scott Fitzgerald captured the moment best at the conclusion of *The Great Gatsby* when his narrator imagines what the first Dutch explorers must have thought and felt: "for a transitory enchanted moment man must have held his breath in the presence of this continent, compelled into an aesthetic contemplation he neither understood nor desired, face to face for the last time in history with something commensurate to his capacity for wonder."

The first literature inspired by the newfound land was strictly utilitarian: what did the country look like, who lived there, what treasures were there, and what were the prospects for trade and settlement. Published in Europe (and in Mexico after the establishment of the first printing press in the Americas there in 1539), these travel chronicles in the form of letters, journals, and narratives served as guides for the colonists who followed. In the fifty years after Columbus's initial voyage in 1492, the Spanish had ringed the Gulf of Mexico, pushed into the Southwest, and advanced to the Pacific Coast. The French established a sphere of influence in the north and along the inland waterways to the west. In the early seventeenth century, the English began colonizing along the eastern coastal plain bordered to the west by the Alleghenies.

The first permanent colony at Jamestown in Virginia in 1607 was founded for profit. Raw materials and crops, particularly tobacco, were exchanged for manufactured goods in England. This mercantile policy fostered the growth in the southern colonies of a plantation system under which a small number of privileged landowners depended upon slave labor. Anglican, agrarian, and royalist, the southern colonists differed markedly from those who settled New England. The Pilgrims who established their colony at Plymouth in 1620 were a nonconformist, separatist Protestant sect fleeing religious persecution in England and determined to create a better society in America. Theirs would be the first American settlement based on a social contract, outlined in the Mayflower Compact, establishing a community of believers committed to their mutual welfare. The Puritans, who wanted to reform rather than separate from the Church of England, followed in 1630, absorbing the initial Plymouth settlement into the Massachusetts Bay Company, centered in Boston, the city they founded. The Puritans were far more complex than their reputation as dour, narrow-minded religious fanatics, obsessed with Calvinistic gloom and damnation. Although their impact for good and ill in shaping American institutions, literature, and character was considerable, their opposition to any leisure activity was hardly conducive to the development of a secular literary tradition. Yet the Puritan conviction that an individual's personal salvation required directly attending to God's word as contained in the Bible or as interpreted by the devout and learned promoted literacy and education, two essential ingredients for the creation of a literary culture. Puritan society, therefore, perhaps more than any other at the time, was a reading society. The Puritans established the first public school in America (Boston Public Latin School in 1635), founded the first institution of higher learning in North America (Harvard in 1635), and set up the first printing press (in Cambridge in 1639). As a result, although Puritan society was far too rigid to tolerate dissent or diversity, Puritans were responsible for the bulk of literary work produced during the seventeenth century in the fledgling American colonies.

Toleration and diversity were the singular characteristics of the Middle Colonies. The Dutch, French, Germans, and Swedes mixed with the English in New York, New Jersey, Delaware, and Pennsylvania, establishing for the first time the melting pot of the American myth. The enhancement of individual liberty was seen as a principal goal of government by the visionary William Penn and his Quaker followers who settled Pennsylvania. The Quakers insisted on the preeminence of the individual in matters of faith and extended that concept to embrace tolerance of differing viewpoints, values, and races. This would have an incalculable impact in shaping American democracy and American cultural as pluralistic and adaptive.

Given the practical difficulties of surviving in a wilderness, the early American colonists had little time to produce works of literature or to encourage their creation. What was written and published in the seventeenth century was almost exclusively religious or utilitarian in nature, with little distinction between the two. Following an initial broadside, the *Freeman's Oath*, the first significant work printed on Boston's new press in 1639 was an almanac, a miscellany of practical and moral advice that would serve as a prototype for the only kind of reading material in most colonial households other than the Bible. The first book published in the American colonies was the *Bay Psalm Book* in 1640, the accepted hymnal of the Massachusetts Bay colony. This essential tool of worship was followed by sermons, devotional essays, and works of moral instruction by a distinguished group of Puritan clerics, including Thomas Hooker, John Cotton, Thomas Shepard, John Eliot, the Mathers (Richard, Increase, and Cotton), and Puritan dissenters such as Roger Williams. The most significant secular prose of the seventeenth century would be published much later: William Bradford's *History of Plimmoth Plantation* (written between 1630 and 1651 but not published until 1856), John Winthrop's *Journal* (begun in 1630 and published as *The History of New England* in 1825–1826), and Samuel Sewell's remarkable *Diary* (written between 1674 and 1729 and published in 1878–1882). The best-selling secular work actually published during the seventeenth century was the *Narrative of the Captivity and Restauration of Mrs. Mary Rowlandson* (1682), the first of many Indian captivity narratives.

Poetry in America began with Anne Bradstreet's domestic and devotional verses collected without her approval by her brother-in-law and published in London as *The Tenth Muse Lately Sprung Up in America* (1650). This was one of the first books of poetry ever published by a woman in English. The first book of poems published in America and the first American bestseller was Michael Wigglesworth's *The Day of Doom* (1662), a narrative poem depicting the Last Judgment. The greatest seventeenth-century poet, however, was the Westfield, Massachusetts, clergyman Edward Taylor, whose intense and metaphysical verse written as part of his private devotions remained in manuscript until they were discovered in the Yale Library and published in 1939. Today Taylor is generally regarded as the greatest American poet before the nineteenth century.

By 1700 there were half a million European Americans in all the colonies. Boston was the largest city, with a population of seven thousand. The first half of the century would begin to show the loosening of the religious grip by the Puritans on New England and the emergence of Yankee secular society. Although Puritan control and influence were clearly waning, the period still produced some of Puritanism's greatest literary achievements, most notably Cotton Mather's epic ecclesiastical history of New England, *Magnalia Christi Americana* (1702), and the works of the last great Puritan theologian, Jonathan Edwards. His "Sinners in the Hands of an Angry God" (1741) is arguably the most famous sermon ever written by an American, and his theological work *A Careful and Strict Enquiry into the Prevailing Notions of Freedom of Will* (1754) is one of the foundational documents of American philosophy, anticipating some of the main tenets of Transcendentalism. Yet the Puritans' spiritual interpretation of the world was challenged, as the century progressed, by a rational, scientific worldview advanced by Enlightenment thinkers such as John Locke, Jean Jacques Rousseau, and Voltaire. This conflict between idealism and pragmatism is a dominant theme in American thought. The exemplar of the evolving American character was unquestionably Benjamin Franklin. Born in Boston, Franklin moved to Philadelphia, which by 1750 was the unofficial capital of the colonies, the "Athens of America," second only to London as a commercial center. As a printer, Franklin played a key role in creating and producing the literature that captured the spirit of the times and moved the country toward independence. He produced the first series of periodical essays (*The Dogood Papers*, 1721–1723). His newspaper, the *Pennsylvania Gazette* (1729–1766), carried his *Busy-Body Papers* and in 1754 printed the first

American political cartoon, which Franklin probably drew (a snake in eight parts representing the colonies with the caption "Join or die"). He produced the most popular almanac in America, *Poor Richard's Almanack* (1733–1758), and the first successful American magazine (the *General Magazine* in 1741). Self-educated, a scientist and inventor, Franklin perhaps more than anyone else during the period typified many of the adages he coined for his almanac: that with persistence and application virtually anything could be accomplished. Increasingly, he was asked to apply his many talents to nation building.

Beginning in the 1750s momentum began to bind the loose assembly of colonies into a confederation. Resentment over British trade and taxation policies gradually drove the colonists toward union and independence. The Stamp Act of 1764, the Boston Massacre of 1770, the Boston Tea Party of 1773, and the first shots fired at Lexington and Concord were the milestones leading to revolution. Letters, essays, pamphlets, and editorials framed the question whether Britain had the right to tax colonists without their consent. Independence, which for many was once inconceivable, began to sound inevitable, particularly as urged by Tom Paine in *Common Sense* (1776). Thomas Jefferson soon distilled this best-selling statement of the case for separation into one of the greatest political documents ever created, the Declaration of Independence.

Even before the Revolution, writers and particularly poets began to express what made American culture distinct. The first secular verses began to appear, celebrating American scenes, such as Richard Lewis's "A Journey from Petapsco to Annapolis, April 4, 1730," and American themes, such as Ebenezer Cook's satirical "The Sot-Weed Factor" (1708). The first book by an African American was published, *Poems on Various Subjects, Religious and Moral* (1773), by the former slave Phillis Wheatley. During the Revolution, poets contributed to the war effort in works such as Francis Hopkinson's "The Battle of the Kegs" (1778) and John Trumbull's mock-epic attack on American Loyalists, *M'Fingal* (1775–1776 and 1782). Other poets commemorated American achievements and destiny in works such as Timothy Dwight's *Conquest of Canaan* (1785) and Joel Barlow's *The Vision of Columbus* (1787), his first version of an attempted American epic that would be expanded into *The Columbiad* in 1807. Philip Freneau was unquestionably the most accomplished poet of the Revolutionary period. The author of the visionary "The Rising Glory of America" (1772),

the bitingly satirical "General Gage's Confession" (1775), and the powerful "The British Prison Ship" (1781), based on his incarceration by the British, Freneau was an important transitional figure between the neoclassical style of most eighteenth-century verse written in America and what would follow: a uniquely American version of Romanticism.

Although the novel in England began with Daniel Defoe's *Robinson Crusoe* in 1719, the consensus choice for the first American novel, William Hill Brown's *The Power of Sympathy*, was not published until 1789. A moralistic, epistolary novel set in Boston and drawing on distinctly local affairs, Brown's novel marks the beginning of American fiction.

Drama, like fiction, suffered in colonial America from Puritan disapproval. There were, however, amateur productions of plays mounted at Harvard, Yale, and William and Mary early in the seventeenth century. Benjamin Coleman is generally regarded as the first American playwright for his historical drama *Gustavus Vasa* (1690). The first professional acting company from Britain performed Shakespeare's *The Merchant of Venice* and Ben Jonson's *The Alchemist* in Williamsburg in 1752. The company subsequently toured New York, Philadelphia, and Charleston. Reconstituted in 1763 as the American Company, it staged the first drama by an American to be professionally produced — Thomas Godfrey's *The Prince of Parthia* — in Philadelphia in 1767. The first play with a distinctly American setting and theme was Robert Rogers's Indian tragedy *Ponteach* (1766). During the Revolution plays satirized both sides in the conflict. British general John Burgoyne's play *The Blockade* (1775), ridiculing the rebel soldiers, was performed in Boston during the occupation. It was answered by *The Blockheads* (1776), attributed to America's first woman playwright, Mercy Otis Warren, author of the political satires in dramatic form *The Adulateur* (1773) and *The Group* (1775). America's first comedy of manners was Royall Tyler's *The Contrast* (1787), notable for its depiction of class and social differences in the fledgling democracy and for introducing one of the most durable of stage figures, the homespun but shrewd Yankee.

As George Washington took the oath of office as the first president of the United States in 1789, Americans had won their independence, but the greater challenge of governing lay ahead. Similarly, American literature in its first two centuries had produced its initial, distinctive responses to the phenomenon of America, but it had yet to achieve greatness.

BIRTHS, 1550–1599

Births

c. 1552	Richard Hakluyt (d. 1616), geographer and writer
1560	Thomas Hariot (d. 1621), mathematician, geographer, and writer
1572	John Pory (d. 1636), colonist and writer
	William Strachey (d. 1621), colonist and writer
c. 1575	Samuel Purchas (d. 1626), clergyman and author
	James Rosier (d. 1635), explorer and writer
1577	Robert Cushman (d. 1625), clergyman and writer
1578	George Sandys (d. 1644), writer and translator
c. 1579	Andrew White (d. 1656), colonist and writer
1580	George Percy (d. 1632), colonist and writer
c. 1580	John Smith (d. 1631), colonial leader and writer
1585	John Cotton (d. 1652), religious leader
	Alexander Whitaker (d. c. 1617), clergyman and writer
1586	Thomas Hooker (d. 1647), religious leader and author
	Francis Higginson (d. 1630), clergyman and author
1588	John Winthrop (d. 1649), colonial leader and author
1590	William Bradford (d. 1657), colonial leader and author
c. 1590	Thomas Morton (d. 1647), colonist and writer
c. 1591	John Wilson (d. 1667), clergyman and poet
1592	Charles Chauncy (d. 1672), clergyman, Harvard president, and writer
	Samuel Gorton (d. 1677), colonist and writer
1595	Thomas Parker (d. 1677), clergyman, colonist, and writer
	Thomas Weld (d. 1660), clergyman and author
	Edward Winslow (d. 1655), colonist and writer
1596	Richard Mather (d. 1669), religious leader and writer
1597	John Davenport (d. 1670), clergyman, colonist, and writer
1598	Edward Johnson (d. 1672), clergyman and author

1582

Nonfiction

RICHARD HAKLUYT (c. 1552–1616): *Divers Voyages Touching the Discoverie of America.* The first of the British geographer's compilations of exploration narratives dealing with America. Other important volumes would follow, and his unpublished papers would be collected by English travel writer-editor Samuel Purchas (1575?–1626) in *Hakluytus Posthumus* (1625).

1588

Nonfiction

THOMAS HARIOT (1560–1621): *Briefe and True Report of the New-Found Land of Virginia.* The English mathematician and geographer provides an account of his two years serving on Grenville's second expedition to Virginia. The 1590 edition would include watercolor drawings by fellow colonist John White (fl. 1585–1593).

1598

Nonfiction

RICHARD HAKLUYT: *The Principall Navigations, Voyages, Traffiques, and Discoveries of the English Nation.* The British geographer's greatest literary achievement is this collection of exploration narratives treating the voyages of Hawkins, Drake, Frobisher, Raleigh, and others.

1602

Nonfiction

JOHN BRIERTON (fl. 1572–1619): *A Briefe and True Relation of the Discoverie of the North Part of Virginia.* The clergyman who had participated in the expedition along "the North Part of Virginia" (the New England coast) led by Bartholomew Gosnold publishes this early account of the region.

1605

Nonfiction

JAMES ROSIER (c. 1575–1635): *A True Relation of the Most Prosperous Voyage Made This Present Yeere 1605 by Captain George Waymouth.* The explorer chronicles Waymouth's voyage to find for Sir Thomas Arundel a refuge for Catholics along the east coast of America. It contains the first published descriptions of Maine.

1606

Nonfiction

GEORGE PERCY (1580–1632): *Observations gathered out of a Discourse of the Plantation of the Southerne Colonie in Virginia by the English.* Percy, one of the original Virginia colonists, writes a firsthand account of their voyage. He also describes the landscape outside Jamestown and their trips up the James River by boat to visit with the Indians. The work would be published in 1625 by Samuel Purchas.

1608

Nonfiction

JOHN SMITH (1580–1631): *A True Relation of such occurrences and accidents of noate as hath hapned in Virginia since the first planting of that Colony.* Captain Smith provides the earliest primary account of the Virginia settlement. There is no mention of his rescue by the Indian princess Pocahontas, however.

1609

Diaries, Journals, and Letters

WILLIAM STRACHEY (1572–1621): "A True Reportory of the Wreck and Redemption of Sir Thomas Gates, Knight." Survivor Strachey's letter about the wreck of the *Sea*

BIRTHS AND DEATHS, 1600–1649

Births

1602 Samuel Stone (d. 1663), clergyman and writer

c. 1603 Roger Williams (d. 1683), colonist, clergyman, and writer

1604 John Eliot (d. 1690), religious leader and writer

1605 Thomas Shepard (d. 1649), theologian and author

1606 John Norton (d. 1663), clergyman and writer

1607 Isaac Joques (d. 1646), author of first book describing Manhattan

1608 Abraham Pierson (d. 1678), poet and author of Indian catechism

1609 John Clarke (d. 1676), author and a founder of Newport, Rhode Island

1612 Anne Bradstreet (d. 1672), poet
Ezekiel Cheever (d. 1708), educator and author of earliest American schoolbooks
Daniel Gookin (d. 1687), colonist and author of books on Native American life

1613 Nathaniel Morton (d. 1686), historian of New England
John Woodbridge (d. 1695), author of banking and currency tracts

1616 John Higginson (d. 1708), clergyman and author
Jacob Steendam (d. c. 1672), poet

1617 Peter Folger (d. 1690), poet and grandfather of Benjamin Franklin

1620 Thomas Thacher (d. 1678), author of medical texts

1626 Samuel Danforth (d. 1674), clergyman and poet

1631 Urian Oakes (d. 1681), poet
William Stoughton (d. 1701), clergyman and presiding judge of Salem witchcraft trials
Michael Wigglesworth (d. 1705), clergyman and poet

1632 Samuel Torrey (d. 1707), clergyman and author

1635 Mary White Rowlandson (d. 1678), writer

1639 Increase Mather (d. 1723), religious leader and writer

1640 John Cotton II (d. 1699), clergyman and poet
Samuel Willard (d. 1707), clergyman and writer

1641 Sarah Whipple Goodhue (d. 1681), poet

1642 Edward Taylor (d. 1729), minister and poet
Benjamin Tompson (d. 1714), poet

1643 Solomon Stoddard (d. 1729), clergyman and author

1644 William Penn (d. 1718), religious leader and founder of Pennsylvania; author

1647 Nicholas Noyes (d. 1717), poet
John Richardson (d. 1696), poet

1648 Robert Calef (d. 1719), merchant and author
John Rogers (d. 1721), clergyman and author

Deaths

1616 Richard Hakluyt (b. c. 1552), geographer and writer

1621 Thomas Hariot (b. 1560), mathematician, geographer, and writer
William Strachey (b. 1572), colonist and writer

1625 Robert Cushman (b. 1577), clergyman and writer

1626 Samuel Purchas (b. c. 1575), clergyman and author

1630 Francis Higginson (b. 1686), clergyman and writer

1631 John Smith (b. c. 1580), colonial leader and writer

1632 George Percy (b. 1580), colonist and writer

1635 James Rosier (b. c. 1575), explorer and writer

1636 John Pory (b. 1572), colonist and writer

1644 George Sandys (b. 1578), writer and translator

1647 Thomas Hooker (b. 1586), religious leader and author
Isaac Joques (b. 1607), author of first book describing Manhattan
Thomas Morton (b. c. 1590), colonist and writer

1649 Thomas Shepard (b. 1605), theologian and author
John Winthrop (b. 1588), colonial leader and author

Adventure off Bermuda is believed to be a possible source for Shakespeare's *The Tempest* (1611). Strachy would serve as the first secretary and recorder of the Virginia colony until 1611.

Nonfiction

ROBERT JONSON (fl. 1609–1612): *Nova Britannia: offeringe most excellent Fruits by Planting in Virginia.* Jonson's tract promotes colonization and investment in Virginia. A later work, *The New Life of Virginia* (1612), is also attributed to him.

Sermons and Religious Writing

ROBERT GRAY (fl. 1609): "A Good Speed to Virginia." Gray's sermon promotes colonization in Virginia as a solution to England's overpopulation. It is the third printed work related to the colony after Smith's *A True Relation*

(1608) and Jonson's *Nova Britannia.* Virtually nothing is known about Gray, who might have served as rector of a London church.

1610

Diaries, Journals, and Letters

WILLIAM STRACHEY: "Letter to an Excellent Lady." Although it would not be printed until 1625 by Purchas in *Hakluytus Posthumus*, Strachey's description of the 1609 shipwreck of the *Sea Adventure* is considered one of the possible sources for Shakespeare's *The Tempest.*

Poetry, Fiction, and Drama

RICHARD RICH (fl. 1609–1610): "Newes from Virginia." An English soldier who sailed with Somers's fleet in 1609 and participated in the near-abandonment of the Virginia colony in 1610 composes this ballad based on his experiences. It is the first published poem about America, and it has been suggested as another possible source for Shakespeare's *The Tempest*.

GASPAR PERÉZ DE VILLAGRÁ (c. 1555–c. 1620): *Historia de la Nueva Mexico* (History of New Mexico). The explorer, who participated in Juan de Onate's expedition that claimed New Mexico for Spain and ventured into parts of present-day Oklahoma and Kansas, publishes this epic poem based on his experiences. It would be translated into English in 1933.

1611
Nonfiction

THOMAS WEST, BARON DE LA WARR (1577–1618): *Relation . . . of the Colonie, Planted in Virginia.* The first colonial governor of Virginia writes in support of further colonization.

1612
Nonfiction

JOHN SMITH: *A Map Of Virginia with a Description of the Country.* Smith continues his account of the Jamestown settlement during his governorship.

WILLIAM STRACHEY: *For the Colony of Virginea Britannia: Lawes Divine, Morall, and Martiall.* Strachey's work provides the first codification of laws for Virginia.

1613
Sermons and Religious Writing

SAMUEL PURCHAS (c. 1575–1626): *Purchas his Pilgrimage; or, Relations of the World and the Religions observed in all Ages and places discovered, from the Creation unto this Present.* This first collection of the religious writings of the London clergyman was revised in 1626 and served as a supplement to his *Hakluytus Posthumus* (1625), a compilation of exploration narratives.

ALEXANDER WHITAKER (1585–c. 1617): "Good News from Virginia." This clergyman, who immigrated to Virginia in 1611 and is best known for his religious instruction and conversion of the Indian princess Pocahontas, publishes a sermon urging more British support for the colony along with descriptions of the climate and the native population.

1616
Nonfiction

JOHN SMITH: *A Description of New England: or the Observations and Discoveries of Captain John Smith.* Smith offers an account of his second exploration in North America during which he mapped the coastline of New England.

1618
Nonfiction

WILLIAM STRACHEY: *Historie of Travaile into Virginia Brittania.* Strachey offers an eyewitness account of the shipwreck of the *Sea Adventure* (1609) and life in Jamestown, featuring close observation of the language and beliefs of the surrounding Indian population.

1619
Sermons and Religious Writing

SAMUEL PURCHAS: *Purchas his Pilgrim, Microcosmus, or the histories of Man.* Purchas's best-known collection of his own religious writings.

1620
Nonfiction

JOHN SMITH: *New Englands Trials.* Smith recommends New England as a site for colonization. In an expanded edition in 1622 he would describe the Pilgrims' doubtful prospects and how they might better succeed if they would take instruction from him.

1621
Sermons and Religious Writing

ROBERT CUSHMAN (1577–1625): "The Sin and Danger of Self-Love, Described in a Sermon Preached at Plymouth, in New England, 1621." Written for the Plymouth congregation, the sermon addresses the problem

Captain John Smith

of individualism in a colony founded on the principles of community and cooperation.

c. 1622
Diaries, Journals, and Letters

PHINEAS PRATT (c. 1572–1680): *Phineas Pratt's Narrative.* The work describes Pratt's journey from Wessagusset to Plymouth to inform residents of the plight of his fellow settlers and the danger of Indian attack.

1622
Diaries, Journals, and Letters

EDWARD WINSLOW (1595–1655) AND WILLIAM BRADFORD (1590–1657): *A Relation or Journal of the Beginning and Proceedings of the English Plantation Setled at Plimoth in New England.* The first account of the Plymouth settlement, recording the Mayflower Compact and the earliest days of the colony. It is conjectured that William Bradford and Edward Winslow prepared the account. Published anonymously, the book is commonly known as *Mourt's Relation*, based on the signature of "G. Mourt," attributed to George Morton (1585–1624), who may have been responsible only for the book's publication.

Nonfiction

SIR FERDINANDO GORGES (c. 1566–1647): *A Briefe Relation of the Discovery and Plantation of New England.* Although this English landowner of American territory never visited America, Gorges would be called "the father of American colonization" for his efforts to promote settlement in what he describes as "the most commodious

country for the benefit of our Nation, that ever hath been found."

1624
Diaries, Journals, and Letters

EDWARD WINSLOW: *Good News From New England; or, A True Relation of Things Very Remarkable at the Plantation of Plymouth in New England.* Winslow continues the journal chronicle of the Plymouth colony begun in *Mourt's Relation* (1622) up to September 1623.

Nonfiction

JOHN SMITH: *The General Historie of Virginia, New England, and the Summer Isles.* Smith chronicles the colonization of Virginia, going into more detail than in his earlier, shorter history of 1608. Included is an extensive treatment of the Pocahontas story.

1625
Nonfiction

SAMUEL PURCHAS: *Hakluytus Posthumus; or, Purchas his Pilgrimes, conttayning a History of the World in Sea Voyages and Lande Travells, by Englishmen and others.* Purchas continues Richard Hakluyt's compilation of exploration narratives in four volumes, with the second half devoted to voyages to America.

Poetry, Fiction, and Drama

WILLIAM MORRELL (fl. 1623–1625): "Nova Anglia." Morrell, a member of the ill-fated Maine colony sponsored by Ferdinando Gorges (c. 1566–1647), composes

The Mayflower Compact, taken from Bradford's *History of Plimmoth Plantation*

this poem in Latin hexameters with an English translation into heroic couplets, describing the country and its Indian population.

1626
Diaries, Journals, and Letters

JOHN PORY (1572–1636), EMMANUEL ALTHAM (fl. 1620s), AND ISAACK DE RASIERES (fl. 1620s): *Three Visitors to Early Plymouth*. Letters about the settlement of Plymouth by Pilgrims during its first seven years, published between 1626 and 1628.

Nonfiction

JOHN SMITH: *An Accidence, or The Pathway to Experience Necessary for all Young Seamen*. Smith's manual of seamanship is illustrated with incidents from his own experiences. It would be enlarged as *A Sea Grammar* in 1627.

Poetry, Fiction, and Drama

GEORGE SANDYS (1578–1644): Translation of Ovid's *Metamorphoses*. The Virginia colonist produces the first American translation of a classical work. It includes many references to America.

JOHN WILSON (c. 1591–1667): *A Song, or Story, for the Lasting Remembrance of Divers Famous Works*. Before immigrating to Boston in America, this minister publishes this poem in ballad meter written to teach English history

to children. It would be reissued as *A Song of Deliverance* in 1680.

1629
Diaries, Journals, and Letters

FRANCIS HIGGINSON (1586–1630): *New Englands Plantation*. A journal description of Higginson's arrival in New England and early experience in Salem, where he became the town's first Congregational minister.

1630
Nonfiction

WILLIAM BRADFORD: *History of Plimmoth Plantation*. Bradford begins his historical chronicle by tracing the origin of the Separatist movement, the flight from England to Holland, the plans for the settlement in New England, the *Mayflower* voyage, and the early struggles up to the construction of the first house in Plymouth. The second volume, completed in 1651, describes the Pilgrim community from 1620 to 1646. Of major historical importance, the work is also a model of vigorous prose. With John Winthrop's *Journal*, it is considered the most important nonclerical prose writing of early New England.

JOHN SMITH: *The True Travels, Adventures, and Observations of Captaine John Smith in Europe, Asia, Africa, and America . . . from 1593 to 1629*. Smith provides an account of his early life and his subsequent adventures in a fascinating, though unreliable, autobiography.

John Winthrop

Poetry, Fiction, and Drama

Anonymous: "New England's Annoyances." This poem describing the hardships of colonial life is believed to be the first verse by an American colonist.

Sermons and Religious Writing

JOHN WINTHROP (1588–1649): "A Modell of Christian Charity." Delivered on his way to America, this sermon asserts Winthrop's plan for the colony and warns the colonists of what might lie ahead. Winthrop also begins his most famous work, his *Journal*, which he would continue until his death. A vital record of activities in the colonies, the *Journal*, along with William Bradford's *History of Plimmoth Plantation*, would come to be valued as the most significant secular prose writing of early New England. The first two parts would be published in 1790, and the complete work would appear as *The History of New England* in 1825–1826.

1631
Nonfiction

JOHN SMITH: *Advertisements for the Unexperienced Planters of New England*. Written shortly before Smith's death, this work offers practical advice to the Massa-

chusetts settlers and includes an autobiographical poem, "The Sea-Mark."

1633
Nonfiction

ANDREW WHITE (c. 1579–1656): *Relatio Itineris in Marilandiam* (published in part in 1634 as *A relation of the Successful Beginnings of Lord Baltimore's Plantation in Maryland*). In an official record and an advertisement for attracting colonists, White, an English Jesuit priest, provides a lively firsthand account of the Maryland settlement. He expresses his belief that the conversion of the Indians to Christianity is the noble purpose of colonization.

1634
Nonfiction

WILLIAM WOOD (fl. 1629–1635): *New Englands Prospect*. This work by the Massachusetts poet and pamphleteer contains the first detailed map of the southern region of the New England colony of Massachusetts Bay. Descriptions of flora and fauna and the Indian tribes are interspersed with the author's verses.

1635
Publications and Events

Boston Public Latin School. Founded on April 13, it is the first public school in America.

1637
Nonfiction

THOMAS MORTON (c. 1590–1647): *New English Canaan*. After his second deportation back to England, colonist, trader, and writer Morton, representing the Anglican and anti-Puritan faction, provides a description of New England, its topography, settlements, and Indians, as well as a satirical account of the Plymouth colonists' attack on Morton's colony at Merry Mount. Myles Standish, the Pilgrim leader, is depicted as Captain Shrimp. The work is regarded as one of the earliest examples of American humor.

Sermons and Religious Writing

THOMAS HOOKER (1586–1647): "The Soules Humiliation," "The Soules Implantation," "The Soules Ingrafting into Christ," and "The Soules Effectuall Calling to Christ." Having immigrated to America in 1633, Hooker had served as the pastor of Cambridge for three years and then led his congregation of more than one hundred families to establish the Connecticut colony at Hartford.

He is regarded as one of the greatest preachers of his generation in early New England, and his considerable oratorical power is demonstrated in these sermons.

1638
Nonfiction

JOHN UNDERHILL (c. 1597–1672): *Newes from America.* The professional soldier who had come to Boston in 1630 to organize its militia provides an account of the English colonists' war against the Pequod Indians and against the Dutch in New Netherlands. He would later be the subject of the poem "John Underhill" by John Greenleaf Whittier, published in *Hazel Blossoms* (1875).

1639
Nonfiction

JOHN WINTHROP AND JOHN COTTON (1584–1652): *The Wicked Capitalism of Robert Keayne.* A rebuke of merchant Robert Keayne for his sharp business practices in Boston. Keayne is soundly attacked for overcharging in the Massachusetts Bay colony at a time when the colonists believe that this practice violates their covenant with God.

Publications and Events

An Almanack for New England for the Year 1639. The first American almanac is compiled by William Pierce (fl. 1640s) and printed in Boston by Stephen Daye (1594–1688), who brought the first printing press to the English colonies. It is considered the first substantial work printed in the English colonies.

Oath of a Free Man. This broadside, which challenges the power of English law over the colonists, is the first work printed in the American colonies. It is printed by Stephen Daye. It has not survived but is described in Major John Child's *New England's Jonas Cast Up at London* (1647).

1640
Sermons and Religious Writing

THOMAS WELD (1595–1660), RICHARD MATHER (1596–1669), AND JOHN ELIOT (1604–1690): *The Whole Book of Psalmes, Faithfully Translated into English Metre.* Better known as the *Bay Psalm Book*, the work, translated mainly by these three clergymen but assisted by others, is considered the first bound book produced in America. It becomes the accepted hymnal of the Massachusetts Bay colony.

The title page from *The Bay Psalm Book*

1641
Nonfiction

NATHANIEL WARD (c. 1578–1652): *The Liberties of the Massachusetts Colony in New England.* The Congregational minister at Agawam (now Ipswich) contributes to the legal code of Massachusetts its first code of law. It is incorporated in "The Body of Liberties," a bill of rights for the colony that is considered one of the fundamental works in American constitutional history.

Sermons and Religious Writing

THOMAS SHEPARD (1605–1649): *The Sincere Convert.* Shepard's most popular work would go through twenty editions up to 1812 and would be translated into Massachusett, an Algonquian Indian language, by John Eliot in 1689. It stresses God's infinite love and compassion and the salvation of all who accept him.

1642
Sermons and Religious Writing

JOHN COTTON (1583–1652): "The Powering Out of the Seven Vials." The influential New England church leader's sermon predicts that the destruction of iniquity and the coming of the millennium are at hand. In "The Church Resurrected," he urges New Englanders not to return to England but to recommit themselves to the Puritan revolution.

1643

Nonfiction

THOMAS WELD AND HUGH PETER (1598–1660): *New England's First Fruits.* This publicity tract, published in London, describes New England's topography, climate, and religion and is reputed to be the first published account of the founding of Harvard College. Weld was one of the ministers who compiled the *Bay Psalm Book* (1640); Peter, who would follow Roger Williams as pastor of Salem, helped found Harvard.

ROGER WILLIAMS (c. 1603–1683): *A Key into the Language of America.* The first published work of Williams, the clergyman and founder of Rhode Island, is based on his missionary efforts among the Indians and describes Indian customs "from the Birth to their Burialls." The work helped spark more missionary endeavors among the Indians.

Sermons and Religious Writing

JOHN COTTON: *God's Promise to His Plantation.* This religious tract by one of the era's most formidable Puritan divines explains the author's justification for the founding of New England.

RICHARD MATHER: *Church-Government and Church-Covenant Discussed.* Mather's second publication is the earliest comprehensive presentation of New England Puritan church doctrine. *Apologie of the Churches in New-England for Church Covenant* also appears, serving as a standard justification for church policy and action.

1644

Diaries, Journals, and Letters

THOMAS PARKER (1595–1677): "The True Copy of a Letter Written by Mr. T. Parker." The Calvinist minister's most controversial work, written after his arrival in New England in 1635, is a critique of Congregationalism, denouncing the democratic forces within the church. His only printed book, *The Visions and Prophecies of Daniel Expounded* (1646), first issued in Newbury, Massachusetts, the town he founded, is an interpretation of biblical prophecies.

Essays and Philosophy

THOMAS WELD: *An Answer to W. R.* After returning to England in 1641, Weld remained active in New England's religious and political affairs as evident in this attack on William Rathband's criticism of New England churches.

JOHN WINTHROP: *Arbitrary Government.* Winthrop's discourse supports the absolute power of the Puritan government. It so inflames his constituents that he is

Roger Williams

impeached as governor. Nonetheless, he would avoid conviction by delivering a rousing speech on liberty and would be reelected governor annually until his death in 1649.

Nonfiction

ISAAC JOQUES (1607–1646): *A Description of New Amsterdam.* Written by a Jesuit, this account includes one of the first published descriptions of Manhattan Island and its native inhabitants.

JOHN WINTHROP: *Antinomians and Familists Condemned by the Synod of elders in New England.* Better known by the title of its second edition, *A Short Story of the Rise, Reign, and Ruin of the Antinomians...*, Winthrop's only historical book published during his lifetime is a collection of materials related to the Antinomian controversy and a defense of his banishment of Anne Hutchinson (1591–1643) from Massachusetts.

Sermons and Religious Writing

JOHN COTTON: *The Keyes of the Kingdom of Heaven.* Cotton's religious treatise becomes the standard guide of the New England Congregational Church until the acceptance of the *Cambridge Platform* (1648).

ROGER WILLIAMS: *The Bloudy Tenent of Persecution.* Williams's most celebrated work is this pamphlet, presenting a dialogue between Truth and Peace in which the author argues for religious tolerance and the separation of church and state. It would prompt John Cotton's rebuttal, *The Bloudy Tenent Washed and Made White in the Bloud of the Lamb* in 1647, and Williams's counterattack, *The Bloudy Tenent Yet More Bloudy . . .* in 1652. In 1644, Williams also issues *Queries of Highest Consideration*, his address to Parliament opposing the establishment of a national church, and *Mr. Cotton's Letter Lately Printed, Examined and Answered*, his response to Cotton's justification of Williams's banishment from the Massachusetts colony in 1635.

1645
Essays and Philosophy

JOHN WHEELWRIGHT (c. 1592–1679): *Mercurius Americanus.* The brother-in-law of Anne Hutchinson comes to her defense in the Antinomian controversy.

JOHN WINTHROP: *On Liberty.* Winthrop discusses the political liberties demanded by the colonists when challenged by the magistrates. In the same year Winthrop publishes *A Declaration of Former Passages and Proceedings Betwixt the English and the Narrowgansets*, a pamphlet expressing his concern that the colonists would soon have to punish the Rhode Island Indians at war with the Mohegans.

Nonfiction

EZEKIEL CHEEVER (1615–1708): *Accidence: A Short Introduction to the Latin Tongue.* Written by the New Haven schoolteacher and clergyman, Cheever's pamphlet becomes the primary handbook for Latin instruction throughout the colonies, reprinted in twenty subsequent editions by 1785 and still in use as late as 1838.

Sermons and Religious Writing

JOHN COTTON: *The Way of the Churches of Christ in New-England.* One of Cotton's most important works is a full-scale description and justification of Congregational Church government and the "New England Way" of cooperation between church and state. Included is a valuable, detailed description of how the church operated in its earliest days in New England.

THOMAS SHEPARD: "New England's Lamentation for Old England's Present Errours." Shepard's sermon, written for the church in Cambridge, Massachusetts, exemplifies his nonconformity and his contribution to contemporary theological debate.

THOMAS WELD: *A Brief Narration of the Practices of the Churches in New-England.* This ecclesiastical treatise is the last work about the colonies by the Puritan divine and one of the compilers of the *Bay Psalm Book*.

ROGER WILLIAMS: *Christenings Make Not Christians.* This polemic against the Puritan church in New England demonstrates Williams's rhetorical skills and the opinions that led to his banishment from Massachusetts.

1646
Diaries, Journals, and Letters

EDWARD WINSLOW: *Hyprocrisie Unmasked by the True Relation of the proceedings of the Governour and Company of the Massachusetts Against Samuel Gorton. . . .* Winslow, coauthor of *Mourt's Relation* (1622) and *Good News from New England* (1624), defends the colony's religious and political policies against the charges of Samuel Gorton (c. 1592–1677), who had been imprisoned for his Antinomian beliefs in 1644.

Sermons and Religious Writing

SAMUEL GORTON (c. 1592–1677): *Simplicities Defence against Seven-Headed Policy.* Imprisoned in 1644 as an enemy of "civil authority among the people of God," Gorton sets out his unorthodox religious views in a reply to Edward Winslow's *Hypocrisie Unmasked* (1646). After four years of exile in England, he would return in 1648 to Shawomet, Rhode Island, the town he founded in 1643, renaming it Warwick in honor of his protector.

1647
Essays and Philosophy

NATHANIEL WARD: *The Simple Cobler of Aggawam in America.* This pamphlet, one of the earliest examples of American humor and satire, warns New Englanders of the danger of religious dissenters and attacks women's frivolity and men's foppish fashions. Published first in England under the pseudonym "Theodore de la Guard," it is reprinted in America. Ward also publishes *A Word to Mr. Peters and Two Words to the Parliament and Kingdom*, an expression of his political philosophy, and *A Religious Retreat Sounded to a Religious Army*, a jeremiad calling for spiritual vigilance and devotion to Puritan doctrine.

EDWARD WINSLOW: *New-Englands Salamander Discovered by an Irreligious and Scornfull Pamphlet.* Winslow replies to an attack by Major John Child in *New-Englands Jonas Cast Up in London* (1647) on the Puritan regime in general and Winslow in particular. The war of words over religious and civil liberty anticipates what would become a central debate among colonial writers.

Nonfiction

SIR FERDINANDO GORGES: *The Briefe Narration of the Original Undertakings of the Advancement of Plantations into Parts of America.* Gorges's final prospectus to establish an aristocratic Anglican settlement in New England fails to win financial and political support due to the growing power of the Puritans in England. Completed shortly before Gorges's death, the work expresses his regrets at past colonizing failures but confidently predicts a bright future for the land he never visited.

Poetry, Fiction, and Drama

SAMUEL DANFORTH (1626–1674): *An Almanack for the Year of Our Lord 1646.* Included in Danforth's almanac is one of the earliest collections of nonreligious poems printed in the colonies. Danforth was a Roxbury, Massachusetts, clergyman well known for his pious sermons.

Sermons and Religious Writing

JOHN COTTON: *The Bloudy Tenent Washed and Made White in the Bloud of the Lamb.* Cotton replies to Roger Williams's *The Bloudy Tenent of Persecution* (1644) with a defense of Puritan religious and political orthodoxy whereby church and state act not as separate entities but as cooperating partners. Cotton describes Massachusetts as analogous to ancient Israel, with its magistrates like Israel's ancient kings. It would prompt a return salvo from Williams, *The Bloudy Tenent Yet More Bloudy* (1652).

1648
Essays and Philosophy

WILLIAM BRADFORD: *A Dialogue; or, The Sum of a Conference Between Some Young Man Born in New England and Sundry Ancient Men That Came Out of Holland and Old England.* In this dialogue, Bradford attempts to instruct second-generation Puritans in the history of Puritan beliefs, including the origins of the Congregational Church. A second dialogue, written in 1652, contrasts four different forms of church government — Papist, Episcopal, Presbyterian, and Independent — arguing in favor of the latter as being closer to the original Christian church.

Sermons and Religious Writing

JOHN COTTON: *The Way of the Congregational Churches Cleared.* Cotton compares Congregationalism with Presbyterianism in order to differentiate the New England church from the radical nonconformists.

THOMAS HOOKER: *A Survey of the Summe of Church Discipline.* A posthumously published defense of New England Congregationalism by the founder of the Con-

necticut colony. A second volume would be written by John Cotton and also published in 1648.

JOHN NORTON (1606–1663): *Responsio ad Guliel.* Norton, a leading opponent of the Antinomians, a drafter of the *Cambridge Platform*, and the pastor of the First Church of Boston, offers a Latin treatise on New England church governance.

THOMAS SHEPARD: *The Clear Sun-shine of the Gospel Breaking Forth Upon the Indians.* Shepard describes the conversion work of John Eliot (1604–1690) among the Naticks, a Massachusetts branch of the Algonquians, which includes the establishment of independent Indian communities of converted "Praying Indians," schools, and seminaries.

1649
Diaries, Journals, and Letters

THOMAS MAYHEW (C. 1621–1657): *The Glorious Progress of the Gospel, Amongst the Indians in New England.* In this collection of documents gathered by Edward Winslow, Mayhew's letter describes the Indians' voluntarily acceptance of Christianity due to "their noble reason, judgment, and capacitie." The volume is intended to muster parliamentary support for financing Indian missions. Parliament would respond by creating the Society for the Propagation of the Gospel.

JONATHAN MITCHEL (1624–1668): "Letter to His Brother." Mitchel's letter offers spiritual advice to his brother. Cotton Mather would call the Cambridge pastor and the Harvard fellow's work "one of the most consummate pieces, in the methods of addressing a troubled mind."

Nonfiction

EZEKIEL CHEEVER: *A Short Introduction to the Latin Tongue.* Developed for Cheever's students, this is one of the earliest schoolbooks published in America. It would go through twenty editions and be used for more than a century.

Sermons and Religious Writing

RICHARD MATHER: *A Platform of Church-Discipline Gathered Out of the Word of God, Mather, John Cotton, and others.* A series of responses to critics of the New England church who favored a Presbyterian church structure. Known as the *Cambridge Platform*, it was adopted by a church synod in 1648 and served as the basic tenets of New England Congregationalism until the adoption of the *Saybrook Platform* in 1708.

THOMAS SHEPARD: *Theses Sabbaticae.* According to Cotton Mather, Shepard in these rules for New England

BIRTHS AND DEATHS, 1650–1699

Births

1651 Francis Daniel Pastorius (d. c. 1720), Quaker settler and poet

1652 Samuel Sewall (d. 1730), merchant, colonial magistrate, and author
Sarah Symmes Fiske (d. 1692), Puritan author

1655 James Blair (d. 1743), clergyman and author

1656 Thomas Bray (d. 1730), Anglican clergyman and author

1659 John Dunton (d. 1733), author and bookseller

1662 William Brattle (d. 1717), clergyman and author

1663 Cotton Mather (d. 1728), clergyman and writer

1664 John Williams (d. 1729), Congregational clergyman and author

1665 Samuel Penhallow (d. 1726), historian

1666 Sarah Kemble Knight (d. 1727), teacher and author

1671 (c.) Ebenezer Cook (d. 1732), poet

1673 Robert Beverley (d. 1722), colonial official and historian
Benjamin Colman (d. 1747), clergyman and poet
Daniel Coxe (d. 1739), landowner, politician, and writer
Experience Mayhew (d. 1758), missionary, translator, and author

1674 William Byrd (d. 1744), colonial official and author
James Logan (d. 1751), colonial statesman and author
Samuel Niles (d. 1762), clergyman and historian

1675 Thomas Chalkley (d. 1741), clergyman and writer

1679 Roger Wolcott (d. 1767), poet

1680 John Checkley (d. 1754), clergyman and author

1681 John Barnard (d. 1770), clergyman and author
Jeremiah Dummer (d. 1739), colonial agent and author

1683 Mark Catesby (d. 1749), naturalist author
Judah Monis (d. 1764), Hebrew scholar and educator

1684 Elizabeth Hanson (d. 1737), writer

1685 Jared Eliot (d. 1763), clergyman, physician, and author

1687 Thomas Prince (d. 1758), theologian, scholar, and author

1688 Cadwallader Colden (d. 1776), scientist, philosopher, and author
Samuel Keimer (d. 1739), printer and writer

1691 William Douglass (d. 1752), physician and author

1694 Jane Fenn Hoskens (d. c. 1750), traveling minister and author
William Shirley (d. 1771), colonial official, lawyer, and author

1696 Ebenezer Gay (d. 1787), clergyman and author
Thomas Walker (d. 1725), clergyman and poet

1697 John Peter Zenger (d. 1746), printer and journalist

1699 John Bartram (d. 1777), botanist and author

Deaths

1652 John Cotton (b. 1585), religious leader
Nathaniel Ward (b. c. 1578), clergyman and author

1655 Edward Winslow (b. 1595), colonist and writer

1656 Andrew White (b. c. 1579), colonist and writer

1657 William Bradford (b. 1590), colonial leader and author

1663 John Norton (b. 1606), clergyman and writer
Samuel Stone (b. 1602), clergyman and writer

1667 John Wilson (b. c. 1591), clergyman and poet

1669 Richard Mather (b. 1596), religious leader and writer

1670 John Davenport (b. 1597), clergyman, colonist, and writer

1672 Anne Bradstreet (b. 1612), poet
Charles Chauncy (b. 1592), clergyman, Harvard president, and writer
Edward Johnson (b. 1598), clergyman and author
John Steendam (b. c. 1615), poet

1674 Samuel Danforth (b. 1626), poet

1676 John Clarke (b. 1609), author and a founder of Newport, Rhode Island

1677 Samuel Gorton (b. 1592), colonist and writer
Thomas Parker (b. 1595), clergyman, colonist, and writer

1678 Abraham Pierson (b. 1608), poet and author of Indian catechism
Mary White Rowlandson (b. c. 1631), writer
Thomas Thacher (b. 1620), author of medical texts

1681 Sarah Whipple Goodhue (b. 1641), poet
Urian Oakes (b. 1631), poet

1683 Roger Williams (b. c. 1603), colonist, clergyman, and writer

1686 Nathaniel Morton (b. 1613), historian of New England

1690 Peter Folger (b. 1617), poet and grandfather of Benjamin Franklin

1692 Sarah Symmes Fiske (b. 1652), Puritan author

1695 John Woodbridge (b. 1613), author of banking and currency tracts

1696 John Richardson (b. 1647), poet

1699 John Cotton II (b. 1640), clergyman and poet

---

religious life "hath handled the morality of the Sabbath, with a degree of reason, reading, and religion, which is truly extraordinary." This work is also important for its description of life and customs of the period.

1650
Diaries, Journals, and Letters

THOMAS SHEPARD: *Three Valuable Pieces . . . and a Private Diary; Containing Meditations and Experiences Never* *Before Published.* Shepard's literary reputation is based largely on these journal entries reflecting his religious experience and published for the first time here.

Poetry, Fiction, and Drama

ANNE BRADSTREET (c. 1612–1672): *The Tenth Muse Lately Sprung Up in America.* Bradstreet's first collection of poetry is published, without her knowledge, in London by her brother-in-law. The collection includes rhymed

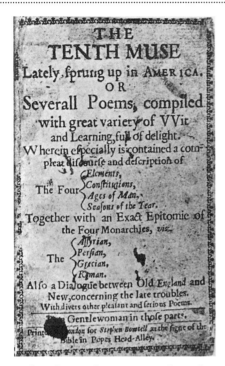

The title page from Anne Bradstreet's
The Tenth Muse

discourses and chronicles. Her modern reputation as the first noteworthy American poet is based mainly on her intimate verse exploration of religious and domestic experience, written primarily after 1650 and published in 1678 in a posthumous second edition of her work.

1651
Nonfiction

WILLIAM BRADFORD: *History of Plimmoth Plantation.* Bradford completes his crucial history begun in 1630. His second book, written between 1646 and 1650, covers the period 1620 to 1646 and chronicles virtually every aspect of Pilgrim life. The manuscript would be consulted and quoted from by five important colonial historians before 1730. Though deposited in the "New England Library," the steeple room of Boston's Old South Church, the history disappeared for nearly a century, resurfacing in the library of the bishop of Oxford. The first complete edition of the work appeared in 1856, and in 1897 the original was finally returned to Massachusetts.

1652
Sermons and Religious Writing

JOHN CLARKE (1609–1676): *Ill News from New England.* A supporter of Anne Hutchinson in the Antinomian controversy and one of the founders of Newport, Rhode Island, Clarke attacks the intolerance of Massachusetts leaders and their suppression of religious liberty.

RICHARD MATHER: *The Summe of Certain Sermons Upon Genes. 15.6.* This is Mather's only published collection of sermons. His style has been described as simple and practical, and his views show moderation concerning the various religious disputes of the era.

SAMUEL STONE (1602–1663): *A Congregational Church Is a Catholike Visible Church.* The controversial Hartford minister, whose unorthodox beliefs brought him into conflict with Cotton Mather and others, publishes his only book outlining his Presbyterian-leaning views.

ROGER WILLIAMS: *The Bloudy Tenent Yet More Bloudy.* Williams reiterates his argument for the separation of civil and religious administration to ensure personal and religious liberty. He condemns the Puritan doctrine of persecution by which the civil administration enforces orthodoxy as "one of the most Seditious, Destructive, Blasphemous, and Bloudiest in any or in all Nations of the World." He also publishes *The Hireling Ministry None of Christs*, an attack on mercenary clergy, and "Experiments of Spiritual Life and Health," a devotional letter to his wife, consoling her after an illness and religious doubt.

1653
Diaries, Journals, and Letters

MICHAEL WIGGLESWORTH (1631–1705): *The Diary of Michael Wigglesworth, 1653–1657; the conscience of a Puritan.* The poet and minister begins writing this diary during a long illness.

Nonfiction

JOHN ELIOT (1604–1690): *Tears of Repentance.* This is the first of Eliot's many tracts reporting on the progress of Indian conversion to Christianity. Included also is a letter from Thomas Mayhew. It would be followed by *A Late and Further Manifestation* (1655), *A Further Account* (1660), and *A Brief Narration* (1671).

Sermons and Religious Writing

JOHN NORTON: *A Discussion of that Great Point in Divinity, the Sufferings of Christ.* Norton, a prolific writer and Puritan clergyman who succeeded John Cotton as pastor of First Church in Boston, mounts an attack on the heresy of William Pynchon, who denied that Christ suffered the torment of hell.

SAMUEL WHITING (1597–1679): "Concerning the Life of the Famous Mr. Cotton. . . ." Whiting, the minister to the Massachusetts town of Saugus, produces one of the earliest spiritual biographies. Though not published until 1769, the sketch would be consulted by John Norton and Cotton Mather for their more extensive biographies of Cotton.

1654
Nonfiction

EDWARD JOHNSON (1598–1672): *A History of New-England.* Better known by its subtitle, *The Wonder-Working Providence of Sions Saviour in New England*, this first detailed history of the New England colonial experience by the Massachusetts colonist and captain of militia in Boston covers the period 1628 to 1652 and depicts the colonists as spiritual crusaders. Johnson's vigorous prose is interspersed with verse tributes to contemporary figures and events.

Sermons and Religious Writing

JOHN ELIOT: *A Primer or Catechism in the Massachusetts Indian Language.* Eliot produces the first Indian-language catechism. No copy has survived.

JOHN NORTON: *The Orthodox Evangelist.* Norton's most famous work is an important theological treatise endorsed by John Cotton, who had provided a prefatory epistle.

1655
Sermons and Religious Writing

CHARLES CHAUNCY (1592–1672): "God's Mercy, Shewed to His People." The second president of Harvard College delivers this sermon after the first commencement of his presidency, advocating colleges for the training of ministers and the inclusion of secular subjects in the curriculum.

1656
Essays and Philosophy

JOHN HAMMOND (fl. 1635–1656): *Leah and Rachel; or, The Two Fruitfull Sisters, Virginia and Maryland.* This pamphlet by a colonist who lived in Virginia and Maryland from 1635 to 1656 contrasts living conditions in England and the colonies and advocates relocation of Britain's poor to America.

1657
Sermons and Religious Writing

JOHN FISKE (c. 1608–1677): *The Watering of the Olive Plant in Christs Garden.* The only published work during the physician and minister's lifetime is a catechism for children of his church in Chelmsford, Massachusetts. Fiske's poetry would be later discovered in a commonplace book at Brown University and first published in 1943 to critical acclaim.

THOMAS HOOKER: *The Application of Redemption.* Hooker's series of sermons describing the soul's progress from contrition to humiliation, vocation, justification, adoption, sanctification, and glorification would be called his masterpiece by twentieth-century scholar Perry Miller.

RICHARD MATHER: "A Farewell Exhortation to the Church and People of Dorchester in New England." A sermon on the loss of piety and a call for renewed commitment to God.

1658
Nonfiction

JOHN NORTON: *Abel Being Dead Yet Speaketh; or, The Life and Death of . . . John Cotton.* This is the first separately published biography in America.

Sermons and Religious Writing

ABRAHAM PIERSON (c. 1608–1678): *Some Helps for the Indians.* This prose catechism by the Branford, Connecticut, pastor and Indian missionary, written in an Indian dialect, is one of Pierson's two published works. The other is the poem "Lines on the Death of Theophilus Eaton," a long eulogy for his friend.

1659
Poetry, Fiction, and Drama

JOHN STEENDAM (c. 1615–c. 1672): *Klacht von Nieuw Nederlandt tot Haar Moeder* (Complaint of New Netherland to Her Mother). Steendam, who is regarded as the first poet published in America, supplies an allegorical history of the Dutch colony and appeals to the government for adequate protection against the local Indians.

Sermons and Religious Writing

JOHN ELIOT: *The Christian Commonwealth.* This theological tract is the first American book to be suppressed. Massachusetts colonial authorities fear that Eliot's radical conception of a Christian utopia, which replaces all civil authority with religious laws, will anger the restored English monarch. Consequently, they suppress the book and force Eliot to make a public apology.

JOHN NORTON: *The Heart of N-England Rent at the Blasphemies of the Present Generation.* Another of Norton's works dealing with theological controversies in which he expresses his opposition to Quakers and advocates the death penalty.

1660
Nonfiction

SAMUEL MAVERICK (c. 1602–1676): *A Briefe Description of New England and the Severall Townes Therein.* This account of the topography and settlements of New England by an associate of Ferdinando Gorges is distinguished by keen observation, but its objectivity is undermined by Maverick's evident hostility toward the Puritans. His call for more supervision of New England's affairs by English authorities anticipates the central question of who should rule the colonies, which will eventually lead to the Revolution.

Sermons and Religious Writing

THOMAS SHEPARD: *The Parable of Ten Virgins Opened and Applied.* This posthumous transcription of sermons written from 1636 to 1640 provides insights into important theological controversies of the period. The theme of hypocrisy among the elect is repeated throughout Shepard's writings.

1661
Poetry, Fiction, and Drama

JOHN STEENDAM: *'T Lof von Nieuw Nederlandt* (The Praise of New Netherlands). Steendam's Dutch poem describes the New World, praising the land as a paradise: "a very Eden . . . the masterpiece of nature's land."

Sermons and Religious Writing

JOHN ELIOT: *The New Testament.* Eliot, the Puritan leader and missionary to the Indians, translates into an Algonquian language the first half of what would become in 1663 the first complete Bible in any language printed in America.

THOMAS HOOKER: *The Saints Dignitie, and Duty.* The sermons in this posthumously published collection were likely delivered during and after the trial of Anne Hutchinson in the 1630s since they all deal with aspects of the Antinomian controversy.

1662
Poetry, Fiction, and Drama

JACOB STEENDAM: *Spurring Verses.* Steendam's poems precede a prospectus to promote colonization of the Delaware River area and recapitulate the poet's previous praise for the land and its potential.

MICHAEL WIGGLESWORTH: *The Day of Doom; or, A Description of the Great and Last Judgment.* Wigglesworth's theological poem in ballad meter treats the Puritan concept of predestination, original sin, and God's grace and wrath in what has been described as the first American bestseller. Its first edition of eighteen thousand copies sells out in a year, and it would be reprinted so frequently that it is estimated that one of every twenty New Englanders and one of every forty-five colonists owned a copy. Wigglesworth also writes *God's Controversy with New England.* Unpublished until 1873, it is a verse jeremiad that considers the serious drought of 1662 as a divine punishment and urges New Englanders to strengthen their spiritual lives.

1663
Diaries, Journals, and Letters

THOMAS SHEPARD: "Church Membership of Children and Their Right to Baptisme." Shepard's letter, written to the congregation in Cambridge, Massachusetts, addresses the question of infant baptism.

Essays and Philosophy

JOHN DAVENPORT (1597–1670): *A Discourse About Civil Government in a New Plantation Whose Design is Religion.* One of the founders of the New Haven colony publishes this defense of theocracy.

Sermons and Religious Writing

JOHN ELIOT: *The Holy Bible . . . Translated into the Indian Language.* Eliot completes one of the greatest works of scholarship in early American history, finishing his translation of the Bible into an Algonquian language, which had been preceded by his New Testament translation in 1661. He had faced considerable challenges such as the absence in this Indian language of the verb *to be*. It is the first complete Bible published in America. A copy is presented to King Charles II, and this Bible would remain in use into the early nineteenth century.

JOHN HIGGINSON (1616–1708): "The Cause of God and His People in New-England." The Salem, Massachusetts, minister's election sermon, an address delivered throughout colonial New England before elections to heighten the sense of responsibility among candidates and voters, is the first printed in New England. It pleads for a return to the piety of the Puritan founders.

1664
Sermons and Religious Writing

ANNE BRADSTREET: *Meditations.* At the request of her son, Bradstreet collects her prose devotional writings, which draw on her daily experiences.

JOHN NORTON: *Three Choice and Profitable Sermons Upon Severall Texts of Scripture.* This is the final, and posthumously published, collection of Norton's religious writing, containing "Sion the Out-cast," "The Believer's Consolation," and "The Evangelical Worshipper."

1665
Poetry, Fiction, and Drama

CORNELIUS WATKINSON (fl. 1660s), PHILIP HOWARD (fl. 1660s), AND WILLIAM DARBY (fl. 1660s): *Ye Beare and Ye Cub.* In what is believed to be the first record of a play performed in English in America, three residents of Accomac County, Virginia, write and perform this play and are charged with licentiousness. They perform the work at their trial and are found not guilty. The play has not survived.

Sermons and Religious Writing

SAMUEL DANFORTH: *An Astronomical Description of the late Comet or Blazing Star. . . .* This work attempts to reconcile science and religion while justifying the study of astronomy by theologians.

JOHN ELIOT: *The Communion of Churches.* The work includes reports on the conversion progress among the Indians. It is considered the first privately printed American book.

1666
Nonfiction

JOHN ELIOT: *The Indian Grammar.* The first of Eliot's books on, and in, an Algonquian language written to assist in the conversion work among the Indians. Described as "Some Bones and Ribs preparation for such a work," the *Grammar* is intended for missionaries who wish to learn the Massachusett dialect of Algonquian. It would be followed by *The Indian Primer* (1669), a compilation of catechistic exercises to aid converted Indians; *Indian Dialogues* (1671), to help Indians to convert their fellows; and *The Logic Primer* (1672), a guide to help the converted deduce lessons from scripture.

ROBERT HORNE (fl. 1660s): *A Description of Carolina.* One of the earliest descriptions of the Carolina settlement, intended to attract English migration. It is published by Robert Horne in London (although he may not have been the author).

Poetry, Fiction, and Drama

GEORGE ALSOP (1636–?): *A Character of the Province of Mary-land.* The travel writer who came to America in 1638 produces this promotional account of Maryland in verse and prose that mixes jocularity and seriousness. Although the work exaggerates the idyllic nature of the colony, it provides descriptions of the country and its Indian population.

Sermons and Religious Writing

SAMUEL WHITING: *Abraham's Humble Intercession for Sodom. . . .* The popularity of Whiting's sermon notes for *A Discourse of the Last Judgment . . .* (1664) prompts him to write this more substantial articulation of his religious views, which reflects his mild and introspective nature.

1668
Poetry, Fiction, and Drama

PHILIP PAIN (fl. 1660s): *Daily Meditation.* Nothing is known about the poet of these reflective lyrics reminiscent of the metaphysical poets other than the indication on the title page that he "lately suffering shipwrack, was drowned." Because the book was published in Massachusetts, it is assumed that Pain was American, and as such the work is considered the earliest American lyrical poetry published in the colonies.

1669
Essays and Philosophy

WILLIAM PENN (1644–1718): *No Cross, No Crown.* Penn's tract *The Sandy Foundation Shaken* (1668), which attacks the doctrine of the Trinity, had resulted in his being imprisoned in the Tower of London. There he writes this first of his major works: a defense of his faith and an attack on the clergy. He also begins *My Irish Journal,*

1669–1670, an account of his experience with nonconformity and his conversion to Quakerism.

Nonfiction

NATHANIEL MORTON (1613–1686): *New England's Memorial.* This work by the secretary of the Plymouth colony, who drew on the papers of William Bradford and Edward Winslow, is the first extensive historical narrative published in Massachusetts. The discovery of the lost manuscript of Bradford's *History of Plimmoth Plantation* in 1855 would show that Morton had transcribed many of Bradford's passages verbatim.

Sermons and Religious Writing

JOHN DAVENPORT: "Gods Call to His People to Turn Unto Him." Davenport's election sermon typifies the style and sermon structure of first-generation Puritan preachers and foreshadows the jeremiads (sermons chastising congregations for lack of piety and interpreting various events as signs of God's wrath) of the second generation.

INCREASE MATHER (1639–1723): "The Mystery of Israel's Salvation." Mather's first published work is a sermon that expresses his belief in the imminent arrival of the kingdom of Christ.

THOMAS WALLEY (1618–1679): "Balm in Gilead to Heal Sions Wounds." Walley's single contribution to American literature is this election sermon, a notable example of Puritan plain style and the articulation of the unity of church and state in early New England. Walley instructs magistrates to "be Healers to a poor sick country," and the sermon features an extended conceit equating sin to illness.

1670
Essays and Philosophy

WILLIAM PENN: "The Great Cause of Liberty of Conscience." Penn's essay asserts his absolute commitment to freedom of conscience in the face of religious persecution in Restoration England. In it he develops an unusual theory that conscience is a part of property that must be protected and that persecution and good government are irreconcilable. Penn's ideas anticipate those of Thomas Jefferson's Virginia statute of religious freedom.

Nonfiction

DANIEL DENTON (c. 1640–1696): *A Brief Description of New-York.* This is the first detailed description of New York written in English. Denton, a landowner and politician, was born in Connecticut and settled in New York soon after the English took possession from the Dutch.

INCREASE MATHER: *The Life and Death . . . of Richard Mather.* Mather produces a biography of his illustrious father. It is characteristic of Puritan biographies, more hagiography than an accurate portrait based on verifiable facts.

Poetry, Fiction, and Drama

JOHN RICHARDSON (1647–1696): *An Almanack . . . for . . . 1670.* Contains the poem "The Country-man's Apocrypha" in which the poet pokes fun at rustic superstition. Its statement that "The Moon is habitable, some aver me; / And that some Creatures have their dwelling there" has been cited as the first hint of science fiction in American literature.

MICHAEL WIGGLESWORTH: *Meat Out of the Eater.* Wigglesworth's final major poetic effort is a collection of songs and meditations. The most introspective and personal of the poet's verses, they provide solace for those suffering the trials and tribulations of daily life in Puritan New England. Wigglesworth would add new works to the fourth edition of the volume (1689).

Sermons and Religious Writing

JOHN OXENBRIDGE (1609–1674): "A Quickening Word." The first of Oxenbridge's two published sermons is delivered to Boston merchants, who are told that a wise trader would take advantage of Christ's offer of salvation. It would be followed by "New-England Freemen Warned and Warmed" (1673), instructing members of the legislature on their religious duties.

WILLIAM STOUGHTON (1631–1701): "New Englands True Interest." This sermon by the future presiding judge at the Salem witchcraft trials describes the special qualities and responsibilities of the Massachusetts colonists.

1671
Sermons and Religious Writing

SAMUEL DANFORTH: "A Brief Recognition of New-Englands Errand into the Wilderness." Danforth's election sermon, his most notable work, is a jeremiad denouncing the decline of piety in Massachusetts.

JONATHAN MITCHEL: "Nehemiah on the Wall in Troublesome Times." Mitchel's election sermon exhorts civil leaders to glorify God by aiding the welfare of the people. It follows the basic formula of the Puritan jeremiad, dealing first with sin and punishment, then reform and salvation. It is included in Mitchel's posthumous collection of sermons, *A Discourse of the Glory to which God hath called believers by Jesus Christ* (1677).

Two pages from Increase Mather's diaries

1672

Nonfiction

JOHN JOSSELYN (fl. 1638–1675): *New-England Rarities Discovered*. The English naturalist supplies one of the earliest works of natural history, mixing descriptions of flora and fauna with practical advice for settlers and local history and fanciful claims, such as the existence of mermen and Indians who speak in perfect hexameter. *An Account of Two Voyages to New-England* would follow in 1674.

Sermons and Religious Writing

JAMES FITCH (1622–1702): "Peace the End of the Perfect and Upright." Cited by scholar David Stannard as the oldest extant funeral sermon in New England.

1673

Sermons and Religious Writing

INCREASE MATHER: "The Day of Trouble is Near" and "Wo to Drunkards." In the first of these sermons, Mather defends Puritan theology and calls on his congregants to observe their covenant with God with renewed piety. In "Wo to Drunkards," he decries drinking. Mather's later published sermons include "The Wicked Mans Portion" (1675), "Truth Tending to Promote the Power of Godliness" (1682), "A Testimony Against Several Profane and Superstitious Customs" (1687), and "The Folly of Sinning, Opened & Applyed" (1699). They criticize behaviors Mather considered wayward: playing games of dice and cards, keeping Christmas, and giving gifts at the New Year.

URIAN OAKES (c. 1631–1681): "New-England Pleaded With, and Pressed to Consider the Things Which Concern Her Peace." Oakes's first sermon, "The Unconquerable, All-Conquering & More-Than-Conquering Souldier" (delivered in 1672, published in 1674), is considered so eloquent that he is invited to deliver the annual Boston election sermon in 1673. In this jeremiad he calls for an end to "rebelliousness" and submission to authority.

WILLIAM PENN: *Quakerism: A New Nick-Name for Old Christianity*. One of Penn's many tracts written between 1672 and 1675, responding to critics of the Society of Friends. It explains Quaker thought and practices and makes a case that Quaker beliefs are closer to those of the original Christians.

THOMAS SHEPARD II (1635–1677): "Eye-Salve, or A Watch-Word for Our Lord Jesus Christ Unto His Churches." Shepard's only published sermon is a Massachusetts election address that typifies the second-generation Puritans' sense of the decline of the ideals of the founders. As a central metaphor for religious awakening, it draws on Shepard's own childhood eye affliction that left him temporarily blind.

SAMUEL WILLARD (1640–1707): *Useful Instructions for a Professing People in Times of Great Security and Degeneracy: Delivered in Several Sermons on Solemn Occasions*. A defense of the traditional Puritan way of life at a time when social and cultural forces threatened change

Willard was a Congregational clergyman and served for a time as vice president of Harvard.

1674
Diaries, Journals, and Letters

SAMUEL SEWALL (1652–1730): *Diary*. Jurist and government official Sewell commences his remarkable and invaluable record of his daily activities and observations that, except for a gap between 1677 and 1685, continues until 1729 and earns him the sobriquet "the American Pepys." The *Diary* would be first published in 1878–1882.

Nonfiction

DANIEL GOOKIN (c. 1612–1687): *Historical Collections of the Indians in New England of the Several Nations, Numbers, Customs, Manners, Religion and Government Before the English Planted There*. A thorough account of Indian religious, political, and cultural life as observed by the author while serving as superintendent of Indians in Massachusetts. Although Gookin was a prominent member of the New England colony, his sympathetic views of the Indians were unpopular. The work would be first published in 1792.

JOHN JOSSELYN: *An Account of Two Voyages to New-England*. This collection of observations on the flora and fauna of New England is among the earliest works on the natural history of the region.

Sermons and Religious Writing

JOSHUA MOODEY (1633–1697): "Souldiery Spiritualized." Moodey's most famous sermon, one of the first artillery election sermons published in New England, is preached before soldiers on the day of their election to their ranks. It argues the connection between the Christian and the soldier, employing a succession of military terms.

SAMUEL TORREY (1632–1707): "An Exhortation unto Reformation. . . ." Torrey's first publication, his election sermon, establishes his reputation as one of the leading voices supporting reform of the era. Along with his subsequent publications, "A Plea for the Life of Dying Religion" (1683) and "Man's Extremity, God's Opportunity" (1695), it is a notable expression of the ideas and issues faced by late-seventeenth-century Puritans.

1675
Sermons and Religious Writing

INCREASE MATHER: *A Discourse Concerning the Subject of Baptisme and The First Principles of New-England. . . .* Mather writes in support of the Half-Way Covenant, which extends church membership by allowing the baptism of children of the uncovenanted — those who have not made the public professions necessary for full church membership.

1676
Nonfiction

INCREASE MATHER: *A Brief History of the War with the Indians*. This is the earliest published historical account of King Philip's War, a conflict between Indians and colonists concerning ownership of land, which concluded in this year with the death of Metacomet (King Philip) and a colonist victory.

Poetry, Fiction, and Drama

PETER FOLGER (1617–1690): *A Looking-Glass for the Times*. The grandfather of Benjamin Franklin pens this collection of rough ballads defending religious liberty and stating that the recent Indian wars are divine punishment for religious intolerance in Massachusetts.

BENJAMIN TOMPSON (1642–1714): *New Englands Crisis; or A Brief Narrative, of New Englands Lamentable Estate at Present. . . .* and *New-Englands Tears for Her Present Miseries*. Tompson, the first known native-born New England poet, provides in *New Englands Crisis* a satirical treatment in heroic couplets of King Philip's War and its causes — moral and spiritual decline. It is the first imaginative account of war in America. It is incorporated in the longer work *New-Englands Tears for Her Present Miseries*.

Sermons and Religious Writing

WILLIAM HUBBARD (c. 1621–1704): "The Happiness of a People in the Wisdome of Their Rulers." Hubbard's first publication, his election sermon, has been called by literary historian Perry Miller "the finest prose of the decade, which rises to a lofty hymn to order."

ROGER WILLIAMS: *George Fox Digg'd out of His Burrowes*. Although Williams was known for his principles of religious tolerance, here he provides scathing criticism of the Quakers and their leader.

1677
Nonfiction

DANIEL GOOKIN: *An Historical Account of the Doings and Sufferings of the Christian Indians in New England in the Years 1675, 1676, 1677*. In marked contrast to the histories of King Philip's War written by William Hubbard and Increase Mather, Gookin reveals the injustices, imprisonment, and murder of the "Praying Indians" (Indians who had converted to Christianity) during the conflict.

WILLIAM HUBBARD: *Narrative of the Troubles with the Indians in New-England.* In this popular account of King Philip's War, the historian and clergyman makes it clear who he believes is to blame for the recent conflict, calling the Indians "treacherous villains" and the "dross of mankind."

INCREASE MATHER: *A Relation of the Troubles Which Have Hapned in New-England, By Reason of the Indians there....* Mather's second Indian history is a litany of Indian atrocities and betrayals, typifying the feelings of many colonists during the period.

THOMAS THACHER (1620–1678): *A Brief Rule to Guide the Common People of New-England How to Order Themselves and Theirs in the Small Pocks, or Measels.* Thacher, not a physician but "a well-wisher to the sick," issues the first medical treatise published in America. Addressing the 1677 epidemic that killed at least seven hundred, Thacher gives advice based on Thomas Sydenham's research in England. The book would become one of the best-known texts in New England, reprinted during subsequent epidemics in 1702 and 1721.

Poetry, Fiction, and Drama

URIAN OAKES: "Elegie Upon the Death of the Reverend Mr. Thomas Shepard." Oakes's single published poem is one of the most praised by an American colonial poet. He interprets Shepard's death at the age of forty-two from smallpox as divine punishment, stating that "Our sins have slain our Shepard! We have bought, / And dearly paid for, our Enormities."

Sermons and Religious Writing

SARAH SYMMES FISKE (1652–1692): *A Confession of Faith: or, A Summary of Divinity. Drawn Up By a Young Gentle-Woman, in the Twenty-Fifth Year of Her Age.* Fiske's well-written and only known literary work is composed in 1677 but would not be published until 1704. The work is a spiritual biography that emphasizes Puritan theology and argument, an uncommon topic for a woman at the time.

SAMUEL HOOKER (1635–1697): *Righteousness Rained from Heaven.* The son of Thomas Hooker delivers this jeremiad to Connecticut voters, decrying the "declension" of the current generation from the founders' piety.

1678
Poetry, Fiction, and Drama

ANNE BRADSTREET: *Severall Poems Compiled with great variety of Wit and Learning.* This posthumous second edition of Bradstreet's poems includes revisions of her earlier works and a dozen new works found among her papers after her death, including "The Flesh and the Spirit"; "On the Burning of Her Home," a short spiritual autobiography in prose; "Religious Experience"; and "Contemplation," regarded by many as her greatest poetic achievement.

JOHN COTTON II (1640–1699): "Verses Upon the Death of Noah Newman." The first of the verse elegies published by the son of the illustrious Puritan divine. It would be followed by "Poem Occasioned by the Death of . . . John Alden" in 1687.

Sermons and Religious Writing

JOHN ELIOT: *The Harmony of the Gospels.* This book of biblical reflections on Christ's suffering and *A Brief Answer to a Small Book Written by John Norcot Against Infant-Baptisme* (1679), defending the practice of infant baptism, are the final publications of the "Apostle to the Indians."

SAMUEL NOWELL (1634–1688): "Abraham in Arms." Nowell's single publication, his election sermon, is regarded as one of the most stirring and important Puritan sermons produced during the second half of the seventeenth century. It is notable for Nowell's elaborate use of images of war and soldiering while trying to put into a wider religious context the recently concluded Indian war.

1679
Diaries, Journals, and Letters

CLAUDE JEAN ALLOUEZ (1622–1689): *Recit d'un 3e voyage fait aux Illinois.* Published in part in *Jesuit Relations,* this prayer book/journal chronicles the French Jesuit missionary Allouez's observations of American Indians. It is an invaluable ethnographic source.

Sermons and Religious Writing

JAMES FITCH (1622–1702): *The First Principles of the Doctrine of Christ.* Historian Perry Miller has called Fitch's first important publication "the best succinct summary of the creed and philosophy of the New England variety of Calvinism." Fitch was the first minister of Norwich, Connecticut, who preached to the Mohegan Indians in their own tongue.

JOHN RICHARDSON: "The Necessity of a Well Experienced Souldiery." Richardson's sermon urges military readiness against the Indians. He argues that "War is an Ordinance appoynted by God for subduing and destroying the Churches enemies here on Earth."

1680

Nonfiction

WILLIAM HUBBARD: *A General History of New England from the Discovery to MDLLXXX*. First published in 1815, Hubbard's history draws on Morton's *Memorial* and Winthrop's *Journal* as well as his own original research. Cotton Mather and Thomas Prince would consult it to produce their later histories.

Sermons and Religious Writing

SAMUEL WILLARD: "The Duty of a People That Have Renewed Their Covenant With God." Willard's sermon typifies his position as a staunch defender of Puritan orthodoxy. Nevertheless, he shows flexibility on certain matters of church membership, particularly in his willingness to open his church for Anglican services.

1681

Diaries, Journals, and Letters

SARAH WHIPPLE GOODHUE (1641–1681): "Valedictory and Monitory-Writing." Goodhue's letter to provide spiritual guidance to her family would be read for inspiration through the nineteenth century. The Ipswich, Massachusetts, native had written the work anticipating that she might die in childbirth. It offers advice to her husband and children and remains interesting for the light it sheds on colonial family life.

Nonfiction

JOHN WOODBRIDGE (1613–1695): *Severals Relating to the Fund Printed Divers Reasons, As May Appear*. This explanation and defense of the land banks in Massachusetts form the earliest American tract on banking and currency.

1682

Diaries, Journals, and Letters

MARY WHITE ROWLANDSON (c. 1635–c. 1678): *The Sovereignty & the Goodness of God . . . Being a Narrative of the Captivity and Restauration of Mrs. Mary Rowlandson*. One of the most famous and popular examples of colonial American prose chronicles Rowlandson's spiritual and physicial travails after her eleven-week captivity among Indians in 1676. It is the first best-selling book written by a woman and sets the standard for subsequent captivity narratives.

Nonfiction

WILLIAM PENN: *The Frame of the Government of the Province of Pennsylvania*. This is the constitution for the

The title page from *The Sovereignty & the Goodness of God, Together With the Faithfulness of His Promises Displayed: Being a Narrative of the Captivity and Restauration of Mrs. Mary Rowlandson*

colony of Pennsylvania, written in preparation for the arrival of the settlers to the Quaker colony.

Poetry, Fiction, and Drama

COTTON MATHER (1663–1728): "Poem Dedicated to . . . Urian Oakes." Mather's first published work is a funeral elegy on the recently deceased clergyman and Harvard president, summarizing his virtues and the impact of his death on his family, friends, and the community. Mather, the son of Increase Mather, would produce a comparable poem, "Elegy on . . . Nathanael Collins," in 1685.

EDWARD TAYLOR (1642–1729): *Preparatory Meditations*. It is believed that in this year Taylor begins his series of more than two hundred poems, written every two months until 1725, as private spiritual exercises prior to communion services. They represent the major poetic achievement of colonial America and some of the finest English-language poetry of the late seventeenth and early eighteenth centuries. It is also thought that around this time Taylor begins work on his other major poetic work, *Gods Determinations Touching his Elect*, a justification of God's ways to man from the Calvinist perspective. Taylor's *Poetical Works* would be discovered and first published in 1939.

William Penn making peace with the Native Americans

Sermons and Religious Writing

URIAN OAKES: "The Soveraign Efficacy of Divine Providence. . . ." Oakes's sermon attempts to reconcile religion and science according to orthodox Puritan principles. It is published posthumously with a lengthy preface by Increase Mather, extolling Oakes's merits as a divine and a scholar.

1683

Diaries, Journals, and Letters

JASPER DANCKAERTS (1639–c. 1703): *Journal of a Voyage to New York.* This is the Dutch author's account of conditions in the colonies, with descriptions of the environment and the settled communities in New York, New Jersey, Delaware, Maryland, and Massachusetts.

Nonfiction

LOUIS HENNEPIN (1640–c. 1710): *Description de la Louisiane* (Description of Louisiana). The chaplain on La Salle's expedition to the Great Lakes and a participant of the first exploration of the Upper Mississippi Valley provides an account of his experiences. (It would be translated into English in 1880.) *Nouveau voyage* would follow in 1698.

Poetry, Fiction, and Drama

EDWARD TAYLOR: "Upon the Sweeping Flood, April 13 14, 1683." Taylor's only poem that can be precisely dated is this allegorical response to a spring flood, which the poet uses as a lesson of divine punishment for man' sinfulness.

Publications and Events

The New England Primer. The Calvinist schoolbook for teaching children the alphabet. In rhymed couplets, i presents simple moral and religious lessons ("In Adam' fall / we sinned all"), and it includes the prayer "Now I Lay Me Down to Sleep." The book is published by Benjamin Harris (fl. 1673–1716). Though the year of its first appearance is disputed, it is estimated to have sold more than five million copies.

Sermons and Religious Writing

JAMES FITCH: *An Explanation of the Solemn Advice. . .* The last published work of the Connecticut clergyman castigates the "vile Examples" of white settler and absolves the Indians from blame in New England' calamities.

SAMUEL TORREY: "A Plea for the Life of the Dying Religion." Torrey's election sermon establishes one of the dominant themes of clergy during the period: that the original purpose of New England's settlement, the establishment of a "plantation Religious," has been undermined by the backsliding, or "Declension," of the Christians.

1684
Essays and Philosophy

INCREASE MATHER: "An Essay for the Recording of Illustrious Providences." One of Mather's most important works, the treatise better known as "Remarkable Providences" draws upon both scientific knowledge and faith to report on supernatural incidents in New England's history.

Nonfiction

THOMAS GAGE (c. 1596–1656): *The English-American: His Travail by sea and land.* The English Catholic missionary who traveled in Mexico and Central America helps stimulate English exploration with this account of the wealth of the region.

Poetry, Fiction, and Drama

RICHARD STEERE (1643–1721): *A Monumental Memorial for Marine Mercy.* Literary historians consider Steere's poem one of the finest celebrating a sea deliverance. Prompted by a nearly disastrous voyage to London in 1683, it interprets events as an allegory of the soul's redemption.

1685
Nonfiction

THOMAS BUDD (?–1698): *Good Order Established in Pennsylvania and New Jersey.* Budd, a prominent Quaker, proposes a comprehensive plan for public education, which would be largely adopted.

Sermons and Religious Writing

EZEKIEL CHEEVER: *Scripture Prophecies Explained.* A collection of three essays of biblical interpretation and Cheever's millennial beliefs that the world will not be destroyed but "perfected" and that Christ will return a thousand years before the Last Judgment to establish an "outward glorious visible kingdom."

1686
Sermons and Religious Writing

JOHN HIGGINSON: "Our Dying Saviour's Legacy of Peace." The first of Higginson's two long sermons on

Puritan devotions that assert the need for preserving religious orthodoxy. It would be followed by "A Testimony to the Order of the Gospel" (1701), which has been described as a model of conservative Puritan ideology.

COTTON MATHER: "The Call of the Gospel." The first of Mather's published sermons is addressed to a condemned murderer who repented. The notoriety of the case helps establish Mather as one of the era's distinctive voices.

1687
Publications and Events

Tulley's Almanac. John Tulley (c. 1639–1701) launches the first in an annual series of almanacs that would continue until his death, the first such continuous publication in America. It includes what is believed to be the earliest New England road map, as well as prose, verse, practical advice, and jokes, thus beginning the humorous almanac tradition in America.

1688
Essays and Philosophy

INCREASE MATHER: "A Narrative of the Miseries of New England." Mather's political essay speaks out against the threat to autonomous Puritan rule represented by the revocation of the Massachusetts Bay colony's charter. He would continue the subject in 1689 with "A Brief Relation of the State of New England, New-England Vindicated" and "The Present State of Affairs."

1689
Essays and Philosophy

COTTON MATHER: *Memorable Providences, Relating to Witchcrafts and Possessions* and *The Declaration of the Gentlemen, Merchants,* and *Inhabitants of Boston.* The first provides Mather's reflections on one of the accused in the Salem witchcraft trials, whom he took into his home for observation. The second is a manifesto against Governor Edmund Andros (1637–1714), which helps incite the uprising that contributes to the governor's dismissal.

1690
Poetry, Fiction, and Drama

BENJAMIN COLMAN (1673–1747): *Gustavus Vasa.* This play by the liberal Congregational Boston minister, said to have been produced at Harvard, has traditionally been considered the first performed play by an American-born writer.

Cotton Mather

Publications and Events

Publick Occurrences, Both Foreign and Domestick. The first newspaper published in America is issued by Benjamin Harris in Boston. Because it is unlicensed, it is suppressed after only one issue.

1691
Diaries, Journals, and Letters

THOMAS SAVAGE (1640–1705): "Account of the Late Action . . . Against the French at Canada." In a richly detailed and accurate letter to his brother in London, Savage, who served as a major under Sir William Phips who led the colonial attack on the French, provides a valuable firsthand account of the failed military expedition against Quebec in 1690.

Nonfiction

SAMUEL SEWALL: *The Revolution in New England Justified.* Sewall provides a defense of the uprising that deposed Governor Edmund Andros.

Sermons and Religious Writing

COTTON MATHER: "Little Flocks Guarded Against Grievous Wolves: An Address Unto those Parts of New-England which are most Exposed unto Assaults, from the Modern Teachers of the misled Quakers." Mather warns his readers to be prepared to confront the Quakers with scripture.

JOSHUA SCOTTOW (c. 1618–1698): "Old Men Tears for Their Own Declension." The Boston merchant offers a model jeremiad on the theme of the second-generation Puritans' failure to live up to the mission set by the first.

SAMUEL WILLARD: *The Barren Fig Trees Down.* One of the clergyman's most notable sermon collections supports his contention that church membership is "not only a title of dignity, but also an obligation to Service."

1692
Nonfiction

INCREASE MATHER: *The Autobiography of Increase Mather.* Written for his family, Mather relates how his faith has helped him through life's spiritual tribulations.

FRANCIS DANIEL PASTORIUS (1651–c. 1719): *A Particular Geographical Description of the Lately Discovered Province of Pennsylvania.* The German-born theologian, lawyer, historian, and poet provides a geographical description of Pennsylvania and an evaluation of the colony's suitability for settlement.

SAMUEL WILLARD: *Some Miscellany Observations on . . . Witchcrafts.* A critical analysis of the Salem witch trials and an argument against the use of spectral (supernatural, and therefore not empirically verifiable) evidence to prove demonic possession.

Samuel Sewall

Poetry, Fiction, and Drama

RICHARD FRAME (fl. 1692): *A Short Description of Pennsylvania.* To attract settlers and investment, Frame offers a verse description of "what things are known, enjoyed, and like to be discovered" in Pennsylvania.

COTTON MATHER: *Political Fables.* Three allegorical tales supporting the new charter for the New England colonies and the new governor, Sir William Phips, is circulated in manuscript and would be first published in 1868.

1693
Essays and Philosophy

GEORGE KEITH (1638–1716): *Exhortation and Cautions to Friends.* Keith, the Scottish-born clergyman who organized a sect called Keithians, or Christian Quakers, issues what is believed to be the first antislavery document printed in the colonies.

COTTON MATHER: *The Wonders of the Visible World.* Mather provides a narrative account of some of the Salem witchcraft trials along with his comments on demonic possession. It would prompt a satirical reply by Robert Calef (1648–1719), *More Wonders of the Invisible World* (1700), condemning the trials and Mather's part in them, which would provoke a response from Mather, *Some Remarks Upon a Scandalous Book* (1701).

WILLIAM PENN: "An Essay Towards the Present and Future Peace of Europe. . . ." and *Some Fruits of Solitude.* Penn's essay presents a vision of a peacefully united world achieved by applying advanced legal, social, and moral theories. It envisions a United Nations–like parliament of nations and global disarmament. He also publishes *Some Fruits of Solitude,* a collection of maxims and aphorisms that record his mature philosophy of life. It would be followed by *More Fruits of Solitude* (1702).

Nonfiction

INCREASE MATHER: *Cases of Conscience Concerning Evil Spirits.* A study of the Salem witch trials in which Mather questions using spectral evidence to prove possession by Satan.

1694
Nonfiction

WILLIAM PENN: *An Account of W. Penn's Travails in Holland and Germany.* Penn provides a record of his second journey to Holland and Germany accompanied by a group of prominent Quakers. The work illustrates his religious enthusiasm. With several accounts of conversion experience, he records his contacts with wealthy patrons who would later invest in Pennsylvania. Penn

also publishes "Primitive Christianity Revived," one of his most significant essays. It expresses his insistence on individual liberty and the conscience as the reliable guide to moral action.

Sermons and Religious Writing

FRANCIS MAKEMIE (c. 1658–1708): *An answer to George Keith's Libel.* Makemie's *A Catechism* (1691) had attacked the tenets of the Quakers. Here he responds to Quaker George Keith's rebuttal to vindicate his orthodox doctrinal views.

JOSHUA SCOTTOW: *A Narrative of the Planting of the Massachusetts Colony Anno 1628. . . .* Scottow recasts political and social events in the colony's history to form a spiritual narrative about the decline in religious piety and Puritan sense of mission.

1695
Sermons and Religious Writing

WILLIAM PENN: *A Brief Account of the Rise and Progress of the People Called Quakers.* Penn's account is noteworthy both as a religious history and an expression of Penn's passionate advocacy for individual liberty and the reliance on the conscience as the fundamental guide to moral action.

1697
Essays and Philosophy

JAMES BLAIR (1655–1743): *The Present State of Virginia and the College.* The founder and first president of the College of William and Mary issues this report, co-written with Henry Hartwell and Edward Chilton. It would languish in a government file until its publication in 1727. Its sociopolitical approach provides a significant view of developing political attitudes in Virginia during the period.

FRANCIS DANIEL PASTORIUS: *Four Boasting Disputers of This World Briefly Rebuked.* A respected work in which Pastorius offers his reflections on politics and theology.

SAMUEL SEWALL: *Phaenomena quaedam apocalyptica. . . .* The work is Sewall's statement about and apology for his role as a judge of the Salem witch trials. He was the only judge publicly to lament the trials. The work predicts that New England will become the New Jerusalem and will be the subject of John Greenleaf Whittier's poem "The Prophecy of Samuel Sewall."

1698
Diaries, Journals, and Letters

THOMAS BRAY (c. 1658–1730): *A General View of English Colonies in America with Respect to Religion.* One of several accounts of Bray's activities in America in which he makes clear his support for the establishment of the Anglican Church in Maryland and the need for missionaries for the colonies.

Nonfiction

WILLIAM BRADFORD (1663–1752): *The Secretary's Guide; or, Young Man's Companion.* The printer who had introduced printing to the Middle Colonies, had established the first paper mill (1690), and would print the first legislative proceedings in America (1698) and the first American-written drama (1714), publishes his best-known work, a spelling guide that would stand as a standard educational tool for several decades.

FRANCIS DANIEL PASTORIUS: *A New Primmer or Methodical Directions to attain the True Spelling, Reading & Writing of English.* This is believed to be the first textbook used in Pennsylvania schools.

GABRIEL THOMAS (1661–1714): *An Historical and Geographical Account of Pennsylvania and of West-New-Jersey.* Written to promote the settlement of Pennsylvania, this book describes in a favorable light the area and the opportunities it presents. Thomas was a member of the first group of William Penn's Quaker colonists, and his promotional tract is generally regarded as the best of those written about the Pennsylvania colony.

1699
Nonfiction

COTTON MATHER: *Decennium luctuosum.* Mather chronicles Indian affairs from 1688 to 1698, which he presents as mainly a conflict between good and evil, with the Indians depicted as descendants of Satan and the enemies of God.

Sermons and Religious Writing

FRANCIS MAKEMIE: *Truth in a True Light.* Makemie defends Presbyterianism against charges that it has deviated too far from the Westminster Confession, the tenets of Presbyterian faith established in 1646.

1700
Diaries, Journals, and Letters

THOMAS BRAY: *A Memorial Representing the State of Religion on the Continent of North America.* This work is based on Bray's letters circulated among the Anglican ministry in America. His writing, covering subjects ranging from church dogma to opposition to the Catholic Church, would have a significant impact on religion in the English colonies in North America. *The Acts of Dr.*

Bray's Visitation at Annapolis also appears, a work based on his circular letters to the Anglican clergy in Maryland, seeking to draw attention to the plight of Africans and Native Americans and influence the founding of Georgia.

Nonfiction

ROBERT CALEF (1648–1719): *More Wonders of the Invisible World.* A Boston dissenter's satiric attack on the colony's clergy, particularly Cotton Mather, for their role in the Salem witchcraft trials of 1692. Mather would respond in *Some Few Remarks upon a Scandalous Book* (1701), and Increase Mather is said to have ordered the book burned in Harvard Yard.

SAMUEL SEWALL: *The Selling of Joseph.* Sewall's anti-slavery tract, one of the earliest published in the colonies, condemns slavery based on the doctrine that both blacks and whites descended from Adam and Eve.

Sermons and Religious Writing

THOMAS BRAY: "The Necessity of an Early Religion." Bray's most famous sermon, the first to be published in America in the eighteenth century, expresses his faith in rationality and advocates building schools and libraries to develop the intellect of the young.

SOLOMON STODDARD (1643–1729): *The Doctrine of Instituted Churches Explained and Proved from the Word of God.* Written to advocate a national church governed by a synod, this work is an important contribution to the theological and ecclesiastical history of New England.

1701
Sermons and Religious Writing

COTTON MATHER: *Some Few Remarks Upon A Scandalous Book, against the Government and Ministry of New-England . . . by One Robert Calef.* Mather responds to Calef's charge in *More Wonders of the Invisible World* (1700) that Mather was responsible for the witchcraft trials in Salem.

1702
Nonfiction

JOHN HALE (1636–1700): *A Modest Enquiry into the Nature of Witchcraft.* One of the prosecutors in the witchcraft trials of the 1690s reassesses the notion of witchcraft after his own wife is charged with sorcery. He now finds natural explanations for what in 1692 was accepted as proof for possession. The work is important for the light it sheds on the witchcraft hysteria of the 1690s.

BIRTHS AND DEATHS, 1700–1749

Births

1700 David French (d. 1742), poet
1701 James Sterling (d. 1763), poet
1702 Isaac Greenwood (d. 1745), scholar and textbook writer
1703 Jonathan Edwards (d. 1758), clergyman, philosopher, and author
1704 John Adams (d. 1740), clergyman and poet
William Dawson (d. 1752), poet
1705 Francis Alison (d. 1779), educator and scholar
Charles Chauncy (d. 1787), clergyman and author
1706 Benjamin Franklin (d. 1790), printer, writer, inventor, and public official
Joseph Green (d. 1780), merchant and poet
1707 Mather Byles (d. 1788), clergyman and poet
1708 John Seccomb (d. 1792), clergyman and poet
1709 James Adair (d. c. 1783), Indian trader and writer
1710 Richard Bland (d. 1776), colonial statesman and author
Jonathan Carver (d. 1780), travel writer
1711 Thomas Hutchinson (d. 1780), writer and colonial official
1713 Anthony Benezet (d. 1784), author and teacher
1715 Samuel Finley (d. 1766), clergyman and author
1718 David Brainerd (d. 1747), missionary and author
1719 Joseph Bellamy (d. 1790), clergyman and author
1720 Charlotte Ramsay Lennox (d. 1804), novelist and playwright
Jonathan Mayhew (d. 1766), clergyman and author
John Woolman (d. 1772), clergyman and author
1721 Samuel Hopkins (d. 1803), writer and minister
1722 Samuel Adams (d. 1803), patriot and writer
Lemuel Briant (d. 1754), clergyman and author
Jacob Green (d. 1790), clergyman and author
1723 Samuel Davies (d. 1761), clergyman, author, and poet
William Livingston (d. 1790), public official, poet, and writer
1724 Isaac Backus (d. 1806), clergyman and author
1727 William Smith (d. 1803), educator, theologian, poet, and historian
Ezra Stiles (d. 1795), clergyman and diarist
1728 Jonathan Sewall (d. 1796), playwright
Mercy Otis Warren (d. 1814), playwright, poet, and historian
1729 Samuel Seabury (d. 1796), clergyman and essayist
1731 Robert Rogers (d. 1795), soldier, writer, and playwright
1732 John Dickinson (d. 1808), colonial statesman and author
1735 John Adams (d. 1826), political figure and writer
1736 Thomas Godfrey (d. 1763), poet and playwright
1737 Francis Hopkinson (d. 1791), poet, essayist, musician, and judge
Jonathan Odell (d. 1818), poet and physician
Thomas Paine (d. 1809), author and revolutionary agitator
1738 Ethan Allen (d. 1789), patriot and writer
1739 William Bartram (d. 1823), naturalist and author
1742 Nathaniel Evans (d. 1767), clergyman and poet
1743 Thomas Jefferson (d. 1826), president of the United States, scientist, diplomat, and author

1744 Abigail Adams (d. 1818), correspondent, wife of President John Adams
Jeremy Belknap (d. 1798), clergyman and historian
Enos Hitchcock (d. 1803), novelist
1745 John Jay (d. 1829), public official and contributor to the *Federalist Papers*
1748 Hugh Henry Brackenridge (d. 1816), novelist, poet, and judge

Deaths

1701 William Stoughton (b. 1631), clergyman and presiding judge of Salem witchcraft trials
1705 Michael Wigglesworth (b. 1631), clergyman and poet
1707 Samuel Torrey (b. 1632), clergyman and author
Samuel Willard (b. 1640), clergyman and writer
1708 Ezekiel Cheever (b. 1612), educator and textbook author
John Higginson (b. 1616), clergyman and author
1714 Benjamin Tompson (b. 1642), poet
1717 William Brattle (b. 1662), clergyman and author
1718 William Penn (b. 1644), religious leader and founder of Pennsylvania; author
1719 Robert Calef (b. 1648), merchant and author
1721 John Rogers (b. 1648), clergyman and author
1722 Robert Beverley (b. 1673), colonial official and historian
1723 Increase Mather (b. 1639), religious leader and writer
1725 Thomas Walker (b. 1696), clergyman and poet
1726 Samuel Penhallow (b. 1665), historian
1727 Sarah Kemble Knight (b. 1666), teacher and author
1728 Cotton Mather (b. 1663), clergyman and writer
1729 Edward Taylor (b. 1642), minister and poet
Solomon Stoddard (b. 1643), clergyman and author
John Williams (b. 1664), Congregational clergyman and author
1730 Thomas Bray (b. 1656), Anglican clergyman and author
Samuel Sewall (b. 1652), merchant, colonial magistrate, and author
1732 Ebenezer Cook (b. c. 1671), poet
1733 John Dunton (b. 1659), author and bookseller
Richard Lewis (b. c. 1699), poet
1734 Richard Lewis (b. c. 1700), poet and author
1737 Elizabeth Hanson (b. 1684), writer
1739 Daniel Coxe (b. 1673), landowner, politician, and writer
Jeremiah Dummer (b. 1681), colonial agent and author
Samuel Keimer (b. 1688), printer and writer
1740 John Adams (b. 1704), clergyman and poet
1741 Thomas Chalkley (b. 1675), clergyman and writer
1742 David French (b. 1700), poet
1743 James Blair (b. 1655), clergyman and author
1744 William Byrd (b. 1674), colonial official and author
1745 Isaac Greenwood (b. 1702), scholar and textbook writer
1746 John Peter Zenger (b. 1797), printer and journalist
1747 Benjamin Colman (b. 1673), clergyman and poet
David Brainerd (b. 1718), missionary and author
1749 Mark Catesby (b. 1683), naturalist author

POPULAR BOOKS, 1701–1750*

Horace Lyricae by Isaac Watts (First English Printing, 1706; First American Printing, 1741)

The Redeemed Captive Returned to Zion by John Williams (First American Printing, 1707)

Iliad Translated by Alexander Pope (First English Printing, 1715; First American Printing, 1795)

Divine Songs for Children by Isaac Watts (First English Printing, 1715; First American Printing, 1719)

Robinson Crusoe by Daniel Defoe (First English Printing, 1719; First American Printing, 1775)

Odyssey Translated by Alexander Pope (First English Printing, 1725; First American Printing, 1813)

Gulliver's Travels by Jonathan Swift (First English Printing, 1726; First American Printing, 1793)

Poor Richard's Almanack by Benjamin Franklin (First American Printing, 1732)

Poor Richard Improved by Benjamin Franklin (First American Printing, 1748)

Pamela by Samuel Richardson (First English Printing, 1740; First American Printing, 1744)

Joseph Andrews by Henry Fielding (First English Printing, 1742; First American Printing, 1786)

The Grave by Robert Blair (First English Printing, 1743; First American Printing, 1753)

Clarissa Harlowe by Samuel Richardson (First English Printing, 1747; First American Printing, 1786)

Tom Jones by Henry Fielding (First English Printing, 1749; First American Printing, 1786)

* The books listed here were the most widely read books in this time period. Most were printed outside of the colonies and imported by colonists from their native country.

Poetry, Fiction, and Drama

NICHOLAS NOYES (1647–1717): "A Prefatory Poem." The preface for Mather's *Magnalia* and the best-known work by one of the prosecuting judges of the Salem witchcraft trials.

Sermons and Religious Writing

COTTON MATHER: *Magnalia Christi Americana.* Mather's most ambitious work, this history of the New England church aspires to the comprehensiveness of a Puritan epic, explaining theological points and justifying church actions. It incorporates many of Mather's previous religious writings and includes biographical portraits of governors and clergy, as well as a history of Harvard College and an account of several of its graduates.

INCREASE MATHER: "Ichabod. Or . . . the Glory of the Lord, is Departing from New-England." The greatest of Mather's sermons, and one of the greatest Puritan jeremiads, indicts the backsliding of current Puritans, including

the clergy: "Look unto the Pulpits, and see if there is such a Glory there, as once there was? . . . The Glory is Gone!"

1703
Nonfiction

LOUIS-ARMAND, BARON DE LAHONTAN (1666–c. 1713): *Nouveaux voyages.* The French explorer's account of his journeys and encounters with the Indians is translated into English, with an added series of "Dialogues" with a Huron chief. The volume provides important information on Indian customs and contributes to the concept of the noble savage that would influence writers such as Chateaubriand and Jean Jacques Rousseau.

Sermons and Religious Writing

COTTON MATHER: *Meat Out of the Eater or, Funeral Discourses Occasioned By the Death of Several Relatives.* This is a series of five sermons preached on the death of Mather's wife and his children. The title refers to the biblical Samson's riddle: "Out of the eater came forth meat, And out the strong came forth sweetness."

SOLOMON STODDARD: "God's Fervor in the Death of Usefull Men." Stoddard's later sermons, such as this one, show his increasingly pessimistic views on the materialism and immorality of the period, a theme best expressed in "The Danger of Speedy Degeneracy" (1705), which tells of his doubts about the goals of recent Puritan generations.

1704
Diaries, Journals, and Letters

SARAH KEMBLE KNIGHT (1666–1727): *The Journals of Madam Knight.* A record of Knight's trip by horseback from Boston to New York. The author's journal is considered a classic of early American literature, one of the first to employ dialect and humorously outrageous similes.

Publications and Events

The *Boston News-Letter.* The first printed version of a formerly handwritten newsletter sent to New England governors by the Boston postmaster is published. It offers local information and foreign news reprinted from English papers. It would continue until 1776 as a mouthpiece for the governor and the Loyalists.

1705
Diaries, Journals, and Letters

INCREASE MATHER: "A Letter About The Present State Of Christianity, Among the Christianized Indians of

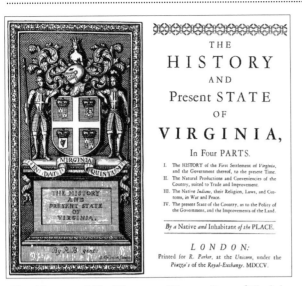

The title page of *The History and Present State of Virginia*

New-England." A letter to London, explaining efforts to promote piety and religion among the Indians.

Nonfiction

ROBERT BEVERLEY (c. 1673–1722): *The History and Present State of Virginia*. The Virginia planter and politician supplies a history of the colony and description of the region and its Indian population. It is a response to a negative account written by British historian John Oldmixon. Later, literary historian Jay Hubbell would call it "a minor but genuine American classic." An enlarged edition would appear in 1722.

JOHN DUNTON (1659–1733): *Life and Errors of John Dunton*. The English bookseller, who came to Boston in 1686 and traveled to neighboring towns selling his wares, describes his visit, providing an authentic portrait of the period and its customs.

FRANCIS MAKEMIE: *A Plain and Friendly Perswasive to the Inhabitants of Virginia and Maryland for Promoting Towns an Cohabitation*. The only one of Makemie's published works dealing entirely with secular matters points out the advantages of forming towns for commerce, education, and worship. It is addressed to the new governor of Virginia, Edward Nott, and contains valuable details on the current state of the region.

1706
Poetry, Fiction, and Drama

NICHOLAS NOYES: "On Cotton Mather's Endeavors Toward the Christian Education of Negro Slaves." Noyes's verse praising Mather's attempt to educate and convert slaves is an important expression of Puritan views on racial matters.

Sermons and Religious Writing

COTTON MATHER: *The Negro Christianized*. Although Mather kept slaves and believed that Christian law allowed slavery, he argues here for the humane treatment of slaves, stating that they are "Men, and not Beasts, that you have bought." He also argues against the notion that slaves should not be converted because it is unlawful for Christians to own other Christians.

1707
Essays and Philosophy

FRANCIS MAKEMIE: *A Narrative of a New and Unusual American Imprisonment*. The clergyman relates his experiences of being arrested for preaching without a license in New York in this pamphlet, which helped end this restriction.

COTTON MATHER: *A Memorial of the Present Deplorable State of New-England*. Published anonymously, Mather's pamphlet lists charges against Governor Dudley and calls for his dismissal. Mather would continue his attack in 1708 in *The Deplorable State of New-England*.

JOHN WILLIAMS (1664–1729): *The Redeemed Captive Returning to Zion*. Williams's account of his experiences, as pastor of the Congregational church in Deerfield, Massachusetts, of being taken captive by the Mohawk Indians and brought to Canada. Written with Cotton Mather, the account treats Williams's two-year captivity and his resistance to the French Jesuits' attempts to convert him.

Poetry, Fiction, and Drama

BENJAMIN COLMAN (1673–1747): "A Poem on Elijah's Translation, occasioned by the death of Rev. Samuel Willard." Delivered as a funeral sermon, this is the longest of Colman's poetic efforts.

Sermons and Religious Writing

BENJAMIN COLMAN: "A Practical Discourse on the Parable of the Ten Virgins." Colman's most renowned sermon is a review of Calvinist teachings, employing the parable of the virgins to illustrate the essential doctrines of preparation, repentance, conversion, election, judgment, and redemption. Colman also publishes the sermon "The Government and Improvement of Mirth," on the benefits of religious joy.

COTTON MATHER: *Manly Christianity: A Brief Essay on the Signs of Growth and Strength in the most Lovely*

Christianity. Issued anonymously, the work was later published under Mather's name. It was intended to impart "Things which are of great Importance to be inculcated on our Christians."

1708
Nonfiction

JOHN OLDMIXON (1673–1742): *British Empire in America*. The English historian supplies the first study of the British settlements on the American coast as a unified political entity.

Poetry, Fiction, and Drama

EBENEZER COOK (fl. 1708): "The Sot-Weed Factor." The Maryland poet's most famous work is a satirical poem treating the experiences of an agent of a British tobacco merchant in Maryland. Its range (and tone) is indicated by its subtitle: "The Laws, Government, Courts, and Constitution of the Country; and also the Buildings, Feasts, Frolics, Entertainments, and Drunken Humours of the Inhabitants of that Part of America."

Sermons and Religious Writing

COTTON MATHER: *The Way of Truth, Laid out....* Mather's catechism for children is written in a style that is "rendered now a little more easy and proper for children of the smallest capacity."

SOLOMON STODDARD: "The Inexcusableness of Neglecting the Worship of God: Under a Pretence of Being in an Unconverted Condition." In this sermon Stoddard forcefully opposes excesses in daily life.

1709
Nonfiction

JOHN LAWSON (?–1711): *A New Voyage to Carolina*. The English explorer who charted the unexplored regions of the Carolinas and Georgia provides this record of his discoveries, reprinted as *The History of Carolina* (1714). One of the best of the early travel writers, Lawson is noteworthy for his sympathetic attitude toward the Indians.

Sermons and Religious Writing

EXPERIENCE MAYHEW (1673–1758): *Massachusee Psalter*. Mayhew, a Massachusetts missionary to the Martha's Vineyard Indians, translates the Psalms and the Gospel of John into the Massachusett language in a work that is second only to John Eliot's Indian Bible as the most significant Indian-language translation in colonial New England.

GRINDALL RAWSON (1659–1715): "The Necessity of a Speedy and Thorough Reformation." Rawson's sermon contains a critique of the Puritan jeremiad, an established form whereby a preacher makes a sustained complaint about the times and the failure of the congregation to live up to its spiritual ideals.

SOLOMON STODDARD: "An Appeal to the Learned." Stoddard's sermon advocates a more liberal position on church membership, calling for only a profession of faith and not the personal experience of grace insisted upon by Puritan clergymen such as Increase Mather.

1710
Essays and Philosophy

COTTON MATHER: *Bonifacius*. This handbook on moral behavior, commonly known as *Essays To Do Good*, is one of Mather's most popular works. Benjamin Franklin would claim it directed his conduct through life and helped make him a useful citizen of the world; he would imitate the work in his *Dogood Papers*.

Sermons and Religious Writing

COTTON MATHER: *Man Eating the Food of Angels: The Gospel of the Manna to be Gathered in the Morning*. The work demonstrates Mather's use of anecdotes to identify ideals and examples for young children to imitate.

JOHN WISE (1652–1725): *The Churches Quarrel Espoused*. The Congregational minister who would be tried, condemned, and imprisoned for protests against arbitrary taxation produces a religious pamphlet responding to arguments laid out by Increase and Cotton Mather in 1705, which attempt to bolster orthodoxy by establishing a council to govern ministerial appointments and arbitrate disputes of church discipline. Wise claims that these proposals are authoritarian and defends the power of each congregation to govern itself. Because of its democratic theme, it would be republished in 1772 and again before the Civil War.

1712
Diaries, Journals, and Letters

WILLIAM BYRD (1674–1744): *The Secret Diary*. The Virginia planter and colonial government official completes his first diary, covering the years 1709 to 1712 and detailing day-to-day activities among the Virginia planter class. Topics range from prayers to diet, family affairs, exercise, and even sexual intercourse.

COTTON MATHER: *Curiosa Americana*. Mather collects his scientific letters to the Royal Society reporting on "all

William Byrd

New and Rare Occurences of Nature, in these parts of the World."

Poetry, Fiction, and Drama

ANTHONY ASTON (c. 1682–c. 1753): *Pastora*. Originally published in 1709 as *The Coy Shepherdess*, this play is a pastoral composed in rhyming couplets about the comical situations of three groups of lovers. The play—only twenty pages long—is one of the author's most important works, displaying his biting humor and optimistic view of life. Aston is sometimes referred to as the "first professional actor in America," and his impoverished life of travel anticipates the lot of itinerant performers of the 1700s.

Sermons and Religious Writing

SAMUEL CHEEVER (1639–1724): "Gods Sovereign Government." An election sermon delivered with Governor Joseph Dudley in attendance. Cheever insists on God's preeminence over government leaders, which is a prominent theme in election sermons of the day as government

officials gradually distance themselves from church influence.

1713
Poetry, Fiction, and Drama

RICHARD STEERE: *The Daniel Catcher*. Steere's most important poetic work includes "Earth Felicities," a poem in blank verse, unusual at the time, and "Caelestial Embassy," a nativity poem that argues against Puritan rejection of Christmas as a pagan practice of the Catholic Church.

Sermons and Religious Writing

JOSEPH MORGAN (1671–c. 1745): *The Portsmouth Disputation Examined*. Morgan, a Connecticut-born clergyman, refutes Quaker objections to Calvinism, contending that a rational Christian must accept the doctrines of election, infant baptism, and professional clergy.

SOLOMON STODDARD: *The Efficacy of Fear of Hell to Restrain Men from Sin*. This pamphlet from one of Massachusetts' most influential clergymen lays out his belief that ministers should frighten their listeners with warnings of damnation to bring about moral order amongst their flock. He would repeat the theme in *A Guide to Christ* (1714).

1714
Poetry, Fiction, and Drama

ROBERT HUNTER (?–1734): *Androboros*. The first printed American play is an unproduced political satire written by Hunter while he is the governor of New York. It attacks the colonial administration and military leader Francis Nicholson (1655–1728), who is represented by the title character, a braggart who indulges in vituperations against the French rather than taking practical action.

Sermons and Religious Writing

JOHN BARNARD (1681–1770): "The Hazard and the Unprofitableness of Losing a Soul for the Sake of Gaining the World." A sermon reminding the political leaders of Massachusetts that, while government is ordained by God, only a government founded on reason and understanding is a godly government. Barnard preaches this message on the day of the governor's election, thus putting forth his own political message.

1715
Essays and Philosophy

JOHN HEPBURN (fl. 1715–c. 1745): *The American Defence of the Christian Golden Rule*. This early antislavery tract presents a debate between a slaveholder and a "True Christian." The slaveholder claims that slavery brings religion to the heathens, while his counterpart refutes this and all the slaveholder's other claims.

Sermons and Religious Writing

JOSEPH MORGAN: *The History of the Kingdom of Basaruah.* Morgan's major literary contribution is this allegory presenting the Calvinist view of humanity's fall and redemption from the perspective of a covenant nation, unlike the emphasis on the individual in John Bunyan's (1628–1688) *Pilgrim's Progress.*

THOMAS SHEPARD (1648–1720): "God's Conduct of His Church Through the Wilderness." Shepard's most important sermon marks a shift in the traditional jeremiad, from an emphasis on damnation to consolation.

1716
Nonfiction

THOMAS CHURCH (1673–1748): *Entertaining Passages Relating to King Philip's War....* Written from the memoirs and memory of Church's father, Benjamin Church (1639–1718), this lively account retells the stories and personal impressions of various Indian leaders from the most successful Indian fighter of his time. A bestseller, the book attracts a varied audience of colonial Americans.

Sermons and Religious Writing

BENJAMIN WADSWORTH (1670–1737): "Rulers Feeding, and Guiding Their People, with Integrity and Skilfulness." The future eighth president of Harvard delivers this sermon before the Great and General Court of the Massachusetts Bay colony to inspire members of government to serve both church and state.

1717
Essays and Philosophy

JOHN WISE: *A Vindication of the Government of New-England Churches.* Wise continues the theme of his earlier writings on the resistance to authoritarianism in regulating the churches. Wise draws comparisons between civil governments — which prosper under democratic rule — and churches — which prosper under independent self-governance. Reissued in 1772, it is widely noted as a forerunner to writings that will sanction revolution and independence.

Sermons and Religious Writing

JOSEPH SEWALL (1688–1769): "The Character and Blessedness of the Upright." After a Boston youth is killed in a duel, Sewall, a pastor of Boston's Old South Church, which became known as "Dr. Sewall's Meeting House," uses the occasion to catalog the sins to be avoided by Boston's impetuous youth.

1718
Poetry, Fiction, and Drama

DAVID FRENCH (1700–1742): *Ovid's Elegies and Anacreon's Odes.* The Delaware lawyer and governmental official's translations, among the earliest undertaken in the Middle Colonies, are preserved by John Parke (1754–1789) in his volume entitled *The Lyric Works of Horace* (1786). They represent some of the best colonial verse translation.

COTTON MATHER: *Psalterium Americanum: The Book of Psalms in a Translation Exactly Conformed unto the Original, but All in Blank Verse.* Mather's major poetic contribution is this blank-verse translation with his analysis of poetry that demonstrates a considerable understanding of contemporary poetics.

Sermons and Religious Writing

THOMAS FOXCROFT (1697–1769): "A Practical Discourse Relating to the Gospel Ministry." Foxcroft's ordination sermon claims to justify the use of shocking language and rhetoric to "breathe heavenly fire to melt and enliven ... dead affections." It demonstrates the style that would come to characterize this popular preacher.

SAMUEL KEIMER (1688–1739): *A Brand Pluck'd from the Burning.* The first of the religious writings by the Philadelphia printer who first employed Benjamin Franklin is followed by *A Search After Religion*, chronicling Keimer's involvement with various religious sects.

1719
Publications and Events

Songs for the Nursery; or, Mother Goose's Melodies. This collection of nursery rhymes was at one time believed to have been published in this year in Boston by Thomas Fleet, based on the verses of Fleet's mother-in-law, Mrs. Elizabeth Goose or Vergoose. However, many scholars now believe that it was first published in London in 1760 by an unknown author and drawn from English and French sources.

The *American Weekly Mercury.* The first newspaper of the Middle Colonies is launched in Philadelphia by Andrew Bradford (1686–1742). It would publish six of Franklin's "Busy-Body Papers" in 1729 and continue publication until 1746.

A reproduction of the front page from the
March 7, 1719, edition of the *Boston Gazette*

The *Boston Gazette*. The second newspaper in Boston is launched by William Brooker (fl. 1715–1720) and printed by Benjamin Franklin's older half-brother, James Franklin (1697–1735). The paper would become the official organ of the government and continue until 1741.

Sermons and Religious Writing

SOLOMON STODDARD: *A Treatise Concerning the Nature of Saving Conversion*. Stoddard displays the evangelical zeal and liberalization of Puritanism that would influence the young ministers of the Connecticut Valley and culminate in the religious revivals of 1735 and 1740.

1720
Nonfiction

DANIEL NEAL (1678–1743): *History of New England . . . to . . . 1700*. The English clergyman and historian issues

this two-volume study that is strongly critical of the Mathers and their part in the witchcraft trials.

Poetry, Fiction, and Drama

JONATHAN BURT (c. 1632–1715): *A Lamentation Occasion'd by the Great Sickness & Lamented Deaths of Divers Eminent Persons in Springfield*. This poem, composed in hymnal meter, is the only known work by Burt. A jeremiad, it recalls the author's grief over the deaths of certain leading members of Springfield society. The poem interprets the unknown disease that killed many in 1712 as evidence of God's displeasure, but rather than harangue his readers for their sins, he chooses to explore the benefits and virtues of righteous living.

Sermons and Religious Writing

JOHN CHECKLEY (1680–1754): *Choice Dialogues*. Along with other contemporaries, Checkley sets the stage for Anglican and Puritan debates for the next fifty years. In *Choice Dialogues*, he speaks out against predestination, calling it a figment of an overactive Puritan imagination.

JOHN ROGERS (1648–1721): *The Book of Revelation of Jesus Christ*. The Connecticut founder of the Rogerene sect, opposed to formal clergy, prayers, church meetings, and any connection between church and state, defends his unorthodox beliefs in his most important work.

THOMAS WALTER (1696–1725): *A Choice Dialogue Between John Faustus, a Conjurer, and Jack Terry, His Friend*. Walter, a Massachusetts Congregational minister, publishes this attack on clergymen who uphold radical views of theology. He uses materials provided by his better-known uncle, Cotton Mather.

1721
Diaries, Journals, and Letters

WILLIAM BYRD: *The Secret Diary*. Byrd's second diary chronicles the years 1717 to 1721, detailing his daily rounds of business, social gatherings, and chocolate drinking in addition to his evenings of sex with a variety of women.

Essays and Philosophy

WILLIAM BYRD: *A Discourse Concerning Plague, With Some Preservatives Against It*. This pamphlet, published anonymously, praises the supposed medicinal qualities of tobacco. Later it would be attributed to the famous diarist Byrd, making it the only piece of his extensive writings to be published during his lifetime.

JEREMIAH DUMMER (1681–1739): *Defence of the New England Charters*. Dummer supplies a legal response to proposals that colonial charters be revoked and the colonies be governed by fiat from England. Dummer's rationale for colonial autonomy would influence future leaders of the Revolution.

COTTON MATHER: *The Christian Philosopher*. Mather's most important scientific work surveys the fields of astronomy, physics, meteorology, geology, geography, and biology, attempting to reconcile scriptural and natural truths. He claims that all that is wondrous and beautiful is created by God and that science is able to locate the deeper meaning in these things.

INCREASE MATHER: *Several Reasons Proving that Inoculating . . . the Small Pox Is a Lawful Practice*. Mather weighs in on the inoculation controversy, offering both scientific and religious justification for the practice.

SAMUEL SEWALL: *A Memorial Relating to the Kennebeck Indians*. Sewall argues on behalf of humane treatment of the Indians.

JOHN WILLIAMS: *Several Arguments, Proving, that Inoculating the Small Pox is not Contained in the Law of Physick, Either Natural or Divine, and Therefore Unlawful*. In this essay the minister and author of the well-known *The Redeemed Captive Returning to Zion* (1707) contributes to the debate concerning smallpox inoculation, which he opposes on the grounds that the process goes against both what is natural and divine.

JOHN WISE: *A Word of Comfort to a Melancholy Country*. Wise's last public writing is a pamphlet arguing for the establishment of Massachusetts land banks to issue paper currency. Wise fears that a reliance on coin currency will retard economic development.

Nonfiction

ZABDIEL BOYLSTON (1679–1766): *Some Account of What Is Said of Inoculation or Transplanting the Small Pox*. Responding to Boston's smallpox epidemic, Boylston, encouraged by Cotton Mather (who, it is believed, collaborated on this account), experiments on his son and slaves in inoculating them against the disease. Boylston would receive international recognition for this pioneering work. Many at the time viewed the procedure as deadly and a violation of God's will, and both Boylston and Mather were accused of murder and threatened. Boylston's more thorough treatise, *An Historical Account of the Smallpox Inoculated in New England*, would appear in 1726.

THOMAS WALTER: *The Grounds and Rules of Musick Explained; or, an Introduction to the Art of Singing by Note*. In the first practical American music instruction book, Walter attempts to correct the "horrid medley of confused and disorderly sound" in New England churches

by introducing the concept of singing based on uniform notes. The first book employing bar lines, it is printed by James Franklin while his brother Benjamin serves as apprentice.

Publications and Events

The Hell-fire Club (1721–1744): This Boston literary circle is formed; its founding members include Benjamin Franklin and William Douglass. Often meeting in James Franklin's office at the *New England Courant*, the group contributed writings to the publication frequently. The club received its name from the Mathers, drawing a parallel between them and a notorious London organization of the same name. The Hell-fire Club brought a coffee-house environment to Boston and opposed reactionary thought.

The *New England Courant*. The first edition of the third Boston newspaper is published by the printer James Franklin (the older half-brother of Benjamin Franklin) on August 7. Prior to the *Courant*, newspapers had provided only a few sentences of editorial commentary at the bottom of an article. Franklin made a conscious decision to break away from this practice by featuring longer editorials. In 1723, Benjamin would take over as publisher of the *Courant*, which continued until 1726.

1722
Essays and Philosophy

BENJAMIN FRANKLIN (1706–1790): *The Dogood Papers*. Franklin's first publication is a series of articles published in his brother James's newspaper, the *New England Courant*. He attacks the Puritan establishment in general and Cotton Mather in particular, commenting on topics such as hoop petticoats, drunkenness, and freedom of thought. Using the pseudonym "Silence Dogood," Franklin assumes the identity of a levelheaded goodwife, a break from James Franklin's editorial policy of never permitting a woman to stand as the voice of reason.

SOLOMON STODDARD: *An Answer to Some Cases of Conscience Respecting the Country*. The Congregational clergyman of Northampton, Massachusetts, Stoddard mounts an attack on contemporary customs, including immorality, wig wearing, lavish dress, and drunkenness.

Nonfiction

DANIEL COXE (1673–1739): *A Description of the English Province of Carolana, by the Spaniards called Florida, and by the French La Louisiane. . . .* The preface of this significant book suggests that the colonies unify under a single government that includes representatives from each colony. It is probably the earliest record of this idea.

Intending the book to serve as a navigational guide, with travel and military movements in mind, Coxe also discusses the dangers of French settlements to the future of Britain's North American colonies.

COTTON MATHER: *The Angel of Bethesda, Visiting the Invalids of a Miserable World.* Demonstrating Mather's sustained interest in science, this work discusses common illnesses and possible cures and is regarded as the first significant treatise on colonial medicine. Mather also publishes *An Account . . . of the Inoculating the Small-Pox,* defending the practice.

Sermons and Religious Writing

JAMES BLAIR: *Our Savior's Divine Sermon on the Mount.* A five-volume collection of sermons that Blair, the founder of the College of William and Mary in Virginia, had preached from 1707 to 1721. Blair was instrumental in reviving and reforming the Anglican Church in Virginia.

JUDAH MONIS (1683–1764): *The Truth, The Whole Truth,* and *Nothing But the Truth.* Monis publishes these three tracts as a defense of New England Congregationalism based on Jewish writings. The tracts are unique in their use of the Talmud, the writings of Maimonides, and the works of cabalistic writers to justify Puritan theology.

1723
Diaries, Journals, and Letters

SAMUEL CHECKLEY (1696–1769): *The Diary of the Rev. Samuel Checkley.* Spanning the years 1723 through 1768, this diary recounts the life and struggles of a more liberal New England divine. Much like his sermons, it displays the minister's fervor as the moral conscience of his community, especially promoting the idea of a unified family living within an orderly and industrious society.

Poetry, Fiction, and Drama

SAMUEL KEIMER: *Elegy on the Much Lamented Death of . . . Aquila Rose.* The Philadelphia printer's verse memorial is chiefly memorable for having been set in type by Benjamin Franklin, who was employed by Keimer when he first arrived in the city.

EDWARD TAYLOR: "A Funerall Teare . . ." Taylor composes an elegy on Increase Mather, who is represented as a champion of Puritan orthodoxy against numerous challenges.

Publications and Events

The *New England Courant.* Ann Smith Franklin (1696–1793) takes over the role of assistant printer and shopkeeper for her husband's publication after James Franklin

has a falling out with his brother Benjamin Franklin, who leaves Boston for Philadelphia. Ann thus becomes one of the first women printers in the colonies.

Sermons and Religious Writing

BENJAMIN COLMAN: "God Deals with Us as Rational Creatures." Colman's sermon comes to the defense of Dr. Zabdiel Boylston in the controversy over smallpox inoculation and demonstrates the growing trend to blend Puritan and Enlightenment thought.

1724
Diaries, Journals, and Letters

COTTON MATHER: *Diary of Cotton Mather, 1681–1724.* Although he would remain an active writer until his death, Mather ceases to keep a thorough diary after 1724. The complete diary, not published until 1911, is perhaps Mather's most important literary contribution, detailing crucial historical events colored with his introspection and personal insights.

Nonfiction

HUGH JONES (c. 1670–1760): *An Accidence to the English Tongue.* The Virginia minister and mathematician produces the first English grammar printed in America. He also writes *The Present State of Virginia,* a valuable account of contemporary life in the colony.

COTTON MATHER: *Parentator.* Mather supplies the first biography of his famed Puritan father, Increase Mather.

Sermons and Religious Writing

THOMAS SYMMES: *Utile Dulci. Or, A Joco-Serious Dialogue, Concerning Regular Singing.* A debate between a minister and a parishioner over new-style hymn singing by regulated notes and the older chanted response by congregants based on whatever manner they preferred. The minister favors the new style, but the parishioner is reluctant to change. Symmes also publishes *The People's Interest,* a scathing indictment of the parsimony of New Englanders toward their pastors. In it, Symmes compares the standard of living of the time for ministers, lawyers, and physicians.

1725
Essays and Philosophy

BENJAMIN FRANKLIN: *A Dissertation on Liberty and Necessity, Pleasure and Pain.* Written while abroad in London and published anonymously, Franklin's first pamphlet questions the existence of God. This satirical work amounts to an attack on contemporary religion in the English-speaking world. Franklin would quickly regret the work and attempted to destroy the one hundred copies printed. Some hold that the young Franklin was merely showing off his intellectual prowess in the treatise, doing nothing more than playing devil's advocate.

Nonfiction

PAUL DUDLEY (1675–1751): "On the Natural History of Whales." In what is considered among the best nature reporting of the colonial era, Dudley, the Massachusetts naturalist, elected as a fellow of the Royal Society of London in 1721, supplies his observations on the great mammals.

Poetry, Fiction, and Drama

PETER FOLGER: "A Looking-Glass for the Times." Praised by Benjamin Franklin, among others, the rough ballad stanzas of Folger's work deliver a plea for religious freedom. Written in 1676, the poem's call for toleration represents a hallmark of seventeenth-century New England dissent. Its delayed publication demonstrates the radical nature of Folger's poetry and ideas.

EDWARD TAYLOR: *Preparatory Meditations.* Taylor concludes his private spiritual verse diary, which he had started in 1682. Containing over two hundred poems composed in preparation for the administering of communion, many believe it to be his most powerful work.

ROGER WOLCOTT (1679–1767): *Poetical Meditations.* A collection of poetry that notably includes "A Brief Account of the Agency of the Honorable John Winthrop," about Winthrop's struggle to gain the Connecticut charter. It combines elements of the New England elegies and anticipates the epic qualities of the Connecticut Wits, an informal group of Yale students and rectors who would come to prominence in the late eighteenth century.

Publications and Events

An Astronomical Diary, or An Almanack. Nathaniel Ames (1708–1764) begins his series three years before James Franklin's *Rhode Island Almanack* and eight years before Benjamin Franklin's *Poor Richard's Almanack. An Astronomical Diary* sold sixty thousand copies a year and was a valuable resource for contemporary humor, verse, and a variety of issues. Ames would continue to publish this work annually until his death in 1764.

The *New York Gazette.* Edited and published by William Bradford, the *New York Gazette* is the first newspaper to be published in New York City. It would chronicle current events until 1744.

1726
Diaries, Journals, and Letters

BENJAMIN FRANKLIN: *Journal of a Voyage from London to Philadelphia.* Franklin describes his Atlantic crossing, a fascinating record of transatlantic travel and Franklin's interests.

Nonfiction

ZABDIEL BOYLSTON: *An Historical Account of the Smallpox Inoculated in New England.* Boylston details his experiments with smallpox inoculation in Boston, in which only 6 of his 244 patients die of the disease. This is a remarkable figure compared with the 844 out of 5,757 Bostonians who died of smallpox naturally during the same epidemic. One of the first of its kind written by an American physician, Boylston's well-documented work is received favorably by prestigious British societies and is responsible for validating inoculation to officials in several other colonies and countries. It also pioneers the use of medical statistics.

ISAAC GREENWOOD (1702–1745): *An Experimental Course on Mechanical Philosophy.* Greenwood, a principal participant in the 1721 Boston smallpox controversy, is responsible for the first printed coursebook in popular science published in America. On October 26, he delivers the first lecture course on science in New England.

SAMUEL PENHALLOW (1665–1726): *History of the Wars of New-England with the Eastern Indians.* Penhallow's account of the Indian wars mixes realistic descriptions with idealistic ones and asserts that the conflict represented a divine judgment on the sin of the Puritans, particularly their failure to convert the Indians.

Poetry, Fiction, and Drama

EBENEZER COOK: "An ELOGY on the Death of Thomas Bordley, Esq." This is the first of the four elegies attributed to Cook. It would be followed by "An Elegy on . . . Nicholas Lowe" (1728), "An Elegy on . . . William Lock" (1732), and "In Memory of . . . Benedict Leonard Calvert" (1732).

Sermons and Religious Writing

COTTON MATHER: *Manuductio ad ministerium.* Mather writes a handbook addressed to his son, concerning the proper education for a minister. It includes Mather's insights on reading and writing and his definition of the proper writing style: "Vigour sensible in every Sentence."

SAMUEL WILLARD: *A Compleat Body of Divinity.* Willard's most famous publication and, when first published, the longest single work ever printed by an American colonial press, consists of more than 250 monthly sermons given from 1688 to 1703. The author upholds Puritan values against the forces that lead to what some historians term the shift from a "Puritan" to a "Yankee" society.

1727
Essays and Philosophy
EXPERIENCE MAYHEW: *Indian Converts*. Mayhew defends his preaching to the Indians of Martha's Vineyard.

Nonfiction
CADWALLADER COLDEN (1688–1776): *History of the Five Nations*. Colden's greatest achievement is this tribal history of the Iroquois Indians based on firsthand observation. An important source on the settlers' relationship with the Iroquois in the seventeenth and eighteenth centuries, the book would be expanded as *The Five Nations of Canada* in 1747.

Poetry, Fiction, and Drama
MATHER BYLES (1707–1788): "A Poem on the Death of His Late Majesty King George...." Byles's first published poem. He would continue writing his formal, neoclassical poetry influenced by English poet Alexander Pope until the death of his first wife, collecting thirty-one poems in *Poems on Several Occasions* (1744).

Publications and Events
The Junto Club. Founded by Benjamin Franklin in Philadelphia, this debate and social club is restricted to twelve of his friends, all of them workingmen. In 1731, it would form the first public library in America.

The *Maryland Gazette*. The first newspaper in Maryland is founded and edited by William Parks (?–1750), an Englishman who lived in Annapolis until 1736; he would then move to Virginia to form the *Virginia Gazette*.

The *New England Weekly Journal*. This newspaper, edited by Samuel Kneeland (1697–1769) and published until 1741, replaces the defunct *New England Courant*, which had been published by James Franklin. Kneeland followed Franklin's precedent, publishing the *Journal* mainly as a literary paper with some news pieces. However, unlike Franklin, Kneeland did not use his paper as a political organ.

The Proteus Echo Series. A set of instructional poems and essays written by Mather Byles (1706–1778), the Congregational clergyman and poet; John Adams (1704–1740), the Newport, Rhode Island, minister; and Matthew

Adams (c. 1694–1753); it is published in Boston's *New England Weekly Journal*. Proteus Echo is the founder of a "club," and the point of the essays is to illuminate the follies of the day to his fellow club members, the readers of the *Journal*. With an air of self-importance, the essays reject the satire and coarseness of the Restoration writers and reflect the instructional tone of Puritan writing.

Sermons and Religious Writing
JAMES ALLIN (1692–1747): "Thunder and Earthquake." This jeremiad recounts the earthquake that startled New Englanders on October 29, detailing the effects of the tremors on the citizens of Brookline, discussing the scientific reasons behind earthquakes, and warning that God brings about such natural disasters for a reason. Minister Allin uses the natural event to highlight his plea for repentance and reformation. Works such as this one prefigure the dramatic devices used by the preachers of the Great Awakening.

COTTON MATHER: *Agricola, or The Religious Husbandman*. Mather uses aspects of nature to reveal spiritual truths. This important work employs Mather's characteristic method of "reading" the world allegorically.

THOMAS PRINCE (1687–1758): *Earthquakes Are the Works of God and Tokens of His Just Displeasure*. Prince's erudition is evident in this treatise on earthquakes. While the writing reflects the influence of the Enlightenment, the author nevertheless stresses the moral purpose behind natural phenomena. Through earthquakes or outbreaks of disease, Prince contends, God reveals his unhappiness with the behavior of the people of New England.

1728
Diaries, Journals, and Letters
WILLIAM BYRD: *History of the Dividing Line*. Written in 1728, but not published until 1841, this excerpt from the author's journal reveals his daily observations while surveying the border of Virginia and North Carolina. It also demonstrates Byrd's humor and sharp intellect, especially his biting commentary about the residents of North Carolina.

Nonfiction
ELIZABETH HANSON (1684–1737): *God's Mercy Surmounting Man's Cruelty*. An account of Hanson's capture by the French and Indians that differs from both Mary Rowlandson's famous captivity narrative and the Reverend John Williams's account of the Deerfield Raid by

its polished literary style. The work would be reprinted frequently.

Poetry, Fiction, and Drama

RICHARD LEWIS (c. 1699–c. 1733): *Muscipula.* Lewis, a poet from Maryland best known for his descriptions of nature, publishes a translation of Edward Holdsworth's popular Latin satire on the Welsh.

JACOB TAYLOR (?–1746): "Pennsylvania." The longest poem from the renowned almanac author focuses on the link between divine providence and the abundance and fertility of the colony.

Sermons and Religious Writing

JOHN ADAMS (1704–1740): "Jesus Christ, an Example to His Ministers." The only published sermon from the minister and poet, it is delivered at his ordination in Providence, Rhode Island. The work displays a classical bent, even referring directly to Platonism, a risky endeavor for any minister. The sermon demonstrates Adams's unusually strong tie to his classical training, which also provides the foundation of his poetry.

BENJAMIN FRANKLIN: *Articles of Belief and Acts of Religion.* Franklin produces a personal devotional book recording his spiritual beliefs, a mixture of deistic and polytheistical tenets.

JOSHUA GEE (1698–1748): "Israel's Mourning for Aaron's Death." A eulogy in honor of Cotton Mather, who according to Gee had exemplified everything worthy in a New England minister — a view shared by many of his contemporaries. The work is a fitting testament to the life of the influential minister and would be followed by two of Gee's doctrinal sermons, "The Strait Gait" and "The Narrow Way," in 1729.

1729
Diaries, Journals, and Letters

SAMUEL SEWALL: *Diary.* Begun in 1674, with a break from 1677 to 1685, Sewall's major work is concluded. The *Diary* portrays life in Massachusetts during that colony's transition from a religious experiment to a thriving, more secular community. Unlike many Puritan journals, it is not a record of a spiritual odyssey. Sewall's writings reflect the life of a wealthy merchant, banker, landowner, councilman, and judge, and they are filled with local news events: the death of major figures, important political elections, legislative and judicial decisions, business transactions, and social happenings. The diary would be first published in 1878–1882.

Essays and Philosophy

BENJAMIN FRANKLIN: *A Modest Enquiry into the Nature and Necessity of a Paper Currency.* Franklin publishes the first of his economic treatises that proposes an economic stimulus by increasing the money supply.

Nonfiction

SAMUEL MATHER (1706–1785): *Life of the Very Reverend and Learned Cotton Mather.* Following Increase Mather's biography of Richard Mather and Cotton Mather's biography of Increase Mather, Samuel Mather continues the family tradition of sons producing biographies of their esteemed fathers.

Publications and Events

Philadephische Zeitung. Benjamin Franklin launches the first foreign-language newspaper in America. It fails after six weeks.

Sermons and Religious Writing

THOMAS BUCKINGHAM (1671–1731): "Moses and Aaron." An election sermon on the theme that God supports his chosen people by guiding them into the ministry. The choice of this topic alone signifies Buckingham's traditionalism. Articulate and powerful, the work sanctions essential Puritan themes and is valuable both historically and artistically.

1730
Essays and Philosophy

WILLIAM DOUGLASS (c. 1691–1752): "Practical Essay Concerning the Small Pox." An essay by the Scottish-born Boston doctor, a key voice in the debate over smallpox inoculation in Massachusetts in 1721 and 1722. He had objected not to inoculation but to the dangerous experimental method of Zabdiel Boylston, particularly his refusal to isolate inoculated patients from the uninoculated.

BENJAMIN FRANKLIN: "A Witch Trial at Mount Holly." Franklin's satire reports on a ludicrous witchcraft trial, playing on the contemporary suspicion that witchcraft was practiced among the Quakers. The *English Gentleman's Magazine* would report details from the fanciful trial as fact.

Poetry, Fiction, and Drama

EBENEZER COOK: "Sotweed Redivivus; or, The Planters Looking-Glass by E. C. Gent." This verse treatise concerning tobacco cultivation and the problems facing the planters of Maryland is thought to be by the author of

The Sot-Weed Factor (1708), though its tone is markedly different.

RICHARD LEWIS: "A Journey from Patapsco to Annapolis, April 4, 1730." Lewis's major literary work, this poem is considered one of the best nature poems in colonial literature.

JAMES RALPH (c. 1705–1762): *The Fashionable Lady.* Ralph's ballad opera is the first American play produced in London. Ralph, a poet, historian, and dramatist, was a friend of Benjamin Franklin who accompanied him to London in 1724.

Publications and Events

The *Pennsylvania Packet.* After attacking the owner of the *Packet* in a series of essays, Benjamin Franklin is able to buy the paper at a very low cost. Under his leadership, the *Packet* is successful in gaining both readership and reputation, laying the foundation for the printer's other endeavors, such as *Poor Richard's Almanack.*

Sermons and Religious Writing

THOMAS FOXCROFT: *Observations, Historical and Practical, on the Rise and Primitive State of New-England.* The popular Boston minister's fullest expression of his orthodox Puritan beliefs in the face of growing liberalism and evangelicalism.

JOSIAH SMITH (1704–1781): *The Greatest Sufferers.* This foremost religious figure in colonial South Carolina provides an orthodox interpretation of natural disasters, using a New England earthquake as a warning to the sinful of Charleston.

1731
Nonfiction

MARK CATESBY (1683–1749): *The Natural History of Carolina, Florida and the Bahama Islands.* The naturalist, explorer, and writer begins his landmark study of southern flora and fauna (completed in 1747) that would set the standard for subsequent works in America and abroad.

Poetry, Fiction, and Drama

ANTHONY ASTON: *The Fool's Opera.* Aston's dramatic parody of John Gay's *The Beggar's Opera* follows the actions of a Fool and a Poet, who attempt to humiliate each other. Following his normal practice, Aston demonstrates his playful wit at the conclusion of the work as he begs for money.

EBENEZER COOK: "The History of Colonel Nathaniel Bacon's Rebellion." Believed to be the work of Cook, this mock-epic appears in the collection *The Maryland Muse*

and satirizes all sides of Bacon's Rebellion, which took place in Virginia in 1696.

RICHARD LEWIS: *Food for Criticks.* Upset that colonial Americans did not respect and revere the land as did the Native Americans who had lived on it previously, the foremost nature poet in the colonies criticizes the "throng at Harvard" for their selfish ignorance. However, he does not appear to disagree with the removal of Indians from the lands in the first place.

JOHN SECCOMB (1708–1792): "Father Abbey's Will." Written while he was a Harvard student, Seccomb's popular humorous verse, about one of the college's bedmakers and custodians, prompts a sequel, "A Letter of Courtship," addressed to Father Abbey's widow from a custodian at Yale. It is the first imaginative treatment of the rivalry between the two schools.

Publications and Events

The *Weekly Rehearsal.* The Boston newspaper founded by Jeremy Gridley (c. 1701–1767) features essays in the witty, urbane style of English essayist and poet Joseph Addison until it is taken over by Gridley's partner, Thomas Fleet, who emphasizes politics. It would continue publication until 1735.

The Library Company of Philadelphia. The first subscription library in America. Benjamin Franklin, as the Library Company's first president, writes its articles of association on July 1.

Sermons and Religious Writing

JONATHAN EDWARDS (1703–1758): "God Glorified in the Work of Redemption." Edwards's first publication is the text of a public lecture delivered in Boston, a forceful defense of divine power and the ways of salvation.

ISAAC GREENWOOD: *A Philosophical Discourse Concerning the Mutability and Changes in the Material World.* Greenwood composes this work upon the death of Thomas Hollis, a benefactor of Harvard, describing the unity of man and God, man and his soul, and man and nature, which he finds are all governed by the laws of perpetual motion. The text demonstrates how American thinkers are coming to rely on science to explain life and events in the eighteenth century.

1732
Diaries, Journals, and Letters

WILLIAM BYRD: *Journey to the Land of Eden.* Another witty excerpt from Byrd's journal, with observations on Native Americans and coarse frontiersmen, would not be published until 1841. Byrd's writing covers his trip to

"Eden" — his piece of land near the River Dan in North Carolina.

Essays and Philosophy

ELIHU COLEMAN (1699–1789): *A Testimony Against the Antichristian Practice of Making Slaves of Men.* In this antislavery tract, a Quaker minister tries to raise support for abolitionism among fellow Quakers. Coleman uses the Bible to demonstrate how one cannot be a Christian and own another human simultaneously. Rather moderate in tone, the work is notable for its time.

BENJAMIN FRANKLIN: "On Literary Style." Franklin's essay, published in the *Pennsylvania Gazette*, contains his definition of a good writing style: "smooth, clear and short."

Nonfiction

WILLIAM BYRD: *A Progress to the Mines.* Byrd records his visit to Alexander Spotswood's iron works near Fredericksburg, Virginia. First published in 1841, the work, like all of Byrd's, provides a fascinating look at the region.

DANIEL NEAL (1678–1743): *A History of the Puritans.* The English historian issues the first of his four-volume history (to be completed in 1738), which chronicles the activities of the Puritans in New England until 1689.

JAMES EDWARD OGLETHORPE (1696–1785): *A New and Accurate Account of the Provinces of South-Carolina and Georgia.* The English general, having gained a charter to found a colony in Georgia for persecuted Protestants and debtors, issues this prospectus to raise funds for the venture.

Poetry, Fiction, and Drama

JOSEPH GREEN (1706–1780): "Parody of a Psalm by Byles." As Mather Byles publishes his poetry, Green immediately writes a parody. For example, he turns Byles's "A Psalm at Sea," an ode to the wonders of the sea, into a poem about a bout of seasickness, "Parody of a Psalm by Byles." Green's parodies mock Byles's vanity and his quest for literary fame. He also publishes "The Poet's Lamentation for the Loss of His Cat." The poem assumes that Byles uses his cat, named Muse, as a source of inspiration for his poetry, declaring that when Byles can't find inspiration in the purring of his pet, "Oft to the well-known volumes I have gone, / And stole a line from Pope or Addison."

Publications and Events

The *New-York Weekly Journal.* John Peter Zenger (1697–1746) launches this newspaper to oppose the official political views of the *New York Gazette.* His polemical articles and rhymes caused him to be arrested and tried for libel in 1735. His acquittal would establish an important precedent for American freedom of the press.

Poor Richard's Almanack. Benjamin Franklin publishes the first volume of his serial of commonsense philosophy and witty maxims. For the next twenty-five years it would be one of the most widely read journals in the British colonies and the most famous American almanac. Franklin stopped writing for the almanac by 1748 and sold it in 1758. It continued to be published until 1796.

Sermons and Religious Writing

JONATHAN EDWARDS: "Narrative of Surprising Conversions." In this sermon, the young minister records the outbreak of the first major religious revival in American history, around Northampton, Massachusetts. Stating that the consciences of the young, who previously did nothing but "frolick," are being stirred, he relates various stories of great emotion and strange delusions, all of which end with the participants coming closer to God.

SAMUEL WIGGLESWORTH (1689–1768): "An Essay for Reviving Religion." The son of clergyman and poet Michael Wigglesworth predicts a calamity for New England unless there is a return to the religious devotion of the first Puritan generation.

1734
Poetry, Fiction, and Drama

RICHARD LEWIS: *Upon Prince Madoc's Expedition to the Country now called America, in the 12th Century.* Lewis creates a fictionalized poetic tale of a valiant Welshman named Prince Madoc. Madoc dreams of a great new empire arising in the New World. The poem further enhances Lewis's excellent literary reputation in England as well as in the colonies.

Sermons and Religious Writing

JOHN BARNARD: "The Throne Established by Righteousness." A sermon prefiguring the Enlightenment theory of government as a contract between rulers and the people. Barnard, recognized as one of the premier sermonizers of his day, proposes that while government is fated by God, authority also comes from the people; therefore government positions must go to representatives who demonstrate the ability to uphold the good of the community.

JONATHAN EDWARDS: "A Divine and Supernatural Light." One of Edwards's most important early works, this sermon attempts to distinguish the true spirit of the divine from the false and "the reality of the spiritual light."

1735
Essays and Philosophy

ANN SMITH FRANKLIN: "A Brief Essay on the Number Seven." The first solo publication from one of the first women printers in the American colonies, this essay deals with the possible biblical significance of the number seven.

Nonfiction

WILLIAM BRATTLE (1662–1717): *Compendium Logicae Secundum Pricipia D. Renati Cartesii.* Published in numerous editions, this work would be a standard text at Harvard until the 1770s. In it, Brattle treats the mind as a machine for thinking. Following the philosopher Descartes, he writes that the way to remove uncertainty from thinking is to study the simplest components of an idea. The work shows Brattle's reaction against Puritan theology by rejecting orthodoxy and tradition as determinants of thought.

JUDAH MONIS: *Grammar of the Hebrew Tongue.* Monis, the first instructor of Hebrew at Harvard, issues his long-awaited book, the first published in Hebrew in America.

Poetry, Fiction, and Drama

JAMES LOGAN (1674–1751): *Cato's Moral Distichs.* The first of the scholar's verse translations prompts its printer, Benjamin Franklin, to call it the first translation of a classic both made and printed in the British colonies. It would be followed by *M. T. Cicero's Cato Major* (1744).

JANE TURELL (1708–1735): *Reliquiae Turellae.* The daughter of Benjamin Colman produces a collection of pious poems, reprinted as *Memoirs* (1741), a volume that also includes secular verses.

Sermons and Religious Writing

BENJAMIN COLMAN: *Reliquiae Turellae et Lachrymae Paternae* (The father's tears over his daughter's remains). A moving funeral sermon for Colman's twenty-seven-year-old daughter. During his thriving career as a popular clergyman, he introduced a sophisticated, clever, and expressive tone to the pulpit of the Brattle Street Church in Cambridge, Massachusetts. He is famous for his sermons and his work on church doctrine.

1736
Essays and Philosophy

WILLIAM DOUGLASS: "The Practical History of a New Epidemical Eruptive Miliary Fever. . . ." A clinical description of scarlet fever, published twelve years before the more famous English essay on the disease ("Account of the Sore Throat Attended with Ulcers") by John Fothergill.

Nonfiction

JOHN GYLES (c. 1678–1755): *Memoirs of Odd Adventures, Strange Deliverances, Etc. in the Captivity of John Gyles, Esq.* One of the most popular captivity narratives of the eighteenth century, this memoir is less religious and more entertaining in tone than many comparable works, designed to provide factual information about an uncommon personal experience. The memoir also records the attitudes of the British and the French during King William's War of 1689. The Maine man was for six years until his ransom in 1695 an Indian captive. His work is regarded as a precursor to the frontier romances of James Fenimore Cooper, William Gilmore Simms, and Robert Montgomery Bird.

JOHN MASON (c. 1600–1672): *A Brief History of the Pequot War . . . in 1637.* The military hero of the Pequot War provides his account, which had first appeared in Increase Mather's *A Relation of the Troubles Which Have Hapned in New-England* (1677), where it was attributed to another writer.

THOMAS PRINCE: *A Chronological History of New England in the Form of Annals.* The first of two volumes from the noted New England pastor. Prince's history attempts to cover the period "from the Creation . . . to the discovery of New-England." The first volume was poorly received, and Prince would not finish the second volume until 1755.

JOHN PETER ZENGER: *A Brief Narrative of the Case and Tryal of John Peter Zenger.* Zenger explains the story of the court case that links his name to the notion of freedom of the press. Arrested for alleged libelous statements made in several issues of the *New-York Weekly Journal* in 1734, Zenger had been brought to trial in 1735. The jury found him not guilty, and the acquittal gained an important precedent for American freedom of the press.

Poetry, Fiction, and Drama

WILLIAM DAWSON (1704–1752): *Poems on Several Occasions.* Dawson, a professor at William and Mary College and later its president (1743–1752), anonymously issues this verse collection showing the influence of English poet Alexander Pope.

Publications and Events

ANN SMITH FRANKLIN is named the official printer of the Rhode Island Assembly. Considering the common belief of the time that women had no capacity for politics, it is remarkable that this political body entrusted a woman with its publications. Franklin would retain this profitable position until her death in 1763.

The *Rhode Island Almanack*. Following her husband's death in 1735, Anne Smith Franklin assumes sole control of the first paper in the colony and uses the pseudonym Poor Robin; thus, the publication is also known as *Poor Robin's Almanack*. By 1738, Franklin would be writing the material for the paper herself and assuming the responsibilities of a master craftsman by training her two daughters as typesetters and shopkeepers—all highly unusual events for the eighteenth century.

The *Virginia Gazette*. The first Virginia newspaper is founded by William Parks (?–1750) at Williamsburg. Notable for its essays on London life, it would continue until 1766 when another paper of the same name, but independent of governmental control, began publishing until 1777.

1737
Nonfiction

JOHN BRICKELL (c. 1710–c. 1745): *The Natural History of North-Carolina*. Most of this work by the North Carolina physician and scientist concerns agricultural information and mimics the form of colonial promotional literature, giving a geographical overview, a history of the government and legal system, and a breakdown of the population. However, the final part of the book deals with "An Account of the Indians of North Carolina." The book, like many travel and geographic works of this time, is largely plagiarized from other sources. It appears to be mainly drawn from John Lawson's *A New Voyage to Carolina* (1709).

JOHN MERCER (1704–1768): *An Exact Abridgment of the Public Acts of the Assembly of Virginia*. The value of this work by the Irish-born Virginian political and legal theorist is instantly realized by every justice in the country. Modeled on the *Abridgment of English Statutes* by Edmund Wingate (1596–1656), it is the first comprehensive compilation of legal statutes in the colonies. Mercer lists legal acts alphabetically, giving the year, the chapters, and the pages of the laws, making this reference very useful. He includes laws, punishments, and fines in place for public and private acts. Additional material would appear in 1739 and 1759, when the book is reissued as *A Continuation of the Abridgment and An Exact Abridgment*.

Poetry, Fiction, and Drama

WILLIAM DAWSON: *Poems on Several Occasions*. One of the earliest publications from a southern poet and the first volume of poetry published in Virginia. The collection shows Dawson's familiarity with contemporary and classical poetry.

Sermons and Religious Writing

JOHN BARNARD: "A Call to Parents." A sermon calling for the accountability of parents in the religious upbringing of their children. Reason, wisdom, and good sense are cited as the basis for leading children to God. While Barnard's writing does not explicitly criticize the revivalists, his subject matter and ideology show that he stands opposed to many of the trends that would culminate in the Great Awakening.

1738
Sermons and Religious Writing

ELIPHALET ADAMS (1677–1753): "A Sermon Preached on the Occasion of the Execution of Katherine Garret. . . ." Adams's sermon uses the example of the execution of an Indian servant who murdered her illegitimate infant to warn his congregation to "take heed and beware of loose living."

GEORGE WHITEFIELD (1714–1770): "The Eternity of Hell Torments." One of nearly eighteen thousand sermons produced by the famed English minister, who visits America for the first time in 1738 and would be largely responsible for the Great Awakening, the wave of religious revivalism that would sweep through the colonies during the 1740s. In the sermon, Whitfield expresses his resolute belief in predestination, which forms the foundation of his faith.

1739
Diaries, Journals, and Letters

ELIZA LUCAS PINCKNEY (c. 1722–1793): *Journal and Letters of Eliza Lucas*. The life chronicle of one of the leading women of the colonial era, a prominent South Carolina planter and mother of political figure Charles Pinckney (1757–1824). Not published until 1850, it gives an intimate look at a lively, confident, and intellectually curious

George Whitefield

woman and an able businessperson of the eighteenth century.

Essays and Philosophy

WILLIAM DOUGLASS: *A Discourse Concerning the Currencies of the British Plantations in America*. This pamphlet identifies the currency struggles in the colonies and opposes the irresponsible ways that legislatures create and use paper money. Adam Smith would later refer to this pamphlet in *The Wealth of Nations*.

Sermons and Religious Writing

JOHN CALLENDER (1706–1748): "An Historical Discourse on the Civil and Religious Affairs of the Colony of Rhode-Island and Providence Plantations." A sermon presenting Callender's belief that God has blessed the development of Rhode Island and that the destruction of Native Americans is preordained by God. Like many other documents of the seventeenth and eighteenth centuries, this sermon justifies the removal of Indians from New England.

GEORGE WHITEFIELD: "Thankfulness for Mercies Received a Necessary Duty" and "The Heinous Sin of Drunkenness." In these two sermons, Whitefield states his belief in predestination and in regeneration through

a "new birth" while ignoring the various labels that divide the different religious sects. Whitefield once said to an audience, "Tell me you are a Christian, that is all I want." This view would open religion to many who felt alienated by the rules and regulations of certain sects and, in part, explains the great attraction of revivalism.

1740
Diaries, Journals, and Letters

JONATHAN EDWARDS: *Personal Narrative*. Edwards begins this journal, which is less a chronological account of events in his life than a record of his inner life and spiritual development. It provides an invaluable window into Edwards's mental landscape and would be first published in 1765.

Poetry, Fiction, and Drama

AQUILA ROSE (c. 1695–1723): *Poems on Several Occasions*. An English-born typographer, this poet had moved to Philadelphia prior to 1717. There he worked in Andrew Bradford's printing office, which would be run by Benjamin Franklin after Bradford's death. Rose's poetry, collected here by his son Joseph, displays an amateur versifier steeped in the neoclassical tradition.

Sermons and Religious Writing

GILBERT TENNENT (1703–1764): "The Danger of an Unconverted Ministry." Considered one of the defining American sermons of the eighteenth century, Tennent's attack on ministers who do not heed the revival call is the most important document produced by the Great Awakening in the Middle Colonies.

1741
Diaries, Journals, and Letters

ISAAC BACKUS (1724–1806): *The Diary of Isaac Backus*. Backus, who would become one of the colonial period's leading Baptist authorities, begins a chronicle of his daily life.

WILLIAM BYRD: *The Secret Diary*. Byrd's final diary, covering the period from 1739 to 1741, is completed. It reveals more details about the author's lifelong indulgences — reading and sex.

GEORGE WHITEFIELD: "Letter to John Wesley." Dated December 24, 1740, but published in 1741, this letter represents the author's response to Wesley's sermon entitled "Free Grace" (1739). From the moment of his conversion in 1735, Whitefield had been convinced of the total depravity of humanity, the need for a new birth, and that only God can save. Whitefield disagrees with a number of doctrinal points in Wesley's sermon, most especially Wesley's understanding of new birth and salvation.

Poetry, Fiction, and Drama

SARAH PARSONS MOORHEAD (fl. 1741–1742): "Lines . . . Dedicated to the Rev. Mr. George Tennent." Moorhead's poem sharply criticizes the evangelical clergyman: "O dear sacred TENNENT, pray beware. / Lest too much Terror, prove to some a Snare." She believed that the religious revivalism of the period had become "the Drunkard's song." Little is known about Moorhead beyond her residence in Boston during the 1740s and her criticism of the excesses of the Great Awakening.

PATRICK TAILFER (fl. 1741), Hugh Anderson (?–1748), David Douglas (fl. 1741), and others: *A True and Historical Narrative of the Colony of Georgia.* A humorous satire by several irritated settlers, lauding Georgia's founder, General James Oglethorpe, for keeping them poor and overworked.

Publications and Events

The *American Magazine.* The first magazine published in the American colonies, edited by John Webbe (fl. 1730–1750) in Philadelphia, precedes Benjamin Franklin's *General Magazine* by three days to claim the distinction. In print for only three months, this monthly periodical covered the proceedings of colonial government, as well as moral, political, and historical topics.

The *General Magazine.* Benjamin Franklin conceives the first American magazine, but it would become the second published in the colonies because the *American Magazine* had debuted in Philadelphia three days before the launch of the *General Magazine.* Reporting on the war with Spain, the French and Indian alliance, and other domestic and international current affairs, the magazine remained in circulation for six months.

Sermons and Religious Writing

JONATHAN EDWARDS: "Sinners in the Hands of an Angry God." A sermon aimed at stirring listeners from their sinful ways, centering on the metaphor of a spider and its prey. Proving to be one of the fiery minister's most popular and important sermons, it describes in vivid detail the prospects of eternal damnation for the nonelect.

SAMUEL FINLEY (1715–1766): "Christ Triumphing and Satan Raging." Written by the itinerant evangelist, Pennsylvania clergyman, and controversial participant in the Great Awakening, Finley's first published sermon

Jonathan Edwards

is a rousing expression of Great Awakening zeal that is praised by George Whitefield.

1742
Poetry, Fiction, and Drama

SARAH PARSONS MOORHEAD: "To the Reverend Mr. James Davenport on His Departure from Boston." Moorhead's poem continues her criticism of the evangelical clergy, imagining a dream vision in which Davenport acknowledges his pride and asks pardon for the church he has "rashly rent." Moorhead's criticism of contemporary issues is unique among American women writers in the eighteenth century.

Publications and Events

The *American Weekly Mercury.* Following the death of her husband Andrew, Cornelia Smith Bradford (c. 1700–1755) chooses to take over the responsibilities for the *American Weekly Mercury.* From 1742 until 1744, she published the paper with the help of one assistant. After 1744, she became the sole editor and printer until the paper folded in 1746.

Sermons and Religious Writing

CHARLES CHAUNCY (1705–1787): *Enthusiasm Described and Caution'd Against.* The pastor of the First Church of Boston, speaking as the voice of reason opposing hysteria, upholds orthodoxy and warns against the effects of the Great Awakening.

JONATHAN EDWARDS: *Some Thoughts Concerning the Present Revival of Religion.* A book modeled on the conversion of Edwards's wife, Sarah. The work further explains how revivalism filled the hearts of many Americans at the time with light, love, and comfort.

1743

Essays and Philosophy

JOSEPH SECCOMBE (1706–1760): *Business and Diversion Inoffensive to God, and Necessary for the Comfort and Support of Human Society.* Seccombe, an Indian missionary, poet, and clergyman, provides the first published American work on sports in this defense of fishing as "very friendly to Religion," noting that, after all, the Apostles were "fishers of men."

Nonfiction

JOHN CLAYTON (1694–1774): *Flora Virginica.* A sequel to the first part published in 1739, this volume describes plants of Virginia and their medicinal virtues, and it includes an ethnographic discussion detailing how Indians and white settlers use the plants differently. The work by the Virginia botanist would be reissued in 1762, gaining greater recognition. Written in Latin, the work is undervalued today because of the lack of an English translation.

Poetry, Fiction, and Drama

JOSEPH GREEN: "The Disappointed Cooper." Green, a Harvard-educated writer, had emerged as the leading tavern wit of the 1720s, proudly calling himself New England's "anti-laureate." "The Disappointed Cooper" cleverly mocks an old man's marriage to a young redheaded woman half his age. The poem criticizes the self-righteousness and sexual hypocrisy of some New Light ministers, whose behavior thoroughly repulsed Green, a very religious man despite his love of bawdy verse.

Publications and Events

American Philosophical Society. Established in Philadelphia by Benjamin Franklin, who became its first president, the scientific society is the first of its kind in America.

CHRISTOPHER SOWER (1693–1758), the Pennsylvania printer, issues a German-language Bible, the second complete Bible printed in America, following John Eliot's Indian-language Bible (1663). Since printers in Britain held the monopoly on English-language Bibles, none were printed in America before the Revolution.

Sermons and Religious Writing

CHARLES CHAUNCY: *Seasonable Thoughts on the State of Religion in New-England.* Chauncy, one of the most outspoken and popular voices opposing the Great Awakening, offers an extensive refutation of Jonathan Edwards's defense of revivalism based on the superiority of reason over passion in directing spiritual belief.

BENJAMIN DOOLITTLE (1695–1749): *An Enquiry into Enthusiasm.* In this essay, Doolittle, a Congregational minister, expresses one of the more conservative reactions to the emotional fervor of the Great Awakening. He declares that too many preachers are guilty of excessive pride when they acknowledge "some great and wonderful communication from God."

1744

Diaries, Journals, and Letters

CHARLES CHAUNCY: *Letters to Whitefield.* Chauncy opposes the religious revivalism and enthusiasm of the Great Awakening and its main advocate, George Whitefield. He sees revivalism as unnatural excess and espouses a more rational Congregational Church founded on the benevolence of God.

DR. ALEXANDER HAMILTON (1715–1756): *Itinerarium.* A travel diary of the doctor's trip from Maryland to Boston and back in 1744. The scholar Leo Lemay stated that the diary is "the best single portrait of men and manners, of rural and urban life, of the wide range of society and scenery in colonial America." Hamilton has a special knack for characterization, and while the diary represents only four months of travel, it divulges a lifetime of information.

Essays and Philosophy

JAMES LOGAN: *M. T. Cicero's Cato Major; or, His Discourse of Old Age.* Benjamin Franklin, who prints Logan's translation of Cicero, declares it "a happy omen that Philadelphia shall become the seat of the American muse."

Poetry, Fiction, and Drama

MATHER BYLES: *Poems on Several Occasions*. This is Byles's collection of thirty-one poems written since 1727. Although he dismisses his verse as "Amusements of Looser Hours," Byles's range of poetic forms and imitations of neoclassical models made him one of the most ambitious and accomplished of the early American poets.

Sermons and Religious Writing

SAMUEL BLAIR (1712–1751): *A Short and Faithful Narrative of the Late Remarkable Revival of Religion*. Blair, a Presbyterian pastor in New Jersey and Pennsylvania, provides one of the best contemporary descriptions of an actual revival during the Great Awakening.

ANDREW ELIOT (1718–1778): "An Inordinate Love of the World...." The theme of this sermon is one that the minister of Boston's New North Church would return to time and again: religious commitments must be rekindled immediately to combat worldly influences. In this work, Eliot uses nine examples of people choosing worldly affairs over God to demonstrate the belief of many ministers of this time: a religious decline is taking place.

EXPERIENCE MAYHEW: *Grace Defended*. In this most ambitious of the clergyman's religious writings that summarizes his liberal views, Mayhew challenges Calvinist doctrine by granting the individual a modicum of free will.

THOMAS PRINCE: *The Christian History*. The clergyman and historian describes his enthusiasm for the revivalist teaching of George Whitefield and the evangelical fervor of the Great Awakening.

1745
Essays and Philosophy

CADWALLADER COLDEN: *Explication of the First Causes of Action in Matter, and, of the Causes of Gravitation*. In this scientific critique, Colden takes on Newtonian physics by claiming to have discovered the cause of gravity. Colden's contemporaries are baffled by his logic and subsequent scholars have dismissed his ideas. *Plantae Coldenghamiae*, a treatise on medicine, moral philosophy, and natural science, would follow it in 1749.

Poetry, Fiction, and Drama

JOHN ADAMS: *Poems on Several Occasions*. Containing biblical verse paraphrases and devotional works, as well as nonreligious poems, Adams's collection is one of the first by a New England author to demonstrate a shift away from the notion that all literary works should serve only religious ends.

BENJAMIN FRANKLIN: "Advice to a Young Man on Choosing a Mistress." Franklin's witty satire concerning a rake's perspective on sex argues the advantages of an older mistress over a younger one.

Publications and Events

The Tuesday Club of Annapolis. Founded by Dr. Alexander Hamilton and Jacob Green, editor of the *Maryland Gazette*, this literary and intellectual group typifies the colonial coffeehouse gatherings of the times.

Sermons and Religious Writing

THOMAS PRINCE: *Extraordinary Events in the Doings of God, A sermon celebrating British military victories over European rivals*. Prince delivers several noted sermons on this topic in the 1740s. These essays, unlike his works on "scientific" topics that demonstrate God's displeasure, describe the fruits of divine approval for the people of New England.

1746
Diaries, Journals, and Letters

DAVID BRAINERD (1718–1747): *Mirabilia Dei Inter Indicos* and *Divine Grace Displayed*. The Calvinist missionary to the Indians in Connecticut, New York, and New Jersey publishes these selections from his diary. Jonathan Edwards would publish the complete journal as *An Account of the Life of the Late Reverend Mr. David Brainerd* in 1749.

WILLIAM SHIRLEY (1694–1771): *Journal of the Siege of Louisbourg*. The colonial governor and commander provides a valuable firsthand account of the 1745 battle at Cape Breton, Nova Scotia.

Poetry, Fiction, and Drama

LUCY TERRY (c. 1730–1821): "Bars Fight, August 28, 1746." The first known poem by an African American chronicles an Indian massacre of two white families in Deerfield, Massachusetts. Handed down orally for a century, the ballad would be first printed in 1855.

Publications and Events

The final printing of Jacob Taylor's almanac. Since 1700, Taylor had provided monthly astrological calculations, anecdotes, weather predictions, and even, in 1741, selections from Milton's *Paradise Lost*. Many editions contain examples of Taylor's own poetry, which won praise from many of his contemporaries.

Sermons and Religious Writing

JONATHAN EDWARDS: *A Treatise Concerning Religious Affections.* Edwards's most popular work defends the evangelical and emotional zeal of the Great Awakening.

GEORGE WHITEFIELD: "A Short Account of God's Dealings with the Rev. Mr. George Whitefield." This sermon from the renowned minister typifies Whitefield's tendency to speak with unchecked passion and eagerness about his personal relationship with God, a tendency that moved some members of his congregation but upset others.

1747

Diaries, Journals, and Letters

THOMAS SHEPARD: *Three Valuable Pieces.* While Shepard's sermons were more well known in his day, his modern reputation rests upon his journal, published in this collection. The journal deals with the fundamental question in Puritan life: how do I know that I am saved? To explicate the answer, Shepard recites his own conversion journey, pointing out that dangers, such as Indians and Antinomian heresies, are chances for God to deliver him safely.

Nonfiction

MARK CATESBY: *The Natural History of Carolina, Florida and the Bahama Islands.* Catesby had sold his magnum opus piece by piece, beginning in 1731; the last section is completed in 1747. He had distributed the work twenty plates at a time, which in the end totaled two hundred regular plates and twenty more appendix plates. Catesby spent the years from 1722 through 1726 traveling through the southern colonies and the Bahamas to research what would become a milestone work in nature writing, earning the author a place in the Royal Society of London in 1733.

JOHN NORTON (1715–1778): *The Redeemed Captive.* A captivity narrative detailing the trials and tribulations of Norton's capture by a French and Indian war party during King George's War in 1746. Upholding the traditional Puritan belief that God delivers the true Christian from heathens and papists, Norton's tale is one of the most famous examples of the genre.

WILLIAM STITH (1707–1755): *The History of the First Discovery and Settlement of Virginia.* Based on the writings of John Smith and Robert Beverley, this is the earliest secondary account of the Virginia colony up to 1624.

Stith, a Virginia clergyman, would become president of William and Mary College in 1752.

Poetry, Fiction, and Drama

BENJAMIN FRANKLIN: "The Speech of Polly Baker." Published anonymously in the *General Advertiser,* Franklin's monologue by a woman called into court for her fifth illegitimate offspring is a witty attack on sexual hypocrisy. Widely accepted at the time as a true account, it has subsequently been called the first American short story.

WILLIAM LIVINGSTON (1723–1790): *Philosophic Solitude; or, The Choice of a Rural Life.* In a celebration of the agrarian lifestyle, the book portrays nature as a refuge from the congestion and disorder of urban life. An excellent example of American Augustan verse, this very popular work would go through five printings in Livingston's lifetime. It would also be selected for the first anthology of American poetry, *American Poetry, American Poems, Selected and Original* (1793), edited by Elihu Hubbard Smith.

SAMUEL NILES (1674–1762): *A Brief and Plain Essay on God's Wonder Working Providence for New-England....* Niles, a clergyman, historian, and poet of Braintree, Massachusetts, provides a rhymed account of the siege and capture of Louisburg on Cape Breton in Nova Scotia as a sign of God's favor toward the conquerors.

1748

Essays and Philosophy

JARED ELIOT (1685–1763): *Essays on Field Husbandry in New England.* The first of Eliot's sets of six essays on agriculture published between 1748 and 1759. They represent the first agricultural treatises printed in America. Eliot states his belief that experimentation founded upon past research is the only way to create progress in agricultural science.

1749

Diaries, Journals, and Letters

DAVID BRAINERD: *An Account of the Life of the Late Reverend Mr. David Brainerd.* This journal, edited by Jonathan Edwards, extends from 1746 until Brainerd's death in 1749. It represents the second installment of his diary (the first part, covering 1745–1746, had been published in 1746 under the title *Mirabilia Dei Inter Indicos*). His entries provide valuable information on the evangelical network in New England and the Middle Colonies and its members' verve in converting Native Americans.

THOMAS CHALKLEY (1675–1741): *Journal.* The Quaker sea captain and preacher's posthumously published account of his travels and devotions is widely admired by his fellow Quakers.

Essays and Philosophy

BENJAMIN FRANKLIN: *Proposals Relating to the Education of Youth in Pennsylvania.* Franklin's education proposals would result in the establishment in 1751 of the Philadelphia Academy (later the University of Pennsylvania).

Nonfiction

WILLIAM DOUGLASS: *A Summary, Historical and Political, of the First Planting, Progressive Improvements, and Present State of the British Settlements in North America.* The first of a two-volume history of the colonies (to be completed in 1751) that is critical of other colonial historians, such as Cotton Mather. Overall, Douglass strongly supports the Crown's authority in the management and governance of the empire. Douglass's two beloved topics, medicine and currency, play vital roles in this ambitious history.

Poetry, Fiction, and Drama

JOSEPH DUMBLETON (fl. 1740–1750): "A RHAPSODY on RUM." This very popular poem by the newspaper versifier in Virginia and South Carolina describes how rum destroys a drinker's self-worth. First published in the *South Carolina Gazette,* the solemn poem is reprinted by numerous newspapers throughout the colonies and becomes Dumbleton's most popular work.

Sermons and Religious Writing

LEMUEL BRIANT (1722–1754): "The Absurdity and Blasphemy of Depreciating Moral Virtue." Briant's sermon causes controversy by asserting that most preachers distort the word of God. His position is vigorously attacked, prompting Briant's rebuttals in "Some Friendly Remarks" (1750) and "Some More Friendly Remarks" (1751).

JONATHAN EDWARDS: *An Humble Inquiry into the Rules of the Word of God Concerning . . . Communion.* Edwards's strict requirement of church membership for participation in communion had provoked a conflict with his Northampton, Massachusetts, congregation. This treatise defends his position but does not prevent his dismissal. He also publishes *An Account of the Life of the Late Reverend Mr. David Brainerd.*

1750
Diaries, Journals, and Letters

BENJAMIN DOOLITTLE: *A Short Narrative of Mischief Done by the French and Indian Enemy.* Published posthumously, this brief pamphlet outlines in great detail the happenings in and around Northfield, Deerfield, and Fort Massachusetts from 1744 to 1749. Written in journal form, the work provides a firsthand look at these New England frontier sites during King George's War.

Essays and Philosophy

CHRISTOPHER DOCK (c. 1698–1771): *School Management.* The noted educator, called the "Father of American Pedagogy," finishes this book, detailing his philosophy of education. A unique section discusses how parents can be involved in their children's learning. Dock insists, however, that the work not be published in his lifetime, and it would not be printed until 1770, shortly before his death.

Poetry, Fiction, and Drama

CHARLOTTE RAMSAY LENNOX (1720–1804): *The Life of Harriet Stuart.* Lennox, born in New York and sent to England at the age of fifteen for schooling, remains there for the rest of her life and gets credit for publishing the first novel written by an American-born writer. It is also the first novel with American settings, such as the Hudson River, Albany, and the Mohawk Valley.

Sermons and Religious Writing

JOSEPH BELLAMY (1719–1790): *True Religion Delineated.* An associate of Jonathan Edwards and an important figure in the Great Awakening produces this religious treatise, his most important work. Harriet Beecher Stowe in *Oldtime Folks* (1869) would assert that it represents the gospel of New England religious culture as it existed for more than a century.

JONATHAN MAYHEW (1720–1766): *A Discourse Concerning Unlimited Submission and Non-Resistance to the Higher Powers.* Mayhew, a Harvard graduate, considered himself a liberal minister, but he did not wholly support the Great Awakening. After witnessing the wild gestures and extreme emotions of a revival meeting, Mayhew, in this discourse, speaks in favor of "rational religion."

1751
Diaries, Journals, and Letters

BENJAMIN FRANKLIN: *Experiments and Observations on Electricity.* Franklin kept an active correspondence with many of the leading figures in science. His scientific findings are deemed so important that his letters,

BIRTHS AND DEATHS, 1750–1789

Births

1750 John Trumbull (d. 1831), poet and judge
Lemuel Hopkins (d. 1801), poet and satirist

1751 James Madison (d. 1836), president of the United States and contributor to *The Federalist Papers*
Judith Sargent Murray (d. 1820), author

1752 Ann Eliza Bleecker (d. 1783), poet
Hannah Mather Crocker (d. 1829), author and women's rights advocate
Philip Freneau (d. 1832), poet and editor
Timothy Dwight (d. 1817), religious leader and poet

1754 Joel Barlow (d. 1812), poet

1755 Hannah Adams (d. 1831), author

1757 Royall Tyler (d. 1826), playwright

1758 Noah Webster (d. 1843), lexicographer

1759 Hannah Webster Foster (d. 1840), novelist
Sarah Wentworth Morton (d. 1846), novelist
Sarah Sayward Barrell Keating Wood (d. 1855), novelist
Mason Locke Weems (d. 1825), clergyman and author

1761 Richard Alsop (d. 1815), poet and satirist

1762 Susanna Haswell Rowson (d. 1824), novelist, poet, and playwright
Tabitha Gilman Tenney (d. 1837), novelist

1765 William Hill Brown (d. 1793), novelist

1766 William Dunlap (d. 1839), playwright and historian
Alexander Wilson (d. 1813), nature writer and poet

1768 Joseph Dennie (d. 1812), essayist and editor

1771 Charles Brockden Brown (d. 1810), novelist
Thomas Green Fessenden (d. 1837), poet and journalist
Elihu Hubbard Smith (d. 1798), poet and editor

1772 William Cliffton (d. 1799), poet
William Wirt (d. 1834), author and lawyer

1773 Robert Treat Paine (d. 1811), poet and editor

1774 Isaac Story (d. 1803), poet and essayist

1775 Paul Allen (d. 1826), poet and editor
George Tucker (d. 1861), economist, historian, and author

1777 John Blair Linn (d. 1804), clergyman and poet

1778 James Kirke Paulding (d. 1860), novelist and short story writer
William Austin (d. 1841), short story writer

1780 William Ellery Channing (d. 1842), clergyman and author
Timothy Flint (d. 1840), missionary and writer
William Ioor (d. 1830), playwright

1783 Washington Irving (d. 1859), writer and diplomat

1784 James Nelson Barker (d. 1858), playwright

1785 James McHenry (d. 1845), poet and novelist
Mordecai Manuel Noah (d. 1851), playwright and journalist

1788 Sarah Josepha Buell Hale (d. 1879), novelist, poet, and editor

1789 James Fenimore Cooper (d. 1851), novelist
Asa Greene (d. 1838), novelist
James Abraham Hillhouse (d. 1841), poet and playwright
Catharine Maria Sedgwick (d. 1867), novelist

Deaths

1751 James Logan (b. 1674), colonial statesman and author

1752 William Dawson (d. 1752), poet
William Douglass (b. 1691), physician and author

1754 Lemuel Briant (b. 1722), clergyman and author
John Checkley (b. 1680), clergyman and author

1758 Jonathan Edwards (b. 1703), clergyman, philosopher, and author
Experience Mayhew (b. 1673), missionary, translator, and author
Thomas Prince (b. 1687), theologian, scholar, and author

1761 Samuel Davies (b. 1722), clergyman, author, and poet

1762 Samuel Niles (b. 1674), clergyman and historian

1763 Jared Eliot (b. 1685), clergyman and author
Thomas Godfrey (b. 1736), poet and playwright
James Sterling (b. 1701), poet

1764 Judah Monis (b. 1683), Hebrew scholar and educator

1766 Samuel Finley (b. 1715), clergyman and author
Jonathan Mayhew (b. 1720), clergyman and author

1767 Nathaniel Evans (b. 1742), clergyman and poet
Roger Wolcott (b. 1679), poet

1770 John Barnard (b. 1681), clergyman and author

1771 Christopher Dock (b. c. 1698), educator and author
William Shirley (b. 1694), colonial official, lawyer, and author

1772 John Woolman (b. 1720), clergyman and author

1776 Richard Bland (b. 1710), colonial statesman and author
Cadwallader Colden (b. 1688), scientist, philosopher, and author

1777 John Bartram (b. 1699), botanist and author

1779 Francis Alison (b. 1705), educator and scholar

1780 Jonathan Carver (b. 1710), travel writer
Joseph Green (b. 1706), merchant and poet
Thomas Hutchinson (b. 1711), writer and colonial official

1783 Ann Eliza Bleecker (b. 1752), poet
Thomas Burke (b. c. 1744), colonial governor and poet

1784 Anthony Benezet (b. 1713), author and teacher
Robert Munford (b. c. 1737), playwright
Phillis Wheatley (b. c. 1753), poet

1787 Charles Chauncy (b. 1705), clergyman and author
Ebenezer Gay (b. 1696), clergyman and author

1788 Mather Byles (b. 1707), clergyman and poet

1789 Ethan Allen (b. 1738), patriot and writer

POPULAR BOOKS, 1751–1789*

History of England by George Tobias Smollett (First English Printing, 1757; First American Printing, 1796)

Tristram Shandy by Laurence Sterne (First English Printing, 1760–67; First American Printing, 1774)

New Elosia by Jean Jacques Rousseau (First English Printing, 1761; First American Printing, 1796)

Castle of Otranto by Horace Walpole (First English Printing, 1764; First American Printing, 1854)

The Vicar of Wakefield by Oliver Goldsmith (First English Printing, 1766; First American Printing, 1769)

Letters from a Farmer in Pennsylvania by John Dickinson (First American Printing, 1768)

A Sentimental Journey by Laurence Sterne (First English Printing, 1768; First American Printing, 1771)

History of the Reign of Charles V by William Robertson (First English Printing, 1769; First American Printing, 1770)

The Deserted Village by Oliver Goldsmith (First English Printing, 1770; First American Printing, 1771)

An History of the Earth, and Animated Nature by Oliver Goldsmith (First English Printing, 1774; First American Printing, 1795)

Apology for the Bible by Richard Watson (First English Printing, 1776; First American Printing, 1796)

The Sorrows of Young Werther by Johann Wolfgang Goethe (First English Printing, 1779; First American Printing, 1796)

American Spelling Book by Noah Webster (First American Printing, 1783)

* The books listed here were the most widely read books in this time period. Most were printed outside of the colonies and imported by colonists from their native country.

specifically those to British naturalist Peter Collinson (1694–1768), are published in this volume. In 1752, Franklin would devise and perform his kite experiment proving that lightning is electric. He would report on his later findings in *Supplemental Experiments and Observations* (1753) and *New Experiments and Observations on Electricity* (1754).

Nonfiction

JOHN BARTRAM (1699–1777): *Observations on the Inhabitants, Climate, Soil… From Pennsylvania to Lake Ontario.* A two-volume report discussing plants, animal life, insects, geology, and fossils of the region as studied by Bartram, "the father of American botany."

Sermons and Religious Writing

JONATHAN EDWARDS: "A Farewell Sermon Preached at the First Precinct in Northampton." Having been dismissed from his parish in a conflict over church mem-

bership, Edwards produces one of his most moving sermons before departing for a frontier parish at Stockbridge.

1752
Diaries, Journals, and Letters

LANDON CARTER (1710–1778): *The Diary of Colonel Landon Carter.* Covering the years from 1752 through 1778, *The Diary* documents the life and thoughts of one of Virginia's wealthiest and most influential men, with telling insight into the society of pre-Revolutionary Virginia gentry.

Essays and Philosophy

WILLIAM SMITH (1727–1803): *Some Thoughts on Education.* With this anonymous pamphlet, Smith, later one of the most recognizable names in education in America, becomes involved in the debate over the creation of King's College (later renamed Columbia University). Here, he supports the establishment of the college but insists that it become an Anglican institution.

Nonfiction

MARTHA DANIELL LOGAN (1704–1779): "Gardener's Kalendar." The Charleston, South Carolina, plantation owner, schoolteacher, and horticulturist's reputation largely rests upon this work that first appears in the *South Carolina Almanack*, published by John Tobler. Her work is significant as the first American treatise on gardening and because Logan is one of a few women involved in horticulture, a field dominated by men like John Bartram.

Poetry, Fiction, and Drama

SAMUEL DAVIES (1723–1761): *Miscellaneous Poems, Chiefly on Divine Subjects.* Previously published in the *Virginia Gazette*, Davies's slight and sentimental verses are chiefly noteworthy for being some of the first poems published in Virginia.

CHARLOTTE RAMSAY LENNOX: *The Female Quixote; or, The Adventures of Arabella.* Lennox's most popular novel satirizes the idealized conventions of French romances. Lennox depicts a heroine who regards the romances as true chronicles and guides for her conduct, only to discover the difference between fiction and reality. Ramsay would dramatize the novel as *Angelica; or Quixote in Petticoats* in 1758.

JAMES STERLING (1701–1763): *An Epistle to the Hon. Arthur Dobbs.* The Maryland clergyman's verse epistle addressed to the seeker of the Northwest Passage declares that Britain's future depends on America. The neoclassical-style poem is Sterling's most accomplished verse.

Publications and Events

The *Independent Reflector*. Along with fellow lawyers John Morin Scott (1730–1784) and William Smith (1728–1793), William Livingston sets up this weekly newspaper. The newspaper claimed to be politically neutral but nonetheless displayed a very liberal slant. The editors supported the cause of "truth and liberty" and opposed tyranny and dishonesty in public office.

Sermons and Religious Writing

JOHN BARNARD: *A New Version of the Psalms*. A notable revision of the classic *Bay Psalm Book* (1640) that yields to new literary fashions by omitting many of the original Puritan literary devices.

1753
Essays and Philosophy

WILLIAM SMITH: *A General Idea of the College of Mirania*. Smith proposes a theory of education with two main curriculums. The first prepares young men for professional careers by requiring a liberal education of history, religion, and language. The second is geared to mechanics and stresses more practical subjects. They reflect his vision of American colleges serving as safe havens for English culture.

Poetry, Fiction, and Drama

WILLIAM SMITH: "A Poem on Visiting the Academy of Philadelphia, June 1753." The poem records the author's visit to the academy, having been invited by Benjamin Franklin. To this day, it is the most memorable poem about the institution that would become the University of Pennsylvania. Smith would soon be hired as an instructor, and, in 1754, he helped transform the academy into the College of Philadelphia, where he would serve as its first provost.

Sermons and Religious Writing

ELIZABETH SAMPSON ASHBRIDGE (1713–1755): *Some Account of the Fore Part of the Life of Elizabeth Ashbridge*. Ashbridge finishes a moving account of her life, especially concerning her spiritual development. An ordained Quaker minister, she hints that the ability to free herself from male authority depends on her ability to

accept God's authority. The work would be first published in 1774.

JOHN WITHERSPOON: *Ecclesiastical Characteristics*. Witherspoon's satire on religious liberals becomes a bestseller, going through seven editions. It would be followed by his Swiftian satire on church history, *History of a Corporation* (1765).

1754
Diaries, Journals, and Letters

ESTHER EDWARDS BURR (1732–1758): *Journal*. Burr chronicles daily life from 1754 to 1757, giving information on topics such as the founding of Princeton College, religious revivals, childbearing practices, the French and Indian War, and women's roles during the period. It would be published in several editions by Jeremiah Eames Rankin (1828–1904) as *Esther Burr's Journal*.

CHRISTOPHER GIST (1705–1759): *Journals*. The soldier and explorer who journeyed into regions of Kentucky and Ohio ahead of Daniel Boone completes his journals, begun in 1750. It is one of the best sources of information on the region between the Alleghenies and Ohio in the 1750s. Thomas Jefferson would use Gist's maps and journals extensively for his *Notes on the State of Virginia*. They would be published in 1893.

GEORGE WASHINGTON (1732–1799): *The Journal of Major George Washington*. Washington provides an account of his first military experience in 1753 in the Ohio territory against the French and the Indians. Of his first combat experience, the young lieutenant observes, "I heard the bullets whistle, and believe me, there is something charming in the sound."

Essays and Philosophy

ANTHONY BENEZET (1713–1784): *An Epistle of Caution and Advice*. The French-born teacher who came to Pennsylvania and became a Quaker and associate of John Woolman produces this pamphlet credited with helping convince the Quakers to renounce slavery.

JONATHAN EDWARDS: *A Careful and Strict Enquiry into the Modern Prevailing Notions of Freedom of Will*. Here Edwards links the divine and nature and joins reason to mysticism while radically separating the divine from the human and insisting that only the grace of God can bridge the chasm.

WILLIAM LIVINGSTON: *The Watch Tower*. A series of essays written from 1754 to 1756 about the fight for a "free college." Livingston vehemently opposes Anglican control of King's College (later Columbia University) and the establishment of the Anglican Church in New York in general.

JOHN WOOLMAN (1720–1772): *Some Considerations on the Keeping of Negroes*. The Quaker preacher issues the first part of his antislavery essay, to be completed in 1762. Abolitionists in the nineteenth century later would cite it as predicting the Civil War. It is one of the first documents to argue that slavery demoralizes and enslaves both blacks and whites.

Nonfiction

BENJAMIN FRANKLIN: "Plan of the Union." Appointed as a delegate to the Albany Congress, Franklin calls for official coordination among the colonies. While the state legislatures fail to approve it, the plan establishes Franklin as an advocate for the American colonies.

Poetry, Fiction, and Drama

JOHN MERCER: *The Dinwiddianae Poems and Prose*. Mercer is probably the writer of this satiric series of poems, which attack the policies of Virginia governor Robert Dinwiddie (1693–1770) and General Edward Braddock (1695–1755). The two would suffer frontier losses to the French at the beginning of the French and Indian War. The series, which uses an entertaining mixture of puns, mock-heroics, and invective, would continue until 1757.

Sermons and Religious Writing

SAMUEL FINLEY (1715–1766): *The Madness of Mankind*. The Pennsylvania minister attacks all denominations that deny the need for divine revelation, defining madness as "impiety, superficiality, and irreligiousness."

1755
Diaries, Journals, and Letters

JOHN ADAMS (1735–1826): *Diary of John Adams*. On November 18, the patriot and future president makes the first entry into his new diary. Over the next forty years Adams's diary grows from brief notes about the weather to more detailed and highly personal commentaries on numerous subjects and individuals. Adams's diary is one of the most important firsthand records of life and politics during the late colonial and Revolutionary eras. It would not be widely available until 1961 when published as part of the first volume of the Adams's family papers.

Essays and Philosophy

LEWIS EVANS (c. 1700–1756): *Geographical, Historical, Political, Philosophical, and Mechanical Essays*. Evans's essays mark a shift in American travel writing from an emphasis on adventure to an emphasis on scientific, political, and economic regional issues. Samuel Johnson in his review praises Evans's "elegance . . . tho' not without some mixture of the American dialect" and suggests that the essays show that "literature apparently gains ground" in America. Evans was a surveyor and draughtsman who produced a series of maps published between 1749 and 1755.

WILLIAM SMITH: *A Brief State of the Province of Pennsylvania*. Smith criticizes the Pennsylvania government's hesitancy to support the military campaign in what would become the French and Indian War. His ideas isolate non-English settlers as scapegoats and propose that every member of the assembly should pledge allegiance to the English king. He also suggests banning foreign-language newspapers and denying suffrage to German immigrants until they become anglicized. Smith's blatant nativism spurs a number of angry responses, which he would counter in *A Brief View of the Conduct of Pennsylvania* (1756).

Nonfiction

STEPHEN HOPKINS (1707–1785): *A True Representation of the Plan Formed at Albany for Uniting All the British Northern Colonies*. Hopkins, governor of Rhode Island from 1755 to 1768 and a Rhode Island delegate, provides a valuable account of this meeting to discuss a union of the colonies to ensure mutual defense, cooperation, and regulation of further settlement.

JOHN MITCHELL (1680?–1768): *Map of the British and French Dominions in North America*. Mitchell, a physician, naturalist, and cartographer who settled in Virginia between 1700 and 1725, produces the most reliable map of the period. It is still consulted today for settling boundary disputes.

THOMAS PRINCE: *Chronological History of New England in the Form of Annals*. Following the disappointing reception of his first volume of history, Prince takes almost twenty years to publish the second volume, which never gets beyond the year 1633, when the Puritans began their colony at Massachusetts Bay.

Poetry, Fiction, and Drama

MATHER BYLES: *The Conflagration*. Byles's most daring work is a long poem written in heroic couplets describing the physical phenomena of Judgment Day.

Publications and Events

The *Boston Gazette and Country Journal*, formerly the *Boston Gazette*, is taken over by Benjamin Edes

(1732–1803) and John Gill (1732–1785) and no longer serves as the official paper of the colonial government.

Sermons and Religious Writing

AARON BURR (1716–1757): "A Discourse Delivered at New-Ark. . . ." The son-in-law of Jonathan Edwards and the father of the notorious politician publishes this sermon, arguing for both a vigorous military defense against the potential threat of the French and a change in colonists' behavior.

THOMAS STEPHEN CLAP (1703–1767): *A Brief History and Vindication of the Doctrines Received and Established in the Churches of New England.* Clap, the first president of Yale (1745) and author of *Annals; or, History of Yale College* (1766), the first history of Yale, publishes a polemic in support of traditional Puritan values. This work stands in stark opposition to the spirit of toleration unleashed by the Great Awakening in the 1740s.

SARAH HAGGAR OSBORN (1714–1796): *The Nature, Certainty, and Evidence of True Christianity.* This work begins as a series of letters to a friend and represents a look back on Osborn's spiritual awakening. This emotional account stands in sharp contrast to sober spiritual autobiographies written by other New England women. In 1799, Osborn would expand her letters into *Memoirs of the Life of Mrs. Sarah Osborn.*

ISAAC STILES (1697–?): "The Character and Duty of Soldiers." Stiles preaches this sermon before a company of New Haven soldiers before their departure to fight the French. Representative of the period sentiment supporting the war, it stresses the moral responsibility of the soldiers.

1756

Poetry, Fiction, and Drama

JACOB DUCHÉ (1737–1798): "Pennsylvania: A Poem." Composed when Duché is only eighteen, this work displays his love of the natural wonders of Pennsylvania. It also conveys his appreciation for the British struggles in the French and Indian War and his hopes that the success of the colonies will work for the betterment of England.

Sermons and Religious Writing

GEORGE HUNTER, S. J. (1713–1779): *A Short Account of the Roman Catholics in the Province of Maryland.* This essay provides insight into the problems of Catholics in the colonies. Having fled England to avoid persecution, the Catholics in Maryland are taxed for not being in the militia, a service that they are prohibited from joining by law. This double-tax depopulates the colony, according

to Hunter. It is an early manifestation of the taxation squabbles eventually shared by religious sects throughout the colonies.

1757

Poetry, Fiction, and Drama

MARTHA WADSWORTH BREWSTER (fl. 1725–1757): *Poems on Divers Subjects.* One of only four volumes of poetry published by colonial women, this work by a resident of Lebanon, Connecticut, contains poems, acrostics, several letters, and some prose works. Brewster tackles radical subject matter for an eighteenth-century woman, including military events and the brutality of war. When the book first appears, Brewster has to demonstrate her authorship to a public skeptical that a woman could write poetry by publicly paraphrasing a psalm into verse.

BENJAMIN CHURCH (1734–1778): *The Choice.* Modeled after the English poet John Pomfret's work of the same title, this poem describes the aristocratic aspirations of the eighteenth century—the education and promotion of a man of leisure. The work provides a number of choices for an American gentlemen, but it is clear that the best path is moral and religious. The poem is important for its depiction of eighteenth-century Americans and its use of American subjects for poetry.

Publications and Events

The *American Magazine and Monthly Chronicle.* A monthly magazine established by William Smith and published by William Bradford. As provost of the College of Philadelphia, Smith had founded an intellectual group called the Swains. The *American Magazine* served as its literary outlet. This was in line with Smith's original plan for the publication, which he dreamed would encourage the genius of America and showcase the colonies' capability for independent rule.

1758

Diaries, Journals, and Letters

ELIZABETH SANDWITH DRINKER (1734–1807): *Diary.* Drinker begins her diary (continued until 1787), which provides an in-depth portrait of an elite urban woman from Philadelphia in the late eighteenth century. Excerpts of the diary would be first published in 1889.

Nonfiction

BENJAMIN FRANKLIN: *Father Abraham's Speech.* Franklin's preface to his final edition of *Poor Richard's Almanack* is a collection of aphorisms from previous almanacs, outlining the recipe for a successful financial life. It proves to be Franklin's most popular work, widely reprinted and translated as *The Way to Wealth*.

WILLIAM SHIRLEY: *Memoirs of the Principal Transactions of the Last War Between the English and French in North-America*. Shirley's historical account of the war is less revealing and more self-serving than his previous firsthand account, *Journal of the Siege of Louisbourg* (1746), a vivid, day-to-day chronicle of the 1745 battle at Cape Breton, Nova Scotia.

Poetry, Fiction, and Drama

CHARLOTTE RAMSAY LENNOX: *Henrietta*. This novel concerns an orphaned French girl's adventures. It would be adapted by the author as the drama *The Sister* in 1769.

JOHN MAYLEM (1739–?): "The Conquest of Louisburg" and "Gallic Perfidy." This New England soldier provides a rousing account of his experiences in rough heroic couplets. The second poem treats Maylem's capture by the French and Indians under Montcalm.

THOMAS PRINCE: *The Psalms, Hymns, & Spiritual Songs of the Old and New Testaments*. Prince's metrical translations of verses from the Bible are noteworthy for being nearly unsingable, a testimony to Prince's literalness of wording rather than his poetic skills.

ANNIS BOUDINOT STOCKTON (1735–1801): "Epistle to Mr. S." One of Stockton's earliest poems and possibly the first poetry published by a New Jersey woman. The poem originally appeared in the *New York Mercury* and reveals a period of great sadness in Stockton's life — the time of her husband's extended and final illness. Stockton would become one of the most published American women writers of the century, with at least twenty-one of her poems appearing in prestigious newspapers and magazines.

Publications and Events

The *Newport Mercury*. The second newspaper established in Rhode Island is founded by James Franklin Jr., Benjamin Franklin's nephew. With the exception of three years during the Revolution, when it was forced to move to Massachusetts due to British occupation, the newspaper would be continuously published until 1928; it then merged with another paper to become the *Newport Mercury and Weekly News*.

Sermons and Religious Writing

FRANCIS ALISON (1705–1779): "Peace and Union Recommended." One of the best examples of a sermon intended to reconcile a divided denomination. Alison achieves recognition in Pennsylvania during the Great Awakening as one of the few who try to heal the divisions created by revivalism.

SAMUEL DAVIES: "The Curse of Cowardice." The Virginia minister uses his pulpit to recruit militiamen from Virginia during the French and Indian War. Usually the Great Awakening sentiment is associated with New England; here Davies's revival skills show that it is far more geographically extensive.

JONATHAN EDWARDS: *The Great Christian Doctrine of Original Sin Defended*. Published posthumously, Edwards's last major theological work is a lengthy defense of the doctrine of original sin that makes clear humanity's natural propensity to sinfulness and the divine plan for salvation.

1759
Poetry, Fiction, and Drama

FRANCIS HOPKINSON (1737–1791): "My Days Have Been So Wondrous Free." Likely the earliest song written by a native-born American. Hopkinson would become one of the most popular songwriters during the Revolution.

Sermons and Religious Writing

EBENEZER GAY (1696–1787): "Natural Religion." Gay, who would be called the "father of American Unitarianism," articulates his religious beliefs in this influential Harvard lecture that synthesizes the theories of Hobbes and Locke and applies them to religious faith. Gay defines natural religion as "that which bare Reason discourses and dictates."

SAMUEL HOPKINS: *Sin, Thro' Divine Interpretation*. The most noted of Jonathan Edwards's students, and one of the leading Calvinist theologians in late-eighteenth-century New England, publishes the first of his three major theological treatises, a defense of the existence of sin in the world as part of God's divine plan for humanity's salvation. It would be followed by *An Inquiry into the Promises of the Gospel* (1765) and *An Inquiry into the Nature of True Holiness* (1773).

1760
Essays and Philosophy

BENJAMIN FRANKLIN: *The Interest of Great Britain Considered with Regard to Her Colonies*. This collection of essays states that the colonies should be treated as vital and equal partners of the imperial system since they are economically and militarily important to England.

JAMES OTIS (1725–1783): *The Rudiments of Latin Prosody*. Otis publishes the first of two treatises on prosody, and his alma mater, Harvard, eventually adapts it as a textbook. Otis was one of the most famous opponents of British colonialism during his time.

Nonfiction

BRITON HAMMON (fl. 1747–1760): *A Narrative of the Uncommon Sufferings and Surprising Deliverance of Briton Hammon.* An important work in the history of African American literature, this narrative is one of the few Indian captivity accounts penned by a black author, one of the earliest publications by a black American author, and the oldest extant black American autobiography.

Poetry, Fiction, and Drama

GEORGE COCKINGS (fl. 1767–1802): *War, an Heroic Poem, from the Taking of* Minorca *by the French to the Reduction of the* Havannah. Cockings passionately expresses his support of British generals in a twenty-eight-page poem with erudite references to both biblical and Greek figures. His style attracts many readers; the poem would be published in four editions by 1765.

JUPITER HAMMON (1711–c. 1800): "An Evening Thought." The first poem published by an African American in America appears in a broadside. Typical of Hammon's style, its meter is common in Great Awakening sermons and in African American a cappella hymns. It asserts that God will redeem all seeking His blessings and not just a select few.

Sermons and Religious Writing

EZRA STILES (1727–1795): "A Discourse on the Christian Union." Stiles's influence within the Congregational community grows largely from this sermon, preached in 1760 and published in 1761. It pleads for a reconciliation of a denomination deeply divided during the Great Awakening of the 1730s and 1740s. His call for reunification is crucial as Stiles is the first "Old Light" minister to advocate an end to the factional tensions between "Old" and "New Light" congregations.

1761
Diaries, Journals, and Letters

ABIGAIL ADAMS (1744–1818): *Letters of Mrs. Adams, the Wife of John Adams.* Not published until the 1840s, these letters, starting in 1761 and ending in 1814, span the Revolutionary and post-Revolutionary eras. Adams displays her sharp intellect and a rather strong feminist bent throughout the years. Her letters clearly set her among the heroes of the Revolution.

Nonfiction

JOHN WINTHROP (1714–1779): *Relation of the Voyage from Boston to Newfoundland for the Observation of the Transit of Venus.* Winthrop records his experiences on the first scientific expedition sponsored by a colonial college or government (Harvard and Massachusetts) to observe the parallax of the sun.

Poetry, Fiction, and Drama

NATHANIEL EVANS (1742–1767): *Ode on the Prospect of Peace.* Evans's greatest poetic achievement predicts the arrival of the muse of poetry in America after its abandonment of England. The poem would be posthumously collected with Evans's other works, mainly imitations of English poets such as Milton, Cowley, Gray, Pope, and Dryden, in *Poems on Several Occasions* (1772).

FRANCIS HOPKINSON: *An Exercise Containing a Dialogue and Ode Sacred to the Memory of . . . George II and The Treaty.* The first student to enroll and graduate from the Academy of Philadelphia (and who would become one of the best-known writers during the Revolution) publishes his first poetry.

JAMES LYON (1735–1794): *Urania, or A Choice Collection of Psalm-Tunes, Anthems, and Hymns.* The psalmodist, one of the earliest American composers, publishes this collection, which initiated a new epoch in church music and would be in use for a century.

1762
Diaries, Journals, and Letters

ELIZA LUCAS PINCKNEY: *The Letterbook of Eliza Lucas Pinckney, 1739–1762.* This correspondence of one of the most distinguished women of colonial America details Pinckney's life, including her changing politics, novel ideas on slave education, voracious reading habits, an unusually happy marriage, and her devotion to her children. Eliza manages her father's large plantation holdings, pioneers large-scale cultivation of indigo in South Carolina, and develops into a fervent patriot. The collection would not be published in complete form until 1972.

Essays and Philosophy

CHRISTOPHER GADSDEN (1724–1805): *Observations on Two Campaigns Against the Cherokees.* Gadsden, a captain of a militia unit in the Cherokee battles of 1760 and 1761, returns to South Carolina to find a leader of British soldiers making derogatory remarks about the colonial militiamen. Gadsden responds in this lively piece, which demonstrates the tensions between the British and

Americans even when fighting a "common" enemy, the Indians.

JAMES OTIS: *A Vindication of the Conduct of the House of Representatives....* The first political publication by Otis. Here he uses an example of an expenditure not sanctioned by the colonial legislature as the foundation of his theory that taxes can be charged only by a representative government. In effect, he summarizes the argument that would have a central place in Revolutionary rhetoric. This begins the career of one of the most famous Revolutionary pamphleteers.

JOHN WOOLMAN: *Some Considerations on the Keeping of Negroes.* Published in two parts (the first in 1754), this essay would have a lasting effect on the antislavery movement for the following one hundred years. The author appeals to all Christians in an attempt to change their understanding of slavery. Woolman's call for abolition is based mainly on moral and religious reasoning and seeks to end slavery through voluntary reform.

Poetry, Fiction, and Drama

THOMAS GODFREY (1736–1763): "The Court of Fancy: A Poem." The first published poem of the author of the first American tragedy performed on the professional stage, *The Prince of Parthia* (1767). The poem shows the influence of both Geoffrey Chaucer and Alexander Pope and would be collected in the posthumous collection *Juvenile Poems on Various Subjects* (1765).

FRANCIS HOPKINSON: "Science: A Poem." Hopkinson's poem celebrates the College of Philadelphia and its contribution to American culture. Hopkinson praises "Fair Science soft'ning with reforming Hand / The native Rudeness of a barb'rous Land."

Publications and Events

The *Providence Gazette.* The printer William Goddard (1740–1817) establishes the first printing shop in Providence and prints the first issue of the *Gazette* there. This begins a long involvement of the Goddard family in American publishing.

Sermons and Religious Writing

CHARLES CHAUNCY: *The Dudleian Lecture.* The influential New England minister lays out his opposition to the episcopacy (an attempt by the British to force Anglican bishops on the colonies).

1763
Essays and Philosophy

JOHN WOOLMAN: *A Plea for the Poor.* In this treatise concerning poverty and slavery, Woolman shows that his concern with oppression goes beyond slavery to economic considerations as well. Not published until 1793, it emphasizes a religious solution to the problems raised.

Nonfiction

ELEAZAR WHEELOCK (1711–1779): *Plain and Faithful Narrative of the... Indian Charity-School at Lebanon.* The future first president of Dartmouth College (1769–1779) describes the Indian school he founded in 1754 in Lebanon, New Hampshire. A continuation of the work would appear in 1765.

Publications and Events

The American Company. The most prominent theater company in the American colonies, founded in 1752 by London theater manager William Hallam and his brother Lewis, is reorganized by David Douglas (?–1786) in 1758, and it becomes the American Company of Comedians in 1763. It toured until 1774 and went to Jamaica for the duration of the Revolution, returning in 1784. Operating until 1805, the company employed virtually every important performer in America and became the first professional ensemble to present an American play (Thomas Godfrey's *The Prince of Parthia*) in 1767.

1764
Essays and Philosophy

RICHARD BLAND (1710–1776): *The Colonel Dismounted; or the Rector Vindicated.* In one of the first pamphlets delineating the rights of colonists within the British Empire, Bland distinguishes between external and internal governments, claiming that the British authorities would never overstep these boundaries. Bland, born into the planter class of Virginia, was an expert in colonial legal history and a leading defender of American liberties before the careers of Patrick Henry and Thomas Jefferson.

THOMAS FITCH (1700–1774): *Reasons Why the British Colonies in America Should Not be Charged with Internal Taxes.* The first of Fitch's two pamphlets dealing with the Stamp Act, to be followed by *Some Reasons That Influenced the Governor* (1766). In both, he offers a conciliatory conservative view that does not question parliamentary power or authority but cautions that arbitrary exercises of both would take away the colonies' longstanding autonomy.

BENJAMIN FRANKLIN: *A Narrative of the Late Massacres.* In one of Franklin's most powerful and indignant works, he denounces the Paxton Boys, a gang that had murdered a band of peaceful Indians, and calls for their prosecution. Riots ensue, and Franklin organizes a successful defense of other Indians. Franklin also publishes *Cool Thoughts on the Present Situation of Our Public Affairs* and *Preface to the Speech of Joseph Galloway* in support of a royal charter for Pennsylvania to replace the proprietary government.

THOMAS JEFFERSON (1743–1826): *The Literary Bible of Thomas Jefferson.* The author begins to compile notes that display his strong grounding in Roman and Greek classics as well as his penchant for natural philosophy. Complete through 1772, the collection would not be published until the twentieth century.

JAMES OTIS: *The Rights of the British Colonies Asserted and Proved.* This pamphlet sets down another important philosophy underpinning the Revolutionary debate: it asserts that rights are not derived from human institutions, but from nature and God. Thus, government does not exist to please monarchs, but to promote the good of the entire society.

THOMAS POWNALL (1722–1805): *The Administration of the Colonies.* The former Massachusetts governor (1757–1759) writes in favor of a centralized organization of all British possessions, based on commercial interests.

Nonfiction

THOMAS BARTON (1730–1780): *The Conduct of Paxton-Men.* A pamphlet from the itinerant Anglican minister on the Paxton riots in Pennsylvania. When government officials attempted to arrest those responsible for killing Indians who were living under government security, the people in backcountry Pennsylvania, who felt the government had long ignored their concerns, were outraged. Their march on Philadelphia spurred a drawn-out public debate. *The Conduct of Paxton-Men* is the most spirited defense of the marchers' activities and provides eloquent insights into backcountry ideology and problems that would continue through the next century.

THOMAS HUTCHINSON (1711–1780): *The History of the Colony of Massachusetts Bay.* The first of three volumes (to be completed in 1767) that form Hutchinson's literary legacy. He disliked extremism of any sort, whether the political frenzy of the Revolution or the religious agitation of the Salem witch trials. His scholarly tomes are infused with Hutchinson's conservative views. The first volume puts forth his central political thesis — that the colonists' view of their role within the empire was misguided from the beginning. Here he states that the founders of the colony cannot benefit from British protection and claim the rights of Englishmen if they refuse loyalty to the king.

Poetry, Fiction, and Drama

BENJAMIN YOUNGS PRIME (1733–1791): *The Patriot Muse.* A series of poems on the French and Indian War by a New York physician. During the Revolution, Prime would write several popular political songs and a poetical review of the war called *Columbia's Glory* (1791).

Sermons and Religious Writing

FRANCIS ALISON (1705–1779) AND JOHN EWING (1732–1802): *An Address of Thanks to the Wardens of Christ-Church.* Alison's collaboration with fellow minister Ewing expresses gratitude to the Anglican Church of Pennsylvania for allowing Presbyterians to worship in their churches in 1764. Anglicans and Presbyterians were united during the French and Indian War by their mutual antagonism toward the pacifism of the Quakers, but they would split again over the proposal to establish Anglican bishops in America.

ROBERT SANDEMAN (1718–1771): *Some Thoughts on Christianity.* The Scottish religious leader and founder of the Sandemanian sect (advocates of the strict separation of church and state) immigrates to New England in 1764 and publishes this treatise on his beliefs to assist in establishing his sect there.

1765
Diaries, Journals, and Letters

MARTIN HOWARD (fl. 1765–1781): *A Letter from a Gentleman at Halifax to His Friend in Rhode Island.* The Loyalist Howard responds to Stephen Hopkins's *The Rights of the Colonies Examined* (1765) and to Hopkins's retort in *A Defense of the Letter from a Gentleman at Halifax to His Friend in Rhode Island.*

ROBERT ROGERS (1731–1795): *Journals.* The explorer, frontiersman, and military leader of Rogers's Rangers describes his travels and military engagements against the French and the Indians. He also publishes *A Concise Account of North America,* the first account in English of America's western frontier.

Essays and Philosophy

JOHN ADAMS: *A Dissertation on the Canon and Feudal Laws.* An essay arguing that the experiences of ancient Greece and Rome should be the models for understanding democracy and tyranny.

JOHN DICKINSON (1732–1808): *Declaration of Rights and Grievances.* A pamphlet written by the Pennsylvania patriot and public official, which outlines the wrongs of the Stamp Act, recently imposed by the British. Because of his pamphlet, the Pennsylvannia legislature appoints Dickinson to the Stamp Act Congress, where he helps

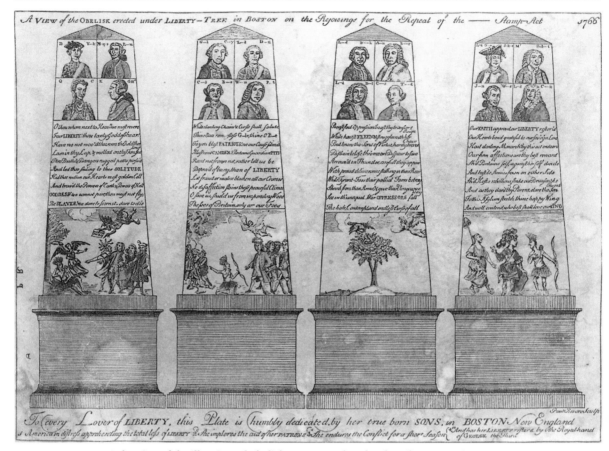

A drawing of the illuminated obelisk constructed under the Liberty Tree in Boston
to celebrate the Stamp Act's downfall

draft the resolution of grievances. In *The Late Regulations Respecting the British Colonies* Dickinson warns of possible rebellion and says that British merchants will suffer from the American boycott on British goods. This pamphlet is Dickinson's first important political publication. It takes the form of a letter from a gentleman in Philadelphia to a friend in London, stating that "we can never be made an independent people, except it be by Great-Britain herself; and the only way for her to do it, is to make us frugal, ingenious, united, and discontented."

DANIEL DULANY (1722–1797): *Considerations on the Propriety of Imposing Taxes in the British Colonies*. The Maryland lawyer offers here the legal grounds for opposing the Stamp Act, and he recommends a boycott of British goods.

STEPHEN HOPKINS (1707–1785): *The Rights of the Colonies Examined*. The governor of Rhode Island and a future signer of the Declaration of Independence issues this

influential pamphlet critiquing parliamentary authority and justifying colonial opposition.

ISAAC HUNT (1742–1809): *A Humble Attempt at Scurrility*. The first in a series of satires aimed at the administration of the Academy of Philadelphia (later the University of Pennsylvania). The college responds by denying Hunt his degree until 1771.

JAMES OTIS: *Considerations on Behalf of the Colonists*. This pamphlet expands the author's argument from *The Rights of the British Colonies Asserted and Proved* (1764). He furthers the notion of natural rights by linking it to the theory of equal representation. In this year he also authors the pamphlets *Vindication of the British Colonies* and *Brief Remarks on the Defence of the Halifax Libel*, Otis's last. Contradicting his earlier statements, Otis now is pleased to grant Parliament complete authority over the colonies. Scholars have settled on two explanations for his drastic reversal: Otis either temporarily became mentally ill, or he intended to use these pieces to defend himself against charges of treason.

Nonfiction

NATHAN COLE (1711–1783): "The Spiritual Travels of Nathan Cole." This is a classic account of the author's twelve-mile journey to hear George Whitfield preach in Middletown, Connecticut. The piece is culturally valuable for its layperson's depiction of the experience of listening to the theatrical preacher.

SAMUEL HOPKINS (1721–1803): *The Life of the Late Reverend Jonathan Edwards.* The first biography of the famous minister. As keeper and editor of Edwards's manuscripts, Hopkins, a Connecticut-born clergyman and theologian and disciple of Edwards, draws heavily from primary documents for his narrative.

JOHN MORGAN (1735–1789): *A Discourse upon the Institution of Medical Schools in America.* The Philadelphia physician who founds the University of Pennsylvania's medical school in 1765 justifies his actions and describes a plan for medical instruction in America.

SAMUEL SMITH (1720–1776): *The History of the Colony of Nova-Caesaria, or New Jersey . . . to the Year 1721.* The Quaker government official provides an early history of the state, concentrating on developments in the seventeenth century.

WILLIAM SMITH (1727–1803): *An Historical Account of the Expedition Against the Ohio Indians in 1764.* A celebratory history of the English victory in the French and Indian War. The account of Smith, an ardent Anglophile living in Philadelphia, demonstrates that while some in the colonies were beginning to question their relationship with Britain, many wanted to strengthen and even celebrate the British government, military, and culture.

Poetry, Fiction, and Drama

JOHN BEVERIDGE (1703–1767): *Epistolae Familiares.* A collection of verse from Philadelphia's leading eighteenth-century Latin poet, wherein he demonstrates his mastery of Latin poetic forms.

THOMAS GODFREY: *Juvenile Poems on Various Subjects.* Godfrey's posthumous collection of early works also contains his blank-verse romantic tragedy, *The Prince of Parthia, a Tragedy*, written in 1759, which would become the first American play professionally performed in 1767.

Sermons and Religious Writing

JONATHAN EDWARDS: *Two Dissertations.* Published posthumously, this collection is made up of "The Nature of True Virtue" and "Concerning the End for Which God Created the World." It anticipates many key tenets of Transcendentalism.

SAMUEL HOPKINS: *An Inquiry into the Promises of the Gospel.* A reinterpretation of the value of prayer and attending church. Hopkins claims that they play less of a role in renewal than inner faith does.

1766
Diaries, Journals, and Letters

CHARLES WOODMASON (c. 1720–c. 1776): *The Carolina Backcountry on the Eve of the Revolution: The Journal and Other Writings of Charles Woodmason, Anglican Itinerant.* The journal of a backcountry minister, kept during his years of proselytizing on the frontier. This record is, according to Richard J. Hooker, "probably the fullest extant account of any American colonial frontier." Woodmason depicts the Carolina backcountry as an impoverished, disease-ridden land filled with crude, lazy men and women whose religious nonconformity paves the way for immorality and barbarism. The journal would be published in 1953.

Essays and Philosophy

ANTHONY BENEZET (1713–1784): *A Caution and Warning to Great Britain on the Calamitous State of the Enslaved Negro.* A pamphlet warning of the tragic consequences that would follow a slave rebellion. Benezet urges his readers to realize that African Americans are humane, hardworking men and women.

RICHARD BLAND: *An Enquiry into the Rights of the British Colonies.* In a condemnation of the Stamp Tax, Bland asserts that the colonies owe their ultimate allegiance to the British Crown and not to the British Parliament.

JOHN DICKINSON: *An Address to the Committee of Correspondence in Barbados.* The pamphleteer denies that defiance of the Stamp Act is equivalent to rebellion.

Nonfiction

THOMAS STEPHEN CLAP: *The Annals or History of Yale College.* The first published history of Yale is still used today as an important source on the institution's early history. Written in the form of annals, the work also contains a number of source materials printed in full.

Poetry, Fiction, and Drama

BENJAMIN CHURCH: "An Elegy on the Death of the Reverend Jonathan Mayhew." This poem celebrates the life of one of the famed ministers of the era. The poet builds a heroic figure of Mayhew and invites others to model themselves after him.

JOSEPH GREEN: "An Eclogue Sacred to the Memory of . . . . Jonathan Mayhew." This poem reflects a different side of New England's satirical master. Green demonstrates his capacity to write poetry of profound spirituality in this pastoral elegy.

ROBERT ROGERS: *Ponteach; or, The Savages of America.* Rogers's blank-verse play is the first tragedy about the Indians and is believed to be the first tragedy with an American theme. It depicts the nobility of Indian fighters during Pontiac's Rebellion and chastises the British for crude military tactics. It does not appear to have been performed. Francis Parkman (1823–1893) would use this play as a source when writing the *History of the Conspiracy of Pontiac* (1851).

Publications and Events

The *Providence Gazette.* After the departure from Providence of her son William in 1765, Sarah Updike Goddard (c. 1700–1770), now a widow in her sixties, manages the city's first print shop alone and decides to revive the *Gazette*, which had failed during her son's first attempt in 1762. For the next two years, she would publish the weekly newspaper, run a bookstore, and establish a book-bindery — creating a printing business successful enough to be sold at a profit in 1768.

Sermons and Religious Writing

JONATHAN MAYHEW: "The Snare Broken: A Thanksgiving Discourse." Mayhew's political sermon warns of the threat from Britain to the colonists' natural rights.

1767
Diaries, Journals, and Letters

JOHN DICKINSON: *Letters from a Farmer in Pennsylvania.* Dickinson begins a series of twelve letters to the public, published in the *Pennsylvania Chronicle*, warning of pending danger to the colonies, examining the worsening relationship between the colonies and the mother country, and urging his fellow countrymen to remain unified. Dickinson advocates opposing arbitrary taxation by legal petition, boycott, and finally, if all else fails, by force of arms.

Essays and Philosophy

CHARLES WOODMASON: *A Remonstrance Presented to the Commons House of Assembly of South Carolina, by the Upper Inhabitants of the said Province, November 1767.* This essay is Woodmason's clearest political statement in favor of law and order. It voices similar political views

attributed to the Regulators, a group of South Carolina backcountry settlers who tried to establish law and order and institutions of local government. A few years later, when the Revolution breaks out, Woodmason would remain faithful to the king — and to his church, leaving America for London in 1774 as a Loyalist refugee.

Nonfiction

THOMAS HUTCHINSON: *The History of the Province of Massachusets-Bay, from the Charter of King William and Queen Mary, in 1691, until the year 1750.* The second volume of Hutchinson's history of Massachusetts, written largely from manuscript sources. Here he narrates the imperial wars of the seventeenth and eighteenth centuries and the power struggles between royal governors and local assemblies. The first volume had concluded with an appeal to preserve the rights of Englishmen in the colony; this second volume ends with an appeal to colonists to follow British trade regulations.

Poetry, Fiction, and Drama

Anonymous: *The Female American; or, The Adventures of Unca Eliza Winkfield.* An adventure story depicting Virginia settlers, relations with the Indians, and the heroine's education in England, shipwreck, and work as a missionary.

THOMAS FORREST (fl. 1760s): *The Disappointed; or, The Force of Credulity.* This comic opera by Andrew Barton (attributed to Forrest) had been scheduled to be performed a few days before Godfrey's *The Prince of Parthia.* This would have made it the first American play professionally performed, but it was withdrawn because of its satire. It concerns the contemporary mania for searching for the supposed buried treasure of the pirate Blackbeard.

THOMAS GODFREY: *The Prince of Parthia.* Believed to be the first tragedy written (1759) and published (1765) by a native-born American, this work is also the first American play to be professionally performed. Godfrey had intended to finish the play in time for a 1759 performance by an English company. However, he did not meet the deadline, and the five-act play based on Parthian history is performed in this year; Godfrey had died in 1763.

PHILLIS WHEATLEY (c. 1753–1784): "On Messrs. Hussey and Coffin." The first African American woman to publish a poetry collection in North America, Wheatley had arrived in the colonies in 1761 as a slave purchased by the Wheatley family of Boston, who immediately noticed her talent for language. Educated along with the Wheatleys' own children, she soon displayed a penchant for poetry. "On Messrs. Hussey and Coffin," her first major publication, appears in the *Rhode Island Newport Mercury.*

Publications and Events

The *Maryland Gazette*. Following the death of her husband, Anne Catherine Hoof Green (c. 1720–1775) quickly takes over the printing of the weekly newspaper of the colony, with the help of her son, William. The masthead reads "Anne Catharine Green & Son," and, by the end of the year, she would be acknowledged as the "printer to the province of Maryland"—a position formerly held by her late husband.

The *Pennsylvania Chronicle*. This Philadelphia newspaper, established to challenge the power of William Penn's heirs for control of the colonies, is chiefly noteworthy for publishing John Dickinson's *Letters from a Farmer in Pennsylvania* (1767–1768).

Sermons and Religious Writing

THOMAS BRADBURY CHANDLER (1726–1790): *An Appeal to the Public, in Behalf of the Church of England in America*. Chandler summarizes another frustration with British control, arguing for the appointment of an American bishop.

1768
Diaries, Journals, and Letters

CHARLES CLINTON BEATTY (c. 1715–1772): *The Journal of a Two Months Tour*. An account by the Presbyterian minister of his journey through the Ohio country. The journal is valuable for its description of the Delaware Indians, including numerous descriptions of the relationships between Indians and whites. The author includes a letter in support of the notion that Indians are related to the Ten Tribes of Israel, a notion later to be promoted by James Adair.

ARTHUR LEE (1740–1792): "The Monitor's Letters." The friend of John Dickinson publishes a complementary series of letters to his *Letters from a Farmer in Pennsylvania* (1767–1768) in the *Virginia Gazette*. They would be included with Dickinson's letters in the pamphlet *The Farmer's and Monitor's Letters* (1769). Lee would write at least thirty-one additional "Monitor's Letters" for newspapers over the next eight years.

Essays and Philosophy

JOHN ADAMS: "An Essay on Canon and Federal Law." Among Adams's earliest publications, this essay uses the New England Puritans' rejection of the "unlimited submission to a monolithic church" to attack British claims to establish total control over the colonies.

CHARLES CHAUNCY: *The Appeal to the Public Answered, in Behalf of the Non-Episcopal Churches in America*. Chauncy warns of the incursion of the Church of England on the liberties of the colonial churches.

BENJAMIN FRANKLIN: *Causes of the American Discontents before 1768*. Franklin summarizes relations between Britain and the American colonies.

JOHN WOOLMAN: "Considerations on Pure Wisdom and Human Policy." An essay on the corruption of wealth and the need for charity. Woolman had spent most of his life spreading his message that all problems have religious answers. Like most of his writing, this essay is passionate and unwavering in its support for the downtrodden.

Poetry, Fiction, and Drama

JOHN DICKINSON: "The Liberty Song" (also called "American Liberty Song"). At the same time that the author publishes his famed *Letters from a Farmer*, he writes these ten stanzas that deal with common issues of his day: slavery or freedom; the original settlers and their pursuit of freedom; the need for unification; and the sweet spoils of victory. The song, which would become the anthem of the Sons of Liberty, was soon one of the most popular of its time and was reprinted extensively.

ELIZABETH GRAEME FERGUSSON (1737–1801): "The Dream of the Patriotic Philosophical Farmer." Fergusson's poem, signed by "Laura," argues for an American embargo on British goods. The Philadelphian was the hostess of the most distinguished literary salon in colonial America.

Sermons and Religious Writing

AMOS ADAMS (1728–1775): "Religious Liberty." The influential minister in Roxbury, Massachusetts, sermonizes on the history of the reform movement in the Church of England. This work focuses on Christ as the only true head of any church, implying that monarchs and politicians should have no say in religious matters.

JOHN WITHERSPOON (1723–1794): *Practical Discourse on the Leading Truths of the Gospel*. The Scottish-born Presbyterian minister who comes to America in 1768 to accept the presidency of the College of New Jersey (later Princeton University) publishes this theological treatise.

1769
Diaries, Journals, and Letters

EZRA STILES: *Literary Diary*. Stiles's greatest achievement is this record of his experiences, readings, and reflections on public events, composed from 1769 until his death. It is an invaluable source of information, particularly on events and participants in the Revolution.

Essays and Philosophy

SAMUEL ADAMS (1722–1803): *An Appeal to the World; or, A Vindication of the Town of Boston from Many False and Malicious Aspersions.* The only published pamphlet from the incendiary Revolutionary leader agitates against British troops in Boston and contributes to the tension that would lead to the Boston Massacre (1770).

TIMOTHY DWIGHT (1752–1817) AND JOHN TRUMBULL (1750–1831): *The Meddler.* A series of essays published from September 1769 to January 1770 in the *Boston Chronicle.* The authors — writers and poets associated with Yale University and subsequently among the Connecticut Wits — cover a wide range of subjects such as religion, comedy, flirting, language, and sin. Trumbull probably wrote most of the essays, noteworthy for their witty criticism.

Nonfiction

AMOS ADAMS: *A Concise, Historical View of New England.* This history from the liberal minister deals with the Pilgrims' fight for liberty and details other such battles through Adams's own time. The minister proposes that the good grace of God justifies the growth and success of the American colonies, a popular theory later used to support Manifest Destiny.

JOHN BARTRAM: *Description of Eastern Florida.* Bartram, the leading American naturalist, makes a trip to Florida under his new appointment as botanist to the king. The book is based on his journal from his trip in 1765–1766.

THOMAS HUTCHINSON: *A Collection of Original Papers Relative to the History of the Colony of Massachusetts-Bay.* Hutchinson's compilation of seventeenth-century documents makes him the premier American historical editor of his day.

Poetry, Fiction, and Drama

ELIZABETH GRAEME FERGUSSON: *Telemachus.* Possibly the first English translation of François Fénelon's *Télémaque.* Fergusson, a poet and a literary salon hostess, is almost certainly the first American woman to undertake such a major job of translation. She had begun the project in 1766 and continued it for the next three years. Fergusson was unsuccessful, however, in finding a publisher for this project, which remains unpublished.

Publications and Events

ABEL BUELL (1742–1822) sells the first type font designed and manufactured in America. The printer also builds the colonies' first type foundry, in New Haven, with backing from the Connecticut assembly.

1770

Essays and Philosophy

HERMAN HUSBAND (1724–1795): *An Impartial Relation of the First Rise & Cause of the Recent Difficulties, in Public Affairs, in the Province of North Carolina.* Husband uses the Christian tradition and the British Constitution to uphold the farmers' protest in North Carolina known as the Regulator Movement. He adamantly states that colonial officials were committing political crimes such as wrongful taxation, the denial of majority rule, and the interruption of citizens' gatherings and assemblies. In *A Continuation of the Impartial Relation,* Husband provides a detailed analysis of the flaws of the colonial legal system and proposes reforming the jury system by permitting juries to decide law as well as "fact."

JOHN TRUMBULL: "An Essay on the Uses and Advantages of the Fine Arts." Trumbull's valedictory oration at Yale urges a liberalization of the college curriculum and concludes with the patriotic verses "Prospect of the Future Glory of America."

Nonfiction

JAMES ALBERT UKAWSAW GRONNIOSAW (c. 1710–?): *A Narrative of the Most Remarkable Particulars in the Life of James Albert Gronniosaw, an African Prince, as Related by Himself.* This spiritual slave narrative, modeled on the Puritan religious writers that influenced Gronniosaw, became a widely read and influential work and established the style of subsequent slave narratives.

PETER KALM (1716–1779): *Travels into North America.* Sent to America by the Swedish Academy of Science, Kalm publishes this important account of his journeys and his observations of the American colonies.

GUILLAUME THOMAS FRANÇOIS REYNAL (1713–1796): *L'Histoire philosophique et politique des établissements et du commerce des Européens dans les deux Indes.* The French author's four-volume history attacks the British Crown and praises the colonists. It is enthusiastically received by American supporters of democracy.

Poetry, Fiction, and Drama

WILLIAM BILLINGS (1746–1800): *The New England Psalm-Singer.* The Boston tanner-turned-composer sets out to revitalize the tedious psalmody of the day and issues this collection of his compositions.

ROBERT MUNFORD (c. 1730–1784): *The Candidates.* Munford, who is regarded as the first American comic dramatist, satirizes in this unproduced play local elections in Virginia. It is believed to be the first American play to feature a black character.

PHILLIS WHEATLEY: "An Elegiac Poem, on the Death of That Celebrated Divine, and Eminent Servant of Jesus Christ, the Reverend and Learned George Whitefield." Wheatley's moving tribute to the leading minister of the religious revivalist movement of the 1740s and 1750s, known as the Great Awakening, earns her the attention of Boston's literary elite and establishes her as a literary prodigy.

Publications and Events

The *Massachusetts Spy.* Isaiah Thomas (1749–1831) launches this Boston newspaper as a nonpartisan journal, but it eventually would serve the Revolutionary cause. It features agricultural articles by Crèvecoeur and Robertson's *History of America*. Thomas remained at its helm until 1815, and the paper continued to be published until 1904.

Sermons and Religious Writing

JANE FENN HOSKENS (1694–c. 1750): *The Life and Spiritual Sufferings of that Faithful Servant of Christ, Jane Hoskens, a Public Preacher among the People called Quakers.* Like other traveling ministers, Hoskens believes her mission is to share the Quaker gospel with the largest possible audience, and she depends on other Quaker women for a female support network. This spiritual autobiography is a superb example of one of the first literary forms to permit women public expression.

1771

Diaries, Journals, and Letters

WILLIAM HENRY DRAYTON (1742–1779): *The Letters of Freeman.* In this pamphlet published in London, Drayton, a South Carolina jurist, defends British authority in America through letters that he had sent earlier to the *South Carolina Gazette,* using the pseudonym "Freeman." Drayton does not, however, include the responses from the working people of South Carolina, who harshly criticize his Loyalist leanings. He justifies this omission by saying that the words from the "meaner sort of people" are not to be taken seriously.

Essays and Philosophy

ANTHONY BENEZET: *Some Historical Account of Guinea.* An extensive pamphlet detailing the civilization of this African region and documenting the horrors of the slave trade and its effect on African cultures. Benezet's work demonstrates that while slavery was accepted by the country as a whole, significant resistance to the practice existed.

Nonfiction

EDWARD ANTILL (1701–1770): "An Essay on the Cultivation of the Vine, and the Making and Preserving of Wine, Suited to the Different Climates in North America." Published in the American Philosophical Society's journal *Transactions* and designed to help American farmers improve their current practices, this essay is an example of the "how-to" articles that colonists turned to when lacking knowledge in certain fields.

BENJAMIN FRANKLIN: *Autobiography.* Franklin begins to write his most important work, a chronicle of his life that took him nearly twenty years to finish. He writes the first five chapters in England in 1771, resuming again thirteen years later (1784–1785) in Paris, and once again in 1788 in the United States. The book ends in 1757, when Franklin is fifty-one years old.

DAVID RITTENHOUSE (1732–1796): *The Transactions of the American Philosophical Society.* The American Philosophical Society publishes the first of four volumes on astronomy, the physical sciences, and mathematics. This first volume contributes to Rittenhouse's growing fame as an astronomer at home and abroad.

Poetry, Fiction, and Drama

PHILIP FRENEAU (1752–1832) AND HUGH HENRY BRACKENRIDGE (1748–1816): "The Rising Glory of America." This poem, read at the authors' graduation ceremony from the College of New Jersey (later renamed Princeton University), strongly expresses national pride in a time of tense relations with the British. The poem would be published in 1772, the first publication for both men.

Publications and Events

The *Pennsylvania Packet or the General Advertiser.* John Dunlop (1747–1812) establishes this weekly newspaper in Philadelphia, which in 1784 would become a daily paper and the first paper to print Washington's "Farewell Address." It would continue until 1839.

Sermons and Religious Writing

ISAAC BACKUS: "The Doctrine of Sovereign Grace." The widely traveled Baptist minister delivers a sermon, in his trademark clear and powerful language, that grapples with the meaning of grace.

CHARLES CHAUNCY: "A Compleat View of Episcopacy." The minister reveals in this sermon that his patriotic

Samuel Adams

fervor is grounded in his opposition to the foundation of the episcopacy in America. He sees the move as a British attempt to reduce the native autonomy of Congregationalism.

GEORGE WHITEFIELD: *The Works of Reverend George Whitefield*. Six volumes of Whitefield's writings are collected and published the year after he dies. As the fervor of the Great Awakening lessened, people came to remember Whitefield more for his theatrical preaching style than for his message. His popularity, however, remained high.

1772
Diaries, Journals, and Letters

THOMAS HUTCHINSON: *The Hutchinson Letters*. Letters from the last royal governor of the Massachusetts Bay Company (1771–1774) to the secretary of the British foreign secretary, urging repression of colonial liberties. Benjamin Franklin discovers and publishes these letters against Hutchinson's instructions, resulting in a scandal that would remove Franklin from his position as deputy postmaster general and generate great hatred for Hutchinson in the colonies.

Essays and Philosophy

SAMUEL ADAMS: *The Rights of the Colonists*. A report from the Committee of Correspondence, this document, believed to be mainly the work of Adams, keeps the idea of independence from England in the public mind. Basing his arguments on the natural rights of man, Adams demonstrates the depth of his education and reading.

BENJAMIN FRANKLIN: *The Sommersett Case and the Slave Trade*. Having come to believe that slavery is inherently evil and after freeing his two slaves during the 1760s, Franklin produces his first writing against the institution of slavery.

Poetry, Fiction, and Drama

JAMES ALLEN (1739–1808): "The Poem Which the Committee of the Town of Boston Had Voted Unanimously to Be Published." The son of a wealthy Boston merchant, Allen composes this poem as a memorial to the Boston Massacre and for publication in a pamphlet on the same subject by James Warren. While the work is initially celebrated, rumors of Allen's Loyalist leanings result in city-wide censoring of the poem. The controversy does little to devalue the author's witty satire.

JOHN TRUMBULL: "The Progress of Dulness." The author's most popular work is a verse satire published in three parts and completed in 1773. Trumbull mocks Yale's educational system as well as its techniques for instructing ministers. The main characters, Tom Brainless, Dick Hairbrain, and Harriet Simper, typify the horrific, if humorous, results of Yale pedagogy.

Sermons and Religious Writing

SAMSON OCCOM (1732–1792): "A Sermon Preached at the Execution of Moses Paul, an Indian Who Was Executed at New Haven." The first publication in America by a Native American is a sermon warning of the evils of alcohol, based on an incident in which an Indian killed a white man while drunk. Occom also condemns racial intolerance, which he says corrupts the minds of both whites and Indians.

1773
Diaries, Journals, and Letters

PHILIP VICKERS FITHIAN (1747–1776): *Journal and Letters of Philip Vickers Fithian*. Fithian's observations on life in Virginia, his career as a traveling minister, and his service as a military chaplain. The most famous portion of his diary records his reactions to the harsh treatment of slaves. One of the few records of this time that observes

John Trumbull

life and society in the rural south, the journal would be published in part in 1934 and as a whole in 1968.

MARTHA LAURENS RAMSAY (1759–1811): *Memoirs of Martha Laurens Ramsay.* The South Carolinian and future wife of historian David Ramsay begins her journal of spiritual and psychological self-analysis. Along with her letters, it would be published upon her death in 1811 and frequently reprinted throughout the nineteenth century.

Essays and Philosophy

JOHN ALLEN (fl. 1764–1788): "An Oration, Upon the Beauties of Liberty." This oration by the Boston Baptist preacher, delivered on Thanksgiving Day, fast becomes the sixth-best-selling pamphlet in the colonies prior to the publication of the Declaration of Independence. It is a spirited defense of the rights of the American people. *The American Alarm* (1773) and *The Watchman's Alarm* (1774), rousing polemical works on behalf of independence, would follow.

TIMOTHY DWIGHT AND JOHN TRUMBULL: *The Correspondent.* Dwight and Trumbull collaborate once again on a series of essays, some of which are published in 1770 and the rest in 1773. Trumbull writes the majority of the essays, and his tone in *The Correspondent* is more sincere than it had been in *The Meddler* (1769). However, both series share Trumbull's characteristically witty critiques and reflections.

BENJAMIN FRANKLIN: *Rules by Which a Great Empire May be Reduced to a Small One.* Franklin's essay is a thinly disguised satire of Britain's colonial policies, summarizing American grievances. As his satire circulates in England, Franklin writes to his sister, "I have held up a Looking-Glass in which some of the Ministers may see their ugly faces, and the Nation its Injustice."

BENJAMIN RUSH (1745–1813): *An Address to the Inhabitants of the British Settlements in America, Upon Slave-Keeping.* In a biting attack on the slave trade and the entire institution of slavery, Rush, the Philadelphia-born physician, public official, and writer who suggested to Thomas Paine the writing of *Common Sense,* combines the philosophy of natural rights with the ideas of the Great Awakening.

Poetry, Fiction, and Drama

BRIDGET RICHARDSON FLETCHER (1726–1770): *Hymns and Spiritual Songs.* This posthumously published collection, presumed to be written by a Massachusetts woman, includes verses in uniform ballad stanzas that are suitable for singing but unimpressive as poetry. The book's editor asks readers "to make allowances for the many inaccuracies of a female pen."

MERCY OTIS WARREN (1728–1814): *The Adulateur.* The Boston poet, dramatist, and historian makes her most noted contribution as a writer of political satires in dramatic form. Published in the manner of all her plays — anonymously in newspapers or as broadsides and not meant to be performed — the drama attacks the colonial government and especially Thomas Hutchinson, calling him Rapatio, a name that haunts him until he leaves Boston. She continues her attack on Rapatio in *The Defeat,* depicting Rapatio and his court as a faction of inept conspirators. To avoid libel and sedition laws, Warren writes anonymously and masks her targets with thinly veiled pseudonyms.

PHILLIS WHEATLEY: *Poems on Various Subjects, Religious and Moral.* After being freed by the Wheatley family in 1772, the poet takes a trip financed by her former owners to England, where she is celebrated by the nobility and in literary circles. Though she had not been able to secure a publisher for her work in America, a British publisher is eager to print this defining collection of her poems. It is the first published poetry collection by an African American. Included is "On Being Brought from Africa to America." Wheatley's poem recounts her fortune as a slave in America. In it she recalls, "'Twas mercy brought me from my Pagan land, / Taught my benighted soul to understand / That there's a God, that there's a Saviour too: / Once I redemption neither sought nor knew."

Publications and Events

The *Maryland Journal.* When William Goddard decides to open a printing shop in Baltimore and publish the city's first newspaper, he asks his sister, Mary Katherine Goddard (1738–1816), to take care of both businesses. By May 1775, the masthead reads, "Published by M. K. Goddard." Mary Katherine served as Baltimore's only printer during the Revolution.

Rivington's New-York Gazetteer or the Connecticut, Hudson's River, New-Jersey, and Quebec Weekly Advertiser. James Rivington (c. 1724–1802), the most influential Loyalist editor of the American Revolution, begins publishing this newspaper. It sparked the ire of some Americans, and in 1775 a mob destroyed his printing shop and press. Rivington set up shop again a few months later only to see his press demolished once again. He began publishing again in 1777 with *Rivington's New-York Loyal Gazette.*

Sermons and Religious Writing

ISAAC BACKUS: "An Appeal to the Public for Religious Liberty." This important sermon helps clarify and define the Baptist faith in the late colonial era.

BENJAMIN CHURCH: "An Oration . . . to Commemorate the Bloody Tragedy of the Fifth of March, 1770." Church delivers a powerful sermon meant to rally support for the patriots' cause on the third anniversary of the Boston Massacre.

SAMUEL HOPKINS: *An Inquiry into the Nature of True Holiness.* In his third and most important theological work, Hopkins states his belief in the need for selflessness among Christians. He holds that people should not be concerned with their own salvation but must devote themselves to a higher cause.

1774

Diaries, Journals, and Letters

WILLIAM HENRY DRAYTON: *A Letter From Freeman of South-Carolina.* The most important of Drayton's pamphlets demonstrates his conversion from Loyalist to patriot. Written to the First Continental Congress in response to the Intolerable Acts, it declares that Americans should be rebellious in their actions and, although similarities exist between 1774 and 1688 (the Glorious Revolution in England), the grievances of Americans are far more severe.

JANET SCHAW (c. 1735–c. 1801): *Journal of a Lady of Quality; Being a Narrative of a Journey from Scotland to the West Indies, North Carolina, and Portugal, in the Years 1774 to 1776.* Published in 1921, this collection of letters by the Scottish-born travel writer includes a travel account, diary, and literary opinions. It is of particular interest for its views of North Carolina during the period.

Essays and Philosophy

ETHAN ALLEN (1738–1789): *A Brief Narrative of the Proceedings of the Government of New York.* Allen's vindication of the Vermont settlers in their dispute over property rights with the government of New York is based on John Locke's *Second Treatise of Government.*

ANTHONY BENEZET: *The Mighty Destroyer Displayed.* The most important of Benezet's tracts against alcohol.

MYLES COOPER (1735–1785): *The American Querist and A Friendly Address to All Reasonable Americans.* The president of King's College (1763–1775) presents the Loyalist position in the growing dispute.

JOHN DICKINSON: "An Essay on the Constitutional Power of Great Britain." A well-documented essay arguing the need to define clearly the powers of Parliament and the powers of the colonial legislatures.

JACOB DUCHÉ: *Caspina's Letters.* This work (first published in the *Pennsylvania Packet* as "Observations on a Variety of Subjects, Literary, Moral, and Religious") takes the form of a foreigner, Tamoc Caspina, commenting on America in letters to his friends in England. The writer is clearly sympathetic to British ideas and actions.

JOSEPH GALLOWAY (c. 1731–1803): *Plan of a Proposed Union Between Great Britain and the Colonies.* The Philadelphia Loyalist tries to halt the growing drift toward separation by drawing up a home-rule plan for America, which anticipates Britain's policies in the nineteenth century.

ALEXANDER HAMILTON (1755–1804): *A Full Vindication of the Measures of the Congress.* A reply to Samuel Seabury's *Free Thoughts on the Proceedings of the Continental Congress*, which displays the author's exemplary logic and expository power in supporting the colonists' boycott of British goods. Yet even Hamilton avoids using the word *independence*, as most colonial leaders do for some time.

JOHN JAY (1745–1829): *An Address to the People of Great Britain.* Jay's plea to the British on behalf of the First Continental Congress to remove parliamentary restrictions on colonial society. It alternates between conciliation and unwavering statements of principle. Thomas Jefferson lauds it as "a production certainly of the finest pen in America."

THOMAS JEFFERSON: "A Summary View of the Rights of British America." Following the Boston Tea Party and the subsequent closing of the port of Boston, Jefferson makes his first significant foray in political writing. He states that natural rights supersede any rights put forth by civil law. The essay is considered a precursor to the Declaration of Independence as it challenges the authority of Parliament in the colonies.

ARTHUR LEE: *An Appeal to the Justice and Interests of the People of Great Britain.* The best known of Lee's many pamphlets opposes Britain's taxation policies based on principle and expediency and appeals to the British sense of fair play. A *Second Appeal* would appear in 1775.

JOSIAH QUINCY (1744–1775): *Observations on the Act of Parliament Commonly Called the Boston Port-Bill.* A response to the closing of Boston Harbor following the Boston Tea Party, the pamphlet accuses the British government of corruption and repression.

SAMUEL SEABURY (1729–1796): "Free Thoughts on the Proceedings of the Continental Congress. . . ." The first in a famous series of essays by the staunch Loyalist author. Published as a pamphlet and signed by "A Westchester Farmer," it is so persuasive that radicals in New York fear its political impact. The essay contains figures of speech familiar to colonial farmers and cautions that Congress's move to boycott English goods will bankrupt farmers while making urban craftsmen rich. In *The Congress Canvassed*, Seabury speaks to New York City merchants, stating that revolutionary enforcement committees will economically impair them.

JAMES WILSON (1742–1798): *Considerations on the Nature and Extent of the Legislative Authority of the British Parliament.* The Scottish-born jurist contends that Parliament has no authority over the colonies since they are separate states connected only by a common monarch.

Poetry, Fiction, and Drama

FRANCIS HOPKINSON: *A Pretty Story.* Hopkinson, known primarily as a poet until now, publishes this allegorical satire tracing the events leading up to the First Continental Congress. It launches his career as a politician and political critic. He would eventually become a signer of the Declaration of Independence, and George Washington would appoint him a justice of the U.S. district court in Pennsylvania.

JONATHAN SEWALL (1728–1796): "The Association of the Delegates." Sewall, known for his defense of Crown policy, takes a satirical look at the Nonintercourse (or boycott resolutions) set by the First Continental Congress. The poem mimics the original document; however, Sewall uses a simple-minded patriot chronicler to attack congressional policy.

JOHN TRUMBULL: "An Elegy for the Times." While studying law in John Adams's Boston office, Trumbull produces this patriotic poem.

MERCY OTIS WARREN: "The Squabble of the Sea Nymphs; or, The Sacrifice of the Tuscaroroes." Demonstrating Warren's skill and importance as a satirist and critic during the Revolution, the poem commemorates the Boston Tea Party while critiquing the role of the British and the colonial government.

Publications and Events

The First Book of the American Chronicles of the Times. This anonymous burlesque, written by a Philadelphian and satirizing American history, begins to appear serially, continuing into 1775.

Sermons and Religious Writing

ELIZABETH SAMPSON ASHBRIDGE: *Some Account of the Fore-Part of the Life of Elizabeth Ashbridge.* Written from 1746 to 1753, one of the most readable and interesting of the Quaker journals and among the earliest autobiographies by an American woman is published; Ashbridge had died in 1755.

SAMSON OCCOM: *A Choice Collection of Hymns and Spiritual Songs; Intended for the Edification of Sincere Christians, of All Denominations.* The second and final published work from the first Native American to publish in America. This is a compilation of spiritual music that Occom thought appropriate for Christian worship.

1775
Diaries, Journals, and Letters

OLIVER HART (1723–1795): *Diary to the Backcountry.* During a three-month stretch, the fervent patriot traveled through western Carolina, trying to convince backcountry settlers to support independence. His diary gives a rare look into the politics of the frontier. It would be first published as *Oliver Hart's Diary to the Backcountry* in 1975.

JOHN HOWE (fl. 1753–1812): *The Journal Kept by John Howe While He Was Employed as a British Spy; Also While He Was Engaged in the Smuggling Business.* Not published until 1827, the journal details the secretive life of the elusive John Howe. The work is an entertaining read as well as an interesting look into the life of a spy during the American Revolution.

Essays and Philosophy

JOHN DICKINSON: *A Declaration by the Representatives of the United Colonies. . . .* Drafted chiefly by John

Dickinson, this is the most radical statement adapted by colonial leaders prior to the Declaration of Independence.

BENJAMIN FRANKLIN: *Proposed Articles of Confederation.* Franklin presents his plan for an American nation called "The United Colonies of North America," with a Congress of limited powers. The Second Continental Congress would not accept it.

JOSEPH GALLOWAY: *A Candid Examination of the Mutual Claims of Great Britain and the Colonies....* The well-known Loyalist supports Parliament's authority to rule the colonies but refutes the wisdom of taxation. As an alternative to American representation in Parliament, Galloway proposes the formation of an American legislature to wield concurrent powers with Parliament. The colonists reject the idea, further escalating tensions.

ALEXANDER HAMILTON: *The Farmer Refuted.* Hamilton rebuts the Reverend Samuel Seabury's denunciation of the boycott of British goods. He daringly argues that since the colonists are not represented in Parliament, the British cannot claim the right to regulate colonial trade.

PATRICK HENRY (1736–1799): "Give Me Liberty or Give Me Death." The fiery orator combines radical visions with wit to convey his message in this speech, given to the members of the second Virginia Convention. It urges rebellion against Great Britain and, as legend reports, ends with the exclamation "I know not what course others may take, but as for me, give me Liberty or give me death!" All of Henry's speeches would be compiled from fragments by his first biographer, William Wirt, in 1817.

ISAAC HUNT: *The Political Family....* Hunt argues in favor of continued union with Great Britain. He was forced to flee to England, where he stuggled to survive as a preacher and tutor.

JOHN JAY: "Olive Branch Petition." In June, Jay composes the first draft of Congress's attempt to reconcile with the British. He recognizes the right of Parliament to regulate colonial commerce and renounces the thought of independence from Britain. These sentiments were genuine, for as late as July 1776, Jay still preferred reconciliation to independence.

THOMAS PAINE: "African Slavery in America." This essay advocates the abolition of slavery in America. While Paine is not the first to propose the idea, he is one of the most influential. A few weeks after his essay appeared in the *Pennsylvania Journal and the Weekly Advertiser,* the first antislavery society in America was founded in Philadelphia.

SAMUEL SEABURY: *An Alarm to the Legislature of the Province of New York.* Here the Loyalist author repeats his reply to Alexander Hamilton's *A View of the Controversy* and again outlines his idea for a compromise between Britain and the American colonies. Seabury proposes that Parliament sanction a constitution for the colonies.

Nonfiction

JAMES ADAIR (c. 1709–c. 1783): *The History of the American Indians.* Completed in 1768, this important chronicle of the Irish-born author's firsthand observations as a trader with the Indians in the South, concerning Indian customs, languages, daily life, and crucial events, is finally published. The account is marred only by Adair's theory that Native Americans are descendants of the ancient Jews.

DAVID RITTENHOUSE: "An Oration Delivered February 24, 1775, Before the American Philosophical Society." The famous astronomer and patriot argues for the existence of a moral universe that will become evident through scientific study. He writes that science will verify the perfection of divine creation. He also hopes for America's permanent separation from Europe.

BERNARD ROMANS (c. 1720–c. 1748): *A Concise Natural History of East and West Florida.* The king's botanist in the province of Florida produces this early natural history of the region.

Poetry, Fiction, and Drama

GENERAL JOHN BURGOYNE (1722–1792): *The Blockade.* A play by the British commander, ridiculing American soldiers and performed in Boston during the British occupation. When the British leave, a burlesque, *The Blockheads,* attributed by some to Mercy Otis Warren, would be performed in response, ridiculing the British.

THOMAS COOMBE (1747–1822): *Edwin; or, The Emigrant, an Eclogue, to Which Are Added Three Other Poetical Sketches.* Coombe, a Philadelphia clergyman, had retracted his former patriotic views in favor of his ordination oath of loyalty; this forced his banishment to England. The title poem of this collection details the life of a man who loses everything. His landlord takes his land, his wife and sons perish on the way to America, and then his daughter is captured by Indians. Coombe makes the point that a man's afflictions make him heroic.

THOMAS ATWOOD DIGGES (1741–1821): *Adventures of Alonso....* Often considered the first American novel, this work is written by an author born in Maryland and educated in England; he composed the novel while in Portugal. Digges portrays Portuguese characters and foreign settings in this sentimental, travel-based romance.

PHILIP FRENEAU: "General Gage's Soliloquy," "General Gage's Confession," "A Voyage to Boston," "American Liberty," and "A Political Litany." Freneau produces this series of satirical and patriotic poems to aid the war effort at the outbreak of the Revolution.

JONATHAN SEWALL: *A Cure for the Spleen, or Amusement for a Winter's Evening, being the Substance of a Conversation on the Times, over a Friendly Tankard and Pipe.* A play from the politically conservative author, based on a debate that takes place in a tavern where the characters voice all the American grievances against the British. The hero, the smart Reverend Sharp, expresses Sewall's belief that the Americans are acting out of selfishness, thwarted ambitions, and an admiration of demagoguery.

ANNA YOUNG SMITH (1756–1780): "An Elegy to the Memory of the American Volunteers." The Philadelphia poet's only published poem is a tribute to the American heroes at Lexington and Concord.

JOHN TRUMBULL: *M'Fingal.* Trumbull issues the first part of his greatest achievement, a mock-epic in tetrameter couplets modeled on Samuel Butler's *Hudibras* (1663). It satirizes the events of 1775 and leading figures through the experiences of the title figure, a blundering Loyalist who inadvertently proves the patriots' case. Divided into two cantos in 1776, the complete four-canto work would be completed in 1782.

MERCY OTIS WARREN: *The Group.* Warren's best political satire from her early period. Warren criticizes the Massachusetts Government Act, one of the so-called Intolerable Acts, which for practical purposes suspended the existing provincial government.

Publications and Events

The *Pennsylvania Evening Post.* After opening his own publishing shop in 1774, Benjamin Towne (c. 1740–1793) attempts to break into the crowded Philadelphia newspaper market the following year. To beat the five other weekly papers, he publishes the *Post* on a triweekly basis. The paper quickly becomes a leading voice for the patriot cause, but Towne switched to the Tory side when the British occupied the city. The move pays off when, after the British evacuated, Towne becomes the sole printer left in the city. He thus secured contracts from the Continental Congress and the state government.

Sermons and Religious Writing

JACOB DUCHÉ: "The Duty of Standing Fast in Our Spiritual and Temporal Liberties." The minister delivers his most famous sermon to the Revolutionary soldiers after the Battle of Bunker Hill, to stiffen their morale.

OWEN NOBLE (1733–1792): "Some Strictures Upon the Sacred Story Recorded in the Book of Esther." This is the most memorable and popular of Noble's sermons, which commemorates the Boston Massacre. It draws a parallel between the contemporary situation and the biblical story of Esther.

WILLIAM SMITH: *A Sermon on the Present Situation of American Affairs.* Previously Smith had questioned the legality of the Stamp Act and denied the right of Americans to rebel. In this sermon, he is torn between his love of England and his vision for America. He acknowledges the validity of American objections, yet seeks some form of compromise. His quasi-Loyalism would cost him his position at the College of Philadelphia in 1779, after which he would accept a parish posting in Maryland.

1776
Diaries, Journals, and Letters

CHARLES CARROLL (1737–1832): *Journal.* This journal, written in 1776 but not published until 1876, details Carroll's travels while on a congressional trip from Philadelphia to Montreal. His companions were Benjamin Franklin and John Carroll, and his entries describe New York's waterways and express hope that the nation will grow and prosper. The Maryland patriot and government official would become the last surviving signer of the Declaration of Independence.

Essays and Philosophy

JOHN ADAMS: *Thoughts on Government: Applicable to the Present State of the American Colonies.* Adams attempts to find the balance between New England republicanism and southern democratic skepticism. He presents the advantages of a bicameral legislature that would provide checks and balances on the power of any group.

JACOB GREEN (1722–1790): *Observations on the Reconciliation of Great-Britain and the Colonies.* One of the most successful and influential of the patriot preachers during the Revolution speaks out in favor of an independent America and predicts "an asylum for all noble spirits and sons of liberty from all parts of the world."

SAMUEL HOPKINS: *A Dialogue Concerning the Slavery of the Africans.* The minister, who freed his own slaves, predicts that the Revolution will inspire social reform — especially the abolition of slavery. He hopes that the era of self-interest will give way to one of benevolence. Harriet Beecher Stowe would make Hopkins the hero of *The Minister's Wooing* (1854).

CHARLES INGLIS (1734–1816): *The True Interest of America Impartially Stated in Certain Strictures on a Pamphlet*

Entitled Common Sense. This pamphlet from the Loyalist and Anglican minister is a response to Thomas Paine's call for rebellion. Inglis states several reasons for reconciliation with Great Britain and then lists the dire consequences of not reconciling.

JOHN JAY: *An Address of the Convention of the Representatives of the State of New York.* This pamphlet addresses the Continental army after its loss at Fort Lee and subsequent retreat deeper into New Jersey. Jay tries to buoy their spirits — "If success crown your efforts, all the blessings of Freedom will be your reward. If you fail in this contest, you will be happy with God and Liberty in Heaven."

SAMUEL LOUDON (c. 1727–1813): *The Deceiver Unmasked; or, Loyalty and Interest United.* The New York printer and publisher responds critically to Thomas Paine's *Common Sense.* As a result his shop is looted, and he is forced to flee from New York City to Fishkill.

THOMAS PAINE: *Common Sense.* Believing that independence will bring about a new era devoid of class and social distinctions, Paine writes the most popular pamphlet of the American Revolution. He reasons that monarchies undermine the natural order; thus, Americans have a duty to break free from British rule. Only then can a virtuous society exist. Sales of *Common Sense* exceed even those of the Bible for the year, with more than 100,000 copies sold in its first three months. It sparks numerous responses from London, Inglis, and other Loyalists. Paine also writes *The American Crisis.* After joining the Continental army as an aide-de-camp, Paine is stationed with the troops of General George Washington in late 1776. The author begins this pamphlet series of sixteen essays in December. It is an inspiring narrative of Washington's soldiers as they retreat from New York, and it quickly becomes the rallying cry for the American cause. "These are the times that try men's souls" is the essay's most recognizable line. Washington had the pamphlet read to his troops to bolster morale.

WILLIAM SMITH (1723–1793): *Plain Truth.* Smith, the New York lawyer who had authored *A Review of the Military Operations in North America . . . 1753–1756* (1757) and *The History of the Province of New York* (1757), responds to Paine's *Common Sense* with sentiments made clear by the subtitle "Independence Is Ruinous, Delusive, and Impractical." Forced to flee to Canada, Smith would become a prominent historian and jurist.

Poetry, Fiction, and Drama

Anonymous. *The Blockheads; or, The Affrighted Officers.* An anti-British satire published anonymously in Boston, which depicts the British as a bungling army of occupation. It is as an excellent example of patriot propaganda during this first phase of the American Revolution. Historians and literary critics are divided over authorship. Some believe its author to be Mercy Otis Warren, the important Revolutionary-era playwright, poet, and political critic. Critics who dispute attribution to Warren point out that the satire is too coarse for a woman of her station.

HUGH HENRY BRACKENRIDGE: "The Battle of Bunker Hill." Brackenridge writes this blank-verse tragedy for performance by his students at the Somerset Academy in Maryland, where he is a master. It features contrasting views by Revolutionary leaders and the British.

PHILIP FRENEAU: "The Beauties of Santa Cruz." Freneau, serving as the secretary to a West Indies planter, extols the beauty of the tropics, which is marred by the horrors of slavery, in this poem. He also writes "The Jamaican Funeral," a satire on the clergy about a minister who beats a man for objecting to collection of parish dues from mourners.

JOHN LEACOCK (1729–1802): *The Fall of the British Tyranny; or, American Liberty Triumphant.* Considered the earliest American chronicle play and the first to portray George Washington in a drama, Leacock's sprawling drama depicts the opening of the Revolution. It includes the Battle of Lexington and warfare in Virginia, with descriptions of many of the participants, including Hutchinson, Gage, Howe, and Burgoyne. There is no record that the play was ever produced. It is believed that Leacock was a Philadelphia silversmith, one of the Sons of Liberty, and an associate of John Dickinson and Benjamin Franklin.

JONATHAN ODELL (1737–1818): "A Birthday Song." Along with Joseph Stansbury (1742–1809), Odell was the most prominent Loyalist poet during the Revolution. Here the New Jersey minister offers verses in honor of the king, attacking the disloyalty of the patriots.

PHILLIS WHEATLEY: "To His Excellency General Washington." A celebratory poem to George Washington upon his appointment as the head of the army. The former slave wishes the virtuous Washington the best of fortune: "Proceed, great chief, with virtue on thy side, / Thy ev'ry action let the goddess guide. / A crown, a mansion, and a throne that shine, / With gold unfading, WASHINGTON! be thine."

Publications and Events

The Declaration of Independence. One of the most influential political documents ever written, the formal proclamation of the colonies' separation from Britain is adopted on July 4 by the Continental Congress and signed by the fifty-six representatives on August 2. It is mainly the work of Thomas Jefferson with revisions by John Adams, Benjamin Franklin, and other members of the Continental Congress.

The *Independent Chronicle*. This Boston newspaper in favor of the American cause begins publication. John Hancock and Samuel Adams are early contributors. It would continue publication until 1819.

Sermons and Religious Writing

JOHN WITHERSPOON (1723–1794): "The Dominion of Providence over the Passions of Men." Witherspoon delivers his most memorable sermon in Princeton, New Jersey, on May 17, an eloquent statement on behalf of independence. He served as a member of the Continental Congress and signed the Declaration of Independence.

1777
Essays and Philosophy

FRANCIS HOPKINSON: *A Letter to Lord Howe*. After writing in support of the Revolutionary cause along with Thomas Paine in the *Pennsylvania Magazine, or American Monthly Museum*, Hopkinson publishes several notable pamphlets. *A Letter* protests the British treatment of civilians during the war.

Nonfiction

ISAAC BACKUS: *History of New England, with Particular Reference to the Denomination of Christians Called Baptists*. Backus publishes the first installment of the three-volume series (to be completed in 1796) of notable early historical scholarship, still important today as a source on colonial New England.

WILLIAM ROBERTSON (1721–1793): *The History of America*. The Scottish historian issues a popular two-volume history.

Poetry, Fiction, and Drama

HUGH HENRY BRACKENRIDGE: *The Death of General Montgomery at the Siege of Quebec*. Brackenridge's second patriotic drama for production at Maryland's Somerset Academy, where he was a master, is about the ill-fated attack on Quebec.

FRANCIS HOPKINSON: "Camp Ballad." This is one of Hopkinson's best-known ballads, written to be sung by American troops to boost morale. He expresses his faith in the new nation: "Make room for America, another great nation, / Arises to claim in your council a state."

ROBERT MUMFORD (c. 1737–1783): *The Patriots*. Written between 1777 and 1779, Mumford's unproduced play is a satire on American radicals intoxicated with "liberty without constraint"; he accuses moderates of being disloyal.

Publications and Events

MARY KATHERINE GODDARD: The Baltimore printer publishes the first copy of the Declaration of Independence, including the names of all the signers.

Sermons and Religious Writing

NATHANIEL WHITAKER (1730–1795): "An Antidote Against Toryism." Whitaker's sermon asserts that the cause of liberty is the cause of God and truth and that it is lawful to wage war even against those not in uniform.

OLIVER HART: "The Character of a Truly Great Man Delineated, and His Death Deplored as a Public Loss. Occasioned by the Death of the Rev. William Tennant." Hart—the most influential Baptist minister in revolutionary South Carolina and an outspoken supporter of interdenominational cooperation—publishes this sermon supporting the disestablishment of the Anglican Church in South Carolina. The work displays the limits of Hart's belief in religious diversity and demonstrates his ardent nationalism.

1778
Diaries, Journals, and Letters

FRANCIS HOPKINSON: *Letter to Joseph Galloway*. Another important pamphlet from the now notable patriot, which criticizes those who are loyal to the British cause.

SARAH WISTER (1761–1804): *Sally Wister's Journal*. Though the Pennsylvania Quaker author tried her hand at many styles of writing, it is her journal covering the period 1777 to 1778 that solidifies her place in American literature. It is one of the most valued looks into the daily life of a typical Quaker teenager of the period.

Essays and Philosophy

SILAS DEANE (1737–1789): *To the Free and Virtuous Citizens of America*. The Connecticut Continental Congressman who served with Benjamin Franklin and Arthur Lee as American commissioners in France defends himself against charges that he exceeded his instructions. The work sparks one of the biggest scandals of the Revolution by revealing to the American public for the first time the nasty factionalization of the Americans in Paris, the secret role the French played in aiding the Americans, and strong sectional disagreements within Congress.

MOLLY GUTRIDGE (fl. 1778): *A New Touch on the Times.* This poetic broadside describes three things about American life during the Revolutionary War: the absence of men and the hardships borne by women as a result; the economic troubles of life during war; and the faith that God had placed these hardships on Americans but will someday reward the new nation. It is a highly unusual record from a woman who was most probably not wealthy and added a new perspective on the lives of women during the Revolution. Little is known of Gutridge beyond her residence in Marblehead, Massachusetts, during the Revolution.

Nonfiction

JONATHAN CARVER (1710–1780): *Travels Through the Interior Parts of North America in the Years 1766, 1767, and 1768.* Travel stories and tall tales combine in what is perhaps the most famous travel book to be published in colonial America.

THOMAS HUTCHINSON: *The History of the Province of Massachusetts-Bay, from 1749 to 1774.* The final volume in Hutchinson's trilogy. Hutchinson, now in exile, details his own administration and claims that the Revolution is a conspiracy of a tiny group of overambitious malcontents, led by James Otis Sr., who have fooled the people and ruined an empire.

BENJAMIN RUSH: *Directions for Preserving the Health of Soldiers: Recommended to the Consideration of the Officers in the Army of the United States of America.* Rush, the surgeon general of the Middle Department of the army during the Revolution, is outraged by the conditions he uncovers in army hospitals. His attempt to remedy this situation through director general Dr. Shippen (his former teacher) fails. General George Washington refers Rush's protest to Congress, which rules in favor of Shippen. Rush resigns his commission. His recommendations are published in this tract.

Poetry, Fiction, and Drama

JOEL BARLOW (1754–1812): "The Prospect of Peace." Barlow's first published poem and his Yale graduation address, clocked at twelve minutes by an impatient, unappreciative Yale president. It is a conventional ceremonial poem, significant for announcing Barlow's intention to celebrate the American experience in his writing.

WILLIAM BILLINGS: "Chester." The psalmodist composes his best-known patriotic anthem, which becomes a rallying song for the American troops. Billings also publishes "The Singing Master's Assistant"; or, "Key to Practical Music."

JUPITER HAMMON: *An Address to Miss Phillis Wheatly, Ethiopian Poetess, in Boston, Who Came from Africa at Eight Years of Age, and Soon Became Acquainted with the Gospel of Jesus Christ.* Here Hammon challenges the young poet and former slave Phillis Wheatley to be a role model for the youth of Boston by displaying that God's salvation is available to all.

FRANCIS HOPKINSON: "The Battle of the Kegs." This famous poem retells the story of how the British struggled endlessly with the armada of explosive kegs that Americans sent down the Delaware River toward the British encampments. This, and Hopkinson's other poems, become so popular that they are praised even in England.

WILLIAM LIVINGSTON: "Ode of General Washington." A poem written in blank verse celebrating the virtues of General George Washington. Livingston would become a member of the American Philosophical Society in 1781.

Publications and Events

Thomas's Massachusetts Spy. During the British occupation of Boston, Isaiah Thomas's original newspaper, the *Massachusetts Spy*, had fallen on difficult times. However, in 1778 the paper returns, revitalized. Like its publisher, it is outspoken, brazen, and dynamic. Opponents damn the publication as a "sedition factory," but prominent patriots such as James Otis, Paul Revere, and John Hancock anonymously contribute articles. Thomas's partisanship wins the *Spy* a large readership.

Sermons and Religious Writing

OLIVER HART: "Dancing Exploded." This sermon displays the famous minister's tendency to dictate moral principles. Here he warns the residents of Charlestown, South Carolina, against the decadence of balls and social gatherings, which are dear to the social life of Charleston's elite. Hart reminds them that a war is going on, a time to give up the "vanities of life."

1779
Diaries, Journals, and Letters

GEORGE ROGERS CLARK (1752–1818): "Clark's Mason Letter." The author writes this letter on November 19, after returning from his Northwest campaign of 1778 and 1779. Addressed to Clark's friend Colonel George Mason, it explains the many facets of his trek. The letter reveals some vivid exploits of the American Revolution, including the defense of Kentucky and an incursion into Illinois. Lost for decades, the letter would be found in the nineteenth century and published in 1869.

JOHN CHURCHMAN (1705–1775): *An Account of the Gospel of Labours and Christian Experiences of Christ.* A spiritual journal from a Pennsylvania Quaker. While such journals often served as moral guides for their readers, Churchman generalizes and moralizes from almost every incident. He truly reflects the Quaker belief that all of life should be lived conscientiously.

JOHN JAY: "A Circular Letter from the Congress of the United States of America to their Constituents." After leaving his post as the first chief justice of New York's Supreme Court, Jay is appointed president of the Continental Congress. Shortly thereafter, Congress adapts his draft of "A Circular Letter." In it, Jay upholds the Articles of Confederation as the best means to safeguard the principles of the Declaration of Independence.

Essays and Philosophy

JONATHAN CARVER: *A Treatise on the Culture of the Tobacco Plant. . . .* Discussing the cultivation of tobacco, the piece proposes possible adaptations for tobacco cultivation in colder climates of Great Britain, thought to be impossible at the time.

BENJAMIN FRANKLIN: *Political, Miscellaneous, and Philosophical Pieces.* The first compilation of Franklin's nonscientific writings is published in London.

THOMAS JEFFERSON: "Act for Establishing Religious Freedom." Written during his first term as governor of Virginia, this historic legislation argues that individual conscience is preferable to mandated religion. The act establishes the separation of church and state and is one of the author's most cherished writings. It would become law in 1786.

GOUVERNEUR MORRIS (1752–1816): *Observations on the American Revolution.* Published by Congress, this work by the eloquent New York statesman praises the new nation, claiming that America will be an example and a haven of freedom for the entire world.

JUDITH SARGENT MURRAY (1751–1820): "On the Equality of the Sexes." A description of women's involvement in history and literature. The essay traces women's contributions to public events in the world just as the new American nation debates the limitations of women's sphere. Murray finishes her essay before Mary Wollstonecraft (1759–1797) completes her *Vindication of the Rights of Woman* (1792); Murray's account would be published in 1790.

PELATIAH WEBSTER (1725–1795): "An Essay on Free Trade and Finance." Webster, who would become one of the outstanding political economists of the early Republic, publishes his first essay in support of a free trade policy by arguing that any restraints on commerce are unjust and self-defeating.

Nonfiction

ETHAN ALLEN: *A Narrative of Colonel Ethan Allen's Captivity.* A best-selling account of Allen's failed attack on Montreal and his subsequent capture and imprisonment from 1775 to 1778. His brash celebration of the underdog boosts the morale of the American army during the Revolution.

JOHN DODGE (1751–1800): *A Narrative of the Capture and Treatment of John Dodge.* Dodge was a successful Indian trader along the Great Lakes, and the British feared his influence over the Indians, arresting him twice during the period from 1776 to 1778. The first time he was released; the second time he escaped from prison in Quebec. His narrative, a very successful piece of anti-British propaganda, retells the story of his mistreatment at the hands of the British and of the British incitement of the Indians against the colonists. George Washington, taken by Dodge's account, would ask Dodge to report to Congress.

ALEXANDER HEWAT (c. 1745–1829): *An Historical Account of the Rise and Progress of the Colonies of South Carolina and Georgia.* Hewat, a South Carolina Loyalist, produces this social and natural history of the region. His account of its political history is criticized for its Loyalist bias.

Poetry, Fiction, and Drama

PHILIP FRENEAU: "The House of Night." Freneau's allegorical poem describing the death of Death has been interpreted as reflecting in part his guilt over his residence in the West Indies during the Revolution. An expanded version would appear in his *Poems* (1786).

JONATHAN ODELL: "Word of Congress." The Loyalist poet produces one of his most powerful invectives aimed at the duplicity of the Continental Congress.

MERCY OTIS WARREN: *The Motley Assembly.* This farce, which attacks Bostonians who oppose the Revolution, has been attributed to Warren, though the evidence for and against this attribution is inconclusive.

Publications and Events

The *United States Magazine.* Edited by Hugh Henry Brackenridge during its twelve-month run, this monthly Philadelphia periodical included a satire on James Rivington by John Witherspoon and Freneau's parody of Psalm 137.

Sermons and Religious Writing

SIMEON HOWARD (1733–1804): "A Sermon on Brotherly Love." This sermon demonstrates the political, military, and emotional concerns of ministers during the Revolutionary War. Delivered to the Masons, it emphasizes the need to be giving to and understanding of soldiers' families.

1780

Essays and Philosophy

JOSEPH GALLOWAY: *Historical and Political Reflections on the Rise & Progress of the American Rebellion*. Writing in exile, the Loyalist apologist continues to make a case for a written constitution that places limits on Parliament to reconcile it with the American colonists. Cornwallis's surrender at Yorktown soon would make his suggestion moot.

Poetry, Fiction, and Drama

DAVID HUMPHREYS (1752–1818): "A Poem Addressed to the Armies of the United States." Washington's aide-de-camp produces this patriotic verse, the first published poem to use the name of the new country in its title.

JONATHAN ODELL: "The American Times." Published under the pseudonym "Camillo Querno" but attributed to the Loyalist writer, the poem is an invective aimed at the American leaders of the Revolution.

1781

Diaries, Journals, and Letters

JOSIAH ATKINS (c. 1749–1781): *Diary of Josiah Atkins*. An impressive record of an American soldier during the Revolutionary War. Atkins's writing leans toward the spiritual, and it is clear that the only reason he joins the army is because he believes that the American cause is divinely sanctioned. The diary details his questioning of these beliefs, such as when he sees slaves at George Washington's plantation and wonders how "persons who pretend to stand for the rights of mankind . . . can delight in oppression." The diary would not be published until 1975.

Essays and Philosophy

ANTHONY BENEZET: *Short Observations on Slavery*. A pamphlet about Benezet's many years teaching African American students. Unlike Thomas Jefferson, Benezet concludes that there is no difference in intellectual capacity between African Americans and whites.

JOHN WITHERSPOON: *The Druid*. The first systematic analysis of the usage of English in America and its

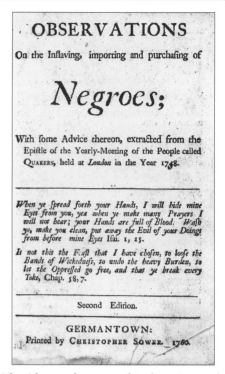

The title page from one of Anthony Benezet's many books and pamphlets

divergence from its English source, a trend that Witherspoon decried. It is noteworthy as well for its coinage of the term *Americanism*.

Nonfiction

SAMUEL ANDREW PETERS (1735–1826): *General History of Connecticut, by a Gentleman of the Province*. The Connecticut Loyalist issues this largely derogatory history that misrepresents colonial blue laws, errors repeated by later historians.

Poetry, Fiction, and Drama

PHILIP FRENEAU: "The British Prison Ship." In what has been called the angriest poem ever written by an American, Freneau chronicles his captivity and brutal imprisonment by the British in a prison ship in New York Harbor.

FRANCIS HOPKINSON: *The Temple of Minerva*. Hopkinson's "dramatic allegorical cantata" celebrates America's alliance with France.

Sermons and Religious Writing

MOSES HEMMENWAY (1735–1811): *A Discourse on the Nature . . . of . . . Baptism*. A popular publication that defends liberal religious principles from a lifelong friend of John Adams. Hemmenway supports adult baptism and infant baptism. The volume would be reprinted four times and was adopted, in abridged form, as doctrine by the Methodist Episcopal Church.

1782
Essays and Philosophy

MICHEL-GUILLAUME JEAN DE CRÈVECOEUR (1731–1813): *Letters from an American Farmer*. The French-born surveyor who settled in Orange County, New York, produces this classic collection of twelve essays that reflect on the nature of American life, particularly its customs and manners. Crèvecoeur celebrates America's religious diversity alongside its plainness and attempts to answer this question: what is an American? His description of bountiful American lands spurs many French people to immigrate to America.

BENJAMIN FRANKLIN: "Information to Those Who Would Remove to America." An essay describing life in the colonies as superior to life in Europe due to less poverty and more land.

Poetry, Fiction, and Drama

THOMAS BURKE (c. 1744–1783): *The Poems of Governor Thomas Burke of North Carolina*. A collection of poems not published until 1961. The verses written between 1764 and 1782 develop pastoral, love, and patriotic themes. The author also attacks certain well-known colonial figures; for example, Thomas Paine is the beneficiary of one of Burke's outbursts: "great Common Sense surely did come / From out the Crack in grizzly Pluto's Bum."

JOHN TRUMBULL: *M'Fingal: A Modern Epic Poem in Four Cantos*. Trumbull completes his masterpiece, a comic satire on the events of 1775 from the perspective of a blundering Loyalist. After M'Fingal is tarred and feathered, he attends a Tory meeting where he predicts the British defeat and the rise of the American nation.

MERCY OTIS WARREN: "To a Young Gentleman, Residing in France." An instructional poem in which Warren offers advice to her son about avoiding the temptations young men from America may encounter when they are away from home.

Publications and Events

The *Aitken Bible*. Following his New Testament issued in 1777, Robert Aitken (1734–1802), a Scottish-born publisher, issues the first complete English-language Bible printed in America. Prior to the Revolution, American printers had been prohibited from publishing Bibles in English since a monopoly was held by printers in Britain.

1783
Nonfiction

JOHN LEDYARD (1751–1789): *A Journal of Captain Cook's Last Voyage to the Pacific Ocean*. Ledyard provides his perspective as a member of Cook's expedition to the Sandwich Islands, which includes the only eyewitness account of Cook's murder.

NOAH WEBSTER (1758–1843): *A Grammatical Institute of the English Language*. The author's first speller. In 1784 and 1785 Webster would enlarge the speller, adding a grammar and a reader; the book would eventually include American spellings and geographic and historical references. To better reflect its contents, later editions used revised titles, which emphasized their nationalist bent — *The American Spelling Book* and, for the enlarged version, *An American Selection of Lessons in Reading and Speaking*. Webster's first edition sold five thousand copies. More than fifteen million copies were sold by 1837 and, by the close of the nineteenth century, more than sixty million.

PELATIAH WEBSTER: *Dissertation on the Political Union*. The political economist argues that a central government must have taxation power. Some have argued that Webster was an important architect of the Constitution, but others have noted that he failed to anticipate some of its key features and that the drafters ignored several of his specific proposals.

Poetry, Fiction, and Drama

DAVID HUMPHREYS: *The Glory of America; or, Peace Triumphant Over War and Poem on the Industry of the United States of America*. Humphreys continues his patriotic verses in celebration of the American victory and its bright economic future.

Publications and Events

The *New York Independent Journal*. The newspaper begins publication. In 1787 and 1788 it publishes the documents that would become *The Federalist Papers*. In 1788 it would become the *New York Daily Gazette*.

Sermons and Religious Writing

EZRA STILES: "The United States Elevated to Glory and Honor." Another significant sermon from the New England minister. Here he argues that America is fated for greatness since God granted it recent victory over Britain. Stiles goes on to predict correctly the westward

John Adams

expansion and demographic explosion of the next century. While there is almost no place in his vision of America for African Americans or Indians, Stiles, a slave owner himself, espouses moving all slaves and freed people to Africa.

1784

Diaries, Journals, and Letters

ALEXANDER HAMILTON: *Letters from "Phocion."* Hamilton publishes two pamphlets protesting state legislative acts punishing Loyalists.

Essays and Philosophy

HANNAH ADAMS (1755–1831): *An Alphabetical Compendium of the Various Sects.* Adams, the first American woman to earn a living by writing, produces her most significant work, a reference to modern religions intended to "avoid giving the least preference of any denomination over another." Revised editions would appear in 1791, 1801, and 1817 as *A Dictionary of All Religions*, and the work is an indispensable resource in registering the changes in religious views in America from 1784 to 1817.

JOHN ADAMS: *History of the Dispute with America.* A collection of newspaper essays originally published in 1774 and 1775 in response to essays by "Massachuset-

tensis" (identified as Daniel Leonard). Adams holds that the legal standing of the colonies—including semi-autonomy from Parliament—is established by precedents within the colonial charters.

ISAAC BACKUS: *History of New England, with Particular Reference to the Denomination of Christians Called Baptists.* The second volume of the three-volume series is published. The first volume of this important source on colonial New England had been published in 1777.

JEREMY BELKNAP (1744–1798): *The History of New Hampshire.* The first volume of the Boston clergyman and historian's three-volume history (to be completed in 1792). It is notable for its use of original documents and eyewitness accounts—a rare practice among early American historians.

ROBERT BELL (c. 1732–1784): "Bell's Address to Every Free-Man." An essay by the famous publisher, attacking the new restrictions the Pennsylvania assembly had placed on the auctioneering of books. In *Memorial on the Free Sale of Books*, Bell claims that access to reading material is an essential element of a free society. Bell died while traveling to an out-of-state book auction.

ANTHONY BENEZET: *Some Observations on the Indian Nations of This Continent.* The Quaker social reformer attempts to do for Native Americans what he had attempted for African Americans, humanizing them and asserting that they possess a valuable culture that should be appreciated and respected.

JOHN FILSON (c. 1747–1788): *The Discovery, Settlement, and Present State of Kentucke. . . .* The Pennsylvania-born explorer and historian produces the first published history of Kentucky, with details on soil and climate. The appendix, "The Adventures of Col. Daniel Boon," establishes the legendary reputation of Daniel Boone.

THOMAS JEFFERSON: *Report of Government for the Western Territories.* Jefferson submits this report to Congress. This historic document declares that all new states should enter the union on equal grounds with the original thirteen states; that any person with a hereditary title must forfeit the title before becoming a citizen; that new states must stay in the union "forever"; and that slavery should be banned from all new states after 1800. Congress passes the Ordinance of 1784 based on Jefferson's report but removes the last two of Jefferson's suggestions. Jefferson also writes *Notes on the State of Virginia*, his only full-length book. It contains detailed descriptions of the natural scenery of his home state and refutes the claim of French naturalist Buffon that every species found in both Europe and America grows to a larger size in Europe. The author defends freedom of religion with great eloquence in this book; however, he also details his theories in support of white racial superiority.

JEDIDIAH MORSE (1761–1826): *Geography Made Easy.* The first geography text published in the United States. This volume and his subsequent works in the field would win him recognition as the "father of American geography."

Poetry, Fiction, and Drama

PETER MARKOE (c. 1752–1792): *The Patriot Chief.* The first of Markoe's two theatrical pieces is a drama about a rebellion against a Lydian king, written, as Markoe asserts, "to call attention to the dangers of aristocracy." He would subsequently create a comic opera, *The Reconciliation* (1790). Neither play was produced during Markoe's lifetime.

PHILLIS WHEATLEY: "Liberty and Peace: A Poem." Wheatley's final publication. Wheatley had married John Peters, a free black Bostonian, in 1778. Their union was marked by constant financial difficulties, and after her husband was jailed for debt, Wheatley found herself without friends to help her. She supported herself and her family as a laundress in a boardinghouse that catered to blacks. This poem, her last attempt to regain public notice, was unsuccessful. Sick and overworked, Wheatley died on December 5.

Publications and Events

ABEL BUELL, a Connecticut printer, publishes the first map of the United States that shows the boundaries negotiated under the Treaty of Paris.

The *Massachusetts Sentinel and the Republican Journal.* The Boston newspaper is launched. Known for its political cartoons, it also would feature John Quincy Adams's series of essays attacking Thomas Paine. In 1790, its name changed to the *Columbian Centinel.*

Sermons and Religious Writing

ETHAN ALLEN: *Reason the Only Oracle of Man, or a Compendious System of Natural Religion.* Scholars have suggested that Allen's deistic treatise, commonly known as "Ethan Allen's Bible," was actually the work of Dr. Thomas Young (1732–1777), whose manuscript Allen published.

CHARLES CHAUNCY: "The Benevolence of the Deity." A sermon in which Chauncy states his belief in a liberal Congregational church founded upon the idea of a benevolent God.

1785
Essays and Philosophy

JAMES MADISON (1751–1836): *Memorial and Remonstrance, Presented to the General Assembly, of the State of Virginia, at Their Session in 1785, in consequence of a Bill Brought into that Assembly for the Establishment of Religion by Law.* A successful attack to thwart Patrick Henry's attempt to establish a state-supported church in Virginia. Madison would write to Thomas Jefferson in 1786, "I flatter myself I have in this Country extinguished forever the ambitious hope of making laws for the human mind."

NOAH WEBSTER: *Sketches of American Policy.* Webster's speller and reader had made him a household name. However, his works fell prey to unauthorized reprinting, leading Webster to fight for practical copyright laws at the state level. This drew him to the nationalist cause, and as early as 1783 he became a crucial supporter of the Federalist movement. Following a series of Federalist articles in the *Connecticut Courant,* he issues this pamphlet in support of his newfound position.

Nonfiction

JOHN MARRANT (1755–1791): *A Narrative of the Lord's Wonderful Dealings with John Marrant, a Black.* The narrative tells of the early life and conversion of Marrant, a black minister from New York. An immensely popular work, it would be reprinted at least nineteen times before 1825. Marrant would continue his life story in *A Journal of the Rev. John Marrant,* published in 1790.

HUMPHREY MARSHALL (1722–1801): *Arbustrum Americanum: The American Grove.* The Philadelphia botanist publishes what is believed to be the first botanical treatise by an American published in the United States.

DAVID RAMSAY (1749–1815): *History of the Revolution of South Carolina.* The acclaimed first historical account of the war in South Carolina. Ramsay would follow it with the more ambitious *History of South Carolina from Its First Settlement in 1670, to . . . 1808* (1809).

ISAIAH THOMAS: *A Specimen of Types.* The printer and publisher of Worcester, Massachusetts, called by Benjamin Franklin "the Baskerville of America," publishes a sample of his typefaces, which reveals important information about early American printing.

Poetry, Fiction, and Drama

TIMOTHY DWIGHT: *The Conquest of Canaan.* According to Dwight, his allegorical reflection of the American Revolution through Joshua's conquest of Canaan is "the first epic poem to have appeared in America."

Timothy Dwight in an engraving by J. B. Forrest
based on an original painting by John Trumbull

MERCY OTIS WARREN: *Sans Souci*. A biting satire of
elite society in Boston after the Revolution. This social
critique of fashion and manners uses many of Mercy Otis
Warren's literary hallmarks, though she never claimed
authorship. Modern scholars remain divided over the
attribution to Warren.

Publications and Events

The *Pennsylvania Evening Herald*. The first edition of
a pro-Irish paper covering the political proceedings and
debates of the Pennsylvania assembly is published by
Mathew Carey (1760–1839).

Sermons and Religious Writing

JONATHAN EDWARDS JR. (1745–1801): *Three Sermons
on the Necessity of the Atonement*. Here the son of the
famous minister demonstrates that God's grace is available to more people than even his father professed. These
sermons, given before the General Assembly of Connecticut, argue that the death of Christ signifies that sin will
be punished and that anyone can be a sinner.

1786
Essays and Philosophy

FRANCIS HOPKINSON: "A Plan for the Improvement of
the Art of Paper War." Hopkinson's essay ridicules the
battles among rival newspapers.

Poetry, Fiction, and Drama

JOSEPH BROWN (1764–1786): *Ladd: The Poems of
Arouet*. The Rhode Island physician publishes this col-
lection, which anticipates the style and subjects of the
Romantics.

CONNECTICUT WITS: "The Anarchiad: A New England Poem." A mock-heroic satirical poem that attacks
the states' sluggishness in ratifying the Constitution. The
Connecticut Wits were an informal association of former
Yale students including David Humphrey, John Trumbull, Timothy Dwight, and Joel Barlow. The poem appears anonymously in the *New Haven Gazette* and the
Connecticut Magazine between 1786 and 1787.

PHILIP FRENEAU: *The Poems of Philip Freneau, Written
Chiefly During the Late War*. A volume containing 111
poems, 98 of which have obvious American or patriotic
themes. This work earns Freneau the title "poet of the
Revolution." It includes one of his greatest nature poems,
"The Wild Honey Suckle."

JOHN PARKE (1754–1789): *The Lyric Works of Horace
. . . to Which Are Added, a Number of Original Poems*.
Published anonymously by a Delaware soldier of the
Continental army, the volume adapts Horace's poems
to American history and substitutes Americans for the
Roman originals (e.g., Washington for Augustus). Included as well is a pastoral drama, *Virginia*.

SUSANNA HASWELL ROWSON (c. 1762–1824): *Victoria*.
Rowson's first novel is published by subscription. It is a
sentimental tale of seduction, in which the title character
is tricked into a sham marriage, becomes pregnant, is
abandoned, and goes insane before dying.

Publications and Events

The *Columbian Magazine*. A publication based on
Britain's popular *Gentleman's Magazine* begins publication in Philadelphia. Carrying foreign and domestic
news, poems, and historical notes, it published Jeremy
Belknap's *The Foresters* and C. B. Brown's "The Rhap-
sodist." It continued until 1792.

The *Massachusetts Centinel*. Upon the death of his
partner, William Warden (1761–1786), Benjamin Russell
(1761–1845) becomes the sole proprietor, editor, and publisher of the *Centinel*. A journalistic pioneer, he would
change the face of editorials, which had always reflected

letters submitted by subscribers, to include the undisguised opinion of the editor. The *Centinel* mirrored Russell's own Federalist stance, for instance, on the constitutional debate.

1787
Essays and Philosophy

JOHN ADAMS: *A Defence of the Constitutions of the United States of America Against the Attack of Mr. Turgot.* Adams begins his three-volume response to the British critics who questioned the political and economic promise of the United States (to be completed in 1788).

GEORGE CLINTON (1739–1812): "Letters of Cato." Clinton begins his series of seven anti-Federalist letters published in the *New York Journal* and completed in 1788. Clinton, using the pseudonym "Cato," believes that the new Constitution threatens liberty and happiness. He writes that soon Americans will come to their senses and not support a government "founded in usurpation." The letters are one of the finest examples of anti-Federalist thought and help spur Alexander Hamilton, John Jay, and James Madison to write their famous *Federalist Papers.*

ALEXANDER HAMILTON: *The Federalist Papers.* Along with James Madison and John Jay, Hamilton attempts to persuade the voters at the New York state convention to ratify the Constitution. Under the pseudonym "Publius," they write eighty-five essays. Hamilton writes fifty-one and collaborates with Madison on another three. Hamilton argues that the creation of federal courts with power over the legislature — a system known as judicial review — will protect against potential excesses of government. In Number 78, he writes, "The courts were designed to be an intermediate body between the people and the legislature." *The Federalist Papers* remains the most elaborate explanation of the Constitution and the most well known writings on American government.

JUPITER HAMMON: *An Address to the Negroes in the State of New York.* Hammon proclaims that faith in God is the only means for African Americans to combat slavery, without discounting the earthly benefits of freedom and liberty.

RICHARD HENRY LEE (1732–1794): *Observations.* The first of two pamphlets containing Lee's "Letters of the Federal Farmer," in opposition to *The Federalist. An Addition and Number of Letters* would follow in 1788.

JAMES MADISON: *The Federalist Papers.* Madison contributes twenty-six of the eighty-five essays that comprise this famous attempt to rally support for the Constitution. His important Number 10 argues that the framework of the new government will not allow any single faction in America to overpower another. Madison's essays, Numbers 37 through 58, clearly define the separation of powers within the several branches of government.

BENJAMIN RUSH: *Thoughts Upon Female Education, Accommodated to the Present State of Society, Manners, and Government in the United States of America.* Rush increasingly sees the need for a variety of social reforms. The education of women is just one on his list, which also includes better treatment of prisoners and abolition. Rush is one of the first civic leaders to promote free public education funded by a property tax in Philadelphia, believing "a republican nation can never be long free and happy" without an educated population.

Poetry, Fiction, and Drama

JOEL BARLOW (1754–1812): *The Vision of Columbus.* A nine-book poem depicting a prosperous, progressive America and intended, according to Barlow's preface, to encourage "the love of national liberty." The work is the precursor to his 1807 magnum opus, *The Columbiad.*

WILLIAM DUNLAP (1766–1839): *The Modest Soldier; or, Love in New York.* The first drama by America's first major playwright. Inspired by Royall Tyler's *The Contrast*, it was never produced.

FRANCIS HOPKINSON: "The New Roof." Hopkinson's best-known later work uses the allegorical technique of *A Pretty Story* (1774) to advance the cause of the Constitution (the "new roof").

PETER MARKOE: *The Algerine Spy in Pennsylvania.* This epistolary novel presenting a non-Christian foreign visitor's observations about America has been attributed to Markoe. His *Miscellaneous Poems* also appears.

ROYALL TYLER (1757–1826): *The Contrast.* The second drama by an American playwright that is professionally staged. Tyler's comedy of manners examines the differences between America and Europe. The play features the first appearance of a typical Yankee, soon to be a stock character in drama. *May Day in Town; or New York in an Uproar*, Tyler's second play, is not as well received as his first and is not published. He draws heavily on the style of Molière, the master of French social comedy. This style is also the hallmark of Mercy Otis Warren, the American author who undeniably has influenced Tyler.

Publications and Events

The *American Magazine.* A second magazine with this name begins publication in New York, edited by Noah Webster and featuring articles of interest to women and

Royall Tyler

contributions from the Connecticut Wits. It is staunchly Federalist.

The *American Museum*. A monthly magazine, edited by Mathew Carey, debuts in Philadelphia. It features contributions from Franklin, Hopkinson, Rush, and the Connecticut Wits.

The Constitution of the United States. On May 25 the Constitutional Convention convened in Philadelphia "to render the Constitution of the federal government adequate to the exigencies of the union" and on September 17, the provisions to establish congressional, presidential, and judicial powers were accepted by the delegates and ratified by June 21, 1788, taking effect on March 4, 1789. The first ten amendments, the Bill of Rights, would be adopted by Congress in 1791.

The *Kentucky* [or *Kentucke*] *Gazette*. John Bradford (1749–1830) publishes the first issue of his newspaper in August. The publication promoted statehood but also demonstrated Bradford's fear of a strong federal government.

Sermons and Religious Writing

FRANCIS ASBURY (1745–1816): *A Form of Discipline*. The most noted of Asbury's writings poses and responds to eighty-one questions about everything from clerical conduct to slavery. Still in use today by the United Methodist Church, the popularity of the work aids the formation of the Methodist Publishing House.

1788
Essays and Philosophy

JOHN DICKINSON: *Letters of Fabius*. Dickinson begins the first of two series of letters written in favor of the Constitution. The second series would appear in 1797.

PATRICK HENRY: "Shall Liberty or Empire be Sought?" A speech from the famous Virginian to the state convention in charge of ratifying the Constitution of the United States. Here he uses his oratory flair to question the ratification, charging that the document will merely replace the king with a president. This is one of Henry's several anti-Federalist statements made at this time.

JOHN JAY: *An Address to the People of the State of New York*. A year after he contributes five essays to *The Federalist Papers*, Jay renews his defense of the Constitution. He criticizes the current political and economic disarray of the country and pleads with New Yorkers to promptly accept the Constitution. George Washington, James Madison, and Noah Webster all read this address with great excitement.

Nonfiction

JOHN BRADFORD: *Kentucky Almanac*. The first edition is printed. It is one of the first books printed in the state of Kentucky.

WILLIAM GORDON (1728–1807): *History of the Rise, Progress, and Establishment of the Independence of the United States*. The three volumes of Gordon's history are published first in London and then, the following year, in New York. This massive history takes the form of an epistolary discussion between an American and his British friends, beginning in 1771 and ending in 1783. The history gives fresh voice to the passion and urgency of the American Revolution.

GEORGE RICHARDS MINOT (1758–1802): *The History of the Insurrection in Massachusetts in the Year 1786*. Minot publishes a highly critical account of Shays's Rebellion, a revolt to protest the government's indifference to the economic plight of farmers.

Poetry, Fiction, and Drama

TIMOTHY DWIGHT: "The Triumph of Infidelity." Dwight's satiric poem, written in heroic couplets and published anonymously, upholds Calvinist orthodoxy while lambasting Voltaire, Hume, Priestley, and their "infidel" followers.

PHILIP FRENEAU: *The Miscellaneous Works of Mr. Philip Freneau, Containing His Essays and Additional Poems.* This compilation further displays Freneau's skill for satire, humor, and moral convictions. It includes "The Indian Burying Ground" and "The Indian Student," two sympathetic portraits of Native Americans.

FRANCIS HOPKINSON: *Seven Songs.* This is considered the first book of music published by an American composer.

PETER MARKOE: "The Times." Markoe's poem satirizes prominent figures of Philadelphia society. "The Storm," a descriptive poem that also appears in 1788, has been attributed to him.

SUSANNA HASWELL ROWSON: "A Trip to Parnassus." Rowson criticizes in verse the contemporary stage. She also publishes *Poems on Various Subjects* and *The Inquisitor.* In a loosely related collection of scenes from domestic life modeled on Laurence Sterne's *A Sentimental Journey,* Rowson expresses her opposition to the excessively contrived, idealized fiction of the day.

1789

Diaries, Journals, and Letters

JOHN ADAMS: *Twenty-six Letters; upon Interesting Subjects Respecting the Revolution of America.* This collection of letters from 1780 displays Adams's fervor for the American Revolution while discussing the opportunities and problems of independence.

Essays and Philosophy

JAMES MADISON: Bill of Rights. Patrick Henry leads an opposition to the ratification of the Constitution in Virginia, claiming that it endangers the principle of democratic self-government. Madison and his supporters defeat Henry by promising to add the Bill of Rights. The promise is delivered when Madison, in Congress, writes the first ten amendments to the Constitution. They would be ratified by the states in 1791.

THOMAS PAINE: *Public Good.* Paine continues his call for a strong federal union in this pamphlet criticizing Virginia's claim to western land.

NOAH WEBSTER: *Dissertations on the English Language.* Webster, one of the most-traveled Americans of his day, journeys extensively through the new nation, promoting standardized copyright legislation and his books, and financing his way by teaching classes and giving public lectures. The five lectures published here exhort Americans to "seize the present moment and establish a national language as well as a national government" by standardizing American English.

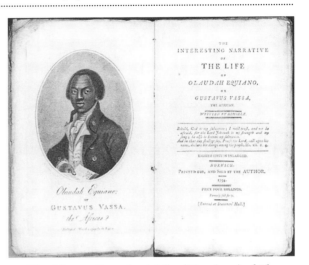

The title page from the eighth edition (1794) of *The Interesting Narrative of the Life of Olaudah Equiano, or Gustavus Vassa, the African*

Nonfiction

WILLIAM BARTRAM: *Observations on the Creek and Cherokee Indians.* A firsthand account of the customs of various Indian groups in the Southeast made during Bartram's collection trips as a botanist. It is one of the earliest accounts to examine the customs of the Creek and Cherokee.

OLAUDAH EQUIANO (c. 1745–c. 1801): *The Interesting Narrative of the Life of Olaudah Equiano, or Gustavus Vassa, the African.* An autobiography about being forced from Africa as an adolescent into slavery. In one of the first slave narratives, Equiano transcends the inhumanity of bondage and writes an insightful narrative.

DAVID RAMSAY: *History of the American Revolution.* Ramsay's best-known historical work has been described by literary historian Page Smith as "the best interpretation of the causes of the Revolution."

BENJAMIN RUSH: *Medical Inquiries and Observations.* The first of five volumes is a collection of the physician's medical papers on topics ranging from smallpox to the effect of alcohol on the aging process. These essays gain Rush admittance into the American Philosophical Society.

Poetry, Fiction, and Drama

WILLIAM HILL BROWN (1765–1793): *The Power of Sympathy.* In one of the earliest American novels, Brown bases this romance on the contemporary scandal of Perez and Sarah Morton, whose sister committed suicide; it was later discovered that Sarah's sister had a child by Perez Morton. The novel would be attributed to Sarah Wentworth Morgan for many years, and not until the end of the nineteenth century was Brown credited as its true author.

WILLIAM DUNLAP: *The Father; or, American Shandyism.* Dunlap's comedy of manners contrasting love among masters and servants is produced by the American Company to much critical acclaim. It is Dunlap's first produced play.

SUSANNA HASWELL ROWSON: *Mary; or, The Test of Honour.* Rowson's novel depicts a spirited heroine who demonstrates that her moral sense is superior to that of the wealthy aristocrat who refuses to let his son marry her.

Publications and Events

The *Gazette of the United States.* A newspaper intended to be the political organ of the Federalists is launched by John Fenno (1751–1798) in time to announce preparations for Washington's inauguration.

Sermons and Religious Writing

OLIVER HART: *America's Remembrancer.* The final published work from the Baptist minister who had moved to New Jersey from South Carolina when the British captured Charleston in 1780. The work praises the Revolution as America's fate, a mark of God's will in history.

GERSHOM MENDEZ SEXIAS (1745–1816): "A Religious Discourse: Thanksgiving Day Sermon, November 26, 1789." A sermon from the man often called the "Patriot Jewish minister of the American Revolution." He attacks certain Calvinist ideas and contends that Jews will be rewarded for their right actions when God gives them a political nation of their own someday. Central to Sexias's discourse is his belief that Jews must feel and express gratitude for the new nation and its freedoms. This sermon is one of only two published by the author.

II

Nationalism and Romanticism

1790–1860

IN 1837 RALPH WALDO EMERSON delivered to Harvard's Phi Beta Kappa Society the speech "The American Scholar," which Oliver Wendell Holmes called "an intellectual Declaration of Independence." In it Emerson stated that "Perhaps the time is already come . . . when the sluggard intellect of this continent will look from under its iron lids, and fill the postponed expectation of the world with something better than the exertions of mechanical skill. Our day of dependence, or long apprenticeship to the learning of other lands, draws to a close. The millions that around us are rushing into life, cannot always be fed on the sere remains of foreign harvests. Who can doubt, that poetry will revive and lead in a new age." Emerson urged his audience to participate in the creation of a distinctive American literary tradition, and the first seventy years in the national literature of the United States show both the causes that prompted Emerson's critique and the responses that were America's first great literary achievements.

If the Revolutionary period had defined what Americans were not — subjects of England — the overriding challenge during these decisive years was to articulate what in fact America and Americans were, during a period of unprecedented territorial expansion, population growth, and technological change. Between 1790 and 1860 the American population grew from 3.9 million to 31 million. The thirteen original colonies had grown to thirty-three states by 1860. By 1830 almost half of the U.S. population of 11 million had pushed west of the Alleghenies, the western border of the American colonies. Twelve percent were recent immigrants, part of a steady flow of Europeans to work the new farmlands in the West and to supply labor for the new steam-driven factories in the Northeast, which already were beginning to transform a rural, agrarian country into a modern, urbanized industrial nation. The steamboat, railroad, and telegraph shrank the nation even as its boundaries expanded and stretched across the continent to the Pacific. Vast western territories were acquired in the Louisiana Purchase; Florida was gained from Spain; and Texas, the Southwest, and California were wrested from Mexico. Between 1790 and 1860, the United States fought another war with Britain, tangled diplomatically with the French, and subdued the pirates of Tripoli and Algiers, all to protect its sovereignty at home and abroad. It also conducted what many regarded as its first war of conquest, against Mexico. Throughout the period, writers struggled to comprehend the new America that was evolving beyond the boundaries, culture, and traditions of its founding while also trying to reconcile the nation's new realities with its professed ideals. As the wilderness receded westward, the environment that had shaped American values changed. Just as important, the unresolved contradiction between the principles of liberty and the fact of institutionalized slavery drove Americans apart.

Many besides Emerson urged American writers to play a prominent role in chronicling and celebrating the ongoing national drama. Many felt the need for a literature to match the uniqueness of the country and its aspirations. However, if the nation had won its independence from Britain, its literature was still mainly subservient to English models and depreciated as secondhand and second rate. In 1820 the British critic Sydney Smith declared, with some justification: "In the four quarters of the globe, who reads an American book? Or goes to an American play? Or looks at an American picture or statue?"

In the first two decades of America's national history there is little to challenge Smith's view. In poetry, Americans mainly imitated English neoclassical models or the more recent works of the English Romantics, such as William Wordsworth, Samuel Taylor Coleridge, and Lord Byron, as well as Sir Walter Scott. The most gifted of the American poets of this period was William Cullen Bryant, whose "Thanatopsis" was written when he was seventeen and whose first collection in 1821 showed the influence of the poets he most admired, including Wordsworth, Scott, Alexander Pope, Thomas Gray, and Robert Burns.

In drama, the period 1790–1820 saw the emergence of America's first professional playwright, William Dunlap, who achieved some success in adapting German and French romantic comedies and melodramas, such as *The Stranger* in 1798, or in Shakespearean-influenced domestic tragedies such as *Leicester* (1807). One of the most successful of the early national dramatists was the prodigy John Howard Payne, whose first play, *Julia; or, The Wanderer* (1806), appeared when he was not quite fifteen years old. Like Dunlap, Payne's stock-in-trade was the adaptation of European stage material.

In fiction, Susanna Haswell Rowson produced the first best-selling American novel, *Charlotte Temple* (1794), modeled on the English novel of domestic sentiment. Hugh Henry Brackenridge's *Modern Chivalry* (1792, 1815) adapted the English picaresque, satirical novel derived from Henry Fielding, and the best of the earliest American novelists, Charles Brockden Brown, transferred the English gothic romance to an American setting. Brown's remarkable string of novels before his early death — *Wieland* (1798), *Arthur Mervyn* (1799), *Ormond* (1799), and *Arthur Huntley* (1799) — employ supernatural elements to serve psychological and social purposes. Brown helped define the romance tradition of the American novel, which was to be a significant influence on subsequent writers such as Edgar Allan Poe and Nathaniel Hawthorne.

The economic conditions of American book publishing contributed significantly to the struggles of American writers as they attempted to emerge from the long shadow cast by the British. Although a national copyright law was enacted in 1790, international copyright protection was not established until 1891, leaving American printers free to pirate the latest works of popular British writers such as Walter Scott and Charles Dickens. Because American readers could read the best of British writers in cheap reprints, there was scant economic incentive for publishers to support American writers who expected to be paid. Most American writers consequently found it difficult to survive by their writing; only those who produced works of exceptional distinction and popularity were rewarded.

The first significant challenges to the domination of British authors came from two New Yorkers, Washington Irving and James Fenimore Cooper. By 1800 New York City, with its population of sixty thousand, had become the largest city in the United States and its literary capital. Washington Irving, part of the city's sophisticated cultural elite, achieved his initial success with a witty and satirical look back at New York's Dutch past in *The History of New York* (1809) and went on to become the first American writer to achieve international renown with *The Sketch Book of Geoffrey Crayon* (1819–1820). Included among its depictions of English scenes are two tales set in rural New York — "Rip Van Winkle" and "The Legend of Sleepy Hollow" — that first demonstrate the imaginative possibilities of American themes, its past, and its setting. Irving's popular success spawned a host of imitators and a market for American writing, while his subsequent histories, travel books, and biographies, along with his sketches and tales, helped establish and legitimize a distinctive American literary voice and subject matter.

Like Irving, James Fenimore Cooper achieved his initial success by re-creating America's past. Capitalizing on the popularity of Walter Scott's historical novels, Cooper gained an audience with his initial best-selling novel, *The Spy* (1821), the first historical romance treating the American Revolution. *The Pioneers* (1823) initiated Cooper's greatest achievement, the series of five Leatherstocking Tales chronicling the career of the prototypical American frontiersman, Natty Bumppo, and his Indian companion, Chingachgook, against a background of American history of the mid–eighteenth century. More than any other writer of the period, Cooper tapped into the mythic reservoir of the American landscape and the archetypal American conflicts between the red man and the white, the individual and the community, nature and civilization.

If Irving and Cooper by their success showed that an American writer could compete with the best of Europe by exploring the thematic and poetic possibilities of America, a third figure, Edgar Allan Poe, helped raise the standard for artistry while formulating distinctive new imaginative forms. Essayist, editor, reviewer, poet, and fiction writer, Poe was America's first literary theorist as well as practitioner. While inventing detective fiction and science fiction, Poe refined an expressive symbolic theory of poetry. He was one of the first to recognize the genius of Nathaniel Hawthorne, and his review of Hawthorne's *Twice-Told Tales* (1842) helped codify the aesthetic of the prose tale or sketch, which he applied to his own works, establishing a uniquely American contribution to narrative fiction, the short story.

If Irving, Cooper, and Poe represented an initial testing of the American imagination against dominant European modes of expression, the first breakthrough for

American literature came from New England. There the particularly American strain of Romanticism known as Transcendentalism emerged. Influenced by British writers such as Wordsworth, Coleridge, and Thomas Carlyle, as well as German idealistic philosophers such as Immanuel Kant, the Transcendentalists rejected a narrow materialistic, rationalistic conception of the world in favor of a secular spirituality emphasizing the primacy of the individual in a direct relationship with the forces of Nature. Ralph Waldo Emerson's first book, *Nature* (1836), contains the first significant statements of Transcendentalism. He refined his views in *Essays* (1841) and *Essays: Second Series* (1844), solidifying his reputation as America's leading philosopher and cultural critic. Transcendentalism was less a coherent or consistent philosophical system than a call to creative self-expression and a liberation of personal authority. Because it rejected dogma and promoted intellectual and artistic risk taking, Transcendentalism embodied American notions of individualism, self-reliance, and equality. Whitman observed that it was Emerson who had brought him to a boil, and the creative energies released by Emerson and the Transcendentalists helped produce arguably the greatest creative decade in American literary history.

The artistic achievement of the 1850s began with Nathaniel Hawthorne's *The Scarlet Letter* (1850), which combines elements of the historical and gothic romance with a philosophical exploration of the nature of sin, guilt, and redemption, derived from the Puritan past. There had never been anything quite like Hawthorne's metaphysical drama in American fiction before — a rich evocation of internal states cast in a historical setting that is both sharply imagined and symbolically suggestive. Hawthorne's achievement prompted Herman Melville to call him the "American Shakespeare." Indeed, Hawthorne's influence on Melville is evident in *Moby-Dick* (1852), an unprecedented experimental novel blending narrative, metaphysical, dramatic, and documentary elements into what one contemporary reviewer called a "salmagundi of fact, fiction, and philosophy." In its own way, Henry David Thoreau's *Walden* (1854) is no less a daring hybrid, combining the author's account of his stay at Walden Pond in Concord from 1845 to 1847 with social commentary and philosophical speculation. Most daring of all is Walt Whitman's *Leaves of Grass* (1855), the first installment of his ongoing American epic. In it Whitman broke all the rules of poetic form and content, abandoning traditional meter for a rhythmical free verse, as flexible as the spoken voice with a perspective wide enough to comprehend the "aggregated, inseparable, unprecedented, vast, composite, electric *Democratic Nationality.*"

In hindsight, Emerson's essays, the novels of Hawthorne and Melville, Thoreau's prose, and Whitman's poetry marked the emergence of a distinctive national literature. But at the time only *The Scarlet Letter* was a bestseller. *Moby-Dick* puzzled and disappointed his first readers, and Melville rapidly slipped into obscurity; Thoreau was dismissed as an eccentric crank and would publish no other books in his lifetime, while Whitman's first collection was self-published and largely unread. Their messages and achievement were in part obscured by the political crisis that split the nation.

As America expanded westward, the opening up of each new territory threatened the delicate balance between free and slave states, exacerbating animosity between North and South and pushing the nation closer to conflict. Abolitionists in Britain and America helped publish dozens of slave narratives documenting the abuses of slavery, the most popular of which was the *Narrative of the Life of Frederick Douglass* (1845). During the 1850s, the first novel written by an African American, William Wells Brown's *Clotel; or, The President's Daughter* (1853), depicting the slave daughter of Thomas Jefferson, was published in London. The first novel by an African American published in the United States is Harriet Wilson's *Our Nig; or, Sketches from the Life of a Free Black* (1859). Harriet Beecher Stowe's *Uncle Tom's Cabin* (1852), the biggest-selling American novel in the nineteenth century and the most controversial book published in the United States up to that time, did more than any other literary work to engage the nation in the debate over slavery. Applauded by abolitionists worldwide and reviled by slaveholders, the novel, like the institution it attacked, divided the nation. North and South, free and slave states seemed on either side of an unbridgeable and widening chasm.

Like the nation itself, American literature between 1790 and 1860 came of age, discovering distinctive voices and subjects, drawing on both what united and divided Americans. This section of the *Chronology* closes like the first, with the election of a president. While the inauguration of the great Revolutionary War hero George Washington united the new nation, the election of Abraham Lincoln precipitated its division. Lincoln had earlier stated that "a house divided against itself cannot stand." He and the nation would shortly face the sobering reality of that assertion.

BIRTHS AND DEATHS, 1790–1799	

Births

1790 Peter Force (d. 1868), historian
Francis Walker Gilmer (d. 1826), lawyer and author
Fitz-Greene Halleck (d. 1867), poet
Augustus Baldwin Longstreet (d. 1870), short story writer

1791 John Howard Payne (d. 1852), playwright
Lydia Huntley Sigourney (d. 1865), poet and author

1792 James Ewell Heath (d. 1862), novelist
Seba Smith (d. 1868), journalist and humorist

1793 Samuel Griswold Goodrich (d. 1860), children's writer
John Neal (d. 1876), novelist
James Hall (d. 1868), novelist, author, and short story writer
Henry Rowe Schoolcraft (d. 1864), writer and ethnologist

1794 William Cullen Bryant (d. 1878), poet and editor
Caroline Howard Gilman (d. 1888), poet and novelist

1795 Joseph Rodman Drake (d. 1820), poet
John Pendleton Kennedy (d. 1870), novelist and statesman
James Gates Percival (d. 1856), poet
Daniel Pierce Thompson (d. 1868), novelist

1796 Thomas Bulfinch (d. 1867), novelist
William Hickling Prescott (d. 1859), historian

1797 William Ware (d. 1852), clergyman and novelist

1798 McDonald Clarke (d. 1842), poet

1799 Amos Bronson Alcott (d. 1888), author and educator
James Lawson (d. 1880), poet
Grenville Mellen (d. 1841), short story writer and poet
Richard Penn Smith (d. 1854), playwright

Deaths

1790 Joseph Bellamy (b. 1719), clergyman and author
Benjamin Franklin (b. 1706), printer, writer, inventor, and public official
Jacob Green (b. 1722), clergyman and author
William Livingston (b. 1723), public official, poet, and writer

1791 Francis Hopkinson (b. 1737), poet, essayist, musician, and judge

1792 John Seccomb (b. 1708), clergyman and poet

1793 William Hill Brown (b. 1765), novelist

1795 Robert Rogers (b. 1731), soldier, writer, and playwright
Ezra Stiles (b. 1727), clergyman and diarist

1796 Samuel Seabury (b. 1729), clergyman and essayist
Jonathan Sewall (b. 1728), playwright

1798 Jeremy Belknap (b. 1744), clergyman and historian
Elihu Hubbard Smith (b. 1771), poet and editor

1799 William Cliffton (b. 1772), poet

1790

Drama and Theater

DAVID HUMPHREYS (1752–1818): *The Widow of Malabar.* A romantic play set in India and based on *La Veuve du Malabar*, by Antoine Le Mierre. The drama follows a woman about to be burned on the funeral pyre of her husband, whom she did not love. The tragic play ends happily when a French general saves her. The epilogue of the popular play is written by Jonathan Trumbull.

PETER MARKOE: *The Reconciliation; or, The Triumph of Nature.* An unproduced comic opera that is one of the first ballad operas written in the United States.

Fiction

ENOS HITCHCOCK (1744–1803): *Memoirs of the Bloomsgrove Family.* An epistolary narrative of the Bloomsgrove children by the former Revolutionary War chaplain and Rhode Island minister, describing the three stages of childhood education and arguing for educational reform that would suit the "state of society." It is praised for its progressive educational doctrines and noted for its early protest against the imitation of British customs. Hitchcock's contribution to American literature rests largely on this work, which is considered the second American novel published in book form.

Nonfiction

JOHN ADAMS: *Discourses on Davila.* A political manifesto controversial for Adams's support of a monarchy and aristocracy in countries such as France and his denunciation of equality based on his belief that humans naturally have "a passion for distinction."

BENJAMIN FRANKLIN: "Sidi Mehemet Ibrahim on the Slave Trade, March 23, 1790." Written shortly before his death, Franklin's last public writing satirizes proslavery rhetoric in Congress. Ibrahim, a Muslim who kidnaps Christians along the African coast, rejects a petition to abolish the enslavement of whites.

ALEXANDER HAMILTON: *Report on Public Credit.* Hamilton argues for the federal government's redemption of Confederation government securities, assumption of states' Revolutionary War debts, and a tax to pay for the assumed debts. Although this work is criticized by anti-Federalists, Congress would eventually accept the report from the secretary of the U.S. Treasury.

JOHN WINTHROP: *A Journal of the Transactions and Occurrences in the Settlement of Massachusetts and the Other New England Colonies from the Year 1630 to 1644.* The first publication of Winthrop's journal, a major primary source of New England history, including documentation of political, social, and religious life in the Massachusetts Bay colony.

POPULAR BOOKS, 1790–1825

Charlotte Temple, a Tale of Truth by Susanna Haswell Rowson (First American Printing, 1791)

Modern Chivalry by Hugh Henry Brackenridge (First American Printing, 1792)

Ruins by Constantin Volney (First English Printing, 1792; First American Printing, 1796)

Autobiography by Benjamin Franklin (First English Printing, 1794; First American Printing, 1818)

The Mysteries of Udolpho by Mrs. Ann Radcliffe (First American Printing, 1794)

The Monk by Matthew Gregory Lewis (First English Printing, 1796; First American Printing, 1799)

The Coquette by Mrs. Hannah Foster (First American Printing, 1797)

Pleasures of Hope by Thomas Campbell (First English Printing, 1799; First American Printing, 1810)

The Life and Memorable Actions of George Washington by Mason Locke Weems (First American Printing, 1800)

Thaddeus of Warsaw by Jane Porter (First American Printing, 1803)

The Lay of the Last Minstrel by Sir Walter Scott (First American Printing, 1805)

Hours of Idleness by George Gordon Byron (First American Printing, 1807)

Marmion by Sir Walter Scott (First American Printing, 1808)

Gertrude of Wyoming by Thomas Campbell (First American Printing, 1809)

History of New York by Washington Irving (First American Printing, 1809)

The Scottish Chiefs by Jane Porter (First American Printing, 1810)

The Lady of the Lake by Sir Walter Scott (First American Printing, 1810)

The Asylum; or, Alonzo and Melissa by Isaac Mitchell (First American Printing, 1811)

Childe Harold by George Gordon Byron (First American Printing, 1812)

Bride of Abydoa by George Gordon Byron (First American Printing, 1813)

Giaour by George Gordon Byron (First American Printing, 1813)

Waverly by Sir Walter Scott (First American Printing, 1814)

Guy Mannering by Sir Walter Scott (First American Printing, 1815)

Moral Pieces in Prose and Verse (First American Printing, 1815)

Manfred by George Gordon Byron (First American Printing, 1817)

Lalla Rookh by Thomas Moore (First American Printing, 1817)

Rob Roy by Sir Walter Scott (First American Printing, 1817)

The Sketch Book by Washington Irving (First American Printing, 1819)

Ivanhoe by Sir Walter Scott (First American Printing, 1819)

The Abott by Sir Walter Scott (First American Printing, 1820)

The Spy by James Fenimore Cooper (First American Printing, 1821)

Kenilworth by Sir Walter Scott (First American Printing, 1821)

The Pirate by Sir Walter Scott (First American Printing, 1821)

Bracebridge Hall by Washington Irving (First American Printing, 1822)

The Fortunes of Nigel by Sir Walter Scott (First American Printing, 1822)

The Pilot by James Fenimore Cooper (First American Printing, 1823)

The Pioneers by James Fenimore Cooper (First American Printing, 1823)

Peveril of the Peak by Sir Walter Scott (First American Printing, 1823)

Quentin Durward by Sir Walter Scott (First American Printing, 1823)

A Narrative of the Life of Mrs. Mary Jemison by James E. Seaver (First American Printing, 1824)

Lionel Lincoln by James Fenimore Cooper (First American Printing, 1825)

Poetry

SARAH WENTWORTH MORTON (1759–1846): *Ouabi; or, The Virtues of Nature.* The Boston writer known as the American Sappho treats a love triangle between an Illinois chief, his wife, and a European aristocrat. The narrative poem is notable for its historically researched representation of Indian life. It would be set to music by Hans Graham in 1793 and would inspire Louis James Bacon's play *The American Indian* (1795).

MERCY OTIS WARREN: *Poems, Dramatic and Miscellaneous.* In the first work printed under her own name, Warren produces verse tragedies and other poems extolling republican virtues and confirming women as moral authorities. The work renews Warren's position in the political and literary mainstream.

1791
Fiction

SUSANNA HASWELL ROWSON: *Mentoria; or, The Young Lady's Friend.* A collection of letters, stories, and an essay; their topics range from charity and the pratfalls of social ambition to obedience and moral conduct. Helena Askam is mentor to four sisters, and each of her letters instructs the girls toward the best decisions. The work would be popular into the next century.

Nonfiction

JOHN QUINCY ADAMS (1767–1848): *An Answer to Paine's* Rights of Man. Adams begins a series of articles, published in the *Columbian Sentinel* under the signature "Publicola," that defends the rights of the

Alexander Hamilton

minority against Thomas Paine's insistence on the absolute power of the majority. Adams defines the Federalist argument for a strong judiciary to protect minority rights.

DAVID AUSTIN (1759–1831): *The American Preacher; or, A Collection of Sermons from Some of the Most Eminent Preachers Now Living in the United States.* An anthology of sermons from notable evangelists, offered by subscription. In it, Austin strives to unite the many Christian denominations into a single community of the faithful. The publication includes sermons by Moses Mather, Samuel Stanhope Smith, and James Dana.

WILLIAM BARTRAM: *Travels Through North and South Carolina, Georgia, East and West Florida, the Cherokee Country, the Extensive Territories of Muscogulges, or Creek Confederacy, and the Country of the Choctaws.* Roughly transcribed from field notes, the book contains passionate descriptions and illustrations based on four years of travel. The famous American naturalist's book was popular in Europe, especially impressing William Wordsworth and Samuel Coleridge, but many in America found it overly enthusiastic.

JONATHAN EDWARDS JR.: *The Injustice and Impolicy of the Slave Trade and Slavery.* One of the first antislavery

treatises by a New England clergyman argues that slavery is a sin and advises that Christians are "obligated" to free their slaves at once.

BENJAMIN FRANKLIN: *Mémoires de la vie privée… écrits par lui-même.* The first edition of Franklin's *Autobiography,* his only book, appears in France. The first American edition would appear in 1818.

ALEXANDER HAMILTON: *Report on Manufactures.* Hamilton urges the federal government to encourage manufactures and proposes protective laws for fledgling industries to ensure the preservation of the home market. Although this important political document in American history provides the most complete description of Hamilton's economic vision and his opposition to southern agrarian economic philosophy, anti-Federalist rivals in Congress do not act on the Treasury secretary's proposals.

THOMAS MORRIS (c. 1732–c. 1802): *Miscellanies in Prose and Verse.* This collection contains the author's most important work, "Journal of Captain Thomas Morris of His Majesty's XVII Regiment of Infantry," which he writes to win a pension after losing property in speculation. The journal details his expedition from Cedar Point, Ohio, to Detroit, where he had hoped to influence the Midwest Indians to support the English rather than the French. It includes descriptions of his dangerous experiences and Indian customs as well as humorous anecdotes.

THOMAS PAINE: *The Rights of Man.* A defense of the French Revolution and an appeal against hereditary monarchy that asserts the people's right to shape their own government. Highly praised by Democrats and condemned by Federalists in the United States, it would become what one journalist called "the veritable Bible of radicals and revolutionaries." After the publication of this work, Paine would flee from England to France, where revolutionaries regard him as a hero.

JOSEPH PRIESTLEY (1733–1804): *Letters to… Edmund Burke.* A collection of incendiary remarks made on the political situations in France and America. The publication expresses support for the freedom movements in both countries and thus enraged his fellow Britons. A mob ransacked Priestley's home and science laboratories, and he fled in 1794 to Philadelphia, where he was exuberantly welcomed.

NOAH WEBSTER: *The Prompter; or, A Commentary on Common Sayings and Subjects.* A popular series of essays in the style of Benjamin Franklin's "Poor Richard." Webster imparts moral, political, and life lessons through humorous and satirical commentaries and stories.

Poetry

RICHARD ALSOP (1761–1815), THEODORE DWIGHT, ELIHU HUBBARD SMITH (1771–1798), LEMUEL HOPKINS (1750–1801), AND MASON COGSWELL (1761–1830): *The Echo.* A Federalist verse satire first published in twenty sections of the *American Mercury.* The satire ridicules Jefferson and other anti-Federalists.

BENJAMIN YOUNGS PRIME (1733–1791): *Columbia's Glory.* A poetical recounting of the Revolutionary War in which Columbia personifies the new nation. The only of Prime's works to be published under his name, it is a precursor of the doctrine of manifest destiny.

Publications and Events

The *National Gazette.* First appearance of this semi-weekly newspaper founded and edited by Philip Freneau and financially supported by Thomas Jefferson to advocate the Democratic Republican Party. It exchanged angry political attacks with the pro-Hamilton *Federalist Gazette of the United States* but would be suspended in 1793 after Jefferson's resignation as secretary of state.

1792
Fiction

JEREMY BELKNAP (1744–1798): *The Foresters, an American Tale, Being a Sequel to the History of John Bull the Clothier.* A historical allegory in a series of sixteen letters that tell the story of the settling and growth of the British colonies in America. Belknap, a Congregational minister and a historian, attacks the English and praises the common sense of American settlers and patriots in the letters.

HUGH HENRY BRACKENRIDGE: *Modern Chivalry.* The first two parts of Brackenridge's satirical picaresque novel appear. Widely read, it is the first important fictional work about the American frontier and called "to the West what Don Quixote was to Europe." Third and fourth sections would appear in 1793 and 1797, with a revision in 1805 and a final addition in 1815.

Nonfiction

JOEL BARLOW: *A Letter to the National Convention of France.* Barlow urges the French to develop a more radical revolutionary constitution eliminating the monarchy, the national church, and property requirements for voting, and instituting annual elections. A member of the "Connecticut Wits" and a future diplomat, Barlow is made an honorary citizen of France for this work. The same year he publishes *Advice to the Privileged Orders in the Several States of Europe Resulting from the Necessity and Propriety of a General Revolution in the Principle of Government,* a complementary work to Paine's *Rights of Man,* asserting the state's responsibility for all society. The British government considers the document seditious.

CALEB BINGHAM (1757–1817): *The Child's Companion: Being a Concise Spelling Book.* Although outsold by Noah Webster's *American Spelling Book* (1787), Bingham's second book, a popular reader and speller, would appear in at least eleven editions through the late 1830s.

DANIEL GOOKIN (1612–1687): *Historical Collections of the Indians in New England.* A description of the customs, trade, religion, politics, and agriculture of the Native American people, with a discussion of New England missionaries' attempts to convert Indians to Christianity. Completed in 1674 and published in *Massachusetts Historical Society Collections* in 1792, the work is considered one of the best studies of Native Americans by a Massachusetts Puritan.

EBENEZER HAZARD (1744–1817): *Historical Collections, State Papers, and Other Authentic Documents.* One of the earliest attempts to preserve American source materials, this collection would have an impact on the writings of historian Jeremy Belknap. As postmaster of New York City, surveyor general of the Continental Post Office, and postmaster general, Hazard had become familiar with the colonies and collected materials he thought would later be important to historians.

FRANCIS HOPKINSON: *The Miscellaneous Essays and Occasional Writings of Francis Hopkinson.* Writings collected just before Hopkinson's death. The dated nature and harsh satire of some of the writings incite this criticism from the *Columbian Magazine:* "In our opinion these cast a shade over the splendour of his works."

GILBERT IMLAY (1754–c. 1828): *A Topographical Description of the Western Territories of North America.* Eleven letters addressed to a probably fictitious "friend in England," describing American settlement history, climate, natural resources, flora and fauna, and customs and manners of the settlers. A novelist, land surveyor in Kentucky, and captain in the Revolutionary War, Imlay celebrates the United States. According to the Irish poet Thomas Moore, the work "would seduce us into a belief that innocence, peace, and freedom had deserted the rest of the world for Martha's Vineyard and the banks of the Ohio."

BENJAMIN RUSH: *Considerations on the Injustice and Impolicy of Punishing Murder by Death.* An argument against capital punishment, which contends that the death penalty increases criminal behavior and amounts

Benjamin Rush

to state-assisted suicide. Rush also asserts that crime stems from a mental disease. First outlined in an essay in the July 1788 *American Museum*, Rush's beliefs had received harsh criticism and prompted him to add material and publish it in book form in 1792 and then again in a book of his essays in 1798, under the title "An Enquiry Into the Consistency of the Punishment of Murder by Death." Rush's writings had won support from Benjamin Franklin and Philadelphia attorney general William Bradford.

WILLIAM SMITH: *Eulogium on Benjamin Franklin.* Smith had delivered this eloquent, lengthy, and praise-filled eulogy before the American Philosophical Society on March 1, 1791, a year after Franklin's death. Franklin and Smith were the original administrators of the Academy and College of Philadelphia, but a rift had formed between them over regional politics.

Poetry

THOMAS ODIORNE (1769–1851): "The Progress of Refinement." A lengthy poem that uses philosophy to discuss the relationship between man and nature. The author, a Romantic poet who predated the Romantic movement, uses the ideas of John Locke and David Hartley to illustrate the harmony between humanity and the environment.

1793
Fiction

ANONYMOUS: *The Hapless Orphan; or, Innocent Victim of Revenge.* This sentimental didactic novel written by "an American Lady" concerns a self-centered Philadelphia girl whose attachment to another's fiancé leads to the hero's suicide and a vendetta by her rival.

GILBERT IMLAY: *The Emigrants.* An epistolary tale of an English family on the American frontier near Pittsburgh, it advocates women's rights. Some critics question Imlay's authorship, crediting the English author and feminist Mary Wollstonecraft (1759–1797) instead.

Nonfiction

ANN ELIZA BLEECKER (1752–1783): *The Posthumous Works of Ann Eliza Bleecker.* A collection of letters, poems, and prose published by Bleecker's daughter, the writer Margaretta Faugères (1771–1801), detailing life on the front lines of the American Revolution and the death of Bleecker's daughter Abella. As a poet, fiction writer, and correspondent, Bleecker provides firsthand accounts of women's life during the Revolution.

SAMUEL HOPKINS (1721–1803): *The System of Doctrines Contained in Divine Revelation.* A complete description of the New Divinity, or the New England School of Theology, which was being widely followed in New England at the end of the eighteenth century. It calls believers to take their places in the divine order and to love God alone, without personal considerations. The theologian's masterpiece, it would sell twelve hundred copies.

ROBERT BAILEY THOMAS (1766–1846): *Farmer's Almanack.* A Massachusetts almanac that provides an annual collection of weather forecasts, fish and game laws, recipes, and more. The almanac continues to be published in the twenty-first century, under Thomas's name as original editor. It is called *The Old Farmer's Almanac* to distinguish it as the original among many imitators.

JOHN WOOLMAN: *A Plea for the Poor; or, A Word of Remembrance and Caution to the Rich.* Published thirty years after its composition, this is the Quaker minister's plea for simple living and freedom from the spiritual constraints of worldly gains. Radical in its positions on the lower classes and slavery, the influential work would be republished more than a hundred years later by the Fabian Society.

Poetry

ELIHU HUBBARD SMITH (1771–1798): *American Poems.* The first notable anthology of American poetry,

Susanna Haswell Rowson

primarily devoted to the works of the Connecticut Wits but also including poems by Philip Freneau, William Livingston, Sarah Wentworth Morton, and Robert Treat Paine.

Publications and Events

The *American Minerva*. New York Federalist daily edited by Noah Webster to curb the propagation of French thought in the United States. The paper's name was changed to the *Commercial Advertiser* in 1797, and Webster remained editor until 1803. His successors included Robert Charles Sands, Turlow Weed, Parke Godwin, and William Leete Stone. The *Commercial Advertiser* merged with the *New York Globe* in 1904 and was called the *Globe and Commercial Advertiser* until the *New York Sun* purchased it in 1923.

The *Aurora*. The Philadelphia anti-Federalist newspaper under the editorship of B. F. Bache (1769–1798) debuts. Bache, one of the first journalists to provide extensive reports on congressional debates, took such a strong anti-Washington stance that veterans of Washington's army wrecked the newspaper's offices in 1797, and the Alien Act and Sedition Act were instituted in part to silence Bache and the *Aurora*.

The *Eagle; or, Dartmouth Centinel*. The Hanover, New Hampshire, newspaper is established by Josiah Dunham

(fl. 1790s) and noted for its literary style and early contributions from Joseph Dennie (1768–1812) and Royall Tyler (1757–1826). It ceased publication in 1799.

1794

Drama and Theater

WILLIAM DUNLAP (1766–1839): *The Fatal Deception; or, The Progress of Guilt*. Dunlap's gothic drama in blank verse tells the story of a warrior, Leicester, whose wife has taken a lover. The play's success bolsters Dunlap's argument that American playwrights are capable of writing tragedy.

ANNE KEMBLE HATTON (c. 1757–c. 1796): *Tammany; or, The Indian Chief*. The earliest drama about American Indians; the title character rescues his beloved from Spanish kidnappers.

SUSANNA HASWELL ROWSON: *Slaves in Algiers; or, A Struggle for Freedom*. The first play by a woman successfully produced in America and Rowson's only drama surviving in complete form utilizes the Barbary pirates' raids on American ships to demonstrate tyranny. The author would perform in this play and her subsequent dramas, including *The Female Patriot* (1795), *The Volunteers* (1795), and *Americans in England* (1797).

Fiction

SUSANNA HASWELL ROWSON: *Charlotte Temple: A Tale of Truth*. One of the first American bestsellers, this novel tells the story of an English girl seduced by a British officer, Montraville. Charlotte follows Montraville to New York, where he abandons her and she dies in childbirth. The supposedly true story exemplifies Rowson's argument for the importance of the education of young women. It had been first published in England in 1791. A sequel, *Charlotte's Daughter*, would be published in 1828.

Nonfiction

JEREMY BELKNAP: *American Biography*. These essays on distinguished Americans, arranged in chronological order, are compiled and written in a scientific and analytical manner and attempt to provide an objective representation. It would be the model for later biographical works by U.S. writers.

CALEB BINGHAM: *The American Preceptor*. A children's book that uses moral but entertaining poetry and prose to teach reading. Bingham's most popular book, it would be published in at least seventy editions.

ELIAS BOUDINOT (1740–1821): *The Age of Revelation*. An anti-deist reply to Paine's *The Age of Reason* in which the author, the first president of the American Bible Society,

A British cartoon picturing writer and philosopher Thomas Paine asleep but plagued by a nightmare in which three faceless judges uncoil scrolls with charges and punishments on them, and gallows and stocks in the background predict his future

refutes the skepticism of Paine's writing and censures the French Revolution's lack of spirituality.

ALEXANDER HAMILTON: *"Americanus" Essays.* Hamilton's two essays criticizing France and its American supporters appear in Dunlap and Claypoole's *American Daily Advertiser.*

THOMAS PAINE: *The Age of Reason.* In his most controversial work, Paine endorses deism and argues that morality should be based on knowledge of God in nature and not on human inventions, such as religious institutions. He suggests that the Bible is fallible.

EZRA STILES: *A History of Three Judges of King Charles I.* This memoir of the judges who condemned Charles I to death and fled to New England defends tyrannicide and argues that people are their own best rulers. Stiles was the president of Yale at the time of publication.

Poetry

TIMOTHY DWIGHT: *Greenfield Hill: A Poem in Seven Parts.* An imitation of John Denham's *Cooper's Hill,* the poem contrasts the virtues of American village life to European depravity. Written after Dwight had become a minister in Greenfield, Connecticut, it includes accounts of historical events.

Publications and Events

The *Federal Orrery.* Robert Treat Paine (1773–1811) begins to publish this semiweekly Federalist journal in Boston. It features poetry, satire, and criticism, with contributions from Joseph Dennie and Sarah Wentworth Morton.

1795
Drama and Theater

WILLIAM DUNLAP: *Fontainville Abbey.* A tragedy written in gothic form, presenting mysterious, seemingly supernatural incidents that are eventually explained as having natural causes. It is based on Ann Radcliffe's (1764–1823) *Romance of the Forest* and opens in New York to warm praise.

MARGARETTA V. BLEECKER FAUGÈRES (1771–1801): *Belisarius: A Tragedy.* Faugères's blank-verse tragedy is her major literary achievement, echoing Shakespeare's *King Lear.* Faugères was the daughter of poetess Ann Eliza Bleecker; she edited her mother's posthumous prose and verse, adding some of her own poems and essays to Bleecker's *Posthumous Works* (1793).

JOHN MURDOCK (1748–1834): *The Triumphs of Love; or, Happy Reconciliation.* The author's first and only produced play is a comedy satirizing Quaker marriage customs and includes the first native black character on the American stage. The play is performed at the New Theatre in Philadelphia on May 22, wins positive reviews, and is printed for a long subscription list, including Dr. Benjamin Rush and Governor Thomas Mifflin (1744–1800). The management of the theater, however, opts not to produce the play again, possibly because of the cost of royalties and the fact that Sambo, the black character, is freed by his master in the third act. Murdock is said to have been a Philadelphia barber who self-published this drama along with *The Politicians* (1798) and *The Beau Metamorphosized* (1800).

SUSANNA HASWELL ROWSON: *The Volunteers.* A "musical entertainment" concerning the Whiskey Rebellion in western Pennsylvania. The score, with Rowson's lyrics set to music by Alexander Reinagle (1756–1809), is all that now survives of the play.

Fiction

EBENEZER BRADFORD (1746–1801): *The Art of Courting.* A didactic novel describing seven model courtships,

William Dunlap

it suggests that religion is the most important component in marriage. Although the work was criticized in the *Massachusetts Magazine* for its "scenes of courtship that are detailed without spirit till vapid narration ends in marriage," the Massachusets writer is chiefly remembered for this contribution to the epistolary novel form.

SUSANNA HASWELL ROWSON: *Trials of the Human Heart.* A novel describing sixteen years of suffering by Meriel Howard. Rowson's first novel written in America wins an impressive list of subscribers, including Martha Washington, members of prominent Philadelphia families, and members of the New Theatre Company, but critics consider it among her least successful works.

Literary Criticism and Scholarship

LINDLEY MURRAY (1745–1826): *Grammar of the English Language.* The Pennsylvania Quaker's most popular book, which was originally written for a Friends' school, becomes the first standard English grammar book in the country. Known as "the father of English grammar," Murray would follow this book with *Exercises and Key* (1797), *English Reader* (1799), and *An English Spelling Book* (1804), all extensively used in the United States.

Nonfiction

HUGH HENRY BRACKENRIDGE: *Incidents of the Insurrection in the Western Parts of Pennsylvania.* Brackenridge describes the conflict between the federal government and the local insurgents during the Whiskey Rebellion.

WILLIAM COBBETT (1763–1835): *A Bone to Gnaw for the Democrats* and *A Kick for a Bite.* The British journalist, having fled to Philadelphia to avoid a fraud charge, issues the first two in a series of Federalist pamphlets attacking the Republicans. It would be followed by *The Scare-Crow* (1796) and the scurrilous *Life of Tom Paine* (1796).

Poetry

PHILIP FRENEAU: *Poems Written Between the Years 1768 and 1794.* Freneau intends this collection of 287 poems, manufactured on his own printing press, to be his "authorized edition." It includes never-before-published poems as well as revisions of earlier poems, omitting Latin mottoes to speak more directly to the common man. Though Freneau and booksellers have anticipated great sales from the publication, it is poorly received.

ROBERT TREAT PAINE (1773–1811): "The Invention of Letters." A commencement verse delivered at Harvard University, recording the history of thought and including a eulogy of Washington and an attack on Jacobins.

A well-regarded poet, drama critic, editor, and lawyer, Paine was the second son of Robert Treat Paine the elder, a signer of the Declaration of Independence.

1796

Drama and Theater

WILLIAM DUNLAP: *The Archers; or, The Mountaineers of Switzerland.* One of America's first musical plays, this opera adapts Friedrich von Schiller's *William Tell* and concerns the contrasting ideas of liberty and anarchy.

SUSANNA HASWELL ROWSON: *Americans in England.* One of the first works exploring the "international theme," Rowson's social comedy would be revised by the author as *The Columbian Daughter* in 1800.

ELIHU HUBBARD SMITH: *Edwin and Angelina; or, The Banditti.* Smith's musical dramatization of Oliver Goldsmith's ballad "The Hermit" is one of the earliest American comic operas.

Nonfiction

JOSEPH DENNIE (1768–1812): *The Lay Preacher; or, Short Sermons for Idle Readers.* This collection of essays combining scripture with a variety of subjects gains a wide readership. The English traveler John Davis calls it "the most popular work on the American continent." By the beginning of the nineteenth century, Dennie would be regarded as one of the nation's most distinguished men of letters.

ROBERT FULTON (1765–1815): *Observations on the Various Systems of Canal Navigation, with Inferences Practical and Mathematical....* Written more than a decade before Fulton's commercially successful steamship design, the work establishes its author as an innovative engineer. It argues for a cost-effective system of canals for small boats. Critics view the work as visionary but impractical.

THOMAS PAINE: *A Letter to George Washington.* Paine's angry letter attacking Washington and others whom he held as partially responsible for his imprisonment in France by Robespierre, during the Reign of Terror, creates an uproar in America and severely damages Paine's reputation.

ST. GEORGE TUCKER (1752–1827): *Dissertation on Slavery.* A widely read pamphlet advocating the emancipation of children born to slave mothers. Tucker, a native of Bermuda, had gone to Virginia to study law with George Wythe, had served in the Virginia militia, and after the American Revolution had become a distinguished lawyer, judge, and teacher of law.

ROBERT JAMES TURNBULL (1775–1833): *A Visit to a Philadelphia Prison.* Originally published in French, the

A facsimile of the opening manuscript page for the first draft of the mock-epic poem "The Hasty-Pudding"

work by the South Carolina writer draws extensive national and international attention for its thoughts on the penitentiary system of Pennsylvania and the injustice of capital punishment.

GEORGE WASHINGTON: *The Speech of George Washington, Esq., Late President of the United States of America: On His Resignation of That Important Office.* Commonly known as the "Farewell Address," the speech had probably been written with the aid of Alexander Hamilton and James Madison. In it, Washington discusses his presidency; stresses the importance of national unity; warns against party conflicts; emphasizes the value of religion, morality, and education; and advises against "entangling alliances" with foreign governments.

Poetry

JOEL BARLOW: "The Hasty-Pudding." A mock-epic about a serving of New England hasty pudding that inspires nostalgic remembrances of Barlow's boyhood in Connecticut. The three cantos in heroic couplets describing the American dish become his most popular poem.

George Washington working the slaves on his farm in Mount Vernon

WILLIAM CLIFFTON (1772–1799): *The Group; or, An Elegant Representation.* The Pennsylvania poet collects political verses defending Jay's Treaty and a satire in which tradesmen and mechanics ignorantly discuss politics and the state. The poem is Clifiton's longest work in support of England, and though the verse is at times sophisticated, its subject matter is considered "the coarse material of Jacobism." Jay's Treaty, signed in 1794, regulated commerce and navigation between the United States and Great Britain.

LEMUEL HOPKINS (1750–1801): "The Guillotina; or, A Democratic Dirge." A 1796 New Year's poem attacking Jefferson and the Democrats, praising Hamilton, and paying tribute to George Washington. In addition to being a member of the Connecticut Wits, Hopkins was also one of the most advanced and distinguished physicians of his time.

THOMAS MORRIS: *Quashy; or, The Coal-Black Maid.* Morris's longest and most notable poem depicts the life of the title character, a black slave in St. Pierre on Martinique, and rebukes the French and British systems of human bondage.

ROBERT TREAT PAINE: "The Ruling Passion." Paine's longest and best poem praises "private virtue ripening public love." Biographer Charles Prentiss proclaims, "We know of no satire, of Horace, of Juvenal, Boileau or Pope that surpasses it."

ISAAC STORY (1774–1803): "All the World's a Stage." Published under the pseudonym "The Stranger" and notable for its sophisticated blank verse, the poem includes highly popular satirical sketches. Story, like many young lawyers of the day, would contribute miscellaneous writings to newspapers between jobs.

ST. GEORGE TUCKER: *The Probationary Odes of Jonathan Pindar.* A popular collection of anti-Federalist satires of Alexander Hamilton, John Adams, and others. It is written in the style of John Wolcot (1738–1819), an English writer who published under the name "Peter Pindar." First published in Philip Freneau's *National Gazette* in 1793, the odes have been mistakenly attributed to Freneau.

1797
Drama and Theater

WILLIAM HILL BROWN: *West Point Preserved.* Brown's posthumous tragedy about Major André receives five professional performances with positive response from critics. Most known in American literature as the author of probably the first American novel, *The Power of Sympathy* (1789), Brown also maintained a favorable reputation as a dramatist.

JOHN DALY BURK (c. 1772–1808): *Bunker Hill; or, The Death of General Warren.* This blank-verse drama wins large audiences due to its patriotic theme and elaborate battle scene, but it is critically condemned and called "vile trash" by William Dunlap. A political refugee from Ireland, Burk had founded and edited two failed papers in the United States, the *Polar Star and Boston Daily Advertiser* and the *Time Piece.*

JOHN BLAIR LINN (1777–1804): *Bourville Castle.* A drama written during Linn's first year as a law student and revised by fellow authors Charles Brockden Brown and William Dunlap. Brown would say of the play, "Its success was such as had been sufficient to have fixed the literary destiny of some minds."

ROYALL TYLER: *The Georgia Spec; or, Land in the Moon.* A three-act comedy, now lost but popular in its time, that satirizes the famous land speculation frauds in Yazoo County. The comedy appears several times in Boston and New York.

Fiction

ANN ELIZA BLEECKER: *The History of Maria Kittle.* This posthumously published epistolary, a captivity narrative set during the French and Indian War, is a fictionalized elaboration of the author's own experiences. It is thought to be the first American fictional account focusing on Native Americans, presenting them as brutal and vicious. Typical of Bleecker's writing, the horrific descriptions of the Indian attack and an earthquake are contrasted with tranquil rural scenes.

JAMES BUTLER (c. 1755–1842): *Fortune's Foot-ball; or, The Adventures of Mercutio.* The Pennsylvania writer's romantic novel concerns the importance of destiny as illustrated through the experiences of Mercutio as he encounters melodramatic situations, including the Algerian slave trade and impressment of British sailors.

HANNAH WEBSTER FOSTER (1759–1840): *The Coquette; or, The History of Eliza Wharton.* An epistolary novel based on the alleged seduction of Foster's distant cousin, Elizabeth Whitman, by Pierpont Edwards, and her death in childbirth. Wildly popular, the novel would appear in numerous editions, with early editions attributed to "A Lady of Massachusetts."

ROYALL TYLER: *The Algerine Captive; or, The Life and Adventures of Doctor Updike Underhill.* A picaresque tale of a young doctor, which draws on the American interest in the Barbary Coast to satirize frontier medicine and college education in New England and to denounce slavery. Tyler, an attorney who would later become chief justice of the Vermont supreme court, was also a playwright. *The Algerine Captive* is his most popular novel.

Nonfiction

CALEB BINGHAM: *The Columbian Orator.* A reader and elocution manual containing exercises to teach reading and recitation to children. Although less popular than his earlier work, *The American Preceptor*, it would remain in use until the 1860s.

JONATHAN BOUCHER (1738–1804): *A View of the Causes and Consequences of the American Revolution.* Thirteen sermons written by the English-born clergyman and originally delivered to his parish in Virginia. The sermons assert that good Christians are also good subjects of the British monarch. His Loyalist opinions forced him to flee the colonies for England, where he published the sermons.

THOMAS PAINE: *Agrarian Justice, Opposed to Agrarian Law, and to Agrarian Monopoly.* A pamphlet written during his time in France that further reveals Paine's visionary thinking and desire to bring social justice to an imperfect political system. Paine suggests a way simultaneously to support the poor, improve the other classes of society, and make real the natural rights of man to own property.

ROBERT PROUD (1728–1813): *The History of Pennsylvania.* The first volume of a chronicle of the state focuses primarily on political and religious subjects and includes an introduction to the life of William Penn. A second volume would appear in 1798. Although a valuable resource, it fails financially. A historian and educator who was a master of the Friends Public School, Proud received financial assistance from former students to continue his work on the history. He spent the last years of his life in poverty and seclusion.

DEBORAH SAMPSON (1760–1827): *The Female Review; or, Life of Deborah Sampson.* An embellished autobiography detailing Sampson's experiences in the American Revolution, in which she had dressed as a man and served in the Massachusetts militia and Continental army. Although she had lost her wartime diary, she told her tale to Herman Man, who wrote and published it.

BENJAMIN TRUMBULL (1735–1820): *A Complete History of Connecticut.* The Connecticut minister's chronicle of the state remains one of the most valuable writings on Connecticut history. Trumbull imbues it with the Puritan understandings of God's presence in history and romantic characteristics stemming from the author's love of his state.

Poetry

SARAH WENTWORTH MORTON: *Beacon Hill: A Local Poem, Historic and Descriptive.* A poetical record of the

Deborah Sampson

American Revolution. Although the verse is conventional, it illustrates the use of neoclassical forms to convey national pride.

Publications and Events

Porcupine's Gazette and Daily Advertiser. William Cobbett begins publishing this pro-British, Federalist daily newspaper in Philadelphia. After battling with the anti-Federalist *Aurora* and losing a $5,000 libel judgment against Benjamin Rush, the paper ceased publication in 1799.

1798
Drama and Theater

JOHN DALY BURK: *Female Patriotism; or, The Death of Joan d'Arc.* A play concerning an Enlightenment heroine. One of the best early American plays, it nonetheless would open inauspiciously amid generally negative attitudes toward the French and a low caliber of acting.

WILLIAM DUNLAP: *André: A Tragedy.* A blank-verse tragedy about the British spy's execution, it is considered superior to most other historical dramas of the time. Dunlap's evenhanded treatment of both sides in the conflict upset some playgoers. The playwright would adapt the drama into a patriotic extravaganza, *The Glory of Columbia,* in 1803.

ROBERT MUNFORD (c. 1737–1784): *The Candidates; or, The Humours of a Virginia Election.* A three-act satire about the conduct of elections in colonial Virginia. Historians consider it the first American farce. Munford was a Virginia planter and a legislator who served as a county official and also in the House of Burgesses and the General Assembly. His works do not appear in print until after his death, when his son William assembles his *Collection of Plays and Poems.*

Fiction

CHARLES BROCKDEN BROWN (1771–1810): *Wieland; or, The Transformation.* The story of Theodore Wieland, who murders his family after hearing what he believes are heavenly voices, which are actually produced by an evil ventriloquist. The book questions the reliability of the senses and finds favor with many authors, especially John Keats (1795–1821).

SUSANNA HASWELL ROWSON: *Reuben and Rachel; or, Tales of Old Times.* A romantic novel that surveys the history of Western civilization and attempts to inspire young women toward an interest in history. It is Rowson's transitional work from fiction to pedagogy.

Nonfiction

CHARLES BROCKDEN BROWN: *Alcuin: A Dialogue.* A discussion on women's education and political equality. Brown would later become one of the first professional novelists in the United States.

HANNAH WEBSTER FOSTER: *The Boarding School; or, Lessons of a Preceptress to Her Pupils.* Moral and domestic lectures, which contemporaries criticize as dull and rigid but some modern critics value for Foster's feminist philosophies, including her advocacy of female education and criticism of sexual double standards.

ABIEL HOLMES (1763–1837): *The Life of Ezra Stiles.* A biography of the president of Yale and the author's father-in-law. Holmes, the father of writer Oliver Wendell Holmes, had great respect for his father-in-law; this highly laudatory biography has been called "a work of genuine worth and character."

JUDITH SARGENT MURRAY (1751–1820): *The Gleaner.* One of the earliest woman essayists in America collects her works published between 1792 and 1794 in three volumes. The collection contains essays on history, guidelines for women's conduct, discussion of education and politics, and poems. Originally published under the guise of male authorship to maintain an impartial readership, the essays attempt to prove the capability of women writers.

Judith Sargent Murray

GEORGE VANCOUVER (1757–1798): *Voyage of Discovery to the North Pacific Ocean and Round the World.* An account, with an atlas of maps and plates, of the Englishman's exploration of the northwest coast of America from 1792 to 1794, during which he circumnavigated Vancouver Island. After Vancouver's death his brother had completed the book, which is printed at government expense and soon translated into French, German, and Swedish.

Poetry

JOSEPH HOPKINSON (1770–1842): "Hail Columbia." A popular patriotic song that refers to England and France but avoids partisanship. Hopkinson, a successful lawyer and future U.S. congressman, writes the song for the actor Gilbert Fox during a time of war fever against France.

WILLIAM MUNFORD (1775–1825): *Poems and Prose on Several Occasions.* A collection of juvenile writings, including a tragedy, versifications of Ossian, translations from Horace, as well as other poems notable for their insights into the interests of a literary young man. Scholar

Frank Shuffleton commends them for their "flashes of wit and intelligence."

ROBERT TREAT PAINE: "Adams and Liberty." The verse, written for the Massachusetts Charitable Fire Society, praises post-Revolutionary America's triumph over European oppression. It is Paine's most famous work, sung throughout America.

Publications and Events

The *Ulster County Gazette.* This New York Federalist newspaper, which would last until 1822, makes its debut and becomes widely known for its issue of January 4, 1800, featuring an account of George Washington's funeral and the congressional proceedings that followed. No known original copy of this issue exists, but twenty-one unauthenticated reprints have sold for high prices.

1799
Drama and Theater

WILLIAM DUNLAP: *The Italian Father.* A drama about a father who disguises himself to follow and monitor his delinquent daughter. Based on Thomas Dekker's (c. 1572–1632) *The Honest Whore, Part II,* the play is acclaimed by contemporary audiences as well as modern critics. Dunlap considered it the best of his numerous plays.

Fiction

CHARLES BROCKDEN BROWN: *Arthur Mervyn; or, Memoirs of the Year 1793.* A complex novel about the misadventures of the eighteen-year-old Mervyn, who has been banished from his country home. It is most notable for its descriptions of the yellow fever epidemic of 1793. He also publishes two more novels. *Edgar Huntley; or, Memoirs of a Sleep-Walker* is called a "fine detective story" by the twentieth-century literary historian and Brown scholar Alexander Cowie. This psychological novel concerns a young man whose attempts at benevolence bring disaster. *Ormond; or, The Secret Witness* is a seduction novel in which an educated and moral heroine kills the radical who attempts to rape her. According to Thomas Love Peacock, Percy Bysse Shelley (1792–1822) called the work "a perfect combination of the purely ideal and the possibly real," though others criticized it as incoherent and overly reliant on coincidence.

HELENA WELLS (c. 1760–c. 1809): *The Stepmother.* The story of an independent woman who manages her own finances and property after the death of her husband; it includes detailed descriptions of the conduct of a sensible woman. The daughter of a Loyalist bookseller and publisher, Wells was a novelist and educator who operated, with her sister, a boarding school for girls in London and worked as a governess.

Literary Criticism and Scholarship

LINDLEY MURRAY: *The English Reader; or, Pieces in Prose and Verse Selected from the Best Writers.* The final volume of Murray's English Grammar series contains selections by important writers, including Joseph Addison and David Hume. The work receives numerous favorable reviews and would go through many English and American editions.

Nonfiction

HANNAH ADAMS (1755–1831): *A Summary History of New England.* An objective account of important events from the sailing of the *Mayflower* to the establishment of the Constitution, based on primary sources from state archives and newspapers. Commonly considered "the first professional women writer in America," Adams had conducted much of her research in bookshops because she could not afford to purchase books.

THOMAS COOPER (1759–1839): *Political Essays.* A collection of essays attacking the Federalists. Cooper, an agitator, scientist, and educator, had allied himself with the Jeffersonians and become a vociferous pamphleteer, speaking out against tyranny. These collected essays are considered among his most significant works.

PHILIP FRENEAU: *Letters on Various Interesting and Important Subjects.* Freneau's most popular nonfiction work, published under the name "Robert Slender," a supposedly simple man whose understanding of politics comes only from reading the newspaper. The letters discuss state, national, and European politics, denounce war, and appeal for a return to true republican values.

SAMUEL KNOX (1756–1832): *An Essay on the Best System of Liberal Education, Adapted to the Genius of the Government of the United States.* The Scottish-born minister and educator's most significant work outlines a system for education in America that includes a college for each state, elementary schools for male and female pupils, training for teachers, and a university press. The essay would win an American Philosophical Society contest and influence Jefferson's plans for the University of Virginia.

JAMES SMITH (c. 1737–c. 1814): *An Account of Remarkable Occurrences in the Life and Travels of Col. James Smith, During His Captivity with the Indians.* The Pennsylva-

Philip Freneau

nia frontiersman and Indian fighter provides a primary source on frontier life in the Ohio Valley, describing Smith's experiences among the Indians.

Poetry

RICHARD ALSOP, with Lemuel Hopkins and Theodore Dwight: *The Political Greenhouse.* A popular verse satire that gains a great deal of attention for its Federalist attack on Thomas Jefferson, the Democrats, France, and the Jacobins. The poem, which had first appeared in the *Connecticut Courant,* was quoted in Congress to illustrate Connecticut's intent to involve the United States in a war against France.

SARAH WENTWORTH MURRAY: *The Virtues of Society.* Murray adapts part of her *Beacon Hill* (1797) as a narrative poem concerning a wounded British officer and his wife.

Publications and Events

The *Monthly Magazine and American Review.* The New York literary periodical edited by Charles Brockden Brown appears, featuring articles on current events, science, as well as poems, tales, essays, and book reviews. Brown included part of *Edgar Huntley* in its pages in 1799. In 1801 he transformed it into the quarterly *American Review and Literary Journal.*

BIRTHS AND DEATHS, 1800–1809

Births

1800 George Bancroft (d. 1891), historian and diplomat
Catharine Esther Beecher (d. 1878), author
Charles James Cannon (d. 1860), playwright

1802 Lydia Maria Child (d. 1880), novelist and social reformer

1803 Jacob Abbott (d. 1879), clergyman and children's author
Ralph Waldo Emerson (d. 1882), essayist and poet

1804 Nathaniel Hawthorne (d. 1864), novelist
Charles Frederick Briggs (d. 1877), journalist, novelist, and editor

1805 William Lloyd Garrison (d. 1879), abolitionist and author
Joseph Smith (d. 1844), founder of the Mormon Church and responsible for *The Book of Mormon*

1806 Robert Montgomery Bird (d. 1854), playwright and novelist
Charles Fenno Hoffman (d. 1884), poet, novelist, and editor
William Gilmore Simms (d. 1870), novelist and poet
Nathaniel Parker Willis (d. 1867), journalist, editor, and novelist

1807 Henry Wadsworth Longfellow (d. 1882), poet
John Greenleaf Whittier (d. 1892), poet

1808 William Davis Gallagher (d. 1894), poet
Samuel Francis Smith (d. 1895), poet

1809 Timothy Shay Arthur (d. 1885), novelist and short story writer
Thomas Holley Chivers (d. 1858), poet
Oliver Wendell Holmes (d. 1894), poet, novelist, and physician
Joseph Holt Ingraham (d. 1860), novelist
Edgar Allan Poe (d. 1849), poet, short story writer, and critic

Deaths

1801 Lemuel Hopkins (b.1750), poet and satirist

1803 Samuel Hopkins (b. 1721), writer and minister
William Smith (b. 1727), educator, theologian, poet, and historian
Isaac Story (b. 1774), poet and essayist

1804 Charlotte Ramsay Lennox (b. 1720), novelist and playwright
Enos Hitchcock (b. 1744), novelist
John Blair Linn (b. 1777), clergyman and poet

1806 Isaac Backus (b. 1724), clergyman and author

1808 John Dickinson (b. 1732), colonial statesman and author

1809 Thomas Paine (b. 1737), author and Revolutionary agitator

1800

Fiction

JOHN DAVIS (1775–1854): *The Farmer of New Jersey.* The former English sailor's walking trip through fifteen states provides the material for the first of three novels. It would be followed by *The Wanderings of William* (1801) and *Walter Kennedy* (1808). A travel account of his journey would appear as *Travels in America* (1803).

HELENA WELLS: *Constantia Neville; or, The West Indian.* This novel about education promotes Christianity in arguments with deists and Unitarians and includes an attack on English author and feminist Mary Wollstonecraft.

SARAH SAYWARD BARRELL KEATING WOOD (1759–1855): *Julia and the Illuminated Baron.* The gothic story of an intrepid young woman who resists an atheistic baron during the French Revolution. Known as "Madam Wood," the author is Maine's first novelist. Most of her work consists of sentimental novels and gothic melodramas.

Nonfiction

ALEXANDER HAMILTON: "Letter . . . Concerning the Public Conduct and Character of John Adams." In a note privately circulated to Federalist leaders, Hamilton justifies his opposition to Adams's reelection. Although calling him an unquestioned patriot, Hamilton criticizes Adams as "a man of an imagination sublimated and eccentric; propitious neither to the regular display of sound judgment, nor to steady perseverance in a systematic plan of conduct."

MASON LOCKE WEEMS (1759–1825): *The Life and Memorable Actions of George Washington.* Published anonymously in its first edition the year following Washington's death, this immensely popular biography would undergo continual expansions and revisions during the author's lifetime, with a twenty-ninth edition published the year of Weems's death. Not a model of strict factual biography, the work originates many of the Washington myths, including the cherry-tree story, which first appears in the fifth edition (1806). Weems also publishes *Hymen's Recruiting Sergeant*, the first of his popular moralistic pamphlets, to be followed by *God's Revenge Against Murder* (1807), *The Devil in Petticoats* (1810), *God's Revenge Against Gambling* (1815), and *God's Revenge Against Dueling* (1820).

Poetry

RICHARD ALSOP: "A Poem, Sacred to the Memory of George Washington." Among the most widely read of the poetic eulogies of Washington, the poem is dedicated to Martha Washington and recalls the first president's service to the country and his nature.

WILLIAM CLIFFTON: *Poems, Chiefly Occasional.* A collection of verse published in New York a year after the author's death. John Dickinson, writing for *The Dictionary*

of American Biography, claims that Cliffton "had perhaps more feeling, more quality than any other American writers of his day save Freneau."

JOHN BLAIR LINN: *The Death of Washington: A Poem, in Imitation of the Manner of Ossian*. Linn's book-length elegy draws criticism for its treatment of the American national hero in the mystical style of the Celtic bard.

Publications and Events

The *National Intelligencer and Washington Advertiser*. Founded by S. H. Smith in Washington, D.C., this newspaper would become the recognized organ of the administrations of Jefferson, Madison, Monroe, Polk, and Fillmore, and until 1825 it provided the only printed record of congressional debates and proceedings. An outlet for many of the writings of Webster, Clay, and Calhoun, the newspaper ceased publication in 1870.

1801
Fiction

CHARLES BROCKDEN BROWN: *Clara Howard*. This novel examines the ambiguity of morality and the unreliability of appearances. In it, Edward Hartley loves Clara Howard but is engaged to Mary Wilmot. Clara insists that he marry his betrothed, not realizing that Mary does not love Edward. Brown also publishes *Jane Talbot*, the story of two lovers who are kept apart by misunderstandings and deceptions. Less interesting than his earlier novels, these works are often cited as marking the end of Brown's literary powers.

TABITHA TENNEY (1762–1837): *Female Quixotism*. A best-selling satire about a young girl who reads novels and attempts to live her life according to them. She rejects suitors for failing to be appropriately romantic and ends up a spinster. A novelist and anthologist, Tenney was the wife of Dr. Samuel Tenney, a surgeon in the Continental army and a congressman from 1800 to 1807. She helped pioneer the gothic style that would be employed by writers such as Washington Irving.

SARAH SAYWARD BARRELL KEATING WOOD: *Dorval; or, The Speculator*. A suspenseful novel in which a virtuous heroine overcomes a villain who convinces the other characters to participate in land speculation, which leads them to ruin.

Nonfiction

MICHEL-GUILLAUME JEAN DE CRÈVECOEUR: *Voyage dans la Haute-Pennsylvanie et dans l'état de New York*. A travel book based on Crèvecoeur's experiences in colo-nial America, it is less popular than his earlier work *Letters of an American Farmer*.

NATHAN FISKE (1733–1799): *The Moral Monitor*. Essays collected soon after Fiske's death that would become widely read school texts. A Massachusetts clergyman, Fiske had originally published his essays in the *Massachusetts Spy* under the pen name "The Neighbor."

ALEXANDER HAMILTON: *An Address to the Electors of the State of New York*. Writing in support of the Federalist candidate for governor, Hamilton summarizes Federalist and Republican positions and programs and calls the election "a contest between the tyranny of jacobinism . . . and the mild reign of rational liberty."

MARTHA MEREDITH READ (fl. early nineteenth century): *A Second Vindication of the Rights of Women*. In one of the earliest American feminist treatises, Read supports and elaborates on Mary Wollstonecraft's work on women's rights, topics she would also take up in her two known novels, *Monima* (1802) and *Margaretta* (1807).

Poetry

PAUL ALLEN (1775–1826): *Original Poems, Serious and Entertaining*. A collection of early American lyric poems influenced by the English style. Although lacking much critical or commercial success at publication, they have since been noted for their grace. Allen, a journalist, editor, and poet, was especially known for his oratory abilities while a student at Brown.

JOHN BLAIR LINN: *The Powers of Genius*. A popular poem consisting of heroic couplets in three parts, which describe genius and writers who attained it.

JONATHAN MITCHELL SEWALL (1748–1808): *Miscellaneous Poems*. A collection of poems, often patriotic and political, including "Profiles of Eminent Men" that offers descriptions, predominately of writers, from Homer through those of the eighteenth century. A lawyer, poet, and fervent Federalist, Sewall was often called upon to deliver speeches at Federalist events. His most important work was the ballad "War and Washington," sung by American soldiers during the Revolution.

ISAAC STORY: *A Parnassian Shop, Opened in the Pindaric Stile; by Peter Quince, Esq*. A collection of satirical verses against the Democrats. Fashioned after the style of the English "Peter Pindar" (John Wolcot), it became Story's best-known and most popular work.

Publications and Events

The *Hudson Balance*. This Federalist newspaper, published until 1809, makes its debut. Alexander Hamilton would unsuccessfully defend its editor, Harry Croswell, in a libel suit caused by the paper's attacks on Thomas Jefferson.

The *New York Evening Post.* Founded as a Federalist organ, the newspaper first features biased political discussion rather than news, advocating Jacksonian democracy and later the Free-Soil and Republican Parties under the editorship of William Cullen Bryant (1794–1878). During the early twentieth century it crusaded against jingoism and political corruption, and its editors included reformer Carl Schurz (1829–1906). Eventually the word *Evening* was dropped from its title, and it became the *New York Post.*

The *Port Folio.* Lawyer and essayist Joseph Dennie founds and edits this Philadelphia literary magazine, which reflects his political and literary conservatism. Its contributors would include Royall Tyler, John Quincy Adams, and Gouverneur Morris. A number of editors headed the magazine before it declined in popularity and folded in 1827.

1802
Fiction

MARTHA MEREDITH READ: *Monima; or, The Beggar Girl.* Published anonymously by "an American Lady," Read's first of two novels (*Margaretta* would follow in 1807) is a socially conscious melodrama about a heroine living on the fringe of Philadelphia society who is kidnapped, imprisoned for theft, stricken by yellow fever, and endures additional disasters brought on by her poverty and gender.

SARAH SAYWARD BARRELL KEATING WOOD: *Amelia; or, The Influence of Virtue.* The story of an orphan girl who marries the son of the wealthy aristocrat who shelters her. She then suffers through his infidelity but rears his illegitimate children. Her virtue is eventually rewarded with marriage to a man she loves.

Nonfiction

NATHANIEL BOWDITCH (1773–1838): *The New American Practical Navigator.* Immensely popular, this revision of J. Hamilton Moore's *Practical Navigator* would appear in more than sixty editions, and according to literary historian Van Wyck Brooks "saved countless lives and made American ships the swiftest that ever sailed." Bowditch was a self-taught mathematician and astronomer.

JAMES CHEETHAM (1772–1810): *View of the Political Conduct of Aaron Burr.* A harsh criticism of Burr's behavior in the 1800 presidential election. This resulted in a hostile newspaper battle among Cheetham, editor Peter Irving of the *New York Morning Chronicle,* and others.

Washington Irving

TIMOTHY DEXTER (1747–1806): *A Pickle for the Knowing Ones; or, Plain Truths in a Homespun Dress.* A humorous description of the author's own experiences and beliefs on a variety of unrelated topics. The privately printed book is famous for its lack of punctuation. The author responded to critics by including one page of miscellaneous punctuation marks at the end of the second edition so that readers could "pepers and solt it as they please."

ALEXANDER HAMILTON: *The Examination of the President's Message, at the Opening of Congress, December 7, 1801.* Hamilton's last major publication, a series of articles first published in his *New York Evening Post* under the pseudonym "Lucius Crassus," criticizes Jefferson's proposals on war, revenue, immigration, and the judiciary.

WASHINGTON IRVING (1783–1859): *Letters of Jonathan Oldstyle, Gent.* A collection of satires of social life in New York, mostly devoted to the theater. Written when Irving was only nineteen, the essays win him his first recognition. A New York publisher pirated the essays in 1824, and five editions are attributed to "the Author of the Sketch Book."

1803
Drama and Theater

WILLIAM DUNLAP: *The Glory of Columbia.* Dunlap revises his blank-verse tragedy *André* (1798) into this musical patriotic spectacular for holiday performance.

Nonfiction

JOHN DAVIS: *Travels of Four Years and a Half in the United States*. A record of the former English sailor's journeys on the eastern seaboard, written especially to cater to Americans' desire for travel literature. The writing offers more about the author than about his observations and also includes descriptions of Jefferson's inauguration and inaugural address, a version of the Pocahontas story, and the tale of "Dick the Negro."

SAMUEL MILLER (1769–1850): *A Brief Retrospect of the Eighteenth Century*. Although based on previous publications, the work is a judicious and thorough history of the progress of agriculture, art, science, medicine, education, and other fields and is lauded by the *North American Review* as "a comprehensive, entertaining, and instructive survey of the progress of the human mind during that period."

WILLIAM WIRT (1772–1834): *Letters of the British Spy*. Popular essays written in the style of James Addison, describing the southern way of life and defending American eloquence. The collection is published anonymously, purporting to be the writings of a traveling Englishman. Wirt, a successful lawyer, would later serve as attorney general of the United States (1817–1829).

Poetry

THOMAS GREEN FESSENDEN (1771–1837): *Terrible Tractoration!* Satire in defense of Elisha Perkins's "metallic tractors," devices used to treat disease by Galvanism, an electricity-based therapy. Fessenden was a successful lawyer and also a journalist.

Publications and Events

The *Literary Magazine and American Register*. This Philadephia monthly, edited until 1807 by Charles Brockden Brown, debuts. It featured both scientific and literary articles, including contributions by Brown such as "Memoirs of Carwin, the Biloquist." In 1807 it became a semiannual almanac called the *American Register*, which folded in 1810.

1804
Fiction

SARAH SAYWARD BARRELL KEATING WOOD: *Ferdinand and Elmira: A Russian Story*. An adventure story set in Russia concerning the history of an extended family and the villany of absolute monarchy. More complex than her earlier novels and lacking a single central female character, it would be Wood's last publication before she married General Abiel Wood. She ceased writing until his death in 1811.

Nonfiction

HANNAH ADAMS: *The Truth and Excellence of the Christian Religion Exhibited*. An outline of the responsibility laypeople had taken in religion since the seventeenth century, the book contains short biographies of prominent men who embody Christian values and selections that serve in her words as "Evidence in Favor of Revealed Religion."

WILLIAM AUSTIN (1778–1841): *Letters from London*. The future successful Boston lawyer, legislator, and writer of tales supplies descriptions of British lawyers and statesmen as viewed by a New Englander, based on Austin's own observations while studying law abroad.

HOSEA BALLOU (1771–1852): *Notes on the Parables*. A theological work emphasizing that people should not try to acquire "eternal life through legal righteousness." Ballou, a theologian and clergyman, developed and clarified American Universalist doctrine.

JOHN DALY BURK: *The History of Virginia*. The first history of Virginia after it became a state is written from a Jeffersonian stance, which wins it a positive reception. The work remains a valuable history because of Burk's access to Jefferson's library of old newspapers and legal manuscripts. The history was unfinished when Burk died in a duel in 1808 and was continued by Skelton Jones, who was also killed in a duel before finishing the history. Louis Hue Girardin (Louis-François Picot) completed the book in 1816.

JOHN MARSHALL (1755–1835): *Life of Washington*. Marshall, chief justice of the Supreme Court, publishes this biography in five volumes from 1804 to 1807. Its Federalist view of Washington's presidency receives mixed reviews. Although the work contains many insights garnered from primary resources provided by Washington's family, Marshall would always regret rushing the production with little revision.

JEDIDIAH MORSE AND ELIJAH PARISH (1762–1825): *A Compendious History of New England*. The Connecticut Congregational clergymen's account provokes Hannah Adams to accuse them of plagiarism. Morse was best known for his *Geography Made Easy* (1784), the first geography published in the United States.

WILLIAM WIRT: *The Rainbow*. A collection of philosophical essays first published in the *Richmond Enquirer* by the Rainbow Association, a Virginia literary and intellectual club. Wirt wrote ten of the essays, including "On the Condition of Women" and "On Forensic Eloquence."

Poetry

THOMAS GREEN FESSENDEN: *Original Poems*. A collection of Fessenden's earlier newspaper contributions,

John Marshall

consisting mostly of humorous anti-Jacobin and literary satires. The verses sell well in America, and one poem, "The Country Lovers," becomes very popular. *The Dictionary of American Biography* calls Fessenden "the most important American satirist in verse between Trumbull and Lowell."

SUSANNA HASWELL ROWSON: *Miscellaneous Poems.* Her second and last collection of poetry, ranging from short occasional poems to songs set to music and lengthy patriotic works, would remain popular in her time though never win critical acclaim. Evert and George Duyckinck, who anthologized the poems forty years later, described them as "expressive of [a] generous women's heart."

JOHN WILLIAMS (1761–1818): *The Hamiltoniad.* Writing as "Anthony Pasquin," Williams produces a three-canto poem containing many harsh criticisms of Alexander Hamilton and other Federalists. The satiric tone is further notable for its extensive footnotes, including Latin and French quotations and exerpts from correspondence between Hamilton and Aaron Burr.

1805
Drama and Theater

WILLIAM IOOR (c. 1780–1830): *Independence; or, Which Do You Like Best, the Peer or the Farmer?* One of the first comedies of manners popular in early-nineteenth-

century America, this play helps establish Charleston, South Carolina, as a theatrical center. Based on an English novel, *The Independent,* said to be by Andrew McDonald but attributed to "anonimous" in Ioor's preface, it praises America's unrefined virtues.

Fiction

JOHN DAVIS: *The Post Captain; or, The Wooden Walls Well Manned.* A popular sentimental novel that initiates the nautical literary genre, serving as a model for authors such as Frederick Marryat (1792–1848) and Frederick Chamier, whose naval adventure stories would become popular in the late nineteenth century. Davis also publishes *The First Settlers of Virginia,* an expansion of the popular story of John Smith and Pocahontas published in Davis's *Travels* (1803). In this idealistic romance, Pocahontas saves the captured Smith by placing her head on his on the chopping block. The book is the first fully developed fictional account of the legend. Although Davis had plagiarized much of the story from Belknap's *American Biography* (1794), he is credited with cultivating the popular American story.

CAROLINE MATILDA WARREN (c. 1787–1844): *The Gamesters; or, Ruins of Innocence.* A sentimental, moralistic novel concerning the evils of gambling and the corruption of an orphan. The New England schoolteacher's novel would be reprinted in numerous editions.

Nonfiction

HOSEA BALLOU: *A Treatise on Atonement.* Ballou's most significant work reconsiders John Murray's Universalism, argues against the idea of punishment after death, and denies the existence of the Trinity. John Coleman Adams, in the introduction to the fourteenth edition, would call it "the first American book to anticipate all the essential points of . . . liberal theology."

JOEL BARLOW: *Prospectus of a National Institution.* A proposal for a federally funded institution for research and instruction in the arts and sciences. Not implemented due to cost and Federalist political skepticism about it, Barlow's plan would affect the educational institutions established in each state under the Morrill Act in the mid-1800s.

MERCY OTIS WARREN: *History of the Rise, Progress, and Termination of the American Revolution.* A history whose merit lies in Warren's descriptions of participants in the war, many of whom she was acquainted with or corresponded with personally. Although less successful than expected during her lifetime, it would endure as a resource for later writers.

Mercy Otis Warren

Poetry

THOMAS GREEN FESSENDEN: *Democracy Unveiled.* The most famous poetic attack on Thomas Jefferson and other Democratic leaders. In mock-heroic couplets with numerous footnotes, the six cantos are a "call to arms against the demagogues of the new Republic." In it the author compares Democrats to Illuminists and Jacobins and describes mob law in America as a caricature of the Democratic Party.

JOHN BLAIR LINN: *Valerian.* An epic poem about the persecution of early Christians and the impact of Christianity on the "Manners of Nations." Although intended to be his masterpiece, Linn had died of tuberculosis before finishing it. It is published posthumously with an introduction by his brother-in-law, Charles Brockden Brown.

ALEXANDER WILSON (1766–1813): *The Foresters.* A poetical description of nature and adventure as experienced on a walking trip from Philadelphia to Niagara Falls and back. Wilson, who would become most known for his

American Ornithology (1808), is notable for his contribution to the beginnings of American nature literature.

Publications and Events

The Boston Athenaeum. The Anthology Club founds this library, museum, and laboratory. In 1845 it would move to its own large building. Mentioned in Hawthorne's *American Notebooks*, it serves as the setting for Hawthorne's story "The Ghost of Doctor Harris."

1806
Drama and Theater

JOHN HOWARD PAYNE (1791–1852): *Julia; or, The Wanderer.* Melodrama concerning a heroine kidnapped by her brother in an attempt to win the family's property. Although conventional in form, it is Payne's first play, written at the age of fifteen. He edited the weekly theatrical paper, the *Thesbian Mirror* (1805–1806) when he was fourteen.

Nonfiction

WILLIAM LITTELL (1768–1824): *An Epistle from William, Surnamed Littell, to the People of the Realm of Kentucky.* A volume of essays satirizing government officials. Previously known for his compilation of law books, Littell shocks his colleagues with the publication of this work. It has lasted as an illustration of early frontier humor.

NOAH WEBSTER: *A Compendious Dictionary of the English Language.* The author's first dictionary contains five thousand words never before included in dictionaries, such as *lengthy, sot, spry, gunning, belittle,* and *caucus;* Webster considers them the result of American social life and customs.

1807
Drama and Theater

JAMES NELSON BARKER (1784–1858): *Tears and Smiles.* A comedy concerning Philadelphia manners and presenting the theme of American superiority over European lifestyles. Barker is one of the first American playwrights to use American material and themes in his plays.

WILLIAM IOOR: *The Battle of Eutaw Springs.* A patriotic historical play concerning the South Carolina battle of 1781 in which General Nathanael Greene forced the British to withdraw northward. Like Ioor's other plays, it lauds simple American virtues and condemns the affectations of the English. Not as popular as his earlier plays, it is nonetheless well received and further distinguishes South Carolina as a theatrical center in the early nineteenth century.

Fiction

WILLIAM HILL BROWN: *Ira and Isabella; or, The Natural Children.* In a variation on the plot of his first novel, *The Power of Sympathy* (1789), Brown allows for a happy ending by revealing that Ira and Isabella are not in fact related, so their marriage is not incestuous.

MARTHA MEREDITH READ: *Margaretta; or, The Intricacies of the Heart.* The second of Read's two known novels dramatizes the perils of a wealthy single woman. It incorporates many of Read's opinions about the contemporary status of women contained in her early feminist treatise *A Second Vindication of the Rights of Women.*

Nonfiction

WASHINGTON IRVING: *Salmagundi; or, The Whim-Whams and Opinions of Launcelot Langstaff, Esq., and Others.* Written with William Irving (1766–1821) and James Kirke Paulding (1778–1860), the miscellany includes political satires and critiques of theater, music, fashion, Jeffersonian democracy, and New York society. Named for a spicy salad, *Salmagundi* is the first collection of its kind in the United States and becomes instantly popular.

Poetry

JOEL BARLOW: *The Columbiad.* In an expansive revision of *The Vision of Columbus* (1787) written in heroic couplets, Barlow produces the Miltonic epic that he would regard as his masterpiece. In it Columbus, an old man dying in prison, has a vision of the future and the glories of America. They include Barlow's predictions of the building of the Panama Canal, airplanes, submarines, and an organization similar to the United Nations.

1808

Drama and Theater

JAMES NELSON BARKER: *The Indian Princess; or, La Belle Sauvage.* A comedy with songs about the Pocahontas story. It is the first play about American Indians by an American playwright and the first play produced in America to be performed in England. Also produced is Barker's *The Embargo; or, What News?* Barker's drama in support of the Embargo Acts and the Jefferson administration causes opponents to riot against both when it is performed in Philadelphia.

Nonfiction

SAMUEL BARD (1742–1821): *A Compendium of the Theory and Practice of Midwifery.* The first obstetrics textbook written by an American, it becomes America's

An illustration drawn by Alexander Wilson
from *American Ornithology*

standard work on the subject and goes through five editions.

ANNE MacVICAR GRANT (1755–1838): *Memoirs of an American Lady.* Published anonymously, this record of the memoirist's experiences as a girl living near Albany, New York, is notable for its accurate description of colonial life and manners.

ALEXANDER WILSON: *American Ornithology.* An accurate and thorough description of birds of the eastern United States, north of Florida. Wilson, a schoolmaster, had devoted ten years to gathering materials. Over the next hundred years, only twenty-three more land bird species would be identified by ornithologists. Although Wilson did not live to receive financial or critical success, the book is considered a classic in the field.

Poetry

WILLIAM CULLEN BRYANT (1794–1878): "The Embargo; or, Sketches of the Time, a Satire; by a Youth of Thirteen." A verse satire against Jefferson's trade restrictions. Bryant's father publishes the poem in pamphlet form, and it wins regional popularity. Its success and the fact that Dr. Bryant wanted his son to receive credit for

BIRTHS AND DEATHS, 1810–1819

Births

1810　Margaret Fuller (d. 1850), essayist, critic, and social reformer
　　　Ann Sophia Stephens (d. 1886), novelist and editor

1811　William Starbuck Mayo (d. 1895), novelist
　　　Harriet Beecher Stowe (d. 1896), novelist
　　　Alfred Billings Street (d. 1881), poet
　　　Sara Payson Willis (d. 1872), novelist

1813　Nathaniel Bannister (d. 1847), playwright and actor
　　　Henry Ward Beecher (d. 1887), theologian, writer, and editor
　　　Epes Sargent (d. 1880), playwright
　　　Jones Very (d. 1880), poet

1814　John Lothrop Motley (d. 1877), historian
　　　Benjamin Penhallow Shillaber (d. 1890), humorist and editor

1815　Richard Henry Dana Jr. (d. 1882), novelist
　　　Elizabeth Stuart Phelps (d. 1852), novelist
　　　Thomas Bangs Thorpe (d. 1878), painter and humorist

1816　Philip Pendleton Cooke (d. 1850), poet

1817　Henry David Thoreau (d. 1862), philosopher and author
　　　William Ellery Channing [II] (d. 1901), poet

1818　Henry Wheeler Shaw (d. 1885), humorist

1819　James Russell Lowell (d. 1891), essayist, poet, editor, and educator
　　　Herman Melville (d. 1891), novelist
　　　Anna Cora Mowatt (d. 1870), actor and playwright
　　　E.D.E.N. Southworth (d. 1899), novelist
　　　Walt Whitman (d. 1892), poet

Deaths

1810　Charles Brockden Brown (b. 1771), novelist

1811　Robert Treat Paine (b. 1773), poet and editor

1812　Joel Barlow (b. 1754), poet
　　　Joseph Dennie (b. 1768), essayist and editor

1813　Alexander Wilson (b. 1766), nature writer and poet

1814　Mercy Otis Warren (b. 1728), playwright, poet, and historian

1815　Richard Alsop (b. 1761), poet and satirist

1816　Hugh Henry Brackenridge (b. 1748), novelist, poet, and judge

1817　Timothy Dwight (b. 1752), religious leader and poet

1818　Abigail Adams (b. 1744), correspondent, wife of President John Adams
　　　Jonathan Odell (b. 1737), poet and physician

the poem would lead to a second volume of poems in 1809.

1809

Drama and Theater

JOHN HOWARD PAYNE: *Lover's Vow.* Payne adapts August von Kotzebue's *Das Kind der Liebe.*

Fiction

WASHINGTON IRVING: *A History of New York, from the Beginning of the World to the End of the Dutch Dynasty, by Diedrich Knickerbocker.* A satirical record of the history of the Dutch settlement and a criticism of Jeffersonian democracy. The story introduces readers to Knickerbocker, who would become a famous American literary character. It is widely considered the first great book of comic literature written by an American.

ROYALL TYLER: *The Yankey in London.* A series of patriotic letters, purportedly from London, to a friend and sister in the United States. The letters comment on British life, finding English manners and customs artificial compared with those of Americans.

Nonfiction

WILLIAM ALLEN (1784–1868): *American Biographical and Historical Dictionary.* A comprehensive biographical dictionary containing seven hundred entries in the first edition and expanded to seven thousand entries by the 1857 edition. Allen was a clergyman, educator, and historian, well known in New England as one of the most erudite scholars of his time. He compiled the first edition of the dictionary during his six years as assistant librarian and regent of Harvard.

FISHER AMES (1758–1808): *Works.* A posthumous collection of essays and political tracts from a staunchly Federalist statesman. Ames supported Hamilton and attacked Jeffersonian politics, which he saw as rule by the masses of the poor and ferocious. Having won a large audience, the book would be republished in an expanded edition in 1854.

JAMES CHEETHAM: *Life of Thomas Paine.* A derisive and partisan biography of the man whose acquaintance he called "more frequent than agreeable." Cheetham, a journalist and biographer, owned a part of the *American Citizen*, a New York daily that supported Republicans.

DAVID RAMSAY: *History of South Carolina from Its First Settlement in 1670 to the Year 1808.* Ramsay's most enduring work, significant for his research method of sending questionnaires to prominent men in each parish or district. The first volume contains basic demographics, history of the proprietary period, studies of the revolutions of 1719 (by which South Carolina became a royal colony) and 1776, and a military history of the state. The second volume provides social, economic, and civil history as well as biographical sketches.

SAMUEL STANHOPE SMITH (1751–1819): *Lectures on the Evidences of the Christian Religion.* A widely read book that furthers the pragmatic philosophy and realism of John Witherspoon. Smith, a Presbyterian clergyman, had raised the standards of the College of New Jersey (now Princeton) where he was president from 1795 to 1819.

Poetry

THOMAS CAMPBELL (1777–1844): *Gertrude of Wyoming.* The first popular English poem set in the United States and including Native American characters, this long narrative work tells of Gertrude's life and tragic death in her lover's arms after an Indian attack. The poem meets with mixed reviews but finds favor with Washington Irving, Oliver Wendell Holmes, and much of the American and British public, selling out three British editions and one American edition in two years.

Publications and Events

The *Literary Gazette.* This Philadelphia journal debuts; it later becomes the *Analectic Magazine* under the editorship of Washington Irving (1813–1814), who also contributes some of his writings to it. By 1817 it had become a service magazine of the U.S. Navy and later published book reviews until it ceased publication in 1821.

1810
Nonfiction

WILLIAM COOPER (1754–1809): *A Guide to the Wilderness.* Posthumously published as an aid to new settlers, this is both an autobiographical account of the founding of Cooperstown, New York, and a meditation on salutary business practices written by the father of James Fenimore Cooper.

CHARLES JARED INGERSOLL (1782–1862): *Inchiquin: The Jesuit's Letters on American Literature and Politics.* A widely read pamphlet containing a collection of letters supposedly written by a Jesuit traveler in the United States. The pamphlet calls for intellectual independence and stimulates a sense of national self-sufficiency. Negative criticism in the *English Quarterly Review* led American defenses of the book, such as Timothy Dwight's *Remarks on the Review of Inchiquin's Letters* (1815) and James Kirke Paulding's *The United States and England.* Ingersoll, a lawyer, was a Jacksonian Democrat who served in Congress as chairman of the Judiciary Committee and a member of the Foreign Relations Committee.

Zebulon Montgomery Pike

WASHINGTON IRVING: *Biographical Sketch of Thomas Campbell.* Irving supplies a biographical profile of the Scottish poet whose work Irving had compiled.

ZEBULON MONTGOMERY PIKE (1779–1813): *Account of an Expedition to the Sources of the Mississippi and Through the Western Parts of Louisiana from 1805–1807, and a Tour Through the Interior Parts of New Spain, When Conducted Through These Provinces by Order of the Captain-General in the Year 1807.* A diary detailing the expeditions of Pike, an explorer and army officer, during which he was taken prisoner by the Spanish and first sighted the peak that would be named for him.

JOHN TAYLOR (1753–1824): *The Arator.* A collection of essays originally published in the newspaper the *Spirit of Seventy-Six* from 1810 to 1811 and in book form in 1813. They are Taylor's most widely read works and advocate a system in which all decisions and policies of government should support the agrarian way of life. The author also promotes crop rotation and soil fertilization methods not yet recognized as useful.

ISAIAH THOMAS (1785–1866): *History of Printing in America.* The most important early work on the topic. Thomas had written the history in retirement, compiling a vast personal library of early American newspapers and pamphlets. The foremost publisher of his time, he produced the *Massachusetts Spy* and the *Royal American Magazine.*

BENJAMIN TRUMBULL: *General History of the United States.* Trumbull completes one volume of a history that is judged inferior to his book on Connecticut (*A Complete History of Connecticut*, 1797). Achieving neither literary nor financial success, Trumbull would abandon the project after beginning a second volume.

GEORGE WHITE: *Brief Account.* White is believed to be the first African American to write the story of his own enslavement.

1811
Fiction

ISAAC MITCHELL (C. 1759–1812): *The Asylum; or, Alonzo and Melissa.* A gothic tale set during the Revolution, in which Melissa's father keeps her from her love, Alonzo, because he is poor. The two overcome great adversity, including the false report of Melissa's death and Alonzo's capture by the British, before they eventually reunite in Charleston. A verbatim plagiarism, attributed to Daniel Jackson (fl. 1790–1811), appears in the same year, titled *Alonzo and Melissa; or, The Unfeeling Father.* Mitchell died before he could sue for damages.

Publications and Events

Niles' Weekly Register. This Baltimore journal debuts, published by economic nationalist Hezekiah Niles (1777–1839). Titled *Niles' National Register* from 1836 to 1839, the paper published a generally unbiased record of current events and stayed in business until 1849.

1812
Drama and Theater

JAMES NELSON BARKER: *Marmion; or, The Battle of Flodden Field.* A blank-verse dramatization of Sir Walter Scott's poem concerning the dispute between James IV of Scotland and Henry VII of England; it echoes the issues leading to the War of 1812. At first its writing was intentionally attributed to the English dramatist Thomas Morton, out of fear that audiences would disregard a play by an American. It succeeded and was staged until as late as 1848.

WILLIAM DUNLAP: *Yankee Chronology.* A very popular patriotic play produced at the height of the War of 1812. American sailor Ben Bundle recounts the naval battle between the *Constitution* and the British *Guerriere*, a battle that took place less than three weeks before the production. The play also includes a song of the same name, chronicling the entire American Revolution.

MORDECAI MANUEL NOAH (1785–1851): *Paul and Alexis.* The first play of one of the earliest Jewish American writers is an adaptation of René-Charles Guilbert de Pixérécourt's (1773–1844) *Le Pèlerin blanc.* It ran in Charleston prior to Noah's departure to serve as consul in Tunis.

Fiction

REBECCA RUSH (1779–?): *Kelroy.* A novel about a young man whose father dies, leaving the family in financial ruin, and his love for a girl, Emily. Her father's death has also left her family in economic danger. To ensure her children's wealth and her own expensive lifestyle, Emily's mother plans to marry her daughters to rich husbands and schemes to keep Emily and Kelroy apart. Considered by many to be one of the best fictional works of the early United States, it did not win acclaim in its time, possibly because it was published at the start of the War of 1812.

JAMES KIRKE PAULDING: *The Diverting History of John Bull and Brother Jonathan.* A comedy about the settlement and revolution of the thirteen colonies, inspired by the sentiments leading to the War of 1812. Numerous editions were published in the United States; it would be followed by an inferior sequel, *The History of Uncle Sam and His Boys* (1835).

Nonfiction

HANNAH ADAMS: *The History of the Jews from the Destruction of Jerusalem to the Present Time.* A sympathetic description of the oppression and persecution of the Jews. Adams cites several writers who propose restoration of the Jews to their ancestral country, but she also encourages efforts towards conversion to Christianity.

JOHN MELISH (1771–1822): *Travels in the U.S. of America in the Years 1806 and 1807, and 1809, 1810, and 1811.* Published in two volumes and later twice republished under slightly different titles, this work is the author's attempt to promote British immigration to the United States. Critically lauded as an objective and fair look at the country and its inhabitants, it includes eight maps by the author. Melish, a Scottish textile manufacturer, had settled in Philadelphia in 1811.

JOHN MURRAY (1741–1815). *Letters and Sketches of Sermons.* The founder of Universalism in America begins publication of his sermons and religious writings (completed in 1813 in three volumes). His autobiography, *Records*, would appear posthumously in 1816.

BENJAMIN RUSH: *Medical Inquiries and Observations upon the Diseases of the Mind.* Rush's most famous work is one of the earliest significant American works on psychiatry and suggests some understanding of what would become the theories of psychoanalysis. The book would be reprinted four times by 1835. The first American physician to win literary acclaim, Rush was hailed "the father of American psychiatry."

JAMES SMITH: *A Treatise on the Mode and Manner of Indian War, Their Tactics, Discipline and Encampments.* Taken primarily from Smith's earlier *Account of the Remarkable Occurrences in the Life and Travels of Col. James Smith* (1799), the work shows his understanding of Indian warfare, describing the Indians as disciplined soldiers with organized strategies.

SAMUEL STANHOPE SMITH: *Lectures on Moral and Political Philosophy.* Lectures based on traditional ideology but expressing liberal opinions, especially concerning marriage. Smith advocates polygamy in some cases and the eventual freedom of all slaves. The popular Presbyterian minister publishes the lectures in the same year he resigns as president of Princeton.

WILLIAM WIRT: *The Old Bachelor.* A series of essays in the manner of the *Spectator*, extolling virtues and discussing popular topics such as undue condemnation of America by condescending English travelers, female education, manners and customs in Virginia, and the fine arts. Others who contributed to the work include Dabney Carr, Dr. Frank Carr, Richard E. Parker, Dr. Louis Hue Girardin, Judge Tucker, David Watson, and George Tucker. The essays would reach a third edition by 1818, though they never won the popularity of Wirt's earlier *Letters of the British Spy.*

Poetry

ROBERT TREAT PAINE: *Works.* A posthumous collection gathered by the editor Charles Prentiss that displays the author's versatility with various genres, including political satire, drama criticism, neoclassical verse, and spiritual prose.

JOHN PIERPONT (1785–1866): *The Portrait.* Pierpont's poetic debut is a Federalist poem praising Washington and Hamilton and vilifying Jefferson. He would in 1818 become a Boston minister and advocate of abolition, pacifism, and temperance, and subsequently published *The Anti-Slavery Poems of John Pierpont* (1843).

Publications and Events

The American Antiquarian Society. Founded by Isaiah Thomas in Worcester, Massachusetts, this institution would build an impressive collection of Americana up to 1876. A private institution, it has about five hundred elected members.

The *General Repository and Review.* This Boston quarterly journal, affiliated with Harvard, debuts and lasts only until 1813. Under the editorship of biblical scholar Andrews Norton (1786–1853), it championed Unitarianism.

1813
Fiction

SUSANNA HASWELL ROWSON: *Sarah; or, The Exemplary Wife.* A domestic novel about a wife who remains dutiful to her husband even though he is unfaithful and cruel. Unlike the experience of heroines in other novels of the time, Sarah's virtue is not rewarded. The last novel published during Rowson's lifetime, it is somewhat autobiographical, and the message in the prologue, "Do not marry a fool," is based on her own experience.

Nonfiction

WILLIAM DUNLAP: *Memoirs of the Life of George Frederick Cooke, Esquire.* Two volumes of memoirs are published after the famous author's death. Dunlap, Cooke's former assistant, had been granted access to his journal and presents a frank look at a man rocketed to fame by great talent and brought low by alcoholism.

Poetry

WASHINGTON ALLSTON (1779–1843): *The Sylphs of the Seasons.* A collection of sentimental and satirical poems lauded by William Wordsworth and Robert Southey and written while the poet is a student at Harvard. Allston, a painter as well as an author, publishes the poems during convalescence related to an illness from which he never fully recovers.

EDWIN CLIFFORD HOLLAND (c. 1794–1824): *Odes, Naval Songs, and Other Occasional Poems.* The distinctive work of the Charleston poet, also an author and editor of the *Charleston Times*, marks the beginning of Romantic poetry written in South Carolina.

JAMES KIRKE PAULDING: *The Lay of the Scottish Fiddle: A Tale of Havre de Grace, Supposed to Be Written by Walter Scott, Esq.* A parody of Sir Walter Scott's *Lay of the Last Minstrel*, the work condemns the British invasion of Chesapeake Bay. Although the work is published in England with a preface complimenting Paulding, the poet is heavily criticized for it in the *London Quarterly.*

Publications and Events

The *Boston Daily Advertiser.* The first successful daily newspaper in New England debuts and by midcentury had become nationally prominent despite accusations of its deference to the interests of upper-class Bostonians. The paper was purchased by William Randolph Hearst in 1917, became an illustrated tabloid in 1921, and folded in 1929.

The *Christian Disciple*. This Boston magazine and Unitarian organ debuts. The leading religious review of its time, it was retitled the *Christian Examiner* in 1823. By 1857 it was more liberal, advocating Transcendentalism, but after its removal to New York (1866), the magazine's theological views became conservative, its influence declined, and in 1869 it ceased publication.

1814

Drama and Theater

DAVID HUMPHREYS: *The Yankey in England*. A drama introducing Doolittle, a model of Yankee characteristics: simple, inquisitive, credulous, and also suspicious, prejudiced, and obstinate. So that his accurately replicated dialect could be understood, Humphreys appends a glossary of three hundred Yankee terms to published editions of the play.

Nonfiction

NICHOLAS BIDDLE (1786–1844) AND PAUL ALLEN (1775–1826): *History of the Expedition of Captains Lewis and Clark*. The first authentic history of the expedition based on the explorers' own papers and notes. The history includes a preface by Thomas Jefferson. Biddle was a Philadelphia financier and editor of the *Port Folio* (1812). Allen was a well-known magazine contributor whose works included *Original Poems, Serious and Entertaining* (1801).

HENRY MARIE BRACKENRIDGE (1786–1871): *Views of Louisiana*. A compilation of various articles, including Brackenridge's journal of his voyage up the Missouri River and a period in New Orleans studying Spanish law and researching territorial subjects. The work supports the American administration's opinions on Louisiana's boundaries. Parts of it would be used as a source by Washington Irving for *Astoria* (1836).

HUGH HENRY BRACKENRIDGE: *Law Miscellanies*. Essays concerning Pennsylvania law, federal statutes, judgments of the U.S. Supreme Court, and the employment of English common law in the American legal system. The work was written while Brackenridge was a justice of the Pennsylvania Supreme Court and is an important source in the history of American jurisprudence.

MATTHEW CAREY (1760–1839): *The Olive Branch; or, Faults on Both Sides, Federal and Democratic*. A nonpartisan treatise written in response to the New England states' threat to secede from the Union. It is the most widely read political pamphlet since *Common Sense*, reproduced in ten editions. Carey was born in Ireland, and his pamphlet in defense of Irish Catholics led to his exile to France, where he worked in Benjamin Franklin's printing office in Passy.

JOHN TAYLOR: *An Inquiry into the Principles and Policy of the Government of the United States*. Treatise disavowing "a natural aristocracy," denouncing Hamilton's economic system, and arguing for shorter presidential and senatorial terms. Originally written as a response to John Adams's *A Defence of the Constitutions of the Government of the United States of America* (1787–1788), it is ranked by scholar Charles A. Beard as "among the two or three really historic contributions to political science which have been produced in the United States."

NOAH WORCESTER (1758–1837): *A Solemn Review of the Custom of War*. The New Hampshire clergyman and editor explains his pacifist views in this book written under the pseudonym "Philo Pacificus."

Poetry

FRANCIS SCOTT KEY (1779–1843): "The Star-Spangled Banner." Key had written his celebrated poem while detained by the British during the War of 1812; at that time he witnessed the bombardment of Baltimore's Fort McHenry. Set to the music of the English drinking song "To Anacreon in Heaven," by John Stafford Smith (1750–1836), "The Star-Spangled Banner" would be established as the national anthem by an act of Congress in 1931.

WILLIAM LITTELL: *Festoons of Fancy, Consisting of Compositions Amatory, Sentimental and Humorous in Verse and Prose*. A collection of poetry containing mostly verses on love and women, it is most notable for its satires on government officials, the recently passed divorce law, which favored men, and the electoral process.

Publications and Events

New Harmony. Founded by the Rappists, a German communal religious sect, this socialized community on the Wabash River in Indiana eventually failed and in 1825 was purchased by Robert Dale Owen (1801–1877) for use in applying his own communal theories. The commune attracted some one thousand settlers and spawned a periodical, the *New-Harmony Gazette*, later entitled the *Free Enquirer*. Ineffective leadership, group dissension, and secession led to dissolution of the community in 1828.

1815

Fiction

HUGH HENRY BRACKENRIDGE: *Modern Chivalry*. Brackenridge completes the final additions to his four-

A view of the bombardment of Fort McHenry in Baltimore, Maryland, during the War of 1812,
an event inspiring Francis Scott Key's poem "The Star-Spangled Banner"

volume novel, begun in 1792, satirizing American politics and depicting the American frontier experience. Henry Adams would call the novel "a more thoroughly American book than any written before 1833."

Nonfiction

HANNAH MATHER CROCKER (1752–1829): *Series of Letters on Free Masonry.* Attributed to "A Lady of Boston," the letters defend the Society of Free Masons against charges of excessive revelry in Boston pubs. One of the earliest advocates of women's rights in the United States, Crocker, the granddaughter of Cotton Mather, acknowledges "that it will be thought by many, a bold attempt for a female to even dare enter on the subject at all."

DANIEL DRAKE (1785–1852): *Picture of Cincinnati in 1815.* A description of the natural and social history of the city and its environs, it was one of the first works to draw attention to the Ohio Valley. Drake was a physician, educator, and civic leader in Cincinnati who would found the Ohio Medical College in 1819.

WILLIAM DUNLAP: *The Life of Charles Brockden Brown.* The book contains Brown's lectures and correspondence, with transitions and critical remarks by Dunlap. Although considered Dunlap's worst work, with poor organization and lack of a clear focus, it is the primary

source of biographical information on Brown and his only biography published before 1949.

TIMOTHY DWIGHT: *Remarks on the Review of Inchiquin's Letters.* Dwight comes to the defense of Charles Ingersoll's *Inchiquin, the Jesuit's Letters* (1810) after it is harshly attacked in the *English Quarterly Review.*

JAMES KIRKE PAULDING: *The United States and England.* A passionate defense of the ethics, conduct, literature, and institutions of the United States. After its publication, President James Madison appoints Paulding as secretary of the Board of Navy Commissioners, beginning Paulding's association with the navy, which would last until 1841.

DAVID PORTER (1780–1843): *A Journal of a Cruise Made to the Pacific Ocean.* A factual account of the naval officer's service in the Pacific protecting American trade during the War of 1812. The *Journal* includes a passage Herman Melville would use in *The Encantadas.*

Poetry

WILLIAM CULLEN BRYANT: "To a Waterfowl." A very popular and frequently anthologized poem expressing the poet's doubt and uncertainty, relieved when the sight of a bird flying alone across the sky inspires him to believe in the guidance of a divine power. It would be first published in the *North American Review* in March 1818 and called "the best short poem in the language" by Matthew Arnold.

PHILIP FRENEAU: *A Collection of Poems, on American Affairs.* A two-volume collection of previously unpublished works released in response to the War of 1812. The poems reflect the author's strong patriotic fervor and, though repetitive, show the mature Freneau to be a calm, self-assured poet.

LYDIA HUNTLEY SIGOURNEY (1791–1865): *Moral Pieces in Prose and Verse.* The Connecticut poet's first work contains material she had written as reading exercises for her students. Rufus Wilmot Griswold would write in *The Female Poets of America* (1849), "None of its contents are deserving commendation, but they are all respectable, and the volume procured her an accession of reputation which was probably of much indirect advantage."

Publications and Events

The *North American Review.* This Boston literary, critical, and historical review, closely affiliated with Harvard and Boston Unitarianism, begins as an outgrowth of the *Monthly Anthology.* Its early contributions include Bryant's "Thanatopsis" (1817) and "To a Waterfowl" (1818). By the second decade of the twentieth century it had published the works of numerous celebrated literary figures and essayists, but circulation had declined, and the review ceased publication in 1939. In 1963 it was revived as a quarterly by Cornell University.

1816
Fiction

"Frederick Augustus Fidfaddy": *The Adventures of Uncle Sam, in Search After His Lost Honor.* This allegory, which attacks the Democrats' militant stance during the War of 1812, features the earliest use of the moniker "Uncle Sam" in a book — thought to have originally referred to army inspector Samuel Wilson of Troy, New York, the term had been used derisively by antiwar advocates. The true name of the author of this work is unknown.

SAMUEL WOODWORTH (1785–1842): *The Champion of Freedom.* The only novel by the New York journalist and the editor of the *New-York Mirror* is a fantasy-filled romance set during the War of 1812, featuring the spirit of George Washington, which guides military figures such as Andrew Jackson and William Henry Harrison.

Literary Criticism and Scholarship

JOHN PICKERING (1777–1846): *Vocabulary; or, Collection of Words and Phrases Peculiar to the U.S. of America.*

The first collection of Americanisms. Pickering, a lawyer and philologist, had learned twenty languages and was a recognized authority on some North American Indian tongues. In a letter to Pickering, Noah Webster questioned some of the *Vocabulary's* claims.

Nonfiction

FRANCIS WALKER GILMER (1790–1826): *Sketches of American Orators.* An analysis of the oratorical styles of important lawyers and public figures, including John Marshall, Thomas Addis Emmett, William Pinckney, and Patrick Henry. It is one of the first U.S. studies of oratory. An expanded edition with analysis of John Randolph and Henry Clay would be published as *Sketches, Essays, and Translations* in 1828.

GEORGE TUCKER (1775–1861): *Letters from Virginia.* A satire of the customs and conduct of Virginia, condemning slavery and deriding planters, purportedly written by a traveling Frenchman. The authorship is disputed; it has also been attributed to William Maxwell and James Kirke Paulding.

Poetry

JOSEPH RODMAN DRAKE (1795–1820): "The Culprit Fay." A six-hundred-line poem set in the Hudson River Valley about a fairy who falls in love with a mortal maiden. Drake's attempt to import fairy legends to the United States is best known for its natural descriptions. Dying of tuberculosis in 1820, he asked his wife to destroy the manuscripts of his "trifles in rhyme," but she did not, and the poem would appear in 1835 in *The Culprit Fay and Other Poems.*

JOHN PIERPONT: *Airs of Palestine.* A set of heroic couplets tracing the impact of music on Jewish history and extolling sacred music. Pierpont's first book of poetry, written while he was working as a shopkeeper in Baltimore, becomes very popular and earns him a reputation as one of the top poets of the era.

ALEXANDER WILSON: *Poems; Chiefly in the Scottish Dialect.* A collection of poems with a biographical account of Wilson's life, published posthumously. Although critics consider the verses undistinguished, the poems show a notable devotion to nature.

Publications and Events

The *Portico.* This Baltimore literary magazine is founded by Tobias Watkins and Stephen Simpson for the Delphian Club. It presented a strong bias toward American nationalism and contains favorable reviews of

American literature, while harshly criticizing foreign writers. It continued until 1818.

1817
Drama and Theater

JAMES NELSON BARKER: *How to Try a Lover*. An adaptation of the French picaresque novel *La Folie espagnole* by Pigault-Lebrun (1753–1835) about the testing of the faithfulness of two lovers by their fathers. The play was not produced until 1836 as *The Court of Love*. When asked why, Barker replied, "I am unable to say, as it is the only drama I have written with which I was satisfied."

Fiction

JOHN NEAL (1793–1876): *Keep Cool*. An anti-dueling novel in which the hero kills his insulter in a duel and lives the rest of his life in guilt and remorse. Although not a lasting work or a financial success, it is Neal's first novel and begins to establish his literary reputation.

Nonfiction

MORRIS BIRKBECK (1764–1825): *Notes on a Journey in America from Virginia to the Territory of Illinois*. A popular book that goes through eleven editions in two years, it has great impact in directing settlers to the western prairie lands, where Birkbeck had established a town. The work is harshly criticized by the journalist William Cobbett, paid to do so by eastern land speculators.

AMASA DELANO (1763–1823): *A Narrative of Voyages and Travels in the Northern and Southern Hemispheres, Comprising Three Voyages Round the World*. This account of Delano's experiences in India, China, Polynesia, Africa, and South America illustrates respect and curiosity for a diversity of cultures. It would be reprinted numerous times and is most remembered as the source for Melville's "Benito Cereno."

JAMES KIRKE PAULDING: *Letters from the South*. Paulding offers an agrarian, Jeffersonian defense of Southern values.

WILLIAM WIRT: *Sketches of the Life and Character of Patrick Henry*. A popular biography known for its animated style, providing special insight into Henry's oratory. The work re-creates many of Henry's previously unrecorded speeches, and it is from this work that we know the famous "Give Me Liberty" speech.

Poetry

WILLIAM CULLEN BRYANT: "Thanatopsis." A meditation on death influenced by the reading of Thomas Gray, Henry Kirke White, and Robert Southey, and first

William Cullen Bryant

published in the *North American Review* as fragments that the editors combined under the heading "Thanatopsis." Many readers were skeptical that such a young man could manage such sophisticated and powerful verse (Bryant was not yet twenty when he began to write it).

1818
Drama and Theater

JOHN HOWARD PAYNE: *Brutus; or, The Fall of Tarquin*. A verse tragedy about a consul of the Roman Republic who condemns his son to death for treason. It would become one of the most famous nineteenth-century tragedies in English, staged for seventy years.

Nonfiction

WILLIAM COBBETT: *A Year's Residence in the United States of America*. This is the first of three parts of Cobbett's observations of American life (completed in 1819), combining an agricultural treatise, radical philosophy, and autobiographical reflections. The series would sell 100,000 copies by 1834. Cobbett would also write of his experiences on Long Island, New York, in *The American Gardener* (1821).

HANNAH MATHER CROCKER: *Observations on the Real Rights of Women, with Their Appropriate Duties, Agreeable to Scripture, Reason and Common Sense*. One of the first works on women's rights published in America by an American, it argues for the equality of women and men based on Christian justice and surveys the history of religious and secular women.

TIMOTHY DWIGHT: *Theology; Explained and Defended, in a Series of Sermons . . . with a Memoir of the Life of the Author. . . .* Posthumously published in five volumes, this collection of sermons, presented while the author was president of Yale College, are very popular in their day and remain influential works on religious matters. The author defends his faith with intelligence, eloquence, and originality.

JOHN PENDLETON KENNEDY (1795–1870) AND PETER HOFFMAN CRUSE (c. 1793–1832): *The Red Book.* A series of satirical essays and verses on contemporary subjects published biweekly in 1818 and 1819, eventually comprising two volumes. According to Rufus Griswold's *The Prose Writers of America* (1847), "It was of local and temporary interest, but it contained much neat and playful satire by Kennedy, and some exceedingly clever poetry by Cruse, which will prevent its being forgotten."

THOMAS NUTTALL (1786–1859): *The Genera of North American Plants.* A classic work on plants of the Western Hemisphere by the botanist who participated on an expedition to the Platte and Mandan regions, this book is the first of its kind published in the United States. The comprehensive work fully describes 834 genera and numerous new species names that Nuttall proposes in English rather than Latin.

BENJAMIN TRUMBULL: *A Complete History of Connecticut.* Trumbull issues the second volume of his acclaimed state history, bringing his narrative up to the outbreak of the Revolution. Despite evident political bias, the work is valued for its inclusion of important primary sources.

Poetry

JAMES KIRKE PAULDING: *The Backwoodsman.* Paulding's most significant poem is a narrative in heroic couplets recounting the adventures of a New York pioneer who finds freedom on the frontier of Kentucky.

1819
Drama and Theater

JAMES ABRAHAM HILLHOUSE (1789–1841): *Percy's Masque.* A romantic verse drama based on Bishop Percy's ballad "The Hermit of Warksworth." Hillhouse had written the drama when his plans for a mercantile career were interrupted by the War of 1812. Later a member of Congress and a wealthy merchant, he would remain devoted to theater and verse.

MORDECAI MANUEL NOAH: *She Would Be a Soldier.* Based on the Battle of Chippewa, this play focuses on Christine, who disguises herself as a male and enlists as a soldier to avoid marrying a farmer and to be near her lover, Lenox. She is tried as a spy but is saved in the end by Lenox. The play would hold the stage for many years.

FRANCES WRIGHT (1795–1852): *Altorf, a Tragedy.* Produced soon after the arrival in the United States of the Scottish-born freethinker and future founder of the Nashoba community, the play concerns the war of independence in fourteenth-century Switzerland. Although warmly received at its opening, the play loses its audience to General Andrew Jackson, who arrives in New York the day after its opening. It is revived with success in Philadelphia and again in New York in 1829.

Fiction

WASHINGTON IRVING: *The Sketch Book of Geoffrey Crayon, Gent.* A collection of essays and tales, considered one of the most important books in American literary history and often credited with originating the American short story. The sketches show Irving's transition toward the Romanticism of Sir Walter Scott and his contemporaries. Included are the immensely popular Americanized versions of German folk tales, "Rip Van Winkle" and "The Legend of Sleepy Hollow," and the travel stories "Stratford on Avon" and "Westminster Abbey." The success of the book catapults Irving to celebrity status.

Nonfiction

WILLIAM ELLERY CHANNING (1780–1842): "A Sermon Delivered at the Ordination of the Rev. Jared Sparks." Commonly known as the "Baltimore Sermon" or as "Unitarian Christianity," this famous sermone outlines the main points of the liberal doctrine Channing calls "Unitarian." The teacher and Congregational minister is also known for his influence on New England literary Transcendentalism and on social reform movements, especially abolitionism.

JOHN GOTTLIEB ERNESTUS HECKEWELDER (1743–1823): "An Account of the History, Manners, and Customs of the Indian Nations, Who Once Inhabited Pennsylvania and the Neighboring States." Included in the first volume of *The Transactions of the Historical and Literary Committee of the American Philosophical Society*, the essay provides information on Native Americans garnered during the author's years as a Moravian missionary and tells of his role in removing Indians to Ohio and Canada.

Emma Hart Willard

JAMES KIRKE PAULDING: *Salmagundi, Second Series.* Paulding's solo attempt at a continuation of his immensely popular earlier work, written with Washington Irving and others. Although some of the material is notable, it wins little critical attention.

DAVID RAMSAY: *Universal History Americanized.* Ramsay's most ambitious work. He had spent forty years preparing the volumes, which provide biblical writings, Greek and Latin classics, and a history of humanity written specifically for an American audience, with volumes ten through twelve devoted to the history of the United States. Ramsay was shot by an insane man near his home in Charleston before it was completed. Samuel Stanhope Smith finished and published the history to raise funds for Ramsay's eight children.

ROBERT WALSH (1784–1859): *An Appeal from the Judgments of Great Britain Respecting the U.S.* A staunch defense of the United States against vehement attacks made by British editors and travel writers. For his work, the author is praised in letters by Thomas Jefferson, John Adams, and John Quincy Adams.

EMMA HART WILLARD (1787–1870): *An Address... Proposing a Plan for Improving Female Education.* An appeal for funding girls' schools and equality in educational opportunites for women. Willard had sent her appeal to New York governor DeWitt Clinton and other distinguished men in the United States and had won a sympathetic and fervent response, but her plan did not pass the legislature. Willard, who had earlier established the Middlebury, Vermont, Female Seminary, wrote numerous textbooks, of which her histories are especially noteworthy.

Poetry

JOSEPH RODMAN DRAKE AND FITZ-GREENE HALLECK (1790–1867): *The Croaker Papers.* This collection of Knickerbocker poetry provides light, satirical criticisms, usually of local politicians. The poems had first appeared anonymously in the *New York Evening Post*, and while many praised them, Edgar Allan Poe had criticized them as careless and ephemeral. Drake's early death from tuberculosis in 1820 prompted Halleck to write "On the Death of Joseph Rodman Drake," considered one of the finest elegies by an American.

FITZ-GREENE HALLECK: *Fanny.* Highly praised social commentary concerning a poor merchant and his daughter who unexpectedly rise into high society. Written in the style of Byron's *Beppo*, its success would lead Halleck to add fifty stanzas two years later.

GULIAN CROMMELIN VERPLANCK (1786–1870): *The State Triumvirate.* A collection of seven poetical satires by the New York journalist and politician, originally published in the *New York American*. These hugely popular and critically acclaimed poems rail against New York governor DeWitt Clinton and his administration.

RICHARD HENRY WILDE (1789–1847): *The Lament of the Captive.* The poet and Georgia congressman's intended epic on the Seminole War is notable mainly for the highly praised lyric "My Life Is Like the Summer Rose," nationally reprinted unattributed, without the author's consent. After several poets claim to be its author, Wilde would finally receive credit in 1834.

Publications and Events

The *New York American.* This Whig and National Republican newspaper, influential in New York's aristocratic circles, makes its first appearance. Cofounded by New York lawyer, journalist, politician, and author Gulian Crommelin Verplanck (1786–1870), the paper would be absorbed by the *New York Courier and Enquirer*, a Whig newspaper, in 1845.

1820
Drama and Theater

SAMUEL BENJAMIN HELBERT JUDAH (1804–1876): *The Mountain Torrent.* The first of the New York playwright's melodramas concerns a young woman who marries a

BIRTHS AND DEATHS, 1820–1829

Births

1820 John Bartlett (d. 1905), editor
Dion Boucicault (d. 1890), playwright

1821 Frederick Goddard Tuckerman (d. 1873), poet

1822 William Taylor Adams (d. 1897), novelist
Emerson Bennett (d. 1905), novelist
George Lippard (d. 1854), novelist
Donald Grant Mitchell (d. 1908), novelist
Frederick Law Olmsted (d. 1903), architect and travel writer

1823 George Henry Boker (d. 1890), playwright and poet
Henry Morford (d. 1881), poet
Francis Parkman (d. 1893), historian

1824 George William Curtis (d. 1892), author and orator
William Henry Thomes (d. 1895), novelist

1825 William Clark Falkner (d. 1889), novelist
Harriet Jane Hanson (d. 1911), novelist
Bayard Taylor (d. 1878), travel writer, novelist, and poet

1826 John William DeForest (d. 1906), novelist
Charles H. Smith (d. 1903), humorist

1827 Maria Susanna Cummins (d. 1866), novelist
John Rollin Ridge (d. 1867), novelist
John Townsend Trowbridge (d. 1916), novelist
Lewis Wallace (d. 1905), novelist

1828 Oliver Bell Bunce (d. 1890), playwright
Martha Farquharson Finley (d. 1909), children's author

Henry Timrod (d. 1867), poet
Theodore Winthrop (d. 1861), novelist

1829 Hinton Rowan Helper (d. 1909), businessman and author
Silas Weir Mitchell (d. 1914), novelist, poet, and physician
Charles Dudley Warner (d. 1900), novelist and travel writer

Deaths

1820 Joseph Rodman Drake (b. 1795), poet
Judith Sargent Murray (b. 1751), author

1823 William Bartram (b. 1739), naturalist and author

1824 Susanna Haswell Rowson (b. 1762), novelist, poet, and playwright

1825 Mason Locke Weems (b. 1759), clergyman and author

1826 John Adams (b. 1735), political figure and writer
Paul Allen (b. 1775), poet and editor
Francis Walker Gilmer (b. 1790), lawyer and author
Thomas Jefferson (b. 1743), president of the United States, scientist, diplomat, and author
Royall Tyler (b. 1757), playwright

1828 Gilbert Imlay (b. c. 1754), adventurer and author

1829 Hannah Mather Crocker (b. 1752), author and women's rights advocate
John Jay (b. 1745), public official and contributor to *The Federalist Papers*

man she does not love to save her father from financial ruin. It would be followed by *The Rose of Arragon* and *A Tale of Lexington* (1823), after which Judah abandoned stage work.

MORDECAI MANUEL NOAH: *The Siege of Tripoli*. A successful play with a national theme. On its third night at New York City's Park Theatre, a disastrous fire left the theater in ruins, and Noah donated his full $400 profit to the members of the company. Later staged in Philadelphia under the title *Yusef Caramalli*, the play has not survived.

Fiction

JAMES FENIMORE COOPER (1789–1851): *Precaution; or, Prevention Is Better Than a Cure*. The novel that launched Cooper's literary career is a novel of manners concerning English high society that receives some critical acclaim but sells poorly. Cooper had written the book after his wife expressed doubt in his declaration that he could write a better book than the English novel he was reading to her.

PETER IRVING (1771–1838): *Giovanni Sbogarro*. A historical romance set in Venice, attributed to "Percival G." and adapted from a French story by Charles Nodier. The only novel published by Washington Irving's older brother, the editor and proprietor of the *Morning Chronicle*, it is considered a failure.

Literary Criticism and Scholarship

SYDNEY SMITH (1771–1845): "Who Reads an American Book?" A notorious review of Adam Seybert's *Annals of the United States* by the famous critic for the *Edinburgh Review*, which asks, "In the four quarters of the globe, who reads an American book? or goes to an American play? or looks at an American picture or statue?" Several American writers respond to the review, including Herman Melville, who suggests in his "Hawthorne and His Mosses" (1850), "The day will come when you shall say, who reads a book by an Englishman that is a modern?"

Nonfiction

WILLIAM ELLERY CHANNING: *The Moral Argument Against Calvinism*. An elaboration of the liberal theology Channing pronounced in 1819, denying the Calvinistic doctrine of humanity's essential corruption because this would suggest that God also is corrupt. Channing's linkage between humanity and God has great influence on Ralph Waldo Emerson and helps stimulate the Transcendentalist movement.

RAYMOND DANIEL (1786–c. 1849): *Thoughts on Political Economy.* The first analytical thesis on political economy written in the United States. The work specifically addresses American economics and argues against individualism, banks, and paper money, and for government authority and a protective system.

PETER FORCE (1790–1868): *National Calendar and Annals of the United States.* The Washington, D.C., printer, archivist, and historian begins an annual compilation of historical and statistical information (through 1824 and again from 1828 to 1836).

JOHN GOTTLIEB ERNESTUS HECKEWELDER: *A Narrative of the Mission of the United Brethren Among the Delaware and Mohegan Indians.* The Moravian missionary to the Indians presents a study that would become a major source for James Fenimore Cooper, contributing to the novelist's partiality for the Delawares and hostility toward the Iroquois, which reflects Heckewelder's biases.

JOHN TAYLOR: *Construction Construed and Constitutions Vindicated.* Taylor argues against the Supreme Court's jurisdiction over appeals from state courts. His further views on constitutional government would appear in *New Views of the Constitution* (1823).

HENRY WARE (1764–1845): *Letters Addressed to Trinitarians and Calvinists, Occasioned by Dr. Woods' Letters to Unitarians.* After fifteen years of relative silence on the controversy over his election to the Hollis Professorship of Divinity at Harvard College, Ware, a liberal Congregationalist, writes this letter, sparking what has become known as the "Wood 'n' Ware Controversy." The conflict between the liberal and orthodox Congregationalists eventually led the Unitarians to separate from the Congregationalists and form an independent denomination.

Poetry

MARIA GOWEN BROOKS (c. 1795–1845): *Judith, Esther, and Other Poems.* In the Massachusetts poet's first collection of verse, the two title poems concern the psychological characteristics of the biblical heroines. English poet Robert Southey acclaims the collection and names her "Maria of the West," a name she would later use as a pseudonym.

JAMES WALLIS EASTBURN (1797–1819) AND ROBERT CHARLES SANDS (1799–1832): *Yamoyden.* Six cantos about "King Philip" (the Indian leader Metacomet), using some material from William Hubbard's *Narrative of the Troubles with the Indians in New England* (1677) and depicting Philip as wise and courageous. Enormously popular in its day, the poem pioneered the romantic treatment of the Indian in literature. Eastburn, a Virginia clergyman,

had died before revisions to the poem were complete, and Sands finished and published it as a memorial to his friend.

Publications and Events

The *Providence Journal.* This Rhode Island newspaper first appears. Founded as a nonpartisan paper, it has frequently been referred to as "the conscience of Rhode Island."

1821
Drama and Theater

JOSEPH DODDRIDGE (1769–1826): *Logan.* Winning the frontier clergyman moderate acclaim, this unproduced drama urges justice for a Native American leader who led raids on white settlements after his family had been slaughtered during the Yellow Creek Massacre.

MORDECAI MANUEL NOAH: *Marion; or, The Hero of Lake George.* A drama concerning the dangerous life of a patriotic leader during the Battle of Saratoga; his wife dresses as a man to save him from prison. The play would be popular in Boston, New York, and Philadelphia for ten years.

JOHN HOWARD PAYNE: *Therese, the Orphan of Geneva.* An adaptation of Victor Ducange's *Thérèse, ou l'orpheline de Genève.* The successful melodrama was written while Payne was imprisoned in the London Fleet debtors' prison and concerns a villain who attempts to murder a seemingly illegitimate girl so that he might keep the inheritance he knows belongs to her. He mistakenly kills the wrong woman, and when he realizes that his intended victim is still alive, he is so shocked that he confesses.

Fiction

JAMES FENIMORE COOPER: *The Spy: A Tale of the Neutral Ground.* A novel concerning a Yankee who serves George Washington by passing behind enemy lines disguised as a peddler. Employing the style of Sir Walter Scott, it is based on a true story with added romantic embellishments, set in America. The novel's success establishes Cooper's literary career.

Nonfiction

WILLIAM HENRY DRAYTON: *Memoirs of the American Revolution.* The South Carolina jurist and one of the first important advocates of American nationhood offers his recollections of the Revolution, edited from his papers by his son.

TIMOTHY DWIGHT: *Travels in New-England and New-York.* Dwight's most famous prose work details and

James Fenimore Cooper

comments upon the scenery, history, religious organization, public education, and statistics gathered from travels during his academic vacations in the years 1796–1815.

HENRY ROWE SCHOOLCRAFT (1793–1864): *Narrative Journal of Travels Throughout the Northwestern Regions of the United States.* An account of the geologist's experiences traveling with Lewis Cass on his expedition to survey the copper regions and explore other parts of the Upper Mississippi, northern Michigan, and Lake Superior. Schoolcraft, the first Caucasian to translate Indian poetry, provides detailed and respectful descriptions of Indian legends and religious practices.

WILLIAM TUDOR (1779–1830): *Miscellanies.* A diverse collection of Tudor's essay submissions to the *Monthly Anthology* and the *North American Review*, illustrating the author's light, playful, but intelligent humor. The subjects range from the "Secret Causes of the American and French Revolutions" to human misery, purring cats, and cranberry sauce. Tudor was a Boston merchant and literary figure who founded the Anthology Club and was the first editor of the *North American Review*.

FRANCES WRIGHT: *Views of Society and Manners in America.* A collection of correspondence written during travels with her sister on the Hudson River, in the Mohawk Valley, around New England, and in Philadelphia, New Jersey, and Washington, D.C. The book sells well and is soon translated into French and Dutch. Literary historians consider Wright's book to be one of the first important travel books about the United States. Free of the critical tone of other British travel accounts during the period, it praises Americans' openness and friendliness and what Wright sees as their enlightened views on women.

Poetry

PAUL ALLEN: *Noah.* A poem treating the biblical story and expressing America's place in divine providence. The poem attacks slavery and is most notable for illustrating the slavery debate in the early United States. In a private letter, Jefferson called Allen one of the two best writers in America.

WILLIAM CULLEN BRYANT: *Poems.* A collection of eight poems issued by Richard Henry Dana, Edward Channing, and Willard Phillips, who were impressed with Bryant's "The Ages." Delivered at the Harvard commencement, "The Ages" consists of Spenserian stanzas surveying the history of mankind and presenting a positive outlook for the future. *Poems* includes it and the last major revision of "Thanatopsis." Although the volume does not sell well, it brings critical acclaim and publicly confirms Bryant as one of the finest American poets.

JAMES GATES PERCIVAL (1795–1856): *Poems.* This well-received collection of poems includes the first part of Percival's highly acclaimed "Prometheus." Percival, a medical officer and chemistry teacher at West Point, begins his formal literary career with this publication, although in the same year he attempts suicide after his marriage proposal is declined and his medical practice fails.

Publications and Events

The *Saturday Evening Post.* Founded by Philadelphia printers Charles Alexander and William Coate Atkinson, the *Post* featured news, household tips, essays, and poems for light Sunday reading before the existence of Sunday newspapers. Its popularity grew after the owners acquired several competitors and installed Henry Peterson as editor in 1846. It featured contributions from Emma Dorothy Eliza Nevitte Southworth, Emerson Bennett, "Fanny Fern" (Sarah Payson Willis), and other popular writers. Its trademark cover woodcuts first appeared in 1863. After a sharp decline, the *Post* was sold to Cyrus H. K. Curtis in 1897, who increased circulation into the millions with aggressive subscription sales and advertising.

Curtis played up the legend that Benjamin Franklin had been involved with the magazine's founding, altering the founding date from 1821 to 1728 and the magazine's volume 77 to 170. The *Post* remained successful until 1962, when it lost $4 million, and it was finally suspended in 1969. Revived in 1971, it was offered bimonthly.

1822
Drama and Theater

CHARLES POWELL CLINCH (1797–1880): *The Spy, a Tale of the Neutral Ground.* Clinch's adaptation of James Fenimore Cooper's novel is believed to be the first successful dramatization of an American novel. Its success prompts subsequent dramatizations of Cooper's works and those of other American novelists.

MORDECAI MANUEL NOAH: *The Grecian Captive.* A loose adaptation of the French *Mahomet II* by Pierre-Joseph Charrin. Set in a foreign country, it is popular for its patriotic sentiments regarding a country fighting for its independence. Its production is marked by unsuccessful dramatic innovations such as providing the audience with a copy of the play (upsetting actors who had lacked time to master their lines) and the use of live animals, even an elephant, on stage.

Fiction

WASHINGTON IRVING: *Bracebridge Hall; or, The Humorists.* A collection of forty-nine sketches and stories in the manner of his earlier *Sketch Book* with the same narrator, Geoffrey Crayon. It is chiefly remembered for "Dolph Heyliger," "The Storm Ship," "The Stout Gentleman," and "Student of Salamanca." Although widely read, it wins only moderate critical acclaim.

JOHN NEAL: *Logan, A Family History.* The first of Neal's six greatest romances, all written and published in five years, is a fictionalized story about an Englishman who marries an Indian queen. In it Neal speaks out against Indian regulations, the death penalty, and debtors' prisons.

CATHARINE MARIA SEDGWICK (1789–1867): *A New-England Tale.* Initially intending to write a tract comparing the virtues of Unitarianism to the spiritual limitations of Calvinism, Sedgwick instead composed this novel about an orphan who is poorly treated by her Calvinist aunt. It is acknowledged today for its innovation in use of characters, manners, and New England dialect. The Massachusetts writer is now considered a premier author of her time, though earlier critics had dismissed her writing as sentimental.

FRANCES WRIGHT: *A Few Days in Athens.* Wright's novel about a young disciple of Epicurus would later be called by Walt Whitman his "daily food."

Nonfiction

ALEXANDER HILL EVERETT (1790–1847): *Europe: or, A General Survey of the Present Situation of the Principle.* An overview of European politics since the fall of Napoleon. It is most notable for its effort to determine the political trends and events that led to the birth of America. Everett was a Boston diplomat who served in Russia, Holland, and Spain between 1809 and 1829.

JEDIDIAH MORSE: *Report to the Secretary of War of the United States, on Indian Affairs.* Commissioned to study conditions of Indian nations, Morse (also secretary of the Society for Propagating the Gospel Among the Indians and Others in North America) urges that American Indians "be raised gradually and ultimately, to the rank and to the enjoyment of all the rights and privileges of freemen, and citizens of the United States."

JAMES KIRKE PAULDING: *A Sketch of Old England, by a New England Man.* An account of a purported tour of England that begins with comedic travel adventures but is mostly devoted to a discussion of the differences between the two countries and an attack on the British who misrepresent America.

JOHN TAYLOR: *Tyranny Unmasked.* The third of his highly agrarian political writings, this forceful pamphlet attacks the high protective tariffs that were developed to promote American industry during the previous few years. Taylor finds the protective tariff unconstitutional and fears it will create privilege and decrease profits.

Poetry

HEW AINSLIE (1792–1878): *A Pilgrimage to the Land of Burns.* An anonymously published travel diary detailing a tour of Scotland (Ayrshire) with elaborate descriptions of scenes and poetry inspired by the experience. The two friends Ainslie had traveled with took pseudonyms from Sir Walter Scott's *Antiquary.* The book receives good reviews, but Scott finds it "wanting originality." It is published in the same year that Ainslie immigrated to the United States. He would become a member of the New Harmony colony and publish a collection of dialect poems, *Scottish Songs, Ballads, and Poems* (1855).

McDONALD CLARKE (1798–1842): *Elixir of Moonshine, Being a Collection of Prose and Poetry by the Mad Poet.* A collection containing the only couplet for which the so-called Mad Poet is remembered: "Now twilight lets her curtain down / And Pins it with a star." Clarke is called "the Mad Poet of Broadway" because of his eccentric behavior there, sporting a dark blue coat and red neckerchief. His mild insanity, which caused impulsive and dramatic responses to music, society, and fashion, would progress later in life.

JAMES LAWSON (1799–1880): "Ontwa, the Son of the Forest." A poem by the New York businessman and author describing the life of the Erie Indians. It contains notes by Lewis Cass, Michigan's territorial governor. The poem would be included in *Columbian Lyre; or, Specimens of Transatlantic Poetry*, published in Glasgow in 1828.

JAMES MCHENRY (1785–1845): *The Pleasures of Friendship*. A collection by the Irish-born poet and novelist who immigrated to Pennsylvania in 1817, containing short lyric poems and a twelve-hundred-line title poem extolling the healing powers of friendship. McHenry would add more minor poems in each of the succeeding nine American and English editions published in his lifetime.

JAMES GATES PERCIVAL: *Clio*. Percival issues the first two volumes of what would become his three-volume collection of poetic soliloquies (completed in 1827).

1823

Drama and Theater

JOHN HOWARD PAYNE: *Clari; or, The Maid of Milan*. A popular opera concerning a virtuous rural maid and a duke who eventually marries her. The play is most memorable for its song "Home, Sweet Home," which is set to music by Henry Bishop and becomes one of the most popular American songs ever written.

Fiction

JAMES FENIMORE COOPER: *The Pilot: A Tale of the Sea*. An immediately popular patriotic and romantic novel dealing with the conflict between freedom and authority and employing a character based on John Paul Jones. Cooper, a former sailor, had written the book to demonstrate that he could write a better nautical novel than Sir Walter Scott had in *The Pirate* (1822). Cooper also publishes *Tales for Fifteen; or, Imagination and Heart*, two short tales for young readers, under the pseudonym of "Jane Morgan," as well as *The Pioneers; or, The Source of the Susquehanna*. This somewhat autobiographical novel examines the conflict between civilization, represented by Judge Marmaduke Temple, who is establishing the village of Templeton, and wilderness values, personified in Natty Bumppo. In the preface, Cooper claims to have written the novel "exclusively to please myself: so it would be no wonder if it displeased every body else," but it proves a great success, selling thirty-five hundred copies before noon on the first day of its publication. Some modern scholars consider it the best of all his novels; it is the first of Cooper's Leatherstocking Tales.

JAMES MCHENRY: *The Wilderness; or, Braddock's Time*. A romance portraying the first Ulster immigrant family in American fiction, set in Pennsylvania during the French and Indian War. A youthful George Washington is a central character, and the novel suggests that his devotion to the country was due to unrequited love for the novel's heroine. It sells fifteen hundred copies, but many critics argue it is not an American novel since most of the characters are foreign. McHenry also publishes *The Spectre of the Forest; or, Annals of the Housatonic*, one of his most famous novels, a historical romance about the witchcraft terror in the seventeenth century.

JOHN NEAL: *Randolph, a Novel*. Published after a twelve-month flurry of writing that led to three of Neal's finest works, the novel critiques writers and other public figures, including himself. His comments on William Pinkney incited his son, Edward Coote Pinkney, to challenge Neal to a duel. When Neal refused, Pinkney publicly called him "craven." Neal treats the experience in his next novel, *Errata; or, The Works of Will Adams*. Neal also publishes *Seventy-Six*. Written in twenty-seven days during his three-novel year, this historical romance of the Revolutionary War is considered Neal's best work by critics and the author himself, who pronounced it "to be one of the best romances of the age."

JAMES KIRKE PAULDING: *Königsmarke, the Long Finne: A Story of the New World*. A historical novel about a Finnish immigrant in the colony of New Sweden on the Delaware River. Each volume of the novel begins with an author's commentary.

Nonfiction

SARAH WENTWORTH MORTON: *My Mind and Its Thoughts, in Sketches, Fragments, and Essays*. This collection of aphorisms, poetry, and prose is Morton's last published work and the only one published under her own name. It demonstrates her patriotism, Christianity, and sentimentality.

JAMES THACHER (1754–1844): *A Military Journal During the American Revolutionary War*. Considered one of the best firsthand narratives of the Revolution, the book is especially notable because the author, a physician, witnessed and wrote about several of the most important events of the war, including his experience treating soldiers wounded at Bunker Hill and Saratoga, the execution of Major André, and the surrender of Cornwallis.

Clement Clarke Moore

WILLIAM TUDOR: *The Life of James Otis of Massachusetts.* An energetic account of James Otis, a Boston political activist who helped organize the colonists' protests against the British government in the 1760s. It is considered Tudor's best work. Tudor also issues *Letters on the Eastern States*, a critique of eastern society, which according to Edward Everett's review in the *North American Review* is "The work evidently of a scholar and a gentleman, of an impartial observer, a temperate champion, a liberal opponent and a correct writer."

Poetry

FITZ-GREENE HALLECK: "Alnwick Castle." One of Halleck's most significant poems is a meditation set in Scotland that contrasts the romantic past with the present "bank-note world."

JAMES MCHENRY: "Waltham." One of the earliest poetic treatments of an American patriotic theme, this poem in three cantos treats George Washington's experience at Valley Forge.

CLEMENT CLARKE MOORE (1779–1863): "A Visit from St. Nicholas." Commonly known as "'Twas the Night Before Christmas," Moore's enduring Christmas poem first appears anonymously in the *Troy Sentinel* and is published in numerous later editions. It marks a division between the Puritan antipathy toward Christmas and acceptance of the holiday. The work is attributed to Moore, who claimed to have written the poem for his children, but his authorship has been questioned; some believe it to be the work of Major Henry Livingston Jr.

Publications and Events

The *New York Mirror.* A weekly newspaper featuring society, art, and literary news is founded by Samuel Woodworth (1785–1842). Numerous significant authors of the day contribute, including Cooper, Irving, and Whittier. The *Mirror* purchased the *American Monthly Magazine* in 1831, and Nathaniel Parker Willis became the associate editor. The name was changed in 1842 to the *New Mirror* and again in 1844 to the *Evening Mirror*, when it became a daily with Edgar Allan Poe as literary critic.

1824
Drama and Theater

JAMES NELSON BARKER: *Superstition; or, The Fanatic Father.* Barker's most important play, considered one of the most significant dramas of the time for its mingling of psychology, religious intolerance, witchcraft, and regicide (of King Charles I). It concerns the clergyman Ravensworth, who attempts to kill Isabella and her son Charles for failing to properly regard him.

JOHN HOWARD PAYNE AND WASHINGTON IRVING: *Charles the Second; or, The Merry Monarch.* A comedy adapted from Alexandre Duval's "La Jeunesse de Henri V," in which the earl of Rochester must reform King Charles II to be rewarded with the hand of Lady Clara. It was the first play on which Payne collaborated with Washington Irving, and many consider his best work.

SAMUEL WOODWORTH: *Lafayette; or, The Castle of Olmutz.* Woodworth's first serious drama is a romantic depiction of the imprisonment in Germany that Lafayette, the French hero of the Revolution, had endured in 1792.

Fiction

WILLIAM AUSTIN: *Peter Rugg, the Missing Man.* A fable about a Boston man whose attempt to drive to the city in a storm takes him fifty years. Austin's best-known story, it becomes a part of New England folklore, is later used by Louise Imogen Guiney and Amy Lowell, and may have influenced Hawthorne.

LYDIA MARIA CHILD (1802–1880): *Hobomok: A Tale of Early Times.* A story about a young girl who marries and has a child with the Indian Hobomok after hearing that her fiancé has died. Hobomok relinquishes her when her fiancé returns, and she and her new husband raise the half-Indian child together. It is purportedly based on an early Puritan manuscript and influenced by the

Catharine Maria Sedgwick portrayed in an engraving by A. B. Durand based on a painting by Charles Ingham

clergyman and editor J. G. Palfrey's advocacy of American writers working on American themes. The theme of assimilation earns the novel harsh reviews, stating that it is "unnatural" and "revolting," but the scandalous subject matter helps boost interest in the book.

WASHINGTON IRVING: *Tales of a Traveller.* Irving's only collection composed entirely of fiction receives unfavorable reviews until later lauded by Edgar Allan Poe and Henry Wadsworth Longfellow. The thirty-two stories are divided into four sections: the first is told by Englishmen, the second is about a young man who wants to be a writer, the third is about Italian bandits, and the final contains "The Devil and Tom Walker," one of Irving's finest stories.

CATHARINE MARIA SEDGWICK: *Redwood.* The story of Ellen Bruce, a young woman of mysterious parentage, who learns that her father is the southern slave owner Redwood, who has been kept from her because of the anti-Christian beliefs he picked up by studying Voltaire and David Hume. The novel ends with Redwood's religious conversion and Ellen's marriage to a Southern gentleman. William Cullen Bryant praises the book but notes that domestic fiction cannot contend with stories of adventure and war.

MARGARET BAYARD SMITH (1778–1844): *A Winter in Washington.* The first novel of the Washington socialite, it draws on her own experiences to detail life in the nation's captital and the changing morals and manners of society.

GEORGE TUCKER: *The Valley of Shenandoah.* Tucker's first and best novel details plantation life in the valley and cautions young men against mismanaging their finances and young women against possible seducers. The book's financial failure would influence Tucker's decision to become professor of moral philosophy at the University of Virginia, a post offered to him by Thomas Jefferson.

Literary Criticism and Scholarship

JOHN NEAL: *American Writers.* A collection of critical papers dealing with 135 American authors, first published as a series of essays in *Blackwood's Magazine.* Varying in quality from the inane to the brilliant, Neal provides expert criticism but gives the most space to his own writing and is said to have treated James Fenimore Cooper unfairly. The work is significant for being the first attempted history of American literature.

Nonfiction

JOSEPH DODDRIDGE: *Notes on the Settlement and Indian Wars of the Western Parts of Virginia and Pennsylvania, from 1763 to 1783 Inclusive.* An accurate description of the land and people taken from the author's experience on the frontier where he had lived since his childhood.

JAMES E. SEAVER (1787–1827): *A Narrative of the Life of Mrs. Mary Jemison.* Among the most popular Indian captivity narratives of the early nineteenth century, the book details the capture of Mary Jemison (1743–1833), called "the White Woman of the Genesee," who was abducted at age fifteen by a war party during the French and Indian War in western Pennsylvania in 1758. She married into the Delaware tribe and chose to remain among the Delaware for the rest of her life.

Poetry

WILLIAM CULLEN BRYANT: "Monument Mountain." Bryant's popular blank-verse poem tells the story of an Indian princess who kills herself after falling in love with her cousin.

ROYALL TYLER: *The Chestnut Tree.* Tyler's longest poem contains sketches of people who pass beneath a chestnut tree, which the protagonist had planted two hundred years earlier. The poem is notable for its illustration of village life and the foretelling of the outcomes of the machine age, though it is criticized as monotonous and lacking a unifying theme.

Publications and Events

The *Springfield Republican.* Founded by Samuel Bowles and continued by his son, this Massachusetts newspaper originally supported the Whigs, became politically independent to oppose slavery and the Mexican War, supported Lincoln during the Civil War, and attacked the corruption of the Grant administration.

The *United States Literary Gazette.* A semimonthly literary magazine edited primarily by James G. Carter featured book reviews, announcements, and literary news. It is particularly significant for the poetry that appeared in its pages, including works by Longfellow and Bryant. The magazine joined with the *New York Review and Athenaeum Magazine* in 1826 and would continue for one year as the *United States Review and Literary Gazette* under editor Charles Folsom.

1825

Drama and Theater

JAMES ABRAHAM HILLHOUSE: *Hadad.* A blank-verse biblical drama based on Absalom's rebellion, it is Hillhouse's longest and most ostentatious drama. His contemporaries consider it his best work.

SAMUEL WOODWORTH: *The Forest Rose; or, American Farmers: A Pastoral Opera.* A successful domestic play, most notable for its character Jonathan Ploughboy, who popularized the Yankee stock character. The Yankee stereotype had been introduced in Royall Tyler's *The Contrast* (1790) and was often imitated.

Fiction

LYDIA MARIA CHILD: *The Rebels; or, Boston Before the Revolution.* This novel, depicting the events that led to the American Revolution, receives a warm critical reception and wide readership.

JAMES FENIMORE COOPER: *Lionel Lincoln; or, The Leaguer of Boston.* This story of a British officer with a mysterious family history details the first months of the Revolution, with descriptions of the Battles of Lexington, Concord, and Bunker Hill. Intended as the first in a series of Revolutionary stories, it receives a poor response.

NICHOLAS MARCELLUS HENTZ (1797–1856): *Tadeuskund, the Last King of the Lenape.* A melodramatic novel concerning the Delaware Indians, in the style of James Fenimore Cooper. This is the most famous work of the French-born novelist.

JOHN NEAL: *Brother Jonathan.* Neal's historical romance is set in New England prior to the Revolution.

JAMES KIRKE PAULDING: *John Bull in America; or, The New Munchausen.* Paulding's final published defense of America against the scorn of English travelers, this work recounts the adventures of a Cockney traveler, satirically illustrating his failure to view America with an open mind and his reliance on the *Quarterly Review*, which was publishing biased attacks of America by British travelers.

Literary Criticism and Scholarship

WILLIAM CULLEN BRYANT: *Lectures on Poetry.* Bryant's series of four lectures delivered at the New York Athenaeum puts forward his theory of poetry, influenced by the English Romantic poets, and his denial of assertions that America is lacking in poetic material, that the American language is too primitive for poetry, and that American society is too materialistic and pragmatic to support poetry.

Nonfiction

DANIEL WEBSTER (1782–1852): "Bunker Hill Oration." A famous speech commemorating one of the earliest battles of the Revolutionary War, given at the laying of the cornerstone for the Bunker Hill Monument. In the speech Webster presents a vivid description of the battle and praises representative government. The speech wins him wide acclaim for his oratorical skills. He would give another famous speech at the dedication of the finished monument in 1843.

JOHN WINTHROP (1588–1649): *A History of New England from 1630–1649.* An expanded version of Winthrop's *Journal* (1790) after his third notebook is found in the tower of Boston's Old South Church. The manuscript had been edited by James Savage, who publishes the complete journal with corrections and modernized spellings.

Poetry

JOHN GARDINER CALKINS BRAINARD (1776–1828): *Occasional Pieces of Poetry.* A warmly received collection of poetry taken in part from the verses Brainard had contributed to the *Connecticut Mirror*, which he edited from 1822 to 1827. Though highly regarded as a poet by his contemporaries, this is the only significant book of Brainard's work published in his lifetime.

WILLIAM CULLEN BRYANT: "A Forest Hymn." A blank-verse nature poem exhibiting Bryant's beliefs about the universe. The poet in the forest expresses faith in a personal creator, but the poem is also suggestive of pantheism and reminiscent of Wordsworth's early verse. It is considered one of Bryant's best poems.

FITZ-GREENE HALLECK: "Marco Bozzaris." The poem is inspired by the death of the Greek hero of the war of independence against the Turks. The poem would appear in several periodicals and win praise from critics, despite Edgar Allan Poe's claim that it lacks lyricism.

WILLIAM LEGGETT (c. 1802–1839): *Leisure Hours at Sea.* The first of Leggett's two volumes of verse based on his experiences as a midshipman. It would be followed by *Journals of the Ocean* (1826) and the prose collection *Naval Stories* (1834).

EDWARD COOTE PINKNEY (1802–1828): *Poems.* A collection of verse that prompts the *North American Review* to declare that "Some of the small pieces in this very small volume are really exquisite." The longest poem, "Rodolph, a Fragment," a Byronic poem about a man who kills his lover's husband, receives mixed reviews, however.

Publications and Events

The *Biblical Repertory.* This magazine of Presbyterianism makes its debut and becomes the most important Presbyterian periodical until 1878, when it was rechristened the *Princeton Review* and its emphasis shifted to compete with the *North American Review.* It suspended publication in 1884 but was revived as the *New Princeton Review* (1886). It featured contributors such as Theodore Roosevelt and Woodrow Wilson until its demise in 1888.

The *New-Harmony Gazette.* A weekly periodical founded to interpret and record the progress of the New Harmony commune. It broadened in scope after the commune's dissolution in 1828 and in 1829 became the *Free Enquirer,* promoting socialist and agnostic views.

The *New York Review and Athenaeum Magazine.* A monthly literary periodical supplanting the *Atlantic Magazine* and edited by William Cullen Bryant, Robert Charles Sands, and Henry J. Anderson. The magazine featured book reviews and essays on science, literature, and the arts, as well as poetry. Notable contributors included Fitz-Greene Halleck, Henry Wadsworth Longfellow, Richard Henry Dana, and George Bancroft. It merged with the *United States Literary Gazette* in 1826.

1826

Drama and Theater

GEORGE POPE MORRIS (1802–1864): *Brier Cliff.* This drama about the American Revolution has a long run and earns the author $3,500 and a notable, though temporary, reputation. The play would never be published. Morris founded the *New York Mirror.* His best-known prose work is *The Little Frenchman and His Water Lots* (1839), a collection of short stories.

JOHN HOWARD PAYNE: *Richelieu: A Domestic Tragedy.* This drama about the seduction of a merchant's wife by a French nobleman is an adaptation of Alexandre Duval's *La Jeunesse du duc de Richelieu, ou le Lovelace français* (1796). Payne dedicates the work to Washington Irving, who had assisted with the writing. Very successful in the United States, it would play until at least 1850 in a version titled *Remorse,* but its English reception was marred when a descendant of Richelieu protested against his ancestor's role as a villain.

Fiction

JAMES FENIMORE COOPER: *The Last of the Mohicans.* The second Leatherstocking Tale is set during the French and Indian War. Natty Bumppo and the two remaining Mohican Indians, Chingachgook and his son Uncas, guide two daughters of a British commander to Fort William Henry, saving them from the treacherous Indian Magua, who is secretly working for the French.

TIMOTHY FLINT (1780–1840): *Francis Berrian; or, The Mexican Patriot.* The first English-language novel set in the Southwest tells the story of a New England Puritan who travels to Mexico during the Mexican Revolution, where he encounters the Comanches, finds romance, and wins battles. The Massachusetts writer traveled as a missionary into Arkansas and Missouri, recounting his experiences in *Recollections of the Last Ten Years* (1826).

JAMES KIRKE PAULDING: *The Merry Tales of the Three Wise Men of Gotham.* The first in a series of short story collections, to be followed by *Tales of the Good Woman* (1829), *Chronicles of Gotham* (1830), and *The Book of St. Nicholas* (1836). All earn praise from critics and writers such as Poe and are valued as early achievements in short fiction.

Nonfiction

TIMOTHY FLINT: *Recollections of the Last Ten Years, Passed in Occasional Residences and Journeyings in the Valley of Mississippi.* An account of Flint's missionary travels into Ohio, Kentucky, and Missouri on commission from the Missionary Society of Connecticut. The work comprises letters to his cousin in Salem, Massachusetts, and describes the places he and his family visit.

ABIEL HOLMES: *The Annals of America.* A chronological collection of important facts and events, these annals are the first effort to create an organized, linear history of the country and represent a significant contribution to American historiography. A second edition would be published in 1829.

JAMES KENT (1763–1847): *Commentaries on American Law.* A Federalist discussion of international law, the Constitution, U.S. government, state laws, people's

POPULAR BOOKS, 1826–1849

The Last of the Mohicans by James Fenimore Cooper (First American Printing, 1826)

Woodstock by Sir Walter Scott (First American Printing, 1826)

The Prairie by James Fenimore Cooper (First American Printing, 1827)

The Red Rover by James Fenimore Cooper (First American Printing, 1827)

Pelham by Edward Bulwer Lytton (First American Printing, 1828)

Lucy Temple by Susanna Haswell Rowson (First American Printing, 1828)

The Conquest of Granada by Washington Irving (First American Printing, 1829)

Richelieu by G.P.R. James (First American Printing, 1829)

The Dutchman's Fireside by James Kirke Paulding (First American Printing, 1831)

The Alhambra by Washington Irving (First American Printing, 1832)

My Mother's Gold Ring by Lucius Manlius Sargent (First American Printing, 1833)

The Life and Writings of Major Jack Downing by Seba Smith (First American Printing, 1833)

The Hunchback of Notre Dame by Victor Hugo (First American Printing, 1834)

Outre-Mer by Henry Wadsworth Longfellow (First American Printing, 1834)

The Last Days of Pompeii by Edward Bulwer Lytton (First American Printing, 1834)

A Tour on the Prairies by Washington Irving (First American Printing, 1835)

Horse-Shoe Robinson by John Pendleton Kennedy (First American Printing, 1835)

The Yemassee by William Gilmore Simms (First American Printing, 1835)

The Slave; or, Memoirs of Archy Moore by Richard Hildreth (First American Printing, 1836)

Astoria by Washington Irving (First American Printing, 1836)

Awful Disclosures by Maria Monk (First American Printing, 1836)

Nick of the Woods by Robert Montgomery Bird (First American Printing, 1837)

Pickwick Papers by Charles Dickens (First American Printing, 1837)

Life of Washington by Jared Sparks (First American Printing, 1837)

Zenobia by William Ware (First American Printing, 1837)

Oliver Twist by Charles Dickens (First American Printing, 1838)

The Robber by G.P.R. James (First American Printing, 1838)

Life of Scott by John Gibson Lockhart (First American Printing, 1838)

Selections from the American Poets by William Cullen Bryant (First American Printing, 1839)

Nicholas Nickleby by Charles Dickens (First American Printing, 1839)

The Gentleman of the Old School by G.P.R. James (First American Printing, 1839)

The Green Mountain Boys by Daniel P. Thompson (First American Printing, 1839)

The Old Curiosity Shop by Charles Dickens (First American Printing, 1841)

The Ancient Regime by G.P.R. James (First American Printing, 1841)

American Notes by Charles Dickens (First American Printing, 1842)

Zanoni by Edward Bulwer Lytton (First American Printing, 1842)

Ned Myers by James Fenimore Cooper (First American Printing, 1843)

A Christmas Carol by Charles Dickens (First American Printing, 1843)

Martin Chuzzlewit by Charles Dickens (First American Printing, 1844)

The Monks of Monk Hall by George Lippard (First American Printing, 1844)

Festus by Philip James Bailey (First American Printing, 1845)

Satanstoe by James Fenimore Cooper (First American Printing, 1845)

The Count of Monte Cristo by Alexandre Dumas (First American Printing, 1845)

The Smuggler by G.P.R. James (First American Printing, 1845)

Napoleon and His Marshals by Joel Tyler Headley (First American Printing, 1846)

Home Influence, a Tale for Mothers and Daughters by Grace Aguilar (First American Printing, 1847)

Jane Eyre by Charlotte Brontë (First American Printing, 1847)

Dombey and Son by Charles Dickens (First American Printing, 1848)

Vanity Fair by William Makepeace Thackeray (First American Printing, 1848)

The Female Poets of America by Rufus Wilmot Griswold (First American Printing, 1849)

Kavanagh by Henry Wadsworth Longfellow (First American Printing, 1849)

rights, personal property, and real property. Kent served as a jurist, professor of law, chief justice of New York, and chancellor of the New York Court of Chancery and is known as "the American Blackstone."

JOHN PICKERING (1777–1846): *Comprehensive Lexicon of the Greek Language.* The best Greek-English dictionary of its time, written to promote the study of Greek in the United States. The Massachusetts lawyer, diplomat, and linguist produced the first formal work on American language, *A Vocabulary; or, Collection of Words and Phrases Which Have Been Supposed to Be Peculiar to the U.S. of America* (1816).

SAMPSON REED (1800–1880): *Observations on the Growth of the Mind.* The most important work of the author, a proponent of the principles of Emanuel Swedenborg (1688–1772), widely considered the foundation of Transcendentalist aesthetic theory. Although some critics disparage the work, Emerson praises it and its author; Emerson would be especially influenced by the book's concept of a "correspondence" between the natural and spiritual dimensions.

ANN NEWPORT ROYALL (1769–1854): *Sketches of History, Life and Manners in the United States, by a Traveller.* Considered the best of the writer's numerous travel books, it chronicles her journey from Alabama to New England. The work includes statistics, interviews with important citizens, and discussions on libraries, hospitals, prisons, schools, and other social institutions.

Poetry

SAMUEL WOODWORTH: *Melodies, Duets, Songs, and Ballads.* Woodworth's collection includes his best-known poem, "The Old Oaken Bucket," and "The Hunters of Kentucky," a ballad celebrating the frontiersmen who helped General Andrew Jackson win the Battle of New Orleans.

Publications and Events

Graham's Magazine. Begun as *Atkinson's Casket,* this monthly magazine with puzzles, jokes, and article reprints from other periodicals was purchased by George Rex Graham in 1839 and merged with Burton's *Gentleman's Magazine.* Graham's generous payments attracted prominent writers such as Cooper, Longfellow, Nathaniel Parker Willis, and James Kirke Paulding, and romance writers such as Emma C. Embury and Ann Sophia Stephens. Edgar Allan Poe served as literary editor from 1841 to 1842 and contributed "The Murders in the Rue Morgue," "The Masque of the Red Death," and "To Helen."

1827
Drama and Theater

GEORGE WASHINGTON PARKE CUSTIS (1781–1857): *The Indian Prophecy, a National Drama in Two Acts, Founded on the Life of George Washington.* The grandson of Martha Washington produces this patriotic drama.

Fiction

JAMES FENIMORE COOPER: *The Prairie.* A Leatherstocking Tale in which Natty Bumppo saves an immigrant train from an Indian raid, rescues the betrothed of Duncan Uncas Middleton (a descendant of his friend in *The Last of the Mohicans*) from kidnappers, and rescues them all again from capture by the Sioux, while surviving a prairie fire and buffalo stampede before his own death. Cooper also publishes *The Red Rover,* a sea novel concerning Lieutenant Henry Ark's search for the infamous pirate Red Rover. Ark learns that Rover had become a pirate after escaping from the Royal Navy due to his allegiance to the colonies and that he later renounced piracy and became an honorable patriot. According to the March 1850 issue of *United States Democratic Review,* it is "the most popular of all Mr. Cooper's works."

SAMUEL GRISWOLD GOODRICH (1793–1860): *The Tales of Peter Parley About America.* The first of Goodrich's more than one hundred Peter Parley books in which an elderly man tells stories about history, society, geography, and biography to children. Elementary schools use them as textbooks, and they sell millions of copies.

SARAH JOSEPHA BUELL HALE (1788–1879): *Northwood: A Tale of New England.* One of the earliest American novels to portray everyday life realistically, the book details social customs in New England, contrasts life in the North and the South, and illustrates Hale's belief in the importance of women's domestic role as it affects the politics of the nation. Hale, a widow with five children, had turned to writing to support her family. The success of *Northwood* would lead her to the editorship of the *Boston Ladies' Magazine.*

SAMUEL BENJAMIN HELBERT JUDAH: *The Buccaneers, A Romance of Our Own Country in Its Ancient Day.* A romance and one of the first novels to employ the legend surrounding Captain Kidd. It is published under the pseudonym "Terentius Phlogobombos."

ANNE NEWPORT ROYALL: *The Tennessean.* Royall's single novel set in Boston and New Orleans has been called by critic Helen Beal Woodward "the worst American novel of all time."

CATHARINE MARIA SEDGWICK: *Hope Leslie; or, Early Times in the Massachusetts.* This historical romance set during the Pequod War in Massachusetts scrutinizes the Puritans' treatment of the Native Americans and considers female identity through the two main characters, Hope Leslie, a Puritan, and the Native American Magawisca. It is Sedgwick's most popular work.

GEORGE TUCKER: *A Voyage to the Moon.* A science fiction satire published under the pseudonym "Joseph Atterly," mocking typical objects of satire, including quack physicians, inept attorneys, and fashion-crazed women.

SARAH SAYWARD BARRELL KEATING WOOD: *Tales of the Night.* Contains "Storms and Sunshine," a romance about a family who loses everything and gains it back again, significant for its realistic representation of early American life, and "The Hermitage," a story of a servant girl's rise to the aristocracy and happiness in marriage.

An engraving of the American white pelican from Audubon's book *The Birds of America*

Nonfiction

JOHN JAMES AUDUBON (1785–1851): *The Birds of America*. Audubon's classic contains more than one thousand color illustrations identifying more than five hundred bird species. With the engravings by Robert Havell Jr. and text help from William MacGillivray, Audubon issued the work as *Ornithological Biography* from 1831 to 1839. Although the scientific accuracy of Audubon's bird paintings has been questioned, they are renowned for their natural settings.

BENJAMIN DRAKE (c. 1795–1841): *Cincinnati in 1826*. A description of the city, providing statistics and information about churches, schools, culture, agriculture, and economy. Later published in London and Germany, it would serve as a guide for immigrants. Drake would follow it with another valuable book on Cincinnati history, *Tales and Sketches from the Queen City* (1838).

ALEXANDER HILL EVERETT: *America; or, A General Survey of the Political Situation of the Several Powers of the Western Continent, with Conjectures on Their Future Prospects*. This well-received work lucidly contemplates the political role of the United States and would be translated into several languages. Conservative in spirit, it shows disdain for radical experiments in ideas such as gender equality but defies expectations by criticizing slavery.

ELIZA LESLIE (1787–1858): *Seventy-Five Receipts for Pastry, Cakes, and Sweetmeats*. An early American cookbook compiled from recipes the Philadelphia short story writer had collected. The success of the book prompts her to take on other works on domestic life, which would make her a celebrity by the time of her death.

CHARLES SEALSFIELD (1793–1864): *Die Vereinigten Staaten von Nordamerika . . .* (translated as *The United States as They Are, and the Americans as They Are; Described in a Tour Through the Valley of the Mississippi*). This travelogue, based on the German writer's first stay in the United States, extols simple western life. The work is first published in German; the author would translate it into English the following year. Sealsfield, a Moravian-born monk whose birth name is Karl Anton Postl, fled his monastery to become a writer and is most famous for his depiction of Southwestern frontier life.

ROBERT JAMES TURNBULL (fl. 1820s): *The Crisis: or, Essays on the Usurpations of the Federal Government*. The author's most important work is a notable defense of South Carolina's doctrine of nullification, the theory that held that a state could suspend within its boundary a federal law. Two thirds of the included essays had previously appeared in the *Charleston Mercury*, attributed to "Brutus." The work inspires the state's citizens to defend anew state powers against those of the federal government.

Poetry

SUMNER LINCOLN FAIRFIELD (1803–1844): "The Cities of the Plain." A narrative poem depicting the destruction of Sodom and Gomorrah. The Massachusetts-born poet is best remembered for *The Last Night of Pompeii* (1832).

FITZ-GREENE HALLECK: *Alnwick Castle, with Other Poems*. Halleck's first collection of verse contains his highly acclaimed tribute to Robert Burns. The collection is well received and sells rapidly.

EDGAR ALLAN POE (1809–1849): *Tamerlane and Other Poems*. Poe's first collection of verse is published anonymously. The Byronic title poem concerns the Mongol conqueror's dying confession of a love affair and is based on Poe's relationship with Sarah Elmira Royster. Also included are "Visit of the Dead," "The Lake," "Evening Star," and "Imitation."

WILLIAM GILMORE SIMMS (1806–1870): *Lyrical and Other Poems* and *Early Lays*. Simms debuts with Romantic verses in the manner of Byron. These two collections would be followed by *The Vision of Cortes, Cain, and Other Poems* (1829).

NATHANIEL PARKER WILLIS (1806–1867): *Sketches*. Published the year Willis graduates from Yale, this is his first volume of poetry and is predominantly comprised of biblical paraphrases, which had won favor with magazine-reading audiences. The success of the verses earns him offers to write for some of the leading magazines of the day, including Philadelphia's *Atlantic Souvenir* and the *New York Review*, as well as the collection *The Token*.

Publications and Events

The Token. This gift book, published in Boston by S. G. Goodrich, contains the first publication of many of what would become Hawthorne's *Twice-Told Tales*. Appearing annually until 1842, *The Token* featured contributors such as Harriet Beecher Stowe, Oliver Wendell Holmes, and James Russell Lowell.

The *Youth's Companion*. A children's magazine founded by Nathaniel Parker Willis and Asa Rand features contributions by notables such as Willis and Lydia Huntley Sigourney. In 1857, the magazine was bought by Daniel Sharp Ford and began including articles for adults. Contributions by Harriet Beecher Stowe, Alfred Lord Tennyson, Louisa May Alcott, and Jack London helped boost circulation from 4,000 subscribers to more than 500,000 by 1899. Suffering financially in the twentieth century, it merged with the *American Boy* in 1929 and completely folded in 1941. *Youth's Companion Anthology* was published in 1954.

1828
Drama and Theater

ROBERT MONTGOMERY BIRD (1806–1854): *The City Looking Glass*. The novelist and dramatist's first drama is a comedy of Philadelphia life notable for its characters Ravin and Ringfinger, early examples of big-city scoundrels.

WILLIAM DUNLAP: *A Trip to Niagara; or, Travellers in America*. This play, about an English visitor whose constant complaints about America gradually give way to admiration, features panoramic set designs that make it

one of the earliest important American theatrical spectacles, giving Dunlap his greatest commercial success.

T. D. RICE (1806–1860): Rice, "the father of American minstrelsy," allegedly observes the singing and dancing of a crippled slave named Jim Crow. Rice imitates him in his popular blackface performance as an "Ethiopian delineator." His one-man performances would lead to full-length "Ethiopian operas," or minstrel shows, begun in 1843 when the Virginia Minstrels, founded by Dan Emmett, appeared in New York City.

Fiction

NATHANIEL HAWTHORNE (1804–1864): *Fanshawe*. Hawthorne's first novel concerns the attempted seduction of Ellen Langdon and her rescue by Fanshawe, a rigidly formal scholar. She offers to marry him, but he refuses because of their incompatibility, and he dies soon thereafter. The hero and the setting are loosely based on Hawthorne himself and his alma mater, Bowdoin College. Although the immature novel goes largely unnoticed and Hawthorne even attempts to have the book recalled and all copies destroyed, it leads to important contacts. Publisher Samuel Griswold Goodrich introduces Hawthorne to the editors of the *New England Magazine*, where he would publish many later works.

JAMES EWELL HEATH (1792–1862): *Edge-Hill; or, The Family of the Fitzroyals*. Set in Virginia at the end of the American Revolution, this is one of the earliest plantation novels. Notable for its historical description of Virginia and depiction of social strata, the novel would win praise from Edgar Allan Poe. Though George Tucker compares it to the novels of James Fenimore Cooper, it does not sell well.

GRENVILLE MELLEN (1799–1841): *Sad Tales and Glad Tales*. A collection of short stories influenced by Washington Irving and published under the pseudonym "Reginald Reverie." Mellen, a lawyer, poet, storyteller, editor, and historian, had first published his stories in the *United States Literary Gazette*. They foreshadow the short story form utilized by Poe and Hawthorne.

JOHN NEAL: *Rachel Dyer*. Considered among Neal's finest works, the novel concerns the life of a Salem witch and accurately describes the customs and injustices of the time.

JAMES KIRKE PAULDING: *The New Mirror for Travellers and a Guide to the Springs*. An earnest satire of the day's many bombastic travel journals and guidebooks. When mistaken publicly and critically for a serious work, it is hailed as "The New Pilgrim's Progress." The work parodies the rules and manners appropriate for various groups and contains sketches, short fiction, and references to people and places well known at the time.

SUSANNA HASWELL ROWSON: *Charlotte's Daughter; or, The Three Orphans.* Commonly known as *Lucy Temple,* this is a sequel to *Charlotte: A Tale of Truth* (1791). Set eighteen years after the first novel, it deals with the coming of age of Charlotte's daughter, Lucy, and two other orphans, who are all in the care of the kindhearted Reverend Matthews. Lucy narrowly avoids marrying her half-brother, the son of Charlotte's seducer, and chooses never to marry.

CHARLES SEALSFIELD: *Tokeah; or, The White Rose.* Published anonymously in two volumes, this is the only of Sealsfield's novels written in English, and it features conflict between whites and Indians on the Jacksonian frontier. Sealsfield calls it an "ethnographic novel," which reveals a group of people through the portrayal of specific characters.

Nonfiction

JOHN C. CALHOUN (1782–1850): *South Carolina Exposition and Protest.* A report drafted at the request of the South Carolina legislature in response to federal protective tariffs deemed harmful to Southern states. Outlining a doctrine later to be termed *nullification,* Calhoun opposes President Jackson's nationalist agenda. Jackson's vice president at the time, Calhoun writes the paper secretly but would break openly with Jackson later and resign as vice president in 1832.

JAMES FENIMORE COOPER: *Notions of the Americans, Picked Up by a Travelling Bachelor.* Written for General Lafayette, who had requested an account of his travels in the United States from 1824 to 1825, this book purportedly recounts the travels of an Englishman, occurring at the same time as Lafayette's trip. The book glorifies the United States and insults England. It is ill received in both England and the United States, and to it Cooper traces the deterioration of his literary prosperity.

JAMES HALL (1793–1868): *Letters from the West: Containing Sketches of Scenery, Manners, and Customs; and Anecdotes Connected with the First Settlements of the Western Sections of the United States.* A youthful account of the land and people Hall had encountered on his travels down the Ohio River to Shawneetown. The tales and sketches win him a reputation as a Western writer, though he is castigated in English reviews for his anti-British sentiments. Hall would never allow the work to be republished. Hall founded and edited the *Illinois Monthly Magazine* (1832–1836), the first Western literary periodical.

WASHINGTON IRVING: *History of the Life and Voyages of Christopher Columbus.* A very popular biography based mostly on the work of the Spanish scholar Navarrete and written during Irving's time as diplomatic attaché in Spain. Highly acclaimed by reviewers, the book bolsters Irving's reputation and earns him an honorary LL.D. degree from Oxford and the gold medal of the Royal Society of Literature in 1830. It is the first of Irving's books not published under a pseudonym.

JESSE OLNEY (1798–1872): *Practical System of Modern Geography.* The Connecticut educator's book would become the standard American text on geography during the nineteenth century.

ANNE NEWPORT ROYALL: *The Black Book.* The travel writer issues the first volume of her popular three-volume collection (completed in 1829) of her travels, mainly in New England.

CHARLES SEALSFIELD: *The Americans As They Are.* The first of the Moravian-born monk's observations based on his travels in America are published in English.

JARED SPARKS (1789–1866): *The Life of John Ledyard, the American Traveller; Comprising Selections from His Journals and Correspondence.* A biography of the explorer who had lived among the Iroquois, traveled to Russia and Alaska, and journeyed with Captain James Cook on his last voyage around the world. Sparks's ten years of extensive research and travels to foreign archives set a precedent in historical research. The work receives a positive reception and advances the reputation of the Harvard professor and editor of the *North American Review* who would become Harvard's president in 1849.

JAMES THACHER: *American Medical Biography.* A pioneering record of American medicine. The first medical biography of the United States, notable for its accurate and unprejudiced descriptions, it serves as a valuable source on medicine in early America.

NOAH WEBSTER: *An American Dictionary of the English Language.* The authoritative American English dictionary, with five thousand words never before included in English dictionaries, as well as unique Americanisms. The definitions are based on American and English usage, but the work clearly defines an American language, with a standardized pronunciation.

Poetry

CARLOS WILCOX (1794–1827): *Ramains.* Comprising fourteen sermons and two poems, "The Age of Benevolence" and "The Religion of Taste," the volume by the

A portrait of Noah Webster superimposed on a page of his original handwritten manuscript, *American Dictionary of the English Language*, with some of his other books

Connecticut Congregational clergyman is notable for praiseworthy verse that accurately depicts the natural world.

Publications and Events

The *Southern Review*. This Charleston quarterly literary magazine, edited by Stephen Elliott and Hugh Swinton Legare to champion Southern culture and literature, begins publication. Contributors included the editors, as well as other prominent South Carolinians, such as Senator Robert Y. Hayne and Thomas Cooper, president of the College of South Carolina.

1829

Drama and Theater

RICHARD PENN SMITH (1799–1854): *The Eighth of January*. One of the earliest of the Philadelphia playwright's

works is a popular melodrama about Andrew Jackson's victory at the Battle of New Orleans in 1815. Written to celebrate Jackson's recent election to the presidency, the play dramatizes the sentiment of many Americans who are pleased to see a "popular" government overtake the "Adams dynasty." It is an adaptation of "Le Maréchal de Luxembourg" (1812), by Frédéric and Boirie. Smith also writes *The Sentinels; or, The Two Sergeants*. In an update of the Damon and Pythias myth, adapted from Théodore d'Aubigny's *Les Deux Sergents*, this successful drama follows two sergeants condemned to death for letting a woman and child from a yellow-fever district pass their checkpoint. A story of love, jealousy, friendship, and justice unfolds, and the well-constructed play ends happily with the soldiers' vindication. Smith also completes a melodrama, *William Penn; or, The Elm Tree*. Set in colonial times, it would be produced as late as 1842. The narrative is a tale of sacrifice, rescue, murder, and ultimate conciliation between two Indian tribes; the famous Quaker Penn helps resolve the crisis.

JOHN AUGUSTUS STONE (1800–1834): *Metamora; or, The Last of the Wampanoags*. The hugely successful romantic melodrama depicts the Indian leader "King Philip" (Matacomet, or Metamora) as a noble savage victimized by British colonists. The play won the actor Edwin Forrest's $500 prize for the best five-act tragedy with an American aboriginal hero; playing the role of Metamora helped maintain Forrest's fame for forty years, but the role would be burlesqued by John Brougham in *Metamora; or, The Last of the Pollywoags* (1847).

Fiction

JAMES FENIMORE COOPER: *The Wept of Wish-ton-Wish: A Tale*. The story of Conanchet, a young captive Indian who lives with the Heathcote family and flees during an Indian attack, taking the young Heathcote daughter, Ruth, with him. Ruth becomes known as Narra-mattah and marries Conanchet, and together they save the Heathcote family from another attack years later during King Philip's War. Although the only American review of the book called it "a failure," the book is important to modern critics, who disagree as to Cooper's intentions in the novel, some believing that it upholds prejudices of his time and others arguing that it challenges them.

SARAH JOSEPHA HALE: *Sketches of American Character*. Hale's collection focuses on "the morals, manners, and habits of the citizens of our republic."

WASHINGTON IRVING: *A Chronicle of the Conquest of Granada*. A recounting of the battles that ended Muslim power in Spain in the fifteenth century. Based on thorough research and highly regarded for its accuracy, Irving's book employs a fictional narrator to present history in the form of tales.

JAMES ATHEARN JONES (1791–1854): *Tales of an Indian Camp*. This three-volume collection of legends by the Massachusetts author and editor is noteworthy as the first major attempt to preserve the folklore of American Indians. It is published in England and quickly translated into German, but not published in the United States. It would be reissued as *Traditions of the North American Indian* in 1830.

WILLIAM LEGGETT: *Tales and Sketches by a Country Schoolmaster*. A collection mainly comprising stories that the poet and editor Leggett had contributed to magazines. It is notable for the popular tale "The Rifle," an accurate depiction of manner and speech on the Illinois frontier, which had been originally published in the gift book *Atlantic Souvenir*.

WILLIAM TUDOR: *Gebel Teir*. An anonymously published satire on international politics in which a council of birds, each representing regions of the United States, Spain, England, France, and the Elysian Fields, gathers to discuss politics. Tudor had written the book in Rio de Janeiro, where he would die of a fever in 1830.

Literary Criticism and Scholarship

SAMUEL LORENZO KNAPP (1783–1838): *Lectures on American Literature, with Remarks on Some Passages in American History*. A pioneering effort toward a comprehensive study of the history of American literature. The popular hack writer runs short of substantive material and expands the work with chapters on loosely relevant topics, such as "The Naval Character of Our Country."

Nonfiction

WILLIAM APES (1798–1839): *A Son of the Forest*. Apes's autobiography details the conversion experience that led to his missionary work and preaching to fellow Indians. The work provides a history and character descriptions of Native Americans and argues for their equal treatment.

LYDIA MARIA CHILD: *The Frugal Housewife*. One of the first American books providing suggestions and ideas for maintaining a household, the work is enormously popular and goes through twenty editions in seven years. Child would follow it with *The Mother's Book* and *The Little Girl's Own Book* (1831), both volumes of domestic guidance that helped Child achieve international acclaim.

JAMES MARSH (1794–1842): *Aids to Reflection*. Marsh is most remembered for editing this first American edition of Samuel Taylor Coleridge's essays on faith. The volume, especially Marsh's own "Preliminary Essay," makes Coleridge's ideas more accessible to American readers. Its explanation of religion, philosophy, reason, and understanding would have an impact on American Transcendentalism.

JARED SPARKS: *The Diplomatic Correspondence of the American Revolution*. Twelve volumes of letters of various prominent men of the Revolution, including Benjamin Franklin, John Adams, John Jay, Arthur Lee, and others, up to the year 1783. The work would be respected for many years and earned Sparks a great profit, but in the late 1880s Sparks's choice of documents and his editing and revising of the letters would be criticized. After a congressional investigation, Francis Wharton prepared a new edition, and Francis P. Blair and John C. Rives were hired to extend the correspondence from 1783 to 1789.

Lydia Maria Child (bottom) with other prominent figures
of the early women's rights movement

DAVID WALKER (1785–1830): *Walker's Appeal.* A pamphlet that is outlawed in the South for its strong antislavery stance. Walker, the son of a free mother and slave father, owned a clothing store in Boston and had the pamphlet smuggled into the South by sailors. Its radical message prompted a bounty on the author's head, but Walker refused to flee and was found dead near his shop; many believed he had been poisoned.

Poetry

GEORGE MOSES HORTON (c. 1797–1883): *The Hope of Liberty.* The first book of African American poetry in more than fifty years and the first by a black from the South, Horton's collection of twenty-three poems includes three dealing with the poet's feelings about being a slave. Two later collections — *The Colored Bard of North Carolina* (1845) and *Naked Genius* (1865) — would follow.

SAMUEL KETTELL (1800–1855): *Specimens of American Poetry, with Critical and Biographical Notices.* The first comprehensive anthology of American poetry includes 189 poets from Cotton Mather to poets of Kettell's own time along with a historical introduction and chronological listing of American verse beginning with the *Bay Psalm Book* and continuing to 1829. The work was criticized for including minor poets and editorial discrepancies. Samuel Goodrich, who published the work, lost $1,500 on the project and was insulted to learn that it had become known as "Goodrich's Kettle of Poetry."

EDGAR ALLAN POE: *Al Aaraaf, Tamerlane, and Other Poems.* Poe's second collection of poetry contains the humorous poem "Fairyland" and "Al Aaraaf," an allegorical poem depicting Poe's conception of this place from Arabic mythology — a star on which the "Idea of Beauty" was born. The poem concerns Angelo, a passionate young man, who hopes to enter Al Aaraaf, but an earthbound love keeps him from hearing his call from Nesace, the presiding spirit.

Publications and Events

The *American Monthly Magazine*. Founded in Boston by N. P. Willis, this jocular and satirical magazine features essays, fiction, criticism, poetry, and humor, primarily written by the editor. Other contributors included John Lathrop Motley, Richard Hildreth, Lydia Huntley Sigourney, and Albert Pike. After financial difficulties and criticism by Boston's social elite, the magazine was absorbed by the *New York Mirror*.

The *Free Enquirer*. After the dissolution of the New Harmony community in 1828, Frances Wright renames the *New-Harmony Gazette* and widens its focus to express socialist and agnostic views.

1830
Drama and Theater

ROBERT MONTGOMERY BIRD: *Pelopidas*. A historical drama concerning the Theban uprising against Sparta, based on Plutarch's account. Although never produced, the play won $1,000 from the actor Edwin Forrest, who was searching for tragedies to stage in the Northeast.

JAMES KIRKE PAULDING: *The Lion of the West*. A farce written for the actor James H. Hackett, who plays Nimrod Wildfire, a character similar to Davy Crockett and other hunters and frontiersmen. Hackett, an actor and sometime theater director, promoted American drama by offering a prize for the most original comedy by an American; Paulding won the $300. The role made Hackett famous, and the play was staged for many years.

RICHARD PENN SMITH: *The Deformed; or, Woman's Trial*. Originally written as *The Divorce; or, The Mock Cavalier* in 1825, this attempt at romantic comedy is not performed until its 1830 revision and now is considered among Smith's best plays. Based partly on Thomas Dekker's *Honest Whore* and William Dunlap's *Italian Father*, it concerns a father's observations of a daughter whom he has abandoned. It would be staged numerous times at Philadelphia's Chestnut Street Theatre. Smith also produces *The Triumph at Plattsburgh*. Considered his best historical drama, the play concerns the defeat of the British by Thomas Macdonough's fleet at Plattsburgh Bay in September 1814 and Major McCrea's escape from British soldiers. The play would first be published in A. H. Quinn's *Representative American Plays* (1917).

Fiction

JAMES FENIMORE COOPER: *The Water-Witch; or, The Skimmer of the Seas*. A romantic novel set during Queen Anne's War, concerning a brigantine with a witch on board. The captain, "The Skimmer of the Seas," runs an illegal trade into New York. Skimmer has abducted Alinda de Barberie and is pursued by her suitor, Ludlow, the captain of the English sloop *Coquette*. However, the two men battle together against French ships, and Alinda is eventually returned to Ludlow. This story is Cooper's effort to create a New Jersey legend, as Washington Irving had achieved one for New York. The novel would often be successfully adapted for the theater.

TIMOTHY FLINT: *The Shoshonee Valley: A Romance*. The story of a New England seaman and his Chinese wife who go to live among the Indians is arguably the best work of Flint's career and draws thematic comparisons with James Fenimore Cooper's work. It looks favorably on the Shoshone people and laments the destruction and loss caused by the advance of white civilization.

CATHARINE MARIA SEDGWICK: *Clarence; or, A Tale of Our Own Times*. Sedgwick's popular satirical novel deals with New York elite society and extols an aristocracy based on natural ability and merit rather than one founded upon lineage and money. Hawthorne would call Sedgwick "our most truthful novelist."

WILLIAM JOSEPH SNELLING (1804–1848): *Tales of the Northwest; or, Sketches of Indian Life and Character, by a Resident of the Frontier*. A widely read collection of ten stories realistically portraying the Dakota Indians in the present upper Midwestern United States. Snelling had recorded his experiences among the Indians to preserve the memory of traditional Native American life.

Literary Criticism and Scholarship

WILLIAM ELLERY CHANNING: "The Importance and Means of a National Literature." An essay arguing for greater encouragement of American writers and calling for a literary declaration of independence, to free American writers from imitating the British. Channing's most important critical commentary, it had been first presented to the American Philosophical Society in 1823 and is printed in the *Christian Examiner* in 1830.

JOSEPH EMERSON WORCESTER (1784–1865): *A Comprehensive Pronouncing and Explanatory Dictionary of the English Language*. Worcester's first dictionary is more conservative and leans more toward British usage than Webster's. It sparks the "War of Dictionaries" between the two lexicographers when Webster charges Worcester with plagiarism, which he would vehemently deny in *A Gross Literary Fraud Exposed* (1835).

Nonfiction

AMOS BRONSON ALCOTT (1799–1888): *Observations on the Principles and Methods of Infant Instruction.* Written for the *United States Gazette*'s education essay contest, the piece outlines Alcott's method of education, which stresses conversation and play and the teacher's role in a child's morality. Although it did not win the contest, it received acclaim from Philadelphia readers and encouraged Alcott to move there, where he opened experimental schools that ultimately failed.

ANNE NEWPORT ROYALL: *Letters from Alabama.* A collection of letters written by the author to a friend as she traveled on horseback through Alabama, Tennessee, and Kentucky from 1817 to 1822. The letters were her first literary compositions, and with them Royall had discovered her gifts of observation and verbal expression, but she did not publish them until she had become an established author. She also publishes her final travel book, *Mrs. Royall's Southern Tour*, in which she criticizes some aspects of her religion and provides keen observations of life in the South.

JOSEPH SMITH (1805–1844): *The Book of Mormon.* A sacred text of the Church of Jesus Christ of Latter-Day Saints, founded by Smith after several visions and the reported delivery of a book written on golden plates by the angel Moroni, which Smith translated using a device called Urim and Thummim. Smith won a small number of followers and began the church, though clergy and members of other sects rejected claims that the book was divine in origin.

SEBA SMITH (1792–1868): "Major Downing Letters." In his *Portland Courier*, the Maine humorist Smith issues the first in a series of popular letters that feature his Down East Yankee persona. Reprinted nationally, the earlier letters concern local issues but would widen in breadth to deal with national politics when the character Downing becomes a member of Andrew Jackson's cabinet.

Poetry

SARAH JOSEPHA BUELL HALE: *Poems for Our Children.* Written at the request of Lowell Mason, an advocate of music education in American public schools, the collection contains Hale's most famous verse, "Mary Had a Little Lamb." This poem, as well as several others, would be reprinted numerous times in anthologies and in William

The New York home of Mormon founder Joseph Smith

Holmes McGuffey's *Eclectic Readers*, without credit given to Hale.

OLIVER WENDELL HOLMES (1809–1894): "Old Ironsides." The poem is published first in the *Boston Daily Advertiser* after Holmes had been angered to learn that the *Constitution*, the U.S. frigate that had served in the Tripolitan War (1800–1815) and was especially important in the War of 1812, had been declared unseaworthy and was to be broken up and sold. Reprinted throughout the country, the poem wins great public attention and saves the ship from demolition.

GEORGE POPE MORRIS (1802–1864): "Woodman, Spare That Tree!" Morris's most successful poem wins immediate popularity and acclaim from Edgar Allan Poe, who calls it a verse "of which any poet, living or dead, might justly be proud." The poem is frequently included in schoolbooks and often used to support conservation efforts. First published in the *New York Mirror*, it would also be included in *The Deserted Bride and Other Poems* (1838).

Publications and Events

Godey's Lady's Book. The most popular nineteenth-century women's magazine, whose circulation reaches 150,000, begins publication. Started in Philadelphia by Louise Antoine Godey (1804–1878), it contained recipes, book reviews, articles on beauty and health, and much of the sentimental and didactic writing typical of the time, as well as works by Emerson, Longfellow, Holmes, Hawthorne, Poe, and Harriet Beecher Stowe. It is also notable for its color fashion plates and art reproduction engravings. In 1837, Godey purchased Sara Josepha Buell Hale's *Boston Ladies' Magazine* and made Hale editor, launching Godey's most successful years. After Hale's retirement in 1877 and Godey's death in 1878, the magazine moved to New York. It folded in 1898.

The *Illinois Monthly Magazine*. The earliest literary magazine to be published west of Ohio is founded and edited by Judge James Hall, who contributes the majority of its material. The magazine includes regional sketches and articles written to draw more settlers to the area. Hall relocated to Cincinnati in 1832 and changed the title to the *Western Monthly Magazine*.

1831
Drama and Theater

ROBERT MONTGOMERY BIRD: *The Gladiator*. Bird's most popular play. It stars Edwin Forrest as Spartacus, the leader of the first century B.C. Roman slave revolt, and achieves immediate success. Praising its contemporary relevance, Walt Whitman declared that it "was as full of 'abolitionism' as an egg is of meat."

RICHARD PENN SMITH: *Caius Marius*. Smith's most successful play concerns the conflict between democracy and oligarchy. The play, written for the actor Edwin Forrest, has not survived because Forrest, to prevent other theatrical companies from producing it, refused to allow it to be published.

JOHN AUGUSTUS STONE: *Tancred, King of Sicily* and *The Demoniac; or, The Prophet's Bride*. The first of Stone's 1831 productions is a revenge play; the second is a revision of James Kirke Paulding's *The Lion of the West* (1830).

Fiction

JAMES FENIMORE COOPER: *The Bravo: A Tale*. A romantic novel concerning an Italian who pretends to be a hired assassin for the Venetian senate in order to free his father from unjust imprisonment. Cooper's best novel with a European setting, it attempts to show the righteousness of democracy in contrast to rule by aristocracy.

LAUGHTON OSBORN (c. 1809–1878): *Sixty Years of the Life of Jeremy Levis*. A two-volume episodic novel by the New York writer, echoing Laurence Sterne's *Tristam Shandy*. This meandering satire is widely denounced by critics, prompting Osborn's ongoing dialogue with the press. The editor Rufus Griswold (1815–1857), however, found the book "powerfully written and deeply interesting."

JAMES KIRKE PAULDING: *The Dutchman's Fireside*. Set near Albany during the French and Indian War, the novel presents an accurate picture of the life of the old Dutch settlers.

Nonfiction

OLIVER WENDELL HOLMES: "The Autocrat of the Breakfast-Table." Holmes publishes his first essay of what would become his famous series on table talk at a Boston boarding house; the series itself would commence publication in the *Atlantic Monthly* in 1858.

WASHINGTON IRVING: *Voyages and Discoveries of the Companions of Columbus.* Irving publishes a sequel to his Columbus biography, completing the story of the early explorers.

JAMES OHIO PATTIE (1804–c. 1850): *The Personal Narrative of James O. Pattie, of Kentucky, During an Expedition from St. Louis, Through the Vast Regions Between That Place and the Pacific Ocean.* A significant work of frontier literature, comprised of history and fiction, and especially notable for its exciting adventure narrative. Much of the book may have been written by its editor, Timothy Flint. It was plagiarized in 1847 in *The Hunters of Kentucky; or, The Trials and Toils of Trappers and Traders,* by B. Bilson.

JOHN MASON PECK (1789–1858): *Guide for Emigrants Containing Sketches of Illinois, Missouri, and Adjacent Parts.* A collection of the author's reports and articles concerning the western United States. Compiled during Peck's travels as a missionary, the work is considered authoritative and would be expanded in 1836 as *A New Guide for Emigrants.*

MARY PRINCE (c. 1788–?): *The History of Mary Prince, a West Indian Slave, Related by Herself.* Dictated to poet and abolitionist writer Susanna Strickland, this slave narrative is published as an antislavery tract in England. It disappeared from view, was rediscovered in 1987, and is acclaimed as one of the most authentic oral accounts of slavery.

MARIA W. STEWART (1803–1979): *Religion and the Pure Principle of Morality.* One of the earliest known American woman lecturers publishes her first book, calling upon African Americans to organize against slavery in the South and racial restrictions in the North.

NAT TURNER (1800–1831): *The Confessions of Nat Turner.* The leader of the bloodiest slave rebellion during the antebellum period dictates his story to Virginia attorney Thomas Gray while awaiting his execution.

HENRY WHEATON (1785–1848): *History of the Northmen.* Wheaton makes the case for the pre-Columbian discovery of America by the Vikings.

Poetry

WILLIAM CULLEN BRYANT: "Song of Marion's Men." Considered among Bryant's best lyric poetry, the work commends Francis Marion (1732–1795), the Revolutionary soldier known for his guerrilla tactics in South Carolina. The poet and critic Edmund Clarence Stedman would declare in his 1864 essay "Mr. Bryant's 'Thirty Poems'" that the poem "has stirred the pulses of every school-boy in the land."

OLIVER WENDELL HOLMES: "The Last Leaf." Holmes publishes a poem about an aging veteran of the Boston Tea Party.

EDGAR ALLAN POE: *Poems by Edgar Allan Poe, Second Edition.* A collection of verse containing early, unrevised versions of some of Poe's most significant poems, including "To Helen," "Israfel," and "The Doomed City." Although little noticed outside the circle of West Point cadets to whom Poe dedicated the book, biographer Kenneth Silverman notes that its "most marked feature is a preoccupation with death and the afterlife." Also significant is the preface, "Letter to B," in which Poe begins to build his critical theories, borrowing liberally from Coleridge.

SAMUEL FRANCIS SMITH (1808–1895): "America." One of the country's most popular patriotic hymns. Smith wrote the verse at the request of Lowell Mason, an advocate of music education; Smith composed its five stanzas in thirty minutes. Set to the music of the British anthem "God Save the King," it is first sung at a Fourth of July meeting in Boston. It would be published by Mason in *The Choir* (1832).

WILLIAM JOSEPH SNELLING: *Truth: A New Year's Gift for Scribblers.* A notorious verse satire sends up contemporary poets, classifying many as inferior hacks, especially those who portray Native Americans as stereotypes.

JOHN GREENLEAF WHITTIER (1807–1892): *Legends of New-England in Prose and Verse.* Whittier's first book, which receives little attention, is significant as an original endeavor to represent New England folklore. Uneasy with the gothic style of the book, Whittier would suppress it later in life.

EMMA HART WILLARD: *The Fulfillment of a Promise.* This collection of basically undistinguished verse includes the poem "Rocked in the Cradle of the Deep," written on the poet's journey home from Europe. It becomes immensely popular and is set to music by Joseph P. Knight.

Publications and Events

The *Liberator.* Founded in Boston by William Lloyd Garrison (1805–1870), this abolitionist weekly's salutation includes the words "I will be heard!" Its militant stance for immediate abolition and enfranchisement of all American blacks aroused violent opposition in the South, where states passed laws suppressing the

John Greenleaf Whittier

magazine. It ceased publication in 1865, its last issue co-inciding with the ratification of the Thirteenth Amendment.

The *New-England Magazine.* The most significant New England periodical preceding the *Atlantic Monthly* is launched. Edited by Joseph Buckingham (1779–1861) in Boston, its list of prominent contributors included Longfellow, Whittier, Noah Webster, and Holmes. The magazine reached its greatest literary significance under Park Benjamin's editorship in 1835, during which the beginning of Hawthorne's "The Ambitious Guest" was published.

The *Spirit of the Times.* W. T. Porter (1809–1858) founds the popular New York journal devoted to sports and humor. It includes writing by the foremost humorists and sportsmen, including Thomas Bangs Thorpe (most notably "The Big Bear of Arkansas"), Henry William Herbert, Albert Pike, and others, as well as contributions from subscribers on frontier topics. It was purchased by George Wilkes in 1856, though edited by Porter until 1858 under the name *Porter's Spirit of the Times.* In 1859, Wilkes began his own *Spirit of the Times,* which ran until 1902.

1832
Drama and Theater

ROBERT MONTGOMERY BIRD: *Oralloossa.* A tragedy set in Peru just after the Spanish conquest. Bird had thoroughly researched the period and created the character of Oralloossa, who leads a revolt against Pizarro but is betrayed by his own people in the end.

ROBERT TAYLOR CONRAD (1810–1858): *Conrad, King of Naples.* Conrad's first play, though it has not survived, is known to have been written for the actor James E. Murdoch, and it is produced with much success at Philadelphia's Arch Street Theatre. Conrad is remembered as the best dramatist in Philadelphia after Robert Montgomery Bird and Richard Penn Smith.

JOSEPH STEVENS JONES (1809–1877): *The Liberty Tree; or, Boston Boys in '76.* Jones's first successful play celebrates the fiftieth anniversary of the end of the Revolutionary War. The play is staged at Boston's Warren Theatre, with Jones acting as the Yankee character Bill Ball.

Fiction

JACOB ABBOTT (1803–1879): *The Young Christian.* A collection of fiction and nonfiction works for young Christians by the Massachusetts educator and Congregational clergyman. Immediately successful, it becomes Abbott's most widely known book, and the first of nearly two hundred similar works, including the popular Rollo series.

JAMES FENIMORE COOPER: *The Heidenmauer; or, The Benedictines: A Legend of the Rhine.* Cooper's second European novel to present the wickedness of aristocracy. It deals with the social shift from Catholicism to secular rule in sixteenth-century Bavaria.

JAMES HALL: *Legends of the West.* Considered among Hall's most valuable works, this collection of essays and tales depicts life in Illinois. It is especially notable for the realistic piece "The Seventh Son," concerning a doctor who must pretend to be the magical seventh son of an Indian doctor to reassure his western patients, and the four-part series "On the Intercourse of the American People with the Indians."

NATHANIEL HAWTHORNE: "My Kinsman, Major Molineux." First published in *The Token* and to be collected in *The Snow-Image* (1851), Hawthorne's story is a richly symbolic treatment of innocence and experience concerning a country boy's arrival in Boston during demonstrations against British rule.

WASHINGTON IRVING: *The Alhambra.* Considered Irving's *Spanish Sketch Book,* this is a collection of adapted

Andalusian lore, anecdotes, and descriptions of architecture and scenery of the Moorish castle in Spain where Irving lived in 1829. The book would generate an interest in romantic Alhambraism and remain an important document in Granada's history.

JOHN PENDLETON KENNEDY: *Swallow Barn; or, A Sojourn in the Old Dominion.* This series of forty-nine Addisonian sketches of Virginia life is the Baltimore lawyer and political figure's first fiction. Written under the pseudonym of New York outsider "Mark Littleton," it wins critical and financial success and is considered Kennedy's best work and one of the first important fictional depictions of Virginia life. The tales include one of the first portraits of the stereotypical Southern gentleman, gently mock the prevalence of litigation in Virginia, and address the problem of slavery.

JAMES KIRKE PAULDING: *Westward Ho!* Best-selling romance about the adventures of a Virginia family pioneering in Kentucky. The novel contains a love story with Hawthorne-like psychological undertones.

Literary Criticism and Scholarship

WILLIAM DUNLAP: *The History of the American Theatre.* The first history of the American stage, the work is drawn extensively from the author's own life in the theater. It is a wellspring of anecdotes, descriptions of prominent figures, observations on the state of the industry, and rich personal accounts of the dramatic art that Dunlap strove to improve.

Nonfiction

RALPH WALDO EMERSON (1803–1882): *Letter... to the Second Church and Society.* Emerson defends leaving his pastorship after he could not in good conscience meet his various clerical responsibilities. Emerson's reliance on his own conscience as the ultimate guide for his actions has been identified as the beginning of his career as a Transcendentalist.

THEODORE SEDGWICK FAY (1807–1898): *Dreams and Reveries of a Quiet Man.* A collection of Fay's early writings originally published in the *New York Mirror,* which he edited from 1828 to 1833. It includes his popular series The Little Genius and other essays concerning literature, politics, the press, social issues, and the theater.

WILLIAM LLOYD GARRISON: *Thoughts on African Colonization.* In a powerful pamphlet published by the New England Anti-Slavery Society, Garrison argues against the American Colonization Society's plan to relocate freed slaves in Africa, a plan that he had previously supported.

William Lloyd Garrison

SETH LUTHER (fl. 1817): *An Address to the Working-Men of New England.* The first pamphlet by the champion of labor reforms attacks the factory system in which he had witnessed children subjected to a fifteen-hour workday and physical mistreatment. It wins sympathy from the Boston elite and would be partly responsible for the enactment of the first American child-labor law in 1842, in Massachusetts.

JOSEPH STORY: *Commentaries on the Constitution of the United States.* The second in Story's series of legal commentaries, used throughout the country by attorneys with little access to recent reports of cases. An abridged edition would become a widely used textbook in American law schools. Story's other commentaries are *Commentaries on the Law of Bailments* (1832), *The Conflict of Laws* (1834), *On Equity Jurisprudence* (1836), *Equity Pleading* (1838), *Law of Agency* (1839), *Law of Partnership* (1841), *Law of Bills of Exchange* (1843), and *Law of Promissory Notes* (1845).

CHARLES STUART (1783–1865): *The West India Question: Immediate Emancipation Safe and Practical.* The most influential of the Jamaican immigrant's more than two dozen antislavery pamphlets. The famous work becomes the guide for the abolitionist movements in the United States and Great Britain.

BENJAMIN BUSSEY THATCHER (1809–1840): *Indian Biography*. The writer's most famous work attempts an accurate depiction of Native Americans. Comprising two volumes of the *Harpers' Family Library*, the work receives favorable reviews and is followed by *Indian Traits* (1833), a part of Harpers' juvenile series The Boys' and Girls' Library.

FRANCES TROLLOPE (1780–1863): *Domestic Manners of the Americans*. The British author's first published and most important book is a best-selling and controversial work recounting the author's travels during her four-year stay in America, which she castigates for its rudeness, vulgarity, disrespect, and greed. Trollope argues that the problems in America arise from "the lamentable insignificance of the American woman." The work spawns many replies, including the satirical *Travels in America by George Fibbleton* (1833) by Asa Green and *The Americans in Their Moral, Social, and Political Relations* (1837) by Francis J. Grund.

Poetry

WILLIAM CULLENT BRYANT: *Poems*. A collection containing most of Bryant's significant work since 1818. It includes five previously unpublished poems, including "To a Fringed Gentian" and "The Song of Marion's Men." The *North American Review* hails it as "the best volume of American verse that has ever appeared."

THOMAS HOLLEY CHIVERS (1809–1858): *The Path of Sorrow; or, The Lament of Youth*. Chivers's first collection, written while he was studying medicine (1828–1829), is a reflection on his own suffering, in particular the unhappiness of his first marriage. Edgar Allan Poe describes Chivers as "one of the best and one of the worst poets in America." Chivers is chiefly remembered for accusations and counteraccusations of plagiarism exchanged between him and Poe.

SUMNER LINCOLN FAIRFIELD: *The Last Night of Pompeii*. Fairfield's best work is a narrative poem about the strife that existed between Christian and pagan faiths. It comprises three blank-verse cantos. Fairfield would accuse Edward Bulwer-Lytton of plagiarizing his poem in his volume *The Last Days of Pompeii* (1834).

WILLIAM GILMORE SIMMS: "Atlantis: A Story of the Sea." A poem concerning a sea-fairy who is saved from a demon by a Spanish knight, with whom she happily descends into the caves of the ocean. Although it has little lasting literary value, the poem is well received and introduces Simms into New York literary circles.

FREDERICK WILLIAM THOMAS (1806–1866): *The Emigrant*. Thomas's first book is a verse reflection on the Ohio River region. It shows the influence of Wordsworth and Byron. Thomas is better known as a novelist of such works as *Clinton Bradshaw* (1835) and *Howard Pinckney* (1840).

1833
Fiction

JAMES FENIMORE COOPER: *The Headsman; or, The Abbaye des Vignerons*. Cooper's third novel criticizing European feudal society and aristocracy concerns the son of an executioner whose identity is hidden so he will not be forced into his father's profession. He reveals his secret to the woman he loves and later learns that he is actually the son of the doge of Genoa.

ASA GREENE (1789–1838): *The Life and Adventures of Dr. Dodimus Duckworth*. The purported biography of the late New England quack doctor, written in mock-heroic style and employing puns and malapropisms for humor, is Greene's most remembered book. A second 1833 book by Greene, *A Yankee Among the Nullifiers*, is a fictional autobiography of Elnathan Elmwood, who persuades Major Harebrain Harrington, a passionate supporter of states' rights and nullification, to adopt his antislavery, antinullification stance. Based on the author's travels to South Carolina, the book employs the mock-heroic style, figurative language, and wordplay popular in 1830s literature. Greene's third 1833 comic work is *Travels in America by George Fibbleton*, a burlesque on English travel writers' views of America. Critic Walter Blair later cites the three works as the most significant examples of American humor published between 1825 and 1833.

JAMES HALL: *The Harpe's Head*. The western writer's only published novel is an episodic tale set in Kentucky, which features one of his most memorable characters, the archetypal backwoods outlaw Micajah Harpe.

ELIZA LESLIE: *Pencil Sketches; or, Outlines of Characters and Manners*. Considered among Leslie's most impressive fictions, this is a three-volume collection of the Unitarian minister and poet's popular magazine sketches. W.B.O. Peabody's review of the first series found the sketches all to be "written in a correct, easy, spirited style, and exhibit a very keen and nice observation of the various scenes of domestic life, with a happy talent for working up the results in a narrative form."

HENRY WADSWORTH LONGFELLOW (1807–1882): *Outre-Mer: A Pilgrimage Beyond the Sea*. The author's first prose book is a series of travel essays similar to Washington Irving's *Sketch Book*. Drawn from the author's travels in Europe, the book is published anonymously and is well received by the public and critics.

JOHN NEAL: *The Down-Easters*. Regarded among Neal's best novels, this is a melodramatic story in which two men vie for the love of a widow. The work is especially notable for its realistic descriptions of New England and the Yankee character.

EDGAR ALLAN POE: "MS. Found in a Bottle." Poe's tale, based on the legend of the *Flying Dutchman*, depicts a seaman forced to stay at sea until Judgment Day. It wins the *Baltimore Saturday Visitor*'s $50 prize for the best story and introduces Poe to John Pendleton Kennedy, one of the contest's judges, who would assist Poe with his publishing endeavors, most notably by introducing him to the T. W. White, the editor of the newly established *Southern Literary Messenger*.

WILLIAM GILMORE SIMMS: *Martin Faber.* In this novel Martin seduces, and then murders, Emily so that he might marry Constance. The crime is discovered by his friend, who exposes him in a painting hung in the village gallery. Martin is killed after attempting to stab Constance when she visits him in prison. The work is immediately successful though faulted by modern critics as implausible.

SEBA SMITH: *The Life and Writings of Major Jack Downing of Downingville.* A series of letters from a simple Yankee who provides clever commentary on current events, local politics, and Jacksonian democracy. Smith's prototype of the Yankee commentator would often be imitated.

Literary Criticism and Scholarship

GULIAN CROMMELIN VERPLANCK: *Discourses and Addresses on Subjects of American History, Arts, and Literature.* A well-received collection of orations celebrating prominent men and the lofty merits of literature and art. Verplanck toasts the good works of Lord Baltimore, DeWitt Clinton, Gouverneur Morris, Alexander Hamilton, and others, and argues that there is a reciprocal connection between the arts and sciences.

Nonfiction

WILLIAM APES: *The Experiences of Five Christian Indians.* Apes provides Protestant conversion narratives of himself and four Indian women. The work discusses various injustices experienced by Native Americans and ends with the militant essay "An Indian's Looking-Glass for the White Man."

BLACK HAWK (1767–1838): *Autobiography.* Also published as *Life of Ma-Ka-Tai-Me-She-Kia-Kiak*, the book is the Sauk and Fox Indian chief's attempt to present his version of the events of the Black Hawk War (1832). Black Hawk dictated his story to Antoine Le Claire, a government interpreter at Fort Armstrong, and the journalist J. B. Patterson added contemporary literary flourishes for its publication. To settle a dispute over the authenticity

of the autobiography, Donald Jackson published his research in a 1955 edition of the book, concluding that the work did indeed come from Black Hawk. The text is considered invaluable because of its Native American perspective on the war.

LYDIA MARIA CHILD: *Appeal in Favor of That Class of Americans Called Africans.* One of the first books to argue for the immediate emancipation of slaves creates a sensation and influences many. The work launches Child's career as an abolitionist but also incites great antagonism that hurts sales of her other books and forces her to give up the editorship of *Juvenile Miscellany*, which she had founded in 1826.

DAVY CROCKETT (1786–1836): *Sketches and Eccentricities of Col. David Crockett.* The first of the books allegedly written by the frontiersman and congressman that were more likely the work of Whig journalists. It would be followed by *An Account of Col. Crockett's Tour to the North and Down East* (1833) and *Col. Crockett's Exploits and Adventures in Texas* (1836).

CHARLES AUGUSTUS DAVIS (c. 1795–c. 1868): *Letters Written During the President's Tour, "Down East," by Myself, Major Jack Downing, of Downingville.* The New York merchant and journalist "borrows" Seba Smith's "Jack Downing" persona for a similar satire on the Jackson administration from the perspective of a Maine Yankee.

TIMOTHY FLINT: *Memoir of Daniel Boone.* A popular biography of Boone, edited and largely written by Flint, who labels Boone "the Achilles of the West." The work would be reprinted in numerous editions and published under different titles throughout the nineteenth century.

JOHN GREENLEAF WHITTIER: *Justice and Expediency.* Whittier's antislavery tract is written in the same year he was elected as a delegate to the National Anti-Slavery Convention. His verses and other tracts on the subject would be collected in *Poems Written During the Progress of the Abolition Question* (1838).

Poetry

MARIA GOWEN BROOKS: *Zophiël.* The Massachusetts poet's highly emotional verse, influenced by her association with the English Lake poets, prompts Charles Lamb to declare that she could not have been the author: "as if there could have been a woman capable of anything so grand."

RICHARD HENRY DANA SR. (1787–1879): *Poems and Prose Writings.* A highly lauded collection by the Massachusetts poet and founder of the *North American Review*, containing many of his well-known essays and poetry, including "The Buccaneer," one of the most famous poems of the 1830s. An enlarged edition would be published in 1850.

PENINA MOISE (1797–1880): *Fancy's Sketch Book*. This is considered the first poetry collection by a Jewish American published in the United States. The verses by the native of Charleston, South Carolina, include humorous and satirical treatment of love, poverty, and death as well as commentary on the suffering of Jews abroad and calls for Jewish immigration to America. Her other major publication would be *Hymns Written for the Use of Hebrew Congregations* (1856).

Publications and Events

The *American Monthly Magazine*. Literary magazine founded by Henry William Herbert (1807–1858) in New York to rival the *Knickerbocker* debuts. Much of the content was written by Herbert himself, including some significant commentaries on theater, art, and music, as well as a novel, *The Brothers, a Tale of the Fronde*. The magazine absorbed the *New England Magazine* in 1835 and was edited by Charles Fenno Hoffman and Park Benjamin. Contributors included Albert Pike, Edgar Allan Poe, James Hall, and James Kirke Paulding, and the magazine particularly emphasized German literature, the American Lyceum, and the West. In later years the political focus of the magazine increased with writings by Horace Greeley and Henry Clay. It was absorbed by Horace Greeley's *New Yorker* in 1838.

The *Knickerbocker Magazine*. The New York monthly literary magazine debuts. It achieves literary merit and good circulation under Lewis Gaylord Clark and Clement M. Edson. Clark's twin brother, Willis Gaylord Clark, provided much of the writing. Other notable contributors included Irving, Cooper, Bryant, Longfellow, Hawthorne, Whittier, Kirkland, and Parkman. Clark's humorous "Editor's Table" was a notable feature. The quality of the magazine diminished by 1850 and, after several changes in ownership and focus, folded in 1865.

The *New York Sun*. Founded by Benjamin H. Day as a penny daily to feature human interest stories, this newspaper first attracted wide attention with its sensational moon hoax (1835), an article purporting to reveal a discovery by the famous astronomer Sir John Herschel of people and animals on the moon. The paper later merged with the *New York Herald* (1920) and the *World-Telegram* (1950), but labor disputes forced the closing of the newspaper in 1966, although a Sunday edition lingered until 1967.

Parley's Magazine. Samuel G. Goodrich founds this magazine for youth, which covers many diverse areas, such as social sciences, physical education, and art, and includes tales from the Bible, poems, games, and morality stories. It merged with Goodrich's *Merry's Museum for Boys and Girls* in 1844.

1834
Drama and Theater

ROBERT MONTGOMERY BIRD: *The Broker of Bogota*. A domestic drama concerning an honest money lender, Baptista Febro, and his eldest and most beloved son, Ramon, who plots against his father in an attempt to steal from his vaults to win his beloved's hand. Febro is devastated when the truth is revealed in the end, and Ramon commits suicide. This work is Bird's most critically acclaimed drama.

THOMAS HOLLEY CHIVERS: *Conrad and Eudora*. Chivers's verse drama is the first of several works inspired by the celebrated Beauchamp-Sharp murder case, known as the Kentucky Tragedy. Jeroboam Beauchamp had killed his wife's seducer, Colonel Solomon P. Sharp, solicitor general of Kentucky, in 1825. Other treatments of the story include Edgar Allan Poe's *Politian* (1835), Charles Fenno Hoffman's *Greyslaer* (1840), William Gilmore Simms's *Beauchampe* (1842), and Charlotte Mary Sanford Barnes's *Octavia Bragaldi* (1848).

CORNELIUS AMBROSIUS LOGAN (1806–1853): *Yankee Land; or, The Foundling of the Apple Orchard*. The first of the playwright and popular actor-manager's successful farces features his much-repeated Yankee character type, here called Lot Sap Sago. Logan's subsequent plays include *The Wag of Maine* (1835) and *The Vermont Wool Dealer* (1840).

Fiction

ROBERT MONTGOMERY BIRD: *Calavar; or, The Knight of the Conquest*. A historical romance concerning the consequences of Cortez's conquest of the Aztecs. The work is praised by the historian William Hickling Prescott for its historical accuracy. Edgar Allan Poe's review in the *Southern Literary Messenger* notes its "fertility of the imagination rarely possessed by his compeers."

WILLIAM ALEXANDER CARUTHERS (1802–1846): *The Cavaliers of Virginia; or, The Recluse of Jamestown*. The first book-length work devoted to the subject of Nathaniel Bacon's rebellion in 1676 and Caruthers's most extensively reviewed writing, the book incorporates a nationalist, democratic view and portrays Bacon as a symbol of manifest destiny. It gives rise to a number of romances on Bacon's Rebellion and inspires future writing on the folklore of the early Virginians and Cavaliers.

George Bancroft

Caruthers also publishes *The Kentuckian in New York; or, The Adventures of Three Southerners*, an epistolary romance concerning three college friends — two South Carolinians who travel to New York accompanied by an eccentric Kentuckian, and one Virginian who journeys through the Deep South. They record their adventures, contrasting customs in the North and the South. Written while Caruthers was practicing medicine in New York and attending Gotham literary meetings, it received mild critical success but remains significant as one of the first romances to place country protagonists in urban environments and for the Southern writer's advanced ideas on the evils of slavery.

CAROLINE HOWARD GILMAN (1794–1888): *Recollections of a New England Housekeeper*. A popular novel first published serially in Gilman's weekly magazine the *Rose Bud*, under the pseudonym "Clarissa Packard." It is a humorous story of an attorney's wife who educates country women to be her house servants. Gilman proclaims this "the first attempt, in that particular mode, to enter into the recesses of American homes and hearths." She would follow the success of this novel with the similar work *Recollections of a Southern Matron* (1838), also greatly popular. Gilman was a New Englander whose clergyman husband became a pastor in the South, which she came to love.

ASA GREENE: *The Perils of Pearl Street*. A humorous tale of Billy Hazard, an innocent country boy, and his three failed attempts to win fortune in the New York City mercantile business. It provides an in-depth picture of New York merchants and commerce in the 1830s.

JOSEPH C. HART (1798–1855): *Miriam Coffin; or, The Whale Fisherman*. The first novel to deal with whaling. Hart, a lawyer and journalist, wrote it to build congressional support for the whaling industry.

NATHANIEL HAWTHORNE: "Mr. Higginbotham's Catastrophe." First published in *The Token* and to be included in *Twice-Told Tales* (1837), this story about a murder plot is based on an actual case. Despite its subject matter, it is one of Hawthorne's most lighthearted comic stories.

HENRY JUNIUS NOTT (1797–1837): *Novelettes of a Traveller; or, Odds and Ends from the Knapsack of Thomas Singularity*. Humorous picaresque sketches depicting frontier life, taken from the life and experiences of the South Carolina lawyer and teacher.

WILLIAM GILMORE SIMMS: *Guy Rivers*. The first in Simms's series of Border Romances, *Guy Rivers* tells the story of Ralph Colleton's near-demise at the hands of the lawyer-turned-outlaw, Guy Rivers, during the gold rush of the 1820s in the wilds of northern Georgia. Other Border Romances include *Richard Hurdis* (1838); its sequel, *Border Beagles* (1840); and *Beauchampe; or, The Kentucky Tragedy* (1842) and its expansion, *Charlemont; or, The Pride of the Village* (1842).

WILLIAM LEETE STONE (1792–1844): *Tales and Sketches — Such as They Are*. A two-volume collection of exciting and entertaining works that had previously appeared in periodicals by the New York journalist and writer of colonial and Native American life. The author's first notable work, it contains numerous tales that recast popular New England myths and legends.

HARRIET BEECHER STOWE (1811–1896): "Isabelle and Her Sister Kate" and "A New England Sketch." The former is Stowe's first published work, appearing in the February installment of the *Western Monthly Magazine*. The second, appearing in its April issue, wins first prize in its fiction contest and is published in the pamphlet *Prize Tale: A New England Sketch*.

Literary Criticism and Scholarship

PIERRE ÉTIENNE DU PONCEAU (1760–1840): *A Discourse on the Necessity of and Means of Making Our National Literature Independent*. Du Ponceau's early call for the means to encourage a native American literature. Du Ponceau came to the United States from France in 1777, served in the Continental army, and became a member of the Pennsylvania bar. He wrote books on linguistics and history.

Nonfiction

GEORGE BANCROFT (1800–1891): *A History of the United States.* A pioneering history with a democratic, rather than Federalist, point of view, lauding the American people and the republic in general. Bancroft had gathered the information for the history from his massive correspondence and experience in numerous government posts, which included secretary of the navy and minister to Great Britain and Germany.

JAMES FENIMORE COOPER: *Letter to His Countrymen.* Cooper's first publication after returning from seven years in Europe discusses controversies that arose in England from his defense of American ideals and his condemnation of the powerful elite. It also attacks the press, President Jackson, Congress, and Americans. He ends the work with a proclamation that he will quit writing.

DAVY CROCKETT: *A Narrative of the Life of David Crockett of the State of Tennessee.* Purportedly written to correct the outrageous stories printed under Crockett's name in *Sketches and Eccentricities of Col. David Crockett* in 1833, this autobiography, written with the assistance of Thomas Chilton and interspersed with tall tales, presents a more straightforward and more believable image of Crockett as a frontiersman and congressman.

WILLIAM DUNLAP: *History of the Rise and Progress of the Arts of Design in the U.S.* This is the foremost work on early American art, especially valuable for the author's firsthand knowledge and use of original sources. It is the primary resource for most information about early American painters.

JAMES HALL: *Sketches of History, Life, and Manners in the West.* An informal history of expansion into the Ohio Valley, based on Hall's own observations and primary source material. The first volume is published in 1834 by Hubbard and Edmonds, who would go bankrupt before the second volume could appear. The completed two volumes would be published in 1835 by Hall's brother Harrison Hall and are considered among Hall's most important works.

ALBERT PIKE (1809–1891): *Prose Sketches and Poems, Written in the Western Country.* The volume contains prose descriptions of Pike's frontier travels and verse accounts of the scenery of the Southwest, held in high regard by Edgar Allan Poe. Although considered of little interest today as literary art, the work continues to be noteworthy for its vibrant descriptions of the early-nineteenth-century Southwest.

JARED SPARKS: *The Writings of George Washington.* Sparks's greatest work is a series of twelve volumes of Washington's papers and correspondences. Volume one, the last volume written and published (1837), is a highly laudatory biography of Washington. A great financial success, the volumes would remain uncriticized until 1851, when some charged that Sparks had omitted passages in which Washington criticized New England and that Sparks had altered and added to the writings. He defended himself in letters to the *Evening Post* and the *National Intelligencer*, but the work never regained its earlier reputation.

Publications and Events

The *Ladies' Companion.* A monthly magazine mimicking *Godey's Lady's Book* debuts. Edited and published by William W. Snowden, it primarily contained fiction, engravings, music, fashion, and sentimental poetry. Submissions by Paulding, Simms, Longfellow, and Poe (including "The Mystery of Marie Roget") appeared in its pages.

The *Southern Literary Messenger.* Founded in Richmond by Thomas W. White for the Virginia Historical and Philosophical Society, the magazine featured fiction, translations, poems, reviews, legal articles, and Virginia historical notes. Poe began his career with the *Messenger* in March 1835 with the contribution of his poem "Berenice," and he became editor in December of that year. Under Poe's editorship from 1835 to 1837, the *Messenger* was known for his cutting reviews, which created several literary stirs, raising the circulation from five hundred to thirty-five hundred. After Poe was fired for drunkenness, the magazine was edited by White, and after his death in 1843, its popularity greatly declined. The magazine was revived from 1939 to 1944, featuring earlier articles and literature.

1835

Drama and Theater

ROBERT TAYLOR CONRAD: *Jack Cade, the Captain of the Commons.* Sometimes titled *Aylmere*, Conrad's most important play gains him literary prominence in Philadelphia. The blank-verse tragedy concerns the leader of the 1450 rebellion against the government of King Henry VI. The opening performance is delayed because of the leading actor's drunkenness, but it later would star Edwin Forrest and become very successful.

EDGAR ALLAN POE: *Politian: A Tragedy.* Three scenes of Poe's unfinished blank-verse drama based on the Beauchamp-Sharp murder case known as the Kentucky Tragedy but set in sixteenth-century Rome are published in the *Southern Literary Messenger*. It would be published in its entirety in 1923.

Fiction

JACOB ABBOTT: *The Little Scholar Learning to Talk and Rollo Learning to Read.* Abbott, an educator and minister, publishes the first in his Rollo series about a New England farm boy whose experiences at home and abroad provide lessons in self-improvement, prudence, and honesty for young readers.

ROBERT MONTGOMERY BIRD: *The Hawks of Hawks Hollow.* A novel set in the years following the Revolutionary War. The romance recounts the fate of a Pennsylvania family torn apart by the conflict between American patriots and Tories. The well-received novel represents a shift in Bird's writing from romances of great historical periods to a domestic novel of contemporary times. Bird also publishes *The Infidel; or, The Fall of Mexico*, a sequel to *Calavar* (1834). The work is acclaimed by Poe in the *Southern Literary Messenger*.

THEODORE SEDGWICK FAY: *Norman Leslie: A Tale of the Present Times.* The story of a sensational New York murder case in which Leslie is tried and acquitted for the murder of a young girl who disappears and later resurfaces in Paris. Fay's best work, it receives immediate popular and critical praise. However, it is also remembered for Edgar Allan Poe's comment that it is "the most inestimable piece of balderdash with which the common sense of the good people of America were ever so openly or so villainously insulted."

JAMES HALL: *Tales of the Border.* Hall's third collection of short stories in three years contains seven tales, including "The Pioneer," a story of a man who hates the Indians for killing his family and abducting his sister, who, he later realizes, is living happily in the Indian village.

NATHANIEL HAWTHORNE: "The Ambitious Guest." First published in *The Token* and to be included in *Twice-Told Tales* (1837), Hawthorne's allegorical story recalls the confessions of the inhabitants of an isolated cottage in New Hampshire's White Mountains before a landslide hits. Hawthorne also publishes "Young Goodman Brown," a psychological allegory that would become one of Hawthorne's most critically acclaimed stories. Goodman Brown, a young Puritan in Salem, Massachusetts, leaves his wife and discovers a witches' sabbath in the forest, where he finds all of the prominent moral leaders of his community, as well as his wife, Faith. He realizes evil exists inherently in all humanity but can no longer see the good and spends the rest of his life in gloom and isolation. The story is first published in *New England Magazine* and would be included in *Mosses from an Old Manse* (1846).

HENRY WILLIAM HERBERT (1807–1858): *The Brothers: A Tale of the Fronde.* A popular historical romance concerning an English cavalier in France who witnesses a duel between two brothers and marries the woman over whom they were fighting. A review in the *New England Magazine* urges readers "to procure *The Brothers*, at once, and thus secure a valuable addition to their stores of fiction." Herbert immigrated to America from England in 1831, helped found the *American Monthly Magazine*, and, under the name "Frank Forrester," became the first sports writer in the United States.

JOHN PENDLETON KENNEDY: *Horse-Shoe Robinson.* This popular romance set during the American Revolution concerns the daughter of a Tory who secretly marries a patriot. The story is notable for its title protagonist, a crude but resourceful blacksmith, and also for its portrayal of the Battle of King's Mountain.

AUGUSTUS BALDWIN LONGSTREET (1790–1870): *Georgia Scenes, Characters, Incidents, &c. in the First Half Century of the Republic.* A popular collection of sketches on the customs, manner, wit, and dialect of the common frontier people. Attributed to "A Native Georgian," the sketches are based on Longstreet's experiences as a circuit judge, and they provide the first example of Southwestern humor and represent the first alternative to the plantation story in Southern literature.

JOSEPH CLAY NEAL (1807–1847): "Peter Brush, the Great Used Up." A sketch about a man who fails to win a political office and laments on a city curb. The most renowned sketch written by the Philadelphia journalist, who is remembered for his urban Northeast humor, it is published in the *Gentleman's Vade Mecum* and would be often reprinted without credit to the author.

EDGAR ALLAN POE: "Berenice." Poe's first story to be published in the *Southern Literary Messenger* after John Pendleton Kennedy had introduced him to the editor, T. W. White. In the story Egaeus is captivated by the white teeth of his beloved cousin Berenice, and when she falls into a trance after an epileptic seizure, he believes she has died and removes her teeth. Although White feared the story too grotesque for the magazine, Poe had convinced him that articles that are "ludicrous heightened into the grotesque" sell magazines. This initial publication would lead to Poe's numerous story contributions, critical reviews, and editorship of the *Messenger*. Poe also publishes "Morella" in the *Southern Literary Messenger;* it would be later included in *Tales of the Grotesque and Arabesque* (1840). Poe's story, regarded as a preliminary workup of his later work "Ligeia," concerns a dying woman who vows to return to life to punish her unloving husband. Poe's tale "The Unparalleled Adventures of One Hans Pfaal," describing a trip to the moon, is published in the *Southern Literary Messenger* and is one of the earliest examples of American science fiction.

CATHARINE MARIA SEDGWICK: *The Linwoods; or, "Sixty Years Since" in America.* A critically acclaimed historical romance concerning social life in New York City during the last two years of the American Revolution and the conflict between a Loyalist father and rebel son.

WILLIAM GILMORE SIMMS: *The Partisan, a Tale of the Revolution.* The first of Simms's Revolutionary romances concerns a Whig officer, Major Singleton, who leads a partisan effort against the British and Loyalists. The work is praised for its beauty of description by Edgar Allan Poe in the *Southern Literary Messenger.* It is notable for the character Captain Porgy, whom many consider the best comic character in American Romantic fiction, but whom Poe finds "an insufferable bore." The other books in his Revolutionary trilogy are *Mellichampe, a Legend of the Santee* (1836) and *Katharine Walton; or, The Rebel of Dorchester* (1851). Simms also publishes *The Yemassee.* The best known of his series of historical novels that he called "border romances," which deal with Southern frontier life in the eighteenth and nineteenth centuries, concerns the warfare between the Carolina colonists and the Yamasee Indians. It receives praise from the *American Monthly Magazine* for its realistic and sympathetic depictions of Native Americans.

WILLIAM LEETE STONE: *The Mysterious Bridal and Other Tales.* Stone's collection of gothic tales set in colonial New England invites comparisons with Hawthorne and displays his characteristic use of local color, history, and legend.

FREDERICK WILLIAM THOMAS: *Clinton Bradshaw; or, The Adventures of a Lawyer.* Thomas's first novel is an Americanization of the British novelist Edward Bulwer-Lytton's *Pelham* (1828), about upper-class life mixed with crime scenes. It features a courtroom scene that would set a standard for later fictional depictions.

DANIEL PIERCE THOMPSON (1795–1868): "May Martin." The Vermont lawyer and politician achieves his first literary success with this Vermont story, based on a local legend; it wins a prize from the *New-England Galaxy* for best original tale. More than fifty editions of the story would subsequently appear.

Literary Criticism and Scholarship

JOSEPH EMERSON WORCESTER: *A Gross Literary Fraud Exposed.* Noah Webster's accusation of plagiarism against his lexicographer rival prompts the so-called War of Dictionaries and Worcester's self-defense in this pamphlet.

Nonfiction

WILLIAM APES: *Indian Nullification of the Unconstitutional Law of Massachusetts.* Apes presents the Indian viewpoint concerning the Mashpee Revolt of 1833, in which inhabitants of the last surviving Indian town in Massachusetts had protested governmental control and the Indians' lack of autonomy. The work has been described as the first successful Indian rights protest in U.S. history.

HENRY CHARLES CAREY (1793–1879): *Essay on the Rate of Wages.* The author's first published work argues for the laissez-faire school of economics, which embraces the wage-fund theory. Carey opposes the theories of English economist David Ricardo and espouses free trade. He is considered the founder of the American school of economics.

LYDIA MARIA CHILD: *A History of the Condition of Women in Various Ages and Nations.* The final two volumes of Child's *Ladies' Family Library* provide biographical sketches of important women. The work became a source for feminists such as Sarah Grimké, and the popularity of the history, published in twenty editions in seven years, demonstrates the country's increasing interest in feminism.

CHARLES FENNO HOFFMAN (1806–1884): *A Winter in the West.* A collection of letters detailing Hoffman's horseback trip west to Cleveland, Detroit, Chicago, and St. Louis. First printed in the *American Monthly Magazine,* the letters are popular for their descriptions of America's westward expansion.

WASHINGTON IRVING: *A Tour on the Prairies.* The first volume of *The Crayon Miscellany,* which comprises three works published under the pseudonym "Geoffrey Crayon." *A Tour* is an account of Irving's travels westward from Arkansas into what is now Oklahoma and depicts his frontier adventures, including buffalo hunting, in a romantic reflection of western life.

FRANCES ANNE KEMBLE (1809–1895): *Journal.* The English actress who had toured America in 1832 records her observations of American life. She would later marry a Georgia plantation owner; her *Journal of a Residence on a Georgia Plantation,* with critique of slavery, would be published in 1863 to influence British opinion against the Confederacy.

SUSAN PAUL (1809–1841): *Memoir of James Jackson, the Attentive and Obedient Scholar....* The first biography by an African American published in the United States. Unnoticed until its rediscovery in 2000, the biography of a pious black child prodigy by his Boston teacher provides significant information about early African American education, reading, and family life in the North.

JAMES KIRKE PAULDING: *A Life of Washington.* Considered the standard biography of Washington until Irving's biography of the first president (1855). Poe's review exclaims, "There is no better literary manner than the manner of Mr. Paulding."

ELIZABETH PALMER PEABODY (1804–1894): *Record of a School, Exemplifying the General Principles of Spiritual Culture.* A record of the methods of discipline and inductive lessons at Amos Bronson Alcott's experimental Temple School, where Peabody served as an assistant from 1834 to 1836. The work advances the reputation of the school and is an important document in Transcendentalism and a record of Alcott's educational theories. Hawthorne's sister-in-law, whose Boston bookshop became a favorite meeting place for the Transcendentalist Club, Peabody opened the first kindergarten in the United States in 1860.

REMBRANDT PEALE (1778–1860): *A Manual of Drawing and Writing for the Use of Schools and Families.* Based on Peale's belief that drawing should and could be taught to everyone, this work presents a system of instruction. His most popular work, it would go through four editions by 1866 and stay in print for thirty years.

Poetry

JOSEPH RODMAN DRAKE: *The Culprit Fay and Other Poems.* This posthumous selection of Drake's works (he died in 1820) includes his most popular pieces, the title poem and "The American Flag," long a popular recitation.

WILLIAM DAVIS GALLAGHER (1808–1894): *Erato.* Three warmly received collections of verse, two published in 1835 and the last in 1837, that are noteworthy for their descriptions of life and nature in the West. Ralph Leslie Rusk, author of *The Literature of the Middle Western Frontier* (1925), said the collections hold "almost, if not quite, the best verses written on the frontier."

Publications and Events

The *New York Herald.* Founded by James Gordon Bennett (1795–1872) and edited after 1872 by the younger James Gordon Bennett (1841–1918), this daily featured the writings of authors such as Mark Twain and Richard Harding Davis, and it organized and financed explorer-reporter Sir Henry Stanley's expedition to Africa (1869–1872) to find the missionary David Livingstone. It later merged with the *New York Sun* (1920) and the *New-York Tribune* (1924) to create the *New York Herald Tribune,* a

Republican daily noted for its news coverage and columnists, such as Walter Lippmann. Circulation and labor problems forced closure of the newspaper in 1966.

The *Southern Literary Journal and Monthly Magazine.* A Charleston-based review devoted to chronicling Southern life and supporting Southern culture and slavery. Founded and edited by Daniel K. Whitaker, its primary contributor is William Gilmore Simms, whose most notable article is "American Criticism and Critics."

The *Western Messenger.* A monthly magazine, committed to delivering the culture and literature of the American West to the East and bringing New England Transcendentalist topics to the West, begins under the auspices of the Unitarian church. Edited by W. H. Channing, J. F. Clarke, and J. H. Perkins, the magazine featured work by Ralph Waldo Emerson, Margaret Fuller, Jones Very, Elizabeth Palmer Peabody, and Francis Parkman.

1836
Drama and Theater

RICHARD PENN SMITH: *The Actress of Padua.* Smith's last and most successful play is an adaptation of the French writer Victor Hugo's drama *Angelo, Tyran de Padoue.* Produced in 1851, it would run intermittently for twenty years. The melodramatic story is set in sixteenth-century Padua and concerns the passions of Angelo, the deputy of Venice, who is jealous of, but does not love, his wife, Catharina. Angelo is in love with an actress, Thisbe, but both she and Catharina are in love with Rodolpho.

Fiction

ROBERT MONTGOMERY BIRD: *Sheppard Lee.* Bird's anonymously published novel deals with the popular idea of metempsychosis, or reincarnation. The cultural satire follows an unsatisfied farmer who undergoes a spiritual journey in which he overtakes the bodies of men he thinks live better lives than his own. Critically hailed, the novel deftly analyzes and comically portrays many disparate sectors of 1830s America, including the agrarian, political, and aristocratic ways of life in the North and the South.

LYDIA MARIA CHILD: *Philothea.* A romance set in classical Greece, which the literary critic C. C. Felton lauds in the *North American Review,* writing, "Every page of it breathes the inspiration of genius, and shows a highly cultivated taste, in literature and art."

WILLIAM DUNLAP: *Thirty Years Ago; or, The Memoirs of a Water Drinker.* The playwright's only novel is a temperance story about an actor's battle with alcohol.

RICHARD HILDRETH (1807–1865): *The Slave; or, Memoirs of Archy Moore.* The first U.S. antislavery novel deals with an octoroon, the illegitimate son of a Virginia planter, who is torn from his family when he is sold. Although the book is not immediately popular, it would receive greater attention when republished in the 1850s.

JOSEPH HOLT INGRAHAM (1809–1860): *Lafitte: The Pirate of the Gulf.* Based loosely on fact, the novel by the popular Maine author of historical romances is a melodramatic telling of the pirate's adventures at the Battle of New Orleans during the War of 1812. The work wins the author critical and financial success — and the first edition quickly sold out its twenty-five hundred copies — prompting Ingraham to continue writing novels.

SUSAN RIDLEY SEDGWICK (c. 1789–1867): *The Young Emigrants.* A children's story about a family that moves from New York to Ohio. Like her other works, the novel by the sister-in-law of novelist Catharine Maria Sedgwick is sentimental and didactic but is important as one of the first American works of nonreligious children's fiction.

FREDERICK WILLIAM THOMAS: *East and West.* Thomas's second novel relocates elements of the popular English novel to the American setting of western Pennsylvania.

NATHANIEL BEVERLY TUCKER (1784–1851): *George Balcombe.* Although he publishes the book anonymously, Tucker's career as a novelist begins with this realistic story of plantation life. Edgar Allan Poe praises it as "the best American novel." Also, outraged by the effect of the Nullification Proclamation and the Force Bill on the doctrine of state sovereignty, Tucker writes *The Partisan Leader: A Tale of the Future*, hoping this romance will swing the 1836 election away from Martin Van Buren. Set in 1849 and bearing the false imprint date of 1856, the novel depicts Virginia's struggle between loyalty to the Union and the prospect of joining a prosperous Southern Confederacy as Van Buren attempts to win a fourth term as president. Tucker's best-known novel, it is renowned for its prediction of the Civil War, during which it would be distributed as propaganda.

Literary Criticism and Scholarship

EDWARD SHERMAN GOULD (1805–1885): *American Criticism of American Literature.* Gould mounts a reactionary argument against native writing, which he judges inferior to the standard set by English writers. He was a New York writer of fiction and journalistic hack work.

Nonfiction

AMOS BRONSON ALCOTT: "The Doctrine and Discipline of Human Culture." A profession of Alcott's religious faith, which argues that humans can find divine truth without organized religion. Intended to outline his Transcendentalist beliefs, the work would be little noticed until included in his highly controversial *Conversations with Children on the Gospels*, published later that year. This controversial work concerning Alcott's experimental Temple School describes Alcott's liberal theories of education, taken from a transcript of conversations he had held with his students on a variety of topics, including birth and the origins of life. While the work won support from Emerson and J. F. Clarke, many students were removed from the school after its publication, and the *Boston Courier* called the work "obscene and blasphemous."

WILLIAM APES: *Eulogy on King Philip.* In the author's last important public oration, Apes elevates the seventeenth-century Native American chief "King Philip" to the same importance as George Washington as a national hero. Apes compares the Native American cause to the American Revolution and argues that Indian history and culture should not be considered separate from American history.

ORESTES BROWNSON (1803–1876): *New Views of Christianity, Society, and the Church.* Brownson's first book argues against organized Christianity. Brownson, a New England clergyman and editor, was a leading Transcendentalist before converting to Catholicism in 1844.

JAMES FENIMORE COOPER: *Sketches of Switzerland.* Cooper chronicles four tours drawn from his journals, providing lessons in appreciating the picturesque. Creeping into his writing is a lament for the lost pristine American landscape compared to the unspoiled Swiss scenes.

DAVY CROCKETT: *Col. Crockett's Exploits and Adventures in Texas.* Purportedly written by Davy Crockett himself before his death at the Alamo, the book is assumed to be the work of Richard Penn Smith. Ten thousand copies of the book sell within a year, and an English reprint also proves popular.

RALPH WALDO EMERSON: *Nature.* Emerson's first major work brings together all of the basic tenets of Transcendentalism through a discussion of nature and its uses (commodity, beauty, language, discipline). It contends that expansion of the human soul is possible through a reconnection with nature and develops Emerson's idea of the "Over-Soul." Although the essay is published anonymously, many know Emerson to be the author, and it establishes him as the key figure of Transcendentalism.

PETER FORCE: *Tracts and Other Papers Relating Principally to the Origin, Settlement, and Progress of the Colonies in North America.* A four-volume collection of historical

Ralph Waldo Emerson

documents tracing the history of the colonies. The work makes important documents available to the public, including a description of New England by Captain John Smith written in 1616 and Patrick Tailfer's 1741 chronicle of Georgia from its settlement to 1740.

ALBERT GALLATIN (1761–1849): *Synopsis of the Indian Tribes Within the United States, East of the Rocky Mountains and in the British and Russian Possessions in North America.* The most important work of the frontier political leader, it earns Gallatin a reputation as "the father of American ethnology."

DANIEL GOOKIN: *An Historical Account of the Doings and Sufferings of the Christian Indians in New England in the Years 1675, 1676, 1677.* Written in 1677 and published by the American Antiquarian Society Transactions in 1836, this history recounts the disgraceful treatment of John Eliot's converts by anti-Indian groups during King Philip's War. The work is an attempt to present a history of the Christian Indians, which is lacking in other histories of the time, including those by Increase Mather and William Hubbard.

ANGELINA EMILY GRIMKÉ (1805–1879): *An Appeal to the Christian Women of the South.* Angelina, like her sister, Sarah, after moving to Philadelphia becomes an out-spoken opponent of slavery. This is her first publication directed at her former fellow Southerners. Copies are destroyed by Southern postmasters, and Angelina is warned not to return to her home in Charleston, South Carolina.

SARAH MOORE GRIMKÉ (1792–1873): *Epistle to the Clergy of the Southern States.* This is the first publication of the South Carolina–born writer who moved to Philadelphia and, along with her sister, Angelina, becomes an outspoken opponent of slavery. It refutes the biblical justification for slavery offered by Southern ministers.

JAMES HALL AND THOMAS L. MCKENNEY (1785–1859): *History of the Indian Tribes of North America, with Biographical Sketches and Anecdotes of the Principal Chiefs.* This important Native American history brings together portraits of prominent Indians that had been originally painted for the War Department, as well as biographical sketches and historical information, including descriptions of territories, tribal populations and relations, government, and customs. The work is also important because it contains copies of original paintings by Charles King and George Catlin that would be lost in a fire in 1865 at the Smithsonian Institution.

WASHINGTON IRVING: *Astoria; or, Anecdotes of an Enterprise Beyond the Rocky Mountains.* An exciting history of the wealthy merchant John Jacob Astor's Pacific Fur Company (1810–1813), which he had established in Fort Clatsop, Oregon, and sold to British traders during the War of 1812. Astor collaborated with Irving, providing records and helping gather former employees for interviews; the work remains a valuable history of the early fur trade.

JARENA LEE (1783–?): *The Life and Religious Experience of Jarena Lee, Giving an Account of Her Call to Preach the Gospel.* Lee, an itinerant preacher, free-born in Cape May, New Jersey, becomes the first African American woman to publish an extended account of her own life; she is also the first African American woman officially recognized as a preacher by an established church. She would write a longer version, *Religious Experience and Journal of Mrs. Jarena Lee,* in 1849.

WILLIAM HOLMES MCGUFFEY (1800–1873): *Eclectic Readers.* School readers comprised of moral and literary lessons and readings by English writers. They are compiled by the professor of languages, philosophy, and philology at Miami University (Ohio) for the Cincinnati publishers Truman and Smith, who wanted a series of textbooks for the newly added western states of Ohio, Kentucky, and Indiana. The six books in the Eclectic

Reader series (*First and Second 1836, Second and Third 1837, The Speller 1838*, and *The Rhetorical Guide 1841*) are estimated to have sold 122 million copies.

MARIA MONK (c. 1816–c. 1849): *Awful Disclosures of the Hotel Dieu Nunnery of Montreal.* This purported exposé of scandalous activities in a Montreal nunnery by an escaped nun details rapes, torture, and infanticide so luridly that it would be considered by the Kinsey Institute to be the first pornographic text published in America. The anti-Catholic book sells 200,000 copies, becoming one of the bestsellers of the decade. The author's claims are proven fraudulent after an investigation by two Protestant clergymen. The actual identity of the author remains uncertain but has been at different times attributed to George Bourne, J. J. Slocum, and Theodore Dwight.

JAMES KIRKE PAULDING: *Slavery in the United States.* A discussion of the legal, social, and economic aspects of slavery, defending the Southern point of view on the basis of states' rights and preservation of the union.

JARED SPARKS: *The Works of Benjamin Franklin.* Published in ten volumes, Sparks's exhaustive research and skillful search for new material produce a popular and admired work. Republished several times, it flatteringly and uncritically portrays Franklin as a sage.

ROBERT WALSH (1784–1859): *Didactics, Social, Literary, and Political.* A collection of essays on a variety of topics, many of which had been published earlier in the journalist and editor's career. The work and the man are praised by Poe in the *Southern Literary Messenger*, and literary historian William Charvat claims that the work is "a monument to the influence of Scotch philosophy and aesthetics on the American mind."

HENRY WHEATON (1785–1848): *Elements of International Law.* Originally published in French, the sixth edition of this landmark compilation of regulations that govern behaviors between countries would become the diplomatic handbook in the United States when Congress purchased five hundred copies for its diplomats abroad and at home.

NATHANIEL PARKER WILLIS: *Inklings of Adventure.* A popular collection of short sentimental travel sketches and romantic stories attributed to "Philip Slingsby." Originally published as letters to the *New York Mirror*, they are popular for providing a personal acquaintance with fashionable Europe, but many critics condemn them for their indiscretion.

Poetry

ELIZABETH MARGARET CHANDLER (1807–1834): *Poetical Works.* The Quaker writer's antislavery and descriptive verses, including "The Captured Slave" and "The Sunset Hour," are published posthumously, along with her *Essays, Philosophical and Moral.*

OLIVER WENDELL HOLMES: *Poems.* A collection of early verse filled with humor, especially as seen in "Ballad of the Oysterman" and "My Aunt," as well as pathos in "The Last Leaf" and "Old Ironsides." His first collection of poetry, it is published in the same year that he graduates from Harvard Medical School. John Gorham Palfrey's review calls Holmes "a man of genius" and expresses hopes that the positive reception of the book would "induce him to come before the public again."

JOHN GREENLEAF WHITTIER: "Mogg Megone." Whittier's critically acclaimed poem concerns Native American life in Maine and the relationship between Catholic missionaries and Indians. The *North American Review* calls it "a work of real and distinguished power."

Publications and Events

The *Philadelphia Public Ledger.* Founded as the city's first penny paper and edited by W. H. Swain, this newspaper advocated independent voting and a free press, voiced its opposition to the Bank of the United States, and after its sale to G. W. Childs (1864) became well known for its carefully substantiated attacks on war profiteering, monopolies, and debased currency and its editorials on political and moral corruption. The *Philadelphia Inquirer* took over the paper in 1934, renaming it the *Evening Public Ledger.* It ceased publication in 1942.

1837
Drama and Theater

CHARLOTTE MARY SANFORD BARNES (1818–1863): *Octavia Bragaldi; or, The Confession.* The author's first and best-known drama is originally produced in New York City, starring Barnes in the title role. The tragedy in blank verse follows attempts by Edgar Allan Poe and Thomas Holley Chivers to adapt the true events of the Beauchamp murder, which had caused a sensation in Kentucky in 1825. The play, set by Barnes in fifteenth-century Milan, details accumulating acts of deception, seduction, jealousy, and murder, leading to the heroine's suicide.

JOSEPH STEVENS JONES: *The Green Mountain Boy.* Jones's play is noteworthy for providing actor G. H. Hills, the preeminent interpreter of the stage Yankee during the period, one of his most famous roles as Jedediah Homebred, a Yankee servant with an inexhaustible supply of homespun sayings.

EPES SARGENT (1813–1880): *Velasco.* The Boston writer and journalist's most important play deals with Rodrigo

Diaz, the Cid, and a love triangle between Izidora, Hernando, her betrothed, and Velaso, whom she loves. It is rich with fights, revenge plots, and poisonings. Sargent had written the play for the actress Ellen Tree. Also produced is Sargent's *The Bride of Genoa*, a five-act romantic tragedy about the Plebian Revolt in Genoa in 1393. This play had been written for the actress Josephine Clifton, who appeared in it successfully in Boston. It would be later staged in New York and printed in the *New World* in 1842 as *The Genoese*.

NATHANIEL PARKER WILLIS: *Bianca Visconti; or, The Heart Overtasked.* A five-act verse tragedy written in competition for the play best suited to the talents of the actress Josephine Clifton. Well received, even after Clifton left the role, it is set in fifteenth-century Italy and deals with the duke of Milan, Francesco Sforza, and his wife, Bianca Visconti.

Fiction

ROBERT MONTGOMERY BIRD: *Nick of the Woods; or, The Jibbenainosay.* A novel set in Kentucky in the aftermath of the Revolutionary War concerns a man with a split personality who is mockingly known in some circles as "Brother Nathan," for his complete hatred for violence, but who is also revealed to be "Nick of the Woods," the much-feared Indian killer. It is considered Bird's best novel and was immensely popular in its time.

THOMAS CHANDLER HALIBURTON (1796–1865): *The Clockmaker; or, The Sayings and Doings of Samuel Slick, of Slickville.* The Nova Scotia humorist introduces the Yankee peddler Sam Slick, who had first appeared in *The Novascotian*, a Halifax newspaper. This is the first collection of dialect humor celebrating the virtues of America at the expense of the gullible Nova Scotians. The popularity of Haliburton's work would earn him the title "the father of North American humor."

NATHANIEL HAWTHORNE: *Twice-Told Tales.* A collection of thirty-nine previously published stories that Hawthorne believed "seemed best worth offering to the public a second time." The publication was not financially successful, and a second edition in 1842 also fared poorly. Some of Hawthorne's masterpieces, such as "The Minister's Black Veil," "Dr. Heidegger's Experiment," and "The Ambitious Guest," are included. Poe's review of the 1842 edition, recognizing Hawthorne's genius, also includes one of the defining critiques of the short story form.

WASHINGTON IRVING: *The Adventures of Captain Bonneville in the Rocky Mountains and the Far West.* A narrative of Benjamin Louis Eulalie de Bonneville's (1793–1878) trapping expedition in the Rocky Mountains, taken from the explorer's personal maps and papers. The objective novel provides eastern readers with a picture of the American effort on the frontier and shows Irving's sympathy for Native Americans.

VICTOR SEJOUR (1817–1874): "Le Mulatre" (The mulatto). Published in Paris in a journal sponsored by a society of men of color, Sejour's antislavery short story describing the social and psychological impact of life under slavery is considered the earliest known work of African American fiction. The author, a free black man from New Orleans, would later contribute an ode to Napoleon to *Les Cenelles* (1845), the first anthology of African American poetry.

WILLIAM WARE (1797–1852): *Letters of Lucius M. Piso, from Palmyra, to His Friend Marcus Curtius, at Rome* (republished in 1838 as *Zenobia; or, The Fall of Palmyra, an Historical Romance*). First published in the *Knickerbocker Magazine*, the novel by the Unitarian clergyman describes events of third-century Rome and the life of early Christians, presenting a Unitarian point of view. It becomes so widely popular that Ware is motivated to produce a sequel, *Probus*, in 1839. These novels are notable in that they present religious education in the still-suspect novel form.

Nonfiction

RALPH WALDO EMERSON: *The American Scholar.* Address before the Phi Beta Kappa Society of Harvard, characterizing a scholar as one with "self-trust" and calling for the leadership of American thinkers. Oliver Wendell Holmes calls the speech "our intellectual Declaration of Independence," and all five hundred printed copies of the address sell out within one month.

PETER FORCE: *American Archives.* The historian's most important work comprises nine volumes of original documents and correspondence important to American history.

ANGELINA EMILY GRIMKÉ: *Appeal to the Women of the Nominally Free States.* Grimké widens her argument on behalf of abolition to gain support in the North while castigating prejudicial views by nonslaveholders.

JOHN TREAT IRVING (1812–1906): *The Hawk Chief: A Tale of the Indian Country.* An account by the nephew of Washington Irving of his own experiences on an expedition west, led by Henry L. Ellsworth in 1833. It records the "pleasurable excitement" of the travels and notes the customs of some Indian tribes.

ELIZA LESLIE: *Directions for Cookery: Being a System of the Art, in Its Various Branches.* The most popular cookbook of the nineteenth century, going through fifty printings.

John Lloyd Stephens

HARRIET MARTINEAU (1802–1876): *Society in America.* The English social critic evaluates American economic, political, and social institutions based on her travels (which would be chronicled in *Retrospect of Western Travel*, 1838). Her criticism, particularly of the South and slavery, would prompt a harsh personal attack from William Gilmore Simms in *Slavery in America* (1838).

ANDREWS NORTON (1786–1853): *The Evidences of the Genuineness of the Gospels.* An examination of the New Testament canon, using information outside the Bible to defend the idea of divine inspiration. Norton's most important work, it would be published in several editions and helps establish his position in American Unitarianism and his reputation as a scholar. It is one of the earliest American examples of critical studies of biblical literature.

JOHN LLOYD STEPHENS (1805–1852): *Incidents of Travel in Egypt, Arabia, Petraea, and the Holy Land.* An account of the New Jersey author's travels, the book wins immediate popular and critical acclaim. The *London Monthly Review* proclaims, "Perhaps no writer has ever produced a better or more satisfactory book of travels, who had no other guide but the Holy Scriptures and a good general education to pioneer and encourage him." A confidential mission to Central America for President Van Buren

would produce *Incidents of Travel in Central America, Chiapas, and Yucatan* (1841).

CALVIN ELLIS STOWE (1802–1886): *Report on Elementary Instruction in Europe.* A report of Stowe's study of public education in Europe and recommendations of Prussian practices including state-funded teacher preparation. The Ohio legislature, for whom he conducted the study, ordered more than eight thousand copies of the report, placing one in each school district. It would also be printed for the legislatures of Massachusetts, Pennsylvania, Michigan, and other states and subsequently printed in *Common Schools and Teachers' Seminaries* (1839) and *Reports on Education by John Griscom, Victor Cousin, Calvin E. Stowe* (1930), by E. W. Knight. Stowe's work would be influential in defining policies for the development of American Midwestern education. (He had married the future writer Harriet Beecher in 1836.)

GEORGE TUCKER: *The Life of Thomas Jefferson.* The first authorized biography of Jefferson. Though complimentary, it is the fairest nineteenth-century treatment of the former president, based on Tucker's personal acquaintance with the man and his contemporaries, extensive research, and conversations with Jefferson's family.

Poetry

FREDERICK WILLIAM SHELTON (1815–1881): *The Trollopiad; or, Travelling Gentlemen in America.* Shelton's verse satire takes aim at British travel writer Frances Trollope for her harsh views on Americans published in *Domestic Manners of the Americans* (1832).

JOHN GREENLEAF WHITTIER: *Poems Written During the Progress of the Abolition Question in the United States.* Whittier's first collection of poetry is published in an unauthorized edition by Boston abolitionists and the next year expanded by Whittier and published as *Poems*. It contains his attacks on slavery, including "Clerical Oppressors," which assails Southern religious officials who use Christianity to uphold slavery, and "Stanzas," which discusses the irony of America's dual commitment to freedom and the slave system.

Publications and Events

The *Baltimore Sun*. This nonpartisan newspaper makes its debut, attracting wide attention during the Mexican War by publishing news of the capture of Veracruz before the War Department released the information. During the Civil War it favored the South but opposed secession. H. L. Mencken worked on the *Sun* (1906–1916, 1918–1941), and between 1931 and 1949 the paper or its staff members won eight Pulitzer Prizes.

Gentleman's Magazine. This monthly Philadelphia periodical, founded by William Evans Burton (1804–1860), who later added his name to the title, debuts. It featured articles on art, literature, sports, the theater, reprints and translations from English and foreign magazines, and tales of frontier life. Edgar Allan Poe was the magazine's editor from 1839 until 1840 when the magazine merged with *Atkinson's Casket* to become *Graham's Magazine.* Poe contributed some of his short stories, including "The Fall of the House of Usher" and "William Wilson."

The *United States Magazine and Democratic Review.* Monthly magazine featuring authors such as Whittier, Bryant, Poe, Whitman, and Hawthorne debuts. It is notable for its political emphasis, which would increase in 1841 when the periodical moved to New York and overtook Brownson's *Quarterly Review* in 1842. The magazine's most famous years were 1837–1846, when edited by John L. O'Sullivan, who coined the term *manifest destiny* in its pages.

1838
Fiction

ROBERT MONTGOMERY BIRD: *Peter Pilgrim; or, A Rambler's Recollections.* A collection of magazine sketches notable for providing the first detailed description of Mammoth Cave and a vivid account of life on a Mississippi steamboat.

JAMES FENIMORE COOPER: *Homeward Bound; or, The Chase: A Tale of the Sea.* The story of the Effingham family's voyage home after several years in Europe, providing a social commentary through their encounters with the other passengers. It is followed the same year with the sequel *Home as Found.* Cooper had written the novels after he returned to America, following seven years abroad. He found the country, to his great displeasure, much changed. He was particularly frustrated by a controversy with his neighbors over land on Otsego Lake, which led to lawsuits and personal attacks in Whig newspapers.

ELIZA LEE FOLLEN (1787–1860): *Sketches of Married Life.* Unlike other sentimental domestic fiction of the period that advocated submissiveness for wives, Follen's novel presents an independent heroine who supports her family and defies society by going to the hospital to nurse her fiancé. Follen was a Boston writer married to Charles Follen, the first German professor at Harvard. She was active in the antislavery cause, producing the well-known tract *A Letter to Mothers in the Free States* (1855).

CAROLINE HOWARD GILMAN: *Recollections of a Southern Matron.* Following the success of her earlier *Recol-* *lections of a New England Housekeeper* (1834), Gilman publishes this similar novel, an idealistic portrayal of plantation life in a chronicle of a young girl being raised in the South.

NATHANIEL HAWTHORNE: "Lady Eleanor's Mantle." Originally published in the *Democratic Review* and to be included in *Twice-Told Tales* (1842), Hawthorne's story is a moral fable about pride and takes place during a Boston smallpox epidemic.

JOSEPH HOLT INGRAHAM: *Burton; or, The Sieges.* Ingraham capitalizes on the recent death of Aaron Burr with this novel treating Burr's activities during the Revolution, particularly during the sieges of Quebec and New York. The historical adventure alternates with the title character's romantic assaults on three young ladies.

JOHN PENDLETON KENNEDY: *Rob of the Bowl: A Legend of St. Inigoe.* A historical novel concerning the attempted overthrow of the Catholic Lord Baltimore by the Protestants in Maryland in 1681.

JOSEPH CLAY NEAL: *Charcoal Sketches; or, Scenes in a Metropolis.* A collection of urban sketches, which concern comical city men whose faults are revealed through soliloquies. The volume would go through several editions and be reprinted, unattributed, in volume two of *The Pic Nic Papers* (1841), erroneously said to have been edited by Charles Dickens.

LAUGHTON OSBORN: *The Vision of Rubeta.* A historical romance set in New York with vicious assaults on authors such as William Wordsworth and William Leete Stone. It had been written after critics denounced Osborn's earlier work, *The Confessions of a Poet*, which also received much negative criticism; Edgar Allan Poe, however, had extolled the genius of the author in his "Sketches of the Literati."

EDGAR ALLAN POE: "Ligeia." One of Poe's most famous stories and the one its author cited as his best is the tale of a woman who becomes ill and dies, though she has great desire to live. After her husband marries a woman he does not love, Rowena, Ligeia's powerful will to live brings her back into the body of Rowena. First published in the *Baltimore Museum*, it would be included in *Tales of the Grotesque and Arabesque* (1840). Poe also publishes *The Narrative of Arthur Gordon Pym, of Nantucket*, a fictional tale based partially on fact concerning the sea adventures of a young boy who stows away on a New Bedford whaler, which sails from Nantucket to the South Seas in 1827. Poe had used J. N. Reynolds's "Report of the Committee on Naval Affairs" (1836) and Benjamin Morell's *Narrative of Four Voyages to the South Seas and Pacific* (1832) as sources for the work.

WILLIAM WARE: *Probus; or, Rome in the Third Century.* The sequel to Ware's highly successful *Zenobia* (1837) concerns Aurelian's persecution of Christians. The work presents philosophical comparisons of contemporary Boston and third-century Rome and contains Ware's most compelling fictional treatment of slavery's injustice.

Nonfiction

JAMES FENIMORE COOPER: *The American Democrat; or, Hints on the Social and Civic Relations of the United States of America.* A criticism of America written after seven years in Europe, this book presents Cooper's conservative opinion of American government and society. Cooper was attacked in the press for this work and his other post-European writings on America. He won many libel suits against newspapers but lost his fortune in the process.

RALPH WALDO EMERSON: *Divinity School Address.* A lecture given to the senior students at Harvard Divinity School that became Emerson's most controversial proclamation. In it, Emerson criticizes traditional Christianity as empty and calls for a revitalization of spirit. He urges the new ministers to speak the truth of their own experience because they, like Jesus Christ, are capable of the Divine. Printed as an essay later that year and collected in *Nature, Addresses, and Lectures* (1849), the address wins favor from William Ellery Channing and Theodore Parker but is disdained by Andrews Norton, who would assail it in *On the Latest Form of Infidelity* (1839).

CAROLINE HOWARD GILMAN: *Poetry of Travelling in the United States.* This lively work arose from the author's travels in the North and the South. The often humorous work represented Gilman's attempt to unite the two regions under the auspices of goodwill and brotherhood.

SARAH MOORE GRIMKÉ: *Letters on the Equality of the Sexes and the Conditions of Women.* Grimké adds her voice to the cause of women's rights despite being urged by abolitionists not to depart from the focus of the anti-slavery cause.

FRANCIS LIEBER (1800–1872): *Manual of Political Ethics.* This two-volume handbook by the German-born political philosopher who immigrated to the United States in 1827 considers various aspects of ethics and morality for the state and its citizens. Used as a textbook at Harvard and by assorted courts, it is the first methodical study of political science in America and covers a range of topics including public opinion, voting, and political parties. According to the jurist Joseph Story, the work "abounds with profound views of government."

SAMUEL PARKER (1779–1866): *Journal of an Exploring Tour Beyond the Rocky Mountains.* The work that estab-

William Hickling Prescott

lishes Parker's literary reputation is an account of his exploration of Oregon for the American Board of Commissioners for Foreign Missionaries, during which he established friendly relationships with Native Americans. The work goes through several editions and is also published in Great Britain.

WILLIAM HICKLING PRESCOTT (1796–1859): *History of the Reign of Ferdinand and Isabella, the Catholic.* The Massachusetts historian's first published work is an engaging account of a celebrated era in Spanish history. An immediate commercial bestseller, it is acclaimed by scholars internationally and would be followed by his most enduring work, *The History of the Conquest of Mexico* (1843).

OLE RYNNING (1809–1838): *A True Account of America for the Information and Help of Peasant and Commoner.* Rynning's travel book depicts the government, language, physical features, and possibilities for success in America. The Norwegian author's observations would create an enormous stir in his homeland, and some attribute increased numbers of nineteenth-century immigrants from Norway to the book's publication.

JOHN SANDERSON (1783–1844): *Sketches of Paris: In Familiar Letters to His Friends.* An account of the teacher and writer's experiences and perceptions of France, where he had traveled for health reasons in 1835. Noted for its astute and striking descriptions, it became popular in the United States, is published in London as *The American in Paris* (1838), and would be later translated into French by Jules Janin.

WILLIAM GILMORE SIMMS: *Slavery in America*. Simms responds to Harriet Martineau's criticism of the South and its "peculiar institution" in her book *Society in America* (1837) with a vicious ad hominem attack on the Englishwoman's character and deafness.

JOHN LLOYD STEPHENS: *Incidents of Travel in Greece, Turkey, Russia, and Poland*. Motivated by the success of *Incidents of Travel in Egypt, Arabia, Petraea, and the Holy Land* (1837), Stephens publishes this account of his European travels in Greece from Missolonghi to Athens and on to Russia, where he had been appalled by the condition of the serfs, and into Poland, where he had heard a firsthand account of the Battle of Crakow by a young boy. Like the earlier work, this achieves great success, reaching its seventh edition by 1839.

WILLIAM LEETE STONE: *Life of Joseph Brant Thayendanegea: Including the Border Wars of the American Revolution*. A biography of the Mohawk Indian who led the Iroquois against the Revolutionary colonials, the book refutes the popular belief that Brant had participated in the Seneca Massacre of settlers in Wyoming, an argument later proven correct. The work is notable for its unprejudiced treatment of both the Native Americans and colonials and its use of primary sources.

ALEXIS, COMTE DE TOCQUEVILLE (1805–1859): *Democracy in America*. The first American edition of the French writer's astute observations about American traits and tendencies (first published in French as *Démocratie in Amérique*). It is widely regarded as one of the greatest studies of the American character and the implications of democracy on politics, economy, and culture. Tocqueville toured the United States from 1831 to 1832 at the request of the French government to report on the American prison system.

JOHN GREENLEAF WHITTIER: *Narrative of James Williams, an American Slave*. Published anonymously by the American Anti-Slavery Society, this is a transcription and reworking of a slave narrative.

Poetry

JAMES RUSSELL LOWELL (1819–1891): "Class Poem." Lowell's first publication is a satire on new ideas and reforms such as Transcendentalism, abolition, women's rights, and temperance. Lowell would later regret his attempt at humor at the expense of ideas that he later supported. His first collection of apprentice works, *A Year's Life and Other Poems*, would appear in 1841.

GEORGE POPE MORRIS: *The Deserted Bride and Other Poems*. A successful collection of verse to be published in

numerous editions, it contains the author's most popular poem, "Woodman, Spare That Tree!" originally published in the *New York Mirror* in 1830.

1839
Drama and Theater

JAMES EWELL HEATH (1792–1862): *Whigs and Democrats; or, Love of No Politics*. Published anonymously and meant to prove that America holds sufficient topics for drama, the play by the Virginia author and politician is a spirited satire of rural elections in Virginia. It is an example of several contemporary plays depicting conflict between political parties.

JOSEPH STEVENS JONES (1809–1877): *The People's Lawyer*. The Boston actor and playwright's best-known play tells the tale of the defense of Charles Otis, a poor clerk who, framed by his co-worker, is accused of stealing. Its popularity rests on the sharp country Yankee Solon Shingle, who humorously interrupts the action with impertinent remarks. The actor John E. Owens wins great success as the Yankee, making his final performance as Shingle in New York in 1884.

NATHANIEL PARKER WILLIS: *Tortesa; or, The Usurer*. Willis's romantic drama concerns a Florentine moneylender who longs to marry the daughter of a count to gain status but ultimately allows her to be with Angelo, whom she truly loves. The play is held in high regard by Edgar Allan Poe, who calls it the best drama by an American writer to date.

Fiction

CHARLES FREDERICK BRIGGS (1804–1877): *The Adventures of Harry Franco: A Tale of the Great Panic*. Briggs's first novel is a somewhat autobiographical story of a young man's search for gentility, virtue, and success in a large city and at sea. The success of the novel wins Briggs a job writing regularly for the *Knickerbocker Magazine*. He would later go on to edit the *Broadway Journal*, *Putnam's Magazine*, and the *New York Times*.

CAROLINE STANSBURY KIRKLAND (1801–1864): *A New Home—Who'll Follow? Or, Glimpses of Western Life*. A popular novel describing Kirkland's experiences on the frontier in Michigan, written under the pseudonym "Mrs. Mary Clavers." The book provides an amusing and realistic look at a woman's view of the people and customs of the frontier and her transformation from prejudice to participation in this new land. The granddaughter of Joseph Stansbury, Kirkland would become one of the first settlers of Pinckney, Michigan.

HENRY WADSWORTH LONGFELLOW: *Hyperion: A Romance*. The author's most vigorous prose work is

Edgar Allan Poe

autobiographical, proceeding from his study of German Romanticism. The narrative follows Paul Fleming, who travels about Europe in search of the elusive blue rose, a German mythical symbol of the unobtainable. Although achieving only moderate success and sometimes antagonistic reviews at the time, the work would find an audience with later American travelers in Europe.

GEORGE POPE MORRIS: *The Little Frenchman and His Water Lots, with Other Sketches of the Times.* Morris, best known for his sentimental poem "Woodman, Spare That Tree!" offers a collection of realistic contemporary sketches and tales. The title work is one of the earliest fictional portrayals of an unscrupulous New York City realtor.

EDGAR ALLAN POE: "The Fall of the House of Usher." Poe's classic horror story concerns the last remaining members of a cursed family, a twin brother and sister who die simultaneously. It is the most significant work that Poe contributed to *Burton's Gentleman's Magazine*, which he coedited during his most prolific literary period. Poe also publishes "William Wilson." Considered one of Poe's best stories, it concerns a man haunted since his youth by his alter ego, whom he eventually kills in a sword fight. At his death, his double tells Wilson, "In me didst thou exist — and in my death, see by this image, which is thine own, how utterly thou hast murdered thyself." The story would be a source for Robert Louis Stevenson's *The Strange Case of Dr. Jekyll and Mr. Hyde* (1885).

DANIEL PIERCE THOMPSON (fl. 1830s–1840s): *The Green Mountain Boys.* A popular historical romance honoring Ethan Allen's militia, who were organized to defend the "New Hampshire Grants" of Vermont from New York land-jobbers and later captured the fortress of Ticonderoga during the American Revolution.

Nonfiction

JAMES GILLESPIE BIRNEY (1792–1857): *Letter on the Political Obligations of Abolitionists.* In an antislavery report originally published in the *Boston Emancipator*, the southern antislavery leader speaks out against the prevailing policies of the American Anti-Slavery Society and abolitionist William Lloyd Garrison. Birney strongly advocates political action over simple moral argument as the means to achieve the goals of abolitionism.

JAMES FENIMORE COOPER: *History of the Navy.* The first attempted American maritime history studies the beginnings and expansion of the navy, gives vivid accounts of battles, and considers the future of the institution. Although Cooper's account of the Battle of Lake Erie has been questioned regarding its veracity, the overall work is lauded as accurate.

RICHARD HENRY DANA JR. (1815–1882): "Cruelty to Seamen." Dana's first publication appears in the *American Jurist*, announcing the theme he would elaborate in *Two Years Before the Mast* (1840). To regain his health, Dana had sailed to California as a common sailor in 1834 and had vowed to redress the grievances suffered by sailors.

WILLIAM DUNLAP: *History of the New Netherlands, Province of New York, and State of New York.* A meticulous early history of New York, which Evert Augustus Duyckinck's *Cyclopaedia of American Literature* (1875) would call "a work of industry and research." In press at the time of Dunlap's death, it demonstrates Dunlap's disdain of slavery, prejudice, and mistreatment of Native Americans.

ZENAS LEONARD (1809–1857): *Narrative of the Adventures of Zenas Leonard, Fur Trader.* An account of an expedition to Utah, Nevada, and California, led by John Reddeford Walker for Captain Benjamin Eulalie de Bonneville, which Leonard, a fur trapper, had joined in 1833 as the official clerk. First published in serial form in the *Clearfield Republican*, the work remains an important source of information about the expedition, the life of trappers, and the people of Spanish California and the Upper Missouri.

FREDERICK MARRYAT (1792–1848): *Diary in America, with Remarks on Its Institutions.* The British naval captain and popular adventure novelist offers his account of his travels (1837–1839) comparing British and American governments and customs. His often caustic comments would provoke a furor; he was hanged in effigy and his book burned.

ANDREWS NORTON: *Discourses on the Latest Form of Infidelity.* A condemnation of Transcendentalism and Norton's former student Ralph Waldo Emerson. Norton, an important figure in American Unitarianism, argues against Emerson's assertions that the miracles of the New Testament did not truly occur. Norton's attack was embarrassing and made conservative Unitarians uneasy, but it is for this dispute that he is most remembered.

JEREMIAH N. REYNOLDS (c. 1799–1858): "Mocha Dick; or, The White Whale of the Pacific." A report in the *Knickerbocker Magazine* of a white whale that wreaked havoc for seamen. It would be a source for Melville's *Moby-Dick.*

HENRY ROWE SCHOOLCRAFT: *Algic Researches.* A popular collection of Indian myths and legends based on research among tribes from the Alleghenies to the Atlantic during Schoolcraft's tenure as an Indian agent at Sault Sainte Marie and as superintendent of Indian affairs for Michigan.

JONES VERY (1813–1880): *Essays and Poems.* Edited and published by Ralph Waldo Emerson, the collection by the Unitarian minister and poet wins critical acclaim within elite literary circles. Including essays on epic poetry and Shakespeare, and a number of sonnets, the book exhibits many simple but thoughtful meditations on man's relationship with God. The somewhat metaphysical examinations of that relationship draws praise from notables such as William Cullen Bryant and William Ellery Channing.

THEODORE DWIGHT WELD (1803–1895): *American Slavery As It Is: Testimony of a Thousand Witnesses.* A collection of personal accounts and newspaper reports documenting slave life in the South, gathered by the Massachusetts reformer and his wife, Angelina Grimké, but published anonymously. It is among the most influential antislavery pamphlets; Harriet Beecher Stowe would credit the work as her inspiration for *Uncle Tom's Cabin* (1852).

Poetry

RALPH WALDO EMERSON: "Each and All." Emerson's poem calls Nature "the perfect whole." He also publishes "The Humble-Bee," in praise of the "yellow-breeched philosopher" who sips "only what is sweet," and "The Rhodora," with the lines "if eyes were made for seeing / Then Beauty is its own excuse for being."

HENRY WADSWORTH LONGFELLOW: *Voices of the Night.* The author's first book of original poetry is a collection of works previously published in magazines. Containing inspirational poems such as "A Psalm of Life" and "Light of the Stars," the popular book supports Longfellow's opinion that poetry should be "an instrument for improving the condition of society, and advancing the great purpose of human happiness."

EDGAR ALLAN POE: "The Haunted Palace." Written when Poe's financial situation forced him to write tales instead of verse, this is considered one of his best poems. Originally published in the *Baltimore Museum*, it would later be included in "The Fall of the House of Usher." The poem is an allegory of mental states, with the palace taking the form of a human head that is attacked by evil.

Publications and Events

The *Liberty Bell.* This gift book devoted to antislavery literature is published in Boston under the sponsorship of abolitionist Maria Chapman, with volumes appearing nearly annually until 1858. Contributors included Emerson, Longfellow, and Stowe, as well as foreign literary figures such as Elizabeth Barrett Browning and Alexis de Tocqueville.

1840

Drama and Theater

CORNELIUS AMBROSIUS LOGAN: *The Vermont Wool Dealer.* A popular one-act farce about a young woman who uses her guardian, a humorous Yankee character Deuteronomy Dutiful, to make Captain Oakley jealous. The American comedian Dan Marble made his successful debut in the role of Deuteronomy in London.

CORNELIUS MATHEWS (1817–1889): *The Politicians.* Mathews's unproduced comedy of New York City politics depicts two rival candidates who employ unsavory tactics in their attempt to win the office of alderman. The topic and theme would be repeated in Mathew's writing, and the work is a forerunner to comparable attempts at local color fiction.

Fiction

ORESTES BROWNSON: *Charles Elwood; or, The Infidel Converted.* Brownson's autobiographical novel depicts the protagonist's transformation from spiritual infidelity to Unitarian belief. The *Christian Examiner* remarks that the book "will aid many a doubter to a cheerful faith," and Poe praises it highly.

JAMES FENIMORE COOPER: *The Pathfinder; or, The Inland Sea.* A Leather-Stocking Tale in which Mabel Dunham promises to marry Natty Bumppo if he saves her

Births

1840 George Wilbur Peck (d. 1916), novelist
Constance Fenimore Woolson (d. 1894), novelist

1841 Edward Rowland Sill (d. 1887), poet

1842 Ambrose Bierce (d. 1914), short story writer
Bronson Howard (d. 1908), playwright
Sidney Lanier (d. 1881), poet and critic
Steele MacKaye (d. 1894), playwright
Fred Marsden (d. 1888), playwright

1843 Bartley Campbell (d. 1888), playwright
Henry James (d. 1916), novelist
Prentiss Ingraham (d. 1904), novelist
Frank Hitchcock Murdoch (d. 1872), playwright
Charles Warren Stoddard (d. 1909), poet

1844 George Washington Cable (d. 1925), novelist and short
story writer
Richard Watson Gilder (d. 1909), poet and editor
Edward Harrigan (d. 1911), playwright, actor, and producer
Elizabeth Stuart Phelps Ward (d. 1911), novelist

1845 John B. Tabb (d. 1909), poet

1846 Anna Katharine Green (d. 1935), novelist
Julian Hawthorne (d. 1934), novelist and son of Nathaniel
Hawthorne

1847 Mary Catherwood (d. 1902), novelist
Edgar Fawcett (d. 1904), novelist
Mary Hallock Foote (d. 1938), novelist
Archibald Clavering Gunter (d. 1907), novelist and
playwright
Julia A. Moore (d. 1920), poet

1848 H. H. Boyesen (d. 1895), novelist
Joel Chandler Harris (d. 1908), short story writer and
humorist

1849 James Lane Allen (d. 1925), novelist
Frances Hodgson Burnett (d. 1924), children's author and
novelist
Sarah Orne Jewett (d. 1909), novelist and short story
writer
Emma Lazarus (d. 1887), poet and essayist
James Whitcomb Riley (d. 1916), poet

Deaths

1840 Timothy Flint (b. 1780), missionary and writer
Hannah Webster Foster (b. 1759), novelist

1841 William Austin (b. 1778), short story writer
James Abraham Hillhouse (b. 1789), poet and
playwright
Grenville Mellen (b. 1799), short story writer and poet

1842 William Ellery Channing (b. 1780), clergyman and author
McDonald Clarke (b. 1796), poet

1843 Noah Webster (b. 1758), lexicographer

1844 Joseph Smith (b. 1805), founder of the Mormon Church
and author of *The Book of Mormon*

1845 James McHenry (b. 1785), poet and novelist

1846 Sarah Wentworth Morton (b. 1759), novelist

1847 Nathaniel Bannister (b. 1813), playwright and actor

1849 Edgar Allan Poe (b. 1809), poet, short story writer, and
critic

father from an Iroquois attack. Natty saves him but relinquishes Mabel to Jasper Western, whom he knows she loves and who has proved not to be a traitor.

THEODORE SEDGWICK FAY: *The Countess Ida: A Tale of Berlin.* The author's second novel is set partly in Berlin during the French Revolution. It wins much critical praise; the *Mirror* describes it as "the best American novel of the day." The plot concerns a man who shows great bravery in refusing to duel, and the novel is notable for its clever turns of plot and vivid characterizations.

CHARLES FENNO HOFFMAN: *Greyslaer: A Romance of the Mohawk.* Hoffman's only published novel is a popular, fictionalized version of the famous Beauchamp-Sharp murder case in Kentucky. Set during the American Revolution, it concerns a young patriot who cannot marry the woman he loves because of the dishonor of her earlier secret marriage.

JOSEPH HOLT INGRAHAM: *The Quadroone; or, St. Michael's Day.* This is a pioneering attempt to deal with miscegenation in fiction, though the stigma of black blood is removed from the hero and heroine by the novel's climax. It is the first in a string of the prolific Ingraham's

popular novels. Some claim that Ingraham was personally responsible for 10 percent of all American novels published during the 1840s.

JOHN PENDLETON KENNEDY: *Quodlibet: Containing Some Annal Thereof . . . by Solomon Second-Thoughts, Schoolmaster.* A forceful political satire criticizing Jacksonian democracy, published under the pseudonym "Mark Littleton."

EDGAR ALLAN POE: *Tales of the Grotesque and Arabesque.* Poe's first collection contains twenty-five short stories including "MS. Found in a Bottle," "William Wilson," "Ligeia," and "The Fall of the House of Usher." Although favorably received and a boost to Poe's national reputation, slow sales meant that Poe received no royalties. Though the title page reads 1840, the collection is actually published in Philadelphia in 1839. Poe also publishes "The Journals of Julius Rodman, Being an Account of the First Passage Across the Rocky Mountains of North America Ever Achieved by Civilized Man," a work of fiction written by Poe but kept anonymous. The story of exploration beyond the Rocky Mountains is purportedly taken from the journal of Rodman, a fictional

Richard Henry Dana Jr.

English immigrant whose heirs find his writings. The descriptions of land and travel experiences are based largely on Irving's *Astoria* and the accounts of Lewis and Clark and of Sir Alexander Mackenzie. Many readers believe the tale to be nonfiction.

FREDERICK WILLIAM THOMAS: *Howard Pinkney.* Regarded as Thomas's greatest novel, *Howard Pinkney* is noteworthy as an early attempt to incorporate a detective story into an American novel. Poe depreciates his friend's effort, sensing it is too close to his own method.

Nonfiction

ABIGAIL ADAMS: *The Letters of Mrs. Adams, the Wife of John Adams.* The first collection of the former first lady's letters, edited and published by her grandson Charles Francis Adams Sr. The 114 spirited and charming letters win immediate popularity and would be published in three more editions over the next ten years.

AMOS BRONSON ALCOTT: *Orphic Sayings.* In a famously ill-received collection of parables printed in the *Dial*, a Transcendentalist periodical founded to print materials that would be rejected elsewhere, Alcott's sayings comment on many topics, including nature, hope, speech, and conscience. They draw derision from all corners of the literary world; the *Knickerbocker* mocks them as "Gastric Sayings."

ALBERT BRISBANE (1809–1890): *Social Destiny of Man.* A description and translation of the French social theorist Charles Fourier's idea that planned communities with equal economic distribution are superior to capitalist, laissez-faire society. The book converts Horace Greeley to "Fourierism," and approximately eight thousand Americans would invest in "phalanxes," organized Fourierist communities, from Massachusetts to Wisconsin.

RICHARD HENRY DANA JR.: *Two Years Before the Mast.* Taken from the journal he had kept on a hide-trading expedition around the Horn to California in 1834, this is a description of Cape Horn, the land that is now California, and life at sea in general, concentrating on the abuses endured by sailors. The popular work would set a standard of realism in sea literature and prompt maritime reforms.

LYDIA HUNTLEY SIGOURNEY: *Pleasant Memories of Pleasant Lands.* An account of the writer's travels to Europe, which she had undertaken to become acquainted with the European literati. Although not well liked by all whom she visited, many writers had received her, including William Wordsworth and Maria Edgeworth, guaranteeing her success in the United States.

WILLIAM GILMORE SIMMS: *The History of South Carolina.* Simms's state history is devoted primarily to the Revolutionary period, demonstrating his contention, dramatized in his novels, that the Revolution in Carolina was truly a civil war that resulted in more devastation there than in any other of the colonies.

NATHANIEL PARKER WILLIS: *Loiterings of Travel* and *American Scenery.* The first is a collection of European travel sketches; the second a look at American sights. Although Willis sees many "blemishes" in the developing American landscape, he praises the evident vitality of the place, a quality he finds lacking in Europe.

Poetry

PHILIP PENDLETON COOKE (1816–1850): "Florence Vane." A famous and often anthologized ballad, written for Cooke's beloved cousin and first published in Burton's *Gentleman's Magazine* at the request of editor Edgar Allan Poe. Philip, the older brother of the novelist John Esten Cooke, composed poetry while studying law.

Publications and Events

The *Dial.* A quarterly journal devoted to literature and religion founded by Theodore Parker, Bronson Alcott, Orestes Brownson, Margaret Fuller, James Freeman Clarke, and Ralph Waldo Emerson as the mouthpiece of New England Transcendentalism. Edited the first two years by Fuller, it included writings by Thoreau, Emerson, Parker, Christopher Pearse Cranch, and others. In 1842, Emerson assumed the editorship and was responsible for printing excerpts from Eastern religious writings, poetry by W. H. Channing, and "Lectures on the Times" by Emerson himself. The *Dial*'s subscriber list never grew above three hundred, and it received harsh criticism from other periodicals but became one of the most significant periodicals for American literary historians.

National Anti-Slavery Standard. This New York periodical, founded by the American Anti-Slavery Society, staunchly endorsed immediate and complete abolition. Notable contributors included Eliza Lee Follen, Wendell Phillips, and James Russell Lowell, who served as its editor from 1845 to 1849 and published some of the satirical poems that would later become Lowell's *Biglow Papers*. After the Civil War, the periodical took up the cause of women's rights and temperance until its demise in 1872.

1841
Fiction

WASHINGTON ALLSTON: *Monaldi: A Tale.* This gothic romance by the painter and friend of Coleridge and Wordsworth is set in Italy and concerns a successful artist, Monaldi, who is destroyed by his childhood friend whose failure as a poet and rejection by Monaldi's wife has corrupted him with jealousy. Although gothic novels are no longer popular, the book, Allston's only novel, receives positive reviews, especially for its descriptive values and its morality.

JAMES FENIMORE COOPER: *The Deerslayer; or, The First War-Path.* A Leather-Stocking Tale of Natty Bumppo's youth in which he is depicted hunting and fighting the Hurons with the Delaware Indians near Otsego Lake. Judith, whom he has protected from an Iroquois attack, professes her love for Natty, who refuses her, although he always fondly remembers the romantic memories of the relationship, even after she has married a British officer.

JOHN BEAUCHAMP JONES (1810–1866): *Wild Western Scenes.* The frontier writer who was raised in Kentucky and Missouri produces his first novel, a bestseller about a group of easterners who retreat from harsh city life into the wilderness on the Missouri River. The novel features Daniel Boone as a guide through the frontier. When Jones could not find a publisher for the book, he printed it at his own expense and sold 100,000 copies. His other novels include *The Western Merchant* (1849), *Freaks of Fortune* (1854), and *The War Path* (1858).

EDGAR ALLAN POE: "A Descent into the Maelstrom." First published in *Graham's Magazine* and to be included in *Prose Tales* (1843), Poe's adventure story describes a Norwegian sailor and his brother who are drawn into a massive whirlpool. Poe also publishes "The Murders in the Rue Morgue" in *Graham's Lady's and Gentleman's Magazine*, where he is editor. This story is the pioneer work of modern detective fiction. The detective, Auguste Dupin, analyzes evidence to solve the murder of a mother and daughter.

WILLIAM GILMORE SIMMS: *Confession; or, The Blind Heart.* Simms relocates *Othello* to the American frontier in this psychological study of jealousy. Of note is the main female character, Margaret Cooper, who has been described by one critic as "a kind of Margaret Fuller on the frontier." He also publishes *The Kinsmen; or, The Black Riders of Congaree*, a Revolutionary romance in which two brothers are divided by the conflict.

THOMAS BANGS THORPE (1815–1875): "The Big Bear of Arkansas." The most highly acclaimed sketch by the Massachusetts-born writer who wrote tales of the frontier based on his residence in Louisiana from 1833 to 1855 is a tall tale concerning a hunt for a bear of mythic proportions, recounted by an unnamed narrator who has learned the story from a fellow passenger on his trip up the Mississippi from New Orleans. The bear's death symbolizes the loss of the wilderness.

WILLIAM WARE: *Julian; or, Scenes in Judea.* This unprecedented fictionalization of events during the time of Jesus Christ is originally published in the *Christian Examiner* (1839–1840). The narrative follows a Jew who explores Jesus' claim to divinity during turbulent Roman times. The work comes to a Unitarian conclusion that Jesus was not the Messiah. It is one of the earliest fictional portrayals of the Christ story.

Nonfiction

GEORGE CATLIN (1796–1872): *Letters and Notes on the Manners, Customs, and Conditions of the North American Indians.* This two-volume work by the painter of Native American life, illustrated with a number of engravings, contains astute, objective, and respectful observations of the Plains Indians. Winning critical and commercial success, it is Catlin's most famous literary work.

RICHARD HENRY DANA JR.: *The Seaman's Friend.* This reference for sailors on their legal rights and duties and important sea vocabulary and customs would become the standard manual on maritime law in England and the United States. Dana, known as "the sailor's lawyer," had assembled the manual after witnessing cruelty toward sailors.

BENJAMIN DRAKE: *Life of Tecumseh, and his Brother the Prophet, with a Historical Sketch of the Shawnee Indians.* The author's final work remains one of the best biographies of the Indian leader Tecumseh. Drawing on recollections from witnesses, the book's accuracy and concise writing make it an important historical document.

RALPH WALDO EMERSON: "The Method of Nature." Emerson's address is his fullest treatment of his theory of natural development and organic growth, which he applies to society and literature. Also in this year Emerson publishes *Essays,* the first of two collections of essays originally presented as lectures. The twelve compositions study the concepts of friendship, heroism, intellect, and art. The most celebrated is "Self-Reliance," in which the author extols the primacy of the individual.

THEODORE PARKER (1810–1860): "On the Transient and Permanent in Christianity." The Massachusetts clergyman, abolitionist, and writer's controversial sermon rejects scriptures and church authorities for a personal intuition of divinity. It is his first major statement of his unorthodox religious beliefs, which would come to be associated with the Transcendentalists. He would expand on his position in lectures collected in *A Discourse on Matters Pertaining to Religion* (1842).

ANN PLATO: *Essays.* This is the first collection of essays by an African American. Included are four biographical pieces, sixteen short essays, and a selection of poetry. Little is known of Plato's life; it is believed that she was a free black who lived in Hartford, Connecticut.

JOHN LLOYD STEPHENS: *Incidents of Travel in Central America, Chiapas, and Yucatan.* An account of observations made on a diplomatic mission to Central America, with illustrations by Frederick Catherwood, an English artist experienced in archaeology. The work stimulates interest in the area and wins flattering reviews, including one from Poe that calls it "perhaps the most interesting book on travel ever published."

WILLIAM LEETE STONE: *The Life and Times of Red-Jacket, or Sa-go,ye,wat,ha.* A keen biography notable for its voluminous notes and primary materials. It portrays the Iroquois chief Red-Jacket as a champion of his race and a man whose eloquence and leadership greatly benefited his cause, which contrasts with his earlier general reputation for being vain and opportunistic.

DAVID THOMAS VALENTINE (1801–1869): *Manual of the Corporation of the City of New York.* A collection of historical information and numerous illustrations assembled annually from 1841 to 1867 by Valentine, who for many

years served as the clerk of the Common Council of the City of New York. By 1869 the work had become so popular that the *New York Times* called it "almost a necessity among New-Yorkers." It remains a valuable source of information.

ALEXANDER YOUNG (1800–1854): *Chronicles of the Pilgrim Fathers of the Colony of Plymouth, from 1602 to 1625; Now First Collected from Original Records and Contemporaneous Printed Documents, Illustrated with Notes.* A collection of original documents detailing the history of the American Pilgrims that the *North American Review* hails as "exceedingly praiseworthy" and "an important addition to the historical library of America."

Poetry

RALPH WALDO EMERSON: "The Sphinx." First published in the *Dial* and to be included in *Poems* (1847), the poem is paraphrased in Emerson's journal as expressing the concept that "if the mind lives only in particulars . . . then the world addresses to the mind a question it cannot answer."

WILLIAM DAVIS GALLAGHER: *Selections from the Poetical Literature of the West.* One of the earliest regional anthologies is edited by Gallagher and contains work by thirty-eight western poets, including Gallagher's own much-celebrated poem "Miami Woods."

HENRY WADSWORTH LONGFELLOW: *Ballads and Other Poems.* Longfellow's second book of poems includes major and popular works such as "The Village Blacksmith," "The Wreck of the Hesperus," "Elcelsior," and "The Skeleton in Armor," works that help establish him as one of the leading poets of the era.

CORNELIUS MATHEWS: *Wakondah; The Master of Life.* This narrative poem deals with prehistoric Indians.

Publications and Events

The Brook Farm Institute of Agriculture and Education. A cooperative community is established on a two-hundred-acre farm in West Roxbury, Massachusetts, under the leadership of George Ripley (1802–1880). It would continue until 1846, and Hawthorne, who lived there for a time, would write about the community in *The Blithedale Romance* (1852).

The *Brooklyn Eagle.* A daily newspaper founded by Henry Cruse Murphy and Isaac Van Anden and affiliated with the Democratic Party begins publication. The paper runs continuously for 114 years, except for a brief suspension in 1861 when opposition to Lincoln's policies prohibited its mailing. Walt Whitman edited the *Brooklyn Eagle* from 1846 to 1848, and his contributions to the paper were collected in 1920 as *The Gathering of Forces*. Other notable staffers included Edward W. Bok and H. V. Kaltenborn. Always maintaining a local Brooklyn focus, the paper changed ownership several times after Brooklyn became a borough of New York City in 1898. As Brooklyn's economy diminished, so did the paper, and it was finally suspended in 1955 during a New York Newspaper Guild strike.

The *Ladies' Repository*. Monthly magazine founded by Samuel Williams and published by Cincinnati Methodists with the aim of providing a moral alternative to *Godey's Lady's Book* and *Snowden's Lady's Companion*. It featured numerous articles on religion and fashion, and notable contributors included Alice and Phoebe Cary and Frances E. Willard, the founder of the Women's Christian Temperance Union. After 1876 the name was changed to the *National Repository*.

The *New-York Tribune*. This daily newspaper is founded by Horace Greeley, who edited it until his death (1872) and made it famous for trenchant editorials and the journalists he attracted to it, such as H. J. Raymond, who would go on to found the *New York Times* (1851), and George Ripley, who as literary critic (1849–1880) wrote the first daily book reviews in the United States. The paper remained the most distinguished and powerful Republican organ in the nation under the editorship of Whitelaw Reid and his son, Ogden Reid. In 1924 it purchased the *New York Herald*, becoming, until its demise in 1966, the *Herald Tribune*.

1842
Fiction

TIMOTHY SHAY ARTHUR (1809–1885): *Six Nights with the Washingtonians: A Series of Original Temperance Tales*. The editor, author, and social reformer's first important book establishes his pro-temperance reputation. The Washington Temperance Society, which had influenced Arthur, was formed by recovering alcoholics, and their efforts greatly aided the anti-liquor movement. He would go on to write arguably the most famous American temperance melodrama, *Ten Nights in a Bar-Room and What I Saw There* (1854).

JAMES FENIMORE COOPER: *Wing-and-Wing; or, Le Feu-Follet: A Tale*. A romantic sea adventure, set on the island of Elba during the Napoleonic Wars, in which the devout Catholic daughter of the Neapolitan admiral Caraccioli refuses to marry her beloved French privateer because he is an atheist. An account of the infamous execution of Admiral Caraccioli is included.

CAROLINE STANSBURY KIRKLAND: *Forest Life*. This collection of stories and poetry written while the author lived on the Michigan frontier is greeted enthusiastically by critics. Kirkland portrays her Michigan neighbors less harshly than she had in her previous book *A New Home* (1839), but their continued scorn would prompt the Kirklands to move back to New York City.

CORNELIUS MATHEWS: *The Career of Puffer Hopkins*. Mathews's novel satirizing New York City politics would be called by critic Perry Miller "at the head (crude though it be) of long tradition in American writing" — the urban novel.

EDGAR ALLAN POE: "The Masque of the Red Death." One of the author's finest stories is an allegorical tale of Prince Prospero's attempt to escape the plague by hiding away with his friends in an isolated castle. Published in *Graham's Magazine*, it illustrates that death cannot be escaped. The Red Death appears at a masquerade Prospero is holding in his castle and kills everyone in attendance. Poe also publishes "The Mystery of Marie Roget." The sequel to "The Murders in the Rue Morgue," it is a detective story based on an actual New York murder case. Poe's story "Eleonora," a romantic tale about a youth who falls in love with his cousin, also appears in this year.

WILLIAM GILMORE SIMMS: *Beauchampe; or, The Kentucky Tragedy*. A fictionalized account of the famous murder of Kentucky solicitor general Colonel Solomon P. Sharp, by the attorney Jeroboam O. Beauchamp. In the novel, Beauchamp marries Anna Cook, who demands that he kill the man who seduced her, which he does, and is condemned to death. The night before the execution, he and his wife attempt suicide, but his attempt fails and he is hanged. Simms would expand the first part of the novel in 1856 under the title *Charlemont; or, The Pride of the Village*.

ELIZABETH OAKES SMITH (1806–1893): *The Western Captive; or, The Times of Tecumseh*. Taking advantage of the contemporary popularity of Indian stories, Smith's novel, one of the first paperback books published in the United States, treats both governmental hypocrisy regarding Indian affairs and the danger of mixing white and Indian bloodlines.

WALT WHITMAN (1819–1892): *Franklin Evans; or, The Inebriate*. In this conventional temperance novel indicative of Whitman's own beliefs about liquor, the plot concerns a rural Long Island boy who becomes a drunkard when he moves to New York City. He suffers numerous misfortunes and causes the death of two women he loved, but eventually manages to save a drowning boy, gives up drinking, and becomes a success. Although considered hack work, the novel, Whitman's longest work of fiction, is first serialized in the *New World* and sells twenty thousand copies.

Literary Criticism and Scholarship

RUFUS WILMOT GRISWOLD (1815–1857): *The Poets and Poetry of America.* The critic Griswold's most significant anthology solidifies his literary reputation. Although criticized for its inclusion of poets who lacked lasting worth and exclusion of southern and western writers, this book proves popular, and many critics believe it to be, as the *Knickerbocker* said, "the best collection of American poetry that has ever been made."

EDGAR ALLAN POE: "Review of New Books: *Twice-Told Tales.*" Poe's review of Hawthorne's collection sets forth Poe's theory of the short story. He argues that the form is the most "advantageous field of exertion" since a short story can be read in one sitting. He further states that the effect of a tale should be known to the author before commencing, and all should contribute to the "preconceived effect." Poe's analysis supplies the theoretical underpinnings for the evolution of the modern short story.

Nonfiction

CHARLES DICKENS (1812–1870): *American Notes for General Circulation.* Dickens publishes his observations based on his 1842 tour of the United States. His relatively mild criticisms of the American penal system, press, and chewing tobacco prompt American outrage in the press. Dickens would vent his irritation in the more devastating fictional satire in *Martin Chuzzlewit* (1844).

PARKE GODWIN (1816–1904): *Democracy, Constructive and Pacific.* The social reformer argues that unless rural cooperative communities are established throughout the United States to provide an alternative to capitalism for urban workers, class warfare will ensue. Godwin thus anticipates the Marxist concept of class struggle in a capitalist society.

THEODORE PARKER: *A Discourse on the Matters Pertaining to Religion.* An expansion of five lectures on religion that Parker had delivered to large audiences around Boston. It fully outlines his Transcendentalist theology, which argues that the church is less important than a personal relationship with God.

ZADOCK THOMPSON (1796–1856): *History of Vermont, Natural, Civil, and Statistical.* This standard authority on the Green Mountain State by the Vermont historian and naturalist is notable for its breadth of detail. The work is divided into three parts: a natural history, a historical survey, and a revision of the *Gazetteer of the State of Vermont* (which describes the natural features of the state's towns and bodies of water), which he had first published in 1824.

RICHARD HENRY WILDE (1789–1847): *Conjectures and Researches Concerning the Love, Madness, and Imprisonment of Torquato Tasso.* A critical examination by the Georgian poet, lawyer, and congressman of the imprisonment and later release of the Italian poet Tasso, the author of *Jerusalem Delivered* (1575). Wilde discusses the documents concerning the prison sentence, which was officially for madness, and also looks at Tasso's poetry. He concludes that Tasso was not mad but was jailed for being romantically involved with a woman above his social stratum and feigned madness to escape persecution. Wilde's first and only book published during his lifetime is highly acclaimed by critics.

Poetry

WILLIAM CULLEN BRYANT: *The Fountain and Other Poems.* Bryant responds to persistent requests for a longer work with a collection of parts of a larger work of grand design that he never completed.

CHARLES FENNO HOFFMAN: *The Vigil of Faith and Other Poems.* This warmly received collection of Hoffman's popular verse would go through four editions in three years. The title poem concerns an Adirondack Indian legend about a widower who guards the man who killed his wife so that the murderer will not be able to find her in the spirit world.

HENRY WADSWORTH LONGFELLOW: *Poems on Slavery.* A collection of poems written to demonstrate Longfellow's approval of the abolitionist movement, motivated by his Unitarian beliefs. The collection is dedicated to William Ellery Channing, and Longfellow allows the New England Anti-Slavery Tract Society to reprint and distribute the poems freely.

ALFRED BILLINGS STREET (1811–1881): *The Burning of Schenectady, and Other Poems.* A collection of descriptive verses that is one of the New York lawyer and librarian's two famous books (the other is *Fronteac*, 1849). The title piece is a narrative poem on an infamous event in New York history, and the poet's descriptions of nature are widely admired.

Publications and Events

Boston Miscellany of Literature and Fashion. This magazine, an outgrowth of Evert Augustus Duyckinck and Cornelius Mathews's critical magazine *Arcturus*, has an impressive list of contributors, including Poe, Lowell,

Edward Everett Hale, Hawthorne, and Nathaniel Parker Willis.

The *Southern Quarterly Review*. Founded and initially edited by D. K. Whitaker, this magazine was overshadowed by the earlier and better *Southern Review*, but it is remembered as one of the finest Southern reviews published before the war. Published predominantly from Charleston, it supported slavery and states' rights.

1843

Drama and Theater

HENRY WADSWORTH LONGFELLOW: *The Spanish Student*. Longfellow's poetic drama boosts his literary fame. In it, a dancing gypsy is courted by a gentleman who marries her after it is discovered that she is actually the daughter of a nobleman who had been stolen by the gypsies. Edgar Allan Poe's review of the drama accuses Longfellow of plagiarism of his drama *Politian* (1835–1836).

Minstrel shows. The appearance of the Virginia Minstrels, founded by Dan Emmett (1815–1904), at New York's Bowery Amphitheatre on February 6 is widely credited with initiating the American minstrel show tradition.

Fiction

JAMES FENIMORE COOPER: *Ned Myers; or, A Life Before the Mast*. A biography, written as fiction but based on the stories of Cooper's former shipmate. It is his most accurate depiction of life at sea. Cooper also publishes *Wyandotté; or, The Hutted Knoll: A Tale*, a story about the divided loyalties of a New York family during the Revolution and a retired British officer who is ruined for his refusal to choose sides. It is the first of Cooper's works dealing with the conflict between New York's tenant farmers and landowners that escalated into the Anti-Rent War (1839–1846), which Cooper would treat in his *Littlepage Manuscripts* trilogy (1845–1846).

NATHANIEL HAWTHORNE: "The Birthmark." One of Hawthorne's most frequently anthologized stories is first published in *Pioneer* and would be later included in *Mosses from an Old Manse* (1846). The allegorical tale concerns a scientist whose wife's perfection is flawed by a birthmark; his attempts to remove it kill her. Hawthorne also publishes "The Celestial Railroad," a moral satire. In this modern update of *Pilgrim's Progress*, a railroad leads from the City of Destruction to the Celestial City.

THOMAS LOW NICHOLS (1815–1901): *Ellen Ramsay*. The first of the journalist and reformer's three novels on contemporary life in New York City. It would be followed by *The Lady in Black* (1844) and *Raffle for a Wife* (1845).

EDGAR ALLAN POE: "The Black Cat." One of Poe's finest horror stories is a psychological tale first published in the *U.S. Saturday Post* and later included in *Tales* (1845); it has been much anthologized. In the story a man murders his wife and entombs her in a cellar wall, accidentally enclosing a cat with her. The cat's cries reveal his guilt. Poe also publishes "The Gold Bug," a tale of Captain Kidd's buried treasure on Sullivan's Island, South Carolina, and its discovery by a poor Southern gentleman. The suspenseful tale is one of the first to employ a buried treasure theme and a hidden message in a cipher. It wins a great deal of attention for the struggling author and the $100 first prize in the *Dollar* newspaper literary contest. In the same year "The Pit and the Pendulum" appears in the *Gift*. The story describes the tortures of the Spanish Inquisition in a thrilling horror tale. Poe also publishes "The Tell-Tale Heart," in which a madman betrays his crime when he thinks he hears the beating heart of the man he has murdered.

HARRIET BEECHER STOWE: *The Mayflower; or, Sketches of Scenes and Characters Among the Descendants of the Pilgrims*. Stowe's first collection of stories and sketches features New England characters and a pioneering use of dialect. Many of the stories had been originally written for gatherings of the Semi-Colon Club and published in *Western Monthly Magazine*.

WILLIAM TAPPAN THOMPSON (1812–1882): *Major Jones's Courtship*. Thompson's most popular book is a collection of letters that he had originally submitted to Georgia newspapers from the fictional middle-class planter Joseph Jones, detailing his misadventures and humorously, but realistically, depicting Georgia life. Thompson was born in Ohio but was a longtime Georgia resident and an associate of A. B. Longstreet, whose works Thompson imitated.

Nonfiction

CATHARINE ESTHER BEECHER (1800–1878): *A Treatise on Domestic Economy*. Beecher's most important work affirms the belief that women's role is in the home but stresses the importance of the domestic sphere to society. The work would go through fifteen editions, and the author's sister, Harriet Beecher Stowe, later helped her revise the work as *The American Woman's Home* (1869), which sold almost fifty thousand copies by subscription.

HENRY HIGHLAND GARNET (1815–1882): *Address to the Slaves of the United States*. Garnet's address, better known as the "Call to Rebellion" speech, delivered at the National Negro Convention in Buffalo, New York, calls for violent resistance to end slavery. Strongly denounced by

Frederick Douglass, who supports nonviolent persuasion, Garnet's speech falls short by a single vote of being endorsed as the official resolution of the convention.

JAMES JACKSON JARVES (1818–1888): *History of the Hawaiian or Sandwich Islands.* Much lauded for its scholarship and literary merit, this history of the Hawaiian nation remains an important early source of information. Jarves was the editor of the *Polynesian* (1840–1848), the first Hawaiian newspaper.

GEORGE TUCKER: *Progress of the United States in Population and Wealth in Fifty Years, as Exhibited by the Decennial Census.* A groundbreaking statistical work compiling facts and figures from the decennial censuses. The *United States Democratic Review* says it is "one of the few books that may be set down as indispensable to every American library."

WILLIAM HICKLING PRESCOTT: *The Conquest of Mexico.* A dramatic and well-documented narrative history describing the Aztec civilization and its conquest by Cortez. Prescott's most popular work, it suggests that the fall of the Aztecs resulted from their oppression of other cultures. Its portrayal of Mexicans in 1519 as backward and barbarous was picked up by newspapers and pamphlets to describe the Mexicans during the Mexican War.

JOHN LLOYD STEPHENS: *Incidents of Travel in the Yucatan.* Following the success of his 1841 *Incidents of Travel in Central America, Chiapas, and Yucatan,* Stephens had returned to Central America with the English artist Frederick Catherwood for a more exhaustive study of the land. By the time of Stephens's death, 9,750 copies of the book had been published.

WILLIAM LEETE STONE: *Border Wars of the American Revolution.* Stone's final major history, and his most readable work, treats the war along the frontier of colonial expansion and Native Americans on both sides of the conflict.

Poetry

WILLIAM ELLERY CHANNING [II] (1817–1901): *Poems.* A collection of poems published at the expense of Channing's friend Samuel Gray Ward, admired by Emerson and Thoreau, but attacked by Edgar Allan Poe in his *Graham's* essay "Our Amateur Poets."

THOMAS DUNN ENGLISH (1819–1902): "Ben Bolt." A popular ballad written for Nathaniel Parker Willis and George Pope Morris, who had revived the *New York Mirror* and asked English for a sea chantey. The sentimental verse, fondly recalling childhood and the past, becomes English's most popular work, is set to music numerous

times, and is included in George Washington Cable's *Dr. Sevier* (1885) and in George du Maurier's *Trilby* (1894).

ELIZABETH OAKES SMITH: *The Sinless Child and Other Poems.* A collection of verse that critics, including Poe, acclaim, affirming Smith's literary reputation. The title poem, about an innocent woman's escape from a depraved world through death, had first appeared in the *Southern Literary Messenger.*

JOHN GREENLEAF WHITTIER: *Lays of My Home and Other Poems.* Whittier's return to regional poetry contains some of his best verses, such as "The Merrimack," "The Funeral Tree of the Sokokis," "The Ballad of Cassandra Southwick," and "Massachusetts to Virginia." Many of the poems cover ideas such as acceptance and unity that echo his antislavery works. One of Whittier's most impassioned abolitionist poems responds to those in Virginia who complain that Massachusetts has refused to enforce the Fugitive Slave Law by justifying noncompliance and urging Virginians to remember the ideals of Thomas Jefferson.

Publications and Events

Miss Leslie's Magazine. This periodical of literature and fashion for women debuts. It would include contributions by Lydia Huntley Sigourney, Park Benjamin, and Henry Wadsworth Longfellow. The name was changed to the *Ladies' Magazine* (1844) and *Arthur's Ladies' Magazine* (1845) before the magazine merged with *Godey's Lady's Book* (1846).

The Pioneer. A monthly literary magazine founded by Robert Carter and James Russell Lowell to develop a finer periodical than the popular ladies' magazines. Although critically acclaimed, the *Pioneer* suffered from financial difficulties and poor management by the publisher and subeditor hired after Lowell lost his eyesight. The magazine folded after its third issue. During its short but significant run, it printed Hawthorne's "The Birthmark," Poe's "The Tell-Tale Heart" and "Notes Upon English Verse," as well as writings by Whittier, Elizabeth Barrett, Jones Very, and others.

The Present. This New York monthly was edited by W. H. Channing in support of reform movements. Margaret Fuller, Charles Dana, and James Russell Lowell contributed, and translations of French and German writing also appeared.

1844

Drama and Theater

NATHANIEL BANNISTER (1813–1847): *Putnam, the Iron Son of '76.* The most successful play of the Baltimore actor and playwright is set during the Revolutionary War and is popular for its exciting action featuring the trained horse named Black Vulture. Despite being one of the most well known actor-dramatists of his day, Bannister died a pauper.

WILLIAM HENRY SMITH (1806–1872): *The Drunkard; or, The Fallen Saved.* The most successful of the "temperance plays," which became popular in the 1830s and 1840s as demand for prohibition laws increased. The play attracts large audiences and appeals to many who ordinarily did not attend dramas.

Fiction

CHARLES FREDERICK BRIGGS (1804–1877): *Working a Passage; or, Life in a Liner.* Widely considered one of the author's best works, it draws on Briggs's days as a sailor and explores social and economic inequality. The story unfolds during a voyage to Liverpool and symbolizes class struggle between the sailors and the privileged officers and passengers.

JAMES FENIMORE COOPER: *Afloat and Ashore.* In this novel, two orphaned sons of a Revolutionary naval officer run away to sea with a black slave. They fight Malay pirates and become shipwrecked in Madagascar before returning home to New York. One of the boys, Miles, sets out again, traveling to South America and China and returning to become the master of his own ship. This work is followed later in 1844 with a sequel, *Miles Wallingford*, in which Miles again goes to sea in search of a fortune in trade but instead is imprisoned and pressed into service. He escapes to New York, where he learns that his estate has been seized, and he is imprisoned for debt. In the end, he is bailed out by the woman he loves and realizes that he belongs on the farm he almost lost while seeking riches. Based on Cooper's own experiences, it marks his first use of first-person narration.

CHARLES DICKENS: *Martin Chuzzlewit.* After installment sales falter, Dickens sends his hero off to America for a satirical thrust at the gap between American ideals and reality. The satire reflects Dickens' disillusionment with America based on his 1842 tour and the furor prompted by his mild criticism in *American Notes* (1842).

NATHANIEL HAWTHORNE: "Rappaccini's Daughter." One of Hawthorne's greatest stories concerns a doctor whose intellectual pride leads him to feed his daughter poison to study its effects. When her young lover gives her an antidote to save her, it kills her instead. Hawthorne also publishes "The Artist of the Beautiful" in the *Democratic Review*; it would be included in *Mosses from an Old Manse* (1846). The story concerns the attempt of a watchmaker to create something of great beauty. He manages a mechanical butterfly, but it fails to impress the woman he loves and she marries a coarse blacksmith.

GEORGE LIPPARD (1822–1854): *Quaker City; or, The Monks of Monk Hall.* A sensational novel based on the Singleton Mercer trial of 1843, in which Mercer was acquitted of murdering the man who raped his sister. The book exposes the hypocrisy of the Philadelphia elite, and although many are offended by its pornographic elements, it becomes very popular and would lead to New York's enactment of an antiseduction law in 1849.

EDGAR ALLAN POE: "The Balloon Hoax." Poe's story first appears in the *New York Sun* in the guise of an actual article reporting on a balloon crossing of the Atlantic.

SUSAN RIDLEY SEDGWICK: *Alida; or, Town and Country.* Sedgwick's novel is about the beautiful but willful daughter of a New York merchant who is greatly improved when she and her father move to the country. Critics praise its natural style.

Nonfiction

HENRY WARD BEECHER (1813–1887): *Seven Lectures to Young Men on Various Important Subjects.* A melodramatic advice book warning against idleness, dishonesty, gambling, popular amusements, and other vices by the celebrated Congregational minister and reformer, the brother of Harriet Beecher Stowe. Widely popular, it is noted for its realism and vivid language.

RALPH WALDO EMERSON: *Essays, Second Series.* A collection of essays, more popular than the first, formed from lectures based on Emerson's journals. In it the author investigates experience, manners, politics, and character. In the essay "The Poet," Emerson calls for a literary artist through whom the wonder of America can resonate. The series of essays helps raise the author's status in the United States and Europe.

MARGARET FULLER (1810–1850): *Summer on the Lakes.* Midwestern travel book containing poetry, reflections, and notes from a trip to the Upper Midwest. Although the book is not commercially successful, it wins Fuller the position of literary critic for the *New York Tribune* and is possibly the model for Thoreau's *Week on the Concord and Merrimack Rivers.*

JOSIAH GREGG (1806–1850): *Commerce of the Prairies; or, The Journal of a Santa Fe Trader.* Based on Gregg's nine years of travel as a trader through the plains regions near Santa Fe, the book wins immediate success and would be reprinted numerous times, including in Reuben G. Thwaite's *Early Western Travels* (1905).

GEORGE WILKINS KENDALL (1809–1867): *A Narrative of the Texan Sante Fe Expedition, Comprising a Description of a Tour Through Texas and Across the Great Southwestern Prairies*. An account of a trip Kendall had taken in 1841 to gather proof that New Mexicans desired freedom from Mexico. Along the way he had experienced great adversity, including imprisonment and near death in Mexico. Kendall was a cofounder of the *New Orleans Picayune* and one of the pioneer of war correspondents.

HENRY ROWE SCHOOLCRAFT: *Oneota; or, The Red Race of America*. A collection of miscellaneous essays and poems on Native American characteristics that the *United States Democratic Review* calls "a store house of both fact and fancy [that] will afford rich materials hereafter for the antiquarian, the moralist and the bard."

Poetry

WILLIAM CULLEN BRYANT: *The White-Footed Deer and Other Poems*. A collection of ten poems, some of which had previously been published, that the *United States Democratic Review* credits with "beauty and simplicity."

CHRISTOPHER PEARSE CRANCH (1813–1892): *Poems*. Poe's review of the Unitarian minister's first collection calls him the "least intolerable of the School of Boston transcendentalists," praising his "unusual vivacity of fancy and dexterity of expression." In "The Ocean" Cranch supplies a poetic explanation of Emerson's concept of the Over-Soul. Cranch had also dedicated the collection to Emerson.

WILLIAM H. C. HOSMER (1814–1877): *Yonnondio; or, Warriors of the Genesee*. The upstate New York lawyer's most famous work is a long poem about the marquis de Nonville's attempt to claim the Senecas' land for King Louis XIV in 1687. The poem is composed primarily of octosyllabic couplets, suggestive of the oral tradition of the poem's subjects, and features a sympathetic treatment of the Indians.

EDGAR ALLAN POE: "The Raven." Submitted to the *New York Evening Mirror*, where Poe had been undertaking the menial tasks of a "mechanical paragraphist," the poem concerns the loss of a beloved woman and brings Poe celebrity status. It would be first published in the *American Whig Review* in 1845 and lead to his important critical essay "The Philosophy of Composition," to be published in the April 1846 issue of *Graham's*, in which he describes his writing process.

Publications and Events

Brownson's Quarterly Review. Founded by Orestes Brownson after subscribers' outcry barred his contribu-tions to the *Democratic Review*, the magazine contained Brownson's Catholic thought, including his arguments against "radicalism" and "despotism" in the Church. Brownson was frequently chastised by other Catholic periodicals. He suspended the religious publication in 1864 and began publishing the political "National Series," which lasted one year.

The *Columbian Lady's and Gentleman's Magazine*. A monthly literary magazine and competitor to *Graham's*. Predominately comprising sentimental writings and book reviews, it contained one piece of music in each issue, fashion plates in each issue after 1848, and featured Paulding, Poe, and numerous popular female writers such as Caroline Stansbury Kirkland and Lydia Maria Child.

The *Living Age*. Publisher Eliakim Littel (1797–1870) launches this eclectic magazine of fiction, poetry, and commentary, which he edits until his death. The magazine featured reprints of the best articles from foreign periodicals, but after 1938 and until its demise in 1941, it was surreptitiously financed by the Japanese government for purposes of propaganda.

1845
Drama and Theater

ANNA CORA MOWATT (1819–1870): *Fashion; or, Life in New York*. A social farce concerning the daughter of a wealthy couple who hopes to marry a man posing as a count. Her father wants her to marry a clerk who has uncovered the imposter. Mowatt's best-known play, it wins her respect as an author and popularizes social satires. She began her stage career in 1845, described in *Autobiography of an Actress*.

Fiction

EMERSON BENNETT (1822–1905): *The League of the Miami*. In this story, a young girl is kidnapped by an outlaw (a character based on Aaron Burr), marries her rescuer, and discovers her aristocratic ancestry. One of the most popular works of the prolific romance and western writer, it is first serialized in the *Cincinnati Dollar Weekly Commercial* and would be published as a book in 1850.

WILLIAM ALEXANDER CARUTHERS: *The Knights of Horse-Shoe, a Traditionary Tale of the Cocked Hat Gentry in the Old Dominion*. A romance concerning the career of Lieutenant Governor Sir Alexander Spotswood and his 1716 expedition to the Shenandoah Valley. It is the first comprehensive treatment of Spotswood and a celebration of Virginians.

JAMES FENIMORE COOPER: *Satanstoe; or, The Littlepage Manuscripts: A Tale of the Colony*. The first Littlepage Manuscript, written in response to the Anti-Rent controversy in New York. The trilogy argues against forcing landlords to sell their property through tales that depict the hardships that the Littlepage family endures to secure their settlements. The first tale concerns their struggle to survey lands amid the invasion of the French and the Indians. In the second of the Littlepage Manuscripts, also published in 1845, *The Chainbearer*, the family fights squatters who are stealing timber.

JOHNSON JONES HOOPER (1815–1862): *Some Adventures of Captain Simon Suggs, Late of the Tallapoosa Volunteers*. A humorous novel recounting the adventures of Captain Suggs from age seventeen through age fifty as he promotes his candidacy for sheriff, an effort that actually highlights his inadequacy. The popular sketches sell quickly, making Hooper famous.

SYLVESTER JUDD (1813–1853): *Margaret: A Tale of the Real and Ideal*. Called the only Transcendentalist novel by some critics, this is the story of an orphan, raised by a New England country family, who marries a Transcendentalist and restructures their town to form a Fourierist community. The novel is notable for its regional descriptions and its detailing of Transcendentalism and Fourierism, a plan for a utopian social structure based on independent "phalanxes," or small organized communities. This idea had been developed by the French social theorist Charles Fourier. The Unitarian minister and Augusta, Maine, pastor (1840–1853) would produce a second novel, *Richard Edney and the Governor's Family* (1850), noteworthy for its realistic depiction of Maine life.

CAROLINE STANSBURY KIRKLAND: *Western Clearings*. A popular collection of domestic sketches situated in a western settlement. Poe considers it Kirkland's best work, and it is hailed by the *U.S. Democratic Review* as "among the few home productions of the pen that merit the name American literature, for they belong peculiarly to our soil."

CORNELIUS MATHEWS: *Big Abel, and the Little Manhattan*. Mathews's novel juxtaposes contemporary New York City against its Indian and Dutch heritage. The character Abel Henry Hudson, a great-grandson of the explorer, and the Indian "Little Manhattan" tour the city and consider the changes that they see.

EDGAR ALLAN POE: *Tales*. Evert A. Duyckinck collects Poe's previously printed works, including "The Black Cat" and "The Purloined Letter."

WILLIAM GILMORE SIMMS: *The Wigwam and the Cabin*. Simms's popular story collection combines back-

Frederick Douglass

woods adventures, stories set during the Revolutionary War, Indian lore, and supernatural tales.

WILLIAM TAPPAN THOMPSON: *Chronicles of Pineville*. Thompson's second collection of letters depicts Georgia life through the character of Major Joseph Jones, a Georgia backwoodsman, and the rapid changes that result from the growth of settlement.

CHARLES WILKINS WEBBER (1819–1856): "Jack Long; or, Lynch Law and Vengeance, a Tale of Texas Life." Webber's best-known story, derived from his frontier experience in Texas, appears in the *American Review*. Edgar Allan Poe believes that its construction approaches perfection. Webber died in battle serving with William Walker in Nicaragua.

WALT WHITMAN: *The Half-Breed*. Whitman's novella, his second-longest fictional work after *Franklin Evans* (1842), sympathetically portrays an Indian, wrongfully accused of theft and murder, who accepts his execution with Christ-like forbearance.

NATHANIEL PARKER WILLIS: *Dashes at Life with a Free Pencil*. The *U.S. Democratic Review* calls Willis's final collection of short fiction "As agreeable a book as was ever published to let the mind loose on a holiday excursion in midsummer." The short tales are basically condensed novels that Willis shortened because long fiction had failed to sell in America.

Literary Criticism and Scholarship

WILLIAM HICKLING PRESCOTT: *Biographical and Critical Miscellanies.* A collection of Prescott's most important essays on literary history, including an essay on Cervantes and Italian narrative poetry; analyses of the works of his friends, including George Ticknor and George Bancroft; and a brief "Life of Charles Brockden Brown."

WILLIAM GILMORE SIMMS: *Views and Reviews in American Literature, History, and Fiction.* A collection of literary criticism, lectures, and biographical sketches published in American periodicals during the previous fifteen years. It includes a social commentary on "The Domestic Manners of the Americans," a sketch of Daniel Boone, an essay on Cortez, and criticism of authors such as James Fenimore Cooper and Cornelius Mathews. The *American Whig Review* declares it "the best volume of Mr. Simms' miscellaneous writings."

Nonfiction

HORATIO BRIDGE (1806–1893): *Journal of an African Cruiser.* A collection of observations based on Bridge's service as a naval officer, edited by the author's close friend and Bowdoin classmate Nathaniel Hawthorne, who is often attributed as the author. It is notable for its abundant information on Africa and its widespread use as an antislavery reference in later years.

FREDERICK DOUGLASS (1817–1895): *Narrative of the Life of Frederick Douglass, an American Slave, Written by Himself.* Douglass's autobiography vividly describes his years as a slave. Written after he had escaped north in 1838 and begun work in William Lloyd Garrison's abolitionist movement, the work sells more than eleven thousand copies in its first year and proves to be the most popular and influential of the published slave narratives. Douglass would issue two additional autobiographical works, *My Bondage and Freedom* (1855) and *Life and Times of Frederick Douglass* (1881, revised 1892).

MARGARET FULLER: *Woman in the Nineteenth Century.* A feminist treatise based on Transcendentalist philosophy, arguing that women have the right to advance their individual natures. It surveys the position of women in society from economic, political, intellectual, and sexual viewpoints and is considered the philosophical basis for the American women's rights movement and the Seneca Falls Convention of 1848.

HORACE MANN (1796–1859): *Lectures on Education.* The first of the influential educator's assessments of American education calls for a strong public school system. As the secretary of the Massachusetts Board of Education, Mann had documented educational conditions and practices

Margaret Fuller

in public schools at home and abroad, publishing his findings in twelve *Annual Reports*, which helped shape American educational policies.

HENRY WHEATON: *History of the Law of Nations.* An expansion of a historical outline that prefaced Wheaton's earlier *Elements of International Law* (1836). The work wins honorable mention in a competition sponsored by the French Institute, is hailed throughout Europe, and becomes a standard source on international law.

Poetry

THOMAS HOLLEY CHIVERS: *The Lost Pleiad and Other Poems.* A commercially successful collection of poems written between 1836 and 1844, primarily concerning supernatural themes. "The Lost Pleiad" and "To Allegra Florence in Heaven" are elegies for Chivers's daughter. The latter repeats the word *nevermore* and would lead to accusations that Chivers had plagiarized Poe. However, Poe's review in the *Broadway Journal* shows admiration for the verse.

HENRY BECK HIRST (1817–1874): *The Coming of the Mammoth, The Funeral of Time, and Other Poems.* The Philadelphia poet's first collection of verse, in the words of the *Cyclopaedia of American Literature*, displays "vigor and feeling" and includes a number of well-written sonnets. Hirst, a friend of Poe, would have a falling out with the writer over Hirst's parody of "The Haunted Palace." Hirst would later claim to be the author of "The Raven."

HENRY WADSWORTH LONGFELLOW: *The Belfry of Bruges and Other Poems*. A collection containing many verses published earlier in *Graham's*. Some of the poems were inspired by the author's European travels, including the title poem "The Belfry of Bruges," "Nuremberg," "The Norman Baron," and "Walter von der Vogelweid." Also notable are "The Bridge," in which the poet considers his numerous travels over the Charles River; "The Arsenal at Springfield," which compares a cannon to an organ; and "The Arrow and the Song," in which he compares writing poetry to shooting arrows.

WILLIAM WILBERFORCE LORD (1819–1907): *Poems.* This slim collection of verse is praised by Wordsworth and earns the New York Episcopal clergyman acclaim as "the American Milton." Poe, however, condemns the poems for being "a very ordinary species of talent" and later would write a parody of the verses accusing Lord of plagiarism. The book includes the popular poem "On the Defeat of a Great Man."

EDGAR ALLAN POE: *The Raven and Other Poems.* A collection containing all of Poe's verse to date. Biographer Hervey Allen would write that it "may be said to have been the finest contribution to poetry so far by an American."

Publications and Events

The *American Whig Review.* Founded as a political magazine supporting Henry Clay's bid for the presidency, it continued as a literary journal in opposition to the *Democratic Review.* An ardent supporter of American literature, the periodical featured various articles on New York art and theater, tales, literary criticism, and translations from French and German. Highly noted for its biographies of statesmen, which include engraved plate illustrations, it also published political writings. Contributors included Poe (whose "The Raven" and "Ulalume" and other works appeared in its pages), Horace Greeley, and Daniel Webster.

The *Broadway Journal.* New York literary periodical edited by Charles Frederick Briggs and partially owned by Poe. Within ten months of its founding, Poe became sole owner. In this journal he published many of his arguments against Transcendentalists, accused Longfellow of plagiarism, and reprinted several of his stories, poems, and other writings.

The *National Police Gazette.* This New York weekly initially featured crime stories and criminal biographies. Both police and organized crime disliked it, and the

Gazette offices were assaulted three times, killing nine people. In 1866 it was purchased by New York City chief of police George W. Matsell, who began publishing sensational sex stories. Richard Fox took control in 1877, expanded the sexual content, and began printing the paper on pink stock with woodcut illustrations. Features included "Crimes of the Clergy" and "Vice's Vanities." Although carried by few newsstands, its circulation reached 150,000. Often found in barrooms and barbershops, it earned it the nickname "the barbershop bible."

The *Southern and Western Monthly Magazine and Review.* This Charleston, South Carolina, periodical debuts but within a year is absorbed by the *Southern Literary Messenger.* Its editor and principal contributor was William Gilmore Simms.

1846
Drama and Theater

CORNELIUS MATHEWS: *Witchcraft; or, The Martyrs of Salem.* Mathews's blank-verse tragedy treating the Salem witchcraft trials successfully debuts in Philadelphia and goes on tour across the country. Regarded as one of the strongest of the American dramas written before the Civil War, it helps earn Mathews recognition as "the father of American drama."

Fiction

JAMES FENIMORE COOPER: *The Redskins; or, Indian and Injin: Being the Conclusion of the Littlepage Manuscripts.* Cooper dramatizes an attempted raid on the Littlepage property, Ravensnest, by a group of Anti-Rent agitators disguised as Indians. The novel is Cooper's most aggressive defense of New York's patroon system, supporting feudal-like landowners rather than the claims of the propertyless class, which he felt threatened violence and mob rule.

NATHANIEL HAWTHORNE: *Mosses from an Old Manse.* A collection of tales, sketches, and essays published in two volumes. Several of the author's most notable stories are in this collection, including "Young Goodman Brown," "Rappaccini's Daughter," "The Celestial Railroad," and "The Birthmark." The tales touch on Puritan themes common to Hawthorne's work and were written during his stay in the title's Old Manse, owned by Ralph Waldo Emerson.

HERMAN MELVILLE (1819–1891): *Typee: A Peep at Polynesian Life.* A fictionalized account of the author's experiences as a whaleman who jumps ship from the *Acushnet* and is confined by the cannibalistic Typee tribe in the

Herman Melville

Marquesas Islands. First published in England, it had received warm reviews there, but its U.S. publishers, Wiley and Putnam, made Melville cut thirty pages that disparaged Christian missionaries. The book creates a sensation, and many of Melville's contemporaries, including Margaret Fuller, Washington Irving, Walt Whitman, and Nathaniel Hawthorne, praise it. Others find the depiction of primitive culture vulgar. The book would sell more than twenty thousand copies during Melville's life.

JAMES KIRKE PAULDING: *The Old Continental; or, The Price of Liberty.* Paulding's historical novel, set during the Revolution, provides a realistic portrait of lower-class New Yorkers during the period.

EDGAR ALLAN POE: "The Cask of Amontillado." First published in *Godey's Lady's Book*, the work is the last of Poe's famous and frequently anthologized psychological crime stories. Set in an Italian city during Carnival, it follows Montresor as he leads Fortunato into his underground vaults with promises of a premium wine, but then walls him in to die.

THOMAS BANGS THORPE: *The Mysteries of the Backwoods.* A collection of sketches treating Southern sporting life. Although not financially successful, the sketches are significant for their Americanization of sporting literature.

Literary Criticism and Scholarship

MARGARET FULLER: *Papers on Literature and Art.* A collection of selected literary reviews written when Fuller was a literary critic for the *New York Tribune*. A redoubtable intellectual, Fuller examines various works of art and literature and explores the craft of the literary critic.

EDGAR ALLAN POE: *The Literati of New York.* A series of sketches frankly critiquing the writing, personalities, and appearances of New York authors, including Caroline Stansbury Kirkland, Epes Sargent, the members of the Knickerbocker group, and others. His negative remarks about Thomas Dunn English bring a bristling response; Poe would respond by suing the *New York Mirror* for libel. Poe also publishes "The Philosophy of Composition." Among the most famous works of literary criticism, this essay is published in *Graham's Magazine* and describes the process of writing poetry, primarily discussing Poe's procedures in composing "The Raven." Poe explains the importance of keeping a poem brief enough to read in one sitting and his use of a refrain. He declares that poems should be about beauty, and the death of a beautiful woman is therefore "the most poetical topic in the world."

HENRY THEODORE TUCKERMAN (1813–1871): *Thoughts on Poets.* The New York–based writer and critic supplies a biographical and critical work on twenty-six poets, including Goldsmith, Pope, and Byron, which the *United States Democratic Review* favors over numerous similar works for the author's "cultivated mind" and "honest convictions." The *Review* assures readers that the book will provide "improved taste" and a "wider sphere of knowledge."

Nonfiction

CATHARINE ESTHER BEECHER: *The Evils Suffered by American Women and Children: The Causes and the Remedy.* One of the principal works of the prolific author, this pamphlet is a print version of a lecture that Beecher had delivered in large cities. It outlines the problems of widespread illiteracy, difficulties for women in the school system, and the ills of the Lowell, Massachusetts, factory system.

J. ROSS BROWNE (1821–1875): *Etchings of a Whaling Cruise, with Notes of a Sojourn on the Island of Zanzibar; with a History of the Whale Fishery.* Browne's first book is an account of his sea travels to Zanzibar in 1842–1843 on the whaling ship *Bruce*. The work wins critical recognition and would influence Melville's writing of *Moby-Dick*. Browne served as official reporter for the first Constitutional Convention in California in 1849.

JAMES FENIMORE COOPER: *Lives of Distinguished American Naval Officers*. This complement to Cooper's *History of the Navy* (1836) presents sketches of prominent naval men, including Commodore Woolsey and John Paul Jones, and is highly commended for its historical importance and graceful narrative.

MARK HOPKINS (1802–1887): *Lectures on the Evidences of Christianity*. A published edition of the Massachusetts clergyman and physician's first lectures given at the Lowell Institute in Boston wins great praise and passes through several editions. The nonsectarian treatise argues the truth of Christianity and its connection with nature.

SAMUEL JOSEPH MAY (1797–1871): *The Rights and Conditions of Women*. A defense of women's suffrage and an attempt to transform Americans' definitions of women and men. May is the first American clergyman to openly support women's right to vote.

BAYARD TAYLOR (1825–1878): *Views A-foot; or, Europe Seen with Knapsack and Staff*. An account of the Pennsylvania poet and novelist's two-year walking tour of Europe, which he managed on an extremely limited budget. Written on his return to the United States, the book becomes immediately popular, passing through six printings in one year and acclaimed by the New England literati, including Henry Wadsworth Longfellow and John Greenleaf Whittier.

THOMAS BANGS THORPE: *Our Army on the Rio Grande*. An account of the Mexican War gathered from eyewitnesses of important battles, official military documents, and camp newspapers. Although the work sells poorly, it is credited as the source for subsequent histories of the conflict.

Poetry

OLIVER WENDELL HOLMES: *Poems*. An enlarged edition of his 1836 *Poems* is published in the *New Englander*. *Yale Review* notes that it contains "some of the finest passages to be found in the whole range of American poetry." Holmes would expand his *Poems* in 1852 as *The Poetical Works of Oliver Wendell Holmes*.

ELIJAH KELLOGG (1813–1901): "Spartacus to the Gladiators." First published in the *School Reader*, this declamatory poem by the Maine clergyman would become a favorite recitation piece for schoolchildren throughout the rest of the century.

HENRY WADSWORTH LONGFELLOW: "Seaweed." Longfellow's poem offers the poet's conception of the poetic process in which the "storms of wild emotion" produce "some fragment of a song" like seaweed tossed onto shore.

JAMES RUSSELL LOWELL: *The Biglow Papers*. A political satire in verse that presents Hosea Biglow, a wise Yankee farmer opposed to the Mexican War on the grounds that it is an attempt to expand slavery westward. The papers are considered the best of Lowell's humorous writing. *The Biglow Papers, Second Series* would appear in the *Atlantic Monthly* during the Civil War and be published as a collection in 1867.

HENRY MORFORD (1823–1881): *The Rest of Don Juan*. Considered the New York journalist's best work of poetry, the poem is an imitation of Byron's masterpiece, written as a sequel.

WILLIAM MUNFORD: *Iliad*. The first American translation of the Greek epic, published years after Munford's death. The *Southern Literary Messenger* proclaims that his name is "destined to stand high among the literary men of Virginia."

JOHN GREENLEAF WHITTIER: *Voices of Freedom*. Whittier's final collection of antislavery verse contains his most ardent poem on the subject, "Massachusetts to Virginia," in which he responds to Virginians' attacks on Massachusetts for refusing to enforce the Fugitive Slave Law.

Publications and Events

DeBow's Review. Founded by James Dunwoody Brownson De Bow (1820–1867) and written mainly by him, this monthly magazine was influential in shaping Southern opinion during the antebellum era, through its vigorous support of John C. Calhoun, the protective tariff, and slavery. After the Civil War it was sympathetic toward Reconstruction. It folded in 1880.

The *Home Journal*. Branching off from the *New York Mirror*, this weekly magazine featured a variety of writing, including poetry, essays, and society news and gossip. Founded and edited by Nathaniel Parker Willis until his death in 1867, its name was changed in 1901 to *Town and Country*, which in turn was bought by William Randolph Hearst in 1925 and continues to be published.

1847
Drama and Theater

JOHN BROUGHAM (1810–1880): *Metamora; or, The Last of the Pollywoags*. A popular burlesque of John Augustus Stone's Indian melodrama *Metamora; or, The Last of the Wampanoags* (1829) by the Irish-born actor and playwright. Full of puns and parody, it would hold the American stage for more than thirty years.

JAMES KIRKE PAULDING: *The Bucktails; or, Americans in England.* In Paulding's satirical comedy of manners, several caricatured English types court an American girl before she comes to her senses and accepts her American beau.

Fiction

ALFRED W. ARRINGTON (1810–1867): *The Desperadoes of the Southwest.* This vivid portrait of lynch law, based on the western lawyer's own experiences, is first published in eastern newspapers under the pseudonym "Charles Summerfield." The *United States Democratic Review* calls it "A work of thrilling adventure, recounting, in a graphic and readable style, scenes of murder and lynching."

EMERSON BENNETT: *The Bandits of the Osage: A Western Romance.* The story of a virtuous and strong woman who is twice kidnapped but then rescued by an upper-class man who loves her. It wins Bennett a $500 prize and affirms his popular reputation when published in the *Cincinnati Dollar Weekly Commercial.* More than twenty thousand copies in book form would be sold by the end of 1848.

CHARLES FREDERICK BRIGGS: *The Trippings of Tom Pepper: The Results of Romancing, an Autobiography by Harry Franco.* A literary history parodying many of Briggs's New York contemporaries, including Cornelius Mathews, Evert Augustus Duyckinck, William Gilmore Simms, and Edgar Allan Poe. Many of them took offense, leading Briggs to vow never again to write fiction.

EMILY CHUBBUCK JUDSON (1817–1854): *Alderbrook.* A collection of sketches originally contributed to the *New York Mirror* under the pseudonym "Fanny Forester." Although the newspaper did not pay her for these sentimental tales of village life, she wins a large following, and the collection goes through eleven editions. Judson was the third wife of the Baptist missionary to Burma Adoniram Judson (1788–1850).

HERMAN MELVILLE: *Omoo: A Narrative of Adventures in the South Seas.* This sequel to *Typee* is a fictionalized account of Melville's adventures in Tahiti, which, after the success of *Typee,* publishers were eager to print and readers quick to purchase. The work includes a severe attack on missionaries and French colonials in Polynesia and a great degree of sexuality, which again wins an audience but also results in negative reviews. The *American Whig* declares that Melville is "a man glorifying in his licentiousness."

JOHN S. ROBB (fl. 1847): *Streaks of Squatter Life, and Far-West Scenes.* This popular collection of humorous western sketches, many of which had appeared in the *Spirit of the Times,* contains some of the earliest tales about the legendary frontiersman Mike Fink. Robb was a journeyman printer based in St. Louis who also wrote *Kaam; or, Daylight: A Tale of the Rocky Mountains* (1847).

DANIEL PIERCE THOMPSON: *Locke Amsden; or, The Schoolmaster.* Notable for its accurate depiction of life on the Vermont frontier, this semi-autobiographical story depicts a boy's efforts to educate himself and others. Thompson outlines his own theories on the importance of education for the good of society and the self. The book wins praise from critics and educators, including Horace Mann and Jared Sparks.

Literary Criticism and Scholarship

RUFUS WILMOT GRISWOLD: *The Prose Writers of America.* An anthology of contemporary writers. Griswold, the most important anthologist of his time, praises Hawthorne, Poe, and Emerson, though he gives undue glorification to his literary friends. The work is also important for the author's opening essay, which exalts American literature.

Nonfiction

WILLIAM WELLS BROWN (c. 1814–1884): *Narrative of William W. Brown, a Fugitive Slave, Written by Himself.* An immediate bestseller with more than ten thousand copies sold in two years, Brown's memoir details his life as a slave and escape to the North. Brown would dramatize incidents in his autobiography as *The Escape; or, A Leap to Freedom* (1856) and *Experience; or, How to Give a Northern Man a Backbone* (1856).

HORACE BUSHNELL (1802–1886): *Christian Nurture.* The first important publication of the Congregationalist minister who is sometimes called "the father of American religious liberalism." In it he analyzes the importance of the conversion experience for revivalists.

GEORGE COPWAY (1818–1869): *The Life, History, and Travels of Ka-ge-ga-gah-bowh.* The popular autobiography of the Ojibway chief who becomes a Wesleyan missionary.

ANDREW JACKSON DAVID (1826–1910): *The Principles of Nature, Her Divine Relations, and a Voice to Mankind.* The spiritualist's first book is a sensational collection of lectures on philosophy, psychology, science, and the occult, transcribed while the author was in a trance. Davis was known as the "Poughkeepsie Seer" for his trance revelations, which were popular in abolitionist, feminist, and temperance circles.

HARRIET FARLEY (1817–1907): *Shells from the Strand of the Sea of Genius.* A collection of essays on the social and cultural life of female workers at the textile mills in Lowell, Massachusetts. Some of the essays had been previously published in the *Lowell Offering*, a literary magazine by and for the women textile workers and popular throughout the United States and England that Farley, a factory worker herself, edited. Farley's essays assert the mill women's intelligence.

JOEL PALMER (1810–1881): *Journal of Travels over the Rocky Mountains*. The description of the pioneer's 1845 expedition to Oregon from his Indiana home would serve as a significant guidebook for settlers throughout the next decade. It is noted for its comprehensive chronicle of the Oregon Trail.

WILLIAM HICKLING PRESCOTT: *History of the Conquest of Peru*. A narrative history of Pizarro's invasion of Peru, which Prescott had written after the success of *The Conquest of Mexico* (1843). The work covers Inca culture, the conquests, civil wars between the conquerors, and the discovery and settlement of the country. It remains a standard authority.

LORENZO SABINE (1803–1877): *The American Loyalist; or, Biographical Sketches of Adherents to the British Crown in the War of the Revolution*. A highly commended and unbiased biographical history of American Loyalists in the Revolutionary War, this book is the most important work of the New England historian. He would revise it as *Biographical Sketches of the Loyalists of the American Revolution* (1864), recognized as an important source for many years.

Poetry

PHILIP PENDLETON COOKE: *Froissart's Ballads*. Cooke's only collection of narrative poems, some of which are based on the French poet Jean Froissart's *Chronicles*, fails to sell well despite positive reviews.

RALPH WALDO EMERSON: *Poems*. Emerson's first collection of verse is harshly criticized in some reviews, including one in the *North American Review*, which calls it "the most prosaic and unintelligible stuff." Other critics admire the poems' unique and understated style, and the volume earns the author a modest profit with a sale of 850 copies in one year. Revised and enlarged numerous times, the collection would be issued in 1904 in an edition celebrating the centenary of Emerson's birth. Emerson also publishes "Ode Inscribed to W. H. Channing," a response to the request by William Henry Channing [II] for Emerson's views on slavery. It includes one of his most famous lines: "Things are in the saddle, / And ride mankind."

HENRY WADSWORTH LONGFELLOW: *Evangeline, a Tale of Acadie*. A verse romance of Acadian lovers who are separated on their wedding day when the English expel French Canadian settlers from Nova Scotia. Hugely successful, the poem establishes Longfellow's popular reputation and stands among the most highly praised poems of the nineteenth century.

EPES SARGENT: *Songs of the Sea and Other Poems*. A popular collection of verses, some based on Sargent's travels to Cuba. Many would be later set to music. Numerous critics, including Poe, consider the sonnet section "Shells and Seaweeds" (which depicts a young man's voyage at sea) to be the best of Sargent's poems.

Publications and Events

The *Chicago Tribune*. This newspaper debuts and becomes prominent under the editorship of Joseph Medill (1855–1899), who made it a fervently Republican journal after he helped found the party. The paper continued to be controlled by Medill's descendants, including Colonel Robert Rutherford McCormick (1880–1955), a militaristic, anti-union isolationist.

The *Literary World*. A weekly journal devoted to society and literature that featured sketches, gossip, and numerous book reviews. Editors included both Duyckinck brothers (Evert Augustus and George Long) and Charles Fenno Hoffman. A fire forced it out of business in 1853.

The *Massachusetts Quarterly Review*. This Boston literary, philosophical, and humanitarian journal, edited by Emerson and others, debuts. James Russell Lowell, Julia Ward Howe, and the elder Henry James appeared in its pages before its demise in 1850.

The *North Star*. Frederick Douglass begins this antislavery newspaper in Rochester, New York. In contrast with the *Liberator*, the paper favored peaceful political action to end slavery. It was later called *Frederick Douglass's Paper* and ceased publication in 1864.

The *National Era*. An antislavery journal famous for its notable abolition articles, particularly those on the Compromise of 1850 and John Brown's raid. It also published poems and fiction, including Harriet Beecher Stowe's *Uncle Tom's Cabin* and Hawthorne's "The Great Stone Face."

1848
Drama and Theater

BENJAMIN A. BAKER (1818–1890): *A Glance at New York*. The New York playwright's drama is one of the earliest tour-of-the-city plays, about a country bumpkin's visit to New York. It introduces a Bowery character named Mose who uses contemporary slang, previously unheard on the stage of the day.

CHARLOTTE MAY SANFORD BARNES: *The Forest Princess.* This historical melodrama shows Pocahontas in America and England. Barnes also publishes *Octavia Bragaldi,* a blank-verse drama based on the Beauchamp murder in Kentucky (1825), first produced in 1837.

GEORGE HENRY BOKER (1823–1890): *Calaynos.* Audiences in London, Philadelphia, Chicago, Baltimore, and Albany enjoy Boker's first play, a tragedy about a Spanish nobleman, Calaynos, whose wife is seduced by her husband's guileful friend, who reveals that Calaynos has Moorish ancestry. It is especially notable for its depiction of the racial issues between the Spanish and the Moors.

WILLIAM E. BURTON (1804–1860): *The Toodles.* Burton's comedy about a man beset by a foolish wife with a penchant for buying useless things is a popular success. The English-born comic actor would play the lead role to great acclaim for the rest of his life.

CORNELIUS MATHEWS: *Jacob Leisler.* Set in seventeenth-century New York, Mathews's historical drama concerns a former governor who is executed for defying his successor.

Fiction

EMERSON BENNETT: *Mike Fink: A Legend of the Ohio.* Bennett popularizes the frontier boatman, the self-described "Kaintuck war-horse, the snapping turtle, and Massassip alligator." The book, and Bennett's other 1848 publication *The Renegade: A Historical Romance of Border Life,* both sell fifty thousand copies.

JAMES FENIMORE COOPER: *The Crater; or, Vulcan's Peak: A Tale of the Pacific.* The story of a utopian island in the Pacific that sinks into the sea after clergymen, a lawyer, and an editor create conflict there. It offers Cooper's opinion of government and his diagnosis of the decaying values in American society. *Oak Openings; or, The Bee-Hunter,* Cooper's final wilderness tale, deals with bee-hunting and Indian fighting on Lake Michigan and has a religious theme, affirming Christian faith. Cooper also publishes *The Sea Lions; or, The Lost Sealers,* his last sea tale. It recounts Captain Kidd's life and describes a treasure-hunting expedition in the West Indies based on the island chart found among Kidd's belongings. The work also contains a story of whaling in the Antarctic and again affirms Cooper's Christianity.

ELIZA LESLIE: *Amelia; or, A Young Lady's Vicissitudes.* The only novel of the celebrated writer of cookbooks and domestic science concerns a proper woman who is forced to work as a maidservant at the inn owned by her father and stepmother until her gentility attracts a wealthy man.

ELIZABETH OAKES SMITH: *The Salamander: A Legend for Christmas, Found Amongst the Papers of the Late Ernest Helfenstein.* Based on legends told by ironworkers in the Ramapo Valley, this Christian allegory features a fiery Salamander that takes human form and sacrifices himself for the sake of others. This highly acclaimed publication is considered by many critics to be Smith's finest work because of its complexity and beauty of description. It is also notable because in it Smith announces that she will no longer use her male pseudonym, "Ernest Helfenstein."

WILLIAM TAPPAN THOMPSON: *Sketches of Travel, Comprising the Scenes, Incidents, and Adventures of His Tour from Georgia to Canada.* The third collection of letters detailing the adventures of Major Joseph Jones, a Georgia planter, who this time travels north, providing humorously naive impressions. The letters illustrate the growing conflict between the North and the South and defend slavery.

CHARLES WILKINS WEBBER: *Old Hicks, the Guide; or, Adventures in the Comanche Country in Search of a Gold Mine.* Webber's well-received first book-length work concerns an expedition through Texas to "Peaceful Valley" in search of gold.

Literary Criticism and Scholarship

JOSEPH C. HART: *The Romance of Yachting.* Included in Hart's travel sketches are a number of literary essays, including one of the earliest analyses to claim that Bacon was the real author of Shakespeare's plays.

FREDERIC HENRY HEDGE (1805–1890): *The Prose Writers of Germany.* A critically praised collection of essays by German authors, including Goethe, Luther, and Friedrich Wilhelm Joseph von Schelling, translated and introduced by Hedge. The translations and the introductions familiarize American readers with German literature.

EDGAR ALLAN POE: *The Poetic Principle.* Poe sets forth his precepts of poetry in this 1848 lecture that would be published posthumously in 1850. He asserts the importance of emotion in lyrical endeavors and presents eleven American and English poems that he considers works of art.

WILLIAM FREDERICK POOLE (1821–1894): *An Alphabetical Index to Subjects Treated in the Reviews and Other Periodicals, to Which No Indexes Have Been Published.* Later called *Poole's Index to Periodical Literature,* the foremost American periodical index of the time. Poole had begun to compile the entries while a student at Yale. The index would be updated until 1908, and it remains significant

Theodore Parker

for its bibliographical coverage of 590,000 articles in 479 American and English periodicals.

EDWIN P. WHIPPLE (1819–1886): *Essays and Reviews.* A perceptive and insightful collection of critical essays that confirms the Massachusetts writer and lecturer's reputation as one of the era's foremost critical essayists. The collection includes essays from Whipple's earlier magazine publications and new writings on subjects such as Daniel Webster, Sydney Smith, and Byron.

Nonfiction

WILLIAM HENRY CHANNING (1810–1884): *Memoir of William Ellery Channing, with Extracts from His Correspondence and Manuscripts.* A widely read and frequently republished biography of the author's famous uncle, the writer and Unitarian clergyman. The work lacks numerous significant details of Channing's life but remains important as the only source for many of his papers.

CHARLES FENNO HOFFMAN: *The Pioneers of New York.* Originally offered as a lecture, this highly respected essay on New York's settlers argues against the superiority of New England in American literature.

THEODORE PARKER: *A Letter to the People of the United States Touching the Matter of Slavery.* An antislavery tract written when Parker was speaking at abolitionist conventions. The letter promotes the idea that slavery is economically damaging to the South.

EPHRAIM GEORGE SQUIER (1821–1888): *Ancient Monuments of the Mississippi Valley.* A study of the remains of the Mound Builders, resulting from Squier and Edwin Hamilton Davis's excavation of mounds in Ohio from 1845 to 1847. Their findings appear as volume one of the Smithsonian Institution's *Contributions to Knowledge* and are the first analytical study of ancient American monuments.

ELIZABETH CADY STANTON (1815–1902): "Declaration of Sentiments." Mostly the work of Stanton, this manifesto, modeled on the Declaration of Independence, proclaims that men and women are created equal and enumerates eighteen legal grievances suffered by women. It is also the first public demand by American women for the vote. It is adopted at the first woman's rights convention in Seneca Falls, New York, and would be reintroduced at successive conventions and become the rallying cry in the campaign for equality and enfranchisement.

Poetry

WILLIAM WELLS BROWN: *The Anti-Slavery Harp: A Collection of Songs for Anti-Slavery Meetings.* This popular collection of antislavery songs published to invigorate the abolitionist cause contains verses by John Greenleaf Whittier and James Russell Lowell. "Fling out the Anti-Slavery Flag," the only piece by Brown, is thought to be his first published poetical work.

STEPHEN COLLINS FOSTER (1826–1884): *Songs of the Sable Harmonists.* This collection of songs is published while Foster is working as a bookkeeper in Cincinnati. It includes "Oh! Susannah!" and "Uncle Ned." It gains such widespread popularity that Foster leaves bookkeeping to become the most successful professional songwriter in the country.

JAMES RUSSELL LOWELL: *The Vision of Sir Launfal.* A popular verse parable concerning a knight's discovery that the Holy Grail lies in offering charity to a suffering leper. The work illustrates the author's ability to Americanize a legend. Lowell also publishes anonymously *A Fable for Critics*, a satirical poem about a critic who worships Apollo; he reviews contemporary writers, including Holmes, Emerson, Bryant, Fuller, Irving, Whittier, Hawthorne, Cooper, and others to find the one who will please the god. The fanciful work is noted for its accurate criticism of the authors. Also appearing in book form is *The Biglow Papers.*

EDGAR ALLAN POE: *Eureka: A Prose Poem by Edgar A. Poe.* In a metaphysical treatise inspired by the scientists Isaac Newton and Pierre-Simon Laplace, Poe reconciles conflicting theories of the origin of the universe by suggesting that there is an order to the cosmos, but that

Stephen Collins Foster

annihilation is a component of the order. The work would influence many writers, including France's Paul Valéry.

Publications and Events

The *Independent*. The New York weekly, initially affiliated with the Congregationalists, debuts. Contributors included Whittier, Lowell, and Stowe. It continued until 1928.

Oneida community. John Humphrey Noyes (1811–1886) establishes this utopian socialist community on a nine-hundred-acre farm in central New York. Branch communities would be established throughout the northeastern states, but controversy surrounding the group's concept of "Complex Marriage," combining polygamy and selective breeding, caused Noyes to relocate the community to Canada in 1879.

1849
Drama and Theater

CORNELIUS AMBROSIUS LOGAN: *Chloroform; or, New York a Hundred Years Hence*. In Logan's last known play, Aminadab Slocum awakens after being chloroformed for a pulled tooth into a future New York to confront his descendants.

Fiction

HENRY WADSWORTH LONGFELLOW: *Kavanagh: A Tale*. Longfellow's final major prose publication tells the story of two friends who both fall in love with the village's new pastor. Although it receives mixed reviews and is not considered among his finer works, it wins favor with Emerson and Hawthorne.

WILLIAM STARBUCK MAYO (1811–1895): *Kaloolah; or, Journeyings to the Djébel Kumri*. This romantic novel by the New York physician about a Yankee's marriage to an African princess is the best of Mayo's novels inspired by his travels in Spain and North Africa. It is often likened to Swift's *Gulliver's Travels* and Melville's *Typee*.

HERMAN MELVILLE: *Mardi: And a Voyage Thither*. A romantic and satirical novel that introduces Melville's first questioning protagonist, a seaman who is dissatisfied with his life, deserts his ship, and encounters metaphysical, ethical, and political questions. The book signifies the beginning of Melville's emphasis on psychology and metaphysics and more allegorical, symbolic method. Mellville also publishes *Redburn*, which he considers a "potboiler" and a way to please audiences after their displeasure with *Mardi*. It is based on his first sea voyage, in which the naive protagonist is thrown into the world of Liverpool, learns about the harsh realities of life, and eventually matures.

JAMES KIRKE PAULDING: *The Puritan and His Daughter*. Paulding's popular historical novel treats seventeenth-century American life in Virginia and New England.

E.D.E.N. SOUTHWORTH (EMMA DOROTHY ELIZA NEVITTE SOUTHWORTH, 1819–1899): *Retribution*. Southworth's first novel tells of a pure young woman who works for the freedom of her slaves while her husband is seduced by a more passionate woman. Originally published in the *National Era*, it is praised in the *American Whig Review*, which observes that "The style is eloquent, refined, the plot consistent, and powerful, the characters natural and strongly marked." Southworth would become one of the best-selling female novelists of the era, specializing in fiction of domestic sentimentality.

JOHN GREENLEAF WHITTIER: *Leaves from Margaret Smith's Journal in the Province of Massachusetts Bay, 1678–9*. Originally published anonymously in the *National Era*, this is the author's only novel, written in the form of a diary kept by a young English girl visiting New England. The Margaret Smith character is considered by many, including twentieth-century literary scholar Lewis Leary, one of the earliest "native heroines."

HENRY AUGUSTUS WISE (1819–1869): *Los Gringos; or, An Inside View of Mexico and California, with Wanderings in*

Peru, Chili, and Polynesia. Based on the naval officer's experiences, this work is hailed by the *United States Democratic Review* as the "preeminent" book resulting from the Mexican War "for power and truth of description, for keen-sighted detection of the attractive points of adventure, and whole-souled appreciation of manners, fun, and frolic."

Literary Criticism and Scholarship

HENRY THEODORE TUCKERMAN: *Characteristics of Literature, Illustrated by the Genius of Distinguished Men.* Biographical sketches of authors who represent different types of literature. A second series of sketches would be published in 1851, and both volumes are highly regarded. The *Living Age* describes the essays as "marked by a clearness of outline, a vividness of coloring, a felicity of arrangement, and a fidelity to reality that denote genius and skill of no common order."

Nonfiction

HORACE BUSHNELL: *God in Christ.* A criticism of the established belief in Christ's death as atonement for human sins and a discussion of the relationship of language to religion. Some readers accuse Bushnell of heresy. He would respond to the accusations in *Christ in Theology* (1851).

MARY HENDERSON EASTMAN (1818–1880): *Dacotah; or, Life and Legends of the Sioux Around Fort Snelling.* Eastman's first and most significant work recounts Sioux legends as told to her by Chequered Cloud, a "medicine woman and legend-teller." Based on firsthand observations, the work also describes Sioux culture, especially the devout spirituality and the degradation of women. Eastman's familiarity with Indian life resulted from accompanying her soldier husband to his frontier posts in the West.

JOSIAH HENSON (1789–1881): *The Life of Josiah Henson.* The dictated autobiography of an escaped slave who fled to Canada, set up a cooperative community, and became a Methodist preacher. Later editions of the book, titled *Truth Stranger Than Fiction* (1858) and *Truth Is Stranger Than Fiction* (1879), would feature introductions by Harriet Beecher Stowe, who cites Henson as the basis for her character Uncle Tom.

RICHARD HILDRETH: *History of the United States.* A six-volume history up to 1821. Told from a Federalist perspective, it is criticized as dull and lacking philosophy in its day but would later prove more influential than the more popular histories of the time.

JOHN PENDLETON KENNEDY: *Memoir of the Life of William Wirt.* Kennedy's final important literary pro-

Francis Parkman

duction offers a highly detailed, authoritative biography of the author of *Letters of the British Spy* (1803), who also served as attorney general under Presidents James Monroe and John Quincy Adams. The work receives positive reviews and goes through six printings.

FRANCIS PARKMAN (1823–1893): *The California and Oregon Trail; Being Sketches of Prairie and Rocky Mountain Life.* A classic account of the historian's western excursion with his cousin Quincy Adams Shaw from St. Louis to Fort Laramie and his weeks spent living among Sioux Indians in 1846. The book describes prairies, Indians, pioneers, and buffalo. It had been first serialized in the *Knickerbocker* in 1847 as *The Oregon Trail.*

ALEXANDER ROSS (1782–1856): *Adventures of the First Settlers on the Oregon or Columbia River, 1810–1813.* An autobiographical account of the Scottish-born fur trader's experiences in the Pacific Northwest. The book contains important details on the life of fur traders as well as ethnography of Chinook, Okanogan, and other Native Americans. A sequel, *The Fur Hunters of the Far West,* would appear in 1855.

HENRY DAVID THOREAU (1817–1862): *A Week on the Concord and Merrimack Rivers.* Thoreau's first book, organized around a river journey that the author had taken with his brother in 1839, contains a humorous recounting of events and brilliant contemplations on philosophy, religion, history, literature, and science. It does not sell, however. Thoreau also publishes the essay "Resistance to

Civil Government" in Elizabeth Palmer Peabody's journal *Aesthetic Papers.* The essay concerns the primacy of the individual over government and had been written after the author spent a night in jail for refusing to pay a poll tax that he considered immoral. The essay would go unnoticed until republished in 1866 under the title "Civil Disobedience."

Poetry

ALICE CARY (1820–1871) AND PHOEBE CARY (1824–1871): *Poems.* This first volume of verse by two sisters from the Ohio frontier wins them $100 from the publisher and an introduction to the intellectual society of New York.

HENRY WADSWORTH LONGFELLOW: *Seaside and the Fireside.* Longfellow's popular collection contains "The Fire of Driftwood," "The Secret of the Sea," and, most notably, "The Building of the Ship," a pro-Union allegory, which would win fame in dramatic readings by Fanny Kemble and attract the favor of Abraham Lincoln. Thirty thousand copies of the book sell in five years.

ALFRED BILLINGS STREET: *Frontenac; or, The Atotarho of the Iroquois.* One of the author's most famous works is a spirited historical verse of seven thousand lines. In its critique, the *North American Review* hails Street's poems, saying they "abound in native beauties, both of thought and expression."

JOHN GREENLEAF WHITTIER: *Poems.* This expanded edition of his 1838 *Poems* receives wide critical praise; the *American Whig Review* notes, "there is scarcely a modern poet whose admirers would more gladly welcome the scattered lays of their favorite in so fine a form for constant reference."

Publications and Events

The *Spirit of the Age.* William Henry Channing edits this New York weekly journal, which advocates abolition, universal education, pacifism, and temperance. Contributors included Parke Godwin and Henry James Sr. It would continue until April 1850.

1850
Drama and Theater

GEORGE HENRY BOKER: *The Betrothal.* A successful comedy set in Tuscany about the marchioness di Tiburzzi's attempt to marry her daughter to a wealthy merchant although the girl is in love with Count Juranio.

CHARLES JAMES CANNON (1800–1860): *The Oath of Office.* A tragedy set in fifteenth-century Ireland about the mayor of Galway, who must choose between condemning his son to death for murder or breaking his oath.

After choosing to break the oath, he kills his son himself. It is the New York writer's most successful play.

GEORGE HENRY MILES (1824–1871): *Mohammed, the Arabian Prophet.* This blank-verse tragedy by the Maryland dramatist, poet, and religious novelist wins a $1,000 prize for the best tragedy in five acts offered by the actor Edwin Forrest. Although the versification is highly regarded and the *American Whig Review* proclaims it the best since Coleridge, it would not succeed on the stage when produced in 1851.

Fiction

ELIZA ANN DUPUY (1814–1880): *The Conspirator.* Dupuy's highly fictionalized account of the life of Aaron Burr, excerpted in the *Southern Literary Messenger* in 1838 and serialized in the *New World* in 1843, proves a popular success when published in book form, selling more than twenty-four thousand copies.

NATHANIEL HAWTHORNE: *The Scarlet Letter.* Hawthorne's masterpiece, set in seventeenth-century Boston, describes the consequences of sin and guilt as Hester Prynne is forced to wear a scarlet *A* to show her sinful state after committing adultery and bearing a daughter. Her returned husband, Roger Chillingsworth, is determined to expose the outwardly pure clergyman, Arthur Dimmesdale, as the father. The novel combines elements from Puritan life and the gothic romance into a symbolical moral and psychological drama, unmatched in ambition and artistry by any other American novel to date.

CAROLINE LEE WHITING HENTZ (1800–1856): *Linda; or, The Young Pilot of the Belle Creole.* Hentz's sentimental novel of Southern life describes the jealousy of the heroine's lover who vows vengeance on her other suitors. In its equally popular sequel, *Robert Graham* (1855), the hero has learned to control his passion, marries Linda, and takes her to India as a missionary.

HENRY CLAY LEWIS (1825–1850): *Odd Leaves from the Life of a Louisiana "Swamp Doctor."* One of the finest collections of early Southwestern humor contains tales of the young "Madison Tenas," a swamp doctor, taken from the author's own experiences as a physician. Soon after the book is published, Lewis drowned in a flood.

WILLIAM STARBUCK MAYO: *The Berber; or, The Mountaineer of the Atlas.* A popular novel about twin brothers separated as children, one of whom is raised by Barbary pirates, and their reunion and adventures in the Atlas Mountains. The accurate descriptions of people and surroundings reflect Mayo's travels in Spain and North Africa.

BIRTHS AND DEATHS, 1850–1860

Births

1850   Edward Bellamy (d. 1898), novelist
        Lafcadio Hearn (d. 1904), author and critic
        Ella Wilcox (d. 1919), poet

1851   Kate Chopin (d. 1904), short story writer and novelist
        Grace Elizabeth King (d. 1931), novelist
        Albery Allson Whitman (d. 1901), poet

1852   Mary E. Wilkins Freeman (d. 1930), short story writer
        Edwin Markham (d. 1940), poet and editor

1853   William Gillette (d. 1937), actor and playwright
        Jacob Gordon (d. 1909), playwright
        Edgar Watson Howe (d. 1937), novelist
        Thomas Nelson Page (d. 1922), novelist and short story writer

1854   F. Marion Crawford (d. 1909), novelist

1855   H. C. Bunner (d. 1896), short story writer and editor
        Edgar Saltus (d. 1921), novelist and essayist
        George Edward Woodberry (d. 1930), poet and literary critic

1856   L. Frank Baum (d. 1919), children's writer, playwright, and journalist
        Harold Frederic (d. 1898), novelist
        Charles Major (d. 1913), novelist
        Lizette Woodworth Reese (d. 1935), poet
        Booker T. Washington (d. 1915), writer and educator
        Kate Douglas Wiggin (d. 1923), novelist and educator

1857   Gertrude Franklin Atherton (d. 1948), novelist
        Margaret Deland (d. 1945), novelist
        Henry Blake Fuller (d. 1929), novelist
        S. S. McClure (d. 1949), editor and publisher
        Ida Tarbell (d. 1944), journalist, historian, and biographer
        Augustus Thomas (d. 1934), playwright
        Thorstein Veblen (d. 1929), economist and editor

1858   Charles W. Chesnutt (d. 1932), novelist and short story writer

Sam Walter Foss (d. 1911), poet
Agnes Repplier (d. 1950), author and critic
Theodore Roosevelt (d. 1919), writer, historian, and president of the United States
Alfred Henry Lewis (d. 1914), novelist

1859   Irving Bacheller (d. 1950), novelist
        Katherine Lee Bates (d. 1929), poet
        David Belasco (d. 1931), playwright

1860   Hamlin Garland (d. 1940), novelist and short story writer
        Owen Wister (d. 1938), novelist

Deaths

1850   Philip Pendleton Cooke (b. 1816), poet
        Margaret Fuller (b. 1810), essayist, critic, and social reformer

1851   Mordecai Manuel Noah (b. 1785), playwright and journalist
        James Fenimore Cooper (b. 1789), novelist

1852   John Howard Payne (b. 1791), playwright
        Elizabeth Stuart Phelps (b. 1815), novelist
        William Ware (b. 1797), clergyman and novelist

1854   Robert Montgomery Bird (b. 1806), playwright and novelist
        George Lippard (b. 1822), novelist
        Richard Penn Smith (b. 1799), playwright

1855   Sarah Sayward Barrell Keating Wood (b. 1759), novelist

1856   James Gates Percival (b. 1795), poet

1858   James Nelson Barker (b. 1784), playwright
        Thomas Holley Chivers (b. 1809), poet

1859   Washington Irving (b. 1783), writer and diplomat
        William Hickling Prescott (b. 1796), historian

1860   Charles James Cannon (b. 1800), playwright
        Samuel Griswold Goodrich (b. 1793), children's writer
        Joseph Holt Ingraham (b. 1809), novelist
        James Kirke Paulding (b. 1778), novelist and short story writer

HERMAN MELVILLE: *White-Jacket; or, The World in a Man-of-War.* This semi-autobiographical account of Melville's travels from Hawaii to the Atlantic coast with the U.S. Navy includes scenes of flogging, which would be used as propaganda to stop the custom. The work is also noteworthy for its use of symbols, especially the white jacket, which the narrator breaks free of, thus losing his innocence.

DONALD GRANT MITCHELL (1822–1908): *Reveries of a Bachelor; or, A Book of the Heart.* Writing as "Ik Marvel," the Connecticut-born farmer and essayist collects his whimsical essays of a bachelor's musings on marriage, love, and friendship, which had originally appeared in the *Southern Literary Messenger* in 1849. His most popular work, *Reveries* would prompt another collection blending fiction and the essay "Dream Life" (1851).

MAYNE REID (1818–1883): *The Rifle Rangers; or, Adventures of an Officer in Southern Mexico.* The Irish-born writer, actor, dramatist, and Indian fighter's first novel is a popular adventure tale that incorporates his own experiences in the Mexican War, where he had been wounded in the Battle of Chapultepec.

SUSAN BOGERT WARNER (1819–1885): *The Wide, Wide World.* Warner's sentimental domestic novel, written under the pseudonym "Elizabeth Wetherell," concerns the moral development of a young orphan. It becomes the first American novel to sell more than one million copies. Warner's work had been rejected by several publishers, one of whom dismissed it as "fudge."

Literary Criticism and Scholarship

HERMAN MELVILLE: "Hawthorne and His Mosses." Melville's review of Hawthorne's *Mosses from an Old*

POPULAR BOOKS, 1850–1860

David Copperfield by Charles Dickens (First American Printing, 1850)

Reveries of a Bachelor by "Ik Marvel" (First American Printing, 1850)

The Wide, Wide World by Elizabeth Wetherell (Susan Bogert Warner) (First American Printing, 1850)

The Sunny Side; or, The Country Minister's Wife by Elizabeth Stuart Phelps (First American Printing, 1851)

The Curse of Clifton by E.D.E.N. Southworth (First American Printing, 1852)

Uncle Tom's Cabin by Harriet Beecher Stowe (First American Printing, 1852)

A Key to Uncle Tom's Cabin by Harriet Beecher Stowe (First American Printing, 1853)

Fern Leaves from Fanny's Portfolio by "Fanny Fern" (Sara P. Willis) (First American Printing, 1853)

Agnes Sorel by G.P.R. James (First American Printing, 1853)

Heir to Redclyffe by Charlotte Mary Yonge (First American Printing, 1853)

The Lamplighter by Maria Susanna Cummins (First American Printing, 1854)

Hard Times by Charles Dickens (First American Printing, 1854)

Hot Corn by Solon Robinson (First American Printing, 1854)

The Newsboy by Elizabeth Oakes Smith (First American Printing, 1854)

Ruth Hall by "Fanny Fern" (Sara P. Willis) (First American Printing, 1855)

The Prince of the House of David by Joseph Holt Ingraham (First American Printing, 1855)

John Halifax, Gentleman by Dinah Maria Mulock (First American Printing, 1856)

Widow Bedott Papers by Frances Miriam Whitcher (First American Printing, 1856)

Nothing to Wear by William Allen Butler (First American Printing, 1857)

Little Dorrit by Charles Dickens (First American Printing, 1857)

Barchester Towers by Anthony Trollope (First American Printing, 1857)

Bitter-Sweet by Josiah Gilbert Holland (First American Printing, 1858)

Autocrat of the Breakfast-Table by Oliver Wendell Holmes (First American Printing, 1858)

Lord Montague's Page by G.P.R. James (First American Printing, 1858)

Adam Bede by George Eliot (First American Printing, 1859)

The Hidden Hand by E.D.E.N. Southworth (First American Printing, 1859)

The Virginians by William Makepeace Thackeray (First American Printing, 1859)

The Woman in White by William Wilkie Collins (First American Printing, 1860)

Lucile by Owen Meredith (First American Printng, 1860)

Malaeska; or, The Indian Wife of the White Hunter by Ann Sophia Stephens (First American Printing, 1860)

Manse (1846) acknowledges the writer as the "American Shakespeare." While reading the work, Melville had recognized Hawthorne as a kindred spirit, and the younger writer would pursue an acquaintance with Hawthorne that became one of the most significant American literary friendships.

EDWIN P. WHIPPLE: *Lectures on Subjects Connected with Literature and Life.* A collection of the popular lecturer's speeches made on his travels from Boston to Maine and Ohio. The collection would go through three printings in one year and includes two of his most famous lectures from 1843–1849: "Wit and Humor" and "The Ludicrous Side of Life." The other lectures are "Authors in Their Relations to Life," "Novels and Novelists," "Genius," and "Intellectual Health and Disease." He would publish six more lectures in *Character and Characteristic Men* (1866).

Nonfiction

CHARLES FRANCIS ADAMS (1807–1886): *The Works of John Adams.* The first and only comprehensive collection of the papers of John Adams, a ten-volume collection edited by Adams's grandson Charles Francis Adams, the son of John Quincy Adams.

WASHINGTON ALLSTON: *Lectures on Art, and Poems.* Essays outlining Allston's artistic theory, which he had developed during the 1830s, as well as a number of his poems, some of which had never before been published, edited by Richard Henry Dana Jr. Although the book is not popular, it wins favorable critical review, especially for the essays, which constitute the first important American art criticism.

WILLIAM CULLEN BRYANT: *Letters of a Traveller; or, Notes of Things Seen in Europe and America.* This collection of unrevised letters written over fifteen years of travel wins immediate popularity with a public hungry for travel literature. The book would be reprinted the following year as *The Picturesque Souvenir, Letters of a Traveller,* and in 1859 a second series of *Letters of a Traveller* would be published.

WALTER COLTON (1797–1851): *Three Years in California, 1846–1849.* An important account of California's history. In journal-style narration, Colton describes people and events and chronicles the changes in California caused by Anglo settlers. Colton, a navy chaplain and founder of California's first newspaper, the *Californian* (1846), wrote other popular descriptions of his travels, but this is his most significant and lasting work.

SUSAN FENIMORE COOPER (1813–1894): *Rural Hours.* The most famous work of James Fenimore Cooper's daughter describes nature and life in Cooperstown, New York, in writing taken from her journals. Revised editions would appear in 1868 and 1887.

GEORGE COPWAY: *Traditional History of the Ojibway Nation.* An examination of the customs, language, legends, and history of the Ojibway Indians.

DANIEL DRAKE: *A Systematic Treatise, Historical, Etiological and Practical, on the Principal Diseases of the Interior Valley of North America, as They Appear in the Caucasian, African, Indian, and Eskimoux Varieties of Its Population.* A two-volume, 1,863-page collection of geographical, meteorological, and sociological information as well as descriptions of diseases. The *American Journal of Medical Sciences* hails this massive work as "the most valuable and important original production . . . that has yet appeared from the pen of any of our physicians."

RALPH WALDO EMERSON: *Representative Men.* A collection of biographical sketches of Shakespeare, Plato, Goethe, Swedenborg, Napoleon, and Montaigne, which Emerson had delivered from 1845 to 1848. The introductory essay, "On the Uses of Great Men," explains his belief that these men represent their times and countries and illustrate the individual's ability to effect change regardless of environment.

LEWIS H. GARRARD (1829–1887): *Wah-to-yah, and the Taos Trail; or, Prairie Travel and Scalp Dances, with a Look at Los Rancheros from Muleback and the Rocky Mountain Campfire.* An account of the Ohio explorer's ten-month expedition at age seventeen along the Santa Fe and Taos Trails. It is an important source of information about the Cheyenne Indians, traders, and mountain men.

WILLIAM JOHN GRAYSON (1788–1863): *Letter to His Excellency, Whitemarsh B. Seabrook, Governor of the State of South Carolina, on the Dissolution of the Union.* Although a passionate supporter of states' rights and slavery, the South Carolina lawyer, public official, and poet publishes this pamphlet against secession, predicting that "disorder, violence, and civil war" would result from disunion.

SARA JANE CLARKE LIPPINCOTT (1823–1904): *Greenwood Leaves: A Collection of Sketches and Letters.* The popular poet, journalist, and essayist's best-selling collection of letters, sketches, and burlesques of Edgar Allan Poe, Herman Melville, Henry Wadsworth Longfellow, and others had been popular when first published in the *Home Journal* under the pseudonym "Grace Green-

wood." John Greenleaf Whittier praises the author's letters for their "strong individuality" and "freshness." A second series of *Greenwood Leaves* would be published in 1852, followed by *Haps and Mishaps of a Tour in Europe* in 1854.

CHARLES JACOBS PETERSON (1819–1887): *The Naval Heroes of the United States.* This popular history is Peterson's most important book. He would expand on the topic in two later works, *A History of the United States Navy* (1852) and *The American Navy, Being an Authentic History* (1856). An important nineteenth-century editor and publisher, Peterson also edited *Atkinson's Casket* (which became *Graham's Magazine*) and the *Saturday Evening Post*, and he founded the *Ladies' National Magazine*, later known as *Peterson's*.

NANCY PRINCE (1799–?): *A Narrative of the Life and Travels of Mrs. Nancy Prince.* Published in Boston by the author, the book is a remarkable account of this freeborn New England African American woman's travels, including missionary work in Jamaica and time spent at the Russian court, where her husband was a steward.

BAYARD TAYLOR: *Eldorado; or, Adventures in the Path of Empire: Comprising a Voyage to California, via Panama; Life in San Francisco and Monterey; Pictures of the Gold Region, and Experiences of Mexican Travel.* A vibrant account of the gold rush and the establishment of government in California as Taylor observed it when sent west as a reporter for Horace Greeley's *Tribune*. Considered his best travel book, it would be reprinted in 1949 for the centennial of the gold rush.

SOJOURNER TRUTH (C. 1797–1883): *The Narrative of Sojourner Truth.* The ex-slave, preacher, abolitionist, and women's rights advocate had dictated her life story to Olive Gilbert. Seven subsequent editions would appear.

HENRY THEODORE TUCKERMAN: *The Optimist.* A miscellaneous collection of essays on topics ranging from hair to music, travel, and poetry. It is lauded by critics, including the reviewer for the *United States Democratic Review*, who finds the the work "instructive and agreeable" as well as written with "peculiar grace and precision."

DANIEL WEBSTER: "Seventh of March Speech." Also known as "For the Union and Constitution," this Senate speech concerns the expansion of slavery into the land annexed from Mexico. Webster's speech is a response to John C. Calhoun, who had condemned Henry Clay's "Compromise of 1850." Webster argues in support of the compromise to preserve the Union at all costs and suggests that abolitionists temper their own beliefs. Abolitionists are outraged, and John Greenleaf Whittier would respond with one of his finest poems, "Ichabod."

The editorial staff of the *New York Tribune* (*from left to right*): *seated,* George M. Snow, financial editor;
Bayard Taylor; Horace Greeley; George Ripley, literary editor; *standing,* William Hennry Fry, music editor;
Charles A. Dana; and Henry J. Raymond

Poetry

JOHN GREENLEAF WHITTIER: "A Sabbath Scene."
Whittier's most aggressive antislavery poem is written
to oppose the Fugitive Slave Law and speaks out against
religious leaders in the North who believe that the Bible
sanctions slavery. The poem tells of a parson who returns
a runaway slave who is hiding in the church. Whittier also
publishes "Ichabod," whose title in Hebrew means "in-
glorious." The poem expresses the antislavery faction's
disappointment over Daniel Webster's support of the
Compromise of 1850. In the poem "The Lost Occasion"
(1880) Whittier would moderate his view on Webster's
betrayal.

Publications and Events

Harper's Monthly Magazine. Founded in New York by
Harper and Brothers, this literary periodical first featured
British authors such as Dickens and Thackeray. Under
the editorship (1869–1919) of Henry M. Alden, more
Amerian writers appeared, such as Melville, James, and
Howells.

The *International Monthly Magazine of Literature, Arts,
and Science.* Begun as a weekly by Rufus Wilmot Griswold but soon published monthly, this magazine featured
travel and leisure articles as well as fiction, poetry, literary
criticism, and, after 1850, an illustrated fashion section.
A competitor of *Harper's,* it eventually merged with that
publication. Notable contributors included Thackeray,
Dickens, Simms, and Hawthorne.

The Works of the Late Edgar Allan Poe. The first three
volumes of Poe's collected works were rushed into print
by his literary executor Rufus Wilmot Griswold. Griswold
created the myth of a damned and dissolute Poe in his
misleading memoir, included in the collection. A fourth
volume would appear in 1856.

1851

Drama and Theater

JOHN BROUGHAM: *A Row at the Lyceum.* In Brougham's
play-within-a-play, a cast rehearsing a blank-verse
tragedy is interrupted by an actor from the audience, who
jumps onto the stage and provokes a fight, claiming to be

the husband of one of the actresses. The unconventionality of the comedy is striking compared with theatrical standards of the day.

HENRY WADSWORTH LONGFELLOW: *The Golden Legend.* Longfellow completes what would become the middle section of *Christus: A Mystery* (1872), the trilogy of dramatic poems providing an imaginative history of Christianity from its beginning (*The Divine Tragedy*, 1871), through the Middle Ages, to the time of the Puritans (*The New England Tragedies*, 1868).

JAMES PILGRIM (1825–1877): *Harry Burnham.* Set during the Revolution, this jingoistic melodrama is typical of the patriotic spectacles popular in the wake of the Mexican War.

Fiction

NATHANIEL HAWTHORNE: *The House of the Seven Gables.* Hawthorne's novel explores the history of the New England Pyncheon family and their house, fraudulently built on land obtained from a man whom the Puritan Judge Pyncheon had condemned to death for witchcraft. It explores, as the author states in the preface, "The truth, namely, that the wrong-doing of one generation lives into the successive ones, and divesting itself of every temporary advantage, becomes a pure and uncontrollable mischief."

HERMAN MELVILLE: *Moby-Dick; or, The Whale.* Melville's masterpiece converts an account of a whaling voyage into a symbolic existential drama framed by the monomaniacal Captain Ahab's pursuit of a white whale. Described by one reviewer as a "salamagundi of fact, fiction, and philosophy," contemporaries are mainly baffled by the book's techniques and intentions, and its failure to find an appreciative audience embittered Melville. In the twentieth century the novel would be rediscovered and acknowledged as possibly the greatest of all American novels.

ELIZABETH STUART PHELPS (1815–1852): *The Sunny Side; or, The Country Minister's Wife.* The popular Massachusetts author of religious fiction traces Emily Edwards's life from her wedding to her death, providing an accurate and sympathetic rendering of women's lives during the period. Although five publishers had refused the book, it sells over 100,000 copies in its first year, is internationally acclaimed, and establishes Phelps's popularity.

Nonfiction

JOHN C. CALHOUN: *A Disquisition on Government and a Discourse on the Constitution and Government of the United States.* This posthumously published essay attempts to establish a theory of minority rights within the framework of majority rule and argues that government is less important than society. Calhoun served as secretary of war, senator, vice president, and secretary of state, and this essay caps his reputation as one of the South's preeminent political theorists.

HENRY CHARLES CAREY: *Harmony of Interests: Manufacturing and Commercial.* A continuation of the author's opinions on economics, collectively among the first significant American works in that discipline. Carey supports protectionism and warns of the danger English economics might pose to American interests.

LOUISE AMELIA KNAPP SMITH CLAPPE (1819–1906): *Dame Shirley Letters.* Writing as "Dame Shirley," Clappe begins her series (through 1852) of letters from California. First published in San Francisco's *Pioneer Magazine*, they provide a woman's intriguing perspective on the gold rush. They would be collected as *The Shirley Letters* in 1922.

GEORGE WILLIAM CURTIS (1824–1892): *Nile Notes of a Howadji.* The first book published after the author's travels in the Near East as a correspondent for the *New York Tribune* receives popular and critical success and leads to further travel writing assignments from the paper. It would be followed by another critically appreciated account of his travels, *The Howadji in Syria* (1852).

CHARLES ÉTIENNE ARTHUR GAYARRE (1805–1895): *History of Louisiana.* The New Orleans historian begins publishing his most important work, a historically accurate and detailed four-volume narrative history of Louisiana (completed in 1866).

WILLIAM JOHN GRAYSON: *Letters of Curtius.* The South Carolina lawyer, politician, and author offers an economic justification for slavery.

GEORGE WILKINS KENDALL: *The War Between the United States and Mexico.* The cofounder of the *New Orleans Picayune* and one of the earliest American war correspondents provides a vivid account of the Mexican War based on his firsthand observations.

HENRY LEWIS MORGAN (1818–1881): *League of the Ho-de-no-sau-nee, or Iroquois.* The first scientific study of a Native American tribe, written after Morgan, known as "the father of American anthropology," became interested in Indian affairs as a member of the New York secret society the Gordian Knot, later renamed the Grand Order of the Iroquois.

FRANCIS PARKMAN: *History of the Conspiracy of Pontiac, and the War of the North American Tribes Against the English Colonies After the Conquest of Canada.* The first in Parkman's multivolume series about the conflicts between the French and the English for control of colonial

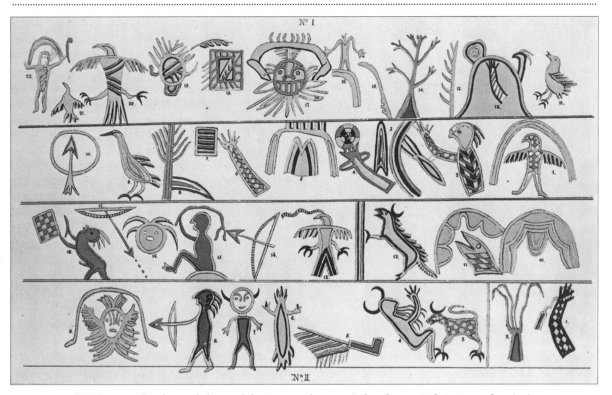

"Meda Songs," a chromolithograph by James Ackerman (taken from a Seth Eastman drawing), appearing in Schoolcraft's six-volume encyclopedia on American Indians published in 1851

America, the work details Pontiac's rebellion against England after France had surrendered its North American territories. The series would include *Pioneers of France in the New World* (1865), *The Jesuits in North America* (1867), *LaSalle and the Discovery of the Great West* (1869), *Count Frontenac and New France Under Louis XIV* (1877), *Montcalm and Wolfe* (1884), and *A Half Century of Conflict* (1892).

HENRY ROWE SCHOOLCRAFT: *Historical and Statistical Information Respecting the History, Condition, and Prospects of the Indian Tribes of the United States.* Written during Schoolcraft's employment at the Bureau of Indian Affairs, this is an agglomeration of facts and articles about Indian tribes and archaeological studies with illustrations by Captain Seth Eastman (1808–1875). The work is qualitatively inconsistent yet contains essential information and remains an important reference on the subject.

ELIZABETH OAKES SMITH: *Woman and Her Needs.* A collection of essays originally published in the *New York Tribune;* they assert female individuality and advocate suffrage.

EPHRAIM GEORGE SQUIER: *Aboriginal Monuments of the State of New York.* Squier's premier work on the subject of American antiquities presents the results of his archaeological study of western New York and is published as a portion of volume two of the Smithsonian's *Contributions to Knowledge.*

SOJOURNER TRUTH: "Ain't I a Woman?" Delivered at a conference on women's rights in Akron, Ohio, Truth's rousing speech calls for a redefinition of *woman* to include working-class and black females. The speech is transcribed for publication by Frances Dana Gage.

Poetry

THOMAS HOLLEY CHIVERS: *Eonchs of Ruby: A Gift of Love.* This collection of verses that experiment with the acoustic effects of words receives positive critical notice until it is suggested that Chivers is imitating Poe's style. Chivers would dispute this claim, stating that Poe had in fact plagiarized him. Although modern literary historians believe that Chivers was probably right, his contemporaries believed he was the plagiarist, and his reputation as a poet was ruined.

WILLIAM WILBERFORCE LORD: *Christ in Hades.* A religious epic significant for its vestiges of Milton, which wins its author the title "the American Milton."

Publications and Events

The *Carpet-Bag*. Under the editorship of B. P. Shillaber, this humorous Boston weekly begins publication. Until its demise in 1853, it featured Shillaber's "Mrs. Partington" sketches. In 1852 a sixteen-year-old Samuel Clemens published his first work, "The Dandy Frightening the Squatter," in its pages.

Gleason's Pictorial Drawing-Room Companion. The Boston weekly modeled on the *London Illustrated News* debuts. Contributors included Sylvanus Cobb, T. S. Arthur, and Horatio Alger. It continued until 1859.

The *New York Times*. The New York daily newspaper with a reputation for accuracy is founded by Henry J. Raymond (1820–1869) as a conservative alternative to the sensational papers of the day. In 1896 it was purchased by Adolph Ochs, and it maintained its reputation as America's preeminent newspaper throughout the twentieth century.

1852
Drama and Theater

GEORGE L. AIKEN (1830–1876): *Uncle Tom's Cabin*. The most popular dramatization of Harriet Beecher Stowe's novel includes minstrel songs and banjo music and is an immediate success, sometimes staged eighteen times in a week. It helps create a positive opinion of the theater for many Americans who had previously disdained it. Aiken was a popular actor as well as a playwright.

JOSEPH STEVENS JONES: *The Silver Spoon; or, Our Own Folks*. Jones's most enduring play concerns a humorous country delegate to the Massachusetts General Court who is tricked by the other characters. It would be revived multiple times and reprinted in 1911.

Fiction

ALICE CARY: *Clovernook; or, Recollections of Our Neighborhood in the West*. A narrative of lasting significance for its descriptions of the harsh conditions of early western life from a woman's point of view. Selling well, it would be pirated in five editions in England.

MARY HENDERSON EASTMAN: *Aunt Phillis's Cabin; or, Southern Life As It Is*. One of the most popular of the proslavery novels written in response to Harriet Beecher Stowe's *Uncle Tom's Cabin* sells eighteen thousand copies in a few weeks. The sentimental work portrays slavery in an idealized light and reveals the author's desire to justify the "necessary evil" of slavery.

BAYNARD RUSH HALL (1798–1863): *Frank Freeman's Barber Shop*. Hall's novel offers one of the earliest fictional treatments of a free African American. Rush was a Presbyterian clergyman and Indiana classics professor who previously published an account of frontier life under the name Robert Carlton, *The New Purchase* (1843).

NATHANIEL HAWTHORNE: *The Blithedale Romance*. One of the author's major romances, the story of Miles Coverdale's unsuccessful attempt at creating a utopia, reflects Hawthorne's own experiences at Brook Farm. Although Hawthorne makes clear in his preface that the characters are not representative of the actual members of the Brook Farm community, many suspect that Zenobia is modeled on Margaret Fuller and Coverdale is Hawthorne himself. The novel wins high praise, with Edwin P. Whipple in particular noting that it is "hardly equaled by anything this country has produced." Hawthorne also publishes *A Wonder-Book for Girls and Boys*, a collection of Greek myths for children. A similar volume, *The Tanglewood Tales*, would follow in 1853.

HERMAN MELVILLE: *Pierre; or, The Ambiguities*. The complicated life story of Pierre Glendinning, the son of a prominent Revolutionary family, as he grows from the security of his youth to the uncertainty of adulthood, the result of a letter from a woman claiming she is his illegitimate half-sister. The work is harshly criticized, and many continue to consider it poor, but it did win favor with some critics after Melville's rediscovery in the twentieth century.

ELIZABETH STUART PHELPS: *The Angel over the Right Shoulder*. The title story of this collection has been much anthologized for its depiction of a woman's self-sacrifice for her domestic responsibilities. Also published is an autobiographical story "A Peep at 'Number Five'; or, A Chapter in the Life of a City Pastor."

MAYNE REID: *The Desert Home; or, The Adventures of a Lost Family in the Wilderness*. The first of Reid's many adventure novels for boys is modeled on *The Swiss Family Robinson* and set in the Mexican desert. Reid had produced it for the Christmas market and would publish at least one new title annually until his death.

E.D.E.N. SOUTHWORTH: *The Curse of Clifton; or, The Widowed Bride*. Among Southworth's most popular works, this rags-to-riches tale concerns Clifton, heir to his family's wealth, his love for Capitola (a poor mountain girl), and his vicious stepmother.

HARRIET BEECHER STOWE: *Uncle Tom's Cabin; or, Life Among the Lowly*. Perhaps the most important American novel of the nineteenth century, Stowe's masterpiece is published serially in the *National Era* in 1851–1852 and as a book in 1852. The primary plot recounts the travails of the faithful slave Uncle Tom as he passes among several

Harriet Beecher Stowe

owners, eventually dying a martyr under the cruel Simon Legree. It is considered the first novel to portray blacks as individuals rather than stereotypes.

MARK TWAIN (Samuel Langhorne Clemens, 1835–1910): "The Dandy Frightening the Squatter." The sixteen-year-old Samuel Clemens publishes his first story in the humorous Boston weekly the *Carpet-Bag.*

SUSAN BOGERT WARNER: *Queechy.* A sentimental, moralistic novel about a young orphan who must sell flowers and garden produce to support her family. Following the success of Warner's *Wide, Wide World* (1850), the work becomes an immediate bestseller though is not as popular as the earlier novel.

CHARLES WILKINS WEBBER: *Tales of the Southern Border.* Called the "first fiction writer of importance to use Texas as his theme," Webber collects his autobiographically derived tales of the Texas frontier in this book.

Nonfiction

LYMAN BEECHER (1775–1863): *Works.* A collection of sermons and previously published magazine articles by the Presbyterian minister and father of Catharine Beecher, Henry Ward Beecher, and Harriet Beecher Stowe. The first president of Cincinnati's Lane Theo-

logical Seminary, Beecher was famous for his vitriolic condemnation of Catholicism and liquor.

WILLIAM WELLS BROWN: *My Three Years in Europe; or, Places I Have Seen and People I Have Met.* This narrative, comprising letters to Brown's friends, including Frederick Douglass, describes Brown's European travels, during which he journeyed for twenty-thousand miles, delivering more than a thousand speeches. The work is widely praised in Europe and the United States.

MARTIN DELANY (1812–1885): *The Condition, Elevation, Emigration, and Destiny of the Colored People of the United States.* Delany, a protégé of Frederick Douglass, analyzes contemporary race relations in America and argues for the immigration of freed blacks to a new, separate state of their creation.

NATHANIEL HAWTHORNE: *The Life of Franklin Pierce.* Hawthorne's campaign biography of his Bowdoin College classmate earns the writer an appointment as consul at Liverpool during the Pierce administration. Hawthorne would live in Europe for the next seven years.

FREDERICK LAW OLMSTED (1822–1903): *Walks and Talks of an American Farmer in England.* The first of the landscape architect's accomplished travel books. Later works would include *A Journey in the Seabord Slave States* (1856), *A Journey Through Texas* (1857), and *A Journey in the Back Country* (1860).

JOHN REYNOLDS (1788–1865): *Pioneer History of Illinois.* The Illinois governor's state history provides a wealth of information on frontier life in Illinois.

JOHN DAWSON GILMARY SHEA (1824–1892): *Discovery and Exploration of the Mississippi Valley.* The Catholic historian's highly acclaimed history wins Shea invitations to join the historical societies of Wisconsin, Maryland, and Massachusetts, a distinction rarely bestowed on Catholics at the time.

Publications and Events

Boston Public Library. The city's central library is founded. It would house one of the most extensive collections of materials on colonial and Revolutionary history and feminist history.

The *Golden Era.* This San Francisco journal and newspaper, noted for its publication of western writers, begins publication. Contributors included Bret Harte, Mark Twain, Alonzo Delano, and Joaquin Miller.

1853
Drama and Theater

GEORGE HENRY BOKER: *Lenor de Guzman.* Considered among the best of Boker's tragedies, the genre for which he is best known, the play is set in Castile in 1350 and concerns a powerful figure in Spain, who is killed by the mother of the succeeding king after the death of King Alfonso XII.

Fiction

JOSEPH GLOVER BALDWIN (1815–1864): *The Flush Times of Alabama and Mississippi.* A collection of satirical but realistic biographical sketches and frontier tales by a judge who lived in Alabama and Mississippi in the 1830s and 1840s, illustrating the humor of the Old Southwest involving a colorful gallery of backwoods lawyers, gamblers, con men, and tellers of tall tales.

WILLIAM WELLS BROWN: *Clotelle; or, The President's Daughter: A Narrative of Slave Life in the United States.* The first novel published by an African American tells the fictionalized story of Thomas Jefferson's slave mistress and depicts the horrors of slavery and racism. Initially published in England, it is brought out in the United States with references to the president removed. Brown would produce three additional revisions and expansions of his novel as *Miralda; or, The Beautiful Quadroon* (1860–61), *Clotelle: A Tale of the Southern States* (1864), and *Clotelle; or, The Colored Heroine* (1867).

GEORGE WILLIAM CURTIS: *The Potiphar Papers.* Seven sketches satirizing New York's fashionable society. Curtis had written the book after his essay "Our Best Society" won great popularity when published in *Putnam's.* Although the book receives poor reviews, it sells five thousand copies in its first month.

FREDERICK DOUGLASS: *The Heroic Slave.* Douglass's only work of fiction is a novella describing a mutiny aboard a slave ship. It is noteworthy for showing Douglass's shift away from a nonviolent stance and his contention that blacks must rely on themselves to gain their freedom.

SAMUEL ADAMS HAMMETT (1816–1865): *A Stray Yankee in Texas.* Writing as "Philip Paxton," Hammett details, in an anecdotal narrative, the natural and urban scenery, the harsh weather, and the dialect of Texas. The work is lauded by reviewers and remains an important contribution to Southwestern literature.

NATHANIEL HAWTHORNE: *The Tanglewood Tales.* Hawthorne's sequel to *A Wonder-Book for Girls and Boys* (1852) retells six additional Greek myths for children, including "The Minotaur" and "The Golden Fleece."

HERMAN MELVILLE: "Bartleby the Scrivener: A Story of Wall Street." Now considered one of the best American short stories, it is first published anonymously in *Putnam's,* receives acclaim, and would be later collected in

The Piazza Tales (1856). The story concerns a Wall Street lawyer who is unable to fire his copyist, who objects to things with the repeated refrain "I would prefer not to." Some suggest the story is an allegory of Melville's own feelings in response to the reception of his novels.

HARRIET BEECHER STOWE: *Uncle Sam's Emancipation.* Stowe collects stories, sketches, and moral essays. The most substantial story is "The Yankee Girl" in which a New England woman rejects a Canadian aristocrat to preserve her independence. In "The Two Altars" Stowe contrasts the ideals of the American Revolution with the realities of contemporary America under the Fugitive Slave Law.

Nonfiction

JOHN ROSS BROWNE: *Yusef . . . a Crusade in the East.* Browne's humorous account of foreign travel anticipates the method and style of Mark Twain's *Innocents Abroad.*

JAMES DUNWOODY BROWNSON DE BOW (1820–1867): *Industrial Resources of the South and West.* A three-volume compilation of the editor and statistician's most significant articles published in *De Bow's Review* provides information and statistics on a variety of topics including slavery, population, agriculture, railroads, and health. The *United States Democratic Review* hails the book as "not only the most extensive, but the most accurate and well-written Cyclopaedia of its kind."

ALONZO DELANO (1802?–1874): *Pen-Knife Sketches; or, Chips of the Old Block.* A collection of frontier sketches originally published in the *Pacific News* and written under Delano's popular nickname, "The Old Block." The sketches solidify Delano's reputation and would be followed by *Old Block's Sketch Book* (1856). Delano made the overland journey to California in 1849, described in *Life on the Plains and Among the Diggings* (1854).

FRANCIS LIEBER: *On Civil Liberty and Self-Government.* Lieber's best-known work is a historical exposition of the components of freedom in relation to law. The work would be used as a college textbook and, taken with his earlier works, represents one of the first methodical studies of political science in America.

JARED SPARKS: *Correspondence of the American Revolution, Being Letters of Eminent Men to George Washington, from the Time of His Taking Command of the Army to the End of His Presidency.* Sparks's final historical work is published the same year that he retires as president of Harvard College. The volume contains approximately a thousand letters from 190 writers, which Sparks edited only for problems in grammar. According to the critic J. G. Palfrey, "The volumes are prepared with the good judgment, good taste, and careful illustration which the public looks for in whatever passes through the hands of Mr. Sparks."

HARRIET BEECHER STOWE: *A Key to Uncle Tom's Cabin.* Written to refute attacks on the validity of Stowe's portrayal of slavery in *Uncle Tom's Cabin*, the volume gathers letters, newspaper articles, court records, and legal information that support her claims.

SARA PAYSON WILLIS (1811–1872): *Fern Leaves from Fanny's Portfolio.* A collection of intelligent and humorous sketches by the sister of N. P. Willis, originally contributed to newspapers under the name "Fanny Fern." This work is her greatest success, selling more than seventy-thousand copies in the United States in its first year. Willis would follow this work with a second series of *Leaves* in 1854 and *Fresh Leaves* in 1857.

Poetry

JAMES M. WHITFIELD (1822–1871): *America and Other Poems.* This is the major collection by the most notable of the antebellum African American antislavery poets. The title work is a parody of a nationalistic hymn, exposing the inconsistency between the institution of slavery and American ideals of liberty.

SARAH HELEN POWER WHITMAN (1803–1878): *Hours of Life and Other Poems.* A collection of Whitman's popular poetry. Sixteen of the poems detail her love for Edgar Allan Poe, to whom she was engaged after the death of her husband. A complete edition of her poetry would be published in 1879.

Publications and Events

Putnam's Monthly Magazine. Founded by the New York publishing firm, this general-interest magazine distinguishes itself from rival publications such as *Harper's* by its emphasis on American writing. The magazine was suspended in 1857 and a second series began in 1868, titled *Putnam's Magazine*, which ran until 1870. Notable contributors would include Melville, Longfellow, Lowell, Henry James, and humorists such as Gelett Burgess before the magazine merged with the *Atlantic Monthly* in 1910.

1854
Drama and Theater

EPES SARGENT: *The Priestess.* Sargent's most ambitious drama is a five-act blank-verse version of Bellini's opera *Norma;* the play fails to please audiences.

Fiction

WILLIAM TAYLOR ADAMS (1822–1897): *The Boat Club; or, The Bunkers of Rippleton.* This melodramatic adventure story in which three teenage boys defeat a gang of ruffians proves immediately popular, and Adams, writing as "Oliver Optic," would follow it with six similar books involving the same characters. The Boat Club series is the first of his many juvenile series.

LOUISA MAY ALCOTT (1832–1888): *Flower Fables.* Written when the author was sixteen, Alcott's first book is a collection of fairy tales and poems dedicated to Ralph Waldo Emerson's daughter Ellen, who first read them.

TIMOTHY SHAY ARTHUR: *Ten Nights in a Barroom and What I Saw There.* This popular melodramatic novel about an alcoholic who leads his family to destruction is often used by temperance lecturers and would be dramatized by William W. Pratt in 1858. The temperance song "Come Home, Father" would be included in the play around 1864.

JOHN ESTEN COOKE (1830–1886): *The Virginia Comedians; or, Old Days in the Old Dominion.* The Virginia writer's finest early novel, winning popular and critical acclaim, depicts colonial life in Virginia while presenting a negative view of the aristocracy and praising the common man. The sequel, *Henry St. John, Gentleman,* would be published in 1859. Cooke also publishes *Leather Stocking and Silk; or, Hunter John Myers and His Times.* This romance of the Virginia Valley early in the nineteenth century tells the story of Hunter John (a character similar to James Fenimore Cooper's Natty Bumppo), his daughter, and a host of love affairs.

MARIA SUSANNA CUMMINS (1827–1866): *The Lamplighter.* This wildly popular didactic romance would compel Hawthorne to remark bitterly about the "d——d mob of scribbling women" dominating publishing industry sales. In the novel, an afflicted orphan is taken in by a compassionate lamplighter, and, having been lovingly raised and taught virtues and religious faith, blossoms into a moralistic woman. In adulthood she is rewarded for her long suffering with marriage to a childhood friend. Translated into a number of languages, its first decade's sales show it to be second only to *Uncle Tom's Cabin* in popularity.

CAROLINE LEE HENTZ (1800–1856): *The Planter's Northern Bride.* One of the most popular sympathetic portraits of Southern life, Hentz's novel responds to *Uncle Tom's Cabin* by presenting slavery in a more positive light. Hentz was a New Englander who moved to the South and attempted to correct northern prejudices against southerners.

HERMAN MELVILLE: "The Encantadas; or, The Enchanted Isles." First published in *Putnam's Monthly* under the pseudonym "Salvator R. Tarnmoor," this collection of ten allegorical sketches of the Galapagos Islands, where Melville had traveled in 1841, would be included in *The Piazza Tales* (1856).

MARY HAYDEN GREEN PIKE (1824–1898): *Ida May.* The story of a white girl who is sold into slavery blends sentimental melodrama with antislavery subjects. It becomes an immediate bestseller, selling sixty thousand copies in two years in the United States. Pike, a Maine novelist, publishes it under the pseudonym "Mary Langdon."

EDMUND QUINCY (1808–1877): *Wensley, a Story Without a Moral.* This acclaimed fictional examination of the idiosyncrasies of early New England life is hailed by John Greenleaf Whittier as "the most readable book of this kind since Hawthorne's *Blithedale Romance.*"

JOHN ROLLIN RIDGE (1827–1867): *The Life and Adventures of Joaquin Murieta, the Celebrated California Bandit.* This immensely popular romance is based on a notorious outlaw in northern California. Ridge, writing as "Yellow Bird," transforms Murieta into a romantic hero. It is the first novel written by an American Indian and also the first published in California.

SOLAN ROBINSON (1803–1880): *Hot Corn: Life Scenes in New York Illustrated.* Robinson's collection of stories about life in New York City's notorious Five Points had first appeared as a series of articles in the *New York Tribune* in 1853. It becomes a runaway bestseller, spawning at least three dramatizations in 1854 that would rival *Uncle Tom's Cabin* at the box office.

BENJAMIN PENHALLOW SHILLABER (1814–1890): *Life and Sayings of Mrs. Partington.* Shillaber scores a popular success with a female counterpart to male comic figures such as Jack Downing and Sam Slick. Mrs. Ruth Partington is a small-town Yankee given to malapropisms and misadventures. She is regarded as the model for Mark Twain's Aunt Polly.

WILLIAM GILMORE SIMMS: *Woodcraft.* Regarded by some as Simms's best book and as the first realistic novel in American literature, *Woodcraft* depicts South Carolina adjustment to peace following the Revolution. Included is a benign portrait of plantation life, representing Simms's answer to *Uncle Tom's Cabin.*

ELIZABETH OAKES SMITH: *The Newsboy.* This novel about life in a city slum would win support for social reforms to aid New York street children. Smith also publishes *Bertha and Lily,* a novel telling the story of Bertha's transition from desolation after her seduction and the loss of her child to happiness in marriage to a man who considers her his equal. The feminist sentiments are popular with reformers in the nineteenth century and would attract the attention of late-twentieth-century literary scholars.

SEBA SMITH: *Way Down East; or, Portraitures of Early Life.* A collection of the author's best stories about Yankee life. *Putnam's* calls "Polly Gray and the Doctors," "Jerry Guttridge," and "Seth Woodsum's Wife" "funny and spirited." It is the author's most widely circulated book.

ANN SOPHIA STEPHENS (1810–1886): *Fashion and Famine.* One of the most popular novels of the prolific writer and her first long work, *Fashion and Famine* contrasts the fashionable society of Saratoga and Newport with the poor of New York. Published by four different publishers in New York, London, and Philadelphia, and translated into German and French, it would be dramatized in 1854. She would produce *Malaeska,* the first dime novel issued in the Beadle Dime Novel series in 1860.

MARY VIRGINIA HAWES TERHUNE (1830–1922): *Alone.* Written when Terhune was sixteen, this is the first and best of her twenty-six moral novels. It chronicles the life of Ida Ross, whose mother dies at age fifteen. Ida is sent to live with a cold and materialistic guardian in Virginia but eventually weds the man she loves, the Reverend Morton Lacy.

THOMAS BANGS THORPE: *The Hive of the Bee-Hunter, a Repository of Sketches, Including Peculiar American Character, Scenery, and Rural Sports.* The author's best work contains revisions of his popular sketches free of the sentimentality and mistakes of his earlier publications. It includes the final version of his best story, "The Big Bear of Arkansas," with illustrations by Felix O. C. Darley. It receives warm critical reviews, further boosting Thorpe's status as a western writer.

Nonfiction

THOMAS HART BENTON (1782–1858): *Thirty Years' View.* This preeminent political autobiography traces Benton's years as a Missouri senator and provides a study of American politics as he had seen it from 1820 to 1850. The work also outlines his concern for the state of the Union, his agrarian philosophy, and his opposition to the extension of slavery.

ALONZO DELANO: *Life on the Plains and Among the Diggings.* Critics consider this account of the author's 1849 overland expedition to California one of the most fascinating chronicles of the western migration.

GEORGE FITZHUGH (1806–1881): *Sociology for the South; or, The Failure of a Free Society.* The first American book with the word *sociology* in the title argues that slavery is natural and advantageous, not only to the slave owners but also to the slaves, who could not survive without white supervision. Troubling to Abraham Lincoln and other northerners, it provokes southerners to be more active in their defense of slavery.

SARAH JOSEPHA BUELL HALE: *Women's Record; or, Sketches of All Distinguished Women from 'The Beginning' til A.D. 1850.* An important biographical encyclopedia that contains twenty-five hundred entries and strives to exhibit the significance of women in history and literature.

SARA JANE CLARKE LIPPINCOTT: *Haps and Mishaps of a Tour in Europe.* A best-selling collection of letters originally sent to periodicals in the United States, detailing Lippincott's European tour with accounts of literary and historical attractions as well as prisons and asylums. The charming letters would remain in print for forty years.

HARRIET BEECHER STOWE: *Sunny Memories of Foreign Lands.* An epistolary travelogue based on Stowe's first voyage to England and the European continent, written in the fashion of the growing field of female travel books popular in the nineteenth century. Americans would use it extensively as a guidebook.

BAYARD TAYLOR: *A Journey to Central Africa; or, Life and Landscapes from Egypt to the Negro Kingdoms of the White Nile.* An account of Taylor's travels to exotic areas seldom traversed by Americans or Europeans. It wins wide commendation; *Putnam's* calls him "clearly the traveller of the nineteenth century." His other books include *The Lands of the Saracen* (1855) and *A Visit to India, China, and Japan, in the Year 1853* (1855).

HENRY DAVID THOREAU: "Slavery in Massachusetts." A lecture published in the *Liberator.* Thoreau, an active abolitionist who occasionally helped slaves escape to freedom in Canada, speaks out against the collusion of the North in slavery. Thoreau also publishes *Walden; or, Life in the Woods.* The landmark book is renowned both for its compelling descriptions and comments on nature and the personal insights of a philosophical man searching for his true self. The book, written after the author lived primitively on a parcel of land on Walden Pond owned by Ralph Waldo Emerson, had gone through seven complete revisions prior to publication, is positively received by critics, but sells only modestly.

BRIGHAM YOUNG (1801–1877): *Journal of Discourses.* The Mormon leader begins publishing what would eventually grow to a twenty-six-volume collection of religious writings (completed in 1886).

Poetry

WILLIAM JOHN GRAYSON: *The Hireling and the Slave.* The work for which Grayson is most remembered is a long poem contrasting the pleasant life of a Southern

Henry David Thoreau

slave against the painful existence of the English pauper and happily depicting the slave's participation in sports and activities.

FRANCES ELLEN WATKINS HARPER (1825–1860): *Poems on Miscellaneous Subjects.* This volume of poetry by the most famous African American poet of the time has an introduction by William Lloyd Garrison. The verses deal with motherhood, death, and antislavery issues. It would sell ten thousand copies in five years and go through at least twenty editions by 1874.

JULIA WARD HOWE (1819–1910): *Passion-Flowers.* Howe's first publication appears anonymously. Her intensely emotional lyrics are a popular success. A second volume, *Words for the Hour*, would follow in 1857, and her final collection, *Later Lyrics*, would be issued in 1866.

Publications and Events

The *Chicago Times.* The newspaper begins operation. Before the Civil War it gained a reputation for advancing Southern Democratic views and denouncing Lincoln. During the war it was a strong Copperhead (pro-Southern) paper. In 1895 it became the *Times-Herald.* Most noteworthy among its contributors was F. P. Dunne, the author of the "Mr. Dooley" papers. It was incorporated into William Randolph Hearst's *Examiner* in 1918.

Frances Ellen Watkins Harper

1855

Drama and Theater

GEORGE HENRY BOKER: *Francesca da Rimini.* Boker's masterpiece, which some scholars rank as the best nineteenth-century American play, is a verse tragedy based on the story of Paolo and Francesca from the fifth canto of Dante's *Inferno.*

JONATHAN BROUGHAM: *Po-ca-hon-tas!: Ye Gentle Savage.* A staple of American theater for thirty years, this excellent parody of popular American dramatic depictions of Native Americans as noble savages is based on the Pocahontas legend. The play is replete with comments on contemporary social and political themes and ideas.

CORNELIUS MATHEWS: *False Pretences; or, Both Sides of Good Society.* Mathews's social satire looks at the hypocrisy in contemporary society.

Fiction

THOMAS BULFINCH (1796–1867): *The Age of Fable.* An immediately successful updated narration of ancient mythologies of the Greek, Roman, Scandinavian, Celtic, and Asian peoples makes significant fables available to the layperson. This book would long remain the standard guide to mythology for young readers and would be followed by the less successful *The Age of Chivalry; or, Legends of King Arthur* (1858) and *Legends of Charlemagne; or, Romance of the Middle Ages* (1863). These three volumes are often referred to as Bulfinch's Mythology, but that title is also sometimes used only for *The Age of Fable.*

CHARLES JAMES CANNON: *Ravellings from the Web of Life.* Written under the pseudonym "Grandfather Greenway," this is a story collection narrated by a family to pass time. The work is warmly received, and a critic from *Brownson's Quarterly* notes the tales' "nice observation, deep feeling, happy descriptive powers and now and then something of the witchery of romance."

GEORGE HORATIO DERBY (1823–1861): *Phoenixiana; or, Sketches and Burlesques.* An immensely popular collection of humorous sketches on subjects ranging from frontier humor to poetry, politics, and frontier life. It would be reprinted more than twenty times by 1890. Mark Twain would deem Derby "the first great modern humorist." Derby's work appeared in various newspapers from 1849 to 1856, during his residence in California.

AUGUSTA JANE EVANS (1835–1909): *Inez: A Tale of the Alamo.* Evans draws on her experiences living in frontier San Antonio just before the outbreak of the war with Mexico to write her first novel, a sentimental, moralistic romance with a strong anti-Catholic, anti-Mexican bias.

JOSEPH HOLT INGRAHAM: *The Prince of the House of David.* A best-selling epistolary novel about a young Jewish girl during the life of Christ, it is the first and most successful of Ingraham's biblical romances, selling more than one million copies in the nineteenth century and remaining in print until 1975. The work helps win wider approval for novels and opens the door for subsequent adaptations of biblical stories.

WASHINGTON IRVING: *Wolfert's Roost.* An enormously popular collection of fables previously published in the *Knickerbocker Magazine.* It includes whimsical Spanish romances and scenes around Westchester County.

HERMAN MELVILLE: *Israel Potter: His Fifty Years in Exile.* Melville's only serialized novel is a historical narrative of a Revolutionary War hero who is captured by the British and lives in exile in England for fifty years, during which he encounters King George III, Benjamin Franklin, and John Paul Jones. The adventurous novel is Melville's attempt to satisfy his displeased readership, though he maintains his criticisms of American politics and philosophies.

WILLIAM GILMORE SIMMS: *The Forayers; or, The Raid of the Dog Days.* This Revolutionary War romance, set in South Carolina at the end of the war, tells the story of Willie Sinclair's defense of his home and that of his beloved against Tory raiders. The story and its sequel,

Iranistan, an oriental-style villa near Bridgeport, Connecticut, was the home of P. T. Barnum during the 1850s

Eutaw (1856), are considered by some critics to be Simms's finest work.

MORTIMER NEAL THOMSON (1831–1875): *Doesticks, What He Says.* A collection of sketches by "Queer Kritter Doesticks." Greatly popular when originally published in the *New York Tribune*, the collection reportedly sells seventy-five hundred copies on the first day it is available. The humorous sketches burlesque aspects of New York life, including Barnum's Museum, boardinghouses, and fire companies. Thomson was a New York writer, one of the first professional American humorists.

SARA PAYSON WILLIS: *Ruth Hall.* Willis's best-selling novel, written under her pseudonym "Fanny Fern," causes a sensation when the author's identity and the autobiographical elements are revealed, including an unflattering portrait of her famous brother Nathaniel Parker Willis. Equally shocking is the book's independently minded female protagonist. Many consider the novel unfeminine, but Elizabeth Cady Stanton praises it for debunking the myth that women must depend on men for economic, legal, and social protection. The novel would later be rediscovered as an important early feminist work. Willis would publish a second and final novel, *Rose Clark*, in 1856.

Literary Criticism and Scholarship

JOHN BARTLETT (1820–1905): *Familiar Quotations.* The Cambridge college bookstore owner issues the first edi-

tion of his popular reference volume of famous quotations from various writers. Nine more editions would be published during Bartlett's lifetime.

EVERT AUGUSTUS DUYCKINCK (1816–1878) AND GEORGE LONG DUYCKINCK (1823–1863): *Cyclopaedia of American Literature.* The landmark literary history encyclopedia provides a comprehensive examination of important American writers. The two volumes are arranged in chronological order by birth date and contain biographical information about each author and selections from their writings. Although it is no longer considered a standard reference, it remains a useful historical document. The brothers edited the *New York Literary World* (1847–1853), the leading weekly literary review of the period.

Nonfiction

JOSEPH GLOVER BALDWIN: *Party Leaders: Sketches of Thomas Jefferson, Alex'r Hamilton, Andrew Jackson, Henry Clay, John Randolph of Roanoke, Including Notices of Many Other Distinguished American Statesmen.* A survey of American political leaders. Baldwin, a humorist, undertakes the writing of this "serious" book to boost his literary reputation. It sells well but is not as popular as his earlier work, *Flush Times* (1853).

P. T. BARNUM (1810–1891): *The Life of P. T. Barnum, Written by Himself.* The first edition of Barnum's frequently revised autobiography detailing his career as a showman. Over the years many editions of the book would describe his exploits. Barnum, who also served as mayor of Bridgeport and a representative in the Connecticut legislature, founded "The Greatest Show on Earth," a circus that premiered in Brooklyn in 1871 and later became Barnum and Bailey's.

RUFUS WILMOT GRISWOLD: *The Republican Court; or, American Society in the Days of Washington.* A social history of the period of George Washington's presidency. The book is commercially successful and include discussions on varying social conventions throughout the country as well as illustrations of some of the prominent women of the day. It is considered Griswold's best work.

HINTON ROWAN HELPER (1829–1909): *Land of Gold: Reality Versus Fiction.* Helper, a North Carolina author who had spent three years in California during the gold rush, provides this critical account of his impressions.

WASHINGTON IRVING: *The Life of George Washington.* A popular biography that presents a broad view of the Revolutionary era as well as descriptions of Washington's contemporaries; it would remain the standard biography of Washington for decades. The final volume is published just weeks before Irving's death.

JAMES PARTON (1822–1891): *The Life of Horace Greeley.* The first biography from Parton, who would become one of the foremost biographers of the nineteenth century.

WILLIAM HICKLING PRESCOTT: *History of the Reign of Philip the Second.* Prescott begins publishing his final major historical work, issuing three volumes between 1855 and 1858 despite ill health and flagging energy. He dies while preparing the fourth volume.

Poetry

THOMAS BAILEY ALDRICH (1836–1907): *The Bells: A Collection of Chimes.* A widely popular and highly acclaimed poem that is praised by members of the New York literati, including Fitz-Greene Halleck and Nathaniel Parker Willis. Originally published in the *Journal of Commerce*, it launches Aldrich's literary career when reprinted in newspapers throughout the country; it would later be collected in *The Ballad of Babie Bell and Other Poems* (1859).

PAUL HAMILTON HAYNE (1830–1886): *Poems.* The South Carolina writer, called "the last literary cavalier," achieves popularity with his nature verses collected here and in *Sonnets and Other Poems* (1857) and *Avolio* (1860).

HENRY WADSWORTH LONGFELLOW: *The Song of Hiawatha.* A narrative poem depicting numerous Indian legends through the adventures of the fictionalized Hiawatha. It is Longfellow's most popular work and would

Poet Walt Whitman (left) seated with his soldier friend, Pete Doyle, in the early 1860s

sell more than fifty thousand copies by 1860. The meter of the poem was adapted from the Finnish epic *Kalevala*. Longfellow used the writings of Henry Rowe Schoolcraft, the Reverend John Heckewelder, and George Catlin as source material.

BAYARD TAYLOR: *Poems of the Orient.* Considered the author's finest and most characteristic book of verse, it contains his most famous poem, "The Bedouin Song," which would be set to music at least six times.

WALT WHITMAN: *Leaves of Grass.* Published at the author's expense and made up of only twelve poems, the collection of experimental free verse celebrates America and the American character. Whitman would revise and expand it nine times. Although it receives lukewarm critical and commercial response, the book contains a preface that is considered one of the most significant works on American nationalism in literature. One of the poems, "Song of Myself," is one of the crowning achievements of Whitman's career.

Publications and Events

The *New York Ledger.* The most popular weekly of its day is an outgrowth of the *Merchants Ledger*, founded in 1847, purchased by Robert Bonner in 1851, and renamed in 1855. The success of the publication was due to Bonner's elaborate advertising and contributions from popular writers, including E.D.E.N. Southworth and Lydia Huntley Sigourney, as well as sophisticated works by Harriet Beecher Stowe, Longfellow, Tennyson, and Dickens. Advice columns by Henry Ward Beecher, Edward Everett, and others were also popular. The *New York Ledger* became a monthly in 1898 and ceased publication in 1903.

1856

Drama and Theater

SIDNEY FRANCES BATEMAN (1823–1881): *Self.* Bateman's comedy of New York society deals with the fashionable Apex family's financial struggles, which are solved by a retired banker. Bateman was also an actress and for a time managed the Lyceum Theatre in London.

CHARLES TIMOTHY BROOKS (1813–1883): *Faust: A Tragedy, Translated from the German of Goethe.* The first English translation of Goethe's work to be published in America, it is particularly noted for maintaining the rhyme and meter of the original German. *Harper's* calls it "far more Goethe's *Faust* than any preceding English version."

JOHN BROUGHTON: *Dred.* The actor and playwright adapts Harriet Beecher Stowe's second novel.

CLIFTON W. TAYLEURE (1831–1887): *Horseshoe Robinson.* Based on John Pendleton Kennedy's 1835 historical romance, Tayleure's dramatic adventure set during the Revolution would remain popular with audiences for the next decade.

Fiction

FREDERICK S. COZZENS (1818–1869): *The Sparrowgrass Papers.* This immediately popular collection of humorous sketches by the New York wine merchant, essayist, and humorist, written under the pseudonym "Richard Haywarde," describes the adventures of a family that moves to the countryside of Yonkers from New York City. The sketches had been originally published in the *Knickerbocker* and *Putnam's.*

CHRISTOPHER PEARSE CRANCH: *The Last of the Huggermuggers.* The first of the children's books by the poet and humorist — among the few original fairy stories written in nineteenth-century America — is a Gulliver-like tale of a shipwrecked sailor on an island inhabited by two giants. *Kobboltzo* (1857), its sequel, deals with an evil dwarf living on the same island.

CAROLINE LEE HENTZ: *Ernest Linwood; or, The Inner Life of the Author.* The author's most autobiographical novel, about a woman married to an insanely jealous man and the struggle between domesticity and having a career as an author, sells twenty thousand copies in its first edition.

MARY JANE HOLMES (1825–1907): *Lena Rivers.* The most famous work of the prolific and popular author concerns a young girl, orphaned when her father disappears, who is accused of wrongdoing and is sent from her country village in Massachusetts to live with wealthy, snobbish relatives in Kentucky.

HERMAN MELVILLE: *The Piazza Tales.* A collection of Melville's finest short stories, which had been previously published in *Putnam's* after the commercial failure of his later novels. "The Piazza," a previously unpublished story, describes Arrowhead, Melville's farmhouse near Pittsfield, Massachusetts, and serves as an introduction to the collection, underscoring the repeated theme in the works in the difference between appearance and reality. The stories are "Bartleby the Scrivener," "The Encantadas," "The Lightning-Rod Man," "The Bell-Tower," and "Benito Cereno," about an innocent American sea captain who believes that the *San Dominick* is a slave ship under the command of captain Benito Cereno, when it is actually under the control of the slaves who have murdered most of the crew. Robert Lowell would adapt the story as a one-act verse play in *The Old Glory* (1965).

ANNA CORA MOWATT: *Mimic Life; or, Before and Behind the Curtain.* A collection of theater tales based on the author's own life. The book sells ten thousand copies and earns moderate critical notices.

MARY HAYDEN GREEN PIKE: *Caste: A Story of Republican Equality.* Among the author's best-known writings, the novel tells the story of a brother and sister who suffer many hardships when their African American ancestry is discovered. The popular book is published under the pseudonym "Sydney A. Story" and is particularly controversial for highlighting prejudice against African Americans in the North.

MAYNE REID: *The Quadroon.* The story of Edward Rutherford's love for a slave of mixed racial heritage, whom he saves from drowning. Unable to buy her at a slave auction, he abducts the slave girl and eventually the two lovers are wed. Reid adapts the novel as a play, and it would become the basis for Dion Boucicault's drama *The Octoroon* (1859).

WILLIAM GILMORE SIMMS: *Charlemont; or, The Pride of the Village.* An expansion of the beginning of his earlier novel *Beauchampe* (1842), detailing the seduction of Margaret Cooper by Wharham Sharp, a young attorney disguised as a theological student. After he breaks his promise of marriage and her illegitimate child dies, she vows to kill Warham. The work is based on the Kentucky crime involving Anna Cook and her husband Jeroboam O. Beauchamp, who killed Colonel Solomon P. Sharp.

HARRIET BEECHER STOWE: *Dred: A Tale of the Great Dismal Swamp.* Stowe's second popular antislavery novel. Not as successful as *Uncle Tom's Cabin*, it focuses on the negative economic and moral effect of slavery on whites.

FRANCES MIRIAM WHITCHER (1814–1852): *The Widow Bedott Papers.* A series of previously published sketches by the popular New York author of sketches and dialect tales goes through twenty-three printings in a decade. The book features two narrators, the widow Prissilly Bedott, an unrefined woman who often receives the brunt of the author's satire, and Aunt Maguire, through whom the author mocks haughty small-town life. The book is notable for its adept handling of local color and colloquial speech.

Literary Criticism and Scholarship

EDWARD TYRRELL CHANNING (1790–1856): *Lectures Read to the Seniors in Harvard College.* The only surviving publication to record the author and educator's rhetorical theories, which influenced his many prominent students, including Ralph Waldo Emerson, Oliver Wendell Holmes, James Russell Lowell, and Henry David Thoreau. The posthumously published book was edited by Richard Henry Dana Jr. and contains essays on rhetoric, composition, criticism, and language.

Sabin's Dictionary. This bibliographical listing of every book and pamphlet in any language related to America is begun by English-born New York City rare-book dealer Joseph Sabin (1821–1891). The first volume in the series was published in 1868, and the last under Sabin's direction, the fourteenth, appeared in 1884. The series concluded with volume twenty-nine in 1936.

Nonfiction

JAMES P. BECKWOURTH (1798–c. 1867): *The Life and Adventures of James P. Beckwourth, Mountaineer, Scout, and Pioneer and Chief of the Crow Nation of the Indians.* An exaggerated and grandiloquent account of the mountaineer's marriage to a Native American and how he became the chief of the Crow Indians. Beckwourth is a legendary character in frontier tales, and this autobiography, dictated to T. D. Bonner, is considered the best information predating 1830 on the Crow, Cheyenne, and Comanche tribes.

GEORGE WILLIAM CURTIS: *Prue and I.* A collection of essays in the style of Irving's *Salmagundi*, employing an old bookkeeper and his practical wife as a means of satirizing life in New York City. The work is well received by popular and critical audiences and would be republished numerous times until 1919. Curtis also publishes "The Duty of the American Scholar to Politics and the Times," his most famous and often-repeated speech, which inspires antislavery sentiments. This speech would be followed by "The Present Aspect of the Slavery Question" (1859) and "Political Infidelity" (1864); both would influence the public's opinion about slavery and the Civil War.

RALPH WALDO EMERSON: *English Traits.* A book of lectures exploring the nature of the English. Emerson investigates the qualities that he asserts mark the English as paragons of excellence, while also objectively illustrating their imperfections. The result of Emerson's stay in England, the book lauds British men, including writers such as Wordsworth, Coleridge, and Carlyle.

SAMUEL GRISWOLD GOODRICH: *Recollections of a Lifetime; or, Men and Things I Have Seen.* A two-volume autobiography of the author and publisher most known for his Peter Parley children's stories. The work remarks on subjects such as society, history, books, and the many authors with whom Goodrich was acquainted, including Nathaniel Hawthorne and Epes Sargent.

ELISHA KENT KANE (1820–1857): *Arctic Explorations: The Second Grinnell Expedition.* An account of the surgeon and explorer's second attempt to locate the missing Arctic explorer Sir John Franklin. Although Franklin was never found, the expedition did result in numerous Arctic discoveries, making Kane the first American hero of the Arctic. This account becomes an immediate bestseller. Kane's first unsuccessful attempt had been detailed in *The U.S. Grinnell Expedition in Search of Sir John Franklin* (1853).

JOHN LOTHROP MOTLEY (1814–1877): *The Rise of the Dutch Republic.* The Massachusetts diplomat and historian's three-volume study of the Netherlands, from the abdication of Charles V to the death of William the Silent in 1584, establishes his reputation as one of the era's leading historians. Volumes of the *History of the United Netherlands* would appear between 1860 and 1868.

FREDERICK LAW OLMSTED: *A Journey in the Seaboard Slave States, with Remarks on Their Economy.* A collection of travel letters previously published in the *New York Times* and new observations made by the author as he again traveled from Virginia to Louisiana. The book includes an impartial look at the economic effects of slavery. Olmsted, the landscape architect who would design Central Park, Golden Gate Park, Boston's "Emerald

Necklace," and the Stanford University campus, is known for his unbiased travel books.

MATTHEW CALBRAITH PERRY (1794–1858): *Narrative of the Expedition of an American Squadron to the China Seas and Japan.* The brother of Oliver Hazard Perry details his travels in China and Japan, where he had negotiated treaties opening up Japan to western trade and establishing the first American consulate.

GEORGE TUCKER: *The History of the United States from Their Colonization to the End of the Twenty-Sixth Congress, in 1841.* A highly detailed four-volume history by an author who had personally known every president of the United States up to that time. Although criticized for its Southern bias and largely forgotten today, this pioneering work looks at American history through a lens of economics and morality and fills the gap between Richard Hildreth's factual American history (1849) and the later published volumes of George Bancroft's monumental work (1834–1875).

Poetry

MORTIMER NEAL THOMSON: *Plu-ri-bus-tah, a Song That's By-No-Author.* A nationally popular parody of Longfellow's *Song of Hiawatha* and a social satire that burlesques many aspects of American life, most notably the desire for money.

GEORGE VASHON (1820–1878): *Autographs of Freedom.* Vashon's verse collection contains "Vincent Oge," the story of the Haitian revolutionary hero, which is considered the first published narrative poem by an African American.

WALT WHITMAN: *Leaves of Grass, second edition.* Whitman expands the original twelve poems of the 1855 first edition to thirty-two, including poems such as "By Blue Ontario's Shore," "Crossing Brooklyn Ferry," and "Song of the Broad-Axe."

JOHN GREENLEAF WHITTIER: *The Panorama and Other Poems.* A verse collection containing some of Whittier's most popular poetry, including the very popular "Barefoot Boy," a nostalgic poem celebrating boyhood in the country; "Maud Muller," a poem about the lost possibility of love; and an antislavery poem, "The Haschich."

1857
Drama and Theater

DION BOUCICAULT (1820–1890): *The Poor of New York.* A social satire following the disparate destinies of two families, the Bloodgoods, who thrive after they receive ill-gotten money, and the downtrodden Fairweathers, victims of the Bloodgoods' thievery. Boucicault also incorporates the contemporary events of the Panic of 1857. This is the Irish-born actor, theater manager, and playwright's first American success, demonstrating his superior ability with the melodramatic form.

OLIVER BELL BUNCE (1828–1890): *Love in '76.* Bunce's "comedietta" concerns the efforts of the daughter of a Tory Loyalist to protect a captain in the American army who is trapped in her home by British troops. Theatrical historian Arthur Hobson Quinn would consider it "the best of the Revolutionary plays"; it would remain popular until the end of the century.

JULIA WARD HOWE: *The World's Own.* Howe's drama about the seduction of a village maiden who extracts merciless revenge on her seducer draws criticism for its unapologetic portrait of an aggressive and powerful female.

Fiction

MARIA SUSANNA CUMMINS: *Mabel Vaughan.* A popular and critically successful follow-up to her bestseller *The Lamplighter* (1854). The novel concerns a woman who loses her wealth but gains morality when she rebuilds her family's life in the Illinois countryside. The *North American Review* finds the book an improvement over *The Lamplighter* and compliments its "strongly conceived" plot and "fresh, vivid, and authentic" descriptions of rural, city, and western life.

CHARLES G. LELAND (1824–1903): "Hans Breitmann's Party." Having published in 1855 his first miscellany, *Meister Karl's Sketch-Book,* the humorist introduces his popular German persona in this story published in *Graham's Magazine* and reprinted across the country. Leland's German-dialect-flavored observations would be later collected in *Hans Breitmann About Town* (1869) and *Hans Breitmann in Church* (1870).

HERMAN MELVILLE: *The Confidence-Man: His Masquerade.* A narrative following a series of con men, or possibly one confidence man in a number of disguises, on board a Mississippi River steamboat on April Fool's Day. The bitterly satiric novel examines the nature of trust and faith in America. Melville's final prose fiction work published during his lifetime, it is a dismal failure.

CATHARINE MARIA SEDGWICK: *Married or Single?* Written to justify single womanhood, this novel considers the various pursuits that can be undertaken by unmarried women, though in the end Sedgwick's heroine finds happiness in matrimony. Sedgwick's final novel is described by the *North American Review* to be "both in an artistical and ethical point of view, the best of the series that bears her name."

JOHN TOWNSEND TROWBRIDGE (1827–1916): *Neighbor Jackwood.* An antislavery novel by the Boston author of juvenile literature about the beautiful Camille Delisard, the daughter of a Frenchman and his slave, who is sold after her father is killed by his wife. She escapes to Vermont, where she is protected from a villain who wants to claim her as a fugitive slave. She then marries her rescuer, Hector Dunbury. The work, Trowbridge's first success, is considered notorious for the marriage between the white hero and the multiracial heroine.

FRANK J. WEBB (fl. 1857): *The Garies and Their Friends.* One of the earliest novels by a black American, portraying a white Southern aristocrat and his mulatto wife and a middle-class black family, is considered the first fictional work to describe free Northern blacks, a lynch mob in a free state, a mixed marriage, and the theme of passing for white.

NATHANIEL PARKER WILLIS: *Paul Fane; or, Parts of a Life Else Untold.* The only novel written by the writer hailed by his contemporaries as a distinguished American poet is the story of a young artist who is cherished by women for his talent, though scorned as a social inferior. It is an allegory of the relationship between American and European society.

Literary Criticism and Scholarship

DELIA BACON (1811–1859): *The Philosophy of the Plays of Shakespeare Unfolded.* This work sets forth the author's belief that Shakespeare's plays were written by a group of eminent men of the time, including Sir Francis Bacon, Edmund Spenser, and Sir Walter Raleigh. The writer's concepts, labeled Baconian theory, suggest that the plays contain a vast concealed wealth of wisdom, hidden in enigmas and puzzles to be deciphered. Her beliefs convince Emerson for a short period, and Nathaniel Hawthorne, though not a convert, wrote a preface, helped finance the book, and would later describe Bacon's insanity during his final years in *Our Old Home* (1863).

Nonfiction

JEAN LOUIS RODOLPHE AGASSIZ (1807–1873): *Contributions to the Natural History of the United States.* The Swiss scientist who had come to the United States in 1846 begins publishing his major work, completing four volumes in 1862. Volume one includes his most important theoretical statement, "Essay in Classification."

THOMAS HART BENTON: *Abridgment of the Debates of Congress from 1789 to 1856.* A sixteen-volume collection of congressional speeches that, according to the *United States Democratic Review*, presents "a thorough digest of all the important actions of our great men, as well as the series of events which have brought us up to the position we occupy at the present time." The highly lauded book makes many important congressional speeches more accessible to citizens, including those of Henry Clay and Daniel Webster concerning the Compromise of 1850.

PETER CARTWRIGHT (1785–1872): *Autobiography of Peter Cartwright, the Backwoods Preacher.* A personal story of the life of the traveling preacher who led frontier camp meetings for fifty years in Kentucky, Tennessee, Ohio, Indiana, and Illinois and unsuccessfully ran for Congress against Abraham Lincoln. Cartwright earns a legendary status in Methodism after the book's publication; it becomes an important source on circuit riders.

HINTON ROWAN HELPER: *The Impending Crisis of the South: How to Meet It.* A sensational work arguing that slavery hinders the economic growth of the South and should be abolished, and all African American men, whom he despises, should be sent back to Africa. Helper attacks Southern political, religious, and literary figures, infuriating the South and leading to suppression of the book in that region. However, it becomes extremely popular in the North, especially with Republicans, who distribute it during Lincoln's 1860 presidential campaign.

FITZ HUGH LUDLOW (1836–1870): *The Hasheesh Eater.* Ludlow achieves a sensation with a confession of his experiences as a drug addict. The first version of the book had appeared as "The Apocalypse of Hasheesh" in *Putnam's Magazine* when Ludlow was an undergraduate at Union College.

JAMES PARTON: *The Life and Times of Aaron Burr.* An objective biography of the much-despised Burr that is considered the best nineteenth-century life of the man because of its careful research. It depicts Burr as smart and able, though brought to ruin by his own shortcomings. The very popular book goes through sixteen printings, and the *North American Review* declares that "it ought to be read by every American who would know the history of his own country."

Poetry

WILLIAM ALLEN BUTLER (1825–1902): *Nothing to Wear.* The satirical poem is originally published anonymously in *Harper's Weekly* then later that year republished as a book without the author's permission. Its success is so great that a number of people claim responsibility for the work. The poem attacks the excessive wastefulness of the day. It recounts the story of Miss Flora M'Flimsy, a woman who has spent six weeks shopping in Paris but feels she has nothing to wear. Butler was a New York lawyer, teacher, and civic leader.

LYDIA MARIA CHILD: "Thanksgiving Day." Child publishes her best-known poem with the still memorable lines: "Over the river and through the wood / To grandmother's house we go."

Publications and Events

The *Atlantic Monthly*. The prestigious literary magazine is founded in Boston by several of New England's literary lights. Oliver Wendell Holmes named the magazine, and James Russell Lowell served as its first editor, with early contributions by Emerson, Whittier, and Longfellow. It published what would become Holmes's *Autocrat of the Breakfast-Table* and Lowell's *The Biglow Papers*, as well as Howe's "The Battle Hymn of the Republic" and Hale's *The Man Without a Country*.

Harper's Weekly. The political and literary journal created by Fletcher Harper of the publishing firm Harper & Brothers, which was also responsible for creating *Harper's Monthly*. Published until 1916, it was best known for its illustrations, particularly by Thomas Nast (1840–1902), who created the familiar symbols of the Democratic donkey and the Republican elephant.

Russell's Magazine. A monthly magazine is founded by William Gilmore Simms and edited by Paul Hamilton Hayne, which grew out of meetings of the Russell's Bookstore Group, a literary association that met at John Russell's bookshop in Charleston. The magazine strongly supported the South.

1858
Drama and Theater

DION BOUCICAULT: *Jessie Brown; or, The Relief of Lucknow*. Set during the Sepoy Rebellion in India, Boucicault's suspenseful drama describes the relief at the last minute of the English garrison of Lucknow. No actor agrees to play the treacherous rebel leader for fear of being hissed off the stage, so the playwright plays the role himself. The melodrama would be performed for the next twenty years.

WILLIAM WELLS BROWN: *The Escape; or, A Leap for Freedom*. The first play published by an African American is a five-act drama about two slaves who secretly marry and escape to Canada. The play is never staged, but Brown's readings of the script at his many lectures are favorably reviewed.

WILLIAM W. PRATT: *Ten Nights in a Barroom*. Based on the 1854 story by Timothy Shay Arthur, Pratt's adaptation would become the most most popular temperance melodrama of the nineteenth century, second in stage popularity only to *Uncle Tom's Cabin* on theatrical circuits.

Fiction

THOMAS BULFINCH: *The Age of Chivalry*. Bulfinch collects Arthurian and Welsh legends.

OLIVER WENDELL HOLMES: *Autocrat of the Breakfast-Table*. Fictionalized conversations on science, theology, and American society among the Autocrat, the Schoolmistress, the Landlady and her Daughter, the Old Gentleman Opposite, the Divinity Student, and the Poor Relation, as they breakfast at a Boston boardinghouse. The work also contains numerous epigrams and several of Holmes's finest poems, including "The Deacon's Masterpiece," "The Chambered Nautilus," "Contentment," and "The Living Temple." Its success would prompt Holmes to write *The Professor of the Breakfast-Table* (1860), *The Poet at the Breakfast-Table* (1872), and *Over Teacups* (1891).

ROBERT TRAILL SPENCE LOWELL (1816–1891): *The New Priest in Conception Bay*. A popular novel about a man who gives up his wife to become a Catholic priest and his reconversion to the Church of England. The widely respected work is notable for its descriptions of Newfoundland, based on Lowell's own experiences as an Episcopal priest in New Brunswick.

FITZ-JAMES O'BRIEN (c. 1828–1862): "The Diamond Lens." O'Brien's most famous and frequently anthologized story is published in the *Atlantic Monthly* and tells of an inventor of a powerful microscope who finds the image of perfect beauty in a sylphlike human in a microworld existing in a drop of water. He is obsessed with her and goes mad when her world evaporates.

HARRIET BEECHER STOWE: *Our Charley, and What to Do with Him*. Stowe publishes a collection of children's stories for mothers to share with their children. Included are "Take Care of the Hook," about a fish who fails to obey his mother, and "A Tale About Birds," about the kindness of God's creatures.

Literary Criticism and Scholarship

SAMUEL AUSTIN ALLIBONE (1816–1889): *A Critical Dictionary of English Literature and British and American Authors*. A pioneering reference work providing a comprehensive listing of works as well as criticism. Compiled by Allibone from 1858 to 1871, with a supplement by John

F. Kirk published in 1896, it provides invaluable information on early American and British writing.

JOSEPH B. COBB (1819–1858): *Leisure Hours.* Cobb's collection of literary and political essays criticizes Longfellow and Nathaniel Parker Willis for their insipid style and failure to develop native subjects. Cobb was a Mississippi writer, whose work included the historical romance *The Creole* (1850) and a collection of sketches, *Mississippi Scenes* (1851).

Nonfiction

HENRY CHARLES CAREY: *The Principles of Social Science.* Published in three volumes, this is a philosophical examination of the relationship between economics and politics. Carey promotes American political economy to a social science and suggests that it is correlated to natural science and in accordance with natural law and moral society.

JOHNSON JONES HOOPER: *Dog and Gun: A Few Loose Chapters on Shooting.* A serious work by the lawyer and journalist most known for his humorous writings. It contains essays on gun purchasing, hunting, and other sporting advice with essays by Hooper, Henry William Herbert, Dr. Egbert B. Johnson, and William T. Stockton. The popular book goes through four editions over the next seven years.

JOHN GORHAM PALFREY (1796–1881): *History of New England.* A sophisticated and highly lauded five-volume study of the region, utilizing every accessible primary source with complete documentation. Although hailed in its day for a lack of bias, its partiality to Massachusetts is now recognized, along with its defense of Puritan fanaticism and its prejudiced opinion of New England as superior to other regions because its population includes descendants of the finest English blood.

Poetry

JAMES THOMAS FIELDS (1817–1881): *A Few Verses for a Few Friends.* A collection of poetry by the Boston publisher, owner of the famous Old Corner Bookstore, and editor of the *Atlantic Monthly* from 1837 to 1871. The poems are praised by the *North American Review* for their "pure thought, genial feeling, tender remembrance, and lambent fancy." The collection contains the long-popular lines "We are lost! the captain shouted, / As he staggered down the stairs."

WILLIAM JOHN GRAYSON: *The Country.* Grayson's poem in heroic couplets, described as a combination of the styles of Pope and Whitman, celebrates the virtues of American rural life. He also publishes "Marion — the

Carolina Partisan," celebrating Francis Marion's military exploits during the Revolution.

JOSIAH GILBERT HOLLAND (1819–1881): *Bitter-Sweet.* A vastly popular, long, melodramatic narrative poem on New England life and the coexistence of good and evil. The reviewer for the *Atlantic Monthly* remarks that the poem is "truly an original poem," "purely American," and "an obstinately charming little book." Holland was an editor of the *Springfield Republican* who became the first editor of *Scribner's Monthly* (1870–1881).

OLIVER WENDELL HOLMES: *The Deacon's Masterpiece; or, The Wonderful "One-Hoss Shay."* First published in the *Atlantic Monthly* and included in *The Autocrat of the Breakfast-Table,* one of Holmes's best poems is a parable about the decline of Calvinism. It concerns a deacon who builds an indestructible carriage with each part of equal strength. Unfortunately, the entire carriage eventually collapses.

HENRY WADSWORTH LONGFELLOW: *The Courtship of Miles Standish.* Narrative poem about the captain of the Plymouth colony who sends his friend John Alden to ask for the hand of Priscilla. Priscilla desires John, and when they hear that Miles has been killed in battle, the couple plan their wedding. On the eve of the nuptials Miles returns but gives his blessing to the betrothed. The poem sells fifteen thousand copies the first day it is available.

Publications and Events

The *Saturday Press.* An experimental New York weekly founded by Henry Clapp and frequently featuring the writings of the Pfaff's Cellar literary group, whose members included Walt Whitman, Fitz-James O'Brien, and Ada Clare. The magazine was suspended in 1860 but revived in 1865. One of its final numbers included Mark Twain's "The Celebrated Jumping Frog of Calaveras County."

1859
Drama and Theater

DION BOUCICAULT: *The Octoroon.* Based on Mayne Reid's 1856 novel, *The Quadroon,* this successful melodrama features a man who falls in love with a slave of mixed race but is forced to sell her to an abhorrent character.

Fiction

JOHN ESTEN COOKE: *Henry St. John, Gentleman.* The sequel to *The Virginia Comedians* (1854), this novel employs some of the same characters but mostly concerns

St. John, the great-grandson of Pocahontas, and his romance with Bonneybel Vane.

MARTIN R. DELANY: *Blake; or, The Huts of America.* Delany's only novel, partially serialized in the *Afro-American Magazine,* fully serialized in the *Weekly Anglo-African* (1861–1862), and published in book form in 1870, describes a slave rebellion in Cuba and the South. Its protagonist is the first fully developed West Indian character in American fiction, and the book is considered the most radical black novel of the nineteenth century. Its themes of militancy and black nationalism anticipate the views of black fiction of the 1960s and 1970s.

AUGUSTA JANE EVANS: *Beulah.* Popular with critics and the public, selling twenty-two thousand copies in its first nine months, this domestic novel concerns a young girl's unrequited love for her guardian. Her religious questioning leads her to read Poe, Emerson, Goethe, Locke, Descartes, Hume, and others.

FRANCES ELLEN WATKINS HARPER: "The Two Offers." The first short story published by an African American is published in the *Anglo-African.* It argues that there are alternatives to married life for intelligent women by juxtaposing the intelligent and self-assured Janette with the beautiful but overindulged Laura, who marries for the wrong reasons and dies of grief.

FITZ-JAMES O'BRIEN: "What Was It? A Mystery." A fantastic tale in which the narrator is attacked by an invisible creature in his bed, forcing him to question reality. O'Brien's most sensational tale, it would influence Guy de Maupassant's writing of "The Horla." First published in *Harper's New Monthly Magazine,* it would be included in O'Brien's *Poems and Stories* (1881). "The Wondersmith," published in the *Atlantic Monthly,* is O'Brien's last important short story. It concerns toys that are turned into evil automatons by gypsies; the idea of the robot is one of O'Brien's most important contributions to science fiction.

E.D.E.N. SOUTHWORTH: *The Hidden Hand.* The author's most popular novel (nearly two million copies sold) had been originally serialized in the *New York Ledger,* is translated into several languages, and would be the basis for a variety of theatrical renditions. In it the orphan Capitola seeks adventure, battles the villainous Black Donald, and eventually realizes that she is the heiress to a great fortune.

HARRIET ELIZABETH PRESCOTT SPOFFORD (1835–1921): "In a Cellar." This mystery story by the New England writer about a stolen diamond is set in Paris. Praised for its vivid description, it launches Spofford's career when first published in the *Atlantic Monthly.* It would

be later included in her collection *The Amber Gods and Other Stories* (1863) and also in Alexander Jessup's *Representative American Short Stories* (1923).

HARRIET BEECHER STOWE: *The Minister's Wooing.* Stowe's first and most complex novel of New England is the story of a Calvinist minister and his courtship of a younger girl who is in love with her cousin but will not marry him because he has not been saved. The novel attacks Calvinism and accurately depicts Puritan life in colonial New England.

HARRIET E. ADAMS WILSON (c. 1827–c. 1863): *Our Nig; or, Sketches from the Life of a Free Black, in a Two-Story White House, North, Showing That Slavery's Shadows Fall Even There.* The first novel published in the United States by a black American goes unnoticed until rediscovered by Henry Louis Gates Jr. in 1983. The slave narrative tells the story of Frado, the daughter of a black man and white woman, who becomes an indentured servant after her father dies and her mother deserts her. It details the many hardships of her life, including abuse by her owner and abandonment by her husband while she is pregnant.

Nonfiction

RICHARD HENRY DANA JR.: *To Cuba and Back.* The author's only travel book. Although he had written it hastily, Dana's descriptive talents provide a lasting picture of Cuban life and culture. Especially notable are his depictions of slave life on a sugar plantation and a bullfight.

JAMES PARTON: *Life of Andrew Jackson.* Parton's most significant biographical work is a three-volume study of the heroic but controversial seventh president. Noteworthy as one of the best biographies of the nineteenth century, it would be often reprinted and is considered an invaluable source for all later books on Jackson.

JAMES REDPATH (1833–1891): *The Roving Editor; or, Talks with Slaves in the Southern States.* The Scottish-born journalist and social reformer collects his investigations on slavery in the South. He also issues *A Handbook to Kansas Territory.*

HARDEN E. TALIAFERRO (1818–1875): *Fisher's River (North Carolina) Scenes and Characters, by "Skitt," "Who Was Raised Thar."* Acclaimed by contemporary critics and twentieth-century literary scholars alike, the book presents humorous sketches of life in Surry County in the mountains of North Carolina. Cratis D. Williams, writing for the *North Carolina Folklore Journal,* calls it "perhaps the most important book portraying the social life and customs of the Southern mountain people to appear before the Civil War."

HENRY DAVID THOREAU: "A Plea for Captain John Brown." A lecture first delivered in Concord, Massachusetts, after Brown's abolitionist raid at Harpers Ferry. Thoreau reportedly had won over a mostly hostile crowd with his philosophical praise for the man widely thought to be a criminal. Together with his essays "The Last Days of John Brown" and "After the Death of John Brown," Thoreau's writing gives voice to his growing acceptance of violent protest in place of civil disobedience.

Publications and Events

Vanity Fair. A comic New York weekly financed by Frank J. Thompson and edited by Louis Henry Stephens, William Allen Stephens, and Henry Louis Stephens. The magazine, which continued until 1863, contained satirical illustrations of politicians, protests against the Civil War and abolitionists, and a variety of poetry, theater, and book reviews. Notable contributors to the influential periodical included Thomas Bailey Aldrich, William Dean Howells, Fitz-James O'Brien, and Charles Farrar Browne, whose "Artemus Ward" writings were especially popular.

1860

Drama and Theater

SIDNEY FRANCES BATEMAN: *Evangeline*. Bateman produces a dramatization of Longfellow's poem (1847).

DION BOUCICAULT: *The Colleen Bawn*. The first of many Irish comedy dramas for which Boucicault is most famous. Based on Gerald Griffin's novel *The Collegians* (1829), it is an account of the attempted murder of Eily O'Connor, whose husband has had an affair to save his estate.

Fiction

EDWARD S. ELLIS (1840–1916): *Seth Jones; or, The Captives of the Frontier*. Ellis's first novel has been described as the "perfect dime novel" of thrilling frontier adventure. After a saturation publicity campaign, it sells 60,000 copies in its first week and 450,000 copies in its first six months. Ellis, an unknown schoolteacher at the time, becomes a full-time writer and provides variants of his most popular story for the next thirty years.

MIRIAM COLES HARRIS (1824–1925): *Rutledge*. Harris's first novel is a best-selling gothic romance about an orphan who falls in love with her provisional guardian, Rutledge, a gloomy older man. After rebelling against the fashionable lifestyle of her new permanent guardian, and an engagement to a murderer, she repents for

Nathaniel Hawthorne

her wrongdoing and is finally united with her beloved Rutledge.

BRET HARTE (1836–1902): *The Work on Red Mountain*. The author's first writing to gain notice is a novelette about a feisty but intelligent and beautiful young girl and the mysterious death of her father in a mining town during the early gold rush years. Published in the 1860 *Golden Era*, it would be expanded in the same periodical in 1863 at the request of readers and titled *M'liss*. The story would be collected in *The Luck of Roaring Camp and Other Sketches* (1870); a film adaptation starring Mary Pickford would appear in 1918.

NATHANIEL HAWTHORNE: *The Marble Faun; or, The Romance of Monte Beni*. Hawthorne's last major romance. Written in England and based in Rome, the novel features characters dealing with moral dilemmas. The book is notable for vibrant descriptions and keen observations of its Roman setting.

OLIVER WENDELL HOLMES: *The Professor at the Breakfast-Table*. Following the pattern of the successful *Autocrat of the Breakfast-Table*, Holmes picks up the conversation of the earlier work but allows another boarder, the Professor, to lead the discussion. The essays in *The*

Professor deal more with religion than do the *Autocrat* sketches, which bring accusations of heresy against Holmes from orthodox Congregationalists. Though the controversy results in a loss of subscribers for the *Atlantic Monthly*, where the essays had been originally published, they gain wide popularity.

HARRIET ELIZABETH PRESCOTT SPOFFORD: *Sir Rohan's Ghost.* Spofford's first novel is a gothic romance about a man who tries to murder his mistress. The well-received work boosts the writer's reputation and is especially notable for her descriptions—that of a wine cellar in the book is so admired that wine aficionados compliment her with bottles of wine for years. Spofford also publishes "Circumstance," a story based on an event in the Prescott family history. It tells of a pioneer woman who protects herself from a mythical creature by singing. Emily Dickinson said of the story, "I read Miss Prescott's 'Circumstance,' but it followed me in the Dark so I avoided her . . . It is the only thing I ever read in my life that I didn't think I could have imagined myself." The story is first published in the *Atlantic Monthly* and later included in *The Amber Gods and Other Stories* (1863). In the story "The Amber Gods," considered Spofford's finest work, Yone and her cousin Lu compete for the love of an artist. Yone narrates the tale from beyond the grave. Spofford contrasts the two characters, giving Yone passionate, dangerous, and sometimes even demonic characteristics, and Lu, who wins the artist, meek and proper traits.

ANN SOPHIA STEPHENS: *Malaeska: The Indian Wife of the White Hunter.* This historical Indian romance is the first of the dime novels published by Erastus Beadle, selling 300,000 copies in its first year. The novel helps Stephens become one of the most popular authors of the mid–nineteenth century.

Literary Criticism and Scholarship

SARAH HELEN POWER WHITMAN: *Edgar Poe and His Critics.* Written in response to a decade of posthumous attacks on Poe, this work defends him as a person and an author. Whitman draws on her personal knowledge of Poe but also reveals her keen understanding of literature.

JOSEPH EMERSON WORCESTER: *A Dictionary of the English Language.* Worcester publishes his last revision of his dictionary.

Nonfiction

LYDIA MARIA CHILD: *Correspondence Between Lydia Maria Child and Gov. Wise and Mrs. Mason, of Virginia.* A pamphlet containing the correspondence of the au-

thor, the Virginia governor, and the wife of James Mason (who authored the Fugitive Slave Act) concerning the actions and treatment of Harpers Ferry raider John Brown. Three hundred thousand copies of the pamphlet are circulated in the North, winning favor for the abolitionist cause.

WILLIAM CRAFT (C. 1826–1900) AND ELLEN CRAFT (1826–1891): *Running a Thousand Miles to Freedom; or, The Escape of William and Ellen Craft from Slavery.* An account of the couple's ingenious escape from slavery in Georgia to freedom in Philadelphia in 1848. They had traveled the thousand miles with the fair-skinned Ellen disguised as an injured man, a bandage covering her face and her arm in a sling so she would not have to sign anything, and William acting as her servant. The book also tells of the hardships they faced in Boston after the passage of the Fugitive Slave Act in 1850, which forced them to flee to England.

RALPH WALDO EMERSON: *The Conduct of Life.* This collection of lectures first delivered between 1851 and 1852 reiterates Emerson's beliefs about fate, power, wealth, and worship, among other topics. The lectures reveal the author's optimism and modification of his Transcendentalist philosophy in the direction of pragmatism. Included are some of his best-known epigrams, such as "Shallow men believe in luck" and "One of the benefits of a college education is to show the boy its little avail."

WILLIAM GILPIN (1813–1894): *The Central Gold Region.* A theoretical work envisioning greatness for the United States, especially in the Mississippi Valley, for its position in the "Isothermal Zodiac." Gilpin, the first territorial governor of Colorado, also argues for more railroads, including intercontinental networks at the Bering Strait and Gibraltar.

WILLIAM DEAN HOWELLS (1837–1920): *Lives and Speeches of Abraham Lincoln and Hannibal Hamlin.* Howells's first prose book is this campaign biography. Rewarded by Lincoln with a consular position in Venice, he remains there during the Civil War.

THOMAS STARR KING (1824–1864): *The White Hills: Their Legends, Landscape, and Poetry.* One of the first American regional studies is a highly detailed description of the natural features of New Hampshire by the clergyman, poet, and editor. Evert Augustus Duyckinck declares that King's writing displays "the fancy of a poet, the minute observation and enthusiasm of an ardent lover of nature, and the spiritual insight of a philosopher."

FREDERICK LAW OLMSTED: *A Journey to the Back Country.* The third volume in a series of observations and ruminations based on the author's travels through slave states. It is a significant contemporary comment on the state of affairs and way of life in the antebellum South.

HENRY JARVIS RAYMOND (1820–1869): *Disunion and Slavery.* One of the founders of the *New York Times* publishes a collection of letters addressed to secessionist William Yancey, contending that secession is unconstitutional and will precipitate war. Raymond would go on to write a campaign work, *History of the Administration of President Lincoln* (1864), which he expanded into *The Life and Public Services of Abraham Lincoln* (1865).

WILLIAM WALKER (1824–1860): *The War in Nicaragua.* The Tennessee adventurer who led an invasion of Nicaragua and became that country's president in 1856 publishes an account of his exploits in the year that he is executed by a Honduran firing squad.

Poetry

ELIZABETH AKERS (1832–1911): "Rock Me to Sleep." Akers's best-known poem, with the lines "Backward, turn backward, O Time, in your flight; / Make me a child again just for tonight," is published under the pseudonym "Florence Percy" in the *Saturday Evening Post* and under Akers's own name in her *Poems* (1866).

WILLIAM TURNER COGGLESHALL: *The Poets and Poetry of the West.* Preceded only by William D. Gallagher's *Selections from the Poetical Literature of the West* (1841), this collection of 159 authors published between 1789 and 1860 is one of the earliest anthologies to celebrate the poetic achievement of Midwestern writers. This work is intended to compensate for the neglect of western authors by eastern critics and anthologists. Coggleshall had pleaded for regionalism in literature in *The Protective Policy of Literature* (1859), and his anthology, which would become his most famous work, is his own contribution to the effort. Coggleshall was an Ohio journalist, novelist, and publisher.

PAUL HAMILTON HAYNE: *Avolio: A Legend of the Island of Cos. With Poems, Lyrical, Miscellaneous, and Dramatic.* A collection of Hayne's best pre–Civil War verses wins warm praise from James Russell Lowell in the *Atlantic Monthly* and William Cullen Bryant in the *Evening Post.*

WILLIAM DEAN HOWELLS AND JOHN JAMES PIATT (1835–1917): *Poems of Two Friends.* A poetic collaboration written while Howells and Piatt worked at the *Ohio State Journal.* Although the work is not a commercial success, James Russell Lowell, editor of the *Atlantic Monthly,*

Frederick Law Olmsted

praises the poems and their authors. *Poems of Two Friends* is Howells's first book of verse.

HENRY WADSWORTH LONGFELLOW: "The Children's Hour." Longfellow's celebration of the delights provided by his small daughters proves to be one of his most popular works.

HENRY TIMROD (1828–1870): *Poems.* Timrod who would be called "the laureate of the Confederacy," issues the only collection published during his lifetime, containing classically influenced nature verses.

FREDERICK GODDARD TUCKERMAN (1821–1873): *Poems.* Tuckerman's only volume of poetry. The reclusive Tuckerman sends copies of the book to significant writers, and Tennyson is said to have favored them. The collection would be reissued in 1864 and 1869 but then fell out of sight until the twentieth century. The poet Witter Bynner rediscovered Tuckerman, whom he described as having "the subtly fine craft of a devout poet." Bynner published *The Sonnets of Frederick Goddard Tuckerman* in 1931.

WALT WHITMAN: *Leaves of Grass, third edition.* Whitman adds 146 new poems, including "Starting from

Paumanok" and "Out of the Cradle Endlessly Rocking," alters and renames previously published poems, and for the first time groups them in several "clusters," including the "Calamus" poems dealing with love between men. It sells more copies and provokes more reviews than did earlier editions.

JOHN GREENLEAF WHITTIER: *Home Ballads and Other Poems.* This collection contains Whittier's popular poems "Skipper Ireson's Ride," a ballad about the punishment of a fisherman who was accused of leaving his rival fisherman to die in a shipwreck, and "Telling the Bees," about a young man who approaches the home of his fiancée and sees the hired girl dressing the hives, an old New England mourning custom, and realizes that his beloved has died.

Publications and Events

Beadle dime novels. With the slogan "a dollar book for a dime," New York publishers Erastus F. Beadle (1821–1894), his brother Irwin, and Robert Adams issue their first dime novel, Ann Sophia Stephens's *Malaeaska, the Indian Wife of the White Hunter.* It would sell more than 300,000 copies and would be followed for the next thirty years by hundreds of similar frontier adventure novels by a stable of writers including Edward S. Ellis, W. F. Cody, Ned Buntline, and Mayne Reid.

III

Realism and Naturalism

1861–1914

H ERMAN MELVILLE IN *Clarel* (1876) called the winter of 1860–1861, the weeks immediately preceding the Civil War, "a sad arch between contrasted eras." The same could be said of the war years as a whole and of the entire era between them and World War I. The Romantic idealism of American writing before 1861 gave way to a realistic perspective on what America had become under the pressure of war and expansion as well as the acceleration of technological, economic, and social change. Those who lived through the Civil War found it increasingly hard to imagine prewar realities. Harvard professor George Ticknor observed in 1868 that the Civil War had opened a "great gulf between what happened before in our century and what has happened since, or what is likely to happen hereafter. It does not seem to me as if I were living in the country in which I was born."

The war put an end to slavery and the Southern plantation aristocracy while setting in motion forces that transformed the nation. Between 1861 and 1914 America metamorphosed from a rural, agrarian, insular nation to an industrialized, urbanized world power. At every stage in this radical transformation, citizens must have looked back on the prewar world as quaint and lost forever while indulging a nostalgia for a simpler America of small villages, stable communities, and shared cultural values. Who Americans were and what America had become were the dominant themes of literature as the first clear outlines of modern American life took shape.

In 1860 the U.S. population was less than 40 million; by 1900 it had doubled, and by 1920 it had swelled to almost 106 million. Before the Civil War the vast majority of the population lived in rural areas, with 60 percent of the work force engaged in farming; by 1900 a third of the population were city dwellers and more worked in industry than in agriculture. To win the Civil War, Northern industries were modernized and expanded—a process that made a few enormously wealthy and set in motion a

scramble for power and gain that worried President Lincoln, who feared that by winning the war the American democracy might be destroyed. He predicted this with uncanny accuracy in a letter discussing the postwar period: "I see in the near future a crisis that unnerves and causes me to tremble for the safety of my country. By the result of the war, corporations have been enthroned, and an era of corruption in high places will follow, and the money power of the country will endeavor to prolong its reign by working upon the prejudices of the people, until all wealth is aggregated in a few hands and the Republic is destroyed." Mark Twain called the postwar era that Lincoln feared the "Gilded Age," others the "Great Barbecue." It was the age of the robber barons, of unchecked accumulation by a few, widespread political corruption, and a widening gap between rich and poor that threatened to turn the democracy into a plutocracy. By 1904, 1 percent of the nation's businesses controlled 40 percent of the industrial production. Cheap labor came from abroad, and by the turn of the century a million immigrants were arriving annually, most living in appalling slum conditions and working in dangerous settings. By 1914 the United States had grown into the industrial powerhouse of the world, eclipsing every other nation in its productivity and resources. Electricity was beginning to power the nation, a rail system connected all regions, horsepower was being replaced by the automobile, and the telephone made communication instantaneous.

No other period in American history brought more dynamic change or anxiety over what America was becoming. Writers developed a new aesthetic to come to terms with the dislocations affecting an increasingly ethnically diverse population caught in the grips of accelerating social change. In the words of literary historian Robert E. Spiller, "Regionalism and realism took the place of imagination and idealism." American literature between the Civil War and the Great War broadened its perspective by incorporating the voices and scenes of its hinterlands and its new urban centers while finding innovative ways to explore contemporary American experience and its implications for the American psyche.

The initial shock to the system was of course the war itself. It was, arguably, *the* defining and shaping event in American history, a war over the full meaning of America itself. By emancipating the slaves, President Lincoln found the principle that helped ennoble what otherwise was senseless carnage. Three million fought in the war, and more than 600,000 (2 percent of the population) died. And yet, although unquestionably the most written-about single event in American history, the Civil War produced relatively few imaginative responses from its participants and eyewitnesses. Among the major literary figures before the war, only Herman Melville (*Battle-Pieces and Aspects of the War*, 1866) and Walt Whitman (*Drum-Taps*, 1865, 1866) produced important poems treating the war experience. The significant postwar writers — Mark Twain, William Dean Howells, and Henry James — sat out the war in safety, respectively, in the West, in Venice, and in Newport and Cambridge. John De Forest's *Miss Ravenel's Conversion from Secession to Loyalty* (1867) was among the few significant fictional achievements by a combatant, based largely on its author's own experiences and observations. The greatest literary treatment of the Civil War, Stephen Crane's *The Red Badge of Courage*, did not appear until 1895, the work of a twenty-four-year-old writer born in 1871 who claimed that he learned about combat on the playing fields of Syracuse University.

For the most part, writers of the period immediately following the war directed their attention closer to home. For the first time in American literature, significant writing began to emerge west of the Mississippi. Mark Twain (*The Celebrated Jumping Frog of Calaveras County*, 1867; *Roughing It*, 1872), Bret Harte (*The Luck of Roaring Camp*, 1868), and Joaquin Miller (*Songs of the Sierras*, 1871) portrayed life in California and the Far West exuberantly and idiomatically. Their stories and poems were the first in a steady stream of literature with distinctive regional characteristics from all parts of the country. Contributors to this proto-realistic movement, dubbed local colorists, include Edward Eggleston, John Hay, Sarah Orne Jewett, Mary Eleanor Wilkins Freeman, Harriet Beecher Stowe, Mary Noailles Murfree (writing as "Charles Egbert Craddock"), and George Washington Cable. These writers tapped into the rich resources of local scenes, speech, and customs to revitalize American writing enervated by

the war while paving the way for an increasingly realistic aesthetic, the dominant mode of American literary expression during the period.

The greatest of the regionalists was Mark Twain. In his masterpiece, *Adventures of Huckleberry Finn* (1884), Twain transformed a boy's adventure tale into what Lionel Trilling called "One of the world's great books and one of the central documents of American culture." With Huck and Jim's trip downriver into the heart of America's racial conflict, Twain tapped the poetic resources of the American vernacular and the dramatic and thematic possibilities of the American landscape, earning his friend William Dean Howells's praise as "the Lincoln of our literature." Although an overstatement, Ernest Hemingway's oft-quoted claim that "All modern American literature comes from one book by Mark Twain called *Huckleberry Finn*" is not far off the mark.

Twain showed his readers what their fellow Americans outside the settled Northeast actually looked and sounded like, while poking holes in the prevailing sentimental and Romantic ethos of the literary establishment. The main theorist and influential supporter of the new realism was William Dean Howells, who as the editor of the prestigious *Atlantic Monthly* (1866–1881) and *Harper's* (1886–1892) helped legitimize the efforts of the regionalists while advocating the refinement of the American novel into a truth-telling instrument. "Let fiction cease to lie about life," he argued; "let it portray men and women as they are, actuated by the motives and passions in the measure we all know." Howells supported fiction that emphasized the commonplace over the exceptional and would apply his theories in novels such as *A Modern Instance* (1882), *The Rise of Silas Lapham* (1885), and *Indian Summer* (1886), which helped raise the standards of realism in American fiction and slowly pushed open the doors to subjects previously off-limits to writers.

The third crucial figure in the realistic refinement of American fiction during the period was Henry James, who by absorbing the lessons of writers such as Honoré de Balzac, Ivan Turgenev, and Gustave Flaubert introduced the techniques and sensibilities of European novelists into American fiction. For James, American life was too unformed, without sufficient past and precedent, lacking the clear lines of European culture and hierarchy desirable for a writer interested in the intricate drama of manners. By transporting the vitality and earnestness of his Americans to Europe to be tested, James found the ideal stage for moral and psychological explorations of consciousness and social values, in works such as *Daisy*

Miller (1879), *The Portrait of a Lady* (1881), and his masterful trio of late novels — *The Wings of the Dove* (1902), *The Ambassadors* (1903), and *The Golden Bowl* (1904) — which anticipated the main preoccupations of modern fiction. James, perhaps more than any other writer, turned the American novel into literature while shifting its focus from the outer world to inner states of consciousness.

The realistic standards that Twain, Howells, and James established for American fiction were extended by the naturalist novelists of the 1890s and 1900s, who threatened the last vestiges of genteel discretion in their clinical treatment of modern life. If the realist insisted on the autonomy of the individual as paramount, the naturalist shifted the attention of the novel to the forces of environment and heredity that controlled destiny and the often brutal instincts needed to survive in a hostile world. Stephen Crane's *Maggie: A Girl of the Streets* (1893), Frank Norris's *McTeague* (1899), Theodore Dreiser's *Sister Carrie* (1900), and Upton Sinclair's *The Jungle* (1906) took their readers into a threatening urban landscape populated by victims and damaged survivors. Such works demonstrated that American fiction had come of age and had become the principal literary tool for critiquing contemporary American life.

While American fiction increasingly focused on harsh realities, the nation's poets, with a few notable exceptions, sought to reassure rather than to provoke. The dominant prewar poets — Longfellow, Lowell, Bryant, and Whittier — remained influential, if increasingly remote from the scenes and attitudes that were transforming America. Whitman attempted to maintain his optimistic faith in American democracy while continuing his epic campaign to bring commonplace life and forbidden subjects such as human sexuality within poetic range. Opposite in every way except for her genius, Emily Dickinson wrote introspective verses, echoing the traditions of the Romantics and her Puritan ancestors and treating the drama of daily life with an existential intensity and psychological realism that greatly influenced modern American poetry. Her poetry was unknown to her contemporaries and only gradually began to appear in the 1890s. By the end of the period, both kinds of poetic realism, Whitman's unrestrained panorama and Dickinson's inner truthfulness, had set the direction for a new American poetry, led by figures such as Edwin Arlington Robinson, Carl Sandburg, Robert Frost, and Ezra Pound, whose first poems began appearing before the Great War.

In drama, realism barely dented the popular appeal of melodrama, with its emphasis on idealized characters and situations. Spectacular stage effects replicated recognizable settings, but artificial treatment of character, plot, and dialogue undermined intentions to achieve psychological and social truthfulness. Exceptions included James A. Herne, whose *Margaret Fleming* (1890) has been called the first truly realistic play of American life; Edward Sheldon's social problem plays *The Nigger* (1910) and *The Boss* (1911); and the cultural and psychologically challenging dramas of William Vaughn Moody, *The Great Divide* (1909) and *The Faith Healer* (1909).

The period saw the emergence of a host of minority voices. Figures such as Paul Laurence Dunbar, Charles W. Chesnutt, Booker T. Washington, and W.E.B. Du Bois reflected the African American experience. One of the first widely read works by a writer of Asian heritage was Sui Sin Far's *Mrs. Spring Fragrance* (1912), and the period saw the first major works by Jewish American writers, most notably Abraham Cahan's *Yekl, a Tale of the New York Ghetto* (1896) and Mary Antin's *The Promised Land* (1912). Two of the most daring assaults on conventional views of the identity and role of women in America were Charlotte Perkins Gilman's "The Yellow Wallpaper" (1892) and Kate Chopin's *The Awakening* (1899).

The Civil War, fought to resolve American sectional differences and determine the scope of American democracy, managed to preserve the Union, and the ambitions, originality, and drive of its citizens during the succeeding decades created a world power. In the process, the evolving American literary aesthetic shifted from entertainment to truth-telling, exploring the divisive issues of social and racial equality and justice.

BIRTHS AND DEATHS, 1861–1869

Births

1861 Louise Imogen Guiney (d. 1920), poet
Henry Harland (d. 1905), novelist
John Luther Long (d. 1927), writer and playwright
Albert Bigelow Paine (d. 1937), author and editor
Frederick Jackson Turner (d. 1932), historian

1862 John Kendrick Bangs (d. 1922), novelist
Sydney Porter (O. Henry) (d. 1910), short story writer
Langdon Mitchell (d. 1935), playwright
Edwin Milton Royle (d. 1942), playwright
Edith Wharton (d. 1937), novelist

1863 Amelie Rives (d. 1945), novelist
George Santayana (d. 1952), philosopher, poet, novelist, and critic
Edward Stratemeyer (d. 1930), children's writer and editor
Gene Stratton Porter (d. 1924), novelist

1864 Richard Harding Davis (d. 1916), journalist, short story writer, and playwright
Thomas Dixon (d. 1946), novelist
Richard Hovey (d. 1900), poet
Paul Elmer More (d. 1937), editor and critic

1865 Robert W. Chambers (d. 1935), novelist
Clyde Fitch (d. 1909), playwright
Paul Leicester Ford (d. 1902), historian and novelist

1866 George Ade (d. 1944), short story writer
George Barr McCutcheon (d. 1928), novelist
William Gilbert Patten (Burt L. Standish, d. 1945), novelist and short story writer
Lincoln Steffens (d. 1936), journalist and social reformer

1867 Charles Klein (d. 1915), playwright
Finley Peter Dunne (d. 1936), novelist
David Graham Phillips (d. 1911), novelist and muckraker

1868 Mary Austin (d. 1934), novelist
W.E.B. Du Bois (d. 1963), historian, educator, and reformer
Robert Herrick (d. 1938), novelist
Edgar Lee Masters (d. 1950), poet
William Allen White (d. 1944), novelist

1869 William Vaughn Moody (d. 1910), playwright
Edwin Arlington Robinson (d. 1935), poet
George Sterling (d. 1926), poet
Booth Tarkington (d. 1946), novelist
Brand Whitlock (d. 1934), novelist

Deaths

1861 George Tucker (b. 1775), economist, historian, and author
Theodore Winthrop (b. 1828), novelist

1862 James Ewell Heath (b. 1792), novelist
Henry David Thoreau (b. 1817), philosopher and author

1864 Nathaniel Hawthorne (b. 1804), novelist
Henry Rowe Schoolcraft (b. 1793), author and ethnologist

1865 George Arnold (b. 1834), poet
Lydia Huntley Sigourney (b. 1791), poet and author

1866 Maria Susanna Cummins (b. 1827), novelist

1867 Charles Farrar Browne (Artemus Ward, b. 1834), humorist
Thomas Bulfinch (b. 1796), novelist
Fitz-Greene Halleck (b. 1790), poet
John Rollin Ridge (b. 1827), novelist
Catharine Maria Sedgwick (b. 1789), novelist
Henry Timrod (b. 1828), poet
Nathaniel Parker Willis (b. 1806), journalist, editor, and novelist

1868 Peter Force (b. 1790), historian
James Hall (b. 1793), novelist and short story writer
Seba Smith (b. 1792), journalist and humorist
Daniel Pierce Thompson (b. 1795), novelist

1861
Fiction

JANE ANDREWS (1833–1887): *The Seven Little Sisters Who Live on a Round Ball That Floats in the Air.* The most popular of the Massachusetts schoolteacher's books for children, which teach geography, history, and natural history through stories. Her other popular titles include *The Boys Who Lived on the Road from Long Ago to Now* (1885) and *The Stories Mother Nature Told Her Children* (1888).

GEORGE WILLIAM CURTIS: *Trumps.* First published in *Harper's Weekly* between 1859 and 1860, the only novel by the Rhode Island–born Near Eastern correspondent for the *New York Tribune* combines a romantic story with a realistic depiction of New York society and politics. According to the *North American Review,* "It seems to us the best of Mr. Curtis's works and among the very best of American novels." Curtis became the editor of *Harper's Weekly* in 1863.

REBECCA HARDING DAVIS (1831–1910): "Life in the Iron Mills." Based on Davis's experiences among mill workers in Wheeling, Virginia (later West Virginia), the story highlights the horrific conditions endured by the workers and contrasts their virtue to the self-serving attitude of the mill owners. First published in the *Atlantic Monthly,* it wins acclaim for Davis and is considered one of the first works of American realism, in which she invited her readers, "Come right down with me — here in the thickest fog and mud and effluvia."

OLIVER WENDELL HOLMES: *Elsie Venner: A Romance of Destiny.* Holmes's first novel, a controversial and popular work, had been originally published in the *Atlantic Monthly* serially beginning in 1859. Drawing on new ideas about genetics and serving as an allegory of original sin and family heritage, the work concerns the title character who is born with serpentlike qualities because her mother had been bitten by a snake while pregnant.

POPULAR BOOKS 1861–1877

Great Expectations by Charles Dickens (First American Printing, 1861)

Silas Marner by George Eliot (Mary Ann Evans, First American Printing, 1861)

East Lynne by Mrs. Henry Wood (First American Printing, 1861)

Lady Audley's Secret by Mary Elizabeth Braddon (First American Printing, 1862)

Les Misérables by Victor Hugo (First American Printing, 1862)

Maum Guinea and Her Plantation Children by Metta Victoria Fuller Victor (First American Printng, 1862)

The Great Rebellion by Joseph T. Headley (First American Printing, 1863)

The Fatal Marriage by E.D.E.N. Southworth (First American Printing, 1863)

The American Conflict by Horace Greeley (First American Printing, 1864)

Cudjo's Cave by John Townsend Trowbridge (First American Printing, 1864)

Joseph II and His Court by Louisa Mühlbach (First American Printing, 1865)

The Secret Service by Albert D. Richardson (First American Printing, 1865)

Griffith Gaunt by Charles Reade (First American Printing, 1866)

Snow-Bound by John Greenleaf Whittier (First American Printing, 1866)

St. Elmo by Augusta Jane Evans (First American Printing, 1867)

Kathrina by Josiah Gilbert Holland (First American Printing, 1867)

The Gates Ajar by Elizabeth Stuart Phelps (First American Printing, 1868)

Little Women by Louisa May Alcott (First American Printing, 1868)

Lorna Doone by Richard Doddridge Blackmore (First American Printing, 1869)

Innocents Abroad by Mark Twain (First American Printing, 1869)

The Mystery of Edwin Drood by Charles Dickens (First American Printing, 1870)

Lothair by Benjamin Disraeli (First American Printing, 1870)

The Hoosier Schoolmaster by Edward Eggleston (First American Printing, 1871)

A Terrible Temptation by Charles Reade (First American Printing, 1871)

Barriers Burned Away by Edward Payson Roe (First American Printing, 1872)

Roughing It by Mark Twain (First American Printing, 1872)

Farm Ballads by Will Carleton (First American Printing, 1873)

The Gilded Age by Mark Twain and Charles Dudley Warner (First American Printing, 1873)

Far from the Madding Crowd by Thomas Hardy (First American Printing, 1874)

Opening a Chestnut Burr by Edward Payson Roe (First American Printing, 1874)

Self-Raised by E.D.E.N. Southworth (First American Printing, 1876)

Tom Sawyer by Mark Twain (First American Printing, 1876)

THEODORE WINTHROP (1828–1861): *Cecil Dreeme.* The Connecticut writer's first published manuscript after he gained posthumous fame as reputedly the first Union soldier killed in the Civil War. The gothic story, about a girl who disguises herself as a man to avoid marriage, immediately becomes popular and goes through three printings in one week and nineteen printings by 1866.

Nonfiction

PAUL BELLONI DU CHAILLU (1835–1903): *Explorations and Adventures in Equatorial Africa.* The French-born explorer who came to the United States in 1852 provides a dramatic account of his travels to Africa's unexplored territory to study plants, animals, and tribal culture. The sensational book sells almost 300,000 copies, becoming the bestseller for the year. It receives harsh criticism, however, from scholars and reviewers who view the book's melodrama and lack of scientific measurements as reason to doubt Du Chaillu's veracity.

HARRIET A. JACOBS (1813–1897): *Incidents in the Life of a Slave Girl: Written by Herself.* The first full-length slave narrative written by a woman and published in America provides one of the most extensive treatments of the sexual exploitation experienced by enslaved women. It would be acclaimed in a 1987 edition as an African American and feminist classic. Jacobs was born in North Carolina and hid from her abusive white master for seven years in a small space in her grandmother's house before escaping with her children to the North in 1842.

FREDERICK LAW OLMSTED (1822–1903): *The Cotton Kingdom.* A compilation of Olmsted's earlier travel books — *A Journey to the Seaboard Slave States* (1856), *A Journey Through Texas* (1857), and *A Journey in the Back Country* (1860) — known for their evenhanded descriptions of the South. This two-volume edition is much praised by the *North American Review* for "enabl[ing] the reader with a much smaller expense of time, not only to acquaint himself with Mr. Olmsted's generalizations, results, and conclusions, but to examine specimens of each class of observations."

LUCIUS MANLIUS SARGENT (1786–1867): *The Ballad of the Abolition Blunderbuss.* The Boston author of temperance tracts (collected as *The Temperance Tales* in six volumes, 1863–1864) defends slavery and ridicules the antislavery sentiment of Emerson and other New Englanders.

WINTHROP SARGENT (1825–1870): *Life and Career of Major John André.* A flattering and exhaustive historical biography by the Philadelphia historian and editor that would remain the authoritative work on André for many years.

Poetry

The Anarchiad: A New England Poem. The mock-heroic verse sequence composed by the Connecticut Wits and published anonymously in 1786–1787 is reissued with notes and appendices.

DANIEL DECATUR EMMETT (1815–1904): "Dixie." This patriotic song, written for the New York Bryant's Minstrel Show, becomes immediately popular throughout the country. Numerous adaptations of the song spring up in both the North and the South, including a version by Albert Pike that is considered one of the best. Pike's verses would become the Confederate battle hymn, urging "To arms! arms! in Dixie / Advance the flag of Dixie!"

HENRY WADSWORTH LONGFELLOW: "Paul Revere's Ride." A narrative poem describing how Revere received the signal from the Old North Church and heralded news of the British approach from Boston to Lexington and Concord. In reality, Revere did not wait for a lantern signal, nor did he announce the British approach in Concord; nevertheless, the ballad grew into an American legend. Opening Longfellow's *Tales of a Wayside Inn* (1863), it would become the most popular piece in the collection.

JAMES RUSSELL LOWELL: "The Washers of the Shroud." One of Lowell's most important poems shows a shift from his previous pacifist views to express his contention that the Union cause and the use of force are justified.

JAMES RYDER RANDALL (1839–1908): "Maryland, My Maryland." This Confederate battle song, set to the tune of the German Christmas carol "O Tannenbaum," urges Marylanders to join the Confederacy. Randall, a Louisiana English professor, had written the song in response to attacks on Union soldiers by anti-Union residents of Baltimore. First printed in the *New Orleans Delta*, it would be widely circulated with numerous variations, including a pro-Union version.

HENRY TIMROD: "Ethnogenesis." Written during the first Confederate Congress, the ode proclaims victory for the new Confederacy and pays homage to the culture, people, and nature of the South. One of Timrod's most famous poems, it is included in the poet's 1873 collection *Poems.* Timrod also publishes "The Cotton Boll," one of the most famous poems by the so-called laureate of the Confederacy. In it a cotton boll symbolizes the South's virtue and suggests that the white cotton fields will halt the advance of Union troops just as the snow had kept Napoleon from conqueing Russia. First published in the *Charleston Mercury*, it would be included in Timrod's *Poems* (1873).

1862
Fiction

CHARLES FARRAR BROWNE (1834–1867): *Artemus Ward, His Book.* The Maine humorist's letters in Yankee dialect had first appeared in the *Cleveland Plain Dealer* in 1858 and later in *Vanity Fair.* In 1861 Browne began touring on the lecture circuit as "Artemus Ward." He sells forty thousand copies of this collection. Other popular collections would follow, including *Artemus Ward, His Travels* (1865), *Artemus Ward Among the Fenians* (1867), *Artemus Ward in London and Other Papers* (1867), *Artemus Ward's Panorama* (1869), *Artemus Ward's Lectures* (1869), and *Artemus Ward: His Works Complete* (1875, 1890, 1910).

REBECCA HARDING DAVIS: "John Lamar." Appearing in the *Atlantic Monthly,* the story concerns a slave who, when incited by an abolitionist, murders his master. It and Davis's subsequent stories, "David Gaunt" (September 1862) and "Paul Becker" (May 1863), are among the first realistic stories inspired by the war. Davis also publishes *Margaret Howth: A Story of Today,* a novel about a young girl forced to work in an Indiana wool mill after she is abandoned by her fiancé. First published in the *Atlantic Monthly,* it receives warm reviews and popular success. It is now considered overly sentimental — a result of the changes editor James T. Fields had required to give the book a "sunny" conclusion.

RICHARD BURLEIGH KIMBALL (1816–1892): *Under-Currents of Wall-Street: A Romance of Business.* The story of a bankrupt merchant who works on Wall Street is critically acclaimed for its realistic depiction of business life. The *Continental Monthly* notes that it has "a truthfulness which is positively startling." The first of the New York lawyer and financier's four novels depicting American wealth and business affairs, it would be followed by *Was He Successful?* (1864), *Henry Powers, Banker* (1868), and *To-Day in New York* (1870).

ROBERT HENRY NEWELL (1836–1901): *The Orpheus C. Kerr Papers.* The first volume of letters the New York journalist and humorist had written for newspapers under the pseudonym "Orpheus C. Kerr" is published (four more volumes would appear by 1871). The pseudonym is a play on the term *office seeker.* Using exaggeration and understatement, Newell provides humorous commentary on current events during the Civil War and Reconstruction.

ELIZABETH DREW BARSTOW STODDARD (1823–1902): *The Morgesons.* Stoddard's partially autobiographical novel about a spirited young girl's maturation into an independent woman receives little attention during wartime, but it would be rediscovered and valued in the twentieth century for its realism and unconventional heroine, who seeks fulfillment outside the roles conventionally prescribed for women of the era.

HARRIET BEECHER STOWE: *Agnes of Sorrento.* Stowe's historical romance, begun in 1859 to entertain her daughters while traveling in Italy, is set during the time of Savonarola in the fifteenth century. Stowe also publishes *The Pearl of Orr's Island: A Story of the Coast of Maine,* the story of the virtuous Mara Lincoln (the pearl of the title), an orphan raised by her grandparents in a Maine village, and her love for her adopted brother Moses, a Spanish boy her grandparents had found in the stormy sea. Mara's love, care, and eventual death elevate Moses and save him from his imprudent lifestyle. Stowe's second New England novel is called by John Greenleaf Whittier "the most charming New England idyll ever written."

METTA VICTORIA VICTOR (1831–1886): *Maum Guinea and Her Plantation Children; or, Christmas Among the Slaves.* This popular dime novel about slavery, with an abolitionist bias, sells 100,000 copies in the United States and circulates widely in Britain. The novel is said to have been acclaimed by Abraham Lincoln and the well-known Congregationalist clergyman Henry Ward Beecher. Victor was married to the publisher of dime novels Orville James Victor (1827–1910).

THEODORE WINTHROP: *Edwin Brothertoft.* This popular romance set in New York during the American Revolution is one of a series of the author's writings published after his death in the Civil War, but it receives less critical acclaim than his other publications. Winthrop's work *John Brent* is also published in 1862, the year after Winthrop died. This popular action-filled narrative follows the title character as he tracks down his kidnapped love in the Rocky Mountains. It is considered one of the first western novels.

Nonfiction

WILLIAM GANNAWAY BROWNLOW (1805–1877): *Sketches of the Rise, Progress, and Decline of Secession.* Published after Brownlow's release from a Confederate prison where he had been held for writing pro-Union sentiments, the Tennessee preacher's best-selling history brings together his own experience, newspaper clippings, and speeches,

winning a large Northern audience and selling more than 100,000 copies in six months.

ALEXANDER CRUMMELL (1819–1898): *The Future of Africa.* The African American Episcopal minister and scholar's first collection of sermons is a treatise on what would later be called black nationalism, supporting immigration to the African state of Liberia. He would return to this theme in *Africa and America* (1891), addressing the concerns of African Americans in post-Reconstruction America.

MARY ABIGAIL DODGE (1833–1896): *Country Living and Country Thinking.* This collection of essays argues that women should consider careers outside of the domestic realm, particularly writing. The book's success would lead to four subsequent volumes published within a decade.

ALBERT PIKE: *Letter to the President of the Confederacy.* Pike, the commander of a Confederate troop of Indian soldiers whose alleged atrocities provoked complaints by other generals, writes this defense of his actions in a published letter to Jefferson Davis. Pike would be relieved of his command and forced to flee for a time to Canada.

WILLIAM WETMORE STORY (1819–1895): *Roba di Roma.* The poet and sculptor's most enduring and popular work is this collection of essays, presenting a lyrical and vivid portrait of Italian culture and history. Although largely ignored today, the collection would be expanded in 1871 and go through several printings and editions during Story's lifetime.

ANTHONY TROLLOPE (1815–1882): *North America.* The British novelist makes amends for the negative comments of his mother, Frances Trollope, in her work *Domestic Manners of the Americans* (1832), by rendering a more favorable account of Americans and their customs. The book includes his comments on the Civil War.

Poetry

JAMES SLOAN GIBBONS (1810–1892): "We Are Coming, Father Abraham, Three Hundred Thousand More." A response in verse to Abraham Lincoln's call for 300,000 volunteer troops, this poem by the Quaker abolitionist is printed in the *New York Evening Post.* Set to music by composers including Stephen Foster and Luther O. Emerson, it becomes a popular Union song.

JULIA WARD HOWE: "The Battle Hymn of the Republic." This patriotic verse is set to the tune of the popular song "John Brown's Body," which Howe had sung along with Union soldiers during a visit to Washington, D.C., after the Battle of Bull Run. The Unitarian leader

Julia Ward Howe

James Freeman Clarke had suggested she compose the new lyrics, which first appear in the *Atlantic Monthly* in February. The song wins immediate acclaim and is sung by American soldiers throughout the Civil War and ensuing conflicts. A subsequent collection of her verse, *Later Lyrics*, would appear in 1866.

JAMES RUSSELL LOWELL: *The Biglow Papers.* The second series of Lowell's satirical verse in Yankee dialect appears in the *Atlantic Monthly* in support of the Union cause. They would be collected in book form in 1867.

BAYARD TAYLOR: *The Poet's Journal.* A collection of verse containing popular poems previously contributed to journals. The *North American Review* deems it "his best" volume of poetry.

1863
Drama and Theater

AUGUSTIN DALY (1838–1899): *Leah, the Forsaken.* The first theatrical success by one of the era's most prolific playwrights and producers is an adaptation of Salomon Herrmann von Mosenthal's German play *Deborah.* It concerns a Jewish woman in love with a Christian who betrays her and an apostate Jew's villainy. An advertisement for the play in James Joyce's *Ulysses* serves to remind Leopold Bloom of his Jewishness.

CLIFTON W. TAYLEURE (1831–1887): *East Lynne.* Tayleure's is the most popular of several dramatic versions of the sensational novel by Mrs. Henry Wood (1814–1887), about an unfaithful woman who, disguised as a governess, returns repentant to her family. The play would be performed almost continually for the remainder of the century by road and stock companies, becoming synonymous with the melodramatic stage fare of the day. Tayleure was the house dramatist for Baltimore's Holliday Street Theatre who would go on to manage several important Broadway theaters.

LESTER WALLACK (1819–1888): *Rosedale; or, The Rifle Ball.* One of Wallack's biggest successes is this complicated melodrama about a widow's inheritance. The son of English actor/manager James William Wallack (1794–1864), he took over the management of Wallack's Theatre and was its principal star.

Fiction

LOUISA MAY ALCOTT: *A Whisper in the Dark.* One of Alcott's early thrillers, published anonymously, tells the story of an heiress imprisoned in an asylum to secure her fortune, echoing Wilkie Collins's *The Woman in White* (1860). Alcott later would comment that the thriller was an example of the kind of lurid stories Jo March writes in *Little Women.* This thriller would be published under Alcott's name in 1889 in the volume *A Modern Mephistopheles and a Whisper in the Dark.*

AUGUSTA JANE EVANS: *Macaria; or, Altars of Sacrifice.* The first part of Evans's novel refutes Stowe's *Uncle Tom's Cabin;* the second memorializes Southern bravery and the Confederate cause. Union general G. H. Thomas declares the work contraband, banning it among his troops and burning confiscated copies.

EDWARD EVERETT HALE (1822–1909): "The Man Without a Country." Hale's story concerns the fictitious Philip Nolan, who, when found guilty of treason for conspiring with Aaron Burr, damns the United States and is exiled to life at sea and allowed no knowledge of his native land. Nolan becomes a loyal patriot while living aboard navy vessels, joins in a battle during the War of 1812, and at his death is happy to learn of the progress of the United States. Written to boost patriotism during the Civil War, it is supposedly based on the exile of Copperhead Clement L. Vallandigham. Originally published anonymously in the *Atlantic Monthly,* the story would be printed as a pamphlet in 1865, included in Hale's *If, Yes,* *and Perhaps* (1868), and eventually adapted for the stage, film, and television.

BRET HARTE: *M'Liss*. Harte's first popular success is an expansion of an earlier story, "The Work on Red Mountain" (1860). The story, about a young girl's adventures in California's gold mining camps, is serialized from 1863 to 1864 and would be included in *The Luck of Roaring Camp and Other Sketches* (1870) and published separately as *M'Liss: An Idyl of Red Mountain* (1873).

HENRY MORFORD: *Shoulder-Straps* and *The Days of Shoddy*. Morford's novels expose corruption and incompetence in the Union army and war-profiteering among army contractors. He would continue these themes in *The Coward* (1864) and provide an account of his own war experiences in *Red-Tape and Pigeon-Hole Generals* (1864).

HARRIET PRESCOTT SPOFFORD: *The Amber Gods and Other Stories*. Included in this popular and critically acclaimed collection of stories, most of which had been previously published in the *Atlantic Monthly*, is "In a Cellar," a detective story; "The Amber Gods," which contrasts the identity of two different women in love with the same man; "The South Breaker," a regional romance; and "Circumstance," about a New England woman who keeps a mythical creature at bay by singing.

ANN SOPHIA STEPHENS: *The Rejected Wife*. Stephens's novel about the early life of Benedict Arnold is commended by the *Continental Monthly* for its accurate characterizations and details of period life. The book would be republished in 1876 as *The Rejected Wife; or, The Ruling Passion*.

BAYARD TAYLOR: *Hannah Thurston*. Taylor's first novel deals with women's rights in the United States. Although popular and described by the *Atlantic Monthly* as an "able pioneer" on the topic, bringing "an appreciable degree of sense, justice, and dignity" to the "Women's Rights question," the novel is now considered, with Taylor's others, to lack distinction. It would be followed by *John Godfrey's Fortune* (1864), depicting New York's contemporary literary scene.

Nonfiction

LOUISA MAY ALCOTT: *Hospital Sketches*. Alcott's memoir, composed from letters written during her time as a nurse at the Union Hotel Hospital in the District of Columbia, wins popular and critical success, earning the author funds for a European trip and encouraging her to write the mature novel *Moods* (1865).

WILLIAM WELLS BROWN: *The Black Man, His Antecedents, His Genius, and His Achievements*. Brown, who had published his personal slave memoir in 1847 and the first novel by an African American in 1853, uses this book to dispel misconceptions of racial inferiority. He compares Anglo-Saxon and African cultures, argues that abolition will be advantageous to the country, and provides biographical sketches of prominent African Americans and Haitians. Although criticized for errors and the exclusion of several important African Americans, the book is moderately successful, resulting in four printings by 1865 and the publication of an expanded edition, *The Rising Son*, in 1873.

GEORGE HENRY CALVERT (1803–1889): *The Gentleman*. This manual by the Baltimore-born author of closet dramas illustrates appropriate behavior by giving historical examples of true gentility. Calvert's gentlemen are Christian, honorable, and "above all things free," and his examples include the French knight Pierre Terrail Bayard and Elizabethan courtier and poet Sir Philip Sidney. The book is widely read during the Civil War, going through four printings.

JOHN ESTEN COOKE: *Life of Stonewall Jackson*. While serving as an officer in the Confederate army, Cooke writes this biography of Jackson, which helps to make him a legend. Cooke would also produce a biography of Robert E. Lee in 1871.

PIERRE DE SMET (1801–1873): *New Indian Sketches*. The Jesuit missionary among the Indians of the Northwest issues his final book of observations concerning the Indians and the West.

ELIZABETH (1766–1866): *Memoir of Old Elizabeth*. Born a slave in Maryland, Elizabeth had begun her life as an itinerant preacher in 1808. Her memoir provides her perspective on the resistance she faced from the established church for becoming an evangelist, thus violating accepted racial and gender roles. After establishing an orphanage in Michigan in the 1840s, she retired to Pennsylvania, where she dictated her narrative.

NATHANIEL HAWTHORNE: *Our Old Home*. This collection of sketches, many previously published in periodicals such as the *Atlantic Monthly*, is based on Hawthorne's time in England as an American consul and tourist. The works reveal the author's appreciation for the country while still criticizing the nation for its class system and poverty. Among the best and most honest pieces of literature on England by an American, it is denounced by British critics.

FRANCES ANNE KEMBLE: *A Journal of a Residence on a Georgian Plantation*. A journal in the form of letters written by the English actress who had come to live on her husband's plantation and witnessed the horrors of slavery. The work records numerous instances of mistreatment, such as women being whipped and forced to work soon after childbirth. Written between 1838 and 1839, it is published to sway British opinion during the Civil War.

FRANCIS LIEBER: *A Code for the Government of Armies.* This standardized code of wartime conduct outlines procedures to minimize destruction, protect civilians, and normalize treatment of prisoners of war. Abraham Lincoln's War Department issues it as General Orders No. 100; it becomes a recognized authority on military law and would influence war conduct for many years.

DONALD GRANT MITCHELL (1822–1908): *My Farm of Edgewood.* Called "a book whose merit can hardly be overpraised" by the *Atlantic Monthly* and based on Mitchell's own experience in his rural Connecticut home, this is the first in a series of romantic portraits of country life written under the author's pseudonym "Ik Marvel." His other books include *Wet Days at Edgewood* (1865) and *Pictures of Edgewood* (1869).

ROBERT DALE OWEN (1801–1877): *The Policy of Emancipation.* The son of social reformer and socialist Robert Owen (1771–1858) provides a treatise on racial matters that reportedly influences Abraham Lincoln. It would be followed by *The Wrong of Slavery* (1864).

HENRY DAVID THOREAU: *Excursions.* A posthumous collection of natural history and travel essays that had previously been published in magazines or expanded from notes in his journal. The essays include "Natural History of Massachusetts," "A Walk to Wachusett," "Wild Apples," "May Days," and "Days and Nights in Concord." A biographical sketch of Thoreau written by Ralph Waldo Emerson is also included. Thoreau's essay "Life Without Principle" is also published. Commenting on "the way in which we spend our lives," the piece originated in a lecture entitled "Getting a Living," which Thoreau had delivered numerous times. It is first published in the *Atlantic Monthly* and later collected in *A Yankee in Canada* (1866).

THEODORE WINTHROP: *Life in the Open Air.* A collection of nature essays, two of which had been published in the *Atlantic Monthly* before Winthrop's death. The *North American Review* hails the work as one of the best in the series of the author's posthumous publications and notes that it "illustrates the versatility of the writer's powers.... The style is fresh, manly, and picturesque; the narrative clear, sparkling, and animated; the criticism genial; and the tone always healthful." Winthrop's work *The Canoe and the Saddle: Adventures Among the Northwestern Rivers and Forests; and Isthmania* is also published. A personal memoir of Winthrop's travels to the Northwest, with an appendix describing a trip to Panama, it is noteworthy for its vibrant descriptions of western scenes, including Puget Sound, the Columbia River, and the Cascades. The popular book would be reprinted in numerous editions.

Poetry

RALPH WALDO EMERSON: "Voluntaries." An elegy commemorating Colonel Robert Gould Shaw, commander of the Fifty-fourth Massachusetts Regiment — the first black regiment — killed in the battle for Fort Wagner. Emerson justifies Shaw's death not for the preservation of the Union but for the abolition of slavery.

HENRY WADSWORTH LONGFELLOW: *Tales of a Wayside Inn.* Longfellow publishes the first of three collections of narrative poems (a second would appear in 1872 and a third in 1874, collected in 1886) told by individuals gathered at a fireside of a New England tavern. Although stories set in Europe predominate, the most popular tales are those with American settings and themes, including "Paul Revere's Ride," which opens the book; "The Birds of Killingworth," about the vengeance a horde of caterpillars takes on Connecticut farmers who kill small birds that destroy their crops; and "The Theologian's Tale," a romance set among the Pennsylvania Quakers.

Publications and Events

ABRAHAM LINCOLN (1809–1865): "Gettysburg Address." Lincoln's three-paragraph speech, given on November 19 to dedicate a national cemetery at the site of the Battle of Gettysburg, is initially overshadowed by the two-hour grandiose address by the featured speaker, clergyman Edward Everett (1794–1865). Following Lincoln's death, it would be recognized as one of the most inspired summaries of American principles, described by H. L. Mencken as the "shortest and most famous oration in American history."

The *Round Table.* The New York weekly begins publication. Until 1869, it featured literary criticism from the American point of view with contributors such as poet R. H. Stoddard, critic Edmund Clarence Stedman, and novelist, poet, and editor Thomas Bailey Aldrich.

1864
Drama and Theater

GEORGE HENRY CALVERT: *Arnold and André.* Calvert's closet drama is a tragedy based on the story of Benedict Arnold and Major André.

Depiction of President Lincoln's Address at Gettysburg

Fiction

LOUISA MAY ALCOTT: *On Picket Duty, and Other Tales.* The title work of this collection of stories concerns a group of soldiers on guard duty discussing their various courtships and marriages. "The Death of John" is based on Alcott's bedside witness of a mortally wounded soldier's last night. Alcott also publishes *The Rose Family: A Fairy Tale*, her second fantasy book, which is a moral tale chronicling the education of three fairy daughters who learn how their faults can harm others. She also publishes *Moods*, her first novel. It tells the story of Sylvia Yule, a dynamic young woman who realizes that she has married a man she does not love and is in fact in love with his best friend. Treating marriage, gender relationships, and the societal pitfalls faced by young women, the novel meets mostly unfavorable criticism. A revised edition, more overt in its criticism of the limitations faced by women, would be released in 1882 after the success of *Little Women* and attain a wide audience.

MARIA SUSANNA CUMMINS: *Haunted Hearts.* The author of the bestseller *The Lamplighter* (1854) fails to find an audience for this novel about a heroine who destroys her life by thoughtless acts. Later critics, such as Nina Baym, would be impressed by Cummins's portrait of a society offering limited possibilities to women, who are given "no power except to injure, and no moral destiny other than silent suffering."

MARY MAPES DODGE (1831–1905): *Irvington Stories.* The first publication by the New York writer and editor of juvenile fiction is a collection of stories for children, many with war themes. Its positive reception encourages her to attempt a second book, the bestseller *Hans Brinker* (1865).

CHARLES GRAHAM HALPINE (1829–1868): *The Life and Adventures, Songs, Services, and Speeches of Private Miles O'Reilly.* This popular collection of witty sketches and verse about the war, written from the point of view of an Irish private, is widely read. Some of the parodies by the Irish-born writer, who became a brigadier general in the Union army, had been taken as factual news when first published in newspapers.

HENRY JAMES (1843–1916): "A Tragedy of Error." James's first story is published. It involves a love triangle set in France. A wife hires a man to kill her husband, who murders her lover instead. It shows the influence of French novelist George Sand, one of James's favorite authors.

RICHARD MALCOLM JOHNSTON (1822–1898): *Georgia Sketches.* The local colorist, influenced by August Baldwin Longstreet, produces a collection of sketches of Georgia life before the arrival of the railroad. A revised and expanded version, *Dukesborough Tales*, would appear in 1871.

DAVID ROSS LOCKE (1833–1888): *The Nasby Papers.* The first book collection of the humorous and satirical letters by Locke's persona "Petroleum V(esuvius) Nasby," which had first appeared in newspapers in 1861. Nasby, an illiterate country preacher, a drunkard, and bigot, ineptly and ludicrously writes in support of the Confederate cause. Locke would continue to write Nasby letters until his death, commenting ironically on the American political scene. Subsequent collections include *Divers Views, Opinions, and Prophecies of Yours Trooly, Petroleum V. Nasby* (1866), *Swingin' Round the Cirkle* (1867), *Inflation at the Cross Roads* (1875), and the complete collection, *The Nasby Letters* (1893).

AUGUSTUS BALDWIN LONGSTREET: *Master William Mitten.* The Georgia jurist and local colorist produces this autobiographically based novel, drawing on his experiences as a youth at the turn of the century.

EPES SARGENT: *Peculiar: A Tale of the Great Transition.* This romantic and spiritual novel about slavery following the Battle of New Orleans and occupation features actual personages, including Abraham Lincoln, Jefferson Davis, Senator Wigfall, and George Saunders. The *Continental Monthly* calls it "a novel of graphic power and sustained interest."

HARRIET PRESCOTT SPOFFORD: *Azarian: An Episode.* A romantic, popular novel about Constant Azarian, a selfish Bostonian who undervalues the love of the innocent Ruth Tetton. Although the book receives acclaim from many reviewers, it is harshly criticized by Henry James in the *North American Review* for its romantic descriptions.

WILLIAM HENRY THOMES (1824–1895): *The Goldhunters' Adventures; or, Life in Australia.* The first of the Maine-born world traveler's popular adventure novels draws on his own experiences at sea and as a gold prospector. It would be followed by *The Bushrangers* (1866), *The Whalesman's Adventures* (1872), *A Slave's Adventures* (1872), and *The Ocean Rivers* (1896). He would chronicle his own adventures in *On Land and Sea* (1883) and *Lewey and I* (1884).

JOHN TOWNSEND TROWBRIDGE: *Cudjo's Cave.* This popular, melodramatic antislavery novel is set at the beginning of the Civil War in Tennessee and concerns a group of abolitionist and Union sympathizers who are threatened by slaveholders and hide in a wilderness cave where they meet two escaped slaves. They are all attacked by the angry Confederates, and the survivors flee to Ohio.

Nonfiction

J. ROSS BROWNE (1821–1875): *Crusoe's Island: A Ramble in the Footsteps of Alexander Selkirk, with Sketches of Adventure in California and Washoe.* A popular narrative of Browne's experiences as a custom house and Indian affairs inspector and as a mines commissioner. The autobiographical sketches are embellished with fictional elements and are said to anticipate Mark Twain's *Roughing It*.

HORACE GREELEY (1811–1872): *The American Conflict: A History of the Great Rebellion in the United States of America.* A rapidly written history of the Civil War and abolition that provides an accurate, albeit one-sided, description of events. Postwar sales of the book would fall, however, after Greeley signed a bond to free Jefferson Davis while the Confederate president awaited trial.

OLIVER WENDELL HOLMES: *Soundings from the Atlantic.* A collection of Holmes's essays originally published in the *Atlantic Monthly.* The review in the *Continental Monthly* commends the work as "full of keen satire, genial humor, and tender pathos," and asks who may compete with Holmes "in varied gifts, or rival the charm of intellectual grace which he breathes at will into all he writes."

JAMES RUSSELL LOWELL: *Fireside Travels.* Lowell's collection of essays, most of which had previously appeared in *Putnam's Monthly* and *Graham's Magazine* with some additional descriptions of his travels in Italy, is praised by the *Continental Monthly* as "a right pleasant book to read."

GEORGE PERKINS MARSH (1801–1882): *Man and Nature: Physical Geography as Modified by Human Action.* A popular and influential environmental treatise demonstrating how humanity's wastefulness affects the natural world. A revised edition, *The Earth as Modified by Human Action*, would be published in 1874. The twentieth-century environmentalist movement would rekindle interest in the work. Marsh was a Vermont lawyer and linguist who served as minister to Turkey from 1849 to 1854 and minister to Italy from 1860 to 1882.

THOMAS LOW NICHOLS: *Forty Years of American Life.* This two-volume account of the social customs, history, and geography of America would be reprinted numerous times. It is considered one of the most engaging and informative descriptions of mid-nineteenth-century American life.

ABEL STEVENS (1815–1897): *History of the Methodist Episcopal Church in the United States.* The Methodist clergyman's highly acclaimed denominational history, outlining the roots of the Methodist Episcopal Church in the United States, is distinguished for its entertaining literary style. It was preceded by *A History of the Religious Movement of the 18th Century Called Methodism* (3 vols., 1858–1861).

HENRY DAVID THOREAU: *The Maine Woods.* Thoreau's posthumously published travel collection describes three of his trips to Maine. "Ktaadn" describes an excursion to Mount Katahdin in 1846; "Chesuncook" treats a journey from Bangor to Chesuncook Lake in 1853; and "The Allegash and East Branch" chronicles a canoe voyage with the Indian guide Joe Polis in 1857.

HENRY THEODORE TUCKERMAN: *America and Her Commentators.* Tuckerman surveys writing about America in an attempt to stimulate a new sense of national unity and patriotism in the wake of the Civil War.

Poetry

GEORGE HENRY BOKER: *Poems of the War.* Boker's collection of Civil War verse prompts the *Continental Monthly* to declare that it is comprised of "truly national poems" and that the verse "should be read at every hearthstone in our land."

HENRY HOWARD BROWNELL (1820–1872): *Lyrics of a Day; or, Newspaper Poetry.* A collection of Civil War verse, primarily written following the battles in which the Connecticut lawyer and newspaper versifier had participated as Admiral David Farragut's secretary. Brownell's work is admired by many prominent literary figures, including Ralph Waldo Emerson and Oliver Wendell Holmes, who names Brownell "Our Battle Laureate." *War Lyrics and Other Poems* would follow in 1866.

WILLIAM CULLEN BRYANT: *Thirty Poems.* Bryant gathers some of his Civil War verses in a slight collection, which does not add appreciably to his reputation but generally confirms his status as a poet whose best work is behind him.

ROBERT TRAILL SPENCE LOWELL (1816–1891): *Poems.* A collection of popular and critically acclaimed verses by the older brother of the more famous writer James Russell Lowell. Many of the poems have patriotic themes, including "The Massachusetts Line" and "The Men of the Cumberland."

THOMAS BUCHANAN READ (1822–1872): "Sheridan's Ride." The most famous work of a poet who is now largely forgotten but was considered a leading American poet before his death. The verse details how General Philip Sheridan marshals the beaten Union troops at the Battle of Cedar Creek in Virginia and leads them to victory. This poem, as well as Read's other patriotic verses, including "The Wagoner of the Alleghenies," are popularized by the renowned actor James E. Murdoch, who recites them on tours throughout the country.

EDMUND CLARENCE STEDMAN (1833–1908): *Alice of Monmouth: An Idyll of the Great War, and Other Poems.* In this collection of verse, the title piece describes the New Jersey countryside, various battlefields, and Virginia hospitals. The *North American Review* calls the book "a permanent contribution to our genuinely native literature."

FREDERICK GODDARD TUCKERMAN: *Poems.* Privately printed initially in 1860, Tuckerman's single collection of sonnets is published. A final edition would appear in 1869, after which Tuckerman would be forgotten until the poet Witter Bynner rediscovered and reissued his work in 1931. Poet and critic Yvor Winters would declare that among the Romantics only Wordsworth surpasses Tuckerman "in the description of natural detail."

JOHN GREENLEAF WHITTIER: *In War Time and Other Poems.* Whittier's collection includes one of his most famous poems, "Barbara Frietchie," relating the suppos-

edly true incident in which a ninety-year-old Unionist dares to raise the Stars and Stripes as Stonewall Jackson enters Frederick, Maryland, declaring these well-known lines: "Shoot if you must, this old gray head, / But spare your country's flag, she said."

1865

Drama and Theater

DION BOUCICAULT: *Arrah na Pogue; or, The Wicklow Wedding.* Boucicault's Irish melodrama treats the complications that arise when a young peasant girl hides a fugitive from the British. It becomes one of the playwright's most popular works and would be revived frequently for the remainder of the century.

DION BOUCICAULT AND JOSEPH JEFFERSON (1829–1905): *Rip Van Winkle.* The playwright and actor collaborate on a successful dramatic adaptation of Washington Irving's story. Jefferson would perform the title role for the next forty years.

Fiction

MARY MAPES DODGE: *Hans Brinker; or, The Silver Skates.* Dodge's classic children's story of two children, Hans and Gretel, in a Dutch village. Happy events of the story include Gretel's victory in a skating contest and their father's treatment by an illustrious doctor.

JOHN PENDLETON KENNEDY: *Mr. Ambrose's Letters on the Rebellion.* Kennedy's final book published in his lifetime is a defense of the Union cause.

HENRY WHEELER SHAW (1818–1885): *Josh Billings, His Sayings.* The Massachusetts-born humorist issues his first book as the Yankee cracker-barrel philosopher "Josh Billings," whose philosophical comments feature misspellings and malapropisms. From 1869 to 1880, he would issue an annual *Allminax*, and his other popular collections include *Josh Billings on Ice and Other Things* (1868), *Everybody's Friend* (1874), *Josh Billings' Trump Kards* (1877), *Old Probability* (1879), *Josh Billings Struggling with Things* (1881), and *Josh Billings, His Works Complete* (1888).

MARK TWAIN (SAMUEL LANGHORNE CLEMENS): "The Celebrated Jumping Frog of Calaveras County." Twain adapts a popular folktale from gold rush mining camps, about how Jim Smiley and his frog, Dan'l Webster, are defeated in a frog-jumping contest by a cheating competitor. It is published under the pseudonym "Mark Twain" in New York's *Saturday Press* under the title "Jim Smiley and His Jumping Frog," in *Beadle's Dime Book of Fun* (1866), and in Twain's first book, *The Celebrated Jumping Frog* (1867).

Nonfiction

BRONSON ALCOTT: *Ralph Waldo Emerson.* Alcott presents a laudatory assessment of Emerson's career and genius.

MARY ABIGAIL DODGE: *A New Atmosphere.* Dodge's book-length essay argues against the view of women that "the great business of their life is marriage" and for greater female self-reliance, active lives, and gender equality.

AUGUSTINE JOSEPH HICKEY DUGANNE (1823–1884): *Camps and Prison.* The most important work of the poet, playwright, and dime novelist is this vivid account of his Civil War experiences as a Union officer.

FRANCIS PARKMAN: *Pioneers of France in the New World.* Parkman returns to his multivolume history of colonial North America with the story of Samuel de Champlain's explorations and the struggle between France and Spain for control of Florida.

HENRY DAVID THOREAU: *Cape Cod.* The posthumously published volume collects Thoreau's accounts of his visits to the Cape in 1849, 1850, and 1855, along with reflections on the Cape's history and inhabitants.

Poetry

BRET HARTE: *Outcroppings.* Harte's first book is an anthology of Californian poetry. His selections create controversy; many regard his subjects and style as low-bred and unrefined.

GEORGE MOSES HORTON (c. 1798–c. 1880): *Naked Genius.* Horton, a slave living in the area of the University of North Carolina, had begun his writing career by ghostwriting love poems for undergraduates. This is his third and final verse collection.

HENRY WADSWORTH LONGFELLOW: *Divine Comedy.* Longfellow issues the first of his blank-verse translations of Dante's poem (completed in 1867). He would meet regularly with James Russell Lowell and Charles Eliot Norton to discuss his work and seek their assistance. The sonnets written to precede and follow each of the three parts of Dante's poem are generally regarded as among Longfellow's best works.

JAMES RUSSELL LOWELL: "Ode Recited at the Commemoration to the Living and Dead Soldiers of Harvard University." One of Lowell's most important works is this Pindaric ode eulogizing Harvard's fallen and the Union cause. After being delivered at Harvard, it is expanded and privately printed in 1865 and published in the revised edition of *The Cathedral* (1877).

RAY PALMER (1808–1887): *Hymns and Sacred Pieces.* The Congregational minister of Maine and New York is best remembered for this collection of original hymns. A second volume, *Hymns of My Holy Hours*, would appear in 1867.

MARGARET JUNKIN PRESTON (1820–1897): *Beechenbrook: A Rhyme of the War.* The Pennsylvania poet of the Confederacy publishes her first collection. It includes her best-known poem, "Under the Shade of the Tree," which takes its title from the dying words of her sister's husband, Confederate general Thomas "Stonewall" Jackson. *Cartoons* would follow in 1875 and *For Love's Sake* in 1886.

THOMAS BUCHANAN READ: *A Summer Story, Sheridan's Ride, and Other Poems.* Included in this collection is Read's best-remembered work, "Sheridan's Ride," an exciting account of General Philip Sheridan's desperate ride to rally the retreating Union army at the Battle of Cedar Creek in Virginia.

WILLIAM ROSS WALLACE (1819–1881): "What Rules the World." Having previously published a popular pro-Union poem, "The Liberty Bell" (1862), which was set to music, the Kentucky poet produces the poem for which he is now remembered. It includes the lines "The hand that rocks the cradle / Is the hand that rules the world."

WALT WHITMAN: *Drum-Taps.* A collection of verse inspired by Whitman's work in military hospitals during the Civil War. The original printing contains his celebration of American ideals, "Pioneers! O Pioneers!" Only a few copies of this work are bound for sale, however. After Lincoln's death, *Sequel to Drum-Taps*, which contains Whitman's elegy on Lincoln, "When Lilacs Last in the Dooryard Bloom'd," is quickly appended to the earlier collection, and the two are sold together. Other poems in the collection include "Hymn of the Dead Soldiers," "The Wound Dresser," and "O Captain! My Captain!" Both *Drum-Taps* and the additional verse in its sequel would be included in the 1867 edition of *Leaves of Grass.*

JOHN GREENLEAF WHITTIER: *National Lyrics.* Whittier reissues the poems of *In War Time* (1863) along with "Laus Deo," a poem commemorating the end of slavery.

Publications and Events

The Nation. Founded by E. L. Godkin (1831–1902) as a New York weekly to cover current events, the magazine would be identified for its reformist and liberal views and prove to be an important outlet for new writing under the editorship of distinguished literary figures such as Carl Van Doren, Mark Van Doren, John Macy, Ludwig Lewisohn, and J. W. Krutch.

Our Young Folks. The juvenile magazine begins publication. Its contributors included Harriet Beecher Stowe,

Horatio Alger, and Elizabeth Stuart Phelps. In 1873, it merged with *St. Nicholas.*

The *Radical.* The chief organ of the Radical Club, an informal association of New England Unitarian and Transcendentalist thinkers opposed to the supernaturalism of Christianity, begins publication. Issued until 1872, the journal included contributors such as Henry James Sr., Thomas Wentworth Higginson, and Moncure Conway.

1866

Drama and Theater

CHARLES M. BARRAS (1826–1873): *The Black Crook.* This musical fantasy by the stage manager turned playwright about the "Arch Fiend" who induces Herzog, the "Black Crook," to deliver a soul to him, proves to be the most successful Broadway play up to its time — the first to run for more than a year. One secret of its success was a chorus line of girls clad in flesh-colored tights.

Fiction

WILLIAM MUMFORD BAKER (1825–1883): *Inside: A Chronicle of Secession.* Baker is best known for this novel published under the pseudonym "Gerald F. Harrison," which is based on his life in the South during the Civil War.

JOHN ESTEN COOKE: *Surry of Eagle's Nest.* Cooke's first and hugely successful postwar novel is illustrated by Winslow Homer. Laboring to remain economically viable to his Northern publishers, the Southern writer crafts a work that portrays virtuous Northerners battling courageous and noble Southerners. It is one of the first fictional works to aid the cause of peace between the North and the South following the war. It would be followed by *Hilt to Hilt* (1869) and *Mohun* (1869).

AUGUSTA JANE EVANS: *St. Elmo.* Evans's greatest success and one of the century's biggest sellers is her third sentimental novel concerning the eventual taming of the Byronic title character by a prudish, erudite young orphan, Edna Earle.

WASHINGTON IRVING: *Spanish Papers and Other Miscellanies.* Irving's collection of Spanish chronicles and legends is published posthumously.

JOHN BEAUCHAMP JONES (1810–1866): *A Rebel War Clerk's Diary at the Confederate Capital.* Regarded as the frontier novelist's most important book, this vivid portrait of life in the Confederacy is based on Jones's own experiences working in the Confederate War Department.

DONALD GRANT MITCHELL: *Dr. Johns.* Mitchell's novel, published under the pseudonym "Ik Marvel," looks at New England village life in the early nineteenth century, particularly the native Calvinist response to the arrival of two Catholic Frenchwomen.

S. WEIR MITCHELL (1829–1914): "The Case of George Dedlow." The Philadelphia physician and medical researcher's first story is published in the *Atlantic Monthly.* Based on Mitchell's own war experiences, it is a Civil War story depicting the psychological distress of an injured army surgeon.

CHARLES H. SMITH (1826–1903): *Bill Arp, So-Called.* In 1861, the Southern humorist began publishing letters signed "Bill Arp" in newspapers, offering the ludicrous opinions of an inept Yankee sympathizer. After the war, Smith had turned his persona into a cracker-barrel philosopher, commenting on topics such as women's suffrage, race relations, and Reconstruction. This first book would be followed by *Bill Arp's Letters* (1868), *Bill Arp's Peace Papers* (1873), *Bill Arp's Scrap Book* (1884), and *Bill Arp: From the Uncivil War to Date* (1903).

BAYARD TAYLOR: *The Story of Kennett.* Regarded as Taylor's best fiction, this novel depicts the life and inhabitants of a Pennsylvania town in the eighteenth century.

METTA VICTORIA VICTOR: *The Dead Letter: An American Romance.* The dime novelist, author of the antislavery *Maum Guinea and Her Plantation Children* (1862), writing under the pseudonym "Seely Regester," has been credited with producing the first detective novel written by a woman, a distinction erroneously credited for a long time to Anna Katharine Green for *The Leavenworth Case* (1878).

CHARLES HENRY WEBB (1834–1905): *Liffith Lank and St. Twel'mo.* The New York humorist, founder of the *Californian* and publisher of his friend Mark Twain's first book, offers parodies of Charles Reade's *Griffith Gaunt* and Augusta Jane Evans's *St. Elmo.*

Nonfiction

ELIHU BURRIT: *Lectures and Speeches.* The so-called Learned Blacksmith, a laborer who had mastered more than forty languages and authored scholarly works, collects various discourses from his speaking engagements in this book.

WILLIAM DEAN HOWELLS: *Venetian Life.* Howells had been rewarded for his campaign biography of Abraham Lincoln by an appointment as consul to Venice, where he sat out the Civil War. Here he revises a series of travel letters he had written for the *Boston Advertiser;* it would be followed by *Italian Journeys* (1867).

WILLIAM DOUGLAS O'CONNOR (1832–1889): *The Good Gray Poet: A Vindication.* After Walt Whitman had been dismissed from his government job for writing "obscene" poetry, his friend O'Connor comes to his defense, supplying the sobriquet that would long be attributed to the poet. O'Connor was a government employee who had helped Whitman gain a position in the Department of the Interior and in the attorney general's office.

HENRY DAVID THOREAU: *A Yankee in Canada.* Thoreau's travel narrative of his 1850 week-long trip from Concord to Montreal and Quebec includes reflections on the comparative manners and customs of Canadians and New Englanders. Having appeared in part in *Putnam's Monthly Magazine* in 1853, it is posthumously issued along with Thoreau's "Anti-Slavery and Reform Papers."

GEORGE ALFRED TOWNSEND (1841–1914): *Campaigns of the Non-Combatant.* The Delaware journalist and one of the first syndicated correspondents collects his Civil War dispatches. They concentrate on the lot of the common soldier and the civilians caught in the path of the war.

Poetry

GEORGE ARNOLD (1834–1865): *Drift: A Sea-Shore Idyl and Other Poems.* The first of two posthumous collections of the New York humorist and author of a number of popular burlesques in verse and prose. It would be followed by *Poems, Grave and Gay* in 1867. Arnold was a member of the bohemian group that gathered at New York City's Pfaff's Beer Cellar.

HERMAN MELVILLE: *Battle-Pieces and Aspects of the War.* Melville's collection of Civil War poems begins with "The Portent," a verse on the death of John Brown, and continues with reflections on most of the significant events of the war, arranged chronologically and finishing with "A Meditation," an elegy to the fallen on both sides. Sales and reviews are poor, but Melville publishes a supplement arguing for Northern benevolence toward the struggling South, which wins the work some favor. Not until the twentieth century would the collection truly gain respect as the only Civil War verses comparable in artistry to Walt Whitman's *Drum-Taps.*

JOHN GREENLEAF WHITTIER: *Snow-Bound, a Winter Idyll.* The poet's masterpiece and most enduring poem is a "Yankee pastoral" that he had promised James Russell Lowell he would write. The primarily iambic tetrameter couplets describe a winter snowstorm blanketing Whittier's childhood farm in Massachusetts. It nostalgically presents images of rural life then waning in America, such as family stories and poems recited by the fire, connection

with nature, and a schoolteacher boarding at the family's home.

Publications and Events

Every Saturday. A weekly illustrated magazine edited in Boston by Thomas Bailey Aldrich begins publication. It folded in 1874.

The *Galaxy.* The New York literary monthly, intended as a rival to the *Atlantic Monthly,* begins publication. Until it ceased publication in 1878, it featured important new works by writers such as Henry James, Walt Whitman, and Mark Twain, who served for a time as its humor editor.

The *New York World.* Beginning as a penny religious daily, the *World* gradually shifted to secular concerns, and, when purchased by Joseph Pulitzer in 1883, became a crusading newspaper for popular causes. In 1894 it introduced the first multicolor comic strip, "Hogan's Alley," featuring a character named the Yellow Kid, who is said to be the basis for the term *yellow journalism,* reflecting the paper's increasing sensationalism. In 1931 it merged with the *New York Telegram* and after other mergers ceased publication in 1967.

1867
Drama and Theater

AUGUSTIN DALY: *Under the Gaslight.* Daly's first original play is a sensational melodrama featuring a climactic scene in which the heroine rescues the hero, who is tied to a railroad track as a train approaches. Possibly borrowed from the 1865 English drama *The Engineer,* the scene would become a staple of melodramas and early films.

Fiction

HORATIO ALGER JR. (1832–1899): *Ragged Dick; or, Street Life in New York.* Alger's first successful fiction is serialized in the *Student and Schoolmaster,* a magazine edited by William Taylor Adams, who as "Oliver Optic" would become Alger's chief rival in supplying juvenile reading matter. *Ragged Dick* would be published as a book in 1868, the beginning of a stream of Alger's novels and series about poor boys who achieve success through hard work, prudence, and pluck. It is estimated that more than twenty million copies of his novels have been printed.

JOHN WILLIAM DE FOREST (1826–1906): *Miss Ravenel's Conversion from Secession to Loyalty.* The best work by the Connecticut-born writer who served as a captain in the Civil War concerns a New Orleans doctor who is faithful to the Union and the abolitionist cause and flees

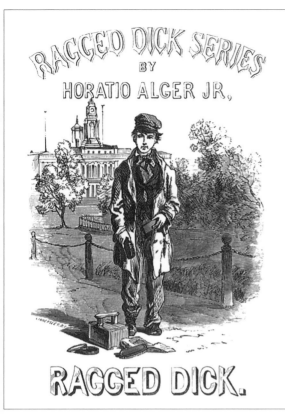

The title page from Horatio Alger's *Ragged Dick*

to Boston with his daughter, Lillie, during the Civil War. The story revolves around Lillie, whose sympathies lie with the South, and the two suitors who court her. Her eventual marriage to the abolitionist lawyer coincides with her growing faith in Christianity and the Union cause.

MARTHA FARQUHARSON FINLEY (1828–1909): *Elsie Dinsmore.* Finley issues the first of twenty-eight popular children's books (completed in 1905) about the meek (and priggish) title character, whose piety and moral rectitude win the affection of her distant father. Other titles include *Elsie's Girlhood* (1872), *Elsie's Womanhood* (1875), *Elsie's Motherhood* (1876), *Elsie's Widowhood* (1880), and *Grandmother Elsie* (1882). Finley would also produce another series, beginning with *Mildred Keith* in 1878, that would comprise seven volumes by 1894.

GEORGE WASHINGTON HARRIS (1814–1869): *Sut Lovingood: Yarns Spun by a "Nat'ral Born Durn'd Fool."* A collection of humorous sketches by the former steamboat captain and political writer depicting a Tennessee backwoodsman with a penchant for whiskey and practical jokes. The volume includes new tales and revisions of Harris's contributions to the *Spirit of the Times*. The book receives high praise from Mark Twain, who commends its use of dialect in the *Califonia Alta*.

BRET HARTE: *Condensed Novels and Other Papers.* First published in the *Golden Era* and the *Californian*, these works blend fiction and commentary in parodying the writing of Charles Dickens, Nathaniel Parker Willis, James Fenimore Cooper, and others. The "novels" bring Harte wide acclaim, and the *North American Review* calls him "a parodist of such genius that he seems a mirror into which novelists may look and be warned." He also publishes *The Lost Galleon and Other Tales,* which includes a collection of his poetry.

OLIVER WENDELL HOLMES: *The Guardian Angel.* The second of the author's "medicated novels," character studies showing Holmes's theories of biological determinism, concerns an orphan girl who rebels from her strict aunt by running away disguised as a boy. It had been preceded by *Elsie Venner* (1861) and would be followed by *A Mortal Antipathy* (1885).

SIDNEY LANIER (1842–1881): *Tiger-Lilies.* The Georgia musician and poet's first publication is a Civil War novel drawing on his own experience as a Confederate soldier, including his four months spent in a Union prison.

NICHOLAS MEYER (1838–1912): *Differences.* Written by one of the earliest Jewish American novelists, the book describes conditions faced by Jews in the South during the Civil War.

WILLIAM GILMORE SIMMS: *Joscelyn: A Tale of the Revolution.* The last of Simms's Revolutionary War tales is published serially. It would be followed by his final fictional works, "The Cub of the Panther" (1869) and "Voltmeier; or, The Mountain Men" (1869).

ELIZABETH OAKES SMITH (1806–1893): *Bald Eagle; or, The Last of the Ramapaughs.* The first of Smith's two novels treating Indian life appears in the Beadle dime novel series. It presents a sympathetic depiction of Tecumseh's attempt to unite the Native American tribes against the U.S. government. It would be followed by *The Sagamore of Saco* (1868), her final work of fiction.

HARRIET BEECHER STOWE: *The Daisy's First Winter, and Other Stories* and *Queer Little People.* These collections of children's stories contain animal fables and realistic moral tales.

MARK TWAIN (SAMUEL LANGHORNE CLEMENS): *The Celebrated Jumping Frog of Calaveras County, and Other Sketches.* Twain's first book is a collection of his sketches and stories assembled on the advice of Twain's friend,

Charles H. Webb (1834–1905), who eventually brought out the book after it had been rejected by several publishers. Despite the popularity of the title story, the book sells poorly and quickly goes out of print.

Literary Criticism and Scholarship

JOHN BURROUGHS (1837–1921): *Notes on Walt Whitman, as Poet and Person.* The first critical biography of Whitman chronicles the publication of *Leaves of Grass,* Whitman's personal interests, and his method. Much of the text is actually written by Whitman himself. Burroughs would later expand the work into *Walt Whitman: A Study* (1896). Burroughs would go on to establish his reputation as a nature writer in volumes such as *Wake-Robin* (1871) and *Birds and Poets* (1877).

Nonfiction

WILLIAM WELLS BROWN: *The Negro in the American Rebellion: His Heroism and His Fidelity.* Brown produces the first military history of African Americans in the United States.

GEORGE CATLIN: *O-Kee-Pa, A Religious Ceremony, and Other Customs of the Mandans.* Written to refute charges that Catlin's earlier observations about Indian life had been invented, he provides a detailed description of a Mandan religious ritual.

DAVID ROSS LOCKE: *Swingin' Round the Cirkle.* This collection of the satirical observations of "Petroleum V. Nasby" takes aim at the racist and pro-Southern policies of the postwar Democratic Party.

FRANCIS PARKMAN: *The Jesuits in North America in the Seventeenth Century.* This installment of Parkman's colonial history of North America looks at the Jesuits' attempt to convert the Indians and the Iroquois retaliation against the converted tribes in the 1670s. Its graphic description of Indian tortures and atrocities makes it a favorite book for schoolboys.

Poetry

CHARLES WARREN STODDARD (1843–1909): *Poems.* Edited by Bret Harte and published by Anton Roman, the San Francisco bookseller and founder of the *Overland Monthly,* this is the first collection and publication by the California author. Sumptuously illustrated by Stoddard's friend William Keith and elegantly bound, it is considered the first example of fine bookmaking to be produced in California.

HENRY TIMROD: "Ode Sung on the Occasion of Decorating the Graves of the Confederate Dead." Considered Timrod's finest poem, this elegy for fallen Confederate soldiers is made up of five quatrains of octosyllabic lines. First delivered at Magnolia Cemetery in Charleston, South Carolina, it would later be included in Timrod's *Poems* (1873).

JOHN TOWNSEND TROWBRIDGE: "Darius Green and His Flying Machine." Trowbridge's best-known poem, first appearing in *Our Young Folks* and collected in *The Vagabonds and Other Poems* (1869), concerns a man's quest to achieve the means of flight.

WALT WHITMAN: *Leaves of Grass,* fourth edition. The so-called workshop edition adds six new poems: "Inscription" (later "One's Self I Sing"), "Small the Theme of My Chant," "The Runner," "Leaves of Grass" number 2 (later "Tears"), "Leaves of Grass" number 3 (later "Aboard at a Ship's Helm"), "When I Read the Book," and "The City of Dead-House."

JOHN GREENLEAF WHITTIER: *The Tent on the Beach and Other Poems.* Whittier's cycle of verse narratives, in the manner of Longfellow's *Tales of a Wayside Inn,* includes "The Eternal Goodness," the poet's expression of his spiritual faith.

Publications and Events

Harper's Bazar. A weekly women's magazine begins publication as a companion to *Harper's Weekly* (1857–1916). In 1901 it became a monthly, and in 1929 its title was changed to *Harper's Bazaar.*

Oliver Optic's Magazine for Boys and Girls. Founded by Boston schoolteacher and writer William Taylor Adams (1822–1897), who, writing as "Oliver Optic," becomes the chief rival of Horatio Alger Jr. in producing juvenile reading matter. Adams wrote nearly a thousand adventure stories; the best of them, "Outward Bound; or, Young America Afloat," appears in the magazine in 1867. His many novels, grouped in series, include the Boat Club series (1854), Woodville series (1861–1867), Army and Navy series (1865–1894), Starry Flag series (1867–1869), Yacht Club series (1872–1900), and Great Western series (1875–1882).

1868
Drama and Theater

AUGUSTIN DALY: *A Flash of Lightning.* The success of this melodrama, featuring a stirring climax aboard a burning steamboat, solidifies Daly's reputation as one of the era's preeminent dramatists and encourages him to form a permanent theatrical company in 1869, based at New York's Fifth Avenue Theatre.

Humpty Dumpty. This musical pantomime is the longest-running musical (483 performances) up to its

Louisa May Alcott

time and represents the high-water mark for traditional pantomime on the American stage.

HENRY WADSWORTH LONGFELLOW: *The New England Tragedies.* This is the third section of Longfellow's verse drama trilogy comprising *Christus* (1872), his history of Christianity in the form of medieval mystery plays. This section consists of two dramas: in "John Endicott," Longfellow traces the persecution of the Quakers by the Puritans; in "Giles Corey of the Salem Farms," Longfellow treats the Salem witchcraft hysteria.

Fiction

LOUISA MAY ALCOTT: *Little Women.* Based on Alcott's New England childhood, the first volume of this juvenile classic details the adventures of four sisters, Meg, Jo, Beth, and Amy March. Written at the request of the Boston editor Thomas Niles, it becomes a bestseller, earning Alcott $200,000 in her lifetime; it has never gone out of print. A second volume would appear in 1869, followed by two sequels, *Little Men* (1871) and *Jo's Boys* (1886). Alcott also publishes *Proverb Stories,* a collection in which each story illustrates a proverbial expression, such as "A stitch in time saves nine" ("Kitty's Class Day"). The book is noteworthy for expressing themes and subjects central to *Little Women.* An expanded edition would appear in 1882.

HENRY WARD BEECHER: *Norwood; or, Village Life in New England.* The brother of Harriet Beecher Stowe publishes his only novel, a sentimental tale noteworthy for its depiction of New England life and for being one of the first fictional works to employ Abraham Lincoln as a character.

REBECCA HARDING DAVIS: *Waiting for the Verdict.* Davis's novel treats the central question of how freed slaves would be integrated into American life. Henry James attacks the novel's gloominess in his review, prompting a defense by Harriet Beecher Stowe.

EDWARD EVERETT HALE: *If, Yes, and Perhaps.* This work collects "Man Without a Country" as well as the whimsical "A Piece of Possible History" and the satirical fantasy "My Double and How He Undid Me." It would be followed by *Sybaris and Other Homes* (1869), a utopian satire on American society.

BRET HARTE: "The Luck of Roaring Camp." Published in the second issue of the *Overland Monthly* (edited by Harte), the story, which has been described as the first example of local-color fiction, becomes immediately popular and wins the author a literary reputation and a national audience for the periodical. The story tells of a rowdy miners' camp, where the birth of Thomas Luck to a prostitute who dies in childbirth motivates the community to improve itself. Later a flood obliterates the camp and kills Thomas Luck. The story would be reprinted in *The Luck of Roaring Camp and Other Sketches* (1870).

ELIZABETH STUART PHELPS WARD (1844–1911): *The Gates Ajar.* This very popular religious novel finds favor with a country suffering after the Civil War. The story concerns the grief-stricken Mary Cabot, whose brother was killed in the war, and records many consoling conversations she has with her aunt, who convinces her that she will be reunited with her brother in the hereafter. The book would be followed by three less successful sequels, *Beyond the Gates* (1883), *The Gates Between* (1887), and *Within the Gates* (1901).

Literary Criticism and Scholarship

JOSEPH SABIN (1821–1881): *Bibliotecca Americana.* The New York antiquarian bookseller produces the first volume, also known as *Sabin's Dictionary,* of the monumental bibliographical listing of every book and pamphlet in all languages related to America. Sabin would complete his final, fourteenth volume in 1881.

Nonfiction

AMOS BRONSON ALCOTT: *Tablets.* A collection of essays and poems arranged in two parts: "Practical" and

"Speculative." They outline Alcott's religious and Transcendentalist philosophy. The work is warmly received and sells well, increasing the author's reputation and demand as a lecturer.

MARY ABIGAIL DODGE: *Woman's Wrongs: A Counter-Irritant*. Dodge provides her first lengthy discussion of suffrage that she would expand into *Woman's Worth and Worthlessness* (1872). Harriet Beecher Stowe describes Dodge's advocacy on behalf of women's rights and expanded role "the brightest, cleverest, healthiest, noblest kind of book."

HORACE GREELEY: *Recollections of a Busy Life*. The newspaper editor, writer, and political figure compiles his memoirs.

NATHANIEL HAWTHORNE: *Passages from the American Notebooks*. The first of the posthumously issued selections from Hawthorne's journals, edited by his wife, appears. It would be followed by *Passages from the English Notebooks* (1870) and *Passages from the French and Italian Notebooks* (1871).

ELIZABETH KECKLEY (c. 1818–1907): *Behind the Scenes; or, Thirty Years a Slave and Four Years in the White House*. Keckley's slave narrative includes an account of her service in the household of Senator Jefferson Davis and the White House of Abraham Lincoln. She creates a controversy by revealing efforts made by Mary Todd Lincoln in 1867 to raise money by selling her personal effects, including jewelry and undergarments, precipitating the "Old Clothes Scandal." Robert Lincoln would successfully pressure the publisher to remove the embarrassing book from sale.

Poetry

ADAH ISAACS MENKEN (1835–1868): *Infelicita*. Having caused a sensation in 1861 by her semi-nude performance in the title role of Byron's *Mazeppa*, the flamboyant actress provides a collection of equally provocative autobiographical poems.

JOAQUIN MILLER (CINCINNATUS HINER, C. 1841–1913): *Specimens*. The western writer's first poetry collection, under the pen name "Joaquin Miller" (from the Mexican bandit Joaquin Murrieta, whom he had helped popularize in his earliest writings). It would be followed by *Joaquin et al* (1869), *Pacific Poems* (1870), and *Songs of the Sierras* (1871), which earned him the title of "the Byron of Oregon."

JOHN ROLLIN RIDGE: *Poems*. This is a posthumous collection of verses by the Cherokee chieftain who wrote as "Yellow Bird." It is generally considered the first collection of poetry published by a Native American.

EDWARD ROWLAND SILL (1841–1887): *The Hermitage and Other Poems*. The only collection of Sill's poetry publicly issued during his lifetime. Sill was born in Connecticut, graduated from Yale, and taught school in California and Ohio.

Publications and Events

The *Aldine*. Beginning as a house publication for a New York printing firm, this journal of art and typography became a general magazine under the editorship of R. H. Stoddard (1871–1875).

Hearth and Home. This weekly journal, aimed at a rural audience, begins publication. Its editors included Harriet Beecher Stowe, Mary Mapes Dodge, Edward Eggleston, and George Cary Eggleston. It serialized Edward Eggleston's *The Hoosier Schoolmaster* from 1870 to 1871, and its contributors included Rebecca Harding Davis and Louisa May Alcott. It ceased publication in 1875.

Lippincott's Magazine. The Philadelphia literary magazine begins publication in competition with the *Atlantic Monthly*. It was the first American magazine to publish Oscar Wilde's *The Picture of Dorian Gray*, Rudyard Kipling's *The Light That Failed*, and the early Sherlock Holmes stories. The magazine relocated to New York in 1915 to become *McBride's Magazine* and merged with *Scribner's* in 1916.

The *Overland Monthly*. The California magazine originally edited by Bret Harte in San Francisco begins publication. Harte published in the magazine the stories and poems that made him famous, including "The Luck of Roaring Camp," which appeared in the second issue. When he left the magazine in 1871, it declined and ceased publication in 1875. Revived in 1883, it published writers such as Frank Norris and Jack London until its final demise in 1935.

The *Revolution*. Susan B. Anthony and Elizabeth Cady Stanton began publishing this women's rights periodical. It continued until 1870.

Vanity Fair. Following the demise of the New York humorous weekly (1859–1863), a second magazine with the name *Vanity Fair* begins publication as "a weekly of political, social, literary, and financial wares." Purchased by Condé Nast in 1913, it became one of the most sophisticated magazines of its day before being absorbed by *Vogue* in 1936.

1869
Drama and Theater

Fifth Avenue Theatre. Playwright and producer Augustin Daly takes over this theater on New York's 24th

Street for his first important acting company. It became known as the "parlor home of comedy," debuting popular plays such as *Frou-Frou*, *Saratoga*, and *Divorce*.

HENRY JAMES: *Pyramus and Thisbe.* James's one-act farce about the romance between a young music teacher and a journalist who live in adjacent rooms in a boardinghouse is published in the *Galaxy*.

Fiction

LOUISA MAY ALCOTT: *Little Women: Part Second.* The second volume of Alcott's immensely popular children's story about the March family. Set three years after the action of the first volume (1868), the novel chronicles the passage of Meg, Jo, and Amy into the adult world. Two sequels would follow: *Little Men* (1871) and *Jo's Boys* (1886).

THOMAS BAILEY ALDRICH: *The Story of a Bad Boy.* Aldrich's popular narrative based on his own experiences growing up in Portsmouth, New Hampshire, appears as a year-long serial in *Our Young Folks;* it would be published in book form in 1870. Aldrich explains that by "bad boy" he actually means "a real human boy."

HORATIO ALGER JR.: *Luck and Pluck.* The first in a series featuring heroes from small rural communities, who are cheated out of their inheritance or who must rise in the world by their own efforts. It would be followed by *Sink or Swim* (1870), *Strong and Steady* (1871), and *Strive and Succeed* (1872).

BRET HARTE: "Tennessee's Partner." Harte's third most frequently anthologized story (behind "The Luck of Roaring Camp" and "The Outcasts of Poker Flat") is a sentimental tale of a gambler and his devoted partner. It is first published in the *Overland Monthly* and would be collected in *The Luck of Roaring Camp and Other Sketches* (1870). Harte also publishes "The Outcasts of Poker Flat," a short story noteworthy for helping develop local-color writing that exploited regional customs, descriptions, and dialects. First published in the *Overland Monthly*, it receives wide acclaim. The plot concerns a gambler, two prostitutes, and a drunk who are thrown out of the Poker Flat mining camp and become trapped in a snowstorm with an innocent couple whose goodness inspires the outcasts. The story would also be collected in *The Luck of Roaring Camp and Other Sketches* (1870).

HENRY JAMES: "Gabrielle de Bergerac." James's short story, published in the *Atlantic Monthly*, is a historical romance set during the French Revolution. It shows the influence of Walter Scott and George Sand on James's early work.

E.Z.C. JUDSON (1823–1886): *Buffalo Bill, the King of the Border Men.* Writing as "Ned Buntline," Judson produces the first of many dime novels celebrating the exploits of William F. Cody, whom Judson had met on a trip west and named "Buffalo Bill." Judson would later write a play about Buffalo Bill, *The Scouts of the Plain* (1873), starring Cody as himself and launching Cody's career as an entertainer.

ELIZABETH PAYSON PRENTISS (1818–1878): *Stepping Heavenward.* The most popular work of the author of religious fiction and books for young people reflects everyday life as recorded in a woman's diary.

WILLIAM GILMORE SIMMS: "Voltmeier; or, The Mountain Men" and "The Cub of the Panther: A Mountain Legend." These two of Simms's border romances are published as magazine stories.

HARRIET BEECHER STOWE: *Oldtown Folks.* Although it receives negative reviews, this novel is noteworthy for its accurate local-color portraits of New England characters just after the Revolutionary War. The work is based on Stowe's own experiences and those of her husband, Calvin Stowe. J. R. Dennet's review in the *Nation* says that Stowe "has succeeded decidedly in depicting typical Massachusetts men and women."

MARK TWAIN (SAMUEL LANGHORNE CLEMENS): *The Innocents Abroad; or, The New Pilgrim's Progress.* Twain's first popular book sells almost eighty thousand copies in sixteen months and becomes one of the most successful travel books of the century. It is drawn from correspondence he had sent to San Francisco's *California Alta* and the *New York Tribune* and *Herald* while traveling on the steamship *Quaker City* through Europe, the Holy Land, and the Near East. The humorous travel narrative presents a patriotic American's views of the sights and pokes fun at fellow travelers, guidebooks, and unfamiliar customs.

Nonfiction

FRANCIS PARKMAN: *The Discovery of the Great West.* Later titled *La Salle and the Discovery of the Great West*, this volume of Parkman's history of colonial North America chronicles La Salle's exploration of the Mississippi Valley.

HARRIET BEECHER STOWE AND CATHARINE E. BEECHER: *The American Woman's Home; or, Principles of Domestic Science: Being a Guide to the Formation and Maintenance of Economical, Healthful, Beautiful, and Christian Homes.* Stowe collaborates with her sister on a revision of the latter's *Treatise on Domestic Economy* (1841), which as a subscription book had sold nearly fifty thousand copies.

HARRIET TUBMAN (c. 1820–1913): *Scenes from the Life of Harriet Tubman.* The former slave, conductor for the

BIRTHS AND DEATHS, 1870–1879

Births

1870 Mary Johnston (d. 1936), novelist
J. Hartley Manners (d. 1928), playwright
Frank Norris (d. 1902), novelist
Alice Hegan Rice (d. 1942), novelist

1871 Winston Churchill (d. 1947), novelist
Stephen Crane (d. 1900), novelist
Theodore Dreiser (d. 1945), novelist
James Weldon Johnson (d. 1938), editor, novelist, poet, and social reformer

1872 Eleanor Hallowell Abbott (d. 1958), novelist and short story writer
Paul Laurence Dunbar (d. 1906), poet, novelist, and short story writer
Zane Grey (d. 1939), western novelist
Sutton E. Griggs (d. 1933), novelist
Harold Bell Wright (d. 1944), novelist

1873 Willa Cather (d. 1947), novelist
Ellen Glasgow (d. 1945), novelist

1874 Robert Frost (d. 1963), poet
Zona Gale (d. 1938), novelist and playwright
Ellen Glasgow (d. 1945), novelist
Amy Lowell (d. 1925), poet and critic
Gertrude Stein (d. 1946), writer, playwright, and critic

1875 Edgar Rice Burroughs (d. 1950), novelist and science fiction author
Alice Ruth Moore Dunbar-Nelson (d. 1935), short story writer and poet

1876 Sherwood Anderson (d. 1941), novelist
Jack London (d. 1916), novelist
Mary Roberts Rinehart (d. 1958), mystery writer

1877 Rex Beach (d. 1949), novelist and short story writer
Lloyd C. Douglas (d. 1951), novelist

1878 James Truslow Adams (d. 1949), historian
Carl Sandburg (d. 1967), poet
Upton Sinclair (d. 1968), novelist and social reformer

1879 James Branch Cabell (d. 1958), novelist
Dorothy Canfield Fisher (d. 1958), novelist
Vachel Lindsay (d. 1931), poet
Wallace Stevens (d. 1955), poet

Deaths

1870 John Pendleton Kennedy (b. 1795), novelist and statesman
Augustus Baldwin Longstreet (b. 1790), short story writer
Anna Cora Mowatt (b. 1819), actor and playwright
William Gilmore Simms (b. 1806), novelist and poet

1872 Frank Hitchcock Murdoch (b. 1843), playwright
Sara Payson Willis (b. 1811), novelist

1873 Frederick Goddard Tuckerman (b. 1821), poet

1875 Mortimer Neal Thomson (b. 1831), journalist and humorist

1876 John Neal (b. 1793), novelist

1877 John Lothrop Motley (b. 1814), historian
Charles Frederick Briggs (b. 1804), journalist, novelist, and editor

1878 Catharine Esther Beecher (b. 1800), author
William Cullen Bryant (b. 1794), poet and editor
Bayard Taylor (b. 1825), travel writer, novelist, and poet
Thomas Bangs Thorpe (b. 1815), painter and humorist

1879 Jacob Abbott (b. 1803), clergyman and children's author
William Lloyd Garrison (b. 1805), abolitionist and author
Sarah Josepha Buell Hale (b. 1788), novelist, poet, and editor

Underground Railroad, Union spy, and nurse narrates the story of her remarkable life to Sarah Elizabeth Bradford. Tubman would use the profits from her biography to establish a home for aged ex-slaves in Auburn, New York.

Poetry

JAMES RUSSELL LOWELL: "The Cathedral." Considered the finest of Lowell's later poems and originally titled "A Day at Chartres," it describes a visit he had made fourteen years earlier to the town and the cathedral. The poem centers on the struggle for balance between science and religion, between New World American qualities and European classicism.

EDMUND CLARENCE STEDMAN: *The Blameless Prince and Other Poems.* This initial collection by the poet and successful Wall Street broker includes his most famous creative work, "Pan in Wall Street." Stedman's *Poetical Works* would be published in 1873.

JOHN GREENLEAF WHITTIER: *Among the Hills and Other Poems.* Whittier's collection, which can be compared with the work of the New England local-color writers, shows an awareness of the darker and solitary side of rural life in New England.

Publications and Events

Appleton's Journal. This weekly magazine of fiction and current affairs begins publication. It became a monthly in 1876 and featured contributions by Rebecca Harding Davis, R. H. Stoddard, and Brander Matthews.

1870

Drama and Theater

AUGUSTIN DALY: *Frou-Frou.* Daly adapts a French play by Henri Meilhac and Ludovic Halevy about the sad end of a flirtatious young wife. It would be revised regularly during the nineteenth century, and the actress Sarah

Bernhardt would perform in it on her American tour in 1880.

CHARLES GUYLER (1820–1892): *Fritz, Our Cousin German.* This play about a German's search for his long-lost sister becomes a reliable vehicle for actor J. K. Emmet (1842–1891), who plays the title role and performs the song known as "Emmet's Lullaby," which brings brother and sister together, for the rest of his life.

BRONSON HOWARD (1842–1908): *Saratoga; or, Pistols for Seven.* Considered the first American to earn a living entirely by playwriting and the "dean of the American drama," Howard achieves his initial New York success with this farce about a man engaged to several women. Regarded as one of the best American comedies of the century, it also becomes one of the first American plays to achieve widespread international popularity.

The Twelve Temptations. This musical spectacle derived from the Walpurgis Night legend, the medieval witches' sabbath, is launched at a cost of $75,000, the most expensive production up to its time. It would remain popular for the next two decades.

Fiction

LOUISA MAY ALCOTT: *An Old Fashioned Girl.* Alcott's children's novel treats the coming of age of the spirited country girl Polly Milton and her experiences among her city cousins, the Shaws. A follow-up to *Little Women* (1868–1869), it is a popular success.

THOMAS BAILEY ALDRICH: *The Story of a Bad Boy.* Originally published serially in *Our Young Folks* (1869), Aldrich's best and most enduring fiction is a semi-autobiographical and nostalgic tale of boyhood. Noted as the first novel to present a realistic portrayal of American boyhood, it would become a classic children's book.

JOHN ESTEN COOKE: *The Heir of Graymount.* In this novel about buried treasure, Cooke weaves elements from his Civil War experience, Poe's "The Gold-Bug," and an argument for an agrarian solution to problems of the postbellum South.

MARTIN R. DELANY: *Blake; or, The Huts of America.* Delany's story, first serialized in part in 1859 and in full between 1861 and 1862, is published in book form. It depicts a West Indian who escapes from slavery in America to lead an insurrection in his homeland.

BRET HARTE: *The Luck of Roaring Camp and Other Sketches.* Harte's second story collection includes his best work, including the title story, "The Outcasts of Poker Flat," "Tennessee's Partner," "Miggles," and "Brown of Calaveras." The stories, along with his comic ballad "Plain Language from Truthful James" (1870), establish Harte's

popular reputation in the United States, prompting the *Atlantic Monthly* to offer him $10,000 for twelve contributions.

HARRIET BEECHER STOWE: *Little Pussy Willow.* Stowe's children's story is a fable contrasting the wholesome life of a country child with the pampered vanity of the daughter of a wealthy city man.

ELIZABETH STUART PHELPS WARD: *Hedged In.* Treating the double standard applied to women who violate conventional moral standards, Ward's novel is the first in a series dealing with women's issues. It would be followed by *The Silent Partner* (1871), about New England mill girls; *The Story of Avis* (1877), about a woman painter; and *Dr. Zay* (1882), about a woman physician.

Literary Criticism and Scholarship

JAMES RUSSELL LOWELL: *Among My Books.* Lowell's first significant critical collection contains six of his finest essays previously contributed to the *North American Review.* It includes reviews of Shakespeare, Dryden, Lessing, and Rousseau as well as two historical works, "Witchcraft" and "New England Two Centuries Ago." The book passes through thirty editions in Lowell's lifetime, and its success motivates him to publish another critical collection, *My Study Windows*, the following year.

Nonfiction

RALPH WALDO EMERSON: *Society and Solitude.* A collection of essays based on Emerson's lectures delivered since 1858. In the title essay, the philosopher argues for a balance between social and solitary ways of living. Other essays include "Civilization," "Art," "Books," and "Old Age."

THOMAS WENTWORTH HIGGINSON (1823–1911): *Army Life in a Black Regiment.* Higginson recounts his experiences as a white officer in the first regiment of black soldiers during the Civil War.

HARRIET BEECHER STOWE: *Lady Byron Vindicated.* Having met Byron's widow abroad, Stowe takes up her cause against her husband, detailing Byron's sexual infidelities and the claim of his incestuous relationship with his sister. The stridently polemical work damages Stowe's reputation.

CHARLES DUDLEY WARNER (1829–1900): *My Summer in a Garden.* Warner's first major work, a series of essays and sketches about his farm, is compared favorably to Washington Irving's sketches. It would go through forty-four editions by 1895. His other essay collections include *Backlog Studies* (1873), *Baddeck* (1874), and *Being a Boy* (1878). Warner, who became the editor of the *Hartford*

Courant in 1861, is best known for his collaboration with his friend Mark Twain that produced the novel *The Gilded Age* (1873).

Poetry

BRET HARTE: "Plain Language from Truthful James." Harte's poem had been originally published in the *Overland Monthly* and became well known as "The Heathen Chinee" when it was pirated under that name. It tells how the gambler Bill Nye attempts to cheat the Chinese character Ah Sin at euchre, a popular card game in the late nineteenth century. Intended to defend the Chinese minority in California, the work is often mistaken for a polemic against that race. Harte would collaborate with Mark Twain on a dramatic version known as *Ah Sin, the Heathen Chinee* (1877).

JOAQUIN MILLER (CINCINNATUS HINER): *Pacific Poems*. Miller's private printing of this collection and *Songs of the Sierras* (1871) in England earns him praise as the "Byron of Oregon," the embodiment of the frontier poet. Included is his best poem, "Kit Carson's Ride," a rousing narrative poem in which the scout rescues his Indian bride from pursuing tribesmen and a prairie fire.

Publications and Events

Scribner's Monthly. Founded by Charles Scribner (1821–1871), the literary journal serialized novels such as Harte's *Gabriel Conroy* and Cable's *The Grandissimes*, short stories by Julian Hawthorne and Helen Hunt Jackson, essays by W. C. Brownell and John Muir, and poetry by Emma Lazarus and Sidney Lanier until 1881. It then continued as the *Century Illustrated Monthly Magazine* (1881–1930).

Woodhull and Claflin's Weekly. Victoria Woodhull (1838–1927) and her sister Tennessee Celeste Claflin (1846–1923) begin publishing this radical journal advocating socialism, women's suffrage, free love, birth control, and vegetarianism. In 1872, it published the first English translation of *The Communist Manifesto*, by Karl Marx and Friedrich Engels. It ceased publication in 1876.

1871
Drama and Theater

AUGUSTIN DALY: *Divorce.* The most successful play of the century explores divorce. Daly had borrowed his plot and characters from Anthony Trollope's novel *He Knew He Was Right.* A smash hit, the comedy runs simultaneously in Boston, Philadelphia, Buffalo, St. Louis, and New York, where it sets the performance record for a comedy at the time. It is the first play performed in Chicago

after the great Chicago fire of 1871. Daly also creates the play *Horizon*, regarded by some as his best. This western drama, influenced by the contemporaneous Indian wars and by the fiction of Bret Harte, features a more complex characterization of Indians than was standard on stage at the time.

T. B. DE WALDEN (1811–1873) AND CLIFTON W. TAYLEURE: *Kit, the Arkansas Traveller.* One of the most popular western dramas of the time concerns a young Arkansas farmer whose wife and daughter are abducted. He encounters the man responsible years later, in a climactic bowie knife fight. De Walden was a London-born actor, playwright, and manager who also authored *The Life and Death of Natty Bumpo.*

HENRY WADSWORTH LONGFELLOW: *The Divine Tragedy.* The last completed but the first section of Longfellow's verse drama trilogy comprising *Christus* (1872), a history of Christianity. It dramatizes Christ's Passion and its effects on key New Testament figures.

JAMES J. MCCLOSKEY (1825–1913): *Across the Continent; or, Scenes from New York Life and the Pacific Railroad.* McCloskey's popular melodrama combines scenes set in New York City's notorious Five Points district with an Indian attack on a Union Pacific railway station. Dismissed as "claptrap" and "rubbish" by reviewers, it thrills audiences with exciting topicality. Born in Canada, McCloskey turned to acting after failing to gain his fortune in the California gold fields. Many of his plays reflect his California experiences.

Fiction

LOUISA MAY ALCOTT: *Little Men: Life at Plumfield with Jo's Boys.* The continuation of the March family trilogy that had begun with *Little Women* (1868–1869) depicts Jo's life with her husband, Professor Bhaer, in the boarding school they open on the grounds of Plumfield, the estate Jo inherited from Aunt March. The novel illustrates Bronson Alcott's pedagogic views and has been of interest to feminist critics in its depiction of Jo as a wife and mother. A sequel, *Jo's Boys*, would appear in 1886.

HORATIO ALGER JR.: *Tattered Tom; or, The Story of a Street Arab.* Alger launches a new series about street life with this novel that features his only female protagonist, a street sweeper who is the writer's most engaging character after Ragged Dick. The novel would be followed by *Paul, the Peddlar* (1871), *Phil, the Fiddler* (1872), and a second Tattered Tom series, beginning in 1874 with *Julius; or, The Street Boy Out West.*

JOHN ESTEN COOKE: *Doctor Vandyke.* The first in a series of historical romances set in colonial America.

It would be followed by *Justin Harley* (1875), *Canolles* (1877), and *My Lady Pokahontas* (1885). Cooke also publishes *Hammer and Rapier,* a novel treating the military engagements of the Civil War from Bull Run to Appomattox.

EDWARD EGGLESTON (1837–1902): *The Hoosier Schoolmaster.* First appearing in *Hearth and Home*, a magazine Eggleston edits, the novel increases sales of the periodical and sells 500,000 copies in book form. The plot, based partly on the author's brother's life, concerns a schoolteacher in rural Indiana whose many adventures include falling in love and being accused and then acquitted of a robbery. Although much of it is sentimental, the work is noteworthy for its realistic depiction of the Indiana backwoods.

HENRY JAMES: "A Passionate Pilgrim." Generally regarded as James's first important fictional work, the story concerns an American claimant to an English estate and introduces what would become James's often-repeated theme of the contrast between American and European values. James would later disparage the story and its theme, calling it the first of his "sops instinctively thrown to the international Cerberus." James's first novel, *Watch and Ward*, also appears in the *Atlantic Monthly*. It is a realistic story of a man who raises an orphaned girl with the intention of marrying her; it would appear in a much revised book form in 1878. James would later belittle the work, calling the later *Roderick Hudson* (1876) his true first novel.

RICHARD MALCOLM JOHNSTON: *Dukesborough Tales.* An expanded and revised edition of Johnston's *Georgia Sketches* (1864), humorously detailing life in the imaginary Dukesborough, Georgia. It would win its author acclaim during the 1880s as local-color writing rose in popularity.

HARRIET BEECHER STOWE: *My Wife and I.* The first of three works that Stowe would call her "society novels" makes a case for a woman's right to a career. A sequel, *We and Our Neighbors*, would appear in 1875. The social satire *Pink and White Tyranny* is also published in 1871.

MARK TWAIN (SAMUEL LANGHORNE CLEMENS): *Mark Twain's (Burlesque) Autobiography and First Romance.* Twain provides a comic genealogy based on his father-in-law's request for character references during Twain's courtship of Olivia Langdon.

Literary Criticism and Scholarship

HORACE HOWARD FURNESS (1833–1912): *New Variorum Shakespeare.* The most important work on Shakespeare in the nineteenth century, this series by the Philadelphia scholar, lecturer, and editor brings together three hundred years of criticism and scholarship, devoting one volume to each of Shakespeare's plays. Furness would cover fourteen plays in his lifetime; the work was continued by his son Horace H. Furness Jr. and after his death by editors and publishers of the Modern Language Association. The work helped gain U.S. criticism and scholarship its first international recognition.

JAMES RUSSELL LOWELL: *My Study Windows.* Lowell's most successful collection of criticism contains essays with a less objective tone than those of his earlier critical volume, *Among My Books* (1870). Many of the essays, which had been first published in the *North American Review*, highlight his contempt for Transcendentalism. He also assails the writings of several authors, including Thomas Carlyle, Henry David Thoreau, and James Gates Percival. The work is popular with American and English audiences and goes through numerous printings and editions.

Nonfiction

CATHARINE E. BEECHER: *Woman Suffrage and Woman's Profession.* Beecher speaks out against voting rights for women, asserting that women's sphere should be exclusively the home.

JOHN BURROUGHS: *Wake-Robin.* The naturalist, essayist, and poet's first collection of popular nature essays would be followed by other much-admired volumes, including *Winter Sunshine* (1875), *Birds and Poets* (1877), *Locusts and Wild Honey* (1879), and *Fresh Fields* (1885).

HENRY GEORGE (1839–1897): *Our Land and Land Policy.* After publishing his first articles in 1868 in the *Overland Monthly* on the negative impact of railroads, the economist George explicates his concept of a single tax on land in this pamphlet. He would further develop this idea in his masterwork, *Progress and Poverty* (1879).

LEWIS HENRY MORGAN (1818–1881): *Systems of Consanguinity and Affinity of the Human Family.* Morgan, "the father of American anthropology," publishes this important work on primitive societies that explicates the kinship system of the Iroquois. His studies would lead to the concept of a common origin and psychology of all races and a theory of social evolution outlined in *Ancient Society; or, Researches in the Lines of Human Progress* (1877).

GEORGE WILBUR PECK (1840–1916): *Adventures of One Terence McGrant.* Peck's comic commentaries on political events written in Irish dialect are collected in his first book. He would later make his reputation with the adventures of "Peck's Bad Boy," first collected in *Peck's Bad Boy and His Pa* (1883).

MARY VIRGINIA TERHUNE: *Common Sense in the Household.* Terhune's book on home economics, the first such work in the United States, sells more than a million copies and establishes her as the leading household authority. She would later write a popular syndicated newspaper column on the subject and produce the popular *National Cookbook* in 1896, an essential book in American homes.

WALT WHITMAN: *Democratic Vistas.* Whitman examines democracy and its problems during the Reconstruction era. He argues for striking a balance between individualism and democracy to attain future greatness, and he suggests that this balance can be best attained by poets and novelists.

VICTORIA WOODHULL (1838–1927): *The Origins, Tendencies, and Principles of Government.* Having declared her candidacy for the presidency in 1870, Woodhull collects her series of articles first published in the *New York Herald*, outlining her principles of women's suffrage, socialism, and free love. Woodhull and her sister Tennessee Celeste Claflin founded the *Woodhull and Claflin's Weekly* (1870–1876) to broadcast her views.

Poetry

BRET HARTE: *East and West Poems.* Harte's collection, like John Hay's *Pike County Ballads* (1871), popularizes the Mississippi River backwoodsman, or "pike," in a series of dialect verses.

JOHN HAY (1838–1905): *Pike County Ballads.* A collection of poems containing the writer's highly successful ballads on Illinois frontier themes, written in dialect. Originally published in the *New York Tribune*, the poems, along with Bret Harte's *East and West Poems* (1871), start a vogue for regional dialect verse. The two most popular of the ballads are "Jim Bludso of the Prairie Belle," about a steamboat operator who sacrifices his life to save passengers during a fire, and "Little Breeches," which tells of the rescue of a young boy from a wagon accident. Hay also publishes a travel book, *Castilian Days.*

EMMA LAZARUS (1849–1887): *Admetus and Other Poems.* After the publication of Lazarus's *Poems and Translations* while she was in her teens, the New York poet's second collection reworks the Admetus-Alcestis and Orpheus stories and the medieval tales of Lohengrin and Tannhäuser. It also contains a sequence of autobiographical lyrics and her earliest poem with a Jewish theme, first printed in 1867, "In the Jewish Synagogue at Newport," a response to Henry Wadsworth Longfellow's "The Jewish Cemetery at Newport." Lazarus asserts that "the sacred shrine" of the oldest extant American synagogue "is holy yet."

WALT WHITMAN: *Leaves of Grass*, 1871–1872 edition. The fifth edition of Whitman's evolving masterwork adds twenty-four new poems and incorporates *Drum-Taps* in a series of new Civil War clusters. Whitman also publishes "Passage to India" in pamphlet form; it would be later included in the 1876 edition of *Leaves of Grass*. The poem celebrates people from around the globe. The work is inspired by the Atlantic telegraph cable, the Suez Canal, and the Union Pacific Railroad, which Whitman suggests will usher in a new era of peace by connecting the material nature of the Western Hemisphere with the spiritual essence of the Eastern Hemisphere.

1872
Drama and Theater

A. C. GUNTER (1847–1907): *Found the True Vein.* The California dramatist's initial success with this play dealing with life in a mining camp prompts Gunter to come east. He would have his first New York success with *Two Nights in Rome* (1880).

HENRY WADSWORTH LONGFELLOW: *Christus: A Mystery.* The poet would regard this dramatic sequence as his greatest achievement. It brings together *The Divine Tragedy* (1871), *The Golden Legend* (1851), and *The New England Tragedies* (1868). Longfellow also publishes the second part of *Tales of a Wayside Inn.*

FRANK H. MURDOCH (1843–1872): *Davy Crockett; or, Be Sure You're Right Then Go Ahead.* Murdoch's most famous play becomes the major stage vehicle for actor Frank Mayo (1839–1896), who for the rest of his career would play the part of the frontiersman who must rescue and protect his sweetheart from various threats; Mayo continually revised Murdoch's drama during his two thousand or more performances of it. Murdoch also is responsible for the anonymous play *Bohemia; or, The Lottery of Love*, a satire on drama critics.

Fiction

LOUISA MAY ALCOTT: *Aunt Jo's Scrap-Bag.* Beginning of a six-volume collection of Alcott's short stories (completed in 1882), narrated from the perspective of Jo March from *Little Women* (1868–1869).

AMELIA E. BARR (1831–1919): *Romance and Reality.* The first of the popular sentimental novels by the English-born novelist who immigrated to Texas in the 1850s appears. It would be followed by *Jan Vedder's Wife* (1885),

The Bow of Orange Ribbon (1886), and *Remember the Alamo* (1888).

JOHN WILLIAM DE FOREST: *Kate Beaumont.* De Forest draws on his experience as the district commander of the Freeman's Bureau for this realistic novel of South Carolina life and manners.

EDWARD EGGLESTON: *The End of the World.* Eggleston's love story is built around Indiana's utopian Millerite community and its anticipation of the coming apocalypse.

NATHANIEL HAWTHORNE: *Septimius Felton; or, The Elixir of Life.* Hawthorne's posthumously published romance, set during the American Revolution, concerns a scholar's attempt to create a potion to attain earthly immortality. Hawthorne had attempted the same theme in the unfinished *Dolliver Romance* (1876).

OLIVER WENDELL HOLMES: *The Poet at the Breakfast-Table.* This is the final work in the Breakfast-Table trilogy, which had begun with *The Autocrat of the Breakfast-Table* (1858) and *The Professor at the Breakfast-Table* (1860). Like the earlier works, it had first appeared in the *Atlantic Monthly* and incorporates similar themes, including creativity, freedom, and love; it also includes events from Holmes's life, such as reforms at Harvard and the sale of his childhood home. This time the poet, a philosophic Old Master, an entomologist, an astronomer, a young female writer, and a lady are assembled.

WILLIAM DEAN HOWELLS: *Their Wedding Journey.* Howells's first novel tells of Basil and Isabel March's honeymoon travels to Niagara Falls, on the St. Lawrence, and in Boston. These characters would reappear in nine more of Howells's works, and many elements of the story are based on his own life. The story, distinguished for its perceptive descriptions of people and places, wins critical and commercial success. Henry Adams, writing for the *North American Review*, declares that the book possesses an "extreme and almost photographic truth to nature, and remarkable delicacy and lightness of touch." Howells returns to the Marches in *Their Silver Wedding Journey* (1899).

PRENTISS INGRAHAM (1843–1904): *The Masked Spy.* The first of the former soldier of fortune's more than six hundred dime novels, including as many as two hundred about his friend William F. "Buffalo Bill" Cody. Ingraham was the son of the popular Maine novelist Joseph Holt Ingraham.

EDWARD PAYSON ROE (1838–1888): *Barriers Burned Away.* Written after the Presbyterian minister visited Chicago after the fire of 1871, this best-selling novel tells the story of Dennis Fleet, an impoverished Christian man who receives little respect from his unreligious European acquaintants. Fleet is a hero during the fire, saving even those people who had treated him badly, and in the end he stands amid the wreckage, ready to begin anew with his love interest, who has converted to Christianity. Roe, one of the most widely read authors of the 1870s and 1880s, would publish eighteen other popular novels.

HARRIET BEECHER STOWE: *Oldtown Fireside Stories.* Material left out of *Oldtown Folks* (1869) had become stories mainly published in the *Atlantic Monthly* and collected here. Narrated in dialect by Yankee Sam Lawson, the collection would be expanded in 1881 as *Sam Lawson's Oldtown Fireside Stories.* Many consider the stories among Stowe's best work.

BAYARD TAYLOR: *Beauty and the Beast and Tales of Home.* Taylor's volume of short stories mainly concerns his home county of Chester, Pennsylvania. Included as well are romantic views of Russia and satires on various contemporary reforms.

MARK TWAIN (SAMUEL LANGHORNE CLEMENS): *Roughing It.* This popular autobiographical narrative tells of Twain's western adventures with his brother Orion. The book mixes truth and fiction to describe his work in mining camps, several acquaintances he made (including Brigham Young), and travels to San Francisco and the Sandwich Islands. Although the book would sell forty thousand copies in just three months, sales later declined, without achieving the success Clemens had anticipated.

SARAH CHAUNCY WOOLSEY (1835–1905): *What Katy Did.* The first of the five-book series of popular novels for girls by the Ohio journalist, poet, and children's writer, written as "Susan Coolidge." The series tracing the maturation of a mischievous young girl would conclude in 1886 with *What Katy Did Next.*

Literary Criticism and Scholarship

JAMES THOMAS FIELDS (1817–1881): *Yesterday Among Authors.* Among Fields's several volumes of recollections, this is considered his best book, recording his literary observations, conversations with other literary figures, and letters.

Nonfiction

AMOS BRONSON ALCOTT: *Concord Days.* Based on his journals, Alcott's memoirs provide an important account of his activities and famous associates, such as Emerson and Channing.

E. H. CLARKE (1820–1877): *Sex in Education; or, A Fair Chance for Girls.* The Boston physician publishes a widely

Sir Henry M. Stanley

circulated book arguing that the rigors of higher education would endanger women's health due to the rest they need during menstruation. His view would be opposed in the volume of essays edited by Julia Ward Howe, *Sex and Education* (1874), and by Mary Putnam Jacobi in *Question of Rest for Women During Menstruation* (1877).

CLARENCE KING (1842–1901): *Mountaineering in the Sierra Nevada.* A commercially successful collection of sketches hailed for being scientifically thoughtful, relevant, and artistically accomplished. First published in the *Atlantic Monthly*, the adventurous tales depict western characters and geology. King completed a cross-country horseback trip after graduating from Yale and worked from 1866 to 1877 surveying the Cordilleran range from eastern Colorado to California.

SIR HENRY M. STANLEY (1841–1904): *How I Found Livingstone: Travels, Adventures, and Discoveries in Central Africa: Including an Account of Four Months' Residence with Dr. Livingstone.* A widely popular book that details the English-born journalist's adventures on an assignment for the *New York Tribune* to locate the Scottish missionary David Livingstone, missing in Africa.

Poetry

PAUL HAMILTON HAYNE (1830–1886): *Legends and Lyrics.* The first of Hayne's three volumes of poetry, which

would lead to his being hailed as the "poet laureate of the South." It would be followed by *The Mountain and the Lovers* (1875) and his collected works, *Poems of Paul Hamilton Hayne* (1882).

CELIA THAXTER (1835–1894): *Poems.* Thaxter's first verse collection reflects her experiences growing up on an island off the coast of New Hampshire. It would be followed by *Among the Isles of Shoals* (1873), *Drift-Weed* (1879), and *Idylls and Pastorals* (1886).

JOHN GREENLEAF WHITTIER: *The Pennsylvania Pilgrim and Other Poems.* The title work is regarded as one of Whittier's most successful narrative poems. It describes the Quaker settlement of Germantown, Pennsylvania, under the leadership of Francis Daniel Pastorius. Also included is "The Brewing of Soma," from which the popular hymn "Dear Lord and Father of Mankind" is taken.

ELLA WHEELER WILCOX (1850–1919): *Drops of Water.* The first of the Wisconsin poet's more than forty volumes of sentimental verse is a collection of temperance poems.

Publications and Events

Publishers Weekly. The trade journal of book publishing and book selling begins publication, founded by Frederick Leypoldt (1835–1884).

1873
Drama and Theater

DION BOUCICAULT: *Led Astray.* Boucicault's play about marital infidelity is described by theatrical historian George Odell as "one of the most famous dramas of its decade in America."

E.Z.C. JUDSON: *The Scouts of the Plain.* Under the name "Ned Buntline," Judson writes this western melodrama to capitalize on the notoriety of frontiersman William F. Cody, whom Judson had named "Buffalo Bill" in 1869 and celebrated in dime novels.

Fiction

LOUISA MAY ALCOTT: *Work: A Story of Experience.* This autobiographical novel depicts aspects of Alcott's life from the age of twenty-one to forty from the perspective of the orphaned heroine Christie Devon, who eventually marries a man who resembles Henry David Thoreau. It is considered the most Dickensian and realistic of Alcott's novels and her most feminist-oriented fictional work.

THOMAS BAILEY ALDRICH: *Marjorie Daw and Other People.* A collection of the Aldrich's most famous short stories. The immensely popular and frequently anthologized title piece concerns Edward Delaney's attempts to help his friend John Fleming recover from an injury by writing him letters about his fictional neighbor, Marjorie Daw. The collection also contains "A Struggle for Life," "A Young Desperado," and "The Friend of My Youth."

AMBROSE BIERCE (1842–C. 1914): *The Fiend's Delight* and *Nuggets and Dust Panned Out in California.* The first collection of sketches, epigrams, and fables by the San Francisco–based journalist, short story writer, poet, and aphorist appears under the pseudonym "Dod Grile." *Cobwebs from an Empty Skull* would follow in 1874.

JOHN ESTEN COOKE: *Her Majesty the Queen.* Cooke's historical romance, his only fictional venture into the seventeenth century, reflects his theory (later debunked) that Virginia was largely settled by Cavaliers, defeated by Cromwell's Puritans.

EDWARD EGGLESTON: *The Mystery of Metropolisville.* Eggleston's melodramic novel concerns the real estate boom in Minnesota. Land-hungry newcomers are victimized by the unscrupulous, whose frauds supply the novel's intrigue.

EDGAR FAWCETT (1847–1904): *Purple and Fine Linen.* Generally regarded as the best of the New York novelist, poet, and essayist's satirical novels on New York society. Others include *An Ambitious Woman* (1884) and *Social Silhouettes* (1885).

BRET HARTE: *Mrs. Skagg's Husbands.* The first in a series of collections of the writer's magazine writings, none of which duplicate the popularity of his earlier work. It would be followed by *Tales of the Argonauts* (1875), *An Heiress of Red Dog and Other Sketches* (1878), *A Sappho of Green Springs and Other Stories* (1891), and *Colonel Starbottle's Client and Some Other People* (1892).

JULIAN HAWTHORNE (1846–1934): *Bressant.* The first of the popular gothic-influenced romances by Nathaniel Hawthorne's son would be followed by works such as *Garth* (1877), *Archibald Malmaison* (1884), and *A Fool of Nature* (1896).

JOSIAH GILBERT HOLLAND (1819–1881): *Arthur Bonnicastle.* The founder and editor of *Scribner's Monthly* provides an autobiographically based novel about a New England youth's life at Yale and in New York.

WILLIAM DEAN HOWELLS: *A Chance Acquaintance.* Howells's second novel is a social comedy in which Kitty Ellison, a New York girl, travels to Quebec and back through Boston. She falls in love with a distinguished Boston gentleman, but she refuses his proposal after she sees that he is embarrassed by her in front of his Boston acquaintances. The novel is noted for its descriptions of the St. Lawrence and Saguenay Rivers and for Kitty's awe on her first glimpse of Boston, taken from the author's own experience of the city.

CHARLES WARREN STODDARD: *South-Sea Idyls.* Stoddard's sketches of Polynesian life help stimulate a vogue for the South Pacific. It would be followed by *Summer Cruising in the South Seas* (1874).

MARK TWAIN (SAMUEL LANGHORNE CLEMENS) AND CHARLES DUDLEY WARNER: *The Gilded Age: A Tale of To-Day.* Twain's first novel is a story of failed speculation schemes, seduction, murder, and crooked politicians. Considered melodramatic and uneven, the novel nonetheless is noteworthy for capturing the avarice of post–Civil War America and for naming that era.

LEW WALLACE (1827–1905): *The Fair God.* Wallace's popular historical novel passed through twenty editions in ten years and was influenced by William Hickling Prescott's *Conquest of Mexico.* Its plot concerns Montezuma's failed attempts to stop Cortez from invading the Aztec empire.

Nonfiction

WILLIAM ELLERY CHANNING [II]: *Thoreau, the Poet-Naturalist.* Channing, nephew of his namesake, the famous Boston clergyman, a friend of Thoreau, and a member of the Concord Circle, produces the first biography of the writer. It features valuable firsthand observations as well as an extended imaginary conversation among Thoreau, Emerson, and the author.

MARIETTA HOLLEY (1836–1926): *My Opinions and Betsy Bobbet's.* Writing as "Josiah Allen's Wife" and "Samantha Allen," Holley publishes her first collection of popular essays of homey, commonsense observations of everyday events. Several volumes — *Samantha at the Centennial* (1877), *Samantha Amongst the Colored Folks* (1892), *Samantha at the World's Fair* (1893), *Samantha in Europe* (1895), and *Josiah Allen on Women's Rights* (1914) — would follow.

JOAQUIN MILLER (CINCINNATUS HINER): *Life Amongst the Modocs: Unwritten History.* Miller's autobiographical narrative describes his relationship with Paquita, the Indian woman he married, who was fatally wounded and died in his arms. Later editions would be issued under the titles *Unwritten History: Life Among the Modocs* (1874), *Paquita: The Indian Heroine* (1881), *My Own Story* (1890), and *Joaquin Miller's Romantic Life Amongst the Indians* (1898). An additional volume of autobiographical reflections, *Memorie and Rime,* would appear in 1884.

SAMUEL SEWALL: "Talitha Cumi." Sewall's eighteenth-century essay arguing against theologians who deny the resurrection of women is finally published. It includes Sewall's provocative statement that "If we should wait till all the ancients are agreed in their opinions, neither men nor women would ever get to heaven."

HARRIET BEECHER STOWE: *Palmetto-Leaves.* In what has been called by Stowe's biographer Forest Wilson "probably the first promotion-writing for Florida ever done," the author describes the state and recommends it for other writers, stating that "Hawthorne ought to have lived in an orange grove in Florida."

Poetry

WILL CARLETON (1845–1912): *Farm Ballads.* The Michigan journalist, short story writer, and poet's first collection of sentimental verses on Michigan farm life contains his best-known poem, "Over the Hill to the Poor House." *Farm Legends* (1875) and *City Ballads* (1885) would follow. The playwright Edward Albee would use some of Carleton's verses in *Quotations from Chairman Mao Tse-Tung* (1968) to typify banality.

HENRY TIMROD: *Poems.* The collected poems of the "poet laureate of the Confederacy" appear posthumously. Included are "Ethnogenesis," hailing the Confederacy and predicting its inevitable victory; "The Cotton Boll," in which a single boll of cotton is made to represent the South; and "Ode," his elegy to the "martyrs of the fallen cause."

Publications and Events

The *Delineator.* The New York monthly devoted to women's fashions begins publication. Theodore Dreiser was its editor from 1907 to 1910. It published articles dealing with women's suffrage, divorce, and women's roles, acquiring a circulation of more than two million before it ceased publication in 1937.

St. Nicholas. A distinguished monthly magazine for children begins publication with Mary Mapes Dodge as its first editor (1873–1905). Contributors included Louisa May Alcott, Frances Hodgson Burnett, Mark Twain, and Rudyard Kipling. Contributions from its juvenile readers included the first appearance in print by William Faulkner, Edna St. Vincent Millay, Robert Benchley, Philip Wylie, E. B. White, and Edmund Wilson. It continued until 1940.

Woman's Home Companion. A women's magazine that included fiction by women writers such as Willa Cather, Zona Gale, and Edna Ferber until it ceased publication in 1957.

1874
Drama and Theater

DION BOUCICAULT: *The Shaughraun.* Considered the best of the playwright's Irish dramas, the play concerns a Fenian under the sentence of death who is saved from the British and a rival by the title character, originally played by Boucicault himself.

J. CHEEVER GOODWIN (1850–1912): *Evangeline; or, The Belle of Acadia.* This musical burlesque of Longfellow's poem was the most performed American musical play of the century, staged continuously for the remainder of the century. The Boston-born actor and writer is considered the first American to achieve a successful career as a librettist.

WILLIAM DEAN HOWELLS: *Samson.* Howells's first drama is a translation of Ippolito D'Aste's *Sansone* written for actor Charles Pope. It was performed for the next twenty-five years.

MARK TWAIN (SAMUEL LANGHORNE CLEMENS): *Colonel Sellers.* Twain's dramatization of *The Gilded Age* runs in New York from September 1874 to January 1875 and subsequently tours the country for the next twelve years. It is based in part on a pirated adaptation by Gilbert B. Densmore, performed in San Francisco. The play reveals Twain's largely untapped potential as a dramatist.

The Two Orphans. This translation by Hart Jackson of the French play *Les Deux Orphelines* by Eugène Cormon and Adolphe d'Ennery, about the harrowing experiences of two sisters separated in Paris, becomes, in the words of theatrical scholar George Odell, "one of the greatest theatrical success of all time in America." It would play almost continuously for the rest of the century.

Fiction

HJALMAR HJORTH BOYESEN (1848–1895): *Gunmar.* The Norwegian-born professor and writer's first novel, a romantic tale of Norwegian life originally serialized in the *Atlantic Monthly,* leads to his lifelong association with William Dean Howells and an increasing realism in subsequent novels, such as *The Mammon of Unrighteousness* (1891), *The Golden Calf* (1892), and *The Social Strugglers* (1893).

CHARLES HEBER CLARK (1847–1915): *Out of the Hurly-Burly; or, Life in an Odd Corner.* The first and best-known of the humorist's collections of sketches appears under the pseudonym "Max Adeler." Popular in the United States and England, the work would be followed by *Elbow Room: A Novel Without a Plot* (1876), *Random Shots* (1878), and *The Fortunate Island and Other Stories* (1882). Nearly one million copies of Clark's works sell during his lifetime.

JOHN ESTEN COOKE: *Pretty Mrs. Gaston and Other Stories.* Cooke's collection about contemporary Virginian society.

REBECCA HARDING DAVIS: *John Andross.* Davis's novel draws on and calls attention to political corruption in the Grant administration. It cites the Whiskey Ring scandal, in which a group of distillers and public officials defrauded the government of liquor taxes.

EDWARD EGGLESTON: *The Circuit Rider.* Noted for its accurate depiction of the rowdiness of the frontier, the novel concerns a Methodist preacher's experiences in the Ohio wilderness in the early nineteenth century. It is based on Eggleston's own experience as well as the autobiography of the renowned circuit rider Jacob Young. The *Atlantic* hails the book as "A noble tragedy, finely set forth."

EMMA LAZARUS: *Alide: An Episode of Goethe's Life.* Lazarus's only novel reworks an incident recorded in Johann Wolfgang von Goethe's *Autobiography* of his brief, idyllic relationship with Frederica Brion. It would be followed by a verse drama, *Spagnoletto*, in 1876.

ALBION W. TOURGÉE (1838–1905): *'Toinette.* Tourgée's first novel treats the antebellum and Civil War South. It would be republished as *A Royal Gentleman* in 1881. A Union officer during the war, Tourgée came to North Carolina as a carpetbagger politician. Many of his works depict Sourthern life during Reconstruction.

Nonfiction

JOHN QUINCY ADAMS: *The Memoirs of John Quincy Adams.* The first of Adams's massive twelve-volume diary is published (completed in 1877). Recording his thoughts and activities for more than sixty years, the memoirs provide a unique perspective on people and events that shaped American history.

HUBERT HOWE BANCROFT (1832–1918): *Native Races of the Pacific Coast.* Bancroft, who founded the West's leading bookstore in San Francisco in the 1850s, and assembled the great collection of regional literature now known as the Bancroft Library, publishes the first of his five-volume history of Native Americans (completed in 1875). It and the many volumes that would follow — *History of the Pacific States* (34 vols., 1882–1890) and *Chronicles of the Builders* (7 vols., 1891–1892) — establish his reputation as the first great historian of the West Coast.

BENJAMIN PAUL BLOOD (1832–1919): *The Anaesthetic Revelation and the Gist of Philosophy.* The poet and philosopher describes his mystical experience, prompted by inhaling nitrous oxide during a dental visit, that led to his pluralistic philosophy. William James would describe Blood's ideas as one of the "stepping-stones" of his own philosophy.

GEORGE ARMSTRONG CUSTER (1839–1876): *My Life on the Plains.* Custer supplies an account of his Indian fighting as lieutenant colonel of the Seventh Cavalry, including his engagements with the Cheyenne at Washita (1868). The book adds to Custer's fame and to the shock of his death at the Battle of the Little Big Horn in 1876.

GEORGE CARY EGGLESTON (1839–1911): *A Rebel's Recollection.* Edward Eggleston's younger brother, whose experiences as a country schoolteacher had provided much of the material for *The Hoosier Schoolmaster*, produces his most important book, a memoir of his experiences serving in the Confederate army.

JOHN FISKE (1842–1901): *The Outlines of Cosmic Philosophy.* A description and defense of the evolutionary philosophy of Englishman Herbert Spencer by the Connecticut-born professor of American history who became the chief popularizer of Victorian science in the United States. The book, which was excoriated by religious periodicals but acclaimed by others, most notably Charles Darwin, argues that evolution is proof of God's existence.

JULIA WARD HOWE: *Sex and Education.* Howe had contributed to and edited this volume produced in response to E. H. Clarke's *Sex in Education; or, A Fair Chance for Girls* (1872), which argues that the rest girls require during menstruation makes higher education and coeducation impractical and dangerous to their procreative capabilities. Howe, along with Mrs. Horace Mann, Elizabeth Stuart Phelps Ward, and others, refutes Clarke's assertions.

FRANCIS PARKMAN: *The Old Regime of Canada.* An installment of Parkman's masterly history of colonial North America, chronicling French rule in Canada.

Poetry

HENRY WADSWORTH LONGFELLOW: *Tales of a Wayside Inn.* The third and final installment of Longfellow's poetic narrative series is published. It contains "Emma and Eginhard," about a king's daughter who outwits her overprotective father.

MARY ASHLEY TOWNSEND (1836–1901): *The Captain's Story, and Other Verse.* The title poem of Townsend's collection creates a controversy with its subject matter: a white man's discovery that his mother was a mulatto. The New York writer drew on her experiences living in New Orleans for her poetry and the novel *The Brother Clerks* (1857).

Publications and Events

The *Congressional Record.* The proceedings of the U.S. Senate and House of Representatives are published in this journal, which follows the *Annals of Congress* (1789–1824), the *Register of Debates* (1825–1837), and the *Congressional Globe* (1834–1873).

1875

Drama and Theater

AUGUSTIN DALY: *The Big Bonanza.* Daly's comedy shows what happens when a professor is given $30,000 to invest successfully. Based on Gustav von Moser's German play *Ultimo,* it receives negative reviews but wins an audience and is performed until the end of the century. Daly also presents *Pique,* about an unhappily married couple brought together by the kidnapping of their child, a story that draws on a recent unsolved child kidnapping case.

STEELE MACKAYE (1842–1894): *Rose Michel.* One of the biggest hits of the decade is this adaptation by the New York acctor and playwright of Ernest Blum's play about a woman who must decide whether to reveal that her husband is a murderer and thereby destroy her daughter's marriage plans.

BENJAMIN E. WOOLF (?–1901): *The Mighty Dollar.* Set in Washington, D.C., at a salon of the rich and powerful called Grabmoor, Woolf's satirical comedy targets the money ethic of the age and features a memorable comic character, Congressman Bardwell Slote.

Fiction

LOUISA MAY ALCOTT: *Eight Cousins; or, The Aunt-Hill.* Written in response to the popular demand for more books like *Little Women* (1868–1869), the story of orphaned Rose Campbell's new life with her adoptive extended family expresses Alcott's ideas about children's education, modern fashion, and gender stereotypes. Henry James declares that it "strikes us as a very ill-chosen sort of entertainment to set before children" because of its satirical tone with "no glow and no fairies; it is all prose, and to our sense rather vulgar prose." A sequel, *Rose in Bloom,* would follow in 1876.

JOHN WILLIAM DE FOREST: *Honest John Vane* and *Playing the Mischief.* De Forest publishes a pair of realistic political novels depicting corruption in Washington during the Grant administration.

JOSIAH GILBERT HOLLAND: *Sevenoaks.* Among Holland's many popular novels, this work concerns the scheming Robert Belcher, who steals a patent from an inventor and becomes a millionaire.

WILLIAM DEAN HOWELLS: *A Foregone Conclusion.* The novel, set in Venice, is first serialized in the *Atlantic Monthly* and gains Howells critical and commercial success. The story concerns an American girl traveling in Italy; she meets a priest who falls in love with her. The critics laud the depth of the priest's character, and the novel's success leads to numerous reprintings and translations and a later dramatization. Howells also begins to publish his novel *Private Theatricals* (completed in 1876) in the *Atlantic Monthly.* It would not appear in book form until after Howells's death, primarily because of the threat of a lawsuit by the owners of the New Hampshire inn where the novel is set. It includes one of Howells's best female characterizations and an attack on the ideals of love and courtship presented in sentimental romances.

HENRY JAMES: *A Passionate Pilgrim and Other Tales.* A collection of stories including the title story, "The Last of the Valerii," "Eugene Pickering," "The Madonna of the Future," "The Praise of Certain Old Clothes," and "Madame de Mauves." James also publishes *Transatlantic Sketches,* a collection of travel essays, some of which would be revised and reprinted in *Foreign Parts* (1883), *English Hours* (1905), and *Italian Hours* (1909).

MAURICE THOMPSON (1844–1901): *Hoosier Mosaics.* The Indiana author's first book is a well-received volume of dialect sketches.

MARK TWAIN (SAMUEL LANGHORNE CLEMENS): *Mark Twain's Sketches, New and Old.* A compilation of humor, satire, social criticism, and philosophy originally sold by subscription. The compilation includes a French translation of Twain's "Jumping Frog" story and the author's witty, literal English retranslation.

CONSTANCE FENIMORE WOOLSON (1840–1894): *Castle Nowhere.* The grandniece of James Fenimore Cooper publishes her first fiction, a story collection about early French settlers near the Great Lakes.

Nonfiction

MARY BAKER EDDY (1821–1910): *Science and Health with Key to the Scriptures.* Eddy is motivated to write this official Christian Science textbook after experiencing the therapies of Dr. Phineas Parkhurst Quimby, studying the Bible, and undertaking her own work in healing. For a time assisted by the Unitarian minister James Henry Wiggin, Eddy would continue to update the book until her death in 1910, at which point more than 400,000 copies had been sold.

WALT WHITMAN: *Memorandum During the War.* Whitman's Civil War memoir had been first printed in articles in the *New York Weekly Graphic* in 1874, is privately printed in 1875, and would be included in the centennial edition of his works and as a section of *Specimen Days* (1882). The work memorializes the war dead and the war's democratic aims, which Whitman saw as under assault by the self-centered business ethos of the Gilded Age.

Sidney Lanier

Poetry

RICHARD WATSON GILDER (1844–1909): *The New Day*. The first of the sixteen poetry collections by the editor of *Scribner's Monthly* and later the *Century* is a sonnet sequence.

SIDNEY LANIER: "The Symphony." Lanier in one of his most acclaimed poems carefully establishes a natural association between poetry and music and strikes against the dehumanizing effects of industrialism. The poem concludes that "Music is Love in search of a word."

HENRY WADSWORTH LONGFELLOW: *The Masque of Pandora*. The collection includes Longfellow's poem "Morituri Salutamus" in heroic couplets. Written for the fiftieth reunion of his class at Bowdoin College, it eulogizes the college and the past and expresses Longfellow's philosophy of seizing all the opportunities that life affords.

Publications and Events

The *Chicago Daily News*. The Chicago daily begins publication. It achieved notoriety in 1876 by being the first newspaper to announce Rutherford B. Hayes's presidential nomination. From 1883 to 1895, it featured Eugene Field's popular "Sharps and Flats" column. It ceased publication in 1978.

Wide Awake. Daniel Lothrop founds this juvenile magazine that, until absorbed by *St. Nicholas* in 1893, would publish works by writers such as James Whitcomb Riley, Sarah Orne Jewett, and "Charles Egbert Craddock" (Mary Noailles Murfree). Lothrop's wife Harriet, under the pen name "Margaret Sidney," first published her popular *The Five Little Peppers and How They Grew* in its pages in 1880.

1876
Drama and Theater

BRET HARTE: *Two Men of Sandy Bar*. Harte attempts to resuscitate his flagging career through drama with his first play, based on his earlier story "Mr. Thompson's Prodigal." It features two of his most successful characters, John Oakhust and Colonel Starbottle, along with a new character, Hop Sing, a Chinese laundryman. The play manages only a month-long run, with one reviewer calling it "the worst failing witnessed on the boards of our theatres for years."

Fiction

LOUISA MAY ALCOTT: *Silver Pitchers and Independence*. Alcott's story collection contains mostly romances featuring plucky, virtuous heroines. It includes the title story, which is a temperance work, and "Transcendental Wild Oats," about a utopian community; it critiques Bronson Alcott's social experiment at Fruitlands (1843–1844).

CHARLES CARLETON COFFIN (1823–1918): *The Boys of '76*. Among the New England journalist's popular stories for boys is this tale of the Revolutionary War. A similar adventure tale, set during the Civil War, *The Boys of '61*, would appear in 1881.

JOHN HABBERTON (1842–1921): *Helen's Babies*. One of the era's biggest sellers is this humorous account by the New York journalist of a bachelor uncle's care for two mischievous boys during their parents' holiday.

BRET HARTE: *Gabriel Conroy*. The longest of Harte's fictions is this novel depicting the early days of the California gold rush, featuring professional gambler Jack Hamlin, who appears in numerous Harte stories. The book is a possible source for the name of James Joyce's protagonist in his short story "The Dead." A second short novel, *Jeff Brigg's Love Story*, would follow in 1880.

NATHANIEL HAWTHORNE: *The Dolliver Romance*. Hawthorne's last major work is this unfinished novel, previously published in part in the *Atlantic Monthly* in 1864 and 1871. It continues the theme of *Septimius Felton* (1872), about the search for the elixir of life.

Mark Twain

HELEN HUNT JACKSON (1830–1885): *Mercy Philbrick's Choice.* Jackson's first novel, published anonymously, is a character study thought to be based on Jackson's Amherst friend, the poet Emily Dickinson. A second novel, *Hetty's Strange History*, would be published in 1877.

HENRY JAMES: *Roderick Hudson.* James's first major work is the story of a young sculptor who goes to Europe to study, supported by the wealthy Rowland Mallet, but whose genius degenerates when he falls in love with Christina Light and disregards his American fiancée. Although the book receives favorable reviews, sales are modest in the United States; it gains a larger readership in England, however.

E.D.E.N. SOUTHWORTH: *Ishmael.* Serialized from 1863 to 1864 as "Self-Made; or, Out of the Depths," Southworth's favorite among her novels is the story of a hero, born into poverty and believed to be illegitimate, who gains success based on the author's concept of the masculine ideal of piety, altruism, and sentimentality. A sequel, *Self-Raised*, also appears in 1876.

MARK TWAIN (SAMUEL LANGHORNE CLEMENS): *The Adventures of Tom Sawyer.* Twain turns for the first time to recollections of his boyhood for the story of the wily Tom Sawyer, his companion Huck Finn, and their adventures. Despite enthusiastic reviews, sales would not pick up until the second printing in 1877. Reprinted frequently ever since, *Tom Sawyer* is regarded as a classic treatment of American boyhood. It includes some of

Twain's most famous scenes, such as Tom's convincing his friends to help him whitewash a fence, the boys' attending their own funeral, the trial of Injun Joe, and Tom and Becky Thatcher's cave experiences. The sequel, *Huckleberry Finn*, would follow in 1884, as well as two lesser novels featuring Tom Sawyer: *Tom Sawyer Abroad* (1894) and *Tom Sawyer, Detective* (1896).

Literary Criticism and Scholarship

RALPH WALDO EMERSON: *Letters and Social Aims.* Emerson's collection contains the long essay "Poetry and the Imagination," his last major restatement and reaffirmation of his symbolizing conception of the literary process, arguing that "A good symbol is the best argument" and that poetry "is the only verity. . . . As a power, it is the perception of the symbolic character of things, and the treating of them as representative."

JAMES RUSSELL LOWELL: *Among My Books, Second Series.* Lowell would consider his final collection of literary criticism "third-rate," but twentieth-century literary critic Thomas Wortham would declare it his most enduring book of criticism. The book contains essays on Dante, Spenser, Milton, and the poetry of Keats and Wordsworth.

Nonfiction

HENRY MARTYN ROBERTS (1837–1923): *Robert's Rules of Order.* Adapting the debate rules of the U.S. House of Representatives, Roberts issues his widely used manual of parliamentary procedures. Roberts was a military engineer who developed his manual from the rules of the U.S. House of Representatives.

Poetry

CHARLES FOLLEN ADAMS (1842–1918): "Leedle Yawcob Strauss." The Massachusetts humorist is best known for this poem written in Pennsylvania Dutch dialect, based on the speech of the German immigrants he encountered while serving in the army during the Civil War.

HERMAN MELVILLE: *Clarel: A Poem and Pilgrimage.* Derived from the author's voyage to the Middle East from 1856 to 1857, Melville's philosophical narrative poem treats a young scholar's search for religious awakening while visiting Holy Land sites and carrying on debates with fellow pilgrims. The book is largely ignored, selling only 478 copies.

JULIA A. MOORE (1847–1920): *The Sweet Singer of Michigan Salutes the Public.* The self-proclaimed "Sweet Singer of Michigan" issues the first of her sentimental verse collections memorializing, in inflated language, both the sublime and the ridiculously mundane. Mark Twain parodies her verse in *Huckleberry Finn* and declares that Moore has "the touch that makes an entertaining, humorous episode pathetic and an intentionally pathetic one funny." A second volume, *A Few Words to the Public with New and Original Poems by Julia A. Moore*, would follow in 1878.

BAYARD TAYLOR: *The Echo Club and Other Literary Diversions*. The "poet laureate of the Gilded Age" assesses the competition in a series of parodies of the works of Whitman and other contemporary poets.

WALT WHITMAN: *Leaves of Grass*, centennial edition. The sixth edition of Whitman's epic work includes the companion volume *Two Rivulets*, a collection of typographical and visual experiments designed to break down "the barriers of form between Prose and Poetry."

ELLA WHEELER WILCOX: *Poems of Passion*. Wilcox achieves a *succès de scandale* when her romantic verse collection is attacked for its immorality.

Publications and Events

Frank Leslie's Popular Monthly. Founded by Frank Leslie (1821–1880), an engraver and publisher of illustrated journals, the magazine featured Leslie's streamlined engraving process, which allowed him to illustrate current events ahead of the competition. It continued operating until 1906 when it became the *American Magazine*.

The *Harvard Lampoon*. The humor magazine produced and published by Harvard students is founded by Ralph W. Curtis, John T. Wheelwright, Samuel Sherwood, and others.

1877
Drama and Theater

BRET HARTE AND MARK TWAIN (SAMUEL LANGHORNE CLEMENS): *Ah Sin, the Heathen Chinee*. The writers collaborate on a dramatic version of Harte's popular narrative poem "Plain Language from Truthful James." It manages only thirty-five performances as the writers could not agree on needed revisions.

WILLIAM DEAN HOWELLS: *A Counterfeit Presentment*. One of Howells's biggest successes as a dramatist is this play about the romance between a woman and an artist who bears a striking resemblance to her former fiancé but who turns out to be a criminal.

FRED MARSDEN (1842–1888): *Zip; or, Point Lynne Light*. Marsden's play, about a young girl who lives with a lighthouse keeper and who foils a plot to sink a passing ship, becomes a standard performance for actress Lotta Crabtree (1847–1924), one of the most popular performers of her day. Crabtree would often enliven her melodramatic roles with banjo playing and dance numbers. Marsden was a former Philadelphia lawyer-turned-playwright who produced melodramas and farces for a number of the leading actors of the day, including Joseph Murphy, Roland Reed, and W. J. Scanlon.

JOAQUIN MILLER (CINCINNATUS HINER): *The Danites in the Sierras*. Miller's play, his best and one of the most popular frontier dramas, concerns a secret sect of Mormons seeking revenge on a young woman who, disguised as a man, seeks refuge in a cabin in the Sierras. The play would be published in 1882.

Fiction

LOUISA MAY ALCOTT: *A Modern Mephistopheles*. Alcott regarded this gothic romance, inspired by Goethe's *Faust* and Hawthorne's *The Scarlet Letter*, the most lurid of the many adult thrillers she published anonymously (discovered and collected by Madeleine B. Stern in *Behind a Mask* [1975] and *Plots and Counterplots* [1976]). The plot treats male pride redeemed by the "female virtues" of purity, patience, and docility.

NOAH BROOKS (1830–1903): *The Boy Emigrants*. One of the most popular of the Maine-born California journalist and editor's books for boys, describing pioneer life during the mid–nineteenth century.

FRANCIS HODGSON BURNETT (1849–1924): *The Lass O'Lowrie's*. The popular children's book writer achieves her first literary success with this adult novel about the Lancashire coal mines. She would follow it with several novels written under the influence of Henry James, including *A Fair Barbarian* (1881), about an American girl in England.

EDWARD EVERETT HALE: *Philip Nolan's Friends: A Story of the Change of Western Empire*. After publishing his best-known story, Hale had learned that there was a real-life Philip Nolan, the name of the fictional protagonist in "The Man Without a Country" (1863). A horse trader and adventurer, the real Nolan was killed on the Mexican border in 1801. The novel offers a fictional version of his story.

JULIAN HAWTHORNE: *Garth*. The most popular work by Nathaniel Hawthorne's son is this novel concerning an Indian curse besetting a New England family.

HENRY JAMES: *The American*. One of the first of James's fictional treatments of his often repeated international theme, the novel concerns a wealthy veteran of the Civil War who travels to France to secure a "quality" wife. The novel establishes James's thematic use of the contrast between the inexperience and simplicity of America and the rich heritage of Europe. Though the book had earned James $1,350 for serial rights, bound editions sell poorly.

SARAH ORNE JEWETT (1849–1909): *Deephaven*. Jewett's sequence of thirteen sketches concerns two young women who summer in a coastal town that is on the decline. The author's first significant work is notable for its early use of local color, Maine speech, and realistic descriptions of the town and citizens. Although many critics hail the work, including John Greenleaf Whittier, who proclaims, "I know of nothing better in our literature of the kind," it is disdained by other reviewers. The *New York Times* critic notes, "it is by some mistake, doubtless, that it got in print at all."

Nonfiction

DAN DE QUILLE (1829–1898): *History of the Big Bonanza*. Using a pen name, Virginia City, Nevada, newspaperman and humorist William Wright supplies a history of the Comstock lode with an introduction by Mark Twain. Twain had become friends with Wright when the latter was the city editor of Virginia City's *Territorial Enterprise*.

MARY PUTNAM JACOBI (1842–1906): *Question of Rest for Women During Menstruation*. Jacobi's scientific study demolishes the myths about menstruation that had been used as an argument against coeducation, particularly by E. H. Clarke in *Sex in Education; or, A Fair Chance for Girls* (1872).

LEWIS HENRY MORGAN: *Ancient Society; or, Researches in the Lines of Human Progress*. Morgan's study of the kinship system among the Iroquois and other Native American tribes led to this treatise. It asserts a common origin of primitive races and a groundbreaking theory of cultural evolution, contributing both to the development of modern anthropology and to the new scientific analysis of "progress."

FRANCIS PARKMAN: *Count Frontenac and New France Under Louis XIV*. Parkman continues his history of French rule in North America with the dynamic efforts of Frontenac to correct the faults of France's autocratic rule and the beginnings of the century-long conflict between New France and the American colonies.

Poetry

SIDNEY LANIER: *Poems*. Lanier's first verse collection is published. Also written in 1877 (published in 1883) is one of the poet's greatest achievements in expressing the musicality of verse, "The Song of the Chattahoochee."

ALBERY ALLSON WHITMAN (1851–1901): *Not a Man and Yet a Man*. The black poet and clergyman's long narrative poem on the state of African Americans is one of the most ambitious works by an African American poet in the nineteenth century.

Publications and Events

Puck. The illustrated humor and satirical weekly magazine begins publication. Largely written and edited by H. C. Bunner from 1878 to 1896, the magazine featured drawings and articles satirizing contemporary society and politics. It continued until 1918.

1878
Drama and Theater

BRONSON HOWARD: *The Banker's Daughter*. One of Howard's biggest successes is this play about a woman, who, despite loving another, marries an older man to support her family. Howard would discuss the origin and evolution of the play in a popular lecture, "An Autobiography of a Play," delivered in 1886 and published in 1914.

WILLIAM DEAN HOWELLS: *Yorick's Love*. Howells's drama is a free adaptation in blank verse of the Spanish dramatist Manuel Tamayo y Baus's play *Un drama nuevo*, which features the jester from Hamlet in a tragic romance.

A. M. PALMER (c. 1838–1905): *A Celebrated Case*. Palmer's adaptation of a French melodrama about a man's unjust imprisonment for the murder of his wife would be frequently performed into the early twentieth century. Palmer was the manager of New York's Union Square Theatre and in 1884 the Madison Square Theatre, which featured new works by American playwrights. In 1888 he would take over Wallack's Theatre, renaming it Palmer's.

Fiction

LOUISA MAY ALCOTT: *Under the Lilacs*. This juvenile domestic novel, written in response to the demand for more works like *Little Women* (1868–1869) and serialized beginning in 1877, is the story of a headstrong boy who runs away from his life in the circus to be domesticated in a respectable home. It is regarded as one of Alcott's weaker efforts, with a bland style and an unconvincing conversion of the novel's protagonist.

EDWARD BELLAMY (1850–1898): *Six to One: A Nantucket Idyl*. The Massachusetts journalist and reformer's first novel is based on his voyage to Hawaii in 1877.

EDWARD EGGLESTON: *Roxy*. This critically and commercially acclaimed tale follows a young religious woman whose faith is tested by her husband's infidelity and illegitimate child. Roxy Adams passes the test as she forgives her spouse and adopts the baby, attaining a greater

POPULAR BOOKS 1878–1894

The Leavenworth Case by Anna Katharine Green (First American Printing, 1878)

Progress and Poverty by Henry George (First American Printing, 1879)

Manliness of Christ by Thomas Hughes (First American Printing, 1880)

A Tramp Abroad by Mark Twain (First American Printing, 1880)

Ben-Hur by Lew Wallace (First American Printing, 1880)

Uncle Remus by Joel Chandler Harris (First American Printing, 1881)

Atlantis: The Antediluvian World by Ignatius Donnelly (First American Printing, 1882)

The Prince and the Pauper by Mark Twain (First American Printing, 1882)

Beyond the Gates by Elizabeth Stuart Phelps Ward (First American Printing, 1883)

Treasure Island by Robert Louis Stevenson (First American Printing, 1883)

A Roman Singer by Francis Marion Crawford (First American Printing, 1884)

Adventures of Huckleberry Finn by Mark Twain (First American Printing, 1884)

Personal Memoirs by Ulysses S. Grant (First American Printing, 1885)

King Solomon's Mines by H. Rider Haggard (First American Printing, 1885)

Little Lord Fauntleroy by Frances Hodgson Burnett (First American Printing, 1886)

The Strange Case of Dr. Jekyll and Mr. Hyde by Robert Louis Stevenson (First American Printing, 1886)

She by H. Rider Haggard (First American Printing, 1887)

The Gates Between by Elizabeth Stuart Phelps Ward (First American Printing, 1887)

Looking Backward by Edward Bellamy (First American Printing, 1888)

Robert Elsmere by Mrs. Humphry Ward (First American Printing, 1888)

A Window in Thrums by J. M. Barrie (First American Printing, 1889)

A Connecticut Yankee in King Arthur's Court by Mark Twain (First American Printing, 1889)

A Cigarette-Maker's Romance by Francis Marion Crawford (First American Printing, 1890)

Barrack-Room Ballads by Rudyard Kipling (First American Printing, 1890)

Caesar's Column by Ignatius Donnelly (First American Printing, 1891)

The Adventures of Sherlock Holmes by Arthur Conan Doyle (First American Printing, 1891)

Don Orsino by Francis Marion Crawford (First American Printing, 1892)

The Sign of the Four by Arthur Conan Doyle (First American Printing, 1893)

The Heavenly Twins by Sarah Grand (First American Printing, 1893)

Pushing to the Front by Orison Swett Marden (First American Printing, 1894)

History of the United States by Bill Nye (First American Printing, 1894)

The Tragedy of Pudd'nhead Wilson by Mark Twain (First American Printing, 1894)

level of religious truth. The novel is now considered Eggleston's best work because, according to Meredith Nicholson in the 1902 *Atlantic Monthly*, "Eggleston shows here for the first time a real capacity for handling a long story."

ANNA KATHARINE GREEN (1846–1935): *The Leavenworth Case.* The great popularity of Green's detective novel heightens the appeal of the mystery genre. Inspector Ebenezer Gryce makes the first of many fictional appearances in her works as he investigates the murder of rich Mr. Leavenworth. The novel was for a long time erroneously considered the first detective novel written by an American woman (Metta Victoria Victor's *The Dead Letter* had appeared earlier, in 1866).

HENRY JAMES: *Daisy Miller.* James's popular international novel is originally published in Britain's *Cornhill Magazine.* The work follows American expatriate Frederick Winterbourne as he is charmed by the socially unsophisticated, innocent American Daisy Miller. The book continues James's theme of the differences between

cultured Europe and naive America. Many pirated copies would sell in the United States prior to its release there. James also publishes *The Europeans: A Sketch*, a kind of opposite companion novel to *The American* (1877). James writes about a group of Europeanized Americans returning home. It features a deft depiction of New England and New Englanders.

KATHERINE SHERWOOD MacDOWELL (1849–1883): *Like unto Like.* The Mississippi local colorist publishes her first novel, an autobiographically based account of life during the Civil War and Reconstruction.

HARRIET BEECHER STOWE: *Poganuc People.* In this novel Stowe treats aspects of her own childhood, drawing on family anecdotes. It is Stowe's contribution to the local-color genre of fiction.

MARK TWAIN (SAMUEL LANGHORNE CLEMENS): "Punch, Brothers, Punch!" Twain's sketch, about a man who becomes a "tottering wreck" when he cannot get a newspaper's catchy jingle out of his head, had originally appeared as "A Literary Nightmare" in the *Atlantic*

Monthly in 1876 and is one of Twain's most popular performance pieces.

Literary Criticism and Scholarship

HENRY JAMES: *French Poets and Novelists.* James's collection of critical essays and reviews of literary figures such as Charles Baudelaire, Honoré de Balzac, George Sand, Gustave Flaubert, and others.

MOSES COIT TYLER (1835–1900): *A History of American Literature, 1607–1765.* The so-called father of American studies produces the first of his pioneering literary histories. This encyclopedic narrative history of the progress of American literature from the Jamestown landing to the eve of the Revolution is the most thorough account yet published on the subject. Tyler would be recognized for his achievement in 1884 by Cornell University, which appointed him the first scholar to hold the position of professor of American history. His second pioneering work, *The Literary History of the American Revolution,* would appear in 1897.

Nonfiction

BRONSON ALCOTT: *Table Talk.* A collection of what Alcott called "Philosophemes," brief topical reflections informed by his speculative philosophy and derived from his conversations.

MARTIN R. DELANY: *Principia of Ethnology: The Origin of Races and Color with an Archaeological Compendium of Ethiopian and Egyptian Civilizations.* Delany's final work counters prevalent notions concerning the inferiority of black people by offering evidence of the intellectual, economic, political, and social contributions of the ancient Ethiopians and Egyptians.

RALPH WALDO EMERSON: *Fortune of the Republic: Lecture Delivered at the Old South Church.* The publication of Emerson's lecture originally delivered in 1862 to boost morale and support the Northern cause.

SIR HENRY M. STANLEY: *Through the Dark Continent; or, The Sources of the Nile, Around the Great Lakes of Equatorial Africa, and Down the Livingstone River to the Atlantic Ocean.* Stanley's account of his second African exploration (1874–1878) becomes an international bestseller. A more accomplished narrative than *How I Found Livingstone* (1872), the book has been subsequently criticized for the distortions of fact that help make it a rousing story.

Poetry

SIDNEY LANIER: "The Marshes of Glynn." Anonymously published in the anthology *A Masque of Poets,* the poem is considered among Lanier's finest. Its description of the sea marshes in Glynn County, Georgia, is his greatest achievement in merging musical and poetical methods. Lanier had intended to write six "Hymns of the Marshes," but besides "Glynn" completed only three: "Sunrise," "Individuality," and "Marsh Song—at Sunset."

HENRY WADSWORTH LONGFELLOW: *Keramos and Other Poems.* The title poem, regarded as among Longfellow's best, links the poet's boyhood interests with his later travels to present his poetic principles.

JOHN GREENLEAF WHITTIER: *The Vision of Echard.* Whittier's collection contains "The Witch of Wenham," one of his best renderings of colonial customs. It displays his knowledge of the psychology of witchcraft and local superstitions. Included as well are "In the 'Old South'" and the courtly love lyric "The Henchman."

1879

Drama and Theater

DAVID BELASCO (1853–1931) AND JAMES A. HERNE (1839–1901): *Hearts of Oak.* Based on an idea suggested by Belasco, Herne achieves his first major success with this drama about an old sailor who raises two orphans, a boy and a girl. He falls in love with the girl but loses her to the boy. The play is unusual for its time in that it lacks a clear villain or hero. Herne would rework the play as *Sag Harbor* in 1899.

BARTLEY CAMPBELL (1843–1888): *My Partner.* Regarded as the Pittsburgh-born playwright and producer's best play, this drama concerns a man wrongfully accused of killing his partner in the waning days of the California gold rush. The play's success allows Campbell also to present *The Galley Slave,* a romantic melodrama in which a man is willing to be wrongfully charged as a thief rather than compromise a lady's honor.

PAULINE E. HOPKINS (1859–1930): *Peculiar Sam; or, The Slaves' Escape.* The Maine-born author becomes the first African American woman playwright to have a play produced when her musical drama, featuring the prominent black performers Sam Lucas (1848–1916) and Anna and Emma Hyers, is staged in New England and goes on tour throughout the North and the Midwest.

NATE SALSBURY (1846–1902): *The Brook; or, A Jolly Day at the Picnic.* First performed by the Salsbury Troubadours of San Francisco, led by Nate Salsbury. The play, depicting a group on a picnic who entertain themselves with song, dance, and comic turns, initiates the genre of farce-comedy, an early form of the musical that is regarded as the beginning of modern American musical theater. Salsbury was the general manager of William F. Cody's *Wild West Show* from 1883 until his death.

Fiction

LOUISA MAY ALCOTT: *Meadow Blossoms, Sparkles for Bright Eyes*, and *Water-Cresses*. These three children's anthologies of Alcott's previously published works are released for the holiday gift-buying market.

EDWARD BELLAMY: *The Duke of Stockbridge*. Bellamy publishes serially this historical romance dealing with Shays's Rebellion. His cousin, Francis Bellamy, would complete and issue it in book form in 1900.

GEORGE WASHINGTON CABLE (1844–1925): *Old Creole Days*. Cable's first book is a collection of short stories depicting Creole life in New Orleans. It advances the American local-color movement and remains one of the most significant collections of that genre. His popular story "Madame Delphine" (1881) would be included in later editions.

THOMAS DETTER (1826–?): *Nellie Brown; or, The Jealous Wife, with Other Sketches*. The first novel published in the American West by an African American is the work of a Nevada journalist, entrepreneur, and community leader. It treats marriage, infidelity, and divorce. The novel and additional writings by Detter would be rediscovered and reissued in 1996.

WILLIAM DEAN HOWELLS: *The Lady of the Aroostook*. Howells's novel tells the story of a naive Massachusetts schoolteacher who sails on the *Aroostook* to Italy, where she is harassed by a drunken man and meets her future husband, the Boston socialite James Staniford. Among Howells's most realistic novels, it questions the morals of an American ingenue amid European culture and customs.

HENRY JAMES: "An International Episode." Originally serialized in Britain's *Cornhill Magazine* (1878–1879), James's lengthy short story concerns an American girl's courtship by an English lord, featuring both American and English settings; James regards the work as a counterpart to *Daisy Miller*. Concerning the hostility it received from English reviewers, James observed, "So long as one serves up Americans for their entertainment it is all right — but hands off the sacred natives!"

JOHN BOYLE O'REILLY (1844–1890): *Monodyne*. The Irish-born writer, who was imprisoned in Australia for his Fenian activities and escaped to the United States, produces a novel reflecting his prison experiences. It helps secure the release of Irish political prisoners in Australia by calling attention to their plight.

FRANK R. STOCKTON (1834–1902): *Rudder Grange*. A whimsical story by the Philadelphia novelist and short story writer of a newlywed couple living aboard a canal boat with a young servant, Pomona. The humorous novel is replete with absurdities typical of Stockton's humor, and its success brings him literary fame and occasions two sequels: *The Rudder Grangers Abroad* (1891) and *Pomona's Travels* (1894).

ALBION W. TOURGÉE: *A Fool's Errand*. Tourgée's novel of a Michigan colonel who moves his family to the South to aid the Reconstruction effort, which he realizes has failed, wins acclaim from reviewers in the North and South and sells 150,000 copies in its first year. It would transfer successfully to the stage by Steele Mac-Kaye in 1881. Tourgée also publishes *Figs and Thistles*, a novel about the Civil War era based on both the author's experiences and on the political career of James Garfield. A sequel, *Bricks Without Straw*, would follow in 1880.

Literary Criticism and Scholarship

HENRY JAMES: *Hawthorne*. James's critical monograph on Hawthorne's life and works deprecates the writer's American milieu and romantic method, judging them inferior to his own European settings and literary realism and asserting that "the flower of art blooms only where the soil is deep, that it takes a great deal of history to produce a little literature, that it needs a complex social machinery to set a writer in motion." The book sparks a hostile outcry by American reviewers, which James would call "a very big tempest in a very small tea-pot."

Nonfiction

HENRY ADAMS (1838–1918): *The Life of Albert Gallatin*. The grandson of John Quincy Adams and son of Charles Francis Adams had previously written an article on Captain John Smith (1867) and a review of Lyell's *Principle of Geology* (1868), as well as other political essays. His four-volume biography initiates the research that would lead to his *History of the United States of America During the Administrations of Thomas Jefferson and James Madison* (9 vols., 1889–1891).

Anonymous: *The Diary of a Public Man*. Published anonymously in the *North American Review*, this diary treating the pre-presidential life of Abraham Lincoln is the source of the famous story that Stephen A. Douglas held Lincoln's hat during the inauguration. The content and the identity of the author stir a controversy. It has been suggested that Samuel Ward (1814–1884), the brother of Julia Ward Howe, is the author.

HENRY GEORGE: *Progress and Poverty.* In his ground-breaking economic analysis, George asserts his theory that poverty increases with prosperity in the United States because of methods of taxation. He proposes a "single tax" on land to replace other taxes, improving conditions for capital and labor. Considered one of the most influential economic treatises ever published, it would be translated into several languages and would shape tax policies throughout the world.

Poetry

ETHEL LYNN BEERS (1827–1879): *All Quiet Along the Potomac, and Other Poems.* The title work, an account of a soldier's death in the Civil War and first published as "The Picket Guard" in 1861, is the New York poet and fiction writer's best-known work.

JOHN WALLACE CRAWFORD (1847–1917): *The Poet Scout.* The Indian fighter and agent who performed his poetry as the "Poet Scout" publishes his first collection.

ABRAM JOSEPH RYAN (1838–1886): *Father Ryan's Poems.* The Maryland priest and supporter of the Confederacy collects the poems that earn him the titles "the poet of the Lost Cause" and "the Tom Moore of Dixie." Included are the poems "Gather the Sacred Dust," "The Conquered Banner," "The Lost Cause," and "The Sword of Robert E. Lee."

Publications and Events

Daly's Theatre. After his Fifth Avenue Theatre was destroyed by fire in 1873, Augustin Daly restores another old New York playhouse, renames it after himself, establishes his second theatrical company, and creates what theatrical historian George Odell calls "one of the most distinguished theatres in the history of the American stage."

1880
Drama and Theater

AUGUSTIN DALY: *Needles and Pins.* Subtitled "A Comedy of the Present," Daly's play is a complicated marital drama involving a pushy mother who wants her weak son to marry a rich woman. Daly also presents *The Last Word,* a comedy about a young woman's defiance of her father's wishes in choosing a husband. It is one of Daly's last major successes.

STEELE MACKAYE: *Hazel Kirke.* A successful domestic play in which Hazel Kirke weds Carringford, a lord in disguise, and angers both of their families. Carringford's

mother convinces Hazel that the marriage is illegitimate. Hazel attempts to drown herself but is rescued by her husband, and the two finally find happiness in their marriage. Despite critical reservations, the play is an immediate hit and manages the longest run (486 performances) for a nonmusical play up to that time. The play would be revived over many years in the United States and in Europe.

Fiction

HENRY ADAMS: *Democracy: An American Novel.* Adams's best-selling satire of Washington politics presents the nation's powerful as seen by a widow from New York who travels to the capital to learn about government and finds it corrupted. Initially published anonymously, the novel portrays many actual Washington figures such as Rutherford B. Hayes and James G. Blaine, creating a sensation among readers as to the true identity of the author and his characters.

LOUISA MAY ALCOTT: *Jack and Jill: A Village Story.* First serialized in *St. Nicholas* in 1879–1880, the novel treats topics such as death and loss, previously considered unsuitable for children, in a series of loosely related incidents in the small village of Harmony. The work reflects many of Alcott's most strongly held beliefs on contemporary issues, including alcohol, gender roles, and education.

EDWARD BELLAMY: *Dr. Heidenhoff's Process.* The first of two romances that recall Hawthorne and show Bellamy's interest in psychic states. It would be followed by *Miss Ludington's Sister* (1884).

GEORGE WASHINGTON CABLE: *The Grandissimes: A Story of Creole Life.* Cable's first novel (and his best) is set at the time of the Louisiana Purchase and concerns the feud between two aristocratic Creole families in New Orleans. Involving white and black half-brothers and a love triangle involving a mulatto, a quadroon woman, and a slave, the novel frankly recognizes miscegenation under slavery. Its theme of a Southern heritage of past crimes and guilt anticipates similar concerns in William Faulkner's novels.

PHILANDER DEMING (1829–1915): *Adirondack Stories.* The New York lawyer converts his knowledge of the region into a collection of realistic Adirondack sketches. It would be followed by *Tompkins and Other Folks* (1885), another realistic look at the region and its inhabitants.

WILLIAM CLARK FALKNER (1825–1889): *The White Rose of Memphis.* The great-grandfather of William Faulkner, and his model for Colonel Sartoris, achieves some literary success with this melodramatic novel. It would

BIRTHS AND DEATHS, 1880–1889

Births

1880 H. L. Mencken (d. 1956), journalist, editor, and critic
Kathleen Norris (d. 1966), novelist
Ernest Poole (d. 1950), novelist and journalist

1881 John Neihardt (d. 1973), poet
Elizabeth Madox Roberts (d. 1941), novelist, short story writer, and poet
T. S. Stribling (d. 1965), novelist

1882 Susan Glaspell (d. 1948), playwright and novelist
Mina Loy (d. 1986), poet
Olive Prouty (d. 1974), novelist
Margaret Wilson (d. 1973), novelist

1883 Max Forrester Eastman (d. 1969), writer, editor, and critic
Martin Flavin (d. 1967), novelist
William Carlos Williams (d. 1963), poet, novelist, and playwright

1884 Damon Runyon (d. 1946), short story writer and columnist
Sara Teasdale (d. 1933), poet
Margaret Widdemer (d. 1978), novelist and poet

1885 Will Durant (d. 1981), historian and philosopher
Edna Ferber (d. 1968), novelist
Ring Lardner (d. 1933), humorist and short story writer
Sinclair Lewis (d. 1951), novelist
Ezra Pound (d. 1972), poet
Carl Van Doren (d. 1950), historian, editor, and critic
Elinor Hoyt Wylie (d. 1928), poet and novelist

1886 Zoe Akins (d. 1958), playwright and poet
Margaret Ayer Barnes (d. 1967), novelist and short story writer
William Rose Benét (d. 1950), poet, author, and editor
Van Wyck Brooks (d. 1963), author and critic
James Gould Fletcher (d. 1950), poet
Douglas Southall Freeman (d. 1953), historian
John Hall Wheelock (d. 1978), poet and editor

1887 Leonard Bacon (d. 1954), poet and critic
Floyd James Dell (d. 1969), novelist, poet, editor, and social critic
Robinson Jeffers (d. 1962), poet
George Kelly (d. 1974), playwright
Marianne Moore (d. 1972), poet
Samuel Eliot Morison (d. 1976), historian

1888 Maxwell Anderson (d. 1959), playwright
James Boyd (d. 1944), novelist
T. S. Eliot (d. 1965), poet

Eugene O'Neill (d. 1953), playwright
John Crowe Ransom (d. 1974), poet and critic
Arthur M. Schlesinger (d. 1965), historian
Alan Seeger (d. 1916), poet
Samuel Shellabarger (d. 1954), novelist

1889 Conrad Aiken (d. 1973), poet, novelist, and critic
Hervey Allen (d. 1949), novelist, biographer, and poet
Fannie Hurst (d. 1968), novelist and short story writer
Walter Lippmann (d. 1974), journalist, editor, and author
Claude McKay (d. 1948), poet

Deaths

1880 Lydia Maria Child (b. 1802), novelist and social reformer
James Lawson (b. 1799), poet
Epes Sargent (b. 1813), playwright
Jones Very (b. 1813), poet

1881 Sidney Lanier (b. 1842), poet and critic
Henry Morford (b. 1823), poet
Alfred Billings Street (b. 1811), poet

1882 Richard Henry Dana Jr. (b. 1815), novelist
Ralph Waldo Emerson (b. 1803), essayist and poet
Henry Wadsworth Longfellow (b. 1807), poet

1884 Charles Fenno Hoffman (b. 1806), poet, novelist, and editor

1885 Timothy Shay Arthur (b. 1809), novelist and short story writer
Helen Hunt Jackson (b. 1830), novelist
Henry Wheeler Shaw (b. 1818), humorist

1886 John Esten Cooke (b. 1830), novelist and poet
Emily Dickinson (b. 1830), poet
Paul Hamilton Hayne (b. 1830), poet
Ann Sophia Stephens (b. 1813), novelist and editor

1887 Jane Andrews (b. 1833), children's author
Henry Ward Beecher (b. 1813), theologian, writer, and editor
Emma Lazarus (b. 1849), poet and essayist
Edward Rowland Sill (b. 1841), poet

1888 Amos Bronson Alcott (b. 1799), author and educator
Louisa May Alcott (b. 1832), novelist
Bartley Campbell (b. 1843), playwright
Caroline Howard Gilman (b. 1794), poet
David Ross Locke (b. 1833), journalist and editor
Fred Marsden (b. 1842), playwright

1889 William Clark Falkner (b. 1825), novelist

be followed by a historical romance, *The Little Brick Church* (1882), offering a Southern response to *Uncle Tom's Cabin*, and a travel book, *Rapid Ramblings in Europe* (1884).

LUCRETIA PEABODY HALE (1820–1900): *The Peterkin Papers*. The sister of Edward Everett Hale gains her own literary reputation with this series of comic stories about a blundering Boston family who are rescued by the commonsensical "lady from Philadelphia." A further volume, *The Last of the Peterkins*, would appear in 1886.

WILLIAM DEAN HOWELLS: *The Undiscovered Country*. One of Howells's best novels treats loss of faith and moral and social disorder during the post–Civil War period. It has been viewed as an updated version of Hawthorne's *The Blithedale Romance*, contrasting false spiritualists with the genuine faith of the Shakers.

HENRY JAMES: *Confidence*. James's short novel, previously serialized in *Scribner's Monthly* (1879–1880), concerns a group of Americans in Europe. Though James would prefer it to *The Europeans* (1878), most critics regard it as his weakest novel. In 1880 James also publishes two short stories: "The Diary of a Man of Fifty," about a retired British general who returns to Florence after twenty-seven years, and "A Bundle of Letters," a rare example of James's use of the epistolary form.

ALBION W. TOURGÉE: *Bricks Without Straw*. The popular sequel to *Fool's Errand* (1879) concerns a schoolteacher from the North whose work in a Reconstruction era African American community in North Carolina infuriates local whites. The title suggests that Southern blacks could not become productive U.S. citizens without the "straw" of a fair social and economic system.

GEORGE ALFRED TOWNSEND: *Tales of the Chesapeake*. Townsend, one of the first syndicated correspondents, publishes his best-known book, a collection of local-color sketches.

LEW WALLACE: *Ben-Hur: A Tale of the Christ*. Wallace's historical romance concerns Judah Ben-Hur, a young Jewish nobleman sent to the galleys after his Roman friend Messala wrongly accuses him of attempting to murder the Roman governor of Judea. After escaping and winning a chariot race against Messala, he frees his mother and sister from imprisonment, and they all convert to Christianity after Jesus cures the women of leprosy. The remarkably popular novel, never yet out of print, would be adapted into a play in 1899 and staged six thousand times over the next twenty-one years. Two successful film versions of the story would be made in 1931 and 1959.

CONSTANCE FENIMORE WOOLSON: *Rodman the Keeper: Southern Sketches*. Based on the author's observations during her residence in the Carolinas and Florida, the collection contrasts the antebellum South with life during Reconstruction.

Literary Criticism and Scholarship

SIDNEY LANIER: *The Science of English Verse*. Lanier's treatise on prosody contains his theories suggesting that the rules governing verse are the same that apply to music.

Nonfiction

WILLIAM WELLS BROWN: *My Southern Home; or, The South and Its People*. The last work of one of first African American men of letters is an autobiographically derived treatment of racial struggles in the South before and after the Civil War.

ADRIEN EMMANUEL ROUQUETTE (1813–1887): *Critical Dialogue Between Aboo and Caboo*. Writing as "E. Junius," Rouquette, the New Orleans priest and poet, attacks George Washington Cable's depiction of Creoles in *The Grandissimes* (1880).

MARK TWAIN (SAMUEL LANGHORNE CLEMENS): *A Tramp Abroad*. Although less successful than his earlier travel works, this chronicle of Twain's 1878 walking tour in Europe with the Reverend Joseph Twichell is noteworthy for several brilliant pieces, including "Baker's Blue-Jay Yarn," in which he discusses the wit of birds. The English critic William Ernest Henley describes the volume as follows: "Of uniform excellence 'A Tramp Abroad' is not; but it is very vigorously and picturesquely written throughout it; it contains some of the writer's happiest work."

Poetry

HENRY WADSWORTH LONGFELLOW: *Ultima Thule*. The collection that Longfellow had intended as his last contains farewell lyrics such as "The Tide Rises, the Tide Falls" and "L'Envoi: The Poet and His Song." Enough uncollected poems would be available, however, to form a second volume, *In the Harbor, Ultima Thule—Part 2*, issued posthumously in 1882. It includes Longfellow's final composition, "The Bells of San Blas."

Publications and Events

The *Dial*. Founded in Chicago as a conservative review, the journal would by 1918 feature advanced ideas by writers such as John Dewey, Thorstein Veblen, and Charles Austin Beard. During the 1920s, it became the leading champion for international modernism, publishing writings by William Butler Yeats, Thomas Mann, and virtually every significant American writer during the period. Marianne Moore served as its editor from 1926 to its demise in 1929.

1881
Drama and Theater

FRANCES HODGSON BURNETT AND WILLIAM GILLETTE (1855–1937): *Esmeralda*. This dramatization of Burnett's novelette about a North Carolina girl whose ambitious mother complicates her love for their neighbor achieves an initial run of 350 performances, one of the longest runs of the era. It would be revived and performed for the next twenty years. Gillette, who made his acting debut in 1875, would achieve his greatest success portraying the title character in *Sherlock Holmes* (1899), which he wrote.

A. C. GUNTER: *Fresh, the American*. Gunter's comedy depicts a brash Yankee schemer who falls in love with an Egyptian harem beauty, whom he rescues.

GEORGE H. JESSOP (?–1915): *Sam'l of Posen; or, The Commercial Drummer.* The Irish-born playwright's drama concerns a Jewish immigrant who gives up life as a traveling salesman to work in a jewelry store, only to lose his job when a coworker is wrongly accused of a crime.

Fiction

JAMES OTIS KALER (1848–1912): *Toby Tyler; or, Ten Weeks with a Circus.* Writing as "James Otis," the Maine writer has his greatest success with this tale of a boy who runs away with a circus. Kaler would produce more than 175 juvenile novels, but none achieved a comparable success.

GEORGE WASHINGTON CABLE: *Madame Delphine.* Cable's novella tells the story of a quadroon woman's attempt to secure an advantageous marriage for her light-skinned daughter by passing her off as white. Southern hostility to the work helps convince Cable to leave the South for Massachusetts.

ROSE TERRY COOKE (1827–1892): *Somebody's Neighbors.* The first collection by the Connecticut short story writer realistically depicts New England mill and village life. Other volumes, *Root-Bound* (1885) and *The Sphinx's Children and Other People's* (1886), would follow. She is considered one of the earliest of the New England local colorists commended by William Dean Howells for writing realistic stories "when truth in art was considered a minor virtue if not a sordid detail."

JOHN WILLIAM DE FOREST: *The Bloody Chasm.* The novel explores the post–Civil War rift between North and South in a domestic allegory that offers a realistic depiction of Charleston in ruins and the lives of freed slaves.

JOEL CHANDLER HARRIS (1848–1908): *Uncle Remus: His Songs and His Sayings.* Harris issues the first of his many fable collections featuring the former slave Uncle Remus, who entertains his employer's young son with dialect stories from black folklore. Included in the collection are the Brer Rabbit, Brer Fox, Brer Wolf, and Tar-Baby stories. Harris declares his aim in the introduction, stating that "However humorous it may be in effect, its intention is perfectly serious . . . to preserve the legends themselves in their original simplicity, and to wed them permanently to the quaint dialect." Several sequels would follow, including *Nights with Uncle Remus* (1883), *Uncle Remus and His Friends* (1892), *Mr. Rabbit at Home* (1895), *The Tar-Baby and Other Rhymes of Uncle Remus* (1904), and *Uncle Remus and Br'er Rabbit* (1906).

WILLIAM DEAN HOWELLS: *Dr. Breen's Practice.* Howells provides an early study of a woman doctor. He also

An illustration from *Uncle Remus* by Joel Chandler Harris

publishes *A Fearful Responsibility and Other Stories*, featuring the title novella, which draws on his experiences as consul to Venice.

HENRY JAMES: *The Portrait of a Lady.* Regarded as the greatest work of James's early period, the novel presents his "conception of a young lady confronting her destiny." In the book Isabel Archer chooses the dilletantish Gilbert Osmond for her husband and suffers the consequences. A richly nuanced work of psychological realism, the novel employs a version of the stream-of-consciousness technique to capture Isabel's state of mind. James also publishes *Washington Square*, which is set in the stylish New York neighborhood of the title, where James himself had lived as a child. The novel concerns Catherine Sloper, the plain daughter of a wealthy doctor. She is heartbroken when she realizes that the man she plans to marry against her father's wishes is interested only in her inheritance, as her father had suspected. The novel would be made into the play *The Heiress* in 1947.

HARRIET M. LOTHROP (1844–1924): *Five Little Peppers and How They Grew.* Originally published in the juvenile magazine *Wide Awake,* under the pen name "Margaret Sidney," Lothrop's highly acclaimed children's story is praised for its moral characters who find happiness although they live in poverty. Lothrop continues the Peppers' story in a series of sequels, including *Five Little Peppers Grow Up* (1892), but this novel is her bestseller, with two million copies sold in fifty years.

SARAH PRATT MCLEAN (1856–1935): *Cape Cod Folks.* The New England local-color writer's first book is a romance set on Cape Cod, treating a schoolteacher's life in a seafaring community.

Nonfiction

SUSAN B. ANTHONY (1820–1906): *History of Woman Suffrage.* The women's rights crusader directs the preservation of the documentary record of the early women's movement in the first installment of what would become a multivolume collection of letters, speeches, reminiscences, and conference papers. Four volumes would be issued by 1887, with two more, compiled by Ida Husted Harper, added by 1922.

JEFFERSON DAVIS (1808–1889): *The Rise and Fall of the Confederate Government.* Davis offers an account of his administration and a defense of his actions as president that is seldom penetrating or self-revealing. It concludes with a call for an end to recriminations. An abridgment, *A Short History of the Confederate States of America,* would appear in 1890.

HELEN HUNT JACKSON: *A Century of Dishonor.* Having previously published poetry collections, children's books, magazine articles, and novels, Jackson issues her first nonfiction book, a powerful indictment of the abuse of Native Americans perpetuated by the U.S. government. One of the first major works to help shift attitudes regarding the injustices experienced by Native Americans, it would serve as a standard reference on the subject for a generation.

Poetry

INA DONNA COOLBRITH (1842–1928): *A Perfect Day.* Born in Illinois, Coolbirth had come to California by covered wagon as a child. This is the initial collection by the woman who would be named the first poet laureate of California. *The Singer of the Sea* (1894) and *Songs from the Golden Gate* (1895) would follow.

WALT WHITMAN: *Leaves of Grass,* seventh edition. The so-called Osgood edition of Whitman's ever-evolving collection is the first distributed by a mainstream publisher, Boston's James R. Osgood and Company. After selling fifteen hundred copies, Osgood withdrew it after a district attorney threatened to prosecute the publisher for selling obscene literature. In the Osgood edition, Whitman had cut thirty-nine poems, added seventeen, and modified hundreds of lines, while regrouping poems into thematic and dramatic clusters.

Publications and Events

American Men of Letters series. Under the editorship of Charles Dudley Warner, this series of critical biographies begins with *Washington Irving.* By 1904, twenty-two volumes would be issued, including studies of Ralph Waldo Emerson, James Fenimore Cooper, and Margaret Fuller.

The *Century Illustrated Monthly Magazine.* A renamed *Scribner's Monthly,* edited from 1881 to 1909 by Richard Watson Gilder, appears. It serialized John George Nicolay and John Hay's biography of Lincoln (1887–1890), William Dean Howells's *A Modern Instance* and *The Rise of Silas Lapham,* Henry James's *The Bostonians,* and Jack London's *The Sea-Wolf.*

The *Critic.* The weekly literary magazine that first published the Uncle Remus stories debuts. Continuing until 1906, its contributors included Walt Whitman, Julia Ward Howe, and Edward Everett Hale.

The *Judge.* This comic weekly is founded by writers and artists defecting from *Puck.* It became an important organ for the Republican Party's political views beginning in 1884, and it continued until 1939.

1882
Drama and Theater

BARTLEY CAMPBELL: *The White Slave.* Campbell's biggest success is this slave drama in which a quadroon girl is threatened by her villainous master to work as a field hand with "a hoe in your hand, rags upon your back," unless she complies with his sexual desires. She responds with the line that brings the house down: "Rags are royal raiment when worn for virtue's sake." The play would be performed as late as 1918.

BRONSON HOWARD: *Young Mrs. Winthrop.* Howard becomes one of the first American playwrights to treat American materialistic values psychologically and morally rather than satirically. The plot concerns a marriage threatened by the husband's business preoccupations and the wife's social climbing, which cause them to neglect their child, who dies as a result.

Fiction

LOUISA MAY ALCOTT: *Proverb Stories.* Alcott expands her 1868 edition of three stories, each illustrating proverbial expressions. Two deal with the Civil War: "Picket Duty," about a Confederate who changes sides (illustrating "Better late than never"), and "My Red Cap," about a disabled veteran honored in an old soldiers' home (illustrating "He who serves well need not fear to ask his wages").

FRANCIS MARION CRAWFORD (1854–1909): *Mr. Isaacs, A Tale of Modern India.* This is the first of Crawford's more than forty novels, many based on his travels around the world. It describes a diamond merchant whom Crawford had met in India and anticipates Rudyard Kipling in introducing India to a Western audience. The nephew of Julia Ward Howe and the son of sculptor Thomas Crawford (1813–1857), Crawford would become one of the most successful American novelists of the era.

EDWARD EGGLESTON: *The Hoosier Schoolboy.* Eggleston's juvenile novel takes to task the conditions of Indiana's rural schools.

WILLIAM DEAN HOWELLS: *A Modern Instance.* The first important American novel to deal realistically with divorce, the work describes the marital collapse of Bartley Hubbard, a newspaper editor given to drinking and philandering, and his wife, Marcia, characterized as irrational and passionate. The work receives mixed reviews, but the reviewer for the *Atlantic Monthly* declares the book "[Howells's] greatest achievement, not in an artistic [sense], but in an ethical apprehension."

FRANK R. STOCKTON: "The Lady or the Tiger." Stockton's most lasting story and the most famous one ever published in the *Century,* the phenomenally popular tale tells of an average man who wins the heart of a princess. As punishment, her father, the king, makes the man choose between two doors; behind one is a beautiful woman whom he must marry and behind the other is a ferocious tiger. The princess directs her lover to the door on the right, but Stockton leaves it up to the reader to decide which fate she has chosen for the man — a source of debate among readers. The story is frequently anthologized.

MARK TWAIN (SAMUEL LANGHORNE CLEMENS): *The Prince and the Pauper.* A pauper and Prince Edward, who bear a striking resemblance to each other, trade clothes and identities in a children's story that illustrates the societal ills of Tudor England. Although critically successful, sales are disappointing.

CONSTANCE FENIMORE WOOLSON: *Anne.* Woolson's first novel tells the story of a simple girl from Michigan's Mackinac Island who is forced to contend with New York society.

Literary Criticism and Scholarship

DANIEL GARRISON BRINTON (1837–1899): *Library of Aboriginal American Literature.* The physician and anthropologist edits the first offering in an eight-volume series (completed in 1890), a major contribution to the preservation of Native American culture and an important resource for those interested in aboriginal arts.

FRANK HAMILTON CUSHING (1857–1900): *Myths of Creation.* The ethnologist, archaeologist, and expert on Zuni culture translates this Zuni epic.

Nonfiction

GEORGE BANCROFT: *History of the Formation of the Constitution.* The historian adds this volume to the final revision of his monumental, multivolume *History of the United States* (1834–1876), revised between 1883 and 1885.

EMMA LAZARUS: "An Epistle to the Hebrews." Lazarus begins a series of fourteen essays to be published in the *American Hebrew* through February 1883, commenting on Jewish history, culture, and the return to Palestine. She excoriates her fellow American Jews for assimilation and taking for granted their privileges and security, and she urges eastern European Jews to immigrate to Palestine.

THEODORE ROOSEVELT (1858–1919): *The Naval War of 1812; or, The History of the United States Navy During the Last War with Great Britain.* Roosevelt's first full-length book would be later described by its author as "dry as a dictionary." However, it goes through three editions in its first year and is placed aboard every ship in the U.S. fleet.

WALT WHITMAN: *Specimen Days and Collect.* Whitman supplies journal entries and autobiographical recollections about his Long Island childhood and the Civil War, as well as musings on nature, thoughts on his recuperation from a stroke, and literary criticism of authors whom he had met on travels to Boston, Canada, and the American West.

Poetry

EMMA LAZARUS: *Songs of a Semite: The Dance to Death and Other Poems.* Reacting to the persecution of Jews in the Russian pogroms of 1882, Lazarus finds her distinctive voice and themes in her defense of the Jewish people. Included are important works such as "The Banner of the Jew," "The Crowing of the Red Cock," and "The Dance to Death." Lazarus's militancy concerning Jewish issues and women's rights are controversial, however.

1883
Drama and Theater

WILLIAM F. CODY (1846–1917): *Wild West Show.* Cody and sharpshooter William F. Carver create an open-air entertainment depicting Indian skirmishes and displays of trick riding and shooting, and enthusiastic audiences throughout America and Europe flock to it for the next three decades. The show often enacts a moral drama in which the whites conquer savagery and bring civilization to the West. Sharpshooter Annie Oakley (1860–1926) would join the troupe in 1885. It merged in 1909 with the chief competition, Pawnee Bill's Historical Far West and Great Far East Show, and finally closed in 1915 due to bankruptcy.

AUGUSTIN DALY: *7-20-8; or, Casting the Boomerang.* The title refers to a painting of a beautiful woman that compels a young man-about-town to seek the original. The play's success rescues Daly's company from bankruptcy.

EDWARD HARRIGAN (1845–1911): *Cordelia's Aspirations.* Considered the songwriter and playwright's best, this drama concerns an Irish immigrant family, the Mulligans, who live in New York's Irish ghetto, and their misadventures when they decide to move uptown. It had been preceded by *The Mulligan Guards' Ball* (1879) and *The Mulligans' Silver Wedding* (1883). Harrigan's works are noteworthy for his realistic depiction of working-class American life.

HENRY JAMES: *Daisy Miller: A Comedy in Three Acts.* James's own dramatization of his 1878 novel, which had appeared in the *Atlantic Monthly* and in book form.

JAMES O'NEILL (1847–1920) first performs, in New York, the title role of Alexandre Dumas's *The Count of Monte Cristo,* adapted by Charles Fechter (1824–1879). In 1885, O'Neill (the father of Eugene O'Neill) would purchase the rights to the adaptation and perform in the play to acclaim for the rest of his career.

WILLIAM YOUNG (1847–1920): *The Rajah; or, Wyncot's Ward.* The Chicago-born lawyer-turned-actor and playwright's biggest dramatic success is this romantic comedy about a feckless young man made the guardian of his uncle's adopted daughter, who falls in love with him. His other major success was his adaptation of Lew Wallace's *Ben-Hur* in 1899.

Fiction

JOHN ESTEN COOKE: *Fanchette by One of Her Admirers.* Cooke attacks religious skepticism, materialism, and an excessive faith in science in this novel. It would be followed by another with similar themes, *The Maurice Mystery* (1885).

MARY HALLOCK FOOTE (1847–1938): *The Led-Horse Claims.* Regarded as one of the first novelists to depict the West realistically, Foote, in her first novel, provides a western version of the Romeo and Juliet story: a feud between rival mines in Colorado. Foote lived in Colorado, Idaho, and California, and Wallace Stegner's *Angle of Repose* (1971) would treat her life.

ROBERT GRANT (1852–1940): *An Average Man.* The Boston-born lawyer and jurist achieves his initial literary success in this first novel, which concerns the contrasting lifestyles and values of two New York lawyers.

JOEL CHANDLER HARRIS: *Nights with Uncle Remus.* Harris's second series of Uncle Remus stories adds African Jack as a storyteller using the Gullah dialect. The tales in this volume, unlike the first, are set during slavery times, and though they do not overly idealize plantation life, they do portray only an affectionate relationship between slave and master. Harris's subsequent collections would be written more and more explicitly for children.

NATHANIEL HAWTHORNE: *Dr. Grimshawe's Secret* and *The Ancestral Footstep.* Hawthorne's unfinished manuscript fragments are edited by his son, Julian, for publication.

EDGAR WATSON HOWE (1853–1937): *The Story of a Country Town.* Howe's first and finest work is, according to William I. McReynolds in the *Dictionary of Literary Biography,* "A pioneering example of realistic fiction." The story highlights the bleakness of the nineteenth-century Midwest. The plot follows a printer, Ned Westlock, whose father had abandoned his family when Ned was young. Westlock also narrates the story of his best friend, Jo, who kills a man because he fears his wife is in love with him. After the novel had been rejected by several eastern printers, Howe prints it himself. It receives high critical acclaim and goes through numerous subsequent printings.

WILLIAM DEAN HOWELLS: *A Woman's Reason.* Composed while Howells was traveling in Europe and judged as one of his weakest efforts, this novel concerns a woman trying to cope with life without a proper education.

HENRY JAMES: *The Siege of London.* The title work in this story collection deals with an American widow's attempt to enter British society. Also included are the stories "The Pension Beauvepas" and "The Point of View."

LAURA JEAN LIBBEY (1862–1924): *A Fatal Wooing.* The first of Libbey's sentimental bestsellers. Others include *Junie's Love Test* (1886), *Miss Middleton's Lover* (1888),

That Pretty Young Girl (1889), *A Mad Betrothal* (1890), *Parted by Fate* (1890), and *We Parted at the Altar* (1892). Over a forty-year career Libbey would produce eighty-two novels that would sell between ten and fifteen million copies.

KATHERINE SHERWOOD MacDOWELL: *Dialect Tales.* The first collection by the Mississippi local colorist. It would be followed by *Suwanee River Tales* (1884).

GEORGE WILBUR PECK: *Peck's Bad Boy and His Pa.* A collection of sketches featuring an unscrupulous Midwestern boy who plays practical jokes, particularly on his father. The articles had been originally published in Peck's Milwaukee newspaper, the *Sun*, and won wide popularity. Numerous collections of Bad Boy stories would follow, including *Peck's Bad Boy and His Pa, No. 2* (1883), *Peck's Boss Book* (1884), *Peck's Irish Friend, Phelan Geohagan* (1887), *Peck's Uncle Ike and the Red-Headed Boy* (1899), and *Peck's Bad Boy with the Cowboys* (1907). Twentieth-century readers would object to the violence and racial prejudice that appear in the sketches.

ALBION W. TOURGÉE: *Hot Plowshares.* Set during Reconstruction, the novel is one of the first to deal with miscegenation with a heroine who is suspected of being part African American.

ELIZABETH STUART PHELPS WARD: *Beyond the Gates.* In the first of several sequels to *The Gates Ajar* (1868), Ward continues her imaginative treatment of the afterlife with the story of a woman who dreams she has gone to heaven. It would be followed by *The Gates Between* (1887) and *Within the Gates* (1901).

CONSTANCE FENIMORE WOOLSON: *For the Major.* Set in North Carolina, the novel treats a wife's sacrifices to help her husband preserve his cherished illusions about the Old South. It is considered one of her best works.

Literary Criticism and Scholarship

SIDNEY LANIER: *The English Novel.* With the subtitle "From Aeschylus to George Eliot: The Development of Personality," Lanier's wide-ranging critical study traces the evolving depiction of human personality by writers such as Geoffrey Chaucer, Émile Zola, and Walt Whitman. Many of Lanier's important aesthetic and social theories are displayed in the work.

Nonfiction

RICHARD MAURICE BUCKE (1837–1901): *Walt Whitman.* The Canadian doctor and devoted friend of the poet (he purportedly committed all of *Leaves of Grass* to memory) writes the first Whitman biography, with the poet's col-

laboration. Bucke would follow it with a critical study, *Walt Whitman, Man and Poet* (1897), and a work on the poet's mysticism, *Cosmic Consciousness* (1901).

HENRY GEORGE: *Social Problems.* George proposes solutions to a variety of social ills, based on the taxation theories he had outlined in *Progress and Poverty* (1879). He would later apply his theories to the topic of tariff laws in *Practices of Free Trade* (1886).

HENRY JAMES: *Portrait of Places.* A collection of travel essays dealing with Italy, France, England, America, and Canada.

PARKER PILLSBURY (1809–1898): *Acts of the Anti-Slavery Apostles.* The Massachusetts abolitionist and women's suffrage leader presents a history of the New England abolition movement.

ROBERT LOUIS STEVENSON (1850–1894): *The Silverado Squatters.* In 1879 the Scottish novelist had come to America by immigrant ship, crossed the country by train, and married an American, Fanny Van de Grift Osbourne. This is the first of his autobiographical narratives recording his experiences in America—in this case, living in a shanty cabin on Mount St. Helena in California. *The Amateur Emigrant*, about his Atlantic crossing, would follow in 1894, along with *Across the Plains*, recounting his transcontinental railroad journey.

MARK TWAIN (SAMUEL LANGHORNE CLEMENS): *Life on the Mississippi.* Twain combines a memoir of his steamboat pilot days with an account of his return to the Mississippi twenty years later, including facts about the river and some unrelated sketches. Despite its lack of focus and unity, the book is considered one of Twain's major works and one of the finest treatments of Mississippi river life. The composition of the book, which had begun in earnest in 1872, also played a significant role in the creation of *Huckleberry Finn*.

SARAH WINNEMUCCA (1844–1891): *Life Among the Piutes: Their Ways and Claims.* Claimed by some to be the first publication in English by a Native American woman, the work includes tribal history, a personal narrative, and a chronicle of white-Indian relations. Winnemucca had written the book to generate support for uniting her tribe on a single reserve of desirable land; this hope would remain unfulfilled.

Poetry

EMMA LAZARUS: *The New Colossus.* Invited to write a poem for a literary auction to raise funds to build a pedestal for the Statue of Liberty, Lazarus creates her most famous work; the sonnet with the famous lines "Give me your tired, your poor, / Your huddled masses yearning to breathe free," which would be inscribed on the statue's pedestal in 1903.

HENRY WADSWORTH LONGFELLOW: *Michael Angelo*. A fragment of a projected poetic drama, Longfellow's last major poem appears posthumously.

JAMES WHITCOMB RILEY (1849–1916): *The Old Swimmin'-Hole and 'Leven More Poems*. The Indiana poet's first book is a collection of country verse in Hoosier dialect originally published in the *Indianapolis Journal* under the name "Benj. F. Johnson, of Boone." The popular collection contains some of his most celebrated poems, including "When the Frost Is on the Punkin" and the title poem; it also introduces Riley's nostalgic themes, which make him the most famous and financially successful poet of the time.

Publications and Events

The *Ladies' Home Journal*. The monthly magazine for the homemaker begins publication. In 1893, it excluded patent-medicine advertising and campaigned for the enactment of the federal Food and Drug Act. It became the first monthly to reach a circulation of one million.

Life. Founded by John Ames Mitchell (1845–1918), the humorous weekly begins competing with *Puck* and *Judge*. Beginning in 1886, it featured the popular drawings of Charles Dana Gibson (1867–1944), who created his "Gibson Girl" for the publication. It became well known for its book and theater reviews and for its editorial campaign against vivisection.

1884
Drama and Theater

DAVID BELASCO: *May Blossom*. Belasco's initial solo New York success is a Civil War melodrama about a soldier who returns home to find that his best friend has married his fiancée, who thought she had been abandoned by him. The soldier's death in battle resolves the dilemma.

WILLIAM F. GILL (fl. 1882–1897): *Adonis*. This "burlesque nightmare" cleverly spoofs both the Pygmalion-Galatea legend and various elements of contemporary drama. With 603 performances, the play sets the record for the longest run on Broadway at that time.

Fiction

HENRY ADAMS: *Esther*. Published under the pseudonym "Francis Snow Compton," Adams's novel, about the collapse of the relationship between a woman artist and a clergyman due to the incompatibility of their religious beliefs, has been read as the author's commentary on his own marriage.

LOUISA MAY ALCOTT: *Spinning-Wheel Stories*. This collection of interconnected tales, first serialized in *St. Nicholas* (1884–1885), features a wise grandmother providing useful moral lessons.

CHARLES E. CARRYL (1841–1920): *Davy and the Goblin*. Inspired by Lewis Carroll, the New York stockbroker and director of railroad companies produces one of the most admired American children's stories of the century, which helps to earn Carryl the title of "the American Lewis Carroll." It describes a journey into a nonsensical fantasy world. *The Admiral's Caravan* would follow in 1892, about a little girl's encounter with wooden figures who come alive on Christmas Eve.

EDWARD EVERETT HALE: *The Fortunes of Rachel*. Hale's novel depicts an orphaned English girl's social career in America.

JOEL CHANDLER HARRIS: *Mingo and Other Sketches in Black and White*. The first of Harris's collections without the character Uncle Remus treats Georgia life from the perspective of a faithful African American servant in the title story and through the experiences of backwoodsmen and moonshiners in "At Teague Poteet's."

JOHN HAY: *The Bread-Winners*. Responding to the 1877 labor strikes, this anti-union novel depicts members of trade unions as ignorant and lazy and labor leaders as scoundrels. Anonymously published in the *Century* and in book form later in 1884, the novel prompts numerous responses, most notably *The Money-Makers* (1885) by Henry Francis Keenan. The authorship of *The Bread-Winners* would remain unknown until after Hay's death.

HELEN HUNT JACKSON: *Ramona*. Written to shed greater light on the plight of Native Americans, the novel is considered Jackson's masterpiece. The romantic novel concerns a half-Indian, half-Scotch girl who marries an Indian. The two suffer prejudice so grave that it drives her husband mad, and he is eventually killed. After Ramona marries her foster brother, they must move to Mexico after their ranch is seized by Americans. Going through more than three hundred printings, the novel prompts both theatrical and film adaptations.

HENRY JAMES: *Tales of Three Cities*. A collection of three short stories: "The Impressions of a Cousin," "Lady Barberina," and "A New England Winter."

SARAH ORNE JEWETT: *A Country Doctor*. Indirectly commenting on her own relationship with her physician father, Jewett in her first novel tells the story of a New England woman who forgoes marriage to become a doctor.

Helen Hunt Jackson

MARY NOAILLES MURFREE (1850–1922): *In the Tennessee Mountains*. In what has been regarded as the first realistic depiction of Southern mountaineers, Murfree, writing as "Charles Egbert Craddock," publishes her first collection of dialect short stories, which had begun appearing in the *Atlantic Monthly* in 1870. The revelation at the time that these earthy stories are the work of a well-educated Tennessee spinster and invalid creates a sensation. Murfree would also publish in 1884 the first in a series of historical romances, *Where the Battle Was Fought*, set during the Civil War. Subsequent story collections include *The Mystery of Witch-Face Mountain* (1895), *The Young Mountaineers* (1897), and *The Frontiersman* (1904).

FRANK R. STOCKTON: *The Lady or the Tiger? and Other Stories*. Stockton adds to his most famous story additional works, including the first of two sequels, "His Wife's Deceased Sister." The second, "The Discourager of Hesitancy," would appear in the *Century* in 1885.

GEORGE ALFRED TOWNSEND: *The Entailed Hat*. Townsend's novel describes the kidnapping and selling of free blacks in Delaware and Maryland before the Civil War.

MARK TWAIN (SAMUEL LANGHORNE CLEMENS): *Adventures of Huckleberry Finn*. Twain's masterpiece about a boy who befriends an escaped slave and their experiences traveling down the Mississippi River. The pic-aresque work has been lauded by critics for its vivid characters and artistic flourishes. Although praised by many as a classic American novel for its humor, its portraits of American life on the Mississippi, and its rich use of vernacular speech, it has also been widely criticized and often banned for its uncouth backwoods characters and deemed by some as unsuitable for children.

Nonfiction

GEORGE WASHINGTON CABLE: *The Creoles of Louisiana*. Cable's history infuriates Creoles by suggesting that they descend from settlers driven to America for profit who married Indians, Africans, and former inmates of French prisons.

FRANCIS PARKMAN: *Montcalm and Wolfe*. In the last chapter of his monumental history, Parkman treats the climax of French power in America, culminating in General Montcalm's defeat by General Wolfe on the Plains of Abraham in Quebec. It is the best-known work in the series.

Poetry

LOUISE IMOGEN GUINEY (1861–1920): *Songs at the Start*. This first collection of verses modeled on English ballads shows the Boston poet's characteristic reliance on traditional metrical forms. A critical and popular success, it would be followed by *Goose-Quill Papers* (1885), an essay collection, and a second verse collection, *The White Sail, and Other Poems* (1887).

SIDNEY LANIER: *Poems*. An expanded edition of Lanier's poetry that includes two of his greatest pieces, "The Symphony" and "The Song of the Chattahoochee."

ALBERY ALLSON WHITMAN: *The Rape of Florida*. Written in Spenserian stanzas, Whitman's narrative poem tells the story of two Seminole chiefs and betrayal by whites. It would be reprinted as *Twasinta's Seminoles* in 1885.

Publications and Events

The American Historical Association. Founded in Saratoga, New York, the association relocated to Washington, D.C., in 1889 and became an important scholarly organization, promoting the study of American history. Its organ, the *American Historical Review*, began in 1895.

The Grolier Club. Established in New York City for the study and promotion of "the arts pertaining to the production of books," the Grolier Club would play a significant role in book preservation and scholarship, issuing a number of books and catalogs documenting American bookmaking and publishing.

1885

Drama and Theater

BRONSON HOWARD: *One of Our Girls.* Howard's play contrasts the openness of an American heiress with the stultifying proprieties of the French.

Fiction

LOUISA MAY ALCOTT: *Lulu's Library.* The first of a three-volume collection of moral, fantasy, and fairy tales for children. The work, which the *Critic* calls "bright, full of fun, and with a great deal of child wisdom," would go through twenty printings and sell more than seventeen thousand copies. A second volume would appear in 1887 and a third in 1889.

GEORGE WASHINGTON CABLE: *Dr. Sevier.* Cable's novel treats antebellum social life in New Orleans from the perspective of a kindly physician and his ambitious protégé.

HENRY HARLAND (1861–1905): *As It Was Written: A Jewish Musician's Story.* Writing as a Jewish immigrant under the pen name "Sidney Luska," Harland publishes the first of his series of novels about Jewish immigrant life. It would be followed by *Mrs. Peixada* (1886), *The Yoke and the Torah* (1887), and *My Uncle Florimond* (1888). Harland was born in New York City but often posed as a Russian-born, European-educated Harvard graduate.

OLIVER WENDELL HOLMES: *A Mortal Antipathy.* The final of Holmes's trio of "medicated novels," character studies in abnormal psychology and heredity, following *Elsie Venner* (1861) and *The Guardian Angel* (1867), concerns a young man who develops an aversion to beautiful young women after being accidentally dropped into a thornbush as an infant by his beautiful young cousin.

WILLIAM DEAN HOWELLS: *The Rise of Silas Lapham.* Howells's novel is a realistic story of an ordinary man's rise to wealth and his family's attempts at joining Boston's elite social circles. Silas loses his affluence but gains morality when he refuses to participate in unethical business practices. The novel is particularly noteworthy for a scene in which Silas embarrasses himself at a dinner party by drinking too much. Although popular in its day, said to be read by one million people in the *Century*, some critics disparaged Howells's relentless realism. Modern critics consider it one of Howells's finest novels and among the best works of American fiction.

THOMAS ALLIBONE JANVIER (1849–1913): *Color Studies.* A collection of stories about Mexico, where Janvier had traveled as a journalist, and about artists in Greenwich Village, taken from earlier submissions to periodicals under the pen name "Ivory Black." Distinguished for its adept characterizations, descriptions, and use of

William Dean Howells

dialect, it is Janvier's first published book, considered his most enduring.

SARAH ORNE JEWETT: *Marsh Island.* Jewett's novel treats the relationship between a rich society painter and a New England farmer's daughter.

HENRY FRANCIS KEENAN (1850–1928): *The Money-Makers.* The most notable response to John Hay's anti-union novel *The Bread-Winners* (1884), the story, published anonymously, attacks capitalists, portraying them as self-serving.

S. WEIR MITCHELL: *In War Time.* Mitchell's first novel depicts the cowardice of a New England doctor during the Civil War. It would be followed by *Roland Blake* (1886), examining combat stress and the neuroses of a possessive woman.

MARY NOAILLES MURFREE: *The Prophet of the Great Smoky Mountains.* This is the first of the author's Tennessee Mountain novels and her best. Written under the pen name "Charles Egbert Craddock," it concerns a heroine in a romantic triangle with a young preacher and a mountaineer.

Literary Criticism and Scholarship

EDMUND CLARENCE STEDMAN: *The Poets of America.* The first critical history of American poetry, Stedman's most important work, remains a penetrating and influential analysis of the genre.

Nonfiction

MATTHEW ARNOLD (1822–1888): *Discourses in America.* The English poet and critic had toured the United States in 1883, delivering the lectures in this collection. Critical of American values, the volume includes an essay on Emerson. Although Arnold considers him neither a great poet, writer, nor philosopher, he ranks Emerson, for his "hopeful, serene, beautiful temper," along with Benjamin Franklin as the "most distinctly and honourably American of your writers." A second essay collection, *Civilization in the United States*, would appear in 1888.

GEORGE WASHINGTON CABLE: *The Silent South.* Having infuriated Creoles with *The Creoles of Louisiana* (1884) by suggesting that they had descended from profit-driven men who had married Indians, Africans, and former inmates of French prisons, Cable next critiques the South in general, arguing for prison reforms, abolition of contract labor, and improved treatment of African Americans. The hostile reaction to this work contributes to his leaving the South for Massachusetts, where he would continue to write on Southern social problems, producing *The Negro Question* (1888) and *The Southern Struggle for Pure Government* (1890).

ULYSSES S. GRANT (1822–1885): *Personal Memoirs.* Written to pay off debts acquired from failed investments and to secure his family's finances, former general and U.S. president Grant completes his memoirs just days before his death. After learning that Grant was intending to write a memoir, Mark Twain had convinced him to allow his firm, Webster and Company, to publish the book. Sold by subscription, the bestseller earns $450,000 for Grant's estate and more than $150,000 for Webster and Company.

HENRY JAMES: *A Little Tour in France.* James's travel essays document his six-week tour of France in 1882 in search of out-of-the-way places, views, and experiences. He also issues in London *Stories Revived*, a collection of fourteen stories in three volumes.

THEODORE ROOSEVELT: *Hunting Trips of a Ranchman.* This is the first of three hunting narratives drawing on Roosevelt's North Dakota ranching experiences. It would be followed by *Ranch Life and the Hunting-Trail* (1888) and *The Wilderness Hunter* (1893). The books' popularity cause Roosevelt to briefly contemplate becoming a full-time writer.

JOSIAH ROYCE (1855–1916): *The Religious Aspect of Philosophy.* The first of the California-born Harvard professor's major treatises develops his Absolutist theory. Royce argues that there is an inherent goodness in all of life and one supreme being in control of that absolute morality.

CHARLES WARREN STODDARD: *The Lepers of Molokai.* Stoddard's book brings the first public attention to the life and work of Father Damien (1840–1889), the Belgian priest working in Hawaii's leper colony.

WOODROW WILSON (1856–1924): *Congressional Government: A Study in American Politics.* Wilson's first book, his doctoral dissertation, analyzes the relationship between the executive and legislative branches. It contains the core of Wilson's political ideas and has been called "one of the truly significant books in the literature of American democracy."

Poetry

JAMES WHITCOMB RILEY: "Little Orphant Annie." One of Riley's most popular poems concerns an orphan girl who tells ghost stories about "gobble-uns" who "gits you ef you Don't Watch Out!"

1886

Drama and Theater

WILLIAM GILLETTE: *Held by the Enemy.* At the time, Gillette's melodrama about a love triangle involving a Union officer, a Southern belle, and a Confederate spy is considered one of the first major dramas depicting the Civil War.

A. C. GUNTER: *Prince Karl.* Written as a serious drama about a penniless prince's scheme to marry a widowed heiress, Gunter's play is turned into a farce by the popular actor Richard Mansfield (1854–1907).

DENMAN THOMPSON (1833–1911): *The Old Homestead.* A popular play about Yankee farming life is based on the Pennsylvania actor and dramatist's earliest play-writing effort, the two-act play *Joshua Whitcomb* (1877). This four-act expansion sustains remarkable success for more than twenty years.

Fiction

LOUISA MAY ALCOTT: *Jo's Boys and How They Turned Out.* The final book of the March family trilogy, preceded by *Little Women* (1868–1869) and *Little Men* (1871), treats the maturation of the Plumfield students. Jo is depicted as a popular writer of "moral pap for the young." It is Alcott's final novel.

AMELIA EDITH BARR: *The Bow of Orange Ribbons.* This popular historical romance set in pre–Revolutionary War New York City is the first in a series of ten novels depicting New York history up to the twentieth century.

H. C. BUNNER (1842–1893): *The Midge.* The best of Bunner's novels is a story of a New York bachelor and his orphan ward. Bunner edited *Puck* from 1878 to 1896.

FRANCES HODGSON BURNETT: *Little Lord Fauntleroy.* The story of Cedric Errol, the young son of an English aristocrat and an American woman, who inherits an

English manor after the death of his father and uncles. The endearing boy charms everyone around him, including his cantankerous grandfather, an earl who disparages Cedric's American mother. The hugely popular book would be staged by Burnett in 1888, and several film versions have been produced.

EDWIN BYNNER (1842–1893): *Agnes Surriage.* The Massachusetts lawyer and author's best-known novel is a historical romance set in eighteenth-century Marblehead.

ROSE TERRY COOKE: *The Sphinx's Children and Other People's.* Some of the Connecticut local colorist's finest stories are collected in this volume, including "Too Late," "Alicedama Sparks," and "Some Account of Thomas Tucker," which Sarah Orne Jewett singles out for particular praise as typifying Cooke's artistry in using regional details to tell universal human stories.

WILLIAM DEAN HOWELLS: *Indian Summer.* Howells considered this novel about a middle-aged man's misdirected love for a widow's young ward as among his best character studies. Mark Twain commends his friend's achievement by declaring, "You are really my only author." The novel has been judged as second only to *The Rise of Silas Lapham* as Howells's greatest achievement as a novelist.

HENRY JAMES: *The Bostonians.* Fulfilling his desire to "write an American story," James's novel, set in Boston, is about the wealthy feminist Olive Chancellor's struggles to win over Verena Tarrant, a young woman with strong oratorical prowess, to the suffragist cause. She eventually loses Verena to marriage and domesticity. Regarded as one of James's important early works, particularly in treating women's issues, the book prompts Mark Twain to write to William Dean Howells that he "would rather be damned to John Bunyan's heaven than read" the novel. James also publishes *The Princess Casamassima.* This novel continues the story of Christina Light from *Roderick Hudson* (1876). She journeys to London, where she gets involved with revolutionaries and an assassination plot. Although an unusual subject for James, the story is narrated, as are many of his mature works, by an observer at a distance from the main action. James regarded the novel as a European companion to his American political novel *The Bostonians.*

SARAH ORNE JEWETT: *A White Heron and Other Stories.* This collection of short stories contains some of Jewett's best work, including the frequently anthologized title story about a young country girl who chooses to secure her bond to nature by choosing not to lead a city ornithologist to the nest of the white heron he is hunting. Another story, "Dulham Ladies," is a humorous story about old women attempting to hide their age under wigs in hopes of improving their social status. Other stories in the collection include "A Marsh Rosemary" and "Farmer Finch."

FRANK R. STOCKTON: *The Casting Away of Mrs. Lecks and Mrs. Aleshire.* Stockton's popular comic novel depicts two New England widows who become shipwrecked on a Pacific island. A sequel, *The Dusantes*, would follow in 1888.

SUI SIN FAR (Edith Eaton, 1865–1914): "A Chinese Feud." Published under the pseudonym "Sui Sin Far," this is believed to be the first short story by a writer of Chinese heritage published in America. Eaton, the daughter of an English father and a Chinese mother, would publish her collected stories, *Mrs. Spring Fragrance*, in 1912.

ELIZABETH STUART PHELPS WARD: *The Madonna of the Tubs.* Ward provides a realistic depiction of the lives of a fishing community in Gloucester, Massachusetts. She would further develop the story in *Jack, the Fisherman* (1887).

CONSTANCE FENIMORE WOOLSON: *East Angels.* Set in a small Florida village, the novel depicts a Northerner who rescues the mistress of a declining plantation from genteel poverty. A popular success, it sells ten thousand copies.

Nonfiction

HENRY WOODFIN GRADY (1850–1889): "The New South." In the celebrated Southern orator's speech to the New England Club in New York City, Grady provides his model of a more democratic and economically diversified South. Grady wins national acclaim by incorporating praise for Abraham Lincoln while taking care not to disgrace the Old South. The address would be published in *The New South and Other Addresses* (1904) and *Complete Orations and Speeches* (1910).

JOHN GILMARY SHEA (1824–1892): *History of the Catholic Church in the U.S.* Called by his biographers "the father of American Catholic history," Shea issues the first installment in his important four-volume history (completed in 1892). Shea, over a forty-year career, would produce more than 240 publications on the Catholic experience in America.

WILL OSBORN STODDARD (1835–1925): *The Lives of the Presidents.* Lincoln's former private secretary issues the first of his ten-volume series (completed in 1889).

Publications and Events

Cosmopolitan. Founded in Rochester, New York, by Joseph N. Hallock, the magazine was relocated to New

York City in 1887 and became one of the most popular periodicals of its day, publishing works by Mark Twain, Henry James, Rudyard Kipling, Arthur Conan Doyle, and many others. In 1965, its new editor, Helen Gurley Brown, shifted its emphasis to fashion and the concerns of single career women.

The *Forum*. A monthly magazine that airs contemporary social concerns begins publication. It absorbed the *Century* in 1930 and merged with *Current History* to become *Current History and Forum* in 1940. It continued publication until 1950.

1887
Drama and Theater

JOSEPH ARTHUR (1848–1906): *The Still Alarm*. Although dismissed by reviewers, Arthur's melodrama is a crowd-pleaser, with a sensational climax in which New York firemen, in a horse-drawn fire engine, rush to a burning building. The Indiana former reporter and foreign correspondent would become one of the era's most successful melodramatists.

DAVID BELASCO AND HENRY C. DE MILLE (c. 1855–1893): *The Wife*. The first of the playwrights' successful collaborations concerns a young woman "on the rebound" who marries a man when she is disappointed by the man she truly loves. De Mille was the father of playwrights William C. De Mille (1878–1955) and Cecil B. De Mille, and grandfather of dancer and choreographer Agnes De Mille (1905–1993).

AUGUSTIN DALY: *The Railroad of Love*. The title refers to the rapid pace of modern courtship, and Daly's comedy, one of his biggest successes, illustrates romantic complications in a high-speed society.

BRONSON HOWARD: *Henrietta*. Howard's comedy-drama treats a son who tries to make his own fortune on Wall Street but threatens his father's financial security. One of Howard's best plays, it continues his interest in American business and material values. It would be regularly revived until the early twentieth century.

STEELE MACKAYE: *Paul Kauver; or, Anarchy*. MacKaye's drama, set during the French Revolution, was inspired by the 1887 trial and execution of anarchists in Chicago.

MARK TWAIN (SAMUEL LANGHORNE CLEMENS) AND WILLIAM DEAN HOWELLS: *Colonel Sellers as Scientist*. The authors collaborate on a sequel to *Colonel Sellers* (1874), the dramatization of *The Gilded Age* (1873). It never plays in New York and is performed only during a single week of one-night stands around the country. Twain would adapt some of its material to produce *The American Claimant* (1892).

Fiction

FRANCIS MARION CRAWFORD: *Saracinesca*. This love story, set amid the Roman upper class in the late nineteenth century, is the first novel in an Italian trilogy, considered Crawford's finest work. The subsequent novels are *Sant' Ilario* (1889) and *Don Orsino* (1892).

HAROLD FREDERIC (1856–1898): *Seth's Brother's Wife*. Frederic's critically acclaimed but unlucrative first novel concerns political corruption and a love triangle in upstate New York. First published in *Scribner's Magazine*, the story is noteworthy for its depiction of country life as dismal and constricting. Frederic was a journalist, editor, and, in 1884, London correspondent for the *New York Times*.

MARY E. WILKINS FREEMAN (1852–1930): *A Humble Romance and Other Stories*. Freeman's first collection of stories for adult readers depicts New England characters constrained by the remnants of Puritanism and a crumbling economy and culture. Representative of her best fiction, it is well received, and although the reviewer William Dean Howells finds the stories sentimental, he says that they are "like the best modern work everywhere in their directness and simplicity." Besides the title work, the volume contains some of Freeman's most admired stories such as "Old Lady Pingree," "Cinnamon Roses," and "An Independent Thinker."

ALICE FRENCH (1850–1934): *Knitters in the Sun*. The first of French's local-color treatments of rural Arkansas, written under the pen name "Octave Thanet." This collection of stories, published in periodicals throughout the 1880s, highlights the author's artistic range, including the fantastical stories "The Ogre of Ha Ha Bay" and "Schopenhauer on Lake Pepin," the dialect tales "Ma' Bowlin'" and "Whitsun Harp, Regulator," and the stories of domestic realism "Mrs. Finlay's Elizabethan Chair" and "Father Quinnailon's Convert." The collection would be followed by *Stories of a Western Town* (1893), *The Missionary Sheriff* (1879), *The Captured Dream* (1899), and *Stories That End Well* (1911).

A. C. GUNTER: *Mr. Barnes of New York*. Gunter's best-known book is this novel about an intrepid adventurer. It sells more than three million copies.

JOEL CHANDLER HARRIS: *Free Joe and Other Georgia Sketches*. A collection of local-color stories that include "Free Joe and the Rest of the World," about a freed slave unable to find a place in society. It is one of Harris's rare believably realistic portraits of race relations.

WILLIAM DEAN HOWELLS: *The Minister's Charge*. In Howells's novel, a minister's excessive praise of a country boy's poetry encourages his literary aspirations, which are dashed. This is the first in a series of novels exploring what Howells calls a doctrine of "complicity," the responsibility one must take for one's actions and the principle that "no one for good or evil, for sorrow or joy, for sickness or health, stood apart from his fellows."

JOSEPH KIRKLAND (1830–1894): *Zury: The Meanest Man in Spring County.* Kirkland, the son of Caroline Stansbury Kirkland, tells the story of a man raised on settlements in rural Illinois who grows simultaneously wealthy and callous until his marriage to a New England schoolteacher makes him become benevolent. Kirkland's first and best novel, it is based on his own settlement observations and praised for its realism. A sequel, *The McVeys*, would appear in 1888.

THOMAS NELSON PAGE (1853–1922): *In Ole Virginia.* Page's first story collection about the antebellum South is said to contain his best work and wins the author wide acclaim. It includes "Marse Chan," a Civil War love story that had been popular when first published in the *Century* in 1884. Page was a Virginia lawyer who produced a string of popular books drawing on Virginia history.

ROWLAND EVANS ROBINSON (1833–1900): *Uncle Lisha's Shop: Life in a Corner of Yankeeland.* This classic in Vermont literature includes local-color depictions of culture in the foothills of the Green Mountains and is considered the prolific writer's best work. Uncle Lisha is a cobbler and the leader of a group of characters who meet at his shop to discuss events, gossip, and tell tales. Robinson was a woodcarver, cartoonist, and writer about Vermont country life.

EDGAR SALTUS (1855–1921): *Mr. Incoul's Misadventure.* Saltus's pessimistic, hedonistic philosophy, expressed in *The Philosophy of Disenchantment* (1885) and *The Anatomy of Negation* (1886), is reflected in the first of his long series of "diabolical" novels. Others include *The Truth About Tritrem Varick* (1888), *The Pace That Kills* (1889), *Madame Sapphira* (1893), and *Enthralled* (1894).

KATE DOUGLAS WIGGIN (1856–1923): *The Birds' Christmas Carol.* Written to earn money for Wiggin's San Francisco Silver Street Kindergarten, one of the first in the United States, the novel is about a child named Carol born on Christmas morning. Carol grows up to be sweet but sickly and dies young but happy after serving a Christmas dinner to her less fortunate neighbors. The popular story, translated into German, Swedish, and Japanese, is said to have sold 750,000 copies.

Literary Criticism and Scholarship

CHARLES F. RICHARDSON (1851–1913): *American Literature, 1607–1885.* The Maine-born teacher, poet, and literary historian issues the first of his pioneering two-volume work (completed in 1889), the first comprehensive American literary history. In his preface, Richardson declares his objectivity and states that the time has come to apply to American writers the same high standards used to measure literature in any age and country.

Nonfiction

BROOKS ADAMS (1848–1927): *The Emancipation of Massachusetts.* The great-grandson of John Adams and brother of Henry Adams offers a sardonic study of the religious prejudices of the Puritans.

NELLIE BLY (1867–1922): *Ten Days in a Mad House.* The journalist (whose real name was Elizabeth Cochrane Seaman) gains her initial notoriety by feigning insanity and having herself committed to New York's Blackwell Island asylum to report firsthand on conditions there.

JOHN DEWEY (1859–1952): *Psychology.* The first of the philosopher and educational reformer's books shows him moving toward experimentalism, emphasizing empirical methods in determining the validity of ideas. The book would be revised twice, in 1889 and 1891, to reflect Dewey's evolving ideas.

GEORGE WILBUR PECK: *How Private Geo. W. Peck Put Down the Rebellion.* Peck treats his Civil War experiences in a series of humorous sketches.

Poetry

PALMER COX (1840–1924): *The Brownies: Their Book.* The first in the popular thirteen-book series of illustrated verse narratives about fairies in an American setting by the Canadian-born author and illustrator who moved to the United States in 1876. Cox's books would sell more than one million copies during his lifetime, and the stage play *Palmer Cox's Brownies* (1895) would run for nearly five years.

EMMA LAZARUS: *By the Waters of Babylon.* Lazarus's poetic sequence is her first and last attempt at free verse. It presents a history of the Jewish diaspora.

LIZETTE WOODWORTH REESE (1856–1935): *A Branch of May.* The first collection by the Baltimore schoolteacher and poet features a spare, lyrical approach that avoids the sentimental inflation of much of the poetry of the period. It would be followed by *A Handful of Lavender* (1891) and *A Quiet Road* (1896).

Publications and Events

The Newberry Library. Founded in Chicago through the estate of banker Walter Loomis Newberry (1804–1868), the library would become an important repository of rare books and manuscripts.

Scribner's Magazine. The magazine founded by Charles Scribner (1854–1930) begins competition with the *Century* and *Harper's.* Its contributors included Henry James, George Washington Cable, Edith Wharton, and Hart Crane, and it was the first important literary magazine to publish the works of Ernest Hemingway and Thomas Wolfe. It ceased publication in 1939.

1888

Drama and Theater

AUGUSTIN DALY: *The Lottery of Love.* Daly's adaptation of a French play takes aim at women's rights advocates in its depiction of a matriarch who makes life miserable for all concerned.

JAMES A. HERNE: *Drifting Apart.* Herne's naturalistic play, depicting the impact of heredity and the environment on character, concerns an alcoholic sailor whose nightmare causes him to give up drinking. The play fails with audiences but wins him attention and praise from literary figures such as Hamlin Garland and William Dean Howells, who encourage Herne to make more efforts in the vein of realism.

BRONSON HOWARD: *Shenandoah.* Howard's finest and most famous drama chronicles the lives of two couples through the whole of the Civil War. The popular play would be revived in 1889 and published in 1897.

Fiction

LOUISA MAY ALCOTT: *A Garland for Girls.* Intended as a companion work to *Spinning-Wheel Stories* (1884), this collection of stories, each named for a flower, illustrates positive moral virtues. Included is a reproof of fashionable values held by young ladies called "Daisy Millers," a jab at Henry James's popular story; James had criticized Alcott's *Moods and Eight Cousins.*

AMELIA EDITH BARR: *Remember the Alamo.* Barr's popular historical romance set during the Texas siege contributes to the heroic myth surrounding the Texas Revolution and the defense of the Alamo. It mixes the historical record with jingoistic sentiment.

EDWARD BELLAMY: *Looking Backward: 2000–1887.* Bellamy's best-selling utopian fantasy novel depicts the character Julian West falling asleep during the turbulence of the nineteenth century and waking at the millennium to find America changed by economic, cultural, and social reforms. The book is acclaimed by prominent figures including John Dewey and Charles Austin Beard.

FRANCES HODGSON BURNETT: *Sara Crewe.* This is the first version of one of Burnett's most popular children's stories about the indignities a young girl suffers when her father dies penniless. It would be reworked in 1902 as the play *A Little Princess* and rewritten as a novel with the same name in 1905.

SYLVANUS COBB JR. (1821–1887): *The Gunmaker of Moscow.* The tirelessly prolific storyteller for the *New York Ledger* ends his career with this best-selling novel about a young Russian commoner beloved by a duchess and advanced, after many adventures, to the nobility by Peter the Great.

MARGARET DELAND (1857–1945): *John Ward, Preacher.* The Pennsylvania writer's first novel treats the marital conflicts between a Calvinist minister and his freethinking wife. It would be followed by two character studies, *Sidney* (1890) and *Philip and His Wife* (1894).

EDWARD EGGLESTON: *The Graysons.* Eggleston's historical romance set on the Illinois frontier adapts the story of Abraham Lincoln's successful defense of "Duff" Armstrong in a murder trial of the 1840s.

WILLIAM DEAN HOWELLS: *Annie Kilburn.* Howells's novel tells of a New England woman's haphazard attempts to save the citizens of her hometown from the negative social and economic effects of industrialism. Eventually she realizes that what the people truly need is justice. The story had been popular when first published in *Harper's Magazine,* and, concerning the book, Edward Everett Hale notes, "It is a pulpit indeed — to write such a book for a million readers." Howells also publishes *April Hopes,* treating the romantic complications between a young woman and her fiancé. It marks Howells's return to the comedy of manners after his focus on socially realistic problem novels.

HENRY JAMES: *The Aspern Papers.* First published in the *Atlantic Monthly,* this novella is reportedly based on a story James heard about Lord Byron's mistress Claire Clairmont. It follows an American editor's obsessive attempts to obtain the papers of the deceased Romantic poet Jeffrey Aspern from the poet's mistress by renting a room in her Venice home. James also publishes *The Reverberator,* a short novel about the scandal caused by a young woman's indiscreet comments to an American newspaper reporter. It is derived from an actual incident involving the daughter of Union general George McClellan.

SARAH ORNE JEWETT: *The King of Folly Island and Other People.* Jewett's collection treats the bleak New England landscape and the quiet desperation of its inhabitants. The title story, about an isolated, antisocial father and his dying daughter who live on a tiny Maine island, is one of the bleakest of Jewett's stories and one of her closet approximations of literary naturalism.

GRACE ELIZABETH KING (1851–1931): *Monsieur Motte.* King, one of the first members of New Orleans Creole

Henry James

society to write about her milieu, publishes her first book, about a young Creole orphan who learns that her benefactor is a former slave. It would be followed by two collections of short fiction — *Tales of a Time and a Place* (1892) and *Balcony Stories* (1893) — mainly concerned with the challenges Southern women faced in the aftermath of the Civil War.

AMELIE RIVES (1863–1945): *The Quick or the Dead?* The Virginia-born novelist, poet, and playwright's first novel is a psychological study of a woman conflicted over her love for her dead husband and for her cousin, who resembles him. A sequel, *Barbara Dering*, would appear in 1892. She also published a romantic novel, *Virginia of Virginia*.

E.D.E.N. SOUTHWORTH: *The Hidden Hand*. Southworth's most popular serialized novel, which had first appeared in 1859, is finally published in book form. It features an intriguing woman protagonist who grows up as a "street boy" in a New York City slum; the work is noteworthy for its critique of conventional gender definitions. The novel proves so popular that it prompts at least forty stage versions.

Literary Criticism and Scholarship

HENRY JAMES: "The Art of Fiction." James's most important artistic pronouncement has been called the "manifesto of fictional realism." It responds to Sir Walter

Besant's assertions, in "Fiction as One of the Fine Arts," that novel writing can be taught and is less an art than a craft and that novels should have a clear moral purpose. James counters that novels must compete with reality in their complexity and should end as unhappily as life does and that a novelist is no less concerned with the pursuit of truth than any other artist. Included is James's famous advice for the prospective novelist: "Try to be one of the people on whom nothing is lost!" The essay is included in the critical collection *Partial Portraits*, which contains other important essays such as "The Life of Emerson," "Daniel Deronda: A Conversation," and "Anthony Trollope."

AGNES REPPLIER (1858–1950): *Books and Men*. The first of the author's many collections of literary essays shows her characteristic genteel, traditional views and preference for the British and European literary tradition. Subsequent collections include *Points of View* (1891), *Essays in Miniature* (1892), and *Essays in Idleness* (1893). Repplier would become known as one of the "Big Four" American women writers around the turn of the century, along with Edith Wharton, Amy Lowell, and Willa Cather.

EDMUND CLARENCE STEDMAN: *A Library of American Literature from the Earliest Settlement to the Present Time.* This critically acclaimed and popular eleven-volume American literary history not only adds to the canon of literature but expands the accepted genres to include travel and political writings, sermons, and other typical early American genres. Stedman had edited the work with Ellen M. Hutchinson, and it is issued by Mark Twain's publishing firm, Charles L. Webster and Company. Although a critical and popular success, the series proves a commercial disaster, contributing to the company's bankruptcy and Twain's scramble to pay off his debtors.

Nonfiction

MATTHEW ARNOLD: *Civilization in the United States.* Arnold's second collection of essays on America contains his provocative statement "Who now reads an American book?" His critique of American culture would trouble American writers and intellectuals for two generations.

JAMES BRYCE (1838–1922): *The American Commonwealth*. The English historian and diplomat publishes his assessment of American government and character in what is regarded, alongside Tocqueville's *Democracy in America*, as a classic analysis. Organized into six segments, the work assesses the federal government, state government, political parties, public opinion, democracy's strengths and weaknesses, and society and culture's influence on the country. The *Atlantic Monthly* notes that "Mr. Bryce's book is of the utmost value to American students of American civilization." A revised edition would appear in 1910.

RUSSELL HERMAN CONWELL (1843–1925): "Acres of Diamonds." Conwell, the founder of Temple University, delivered this inspirational lecture more than six thousand times. It argues that wealth can be attained by anyone and that riches should be sought "in your own backyard."

Poetry

HERMAN MELVILLE: *John Marr and Other Sailors with Some Sea-Pieces.* Melville's collection of sea poems and prose sketches features a section of monologues by mariners, two longer poems concerning tragedies at sea—"The Haglets" and "The Aeolian Harp," and shorter sea lyrics. Privately printed in a limited edition of twenty-five copies, it is distributed to Melville's friends and relatives.

IRWIN RUSSELL (1853–1879): *Poems by Irwin Russell.* Joel Chandler Harris compiled and edited this collection of the Mississippi poet's black dialect verses. An expanded edition, *Christmas-Night in the Quarters,* would appear in 1917. Russell became a lawyer at the age of nineteen and based his verses on life and characters encountered on frequent trips to Texas and New Orleans.

ERNEST LAWRENCE THAYER (1863–1940): "Casey at the Bat." The most famous poem ever written about baseball first appears in the *San Francisco Examiner* on June 3 under the pseudonym "Phin." It describes how the mighty slugger of the Mudville Nine strikes out to lose a game. The actor De Wolf Hopper (1858–1935) would help make the poem famous by reciting it throughout his career during his performances and as part of his curtain calls.

WALT WHITMAN: *November Boughs.* A collection of poetry, essays, and criticism, much of which had been previously published in the *New York Herald.* Most significant is the preface, "A Backward Glance o'er Travel'd Roads," an elucidation of his poetic purpose, which would become the preface to the 1889 edition of *Leaves of Grass.*

Publications and Events

Collier's. The weekly magazine founded by Peter F. Collier begins operation as a vehicle for serialized books. It became a leading liberal and muckracking publication during the first two decades of the twentieth century but folded in 1957.

The Players. The New York City club for actors, writers, painters, sculptors, and musicians is founded by the actor Edwin Booth (1833–1893), who provides his home as a meeting place and serves as the club's president until his death.

1889
Drama and Theater

CHARLES BARNARD (c. 1838–1920): *The County Fair.* In this comedy, a woman saves her New England farm by winning a horse race at a county fair. The play stars the era's leading female impersonator, Neil Burgess (1846–1910). Barnard collaborated with Henry C. De Mille on the play *The Main Line* (1886).

DAVID BELASCO AND HENRY C. DE MILLE: *The Charity Ball.* The play treats the revelation to John Van Buren that his brother has seduced the woman that John has sworn to protect. His confrontation with his brother is regarded, at the time, as one of the most powerful scenes in drama.

AUGUSTUS THOMAS (1857–1934): *The Burglar.* Thomas's first produced play is an adaptation of Frances Hodgson Burnett's novel *Edith's Burglar* (1887). Thomas would go on to write more than sixty plays depicting various aspects of American life and history.

Fiction

ARLO BATES (1850–1918): *The Philistines.* Bates's novel depicts the crippling effects of Boston society on a painter who makes a fashionable marriage.

MARY CATHERWOOD (1847–1902): *The Romance of Dollard.* The first in a series of popular historical romances set in French Canada and the Midwest concerns a noblewoman killed in an Indian attack. It includes a preface by historian Francis Parkman, attesting to the book's authenticity. It would be followed by *The Story of Tonty* (1890), *The Lady of Fort St. John* (1891), *Old Kaskaskia* (1893), *The Spirit of an Illinois Town* (1897), *Spanish Peggy* (1899), and *Lazarre* (1901).

ARTHUR SHERBURNE HARDY (1847–1930): *Passe Rose.* Hardy's best-known novel is a historical romance about a dancing girl at the court of Charlemagne. Hardy was a professor of civil engineering who served as U.S. minister to Persia, Greece, Serbia, and Spain.

LAFCADIO HEARN (1850–1904): *Chita: A Memory of Last Island.* Hearn's novel dramatically describes a tidal wave that obliterates Last Island in the Gulf of Mexico. It had been first published in *Harper's Magazine,* where it attained phenomenal popularity. Hearn, born in the Ionian Islands and educated in France and England, had immigrated to the United States in 1869. His first books — *One of Cleopatra's Nights* (1882) and *Stray Leaves from Strange*

Literature (1884) — were story collections with an emphasis on the fantastic and exotic.

HENRY JAMES: *A London Life.* A collection of four short stories: the title work, "The Patagonia," "The Liar," and "Mrs Temperly."

MARK TWAIN (SAMUEL LANGHORNE CLEMENS): *A Connecticut Yankee in King Arthur's Court.* Twain's fanciful satire of Arthurian legend presents a Yankee manufacturer who awakes in Camelot in the year A.D. 528 after a blow to the head. He attempts to bring progress to Arthurian society by employing nineteenth-century science and technology. Although winning little acclaim in its day and scorned by English reviewers as irreverent, the novel would grow in stature over time.

CONSTANCE FENIMORE WOOLSON: *Jupiter Lights.* Woolson's novel contrasts characteristics of the North and the South in a conflict between sisters-in-law.

Nonfiction

HENRY ADAMS: *History of the United States of America During the Administrations of Thomas Jefferson and James Madison.* Adams's much praised nine-volume history (completed in 1891) would be for years considered the finest description of Jefferson's presidency. Distinguished for its research in primary sources and extensive new information and details, the book has been called by modern scholar Paul Nagel "the finest historical writing ever done by an American."

ANDREW CARNEGIE (1835–1919): *The Gospel of Wealth and Other Timely Essays.* The industrialist Carnegie's collection of essays sets forth his philosophy that the rich have a responsibility to use their affluence for "the improvement of mankind." The idea had been first set down in his article "Wealth," published in the *North American Review.* He would live out the theory by creating endowed institutions, including the Carnegie Endowment for International Peace, the Carnegie Institute at Pittsburgh, and numerous libraries throughout the nation.

LUCY LARCOM (1824–1893): *A New England Girlhood.* The Massachusetts abolitionist and poet provides an autobiographical account of the Lowell textile mills and child labor practices.

THEODORE ROOSEVELT: *The Winning of the West.* Roosevelt's historical account of the post-Revolutionary westward expansion of the United States, in four volumes (completed in 1896), asserts the importance of the westward movement to American identity. Based on primary sources, the works show the influence of historian Francis Parkman.

FRANCIS HOPKINSON SMITH (1838–1915): *A White Umbrella in Mexico.* A collection of colorful stories and

Andrew Carnegie

drawings from the architect, author, and illustrator's travels to Mexico. The *Atlantic Monthly* calls the book "a gay little masterpiece."

Poetry

EUGENE FIELD (1850–1895): *A Little Book of Western Verse.* A collection of the newspaper columnist and poet's best poetry, which, according to the *Critic*, contains "exquisite lullabies, pathetic child-verses, quaint and curious renderings of Horace, and several Western dialect rhymes which abound in wit and hilarity." The book boosts Field's national reputation and would be followed in 1892 by *Second Book of Verse.*

WALT WHITMAN: *Leaves of Grass,* eighth edition. This special pocket-size edition includes the poems of *November Boughs* (1888) and its prose preface, "A Backward Glance o'er Travel'd Roads," in which the poet describes his intention: "to articulate . . . uncompromisingly my own physical, emotional, moral, intellectual, and aesthetic Personality, in the midst of . . . current America."

Publications and Events

The *Business Woman's Journal.* The first American publication to serve working women is launched by Mary Seymour Foot (1846–1893).

Munsey's Weekly. Founded by Frank A. Munsey (1854–1925), this New York weekly devoted to "pictures and art and Good Cheer and human interest" begins publication. It featured serialized fiction and general-interest articles, becoming a monthly in 1891 until its demise in 1929.

1890
Drama and Theater

JOSEPH ARTHUR: *Blue Jeans.* Arthur's play, in which the hero and heroine are lured into a sawmill by the villain, features one of the most sensational and imitated scenes in American melodrama: the unconscious hero on a conveyor belt, slowly moving toward a huge spinning buzz saw.

DAVID BELASCO AND HENRY C. DE MILLE: *Men and Women.* The writing team's fourth and final collaboration uses a celebrated contemporary banking scandal as the backdrop for this melodrama, concerning a theft of bonds that divides four pairs of lovers.

CLYDE FITCH (1865–1909): *Beau Brummell.* The prolific playwright's first major work is this Regency-era drama that becomes a star vehicle for actor Richard Mansfield (1854–1907); he would perform the title role for the rest of his life.

EDWARD HARRIGAN: *Reilly and the Four Hundred.* One of Harrigan's last dramatic successes concerns the immigrant pawnbroker Reilly, whose son's rise into respectable society is threatened by a sausage tycoon who has made it into the "400" and wishes to conceal a dark secret from his past, which is known to Reilly.

JAMES A. HERNE: *Margaret Fleming.* Herne's treatment of adultery is considered a breakthrough in realism for the American stage, the first American "problem play" to show the influence of Henrik Ibsen. No New York producer, however, takes on the play because of its sexual frankness and absence of a happy ending. After Herne revises it, giving it a more positive, upbeat ending, the play is performed frequently.

CHARLES HALE HOYT (1860–1900): *A Texas Steer.* The popular comic dramatist continues his reliance on contemporary social problems begun in *A Midnight Bell* (1889). A farce about political corruption, the play concerns a Texas rancher who buys his way into Congress. Largely ignored at the time, the play proves to be a harbinger of things to come on the American stage in dealing with social issues.

DAVID D. LLOYD (1851–1889) AND SYDNEY ROSENFELD (1855–1931): *The Senator.* After Lloyd dies, Rosenfeld completes this popular comedy, which features one of the era's great comic performances by actor W. H. Crane (1845–1928) as Senator Hannibal Rivers. Rosenfeld was a prolific adapter of foreign plays, often accused of plagiarism, who had nearly fifty plays reach Broadway during his career.

Fiction

KATE CHOPIN (1851–1904): *At Fault.* The first book by the St. Louis native who married a Louisiana cotton trader and would write about Cajun and Creole life is chiefly of interest for anticipating her later themes. The novel concerns a widow who rejects a prospective second husband when she learns that he has divorced his first wife because of her alcoholism. Chopin's portrait of a female alcoholic is daring, as is the book's ambiguous position regarding divorce.

FRANCIS MARION CRAWFORD: *A Cigarette-Maker's Romance.* Crawford's novel describes an impoverished Russian count's love for a working-class Polish girl.

HAROLD FREDERIC: *In the Valley.* This novel is a realistic depiction of the Battle of Oriskany during the American Revolution in 1777. Frederic also publishes *The Lawton Girl*, about a young woman's tarnished reputation in a small New York town.

LAFCADIO HEARN: *Youma.* The last work published before Hearn's move to Japan is a novella based on the actual slave revolt of 1848 in Martinique.

WILLIAM DEAN HOWELLS: *A Hazard of New Fortunes.* Inspired by Tolstoy's *War and Peace*, Howells attempts his largest social canvas in this novel set in New York City, about a recently wealthy farmer who acquires a magazine. It is generally considered among Howells's most important novels. Howells also publishes *The Shadow of a Dream*, an experimental novel that offers a pre-Freudian exploration of the impact of dreams on three characters.

HENRY JAMES: *The Tragic Muse.* James's novel studies the conflict between a young Englishman's desire to become a portrait painter and his family's political ambitions for him.

SARAH ORNE JEWETT: *Strangers and Wayfarers.* Jewett's collection is weakened by her unsuccessful attempt to reproduce black American and Irish dialects. Stories include "A Winter Courtship," "The Mistress of Sydenham Plantation," and "The Town Poor." She also publishes *Tales of New England*, a collection of stories Jewett prized from her previous collections.

AMELIA ETTA HALL JOHNSON (1858–1922): *Clarence and Corinne; or, God's Way.* The second novel published in book form by an African American woman is the first Sunday school book written by a black author.

ALBION W. TOURGÉE: *Pactolus Prime.* This novel treats the theme of miscegenation as a black mother brings up her light-complexioned child as white.

BIRTHS AND DEATHS, 1890–1899

Births

1890 Frederick Lewis Allen (d. 1954), historian and editor
Marc Connelly (d. 1980), playwright
Allan Nevins (d. 1971), historian and editor
Katherine Anne Porter (d. 1980), short story writer and novelist
Conrad Richter (d. 1968), novelist

1891 Esther Forbes (d. 1967), novelist and historian
Henry Miller (d. 1980), novelist

1892 Pearl S. Buck (d. 1973), novelist
Robert P. Tristram Coffin (d. 1955), poet
Frederick Faust (Max Brand, d. 1944), western novelist
Archibald MacLeish (d. 1982), poet
Elmer Rice (d. 1967), playwright and novelist

1893 S. N. Behrman (d. 1973), playwright
Maxwell Bodenheim (d. 1954), poet, playwright, and novelist
J. P. Marquand (d. 1960), novelist
Dorothy Parker (d. 1967), short story writer, poet, and dramatist

1894 E. E. Cummings (d. 1962), poet
Harold L. Davis (d. 1960), novelist
Mark Van Doren (d. 1972), poet, novelist, and critic
Paul Green (d. 1981), playwright and novelist
Dashiell Hammett (d. 1961), mystery writer
Ben Hecht (d. 1964), novelist, playwright, and journalist

1895 Michael Arlen (d. 1956), novelist and short story writer
Robert Hillyer (d. 1961), poet and critic
Lewis Mumford (d. 1990), author, historian, and social critic
Edmund Wilson (d. 1972), author and critic

1896 Louis Bromfield (d. 1956), novelist
John Dos Passos (d. 1970), novelist
F. Scott Fitzgerald (d. 1940), novelist
Marjorie Kinnan Rawlings (d. 1953), novelist
Robert Sherwood (d. 1955), playwright

1897 Louise Bogan (d. 1970), poet and critic
Bernard De Voto (d. 1955), historian and novelist
William Faulkner (d. 1962), novelist
Thornton Wilder (d. 1975), playwright and novelist

1898 Stephen Vincent Benét (d. 1943), poet and short story writer

Thomas Boyd (d. 1935), novelist
Horace Gregory (d. 1982), poet
Melvin B. Tolson (d. 1966), poet

1899 Louis Adamic (d. 1951), novelist and journalist
Léonie Adams (d. 1988), poet
Hart Crane (d. 1932), poet
Ernest Hemingway (d. 1961), novelist
Allen Tate (d. 1979), poet and critic

Deaths

1890 George Henry Boker (b. 1823), playwright and poet
Dion Boucicault (b. 1820), playwright
Oliver Bell Bunce (b. 1828), playwright
Benjamin Penhallow Shillaber (b. 1814), humorist and editor

1891 George Bancroft (b. 1800), historian and diplomat
James Russell Lowell (b. 1819), essayist, poet, editor, and educator
Herman Melville (b. 1819), novelist

1892 George William Curtis (b. 1824), author and orator
Walt Whitman (b. 1819), poet
John Greenleaf Whittier (b. 1807), poet

1893 Francis Parkman (b. 1823), historian

1894 William Davis Gallagher (b. 1808), poet
Oliver Wendell Holmes (b. 1809), poet, novelist, and physician
Joseph Kirkland (b. 1830), novelist
Steele MacKaye (b. 1842), playwright
Constance Fenimore Woolson (b. 1840), novelist

1895 Hjalmar Hjorth Boyesen (b. 1848), novelist
William Starbuck Mayo (b. 1811), novelist
Samuel Francis Smith (b. 1808), poet
William Henry Thomes (b. 1824), novelist

1896 H. C. Bunner (b. 1855), short story writer and editor
Harriet Beecher Stowe (b. 1811), novelist

1897 William Taylor Adams (b. 1822), novelist

1898 Edward Bellamy (b. 1850), novelist
Harold Frederic (b. 1856), novelist

1899 Horatio Alger (b. 1832), novelist and short story writer
Augustin Daly (b. 1838), playwright and producer
E.D.E.N. Southworth (b. 1819), novelist

Nonfiction

NELLIE BLY: *Nellie Bly's Book: Around the World in Seventy-Two Days.* This collection presents newspaper dispatches from Bly's around-the-world race, which she had undertaken to break the "record" of Phileas Fogg, the fictional hero of Jules Verne's *Around the World in Eighty Days* (1873). Bly's progress had been followed avidly by an international audience who read of it in newspaper accounts.

GEORGE WASHINGTON CABLE: *The Negro Question.* In this essay collection, Cable challenges prevailing views by advocating equal access to education for blacks and rejecting the myth of black mental inferiority.

WILLIAM GILPIN: *The Cosmopolitan Railway.* Gilpin calls for the creation of an international rail link between North America and Asia by way of the Bering Strait.

JOHN HAY AND JOHN G. NICOLAY (1832–1901): *Abraham Lincoln: A History.* Lincoln's private secretaries had labored for fifteen years to produce this massive ten-volume political and administrative history of the Lincoln presidency. It covers public acts but reveals little about the president's private life. It had been serialized by the *Century* magazine from 1886 to 1890; the pair were paid an unprecedented $50,000 for serial rights.

WILLIAM DEAN HOWELLS: *A Boy's Town.* This is the first volume (of three) providing an autobiographical account of the writer's life up to his departure for Italy in 1861. It would be followed by *My Year in a Log Cabin* (1893) and *My Literary Passions* (1895).

WILLIAM JAMES (1842–1910): *The Principles of Psychology.* The groundbreaking summary of contemporary views in psychology by the Harvard physiologist and brother of Henry James helps establish the field as a science. The work is immediately adopted as a college textbook. James's chapter "The Stream of Thought" is considered an influence in the eventual development of the stream of consciousness, the literary technique employing a nonlinear, fluid conception of thought and consciousness.

ALFRED THAYER MAHAN (1840–1914): *The Influence of Sea Power Upon History, 1660–1783.* Mahan's theory of naval power, developed in lectures at the Naval War College and presented in this study and its continuation, *The Influence of Sea Power upon the French Revolution and Empire, 1793–1812* (1892), is credited with the growth of the American navy, the maintenance of Britain's naval superiority, and Germany's drive to match England's superiority.

JACOB RIIS (1849–1914): *How the Other Half Lives.* The Danish-born journalist and reformer issues his first important report on slum conditions. It would be followed by other influential studies—*The Children of the Poor* (1892), *Out of Mulberry Street* (1898), *The Battle with the Slum* (1902), and *Children of the Tenements* (1903). All would help raise awareness and prompt reforms.

OCTAVIA V. ROGERS (1824–1890): *The House of Bondage; or, Charlotte Brooks and Other Slaves.* Rogers collects an important volume of slave narratives based on interviews.

SIR HENRY M. STANLEY: *In Darkest Africa.* Stanley provides an account of his last great African adventure, the rescue of Emin Pasha from the followers of the Mahdi in southern Sudan. Stanley elevates what had been, by all objective accounts, a fiasco into a great triumph. The popularity of Stanley's journalistic account prompts Oscar Wilde to comment that "The difference between journalism and literature is, that journalism is unreadable and literature is unread."

Poetry

EMILY DICKINSON (1830–1886): *Poems.* Following Dickinson's death in 1886, nearly two thousand poems had been discovered among her effects. Mabel Loomis Todd (1856–1932) and Thomas Wentworth Higginson selected and edited some poems for publication, adding titles, regularizing the rhymes and meter, and using conventional punctuation. This collection of 115 poems is

Emily Dickinson

the first of three volumes edited by the duo and contains famous works (identified here by their first lines, since Dickinson did not title the poems) such as "I taste a liquor never brewed," "Much Madness is divinest Sense," and "Because I could not stop for Death." *Poems, Second Series* would appear in 1891 and *Poems, Third Series* in 1896. A complete scholarly edition would not be published until 1955.

GEORGE EDWARD WOODBERRY (1855–1930): *North Shore Watch and Other Poems.* The Massachusetts critic, professor, and biographer's first poetry collection applies his concept of Ideality, an insistence that literature should celebrate beauty, sublimity, and the ideal, while ignoring historical reality.

Publications and Events

The *Literary Digest.* The weekly current events magazine, a forerunner of *Time* and *Newsweek*, begins publication. It reached a circulation of nearly two million during the 1920s and continued until 1938, when it was purchased by *Time.*

The *Smart Set.* Founded this year by William D'Alton Mann to chronicle New York society. In 1914, H. L. Mencken and George Jean Nathan became its editors. They helped turn it into a sophisticated literary and cultural magazine that published virtually every important American writer until it ceased publication in 1930.

1891

Drama and Theater

J. CHEEVER GOODWIN: *Wang.* One of the biggest hits of the era is this musical depicting the title character, the conniving regent of Siam, who arranges both a marriage for the prince and himself.

CHARLES HALE HOYT: *A Trip to Chinatown.* Hoyt's biggest stage success is this musical farce, which, despite its San Francisco setting, includes two of the most famous songs about New York City: "The Bowery" and "East Side, West Side." The play would hold the Broadway performance record for a musical until 1919 and is believed to be the longest-running American play of the nineteenth century.

HENRY JAMES: *The American.* James's dramatization of his 1877 novel tours successfully in England, with seventy performances in London.

HARRY B. SMITH (1860–1936) AND REGINALD DE KOVEN (1859–1920): *Robin Hood.* Generally regarded as the first great masterwork of the American musical stage, Smith and De Koven's comic opera is based on the Robin Hood story and would be regularly performed for the next fifty years. In the role of Alan-a-Dale, actress Jessie Bartlett Davis sings the popular song "Oh, Promise Me" in two thousand performances of the play's initial run. Smith, regarded as the most prolific librettist in the history of the American theater, is the author of more than three hundred show scores. De Koven's later scores included *The Knickerbockers* (1892), *Rob Roy* (1894), and *The Highwayman* (1897).

AUGUSTUS THOMAS: *Alabama.* The play depicts an unreconstructed Confederate still at war twenty-five years after the Civil War. Highlighting the continuing sectional differences between North and South, the play is significant for daring to take on relevant social issues. It would remain popular well into the twentieth century.

Fiction

JAMES LANE ALLEN (1849–1925): *Flute and Violins.* The writer's first story collection depicting his native Kentucky. Additional sketches would be collected in *The Blue-Grass Region of Kentucky* (1892).

AMBROSE BIERCE: *Tales of Soldiers and Civilians.* Bierce's first story collection includes realistic and psychologically intense tales such as "A Horse in the Sky," "Chickamauga," "The Middle Toe of the Right Foot," and his most anthologized story, "An Occurrence at Owl

Creek Bridge." In 1898, the collection would be retitled *In the Midst of Life.*

H. C. BUNNER: *"Short Sixes": Stories to Be Read While the Candle Burns.* The first collection of the so-called master of the well-made short story whose specialty was brief, suspenseful tales of incident. Bunner is regarded by some as one of the most important American short story writers in the latter half of the nineteenth century.

S. ALICE CALLAHAN (1868–1894): *Wynema, a Child of the Forest.* Thought to be one of the earliest novels by a Native American, Callahan's only book focuses on the development of a Creek woman, with insights into Creek culture, arguments over women's rights, and reflections on the massacre at Wounded Knee in 1890. Callahan was born in Texas and was a teacher in Oklahoma, and *Wynema* is the first published novel written there.

ROSE TERRY COOKE: *Huckleberries Gathered from New England Hills.* Cooke's final collection of regional stories includes "Clary's Trial," "Odd Miss Todd," and "How Celia Changed Her Mind."

RICHARD HARDING DAVIS (1864–1916): *Gallegher and Other Stories.* The leading reporter for the *New York Sun* publishes this collection of stories about an intrepid newspaper copyboy with a talent for crime detection, which helps make Davis one of the most popular authors in America during the decade. Davis was the son of writer Rebecca H. Davis.

IGNATIUS DONNELLY (1831–1901): *Caesar's Column: A Study of the Twentieth Century.* The Minnesota politician and liberal reformer and future populist presidential candidate provides an anti-Semitic vision of what life would be like in New York City in 1988. Airships, magnetic lights, and instant communication have been invented, and the working class is controlled by an oligarchy of Jews, who through Darwinian selection have developed the cunning and deceit necessary to dominate the city.

MARY ELEANOR WILKINS FREEMAN: *A New England Nun, and Other Stories.* Freeman's story collection is considered her masterpiece, one of the major works of local-color realism. It includes "A Gala Dress," "Sister Liddy," and the title story, about a New England woman who waits fourteen years for her fiancé to return with a fortune to marry her, only to reject him so as not to disturb the domestic routine she has created.

HAMLIN GARLAND (1860–1940): *Main-Travelled Roads.* The Wisconsin-born writer who would draw on his own former experience in his work produces his initial story collection, made up of realistic glimpses of Midwestern

Hamlin Garland

farm life. Additional collections, judged significant in the early American realistic tradition, include *Prairie Folks* (1893), *Wayside Courtships* (1897), *Boy Life on the Prairie* (1899), and *Other Main-Travelled Roads* (1910).

EMMA DUNHAM KELLEY: *Megda.* Under the pseudonym "Forget-Me-Not," Kelley publishes her first novel, the story of a young Christian girl's development that avoids both social protest and race issues while anticipating the feminist spirituality of some African American writers of the latter half of the twentieth century. A second novel, *Four Girls at Cottage City,* would follow in 1895. Little is known of Kelley's life except that she was a mother who had been widowed and probably lived in New England.

JOSEPH KIRKLAND: *The Captain of Company K.* Although Kirkland dismisses this novel as a potboiler, his treatment of his own Civil War experiences in an Illinois infantry company contributes to the development of American realism by accurately depicting camp life and combat.

FRANCIS HOPKINSON SMITH: *Colonel Carter of Cartersville.* Smith's popular comic novella concerns a Virginian stranded without funds in New York. It would be successfully adapted for the stage by Augustus Thomas

in 1892, and a sequel, *Colonel Carter's Christmas,* would appear in 1903.

Literary Criticism and Scholarship

WILLIAM DEAN HOWELLS: *Criticism and Fiction.* Howells's most significant literary pronouncements are taken from his "The Editor's Study" columns in *Harper's Magazine* (1886–1891) and express his views on literary realism, naturalism, and the moral responsibilities of the writer. Additional critical volumes — *Heroines of Fiction* (1901) and *Literature and Life* (1902) — would follow.

CHARLES ELIOT NORTON (1827–1908): The first volume of the Harvard professor of fine arts's prose translation of Dante's *Divine Comedy* (completed in 1892) appears and is acclaimed as a masterpiece. Revised in 1902, it is still considered among the finest English-language prose versions of Dante's poem.

Nonfiction

JOHN FISKE (1842–1901): *The American Revolution.* The most popular (and successful) historian of his day issues this two-volume narrative history.

Poetry

RICHARD HOVEY (1864–1900): *Launcelot and Guenevere: A Poem in Dramas.* The Illinois poet's ambitious initial work initiates a series of poetic dramas based on the *Morte d'Arthur.* Guenevere, Hovey's representation of the "new woman," attempts to emerge from the social limitations imposed on her intellect and instincts.

HERMAN MELVILLE: *Timoleon and Other Ventures in Minor Verse.* The last of Melville's books to appear during his lifetime is privately printed in an edition of twenty-five and consists of poetic meditations on philosophy, history, art, and his own past, as well as poems reflecting his travels to the Mediterranean and the Middle East in 1856–1857.

WALT WHITMAN: *Good-Bye My Fancy.* Whitman's last miscellany of poetry and prose published during his lifetime offers reflections on his art, life, aging, illness, and death.

Publications and Events

International copyright law passed. Previous American copyright laws had applied only to American publications, allowing publishers to reprint European books cheaply without compensating authors, undercutting book prices established by the major publishing firms at a disadvantage to American authors. Although American readers benefited from low book prices, a coalition of authors, publishers, and printers successfully lobbies Congress to pass the first international copyright law.

Review of Reviews. The American counterpart to the English magazine of the same name begins publication. It surveyed current affairs, reprinted articles for other periodicals, and reviewed new books. It continued until 1937.

1892

Drama and Theater

HENRY GUY CARLETON (1856–1910): *A Gilded Fool.* Carleton's comedy concerning an unworldly young man who inherits a fortune is written for the popular stage comedian Nat Goodwin (1857–1919), who achieves acclaim in the role. Carleton, a popular humorist of the day, became the managing editor of *Life* magazine in 1893.

JACOB GORDON (1853–1909): *The Jewish King Lear.* One of the greatest playwrights of the Yiddish American theater produces his most successful play, about a pious immigrant father abused by his heartless American-born daughters. Gordon would follow it with *Mirele Efros* (1898), commonly known as *The Jewish Queen Lear,* and *God, Man and Devil* (1900), based on the story of Faust.

JAMES A. HERNE: *Shore Acres.* The playwright appears in the lead role in this drama, a revision of his *The Hawthornes* (1889), about the rivalry between two brothers. The play's realism is heralded by one reviewer as marking "an epoch in the drama of the American stage."

BRONSON HOWARD: *Aristocracy.* Howard's social comedy contrasts a nouveau riche Californian, a member of New York society, and a European patrician.

Fiction

WOLCOTT BALESTIER (1861–1891): *The Naulahka.* The journalist collaborates with his brother-in-law Rudyard Kipling to create this story of a Californian in India. Balestier, who wrote the American chapters, also publishes a novel of the Colorado mining camps, *Benefits Forgot.*

RICHARD HARDING DAVIS: *Van Bibber and Others.* The volume collects stories concerning Davis's most popular creation, the wealthy man-about-town Courtlandt Van Bibber, who provides a lens on the often ridiculous antics of the rich and famous in Newport and along New York's Park Avenue. *Cinderella and Other Stories* (1896) continues Van Bibber's adventures.

HAMLIN GARLAND: *Jason Edwards: An Average Man.* Garland offers a defense of Henry George's single-tax concept. His other social problem novels published during the year are *A Spoil of Office,* on the Populist

Charlotte Perkins Gilman

movement, and *A Member of the Third House,* concerning the power of the railroads.

CHARLOTTE PERKINS GILMAN (1860–1935): "The Yellow Wallpaper." Gilman's best-known work is the story of a woman's psychological disintegration as she undergoes a course of therapy intended to improve her mental health. Based on the writer's own experiences while being treated for postnatal depression by writer-neurologist S. Weir Mitchell, the story highlights issues in mental health and in the identity and social position of women.

FRANCES ELLEN WATKINS HARPER: *Iola Leroy; or, Shadows Uplifted.* Harper's last and most famous novel is the first widely distributed novel by a black woman writer and the biggest-selling novel by a black writer in the nineteenth century. It tells the story of a light-skinned woman who discovers and accepts her slave ancestry and racial identity. The book is also noteworthy for its depiction of educated and socially committed black characters.

HENRY JAMES: *The Lesson of the Master.* James's short story collection contains some of his best works, including the title story, "The Pupil," and "Brooksmith."

S. WEIR MITCHELL: *Characteristics.* The first of Mitchell's two "conversation novels" (the second is *Dr. North and His Friends,* 1900) made up entirely of dialogue as a doctor, a lawyer, a historian, an artist, and a young woman engage in a wide-ranging discussion that reveals their personalities and values.

MARK TWAIN (SAMUEL LANGHORNE CLEMENS): *The American Claimant*. Twain's novel is based on his play, *Colonel Sellers* (1883), cowritten with William Dean Howells, which in turn is based on a character that had originally appeared in *The Gilded Age* (1873). It concerns a dispute over an English earldom.

Literary Criticism and Scholarship

EDMUND CLARENCE STEDMAN: *The Nature and Elements of Poetry*. Reacting to a comment made by William Dean Howells in a review of *Poets of America*, which had dismissed Stedman's heralding of a revival of fine poetry in America, the critic mounts a defense of poetry against the claims of fictional realism.

Nonfiction

ANNA JULIA HAYWOOD COOPER (c. 1859–1964): *A Voice from the South: By a Black Woman from the South*. Cooper's essays focus on women's rights and the status of black women. In this landmark African American feminist text, she asserts that black men cannot speak for black women and that gender issues are inextricably linked to racial matters. Born in North Carolina the daughter of a slave, Cooper, who lived to be 105, witnessed both the Civil War and the civil rights movement in the 1960s.

THOMAS NELSON PAGE: *The Old South*. This is the first in a series of the author's social studies of Virginia. It would be followed by *Social Life in Old Virginia* (1897) and *The Old Dominion* (1908).

FRANCIS PARKMAN: *A Half-Century of Conflict*. Parkman issues the final installment of his North American colonial history, which treats the events occurring between the Frontenac regime and the beginning of the French and Indian War, including the siege of Louisburg.

JAMES FORD RHODES (1848–1927): *History of the United States*. The first two volumes of Rhodes's popular historical account of American history during the second half of the nineteenth century. It features one of the first objective, nonpartisan, "nationalistic" treatments of the Civil War and Reconstruction. He would complete the series in 1906. Rhodes was a businessman whose histories were done after his retirement.

JOSIAH ROYCE: *The Spirit of Modern Philosophy*. Royce provides a comprehensive survey of the leading trends in modern philosophy.

IDA WELLS-BARNETT (1862–1931): *Southern Horrors: Lynch Law in All Its Phases*. The first of the pamphlets written by the black journalist and social reformer promotes her antilynching campaign. It would be followed by *A Red Record: Tabulated Statistics and Alleged Causes of Lynching in the United States, 1892, 1893, 1894* (1895) and *Mob Rule in New Orleans* (1900).

Poetry

AMBROSE BIERCE: *Black Beetles in Amber*. Bierce, who once remarked that "I am not a poet but an abuser," supplies a collection of satirical verses attacking prominent political figures such as the California politician and railroad magnate Leland Stanford. A second volume, *Shapes of Clay*, would appear in 1903.

EUGENE FIELD: *With Trumpet and Drum*. The humorist and journalist's collection of children's poems includes his most famous — "Little Boy Blue," "The Sugar Plum Tree," and "Wynken, Blynken and Nod." Along with its sequel, *Love-Songs of Childhood* (1894), the work brings Field recognition as "the poet of childhood."

WALT WHITMAN: *Leaves of Grass*. The final ninth, so-called Death-Bed Edition, of Whitman's masterwork adds the poems "Old Age Echoes" and "A Backward Glance o'er Travel'd Roads."

JOHN GREENLEAF WHITTIER: *At Sundown*. Whittier had this final collection printed privately for friends in 1890. Published in 1892, it includes the last poem he wrote for his friend Oliver Wendell Holmes on the occasion of Holmes's eighty-third birthday.

Publications and Events

The *Sewanee Review*. The critical and literary quarterly is founded at the University of the South in Tennessee. Presently, it is the oldest published quarterly in the United States.

1893
Drama and Theater

DAVID BELASCO AND FRANKLIN FYLES (1847–1911): *The Girl I Left Behind Me*. This rousing, suspenseful melodrama concerns an army post under Indian attack. Fyles served as the drama critic for the *New York Sun* for twenty-five years. His subsequent plays included *The Governor of Kentucky* (1896), *Cumberland '61* (1897), and *Kit Carson* (1901).

CHARLES T. DAZEY (1855–1938): *In Old Kentucky*. In Dazey's melodrama, a mountain girl wins her high-born beau when she succeeds in a horse race. The appearance of the heroine in riding breeches creates a stir and helps make the play one of the most popular and frequently performed dramas at the end of the century. Dazey's other plays are *Elsa* (1882) and *The Stranger* (1911).

MARY E. WILKINS FREEMAN: *Giles Corey, Yeoman*. Freeman's only produced play is a six-act tragedy set during the Salem witchcraft trials. The title character

Stephen Crane

is condemned to death by being crushed under stone weights because he refuses to testify at his trials. The play has little success on stage but is more favorably received when published.

AUGUSTUS THOMAS: *In Mizzoura*. Thomas's rural comedy concerns a Missouri sheriff in love with his neighbor's daughter. It shows Thomas's skill in regional mannerisms and dialects and proves to be one of his most well-known efforts, playing for several years.

Fiction

AMBROSE BIERCE: *Can Such Things Be?* Bierce's second story collection treats scenes from the Civil War and the California frontier experience, including works such as "My Favorite Murder," "The Famous Gilson Bequest," and "One Kind Officer."

HJALMAR HJORTH BOYESEN: *The Social Strugglers.* This is Boyesen's final novel and the last in a series of realistic social fiction that includes *The Mammon of the Unrighteous* (1891) and *The Golden Calf* (1892).

STEPHEN CRANE (1871–1900): *Maggie: A Girl of the Street.* Crane's first book is privately printed under the pseudonym "Johnston Smith" and published in 1896. A landmark work in the development of American realism, it depicts tenement life in New York's Bowery and the title character's descent into prostitution and suicide.

VICTORIA EARLE (1861–1907): *Aunt Lindy: A Story Founded on Real Life.* Earle's story portrays a slave owner, injured in a fire, who is nursed by his former slave. It is one of the first attempts to feature a dialect-speaking folk character as a fully plausible protagonist rather than a stock caricature.

HAROLD FREDERIC: *The Copperhead.* This is the first in a series of Frederic's popular novels treating the Civil War from the perspective of noncombatants. It would be followed by *Marsena* (1894) and *In the Sixties* (1897).

HENRY BLAKE FULLER (1857–1929): *The Cliff-Dwellers.* In what has been described as the first significant American urban novel, Fuller treats the daily activities of workers in a Chicago skyscraper. His other works about Chicago life are *With the Procession* (1895), *Under the Skylights* (1901), *On the Stairs* (1918), and *Bertram Copes' Year* (1919).

HAMLIN GARLAND: *Prairie Folks.* Garland considered this collection a companion volume to *Main-Travelled Roads*, as it realistically deals with farm life in a similar fashion and includes many of the same characters. The strongest story is "Sim Burns's Wife," treating the despair of a farm wife.

WILLIAM DEAN HOWELLS: *An Imperative Duty.* Howells provides one of the first fictional treatments of the marriage between a white and a black. A young woman, raised as white, is shocked to learn that her grandmother was a slave, and the doctor who treats her overcomes his prejudice concerning her background and marries her. As a concession to popular prejudice, Howells sends his mixed-race couple to Italy to live. He also publishes *The Quality of Mercy*, a character study of an embezzler, and *The World of Chance*, a satire on publishing in which a young Midwestern newspaperman goes east to sell his novel.

HENRY JAMES: *The Real Thing and Other Tales.* James's story collection includes "The Wheel of Time," "Lord Beaupre," and "The Visit." James also publishes *Picture and Text*, treating art and artists, and *Essays in London and Elsewhere*, on writers, criticism, and travel.

SARAH ORNE JEWETT: *A Native of Winby and Other Tales.* This uneven collection mixes slight and sentimental stories with some of Jewett's best, including "The Failure of David Berry" and "The Flight of Betsey Lane."

MARK TWAIN (SAMUEL LANGHORNE CLEMENS): *The £1,000,000 Bank-Note and Other Stories.* The title story concerns eccentric Englishmen who place a bet on what would happen if a stranger were given a million-pound banknote and no way to explain how he got it. The story explores themes Twain would return to in "The Man

Frederick Jackson Turner

That Corrupted Hadleyburg" (1899) and "The $30,000 Bequest" (1904).

LEW WALLACE: *The Prince of India.* After being appointed by President Garfield (an admirer of Wallace's *Ben-Hur*) as minister to Turkey (1881–1885), Wallace had labored for twelve years to complete this novel, written at Garfield's suggestion, about Constantinople, a massive 300,000-word reworking of the legend of the Wandering Jew.

Literary Criticism and Scholarship

FRANCIS MARION CRAWFORD: *The Novel: What It Is.* Crawford sets forth his concept that the novel should be exclusively a form of popular entertainment, avoiding moralizing and realistic representation.

RALPH WALDO EMERSON: *Natural History of the Intellect and Other Papers.* This posthumous collection of lectures includes "Thoughts on Modern Literature," first published in 1840, in which Emerson identifies three classes of literature: "the highest . . . are those which express the moral element, the next, works of imagination, and the next, works of science."

FREDERICK JACKSON TURNER (1861–1932): "The Significance of the Frontier in American History." The University of Wisconsin history professor delivers his paradigm-setting paper at the American Historical Association. It would become known as Turner's Thesis, which asserts the role of the frontier in the formation of the American character.

Nonfiction

HENRY ADAMS: *Memoirs of Marau Taaroa, Last Queen of Tahiti.* Based on Adams's encounter with a Tahitian woman during his tour of the South Pacific in 1890, the book chronicles Tahitian society before and after Westernization. It shows Adams's interest in women and their influence, a theme that would recur in *Mont-Saint-Michel and Chartes.*

IDA WELLS-BARNETT: *The Reason Why the Colored American Is Not in the Columbian Exposition— The Afro-American's Contribution to Columbia Literature.* Wells-Barnett coauthored and printed this essay to protest the exclusion of African American achievement from the World's Columbian Exposition in Chicago.

Poetry

KATHERINE LEE BATES (1859–1929): "America the Beautiful." Bates's most famous poem is this patriotic verse set to the music of "Materna" by Samuel A. Ward. It would become what many consider the alternative and preferred national anthem. Born in Maine, Bates long served as a professor at Wellesley College.

PAUL LAURENCE DUNBAR (1872–1906): *Oak and Ivy.* The Dayton, Ohio, poet and novelist's first collection of lyrics about African American life appears in a self-published booklet. A second collection, *Majors and Minors* (1895), would come to the attention of William Dean Howells, who promoted Dunbar's works and helped him reach a wider audience.

LOUISE IMOGEN GUINEY: *A Roadside Harp: A Book of Verses.* Guiney's best-known and critically praised collection includes travel-related poems such as "For Isaak Walton" and "The Cherry Bough" and her best chivalric poems— "The Vigil-at-Arms," "The Knight-Errant," and "The Kings."

ALBERY ALLSON WHITMAN: *The World's Fair Poem.* Whitman's two-poem collection includes "The Freedman's Triumphant Song," one of his few works of overt social protest, decrying white stereotypes of African Americans.

Publications and Events

The *Christian Union* (formerly *The Outlook*). The weekly founded in 1879 and edited by Henry Ward Beecher is renamed, with Lyman Beecher as its editor. Its editorial focus shifts to political and social issues, employing Theodore Roosevelt on its staff in 1909.

McClure's Magazine. Founded by S. S. McClure (1857–1949), this monthly featured works by the major writers of the day, including Willa Cather, Ida Tarbell, and Lincoln Steffens. From 1901 to 1912, it published a series of muckraking exposés that prompted social reforms.

The World's Columbian Exposition. This celebration of the four-hundredth anniversary of Columbus's discovery of America takes place in Chicago, with a display of technological, cultural, and architectural achievements. A series of conferences at the exposition demonstrates a growing professionalization of intellectual activity within the academic fields of the social and natural sciences.

1894

Drama and Theater

WILLIAM GILLETTE: *Too Much Johnson.* In one of his rare excursions into comedy, Gillette produces a popularly successful play about a philanderer and inveterate liar.

HENRY JAMES: *Theatricals and Theatricals: Second Series.* James publishes four of his unproduced comedies — *Tennants, Disengaged, The Album,* and *The Reprobate.*

GEORGE W. LEDERER (1861–1938): *The Passing Show.* The theatrical producer mounts the first successful American musical revue, combining topical humor, a chorus line, and musical and dance performances, with a loose story line to tie all together.

Fiction

JAMES LANE ALLEN: *A Kentucky Cardinal.* Allen's most popular work concerns Adam Moss's love for a capricious young woman who demands the present of a bird that Adam has been trying to protect. In the sequel, *Aftermath* (1896), the couple marries.

GERTRUDE ATHERTON (1857–1948): *Before the Gringo Came.* The California writer's first fiction is a sentimental and nostalgic evocation of California life under Mexican rule. It would be revised and retitled *The Splendid Idle Forties* in 1902.

ROBERT W. CHAMBERS (1865–1933): *In the Quarter.* Reflecting the popular taste of the day, this novel tells the story of American and English painters in Paris. During the decade Chambers would also publish *The Red Republic* (1895), *A King and a Few Dukes* (1896), *Lorraine* (1898), and *Ashes of Empire* (1898).

KATE CHOPIN: *Bayou Folk.* Chopin's first collection of sketches and stories of Louisiana life includes "A No-Account Creole" and "La Belle Zoraïde." It also contains one of Chopin's most acclaimed stories, "Désirée's Baby,"

about an aristocrat who marries an orphan girl but turns her out when their child shows evidence of black ancestry; he later discovers that he is responsible for his son's mixed blood.

MARY HALLOCK FOOTE: *Coeur d'Alene.* Foote fictionalizes the violent strike in 1892 at Idaho's Coeur d'Alene mine, showing ruthless union members destroying their opponents.

PAUL LEICESTER FORD (1865–1902): *The Honorable Peter Sterling and What People Thought of Him.* Ford achieves a popular success with this portrait of an idealistic politician whose most famous line is "Votes be damned!" Readers detect a resemblance, which Ford would deny, between the novel's hero and the American president at the time, Grover Cleveland. Ford was a scholar, essayist, and bibliographer responsible for *The Writings of Thomas Jefferson* (10 vols., 1892–1894) and *The True George Washington* (1896).

WILLIAM DEAN HOWELLS: *A Traveler from Altruria.* Howells satirizes contemporary American life from the vantage point of a visitor from a utopian republic, who encounters, at a fashionable summer resort, a representative group of Americans, including a novelist, a banker, a lawyer, and a minister. A sequel, *Through the Eye of the Needle,* would follow in 1907.

MARK TWAIN (SAMUEL LANGHORNE CLEMENS): *The Tragedy of Pudd'nhead Wilson.* Twain deals explicitly with the evils of slavery in the story of a light-skinned slave who exchanges her son with her master's. The deception is finally revealed years later by the eccentric lawyer Wilson, who uses fingerprint evidence to solve the mystery. In the development of the switched children, Twain suggests that traits are learned rather than inherited. Twain also publishes *Tom Sawyer Abroad,* a fanciful and forced tale of travel to Africa and the Middle East.

CHARLES DUDLEY WARNER: *The Golden House.* This is the second of Warner's social satires of the Gilded Age, which had begun with *A Journey in the World* (1889) and would conclude with *That Fortune* (1899).

CONSTANCE FENIMORE WOOLSON: *Horace Chase.* Woolson's final novel concerns the marital conflict between a self-made man and his wife, who looks down on him.

Literary Criticism and Scholarship

BERNARD BERENSON (1865–1959): *Venetian Painters of the Renaissance.* The first of the art historian's studies that would establish his reputation as the leading American authority on Renaissance art. It would be followed by *Florentine Painters of the Renaissance* (1896),

Central Italian Painters of the Renaissance (1897), *Study and Criticism of Italian Arts* (1901), *Venetian Paintings in America* (1916), and *Sienese Paintings* (1918).

HAMLIN GARLAND: *Crumbling Idols.* Garland's critical work presents a manifesto for a new realism and "modern art," including his theory of "veritism," the accurate representation of local truths.

Nonfiction

LAFCADIO HEARN: *Glimpses of Unfamiliar Japan.* Having permanently settled in Japan in 1890, Hearn publishes the first in a series of observations and interpretations of Japanese life and customs. It would be followed by *Out of the East* (1895), *Kokoro* (1896), *In Ghostly Japan* (1899), *Shadowings* (1900), *A Japanese Miscellany* (1901), *Kotto* (1902), *Kwaidon* (1904), *Japan: An Attempt at Interpretation* (1904), and *The Romance of the Milky Way* (1905).

HENRY DEMAREST LLOYD (1847–1903): *Wealth Against Commonwealth.* The best-known work of the social reformer is a treatise suggesting that the control of wealth needs to shifted from the few to the many. Lloyd was a lawyer and the editorial writer for the *Chicago Tribune* from 1873 to 1885 who defended men charged in the Haymarket Riot and Eugene Debs in the Pullman Strike.

JOHN MUIR (1838–1914): *The Mountains of California.* One of the naturalist's most popular books combines new and previously published work on the California wilderness. Designed to elicit support for his conservationist views, the book establishes Muir as one of the chief advocates for the preservation of the American wilderness. A revised, enlarged edition would appear in 1911.

BILL NYE (1850–1896): *Bill Nye's History of the United States.* One of the humorist's most popular works is this burlesque of American history, from Columbus's voyage to the Cleveland presidency.

Poetry

RICHARD HOVEY: *Songs of Vagabondia.* Hovey collaborates with Canadian writer Bliss Carman (1861–1929) on this popular volume of verses celebrating the joys of the tavern, nature, comrades, and the open road. Two sequels would follow: *More Songs from Vagabondia* (1896) and *Last Songs from Vagabondia* (1901).

GEORGE SANTAYANA (1863–1952): *Sonnets and Other Verses.* The Harvard professor of philosophy from 1889 until 1912 publishes his first book, a poetry collection. A second volume, *A Hermit of Carmel and Other Poems*, would appear in 1901.

John Muir

JOHN B. TABB (1845–1909): *Poems.* The Virginia-born Catholic convert who had become a priest is praised for classically modeled lyrics that invite comparison with the metaphysical poets and Emily Dickinson. His subsequent volumes are *An Octave to Mary* (1893), *Lyrics* (1897), *Child Verse* (1899), *Later Lyrics* (1902), *The Rosary in Rhyme* (1904), and *Quips and Quiddits* (1907).

Publications and Events

The *Chap Book.* Established as the house organ of Cambridge publishers Stone and Kimball, it relocated to Chicago and featured contributions by Henry James, Hamlin Garland, and foreign authors such as H. G. Wells, Robert Louis Stevenson, and William Butler Yeats. It continued until 1897.

The Pullman Strike in Chicago. The most violent labor demonstration of the period leads to the founding of the American Socialist Party and becomes a reference point for both radical and conservative writers concerned with the growing problems of industrialization.

Woman's Era. The first newspaper targeted to black women begins publication in Boston by the New Era Club.

1895

Drama and Theater

DAVID BELASCO: *The Heart of Maryland.* Belasco solidifies his reputation as the leading actor, director, and producer of his era in this Civil War melodrama based on Rose Hartwick Thorpe's poem "Curfew Must Not Ring Tonight!" In the play a Maryland belle tries to prevent the execution of her Union lover by stopping the tolling of the bell that signals his end.

WILLIAM GILLETTE: *Secret Service.* Before appearing as Sherlock Holmes, Gillette's most popular role is playing a Union spy in this skillfully constructed Civil War melodrama.

HENRY JAMES: *Guy Domville.* At the premiere of James's drama in London, the playwright is greeted by fifteen minutes of boos and catcalls. With the failure of *Guy Domville*, James decides to abandon his theatrical aspirations.

NATE SALSBURY: *Black America.* Salsbury produces an elaborate stage show, featuring three hundred African American performers to showcase black culture.

Fiction

ALICE BROWN (1857–1948): *Meadow-Grass.* This is the first of the New England local colorist's collections set in the imagined New Hampshire village of Tiverton. It would be followed by *Tiverton Tales* (1899), *Vanishing Points* (1913), and *Homespun and Gold* (1920).

GEORGE WASHINGTON CABLE: *John March, Southerner.* Cable's final social problem novel depicts its title character trying to balance antebellum Southern values with the changes brought by Reconstruction. He would write his subsequent novels — historical romances — mainly to entertain.

ROBERT W. CHAMBERS: *The King in Yellow.* The popular author of historical romances publishes this collection of macabre stories. Together with the works of Edgar Allan Poe and H. P. Lovecraft, it is considered by many critics one of the most important collections of American tales of supernatural terror.

STEPHEN CRANE: *The Red Badge of Courage.* Crane's remarkable evocation of warfare in the Civil War follows the progress of Union infantryman Henry Fleming from panic to resolve. Crane's impressionistic technique marks an influential fictional breakthrough in the American novel, and the story's intensity and authenticity make the twenty-four-year-old writer, who had never been on a battlefield, an international celebrity.

ALICE RUTH MOORE DUNBAR-NELSON (1875–1935): *Violets and Other Tales.* The New Orleans–born African American writer's first collection of stories, poetry, and essays shows her skill in capturing regional life of the period. A second collection, *The Goodness of St. Rocque and Other Stories*, would follow in 1899. Married to writer Paul Laurence Dunbar, she is considered among the first African American women to gain literary distinction.

HENRY BLAKE FULLER: *With the Procession.* Fuller's novel treats the economic boom times in Chicago after the fire of 1871 and shows what happens to those who refuse to "keep up with the procession" of progress and prosperity. The novel deals with ordinary people and chronicles the commonplace events of their lives.

HAMLIN GARLAND: *Rose of Dutcher's Coolly.* Garland's novel offers a prescient portrait of the "new woman" as Rose, a Midwestern farm girl, attends college, goes to Chicago to become a writer, and defers marriage for the sake of her career.

HENRY JAMES: *Terminations.* This short story collection is made up of "The Death of the Lion," "The Coxon Fund," "The Middle Years," and "The Altar of the Dead."

SARAH ORNE JEWETT: *The Life of Nancy.* The title story in Jewett's collection treats the first visit to Boston of a country girl and her long confinement as an invalid. Other stories include "All My Sad Captains," "An Only Rose," and "The Guests of Mrs. Timms."

EDWARD WATERMAN TOWNSEND (1855–1942): *Chimmie Fadden, Major Max, and Other Stories* and *Chimmie Fadden Explains.* Townsend presents scenes of New York street life from the perspective of a young Bowery tough.

Nonfiction

BROOKS ADAMS: *Law of Civilization and Decay.* Adams anticipates the pessimistic thesis of Oswald Spengler's *The Decline of the West* (1918) by positing a deterministic theory of social energy.

ELIZABETH BLACKWELL (1821–1910): *Pioneer Work in Opening the Medical Profession to Women.* The autobiography of the first woman to receive a medical degree in the United States. It gives a vivid account of the bias Blackwell had experienced in her medical training and practice.

ELIZABETH CADY STANTON: *The Women's Bible.* Stanton challenges biblical justification for the subordination of women in a controversial interpretation of scripture. The book becomes a bestseller despite the refusal of libraries to offer it and its being censured by the National American Woman Suffrage Association.

IDA WELLS-BARNETT: *A Red Record: Tabulated Statistics and Alleged Causes of Lynchings in the United States,*

BESTSELLERS, 1895–1899

Fiction*

1895
1. *Beside the Bonnie Brier Bush* by Ian Maclaren
2. *Trilby* by George du Maurier
3. *Adventures of Captain Horn* by Frank R. Stockton
4. *The Manxman* by Hall Caine
5. *Princess Aline* by Richard Harding Davis
6. *Days of Auld Lang Syne* by Ian Maclaren
7. *The Master* by Israel Zangwill
8. *The Prisoner of Zenda* by Anthony Hope
9. *Regeneration* by Max Nordau
10. *My Lady Nobody* by Maarten Maartens

1896
1. *Tom Grogan* by F. Hopkinson Smith
2. *A Lady of Quality* by Frances Hodgson Burnett
3. *The Seats of the Mighty* by Gilbert Parker
4. *A Singular Life* by Elizabeth Stuart Phelps Ward
5. *The Damnation of Theron Ware* by Harold Frederic
6. *A House-Boat on the Styx* by John Kendrick Bangs
7. *Kate Carnegie* by Ian Maclaren
8. *The Red Badge of Courage* by Stephen Crane
9. *Sentimental Tommy* by J. M. Barrie
10. *Beside the Bonnie Brier Bush* by Ian Maclaren

1897
1. *Quo Vadis* by Henryk Sienkiewicz
2. *The Choir Invisible* by James Lane Allen
3. *Soldiers of Fortune* by Richard Harding Davis
4. *On the Face of the Waters* by Flora Annie Steel
5. *Phroso* by Anthony Hope

6. *The Christian* by Hall Caine
7. *Margaret Ogilvy* by J. M. Barrie
8. *Sentimental Tommy* by J. M. Barrie
9. *The Pursuit of the House-Boat* by John Kendrick Bangs
10. *The Honorable Peter Stirling* by Paul Leicester Ford

1898
1. *Caleb West* by F. Hopkinson Smith
2. *Hugh Wynne* by S. Weir Mitchell
3. *Penelope's Progress* by Kate Douglas Wiggin
4. *Helbeck of Bannisdale* by Mrs. Humphry Ward
5. *Quo Vadis* by Henryk Sienkiewicz
6. *The Pride of Jennico* by Agnes and Egerton Castle
7. *The Day's Work* by Rudyard Kipling
8. *Shrewsbury* by Stanley Weyman
9. *Simon Dale* by Anthony Hope
10. *The Adventures of François* by S. Weir Mitchell
11. *The Battle of the Strong* by Gilbert Parker

1899
1. *David Harum* by Edward Noyes Westcott
2. *When Knighthood Was in Flower* by Charles Major
3. *Richard Carvel* by Winston Churchill
4. *The Day's Work* by Rudyard Kipling
5. *Red Rock* by Thomas Nelson Page
6. *Aylwin* by Theodore Watts-Dunton
7. *Janice Meredith* by Paul Leicester Ford
8. *Mr. Dooley in Peace and War* by Finley Peter Dunne
9. *No. 5 John Street* by Richard Whiteing
10. *The Market Place* by Harold Frederic

* During the early years of *Publishers Weekly*'s bestseller lists, fiction and nonfiction were combined. Since fiction far and away outsold nonfiction titles, the top ten sellers were always fiction. In 1912, *Publishers Weekly* added a nonfiction bestseller list, only to drop it in 1914. In 1917, with the rising popularity of books on war, *Publishers Weekly* added a War-Books bestseller list and also reinstated the nonfiction bestseller list. In 1919, the War-Books bestseller list would be dropped.

1892–1893–1894. This first comprehensive statistical study of lynching in America reveals that in 1893, two hundred blacks had been lynched in America.

Poetry

STEPHEN CRANE: *The Black Riders, and Other Lines.* Having set a new standard for American prose fiction with *The Red Badge of Courage*, Crane offers a comparable redefinition of American poetry in a series of experimental poems in free verse, which anticipate the future works of the Imagists and the early Modernists.

PAUL LAURENCE DUNBAR: *Major and Minors.* Dunbar's second verse collection comes to the attention of William Dean Howells, who praises the poet and helps gain Dunbar a wide audience. The collection includes some of his best-known dialect poems as well as conventional lyrics celebrating racial pride and the contributions made by African Americans.

E. PAULINE JOHNSON (1861–1913): *The White Wampum.* The Canadian-born Mohawk, who had toured Canada, the United States, and England as the "Mohawk Princess," becomes the first Indian woman to publish a book of poetry in America. A second collection, *Canadian Born*, would appear in 1903.

HENRY DAVID THOREAU: *Poems of Nature.* The first collection of Thoreau's poetry appears. His *Collected Poetry* would be published in 1964.

Publications and Events

The Actors' Society of America. Formed in reaction to the monopolistic practices of the Theatrical Syndicate and to improve conditions for performers, the society, led by the actor Louis Aldrich (1843–1901), had only limited success and was dissolved in 1913. It was succeeded by Actors' Equity in 1913.

The *American Jewess.* The first national magazine in the United States for Jewish women begins publication, edited by Rosa Sonneschem. It continued until 1899.

The *Bookman.* A monthy devoted to literature and criticism begins publication. Editor Harry Thurston Peck (1856–1914) initiated a list of "Books on Demand," based on sales figures from various bookstores around the country, which became "The Six Best Sellers" in 1903, the forerunner of modern bestseller lists.

The New York Public Library. This institution is created from the consolidation of several previous libraries, including the Astor and Lenox Libraries and the English and American literature collection of Evert Augustus Duyckinck.

BOOKER T. WASHINGTON (1856–1915): "Atlanta Exposition Address." Washington's speech, also called the "Atlanta Compromise," urges African Americans to defer demands for racial equality to concentrate instead on economic and educational progress. His controversial accommodationist view is reflected in the line "In all things that are purely social we can be as separate as the fingers, yet one as the hand in all things essential to mutual progress." The speech secures Washington's national reputation as the preeminent spokesperson for black America for the next twenty years.

The Theatrical Syndicate. Formed by producer Charles Frohman (1860–1915) and booking agents Marc Klaw (1858–1936), and Abraham Erlanger (1860–1930), the syndicate effectively controlled first-class theatrical productions in the United States for the next fifteen years. Operating on the business principle that only plays that generated profits would be produced, it slowed the development of modern drama in America.

1896
Drama and Theater

JOSEPH ARTHUR: *The Cherry Pickers.* Arthur's popular melodrama is set during the Anglo-Afghan War and concerns the rivalry between two officers for a young woman's hand. It is typical of the highly charged, spectacular melodramas of the day.

JOHN PHILIP SOUSA (1854–1932): *El Capitan.* Sousa's most famous song from his operettas, "El Capitan's Song" (later "El Capitan March"), is featured in this comic opera with a libretto by Charles Klein (1867–1915).

Fiction

JOHN KENDRICK BANGS (1862–1922): *A Houseboat on the Styx.* Bangs's most popular work is this extravagant fantasy that collects historical figures such as Shakespeare, Lucrezia Borgia, Napoleon, and George Washing-ton for a comic and satirical encounter. A sequel, *The Pursuit of the Houseboat,* would follow in 1897. Bangs was the editor of *Puck* from 1904 to 1905 and produced collections of farcical tales such as *Tiddledywink Tales* (1891) and *The Idiot* (1895).

ABRAHAM CAHAN (1860–1951): *Yekl, a Tale of the New York Ghetto.* After "Mottke Arbel and His Romance," the first story by the future founder and editor-in-chief of the *Jewish Daily Forward,* had been translated from the Yiddish and published in 1895, William Dean Howells encouraged Cahan to attempt an extended work. This realistic depiction of New York Jewish life is the result. In it, Jake Podgomy attempts to adapt to American culture. The story would serve as the basis for the 1975 film *Hester Street.*

STEPHEN CRANE: *The Little Regiment, and Other Episodes of the American Civil War.* Crane's collection of mainly battlefield stories includes "The Veteran," depicting Henry Fleming, the protagonist of *The Red Badge of Courage,* as an old man. Crane also publishes a novella, *George's Mother,* concerning the devotion of a mother to her less-than-deserving son.

CHESTER BAILEY FERNALD (1869–1938): *The Cat and the Cherub.* The first of Fernald's story collections treats life in San Francisco's Chinatown, based on his firsthand observations. It would be followed by *Chinatown Stories* (1899).

HAROLD FREDERIC: *The Damnation of Theron Ware.* Frederic's most admired work is this novel about a Methodist minister whose faith is shaken under the pressure of modern ideas. Frederic also publishes *March Hare,* a romantic novel of English life.

JOEL CHANDLER HARRIS: *Sister Jane: Her Friends and Acquaintances.* This is the first of Harris's series of four novels depicting life in Georgia before, during, and after the Civil War. It would be followed by *Gabriel Tolliver* (1902), *A Little Union Scout* (1904), and *Shadow Between His Shoulder Blades* (1909).

HENRY JAMES: *Embarrassments.* A collection of four short stories: "The Figure in the Carpet," "Glasses," "The Next Time," and "The Way It Came." James also converts his play *The Other House* into a novel.

SARAH ORNE JEWETT: *The Country of the Pointed Firs.* Jewett's masterpiece is this story sequence set in an isolated Maine seaport in decline. Willa Cather, whom Jewett mentored, would later declare that the volume, along with *The Scarlet Letter* and *Huckleberry Finn,* are the "three American books that have the possibility of a long, long life."

WILLIAM GILBERT PATTEN (1866–1945): *Frank Merriwell.* Boy hero and Yale athlete Frank Merriwell makes his first appearance in stories written by Patten under the pseudonym "Burt L. Standish." The popular series would grow to 208 volumes by 1933 and sell more than 125 million copies. The Maine writer began his career writing Western stories under the pen name "William West Wilder."

CHARLES M. SHELDON (1857–1946): *In His Steps.* Sheldon's novel about a minister who tries to lead his congregation in practicing the teachings of Jesus is first serialized in a Congregational weekly before appearing in book form in 1897. It becomes one of the biggest sellers of the decade. Sheldon was the pastor of a Congregational church in Topeka, Kansas.

MARK TWAIN (SAMUEL LANGHORNE CLEMENS): *Personal Recollections of Joan of Arc.* From boyhood, Twain had been fascinated by the fifteenth-century martyr Joan of Arc, and he supplies this fictionalized biography, supplementing the known facts with the views of fictional characters. Twain also publishes *Tom Sawyer, Detective,* in which Tom and Huck return to the Phelpses' farm, the scene of the conclusion of *Huckleberry Finn,* to unravel a complicated, though uninspired, series of intrigues.

HENRY VAN DYKE (1852–1933): *The Story of the Other Wise Man.* Van Dyke's popular account of the fourth wise man, who sacrifices everything by helping others with the gifts he had intended for Christ, had been originally composed as a Christmas sermon for his church. Van Dyke served as a minister in New Bedford, Rhode Island, and New York City before becoming in 1900 a professor of English at Princeton.

OWEN WISTER (1860–1938): *Red Men and White.* Wister's collection of western stories draws on his summer trips to Wyoming ranches. Two additional collections — *Lin McLean* (1898) and *The Jimmyjohn Boss* (1900) — would follow.

Literary Criticism and Scholarship

GEORGE SANTAYANA: *The Sense of Beauty.* Santayana's initial philosophical work is the first American treatise on aesthetics. It asserts that the beautiful is pleasure objectified.

Nonfiction

W.E.B. DU BOIS (WILLIAM EDWARD BURGHARDT DU BOIS, 1868–1963): *The Suppression of the African Slave-Trade to the United States of America, 1638–1870.* Du Bois, the first African American to receive a doctorate in history at Harvard, publishes his dissertation.

FANNIE FARMER (1857–1915): *Boston Cooking-School Cook Book.* Farmer's popular cookbook is the first to provide standardized measurements. The Boston-born cooking authority became interested in cooking after suffering a paralytic stroke. She managed to attend the Boston Cooking School and became its director in 1891.

MARY VIRGINIA TERHUNE: *National Cookbook.* For many years this cookbook would reign supreme as the essential cooking guidebook in American households.

Poetry

PAUL LAURENCE DUNBAR: *Lyrics of Lowly Life.* The African American poet's third collection constitutes his first major success in treating folk subjects and scenes of plantation life and becomes the best-selling volume of African American poetry before the Harlem Renaissance. *Lyrics of the Hearthside* (1899), *Lyrics of Love and Laughter* (1903), and *Lyrics of Sunshine and Shadow* (1905) would follow.

LIZETTE WOODWORTH REESE: *A Quiet Road.* As in her previous collection, *A Handful of Lavender* (1891), Reese celebrates nature and love but includes an increasingly darker mood and wider philosophical perspective in poems such as "In Time of Grief" and "Growth," which have been compared with poems by Emily Dickinson.

EDWIN ARLINGTON ROBINSON (1869–1935): *The Torrent and the Night Before.* Robinson privately prints his first volume of poems at his own expense. It includes the first portraits of the inhabitants of his imagined Tilbury Town, modeled on his hometown of Gardiner, Maine.

1897
Drama and Theater

HUGH MORTON (C.M.S. MCCLELLAN, 1865–1916): *The Belle of New York.* This musical drama concerns a Salvation Army member, Violet Gray, who attempts to reform a spendthrift young man. His father is so thankful that he tries to force her into a match with his son, who loves another. Violet prevents this by singing a risqué song that offends the father. Only moderately successful in New York, the play becomes the first American musical to achieve success abroad, running for 674 performances in the West End of London. McClellan was a Maine newspaperman whose other plays include *The Jury of Fate* (1906), *Judith Zaraine* (1911), and *The Fountain* (1914).

Fiction

EDWARD BELLAMY: *Equality.* Bellamy's sequel to *Looking Backward* (1888) responds to charges made against the earlier book as well as proposals for instituting his utopian vision.

KATE CHOPIN: *A Night in Acadie.* Chopin's second and final story collection continues to draw on her experiences observing Creole and Cajun life in Louisiana, with an emphasis on gender themes. These concerns are re-vealed in moments of internal conflict in works such as "A Respectable Woman," "Regret," and "Caline."

STEPHEN CRANE: *The Third Violet.* Crane ventures into romantic comedy in his fourth novel, about a poor artist's courtship of a New York belle. Crane confesses to a friend, "It's a pretty rotten work. I used myself up in the accursed 'Red Badge.'"

RICHARD HARDING DAVIS: *Soldiers of Fortune.* The most famous of the writer's many popular adventure romances celebrates the imperialist spirit. It is derived from his travels and experiences as a foreign reporter and war correspondent.

MARY E. WILKINS FREEMAN: *Jerome, a Poor Man.* Free-man is praised for her "photographic realism" in this novel chronicling the travails of a New Englander who doggedly contends with an unending string of setbacks.

HAMLIN GARLAND: *Wayside Courtship.* Garland's col-lection is thematically connected by examining the harsher side of love and romance. Noteworthy stories include "A Preacher's Love Story," "A Stop-over at Tyre," and "An Alien in the Pines."

ELLEN GLASGOW (1874–1945): *The Descendant.* The Richmond, Virginia, writer's first novel, published anonymously, creates a stir by featuring a self-destructive hero and an emancipated heroine who seeks passion rather than marriage. A more conventional second novel, the first published under her name, *Phases of an Inferior Planet*, would appear in 1898.

WILLIAM DEAN HOWELLS: *The Landlord at Lion's Head.* One of Howells's better late novels, this character portrait presents the selfish, amoral, but likable scoundrel Jeff Durgin.

HENRY JAMES: *What Maisie Knew* and *The Spoils of Poynton.* The first of James's 1897 novels is a technical tour de force describing a child's struggle to make sense of her world, split apart by her parents' divorce. The second traces the corrupting influences of possessions on Fleda Vetch and the Gareth family.

ALFRED HENRY LEWIS (1858–1914): *Wolfville.* This is the first in a popular series of story collections by Lewis, set in an Arizona frontier town and narrated by the "Old Cat-tleman" who, as Lewis explains in his introduction, tells "his stories in his own fashion," in a style that is "crude, abrupt, meagre." Six sequels would follow: *Wolfville, Sandburrs* (1900), *Wolfville Days* (1902), *Wolfville Nights* (1902), *The Black Lion Inn* (1903), *Wolfville Folk* (1908), and *Faro Nell and Her Friends* (1913). Lewis was a lawyer and the Cleveland city attorney until 1881, when he be-came a wandering cowboy in the Southwest.

S. WEIR MITCHELL: *Hugh Wynne, Free Quaker.* Mitchell's greatest achievement is this historical novel, set in Philadelphia during the American Revolution. A sequel, *The Red City*, would follow in 1907.

Literary Criticism and Scholarship

MARK TWAIN (SAMUEL LANGHORNE CLEMENS): *How to Tell a Story and Other Essays.* The title essay pro-vides Twain's definition of a "humorous story," which he claims is a unique American invention depending more on the manner of its telling than its subject matter. The essay outlines its leading techniques.

MOSES COIT TYLER: *The Literary History of the Amer-ican Revolution, 1763–1783.* Tyler's seminal and author-itative survey remains an essential account of Ameri-can Revolutionary literature, and its author is praised by critic Howard Mumford Jones as "the supreme master in his field." It is the first attempt at a balanced treatment of the Loyalists.

Nonfiction

EMERSON HOUGH (1857–1923): *The Story of the Cow-boy.* Western outdoorsman and naturalist Hough, who practiced law in New Mexico, gains his first major success with this documentary account of the Southwest cattle industry, which attempts to correct the romantic image of the cowboy popularized in dime novels.

WILLIAM JAMES: *The Will to Believe, and Other Essays in Popular Philosophy.* James's essays are important early indicators of the drift of his thinking, which later would produce *Pragmatism* (1907) and *The Varieties of Religious Experience* (1902).

MARK TWAIN (SAMUEL LANGHORNE CLEMENS): *Fol-lowing the Equator.* Twain's travel book details his gruel-ing 1895 world tour, undertaken to pay off his creditors. The book lacks the spontaneous sparkle of his previous travel books and is considerably darker in tone as Twain reports on the oppression and poverty he observes.

EDITH WHARTON (1874–1945): *The Decoration of Houses.* Wharton's first publication is a treatise on in-terior design written with the architect Ogden Codman, who had helped her redecorate her home in Newport, Rhode Island.

Poetry

SAM WALTER FOSS (1858–1911): *Dreams in Home-spun.* The poet's collection includes his most famous poem, "The House by the Side of the Road," with the well-known lines "Let me live in a house by the side of the road / And be a friend to man."

Edwin Arlington Robinson

EDWIN ARLINGTON ROBINSON: *The Children of the Night.* Robinson's first published volume includes admired poems such as "Richard Corey," "Two Men," and "Luke Havergal." The volume so impresses Theodore Roosevelt that in 1902 he would help the poet gain a sinecure in the New York Custom House.

Publications and Events

The *Survey Graphic.* Founded as the journal of the New York Charity Organization Society, the magazine became a significant liberal periodical.

1898
Drama and Theater

DAVID BELASCO: *Zaza.* Belasco's comedy, adapted from a French play by Pierre Berton and Charles Simon, concerns a prostitute who becomes a music hall entertainer and the mistress of a married man. The play's sexual content and humane depiction of an "immoral" woman create a considerable stir.

BOB COLE (1869–1911): *A Trip to Coontown.* Composer and performer Cole mounts the first musical entirely created and performed by African Americans. His other productions include *Kings of Koontown* (1898), *The Shoofly Regiment* (1907), and *The Red Moon* (1909).

PAUL LAURENCE DUNBAR: *The Origin of the Cake Walk; or, Clorindy.* Dunbar supplies book and lyrics for this musical afterpiece performed at New York's Casino Theatre, the first time a drama written and performed by blacks is presented at a major white theater.

LOTTIE BLAIR PARKER (1868–1937): *Way Down East.* Parker's sentimental melodrama about the travails of a seduced woman, Annie Moore, who is cast out by those who learn her story, proves to be one of the most successful American plays, steadily performed for two decades. Parker, born in Maine, was originally an actress who wrote about a dozen produced plays, including *White Roses* (1892) and *Under Southern Skies* (1901).

PAUL M. POTTER (1853–1921): *The Conquerors.* The English-born former journalist's dramatization of Guy de Maupassant's *Mademoiselle Fifi* features a sensational scene in which the heroine throws a glass of wine in her seducer's face. It prompts the musical hall performers Joe Weber and Lew Fields to mock the scene with a pie-throwing imitation, regarded as the first use of this dependable slapstick device on stage. Potter also writes *Trilby,* a dramatization of George du Maurier's 1894 novel about Svengali's hypnotic power to make a young model into an opera star. The play proves to be one of the most successful dramas of the era and continues to be performed.

HARRY B. SMITH (1860–1936) **AND VICTOR HERBERT** (1859–1924): *The Fortune Teller.* This comic opera with book and lyrics by Smith and music by Herbert establishes the latter as the leading operetta composer.

Fiction

GERTRUDE ATHERTON: *The Californians.* Atherton's novel, regarded by many as her most accomplished work, is her first to treat California in the post-Spanish era. It presents a realistic account of the boom times in San Francisco in the 1880s and their impact on a family's fortune.

EDWARD BELLAMY: *The Blindman's World and Other Stories.* Bellamy's only collection of short stories is published.

ABRAHAM CAHAN: *The Imported Bridegroom and Other Stories of the New York Ghetto.* Cahan publishes an important early story collection documenting Jewish life of the period in New York City.

STEPHEN CRANE: *The Open Boat and Other Tales of Adventure.* The collection contains some of Crane's most admired stories, including the title work based on his experiences during the wreck of the *Commodore*, the steamer he took to Cuba to cover the Spanish-American War, and "The Bride Comes to Yellow Sky," about newlyweds who arrive in a Texas town during an outlaw's drunken shooting spree.

MARGARET DELAND: *Old Chester Tales.* The best of Deland's short fiction, the collection is set in an imagined version of her Pennsylvania hometown outside Pittsburgh, centering on the experiences of the elderly rector Dr. Lavender. Several related collections would follow: *Dr. Lavender's People* (1903), *R. J.'s Mother and Some Other People* (1908), *Around Old Chester* (1913), and *New Friends in Old Chester* (1924).

PAUL LAURENCE DUNBAR: *The Uncalled.* Set in Ohio, Dunbar's first novel deals exclusively with white characters and echoes Nathaniel Hawthorne's *The Scarlet Letter*. It is important chiefly because of its autobiographical elements.

FINLEY PETER DUNNE (1867–1936): *Mr. Dooley in Peace and War.* Dunne's popular creation, the Irish bartender Mr. Dooley, who ventures opinions on diverse subjects, makes his first appearance. Several popular sequels would follow: *Mr. Dooley in the Hearts of His Countrymen* (1898), *What Mr. Dooley Says* (1899), *Mr. Dooley's Philosophy* (1900), *Mr. Dooley's Opinion* (1901), and *Mr. Dooley on Making a Will* (1919). Dunne was a Chicago journalist who would become the editor of *Collier's* from 1918 to 1919.

HARRIET JANE HANSON (1825–1911): *Loom and Spindle; or, Life Among the Early Mill Girls.* The author of the suffragist novels *Captain Mary Miller* (1887) and *The New Pandora* (1889) depicts laboring conditions faced by women in the textile mills.

JOEL CHANDLER HARRIS: *Tales of the Home Folks in Peace and War.* The first of four volumes of local-color stories that mainly feature romanticized portraits of the Southern gentry. It would be followed by *The Chronicles of Aunt Minervy Ann* (1899), *On the Wings of Occasions* (1900), and *The Making of a Statesman and Other Stories* (1902).

HENRY JAMES: *In the Cage.* James's novella concerns a telegraph clerk in a London department store who gets involved with her aristocratic patrons. It is the first of his works that he dictated to a secretary, a development that many critics believe contributed to James's complex mature style. James also publishes *The Turn of the Screw* in the collection *The Two Magics.* This novella becomes his most celebrated psychological ghost story. It concerns a governess who comes to realize that her two young charges are demonically possessed. The ambiguity of the supernatural element, whether it is real or imagined, along with the story's psychological resonance, have made it one of the most debated and interpreted of James's works.

CHARLES MAJOR (1856–1913): *When Knighthood Was in Flower.* The Indiana writer's historical romance set in the early Tudor period is one of the era's biggest sellers and prompts a host of imitators. Major himself would manage only one additional popular success, *Dorothy Vernon of Haddon Hall* (1902).

FRANK NORRIS (1870–1902): *Moran of the Lady Letty.* After publishing his first book, a romantic narrative poem, *Yvernelle: A Tale of Feudal France* (1892), Norris issues his first novel, a romantic adventure tale about the daughter of a fishing schooner captain who, after her father dies, takes command of the boat, assisted by a shanghaied sailor who falls in love with her. Norris was born in Chicago, moved to San Francisco in 1884, studied art in Paris, and began to write stories and sketches as a student at the University of California from 1890 to 1894.

THOMAS NELSON PAGE: *Red Rock.* Page's novel about Southern resistance to the repressive military rule of Reconstruction and the origin of the Ku Klux Klan is critically applauded in the South and dismissed in the North. Edmund Wilson in *Patriotic Gore* describes it as "Page's most ambitious novel," though "boring."

EDWARD NOYES WESTCOTT (1846–898): *David Harum, a Story of American Life.* Published posthumously, Westcott's only novel is about an upstate New York banker given to homely sayings. Westcott himself was a successful Syracuse, New York, banker. Its immediate popular success prompts a 1900 stage version and a film adaptation starring Will Rogers.

Literary Criticism and Scholarship

JOHN JAY CHAPMAN (1862–1933): *Emerson and Other Essays.* The first of Chapman's literary criticism is marked by a fresh and original approach in interpreting Emerson. Edmund Wilson later would call the collection "one of the most brilliant volumes of literary criticism ever written by an American." Chapman's subsequent volumes include *Causes and Consequences* (1898) and *Learning and Other Essays* (1910).

Nonfiction

IDA HUSTED HARPER (1851–1931): *The Life and Work of Susan B. Anthony.* The first two volumes of Anthony's authorized biography appears. It draws upon Anthony's massive archive, collected in her Rochester attic, as well as Harper's close personal relationship with her subject. A third volume would appear in 1908, and, though clearly biased in Anthony's favor, the work has provided the foundation for subsequent biographical and critical studies of Anthony.

THOMAS WENTWORTH HIGGINSON: *Cheerful Yesterdays.* Higginson's memoir is significant for its portraits of virtually every prominent author of his day, including Emily Dickinson, whom Higginson had mentored.

ELIZABETH CADY STANTON: *Eighty Years and More.* Stanton's last major work is an autobiographical account that presents her life in the heroic terms she wished preserved. A revised version would appear as part of *Elizabeth Cady Stanton as Revealed in Her Letters, Diary and Reminiscences*, prepared by her children in 1922.

Poetry

RICHARD HOVEY: *Along the Trail.* Hovey publishes patriotic verses in support of the Spanish-American War, such as "Unmanifest Destiny" and "The Word of the Lord from Havana," as well as the longer poem "Spring."

EDGAR LEE MASTERS (1868–1950): *A Book of Verses.* Masters's first poetry collection is chiefly significant for its contrast with the style and mastery of *Spoon River Anthology* (1915). A second volume, *The Blood of the Prophets*, would be published anonymously in 1905, and Masters would issue two volumes of *Songs and Sonnets* in 1910 and 1912 before his breakthrough in 1915.

MORRIS ROSENFELD (1862–1923): *Songs of the Ghetto.* The Yiddish poet's verses appear in prose translations. Rosenfeld's are some of the earliest and best American Yiddish literature and verse reflections of the Jewish immigrant experience. He immigrated to New York City from Russian Poland in 1886 and worked in sweatshops. His works reflect his experiences and call for social justice.

1899
Drama and Theater

CLYDE FITCH: *Barbara Frietchie.* The playwright transforms the elderly heroine of Whittier's patriotic poem into a young woman, adding a romantic component to this melodrama to cater to his audience's desire for more romance than realism. Fitch's tampering with the image of gray-headed Frietchie proves a mistake, and the play manages only a short initial run, though it would be successfully revived several times.

Florodora. With 505 performances, the New York run of this English musical comedy is the longest in American

William Gillette

theatrical history up to its time. It features the song "Tell Me Pretty Maiden" sung by a chorus, the first Broadway song hit not sung by principal actors.

WILLIAM GILLETTE: *Sherlock Holmes.* Gillette achieves his major theatrical success and discovers his subsequent lifework in his adaptation of Sir Arthur Conan Doyle's detective stories. He would play Holmes on stage regularly until 1931.

JAMES A. HERNE: *The Reverend Griffith Davenport.* Based on Helen H. Gardener's novel *An Unofficial Patriot*, Herne's play depicts a Virginia minister who opposes slavery and assists the Union army during the Civil War. Though critically acclaimed, the play fails with audiences, who are uninspired by the protagonist's betrayal of his home state. Herne's last play, *Sag Harbor*, also appears. It is a version of his earlier 1879 play, *Hearts of Oak*, written with David Belasco, concerning two brothers in love with the same woman.

LANGDON MITCHELL (1862–1935): *Becky Sharp.* Mitchell's popular adaptation of Thackeray's *Vanity Fair* provides one of the greatest successes for Minnie

Maddern Fiske (1865–1932), the major actress of the day. She would perform the title role regularly for the next twenty years.

WILLIAM YOUNG: *Ben-Hur.* Young's dramatization of Lew Wallace's 1880 novel is one of the most spectacular productions ever attempted on Broadway, with a chorus of eighty, 120,000 square feet of scenery, and the use of actual horses for the climactic chariot race. A popular sensation, the play would tour for many years.

Fiction

GEORGE ADE (1866–1944): *Fables in Slang.* Having published his first vernacular moral fable, "The Blond Girl Who Married a Bucket Shop Man" (1898), the Indiana writer repeats his popular formula in the stories that make up the first of several popular collections. It would be followed by *More Fables* (1900), *Forty Modern Fables* (1901), and *Hand-Made Fables* (1920).

AMBROSE BIERCE: *Fantastic Fables.* Bierce collects a number of Aesop-like reflections on contemporary life that are constructed around witty paradoxes and reversals of conventional wisdom and pieties.

GEORGE WASHINGTON CABLE: *Strong Hearts.* The best of the three stories in this collection is "The Solitary," a character study of a man who cures his alcoholism by deliberately marooning himself for a month on a desert island. Although strongly moralistic, the directness and skill of the writing have evoked comparisons with Stephen Crane's "The Open Boat" (1898). A final collection of stories, *The Flower of the Chapdelaines*, would follow in 1918.

CHARLES W. CHESNUTT (1858–1932): *The Conjure Woman.* The African American writer's best-known work is this collection of dialect stories of slavery narrated by an old black gardener to his employer in the North. Chesnutt also publishes a second collection, *The Wife of His Youth*, about a freed slave who is torn between the woman he had married in slavery and the more refined black woman he later meets. Less successful novels — *The House Behind the Cedars* (1900), *The Morrow of Tradition* (1901), and *The Colonel's Dream* (1905) — would follow.

KATE CHOPIN: *The Awakening.* Chopin's novel about the rebellion of wife and mother Edna Pontellier against the confinement of New Orleans social conventions and gender assumptions provokes condemnation that contributes to the end of Chopin's literary career. The novel would be rediscovered in the 1950s and 1960s and recognized as a feminist and artistic masterwork.

WINSTON CHURCHILL (1871–1947): *Richard Carvel.* Churchill's initial popular success, and the first in a series

A poster advertising the 1899 Broadway Theatre production of Lew Wallace's *Ben-Hur* by William Young

of well-received historical novels, is set during the Revolutionary War and depicts a young man who finds himself aboard John Paul Jones's *Bonhomme Richard.* Churchill was born in St. Louis and lived mainly in New Hampshire after graduating from Annapolis.

STEPHEN CRANE: *The Monster and Other Stories.* Crane's collection contains more of his most admired stories, including the title work about a town's ostracism of a maimed black servant and a young boy disfigured in a fire, as well as "The Blue Hotel" and "His New Mittens." Crane also publishes a long, rambling satirical novel, *Active Service*, based on his experiences as a correspondent covering the Greco-Turkish War. It is so contrived that some have suggested that it is a parody of the romantic adventure fiction of the day rather than a potboiler.

PAUL LEICESTER FORD: *Janice Meredith.* Ford's historical novel, set during the American Revolution, proves popular and sparks a fashion trend. Girls imitate the "Janice Meredith curl" as depicted on the novel's cover illustration.

SUTTON E. GRIGGS (1872–1933): *Imperium in Imperio.* Griggs's first and most critically acclaimed novel, about the attempt to establish in Texas an all-black separate country within the United States, anticipates the themes of racial pride, militancy, and separatism expressed by some future African American writers. His other novels, with many of these same themes, are *Overshadowed* (1901), *Unfettered* (1902), *The Hindered Hand* (1903), and *Pointing the Way* (1908).

WILLIAM DEAN HOWELLS: *Ragged Lady.* Howells's novel is chiefly noteworthy for his final use of Italy as a setting. It treats a New England girl who goes to Venice to meet her future husband. Howells also publishes *Their Silver Wedding Journey*, reintroducing the Marches from his first novel, *Their Wedding Journey* (1872).

HENRY JAMES: *The Awkward Age.* The title refers to a girl's transition from adolescence to adulthood. The story depicts Nanda Brookenham's maturation, shaped by her falling in love with the same man her mother loves. It features a dramatic technique by which James allows his characters to act without the narrator's commentary.

SARAH ORNE JEWETT: *The Queen's Twin and Other Stories.* The last collection of Jewett's stories published in her lifetime includes the title story, one of her best, about an old widow who lives alone, surrounded by pictures of Queen Victoria.

CHARLES BERTRAND LEWIS (1842–1924): *Mr. and Mrs. Bowser and Their Varied Experiences and Trials and Troubles of the Bowser Family.* The Ohio humorist and writer for the *Detroit Free Press* publishes the first of several popular volumes about the domestic mishaps of a middle-class family. *Life and Travels of Mr. Bowser* (1902) and *The Humorous Mr. Bowser* (1911) would follow.

FRANK NORRIS: *McTeague.* Norris's naturalistic study that clinically traces the impact of heredity and the environment on characters follows the decline of an unlicensed San Francisco dentist and his miserly wife. Concluding in Death Valley with McTeague handcuffed to the corpse of the former friend he has killed, it is one of the major works of American naturalism, moving from realism to symbolism at its conclusion. Erich von Stroheim would make an epic eight-hour film adaptation of the novel, entitled *Greed*, in 1924. Norris also publishes *Blix*, a sentimental romance with a strong autobiographical basis, about a San Francisco journalist who falls in love with the daughter of a socially prominent family.

EDWARD STRATEMEYER (1863–1930): *The Rover Boys at School.* After initial success with juvenile stories about the Spanish-American War, Stratemeyer launches a series featuring three brothers—Dick, Sam, and Tom Rover—in the first of thirty popular adventures to be published up to 1916. Stratemeyer and the syndicate he founded in 1914 would be responsible for such juvenile literary icons as Tom Swift, the Bobbsey Twins, Nancy Drew, and the Hardy Boys.

BOOTH TARKINGTON (1869–1946): *The Gentleman from Indiana.* The Midwestern novelist and playwright's first novel depicts a crusading newspaper editor fighting corruption in his small Indiana hometown. It becomes the first in a series of Tarkington's novels depicting Midwestern life.

CHARLES DUDLEY WARNER: *That Fortune.* The concluding novel of a trilogy that had begun with *A Little Journey in the World* (1889) and *The Golden House* (1895), satirizing the Gilded Age that Warner and Mark Twain had named in 1873.

ONOTO WATANNA (WINNIFRED EATON, 1875–1954): *Miss Nume of Japan.* The Canadian-born, half-Chinese writer adopts a Japanese literary persona to differentiate her name from the Chinese pseudonym of her sister, Edith Eaton (Sui Sin Far). This story of a romance between a Japanese woman and a Caucasian becomes the first novel by a writer of Chinese ancestry to be published in the United States. It is also the first of the author's seventeen best-selling novels, of which *A Japanese Nightingale* (1901) is the most famous.

EDITH WHARTON: *The Greater Inclination.* Wharton's first fiction appears to positive reviews by English critics who detect echoes of Henry James and a mastery unexpected from an American woman writer. The collection includes three of Wharton's best stories, "The Muse's Tragedy," "The Pelican," and "Souls Belated."

Nonfiction

MARY ANTIN (1881–1949): *From Plotzk to Boston.* At the age of eighteen, Antin publishes her first book, a translation of letters written in Yiddish to her uncle, describing her experiences as a Jewish immigrant in America. Antin immigrated to Boston from Russian Poland in 1894.

JOHN DEWEY: *The School and Society.* This is the first of Dewey's important expressions of his educational philosophy. He would further elaborate his views in *The Child and the Curriculum* (1902), *Moral Principles in Education* (1908), and *Interest and Effort in Education* (1913) before summarizing his position in his masterwork, *Democracy and Education* (1916).

W.E.B. DU BOIS: *The Philadelphia Negro.* Du Bois conducts the first systematic study of a large group of blacks in a major American city. The book shares his findings on the social conditions of blacks in Philadelphia's Seventh Ward.

ELBERT HUBBARD (1856–1915): *A Message to Garcia.* Hubbard's inspirational essay describes an incident in the Spanish-American War in which an American officer faces a series of obstacles to his mission of delivering a message to a Cuban revolutionary leader. The essay's moral of persistence and eventual triumph despite opposition becomes a popular lesson, and an estimated forty million copies of the work would be distributed by 1940. Hubbard founded an artist colony in East Aurora, New York, and edited the inspirational magazine the *Philistine* from 1895 to 1915 and the *Frau* from 1908 to 1917.

THORSTEIN VEBLEN (1857–1929): *The Theory of the Leisure Class.* The first published book by the Wisconsin-born economist and social philosopher is his most important work, an economic and sociological analysis of the creation and perpetuation of a monied class. The work popularizes the term *conspicuous consumption.*

BOOKER T. WASHINGTON: *The Future of the American Negro.* This collection of essays and speeches promulgates Washington's accommodationist views. He urges African Americans to concentrate on education and economic betterment rather than political agitation to combat racial discrimination and inequality. The book has been called by Washington biographer Louis R. Harlan his "most systematic expression of his racial philosophy." It is the first of two dealing directly with U.S. race relations. The other is *The Man Farthest Down: A Record of Observation and Study in Europe* (1912), containing Washington's controversial assertion that black Americans fare better than the dispossessed of Europe.

Poetry

STEPHEN CRANE: *War Is Kind.* Crane's second collection of free verse is more conventional than his first, *The Black Riders* (1895), but it is attacked by reviewers as "a woeful disappointment" and "a joke." Later critics, however, would find some of Crane's greatest work in the volume; the poet John Berryman would call the title poem "one of the major lyrics of the century in America."

PAUL LAURENCE DUNBAR: *Lyrics of the Hearthside.* Divided into romantic lyrics and humorous dialect poems, the collection includes three of Dunbar's best poems on black subject matter: "The Conquerors (The Black Troops in Cuba)," "Alexander Crummell — Dead," and his sonnet memorializing Harriet Beecher Stowe.

EDWIN MARKHAM (1852–1940): *The Man with the Hoe and Other Poems.* The title poem by the California schoolmaster, inspired by the Jean-François Millet painting of

the same name, attacks the exploitation of farm laborers. A remarkable popular success, it would appear, during Markham's lifetime, in more than ten thousand newspapers and magazines throughout the world.

JAMES WHITCOMB RILEY: *Riley Child-Rhymes.* Riley's collection includes one of his most popular poems, "Little Orphant Annie."

GEORGE SANTAYANA: *Lucifer: A Theological Tragedy.* When Santayana's verse drama fails to attract attention, he abandons his poetic ambitions for prose after producing a final collection, *A Hermit of Carmel,* in 1901.

HENRY TIMROD: *Complete Poems.* The complete works of "the poet laureate of the Confederacy" are issued.

Publications and Events

American Boy. Founded as the principal magazine for the Boy Scouts, the magazine became one of the most important souces of juvenile literature. It was published until 1941.

Gideons Society. Founded in Wisconsin by Samuel E. Hill (1867–1936), John H. Nicholson (1859–1946), and William J. Knights (1853–1940), this international association of Christian traveling salesmen sets out to present a Bible for guests' use to each hotel owner in the country. In 1908, the group decided to provide Bibles in each hotel room in the United States.

Pearson's Magazine. The debut of a monthly devoted to literature, politics, and the arts. From 1916 to 1923, it was edited by the literary gadfly Frank Harris (1856–1931) and featured contributions by Upton Sinclair, Eugene Debs, George Bernard Shaw, Maxim Gorky, and others.

1900
Drama and Theater

DAVID BELASCO AND JOHN LUTHER LONG (1861–1927): *Madame Butterfly.* Based on Philadelphia lawyer and writer Long's 1898 short story of the same name, the one-act play, presented as a curtain-closer for Belasco's farce *Naughty Anthony,* is about a geisha, Cho-Cho-San. She falls in love with an American naval officer who betrays her. The play runs for only twenty-four performances. Puccini would adapt it as an opera in 1906.

WILLIAM VAUGHN MOODY (1869–1910): *The Masque of Judgment.* The first of the writer's poetic dramas is the initial play in an unproduced trilogy that includes *The Fire Bringer* (1904) and the incomplete *The Death of Eve* (1912). Moody is regarded as an important figure in the intellectualization of American drama; his early death set back the emergence of serious drama.

BIRTHS, 1900–1914

Births

1900 Taylor Caldwell (d. 1985), novelist
Margaret Mitchell (d. 1949), novelist
Yvor Winters (d. 1968), poet
Thomas Wolfe (d. 1938), novelist

1901 A. B. Guthrie (d. 1991), novelist
Zora Neale Hurston (d. 1960), novelist
Oliver La Farge (d. 1963), novelist and short story writer
Paul Osborn (d. 1988), playwright
Laura Riding (d. 1991), poet

1902 Langston Hughes (d. 1967), poet, novelist, and playwright
Ogden Nash (d. 1971), poet
John Steinbeck (d. 1968), novelist

1903 Kay Boyle (d. 1993), novelist and short story writer
Erskine Caldwell (d. 1987), novelist
James Gould Cozzens (d. 1978), novelist
Countee Cullen (d. 1946), poet and novelist
Paul Horgan (d. 1995), novelist and historian

1904 Hamilton Basso (d. 1964), novelist and journalist
James T. Farrell (d. 1979), novelist
MacKinlay Kantor (d. 1977), novelist
Theodor Seuss Geisel (Dr. Seuss, d. 1991), children's author
Isaac Bashevis Singer (d. 1991), novelist

1905 Lilliam Hellman (d. 1984), playwright
John O'Hara (d. 1970), novelist
Robert Penn Warren (d. 1989), novelist and poet

1906 George Dillon (d. 1968), poet and editor
Sidney Kingsley (d. 1995), playwright
Anne Morrow Lindbergh (d. 2001), author
Clifford Odets (d. 1963), playwright
Henry Roth (d. 1995), novelist

1907 W. H. Auden (d. 1973), poet
Dorothy Dodds Baker (d. 1968), novelist
Rachel Carson (d. 1964), environmental writer
James A. Michener (d. 1997), novelist

Jesse Stuart (d. 1984), poet, novelist, and short story writer
Jessamyn West (d. 1984), novelist and short story writer

1908 Louis L'Amour (d. 1988), western novelist
George Oppen (d. 1984), poet
Theodore Roethke (d. 1963), poet
C. Vann Woodward (d. 1999), historian
Richard Wright (d. 1960), novelist

1909 James Agee (d. 1955), novelist, poet, critic, and screenwriter
Nelson Algren (d. 1981), novelist
Elia Kazan (d. 2003), film director and novelist
Wallace Stegner (d. 1993), novelist
Eudora Welty (d. 2001), novelist and short story writer

1910 Paul Bowles (d. 1999), novelist
Josephine W. Johnson (d. 1990), novelist and short story writer
Wright Morris (d. 1998), novelist
Waters Turpin (d. 1968), novelist

1911 Elizabeth Bishop (d. 1979), poet
Tennessee Williams (d. 1983), playwright

1912 John Cheever (d. 1982), novelist and short story writer
Mary McCarthy (d. 1989), novelist and social critic
Studs Terkel, writer
Barbara Tuchman (d. 1989), historian

1913 William Inge (d. 1973), playwright and novelist
Muriel Rukeyser (d. 1980), poet
Delmore Schwartz (d. 1966), poet

1914 John Berryman (d. 1972), poet
William S. Burroughs (d. 1997), novelist
Ralph Ellison (d. 1994), novelist
Howard Fast (d. 2003), novelist
John Hersey (d. 1993), novelist
David Ignatow (d. 1997), poet
Randall Jarrell (d. 1965), poet
Bernard Malamud (d. 1986), novelist
Budd Schulberg, novelist and screenwriter
William Stafford (d. 1993), poet

AUGUSTUS THOMAS: *Arizona.* Thomas's western melodrama is representative of the drama popular at the turn of the century and is noteworthy for prompting subsequent depictions of the West on the American stage.

Fiction

IRVING BACHELLER (1859–1950): *Eben Holden.* The New York newspaperman's historical novel about an orphan's friendship with a hired man during the years leading up to the Civil War is one of the era's most popular novels.

L. FRANK BAUM (1856–1919): *The Wonderful Wizard of Oz.* Baum introduces his imaginary realm and his American heroine in the first book of a popular children's fantasy series, the first by an American. Baum would produce fourteen sequels, including *The New Wizard of Oz* (1903), *Ozma of Oz* (1907), *The Emerald City of Oz* (1910), and *The Patchwork Girl of Oz* (1913). The Oz franchise was continued with Baum's permission by Ruth Plumly Thompson, who produced an annual Oz book until 1939. The books' illustrator, John R. Neill (1877–1943), added additional books in the series until his death. Baum was born in New York and worked as a poultry farmer, salesman, and newspaperman before establishing his career as a children's book writer with *Father Goose* (1899).

EDWARD BELLAMY: *The Duke of Stockbridge.* Bellamy's historical novel about Shays's Rebellion had been issued serially in 1879; it is finally completed by the writer's cousin Francis Bellamy and brought out in book form after Bellamy's death.

DEATHS, 1900–1914

Deaths

1900 Stephen Crane (b. 1871), novelist
Richard Hovey (b. 1864), poet
Charles Dudley Warner (b. 1829), novelist and travel writer

1901 William Ellery Channing (b. 1818), essayist and clergyman
Ignatius Donnelly (b. 1831), editor and novelist
James A. Herne (b. 1839), playwright
Mary Ashley Townsend (b. 1836), poet
Albery Allson Whitman (b. 1851), poet

1902 Mary Catherwood (b. 1847), novelist
Edward Eggleston (b. 1837), novelist and historian
Paul Leicester Ford (b. 1865), historian and novelist
E. L. Godkin (b. 1831), journalist and editor
Bret Harte (b. 1836), short story writer
Frank Norris (b. 1870), novelist
Frank Stockton (b. 1834), novelist

1903 Frederick Law Olmsted (b. 1822), architect and travel writer
Charles H. Smith (b. 1826), humorist

1904 Edgar Fawcett (b. 1847), novelist
Lafcadio Hearn (b. 1850), author and critic
Kate Chopin (b. 1851), short story writer and novelist
Prentiss Ingraham (b. 1843), novelist

1905 John Bartlett (b. 1820), editor
Emerson Bennett (b. 1822), novelist
Mary Mapes Dodge (b. 1831), children's author
Henry Harland (d. 1905), novelist
John Milton Hay (b. 1838), historian, poet, and statesman
Albion W. Tourgée (b. 1838), novelist, editor, and judge
Lew Wallace (b. 1827), novelist

1906 John William De Forest (b. 1826), novelist
Paul Laurence Dunbar (b. 1872), poet, novelist, and short story writer

1907 Thomas Bailey Aldrich (b. 1836), editor, novelist, poet, and essayist
Archibald Clavering Gunter (b. 1847), novelist and playwright

1908 Joel Chandler Harris (b. 1848), short story writer, novelist, and humorist
Bronson Howard (b. 1828), playwright
Donald Grant Mitchell (b. 1822), novelist
James Ryder Randall (b. 1839), poet
Edmund Clarence Stedman (b. 1833), poet and critic

1909 Francis Marion Crawford (b. 1854), novelist
Augusta Jane Evans (b. 1835), novelist
Martha Farquharson Finley (b. 1828), children's author
Clyde Fitch (b. 1865), playwright
Richard Watson Gilder (b. 1844), poet and editor
Jacob Gordon (b. 1853), playwright
Hinton Rowan Helper (b. 1829), businessman and author
Sarah Orne Jewett (b. 1849), novelist and short story writer
Charles Warren Stoddard (b. 1843), poet
John B. Tabb (b. 1845), poet

1910 Rebecca Harding Davis (b. 1831), novelist and short story writer
O. Henry (William Sydney Porter, b. 1862), short story writer
Mark Twain (Samuel Langhorne Clemens, b. 1835), novelist, short story writer, and humorist
William Vaughn Moody (b. 1868), playwright

1911 Elizabeth Akers (b. 1832), poet
Sam Walter Foss (b. 1858), poet
Harriet Jane Hanson (b. 1825), novelist
Edward Harrigan (b. 1844), playwright, actor, and producer
David Graham Phillips (b. 1867), novelist and muckraker
Denman Thompson (b. 1833), playwright
Elizabeth Stuart Phelps Ward (b. 1844), novelist

1913 Charles Major (b. 1856), novelist
Joaquin Miller (b. 1837), poet

1914 Ambrose Bierce (b. 1842), short story writer
Alfred Henry Lewis (b. 1858), novelist
S. Weir Mitchell (b. 1829), novelist, poet, and physician

CHARLES W. CHESNUTT: *The House Behind the Cedars.* Chesnutt's novel dramatizes the conflict of a light-skinned black woman who must decide between becoming a white man's mistress or a black man's wife.

STEPHEN CRANE: *Whilomville Stories.* This posthumous collection of stories, written during Crane's last years, are mainly tales of childhood set in a small New York town. In contrast to other contemporary fictional treatment of childhood and small-town life, Crane's is remarkably free of sentimentality, anticipating similar approaches by Sherwood Anderson and Ernest Hemingway. Also by Crane, *Wounds in the Rain*, a fictionalized reworking of Crane's reporting from Cuba during the Spanish-American War, is published. The realistic combat sketches include one of his best war stories, "The Price of the Harness."

THEODORE DREISER (1871–1945): *Sister Carrie.* Regarded as a landmark in the development of American realism, Dreiser's first novel charts the opportunistic rise to success of country girl Carrie Meeber and the contrasting decline of her lover, George Hurstwood. Considered immoral in its frank depiction of basic desires, the novel would be withheld by its publisher until 1907.

PAUL LAURENCE DUNBAR: *The Strength of Gideon and Other Stories.* Dunbar's collection includes "The Ingrate," based on his father's slave experiences; "One Man's Fortune," his most extensive treatment of racism and prejudice; and stories of the black migration and lynchings. He also publishes a novel, *The Love of Landry.*

ELLEN GLASGOW: *The Voice of the People.* The first of a series of Glasgow's novels treating the historical and social forces in Virginia from the 1850s and emphasizing

BESTSELLERS, 1900–1904

Fiction*

1900
1. *To Have and to Hold* by Mary Johnston
2. *Red Pottage* by Mary Cholmondeley
3. *Unleavened Bread* by Robert Grant
4. *The Reign of Law* by James Lane Allen
5. *Eben Holden* by Irving Bacheller
6. *Janice Meredith* by Paul Leicester Ford
7. *The Redemption of David Corson* by Charles Frederic Goss
8. *Richard Carvel* by Winston Churchill
9. *When Knighthood Was in Flower* by Charles Major
10. *Alice of Old Vincennes* by Maurice Thompson

1901
1. *The Crisis* by Winston Churchill
2. *Alice of Old Vincennes* by Maurice Thompson
3. *The Helmet of Navarre* by Bertha Runkle
4. *The Right of Way* by Gilbert Parker
5. *Eben Holden* by Irving Bacheller
6. *The Visits of Elizabeth* by Elinor Glyn
7. *The Puppet Crown* by Harold MacGrath
8. *Richard Yea-and-Nay* by Maurice Hewlett
9. *Graustark* by George Barr
10. *D'ri and I* by Irving Bacheller

1902
1. *The Virginian* by Owen Wister
2. *Mrs. Wiggs of the Cabbage Patch* by Alice Caldwell Hegan
3. *Dorothy Vernon of Haddon Hall* by Charles Major
4. *The Mississippi Bubble* by Emerson Hough
5. *Audrey* by Mary Johnston

6. *The Right of Way* by Gilbert Parker
7. *The Hound of the Baskervilles* by Arthur Conan Doyle
8. *The Two Vanrevels* by Booth Tarkington
9. *The Blue Flower* by Henry Van Dyke
10. *Sir Richard Calmady* by Lucas Malet

1903
1. *Lady Rose's Daughter* by Mary Augusta Ward
2. *Gordon Keith* by Thomas Nelson Page
3. *The Pit* by Frank Norris
4. *Lovey Mary* by Alice Hegan Rice
5. *The Virginian* by Owen Wister
6. *Mrs. Wiggs of the Cabbage Patch* by Alice Hegan Rice
7. *The Mettle of the Pasture* by James Lane Allen
8. *Letters of a Self-Made Merchant to His Son* by George Horace Lorimer
9. *The One Woman* by Thomas Dixon
10. *The Little Shepherd of Kingdom Come* by John Fox Jr.

1904
1. *The Crossing* by Winston Churchill
2. *The Deliverance* by Ellen Glasgow
3. *The Masquerader*, anonymous (Katherine Cecil Thurston)
4. *In the Bishop's Carriage* by Miriam Michelson
5. *Sir Mortimer* by Mary Johnston
6. *Beverly of Graustark* by George Barr McCutcheon
7. *The Little Shepherd of Kingdom Come* by John Fox Jr.
8. *Rebecca of Sunnybrook Farm* by Kate Douglas Wiggin
9. *My Friend Prospero* by Henry Harland
10. *The Silent Places* by Stewart Edward White

* During the early years of *Publishers Weekly*'s bestseller lists, fiction and nonfiction were combined. Since fiction far and away outsold nonfiction titles, the top ten sellers were always fiction. In 1912, *Publishers Weekly* added a nonfiction bestseller list, only to drop it in 1914. In 1917, with the rising popularity of books on war, *Publishers Weekly* added a War-Books bestseller list and also reinstated the nonfiction bestseller list. In 1919, the War-Books bestseller list would be dropped.

the clash between tradition and new ideas and emerging social classes. Other such titles include *The Battle-Ground* (1902), *The Deliverance* (1904), *The Wheel of Life* (1906), *The Ancient Law* (1908), *The Romance of a Plain Man* (1909), and *The Miller of Old Church* (1911).

PAULINE E. HOPKINS: *Contending Forces: A Romance of Negro Life North and South.* One of the best-known African American woman writers prior to World War I had published all of her work, except this one, as magazine serials only. The novel is a powerful multigenerational saga of a black family, which provides one of the first fictional examinations of the lot of African American women.

HENRY JAMES: *The Soft Side.* A collection of twelve stories, including "Europe," "The Real Right Thing," "The Great Good Place," and "The Given Case."

MARY JOHNSTON (1870–1936): *To Have and to Hold.* Johnston's second novel, preceded by *Prisoners of Hope*

(1898), is a popular historical romance set in the Jamestown colony in 1621, mixing romance, adventure, and an authentic depiction of early colonial life in America.

JACK LONDON (1876–1916): *The Son of the Wolf.* Having sold his first story, "To the Man on Trail," to San Francisco's *Overland Monthly* and "An Odyssey of the North" to the *Atlantic Monthly* in 1899, London publishes his first collection of Klondike stories to widespread acclaim. His muscular prose and elemental stories energize American fiction. A second collection of Northland stories, *The God of His Fathers*, would be issued in 1901; additional Yukon stories appear in the subsequent collections *Children of the Frost* (1902), *The Faith of Men* (1904), *Love of Life* (1907), *Lost Face* (1910), *Smoke Bellew* (1912), *The Turtles of Tasmin* (1916), and *The Red One* (1918).

FRANK NORRIS: *A Man's Woman.* Written for the popular market to exploit public interest in Arctic

Theodore Dreiser

exploration, Norris's novel deals with an intrepid Arctic explorer who returns from an expedition to claim the love of an independent-minded nurse. Having enough sensational incidents to be regarded a potboiler, the novel is nevertheless noteworthy for showing Norris's attempt to explore the power dynamic in relationships between men and women.

BOOTH TARKINGTON: *Monsieur Beaucaire.* Tarkington achieves a popular success in this historical romance. It features a French duke who goes to England disguised as a barber during the reign of Louis XV.

MAURICE THOMPSON: *Alice of Old Vincennes.* Thompson is best remembered for this historical novel concerning George Rogers Clark's expedition to British-held Vincennes in the Northwest Territory during the American Revolution.

MARK TWAIN (SAMUEL LANGHORNE CLEMENS): *The Man That Corrupted Hadleyburg and Other Stories.* The title story is a moral fable exposing the hypocrisy and greed beneath the surface of small-town American life. A sack of money is deposited with a bank clerk at Hadleyburg, with instructions that it can be claimed by the person who befriended the clerk years before. All the town's prominent men try to claim the treasure, which turns out to be a bag of lead. It is regarded by many as Twain's finest short story.

EDITH WHARTON: *The Touchstone.* Wharton's first extended work is very much in the Jamesian tradition, concerning the ethical conflict between a man's desire to marry for money and his reluctance to sell love letters written to him by a celebrated woman.

OWEN WISTER: *The Jimmyjohn Boss.* Wister's story collection contains one of his first attempts at western fiction, "Hank Wilson." Another story, "Padre Ignazio," is about a parish priest exiled to a California mission.

Literary Criticism and Scholarship

GEORGE SANTAYANA: *Interpretations of Poetry and Religion.* Santayana's first volume of literary criticism explores the connection between the poetic imagination and spirituality. It includes his assessment of Emerson and Whitman.

EDMUND CLARENCE STEDMAN: *An American Anthology, 1787–1900.* Stedman provides examples from virtually every American poet of the period in what is hailed as an authoritative anthology.

BARRETT WENDELL (1855–1921): *A Literary History of America.* The professor who taught the first course at Harvard on American literature produces one of the first comprehensive American literary histories.

Nonfiction

FRANCIS LA FLESCHE (1860–1932): *The Middle Five: Indian Boys at School.* The first Native American to become a professional ethnologist supplies a memoir of his years at a mission school. It is regarded as a classic of Native American childhood biography, along with Charles Eastman's *Indian Boyhood* (1902).

THEODORE ROOSEVELT: *The Strenuous Life: Essays and Addresses.* Roosevelt's essay collection details his muscular philosophy that adversity builds character and that individuals must be tested by danger, hardship, and toil.

JOSIAH ROYCE: *The World and the Individual.* Royce's best-known philosophical work is this series of lectures presenting his theory of the Absolute (a second volume would appear in 1901).

JOSHUA SLOCUM (1844–c. 1909): *Sailing Alone Around the World.* Slocum narrates an account of his three-year voyage in the thirty-six-foot *Spray*, which he had built himself, in a popular work called "the *Walden* of the sea." Slocum was presumably lost at sea during another voyage to the Caribbean in 1909.

IDA TARBELL (1857–1944): *Life of Abraham Lincoln.* Tarbell's popular biography remained the standard work until 1947, when the Lincoln papers were made available to scholars.

Publications and Events

The Shubert Brothers — Sam S. (c. 1876–1905), Lee (1873–1953), and Jacob J. (1878–1963) — begin producing plays and acquiring theaters in New York, challenging the monopoly of the Theatrical Syndicate. Their first production is *The Brixton Burglary* (1901), a failure. But their second, the musical *A Chinese Honeymoon* (1902), succeeds. By 1916 they broke the syndicate's hold and became the most powerful theater managers and producers in America, operating more than a hundred theaters and controlling the bookings for a thousand others.

World's Work. This monthly magazine, founded and edited until 1913 by W. H. Page (1855–1918), celebrated the American way of life and the expanded role of the United States on the world's stage. It continued until 1932.

1901

Drama and Theater

DAVID BELASCO: *Du Berry.* Controversy erupts around Belasco's hit play, about a Parisian milliner who enters French royal circles, when it is charged that the playwright had plagiarized from the French playwright Jean Richepin. Belasco also has a success with the ethnic comedy *The Auctioneer*, about a Jewish peddler on New York's Lower East Side.

CLYDE FITCH: *The Climbers.* Fitch's drama details the corrosive impact of status seeking on a family. The play appears on Broadway simultaneously with three of Fitch's other plays, including *Captain Jinks of the Horse Marines*, which marks the stage debut of Ethel Barrymore.

ALBERT BIGELOW PAINE (1861–1937): *The Great White Way.* Paine, the friend and future biographer of Mark Twain, provides the popular nickname for New York's theater district in this play.

Fiction

IRVING BACHELLER: *D'ri and I.* Bacheller's historical romance set during the War of 1812 concerns a stalwart, raw-boned backwoodsman who accompanies the son of his employer into battle with Admiral Perry on Lake Erie. Based in part on the phenomenal success of *Eben Holden* (1900), the novel quickly sells more than 200,000 copies despite reviews that complain about the novel's improbable plot and wooden characters.

GEORGE WASHINGTON CABLE: *The Cavalier.* Bowing to financial pressure, Cable turns from his unpopular polemical *John March, Southerner* (1893) to a historical romance that becomes so popular that he would adapt it for the stage in 1902. It proves to be his last success; a steady decline in his literary powers would follow.

CHARLES W. CHESNUTT: *The Marrow of Tradition.* Chesnutt's novel, treating black and white half-sisters, is his most extensive analysis of the cause and effects of racial and social problems in the South. The book's failure would cause Chesnutt to observe that "I'm beginning to suspect that the public as a rule does not care for books in which the principal characters are colored people, or written with a striking sympathy with that race as contrasted to the white race."

WINSTON CHURCHILL: *The Crisis.* Set in St. Louis during the Civil War, Churchill's novel concerns a Boston lawyer who falls in love with the daughter of a Southern sympathizer, witnesses some pivotal events of the war, and encounters historical figures such as Lincoln, Grant, and Sherman. A popular and critical success, the novel helps establish Churchill as one of America's foremost novelists of the era.

ROBERT HERRICK (1868–1938): *The Real World.* After two realistic novels — *The Gospel of Freedom* (1898) and *The Web of Life* (1900) — Herrick, who was a professor of English at the University of Chicago from 1893 to 1923, produces the first of three "idealistic" works employing symbolism and allegorical plots to tell "the story of a mind's inner perception of living." It would be followed by similar novels, *A Life for a Life* (1910) and *The Healer* (1911).

HENRY JAMES: *The Sacred Fount.* In what has been viewed as a parody of James's own detached, convoluted narrative method, the novella, set at an English house party, has its narrator test his view that in any relationship the weaker party draws strength while draining the stronger.

SARAH ORNE JEWETT: *The Tory Lover.* Jewett's last major work is a striking departure from her characteristic quiet realism. It is a historical novel set during the American Revolution. Henry James counsels Jewett to return to her "country of the pointed fir," but a fall from a carriage on her fifty-third birthday effectively ends her literary career.

GEORGE BARR McCUTCHEON (1866–1928): *Graustark.* The Indiana writer's first novel borrows from Anthony Hope's popular *Prisoner of Zenda* (1894), sending an American into a mythical kingdom where he falls in love with a princess. Popular sequels — *Beverly of Graustark*

(1904) and *The Prince of Graustark* (1914) — would follow.

S. MITCHELL WEIR: *Circumstance*. Weir's Jamesian social satire studies a large group of characters tested by life's circumstances.

FRANK NORRIS: *The Octopus*. In the first volume of a projected, though uncompleted, trilogy entitled Epic of the Wheat, Norris attempts an American equivalent of the naturalistic studies by Émile Zola in the conflict between California wheat growers and the railroad (the octopus) that entangles their lives. In his review Jack London declares that "the promise of . . . *McTeague* has been realized. Can we ask more?" Critic Charles Child Walcutt regards it as "one of the finest American novels written before 1910. It towers immeasurably far above the sickly sentiments of Norris's contemporaries."

DAVID GRAHAM PHILLIPS (1867–1911): *The Great God Success*. The first of the muckraking journalist's twenty-three social problem novels. He would follow it with other titles exploring contemporary social issues, including *The Master-Rogue* (1903), *The Cost* (1904), *The Deluge* (1905), and *The Plum Tree* (1905).

ALICE HEGAN RICE (1870–1942): *Mrs. Wiggs of the Cabbage Patch*. The Kentucky-born children's book writer's most popular work is her first book about an indomitably optimistic widow living with her children in the tenement section of Louisville, Kentucky, known as "The Cabbage Patch."

UPTON SINCLAIR (1878–1968): *Springtime and Harvest* (retitled *King Midas*). Sinclair's first published novel, like all of his early fiction — *Prince Hugen* (1903), *The Journal of Arthur Stribling* (1903), *A Captain of Industry* (1906), and *The Overman* (1907) — is chiefly significant for reflecting the evolution of his views on social reform. Sinclair began writing to pay his way through New York's City College.

EDITH WHARTON: *Crucial Instances*. Wharton's second story collection is judged inferior to her first, *The Greater Inclination* (1899), but includes at least one important story, "Copy."

Nonfiction

JOHN MUIR: *Our National Parks*. This collection of articles, written to gain support for protecting wilderness lands in the West, is significant as a foundation for the twentieth-century environmentalist movement.

JACOB RIIS: *The Making of an American*. Riis supplies an autobiographical account of his background and career and the formation of his social conscience.

MARK TWAIN (**SAMUEL LANGHORNE CLEMENS**): "To the Person Sitting in Darkness." Regarded as Twain's

Booker T. Washington

most outspoken and significant anti-imperialist polemic, the essay appears in the *North America Review* and is distributed as a pamphlet by the Anti-Imperialist League.

BOOKER T. WASHINGTON: *Up from Slavery*. Washington's version of his life story is intended to inspire, and the details support the book's positivist theme of the struggle for success. Washington's accommodationist position on racial issues sparks ongoing debate over the proper response to racial injustice.

Poetry

EDWARD MARKHAM: *Lincoln and Other Poems*. Markham's second collection includes one of his most celebrated poems, "Lincoln, the Man of the People," which had been printed in virtually every newspaper in America and about which Jack London declares, "If its author had made no other bid for fame, this one bid would suffice."

WILLIAM VAUGHN MOODY: *Poems*. Moody's single poetry collection includes the handful of poems for which he is still remembered, such as "Gloucester Moors," "The Menagerie," "Ode in Time of Hesitation," and "On a Soldier Fallen in the Philippines."

ALBERY ALLSON WHITMAN: *An Idyl of the South: An Epic Poem in Two Parts*. Half of Whitman's narrative poem in ottava rima, "The Octoroon," a tragic love story between a white man and a slave woman, is considered the poet's greatest achievement.

1902

Drama and Theater

DAVID BELASCO AND JOHN LUTHER LONG: *The Darling of the Gods.* After their one-act *Madame Butterfly* (1900), the playwrights collaborate on a full-length romantic drama set in Japan and involving Yo-San's relationship with the outlaw Prince Kara.

PAUL LAURENCE DUNBAR: *In Dahomey.* Dunbar provides the lyrics for this musical by J. A. Shipp, which becomes the first full-length black musical to play at a mainstream New York theater. It establishes Bert Williams and George Walker as stars.

CLYDE FITCH: *The Girl with the Green Eyes.* The first of Fitch's dramatic character studies examines the corrosive effects of jealousy. The play's tragic momentum, however, is abruptly halted by the unrealistic happy ending, which mars the drama.

Fiction

GERTRUDE ATHERTON: *The Conqueror.* Atherton is recognized as pioneering a new fictional genre, the fictional biography, in this treatment of Alexander Hamilton's life, written "as if I stood beside Hamilton throughout his life." In 1952, Van Wyck Brooks would call the novel "perhaps the best of all American historical novels of the decade 1895–1905."

STEPHEN CRANE: *Last Words.* This posthumous collection of stories, sketches, and articles includes at least one important work, the story "An Episode of War."

RICHARD HARDING DAVIS: *Captain Macklin.* Davis adapts his soldier-of-fortune themes in an ambitious attempt to show the psychological development of the novel's protagonists. The book's failure causes Davis to vow to abandon fiction. He also publishes *Ranson's Folly,* a collection of novellas dramatized by Davis in 1904.

THOMAS DIXON (1864–1946): *The Leopard's Spots.* The first installment of Dixon's sensational white supremacist trilogy, treating the Southern response to Reconstruction, is a parody of *Uncle Tom's Cabin* that justifies lynching, Jim Crow segregation laws, and the disenfranchisement of African Americans. It would be followed by *The Clansman* (1905) and *The Traitor* (1907).

PAUL LAURENCE DUNBAR: *The Sport of the Gods.* Dunbar's last novel is his only one dealing exclusively with African American characters. It depicts a butler wrongly accused of theft, who is sentenced to ten years of hard labor and whose family is forced to relocate to New York

Paul Laurence Dunbar

City. It is regarded as Dunbar's major achievement in fiction, the first important protest novel by an African American writer, and the first significant novel to describe the life of blacks in Harlem.

HAMLIN GARLAND: *The Captain of the Gray-Horse Troops.* Garland's novel depicts unjust treatment of the Indians. It would be followed by *Cavanagh, Forest Ranger* (1910), about the conflict between ranchers and conservationists.

JOEL CHANDLER HARRIS: *Gabriel Tolliver: A Story of the Reconstruction.* Harris attempts a social study of the restlessness and uncertainty of newly freed blacks and the newly impoverished Southerners in the years following the Civil War. He also publishes a collection of local-color short stories, *The Making of a Statesman.*

WILLIAM DEAN HOWELLS: *The Kentons.* In this quietly realistic novel, Howells depicts an Ohio family who travel to New York and Europe. Though Henry James praises the book as "miraculously felt and beautifully done," it fails to find an audience.

HENRY JAMES: *The Wings of the Dove.* James's masterfully nuanced novel traces the efforts of Kate Croy to secure the dying Milly Theale's fortune for her unacknowledged fiancé, Merton Densher.

JACK LONDON: *A Daughter of the Snows.* London's first novel is a disjointed work overburdened by ideas. London would later lament, "Lord, Lord, how I squandered into it enough stuff for a dozen novels." He also publishes two collections of juvenilia, *The Cruise of the Dazzler* and *Tales of the Fish Patrol.*

GEORGE BARR McCUTCHEON: *Brewster's Millions.* Mc-Cutcheon's second novel, about an heir who must give away a million dollars, becomes one of the era's biggest-selling books. It would be successfully adapted for the stage by Winchell Smith in 1906.

MARK TWAIN (SAMUEL LANGHORNE CLEMENS): "A Double-Barrelled Detective Story." Twain's burlesque is a send-up of Sir Arthur Conan Doyle's Sherlock Holmes stories and the melodramatic literature of the day.

EDITH WHARTON: *The Valley of Decision.* Wharton's first full-length novel is set in eighteenth-century Italy, pitting the new antireligious beliefs promulgated by Rousseau and Voltaire against the dominant orthodoxy. It illustrates what will become one of the novelist's central themes: the high personal cost of violations of accepted conventions.

BRAND WHITLOCK (1869–1934): *The 13th District.* The first of Whitlock's social criticism novels concerns local political corruption in a Midwestern town as an election is determined in a smoke-filled room; it is based on Whitlock's experiences in Springfield, Illinois. The novel includes fictional portraits of actual figures such as Illinois governor John Peter Altgeld, Clarence Darrow, and William Jennings Bryan.

OWEN WISTER: *The Virginian.* Wister's novel becomes the prototypical western, establishing key ingredients for its many imitators, including the silent but deadly hero, the murderous villain, and the chivalric western code. Wister dedicates the book to his idol and Harvard classmate Theodore Roosevelt, who shares many characteristics of the novel's unnamed protagonist.

Nonfiction

JANE ADDAMS (1860–1935): *Democracy and Social Ethics.* In her first major publication, the founder in 1889 of the Chicago social settlement Hull-House analyzes the effects of American industrialization on immigrants and the urban poor, justifying social activism by calling for a shift in social attitudes from "an age of individualism to one of association." Her subsequent books include *New Ideals of Peace* (1907), outlining her pacifism; *The Spirit of Youth and the City Streets* (1909), on urban sociology; and *A New Conscience to an Ancient Evil* (1912), on the connection between urban poverty and prostitution.

Helen Keller

CHARLES EASTMAN (1858–1939): *Indian Boyhood.* One of the earliest Native American autobiographies captures Eastman's first fifteen years as a traditional hunter and warrior in Minnesota and Canada. The work makes Eastman the most widely known Native American writer in the first decades of the twentieth century. It would be followed by three collections of short stories dealing with Sioux traditions and history — *Red Hunters and the Animal People* (1904), *Old Indian Days* (1907), and *Wigwam Days* (1909) — and a continuation of his autobiography, *From the Deep Woods to Civilization* (1916).

WILLIAM JAMES: *The Varieties of Religious Experiences.* James submits religious states of consciousness to a psychological interpretation, asserting the practical value of religious belief as measured by personal happiness and positive human action.

HELEN KELLER (1880–1968): *The Story of My Life.* Written while she was in college, Keller's autobiographical reflections on her childhood and youth are both candid and inspiring and helped make her a national figure. Additional memoirs — *The World I Live In* (1908), *Out of the Dark* (1913), *My Religion* (1927), *Midstream* (1929), and *Let Us Have Faith* (1940) — would follow.

WOODROW WILSON: *A History of the American People.* Having serialized portions of his popular account of American political history in *Harper's* magazine in 1901, Wilson completes his five-volume survey, written, as he later observed, in order "to find which way we were going." Appointed president of Princeton on June 9, Wilson declares, "I have ceased to be an historian, and have become a man of business."

Poetry

EDWIN ARLINGTON ROBINSON: *Captain Craig.* Robinson's narrative title poem concerns a Tilbury Town vagabond and philosopher who advances the notion that one should learn to "laugh with God." Other significant poems in the collection are "Isaac and Archibald" and "The Book of Annandale."

Publications and Events

The *South Atlantic Quarterly.* Founded at Trinity College (which became Duke University in 1924) by John S. Bassett (its editor until 1905). The journal featured articles on Southern history and culture.

1903

Drama and Theater

GEORGE ADE: *The County Chairman.* Ade's first successful nonmusical play is a comedy about a local election, which displays the writer's skill in capturing colorful eccentrics and sparkling vernacular dialogue. His follow-up, *The College Widow* (1904), introduces collegiate football as a dramatic theme.

DAVID BELASCO: *Sweet Kitty Bellairs.* Belasco's drama depicts an Irish upstart in eighteenth-century Bath who proves herself morally superior to an English highborn lady. It would be adapted as an operetta by Rudolf Frimi (1879–1972) as *Kitty Darlin'* in 1917.

VICTOR HERBERT: *Babes in Toyland.* Herbert's musical fantasy about the adventures of Alan and Jane in Toyland features elaborate sets depicting Mother Goose characters. It is the composer's first great success.

Fiction

ANDY ADAMS (1850–1935): *The Log of a Cowboy.* Based on Adams's own experiences, the novel renders an authentic account of a cattle drive from Texas to Montana in 1882. Adams is regarded as one of the best chroniclers of cowboy and western life, presented in later works such as *The Outlet* (1905), *Cattle Brands* (1906), and *Reed Anthony, Cowman* (1907).

STEPHEN CRANE: *The O'Ruddy.* Written to make money and left unfinished at the time of Crane's death, this historical romance treating the picaresque adventures of an Irishman in England is completed by Canadian writer Robert Barr (1850–1912).

PAUL LAURENCE DUNBAR: *In Old Plantation Days.* This collection of stories romanticizing slavery would prompt a later critical complaint that Dunbar had helped perpetuate the plantation myth of white America. More recent critics have detected in the stories more of a balance between accommodation and protest.

JOHN FOX JR. (1862–1919): *The Little Shepherd of Kingdom Come.* The Kentucky-born writer's first popular success concerns a Cumberland Mountain shepherd loved by two women.

MARY E. WILKINS FREEMAN: *The Wind in the Rose-Bush and Other Stories.* Freeman publishes a collection of ghost stories that would later be praised by fantasy writer H. P. Lovecraft.

WILLIAM DEAN HOWELLS: *Questionable Shapes.* "The dean of American realism" collects three tales dealing with the supernatural. It would be followed in 1907 with *Between the Dark and the Daylight,* treating abnormal psychic states.

HENRY JAMES: *The Ambassadors.* Considered by many to be James's finest novel and the major justification for his complex, mature style, the story follows the mission of American Lambert Strether to reclaim a countryman from European entanglements, an endeavor that tests all of Strether's previous assumptions about Europe and America. James also publishes *The Better Sort.* This collection of stories includes two of James's greatest. "The Birthplace" is about the caretaker of the birthplace of a renowned English poet, who is encouraged to commercialize the place to increase the tourist trade; "The Beast in the Jungle" features the neurotic John Marcher, who mistakenly turns down love while waiting for something special to happen that will make his life extraordinary.

JACK LONDON: *The Call of the Wild.* London's most popular work is set during the Klondike gold rush and concerns the transformation of the domesticated ranch dog Buck from a dominating sled-dog to the leader of a wolf pack. London also publishes *The Kempton-Wace Letters.* Written with Anna Strunsky, a Stanford University student with whom London may or may not have had an affair, this epistolary dialogue on love is published anonymously. Strunsky's persona argues for an idealistic conception of love, whereas London, as a young economics professor, contends that romantic love is nothing but "pre-nuptial madness."

FRANK NORRIS: *A Deal in Wheat and Other Stories of the New and Old West.* The first of Norris's posthumously published works is a collection of stories that appeared in periodicals from 1901 to 1903. A second collection, *The Third Circle,* containing earlier magazine stories, would be issued in 1909. Also published is *The Pit,* the second volume of Norris's unfinished Epic of the Wheat trilogy, which had begun with *The Octopus* (1901). It concerns the attempt by Curtis Jodwin to corner the Chicago wheat market and explores his relationship with his wife, Laura. The novel shows the author shifting from his naturalistic techniques and deterministic philosophy to embrace more popular sentimentality. It becomes Norris's greatest popular success.

EDITH WHARTON: *Sanctuary.* Wharton's novella concerns a young woman who discovers a troubling secret in her fiancé's past, an insight that leads her to recognize the "moral sewage" that surrounds her.

KATE DOUGLAS WIGGIN: *Rebecca of Sunnybrook Farm.* The travails of the plucky, precocious Rebecca Randolph, who comes to live with her two maiden aunts, becomes one of the era's biggest-selling books. A sequel, *New Chronicles of Rebecca,* would follow in 1907; the novel would be first successfully dramatized in 1910.

Literary Criticism and Scholarship

FRANK NORRIS: *The Responsibilities of the Novelist.* Norris's collection of literary criticism is published posthumously. In the title essay, the writer attempts to define his artistic credo, which rejects the notion of art for art's sake or a narrow realism ("the drama of broken teacups") and espouses the essential truths of the human condition.

GEORGE EDWARD WOODBERRY: *America in Literature.* Woodbury's literary history excludes figures such as Mark Twain and Walt Whitman and expresses his hostility to literary realism.

Nonfiction

MARY AUSTIN (1868–1934): *The Land of Little Rain.* This is the first of Austin's highly regarded naturalist studies of the Southwest. Other titles include *The Flock* (1906), *California: The Land of the Sun* (1914), and *The Land of Journey's End* (1924). Born in Illinois, Austin moved to California at the age of eighteen and made a study of Indian life.

W.E.B. DU BOIS: *The Souls of Black Folk.* Du Bois's important collection of essays and sketches portrays black culture and history in its various aspects, including the views of sharecroppers, the music of black churches,

W.E.B. Du Bois

a history of the Freedman's Bureau, and a portrait of Booker T. Washington.

HENRY JAMES: *William Wetmore Story and His Friends.* James's biography of the expatriate American sculptor and writer is chiefly significant for his evocation of the Anglo-American colony in Rome and for the extracts he supplies of letters to Story by his more famous literary friends.

JACK LONDON: *The People of the Abyss.* After spending six weeks living in London's East End disguised as a stranded, down-and-out American seaman, London reports on slum conditions; his work anticipates the New Journalism technique of total immersion and direct experience. London would later state that "No other book of mine took so much of my young heart and tears as that study of the economic degradation of the poor."

MARK TWAIN (SAMUEL LANGHORNE CLEMENS): *My Debut as a Literary Person, and Other Essays and Stories.* The title work had first appeared in the *Century* in 1889 and recounts the events leading up to Twain's first publication in an eastern magazine.

Poetry

PAUL LAURENCE DUNBAR: *Lyrics of Love and Laughter.* Dunbar's collection contains "The Poet," a lament that he is recognized only as a dialect poet; "The Haunted Oak," a poem about lynching; and verse tributes to Lincoln, Robert Gould Shaw, and Booker T. Washington.

H. L. MENCKEN (1880–1956): *Ventures into Verse.* Mencken's first book is a collection of verse echoing Rudyard Kipling's style. The Baltimore journalist would become the editor of the *Evening Herald* from 1905 to 1906 before joining the staff of the *Baltimore Evening Sun.*

GEORGE STERLING (1869–1926): *The Testimony of the Suns and Other Poems.* The volume's title work is Sterling's most ambitious poem, an attempt to formulate a cosmological explanation for human existence and progress. It establishes him as the leading poet of the bohemian literary circle in San Francisco, which also included Ambrose Bierce and Jack London.

Publications and Events

Everybody's. Beginning in 1899 as the house organ of Wanamaker's Department Store, the magazine became an independent periodical in 1903 and one of the principal vehicles for muckrakers such as Upton Sinclair and Lincoln Steffens. It continued publication until 1928.

1904
Drama and Theater

DAVID BELASCO AND JOHN LUTHER LONG: *Adrea.* The playwrights' last collaboration is a romantic tragedy set during the fifth century, which involves a competition between two royal sisters.

GEORGE M. COHAN (1878–1942): *Little Johnny Jones.* Cohan's fifth full-length play establishes him as a popular playwright and performer. Cohan stars as an American jockey who competes in the English Derby. The musical features two of his most famous songs, "Give My Regards to Broadway" and "I'm a Yankee Doodle Dandy."

RICHARD HARDING DAVIS: *The Dictator.* Davis achieves his first theatrical success with this farce set in an imaginary Central American country beset by continual revolutions. He also produces a dramatic adaptation of his 1902 novel *Ransom's Folly.* Two other plays by Davis — *The Galloper* and *Miss Civilization* — would follow in 1905.

CHARLES KLEIN (1867–1915): *The Music Master.* Klein has one of his largest popular successes in this drama about a Viennese conductor's search for his daughter, who is taken from him by his wife when she deserts him for another. Klein was a former actor who wrote librettos, comedies, and melodramas, including *El Capitan* (1896), *Heartsease* (1897), and *The Auctioneer* (1901).

Fiction

B. M. BOWER (1871–1940): *Chip of the Flying U.* The first, and best, of the western novels written by Bertha Bower, who published under her initials to disguise her gender.

JAMES BRANCH CABELL (1879–1958): *The Eagle's Shadow.* Cabell's first novel (and publication) is a romance about modern materialism. A Virginia native, Cabell would base his fiction after his second novel, *Gallantry* (1907), in the imaginary medieval French province of Poictesme, the locus for an immense novel sequence.

WINSTON CHURCHILL: *The Crossing.* Regarded as Churchill's best novel, this historical romance is set during the Revolutionary War along the Kentucky frontier and includes appearances by the frontiersmen George Rogers Clark, Simon Kenton, and Daniel Boone.

CLARENCE DARROW (1857–1938): *Farmington.* The first of the lawyer and social reformer's two novels is based on his autobiography and reflects his social views. The other is *An Eye for an Eye* (1905).

PAUL LAURENCE DUNBAR: *The Heart of Happy Hollow.* Dunbar's final collection of short fiction includes what many consider his best story, "The Scapegoat," about a black party boss who seeks revenge on those who have ousted him from power. It also includes "The Lynching of Jube Benson" and "A Defender of Faith," his only story to describe the realities of a black ghetto in the North.

ELLEN GLASGOW: *The Deliverance.* One of Glasgow's few best-selling novels, which she described as a "big, deep, human document . . . wrung from life itself," considers the dispossessed Southern aristocracy following the Civil War.

O. HENRY (WILLIAM SYDNEY PORTER) (1862–1910): *Cabbages and Kings.* Born in North Carolina, the writer lived for a decade in Texas, writing magazine pieces while working as a bank teller. This is his first book, a loosely joined collection of stories derived from his experiences in Central America, where he had fled after being indicted for embezzlement. He eventually turned himself in, was convicted, and served three years of a five-year sentence in an Ohio penitentiary.

ROBERT HERRICK: *The Common Lot.* Herrick's novel concerns a corrupt young architect whose greed leads him to design unsafe houses.

WILLIAM DEAN HOWELLS: *The Son of Royal Langbrith.* One of the best of Howells's later novels tells the story of a son's delusions about his dead father, who in reality was a scoundrel who tyrannized his wife. The novel presents the ethical dilemma of whether the son should learn the truth.

Jack London working on his manuscript *The Sea-Wolf*

HENRY JAMES: *The Golden Bowl.* James's last completed novel is one of his most masterful explorations of a triangle of relationships. American heiress Maggie Verver, her Italian husband, and her close friend Charlotte Stant cope with loyalty, fidelity, and betrayal.

JACK LONDON: *The Sea-Wolf.* London portrays a version of the Nietzschean superman in schooner captain Wolf Larsen, one of the most memorable characters in American literature.

UPTON SINCLAIR: *Manassas.* Sinclair's historical novel concerning an idealistic Southern abolitionist represents a turning point in Sinclair's career, expressing his willingness to go against his Southern background and endorse a radical response to a social problem. The book would lead to his masterpiece, *The Jungle* (1906); after tackling a historical social problem, he turns his attention to a contemporary assessment of "wage slavery."

EDWARD STRATEMEYER: *The Bobbsey Twins; or, Merry Days Indoors and Out.* Writing under the pen name "Laura Lee Hope," Stratemeyer introduces a popular fictional series for girls featuring two sets of twins — Flossie, Freddie, Nan, and Bert.

GENE STRATTON PORTER (1863–1924): *Freckles.* The Illinois author's most popular work is this juvenile novel set in the Indiana Limberlost swamp country. Her next

book, *A Girl of the Limberlost* (1909), would be equally successful.

EDITH WHARTON: *The Descent of Man and Other Stories.* Wharton's third story collection is called by Wharton biographer R.W.B. Lewis her best, showing her "full maturity as a satirist of American manners." Wharton also publishes her first travel book, *Italian Villas and Their Gardens,* illustrated with the watercolors of Maxfield Parrish (1870–1966).

Nonfiction

HENRY ADAMS: *Mont-Saint-Michel and Chartres.* In the first private printing of this classic study of medieval civilization, which would be published in 1913, Adams contrasts the unified, coherent system of beliefs and culture of the Middle Ages with the confusing modern "multiverse."

EUGENE V. DEBS (1855–1926): *Unionism and Socialism, a Plea for Both.* The best-known pamphlet of the labor activist and socialist politician. Others would follow, including *Industrial Unionism* (1905), *The Growth of Socialism* (1910), *The Children of the Poor* (1911), and *Walls and Bars* (1927), his autobiographical reflections written during his incarceration in an Atlanta penitentiary.

PAUL ELMER MORE (1864–1937): *Shelburne Essays.* The first of a series of collected essays and reviews by the professor of Sanskrit and classics at Harvard and Bryn Mawr that would grow to fourteen volumes by 1936. They elaborate More's views, which made him a leader of the proponents of the New Humanism. More would edit the *Nation* from 1909 to 1914 before resuming his scholarship and teaching at Princeton.

CARRY NATION (1846–1911): *The Use and Need of the Life of Carry Nation.* The memoir of the notorious hatchet-wielding temperance crusader.

LINCOLN STEFFENS (1866–1936): *The Shame of the Cities.* After publishing an article in 1902 on corruption in St. Louis, Steffens widens his investigation to other cities and collects his findings here, in the first of a series of muckracking exposés of corruption that include *The Struggle of Self-Government* (1906) and *Upbuilders* (1909).

IDA TARBELL: *The History of the Standard Oil Company.* Personally motivated by her conviction that her father had been ruined by the company, Tarbell documents a case against Standard Oil and its founder, John D. Rockefeller, in one of the great achievements of the muckracking era. Commenting on the connection between Tarbell's book and the 1911 Supreme Court decision to break up the company, historian Charles D. Hazen

Ida Tarbell

would observe that "Miss Tarbell is the only historian I have ever heard of whose findings were corroborated by the Supreme Court of the United States."

Poetry

WILLIAM STANLEY BRAITHWAITE (1878–1962): *Lyrics of Life and Love.* The first of the African American poet's collections, to be followed by *The House of Falling Leaves* (1908). Braithwaite's reliance on conventional verse forms and his avoidance of social or racial themes sets him apart from trends both in modern poetry and among African American writers.

Publications and Events

American Academy of Arts and Letters. The organization is chartered by an act of Congress to promote American literature. Original members include Henry Adams, Mark Twain, William Dean Howells, and Henry James.

"A National Art Theatre for America." The record of a symposium is published in the *Arena*. Denouncing the commercial policy of the Theatrical Syndicate, prominent critics call for the creation of a national theater. This leads to the opening of the New Theatre in New York City in 1909 and a short-lived attempt to establish a national repertory group to produce the best dramas, both American and foreign.

1905
Drama and Theater

DAVID BELASCO: *The Girl of the Golden West.* Belasco's popular western drama features a schoolmarm/saloon keeper who falls in love with an outlaw and plays cards to decide his fate. Puccini would create an opera based on the story in 1910.

WILLIAM C. DE MILLE (1878–1955): *Strongheart.* De Mille's first produced play features an early sympathetic treatment of a Native American's love for a white woman. De Mille was the son of playwright Henry De Mille and the father of dancer/choreographer Agnes De Mille.

VICTOR HERBERT: *Mlle. Modiste.* Herbert's operetta concerns a shop girl whose love for a higher-born beau is threatened by her employer and his rich uncle. It is regarded at the time as the greatest American musical ever produced. Herbert's biggest commerical success would come a year later, however, with *The Red Mill*, about two Americans stranded in a small Dutch village.

CHARLES KLEIN: *The Lion and the Mouse.* The decade's biggest hit and longest-running play, with 686 performances, is this not-so-veiled dramatization based on Ida Tarbell's muckraking campaign against John D. Rockefeller. Klein would continue to feature social commentary in his dramas, as in his attack on police brutality in his play *The Third Degree* (1909).

EDWIN MILTON ROYLE (1862–1942): *The Squaw Man.* Of the melodramatist's more than thirty productions, this play about an Englishman who immigrates to the American West and falls in love with an Indian is generally regarded as his best. In his career in entertainment, Royle wrote, directed, and acted in plays and composed lyrics for musicals.

Fiction

MARY AUSTIN: *Isidro.* Austin's first novel is a historical romance set in California during Mexican rule.

REX BEACH (1877–1949): *Pardners.* The first of the author's popular Alaskan novels. It would be followed by *The Spoilers* (1906), *The Silver Horde* (1909), and *The Iron Trail* (1913). Beach, from Michigan, spent a number of years in the Klondike.

FRANCES HODGSON BURNETT: *A Little Princess.* This reworking of Burnett's novel *Sara Crewe* (1887), first produced as a play in 1902, is the story of pampered girl who is mistreated at Miss Minchin's Select Seminary for Young Ladies when her father dies destitute. It becomes one of Burnett's best-loved works and would be adapted as a film starring Shirley Temple in 1939.

ELLIS PARKER BUTLER (1869–1937): "Pigs Is Pigs." The Iowa humorist's story published in the *American Magazine* is about a shipping agent who insists that a consignment of guinea pigs be treated as livestock. This provokes a comic dispute in a story that becomes a popular sensation.

JAMES BRANCH CABELL: *The Line of Love.* Cabell's initial short story collection is the first in his series of romantic treatments of the medieval past. Other titles include *Gallantry* (1907) and *Chivalry* (1909).

WILLA CATHER (1873–1947): *The Troll Garden.* Cather publishes her first work of fiction, a story collection dealing with the impact of the insensitive and vulgar on beauty and the imagination. Included are some of Cather's finest stories, such as "The Sculptor's Funeral," "A Wagner Matinée," and, arguably her finest, "Paul's Case."

CHARLES W. CHESNUTT: *The Colonel's Dream.* Chesnutt's final race novel depicts a white idealist who confronts the racial hatred in the South. It represents Chesnutt's most thorough analysis of race issues. The novel's commercial failure leads to his abandoning fiction, and he would subsequently publish only three minor short stories before his death.

THOMAS DIXON: *The Clansman.* Dixon's heroic portrait of Southern white resistance to Reconstruction is widely credited with revitalizing the Ku Klux Klan, which is portrayed as redeeming the South from black domination. It would provide the source for D. W. Griffith's landmark film *The Birth of a Nation* (1915) and is the second of a trilogy on Southern history, preceded by *The Leopard's Spots* (1902) and to be followed by *The Traitor* (1907).

ROBERT HERRICK: *The Memoirs of an American Citizen.* One of Herrick's enduring works is a first-person narrative of an American success story, with an ambiguous depiction of the pursuit of wealth and power.

JACK LONDON: *The Game.* London's novel describes the final bout of a prizefighter whose skill in the ring gives way to an accident that takes his life.

S. WEIR MITCHELL: *Constance Trescott.* A character study of a woman obsessed with gaining revenge for her husband's murder. Weir would regard it as his finest book and the "best American tragic novel."

MARK TWAIN (SAMUEL LANGHORNE CLEMENS): *King Leopold's Soliloquy.* Twain mounts a satirical attack on King Leopold II of Belgium and his brutal regime in the Congo, in a dramatic monologue in which the king delivers an ineffective defense of colonization.

EDITH WHARTON: *The House of Mirth.* The story of Lily Barth's scheme to secure a rich husband provides one of Wharton's richest portraits of New York society and its crippling reliance on wealth and behavioral rules. Diana Trilling would call the novel "one of the most telling indictments of the whole of American society, of a whole social system based on the chance distribution of wealth, that has ever been put on paper."

Literary Criticism and Scholarship

JAMES GIBBON HUNEKER (1860–1921): *Iconoclasts, a Book of Dramatists.* Having previously published his first book of literary essays, *Overtones: A Book of Temperaments* (1904), Huneker establishes his reputation as a leading literary and dramatic critic with this first American book on modern European dramatists such as Henrik Ibsen and George Bernard Shaw.

HENRY JAMES: *The Question of Our Speech and the Lesson of Balzac: Two Lectures.* James gives these two lectures frequently on his 1905 American tour. The first presents his critique of American speech and what it reveals about American culture. The second is his tribute to Balzac, the novelist he calls "the father of us all." James also publishes a collection of travel essays, *English Hours.*

H. L. MENCKEN: *George Bernard Shaw and His Plays.* The first of Mencken's two early critical works is an assessment of the dramatist. The other is *Friedrich Nietzsche* (1908).

Nonfiction

MARY BOYKIN CHESNUT (1823–1886): *A Diary from Dixie.* One of the literary and historical classics of the Civil War is this diary of a prominent South Carolinian who recorded her observations and experiences from 1861 to 1865. The complete text of her diary would be issued in 1982 as *Mary Chesnut's Civil War.*

DANIEL DE LEON (1852–1914): *Socialist Reconstruction of Society.* The major philosophical work of the cofounder, with Eugene Debs, of the Socialist Democratic Party and the Industrial Workers of the World (I.W.W.).

JACK LONDON: *War of the Classes.* In the same year that he receives 981 votes as the Socialist candidate for mayor of Oakland, London issues a collection of essays on sociological topics. *Revolution and Other Essays* would follow in 1910.

GEORGE SANTAYANA: *The Life of Reason.* Santayana's most important early work is this five-volume study (completed in 1906) of rationalism in Western consciousness, institutions, and culture.

EDITH WHARTON: *Italian Backgrounds.* Wharton's first travel book is a compilation of Italian travel sketches. It includes "Sanctuaries of the Pennine Alps," her one major contribution to art history, which reattributes the terra-cotta sculptures at the monastery of San Vivaldo to Giovanni della Robbia. Although the book is generally well received, some reviewers complain that it is too pedantic and not "feminine."

Poetry

TRUMBULL STICKNEY (1874–1904): *Poems.* Having published only a single volume, *Dramatic Verses* (1902), during his lifetime, Stickney is memorialized with this posthumous collection featuring the poems of his previous volume and uncollected works. Neglected as a poet of unfulfilled promise, Stickney would later attract advocates including Conrad Aiken, Edmund Wilson, and most recently, John Hollander, who has argued that "his work appears more central than ever. The interest is not in style, but in the grasp of the visionary moment."

Publications and Events

George Pierce Baker (1866–1935) begins teaching English 47, a playwriting course at Harvard, adding (in 1913) a workshop component to allow students to produce their work. George Abbott, Philip Barry, S. N. Behrman, John Dos Passos, Sidney Howard, Eugene O'Neill, and Thomas Wolfe participated. The course and workshop continued until 1925.

Variety. Sime Silverman (1873–1933) launches the theatrical trade journal that originally concentrates on vaudeville but would expand to cover film, radio, television, and music. It remains a rich source of American slang, popularizing or originating terms such as *high-hat, pushover, belly laugh,* and others.

1906
Drama and Theater

GEORGE BROADHURST (1866–1952): *The Man of the Hour.* Broadhurst, English-born playwright of comedies such as *The Wrong Mr. Wright* (1897) and *Why Smith Left Home* (1899), produces a popular muckraking drama about an idealistic mayor who fights political corruption.

GEORGE M. COHAN: *Forty-Five Minutes from Broadway* and *George Washington, Jr.* These are two of Cohan's biggest hits. The first features the title song and "Mary's a Grand Old Name"; the second stars the playwright and introduces the flag-waving song "You're a Grand Old Flag."

WILLIAM COLLIER (1866–1944) AND GRANT STEWART (1866–1929): *Caught in the Rain.* This farce concerns a gruff Colorado miner who falls in love with a woman he encounters during a downpour. It becomes the season's biggest hit and would be adapted as the musical *Pitter Patter* in 1920. Collier and Stewart were popular actors of the day.

RACHEL CROTHERS (1878–1958): *The Three of Us.* The Illinois-born director and playwright's first theatrical success is about a sister and her two brothers who own a Nevada silver mine. The play is praised for its natural characterization and minimal reliance on stage contrivance.

OWEN DAVIS (1874–1956): *Nellie, the Beautiful Cloak Model.* The most famous of Davis's more than two hundred popular melodramas, written for touring companies at a rate of one per every two or three weeks. Davis features minimal dialogue for the plays' largely immigrant audiences and relies on "noble sentiments so dear to audiences of that class."

JAMES FORBES (1871–1938): *The Chorus Lady.* Forbes's first full-length production concerns a chorus girl's sacrifice of her reputation for her sister. A smash hit, it would be followed by other popular comedies reflecting the current social scene, including *The Traveling Salesman* (1908) and *The Commuters* (1910).

THEODORE KREMER (c. 1871–1923): *Bertha, the Sewing Machine Girl.* This is the most popular of several dramatizations based on a serial, which had appeared in the 1860s in the *New York Weekly*, about the travails of a sweatshop worker who is victimized by her father's murderer. The German-born Kremer produced a number of melodramas with titles such as *The Slaves of the Orient* and *The Great Automobile Mystery.*

LANGDON MITCHELL: *The New York Idea.* Mitchell's chief theatrical achievement is this witty social satire on divorce and marriage. The title is explained by a character's comment: "Marry for whim! That's the New York idea of marriage." The play prompts one critic to call Mitchell "the American Shaw."

WILLIAM VAUGHN MOODY: *The Great Divide.* Originally produced as *A Sabine Woman*, this is the first of Moody's two produced plays and dramatizes the cultural gap between the American East and West. It takes the sensational subject of a prospective rapist who falls in love with his intended victim. Reviewer Walter Prichard Eaton writes, "No other American play has ever gone so deep, has ever seized hold of so powerful an idea."

WINCHELL SMITH (c. 1871–1933): *Brewster's Millions.* A dramatization of George Barr McCutcheon's 1902 comic fantasy about an heir who must spend a million dollars without revealing why. Smith was an actor, director, and playwright of works such as *The Fortune Hunter* (1909), *The Boomerang* (1915), and *Turn to the Right* (1916).

RICHARD WALTON TULLY (1877–1945) AND DAVID BELASCO: *The Rose of the Rancho.* This popular western drama deals with the exploitation of the Spanish in California by lawless Americans.

Fiction

WINSTON CHURCHILL: *Coniston.* Churchill's novel about New England politics in the nineteenth century features one of his greatest characters, the unscrupulous politician Jethro Bass, modeled on an actual New Hampshire political boss. It is the first in a series of social problem novels that includes *Mr. Crewe's Career* (1908), also about politics; *A Modern Chronicle* (1910), on divorce; *The Inside of the Cup* (1913), on the modern church; and *The Dwelling Place of Light* (1917), on industrialization.

MARGARET DELAND: *The Awakening of Helena Richie.* This is the first of a series of Deland's novels dealing with challenges faced by women, in this case, the raising of a homeless boy by a single woman. A sequel, *The Iron Woman* (1911), concerns divorce; it would be followed by *The Rising Tide* (1916), on women's suffrage, and *The Vehement Flame* (1922), examining adultery.

O. HENRY (WILLIAM SYDNEY PORTER): *The Four Million.* The title of this story collection refers to the population of New York City, the subject of many of these portraits of city life. It includes O. Henry's most famous story, "The Gift of the Magi," and "The Furnished Room," which has been called his best. An immense bestseller, the collection establishes O. Henry's reputation nationwide.

JACK LONDON: *White Fang.* London reverses the evolutionary process of *The Call of the Wild* (1903) by depicting a wild dog domesticated through kindness and love. Also published in 1906, *Before Adam* conjures up primitive man in the story of Big Tooth and his mate, Swift One.

ERNEST POOLE (1880–1950): *The Voice of the Street.* After helping Sinclair Lewis with the research for *The Jungle*, Poole publishes his first novel, a documentary of poverty in New York City's Lower East Side.

A poster advertising *The Jungle,* an exposé of the meat-packing industry, by Upton Sinclair

UPTON SINCLAIR: *The Jungle.* Sinclair's exposé of the Chicago meat-packing industry focuses on the destruction of a hardworking immigrant family. The novel creates a sensation, prompting the Roosevelt administration to mount a federal investigation that would result in legislative reforms.

MARK TWAIN (SAMUEL LANGHORNE CLEMENS): *The $30,000 Bequest and Other Stories.* The title story in this collection is a satirical indictment of America's money culture. The volume also includes "Extracts from Adam's Diary," "Eve's Diary," and "A Dog's Tale."

OWEN WISTER: *Lady Baltimore.* Wister's follow-up to *The Virginian* has been called a "Jamesian comedy of manners" set in Charleston, South Carolina. A bestseller, it explores Wister's major theme: the assault of materialism on a traditional way of life.

Literary Criticism and Scholarship

HENRY DAVID THOREAU: *Journal.* Thoreau's journals, regarded by many as his greatest achievement, are first published in fourteen volumes, along with his collected *Writings* (twenty volumes).

HORACE TRAUBEL (1858–1919): *With Walt Whitman in Camden.* The first volume of Traubel's massive diary, recording his almost daily conversations with the poet, appears. Additional volumes would follow in 1908, 1914, 1953, 1963, and 1982. This indefatigable promoter of Whitman's works was one of Whitman's literary executors, the founder of a journal focused on Whitman's works, and a published poet.

Nonfiction

SAMUEL HOPKINS ADAMS (1871–1958): *The Great American Fraud.* Adams's exposé of patent medicines, a significant muckraking book, contributes to the enactment of the Pure Food and Drug Act. He would also raise the subject of quackery in his first novel, *The Clarion* (1914).

AMBROSE BIERCE: *The Cynic's Word Book.* The first edition of Bierce's compilation of his ironic definitions. It would be enlarged and retitled as *The Devil's Dictionary* in 1911.

MARK TWAIN (SAMUEL LANGHORNE CLEMENS): *What Is Man?* Twain's essay, based on a talk delivered in 1883, rewritten in 1899, and privately printed in 1906, takes the form of a Socratic dialogue between a young man and a disillusioned older man who dismisses free will and morality as delusions and suggests that man is a pawn of blind, deterministic forces.

Poetry

WILLIAM ELLERY LEONARD (1876–1944): *Sonnets and Poems.* Leonard's first collection displays both emotional intensity and psychological depth. *The Vaunt of Man* (1912) and *The Lynching Bee* (1920) would follow. Leonard was a longtime professor of English at the University of Wisconsin who produced scholarly works and translations of Lucretius and *Beowulf.*

1907
Drama and Theater

CLYDE FITCH: *The Truth.* Fitch's play is a psychological protrait of a pathological liar. Unappreciated in the United States, the drama is enthusiastically received in Europe, where it is compared with the works of Ibsen.

HENRY JAMES: *The High Bid.* Originally written as the play *Sommersoft* (1895) at the request of actress Ellen Terry, then turned into the short story "Covering End" in 1898, this play gives an account of a courtship complicated by a mortgage on a country house. Successfully produced in Edinburgh, it would run for only a few matinee performances in London in 1909.

MARGARET MAYO (1882–1951): *Polly of the Circus.* This popular drama depicts a romance between a woman circus rider and a minister. Mayo was an actress from 1898 to 1903 before retiring to devote herself to writing a dramatic adaptation of *The Jungle* and original works such as *Baby Mine* (1910) and *Twin Beds* (1914).

AUGUSTUS THOMAS: *The Witching Hour.* Thomas uses telepathy and hypnosis as part of the action surrounding a murder trial in what is regarded as his best work.

FLORENZ ZIEGFELD JR. (1867–1932): *Follies of 1907.* The producer initiates the first in an annual series of stage extravaganzas that would continue until 1925. Each features a chorus line of beautiful girls in sumptuous costumes and the leading musical and comic performers of the day, including Fanny Brice, Eddie Cantor, W. C. Fields, Will Rogers, and many others.

Fiction

O. HENRY (WILLIAM SYDNEY PORTER): *The Trimmed Lamp.* The title story of O. Henry's collection is one of his few stories in which a character undergoes change. It also includes two other noteworthy stories, "Harlem Tragedy" and "The Pendulum." O. Henry also publishes a second collection, *Heart of the West,* which draws on his experiences in Texas.

JACK LONDON: *Love of Life and Other Stories.* London's collection contains two of his best tales, "The Unexpected" and "The Sun-Dog Trail."

S. WEIR MITCHELL: *The Red City: A Novel of the Second Administration of President Washington.* Mitchell's sequel to *Hugh Wynne* (1897) considers the political rivalry between the Federalists and the Republicans.

JOHN G. NEIHARDT (1881–1973): *The Lonesome Trail.* The Illinois-born writer's first book, a collection of short stories, draws on his experiences living among Native Americans in Nebraska from 1897 to 1907. He also publishes a collection of lyrics, *A Bundle of Myrrh.*

EDITH WHARTON: *Madame de Treymes.* Wharton's first book after her move to France explores the cultural differences between Americans and Europeans. She also publishes her only novel of social reform, *The Fruit of the Tree,* set in an American mill town.

BRAND WHITLOCK: *The Turn of the Balance.* The liberal reform mayor of Toledo, Ohio (1905–1913), publishes his most ambitious novel, a wide-ranging indictment of the inequities and injustices of American city life.

HAROLD BELL WRIGHT (1872–1944): *The Shepherd of the Hills.* The first major literary success of the New York–born clergyman who had served churches in Missouri and Kansas. The story of a disillusioned Chicago minister who is reinvigorated when he goes to the Ozark Mountains helps make Wright the most popular novelist of the period. The novel's theme of pastoral nostalgia would be repeated in the successful follow-up, *The Calling of Dan Matthews* (1909).

Literary Criticism and Scholarship

HENRY JAMES: Prefaces to the New York Edition of his novels. The first of the twenty-four volumes of the New York Edition of James's work (completed in 1909) is published with prefaces that offer a remarkable personal critique of his intentions, techniques, and development.

Nonfiction

HENRY ADAMS: *The Education of Henry Adams.* Adams's classic autobiography, subtitled "A Study of Twentieth-Century Multiplicity," is privately printed, to be later published in 1917. Adams provides an analysis of the modern world through a selective account of his own development.

HENRY JAMES: *The American Scene.* After more than twenty years abroad, James had returned to the United States in 1904 for an extended visit and tour. This volume summarizes his rediscovery of his homeland and the changes he observed.

WILLIAM JAMES: *Pragmatism: A New Name for Some Old Ways of Thinking.* Lectures delivered at the Lowell Institute and at Columbia in 1906 and 1907 present James's major philosophical tenets of a "mediating system" that avoids abstractions, "pretended absolutes and origins" toward "facts, towards action, and towards power." A follow-up, *The Meaning of Truth,* would appear in 1909.

JACK LONDON: *The Road.* London's hoboing experiences in 1894 are recounted in this series of recollections. London would later observe that to "this training of my tramp days is due much of my success as a storywriter," since he had learned to tell a convincing story in exchange for food.

WILLIAM GRAHAM SUMNER (1840–1910): *Folkways.* The Yale economist's masterwork analyzes the evolution of social institutions.

MARK TWAIN (SAMUEL LANGHORNE CLEMENS): *Christian Science.* Twain combines his articles (published 1899–1903) that critique Christian Science with new material lampooning the religion's tenets and its leader, Mary Baker Eddy (1821–1910), whom Twain considers dangerous.

Poetry

ROBERT W. SERVICE (1874–1958): "The Shooting of Dan McGrew." Service's most famous poem is a ballad set during the Klondike gold rush. It is collected in the volume

Songs of a Sourdough, the first in a string of comparable ballad collections. The Canadian-born poet and novelist lived for a number of years near the Arctic Circle.

1908

Drama and Theater

EDWARD SHELDON (1886–1946): *Salvation Nell.* The playwright's initial stage success is this drama of a scrubwoman who is rescued by the Salvation Army and in turn reforms her convict boyfriend. The play features a realistic depiction of city squalor.

BOOTH TARKINGTON: *The Man from Home.* Tarkington's jingoistic drama shows a man from Indiana exposing the villainy of an English nobleman. Critic Walter Prichard Eaton calls it "an excellent bad play." It would be performed for six consecutive theatrical seasons for a total of 496 performances.

EUGENE WALTER (1874–1941): *Paid in Full.* Walter achieves his first stage success in this drama about the travails of a woman married to a husband who prostitutes her to save his career. The play is noteworthy for its avoidance of melodrama despite its sensational subject. More than two dozen of Walter's works would reach Broadway, including *The Easiest Way* (1909) and *The Trail of the Lonesome Pine* (1912).

Fiction

GEORGE RANDOLPH CHESTER (1869–1924): *Get-Rich-Quick-Wallingford.* Chester's popular stories, which had first appeared in the *Saturday Evening Post*, concern a con man's shady business dealings. George M. Cohan would adapt the story for stage in 1910. Chester continues Wallingford's misadventures in *Young Wallingford* (1910), *Wallingford and Blackie Daw* (1913), and *Wallingford in His Prime* (1913).

JOHN FOX JR.: *The Trail of the Lonesome Pine.* Fox's novel about an engineer who is caught in the middle of feuding Kentucky mountaineers becomes a bestseller, a play dramatized by Eugene Walter (1912), the title of a popular song (1913), and a silent film (1922).

ZONA GALE (1874–1938): *Friendship Village.* Gale follows her first novel, *Romance Island* (1906), with her first story collection, largely nostalgic reflections of her own small-town upbringing in Wisconsin. Other collections in the local-color tradition were *Yellow Gentians and Blue* (1927) and *Bridal Pond* (1930).

O. HENRY (WILLIAM SYDNEY PORTER): *The Voice of the City* and *The Gentle Grafter.* The first of O. Henry's two 1908 story collections includes one of his best-known

stories, "While the Auto Waits." The second collection draws on his prison experience.

ROBERT HERRICK: *Together.* Here Herrick looks at a number of marriages to explore contemporary economic and political forces. Hailed as a masterpiece, the book solidifies his reputation as one of the era's leading serious novelists. He also publishes his most popular novel, *The Master of the Inn*, describing the search for the cure of modern ills.

HENRY JAMES: "The Jolly Corner." James's admired psychological "ghost" story reflects the writer's own musing on how his life might have been different if he had not lived abroad. James also publishes "Julia Bride," a short story about an American girl who flirtatiously indulges in multiple engagements. Unlike his earlier creation Daisy Miller, an American girl with too little freedom, Julia Bride represents an American girl with far too much.

LUDWIG LEWISOHN (1883–1953): *The Broken Snare.* The first of the German-born writer and critic's novels, published with the help of Theodore Dreiser, concerns a young woman's intellectual, emotional, and sexual development, generating controversy for positively treating the subject of free love.

JACK LONDON: *The Iron Heel.* London's dystopian novel predicts a class war between "The Oligarchy" of entrenched capital and the desperate working class. Its hero, Edward Everhard, is a Nietzchean superman born by chance into the working class.

DAVID GRAHAM PHILLIPS: *Old Wives for New.* The first of a series in which Phillips explores the experience of the "new woman" in love and marriage. Other works include the novels *The Hungry Heart* (1909), *The Husband's Story* (1910), *The Price She Paid* (1912), and the play *The Worth of a Woman* (1908).

MARY ROBERTS RINEHART (1876–1958): *The Circular Staircase.* Rinehart's first mystery establishes her reputation for witty suspense featuring ordinary people as sleuths. She would follow it with the equally successful *The Man in the Lower Ten* (1909). Rinehart would write a number of popular horror and crime stories, plays, and a comic series of novels featuring an old maid named "Tish."

UPTON SINCLAIR: *The Metropolis* and *The Moneychangers.* Sinclair publishes two novels somewhat weakened by the author's moral outrage and crusading zeal. The first targets upper-class New York society; the second reflects the affairs of financier J. P. Morgan.

EDITH WHARTON: *The Hermit and the Wild Woman.* Wharton's story collection mixes the medieval allegory of the title with several stories—"The Pretext," "The Lost Asset," and "In Truth"—about social climbing, male dominance, and failed marital relationships.

Literary Criticism and Scholarship

IRVING BABBITT (1865–1933): *Literature and the American College.* In Babbitt's assessment of current campus trends, he calls for an "inner principle of restraint" to resist the forces of naturalism, materialism, and Romantic excesses, a key principle of the tenets of the New Humanism, with which he would become associated. Babbitt was a professor of French at Harvard from 1894 to 1933.

HENRY JAMES: *Views and Reviews.* James's collection of critical essays and book reviews includes "The Novels of George Eliot," "Mr. Walt Whitman," and "The Limitations of Dickens."

Nonfiction

JOSIAH ROYCE: *The Philosophy of Loyalty.* The philosopher's major contribution to the study of ethics establishes the principle of loyalty, the freely chosen and practical devotion to a cause or goal, as the basic moral law.

WOODROW WILSON: *Constitutional Government in the United States.* The last of Wilson's major works represents a rethinking of many of the key tenets of his masterwork, *Congressional Government: A Study in American Politics* (1885), including a stronger conviction in favor of the power of the executive branch.

Poetry

WILLIAM STANLEY BRAITHWAITE: *The House of Falling Leaves with Other Poems.* Braithwaite's second collection evokes a New England setting and contains a sonnet sequence and "White Magic," a poem celebrating John Greenleaf Whittier's efforts on behalf of abolition. Braithwaite's third collection, *Selected Poems*, would not appear until 1948.

EZRA POUND (1885–1972): *A Lume Spento.* Pound publishes his first poetry collection (the title translates as "a dim light") at his own expense in Venice. With echoes of Robert Browning, Algernon Charles Swinburne, François Villon, William Butler Yeats, and others, the work includes ballads and one of Pound's best-known lyrics, "The Tree."

Publications and Events

The *Christian Science Monitor.* With a mandate to de-emphasize the sensational, this daily newspaper is founded in Boston by Mary Baker Eddy in reaction to the yellow journalism of the day. The paper earns respect for its national and international news coverage.

O. Henry (pseudonym of William Sydney Porter)

1909
Drama and Theater

RACHEL CROTHERS: *A Man's World.* The first of the playwright's dramas about the challenges faced by modern women in marriage and society. It concerns a writer who rears another woman's illegitimate child and refuses to marry her own lover, who is discovered to be the father, because she morally condemns the system that allows men to evade their paternal responsibilities. The play, called by Arthur Hobson Quinn "one of the most significant dramas of the decade," helps establish Crothers as the leading woman playwright of her era.

CLYDE FITCH: *The City: A Modern Play of American Life.* Produced after his death, Fitch's final play is about the contrast between small-town virtue and corrupting city life. He considered it his masterpiece. On opening night, the climactic line "You're a God damn liar!" creates a sensation as the first utterance of the phrase "God damn" on the New York stage.

WILLIAM VAUGHN MOODY: *The Faith Healer.* In the second of Moody's produced dramas, a faith healer's powers are restored when he falls in love.

EDWARD SHELDON: *The Nigger.* In Sheldon's melodrama, a white supremacist Southern governor learns that he is the grandson of a slave. Despite complaints about the play's title and charges that its racial theme is lost amidst the romantic plot, the drama proves to be a popular touring play.

EUGENE WALTER: *The Easiest Way.* This drama about an actress whose past as a rich man's mistress costs her the man she truly loves is, according to critic Burns Mantle, the "first bold denial of the happy ending in [American] drama."

Fiction

ELLEN GLASGOW: *The Romance of a Plain Man.* The novel explores Southern life and manners in transition through the rise of its protagonist, the lower-class Ben Starr, into Richmond's high society.

ROBERT GRANT: *The Chippendales.* One of the best of the Boston-born lawyer and jurist's novels is this saga of a Boston family coping with change at the turn of the century.

O. HENRY (WILLIAM SYDNEY PORTER): *Roads of Destiny.* This story collection includes "Whistling Dick's Christmas Stocking," the first story written under O. Henry's pen name; "The Renaissance at Charleroi," the best of his New Orleans tales; "A Retrieved Reformation," the basis of Paul Armstrong's play *Alias Jimmy Valentine* (1910); and the title story, which is considered one of the most carefully structured of his longer stories. A second, lesser collection, *Options,* also appears in 1909.

JACK LONDON: *Martin Eden.* One of London's most important books is this semi-autobiographical account of a young sailor who struggles to improve himself and achieves eventual success as a writer, but grows disenchanted with fame and wealth. It represents both an indictment of the American dream and an important reflection on London's own background and career.

DAVID GRAHAM PHILLIPS: *The Fashionable Adventures of Joshua Craig.* The first in a trilogy of novels depicting social and political corruption at the national, state, and city levels. *The Conflict* (1911) and *George Helm* (1912) would follow.

GERTRUDE STEIN (1874–1946): *Three Lives.* Stein's first published book is a collection of unconventional character portraits — "The Good Anna," a German-born housekeeper; "Melanctha," a mulatto woman brutalized by her father and abandoned by her black lover; and "The Gentle Lena," a maid. The work is stripped down to simple diction, captures present experience with immediacy, and reflects the spoken rhythms of its subjects. It proves highly influential in shaping the work of writers such as Sherwood Anderson and Ernest Hemingway.

Gertrude Stein

MARK TWAIN (SAMUEL LANGHORNE CLEMENS): *Extracts from Captain Stormfield's Visit to Heaven.* Begun in 1868 and worked on throughout Twain's career, this satirical fable mocking the conventional, sentimental view of the afterlife is one of the last works Twain publishes before his death.

WILLIAM ALLEN WHITE (1868–1944): *A Certain Rich Man.* The first of the Kansas newspaperman's novels is a realistic account of small-town political corruption. *In the Heart of a Fool* (1918) and *The Martial Adventures of Henry and Me* (1918) followed.

Literary Criticism and Scholarship

VAN WYCK BROOKS (1886–1963): *The Wine of the Puritans.* Brooks's first critical book sets forth one of his dominating themes — the impact of Puritanism on the formation of American ideas and culture. Brooks, one of the twentieth century's major American literary critics, would produce critical biographies of Mark Twain and Henry James and his multipart Finders and Makers series of literary and cultural history.

W. C. BROWNELL (1851–1928): *American Prose Masters.* Brownell's companion to his *Victorian Prose Masters* (1901) is a critical study of Cooper, Hawthorne, Emerson, Lowell, Poe, and Henry James. It is noteworthy for its serious consideration of American literary expression compared with that of English masters and its high standard, which avoids the chauvinism of other American literary critics of the period. Poe receives Brownell's harshest criticism; Hawthorne is granted only one perfect work (*The Scarlet Letter*), and James is faulted for desiring "to be precise, not to be clear."

MARK TWAIN (SAMUEL LANGHORNE CLEMENS): *Is Shakepeare Dead?* In the last book published during his lifetime, Twain enters the fray in the Shakespeare–Francis Bacon authorship controversy with a burlesque on the pseudo-scholarship of the day.

Nonfiction

AMBROSE BIERCE: *The Shadow on the Dial.* The volume collects Bierce's social criticism. The first of his twelve-volume *Collected Works* (completed in 1912) is also published, as well as a literary essay, "Write It Right," in which Bierce catalogs the faults of bad writing and defines good writing as "clear thinking made visible."

HERBERT CROLY (1869–1930): *The Promise of American Life.* The first and most influential of the New York editor and social critic's political and social critiques considers the state of modern American democracy and articulates a plan for its revitalization. Theodore Roosevelt would adapt many of the book's tenets and its phrase "New Nationalism" for the platform and the slogan of his 1912 presidential campaign.

W.E.B. DU BOIS: *John Brown.* This sympathetic biographical portrait of the abolitionist leader is chiefly significant for what it reveals about Du Bois's views on militancy in combating white supremacy.

HENRY JAMES: *Italian Hours.* James would describe this collection of mostly previously published Italian travel essays "a lumpish . . . piece of catchpenny bookmaking."

WILLIAM JAMES: *The Meaning of Truth* and *The Pluralistic Universe.* The first is a sequel to *Pragmatism* (1907), which amplifies its tenets and defends James's theories against the attacks prompted by the first book. The second is a further elaboration of his metaphysical beliefs, based on a series of lectures delivered at Oxford in 1908.

Poetry

EZRA POUND: *Personae* and *Exultations.* After publishing his second collection, *A Quinzaine for Yule,* in London in 1908, Pound brings out his first major collections, which include important early works such as "Sestina: Altaforte" and "Ballad of the Goodly Fere."

LIZETTE WOODWORTH REESE: *A Wayside Lute.* Reese's collection includes her best-known poem, "Tears," a sonnet in which the conventional theme of regret is energized by a series of fresh and arresting images.

GEORGE STERLING: *A Wine of Wizardry and Other Poems.* The volume takes its title from Sterling's best-known poem, a striking series of often grotesque images published in 1907.

EDITH WHARTON: *Artemis to Acteon.* This is the first of the writer's two poetry collections. Besides the title work on the Greek myth, the volume contains a sonnet sequence "The Mortal Lease," concerning the author's romantic relationship with William Morton Fullerton, the Boston journalist who worked in the Paris office of the London *Times.* Biographer R.W.B. Lewis calls the collection a "genuine if modest poetic accomplishment" and cites Wharton as one of the few significant American novelists who produced poetry of quality. This collection would be followed by *Twelve Poems* (1926).

Publications and Events

The New Theatre. New York's first major art theater opens as the intended home of an American national repertory theater company. The theater's out-of-the-way location on Central Park West, bad acoustics, and weak productions forced it to close in 1911.

1910
Drama and Theater

PAUL ARMSTRONG (1869–1915): *Alias Jimmy Valentine.* Armstrong scores a success in this melodrama based on the O. Henry story "A Retrieved Reformation," about a professional safe-cracker. Armstrong was a former journalist and sportswriter who wrote a number of melodramas, adaptations, and two popular original plays, *The Deep Purple* (1911) and *The Greyhound* (1912).

VICTOR HERBERT: *Naughty Marietta.* Herbert's operetta set in eighteenth-century New Orleans is generally considered his masterpiece.

MARGARET MAYO: *Baby Mine.* Mayo's comedy concerns a wife's attempt to reclaim her husband's affection by claiming that she is having a baby. The *New York Times* calls it "one of the funniest farces this town has ever seen," and it would become the source for Jerome Kern's 1918 musical *Rock-a-Bye Baby.*

JOSEPHINE PRESTON PEABODY (1874–1922): *The Piper.* The playwright's most famous work is an allegory based on the legend of the Pied Piper of Hamelin. It wins a prize at Stratford-on-Avon and becomes one of the few American works added to the repertory of New York's New Theatre. Peabody studied with poet-dramatist William Vaughn Moody and produced a number of blank-verse dramas with little commercial appeal, such as *Marlowe*

BESTSELLERS, 1910–1914

Fiction*

1910
1. *The Broad Highway* by Jeffrey Farnol
2. *The Prodigal Judge* by Vaughn Kester
3. *The Wild Olive*, anonymous (Basil King)
4. *Max* by Katherine Cecil Thurston
5. *The Kingdom of Slender Swords* by Hallie Erminie Rives
6. *Simon the Jester* by William J. Locke
7. *Lord Loveland Discovers America* by C. N. and A. M. Williamson
8. *The Window at the White Cat* by Mary Roberts Rinehart
9. *Molly Make-Believe* by Eleanor Abbott
10. *When a Man Marries* by Mary Roberts Rinehart

1911
1. *The Broad Highway* by Jeffrey Farnol
2. *The Prodigal Judge* by Vaughn Kester
3. *The Winning of Barbara Worth* by Harold Bell Wright
4. *Queed* by Henry Sydnor Harrison
5. *The Harvester* by Gene Stratton Porter
6. *The Iron Woman* by Margaret Deland
7. *The Long Roll* by Mary Johnston
8. *Molly Make-Believe* by Eleanor Abbott
9. *The Rosary* by Florence Barclay
10. *The Common Law* by Robert W. Chambers

1912
1. *The Harvester* by Gene Stratton Porter
2. *The Street Called Straight* by Basil King
3. *Their Yesterdays* by Harold Bell Wright
4. *The Melting of Molly* by Maria Thompson Davies
5. *A Hoosier Chronicle* by Meredith Nicholson
6. *The Winning of Barbara Worth* by Harold Bell Wright
7. *The Just and the Unjust* by Vaughn Kester
8. *The Net* by Rex Beach
9. *Tante* by Anne Douglas Sedgwick
10. *Fran* by J. Breckenridge Ellis

1913
1. *The Inside of the Cup* by Winston Churchill
2. *V.V.'s Eyes* by Henry Sydnor Harrison
3. *Laddie* by Gene Stratton Porter
4. *The Judgement House* by Sir Gilbert Parker

5. *Heart of the Hills* by John Fox Jr.
6. *The Amateur Gentleman* by Jeffrey Farnol
7. *The Woman Thou Gavest Me* by Hall Caine
8. *Pollyanna* by Eleanor H. Porter
9. *The Valiants of Virginia* by Hallie Erminie Rives
10. *T. Tembarom* by Frances Hodgson Burnett

1914
1. *The Eyes of the World* by Harold Bell Wright
2. *Pollyanna* by Eleanor H. Porter
3. *The Inside of the Cup* by Winston Churchill
4. *The Salamander* by Owen Johnson
5. *The Fortunate Youth* by William J. Locke
6. *T. Tembarom* by Frances Hodgson Burnett
7. *Penrod* by Booth Tarkington
8. *Diane of the Green Van* by Leona Dalrymple
9. *The Devil's Garden* by W. B. Maxwell
10. *The Prince of Graustark* by George Barr McCutcheon

Nonfiction

1912
1. *The Promised Land* by Mary Antin
2. *The Montessori Method* by Maria Montessori
3. *South America* by James Bryce
4. *A New Conscience and an Ancient Evil* by Jane Addams
5. *Three Plays* by Eugne Brieux
6. *Your United States* by Arnold Bennett
7. *Creative Evolution* by Henri Bergson
8. *How to Live on Twenty-Four Hours a Day* by Arnold Bennett
9. *Woman and Labor* by Olive Schreiner
10. *Mark Twain* by Albert Bigelow Paine

1913
1. *Crowds* by Gerald Stanley Lee
2. *Germany and the Germans* by Price Collier
3. *Zone Policeman 88* by Harry A. Franck
4. *The New Freedom* by Woodrow Wilson
5. *South America* by James Bryce
6. *Your United States* by Arnold Bennett
7. *The Promised Land* by Mary Antin
8. *Auction Bridge To-Day* by Milton C. Work
9. *Three Plays* by Eugne Brieux
10. *Psychology and Industrial Efficiency* by Hugo Munsterberg

* During the early years of *Publishers Weekly*'s bestseller lists, fiction and nonfiction were combined. Since fiction far and away outsold nonfiction titles, the top ten sellers were always fiction. In 1912, *Publishers Weekly* added a nonfiction bestseller list, only to drop it in 1914. In 1917, with the rising popularity of books on war, *Publishers Weekly* added a War-Books bestseller list and also reinstated the nonfiction bestseller list. In 1919, the War-Books bestseller list would be dropped.

(1901), *The Wolf of Gobbio* (1913), and *Portrait of Mrs. W.* (1922).

Fiction

MONTAGUE GLASS (1877–1934): *Potash and Perlmutter.* Glass collects his first volume of dialect stories about two Jewish business partners. Other titles in the popular series are *Abe and Mawruss* (1911) and *Potash and Perlmutter*

Settle Things (1919). Stage adaptations would appear in 1913 and 1915. Glass was a New York lawyer who specialized in the humor derived from New York's garment manufacturers.

O. HENRY (**WILLIAM SYDNEY PORTER**): *Strictly Business.* The last story collection published during the author's lifetime includes one of his best works, "A Municipal Report." The first of seven posthumously published volumes, *Whirligigs*, with the much reprinted and ad-mired story "The Ransom of Red Chief," also appears.

ROBERT HERRICK: *A Life for a Life*. Herrick's novel, marking the beginning of his literary decline, carries the subtitle "An Allegory for Today" and concerns an individual beset by financial ambitions and sexual appetites.

HENRY JAMES: *The Finer Grain*. A collection of five short stories — "The Velvet Glove," "Mora Montravers," "A Round of Visits," "Crapy Cornelia," and "The Bench of Desolation." Each, according to James, represents "a moral drama," in which the protagonist "exhibits the finer grain of accessibility . . . to moving experience."

JACK LONDON: *Burning Daylight*. The first of London's three agrarian novels focuses on a Klondike prospector who has come south to match wits with financiers before being persuaded to move to a small ranch. London's other novels exploring the redemptive power of living close to the land are *The Valley of the Moon* (1913) and *The Little Lady of the Big House* (1916). London also publishes *Lost Face*, a story collection that includes London's short fiction masterpiece "To Build a Fire." One of the most widely anthologized works ever produced by an American, it tells the story of a man who perishes off the Yukon trail in the dead of winter because he lacks basic survival skills.

CLARENCE E. MULFORD (1883–1956): *Hopalong Cassidy*. Introduced in Mulford's first book, *Bar-20* (1907), the cowboy hero is featured in the first of twenty-eight western adventure novels by the Illinois writer who, until 1924, had never ventured to the West. Hopalong Cassidy would be portrayed by William Boyd in sixty-six films from 1935 to 1948.

EDWARD STRATEMEYER: *Tom Swift and His Motor-Cycle*. Stratemeyer introduces the plucky boy inventor whom he had modeled on his idol, Henry Ford, in the first of many adventures in this popular juvenile series. Each novel features an ingenious invention, many of which anticipate actual future technology, and a villain attempting to steal Tom's work.

EDITH WHARTON: *Tales of Men and Ghosts*. Wharton attempts versions of the Jamesian psychological ghost stories. "The Eyes," in particular, has been acclaimed as "a small masterpiece."

Literary Criticism and Scholarship

IRVING BABBITT: *The New Laokoon: An Essay on the Confusion of the Arts*. Babbitt assesses the shortcomings of the Romantics, a central tenet of the evolving New Humanism critical movement with which he would become associated.

Jane Addams

JOHN A. LOMAX (1872–1948): *Cowboy Songs and Other Frontier Ballads*. Lomax's first major collection of folk songs is a landmark in the history of American musicology. It saves the signature western anthem, "Home on the Range," from oblivion.

EZRA POUND: *The Spirit of Romance*. Pound's first critical volume examines "certain forces, elements or qualities which were potent in the medieval literature of the Latin tongues, and are, I believe, still potent in our own." Pound includes appreciations of Dante, Guido Cavalcanti, François Villon, and others.

Nonfiction

JANE ADDAMS: *Twenty Years at Hull-House*. Addams interweaves a history of the Chicago settlement home she had founded in 1889 with reflections on her own personal development. A sequel, *The Second Twenty Years at Hull-House*, would appear in 1930.

EMMA GOLDMAN (1869–1940): *Anarchism and Other Essays*. Goldman's first collection of essays explores a variety of radical interpretations of politics, social welfare, and gender issues. Born in Russia, Goldman came to the United States in 1886 and spent a year in prison in 1893 for her anarchist activities. She founded the magazine

Mother Earth in 1906 to broadcast her views on politics, gender issues, and birth control.

JAMES GIBBONS HUNEKER: *Promenades of an Impressionist.* Huneker displays his characteristic impressionistic, personal style in a wide-ranging collection of mainly art criticism.

GUSTAVUS MYERS (1872–1942): *History of the Great American Fortunes.* The muckraking historian and reformer presents a massive three-volume study of American wealth from colonial times.

Poetry

EZRA POUND: *Provença.* Pound's first American publication is a selection from his previous English collections. A reviewer for the *New York Times* describes Pound as a "naive yet sophisticated mystic, with a dash of Rossetti, a good bit of Browning and a trifle of Kipling in him."

EDWIN ARLINGTON ROBINSON: *The Town down the River.* Robinson's third volume contains two of his most popular poems, "Miniver Cheevy" and "How Annandale Went Out."

Publications and Events

The *Crisis.* The monthly magazine of the NAACP is founded by W.E.B. Du Bois, who served as its editor until 1934. Subtitled "A Record of the Darker Races," the magazine, which had by 1918 a circulation of 100,000, reported on news in the black community and provided commentary on culture and politics. When Jessie Redmon Fausset became literary editor in 1921, the magazine became an important vehicle for the work of younger African American writers, including Langston Hughes, who published his first poem here.

The Harvard Classics. The fifty-volume collection of the greatest works from world literature appears. Edited by Charles W. Eliot (1834–1926), it is popularly known as "Dr. Eliot's Five-Foot Shelf of Books."

1911
Drama and Theater

MARY AUSTIN: *The Arrow Maker.* The final production of New York's New Theatre is a sympathetic depiction of Native American life in California before European settlement, which features authentic costumes, chants, and dances.

DAVID BELASCO AND CECIL B. DE MILLE (1881–1959): *The Return of Peter Grimm.* Belasco and De Mille achieve a major popular success with this drama about a man who, after persuading his ward to marry his nephew,

comes back from the dead to prevent a marriage he realizes is a mistake. De Mille would go on to become a successful Hollywood director and producer.

GEORGE BROADHURST: *Bought and Paid For.* Broadhurst's play looks at a marriage in which a drunken husband insists that his wife comply with his every desire.

WILLIAM C. DE MILLE: *The Woman.* One of the most successful of the muckraking dramas of the era concerns a corrupt Illinois politician who tries to ruin the reputation of his idealistic opponent by alleging that he has been unfaithful to his wife.

PERCY MACKAYE (1875–1956): *The Scarecrow.* MacKaye's 1908 dramatic adaptation of Hawthorne's short story "Feathertop" was given a short-lived Broadway production but remains a popular choice for production among amateur and collegiate groups. Son of playwright Steele MacKaye, the dramatist was admired by some but never managed to find a popular audience. His books, *The Playhouse and the Play* (1909) and *The Civic Theatre* (1912), argue for a subsidized, noncommercial American theater.

EDWARD SHELDON: *The Boss.* Sheldon's drama concerns a corrupt political boss whose blackmail leads to his marriage with his victim's daughter. Sheldon's comedy *The Princess Zim-Zim*, about a Coney Island snake charmer, is also produced.

AUGUSTUS THOMAS: *As a Man Thinks.* Thomas's play is a response to Rachel Crothers's *A Man's World* (1909) and defends the double standard that Crothers's play had condemned.

Fiction

FRANCES HODGSON BURNETT: *The Secret Garden.* Burnett's masterpiece is the story of a sickly and spoiled girl who is restored to health and grows up while tending a Yorkshire garden.

THEODORE DREISER: *Jennie Gerhardt.* Dreiser breaks more than a decade of silence, following the controversy surrounding *Sister Carrie* (1900), with his second novel, about the mistress of an Ohio senator and a scion of a wealthy family. It is, like its predecessor, significant for its sexual candor and its playing out of naturalistic theories, which emphasize the role played by heredity and environment in shaping a character's fate.

W.E.B. DU BOIS: *The Quest of the Silver Fleece.* Du Bois's first novel is a romantic melodrama that features a detailed examination of the cotton industry.

ELLEN GLASGOW: *The Miller of Old Church.* Considered the earliest of her mature achievements and among her best books, the novel synthesizes Glasgow's dominant theme of the decay of the Southern gentry.

SUSAN GLASPELL (1882–1948): *The Visioning.* After publishing a conventionally sentimental first novel, *The Glory of the Conquered* (1909), Glaspell begins to take up contemporary social issues including divorce, trade unions, socialism, and gender roles in this novel about the education of Katie Jones, who questions conventional standards. Glaspell, with her husband, George Cram Cook, would found the Provincetown Players in 1915.

HENRY SYDNOR HARRISON (1880–1930): *Queed.* Harrison's best novel tells the story of an idealist who must revisit his opinions when he goes to work on a newspaper. His other novels include *V.V.'s Eyes* (1913), *Angela's Business* (1915), and *Andrew Bride of Paris* (1925).

O. HENRY: *Sixes and Sevens.* The second of O. Henry's posthumously published collections. It would be followed by *Rolling Stones* (1913), *Waifs and Strays* (1917), *Seven Odds and Ends* (1920), *Letters to Lithopolis* (1922), *Postscripts* (1923), and *O. Henry Encore* (1939).

HENRY JAMES: *The Outcry.* James adapts his 1901 drama into a short novel about selling off the great treasures of Europe to American millionaires.

OWEN JOHNSON (1878–1952): *Stover at Yale.* Johnson, the son of poet and editor of the *Century* magazine Robert Underwood Johnson (1853–1937), achieves his greatest success in this novel about the collegiate Dink Stover, Yale freshman, the archetype of the college man of the era. Dink's adventures at prep school are recorded in *The Eternal Boy* (1909), *The Varmint* (1910), and *The Tennessee Shad* (1911).

MARY JOHNSTON: *The Long Roll.* The first of two highly regarded historical novels set during the Civil War. It features a historically accurate background, and the story's climax occurs at the Battle of Chancellorsville. It would be followed by *Cease Firing* (1912), which picks up the story line again and carries it to the war's conclusion.

KATHLEEN NORRIS (1880–1966): *Mother.* The California-born writer's first novel is a sentimental domestic romance about a California family. It becomes a bestseller and typifies the popular literature of the period. Norris would go on to produce more than seventy novels, including what is considered her best, *Certain People of Importance* (1922).

LUCY FITCH PERKINS (1865–1937): *The Dutch Twins.* The first in the author-illustrator's popular juvenile Twins series about children of different nationalities and historical periods. *The Japanese Twins* (1912), *The Irish Twins* (1913), *The Eskimo Twins* (1914), *The Belgian Twins* (1917), *The French Twins* (1918), and others would follow.

ANNE DOUGLAS SEDGWICK (1873–1935): *Tante.* This novel concerns the destructive relationship between a concert pianist and her young protégée. Born in New Jersey, Sedgwick lived abroad after age nine, and her books explore, after the manner of Henry James, the contrasting values of Americans and Europeans.

EDITH WHARTON: *Ethan Frome.* Wharton's novella departs from her characteristic high-society settings to present a stark, ironic tragedy set in rural Massachusetts. Ethan Frome, married to a complaining, hypochondriacal wife, falls in love with his wife's cousin. Their decision to end their lives rather than forgo their love goes awry.

KATE DOUGLAS WIGGIN: *Mother Carey's Chickens.* Wiggin's story of a widow and her children forced from their home due to financial difficulties proves to be her biggest success following *Rebecca of Sunnybrook Farm* (1903).

HAROLD BELL WRIGHT: *The Winning of Barbara Worth.* Wright's western tale of an orphan girl whose true identity resolves her marriage difficulties becomes one of the year's and the era's biggest sellers.

Literary Criticism and Scholarship

J. E. SPINGARN (1899–1911): *The New Criticism.* A reprint of a celebrated lecture that advocates a close reading of a poet's work rather than a consideration of his or her biographical or historical background. The volume anticipates subsequent critical debate and provides the name for the critical movement that would dominate literary analysis from the 1930s to the 1960s. Spingarn was a professor of comparative literature at Columbia University from 1899 to 1911 as well as a poet of volumes such as *The New Hesperides* (1911) and *Poems* (1924).

Nonfiction

AMBROSE BIERCE: *The Devil's Dictionary.* In the last and best of Bierce's major works, the author recasts and retitles *The Cynic's Word Book* (1906) to create a final series of epigrammatic deflations of cherished beliefs and ironic paradoxes, as in these examples: "Prejudice, n. a vagrant opinion without visible means of support"; "Saint, n. a dead sinner revised and edited."

WILLIAM JAMES: *Some Problems of Philosophy: A Beginning of an Introduction to Philosophy.* James's unfinished treatise is published posthumously. It gives an overview of his pragmatic philosophy whereby "empiricism and rationalism may join hands in a concrete view of life."

JACK LONDON: *The Cruise of the Snark.* An account of London's failed attempt to circumnavigate the globe in

Ambrose Bierce

his own boat. Story collections drawing on his experiences, *South Sea Tales* and *When God Laughs and Other Stories*, also are published.

JOHN MUIR: *My First Summer in the Sierra*. The naturalist's account of his work as a shepherd in 1869 celebrates his first encounter with the region that he would make famous in his books.

BOOKER T. WASHINGTON: *My Longer Education: Being Chapters from My Experience*. Washington adds to his reflections on his early life in *Up from Slavery* (1901), providing an account of his years of success and his encounters with famous people.

Poetry

EZRA POUND: *Canzoni*. When Pound presented this collection to Ford Madox Ford, he criticized the poem's stilted language and archaisms. According to Pound, it "saved me at least two years, perhaps more. It set me back toward using the living tongue."

SARA TEASDALE (1884–1933): *Helen of Troy and Other Poems*. Appearing after a private printing of her first collection, *Sonnets to Duse, and Other Poems* (1907), the Missouri-born lyric poet's first publication features the

noteworthy poem "Union Square," about the poet's longing to express her love. The poem's theme of sexual aggression is daring and shocking for the times.

JOHN HALL WHEELOCK (1886–1978): *The Human Fantasy*. After writing with his Harvard classmate Van Wyck Brooks the volume of *Verses of Two Undergraduates* (1905), the New York poet publishes his first solo effort, which brings him critical acclaim. Critic Louis Untermeyer detects in the poems echoes of "Whitman, Shelley, and Edwin Arlington Robinson." Wheelock's follow-up, *The Beloved Adventure* (1912), would also be favorably reviewed.

Publications and Events

The *Masses*. A weekly journal of news and social criticism is launched. Under the editorship of Max Eastman (1883–1969), in 1912 it took on socialist views and was suppressed by the government in 1917.

1912

Drama and Theater

J. HARTLEY MANNERS (1870–1928): *Peg o' My Heart*. Manners's comedy about a poor Irish girl who comes to live with her haughty relatives proves to be one of the most popular plays on the American stage. Closing after 603 performances, it is the longest-running nonmusical play in Broadway history up to that time. Laurette Taylor would perform the role of the Irish waif more than a thousand times, typecast by it until her appearance as Amanda in Tennessee Williams's *The Glass Menagerie* (1945). Manners was a London-born former actor who came to the United States in 1902 as a member of the cast of his own play, *The Crossways*. His other works include *Zira* (1905), *The Harp of Life* (1916), and *Out There* (1917).

EDWARD SHELDON: *The High Road*. Sheldon's drama features a presidential candidate who discovers his wife's disreputable past.

Fiction

GERTRUDE ATHERTON: *Julia France and Her Times*. Atherton portrays the modern woman through the development of her protagonist, who discovers the shortcomings of self-indulgence and the rewards of social activism. The novel features an authentic look at the women's movement in England and is called the "best suffrage book to date."

MARY AUSTIN: *A Woman of Genius*. In what is generally regarded as Austin's best and most important novel, an actress tries to balance her career, marriage, and motherhood. The novel is a significant early attempt to

Gertrude Atherton

investigate the social pressures that constrain women and the forces that punish nonconformity.

THORNTON W. BURGESS (1874–1965): "Little Stories for Bedtime." Burgess begins a syndicated column of children's stories that first popularizes the term *bedtime stories*. The columns would be collected in *The Adventures of Reddy Fox* (1913), the first of the twenty-volume Bedtime Story series (1913–19). Volumes of *Burgess Bedtime Stories* were subsequently issued, containing as many as ten thousand stories.

WILLA CATHER: *Alexander's Bridge.* Cather's first novel presents a romantic triangle—a bridge engineer is divided between his loyalty to his wife and his passion for an old flame. Cather would not value the book very highly, later saying that she had actually written two first novels, this one and *O Pioneers!* (1913), her first to make major use of a Nebraska setting.

THEODORE DREISER: *The Financier.* Dreiser shifts his earlier attention on female protagonists to a male protagonist, Frank Cowperwood, and realistically interprets the American success story. Frank's story is continued in *The Titan* (1914) and concluded in *The Stoic* (1947).

ZANE GREY (1872–1939): *Riders of the Purple Sage.* In what has been called the most famous western ever written, the Ohio dentist achieves his first popular success and establishes his basic formula for more than fifty subsequent best-selling western novels. This is the story of Mormon heiress Jane Withersteen, who is convinced to resist the challenge to her cattle range by Lassiter, a gunman with a mysterious past. A sequel, *The Rainbow Trail*, would appear in 1914. Grey would produce more than sixty books, selling more than 13 million copies during his lifetime.

JAMES WELDON JOHNSON (1871–1938): *The Autobiography of an Ex-Colored Man.* Johnson's novel, published anonymously to lend it greater authenticity as a true story, describes the experiences of a light-skinned black man who can pass for white, which underscore the prejudice and injustice faced by African Americans. The work features one of the most complex psychological characterizations of an African American up to that point. It goes relatively unnoticed, however, at the time.

JACK LONDON: *Smoke Bellew.* London sends a dilletantish San Francisco journalist for some character development in the Klondike, in a series of Northland stories.

JEAN WEBSTER (1876–1916): *Daddy-Long-Legs.* The New York writer's most popular children's book is a sentimental, Cinderella-like orphanage story. She would successfully adapt it for the stage in 1914. She also produced two popular collections of stories for girls, *When Patty Went to College* (1911) and *Just Patty* (1911).

EDITH WHARTON: *The Reef.* One of the author's most Jamesian novels, this is a complex story of sexual entanglements among expatriates in a French château. Daring for the times, the novel depicts the complex personal and social implications of human sexuality.

Literary Criticism and Scholarship

ALBERT BIGELOW PAINE: *Mark Twain: A Biography.* Paine issues his authorized three-volume biography based on his direct involvement with Twain during the last nine years of Twain's life. It would long serve as the standard source on Twain, beginning the debate surrounding his character and career.

Nonfiction

JANE ADDAMS: *A New Conscience and an Ancient Evil.* Addams examines the "white slave" traffic after her experiences working in Chicago's slums. Addams urges better economic conditions, moral education, legal protection for children, and philanthropic and government intervention.

MARY ANTIN: *The Promised Land.* Antin's autobiography tells of her Polish upbringing, the immigration of her family to America, and the challenges of assimilation. It is one of the best treatments of the Jewish immigration experience in the pre–World War I era.

GAMALIEL BRADFORD (1863–1932): *Lee, the American.* The Massachusetts poet, dramatist, and memoirist introduces his biographical method of "psychography," the identification of subjects' essential characteristics from a succession of significant moments in their lives. He would use the method in several subsequent biographical studies, including *Confederate Portraits* (1914), *Portraits of Women* (1916), *Union Portraits* (1916), and *American Portraits* (1922).

WILLIAM JAMES: *Essays in Radical Empiricism.* This posthumously published collection of essays asserts James's central thesis that "the only things that shall be debatable among philosophers shall be things definable in terms drawn from experience."

JOHN MUIR: *The Yosemite.* This recycling of past articles to form a guidebook to Yosemite is noteworthy for its impassioned plea to stop the damming of Hetch Hetchy Valley. Muir's efforts would fail, but his argument, in the words of a later critic, "established the modern argument for wilderness."

Poetry

DONALD EVANS (1884–1921): *Discords.* The first of the journalist and music critic's collections helps make him a popular representative of the Greenwich Village avant-garde. *Sonnets from the Patagonian* (1914), *Two Deaths in the Bronx* (1916), *Nine Poems from a Valetudinarian* (1916), and *Ironica* (1919) would follow.

AMY LOWELL (1874–1925): *A Dome of Many-Coloured Glass.* Lowell's first book is noteworthy for its conventional poems, which contrast with her subsequent experimental poetry.

EDNA ST. VINCENT MILLAY (1892–1950): "Renascence." Millay's first important poem is published as a contest winner in the anthology *The Lyric Year.* In tetrameter couplets, the poem charts the poet's emotional development. It is praised for its freshness, emotional honesty, and what Harriet Monroe calls its "sense of infinity." It would become the centerpiece of Millay's first collection, *Renascence and Other Poems* (1917).

EZRA POUND: *Ripostes.* Besides the important early poem "The Return," the volume features Pound's first use of the term *imagism* and poems reflecting the move-

ment's key principles: direct treatment of a subject; no superfluous words; rhythm based on the musical phrase, not on the "strictness of the metronome." One of his most famous poems, "In a Station of the Metro," illustrates the concept.

Publications and Events

The Actors' Equity Association. This organization is founded to protect actors' rights and to establish a basic contract with producers. Its efforts culminate in a thirty-day strike in 1919, which effectively closes Broadway and ends with an agreement with most producers. Equity established a union shop agreement in 1924, a minimum wage for actors in 1933, and minimum rehearsal pay in 1935.

Authors League of America. An organization founded to protect authors' rights. In 1964, it added the Authors Guild and the Dramatists Guild.

Loeb Classical Library. This series of translations of Greek and Latin texts is initiated by New York banker and scholar James Loeb (1867–1933).

Poetry: A Magazine in Verse. The most important American magazine devoted to poetry is started by Harriet Monroe (1860–1936), who would edit it until her death. It published virtually every important American poet, many for the first time.

1913
Drama and Theater

GEORGE BROADHURST: *Today.* Broadhurst's shocking drama concerns a wife who secretly goes to work in a fashionable brothel when her husband fails in business. A reviewer for the *Times* condemns it as "an indecent, vicious play," but it manages a respectable run of 280 performances because of its notoriety.

RACHEL CROTHERS: *Ourselves.* Crothers dramatizes the social evil of prostitution, which she attributes to a double standard that grants men the indulgence of their sexual appetite while condemning women in the process.

EUGENE O'NEILL (1888–1953): *A Wife for Life.* O'Neill's first play, unproduced during his lifetime and a fairly conventional melodrama. A steady flow of works would follow over the next three years, including *The Web* (1913), about a prostitute with tuberculosis whose pimp forces her to continue working to support his drug habit, and *Bound East for Cardiff* (1916), his first produced play.

EDWARD SHELDON: *Romance.* The playwright achieves his greatest success in this drama about a clergyman's tragic love affair with an opera singer. It would be performed regularly well into the 1920s.

HARRY B. SMITH AND VICTOR HERBERT: *Sweethearts.* One of Herbert's best operettas concerns the long-lost princess of Zilania, who is raised by a laundress.

Fiction

EARL DERR BIGGERS (1884–1933): *Seven Keys to Baldpate.* Biggers's best-known work without Charlie Chan tells the story of a group of people who meet at a mountaintop inn. It is successfully staged by George M. Cohan in 1913 and remains for many years a favorite among amateur companies and summer stock.

JAMES BRANCH CABELL: *The Soul of Melicent.* Cabell initiates one of the most ambitious novel cycles ever attempted by an American. Set in the imaginary medieval province of Poictesme, the series deals with Dom Manuel and his descendents from 1234 to 1750. Subsequent titles include *The Certain Hour* (1916), *Jurgen* (1919), *Figures of Earth* (1921), *The High Place* (1923), *The Silver Stallion* (1926), *Something About Eve* (1927), *The White Robe* (1928), and *The Way of Echen* (1929).

WILLA CATHER: *O Pioneers!* Cather's second novel is her first to reflect her Nebraska childhood. The story concerns Alexandra Bergson, a Swedish immigrant who struggles to keep her family together. Cather wrote in a friend's copy of the novel, "This was the first time I walked off on my own feet — everything before was half real and half imitation of writers whom I admired. In this one I hit the home pasture."

WINSTON CHURCHILL: *Inside the Cup.* Churchill's best-regarded novel dealing with social problems considers the inadequate attempts of the modern church to deal with contemporary realities. It features an out-of-touch minister who is sent to an urban Midwestern parish.

EDNA FERBER (1887–1968): *Roast Beef, Medium.* After publishing a minor novel, *Dawn O'Hara* (1911), and a short story collection, *Buttered Side Down* (1912), Ferber achieves her first success by introducing a new fictional type — the career woman — in the character Emma McChesney. The stories in this collection had begun to appear in 1911. Additional adventures of the divorced mother are collected in *Personality Plus* (1914) and *Emma McChesney and Co.* (1915).

ELLEN GLASGOW: *Virginia.* Glasgow begins a series of novels about women forced to live under a Southern code of behavior that restricts women's roles and options. In this case, the novel examines a wife dealing with her husband's infidelity.

Willa Cather

ROBERT HERRICK: *One Woman's Life.* Herrick's novel is a character study of a female social climber.

WILLIAM DEAN HOWELLS: *New Leaf Mills.* Howells's semi-autobiographical novel reflects his Midwestern boyhood.

JACK LONDON: *The Valley of the Moon.* London's novel suggests that the solution to the problems of modern industrialism is a return to nature. It is generally regarded as the best of his agrarian novels. London also publishes *John Barleycorn,* a cautionary recollection of his drinking life.

ELEANOR H. PORTER (1868–1920): *Pollyanna.* Porter's best-known work is this children's classic, a million-copy seller that would go through forty-seven printings by 1920. The name of the main character has entered the American lexicon to designate irrepressible, and annoying, optimism. Porter would write a sequel, *Pollyanna Grows Up,* in 1915. The New Hampshire–born writer's other books include *Miss Billie* (1911), *Miss Billie — Married* (1914), and *Just David* (1916).

EDITH WHARTON: *The Custom of the Country.* Ranking among Wharton's greatest achievements is this satirical account of Undine Spragg, a nouveau riche social

Ellen Glasgow

climber. Spragg's experiences both puncture the pretensions of provincial Americans and demonstrate the influence of a corrupt society on the individual. The novel is one of Wharton's most expansive social commentaries.

Literary Criticism and Scholarship

MAX EASTMAN (1883–1969): *Enjoyment of Poetry.* Eastman's first book mounts a popular argument that poetry should be primarily enjoyed rather than deciphered or interpreted.

JAMES GIBBONS HUNEKER: *The Pathos of Distance: A Book of a Thousand and One Moments.* Typical of Huneker's style, this book offers a witty and wide-ranging collection of art, music, cultural, and literary criticism, as well as personal recollections.

JOHN MACY (1877–1932): *The Spirit of American Literature.* In this influential survey of major writers from Irving to James, Macy argues that the American vernacular and regionalisms are distinctive features of American literature. Macy was the literary editor of the *Boston Herald* from 1913 to 1914, and of the *Nation* from 1922 to 1923. He was married to Anne Sullivan, the teacher of Helen Keller.

EZRA POUND: "A Few Don'ts by an Imagiste." Pound's essay appears in the March issue of *Poetry* and includes his famous definition of an image: "an intellectual and emotional complex in an instant of time." It also sets out the central tenets of the imagists.

Nonfiction

CHARLES AUSTIN BEARD (1874–1948): *An Economic Interpretation of the Constitution.* This is the first of the Columbia University political scientist's two important early economic analyses that radicallly reinterpret the basis for American democracy. The other is *The Economic Origins of Jeffersonian Democracy* (1915). Both would have a significant impact on subsequent historical approaches to the founding fathers and the evolution of American government and institutions. Beard helped found the New School for Social Research after resigning from Columbia in 1917 to protest the dismissal of pacifist professors.

RANDOLPH SILLIMAN BOURNE (1886–1918): *Youth and Life.* The first of the social critic's books that establishes his reputation as one of the leading radical intellectuals of his time. *The Gary Schools* (1916) and *Education and Living* (1917) would follow.

JOHN JAY CHAPMAN: *William Lloyd Garrison.* Chapman's well-received biography of the abolitionist is valued as a thorough history of the antislavery movement.

THEODORE DREISER: *A Traveler at Forty.* Dreiser offers an account of his European travels and an overall assessment of life from the perspective of his fortieth birthday.

HENRY JAMES: *A Small Boy and Others.* James's first volume of recollections covers his New York boyhood. Though originally conceived as a tribute to his brother William, James extends it to tell the story of his entire family up to 1859.

WALTER LIPPMANN (1889–1974): *A Preface to Politics.* The first in a popular series of Lippmann's social and political critiques. In it, he argues for reform that would allow the state to regulate and direct economic activity and social progress. *Drift and Mastery* (1914), *The Stakes of Diplomacy* (1915), and *The Political Scene* (1919) would follow. Lippmann was associated with the *New Republic* from its inception and would go on to become the leading editorial writer for the *New York World,* the *Herald Tribune,* the *Washington Post,* and *Newsweek.*

JOHN MUIR: *The Story of My Boyhood and Youth.* Muir's Scottish childhood and Wisconsin upbringing are the subjects for this series of recollections that end before the point at which Muir began his career as a roaming naturalist.

THEODORE ROOSEVELT: *An Autobiography.* Roosevelt's selective recollections are often self-justifying and unreliable. His unique voice and personality are, however, clearly evident.

Poetry

ROBERT FROST (1874–1963): *A Boy's Will*. Frost's first publication is issued during his residence in England (1912–1915). Although it contains few of his enduring poems, the collection reflects his characteristic emotional and intellectual intensity and a technical mastery that predicts his future achievement.

VACHEL LINDSAY (1879–1931): *General William Booth Enters into Heaven and Other Poems*. Lindsay's first major collection is built around the title poem, celebrating the ultimate reward of the founder of the Salvation Army. Written in Lindsay's syncopated, chanting rhythm, the collection also includes "The Eagle That Is Forgotten," an elegy to the former liberal governor of Illinois, J. P. Altgeld.

JOHN HALL WHEELOCK: *Love and Liberation*. Wheelock's poetic reputation suffers a blow when this collection is dismissed by critic Louis Untermeyer as "repetition on repetition, sugar on treacle, beauty on banalities."

WILLIAM CARLOS WILLIAMS (1883–1963): *The Tempers*. Following a privately printed first verse collection, *Poems* (1909), Williams's first publication is a series of dramatic monologues showing the influence of his friend Ezra Pound.

Publications and Events

Anthology of Magazine Verse and Year Book of American Poetry. This annual publication under the editorship of William Stanley Braithwaite begins. It closed in 1929.

Armory Show. This exhibition of paintings and sculpture at New York City's Sixty-ninth Regiment Armory introduces Americans to fauvism, cubism, futurism, and expressionism. The event played a critical role in stimulating American modern art and criticism.

Reedy's Mirror. William Marion Reedy (1862–1920) transforms the *St. Louis Sunday Mirror* into a weekly literary and critical magazine that, until it closed in 1920, introduced writers such as Fannie Hurst, Zoe Atkins, and Sara Teasdale. It also first published Edgar Lee Masters's *Spoon River Anthology* serially in 1914.

1914

Drama and Theater

IRVING BERLIN (1888–1989): *Watch Your Step*. This musical features the composer's first complete music score, which relies almost entirely on ragtime tunes. It is one of the first Broadway productions to depend fully on music derived from African American sources.

GEORGE BROADHURST: *Law of the Land*. Broadhurst continues his series of problem plays with a drama about an abused wife who kills her sadistic husband.

JAMES FORBES: *The Show Shop*. An amusing backstage send-up of a Broadway production. Critic Walter Prichard Eaton calls it "the most pungent, arousing, and yet the most kindly satire of stage life and the shams of theatrical productions, yet written by an American."

MARGARET MAYO: *Twin Beds*. In one of the era's most popular comedies, an intoxicated Italian tenor accidently visits a couple's bedroom.

EUGENE O'NEILL: *Thirst and Other One-Act Plays*. O'Neill's first publication, including the plays *Fog*, *Restlessness*, *Warnings*, and *The Web*. *Thirst*, O'Neill's second produced play, is about survivors on a lifeboat and is considered his first experimental work.

ELMER RICE (1892–1967): *On Trial*. Rice's first production, a murder mystery, draws on his experiences as a lawyer. It is distinctive for its accurately depicted trial and for use of flashbacks, enacting scenes that are described by witnesses.

Fiction

EDGAR RICE BURROUGHS (1875–1950): *Tarzan of the Apes*. First introduced in the October 1912 issue of *All-Story*, one of the most famous of all fictional characters, Tarzan, "King of the Jungle," makes his book debut. Burroughs would write twenty-four new Tarzan adventures, making him one of the biggest-selling and most successful writers of the century.

THEODORE DREISER: *The Titan*. The second of Dreiser's Cowperwood trilogy, which had begun with *The Financier* (1912) and would end with *The Stoic* (1947). It explores Cowperwood's drive for power as he rebuilds his fortune in Chicago while his marriage to his former mistress deteriorates.

ROBERT HERRICK: *Clark's Field*. Regarded as one of Herrick's finest novels, the story concerns a farmer's field that, due to urban sprawl, suddenly produces a fortune for the orphan Adelle Clark, who inherits it. After a hedonistic spree, she sees the emptiness of her life and resolves to find a better use for her property.

FANNIE HURST (1889–1968): *Just Around the Corner*. The first of the Ohio-born writer's four consecutive story collections introduces her favorite subjects: working girls in New York City and Jewish immigrants on the Lower East Side. *Every Soul Hath Its Song* (1916), *Gaslight Sonatas* (1918), and *Humoresque* (1919) would follow.

SINCLAIR LEWIS (1885–1951): *Our Mr. Wrenn.* Following a potboiler for boys written under a pseudonym (*Hike and the Aeroplane*, 1912), Lewis's first serious novel concerns a timid clerk whose dream of travel is granted. He tours bohemian London in the company of an expatriate artist before returning home to marry a down-to-earth girl and settle back into his commonplace life.

FRANK NORRIS: *Vandover and the Brute.* One of Norris's earliest works, left unfinished, is published posthumously. It concerns a San Francisco youth who, unable to balance his brutish instincts and his better self, degenerates under the city's economic and social pressures. The novel is notable for its explicit social satire.

EUGENE MANLOVE RHODES (1869–1934): *Bransford in Arcadia.* Rhodes, regarded by many as the best western writer of the early twentieth century, expands his popular story "The Little Eohippus," which had first appeared in the *Saturday Evening Post* in 1912. The resulting novel features cowboy hero Jeff Bransford, who refuses to compromise the woman he loves to clear himself of a murder charge.

GERTRUDE STEIN: *Tender Buttons: Objects, Food, Rooms.* This linguistic experimentation consists of a series of still lifes designed to suggest not the object but its essence and aura. Stein would later explain that she had set out to rid her work of nouns, seeking a "way of naming things that would not invent names, but mean names without naming them." What strikes many as nonsensical babble is widely quoted, if only as a source of ridicule, and helps establish Stein's avant-garde reputation.

BOOTH TARKINGTON: *Penrod.* One of the author's most popular works is a humorous portrait of boyhood in a typical small Midwestern city. It would spawn the sequels *Penrod and Sam* (1916), *Penrod Jashber* (1929), and the omnibus volume *Penrod: His Complete Story* (1931).

Literary Criticism and Scholarship

W. C. BROWNELL: *Criticism.* The literary critic fights an increasingly losing battle to maintain the traditional Victorian literary values of moral earnestness in this essay and his subsequent, aptly named volume, *Standards* (1917).

EMMA GOLDMAN: *The Social Significance of the Modern Drama.* A polemical treatise on the works of George Bernard Shaw, Henrik Ibsen, August Strindberg, and others who "represent the social iconoclasts of our time." Goldman praises their social themes as a means of raising awareness and stimulating reform.

HENRY JAMES: *Notes on Novelists.* Some of James's most revealing comments on the novelist's craft and his peers are collected in this volume of essays, with assessments of Honoré de Balzac, Gustave Flaubert, George Sand, Émile Zola, and others.

Nonfiction

LOUIS BRANDEIS (1856–1941): *Other People's Money.* Here the lawyer and social reformer suggests that the current borrowing system contributes to the concentration of wealth in the United States. His analysis impresses Woodrow Wilson and contributes to Brandeis's appointment to the Supreme Court in 1916.

HENRY JAMES: *Notes of a Son and a Brother.* The second volume of James's recollections concentrates on the period from 1850 to 1870, with revealing portraits of James's father and brother. The other volumes are *A Small Boy and Others* (1913) and *The Middle Years* (1917).

H. L. MENCKEN: *Europe after 8:15.* Mencken collaborates with the *Smart Set* editor W. H. Wright (1888–1939) and drama critic George Jean Nathan (1882–1958) to create this tour of the nightlife of Vienna, Munich, Berlin, London, and Paris.

JOHN REED (1887–1920): *Insurgent Mexico.* The radical journalist's first book is a collection of his dispatches covering the Mexican revolt of Pancho Villa.

THORSTEIN VEBLEN: *The Instinct of Workmanship.* Veblen initiates a series of controversial, polemical economic and cultural analyses of modern institutions. Subsequent volumes include *Imperial Germany in the Industrial Revolution* (1915), *An Inquiry into the Notion of Peace and the Terms for Its Perpetuation* (1917), *The Higher Learning in America* (1918), *The Place of Science in Modern Civilization* (1919), and *The Vested Interest and the State of the Industrial Arts* (1919).

Poetry

EMILY DICKINSON: *The Single Hound.* An important collection of 146 previously unpublished poems, chiefly verses sent to the poet's sister-in-law and Amherst neighbor, Susan Gilbert Dickinson, on various religious, metaphysical, and literary topics.

ARTHUR DAVISON FICKE (1883–1945): *Sonnets of a Portrait-Painter.* The most highly regarded of the poet's fifteen volumes is a sonnet sequence charting the tragic course of love.

ROBERT FROST: *North of Boston.* Frost's second collection brings its author his first considerable attention and recognition as a major American poet. With works of emotional intensity grounded in close observation of its New England setting and inhabitants, the collection includes some of Frost's most enduring poems, including

Amy Lowell

"Mending Wall," "The Death of the Hired Man," "The Wood-Pile," "Home Burial," and "A Servant to Servants."

ARTURO GIOVANNITTI (1884–1959): *Arrows in the Gale.* The labor organizer who had been jailed during the textile strike in Lawrence, Massachusetts, converts his experiences into a poetic appeal for prison and social reform.

JOYCE KILMER (1886–1918): *Trees and Other Poems.* The popularity of Kilmer's poem "Trees," published in *Poetry* in 1913, helps ensure this collection's success. Kilmer would publish only one other volume, *Main Street and Other Poems* (1917), before his death in the second battle of the Marne in World War I — an end that added additional pathos to Kilmer's poetic celebrations of the commonplace.

VACHEL LINDSAY: *The Congo and Other Poems.* Lindsay's second collection solidifies his reputation as one of the leading exponents of the "new poetry." "The Congo," with its syncopated rhythm, is perhaps his most famous and most popular work. Other major poems in the collection include "Abraham Lincoln Walks at Midnight" and "The Sante Fe Trail."

AMY LOWELL: *Sword Blades and Poppy Seed.* The first of two volumes of Lowell's experiments in "polyphonic prose," a version of free verse approximating the "unrhymed cadence" of speech. *Can Grande's Castle* would follow in 1918.

JAMES OPPENHEIM (1882–1932): *Songs for the New Age.* Oppenheim announces his radical break in experimental verses he calls "polyrhythmical poetry," expressing both his indebtedness to Whitman and his radical social and artistic views. Oppenheim was an editor of *The Seven Arts* who produced a story collection, *Dr. Rast* (1909).

Publications and Events

Des Imagistes: An Anthology. Edited by Ezra Pound, the anthology celebrates the works of poets such as Pound, H.D., Amy Lowell, William Carlos Williams, and James Joyce. Pound groups them under the experimental banner of Imagism, countering the methods and the more rustic, pastoral, and sentimental themes of their contemporaries, the Georgian poets.

The *Little Review.* Founded in Chicago by Margaret C. Anderson (1886–1973), this literary monthly became notorious for serializing James Joyce's *Ulysses* (1918–1921) and provided an important outlet for major literary figures such as T. S. Eliot, William Carlos Williams, Amy Lowell, and Carl Sandburg. It continued until 1929.

The *New Republic.* Willard D. Straight (1880–1918) begins the influential liberal magazine that examined current affairs and culture under the editorship of Herbert D. Croly (1869–1930).

The *Unpopular Review.* This conservative quarterly of social, economic, philosophical, and aesthetic issues debuts. Contributors included Brander Matthews, Mary Austin, and Amy Lowell. In 1919, it changed its name to the *Unpartisan Review* and continued publication until 1921.

Vanity Fair. Condé Nast (1873–1942) purchased the fashion magazine *Dress* in 1913 and paid $3,000 for the rights to the name "Vanity Fair," launching *Dress and Vanity Fair* in 1913. Nast hired editor Frank Crowninshield (1872–1947), who in 1914 dropped the magazine's fashion elements and helped turn the periodical into the preeminent literary voice of sophisticated café society until 1935.

IV

The Birth of Modernism

1915–1949

FRAMED BY TWO world wars, the period 1915–1949 is one of the richest and most crucial in American literary history. No other period produced so many masterworks or had such a profound and durable historical, social, and cultural legacy. This thirty-five-year period shaped social and literary policies and practices for the remainder of the twentieth century. Sinclair Lewis, America's first Nobel Prize winner in literature (1930), called the era America's second "coming of age," a period of maturation when poetry, fiction, and drama broke with conventions and achieved unparalleled creative achievement. American expatriate poets such as Ezra Pound and T. S. Eliot forged new methods of modern expression. In fiction there were probably more serious contenders for the mythical title of "Great American Novel" — *The Great Gatsby, An American Tragedy, A Farewell to Arms, U.S.A., Call It Sleep, The Grapes of Wrath, Gone with the Wind, Absalom, Absalom!* — than in any other period in American history. In drama, the first great classics of the American stage were performed. Although the forces of change and innovation were apparent before World War I (1914–1918), it accelerated and intensified those energies.

World War I symbolically divided the nineteenth from the twentieth century. What was unimaginable before 1914 became the reality of the twentieth-century world. Four years of slaughter in the trenches of the Western Front purged Americans' faith in progress and the perfectibility of man and replaced it with a cynicism preoccupied with dislocation, fragmentation, and dehumanization. American participation in the war also marked a fundamental turning point in the nation's emergence as a world power, which by 1945 had been projected into every region of the globe.

Just as America was thrust into the center of international politics, so too its writers and artists emerged as leading intellectual and artistic voices who addressed the shattered confidence in a civilization that seemed hell-bent on self-destruction. It fell to artists and writers to interpret the meaning of total mechanized warfare and America's new role on the world's stage. The result was an explosion of literary achievement far surpassing the first great American literary renaissance of the mid–nineteenth century.

The war also opened the door for European influences. American writers increasingly absorbed, imitated, and transformed the ideas and methods of European modernist masters such as James Joyce and Marcel Proust, and their predecessors, such as Henrik Ibsen, Fyodor Dostoyevsky, Charles Baudelaire, and Joseph Conrad. Modernism originated in an erosion of faith in the social, spiritual, and psychological absolutes of the nineteenth century and a consequent drive to discover new artistic modes of representing reality, new ways of self-understanding and emotional and spiritual renewal. World War I showed conclusively that old beliefs were corrupt and must be replaced. As Ezra Pound wrote in *Hugh Selwyn Mauberley* (1920),

> There died a myriad,
> And of the best, among them,
> For an old bitch gone in the teeth,
> For a botched civilization,
>
> Charm, smiling at the good mouth,
> Quick eyes gone under earth's lid,
>
> For two gross of broken statues,
> For a few thousand battered books.

Pound's rallying cry, "Make It New," defined the modernist agenda: sift the fragments of an exploded culture in search of new and sustaining sources of order, coherence, and faith. New language, new artistic forms, new relations between the artist and society were needed. As Hemingway's protagonist Frederic Henry in *A Farewell to Arms* (1929) says, "I was always embarrassed by the words sacred, glorious, and sacrifice and the expression in vain. . . . I had seen nothing sacred, and the things that were glorious had no glory and the sacrifices were like the stockyards at Chicago if nothing was done with the meat except to bury it. . . . Abstract words such as glory, honor, courage, or hallow were obscene beside the concrete names of villages, the numbers of roads, the names of rivers, the numbers of regiments and the dates." Frederic Henry and his generation needed a new vocabulary and sources of authenticity that the literary modernist attempted to supply.

For the first time in history, Americans would lead the charge. It was an American, T. S. Eliot, who wrote what William Carlos Williams later would describe as the "atomic bomb" of modern poetry, *The Waste Land*. In 1929, William Faulkner would publish the first great American modernist novel, *The Sound and the Fury*, and follow it with a succession of breathtaking literary experiments that helped redefine fiction's possibilities. Hemingway's lean, muscular style revolutionized the novel and short story, and his work became one of America's most influential literary exports. During the period, America also discovered its first great playwright, Eugene O'Neill, who built upon and extended the innovations of the great European modern dramatists, such as Henrik Ibsen, George Bernard Shaw, and August Strindberg. And America's unique contribution to the world's stage, the American musical, achieved mastery. It is also during this period that African American writers pioneered the literary uses of other indigenous cultural forms, the blues and jazz.

The period between the wars saw unprecedented change brought about by urbanization, industrialization, and immigration, as well as by technological innovations such as electricity, the telephone, and the automobile. These things linked the nation and reduced regional distinctions. Formerly silent minority voices were also heard in increasing numbers. Women left the home in unprecedented numbers during the wars and won the right to vote in 1920. African American writers, in particular, voiced their concerns loudly and frankly about racism and black culture, heralding a new and important tributary to the mainstream of American culture.

With these changes came new concepts of American identity, of concepts of justice and success. Magazines, book clubs, radio, motion pictures, and finally television helped create for the first time an American mass culture. The gap created between highbrow and lowbrow, between an audience trained to appreciate the complexity of modernist experiments and an audience demanding

to be entertained, grew more and more pronounced. Writers for the first time became stars like those in Hollywood, in a growing cult of celebrity, feted by and sacrificed to what Norman Mailer called the "bitch-goddess" fame.

Despite these overriding trends, no other literary period is more symmetrically subdivided by its constituent decades. The 1920s, 1930s, and 1940s form distinctly different eras. America emerged from the war as virtually the only great power left standing, and the 1920s became a boom time of prosperity. A remarkable explosion of creative energy captured both the new spirit of youthful rebellion and the conservative traditionalism that still held sway in the American heartland. The 1920s might have been the era of the liberated flapper and gangster, but it was also the period of legislating morality through prohibition. Writers such as F. Scott Fitzgerald (who dubbed the era the Jazz Age), Sherwood Anderson, Theodore Dreiser, John Dos Passos, Sinclair Lewis, and others mined the rich complexity of the American scene for characters and plots that explored the contradictions between the nation's ideals and realities, between its desires and its limitations. In 1929, the stock market crash marked the symbolic end of the party and the beginning of America's greatest social challenge — the Great Depression.

The modernist movement of the 1920s celebrated the artist as a detached observer who produced art for art's sake, but the financial crash and its aftermath led a large segment of the American literary community to shift to a literature of engagement. What had caused the crash? What was the solution? To many writers, the Depression signaled the collapse of capitalism, exposing the system's intractable inequities. The modernist focus had been on the individual consciousness and the innovations necessary to reveal it. But in the 1930s, in masterworks such as Dos Passos's *U.S.A.* and John Steinbeck's *The Grapes of Wrath*, writers began to emphasize theme over formal innovation, putting art in the service of protest and reform. Many embraced radical causes and delivered social realism in the interest of a proletarian literature, rejecting the modernist movement as too detached and too elitist. Others celebrated what they perceived as America's collective greatness and solidarity. If the underlying theme of much of the literature of the 1920s concerned personal liberation, the 1930s forced a concern with economics and politics.

Like the 1929 crash that ended the boom time of the 1920s, the outbreak of war in 1939 brought a shift that characterized the next decade. After the economic deprivation and political unrest of the 1930s, American society united again in the war effort, emerging victorious as an economic and technological powerhouse. The result was a period of unprecedented prosperity for the average American. Yet the Allied victory in 1945 secured an uneasy peace, shadowed by an ongoing cold war and its threat of thermonuclear annihilation. Writers faced a new America. The 1940s became a testing ground both for the generation of prewar writers, who tried to interpret the transformed postwar world, and for the next generation of writers, who had experienced combat or come of age during the bloodiest war in history. Established literary figures such as Hemingway, Faulkner, Dos Passos, and Steinbeck won an audience but not with the strength and power they had enjoyed before the war. A new generation of writers — John Hersey, Norman Mailer, James Jones, and John Hawkes — who focused on combat or at least the war experience — began to gain increasing attention. In poetry the decade produced important works by the great figures of the post–World War I era, such as T. S. Eliot, Ezra Pound, Robert Frost, Wallace Stevens, Marianne Moore, and William Carlos Williams, alongside new voices, such as Robert Lowell, Elizabeth Bishop, and Randall Jarrell. In drama, the 1940s saw Eugene O'Neill's final Broadway production during his lifetime, *The Iceman Cometh* (1946), as well as the failure of *A Moon for the Misbegotten* (1947) to achieve a New York production. By the decade's end, the significant figures of American drama between the wars — O'Neill, Robert Sherwood, Maxwell Anderson, Clifford Odets, Lillian Hellman, S. N. Behrman — were pushed offstage by two new playwrights of distinction: Tennessee Williams and Arthur Miller.

Intellectually and artistically, the postwar era of the 1940s did not generate the explosive creative energy released by the disillusionment that followed World War I and the synthesis of modernist ideas. Rather, it marked the beginning of an age of criticism. The dominant mode of literary analysis at the time, the New Criticism, championed the close examination of literary works without much regard for their biographical or historical influences. Yet a search for moral and social meaning in literature also ensued in response to the collapse of the political and social ideologies of the 1930s. Existentialism, derived from French writers such as Jean-Paul Sartre and Albert Camus, began to influence American writers and thinkers. Writers sifted and resifted the wreckage of traditional beliefs brought into question by the war and searched for its implications about human nature and the meaning of existence. Such preoccupations, at times verging on brooding despair, drove much postwar inquiry and artistic expression. Three titles in particular captured this tone: Saul Bellow's first novel, *Dangling Man* (1944); Ralph Ellison's *Invisible Man*, published in 1952 but mainly composed during the 1940s; and Nelson Algren's *The Man with the Golden Arm* (1949), a novel of addiction and bohemianism that blazed the path for the Beat literature of the 1950s.

By the decade's end, intellectuals and creative writers alike began to sense that the previous prewar ways of understanding the world, including the modernist faith in art and the artistic vision, were inadequate. To chart the literary course out of the 1940s — characterized by both destruction and prosperity — would require new responses and methods as distinctive and as radical as any that emerged in the aftermath of World War I.

1915
Drama and Theater

GUY BOLTON (1884–1979): *Nobody Home*. Its realism makes this comedy about courtship complications, with music by Jerome Kern (1885–1945), one of the pioneer works in the development of the American musical. It is also the first of what would become known as the Princess Theatre musicals, a reference to the intimate Broadway theater where groundbreaking musical dramas were staged. It is followed by the season's smash hit, another Bolton and Kern collaboration, *Very Good Eddie*, about mismatched couples on a Hudson River cruise. Bolton was a prolific librettist and author of stage comedies whose last Broadway production, *Anya*, would appear in 1965.

Fiction

WILLA CATHER: *The Song of the Lark*. Cather's third novel traces the hard-fought struggle of Thea Kronborg of Moonstone, Colorado, to become an international opera singer. The childhood scenes are based on Cather's own, and Thea's youthful aspirations also echo the author's. Cather would later regard the novel as one of her favorites but a failure, particularly in its depiction of Thea's eventual success.

WINSTON CHURCHILL: *A Far Country*. A modern version of the parable of the prodigal son, set in the Midwest of the 1880s during the Robber Baron era. Readers generally resisted the novel as a ponderous, lifeless allegory on the need for business reform and the importance of a social conscience.

BIRTHS AND DEATHS, 1915–1919

Births

1915 Saul Bellow, novelist
Richard Condon (d. 1996), novelist
Arthur Miller, playwright
Jean Stafford (d. 1979), short story writer and novelist
Herman Wouk, novelist

1916 John Ciardi (d. 1986), poet and critic
Horton Foote, playwright and screenwriter
Walker Percy (d. 1990), novelist
Harold Robbins (d. 1997), novelist
Frank Yerby (d. 1991), novelist

1917 Jane Bowles (d. 1973), short story writer, novelist, and playwright
Gwendolyn Brooks (d. 2000), poet and novelist
Robert Lowell (d. 1977), poet
Carson McCullers (d. 1967), novelist
Arthur M. Schlesinger Jr., historian
Peter Taylor (d. 1994), short story writer and novelist

1918 William Bronk (d. 1999), poet
Allen Drury (d. 1998), novelist
Mary Lee Settle, novelist
Mickey Spillane (Frank Morrison), crime novelist

1919 Shirley Jackson (d. 1965), short story writer and novelist
J. D. Salinger, novelist and short story writer
May Swenson (d. 1989), poet

Deaths

1915 Charles Klein (b. 1867), playwright
Booker T. Washington (b. 1856), writer and educator

1916 Richard Harding Davis (b. 1864), journalist, short story writer, and playwright
Henry James (b. 1843), novelist, short story writer, and playwright
Jack London (b. 1876), novelist and short story writer
George Wilbur Peck (b. 1840), novelist
James Whitcomb Riley (b. 1849), poet
John Townsend Trowbridge (b. 1827), novelist
Alan Seeger (b. 1888), poet

1918 Henry Adams (b. 1838), historian and essayist
Joyce Kilmer (b. 1886), poet

1919 Amelia E. Barr (b. 1831), novelist
L. Frank Baum (b. 1856), children's writer, playwright, and journalist
Theodore Roosevelt (b. 1858), writer, historian, and politician
Ella Wilcox (b. 1850), poet

THEODORE DREISER: *The Genius.* Dreiser's novel follows the career of an artist, Eugene Witla, through a succession of relationships. The novel's sexual candor makes it notorious.

CHARLOTTE PERKINS GILMAN: *Herland.* Gilman's utopian novel describes an all-female society (with reproduction by parthenogenesis) in which women's essential qualities of nurturing and caring create a peaceful, prosperous, and rationally ordered world.

SUSAN GLASPELL: *Fidelity.* Glaspell's shocking novel about a young woman who elopes with a married man satirizes the limitations of life in a Midwestern town and the struggle of a "new woman" to achieve autonomy.

ROBERT GRANT (1852–1940): *The High Priestess.* Grant tackles the controversial topic of the career woman in this novel about the complications that result when a woman leaves her domain at home and her duties as a homemaker.

SINCLAIR LEWIS: *The Trail of the Hawk.* Lewis's second mature novel is an idealistic romance about the boyhood, youth, and later career of an adventurer who escapes from his provincial small town in Minnesota to become an aviator.

JACK LONDON: *The Star Rover.* One of London's last major extended works is a science fiction novel concerning the out-of-body experiences of a convicted murderer, Professor Darrell Standing, who is able to project his spirit into past reincarnations. Literary critic Leslie Fiedler has called London's book one of the forgotten classics of American literature.

ERNEST POOLE (1880–1950): *The Harbor.* Poole draws on his own background for this novel, regarded by some as his best, set in New York's harbor area. Its strong socialist message makes the book popular among liberals and activists. It is considered one of the first fictional works to offer a positive view of unions.

BOOTH TARKINGTON: *The Turmoil.* The first novel of a trilogy depicting Midwestern city life. It would be followed by *The Magnificent Ambersons* (1918) and *The Midlander* (1923).

HARRY LEON WILSON (1867–1939): *Ruggles of Red Gap.* The humorist's most popular and best book is this tale of a proper English valet transported to the Wild West. Wilson was the editor of the humorous weekly *Puck* from 1896 to 1902. His earlier novels include *The Spenders* (1902), *The Lions of the Lord* (1903), and *Bunker Bean* (1913).

Literary Criticism and Scholarship

VAN WYCK BROOKS: *America's Coming-of-Age.* Brooks's analysis of American literary culture establishes a dichotomy between the highbrows, idealists who remain aloof from American realities, and the lowbrows, vulgar materialists. He uses this split to explain the failure of American culture, with Whitman as an example of a writer who bridged the gap. The book establishes Brooks's reputation as one of the leading literary and cultural critics of the period.

Fiction*

1915
1. *The Turmoil* by Booth Tarkington
2. *A Far Country* by Winston Churchill
3. *Michael O'Halloran* by Gene Stratton Porter
4. *Pollyanna Grows Up* by Eleanor H. Porter
5. *K* by Mary Roberts Rinehart
6. *Jaffery* by William J. Locke
7. *Felix O'Day* by F. Hopkinson Smith
8. *The Harbor* by Ernest Poole
9. *The Lone Star Ranger* by Zane Grey
10. *Angela's Business* by Henry Sydnor Harrison

1916
1. *Seventeen* by Booth Tarkington
2. *When a Man's a Man* by Harold Bell Wright
3. *Just David* by Eleanor H. Porter
4. *Mr. Britling Sees It Through* by H. G. Wells
5. *Life and Gabriella* by Ellen Glasgow
6. *The Red Adventure* by Henry Kitchell Webster
7. *Bars of Iron* by Ethel M. Dell
8. *Nan of Music Mountain* by Frank H. Spearman
9. *Dear Enemy* by Jean Webster
10. *The Heart of Rachael* by Kathleen Norris

1917
1. *Mr. Britling Sees It Through* by H. G. Wells
2. *The Light in the Clearing* by Irving Bacheller
3. *The Red Planet* by William J. Locke
4. *The Road to Understanding* by Eleanor H. Porter
5. *Wildfire* by Zane Grey
6. *Christine* by Alice Cholmondeley
7. *In the Wilderness* by Robert S. Hichens
8. *His Family* by Ernest Poole
9. *The Definite Object* by Jeffrey Farnol
10. *The Hundredth Chance* by Ethel M. Dell

1918
1. *The U. P. Trail* by Zane Grey
2. *The Tree of Heaven* by May Sinclair
3. *The Amazing Interlude* by Mary Roberts Rinehart
4. *Dere Mable* by Edward Streeter
5. *Oh, Money! Money!* by Eleanor H. Porter
6. *Greatheart* by Ethel M. Dell
7. *The Major* by Ralph Connor
8. *The Pawns Count* by E. Phillips Oppenheim
9. *A Daughter of the Land* by Gene Stratton Porter
10. *Sonia* by Stephen McKenna

1919
1. *The Four Horsemen of the Apocalypse* by V. Blasco Ibañez
2. *The Arrow of Gold* by Joseph Conrad
3. *The Desert of Wheat* by Zane Grey
4. *Dangerous Days* by Mary Roberts Rinehart
5. *The Sky Pilot in No Man's Land* by Ralph Connor
6. *The Re-Creation of Brian Kent* by Harold Bell Wright
7. *Dawn* by Gene Stratton Porter
8. *The Tin Soldier* by Temple Bailey
9. *Christopher and Columbus* by "Elizabeth"
10. *In Secret* by Robert W. Chambers

War-Books

1917
1. *The First Hundred Thousand* by Ian Hay
2. *My Home in the Field of Honor* by Frances W. Huard
3. *A Student in Arms* by Donald Hankey
4. *Over the Top* by Arthur Guy Empey
5. *Carry On* by Coningsby Dawson
6. *Getting Together* by Ian Hay
7. *My Second Year of the War* by Frederick Palmer
8. *The Land of Deepening Shadow* by D. Thoma Curtin
9. *Italy, France, and Britain at War* by H. G. Wells
10. *The Worn Steps* by Margaret Sherwood

1918
1. *My Four Years in Germany* by James W. Gerard
2. *The Glory of the Trenches* by Coningsby Dawson
3. *Over the Top* by Arthur Guy Empey
4. *A Minstrel in France* by Harry Laudner
5. *Private Peat* by Harold R. Peat
6. *Outwitting the Hun* by Lieutenant Pat O'Brien
7. *Face to Face with Kaiserism* by James W. Gerard
8. *Carry On* by Coningsby Dawson
9. *Out to Win* by Coningsby Dawson
10. *Under Fire* by Henri Barbusse

General Nonfiction

1917
1. *Rhymes of the Red Cross Man* by Robert W. Service
2. *The Plattsburg Manual* by O. O. Ellis and E. B. Garey
3. *Raymond* by Sir Oliver Lodge
4. *Poems of Alan Seeger* by Alan Seeger
5. *God the Invisible King* by H. G. Wells
6. *Laugh and Live* by Douglas Fairbanks
7. *Better Meals for Less Money* by Mary Green

1918
1. *Rhymes of a Red Cross Man* by Robert W. Service
2. *Treasury of War Poetry* by G. H. Clark
3. *With the Colors* by Everard J. Appleton
4. *Recollections* by Viscount Morley
5. *Laugh and Live* by Douglas Fairbanks
6. *Mark Twain's Letters* edited by Albert Bigelow Paine
7. *Adventures and Letters of Richard Harding Davis* by Richard Harding Davis
8. *Over Here* by Edgar Guest
9. *Diplomatic Days* by Edith O'Shaughnessy
10. *Poems of Alan Seeger* by Alan Seeger

1919
1. *The Education of Henry Adams* by Henry Adams
2. *The Years Between* by Rudyard Kipling
3. *Belgium* by Brand Whitlock
4. *The Seven Purposes* by Margaret Cameron
5. *In Flanders Fields* by John McCrae
6. *Bolshevism* by John Spargo

* During the early years of *Publishers Weekly*'s bestseller lists, fiction and nonfiction were combined in one list. Since fiction far and away outsold nonfiction titles, the top ten sellers were always fiction. In 1912, *Publishers Weekly* added a nonfiction bestseller list, only to drop it in 1914. In 1917, with the rising popularity of books on war, *Publishers Weekly* added a War-Books bestseller list and also reinstated the nonfiction bestseller list. In 1919, the War-Books bestseller list was dropped.

AWARDS AND PRIZES, 1917–1919

Pulitzer Prizes

1917
History: *With Americans of Past and Present Days* by J. J. Jusserand
Biography/Autobiography: *Julia Ward Howe* by Laura E. Richards, Florence Hall, and Maude H. Elliott

1918
Fiction: *His Family* by Ernest Poole
Drama: *Why Marry?* by Jesse Lynch Williams
History: *History of the Civil War* by James F. Rhodes
Biography/Autobiography: *Benjamin Franklin, Self-Revealed* by William C. Bruce

1919
Fiction: *The Magnificent Ambersons* by Booth Tarkington
Drama: No Prize Awarded
History: No Prize Awarded
Biography/Autobiography: *The Education of Henry Adams* by Henry Adams

JOHN JAY CHAPMAN: *Memories and Milestones.* A miscellaneous collection of essays by the influential critic on literary, dramatic, and cultural topics. Chapman also publishes *Greek Genius and Other Essays*, which includes appreciations of Euripides, Shakespeare, Honoré de Balzac, and others.

JAMES GIBBONS HUNEKER: *Ivory Apes and Peacocks.* This miscellany of literary, artistic, and musical criticism includes a controversial essay on Walt Whitman that deals frankly with the author's homosexuality. Huneker also publishes *The New Cosmopolis*, a comparative study of New York City.

FRED LEWIS PATTEE (1863–1950): *History of American Literature Since 1870.* The first volume of Pattee's most important critical work attempts a paradigm-shifting interpretation that counters the notion of the centrality of New England in the development of American literature. Instead, he insists that what is most distinctively American about the country's literature was generated outside of New England. The book also is one of the first to grant cultural significance to popular works. Pattee, who was a professor at Pennsylvania State College from 1894 to 1928, would complete his survey with *The New American Literature, 1890–1930* (1930) and *The First Century of American Literature, 1770–1870* (1935).

Nonfiction

W.E.B. DU BOIS: *The Negro.* Du Bois's influential compendium of facts about black people around the world includes interpretations of African culture and African American history, serving as "the Bible of Pan-Africanism."

VACHEL LINDSAY: *The Art of the Motion Picture.* The poet supplies one of the earliest examples of film criticism, classifying films and cinema techniques while declaring that "the photoplay cuts deeper into some stratifications of society than the newspaper or the book have ever gone."

JOHN MUIR: *Travels in Alaska.* This posthumous account of Muir's three trips to Alaska in 1879, 1880, and 1890 lacks the intimacy and polish of his other books but has remained one of his most popular works.

LAURA ELIZABETH RICHARDS (1850–1943), FLORENCE HOWE HALL (1845–1922), AND MAUD HOWE ELLIOTT (1854–1948): *Julia Ward Howe.* The first Pulitzer Prize in biography is awarded to this life of Howe, written by her daughters.

ONOTO WATANNA (WINNIFRED EATON): *Me: A Book of Remembrance.* The Canadian-born, half-Chinese writer who adopted a Japanese persona publishes (anonymously) a fictionalized memoir, one of the earliest by an Asian American writer published in the United States.

EDITH WHARTON: *Fighting France, from Dunkerque to Belfort.* Wharton covers the first year of the war from her vantage point in Paris and her visits near the front lines.

CARTER GODWIN WOODSON (1875–1950): *The Education of the Negro Prior to 1861.* The first important work by the African American historian and pioneering scholar of African American studies. He would found and edit the *Journal of Negro History* in 1916 and subsequently publish other important works such as *History of the Negro Church* (1921), *Negro Orators and Their Orations* (1925), *The Mis-Education of the Negro* (1933), and *African Heroes and Heroines* (1939).

Poetry

ADELAIDE CRAPSEY (1878–1914): *Verses.* A posthumous collection featuring the poet's major innovation, the cinquain, a verse form of five unrhymed lines resembling the haiku in its juxtaposition of images. Expanded editions would follow in 1922 and 1934. Crapsey was a literature teacher at private girls' schools and at Smith College. Most of her work was composed during her last year when she was dying of tuberculosis.

JOHN GOULD FLETCHER (1886–1950): *Irradiations: Sands and Spray.* One of the leading American Imagists, Fletcher supplies both a theoretical explanation of the movement and examples in a collection of experimental verses. Fletcher was from Arkansas and lived mainly in Europe from 1908 to 1933. Other volumes include *Goblins and Pagodas* (1916) and *Breakers and Granite* (1921).

AMY LOWELL, EDITOR: *Some Imagist Poets.* The first of three anthologies of Imagist poetry, issued from 1915 to 1917, under the supervision of Amy Lowell. Lowell's preface provides the credo of Imagism (language of common sense, new rhythms, absolute freedom in the choice of subjects, centrality of the image, hard and clear poetry, shunning of the blurred or indefinite, and concentration as the essence of poetry). The anthologies help popularize the movement and fan controversy over its subjects and techniques.

EDGAR LEE MASTERS: *Spoon River Anthology.* First appearing serially in *Reedy's Mirror* in 1914, Masters's collection of verse epitaphs, revealing the secret lives of those buried in a Midwestern town's cemetery, becomes a popular and critical sensation. An expanded edition would be issued in 1916, and a new collection, *The New Spoon River*, appeared in 1924. Masters never duplicated the impact of his 1915 collection, however. He was buried in the cemetery in Lewiston, Illinois, where he derived the names of his subjects from the tombstones.

JOHN NEIHARDT (1881–1973): *The Song of Hugh Glass.* The first volume of Neihardt's five-part epic, tracing the history of the American West and the passing of the Plains Indians, begins in the 1820s with the trappers and mountainmen Glass and Jim Bridger. Subsequent volumes are *The Song of Three Friends* (1919), *The Song of the Indian War* (1923), *The Song of the Messiah* (1935), *The Song of Jed Smith* (1941), together collected as *A Cycle of the West* (1949).

EZRA POUND: *Cathay.* Pound reworks rough translations from the Chinese by Ernest Fenollosa (1853–1908) into polished modernist verses. The collection includes frequently anthologized poems such as "The River Merchant's Wife: A Letter" and "The River Song." The effort forces Pound's realization that the Imagists had "sought the force of Chinese ideo-graphs without knowing it."

SARA TEASDALE: *Rivers to the Sea.* Teasdale's collection features a long dramatic monologue, "Sappho," the last she would produce, and an advance in naturalness and technical artistry. The volume's first printing sells out within three months.

MARGARET WIDDEMER (1884–1978): *The Factories, with Other Lyrics.* The Pennsylvania poet's first collection exposes labor abuses and child labor practices. She also publishes in 1915 a best-selling novel, *The Rose-Garden Husband.*

Publications and Events

The Best Short Stories of 1915. Edward O'Brien (1890–1941) issues the first of an annual series of the best contemporary short stories, which he would select until 1940. Other permanent and guest editors continued the series.

The Provincetown Players. Susan Glaspell and her husband, Georg Cram Cook (1873–1924), found this group in Provincetown, Massachusetts. After two successful summer seasons on the Cape, they took over a Greenwich Village theater and became the most significant little theater in the country, performing important new works by Glaspell, Eugene O'Neill, Theodore Dreiser, E. E. Cummings, and many others until 1929.

The Washington Square Players. Founded by Lawrence Langer (1890–1962), Philip Moeller (1880–1958), Helen Westley (1879–1942), and others, this theater group produced plays by Eugene O'Neill, Elmer Rice, Anton Chekhov, and others until 1918. Many of the group's members then formed the Theatre Guild in 1919.

1916
Drama and Theater

ALICE GERSTENBERG (1885–1972): *Overtones.* One of the season's most talked about dramas is this ingenious production of the Washington Square Players, featuring a four-character interplay of two women and their alter egos, or overtones.

SUSAN GLASPELL: *Trifles.* Glaspell's best-known play is a one-act murder mystery exploiting gender assumptions. The male investigators miss the evidence of why a wife might kill her husband.

CLARE KUMMER (c. 1873–1958): *Good Gracious, Annabelle.* The songwriter's first produced play concerns a group of poor socialites who go to work as servants. It becomes a hit. Kummer's second effort, *A Successful Calamity* (1917), about a millionaire who feigns poverty to evade his family, would also prove popular. *Rollo's Wild Oat* (1920) and *Her Master's Voice* (1933) would follow.

EUGENE O'NEILL: *Bound East for Cardiff.* The first of O'Neill's plays to be performed, this one-act sea drama depicts an injured seaman's death. After reviewing his hard life, he realizes that "this sailor life ain't much to cry about leaving." The play is considered O'Neill's strongest early drama. Other of his one-act plays produced during the year are *Thirst*, about three shipwrecked sailors on a life raft, and *Before Breakfast*, about a shrewish wife who pushes her husband to suicide.

Original members of the Provincetown Players William and Marguerite Zorach (*right*)

EZRA POUND: *Noh; or, Accomplishment: A Study of the Classical Stage of Japan* and *Certain Noh Plays of Japan.* Pound's collaboration with orientalist Ernest Fenollosa results in these two works, which help popularize Japanese drama in America.

Fiction

SHERWOOD ANDERSON (1876–1941): *Windy McPherson's Son.* Anderson's autobiographical first novel concerns life in a small Iowa town and a youth's departure to Chicago to make his fortune. The novel sounds many of Anderson's characteristic themes: the mixed nature of small-town American life, the warping power of material success, and the challenge of male-female relationships.

ELLEN GLASGOW: *Life and Gabriella.* One of the novelist's most popular works is a character study of a strong Southern woman, Gabriella Carr, who is abandoned by her shallow husband and is forced to make her own way in business. Because Gabriella proves that a woman can have both a career and a family, the novel has been seen as an early feminist work.

WILLIAM DEAN HOWELLS: *The Leatherwood God.* Howells's final novel deals with the Ohio of his youth in the 1830s, a subject he also treats in a volume of reminiscences, *Years of My Youth.*

RING LARDNER (1885–1933): *You Know Me Al: A Busher's Letters.* While writing a sports column for the *Chicago Tribune,* Lardner creates the letters of Jack Keefe, a baseball rookie shuttling between the minors and the White Sox, to his Indiana hometown friend, Al Blanchard. Lardner's portrayal of Keefe's experiences in the bigs and out has been called the best use of baseball in American fiction and the most effective dialect humor since *Huckleberry Finn.* Additional letters would be collected in *Treat 'Em Rough* (1918) and *The Real Dope* (1919).

JACK LONDON: *The Little Lady of the Big House.* London's agrarian novel explores a love triangle among a husband and wife and the husband's best friend. London also issues the story collection *The Turtles of Tasman.*

BOOTH TARKINGTON: *Seventeen.* Following his success in capturing boyhood in *Penrod* (1914), Tarkington tackles adolescence and youthful love in this novel about Willie Baxter's infatuation with the baby-talking Lola Pratt. The author's biographer, James Woodress, would call it "one of the superb comedies of adolescence." Another Penrod novel, *Penrod and Sam,* also appears.

MARK TWAIN (SAMUEL LANGHORNE CLEMENS): *The Mysterious Stranger.* Twain's bitterest meditation is this medieval fantasy, written in 1898 out of his despair over his beloved daughter's death, another daughter's incurable epilepsy, his wife's increasing invalidism, and his own struggle to pay off his creditors. In it, Satan instructs an audience of youths about life's fundamental absurdity: "There is no God, no universe, no human race, no earthly

Susan Glaspell

life, no heaven, no hell. It is all a dream — a grotesque and foolish dream."

EDITH WHARTON: *Xingu and Other Stories.* Wharton's story collection includes the title satire on the snobbish hypocrisy of the Hillbridge Lunch Club as well as "Coming Home," about a French collaborator during the war, and "The Bunner Sisters," the story of two spinster sisters who operate a small shop in nineteenth-century New York.

Nonfiction

JOHN DEWEY: *Democracy and Education.* Dewey applies the principles of a democratic society to the problems of public education. It represents the first systematic statement of his educational theories and is considered his masterwork.

THEODORE DREISER: *A Hoosier Holiday.* Dreiser provides an account of a car trip from New York to the Indiana sites of his birth and boyhood, along with commentary on American culture. He also publishes a collection of one-act dramas, *Plays of the Natural and the Supernatural.*

H. L. MENCKEN: *The Book of Burlesques.* Mencken's collection of epigrams, modeled on Ambrose Bierce's *Devil's Dictionary,* contains definitions such as "Evil. What one believes of others," "Love. The delusion that one woman differs from another," and "Immorality. The morality of those who are having a good time."

JOHN MUIR: *A Thousand Mile Walk to the Gulf.* Muir's notebooks of the journey he took on foot in 1867 from Indiana to the Gulf of Mexico has been read both as a conversion narrative of Muir's spiritual awakening and as a portrait of the changes in America following the Civil War.

JOHN REED: *The War in Eastern Europe.* Reed had produced these articles based on his experiences as a war correspondent for the *Metropolitan,* the *Masses,* and the *Seven Arts.* He saw relatively little of the fighting in World War I but a great deal of the social conditions of the Russian people, which he describes convincingly.

AGNES REPPLIER (1855–1950): *Counter-Currents.* In a series of pro-Allied propaganda, the essayist mounts an attack on humanitarians and pacifists, whom she charges with excessive sentimentality.

JOSIAH ROYCE: *The Hope of the Great Community.* The philosopher's final book considers moral questions raised by World War I, including the sinking of the *Lusitania* and the prospects for achieving international peace.

Poetry

CONRAD AIKEN (1889–1973): *The Jig of Forslin: A Symphony.* After two derivative apprentice volumes, *Earth Triumphant* (1914) and *Turns and Movies* (1916), Aiken launches an ambitiously long sequence of "symphonies" blending philosophical and psychological themes in a structure both lyrical and narrative. The sequence would be continued in *The Charnel Rose* (1918), *Senlin: A Biography* (1918), *The House of Dust* (1920), *The Pilgrimage of Festus* (1923), and *Changing Mind* (1925), collected as *The Divine Pilgrim* in 1949.

WITTER BYNNER (1881–1968) AND ARTHUR DAVISON FICKE (1883–1945): *Spectra: A Book of Poetic Experiments.* Written under the pseudonyms "Emanuel Morgan" and "Anne Knish," Bynner and Ficke create a parody of the Vorticists and Imagists, which announces a new poetic movement, Spectric poetry, along with its philosophy and examples. The hoax is taken seriously, and both the *Little Review* and *Poetry* accept Spectric poems, with Alfred Kreymborg's *Others* devoting an entire issue to the movement. Bynner, whose serious poetry collections include *An Ode to Harvard* (1907), *Grenstone Poems* (1917), and *A Canticle of Pan* (1920), would not expose the hoax until 1945.

JOHN GOULD FLETCHER: *Goblins and Pagodas.* Fletcher's second collection of Imagist poems includes the sequence "Symphonies," thought to contain some of his best work and describing the "emotional and intellectual development of an artist."

ROBERT FROST: *Mountain Interval.* Frost's third collection contains some of his most characteristic and finest achievements, such as "The Road Not Taken," "Birches,"

"The Oven Bird," "The Hill Wife," and "An Old Man's Winter Night."

EDDIE GUEST (1881–1959): *A Heap o' Livin'*. The folksy populist poet's most famous line, "It takes a heap o' livin' in a house t' make it home," appears in this volume, which would be followed by other popular, sentimental collections. Guest's poems appeared daily in the *Detroit Free Press* and in wide circulation around the country.

H.D. (HILDA DOOLITTLE, 1886–1961): *Sea Garden*. The poet's first collection establishes her as "the perfect Imagist." It has been said that her friend Ezra Pound conceived the Imagist movement and its principles largely to promote her work. The stark and concrete poems use striking images in nature as the means of exploring consciousness. Admired works in the collection include "Heat" and "Pear Tree." Doolittle was born in Pennsylvania, went to Europe in 1911, and married English writer Richard Aldington.

ROBINSON JEFFERS (1887–1962): *Californians*. After a first collection, *Flagons and Apples* (1912), Jeffers publishes his first narratives and descriptive poems set in California.

ALFRED KREYMBORG (1883–1962): *Mushrooms*. Kreymborg's first collection of experimental free verse, in which, according to one reviewer, "the reader will find the very essence of the new school of ultra poetic expression." Kreymborg also edits the anthology *Others*, featuring new poetry such as Wallace Stevens's "Peter Quince at the Clavier."

AMY LOWELL: *Men, Women, and Ghosts*. Lowell's collection of narrative poems, scenes, and monologues is praised by D. H. Lawrence, who cites as particular achievements "The Cremona Violin," "Reaping," and "Hoops."

EDGAR LEE MASTERS: *Songs and Satires*. Following the phenomenal success of *Spoon River Anthology* (1915), Masters produces the first of five volumes of miscellaneous verse. All are largely dismissed as inferior early work and contribute to his declining reputation. The others are *The Great Valley* (1916), *Toward the Gulf* (1918), *Starved Rock* (1919), and *The Open Sea* (1921).

JOSEPHINE PRESTON PEABODY (1874–1922): *Harvest Moon*. In this collection of mainly war poems, Peabody presents a woman's perspective on the conflict.

EZRA POUND: *Lustra*. Pound's collection includes new and previously published verse, Chinese translations, and the first three of *The Cantos*, Pound's expansive poetic sequence, finally collected in 1970. An expanded American edition appeared in 1917. Pound also publishes in 1916 his memoir of the Vorticist sculptor Gaudier-Brzeska, killed on the battlefield in 1915. It in-cludes Pound's theories of vorticism that established the image as the fundamental poetic element.

EDWIN ARLINGTON ROBINSON: *The Man Against the Sky*. In what is generally regarded as Robinson's most important single collection, Robinson includes the title work, which he claimed summarized his philosophy; "Cassandra," an attack on American capitalism; "Captain Craig," a blank-verse narrative about an eccentric poet and philosopher; and his finest shorter poems, "Hillcrest," "Veteran Sirens," "The Poor Relations," and "Eros Turannos."

CARL SANDBURG (1878–1967): *Chicago Poems*. Sandburg's first recognition had come in 1914, with the publication in *Poetry* of "Chicago," a poem in free verse and colloquial language. It forms the core of his first major collection, which also includes "Fog," "Grass," "Nocturne in a Deserted Brickyard," "I Am the People, the Mob," and "To a Contemporary Bunk Shouter." Throughout, Sandburg echoes Whitman in his celebration of the vitality and diversity of America. Fellow poet Amy Lowell declares the collection "one of the most original books which the age has produced."

ALAN SEEGER (1888–1916): *Poems*. The popularity of the poet's "I Have a Rendezvous with Death" helps make this posthumous collection of his poetry a bestseller. Seeger was a young American who enlisted in the French Foreign Legion at the beginning of the war and was killed in the Battle of the Somme.

Publications and Events

The Seven Arts. This influential little magazine, edited by James Oppenheim, Waldo Frank, and Van Wyck Brooks, featured new American writing by figures such as Sherwood Anderson, Amy Lowell, Robert Frost, and John Dos Passos. Its avowedly pacifist editorial views led to the withdrawal of financial support and its demise in 1917.

Theatre Arts. The first serious magazine devoted to American and world drama is founded in Detroit by Sheldon Cheyney (1886–1980). It was published until 1964.

1917

Drama and Theater

SUSAN GLASPELL: *The People, Close the Book*, and *The Outside*. The first of Glaspell's one-act plays concerns a radical editor's recommitment to the progressive cause; the second looks at free love and radical politics; the third is an experimental drama of ideas. Collectively the works help solidify Glaspell's reputation as one of the key figures in the creation of modern American drama.

EUGENE O'NEILL: *In the Zone.* This Washington Square Players' production is another of the playwright's realistic seagoing dramas, about a crew member aboard the S. S. *Glencairn* suspected of being a spy. O'Neill also writes *The Long Voyage Home*, one of five one-act dramas by the playwright performed by the Provincetown Players in 1917. In it, a Swedish sailor in a sleazy London waterfront bar entertains a dream of returning home, which is shattered when he is shanghaied for another voyage. The other four plays are *Fog*, about lifeboat survivors; *The Sniper*, an antiwar drama; *Ile*, about a mutiny aboard a whaling ship; and *The Rope*, about a senile man's hatred for his son.

RIDGELY TORRENCE (1875–1950): *Grammy Maumee, The Rider of Dreams, and Simon the Cyrenian: Plays for a Negro Theater.* Based on the dramatist's observation of his black neighbors in his native Ohio, these plays represent a groundbreaking realistic portrayal of African American life. Its debut in 1917 would mark the first time black actors appeared on Broadway in dramatic roles.

JESSE LYNCH WILLIAMS (1871–1929): *Why Marry?* The first Pulitzer Prize in drama is awarded to this witty comedy about a woman who decides to live with her scientist fiancé instead of marrying him. Williams's subsequent plays — *Why Not?* (1922) and *Lovely Lady* (1925) — also explore contemporary marriage from controversial angles. Williams began his career writing short stories and in journalism and based his first play, *The Stolen Story* (1906), on his experiences.

Fiction

SHERWOOD ANDERSON: *Marching Men.* Anderson's second novel is an unfocused, poetic meditation on social improvement, set in the Pennsylvania coal-mining country, where an idealist attempts to organize the miners.

MARY AUSTIN: *The Ford.* One of several of the author's social problem novels depicts California farmers contending with urban growth and the real estate frenzy it unleashes.

JAMES BRANCH CABELL: *The Cream of Jest.* Cabell's comic fantasy about an author who escapes into a dream world provides a kind of philosophical coda for his *Dom Manuel* cycle.

ABRAHAM CAHAN: *The Rise of Daniel Levinsky.* The founder and editor of the *Jewish Daily Forward* provides one of the greatest fictional depictions of the Jewish immigrant experience through the material rise but moral fall of the title character, in New York's garment district.

WINSTON CHURCHILL: *The Dwelling-Place of Light.* The novel depicts labor unrest in a Massachusetts mill

Abraham Cahan

town as the I.W.W. calls a strike. It is noteworthy for the realism employed in depicting contemporary labor conditions and the details of the strike.

DOROTHY CANFIELD FISHER (1879–1958): *Understanding Betsy.* The American popularizer of the Montessori educational system illustrates the principles behind the system in this popular children's book about a young girl's development.

JOSEPH HERGESHEIMER (1880–1954): *The Three Black Pennys.* One of Hergesheimer's most popular works is a romantic family saga set in the Pennsylvania iron industry. The Philadelphia-born writer had previously published the novels *The Lay Anthony* (1914) and *Mountain Blood* (1915).

HENRY JAMES: *The Ivory Tower* and *The Sense of the Past.* James's final two unfinished novels are published. The first, set in contemporary America, was intended as an exposé of the corruption of American wealth. When the war broke out, James had found it impossible to deal artistically with the contemporary scene, and he took up, in *The Sense of the Past*, an "international ghost story," begun in 1900 after *The Turn of the Screw*, about an American in London who encounters his eighteenth-century alter ego.

RING LARDNER: *Gullible's Travels, Etc.* Lardner extends his satire beyond the baseball milieu of *Busher's Letters* in this series of adventures in social climbing by an

American Gulliver, a naif who bumbles up the class ladder of the so-called classless American society.

SINCLAIR LEWIS: *The Job.* This is the best of the author's early apprentice works before *Main Street* (1920). It tells the story of a woman's experience in business in New York and anticipates the satire of Lewis's mature work. He also publishes *The Innocents*, about an elderly couple.

CHRISTOPHER MORLEY (1890–1957): *Parnassus on Wheels.* The New York author and journalist's first novel is a whimsical story of an itinerant bookseller. It attains popular success, as would its sequel, *The Haunted Bookshop* (1919).

DAVID GRAHAM PHILLIPS: *Susan Lenox: Her Fall and Rise.* Phillips's greatest literary achievement is this novel, written in 1908 and posthumously published, documenting a country girl's life as a prostitute in the slums of Cincinnati and as an actress in New York. Suppressed as indecent, the work would be eventually accepted as social instruction rather than titillation, earning Phillips the title "the American Balzac" for his frank social portraiture.

ERNEST POOLE: *His Family.* Poole's novel about a man's attempt to understand modern life through the experiences of his three daughters would win the first Pulitzer Prize awarded in fiction.

UPTON SINCLAIR: *King Coal.* As he treated the stockyards in *The Jungle* (1906), Sinclair exposes the unregulated coal-mining camps of Colorado in a documentary novel based on the author's investigations during the great coal strike of 1914–1915.

EDITH WHARTON: *Summer.* This novella is the story of a New England girl, Charity Royall, whose passionate affair gives way to adult responsibilities. Calling it her "hot Ethan," a complement to and contrast with the wintry *Ethan Frome* (1911), Wharton would regard *Summer* as one of her best works.

Literary Criticism and Scholarship

The Cambridge History of American Literature. The first of four volumes (completed in 1921) appears, surveying American writing from the colonial period through the nineteenth century. Written by a distinguished panel of contributors, including V. L. Parrington, Brander Matthews, and Norman Foerster, it is the most comprehensive literary history of the United States attempted up to that time.

T. S. ELIOT (1888–1965): *Ezra Pound: His Metric and Poetry.* Eliot's first critical volume is an anonymously published pamphlet written to help promote Pound's poetry and poetics while Pound was helping Eliot get his poetry published. In Pound's works Eliot detects a tension between freedom and restraint and a reliance on tradition that he finds missing in other contemporaries.

JAMES GIBBONS HUNEKER: *Unicorns.* This collection of essays, written from 1906 to 1917, covers musical, artistic, and literary topics, including critiques of Henry James, George Sand, James Joyce, Oscar Wilde, and others. H. L. Mencken, one of Huneker's champions, declares that Huneker's criticism is worth "not only a whole herd of Harvard poets and essayists, but the whole of Harvard."

AMY LOWELL: *Tendencies in Modern American Poetry.* Having produced an earlier critical volume, *Six French Poets* (1915), Lowell critiques six American poets — Edwin Arlington Robinson, Robert Frost, Edgar Lee Masters, Carl Sandburg, H.D. (Hilda Doolittle), and John Gould Fletcher — while tracing the change in outlook and method that characterizes their art.

H. L. MENCKEN: *A Book of Prefaces.* Mencken's collection of literary essays includes assessments of Conrad and Dreiser and an analysis of Puritanism, in the author's view, a "moral obsession" that sets American literature "off sharply from all other literatures."

CLARK WISSLER (1870–1947): *The American Indian: An Introduction to the Anthropology of the New World.* The anthropologist and curator of the American Museum of Natural History publishes this classic survey of American Indian life and customs.

Nonfiction

HAMLIN GARLAND: *A Son of the Middle Border.* The first of the author's autobiographical narratives provides an account of his life up to the age of thirty-three. He would continue his story and that of his family in *A Daughter of the Middle Border* (1921), as well as in the semifictionalized *Trail-Masters of the Middle Border* (1926) and *Back-Trailers of the Middle Border* (1928).

HENRY JAMES: *The Middle Years.* The concluding volume of James's autobiographical recollections brings his account of his life up to the 1870s. It features portraits of George Eliot, Robert Browning, Tennyson, and others.

JACK LONDON: *The Human Drift.* London's miscellaneous collection contains the title piece, a meditation on the migration of peoples and the rise and fall of races, along with sketches based on London's experiences, and two short plays. He also publishes two dog yarns set in the South Seas: *Jerry of the Islands* and *Michael, Brother of Jerry.*

H. L. MENCKEN: "A Neglected Anniversary." Mencken's mock celebration of American bathroom history prompts the so-called Bathtub Hoax, in which his fancy is taken for truth in subsequent reprints and repetition of the article's "facts."

JAMES FORD RHODES: *History of the Civil War.* The dominant historian of the period between the 1890s and World War I synthesizes, from his massive multivolume history of the United States since 1850, a single-volume history of the Civil War, which wins the Pulitzer Prize.

MARK TWAIN (SAMUEL LANGHORNE CLEMENS): *What Is Man? and Other Essays.* Twain's bitter deterministic dialogue, which had been published anonymously in 1906, appears under Twain's name along with sixteen other essays, including "English as She Is Taught," "The Turning Point of My Life," "William Dean Howells," and "Is Shakespeare Dead?"

Poetry

T. S. ELIOT: *Prufrock and Other Observations.* Eliot's first collection has been likened to *The Lyrical Ballads* of Wordsworth and Coleridge as a turning point in poetic development. "The Love Song of J. Alfred Prufrock," first published in *Poetry* in 1915, is the volume's singular achievement, a dramatic monologue of a man beset by his own timidity and the frustrations and shallowness of modern life. Rendered in a succession of images and a network of allusions, *Prufrock* typifies Eliot's future work and many of the central techniques of modern poetry.

JAMES WELDON JOHNSON: *Fifty Years and Other Poems.* In a collection that includes conventional verse forms and dialect poems, the title work surveys racial history in America, with emphasis on the fifty years since emancipation.

VACHEL LINDSAY: *The Chinese Nightingale and Other Poems.* Some of the poet's strongest works are in this collection, including the title poem, which concerns the poetic vision stimulated by a Chinese laundryman, and "The Ghosts of the Buffaloes," a dream vision of Indian life on the Great Plains before the white man's arrival.

ARCHIBALD MacLEISH (1892–1982): *Tower of Ivory.* MacLeish's first collection, assembled while the poet was serving in the army, registers the disillusioning impact of World War I. The *New York Times* reviewer calls the poems better "than the average run of minor verse." Technically accomplished but conventional, the best is "Our Lady of Troy," a blank-verse play in which Faustus evokes Helen of Troy.

EDNA ST. VINCENT MILLAY: *Renascence and Other Poems.* Millay's first collection features her acclaimed title work; "Interim," a blank-verse monologue in the Browning mode; "Afternoon on a Hill," with the oft-quoted line

"O world, I cannot hold thee close enough!"; and a series of sonnets.

EDWIN ARLINGTON ROBINSON: *Merlin.* This is the initial volume of a modern-verse trilogy treating the Arthurian legend. It would be followed by *Lancelot* (1920) and *Tristram* (1927). In the works Robinson emphasizes the psychology of passion.

SARA TEASDALE: *Love Song.* The poet is awarded a special Pulitzer award for this collection of lyrics, which one reviewer had praised as the work of an "Elizabethan of today; one of the purest and clearest voices in our poetic literature."

WILLIAM CARLOS WILLIAMS: *Al Que Quiere!* Williams's third collection displays the more characteristic open, expressive forms of his mature work. It includes "The Young Housewife," one of his first major poems and one of the first significant achievements of the Imagist method.

Publications and Events

The Dial. Between 1917 and 1929, this literary monthly, which relocated from Chicago to New York, becomes one of the chief publications for new literary writing in America, providing a forum for virtually every significant literary figure during the period.

Pulitzer Prizes in Journalism and Letters. The annual awards are created from a $500,000 bequest of publisher Joseph Pulitzer (1847–1911) to fund annual prizes "for the encouragement of public service, public morals, American literature, and the advancement of education." Besides the journalism prizes, awards in letters are established in four categories — novel, play, U.S. history, and American biography. Poetry would be added in 1922 and general nonfiction in 1962.

1918
Drama and Theater

SUSAN GLASPELL: *A Woman's Honor.* In Glaspell's comedy, a murder suspect refuses to offer an alibi to protect a woman's honor. A chorus of women takes the stage to question his decision and to challenge his gender assumptions. Glaspell also writes *Tickless Time*, about a couple who try to live an unconventional life.

EUGENE O'NEILL: *The Moon of the Caribbees.* O'Neill's one-act drama concerns a knife fight among crew members of the S. S. *Glencairn* at anchor off a West Indies island. The Washington Square Players also perform another one-act play by O'Neill, *Where the Cross Is Made*, about a sea captain's obsession with lost treasure.

WINCHELL SMITH AND FRANK BACON (1864–1922): *Lightnin'.* This popular, sentimental comedy about

"Lightnin'" Bill James, an inveterate liar and proprietor of a hotel straddling the California-Nevada border, becomes, for a time, the longest-running play in American theatrical history, with 1,291 performances.

AUGUSTUS THOMAS: *The Copperhead*. Thomas's historical drama about an Illinois man unjustly accused of Confederate sympathies during the Civil War indirectly comments on the treatment of presumed German sympathizers during World War I.

Fiction

WILLA CATHER: *My Ántonia*. Cather produces one of her most enduring works in this reconstruction of her own Nebraska childhood and youth as reflected by an immigrant Bohemian girl and her friend Jim Burden. Her characters embody both the pioneer past that has been lost and a universal principle of undaunted vitality and regeneration.

THEODORE DREISER: *Free and Other Stories*. Dreiser's first story collection includes both a realistic depiction of a lynching, "Nigger Jeff," and the lyrical "The Lost Phoebe."

MARY E. WILKINS FREEMAN: *Edgewater People*. Freeman's last story collection published during her lifetime contains no enduring work. It is mainly noteworthy as an indicator of changing postwar literary tastes, which no longer respond to Freeman's sentimental, domestic, regional tales. She commented that "Everything is different since the war" and that "I am none too sure of a market for my own wares."

ZONA GALE: *Birth*. Gale's novel is a character study of repression in a small Wisconsin town, portrayed with a grim realism that rivals that of Anderson and Lewis.

JOHNNY GRUELLE (1880–1938): *Raggedy Ann Stories*. The children's book author and illustrator launches a remarkably popular series of stories based on the adventures of a rag doll. Ann's brother would be added in *Raggedy Andy Stories* (1920).

JOSEPH HERGESHEIMER: *Gold and Iron*. These three novellas depict protagonists caught in midlife crises. The best is *Wild Oranges*, frequently anthologized during the 1930s. Hergesheimer would follow this volume with a collection of his short stories, *The Happy End* (1919).

JACK LONDON: *The Red One*. The title work in this posthumously published story collection, about a mysterious spherical object found on a South Sea island, is one of London's major works of science fiction and a possible source for Arthur C. Clarke's *The Sentinel* (1983), which in turn inspired Stanley Kubrick's film *2001: A Space Odyssey* (1968).

ERNEST POOLE: *His Second Wife*. Poole's novel concerns a woman who marries her dead sister's husband and helps restore his artistic vocation. Poole also issues *The Dark People* and *The Village*.

THORNE SMITH (1892–1934): *Biltmore Oswald: The Diary of a Hapless Recruit*. The Maryland humorist achieves a popular success with this fictionalized treatment of his experiences in the navy during World War I.

WILBUR DANIEL STEELE (1886–1970): *Land's End and Other Stories*. Steele's initial story collection includes work he had begun to publish as early as 1910. Half the stories deal with a Portuguese American fishing community like the one on Cape Cod, which Steele knew intimately. All establish his characteristic impressionistic style and melodramatic story lines.

EDWARD STREETER (1891–1976): *Dere Mable: Love Letters of a Rookie*. Streeter's humorous account of army life from the perspective of a typical doughboy sells half a million copies. It would be followed by sequels "*Same Old Bill, eh Mable!*" (1919) and *As You Were, Bill!* (1920). Streeter was a New York banker who became a vice president of the Bank of New York in 1931.

BOOTH TARKINGTON: *The Magnificent Ambersons*. The second novel in a trilogy depicting life in a Midwestern city, which had begun with *The Turmoil* (1915) and would conclude with *The Midlands* (1923). It traces the decline of a complacent American family unable to cope with the changes brought by progress. A winner of the Pulitzer Prize, the novel would be adapted as a film by Orson Welles in 1942, his follow-up to his first film, *Citizen Kane* (1941).

EDITH WHARTON: *The Marne*. Wharton's war novella concerns a young American Francophile who serves in the ambulance corps to aid the French and, in his view, civilization, while participating in the climactic Second Battle of the Marne.

Literary Criticism and Scholarship

BLISS PERRY (1860–1954): *The American Spirit in Literature*. In what has been identified as one of the last critical defenses of the Genteel Tradition, Perry supports sentimentality and avoidance of sexuality in American literature, while ignoring writers such as Theodore Dreiser and Stephen Crane and dismissing others such as Jack London and Frank Norris. The book is savagely attacked by H. L. Mencken and other advocates of the new realism and candor of American writing.

Booth Tarkington

EZRA POUND: *Pavannes and Divisions.* Pound's miscellaneous collection of essays, reviews, notes, and translations includes an explication of his poetic technique as well as critiques of the French writer Rémy de Gourmont and the troubadours of medieval Provence. Critic Louis Untermeyer characterizes Pound's energized approach as one that "begins in being truculent and ends by being tiresome."

MARK TWAIN (SAMUEL LANGHORNE CLEMENS): *Mark Twain's Letters.* The first of several collections of Twain's correspondence, edited by A. B. Paine, becomes a best-seller.

Nonfiction

HENRY JAMES: *Within the Rim and Other Essays: 1914–1915.* In a collection of James's war essays, the title work, published in 1917, compares World War I with the American Civil War and gives James's reaction to both. He closes by calling Germany insolent and deluded for thinking that it could defeat the "unquestionable association of England and America" and their linked "race and tongue, temper and tradition."

Poetry

SHERWOOD ANDERSON: *Mid-American Chants.* Anderson's collection of rough-hewn verses reflects the author's contention that "I do not believe that we people of midwestern America, immersed as we are in affairs, hurried and harried through life by the terrible engine — industrialism — have come to the time of song."

GEORGIA DOUGLAS JOHNSON (1877–1966): *The Heart of a Woman.* The first of four collections by the African American poet and playwright, which would make her the most widely recognized black woman poet since Frances E. W. Harper (1825–1911) and one of the pioneers in reflecting the black experience from a woman's point of view. Her other volumes are *Bronze* (1922), *An Autumn Love* (1928), and *Share My World* (1962).

AMY LOWELL: *Can Grande's Castle.* In this collection of Lowell's experimental "polyphonic prose," the longest work is "The Bronze Horses," depicting scenes in Rome, Constantinople, and Venice through the centuries from the perspective of the horses that adorn the façade of St. Mark's in Venice.

LOLA RIDGE (1871–1941): *The Ghetto and Other Poems.* The Irish-born writer and social activist who had immigrated to the United States in 1907 issues her first collection, a sympathetic look at Jewish life on New York's Lower East Side. Reviewer Francis Hackett praises the title sequence as "the most vivid and sensitive and lovely embodiment that exists in American Literature of that many sided transplantation of Jewish city-dwellers which vulgarity dismisses with a laugh or a jeer." Subsequent politically engaged volumes include *Sun-Up* (1920), *Red Flag* (1927), and *Firehead* (1929).

CARL SANDBURG: *Cornhuskers.* Sandburg's second verse collection includes some of his most characteristic and admired poems, such as "Cool Tombs" and "Prairie." It would receive a special Pulitzer award in 1919.

Publications and Events

Caroline Playmakers. Founded at the University of North Carolina by Professor Frederick Henry Koch (1877–1944), the company became one of the leading producers of regional and folk drama, including the works of Thomas Wolfe and Paul Green.

The O. Henry Prize Stories competition. Begun by the Society of Arts and Sciences, this competition honors the best American short stories published each year.

Stars and Stripes. The official newspaper of the American Expeditionary Force begins publication in France, with John T. Winterich and Alexander Woollcott on its staff. It continued to be printed in the United States from

1919 to 1926 and was resurrected as the newspaper of the U.S. armed forces from 1942 to 1945.

The U.S. Postal Authorities burn copies of the *Little Review* carrying the installment of James Joyce's *Ulysses* in which Gertie McDowell exposes her drawers to the gaze of Leopold Bloom.

1919
Drama and Theater

ZOË AKINS (1886–1958): *Déclassée*. This drama about an English noblewoman who abandons her husband and home after exposing a card cheat whom she loves establishes Akins's reputation as a dramatist. Akins was born in Missouri and came to New York to write plays for the Washington Square Players. Subsequent works include *Daddy's Gone A-Hunting* (1921), *The Varying Shore* (1921), and *The Texas Nightingale* (1922).

WINSTON CHURCHILL: *Dr. Jonathan*. Churchill's unproduced play argues that the significant outcome of the Great War is the vindication of democracy, dramatized by a returning war veteran who applies democratic management ideas to the running of a New England mill.

JAMES FORBES: *The Famous Mrs. Fair*. Regarded as Forbes's greatest achievement, the play is a social comedy about the chastening of an ardent feminist, who returns to her husband and family after four years' service in the war. It is regarded as a significant period piece reflecting contemporary gender issues.

GEORGE GERSHWIN (1898–1937): *La La Lucille*. In 1918 George Gershwin, with his brother Ira (1886–1983), had written the duo's first song, "The Real American Folk Song." In *La La Lucille*, the twenty-one-year-old George Gershwin supplies his first score for a Broadway musical. It helps lead to his writing the scores for George White's *Scandals* (1920–1924) and his unsuccessful solo productions *Our Nell* (1922) and *Little Devil* (1924).

AVERY HOPWOOD (1882–1928): *The Gold Diggers*. This comedy about chorus girls arranging respectable marriages becomes the second-longest-running show in Broadway history, with 727 performances. It would inspire several subsequent Hollywood musicals. Hopwood, one of the era's most successful playwrights, began his career with *Clothes* (1906), *Seven Days* (1909), *Nobody's Widow* (1910), and *Fair and Warmer* (1915).

EDNA ST. VINCENT MILLAY: *Aria da Capo*. Millay's most popular and significant drama is a blank-verse morality play employing elements of the commedia dell'arte to explore human cruelty. It is positively received as an antiwar play and anticipates her later more overtly political writing.

JAMES MONTGOMERY (1882–1966): *Irene*. This musical comedy about a poor shop girl who is loved by a rich man features the popular song "Alice Blue Gown." The play's 670 performances would stand as a Broadway record for a musical until 1939. Montgomery, an actor turned playwright, adapted the musical from his failed play *Irene O'Dare* (1916). His biggest nonmusical success was the farce *Nothing but the Truth* (1916).

EUGENE O'NEILL: *The Dreamy Kid*. O'Neill's one-act drama about a black man's attempt to visit his dying grandmother at the risk of his life is daringly produced with black actors by the Provincetown Players.

BOOTH TARKINGTON: *Clarence*. Tarkington's comedy about a seemingly bumbling ex-soldier who comes to the aid of a family in disarray is hailed by critic Heywood Broun as "the best light comedy which has been written by an American." It features a star-making performance by Alfred Lunt (1892–1980) and typecasts Helen Hayes (1900–1993) as a flapper.

GEORGE WHITE (1890–1968): *Scandals of 1919*. The dancer and theatrical producer mounts the first of thirteen revues (the last in 1939) that feature scores by George Gershwin and introduce African American dance steps such as the Charleston and the Black Bottom to white audiences.

Fiction

SHERWOOD ANDERSON: *Winesburg, Ohio*. Anderson's landmark short story collection provides glimpses of frustrated small-town American life from the perspective of the central consciousness of young reporter George Willard. The stories are linked by their common setting and by Anderson's concept of "grotesques," characters warped by their environment and inwardly divided. The collection's realism, intensity, and criticism of ordinary American life are harbingers of the direction that American fiction would subsequently follow.

JAMES BRANCH CABELL: *Jurgen*. The second of the author's Dom Manuel fantasies, set in the imagined realm of Poictesme, concerns the title character, a poet, who is allowed to relive a year of his youth. The novel's sexual content causes a storm of controversy and is deemed obscene by the New York Society for the Suppression of Vice. Cabel's editor is arrested, and his highly publicized trial in 1922 would result in an acquittal, with Cabell becoming a national celebrity, championed by H. L. Mencken and others.

THEODORE DREISER: *Twelve Men*. Dreiser's series of fictionalized biographical portraits shows his mastery of the short fiction form. Despite enthusiastic reviews, the

Sherwood Anderson

book sells poorly and remains an unjustly overlooked achievement in the Dreiser canon.

FREDERICK FAUST (1892–1944): *The Untamed.* Writing as "Max Brand," Faust publishes his first important western, the story of the archetypal western hero Whistling Dan Barry's transition from innocence to experience, which has elicited comparisons with Melville's character Billy Budd. *Untamed* is considered a classic in the genre. Born in Seattle, Faust wrote *Destry Rides Again* (1930) and the Dr. Kildare series.

ELLEN GLASGOW: *The Builders.* Glasgow assesses the impact of the Great War on Virginia society from the perspective of an idealist, Robert Blackburn, trapped in an unhappy marriage. The novel suggests that the future should be built on the past but also calls for the rejection of outmoded traditions.

JOSEPH HERGESHEIMER: *The Happy End.* Hergesheimer's story collection contains one of his most popular works, "Tol'able David," first published in the *Saturday Evening Post* in 1917, about a West Virginia mountain boy's conflict with a violent Kentucky family. Hergesheimer also publishes *Linda Condon*, regarded as his best novel, a character study of a woman incapable of loving and an artist who is inspired by her beauty. Hergesheimer additionally publishes *Java Head*, a historical novel about a clipper ship captain and his Chinese wife.

FANNIE HURST: *Humoresque.* Hurst's most accomplished short story collection reflects the city life of Jewish immigrants and working girls. The title story, about a violin prodigy, wins the 1919 O. Henry Prize and would be adapted by Hurst as a play in 1923.

HENRY JAMES: *Landscape Painter* and *Travelling Companions.* Two volumes of previously uncollected short stories, the first James had produced.

SINCLAIR LEWIS: *Free Air.* The last of the author's apprentice works before his breakthrough *Main Street* (1920) is a sentimental story of a transcontinental romance, based on a cross-country trip Lewis had made himself. It is chiefly of interest in reflecting source material for his later satirical treatment of American life.

JACK LONDON: *On the Makaloa Mat.* London's posthumously published story collection is unified by both its Hawaiian setting and its use of the ideas of Carl Jung (the first by any literary artist), in which London had become increasingly interested before his death.

UPTON SINCLAIR: *Jimmie Higgins.* Sinclair's ideological novel, about a committed socialist who enlists to fight the Germans but then is driven to insanity when he speaks out against American intervention in Russia, is significant for its display of American socialist views of the war and the Russian Revolution.

ALBERT PAYSON TERHUNE (1872–1942): *Lad: A Dog.* Terhune's best-known book about a courageous collie is the first in a popular juvenile series of dog books. Terhune was the son of popular romantic novelist Mary Virginia Terhune, with whom he collaborated on *Dr. Dade: A Story Without a Moral* (1900).

Literary Criticism and Scholarship

IRVING BABBITT: *Rousseau and Romanticism.* In one of the foundation texts of the New Humanism, Babbitt critiques Jean Jacques Rousseau's philosophy and its negative influences on Romanticism to provide a contrast with his defense of the humanist ideals of classical restraint, moral seriousness, and formalism.

JAMES BRANCH CABELL: *Beyond Life.* In a collection of critical essays, the writer develops a definition of literature through a debate between realism and romance. He asserts that by showing life not as it is but as it ought to be, literature "becomes the demiurge of a higher humanity." His other critical volume that echoes this view is *Preface to the Past* (1936).

H. L. MENCKEN: *The American Language: A Preliminary Inquiry into the Development of English in the United States.* Mencken publishes the first in an ongoing series documenting American English, first begun in columns in the *Baltimore Evening Sun* in 1910. Expanded and revised editions would be issued in 1921, 1923, and 1936, and supplemental volumes in 1945 and 1948.

Nonfiction

RANDOLPH SILLIMAN BOURNE: *Untimely Papers.* Bourne's influential pacifist views are on display in this posthumously published essay collection.

WALDO FRANK (1899–1967): *Our America.* Frank's interpretation of the American character is written to introduce the French to the essentials of America. Frank declares that "Ours is the first generation of Americans consciously engaged in spiritual pioneering," the search for a sustaining belief system that the book explores. The New Jersey–born novelist and critic was a founder and editor of *The Seven Arts.* His poetic, introspective novels included *The Unwelcome Man* (1917), *The Dark Mother* (1920), and *Rahab* (1922).

H. L. MENCKEN: *Prejudices.* The first of six installments of Mencken's iconoclastic views on various topics appears. Subsequent volumes of both literary and cultural criticism would be issued in 1920, 1922, 1924, 1926, and 1927.

FREDERICK O'BRIEN (1869–1932): *White Shadows in the South Seas.* O'Brien's exotic account of his travels in the Marquesas Islands ignites a popular interest in the South Pacific. He would subsequently publish additional travel books about the region, *Mystic Isles of the South Seas* (1921) and *Atolls of the Sun* (1922).

JOHN REED: *Ten Days That Shook the World.* Reed's most important work is this firsthand, sympathetic account of the Russian Revolution, which he describes as "a slice of intensified history." Officially approved by the Soviet government, it would feature an introduction by Vladimir Lenin in subsequent editions.

WILL ROGERS (1879–1935): *The Cowboy Philosopher on the Peace Conference* and *The Cowboy Philosopher on Prohibition.* A regular performer in the Ziegfeld Follies since 1916, Rogers's comic routines featured his commentary on current events, and these are the first collections of his remarks, preserving his "ah-shucks" oral delivery and his commonsense, everyman-style wit. He would begin a syndicated column in 1922 and issue several collections of articles, including *The Illiterate Digest* (1924), *There's Not a Better Suit in Russia* (1927), and *Either and Me* (1929).

EDITH WHARTON: *French Ways and Their Meaning.* Commissioned to make the ways of the French understandable to American servicemen stationed in France after the war, the book treats the country and its values from the perspective of an unapologetic Francophile.

Poetry

BABETTE DEUTSCH (1895–1982): *Banners.* The title poem of the New York poet and critic's first collection celebrates the Russian Revolution. It is praised by critics for its idealism and concrete imagery.

AMY LOWELL: *Pictures of the Floating World.* Lowell's collection contains her adaptations of Chinese and Japanese verse forms and recent lyrics in her experimental "polyphonic" style.

CLAUDE McKAY (1890–1948): "If We Must Die." The Jamaican-born author who immigrated to the United States in 1916 publishes in the *Liberator* an impassioned sonnet reflecting on the 1919 race riots that broke out in several U.S. cities. Its publication has been credited as marking the beginning of the Harlem Renaissance; McKay's pride in African culture and racial self-consciousness helps stimulate African American literary expression. The poem would be read by British Prime Minister Winston Churchill to the British people during World War II.

EZRA POUND: *Quia Pauper Amavi.* Pound's collection features "Homage to Sextus Propertius," a dramatic monologue written in 1917 that deals with aspects of life during the Roman Empire to comment on modern issues, "faced with the infinite and ineffable imbecility of the British Empire."

JOHN CROWE RANSOM (1888–1974): *Poems About God.* After serving in France, Ransom revises his earlier work to form his first collection, meditations on the ways in which God is made manifest. Although the collection is widely and favorably reviewed, the poet, critic, and editor in 1922 of *The Fugitive* would later choose not to include any of its poems in subsequent collections.

LOUIS UNTERMEYER (1885–1977): *Modern American Poetry.* The first of Untermeyer's popular critical anthologies, which introduce poetry to several generations of Americans. Subsequent volumes include *American Poetry from the Beginning to Whitman* (1931), *The Book of Living Verse* (1931), and *New Modern American and British Poetry* (1950).

JOHN HALL WHEELOCK: *Dust and Light.* Like the two collections that would follow — *The Black Panther* (1922) and *The Bright Doom* (1927) — Wheelock's later verses are either welcomed as a return to traditional poetic values or viewed as old-fashioned in their techniques and Romantic idealism.

Publications and Events

The *Liberator.* The editors of the *Masses* begin publishing this weekly journal of radical social criticism. It became affiliated with the Communist Party in 1922, ceased

BIRTHS AND DEATHS, 1920–1929

Births

1920 Isaac Asimov (d. 1992), novelist and short story writer
Ray Bradbury, novelist and short story writer
Charles Bukowski (d. 1994), poet
Amy Clampitt (d. 1994), poet
Howard Nemerov (d. 1991), poet and novelist

1921 Hayden Carruth, poet
Alex Haley (d. 1990), journalist and author
Patricia Highsmith (d. 1995), novelist
James Jones (d. 1977), novelist
Elizabeth Spencer, novelist
Mona Van Duyn, poet
Richard Wilbur, poet

1922 Bernard Bailyn, historian
William Gaddis (d. 1998), novelist
Mark Harris, novelist and biographer
Jack Kerouac (d. 1969), novelist, poet, and essayist
Howard Moss (d. 1987), poet
Kurt Vonnegut, novelist

1923 James Dickey (d. 1997), poet
Alan Dugan, poet
Anthony Hecht, poet
Joseph Heller (d. 1999), novelist
Denise Levertov (d. 1997), poet
Norman Mailer, novelist
James Schuyler (d. 1991), poet
Louis Simpson, poet

1924 James Baldwin (d. 1987), novelist
Edgar Bowers (d. 2000), poet
Truman Capote (d. 1984), novelist

1925 Donald Justice, poet
Kenneth Koch (d. 2002), poet
Maxine Kumin, poet
Flannery O'Connor (d. 1964), novelist and short story writer
William Styron, novelist
Gore Vidal, novelist and playwright

1926 A. R. Ammons (d. 2001), poet
Robert Bly, poet
Allen Ginsberg (d. 1997), poet
Harper Lee, novelist
James Merrill (d. 1995), poet
W. D. Snodgrass, poet

1927 Edward Abbey (d. 1989), novelist and essayist
John Ashbery, poet, critic, and editor

Galway Kinnell, poet
W. S. Merwin, poet
Robert Ludlum (d. 2001), novelist
Neil Simon, playwright
James Wright (d. 1980), poet

1928 Edward Albee, playwright
Maya Angelou, poet
Donald Hall, poet
William Kennedy, novelist
Philip Levine, poet
Cynthia Ozick, short story writer and novelist
Anne Sexton (d. 1974), poet

1929 Marilynn French, novelist and nonfiction writer
Shirley Ann Grau, novelist and short story writer
John Hollander, poet
Richard Howard, poet, critic, and translator
Ursula Le Guin, novelist
Adrienne Rich, poet
Howard Sackler (d. 1982), playwright

Deaths

1920 Louise Imogen Guiney (b. 1861), poet
William Dean Howells (b. 1837), novelist, editor, and critic
Julia A. Moore (b. 1847), poet
John Reed (b. 1887), journalist and political writer
Edgar Saltus (b. 1855), novelist and essayist

1922 John Kendrick Bangs (b. 1862), novelist
Thomas Nelson Page (b. 1853), novelist and short story writer

1923 Kate Douglas Wiggin (b. 1856), novelist and educator

1924 Frances Hodgson Burnett (b. 1849), children's author and novelist
Gene Stratton Porter (b. 1863), novelist

1925 James Lane Allen (b. 1849), novelist
George Washington Cable (b. 1844), novelist and short story writer
Amy Lowell (b. 1874), poet and critic

1926 George Sterling (b. 1869), poet

1927 John L. Long (b. 1861), writer and playwright

1928 George Barr McCutcheon (b. 1866), novelist
J. Hartley Manners (b. 1870), playwright
Elinor Wylie (b. 1885), poet and novelist

1929 Katherine Lee Bates (b. 1859), poet
Henry Blake Fuller (b. 1857), novelist
Thorstein Veblen (b. 1857), economist and editor

publication in 1924, and was revived as the *New Masses* in 1926.

The Theatre Guild. Founded by former members of the defunct Washington Square Players to produce classic and contemporary dramas by subscription, the company becomes the principal producer of the works of Eugene O'Neill, Sherwood Anderson, and Robert Sherwood.

Yale Series of Younger Poets. Yale University issues its first volume in the annual competition to select the best first poetry collection by a writer under the age of forty. Winners have included poets such as Paul Engle, James Agee, Muriel Rukeyser, William Meredith, Adrienne Rich, and John Ashbery.

1920

Drama and Theater

GUY BOLTON: *Sally.* This musical comedy, with music by Jerome Kern, concerns an orphan and a dishwasher who achieves success as a performer in the Ziegfeld

BESTSELLERS, 1920–1929

Fiction

1920
1. *The Man of the Forest* by Zane Grey
2. *Kindred of the Dust* by Peter B. Kyne
3. *The Re-Creation of Brian Kent* by Harold Bell Wright
4. *The River's End* by James Oliver Curwood
5. *A Man for the Ages* by Irving Bacheller
6. *Mary-Marie* by Eleanor H. Porter
7. *The Portygee* by Joseph C. Lincoln
8. *The Great Impersonation* by E. Phillips Oppenheim
9. *The Lamp in the Desert* by Ethel M. Dell
10. *Harriet and the Piper* by Kathleen Norris

1921
1. *Main Street* by Sinclair Lewis
2. *The Brimming Cup* by Dorothy Canfield
3. *The Mysterious Rider* by Zane Grey
4. *The Age of Innocence* by Edith Wharton
5. *The Valley of Silent Men* by James Oliver Curwood
6. *The Sheik* by Edith M. Hull
7. *A Poor Wise Man* by Mary Roberts Rinehart
8. *Her Father's Daughter* by Gene Stratton Porter
9. *The Sisters-in-Law* by Gertrude Atherton
10. *The Kingdom Round the Corner* by Coningsby Dawson

1922
1. *If Winter Comes* by A.S.M. Hutchinson
2. *The Sheik* by Edith M. Hull
3. *Gentle Julia* by Booth Tarkington
4. *The Head of the House of Coombe* by Frances Hodgson Burnett
5. *Simon Called Peter* by Robert Keable
6. *The Breaking Point* by Mary Roberts Rinehart
7. *This Freedom* by A.S.M. Hutchinson
8. *Maria Chapdelaine* by Louis Hémon
9. *To the Last Man* by Zane Grey
10. (tie) *Babbitt* by Sinclair Lewis and *Helen of the Old House* by Harold Bell Wright

1923
1. *Black Oxen* by Gertrude Atherton
2. *His Children's Children* by Arthur Train
3. *The Enchanted April* by "Elizabeth"
4. *Babbitt* by Sinclair Lewis
5. *The Dim Lantern* by Temple Bailey
6. *This Freedom* by A.S.M. Hutchinson
7. *The Mine with the Iron Door* by Harold Bell Wright
8. *The Wanderer of the Wasteland* by Zane Grey
9. *The Sea-Hawk* by Rafael Sabatini
10. *The Breaking Point* by Mary Roberts Rinehart

1924
1. *So Big* by Edna Ferber
2. *The Plastic Age* by Percy Marks
3. *The Little French Girl* by Anne Douglas Sedgwick
4. *The Heirs Apparent* by Philip Gibbs
5. *A Gentleman of Courage* by James Oliver Curwood
6. *The Call of the Canyon* by Zane Grey
7. *The Midlander* by Booth Tarkington
8. *The Coast of Folly* by Coningsby Dawson
9. *Mistress Wilding* by Rafael Sabatini
10. *The Homemaker* by Dorothy Canfield Fisher

1925
1. *Soundings* by A. Hamilton Gibbs
2. *The Constant Nymph* by Margaret Kennedy
3. *The Keeper of the Bees* by Gene Stratton Porter
4. *Glorious Apollo* by E. Barrington
5. *The Green Hat* by Michael Arlen
6. *The Little French Girl* by Anne Douglas Sedgwick
7. *Arrowsmith* by Sinclair Lewis
8. *The Perennial Bachelor* by Anne Parrish
9. *The Carolinian* by Rafael Sabatini
10. *One Increasing Purpose* by A.S.M. Hutchinson

1926
1. *The Private Life of Helen of Troy* by John Erskine
2. *Gentlemen Prefer Blondes* by Anita Loos
3. *Sorrell and Son* by Warwick Deeping
4. *The Hounds of Spring* by Sylvia Thompson
5. *Beau Sabreur* by P. C. Wren
6. *The Silver Spoon* by John Galsworthy
7. *Beau Geste* by P. C. Wren
8. *Show Boat* by Edna Ferber
9. *After Noon* by Susan Ertz
10. *The Blue Window* by Temple Bailey

1927
1. *Elmer Gantry* by Sinclair Lewis
2. *The Plutocrat* by Booth Tarkington
3. *Doomsday* by Warwick Deeping
4. *Sorrell and Son* by Warwick Deeping
5. *Jalna* by Maza de la Roche
6. *Lost Ecstasy* by Mary Roberts Rinehart
7. *Twilight Sleep* by Edith Wharton
8. *Tomorrow Morning* by Anne Parrish
9. *The Old Countess* by Anne Douglas Sedgwick
10. *A Good Woman* by Louis Bromfield

1928
1. *The Bridge of San Luis Rey* by Thornton Wilder
2. *Wintersmoon* by Hugh Walpole
3. *Swan Song* by John Galsworthy
4. *The Greene Murder Case* by S. S. Van Dine
5. *Bad Girl* by Viña Delmar
6. *Claire Ambler* by Booth Tarkington
7. *Old Pybus* by Warwick Deeping
8. *All Kneeling* by Anne Parish
9. *Jalna* by Mazo de la Roche
10. *The Strange Case of Miss Annie Spragg* by Louis Bromfield

1929
1. *All Quiet on the Western Front* by Erich Maria Remarque
2. *Dodworth* by Sinclair Lewis
3. *Dark Hester* by Anne Douglas Sedgwick
4. *The Bishop Murder Case* by S. S. Van Dine
5. *Roper's Row* by Warwick Deeping
6. *Peder Victorious* by O. E. Rölvaag
7. *Mamba's Daughter* by DuBose Heyward
8. *The Galaxy* by Susan Ertz
9. *Scarlet Sister Mary* by Julia Peterkin
10. *Joseph and His Brethren* by W. W. Freeman

General Nonfiction

1920
1. *Now It Can Be Told* by Philip Gibbs
2. *The Economics Consequences of the Peace* by John M. Keynes
3. *Roosevelt's Letters to His Children* edited by Joseph B. Bishop
4. *Theodore Roosevelt* by William Roscoe Thayer
5. *White Shadows in the South Seas* by Frederick O'Brien
6. *An American Idyll* by Cornelia Stratton Parker

1921
1. *The Outline of History* by H. G. Wells
2. *White Shadows in the South Seas* by Frederick O'Brien
3. *The Mirrors of Downing Street* by a Gentleman with a Duster (Harold Begbie)
4. *Mystic Isles of the South Seas* by Frederick O'Brien
5. *The Autobiography of Margot Asquith* by Margot Asquith
6. *Peace Negotiations* by Robert Lansing

1922
1. *The Outline of History* by H. G. Wells
2. *The Story of Mankind* by Hendrick Willem Van Loon
3. *The Americanization of Edward Bok* by Edward Bok
4. *Diet and Health* by Lulu Hunt Peters
5. *The Mind in the Making* by James Harvey Robinson
6. *The Outline of Science* by J. Arthur Thomas
7. *Outwitting Our Nerves* by Josephine A. Jackson and Helen M. Salisbury
8. *Queen Victoria* by Lytton Strachey
9. *Mirrors of Washington*, anonymous
10. *Painted Windows* by a Gentleman with a Duster (Harold Begbie)

1923
1. *Etiquette* Emily Post
2. *The Life of Christ* by Giovanni Papini
3. *The Life and Letters of Walter H. Page* edited by Burton J. Hendrick
4. *The Mind in the Making* by James Harvey Robinson
5. *The Outline of History* by H. G. Wells
6. *Diet and Health* by Lulu Hunt Peters
7. *Self-Mastery Through Conscious Auto-Suggestion* by Emile Coué
8. *The Americanization of Edward Bok* by Edward Bok
9. *The Story of Mankind* by Hendrik Willem Van Loon
10. *A Man from Maine* by Edward Bok

1924
1. *Diet and Health* by Lulu Hunt Peters
2. *The Life of Christ* by Giovanni Papini
3. *The Boston Cooking School Cook Book* edited by Fannie Farmer
4. *Etiquette* by Emily Post
5. *Ariel* by André Maurois
6. *The Cross Word Puzzle Books* by Prosper Buranelli et al.
7. *Mark Twain's Autobiography* by Mark Twain
8. *Saint Joan* by George Bernard Shaw
9. *The New Decalogue of Science* by Albert E. Wiggam
10. *The Americanization of Edward Bok* by Edward Bok

1925
1. *Diet and Health* by Lulu Hunt Peters
2. *The Boston Cooking School Cook Book, Revised Edition* edited by Fannie Farmer
3. *When We Were Very Young* by A. A. Milne
4. *The Man Nobody Knows* by Bruce Barton
5. *The Life of Christ* by Giovanni Papini
6. *Ariel* by André Maurois
7. *Twice Thirty* by Edward Bok
8. *Twenty-Five Years* by Lord Grey
9. *Anatole France Himself* by J. J. Brousson
10. *The Cross Word Puzzle Books* by Prosper Buranelli et al.

1926
1. *The Man Nobody Knows* by Bruce Barton
2. *Why We Behave Like Human Beings* by George A. Dorsey
3. *Diet and Health* by Lulu Hunt Peters
4. *Our Times, Vol. I* by Mark Sullivan
5. *The Boston Cooking School Cook Book, Revised Edition* edited by Fannie Farmer
6. *Auction Bridge Complete* by Milton C. Work
7. *The Book Nobody Knows* by Bruce Barton
8. *The Story of Philosophy* by Will Durant
9. *The Light of Faith* by Edgar A. Guest
10. *Jefferson and Hamilton* by Claude G. Bowers

1927
1. *The Story of Philosophy* by Will Durant
2. *Napoleon* by Emil Ludwig
3. *Revolt in the Desert* by T. E. Lawrence
4. *Trader Horn, Vol. I* by Alfred Aloysius Horn and Ethelreda Lewis
5. *We* by Charles A. Lindbergh
6. *Ask Me Another* by Julian Spafford and Lucien Esty
7. *The Royal Road to Romance* by Richard Halliburton
8. *The Glorious Adventure* by Richard Halliburton
9. *Why We Behave Like Human Beings* by George A. Dorsey
10. *Mother India* by Katherine Mayo

1928
1. *Disraeli* by André Maurois
2. *Mother India* by Katherine Mayo
3. *Trader Horn, Vol. I* by Alfred Aloysius Horn and Ethelreda Lewis
4. *Napoleon* by Emil Ludwig
5. *Strange Interlude* by Eugene O'Neill
6. *We* by Charles Lindbergh
7. *Count Luckner, the Sea Devil* by Lowell Thomas
8. *Goethe* by Emil Ludwig
9. *Skyward* by Richard E. Byrd
10. *The Intelligent Woman's Guide to Socialism and Capitalism* by George Bernard Shaw

1929
1. *The Art of Thinking* by Ernest Dimnet
2. *Henry the Eighth* by Francis Hackett
3. *The Cradle of the Deep* by Joan Lowell
4. *Elizabeth and Essex* by Lytton Strachey
5. *The Specialist* by Chic Sale
6. *A Preface to Morals* by Walter Lippmann
7. *Believe It or Not* by Robert L. Ripley
8. *John Brown's Body* by Stephen Vincent Benét
9. *The Tragic Era* by Claude G. Bowers
10. *The Mansions of Philosophy* by Will Durant

AWARDS AND PRIZES, 1920–1929

Pulitzer Prizes

1920
Fiction: No Prize Awarded
Drama: *Beyond the Horizon* by Eugene O'Neill
History: *The War with Mexico* by Justin H. Smith
Biography/Autobiography: *The Life of John Marshall* by Albert J. Beveridge

1921
Fiction: *The Age of Innocence* by Edith Wharton
Drama: *Miss Lulu Bett* by Zona Gale
History: *The Victory at Sea* by William S. Sims
Biography/Autobiography: *The Americanization of Edward Bok* by Edward Bok

1922
Fiction: *Alice Adams* by Booth Tarkington
Poetry: *Collected Poems* by Edwin Arlington Robinson
Drama: *Anna Christie* by Eugene O'Neill
History: *The Founding of New England* by James Truslow Adams
Biography/Autobiography: *A Daughter of the Middle Border* by Burton J. Hendrick

1923
Fiction: *One of Ours* by Willa Cather
Poetry: *The Ballad of the Harp-Weaver, A Few Figs from Thistles, and Other Poems* by Edna St. Vincent Millay
Drama: *Icebound* by Owen Davis
History: *The Supreme Court in United States History* by Charles Warren
Biography/Autobiography: *The Life and Letters of Walter H. Page* edited by Burton J. Hendrick

1924
Fiction: *The Able McLaughlins* by Margaret Wilson
Poetry: *New Hampshire: A Poem with Notes and Grace Notes* by Robert Frost
Drama: *Hell-Bent for Heaven* by Hatcher Hughes
History: *The American Revolution: A Constitutional Interpretation* by Charles H. McIlwain
Biography/Autobiography: *From Immigrant to Inventor* by Michael Pupin

1925
Fiction: *So Big* by Edna Ferber
Poetry: *The Man Who Died Twice* by Edwin Arlington Robinson
Drama: *They Knew What They Wanted* by Sidney Howard
History: *A History of the American Frontier* by Frederick L. Paxton
Biography/Autobiography: *Barrett Wendell and His Letters* by DeWolfe Howe

1926
Fiction: *Arrowsmith* by Sinclair Lewis (prize declined)
Poetry: *What's O'Clock?* by Amy Lowell
Drama: *Craig's Wife* by George Kelly
History: *History of the United States* by Edward Channing
Biography/Autobiography: *Life of Sir William Osler* by Harvey Cushing

1927
Fiction: *Early Autumn* by Louis Bromfield
Poetry: *Fiddler's Farewell* by Leonora Speyer
Drama: *In Abraham's Bosom* by Paul Green
History: *Pinckney's Treaty* by Samuel F. Bemis
Biography/Autobiography: *Whitman: An Interpretation in Narrative* by Emory Holloway

1928
Fiction: *The Bridge of San Luis Rey* by Thornton Wilder
Poetry: *Tristram* by Edwin Arlington Robinson
Drama: *Strange Interlude* by Eugene O'Neill
History: *Main Currents in American Thought* by Vernon L. Parrington
Biography/Autobiography: *The American Orchestra and Theodore Thomas* by Charles E. Russell

1929
Fiction: *Scarlet Sister Mary* by Julia Peterkin
Poetry: *John Brown's Body* by Stephen Vincent Benét
Drama: *Street Scene* by Elmer L. Rice
History: *The Organization and Administration of the Union Army, 1861–65* by Fred A. Shannon
Biography/Autobiography: *The Training of an American: The Earlier Life and Letters of Walter H. Page* by Burton J. Hendrick

Follies. One of the most popular productions of the decade, it features the songs "Look for the Silver Lining," "Whip-Poor-Will," and "Wild Rose."

RACHEL CROTHERS: *He and She.* First produced in 1911 under the title *The Herfords*, the play concerns husband and wife artists whose marriage is threatened when the wife wins a commission for which both had competed. She (played by Crothers) forgoes the award to save her marriage. The drama is greeted as a thoughtful study of the plight of the emancipated woman and the double standard regarding women's roles. Crothers would follow it with a series of plays exploring gender issues, marriage,

and the "new woman," including *Nice People* (1921), *Mary the Third* (1923), and *Let Us Be Gay* (1929).

ZONA GALE: *Miss Lulu Bett.* Gale's dramatization of her novel (also in 1920) about a spinster's exploitation by her relatives wins a Pulitzer Prize and is praised for its knowing look at Midwestern life. In the novel, Lulu is liberated but faces an uncertain future; in the play she becomes happily married.

ANGELINA WELD GRIMKÉ (1880–1958): *Ruth.* Grimké becomes the first African American woman playwright to publish a work performed by a black cast. The drama, about the effects of lynching on an African American family, had been written in response to the perceived racist views of D. W. Griffith's 1915 film *The Birth of a Nation.*

AVERY HOPWOOD AND MARY ROBERTS RINEHART: *The Bat.* This mystery drama, based on Rinehart's "The Circular Staircase" (1908), concerns a spinster's attempt to solve the puzzle of a banker's disappearance with stolen bank funds. With 867 performances, it is the second-longest-running show on Broadway up to that time.

EUGENE O'NEILL: *Beyond the Horizon.* O'Neill's initial full-length Broadway production wins the first of his four Pulitzer Prizes. In it, two brothers are crippled by fate and frustration, abandoning their dreams. One goes to sea, the other runs the family farm and marries the woman both love. Some critics consider it a turning point in American drama, toward greater psychological realism and emotional intensity. Another of O'Neill's 1920 productions, *Diff'rent*, concerns the sexual repression of a puritanical New England spinster. He also writes *The Emperor Jones*, about an escaped black convict who becomes the dictator of a West Indian island. With its symbolic set and dream-scenes in which Brutus Jones reviews his past, O'Neill introduces expressionism, the attempt to objectify inner experience, to the American theater, while providing the first major lead role for a black actor on the American stage.

Fiction

SHERWOOD ANDERSON: *Poor White.* This story of an Ohio town going through the transition from agriculture to industrialization is regarded by most critics as Anderson's greatest achievement as a novelist.

WILLA CATHER: *Youth and Bright Medusa.* Cather's collection of new stories as well as old favorites, such as "Paul's Case" and "A Wagner Matinée," is organized by the themes of youth and art.

FLOYD DELL (1887–1969): *Moon-Calf.* The first novel by the radical journalist and editor of the *Masses* and the *Liberator* is an autobiographical account of Felix Fay's youth and early journalisim career in Chicago. A sequel, *The Briary-Patch* (1921), would continue his story and present the Chicago literary scene of the period.

JOHN DOS PASSOS (1896–1970): *One Man's Initiation— 1917.* Born in Chicago, Dos Passos went to Europe after graduating from Harvard, and later joined the U.S. medical corps. Dos Passos's first novel draws on his experiences during World War I as a member of the French ambulance service.

F. SCOTT FITZGERALD (1896–1940): *This Side of Paradise.* Fitzgerald's first novel, about Midwesterner Amory Blaine's initiation to life at Princeton and his ill-fated love for Rosaline Connage, makes the writer from St. Paul, Minnesota, an overnight celebrity as a knowing chronicler of the postwar youth culture, which defined the Jazz Age. As Fitzgerald summarizes at the end of the novel: "Here was a new generation . . . dedicated more than the last to the fear of poverty and the worship of success, grown up to find all Gods dead, all wars fought, all faiths in man shaken." Fitzgerald also publishes *Flappers and Philosophers*, his first story collection. It contains two of his finest works: "The Ice Palace," about a Southern girl unable to adapt to life in the North, and "Bernice Bobs Her Hair," about a girl who is dared into trying the radical new hairstyle.

WILLIAM DEAN HOWELLS: *The Vacation of the Kelwyns.* Howells's final novel treats a family's encounter with the Shaker religious sect while vacationing on a farm. It shows the novelist's skill in presenting domestic scenes and is declared by critic Richard Chase as "quite possibly his best" novel.

JAMES GIBBONS HUNEKER: *Painted Veils.* The music and drama critic's only novel is a portrait of New York's art world, which includes appearances by actual figures as well as numerous digressions on artistic subjects. Huneker also publishes his autobiography, *Steeplejack*, in 1920.

SINCLAIR LEWIS: *Main Street.* Lewis's attack on small-town American life, expressed through the frustrations and eventual rebellion of Carol Kennicott in Gopher Prairie, establishes him as an iconoclastic voice of the era. In daring to criticize sanctified topics such as marriage, gender roles, and American values, the book would prompt Lewis's biographer Mark Schorer to declare it "the most sensational event in twentieth-century American publishing history."

EDGAR LEE MASTERS: *Mitch Miller.* Masters's novel about two boys who try to live out the adventures encountered in Twain's *Tom Sawyer* is called by critic William Stanley Braithwaite "the best boy's story in our generation." A sequel, *Skeeters Kirby*, would follow in 1923.

ERNEST POOLE: *Blind.* Poole's autobiographical novel covers tenement life in New York, the Great War, and the Russian Revolution. His other novels of the decade are *Beggar's Gold* (1921), *Millions* (1922), *Danger* (1923), *The Avalanche* (1924), *The Hunter's Moon* (1925), *With Eastern Eyes* (1926), and *Silent Storms* (1927).

Edith Wharton

EDITH WHARTON: *The Age of Innocence.* Generally regarded as Wharton's masterpiece, the novel, set in the New York society world of the 1870s, concerns the fate of Newland Archer, who falls in love with his fiancée's cousin, Ellen Olenska. It is Wharton's most profound character study of desire hemmed in by social restrictions. The novel wins the Pulitzer Prize, the first for fiction by a woman, but Wharton stated that the award should have gone to Sinclair Lewis for *Main Street.* For this generosity, Lewis would dedicate his next novel, *Babbitt*, to Wharton. *The Age of Innocence* would be dramatized by Margaret Ayer Barnes (1886–1967) in 1928.

ANZIA YEZIERSKA (1885–1970): *Hungry Hearts.* Yezierska's first book, a short story collection, documents Jewish immigrant women's lives on New York's Lower East Side. It includes her most acclaimed story, "The Fat of the Land." Her first novel, *Salome of the Tenements*, and a second story collection, *Children of Loneliness*, would follow in 1923. Yezierska was born in Russia and immigrated to the United States in the 1890s.

Literary Criticism and Scholarship

RANDOLPH SILLIMAN BOURNE: *The History of a Literary Radical.* This posthumously published collection of essays by the political maverick and iconoclastic literary critic establishes Bourne's essential positions on various topics, including his opposition to the sentimental in modern literature and an assessment of writers such as Dostoevsky and Dreiser.

VAN WYCK BROOKS: *The Ordeal of Mark Twain.* Brooks's groundbreaking psychological assessment of Twain's character and career helps establish a view of the author that has dominated subsequent biographical and critical debate. As Brooks asserts, "The main idea in the book is that Mark Twain's career was a tragedy — a tragedy for himself and a tragedy for mankind."

T. S. ELIOT: *The Sacred Wood: Essays in Poetry and Criticism.* Eliot's first critical collection is generally regarded as one of the most important and influential critical works of the century. It includes some of Eliot's most famous essays, including "Tradition and the Individual Talent," "Hamlet and His Problems" (defining Eliot's concept of the "objective correlative"), and "The Metaphysical Poets," which helps restore the reputation of seventeenth-century writers such as John Donne.

EZRA POUND: *Instigations.* Pound's critical essays include an appreciation of Henry James. Padraic Colum points out in his review that the essays "badger and bully us out of a state of intellectual backwardness."

FREDERICK JACKSON TURNER: *The Frontier in American History.* Turner's essay collection includes the seminal paper "The Significance of the Frontier in American History," originally presented at the American Historical Association in 1893. It establishes his thesis that the frontier is the determining factor in American development and the formation of American character.

Nonfiction

EDWARD WILLIAM BOK (1863–1930): *The Americanization of Edward Bok.* The influential former editor of the *Ladies Home Journal* provides a bestselling third-person autobiography of his successful career. The book earns the Pulitzer Prize.

ANDREW CARNEGIE: *Autobiography.* Carnegie's posthumously issued memoir is the most reliable of his accounts of his life. His version of the controversies in his career are often self-serving, but he modestly underplays his philanthropical efforts during his retirement. The book is received enthusiastically, with one reviewer calling it and Ulysses S. Grant's *Memoirs* (1885) the two best American autobiographies.

CLARENCE DAY (1874–1935): *This Simian World.* The humorist's first collection of off-beat observations speculates on a world with an alternative evolutionary history.

His other books published during the decade are *The Crow's Nest* (1921) and *Thoughts Without Words* (1928). Day is best known for his autobiographical work, *Life with Father* (1935), evoking family life in nineteenth-century New York City.

JOHN DEWEY: *Reconstruction in Philosophy.* In a series of lectures delivered in Tokyo, Dewey offers, as he explains in his preface, "an interpretation of the reconstruction of ideas and ways of thought now going on in philosophy."

THEODORE DREISER: *Hey-Rub-a-Dub-Dub.* With the subtitle "A Book of the Mystery and Terror and Wonder of Life," the essay collection conveys the writer's naturalistic literary theories as well as the overall philosophy that supports his creative writing.

W.E.B. DU BOIS: *Darkwater: Voices from Within the Veil.* Du Bois's sketches, essays, and poems reflect the perspective of black America and Du Bois's contention that subjugation by whites is the dominating feature of the African American experience.

GEORGE SANTAYANA: *Character and Opinion in the United States.* After leaving America for Europe, Santayana offers his reflections on American values and characteristics, including reminiscences of his former Harvard colleagues William James and Josiah Royce.

UPTON SINCLAIR: *The Brass Check.* This is first of what Sinclair would call his Dead Hand series (in contrast to Adam Smith's "Invisible Hand" of laissez-faire economics) critiquing modern institutions. Sinclair's assessment of contemporary journalism would be followed by *The Goose-Step* (1923), about education, and *Mammonart* (1925), an assessment of art and literature.

EDITH WHARTON: *In Morocco.* Accompanying a French military expedition to Morocco in 1918, Wharton provides this account of her trip, which is generally regarded as the best of her travel books.

WALT WHITMAN: *The Gathering of Forces.* The volume collects Whitman's editorials, essays, and literary and dramatic reviews written when he served as the editor of the *Brooklyn Daily Eagle* in 1846–1847. His *Uncollected Poetry and Prose* would follow in 1921.

Poetry

CONRAD AIKEN: *The House of Dust: A Symphony.* Aiken's complex sequence, regarded as the most successful of his poetic symphonies, develops an analogy between a city and the human body.

STEPHEN VINCENT BENÉT (1889–1943): *Heavens and Earth.* After two volumes of dramatic monologues published while he was a Yale undergraduate — *Five Men and Pompey* (1915) and *Young Adventure* (1918) — Benét publishes his first mature collection. Benét's first novel, *The Beginning of Wisdom*, a college story after F. Scott Fitzgerald, would appear in 1921.

T. S. ELIOT: *Poems.* Eliot's second collection, and his first American publication, includes his Sweeney poems, introducing his version of the representative modern man, in "Mr. Eliot's Sunday Morning Service," "Sweeney Among the Nightingales," and "Sweeney Erect." "Gerontion" anticipates *The Waste Land* in its despairing portrait of the sterility and barrenness of modern life.

VACHEL LINDSAY: *The Golden Whales of California.* Prompted by his fortieth birthday, Lindsay reflects on his past in a series of some of his strongest poems. The volume includes as well his best verses written for children, including "Davey Jones' Door Bell," "The Little Turtle," and "The Sea Serpent Chantey." Also appearing is the volume *The Daniel Jazz and Other Poems*, which prompts reviewers to refer to Lindsay as "the jazz poet," an epithet he disliked.

EDGAR LEE MASTERS: *Domesday Book.* Masters hoped that this novel-in-poetry about the sudden death of a former Red Cross worker would become his masterpiece, a "census spiritual / Taken of our America." In this psychological study, Elenor Murray is seen from various angles, in the manner of Robert Browning's *The Ring and the Book*. Critics find the poem excessively dull and didactic, but Masters would persist with a sequel, *The Fate of the Jury* (1929).

EDNA ST. VINCENT MILLAY: *A Few Figs from Thistles.* Millay's second collection is her first popular success and establishes her image as representative of youthful rebellion and cynicism, best embodied in her most famous lines from the poem "First Fig:" "My candle burns at both ends; / It will not last the night; / But, ah, my foes, and, oh, my friends — / It gives a lovely light." Other admired lyrics include "Recuerdo" and "The Philosopher."

EZRA POUND: *Hugh Selwyn Mauberley.* Pound's poetic sequence represents his farewell to London, assessing the tawdriness of modern culture through the persona of a critic-poet struggling to maintain his artistic mission. Anticipating Eliot's themes and methods in *The Waste Land* (1922), it is considered one of the foundation texts of literary modernism.

EDWIN ARLINGTON ROBINSON: *Lancelot.* The second installment in the poet's Arthurian trilogy and modern interpretation of the legend. The poem concerns the tragic outcome of Lancelot's illicit love for Guinevere. Robinson also issues *The Three Taverns*, a collection that

Edna St. Vincent Millay

includes dramatic monologues and dialogues, such as "Rahel to Varnhagen" and "Rembrandt to Rembrandt," as well as additional Tilbury portraits, most memorably "Mr. Flood's Party."

CARL SANDBURG: *Smoke and Steel.* Sandburg celebrates the working people of industrial America in works such as the title poem, "The Sins of Kalamazoo," and "Prayers of Steel." He also defends his rough-hewed artistry in "Broken Faced Gargoyles."

SARA TEASDALE: *Flame and Shadows.* In a collection of new poems written since 1917, Teasdale reflects a darkening tone based on the war experience and her personal disappointments. The volume also represents its author's mature technical mastery.

WILLIAM CARLOS WILLIAMS: *Kora in Hell.* Williams's series of prose poems in which he attempts "to refine, to clarify, to intensify that eternal moment in which we alone live" had first appeared serially in the *Little Review* in 1919 alongside installments of James Joyce's *Ulysses.* Although it proved an important work in Williams's development of a characteristic American diction and experimental forms, the work baffles the critics and even

his friends: Ezra Pound calls it "incoherent," and H.D. (Hilda Doolittle) complains that it is "un-serious." A second similar volume, *Sour Grapes,* would appear in 1921.

Publications and Events

The *Frontier.* A Northwest regional literary magazine is founded by H. G. Merriam (1883–1981) at Montana State University. It continued until 1939, publishing some of the first work by MacKinlay Kantor, Paul Engle, and Phil Stong.

1921
Drama and Theater

ZOË AKINS: *Daddy's Gone A-Hunting.* Akins's play concerns a man who leaves his wife to pursue a career as a painter. Also appearing is *The Varying Shore,* a play that moves backward in chronological time from the death of an experienced woman to her innocent girlhood.

EUBIE BLAKE (1883–1983): *Shuffle Along.* A popular black musical featuring a score by the Baltimore-born composer and performer. The popular song "I'm Just Wild About Harry" stimulates a rage for black shows, which would continue into the 1930s. This trend prompts criticism in the African American community about the portrayal of blacks on stage only as singers and dancers.

RACHEL CROTHERS: *Nice People.* Crothers's comedy concerns a trio of hedonistic flappers, one of whom decides to settle down to a conventional life to the dismay of the other two. The play is greeted as a lively and knowing reflection of contemporary values.

OWEN DAVIS: *The Detour.* The Maine-born melodramatist would describe this play, about a Long Island truck farmer's family, as his "first attempt to write of life simply and honestly." Despite some critical approval, the play is unsuccessful. Davis penned more than two hundred plays, sometimes at a rate of one or two per month.

SUSAN GLASPELL: *The Inheritors* and *The Verge.* Although neither of these Provincetown Playhouse productions is successful, the playwright earns critical praise for her psychological portraits of women under stress. The first concerns a woman's defense of a radical professor; the second dramatizes the frustrations faced by a woman pushed to the edge of insanity.

SIDNEY HOWARD (1891–1939): *Swords.* The California-born dramatist's first major play is a blank-verse tragedy set in the Middle Ages. It would be followed by adaptations of foreign dramas, including *S. S. Tenacity* (1922),

Casanova (1923), and *Sancho Panza* (1923) before his first success, *They Knew What They Wanted* (1924).

GEORGE S. KAUFMAN (1889–1961) AND MARC CONNELLY (1890–1980): *Dulcy*. The playwrights' first of eight collaborations over the next three years is a successful comedy about a ditzy housewife who blunders into assisting her husband's career. It establishes the career of Lynn Fontanne, who stars in the title role. Kaufman and Connelly were both from Pennsylvania and worked as newspapermen.

EUGENE O'NEILL: *Anna Christie*. O'Neill's rewrite of his earlier play, *Chris Christopherson* (1920), which had failed in tryouts, wins the playwright his second Pulitzer Prize. It is the story of a prostitute's reunion with her father, a coal barge captain, and her redemption at sea. O'Neill would later deprecate the play as "too conventional," a work in which he had "deliberately employed all the Broadway tricks which I had learned in my stage training." His other 1921 dramas are *The Straw*, which deals with the romance between two patients in a tuberculosis sanatorium, and *Gold*, a symbolic drama about the madness of a sea captain destroyed by greed.

SIGMUND ROMBERG (1887–1951): *Blossom Time*. The Hungarian-born composer's operetta, a fictionalized treatment of the life of Franz Schubert, is one of the longest-running musicals of the decade (second only to Romberg's *The Student Prince*, 1924).

Fiction

SAMUEL HOPKINS ADAMS: *Success*. Adams's first novel is a romance set amid the world of modern journalism. Adams was a muckraking journalist whose articles had previously appeared in *McClure's*, *Collier's*, and the *New York Tribune*.

SHERWOOD ANDERSON: *The Triumph of the Egg*. Subtitled "A Book of Impressions from American Life in Tales and Poems," Anderson's glimpses of ordinary life emphasize futility, thwarted instincts, and repressed emotions. The volume includes some of his best stories, such as "The Egg" and "I Want to Know Why."

GERTRUDE ATHERTON: *The Sisters-in-Law*. Atherton offers another in a series of frank portraits of women in this novel about two San Francisco sisters-in-law in love with the same man. It is significant for its depiction of the changing roles of women in the postwar period.

FAITH BALDWIN (1893–1978): *Mavis of the Green Hill*. This is the first of a string of Baldwin's popular romances, which offer insights into gender differences and the way men and women are depicted in popular culture of the period. Other titles include *Those Difficult Years* (1925),

Three Women (1926), *Office Wife* (1930), *White Collar Girl* (1933), *American Family* (1935), *Men Are Such Fools!* (1936), and *Station Wagon* (1939).

GERTRUDE SIMMONS BONNIN (1876–1938): *American Indian Legends*. The Sioux writer also known as Zitkala-Sa collects her autobiographical sketches and stories about Indian life and the displacement caused by assimilation into white Christian society.

DONN BYRNE (1889–1928): *Messer Marco Polo*. Byrne's first popular historical romance describes Marco Polo's trip to China, where he falls in love with the daughter of Kubla Khan. It would be followed by other novels combining history and fancy, including *The Changeling* (1923), *Blind Raftery* (1924), *Hangman's House* (1926), *Brother Saul* (1927), *Crusade* (1928), and *Field of Honor* (1929). Byrne was born in New York, educated in Dublin, and also went by the name of Brian Oswald Donn-Byrne.

JOHN DOS PASSOS: *Three Soldiers*. One of the greatest American fictional responses to World War I is this account of the experiences of three American doughboys — an Italian American, an Indiana farm boy, and a Harvard graduate — who become disillusioned in different ways.

BEN HECHT (1894–1964): *Erik Dorn*. Hecht's first novel captures postwar attitudes in a story of a cynical journalist who abandons his wife and mistress for the excitement of revolutionary Europe. It would be followed by several other story collections and novels, including *1001 Afternoons in Chicago* (1922), *Tales of Chicago Streets and Broken Necks* (1924), *Fantazius Mallare and Gargoyles* (1922), *The Florentine Dagger* (1923), *Humpty Dumpty* (1924), *The Kingdom of Evil* (1924), and *Count Bruga* (1926).

BOOTH TARKINGTON: *Alice Adams*. Tarkington wins his second Pulitzer Prize for this novel about the attempt of a lower-middle-class Midwestern girl to catch a rich husband. The book is praised for its realistic depiction of American life without the idealization that had marred Tarkington's previous work.

Literary Criticism and Scholarship

MICHAEL GOLD (1893–1967): "Towards Proletarian Art." Gold's essay, published in the *Liberator*, offers an influential definition of the aims and methods of proletarian literature. Michael Gold was the pen name of Irving Granich, the editor of the *Masses* and the *New Masses*, whose best-known work was the novel *Jews Without Money* (1930).

HENRY JAMES: *Notes and Reviews*. This collection of previously unsigned book reviews, written from 1864 to 1866, displays James's earliest criticism. Reviewer Brander Matthews observes, "They are interesting because they reveal to us a writer not yet sure of himself, a writer who is sometimes a little over emphatic and even a little overbearing in consequence of his own hesitancy, his own doubt in the sureness of his footing."

LOUISE POUND (1872–1958): *Poetic Origins and the Ballad.* Pound's influential critical study helps establish her reputation as the most prominent woman academic in the United States during the 1920s.

CARL VAN DOREN (1885–1950): *The American Novel.* Van Doren's first critical work is a survey of the nineteenth-century American novel, to be followed by *Contemporary American Novelists, 1900–1920* (1922). Van Doren was the brother of poet and critic Mark Van Doren, a professor at Columbia from 1911 to 1930, and the managing editor of the *Cambridge History of American Literature* (1917–1921).

Nonfiction

JAMES TRUSLOW ADAMS (1878–1949): *The Founding of New England.* The first volume of a trilogy on New England history wins the Pulitzer Prize. It would be followed by *Revolutionary New England* (1923) and *New England in the Republic* (1926). Adams was a successful businessman who served on the House Commission for the Peace Conference following World War I and began to write history on his return from France in 1919.

ROBERT BENCHLEY (1889–1945): *Of All Things.* The first of the humorist's collections of sketches and observations about the absurdities of commonplace life. His other volumes in the decade are *Love Conquers All* (1922), *Pluck and Luck* (1925), *The Early Worm* (1927), and *20,000 Leagues Under the Sea; or, David Copperfield* (1928). Benchley began his career writing advertising copy before doing editorial work for the *New York World, Life,* the *Bookman,* and *The New Yorker.*

DON MARQUIS (1879–1937): *The Old Soak.* The *New York Sun* humor columnist's most famous work is this collection of the misadventures and observations of a town drunk. Marquis would also adapt it as a successful play in 1922 and produce a sequel, *The Old Soak's History of the World* (1924). Marquis's folksy, satirical poetry appeared in such volumes as *Dreams and Dust* (1915), *Noah an' Jonah an' Cap'n Smith* (1921), *Poems and Portraits* (1922), and *The Awakening* (1924).

HAROLD STEARNS (1891–1943): *America and the Young Intellectual.* Stearns attempts to define the postwar generation's attitudes toward contemporary life and literature. Stearns was an expatriate whose critical views were also expressed in the symposium he edited, *Civilization in the United States: An Inquiry by Thirty Americans* (1922).

DONALD OGDEN STEWART (1894–1980): *A Parody Outline of History.* The humorist's first major publication collects irreverent interpretations of major events in tAmerican history as if written by various modern writers, including "Main Street, Plymouth, Mass. in the Manner of Sinclair Lewis," "The Courtship of Miles Standish in the Manner of F. Scott Fitzgerald," and "Custer's Last Stand in the Manner of Edith Wharton." His subsequent popular comic works are *Aunt Polly's Story of Mankind* (1923), *Mr. and Mrs. Haddock Abroad* (1924), *The Crazy Fool* (1925), and *Father William* (1929). Stewart would produce a successful play, *Rebound* (1930), and win an Oscar for his screenplay of Philip Barry's *Philadelphia Story* (1940).

Poetry

JOHN GOULD FLETCHER: *Breakers and Granite.* In this collection of Gould's new and previously published works, he attacks the decay and destruction of modern urban life while celebrating the unravaged natural landscape and a presumed simpler, orderly past.

H.D. (HILDA DOOLITTLE): *Hymen.* This is the first of the poet's collections that explore various classical myths and the personae of figures such as Hymen, Demeter, Circe, and Leda. It would be followed by *Heliodora and Other Poems* (1924), *Hippolytus Temporizes* (1927), and *Red Roses for Bronze* (1931).

VACHEL LINDSAY: "In Praise of Johnny Appleseed." Lindsay's poem, published in the *Century* and to be reprinted in his *Collected Poems* (1923), is the most famous treatment of the life of orchardist John Chapman (1774–1847), whose nomadic, quixotic life is treated by the poet as symbolic of the American spirit.

AMY LOWELL: *Legends.* This collection of dramatic poems based on the folklore of different countries prompts poet Mark Van Doren to declare it "incomparably the best of Amy Lowell so far."

EDNA ST. VINCENT MILLAY: *Second April.* Millay modulates the flippant tone of *A Few Figs from Thistles* (1920) to reveal an increasing seriousness and emotional depth in works such as "Ode to Silence," "The Beanstalk," and her first free-verse poem, "Spring," in which she laments that "Life in itself / Is nothing, / An empty cup, a flight of uncarpeted stairs." Millay also publishes *The Lamp and the Bell,* a poetic drama set during the Elizabethan period, for the fiftieth anniversary of her alma mater, Vassar, and two one-act satirical fantasies, *Aria da Capo* and *Two Slatterns and a King.*

EZRA POUND: *Poems, 1918–1921.* This volume of previously published and new works includes the so-called

Paris Canto (VII), presenting a visionary portrait of the city as an urban hell, which anticipates Eliot's London in *The Waste Land*.

EDWIN ARLINGTON ROBINSON: *Avon's Harvest*. This psychological ghost story tells of a man haunted by his hatred of a persistent enemy. Robinson's other publication of 1921, *Collected Poems*, wins the first Pulitzer Prize awarded for poetry.

YVOR WINTERS (1900–1968): *The Immobile Wind*. The first of Winters's collections contains admired works such as the title poem and "Alone." It would be followed by *The Magpie's Shadow* (1922) and *The Bare Hills* (1927). Winters was a longtime professor of English at Stanford whose many volumes of criticism include *In Defense of Reason* (1947) and *The Function of Criticism* (1957).

ELINOR WYLIE (1885–1928): *Nets to Catch the Wind*. Wylie's first mature poetry collection contains some of her best work, including "A Proud Lady," "Madman's Song," "Velvet Shoes," and "August." It would be followed by *Black Armour* (1923) and four novels—*Jennifer Lorn* (1923), *The Venetian Glass Nephew* (1925), *The Orphan Angel* (1927), and *Mr. Hodge & Mr. Hazard* (1928).

Publications and Events

The *Reviewer*. Edited by Emily Clark and James Branch Cabell, this magazine based in Richmond, Virginia, begins publication to showcase Southern writers. Discoveries included Julia Peterkin, DuBose Heyward, and Paul Green. It continued until 1925.

1922

Drama and Theater

JOHN B. COLTON (1899–1946): *Rain*. Colton's first major success is this adaptation, written with Clemence Randolph, of Somerset Maugham's short story about an American prostitute on a South Sea island and the missionary who falls in love with her. Colton had been the drama critic of the *Minneapolis Tribune* whose first play to reach Broadway was *Drifting* (1922).

GEORGE S. KAUFMAN AND MARC CONNELLY: *To the Ladies*. In their second collaboration, the playwrights atone for their portrayal of a brainless young wife in *Dulcy* (1921) by depicting a sensible woman who helps her befuddled husband succeed in business. The team also adapts Harry Leon Wilson's series from the *Saturday Evening Post*, *Merton of the Movies* (about a country grocery clerk's success in Hollywood) into one of the best satires of the 1920s movie industry.

GEORGE KELLY (1887–1974): *The Torch-Bearers*. Kelly's first major dramatic success is this comedy about the little theater movement, in which a housewife steps in suddenly as the lead in an amateur production. The Philadelphia-born playwright was the brother of vaudevillian Walter C. Kelly and the uncle of the actress and later princess of Monaco, Grace Kelly.

ANNE NICHOLS (1891–1966): *Abie's Irish Rose*. Nichols's sentimental comedy about an Irish Catholic's marriage to a Jew and the couple's attempt to conceal their spouses' ethnicity from their parents is panned by the critics. The playwright, however, then turns to the notorious gangster Arnold Rothstein to bankroll the production until it catches on with the public, eventually setting a new Broadway long-run record of 2,327 performances.

EUGENE O'NEILL: *The Hairy Ape*. O'Neill's expressionistic play, about a stoker on a transatlantic liner who reexamines his dehumanized existence, becomes one of his most popular early plays. His 1922 domestic drama about the impact on a couple of an unwanted pregnancy, *The First Man*, fails.

GERTRUDE STEIN: *Geography and Plays*. Stein's initial collection of experimental "landscape" portraits and theater pieces displays her attempt to liberate language from accepted rules of composition. She would write forty-three plays between 1920 and 1933.

Fiction

WILLA CATHER: *One of Ours*. Cather wins a Pulitzer Prize for this novel about a young man's escape from the stultifying Midwest to redemption at the front during World War I. Her war scenes are criticized by some, including Ernest Hemingway, as overly idealized and unauthentic.

E. E. CUMMINGS (1894–1962): *The Enormous Room*. Cummings's first publication is a fictionalized account of his wartime incarceration in a French prison camp on an erroneous charge of treason. Cummings turns imprisonment into the means for discovering personal freedom, a quest that is echoed by allusions to John Bunyan's *The Pilgrim's Progress*. The work abandons conventional chronology, breaks the rules of normal syntax, and employs slang and improvisational techniques.

F. SCOTT FITZGERALD: *Tales of the Jazz Age*. Fitzgerald's second story collection, though it includes major work such as "The Diamond as Big as the Ritz" and the experimental novella *May Day*, is marred by filler and weak efforts that even Fitzgerald seems to recognize in his depreciatory annotated table of contents. Fitzgerald also publishes *The Beautiful and the Damned*, his second novel. It dramatizes the self-destructive marriage of the rich and glamorous Anthony and Gloria Patch,

Sinclair Lewis

damned by their excesses, and it clearly echoes the author's own marriage and high-flying lifestyle. Although more carefully constructed than *This Side of Paradise*, the novel disappoints reviewers.

ELLEN GLASGOW: *One Man in His Time.* Glasgow continues her portrayal of Richmond, Virginia, in the aftermath of the Great War, as the low-born Gideon Vetch rises to become governor, challenging the vested interests and attitudes of the old Southern aristocracy.

EMERSON HOUGH: *The Covered Wagon.* Hough's most acclaimed work is this historically accurate account of a trip on the Oregon Trail in 1848.

FANNIE HURST: *The Vertical City.* This collection of stories of New York City life includes "She Walks in Beauty," "Back Pay," and "Guilty." Her later collections include *Song of Life* (1927), *Procession* (1929), and *We Are Ten* (1937).

SINCLAIR LEWIS: *Babbitt.* Considered by many Lewis's masterpiece, the novel is a satirical indictment of American provincialism through its portrayal of businessman and booster George Babbitt of Zenith, who desires "to seize something more than motor cars and a house before it's too late," but eventually bows to his conventional, materialistic fate. As Lewis biographer Mark Schorer observes, "Since the publication of *Babbitt* everyone has learned that conformity is the great price that our predominantly commercial culture exacts.... But when *Babbitt* was published, this was its revelation to Americans."

EDGAR LEE MASTERS: *Children of the Market Place.* Masters's novel offers a portrait of American life before the Civil War through the career of political figure Stephen Douglas, as seen by an English immigrant.

CHRISTOPHER MORLEY: *Where the Blue Begins.* One of the humorist's more inventive fantasies is this satire, in which dogs are given human capacities and whose experiences provide commentary on modern life.

CARL SANDBURG: *Rootabaga Stories.* One of Sandburg's eleven books for children, *Rootabaga Stories* is a collection of fables written for his own children. It would be followed by two sequels, *Rootabaga Pigeons* (1923) and *Potato Face* (1930).

ANNE DOUGLAS SEDGWICK: *Adrienne Toner.* Sedgwick continues, in the Jamesian manner, with international themes and settings in this portrait of an American girl among the English.

T. S. STRIBLING (1881–1965): *Birthright.* The Tennessee writer's first novel concerns a Southerner of mixed race who returns home from Harvard to confront Jim Crow laws. It would be called by Jessie Redmon Fauset, who was inspired by the book to attempt her own fiction, "the most significant novel on the Negro written by a white American."

CARL VAN VECHTEN (1880–1964): *Peter Whiffle.* Van Vechten's first novel is a fictionalized autobiography telling of the author's background and his involvement in artistic circles. It would be the first in a series of satirical novels that document the era. Van Vechten was a music and dance critic who gave up writing novels after 1930 for photography.

EDITH WHARTON: *The Glimpses of the Moon.* Wharton's international comedy of manners concerns a parasitical young couple who accepts financial support for their discretion about their host's philandering.

ANZIA YEZIERSKA: *Salome of the Tenements.* Yezierska's first novel describes the relationship between a ghetto girl and a WASP millionaire, which contains elements of the author's relationship with educational theorist John Dewey. It is poorly received but would be later rediscovered and praised for considering the impact of race, class, and gender on the American myth. It would be followed by *Children of Loneliness* (1923), a story collection concerning the children of immigrants struggling to find fulfillment as Americans.

Literary Criticism and Scholarship

JAMES WELDON JOHNSON: *The Book of American Negro Poetry.* In this landmark poetry collection, Johnson supplies a classic analysis of the contributions of African Americans to American literature. An expanded edition would appear in 1931.

AMY LOWELL: *A Critical Fable.* Lowell's witty verse criticism of contemporary poets is patterned on James Russell Lowell's *Fable for Critics* (1848) and includes assessments of H.D., T. S. Eliot, Robert Frost, Ezra Pound, and Carl Sandburg.

Nonfiction

THEODORE DREISER: *A Book About Myself.* Dreiser recounts his early newspaper career. The book would be republished as *Newspaper Days* (1931).

IDA HUSTED HARPER: *The History of Woman Suffrage.* Harper adds the fifth and sixth volumes to the history of the suffrage movement begun by Susan B. Anthony, bringing the account up to 1920.

LUDWIG LEWISOHN: *Upstream.* The writer uses his autobiography to focus on the difficulties faced by Jews in America. He would continue his story in *Mid-Channel* (1929).

EMILY POST (1873–1960): *Etiquette: In Society, in Business, in Politics, and at Home.* Post's guide to good manners establishes her as the leading arbiter of correct behavior for nearly forty years. Her volume goes through multiple editions and is supplemented by a syndicated newspaper column and a radio program. Post was born in Baltimore and had previously published several novels, including *The Flight of the Moth* (1904) and *Purple and Fine Linen* (1906).

GEORGE SANTAYANA: *Soliloquies in England and Later Soliloquies.* The philosopher meditates on diverse topics in this collection of essays written mainly during the war, while he was at Oxford and Cambridge. It also includes some postwar reflections on ethical and political concerns.

Poetry

JOHN PEALE BISHOP (1892–1944) AND EDMUND WILSON (1894–1972): *The Undertaker's Garland.* Wilson's first publication is this collaboration with his *Vanity Fair*

Emily Post

colleague on a series of witty accounts of various funerals. Bishop served as the managing editor of *Vanity Fair* until 1922, when he became a Paris-based expatriate. His Princeton classmate Edmund Wilson would go on to become one of the century's most influential literary and social critics.

JOHN DOS PASSOS: *A Pushcart at the Curb.* Dos Passos's poetry collection provides glimpses of the war, travels in Spain and Italy, and New York City street scenes. He also publishes an impressionistic collection of travel essays on Spanish life and culture, *Rosinante to the Road Again.*

T. S. ELIOT: *The Waste Land.* The most influential poem of the twentieth century is a multivocal poetic sequence interweaving images and allusions around the theme of the barrenness of the modern postwar world. Ezra Pound was responsible for cutting almost half its original length, eliminating exposition and transitions. Positive and negative responses cause one reviewer to refer to the poem as a "battle-field" in which "its adherents see nothing but its virtues; its detractors see nothing but its faults." William Carlos Williams would later call the work the "atom bomb" of modern poetry, establishing the standard by which any attempt to fashion a modern epic poem would have to be measured.

CLAUDE MCKAY: *Harlem Shadows*. McKay's last poetry collection to be published during his lifetime includes his most important works, such as "If We Must Die," "America," "The Harlem Dancer," "Outcast," and "The Lynching."

CARL SANDBURG: *Slabs of the Sunburnt West*. Sandburg's Whitmanesque celebrations of the American landscape include the long poem "The Windy City," commemorating Chicago and showing his developing technique of juxtaposing a succession of images and exploiting the poetic possibility of colloquial language.

GENEVIEVE TAGGARD (1894–1948): *For Eager Lovers*. Taggard's first collection is greeted enthusiastically as announcing the arrival of a major new talent. Mark Van Doren proclaims that the book "places her among the considerable poets of contemporary America." It would be followed by *Hawaiian Hilltop* (1923), reflecting the poet's Hawaiian upbringing. Her other volumes during the decade are *Words for the Chisel* (1926), *Travelling Standing Still* (1928), and *Monologue for Mothers (Aside)* (1929).

Publications and Events

The Fugitive. Poets and writers centered at Vanderbilt University in Nashville, who call themselves the Fugitives, begin a journal for new writing that would until 1925 provide a forum for writers such as Hart Crane, John Crowe Ransom, Allan Tate, and Robert Penn Warren.

The Newbery Medal. The American Library Association institutes this annual prize to honor the best book written for children. It is named for John Newbery (1713–1767), the printer and bookseller who began publishing poems and stories for children in 1744.

The *Reader's Digest*. Founded by DeWitt Wallace (1889–1981) and Lila Bell Acheson Wallace (1889–1984), this monthly, featuring condensations of articles from other periodicals, would become the most widely read magazine in the world. By the 1980s readership had reached 100 million in 163 countries.

1923
Drama and Theater

PHILIP BARRY (1896–1949): *You and I*. Barry's first Broadway success (and the initial display of his characteristic epigrammatic wit) is a drama about a man who gives up his passion for painting to become a successful businessman and tries to persuade his son not to repeat his mistake. It is an ironic inversion of the opposition of Barry's own father to the playwright's decision to pursue a career in drama. After graduating from Yale, Barry enrolled in George Pierce Baker's famous 47 Workshop at Harvard. He would continue to explore his family relations in his second Broadway play, *The Youngest* (1924).

RACHEL CROTHERS: *Mary the Third*. This generational comedy shows a flapper who eventually bows to the pressure to live a conventional life. It is typical of Crothers's shrewd looks at contemporary life from a woman's perspective.

OWEN DAVIS: *Icebound*. Davis's play about a grasping Maine family disinherited by its matriarchal head wins the Pulitzer Prize. It is his last major original work; he would subsequently dramatize the works of others, including *The Great Gatsby* (1926), *The Good Earth* (1932), and *Ethan Frome* (1936).

F. SCOTT FITZGERALD: *The Vegetable; or, From Presidency to Postman*. Fitzgerald's satirical comedy, which he declares "the best American comedy to date and undoubtedly the best thing I have ever written," concerns a postman who becomes president. It closes before reaching Broadway. Critics have suggested that the disappointment over this play was a factor in Fitzgerald's committing to more serious work, which would lead to his masterpiece, *The Great Gatsby*.

LEON GORDON (1895–1960): *White Cargo*. Gordon's sensational drama is about a West Indian plantation owner's relationship with a mulatto woman, whom he marries. Panned by critics, it is one of the decade's biggest hits and Gordon's only Broadway success. Gordon was an actor as well as a playwright who would become a major screenwriter and film producer.

ELMER RICE: *The Adding Machine*. Rice's expressionistic drama about a repressed bookkeeper, Mr. Zero, driven to murder his employer when he is replaced by an adding machine, establishes Rice as a major American dramatist who popularizes experimental dramatic techniques.

LULA VOLLMER (1895–1955): *Sun-Up*. The North Carolina playwright achieves her greatest success with this folk drama about a North Carolina mountain woman who, after her son is killed in the Great War, is tempted to kill a deserter in response. Also produced is Vollmer's *The Shame Woman* about a North Carolina mountain woman who, shunned by her neighbors after being seduced, is pushed to murder.

Fiction

SHERWOOD ANDERSON: *Horses and Men* and *Many Marriages*. The first is a collection of short and longer stories, mainly about horseracing. The second is a novel about a respectable businessman who breaks out of a deadened, conventional lifestyle.

GERTRUDE ATHERTON: *Black Oxen.* Atherton's sexually frank novel about a woman choosing between love and power creates a sensation in its depiction of a liberated woman in the hedonistic 1920s.

DJUNA BARNES (1892–1982): *A Book.* Barnes's first major work is a collection of short plays, stories, and poems. It would be reissued and expanded as *A Night Among the Horses* in 1929. An original member of the Theater Guild who acted in and wrote plays produced by the Provincetown Players, Barnes worked as a journalist and illustrator until 1931.

THOMAS BOYD (1898–1935): *Through the Wheat.* Boyd's most acclaimed work is this World War I novel based on his own war experiences. It is favorably compared, in its authenticity, to John Dos Passos's *Three Soldiers* and Stephen Crane's *Red Badge of Courage.* A sequel, *In Time of Peace* (1935), and a collection of war stories, *Points of Honor* (1925), would follow.

WILLA CATHER: *A Lost Lady.* Some critics have asserted that this novel — about the wife of a railroad pioneer seen through the adoring eyes of a young boy as she coarsens over time — is Cather's masterpiece. It stands as a poignant elegy for the passing of the heroic pioneer age and an indictment of the corruption of modern life, which Cather increasingly lamented. She would observe that for her "the world broke in two in 1922 or thereabouts."

FLOYD DELL: *Janet March.* Dell's psychological study of a modern woman's rebellion against convention and its frank sexuality cause the book to be withdrawn from sale in Massachusetts and New York and earn its author notoriety. Dell would follow it with other portraits of the postwar generation in *Runaway* (1925) and *This Mad Ideal* (1925).

JOHN DOS PASSOS: *Streets of Night.* Dos Passos would call his third novel, about the frustrations of a youth at Harvard, "an effort to recapture the strange stagnation of the intellectual class I'd felt so strangling during college."

ZONA GALE: *Faint Perfume.* The writer continues her realistic documentation of shallow middle-class American life in a depiction of the petty Crumb family.

ELLEN GLASGOW: *The Shadowy Third and Other Stories.* Glasgow's only short story collection emphasizes her interest in the uncanny and the ghostly, as in the acclaimed story "The Past."

ERNEST HEMINGWAY (1899–1961): *Three Stories & Ten Poems.* Hemingway's first publication is brought out by

Fannie Hurst

Robert McAlmon's Paris Contact Publishing Company. The stories included are "Out of Season," "My Old Man," and "Up in Michigan." The first two would become part of *In Our Time* (1925); the third, about a seduction and rape, was removed from this collection at the insistence of the publisher.

FANNIE HURST: *The Lummox.* Hurst would regard this as her favorite novel, a sympathetic portrait of a downtrodden woman, which critic Susan Currier has called "an eloquent tale of an inarticulate heroine from the slums."

OLIVE PROUTY (1882–1974): *Stella Dallas.* The Massachusetts writer's most famous novel dramatizes a mother's sacrifices for her daughter. A bestseller, it would be adapted as a play, a silent film, a talkie, and a weekly radio serial that ran for fifteen years. Her other novels include *Home Port* (1947) and *Fabia* (1951).

WILBUR DANIEL STEELE: *The Shame Dance and Other Stories.* The first of the writer's collections to appear during the decade features stories set in mainly exotic locales. It helps solidify his reputation as a "master narrator." It would be followed by *Urkey Island* (1926), *The Man Who Saw Through Heaven* (1927), and *Tower of Sand* (1929).

JEAN TOOMER (1894–1967): *Cane.* One of the singular achievements of the Harlem Renaissance is this innovative collection, combining stories, poetry, and a play on black life in the North and South. Kenneth Rexroth would call Toomer "the first poet to unite folk culture and the elite culture of the white avant-garde." Toomer would continue to write but published little and eventually abandoned creative writing to become a disciple of the Greek spiritual philosopher George I. Gurdjieff.

CARL VAN VECHTEN: *Blind Bow-Boy*. The first of the writer's satires on New York life during the decade establishes Van Vechten's reputation as one of his era's most insightful cultural critics. His other works include *Firecrackers* (1925) and *Parties* (1930).

EDITH WHARTON: *A Son at the Front*. Drawing on her own wartime experiences in France, Wharton's novel shows an American painter's conversion to the Allied cause based on his son's experiences in battle. Although praised for its psychological acuity, the urgency and relevance of the novel's theme had diminished in the minds of many reviewers.

ELINOR WYLIE: *Jennifer Lorn*. The first of the poet's four novels, a romance set in the eighteenth century, is enthusiastically greeted by the critics, one of whom, Carl Van Vechten, organizes a torchlight parade in Manhattan to celebrate its publication. It would be followed by *The Venetian Glass Nephew* (1925), *The Orphan Angel* (1926), and *Mr. Hodge & Mr. Hazard* (1928).

Literary Criticism and Scholarship

MARY AUSTIN: *The American Rhythm*. Austin's poetic treatise asserts that the roots of true American poetry lie not in Europe but derive from Native American oral tradition. She calls for a freedom of form and language reflecting Native American verse methods.

D. H. LAWRENCE (1885–1930): *Studies in Classic American Literature*. One of the landmark critical treatments of American literature, Lawrence's volume begins with an introductory essay, "The Spirit of the Place," before proceeding to a series of provocative interpretations of the works of James Fenimore Cooper, Edgar Allan Poe, Nathaniel Hawthorne, Herman Melville, and Walt Whitman.

ARTHUR HOBSON QUINN (1875–1960): *A History of the American Drama*. Quinn begins his influential three-volume dramatic history (completed in 1927). It is the first and still one of the best comprehensive treatments of American drama. Quinn was a professor of English and drama at the University of Pennsylvania from 1895 to 1945.

Nonfiction

GAMALIEL BRADFORD: *Damaged Souls*. Bradford's most popular work is an application of his biographical method called "psychography," the isolation of individuals' ruling traits at key moments of their lives. He examines a "group of somewhat discredited figures" from American history, including Aaron Burr, P. T. Barnum, and Thomas Paine.

CARRIE CHAPMAN CATT (1859–1947): *Woman Suffrage and Politics: The Inner Story of the Suffrage Movement*. One of the chief suffrage leaders supplies an insider's look at the effort to gain the vote, from 1848 to the ratification of the Nineteenth Amendment in 1920.

THEODORE DREISER: *The Color of a Great City*. Dreiser provides a collection of sketches of New York City recorded from 1900 to 1915. He would publish a second volume on New York life in *My City* (1929).

EMMA GOLDMAN: *My Disillusionment in Russia*. After being deported to Russia in 1919 for her radical views, Goldman reflects on her two years there, disappointing her liberal colleagues with a negative assessment of life after the Russian Revolution. The book illustrates her contention that "I saw before me the Bolshevik State, formidable, crushing every constructive revolutionary effort, suppressing, debasing, and disintegrating everything." She would follow it with a sequel, *My Further Disillusionment in Russia* (1924), and her autobiography, *Living My Life* (1931).

GEORGE SANTAYANA: *Scepticism and Animal Faith*. With this introductory volume, the philosopher begins his masterwork, the Realms of Being series, made up of *The Realm of Essence* (1927), *The Realm of Matter* (1930), *The Realm of Truth* (1937), and *The Realm of Spirit* (1940).

WILLIAM CARLOS WILLIAMS: *The Great American Novel*. Published in Paris as part of Ezra Pound's series Inquest into the State of Contemporary English Prose, which also includes Ernest Hemingway's *in our time*, Williams's experimental prose work is, in the words of its creator, "about a little Ford falling in love with a truck. It is about an American writer's use of words."

Poetry

STEPHEN VINCENT BENÉT: *The Ballad of William Sycamore*. First published in the *New Republic* in 1922, Benét's popular ballad of a pioneer scout, issued as a pamphlet, anticipates his later achievement in producing mythic portraits based on the American past. He also publishes *King David*, a retelling of the biblical story in a jazzy ballad style, which would win *The Nation*'s poetry prize and generate controversy by its presumed irreverence.

LOUISE BOGAN (1897–1970): *Body of This Death.* The Maine-born critic and poet's first collection shows the influence of the English metaphysical poets, as well as her emotional intensity and control. She is grouped with the "reactionary generation" of poets, who eschewed experimentation but still achieved a modern quality in traditional verse forms. Her second volume published during the decade is *Dark Summer* (1929). Bogan would for many years review poetry in *The New Yorker.*

E. E. CUMMINGS: *Tulips and Chimneys.* Cummings's first collection shows his characteristic eccentric use of grammar and punctuation, though many of the poems are also formally and typographically conventional. Some of his best-known poems are represented, including "All in green went my love riding," "ladies and gentlemen this little girls," and "Buffalo Bill's defunct." The original manuscript was cut down by the publisher, and Cummings privately printed the deleted poems in 1925 in a collection titled *&*.

ROBERT FROST: *New Hampshire.* Frost wins his first Pulitzer Prize for this important collection, which includes a wide range of moods and styles, from the title monologue celebrating New Hampshire to narrative poems such as "The Star-Splitter," "Maple," and "The Axe-Helve." Also included is what has been called his most perfect lyric, "Stopping by Woods on a Snowy Evening."

VACHEL LINDSAY: *Collected Poems.* Bringing together both his earlier published work and previously uncollected poems, the volume includes an autobiographical foreword indicating the occasions that inspired many of Lindsay's compositions.

MINA LOY (1882–1986): *Lunar Baedecker.* Loy's experimental verse collection is published by Robert McAlmon's Contact Press, which was responsible for misspelling *Baedeker*, a reference to the nineteenth-century European guidebooks published by Karl Baedeker. Although now largely forgotten, at the time Loy was ranked as an important American modernist. Critic Yvor Winters would claim that she and William Carlos Williams had the most to offer the next generation of poets.

EDNA ST. VINCENT MILLAY: *The Ballad of the Harp-Weaver* (reprinted as *The Harp Weaver and Other Poems*). Millay wins the Pulitzer Prize for this collection (along with the reissued and expanded *A Few Figs from Thistles* and *Eight Sonnets*). It marks a new seriousness of tone and a growing technical mastery, particularly in its sonnets. The one beginning "Euclid alone has looked on Beauty bare" is one of her most famous and enduring works.

EDWIN ARLINGTON ROBINSON: *Roman Bartholow.* Robinson's narrative poem describes the title character's rescue from despair by his friend, who has designs on Bartholow's wife. The poem's theme and technique baffle many critics, who complain about a lack of clarity in the poem's characterizations and its unfocused drama.

WALLACE STEVENS (1879–1955): *Harmonium.* Stevens's first collection, one of the landmark volumes in American poetry, includes some of the poet's greatest works, including "Sunday Morning," "The Emperor of Ice Cream," "Anecdote of the Jar," "Thirteen Ways of Looking at a Blackbird," "The Comedian as the Letter C," "Le Monocle de Mon Oncle," and "Peter Quince at the Clavier." Despite the astonishing intellectual and emotional range of the poetry, it is largely ignored or dismissed as the work of a dilettante. Stevens would subsequently write little until reissuing the collection, together with new work, in 1931. Born in Reading, Pennsylvania, Stevens was a lawyer who began in 1916 as an executive at the Hartford Accident and Indemnity Company, where he remained until his death.

WILLIAM CARLOS WILLIAMS: *Spring and All.* Published in Paris, this is the poet's most important early collection, containing some of his finest works, including the title poem, "To Elsie," "At the Ballgame," and, perhaps his most famous short poem, "The Red Wheelbarrow." Despite his considerable achievement, Williams would not publish another collection for almost a decade.

ELINOR WYLIE: *Black Armour.* Wylie's second volume continues her identification with the Romantics, particularly Shelley, in a series of explorations of outcasts and wounded sensitivity. In 1923 she also publishes the first of her four novels, *Jennifer Lorn.*

Publications and Events

Time. Founded by Briton Hadden (1898–1929) and Henry R. Luce (1898–1967), this weekly news magazine is targeted at busy Americans who cannot keep abreast of the news in the daily newspaper. It began to turn a profit by 1927 and was imitated by *Newsweek* and *United States News* in 1933. It also helped finance a publishing empire, Time, Inc., which spawned *Fortune, Life,* and *Sports Illustrated.*

1924
Drama and Theater

MAXWELL ANDERSON (1888–1959) AND LAURENCE STALLINGS (1894–1968): *What Price Glory?* Anderson's second play, following *The White Desert* (1923), about marital jealousy, and his first success is this war drama regarded by many as the greatest American play about World War I. It concerns the rivalry between two career American soldiers — Flagg and Quirt — and is based on Stallings's own wartime experiences. At the time, the play's salty language and realism were considered groundbreaking. Anderson had become a playwright after working as a schoolteacher and journalist. Stallings had served after the war as a critic for the *New York World* and also dealt with his war experiences in the novel *Plumes* (1924).

GUY BOLTON: *Lady, Be Good!* The first collaboration of George and Ira Gershwin to reach Broadway features a jazzy, realistic score, a characteristic of musical comedy, which is becoming distinct from operetta. It features standards such as "Fascinating Rhythm" and "Oh, Lady, Be Good!"

RACHEL CROTHERS: *Expressing Willie.* Crothers's comedy about a toothpaste magnate who builds a luxurious mansion on Long Island and attracts a group of spongers and social climbers anticipates some of the themes developed in F. Scott Fitzgerald's *The Great Gatsby* (1925).

DOROTHY DONNELLY (1880–1928) AND SIGMUND ROMBERG: *The Student Prince.* This operetta about the crown prince of Karlsberg who falls in love with a Heidelburg tavern maid becomes the longest-running musical production of the 1920s. Donnelly was an acclaimed actress who played the title roles in the first American productions of Shaw's *Candida* and Yeats's *Cathleen ni Houlihan.*

SIDNEY HOWARD: *They Knew What They Wanted.* Howard's first Broadway success is a Pulitzer Prize–winning drama about an aging Italian winegrower in the Napa Valley. He proposes marriage by mail to a younger woman, using the photo of his younger hired hand as an inducement. The play would be turned into a musical, *The Most Happy Fella*, by Frank Loesser (1910–1969) in 1956.

EDNA FERBER AND GEORGE S. KAUFMAN: *Minick.* After an unsuccessful solo dramatic effort, *The Eldest* (1920), and an equally unsuccessful collaboration with Newman Levy in *$1200 a Year* (1920), Ferber joins forces with Kaufman for the first in a series of hits. Based on one of Ferber's stories, the play concerns an elderly man who must choose between living with his son and daughter-in-law or in an old-folks home.

OTTO HARBACH (1873–1963), OSCAR HAMMERSTEIN II (1895–1960), AND RUDOLF FRIML (1879–1972): *Rose-Marie.* The popularity of this operetta, depicting the romance of a singer and a Mountie in the Canadian Rockies, sparks a revival of traditional operettas, which had, due to their German associations, fallen out of favor during the war.

HATCHER HUGHES (1883–1945): *Hell-Bent for Heaven.* Hughes's melodrama about feuding North Carolina mountain families is a controversial Pulitzer Prize winner after the drama jury's selection of George Kelly's *The Show-Off* is overturned by the Pulitzer board, many of whom are Hughes's colleagues at Columbia University.

GEORGE S. KAUFMAN AND MARC CONNELLY: *Beggar on Horseback.* The playwrights capitalize on the vogue for expressionism in this popular comic fantasy of a young composer's dream about what his life would be like if he submits to a fashionable marriage into a rich, soulless American family. He resorts to murder and contemplates suicide before awakening. A critique of the materialism of the era, the play causes one reviewer to proclaim it "the most searching bit of stage satire yet produced in America."

GEORGE KELLY: *The Show-Off.* Hailed by critic Heywood Broun as "the best comedy which has yet been written by an American," Kelly's play about a braggart's marriage is selected by the Pulitzer Prize drama jury. Their decision, however, is overturned by the Pulitzer board, who award the prize to Hatcher Hughes for his melodrama *Hell-Bent for Heaven*, amid charges of bias in favor of Hughes, a Columbia University professor and colleague of many of the board members.

EUGENE O'NEILL: *Desire Under the Elms.* O'Neill's drama brings obscenity charges from the New York district attorney. It is the story of an aging New England farmer whose young third wife seduces his son and then kills the child she bears by him. O'Neill's other works in a remarkably productive year include *The Ancient Mariner*, a dramatic version of Samuel Taylor Coleridge's poem, and *Welded*, a play about the relationship between a dramatist and an actress. Also, four of the playwright's earlier one-act sea dramas — *The Moon of the Caribbees*, *The Long Voyage Home*, *In the Zone*, and *Bound East for Cardiff* — are staged together to form a single dramatic work, *S. S. Glencairn*, at the Provincetown Playhouse. O'Neill receives threats from the Ku Klux Klan for his drama about miscegenation, *All God's Chillun Got Wings*, depicting the marriage of a black man (played by Paul

Robeson) to a white woman whose repressed racial prejudice leads to insanity. When the New York license commissioner hears that a black man kisses a white woman on stage, he threatens to shut the production down, and child actors are banned from performing.

DOROTHY PARKER (1893–1967) AND ELMER RICE: *Close Harmony.* The first of the poet and short story writer's two plays to reach Broadway, this collaboration with Rice is a comedy about neighbors contemplating leaving their spouses and eloping together. The other is *Ladies of the Corridor* (1953). Neither is a success. Parker had served as the drama critic of *Vanity Fair* from 1917 to 1920 and then at *The New Yorker* after she was fired for overly harsh reviews.

Fiction

SHERWOOD ANDERSON: *A Story Teller's Story.* Anderson begins a fictionalized autobiography, which he would continue in *Tar: A Midwest Childhood* (1926) and conclude with *Sherwood Anderson's Memoirs* (1942).

LOUIS BROMFIELD (1896–1956): *The Green Bay Tree.* The first novel by the Ohio writer initiates a tetralogy, his most popular and acclaimed work, concerning individual attempts in different eras to transcend one's conditions. It would be followed by *Possession* (1925), *Early Autumn* (1926), and *A Good Woman* (1927).

JAMES GOULD COZZENS (1903–78): *Confusion.* Cozzens's first novel, written while he was a nineteen-year-old Harvard undergraduate, is the story of a French girl unable to discover outlets for her talents. Although pretentiously overwritten, the novel does announce Cozzens's central theme, the search for sustaining values that would recur in major works such as *The Just and the Unjust* (1942), *Guard of Honor* (1948), and *By Love Possessed* (1957).

JESSIE REDMON FAUSET (1882–1961): *There Is Confusion.* Fauset's first novel presents the parallel stories of two black middle-class families, one of the first books to take up this subject. It is also noteworthy for its portrayal of the prospects for black women and the discrimination faced by urban blacks in the North. Fauset, believed to be the first African American woman graduate of Cornell University, taught French in a high school in Washington, D.C., and was the literary editor of *Crisis* from 1919 to 1926.

EDNA FERBER: *So Big.* Ferber's popular novel about a mother's sacrifices for her son wins the Pulitzer Prize and contributes to her reputation as the major woman novelist of her day.

Edna Ferber

ERNEST HEMINGWAY: *in our time.* The vignettes that would become the interchapters of *In Our Time* (1925) are published in Paris. To Hemingway, the relationship between these brief scenes typifying contemporary life and the stories in that volume is "Like looking with your eyes at something, say a passing coastline, and then looking at it with 15x binoculars."

JOSEPH HERGESHEIMER: *Balisand.* The author's popular historical romance is set in Virginia during the 1780s and uses the clash between the Jeffersonians and the Federalists as a background to a love story. The novel, one of the author's best, reflects his growing political conservatism during the decade.

RING LARDNER: *How to Write Short Stories.* The book's title and mock critical preface were suggested by F. Scott Fitzgerald, and the collection, with stories such as "Alibi Ike," "My Roomy," "A Caddy's Diary," "Some Like Them Cold," "Champion," and "The Golden Honeymoon," is the first of Lardner's works to receive major critical attention and recognition for its author as a serious literary artist.

HERMAN MELVILLE: *Billy Budd.* Completed during his last five years, Melville's moral allegory pits the handsome and innocent seaman Billy Budd against the malevolent master-at-arms Claggart. When Billy strikes his superior officer, Captain Vere is forced to choose between his duty and his personal sense of Billy's innocence. Melville's last published masterpiece sparks a critical debate over whether the work should be regarded as a bitter depiction of the destruction of virtue or Melville's final acceptance of a Christian consolation.

ANNE DOUGLAS SEDGWICK: *The Little French Girl*. Sedgwick's most popular work continues her characteristic documentation of national differences in the contrast between the French and the English as the daughter of a worldly Frenchwoman goes to England to make a good match.

T. S. STRIBLING: *Teeftallow*. Called by several critics a Southern version of *Main Street*, this satirical novel attacking provincialism and fundamentalism is one of the earliest Southern novels to critique middle-class and poor-white Tennessee hill culture, anticipating the works of Erskine Caldwell, Thomas Wolfe, and Robert Penn Warren.

RUTH SUCKOW (1892–1960): *Country People*. After being encouraged by H. L. Mencken, who helped publish her work in *Smart Set* and *American Mercury*, the Iowa native publishes her first novel, a realistic study of three generations of a German American family. Avoiding striking incidents, the novel is a restrained, documentary-like narrative that shows the writer's characteristic strengths of local color and psychological characterization.

CARL VAN VECHTEN: *The Tattooed Countess*. Van Vechten's novel is a portrait of the author's native Iowa during his boyhood.

GLENWAY WESCOTT (1901–1987): *The Apple of the Eye*. Wescott's first novel begins his reflections on the rural Wisconsin of his childhood in a story that pits a repressed Puritanism against a more sensual appreciation of life.

EDITH WHARTON: *Old New York*. Four separate novellas — *False Dawn*, *The Old Maid*, *The Spark*, and *New Year's Day* — reflect social life during successive decades from 1840 to 1870.

WALTER WHITE (1893–1955): *The Fire in the Flint*. White, a light-skinned black who investigated lynchings for the NAACP by posing as a white reporter, supplies a fictionalized study of the impact of lynching in his first novel. It would be followed by a nonfictional treatment in *Rope and Faggot — A Biography of Judge Lynch* (1929).

Literary Criticism and Scholarship

GILBERT SELDES (1893–1970): *The Seven Lively Arts*. In one of the earliest systematic critiques of popular American culture, the editor and drama critic of the *Dial* examines what he contends are the true creative expressions of the American people in comic strips, movies, vaudeville, and popular songs.

Nonfiction

IRVING BABBITT: *Democracy and Leadership*. Babbitt applies his theories of the New Humanism to political and social issues, characterizing historical eras as naturalistic, religious, or humanistic, with the first two leading to imperialism and tyranny, and the last to democracy.

LEWIS MUMFORD (1895–1990): *Sticks and Stones: A Study of American Architecture and Civilization*. Mumford's second book, following *The Story of Utopias* (1922), interprets American culture through its architecture and city development. The critic, historian, and teacher would subsequently produce cultural and social histories, including *The Golden Days* (1926), *The Brown Decades* (1931), and his four-volume study of city life (1934–1951).

MARK TWAIN: *Autobiography*. Employing a self-described "methodless method," Twain had begun dictating his memoir to Albert Bigelow Paine in 1906 from a set of notes, recording whatever came to his mind at the moment. The result is an unsystematic, though entertaining and often instructive, collection of anecdotes, with the degree of invention the source of subsequent critical debate.

Poetry

WILLIAM FAULKNER (1897–1962): *The Marble Faun*. Faulkner's first book is a collection of pastoral verse that sells so poorly that most of the five-hundred-copy edition is remaindered to a bookstore for ten cents a copy. Sherwood Anderson, whom Faulkner would meet in New Orleans in 1925, helped convince Faulkner that his talent lay in writing prose.

ROBINSON JEFFERS: *Tamar and Other Poems*. In Jeffers's first important collection to sound his characteristic pessimistic themes and narrative method, the title poem transposes the biblical legend to a California setting. Also included is "The Tower Beyond Tragedy," a reinterpretation of the Orestes myth. Significant lyrics include "Night," "Shine, Perishing Republic," and "The Coast Range Christ." Privately printed when a publisher could not be found, the collection would prompt critical comparison with Aeschylus and Shakespeare, and it would be expanded and reissued as *Roan Stallion, Tamar, and Other Poems* in 1925.

ARCHIBALD MacLEISH: *The Happy Marriage and Other Poems.* After two earlier collections—the sonnet cycle *Songs for a Summer's Day* (1915) and *Tower of Ivory* (1917) reflecting his war experiences—MacLeish issues his first mature work in the title poem, a complex meditation that shows the poet working through influences to articulate a personal vision and authority.

EDGAR LEE MASTERS: *The New Spoon River.* Despite returning to the epigraph-portraiture method of his greatest success, *Spoon River Anthology* (1915), Masters fails to achieve a comparable impact with this fierce indictment of modern urban America.

MARIANNE MOORE (1887–1972): *Observations.* After a first collection, *Poems*, had appeared in England without her consent or assistance, Moore makes her own choices among her earlier work in this collection, which includes such admired poems as "Marriage," "An Octopus," and "Sea Unicorns and Land Unicorns."

JOHN CROWE RANSOM: *Chills and Fever.* Ransom's first mature work is collected here to critical acclaim. Louis Untermeyer declares it "the best volume of American verse that has lately come to this reviewer's table," while John McClure insists that Ransom has "developed the intellectually expressive cadence to the point probably not excelled by any American—not even by Eliot, Pound, or Stevens, and certainly not by Frost."

EDWIN ARLINGTON ROBINSON: *The Man Who Died Twice.* Robinson's tragic narrative poem about the destruction of a composer's genius through dissipation wins the Pulitzer Prize.

MARK VAN DOREN (1894–1972): *Spring Thunder, and Other Poems.* The novelist, critic, and poet's first collection is made up of mainly pastoral poems celebrating his Connecticut home, the same themes he would continue in his next two collections, *7 p.m. and Other Poems* (1926) and *Now the Sky and Other Poems* (1928). Van Doren served as literary editor and film critic for the *Nation* during the 1920s.

Publications and Events

The American Mercury is founded by H. L. Mencken and George Jean Nathan as a successor to *Smart Set*, to reflect American culture and to criticize American institutions. Edited by Mencken until 1934, the magazine became a lively forum for critical commentary and would feature work by virtually every important American writer during the 1920s and 1930s. It ceased publication in 1980, after being transformed in 1952 into a right-wing journal.

Commonweal. The weekly review of current events, literature, and social affairs for a Catholic readership debuts.

New York Herald Tribune. The *New York Herald* merges with the *New-York Tribune* to become a Republican-oriented daily featuring columnist Walter Lippmann and *Books*, a Sunday supplement of reviews. It ceased publication in 1966.

The Pierpont Morgan Library. The former private library of J. P. Morgan (1837–1913) is established as a public institution housing an important collection of books, manuscripts, and art works.

The *Saturday Review of Literature.* The magazine begins publication under the editorship of Henry Seidel Canby (1879–1961) as an influential source of book reviews and literary commentary. Retitled the *Saturday Review* in 1952, it continued publication until 1982.

1925
Drama and Theater

JAMES GLEASON (1886–1959) AND GEORGE ABBOTT (1887–1995): *The Fall Guy.* The first of Gleason's two comedies to run during the 1925 season deals with the comic implications of prohibition. The other is *Is Zat So?* about down-on-their-luck boxers who agree to impersonate a butler and a footman. Gleason was a veteran stage actor since childhood; Abbott was an actor, playwright, director, and producer who would be responsible in some capacity for hits such as *Broadway* (1926), *Twentieth Century* (1932), *Pal Joey* (1940), *The Pajama Game* (1954), and *Damn Yankees* (1955).

OTTO HARBACH, OSCAR HAMMERSTEIN II, AND JEROME KERN: *Sunny.* This musical comedy represents the first teaming up of this writing trio.

OTTO HARBACH AND FRANK MANDEL (1884–1958): *No, No, Nanette.* The most successful musical comedy of the decade is this flapper farce set in Atlantic City, with popular songs such as "Tea for Two" and "I Want to Be Happy." Mandel would collaborate on the books for subsequent productions such as *The Desert Song* (1926), *The New Moon* (1928), *Good News!* (1927), and *Follow Thru* (1929).

SIDNEY HOWARD: *Lucky Sam McCarver.* Howard's character study of an ambitious bootlegger's rise as a nightclub owner fails with critics and audiences but would later be seen as one of the significant dramas of the era to explore the materialistic values of the period.

GEORGE S. KAUFMAN: *The Butter and Egg Man.* The playwright achieves his only solo success in this drama about small-time Broadway producers who recruit a naive out-of-town backer. The play's title derives from a phrase coined by nightclub hostess Texas Guinan to designate a hick from the sticks. Kaufman also writes *The Cocoanuts*, a farce with music and lyrics by Irving Berlin. It spoofs the Florida real estate boom through the manic humor of the Marx Brothers. It would be filmed in 1929. Kaufman's second vehicle for the Marxes would be *Animal Crackers* (1928), released as a film in 1930.

GEORGE KELLY: *Craig's Wife*. Kelly's Pulitzer Prize–winning character study concerns an obsessive wife dominated by her possessions. In the play's climax her husband rebels by breaking a favorite knickknack and daring to smoke in the house.

JOHN HOWARD LAWSON (1894–1977): *Processional*. The first in a series of the playwright's proletarian dramas, the play employs expressionistic techniques to depict a West Virginia miners' strike. Lawson's other socialist-leaning works of the decade are *Loud Speaker* (1927) and *The International* (1928). Lawson would eventually leave the theater for Hollywood, where he was a successful screenwriter until he was blacklisted as one of the Hollywood Ten in the 1950s.

EUGENE O'NEILL: *The Fountain*. The futile search of Ponce de León to find eternal youth is O'Neill's subject in this symbolic drama, which ultimately affirms the life-enhancing "eternal becoming" and the idea that "there is no gold but love."

CHANNING POLLOCK (1880–1946): *The Enemy*. This antiwar morality play depicts the devastating impact of World War I on an Austrian family. Pollock was a drama critic and publicist for the Ziegfelds, whose many plays include *Clothes* (1906) and *The Fool* (1922).

Fiction

CONRAD AIKEN: *Bring! Bring! and Other Stories*. The first of the Aiken's short story collections, it would be followed by *Costumes by Eros* (1928) and *Among the Lost People* (1934).

SHERWOOD ANDERSON: *Dark Laughter*. Juxtaposing the sterility of white civilization with the unrepressed lives of blacks, the novel follows a Chicago reporter as he travels the Mississippi and returns to his Indiana hometown. It becomes the only commercial success among Anderson's novels but fails to restore his critical reputation and would inspire Ernest Hemingway's parody, *The Torrents of Spring* (1926). Hemingway later apologized for the attack, stating, "I thought he was going to pot the way he was writing and that I could kid him out of it by showing him how awful it was."

EARL DERR BIGGERS: *The House Without a Key*. Chinese detective Charlie Chan makes his first appearance in this mystery. As critic Margaret J. King would observe, Chan "was in part designed to counteract the image of the sinister or deviously clever Oriental which had dominated foreign adventure novels from the 19th century." Biggers would publish five additional Chan novels, and the detective's career also continued in the movies and on radio.

JAMES BOYD (1888–1944): *Drums*. The first of the author's novels that draws on his experience in World War I, *Drums* takes place during the Revolutionary War. Boyd's other important novel is *Marching On* (1927), about the Civil War. Boyd, born in Pennsylvania and raised in North Carolina, would write a subsequent novel that would treat other eras in American history.

WILLA CATHER: *The Professor's House*. Reflecting the author's increasing disillusionment with the modern world, the novel describes a college professor's midlife crisis, prompted by his move to a new home. Critic Alfred Kazin would consider the novel the "most persistently underrated" of Cather's works, in which her protagonist "is at once the archetype of all her characters and the embodiment of her own beliefs."

JOHN DOS PASSOS: *Manhattan Transfer*. Dos Passos's first attempt at an experimental collective novel interweaves the stories of multiple characters in a series of montage-like episodes to replicate the vibrant, interconnected texture of New York City life. Sinclair Lewis declares that the novel could inaugurate "the vast and blazing dawn we have awaited. It may be the foundation of a whole new school of fiction."

THEODORE DREISER: *An American Tragedy*. Based on an actual murder case, the story of Clyde Griffith shows how someone consumed with the American dream of success could consider killing his pregnant, lower-class girlfriend who threatens his relationship with a socialite. Hailed as a masterpiece, the book brings the writer his first financial success.

F. SCOTT FITZGERALD: *The Great Gatsby*. Self-made Jay Gatsby tries to recapture a romantic past with the now-married Daisy Buchanan. Fitzgerald's masterpiece, the novel is both a lyrical meditation on the American dream and a satiric portrait of the excess and fraudulence of the age. Despite its being considered one of the greatest American novels (T. S. Eliot regarded it as "the first step that American fiction has taken since Henry James"), the book would sell fewer than twenty-nine thousand copies during Fitzgerald's lifetime.

F. Scott Fitzgerald

ELLEN GLASGOW: *Barren Ground.* This novel about the maturation of a Virginia farm girl, Dorinda Oakley, who wins a hard-fought independence and competency, realistically challenges many of the archetypes in previous fictional depictions of the South.

ERNEST HEMINGWAY: *In Our Time.* Readers are introduced to the soon-to-be-famous stripped-down Hemingway style and the character Nick Adams in this masterful collection of fifteen stories, framed by the brief prose vignettes previously published in Paris as *in our time* (1924). The volume, which attempts to characterize what it is like to live "in our time" amid continual violence and threat, includes some of Hemingway's finest stories, such as "Indian Camp," "The Battler," "Soldier's Home," and "Big Two-Hearted River."

RING LARDNER: *What of It?* Lardner's miscellany includes articles about his 1924 trip to Europe, parodies, several of his nonsense plays, and a reprinting of his earlier *The Young Immigrunts* and *Symptoms of Being 35.*

SINCLAIR LEWIS: *Arrowsmith.* Angered that the Columbia University trustees had overturned the Pulitzer Prize fiction jury's selection of *Main Street* (1921) and the Pulitzer committee's neglect of *Babbitt* (1923), Lewis declines the Pulitzer Prize for his novel about an idealistic doctor and scientist who encounters self-interest, corruption, and jealousy at every level of his profession.

ANITA LOOS (1893–1981): *Gentlemen Prefer Blondes.* Subtitled "The Illuminating Diary of a Professional Lady," Loos's bestseller tells the story of a naive young flapper, Lorelei Lee, who uses her charms to coax gifts from her admirers. It is said that Loos, a brunette, was inspired by observing fellow train passengers fawning over a blonde Broadway actress heading to Hollywood for a screen test. The book would be followed by a sequel, *But Gentlemen Marry Brunettes* (1928), and the author's adaptations of the story as a play, musical, and film. Loos, a Californian, was a Hollywood screenwriter at the age of fifteen.

FRANK C. ROBERTSON (1890–1969): *Foreman of the Forty-Bar.* The first of the Idaho farmer's more than two hundred popular western stories. Other titles include *Fall of Buffalo Horn* (1928), *The Hidden Cabin* (1929), and *Riders of the Sunset Trail* (1930).

GERTRUDE STEIN: *The Making of Americans.* Completed in 1908 but deemed unpublishable until brought out in Paris seventeen years later, Stein's nine-hundred-page novel without dialogue or action had begun as a saga of three generations of her family and evolved into a representative portrait of all Americans and of "everyone who ever was or is or will be living." Stein employs simple language, repetition, and description to achieve "a continuous present." Ernest Hemingway arranged serialization with Ford Madox Ford's *transatlantic review* and book publication with Robert McAlmon's Paris Contact Publishing Company. Although he acknowledged Stein's work for teaching him important lessons of prose composition, Hemingway also parodied the book's excesses in "The Passing of a Great Race and the Making and Marring of Americans" from *The Torrents of Spring.*

RUTH SUCKOW: *The Odyssey of a Nice Girl.* Suckow's second novel traces the development of a farm girl frustrated and constrained by family obligations and stultifying social conventions.

EDITH WHARTON: *The Mother's Recompense.* The novel presents a woman's relationship with the daughter she had previously abandoned.

ANZIA YEZIERSKA: *Bread Givers.* Subtitled "A Struggle Between a Father of the Old World and a Daughter of the New," the novel, based on the author's own conflict with her stern traditional father, is regarded as the author's greatest achievement and would be hailed as an important protofeminist work when rediscovered and reissued in 1975.

Literary Criticism and Scholarship

VAN WYCK BROOKS: *The Pilgrimage of Henry James.* In contrast to his thesis in *The Ordeal of Mark Twain* (1920), which asserts the cost of Twain's accepting the confines of American society, Brooks looks at the cost James paid for trying to escape those same confines by living in Europe. *The Life of Emerson* (1932) would present a positive synthesis of the two positions.

V. F. CALVERTON (1900–1940): *The Newer Spirit.* The Marxist critic articulates what he terms "a sociological criticism of literature," in which writing is viewed as an expression of the social system from which it springs. Included is a chapter on Sherwood Anderson and a critique of American criticism. Besides the influential *The Liberation of American Literature* (1932), Calverton's other important works of literary and social criticism are *Sex Expression in Literature* (1926), *For Revolution* (1932), and *The Awakening of America* (1939). "Victor Francis Calverton" is the pseudonym of George Goetz.

ALAIN LOCKE (1886–1954): *The New Negro: An Interpretation.* Locke's anthology of the works of black writers such as Langston Hughes, Countee Cullen, Zora Neale Hurston, Claude McKay, and Jean Toomer is widely credited with providing the first unmistakable evidence of the achievement of the Harlem Renaissance and the beginning of critics' serious consideration of African American writers. W.E.B. Du Bois describes the volume as marking "an epoch," expressing "better than any book that has been published in the last ten years the present state of thought and culture among American Negroes."

AMY LOWELL: *John Keats.* The poet's immense, two-volume, virtually day-to-day record of Keats's life is sustained by Lowell's characteristic enthusiasm and poetical insights.

EDITH WHARTON: *The Writing of Fiction.* Wharton explicates her philosophy of composition, derived from her mentor Henry James, which emphasizes the fundamental veracity of her characters and the situations that they generate.

WILLIAM CARLOS WILLIAMS: *In the American Grain.* In a series of impressionistic prose studies, Williams considers important figures in the development of America, such as Christopher Columbus, Cotton Mather, Benjamin Franklin, Edgar Allan Poe, and Abraham Lincoln,

to "find out for myself what the land of my more or less accidental birth might signify."

Nonfiction

WILLIAM JENNINGS BRYAN (1860–1925): *Memoirs.* Bryan's unfinished memoirs end with his account of the 1912 presidential election. His wife completes the account, also filling in some gaps in the early record.

RICHARD HALIBURTON (1900–1939): *The Royal Road to Romance.* The first of the adventurer and travel writer's bestsellers. Other titles published before he was lost at sea, sailing a Chinese junk from China to San Francisco, are *The Glorious Adventure* (1927), *New Worlds to Conquer* (1929), *The Flying Carpet* (1932), and *A Book of Marvels* (1937).

ALFRED KREYMBORG: *Troubadour.* Kreymborg's autobiography includes reflections on his childhood on the Lower East Side of New York and his involvement with artistic circles in Greenwich Village.

GEORGE SANTAYANA: *Dialogues in Limbo.* The philosopher offers a series of imitative Socratic dialogues on various topics.

Poetry

LÉONIE ADAMS (1899–1988): *Those Not Elect.* Adams's first collection features a style that critic Allen Tate places "somewhere between the eighteenth-century decoration and the fresh intensity of a lyric by Thomas Heyward or Greene." Noteworthy poems include "Death and the Lady," "Discourse with the Heart," and "Thought's End." *High Falcon*, a second volume, would follow in 1929. Adams taught English at New York University, Bennington College, and Columbia.

STEPHEN VINCENT BENÉT: *Tiger Joy.* Combining ballads, sonnets, and lyrics, Benét displays both a growing technical mastery and wider emotional range in this collection. He also achieves a major popular success with the ballad "The Mountain Whippoorwill," which displays his reliance on folk elements and dialect humor.

COUNTEE CULLEN (1903–1946): *Color.* Cullen's first collection is highly praised as one of the major achievements of the Harlem Renaissance. It includes Cullen's most enduring poems, including "Incident," "Heritage," "Yet Do I Marvel," and "The Shroud of Color." About a third deal with racial themes, and most employ the traditional verse forms of the sonnet, rhymed couplet, and ballad stanza.

E. E. CUMMINGS: *XLI Poems.* Cummings's third collection combines a selection of poems from his original *Tulips and Chimneys* manuscript with some newer work. Cummings then arranges for the remaining poems from his manuscript to be privately printed in a volume titled &. Both volumes are well received and establish his reputation for experimentation.

BABETTE DEUTSCH: *Honey Out of the Rock.* Deutsch's second collection is a series of short imagist poems on marriage and motherhood, which reflect influences from Japanese, Greek, and Jewish cultures.

T. S. ELIOT: *The Hollow Men.* Eliot reworks deleted fragments from the first draft of *The Waste Land* into a poetic sequence that meditates on the barrenness of the modern landscape and the search for values to redeem it. Eliot also publishes his collected works, *Poems, 1909–1925.*

H.D. (HILDA DOOLITTLE): *Collected Poems.* H.D. achieves her greatest acclaim in this composite collection of her first three volumes. Mark Van Doren declares that she is "the most perfect women poet alive." H.D. follows this popular success with experimental work in fiction and cinematography, including a number of prose works that pioneer the use of flashbacks and stream-of-consciousness monologues, including *Palimpsest* (1926), *Hedylus* (1928), and *Kora and Ka* (1934).

ROBINSON JEFFERS: *Roan Stallion, Tamar, and Other Poems.* Jeffers's allegorical narrative title poem concerns a dissatisfied California wife's fascination with a red stallion that becomes her means of escape from her brutal husband and sordid life.

WILLIAM ELLERY LEONARD: *Two Lives.* Leonard's most enduring work is this sonnet sequence dealing with his marriage, his wife's suicide, and his increasing bouts of agoraphobia, later detailed in his autobiography, *The Locomotive God* (1927). Leonard was for many years a professor of English at the University of Wisconsin.

AMY LOWELL: *What's O'Clock.* The first of three posthumously published collections is awarded the Pulitzer Prize. It would be followed by *East Wind* (1926) and *Ballads for Sale* (1927).

ARCHIBALD MACLEISH: *The Pot of Earth.* The first of the poet's major modernist works during the decade shows the influence of T. S. Eliot's *The Waste Land* in the story of a woman's sexual awakening, marriage, pregnancy, and death in the context of a mythical fertility cycle.

EZRA POUND: *A Draft of XVI Cantos . . . for the Beginning of a Poem of Some Length.* The first substantial, separate publication of Pound's ever-evolving masterwork appears. Pound would continue to publish sections until the sequence was finally collected in 1970.

EDWIN ARLINGTON ROBINSON: *Dionysius in Doubt.* Both the title poem of this collection and "Demos and Dionysius" attack the materialism of the age, the curtailment of individual liberties, and the weaknesses of democracy, prompted by Robinson's reaction over the passage of the Eighteenth Amendment (prohibition). Reviewers find the volume excessively didactic.

Publications and Events

Guggenheim Fellowships. Established by the John Simon Guggenheim Memorial Foundation, these grants support creative work in the arts and research in various scholarly disciplines. Over the years, a veritable who's who of artists, writers, and academics would receive fellowships to support travel, research, and work.

The New Yorker. Dandy Eustace Tilley makes his first appearance on the cover of the sophisticated weekly magazine. Founded and edited by Harold Ross (1892–1951), it evolved into one of America's greatest literary magazines with a staff that included James Thurber, E. B. White, and John Updike, and contributors who represent the best contemporary fiction and nonfiction writers, including John Hersey, J. D. Salinger, John Cheever, and many more.

The *Virginia Quarterly Review.* This journal, issued at the University of Virginia, features liberal opinions on cultural, social, and economic affairs and would include contributions by Allen Tate, Robert Frost, Thomas Wolfe, and T. S. Eliot.

1926
Drama and Theater

PHILIP BARRY: *White Wings.* Barry leaves his familiar drawing room for this offbeat fantasy about a street cleaner dependent on horse traffic. Archie Inch resists the coming of the automobile, and an actor plays a horse that must be killed before Archie will take a job as a taxi driver. An opera by Douglas Moore (1893–1969) based on the play would appear in 1935.

JOHN B. COLTON: *The Shanghai Gesture.* Colton's sensational melodrama set in a Shanghai brothel is dismissed by critic George Jean Nathan as "box-office drivel," but it proves to be one of the season's biggest hits.

JOHN DOS PASSOS: *The Garbage Man: A Parade with Shouting.* Produced in 1925 as *The Moon Is a Gong*, this experimental play attacks social oppression. It is chiefly significant for previewing the dramatic montage effects Dos Passos would incorporate in his fiction.

PHILIP DUNNING (1891–1968) AND GEORGE ABBOTT: *Broadway.* This crime drama is noteworthy for its treatment of the New York underworld, using contemporary street slang and a hard-boiled, realistic atmosphere. Dunning was an actor and stage manager whose first versions of the play Abbott reworked.

T. S. ELIOT: *Sweeney Agonistes: Fragments of an Aristophanic Melodrama.* Eliot's initial excursion into drama is this first of two fragments featuring his representative figure, Sweeney. "Part One: Fragment of a Prologue" borrows from Fitzgerald's *The Great Gatsby*, which Eliot greatly admired, for its scenes of London postwar party life. The second part, "Fragment of an Agon," with Sweeney as a choral figure commenting on the barren modern landscape, would appear in 1927. The two parts would be combined in 1932 and first performed at Vassar College in 1933.

PAUL GREEN (1894–1981): *In Abraham's Bosom.* The North Carolina playwright wins the Pulitzer Prize for this stirring drama of a Southern black man thwarted in his desire to help his race by opening a school. His next play, *The Field God* (1927), is a domestic tragedy involving a poor farm family.

SIDNEY HOWARD: *Ned McCobb's Daughter* and *The Silver Cord.* Both of Howard's 1926 offerings portray strong women. The first depicts the efforts of a woman to hold together her worthless family; the second concerns a possessive mother determined to wreck her son's engagement.

GEORGE KELLY: *Daisy Mayme.* Kelly's comedy about the romance between a set-in-his-ways middle-aged bachelor and an unfashionable spinster is noteworthy for its trenchant portrait of American snobbery and family dynamics.

ANITA LOOS AND JOHN EMERSON (1874–1956): *Gentlemen Prefer Blondes.* Gold-digger Lorelei Lee from Little Rock makes her stage debut in the author's adaptation (with her husband) of her popular 1925 novel. Loos would also adapt her play as a musical in 1949.

EUGENE O'NEILL: *The Great God Brown.* The playwright continues his expressionistic method, using masks to suggest characters' multiple personalities in a drama of a businessman's self-destruction. With its implied theme of the defeat of the artist in an unsympathetic, materialistic society, O'Neill would regard the play as his favorite among his work.

WILLIS RICHARDSON (1889–1977): *Chip Woman's Fortune.* Richardson's one-act play about charity among the poor in a Southern community becomes the first non-musical play by a black author to be performed on Broadway. Richardson was born in North Carolina and wrote plays for children and adults. He is regarded by critic Bernard L. Peterson Jr., as the "first to make a significant contribution to both the quantity and quality of serious Black American drama."

EDWARD SHELDON AND CHARLES MacARTHUR (1895–1956): *Lulu Belle.* Despite protests from black groups about its sensational treatment of black life, this melodrama about a black prostitute (played by a white actress in blackface) is one of the era's biggest theatrical successes.

MAE WEST (1892–1980): *Sex.* The actress writes, stars in, and is jailed for her earthy portrayal of a prostitute. Her next play, *The Drag* (1927), is the first American drama to depict a homosexual party and would be banned in New York. Her final play of the decade, *Diamond Lil* (1928), is set in a Bowery saloon that also operates a white slave ring and features West's most famous line: "Come up and see me sometime."

Fiction

SAMUEL HOPKINS ADAMS: *Revelry.* Adams's novel about the abuses and scandals of the Harding administration creates its own scandal by alleging that Harding was too small for the job and took his own life.

LOUIS BROMFIELD: *Early Autumn.* The second volume of Bromfield's tetralogy, Escape, dramatizing individuals' struggle from the constrictions imposed by family and tradition, wins the Pulitzer Prize.

WILLA CATHER: *My Mortal Enemy.* In what is perhaps Cather's bitterest novel, Myra Driscoll, an old woman who previously eloped, looks back on her life and regrets ever having married for love.

WILLIAM FAULKNER: *Soldiers' Pay.* Faulkner's first novel, about a disfigured American flyer's painful homecoming to Georgia, is published with the assistance of Sherwood Anderson, who supposedly agreed to recommend it to his publisher under the condition that he would not have to read the book.

EDNA FERBER: *Show Boat.* Ferber's novel centers on Magnolia Hawkes, the daughter of a Mississippi River showboat captain. She marries an irresponsible gambler who takes her away from her life on the river and then deserts her. The story continues with the career of their daughter. The novel features an exploration of miscegenation that was daring for its time and would inspire the popular 1927 musical by Hammerstein and Kern.

F. SCOTT FITZGERALD: *All the Sad Young Men.* Fitzgerald's third collection includes three of his most admired stories, "Winter Dreams," "Absolution," and "The Rich Boy."

ESTHER FORBES (1891–1967): *O Genteel Lady!* This novel, the first in a series of Forbes's well-researched,

Ernest Hemingway

popular historical novels, depicts an independent woman contending with constricting nineteenth-century mores in Boston. It would be followed by *A Mirror for Witches* (1928), *Paradise* (1937), *The General's Lady* (1938), *Johnny Tremain* (1943), *The Running of the Tide* (1948), and *Rainbow on the Road* (1959).

ELLEN GLASGOW: *The Romantic Comedians*. Glasgow's satirical novel of manners concerns a widowed judge who marries an ambitious and unfaithful younger woman.

ERNEST HEMINGWAY: *The Torrents of Spring*. Hemingway's first novel is a labored burlesque of the Chicago school of writers and its leading figure, Sherwood Anderson. Hemingway's second novel, *The Sun Also Rises*, also is published in 1926. It describes the postwar angst and malaise of a group of expatriates who love and quarrel in Paris and Pamplona, Spain, during the annual running of the bulls. Regarded as a prose echoing of T. S. Eliot's *The Waste Land*, the novel helps define the postwar generation and its values and is perhaps Hemingway's greatest accomplishment as a novelist.

RING LARDNER: *The Love Nest and Other Stories*. Some of Lardner's greatest stories, including the title work, "A Day with Conrad Green," and what many consider his finest, "Haircut," are collected here. Evident is a shift away from his usual sports subjects to a darker, more satiric exposure of the hypocrisies of the respectable.

SINCLAIR LEWIS: *Mantrap*. Lewis in "a holiday mood" is the critical consensus concerning this minor novel about a New York lawyer in the Canadian wilderness who is befriended by a backwoodsman and attracted to his flirtatious wife.

LUDWIG LEWISOHN: *The Case of Mr. Crump*. Considered Lewisohn's finest novel, this is a realistic depiction of a failed marriage in which an implacable wife refuses to divorce her husband.

PERCY MARKS (1891–1956): *The Plastic Age*. Marks's realistic treatment of undergraduate life at Stanford, with depictions of gin and petting parties, becomes a controversial bestseller, with some praising its frankness and others decrying its sensationalism. His subsequent novels — *Martha* (1925), *Lord of Himself* (1927, a sequel to *The Plastic Age*), *The Unwilling God* (1929), and several others — would never duplicate the success of his first.

ELIZABETH MADOX ROBERTS (1881–1941): *The Time of Man*. Roberts's first novel introduces her characteristic subject of rural life in her native Kentucky. The story concerns the struggles of a down-and-out sharecropper family that must contend with a charge of barn burning. Roberts had previously published the poetry collections *In the Great Steep's Garden* (1915) and *Under the Tree* (1922).

THORNE SMITH: *Topper*. Smith's most celebrated work is this comic fantasy about two ghosts who complicate the life of the inhibited banker Cosmo Topper.

RUTH SUCKOW: *Iowa Interiors*. As its title indicates, this story collection offers intimate glimpses of Iowa life among small farmers and small-town inhabitants.

S. S. VAN DINE (WILLIAM HUNTINGTON WRIGHT, 1888–1939): *The Benson Murder Case*. The novel marks the debut of Dine's master sleuth, Philo Vance. An immediate popular success, it launches a successful series of crime novels featuring the dilettantish detective; these include *The "Canary" Murder Case* (1927), which would set a sales record for crime fiction up to that time. Wright was an influential art and drama critic during the 1920s.

CARL VAN VECHTEN: *Nigger Heaven*. The writer's sympathetic depiction of African American society and culture in Harlem is one of the first fictional depictions of the area and its inhabitants during the Jazz Age. The title refers to the term for the topmost seats in a theater, a metaphor for uptown Harlem in relationship to the white downtown world.

ERIC WALROND (1898–1966): *Tropic Death*. Walrond's acclaimed story collection deals with life among migratory blacks in Barbados, Panama, and British Guiana in an imagistic style that establishes him as one of the leading experimentalists of the Harlem Renaissance. Walrond was born in British Guiana and immigrated to the United States in 1918. He is regarded as one of the most significant young writers associated with the Harlem Renaissance.

EDITH WHARTON: *Here and Beyond*. Wharton's story collection includes social dramas and character studies set in Brittany, New England, and Morocco as well as ghost stories. It has been judged by Wharton biographer R.W.B. Lewis as the weakest of her story collections.

WALTER WHITE: *Flight*. White's second novel depicts a middle-class African American community in Atlanta and the theme of "passing" for white.

THORNTON WILDER (1897–1975): *The Cabala*. Wilder's first book is an ironic and urbane treatment of a group of Italian aristocrats in the aftermath of the Great War.

ELINOR WYLIE: *The Orphan Angel*. Wylie's inventive novel imagines an alternative to Shelley's death by drowning. The poet is rescued at sea by a Yankee ship and brought to America to reflect on the American scene.

Literary Criticism and Scholarship

HERVEY ALLEN (1889–1949): *Israfel: The Life and Times of Edgar Allan Poe*. Allen's only scholarly work is a popular biography of Poe, which has been both praised for its vividness and criticized for accepting speculation about Poe's life as fact and repeating unsubstantiated gossip about the writer's excesses to bolster the book's psychological theories. After serving in World War I, Allen had taught English in Charleston, South Carolina, and wrote with DuBose Heyward the poetry collection *Carolina Chansons* (1922).

FLOYD DELL: *Intellectual Vagabondage: An Apology for the Intelligentsia*. Dell's major literary criticism is collected in this volume, which takes aim at the waffling of his generation of intellectuals and the weakness of modern literature. In Dell's view, literature fails "to tell the whole truth about our generation" and should be directed to "the relief of the world-wide misery produced by capitalism."

LEWIS MUMFORD: *The Golden Day: A Study in American Experience and Culture*. Mumford's analysis of American cultural history and literature from 1830 to 1860 is one of his best and most influential books. It would help in forming the discipline of American studies during the 1940s. F. O. Matthiessen, whose groundbreaking *American Renaissance* (1941) would echo many of Mumford's

ideas, called the volume a "major event in my experience."

GERTRUDE STEIN: *Composition as Explanation*. Stein explains her literary practices in this series of lectures delivered to Oxford and Cambridge undergraduates. She would further elaborate on her ideas in *How to Write* (1931), *Narration*, and *Lectures in America* (both 1935).

Nonfiction

PAUL DE KRUIF (1890–1971): *Microbe Hunters*. The first of the author's best-selling popular accounts of medical science celebrates the pioneers of bacteriology. It would be followed by *Hunger Fighters* (1928), *Seven Iron Men* (1929), *Men Against Death* (1932), and *The Fight for Life* (1938).

WILL DURANT (1885–1981): *The Story of Philosophy*. Durant had begun his best-selling writing career when asked to adapt his lectures on classical philosophers for the Little Blue Book pamphlet series, developed by E. Haldeman-Julius (1889–1951). The separate booklets are collected in this edition and become the first great success for the fledgling publisher Simon & Schuster. Durant would go on to write the ten-volume series *The Story of Civilization* (1935–1967).

H. L. MENCKEN: *Notes on Democracy*. Mencken mounts a full frontal assault on democracy. In his view, rule by the common man results in a debased form of government that caters to mediocrity.

CARL SANDBURG: *Abraham Lincoln: The Prairie Years*. The initial two volumes of the eventual six in Sandburg's monumental biography cover the first fifty-one years of Lincoln's life, before his presidency. They are written as a kind of prose poem, drawing both praise and censure for their impressionistic method.

MARK SULLIVAN (1874–1952): *Our Times: The United States, 1900–1925*. The first installments of a popular social history of the first quarter of the century appears, eventually growing to six volumes by 1935. Sullivan, a journalist and syndicated columnist, attempts to portray history as it affects the average man, detailing economic conditions, fashions, and amusements. The book remains an important documentary source on life of the period.

Poetry

HART CRANE (1890–1932): *White Buildings*. Crane's first collection contains "My Grandmother's Love Letters" and "Garden Abstract," dealing with his family background and his sexuality, as well as "Praises for an Urn," an elegy asserting the inviolability of art, and "For the

Langston Hughes

Marriage of Faustus and Helen," which Crane considers "an answer to the cultural pessimism" of T. S. Eliot.

E. E. CUMMINGS: *is 5.* The title is the answer to the calculation two-plus-two, indicative of the transformative power of the poet's verse. Included are highly regarded poems such as "nobody loses all the time," "ponder, darling, these busted statues," the antiwar poem "my sweet old etcetera," and the elegy of a conscientious objector, "i sing of Olaf glad and big."

LANGSTON HUGHES (1902–1967): *The Weary Blues.* Hughes's first collection shows his distinctive focus on black experience, musically derived rhythms, and a rich use of vernacular language, qualities that will establish him as the leading poet of the Harlem Renaissance and one of the greatest American poets of the twentieth century. Ironically, the volume and his second collection, *Fine Clothes to the Jews* (1927), would be attacked by black reviewers for what they considered his primitive, dialect style and emphasis on the unflattering aspects of African American life.

ARCHIBALD MACLEISH: *Streets of the Earth.* The volume includes the important long poem "Einstein," a meditation on the physicist's struggle to comprehend the universe, as well as some of MacLeish's enduring short poems, such as "Memorial Rain," "The Silently Slain," and "The Farm."

EDGAR LEE MASTERS: *Lee: A Dramatic Poem.* The poet celebrates Robert E. Lee's life and character in a series of vignettes forming a solemn elegy.

DOROTHY PARKER: *Enough Rope.* Parker's first book of poetry displays her characteristic epigrammatic, sardonic style and includes two of her most-quoted passages: "Men seldom make passes / At girls who wear glasses" ("News Item") and "Guns aren't lawful; / Nooses give; / Gas smells awful; / You might as well live" ("Résumé"). A second volume, *Sunset Gun*, would follow in 1928.

SARA TEASDALE: *Dark of the Moon.* One of the poet's strongest volumes features meditations on age and death, which display a mature mastery of theme and technique.

Publications and Events

Amazing Stories. The first magazine devoted to science fiction is founded by Hugo Gernsback (1884–1967), who popularized the genre and coined the term *science fiction.* The annual Hugo Awards, honoring achievement in the genre, were named in his honor in 1953.

Black Mask. Joseph T. Shaw (1874–1952) assumes the editorship of this "Illustrated Magazine of Detective, Mystery, Adventure, Romance, and Spiritualism," founded in 1920 by H. L. Mencken and George Jean Nathan to support the unprofitable magazine *Smart Set.* Shaw emphasized crime and mystery, publishing the first stories of Dashiell Hammett, Raymond Chandler, Erle Stanley Gardner, and others, and helping establish the genre of the "hard-boiled" detective story. It would continue to be published until 1953, when it was absorbed by the *Ellery Queen Mystery Magazine.*

The Book-of-the-Month Club. This book club begins operation with 4,750 initial subscribers, who agree to receive a book each month selected by a panel of experts as the best currently on offer. By 1946, membership had reached one million, with more than seventy million volumes distributed since 1926. In 1927, the club's major rival, the Literary Guild, would begin operation.

1927
Drama and Theater

MAXWELL ANDERSON: *Saturday's Children.* As the saying goes, Saturday's child must work hard for a living, the theme of Anderson's comedy displaying the sober realities of married life.

PHILIP BARRY: *Paris Bound.* After an earlier 1927 failure, *John*, a biblical drama about John the Baptist, Barry

Philip Barry

returns to more familiar territory in this successful comedy of manners about upper-crust infidelities.

S. N. BEHRMAN (1893–1973): *The Second Man.* The first solo effort and initial success of the playwright, who would be called the "American Congreve" for his witty comedies of manners, concerns a novelist whose marriage plans go awry when a former lover reveals her pregnancy.

E. E. CUMMINGS: *him.* Cummings warns the audience in the program for the Provincetown Playhouse production of his experimental drama, "Don't try to understand it." Most could only comply in a play whose main characters are named Me and Him, women in rocking chairs knit, and an actor playing Mussolini tells a group of adoring homosexuals that he will destroy communism. The play, which manages twenty-seven performances, anticipates the theater of the absurd.

HERBERT FIELDS (1897–1958): *A Connecticut Yankee.* This musical version of Mark Twain's novel features a score by Lorenz Hart and Richard Rodgers. Herbert Fields was the son of comic performer Lew Fields (1867–1941). His other works include *Peggy-Ann* (1926), *Fifty Million Frenchmen* (1929), *DuBarry Was a Lady* (1939), and *Panama Hattie* (1940).

IRA GERSHWIN AND GEORGE GERSHWIN: *Funny Face.* This popular Gershwin brothers' musical features the debut of Fred Astaire dancing on Broadway in top hat and tails.

OSCAR HAMMERSTEIN II AND JEROME KERN: *Show Boat.* One of the greatest and most influential achievements of the American musical is based on Edna Ferber's 1926 novel. Critics consider the play the first true musical play, combining attributes of the operetta and the musical comedy.

OTTO HARBACH, OSCAR HAMMERSTEIN II, AND FRANK MANDEL: *The Desert Song.* No doubt capitalizing on the rage over Rudolph Valentino's performance in *The Sheik*, this operetta set in the Moroccan desert, with music by Sigmund Romberg, is one of the biggest hits of the decade.

DuBOSE HEYWARD (1885–1940) AND DOROTHY HEYWARD (1890–1961): *Porgy.* DuBose Heyward collaborates with his wife on this dramatic adaptation of his 1925 novel about African American life in Charleston's Catfish Row tenement district. This play would be the source for George Gershwin's landmark folk opera, *Porgy and Bess* (1935). DuBose Heyward, a poet, novelist, and playwright, had worked on the docks of his native Charleston. Dorothy Heyward's other plays include *Nancy Ann* (1924), *Love in a Cupboard* (1926), and *Set My People Free* (1948).

GEORGE S. KAUFMAN AND EDNA FERBER: *The Royal Family.* This popular comedy about America's first family of the theater, the Cavendishes, bears such a resemblance to the Barrymores that Ethel Barrymore threatens a lawsuit and would never forgive the playwrights. Years later she turned down Kaufman's request to appear at a benefit, using a line from the play: "But I'm going to have laryngitis that night."

GEORGE KELLY: *Behold the Bridegroom.* Opening on the busiest night in Broadway history (December 27) with ten other plays, Kelly's drama about a disillusioned society woman is considered the playwright's closest approximation of a tragedy.

EDNA ST. VINCENT MILLAY: *The King's Henchman.* Millay's libretto to an opera by Deems Taylor (1885–1966) is set in Saxon England and tells the story of a young knight who falls in love with the woman he is charged with delivering to the king as his bride. Successfully produced in 1927, the published opera would go through eighteen printings in ten months, solidifying Millay's reputation as one of the most successful writers of her era.

EUGENE O'NEILL: *Lazarus Laughed.* O'Neill's "A Play for the Imaginative Theater" is a long philosophical meditation that requires hundreds of actors, forming a masked chorus. Although the work is published, no Broadway producer is willing to take it on. The Pasadena Community Playhouse would stage the only major production in 1928.

ROBERT E. SHERWOOD (1896–1955): *The Road to Rome.* Sherwood's first play is an antiwar drama set during the Punic Wars. The wife of Rome's leader seduces the invader Hannibal and convinces him to withdraw his armies. Sherwood's other 1927 play is a comedy based on Ring Lardner's *The Love Nest.* Sherwood had served on the Western Front and was gassed and wounded in both legs, experiences that shaped his opposition to future wars.

Fiction

CONRAD AIKEN: *Blue Voyage.* Aiken's first novel is a stream-of-consciousness account of a dramatist's voyage to England, presented as a psychological quest for self-knowledge. A short story collection, *Costumes by Eros,* on the vagaries of love, would follow in 1928.

WILLA CATHER: *Death Comes for the Archbishop.* Many regard this novel, based on the life and achievement of Archbishop Lamy of Sante Fe, New Mexico, the author's masterpiece. It is the first of three historical novels she would produce, an episodic novel without a conventional plot but relying on a series of highly visual scenes that the author likened to frescoes.

THEODORE DREISER: *Chains.* With the subtitle "Lesser Novels and Stories by Theodore Dreiser," the collection is regarded as scraps from the writer's workshop, of interest chiefly in providing brief glimpses of Dreiser's social and psychological preoccupations.

WILLIAM FAULKNER: *Mosquitoes.* Faulkner's second novel assembles a mixed group of characters on the yacht of a New Orleans matron for conversations on literature and sex. Daring for its time in its references to masturbation, lesbianism, and syphilis, the book, according to critic Cleanth Brooks, "is Faulkner's least respected novel, and it is easy to see why . . . there is almost no story here; nothing of real consequence happens to any of its characters." The book retains a biographical relevance in expressing Faulkner's view of the New Orleans literary scene.

ERNEST HEMINGWAY: *Men Without Women.* Hemingway's second short story collection contains some of his best work, including "The Undefeated," "The Killers," and what is perhaps the central example of the author's "iceberg principle" of omission, "Hills Like White Elephants," in which a couple "discusses" an abortion and their failed marriage without ever bringing up the subjects.

LOIS LENSKI (1893–1974): *Skipping Village.* The first of the author-illustrator's more than ninety children's books that feature realistic depictions of American farm life and history. She would win Newbery Medals for *Phebe Fairchild* (1936), *Indian Captive* (1941) — her most popular book — and *Strawberry Girl* (1946).

SINCLAIR LEWIS: *Elmer Gantry.* Lewis's satire on American religious fundamentalism provokes an uproar. Gantry is a religious charlatan who trades on his good looks and promotional skills to become a popular evangelist and a leader of a large Midwestern church. The novel is denounced by clergymen of all faiths, and its creator is threatened with violence by those who considers him an agent of the devil.

MOURNING DOVE (HUM-ISHU-MA, 1885–1936): *Cogewea the Half-Blood.* One of the first novels by a Native American woman, the book explores the challenges faced by a mixed-race woman on the Flathead Reservation of Montana at the turn of the century as she tries to live in both the white and the Indian worlds. Mourning Dove was born Christal Quintasket in Idaho, with an Irish father and a mother who was a member of the Colville Confederated Tribes of the Pacific Northwest. Her other major work is *Coyote Stories* (1933).

JULIA PETERKIN (1880–1961): *Black April.* Peterkin's first novel concerns the rivalry between a black foreman of a South Carolina cotton plantation and his illegitimate son. The novel's authenticity derives from the author's firsthand experience as the mistress of a plantation that employed nearly 450 black workers.

ELIZABETH MADOX ROBERTS: *My Heart and My Flesh.* Roberts's second novel is a psychological study of a white Kentucky woman driven to the edge of madness by poverty and revelations about her father's affair with a black woman.

O. E. RÖLVAAG (1876–1931): *Giants in the Earth.* The first and best of the author's epic trilogy of Norwegian immigrants on the American frontier of the Dakotas would be followed by *Peder Victorious* (1929) and *Their Fathers' God* (1931). It would be adapted as an opera by Douglas Moore (1893–1969) in 1951.

UPTON SINCLAIR: *Oil!* Regarded by many as the writer's best novel, this is the story of independent oil operators struggling against monopoly interests. The book reflects the Teapot Dome scandal and the public figures involved in the oil scandals of the Harding administration.

EDWARD STRATEMEYER: *The Tower Treasure.* Under the pseudonym "Franklin W. Dixon," Stratemeyer, "the king of the juveniles," and his syndicate launch a new juvenile detective series featuring teenage sleuths Frank and Joe Hardy, the Hardy Boys. It becomes one of the most popular series in children's fiction.

BOOTH TARKINGTON: *The Plutocrat.* Tarkington's novel depicts a self-made American businessman who travels in Europe. It would be adapted for film as *Business and Pleasure* in 1931.

GLENWAY WESCOTT: *The Grandmothers.* The writer's best-known work is this multigenerational portrait of a rural Wisconsin family. Organized as a meditation on a series of family pictures, the work combines both a probing of the author's own family background and a generalized summary of American themes. Clifton Fadiman suggests that the book "is possibly the first artistically satisfying rendition of the soul of an American pioneer community and its descendants." A collection of similarly autobiographical stories, *Good-bye, Wisconsin,* would appear in 1928.

EDITH WHARTON: *Twilight Sleep.* Wharton critiques contemporary New York society in a blistering account that shows the idle rich anesthetized by self-centeredness and aimless distractions.

THORNTON WILDER: *The Bridge of San Luis Rey.* Wilder's first major success is a Pulitzer Prize–winning novel about the working of fate that leads to the death of five people in a bridge collapse in Peru in 1714. The book sells more than 300,000 copies in its first two years, allowing Wilder to devote himself to writing full-time.

Literary Criticism and Scholarship

COUNTEE CULLEN: *Caroling Dusk: An Anthology of Verse by Negro People.* In his foreword to this important anthology, Cullen expresses his contention that "Negro poets . . . may have more to gain from the rich background of English and American poetry than from any nebulous atavistic yearnings toward an African inheritance."

VERNON PARRINGTON (1871–1929): *Main Currents in American Thought.* Parrington's highly influential two-volume study of American ideas expressed through its literature wins the Pulitzer Prize. A third uncompleted volume would appear posthumously in 1930. In 1927 Parrington would also publish a critical study, *Sinclair Lewis, Our Own Diogenes.* The literary historian was raised in Kansas and taught at the College of Emporia, the University of Oklahoma, and the University of Washington.

CONSTANCE ROURKE (1885–1941): *Trumpets of Jubilee.* In a pioneering work of American Studies, the Cleveland-born teacher, biographer, historian, and critic examines the careers of five Americans who made a significant impact on American popular culture in the nineteenth century — Henry Ward Beecher, Lyman Beecher, Harriet Beecher Stowe, Horace Greeley, and P. T. Barnum. The emphasis on popular culture and the book's interdisciplinary approach, combining history, biography, and literary criticism, anticipate later approaches to studying American ideas and values.

CARL SANDBURG: *The American Songbag.* This compilation of ballads and folk songs makes an important contribution to preserving American folklore.

Nonfiction

RAY S. BAKER (1870–1942): *Woodrow Wilson: Life and Letters.* Wilson's former press secretary publishes the first two volumes of his massive eight-volume documentary biography (completed in 1939). The final two volumes would win the Pulitzer Prize.

CHARLES A. BEARD AND MARY R. BEARD (1876–1958): *The Rise of American Civilization.* This two-volume study, intended for a general audience, is a social and economic analysis of American values and institutions. Sequels, *America in Mid-Passage* (1939) and *The American Spirit* (1943) would follow.

JOHN DOS PASSOS: *Orient Express.* Dos Passos's travel diary of his trip on the Orient Express shows a widening perspective and a growing international social awareness.

RING LARDNER: *The Story of a Wonder Man.* In this witty mock-autobiography, the humorist takes aim at a wide range of subjects.

WILLIAM ELLERY LEONARD: *The Locomotive-God.* The poet's autobiography is a psychoanalytical self-examination that identifies the various phobias of a highly sensitive writer.

CHARLES A. LINDBERGH (1902–1974): *We.* Having completed on May 20–21 the first nonstop airplane flight from New York to Paris, the celebrated aviator provides his own hastily written, factual account of his early flying career and his achievement. Twenty-five years later, Lindbergh would write a far superior version, the Pulitzer Prize–winning *The Spirit of St. Louis* (1953).

Poetry

COUNTEE CULLEN: *Copper Sun.* Cullen's second verse collection contains only two poems on racial themes, "From the Dark Tower" and "Threnody for a Brown

Girl." The work fails to generate the enthusiasm that had greeted *Color* (1925). He also publishes *The Ballad of the Brown Girl*, a rewriting of a traditional black folk ballad in traditional English ballad form.

T. S. ELIOT: "Journey of the Magi." Published in the same year as the poet's Anglican conversion and naturalization as a British citizen, the monologue is the first in a series of poems dealing with spiritual growth that would include "A Song for Simeon" (1928), "Animula" (1929), "Merina" (1930), and "Triumphal March" (1931).

LANGSTON HUGHES: *Fine Clothes to the Jew*. Hughes's second collection presents a realistic depiction of Harlem life and the problems faced by African Americans. It includes some of his most accomplished blues poems, including "Homesick Blues," "Listen Here Blues," and "Young Gal's Blues."

ROBINSON JEFFERS: *The Women at Point Sur*. This narrative poem about a preacher who denounces his faith and sets out to create a new religion provides one of the fullest articulations of the poet's concept of "inhumanism." Jeffers intends the poem to be the "*Faust* of its age," but critics and readers generally find it baffling.

JAMES WELDON JOHNSON: *God's Trombones: Seven Negro Sermons in Verse*. Based on his work as editor of the important song collections *The Book of American Negro Spirituals* (1925) and *The Second Book of Negro Spirituals* (1926), Johnson converts rural black folk sermons, remembered from his childhood, into verse. Many consider it to be his greatest poetic achievement.

DON MARQUIS: *archy and mehitabel*. The popular columnist's humorous verse observations of the contemporary scene are delivered from the perspective of a literary cockroach (who types in lowercase letters because it is unable to work the shift key on a typewriter) and a gadfly cat. Several popular sequels would follow, collected in *The Lives and Times of archy and mehitabel* (1940).

JOHN CROWE RANSOM: *Two Gentlemen in Bonds*. Ransom's fourth verse collection displays his characteristic classically derived, erudite, and sardonic style, in subsequently anthologized works such as "Blue Girls," "Somewhere Is Such a Kingdom," "The Equilibrists," and "Dead Boy."

EDWIN ARLINGTON ROBINSON: *Tristram*. The poet achieves his only major public success with the final volume of his Arthurian trilogy, preceded by *Merlin* (1917) and *Lancelot* (1920). The book-length poetic narrative of the doomed love of Tristram and Isolt wins Robinson his third Pulitzer Prize.

Publications and Events

American Caravan. The initial installment of this annual appears, founded by Paul Rosenfeld (1890–1946), Alfred Kreymborg (1883–1966), Lewis Mumford (1895–1990), and Van Wyck Brooks (1886–1946) to celebrate contemporary American writing. Continuing until 1936, its contributors included Ernest Hemingway, John Dos Passos, Eugene O'Neill, and Gertrude Stein.

Hound and Horn. This little magazine devoted to avant-garde work begins publication. Continuing until 1934, the magazine provided a forum for writers such as Ezra Pound, T. S. Eliot, Gertrude Stein, and many others.

The *Prairie Schooner*. This literary quarterly associated with the University of Nebraska begins publication. Originally featuring a regional emphasis, the magazine later widened its focus, particularly when poet Karl Shapiro took over as editor in 1956.

transition. Founded in Paris by Eugene Jolas (1894–1952) and Elliot Paul (1891–1958), this literary magazine, devoted to experimental works, begins publication. It would continue with interruptions until 1938, providing an important forum for European modernist masters such as James Joyce and Americans such as Gertrude Stein, Ernest Hemingway, Hart Crane, and William Carlos Williams.

1928
Drama and Theater

PHILIP BARRY: *Holiday*. Barry's drama about a young lawyer who decides to abandon his career for a carefree life of pleasure is seen both as a defense of the hedonism of the 1920s and a satire on the idle rich.

J. F. DAVIS (1870–1941): *The Ladder*. Davis's melodrama dealing with reincarnation is panned by critics, but it manages 794 performances, becoming the fourth-longest-running play in Broadway history. This is because millionaire oil man Edgar B. Davis, who believed in reincarnation, had underwritten the play and distributed free tickets. *The Ladder* was the only one of the plays by the journalist from New Bedford, Massachusetts, to reach Broadway.

JOHN DOS PASSOS: *Airways, Inc.* This play, produced in 1929, concerns the tragedy that besets the family of a famous aviator.

BEN HECHT AND CHARLES MACARTHUR: *The Front Page*. The writing team's first collaboration is an American comedy classic, set in the pressroom of the Chicago Criminal Court Building on the eve of an anarchist's execution.

Hecht had drawn on his own newspaper experience to create his portrait of the unscrupulous editor Walter Burns and the intrepid reporter Hildy Johnson.

EUGENE O'NEILL: *Marco Millions.* The first of O'Neill's two 1928 Broadway productions is a dramatic fable attacking materialism, as Marco Polo is shown forgoing love for his commercial ventures. As the play ends, Polo joins the audience as a contemporary businessman exiting to his waiting limousine. Also staged is *Strange Interlude,* a four-hour, nine-act, Freudian-influenced psychodrama, which features extended interior soliloquies contrasting what characters say with what they are thinking. The play, according to critic Joseph Wood Krutch, "brought to the stage certain subtleties which only the novel hitherto seemed capable of suggesting." The season's theatrical sensation, it wins the Pulitzer Prize but is banned in several cities because of its frank sexual content.

SIGMUND ROMBERG: *The New Moon.* Romberg's operetta, set in eighteenth-century New Orleans, is the last of his successes and marks the end of the popularity of operettas on Broadway.

SOPHIE TREADWELL (1890–1970): *Machinal.* In what has been described as "one of the most unusual plays of the 20s," the routinized and dehumanized life of a young woman is depicted in a series of expressionistic scenes and staccato dialogue. The California-born actress's only success, the play features the actor Hal K. Dawson, who would become better known in Hollywood as Clark Gable.

THORNTON WILDER: *The Angel That Troubled the Waters and Other Plays.* Having seen his first play, *The Trumpet Shall Sound,* an allegory on God's forgiveness, produced in 1926, Wilder publishes this collection of short dramatic pieces, mostly with religious themes.

Fiction

DJUNA BARNES: *Ryder.* Barnes's first novel, expurgated in the American edition, is a boldly experimental stream-of-consciousness portrait of a man's disastrous relationships with his wife, mother, and mistress. The novel introduces Barnes's characteristic mixing of moods and styles and helps establish her as an important avant-garde artist.

ROARK BRADFORD (1896–1946): *Ol' Man Adam an' His Chillun.* The Tennessee-born newspaperman's collection of Old and New Testament stories reinterpreted in the context of Southern black life and folklore would be adapted by Marc Connelly in *The Green Pastures* (1930). A sequel, *Ol' King David an' the Philistine Boys,* would

appear in 1930, followed in 1931 by a collection, *John Henry,* about the legendary black hero.

JAMES GOULD COZZENS: *Cock Pit.* Cozzens's third novel, set at a Cuban sugar mill operated by Americans, is an advance over his previous work in its ability to objectify characters and reveal an occupation with convincing familiarity.

VINA DELMAR (1905–1990): *Bad Girl.* This first novel, and Delmar's other books of the decade — *Kept Woman* (1929) and *Loose Ladies* (1929) — are bestsellers, scandalous in their frank depiction of sexual mores of women during the Jazz Age.

W.E.B. DU BOIS: *The Dark Princess: A Romance.* Du Bois's novel concerns the love affair between an African American and an Indian princess and the effort by people of color to resist white domination.

RUDOLPH FISHER (1897–1934): *The Walls of Jericho.* Written on a bet to see if he could blend all of Harlem life into a single story, Fisher's first novel is praised for offering a more balanced view of the black community than previous efforts by Carl Van Vechten in *Nigger Heaven* (1926) and Claude McKay in *Home to Harlem* (1928). Fisher was born in Washington, D.C., and graduated from Brown University and Howard University with a medical degree. His second and last novel, *The Conjure-Man Dies* (1932), is the first American mystery novel entirely populated by black characters.

JOSEPHINE HERBST (1897–1969): *Nothing Is Sacred.* The Iowa writer's first novel is a radically realistic view of the typical American family contending with debt, alcohol, and adultery. Herbst's interest in the collapse of traditional values is evident as well in her next novel, *Money for Love* (1929), about a woman's attempt to extort money from a former lover to arrange a marriage with her current suitor.

NELLA LARSEN (1891–1964): *Quicksand.* The first of the Harlem Renaissance writer's two novels is a character study of a mixed-race woman seeking self-expression and self-respect in the black community. It would be followed by *Passing* (1929), the tragic story of a light-skinned black woman who marries a white man. Both novels feature the most psychologically nuanced characterizations of black women attempted up to that time. In 1930 Larsen would become the first African American woman to receive a Guggenheim fellowship.

SINCLAIR LEWIS: *The Man Who Knew Coolidge.* Lewis continues his documentation of Babbittry in this extended ironic monologue by a businessman whose conventional opinions on many matters make Lewis's satirical points.

CLAUDE McKAY: *Home to Harlem.* McKay's initial novel about a black soldier who deserts, returns to Harlem, and tries to resume his relationship with a prostitute is the first best-selling novel by a black writer. It features realistic depictions of Harlem's cabarets, rent parties, and pool rooms, but is criticized by W.E.B. Du Bois for stressing the baser side of black life rather than its noble aspirations. McKay would follow it with *Banjo: A Story Without a Plot* (1929), about an international collection of black seamen stranded in Marseille.

JULIA PETERKIN: *Scarlet Sister Mary.* The novelist continues her accurate depiction of black Gullah life in her native South Carolina in this Pulitzer Prize–winning work, whose strong black heroine and rich, authentic portrait of black culture win both praise and condemnation in several Southern cities.

ELIZABETH MADOX ROBERTS: *Jingling in the Wind.* Roberts's reliance on folk customs and regional details is evident in this charming novel about a rainmaker.

UPTON SINCLAIR: *Boston.* Sinclair's indignant defense of Sacco and Vanzetti is dramatized through the fictional story of a Boston Brahmin who meets the anarchists and witnesses their arrest and trial.

RUTH SUCKOW: *The Bonney Family.* Suckow is praised for her restrained sympathy and authenticity in this story of a minister's family in a small Iowa town.

CARL VAN VECHTEN: *Spider Boy.* The writer takes on Hollywood in this satirical novel showing a playwright being co-opted and compromised by the movie business.

EDITH WHARTON: *The Children.* Wharton creates one of her most appealing woman characters, Judith Wheater, who tries to keep her family together as her parents contemplate divorce.

WILLIAM CARLOS WILLIAMS: *A Voyage to Pagany.* Williams's first novel is an autobiographical account of a small-town doctor's search for a better life in Europe, providing commentary on the European literary scene.

Literary Criticism and Scholarship

The Dictionary of American Biography. From 1928 to 1936, twenty volumes of biographical portraits of prominent Americans were published under the auspices of the American Council of Learned Societies, financed by the *New York Times.*

NORMAN FOERSTER (1887–1972): *American Criticism* and *The Reinterpretation of American Literature.* These two influential critical works by one of the leaders of the New Humanism help raise the standard for the interpretation of American writing and literary scholarship. Foerster was a professor of English at the University of

North Carolina from 1914 to 1930 and at the University of Iowa from 1930 to 1944.

PAUL ELMER MORE: *The Demon of the Absolute.* More's volume of literary criticism, applying the standards of the New Humanism, argues for the importance of tradition, classicism over Romanticism, and an ethical emphasis in the evaluation of literature.

LAURA RIDING (1901–1991): *Survey of Modernist Poetry.* Written with the British poet Robert Graves, this is an early critical assessment of the works of E. E. Cummings, T. S. Eliot, Marianne Moore, and others. Riding would go on to publish fiction, such as *A Trojan Ending* (1937) and *Lives of Wives* (1939), and her *Collected Poems* (1938).

Nonfiction

RICHARD E. BYRD (1888–1957): *Skyward.* The aviator and polar explorer describes his flying career, including his famous polar and transatlantic flights.

THEODORE DREISER: *Dreiser Looks at Russia.* The writer provides a sympathetic reaction to the Soviet experiment in this account of his tour of the country.

WALDO FRANK: *The Re-discovery of America.* Frank argues that developments in modernist art and modern science promise a restoration of premodern intuitive values in America. Lewis Mumford would call this cultural meditation "one of the most vigorous positive criticisms of our civilization that has been made."

MARGARET MEAD (1901–1978): *Coming of Age in Samoa.* Mead's groundbreaking anthropological study, based on her fieldwork on the Samoan island of T'au, becomes one of the most widely read scholarly works ever written. In it, Mead controversially argues that adolescence is less stressful for Samoan girls than American girls due to more relaxed parenting and sexual permissiveness.

DOROTHY THOMPSON (1894–1961): *The New Russia.* Thompson sparks a controversy and literary squabble when she charges Theodore Dreiser with plagiarizing her report on life in the Soviet Union, in *Dreiser Looks at Russia.* Thompson was a foreign correspondent in the 1920s, a columnist for the *New York Herald Tribune,* and host of a weekly radio news program. In 1928 she married writer Sinclair Lewis.

Poetry

STEPHEN VINCENT BENÉT: *John Brown's Body.* Awarded the Pulitzer Prize, Benét's epic traces the causes and effects of the Civil War from multiple fictional and historical perspectives. It centers on an account of Brown's raid on Harpers Ferry and his ensuing trial and execution. A dramatic version would be produced in 1953.

Margaret Mead

ROBERT FROST: *West-Running Brook.* Frost's fifth volume takes its theme from the title poem about an exceptional brook that flows west rather than east to the Atlantic, a symbol of contrariness, eccentric individualism, and resistance, which the poet admires. The volume includes two other important works in Frost's evolving canon, "Once by the Pacific" and "Tree at My Window."

ROBINSON JEFFERS: *Cawdor and Other Poems.* The title poem is a narrative adapting the story of Phaedra and Hippolytus in a modern setting. The volume also includes some of Jeffers's finest lyrics, such as "Soliloquy" and "The Bird with Dark Plumes."

ARCHIBALD MacLEISH: *The Hamlet of A. MacLeish.* The poet's most elaborate and complex work is a challenging reinterpretation of Hamlet as a reflection of the modern world and the poet's own uncertainties.

JOSEPH MONCURE MARCH (1899–1977): *The Wild Party.* In March's narrative poem, a party is thrown by lovers Queenie and Burns. Queenie's flirtation with a guest leads to his shooting death. The book is banned in Boston for its frank depictions of sex and violence. It would be reissued to acclaim in 1994, with illustrations by Art Spiegelman, who called it "a hardboiled Jazz Age tragedy told in syncopated rhyming couplets." March also publishes in 1928 *The Set-Up,* a similarly rhymed story of an African American prizefighter, which prompts one critic

to declare that March is "to poetry what Mr. Hemingway is to prose."

EDGAR LEE MASTERS: *Jack Kelso.* Masters offers an offbeat reflection of American history in the dramatic monologue of Abraham Lincoln's friend and companion during his days in New Salem, Illinois.

EDNA ST. VINCENT MILLAY: *The Buck in the Snow.* An increasingly bitter tone is evident in this collection of the poet's lyrics and sonnets written since 1924. It reflects Millay's increasing social concerns and her involvement in the Sacco and Vanzetti case.

CARL SANDBURG: *Good Morning, America.* Sandburg echoes Whitman in this lyrical, free-verse evocation of American life, filled with folk elements and a vernacular style that emphasizes the common sense of ordinary Americans.

1929
Drama and Theater

S. N. BEHRMAN: *Serena Blandish* and *Meteor.* The first of the playwright's two 1929 offerings is based on a novel by British author Enid Bagnold (1889–1981), about London high life; the second concerns a ruthless businessman.

RACHEL CROTHERS: *Let Us Be Gay.* One of Crothers's best comedies concerns a divorced woman trying to protect a young girl from the advances of her ex-husband.

EUGENE O'NEILL: *Dynamo.* O'Neill's play, exploring the conflict between science and religion in the machine age, fails. Consequently, the playwright drops his plan to make this the first in a trilogy and retires from the stage until 1931.

ELMER RICE: *Street Scene.* Rice's groundbreaking, realistic depiction of New York tenement life wins the Pulitzer Prize. An operatic version with music by Kurt Weill and lyrics by Langston Hughes would open in 1947. Two other plays by Rice — the expressionistic *The Subway* and *See Naples and Die,* concerning a romantic heiress — are staged unsuccessfully during the year.

EDWARD SHELDON AND MARGARET AYER BARNES (1886–1967): *Jenny.* The first of two collaborations by the playwrights concerns the comic misalliance between a self-righteous businessman and an actress. The other — the final play for both writers — is *Dishonored Lady* (1930), a melodrama in which the heroine poisons one lover to be with another. Barnes is best known for her novels, *Years of Grace* (1930), *Edna, His Wife* (1935), and *Wisdom's Gate* (1938), among others.

PRESTON STURGES (1898–1959): *Strictly Dishonorable.* The future Hollywood writer and director has his only

Broadway success in this witty comedy about a Southern belle abandoned by her escort in a New York speakeasy.

Fiction

ROARK BRADFORD: *This Side of Jordan.* Bradford collects sketches of black life in rural Louisiana.

W. R. BURNETT (1899–1982): *Little Caesar.* Burnett's first novel is an unprecedented insider's look at Chicago gangsters that establishes the author's reputation as a leading writer in the hard-boiled style. The novel would be made into a 1931 film starring Edward G. Robinson, whose memorable Rico helped define the stock character of the Hollywood gangster.

JAMES GOULD COZZENS: *The Son of Perdition.* Drawn from the author's experience in Cuba as the tutor for the children of American employees of a sugar company, the novel concerns an American administrator of the United Sugar Company caught between his business obligations and personal loyalty.

EDWARD DAHLBERG (1900–1977): *Bottom Dogs.* The novelist, poet, and essayist's first novel is based on his troubled childhood in an orphanage and his hobo days. D. H. Lawrence, who provides an introduction, praises it for its ability to penetrate the psychology of society's underclass. Dahlberg's use of vernacular language and realistic descriptions would help define the social realism of the 1930s.

THEODORE DREISER: *A Gallery of Women.* Dreiser offers a two-volume collection of fifteen fictionalized profiles of women who have positively affected his life or whose story he felt compelled to celebrate.

MIGNON G. EBERHART (1899–1996): *The Patient in Room 18.* The first of the writer's nearly seventy popular mysteries features Nurse Sarah Keate, one of the genre's first female sleuths. Born in Nebraska, Eberhart has been called "America's Agatha Christie," one of the most popular mystery writers of the twentieth century.

WALTER EDMONDS (1903–1998): *Rome Haul.* The first of the upstate New York author's meticulously researched and popular historical novels celebrates life along the Erie Canal in the 1850s. Edmonds would return to the setting in *Erie Water* (1933), *Chad Hanna* (1940), and *The Wedding Journey* (1947).

WILLIAM FAULKNER: *Sartoris.* Faulkner's third novel, an abridgment of the unpublished *The Flags in the Dust,* is his first work set in Yoknapatawpha County, the imagined equivalent of the author's native northern Mississippi. It traces Bayard Sartoris's return home from the war, haunted by the death of his twin and his aristocratic Southern family's legacy. The novel introduces themes,

settings, and characters that would dominate Faulkner's books from then on. Faulkner also publishes *The Sound and the Fury,* which presents the disintegration of the Southern patrician Compson family through stream-of-consciousness interior monologues of the three Compson sons—the idiot Benjy, the incestuously haunted Quentin, and the grasping Jason—concerning their relationship with their fallen sister, Caddy. The fourth section is an objective account focusing on the Compson's black cook, Dilsey. It is the first of Faulkner's technically innovative narratives and one of his greatest achievements.

ELLEN GLASGOW: *They Stooped to Folly.* The second of the author's Queensborough trilogy, set in a fictional version of Richmond, Virginia, is subtitled "A Comedy of Morals." Set after the Great War, it concerns a group of disillusioned residents whose unhappiness leads to a series of disastrous liaisons.

DASHIELL HAMMETT (1894–1961): *Red Harvest* and *The Dain Curse.* Hammett's first detective novels, two cases of the unnamed detective "Continental Op," establish his characteristic stripped-down, muscular prose style with authentic dialogue and a gritty, realistic treatment of crime. Raymond Chandler, who credited Hammett with originating the hard-boiled detective story, would remark, "Hammett took murder out of the Venetian case and dropped it into the alley. . . . [He] gave murder back to the kind of people that commit it for reasons, not just to provide a corpse."

ERNEST HEMINGWAY: *A Farewell to Arms.* The author's war wound and love affair with a nurse during World War I in Italy provide the basis for his third novel. Frederic Henry and Catherine Barkley make a separate peace after the disastrous Caporetto retreat (regarded by many as among the greatest fictional depictions of warfare) to Switzerland, but Catherine's death in childbirth makes Hemingway's point that violent death is a constant of the human condition.

OLIVER LA FARGE (1901–1963): *Laughing Boy.* In the first novel about Native American life to win a Pulitzer Prize, ethnologist La Farge tells the story of a Navajo silversmith's unhappiness in marriage due to his wife's affair with a white rancher. La Farge had mastered his subject on archaeological field trips in Arizona.

RING LARDNER: *Round Up.* Lardner's last important short story collection brings together the stories of his two previous collections and adds sixteen stories, allowing the reader to sample the full range of Lardner's achievement. In 1929, Lardner also collaborates with George S. Kaufman in the comedy *June Moon,* about Tin

Pan Alley and based on Lardner's short story "Some Like Them Cold."

SINCLAIR LEWIS: *Dodsworth*. Retired businessman Samuel Dodsworth reassesses his marriage and his life while traveling in Europe. The novel marks a shift from Lewis's previous satirizing of Midwesterners by presenting a sympathetic portrait of his title character. The author would collaborate with Sidney Howard on a dramatic version in 1934.

ELLERY QUEEN: *The Roman Hat Mystery*. "Ellery Queen" is the joint pseudonym of Frederick Dannay (1905–1982) and his cousin Manfred B. Lee (1905–1971) as well as the protagonist (the dapper and cerebral son of a New York detective). Their first mystery is written for a contest, which it wins, gaining the writers a book contract and launching what has been called "the most successful collaboration in the history of prose fiction." In dozens of mystery novels, short stories, omnibus collections, and in *Ellery Queen's Mystery Magazine* (launched in 1941), which they edited, the authors became a dominating force in mystery fiction and popular culture.

JESSIE REDMON FAUSET: *Plum Bun*. Fauset's second novel, generally regarded as her best, concerns a young mulatto woman who passes for white and then develops into an artist who embraces her black heritage.

O. E. RÖLVAAG: *Peder Victorious*. The middle volume of the author's epic trilogy of Norwegian immigrants on the Dakota frontier had been preceded by *Giants in the Earth* (1927) and would be followed by *Their Fathers' God* (1931).

EVELYN SCOTT (1893–1963): *The Wave*. Scott's first important novel is an experimental narrative of the Civil War, using a montage technique of fragmentary episodes, documentary sources, and stream-of-consciousness narration to deliver a symphonic panorama of the conflict. Scott was born in Tennessee, grew up in New Orleans, and was an expatriate living in Brazil. Her previous books include *The Narrow House* (1921), *Narcissus* (1922), and *The Golden Door* (1925).

AGNES SMEDLEY (1892–1950): *Daughter of Earth*. Offering a rare look at the lot of working-class women during the period, Smedley's autobiographical novel chronicles the life of a Wisconsin farm girl. Smedley was born in rural Missouri and spent her childhood in the coal-mining area of southern Colorado. She had worked as a schoolteacher before actively campaigning against injustice and discrimination around the world.

JOHN STEINBECK (1902–1968): *Cup of Gold*. The California writer debuts with this romantic novel based on the career of the pirate Sir Henry Morgan.

Thomas Wolfe

RUTH SUCKOW: *Cora*. The novel describes the Americanization of a German immigrant family in Iowa and the title character's emergence as a modern American woman.

WALLACE HENRY THURMAN (1902–1934): *The Blacker the Berry*. Thurman's is one of the first novels to treat interracial prejudice within the black community, as a dark-skinned black woman is slighted by her family and friends, forcing her to "lighten up." Also, with William Jordan Rapp, Thurman coauthors the play *Harlem*, which deals with the disillusionment of a black family participating in the Great Migration from the South to the urban North. Thurman, born in Salt Lake City, had come to Harlem in 1925 and as editor of the *Messenger* had published the works of Langston Hughes and Zora Neale Hurston.

EDITH WHARTON: *Hudson River Bracketed*. Wharton's novel studies a young Midwestern writer's reactions to sophisticated New York society. A sequel, *The Gods Arrive* (1932), adds a contrast with European society.

EDMUND WILSON: *I Thought of Daisy*. Wilson's first published solo book is a satirical look at New York's bohemian literary circle, where a young man is attracted to two women — Daisy, a chorus girl, and Rita, a young poet. Wilson also publishes in 1929 a collection of verse, *Poets, Farewell!*

THOMAS WOLFE (1900–1938): *Look Homeward, Angel.* Wolfe's masterpiece is an autobiographical account of the coming of age of Eugene Gant. Some credit must go to Wolfe's editor, Maxwell Perkins (1884–1947), who helped cut and shape an enormous, unwieldy manuscript. Wolfe would continue his own and Gant's story in *Of Time and the River* (1935) and discuss his writing and the impact of his first novel's success in *The Story of a Novel* (1936).

LEANE ZUGSMITH (1903–1969): *All Victories Are Alike.* The first of the Kentucky-born proletarian novelist's works concerns the disillusionment of a newspaper columnist. It would be followed by other socially conscious works including *The Reckoning* (1934), about a New York slum child; *A Time to Remember* (1936), about labor conflict; and *The Summer Soldier* (1938), about racism.

Literary Criticism and Scholarship

T. S. ELIOT: *For Lancelot Andrewes: Essays on Style and Order.* Eliot's eclectic collection of essays, first published in England in 1928, includes the title piece on the sermons of the seventeenth-century Anglican bishop; literary essays on Crashaw, Middleton, and Baudelaire; and a critique of Irving Babbitt and the New Humanism. The collection prompts Edmund Wilson to declare that Eliot "has now become perhaps the most important literary critic in the English-speaking world."

ALFRED KREYMBORG: *Our Singing Strength.* The poet and playwright offers one of the first comprehensive surveys of American poetry that establishes the links between an American poetic tradition and contemporary poetry.

Nonfiction

SHERWOOD ANDERSON: *Hello Towns!* and *Nearer the Grass Roots.* The first is a celebration of small-town American life; the second justifies Anderson's retirement to a small Virginia town to become a newspaper editor.

JOHN DEWEY: *The Quest for Certainty.* In a series of lectures Dewey considers the relationship between knowledge and action, calling for a new direction in philosophy that will apply the methods of experimental sciences to conduct and social action.

JOSEPH WOOD KRUTCH (1893–1970): *The Modern Temper.* Krutch's essay collection is a pessimistic assessment of modern life and the damaging effects of science and modern technology. Krutch, a professor of English at

James Thurber

Columbia, was for many years the drama critic for the *Nation.*

WALTER LIPPMANN: *A Preface to Morals.* The political and cultural analyst articulates his social philosophy, which emphasizes rational individualism over collectivism in dealing with the challenges of modern society.

ROBERT S. LYND (1892–1970) AND HELEN MERRELL LYND (1896–1982): *Middletown.* Muncie, Indiana, is the subject of the authors' groundbreaking sociological study of a typical American community, the first in-depth study of American small-town life. The husband and wife team would produce a sequel, *Middletown in Transition* (1937). Helen Lynd issued *Middletown Families: Fifty Years of Change and Continuity* in 1982, the same year that a television documentary series based on the books was produced by Peter Davis (b. 1937).

S. J. PERELMAN (1904–1979): *Dawn Ginsbergh's Revenge.* Perelman's first collection of comic essays and sketches shows his characteristic punning style and reliance on comic reversals drawn from the details of modern life.

JAMES THURBER (1894–1961) AND E. B. WHITE (1899–1985): *Is Sex Necessary? or, Why You Feel the Way You Do.*

Both *New Yorker* writers' first publication is this spoof on popular pseudo-scientific guides and studies of sex delivered in a series of mock lectures, such as "The Nature of the American Male: A Study of Pedestalism" and "What Children Should Tell Their Parents."

Poetry

CONRAD AIKEN: *Selected Poems.* Aiken wins the Pulitzer Prize for this selection from his ten earlier volumes. It establishes him as a critically respected but rarely read (due to the perceived difficulty of his work) modern poet.

MALCOLM COWLEY (1898–1989): *Blue Juniata.* The future literary historian and critic's first publication is this collection of verse describing the author's expatriate experiences in France. The book serves as an important indicator of attitudes of the postwar generation. A second, similar volume, *A Dry Season*, would appear in 1942.

COUNTEE CULLEN: *The Black Christ, and Other Poems.* The title poem of this collection is an affirmation of Christian beliefs as Christ's crucifixion is reflected in the lynching death of a black man. The collection includes Cullen's response, "To Certain Critics," justifying his nonracial themes.

EMILY DICKINSON: *Further Poems.* This is another cache of previously unpublished poems, some of Dickinson's best.

KENNETH FEARING (1902–1961): *Angel Arms.* Fearing's first published volume introduces his characteristic theme of urban, mechanized society in angry, harshly realistic glimpses. Born in Illinois, Fearing would also publish novels, including *The Hospital* (1939) and *The Big Clock* (1946).

ROBINSON JEFFERS: *Dear Judas and Other Poems.* Jeffers provides a striking non-Christian interpretation of Christianity in the title poem: Jesus, Judas, and Mary reflect on the events before and after the crucifixion from the hindsight of twenty centuries. Jeffers's view that misery is one of the principal legacies of Christianity offends many. The volume also features the narrative poem "The Loving Shepherdess," about a doomed woman's devotion to her dead father's flock.

EDWIN ARLINGTON ROBINSON: *Cavender's House.* In this dramatic dialogue between a man and the ghost of the wife he had murdered years before, her voice becomes his conscience.

E. B. WHITE: *The Lady Is Cold.* A collection of verses treating the daily routine of city life. The poems present some of the dominating themes in White's work, namely, his love of New York City, simplicity, and liberty. A

second collection, *The Fox of Peapack*, would follow in 1938.

ELINOR WYLIE: *Angels and Earthly Creatures.* Some of the poet's best work is collected in this posthumously published volume, which includes the intensely introspective sonnet sequence "One Person."

Publications and Events

American Literature. The influential scholarly quarterly begins publication by the Duke University Press.

1930
Drama and Theater

MAXWELL ANDERSON: *Elizabeth the Queen.* Anderson's first blank-verse drama recounts Queen Elizabeth's relationship with Robert Devereux, earl of Essex, and solidifies Anderson's reputation as a major dramatist.

PHILIP BARRY: *Hotel Universe.* Barry shifts from his characteristic comedy of manners to fantasy, as a group of Americans meet at a villa on the Riviera to shed their neuroses through psychological and uncanny means. The play baffles both audiences and critics and manages only eighty-one performances, though it includes some of the playwright's most brilliant dialogue.

GUY BOLTON: *Girl Crazy.* The Gershwins supply the score for this popular musical about a New York operator who flees to an Arizona dude ranch. It features the star-making debut of Ethel Merman and classic songs such as "Embraceable You" and "I Got Rhythm."

MARC CONNELLY: *The Green Pastures.* Based on Roark Bradford's *Ol' Man Adam an' His Chillun* (1928), Connelly's play presents Old and New Testament stories from a Southern black, folkloric perspective.

SUSAN GLASPELL: *Alison's House.* Based on the posthumous fame of poet Emily Dickinson and its impact on her family, Glaspell's drama is called too literary by the critics, and it manages a run of only twenty-five performances. When it unexpectedly wins the Pulitzer Prize, the play is restaged on Broadway but closes after only two weeks.

ZORA NEALE HURSTON (1901–1960) AND LANGSTON HUGHES: *Mule Bone.* The two writers collaborate on a dramatic version of Hurston's short story "Bone of Contention," in which two black men quarrel over a woman's affections. Written in black dialect and full of earthy humor and satire, the play would not be produced or published until 1991 due to the writers' disagreements over authorship and finances.

GEORGE S. KAUFMAN AND MOSS HART (1904–1961): *Once in a Lifetime.* The first of the Kaufman-Hart

BIRTHS AND DEATHS, 1930–1939

Births

1930 John Barth, novelist
Gregory Corso, poet
Stanley Elkin (d. 1995), novelist
Lorraine Hansberry (d. 1965), playwright
Gary Snyder, poet

1931 Allan W. Eckert, novelist
Donald Barthelme (d. 1989), short story writer and novelist
E. L. Doctorow, novelist
Toni Morrison, novelist
Jane Rule, novelist
Tom Wolfe, journalist and novelist

1932 Robert Coover, novelist
John Gregory Dunne, novelist
John Jakes, novelist
Richard E. Kim, novelist
Sylvia Plath (d. 1963), poet
Gay Talese, author and journalist
John Updike, novelist

1933 Jerzy Kosinski (d. 1991), novelist
Cormac McCarthy, novelist
David McCullough, historian
Philip Roth, novelist
Susan Sontag, novelist, critic, and essayist

1934 Amiri Baraka (LeRoi Jones), poet and playwright
Joan Didion, novelist
David Halberstam, author and journalist
N. Scott Momaday, novelist and poet
Carl Sagan (d. 1996), scientist and author
Gloria Steinem, author
Mark Strand, poet

1935 Ellen Gilchrist, short story writer and novelist
Mary Oliver, poet
E. Annie Proulx, novelist and short story writer
Charles Wright, poet

1936 Fred Chappell, novelist and poet
Lucille Clifton, poet
Don De Lillo, novelist
Larry McMurtry, novelist

1937 Thomas Pynchon, novelist
Robert Stone, novelist
John Kennedy Toole (d. 1969), novelist
Joseph Wambaugh, novelist

1938 Raymond Carver (d. 1988), short story writer and poet
John Guare, playwright
Joyce Carol Oates, novelist and short story writer
Ishmael Reed, novelist and poet
Bernice Zamora, poet

1939 Paula Gunn Allen, novelist
Frank Bidart, poet

Charles Fuller, playwright
Thomas McGuane, novelist
Terrence McNally, playwright
Stanley Plumly, poet

Deaths

1930 David Belasco (b. 1859), playwright
Mary Eleanor Wilkins Freeman (b. 1852), short story writer
Edward Stratemeyer (b. 1863), children's writer and editor
George Edward Woodberry (b. 1855), poet and literary critic

1931 Grace Elizabeth King (b. 1851), novelist
Vachel Lindsay (b. 1879), poet

1932 Charles W. Chesnutt (b. 1858), novelist and short story writer
Hart Crane (b. 1899), poet
Frederick Jackson Turner (b. 1861), historian

1933 Sutton E. Griggs (b. 1872), novelist
Ring Lardner (b. 1885), humorist and short story writer
Sara Teasdale (b. 1884), poet

1934 Mary Austin (b. 1868), novelist
Julian Hawthorne (b. 1846), novelist and son of Nathaniel Hawthorne
Augustus Thomas (b. 1857), playwright
Brand Whitlock (b. 1869), novelist

1935 Thomas Boyd (b. 1898), novelist
Robert W. Chambers (b. 1865), novelist
Alice Ruth Moore Dunbar-Nelson (b. 1875), short story writer and poet
Anna Katharine Green (b. 1846), novelist
Langdon Mitchell (b. 1862), playwright
Lizette Woodworth Reese (b. 1856), poet
Edwin Arlington Robinson (b. 1869), poet

1936 Finley Peter Dunne (b. 1867), novelist
Mary Johnston (b. 1870), novelist
Lincoln Steffens (b. 1866), journalist and social reformer

1937 William Gillette (b. 1853), actor and playwright
Edgar Watson Howe (b. 1853), novelist
Paul Elmer More (b. 1864), editor and critic
Albert Bigelow Paine (b. 1861), author and editor
Edith Wharton (b. 1862), novelist

1938 Mary Hallock Foote (b. 1847), novelist
Zona Gale (b. 1874), novelist and playwright
Robert Herrick (b. 1868), novelist
James Weldon Johnson (b. 1871), editor, novelist, poet, and social reformer
Owen Wister (b. 1860), novelist
Thomas Wolfe (b. 1900), novelist

1939 Zane Grey (b. 1872), western novelist

collaborations is a popular Hollywood satire about a vaudeville team that blunders into success in films. The play initiates a series of dramas about the movie industry.

KENYON NICHOLSON (1894–1986) AND CHARLES KNOX ROBINSON (1909–1980): *Sailor, Beware!* This comedy about a sailor who tries to win a hardened nightclub hostess is one of the biggest hits during the Depression. Nicholson's other works include *Honor Bright* (1921) and *The Barker* (1927). Robinson's most successful subsequent play was *Apple of His Eye* (1946).

BESTSELLERS, 1930–1939

Fiction

1930

1. *Cimarron* by Edna Ferber
2. *Exile* by Warwick Deeping
3. *The Woman of Andros* by Thornton Wilder
4. *Years of Grace* by Margaret Ayer Barnes
5. *Angel Pavement* by J. B. Priestley
6. *The Door* by Mary Roberts Rinehart
7. *Rogue Herries* by Hugh Walpole
8. *Chances* by A. Hamilton Gibbs
9. *Young Man of Manhattan* by Katharine Brush
10. *Twenty-Four Hours* by Louis Bromfield

1931

1. *The Good Earth* by Pearl S. Buck
2. *Shadows on the Rock* by Willa Cather
3. *A White Bird Flying* by Bess Streeter Aldrich
4. *Grand Hotel* by Vicki Baum
5. *Years of Grace* by Margaret Ayer Barnes
6. *The Road Back* by Erich Maria Remarque
7. *The Bridge of Desire* by Warwick Deeping
8. *Back Street* by James Truslow Adams
9. *Finch's Fortune* by Mazo de la Roche
10. *Maid in Waiting* by John Galsworthy

1932

1. *The Good Earth* by Pearl S. Buck
2. *The Fountain* by Charles Morgan
3. *Sons* by Pearl S. Buck
4. *Magnolia Street* by Louis Golding
5. *The Sheltered Life* by Ellen Glasgow
6. *Old Wine and New* by Warwick Deeping
7. *Mary's Neck* by Booth Tarkington
8. *Magnificent Obsession* by Lloyd C. Douglas
9. *Inheritance* by Phyllis Bentley
10. *Three Lovers* by A. J. Cronin

1933

1. *Anthony Adverse* by Hervey Allen
2. *As the Earth Turns* by Gladys Hasty Carroll
3. *Ann Vickers* by Sinclair Lewis
4. *Magnificent Obsession* by Lloyd C. Douglas
5. *One More River* by John Galsworthy
6. *Forgive Us Our Trespasses* by Lloyd C. Douglas
7. *The Master of Jalna* by Mazo de la Roche
8. *Miss Bishop* by Bess Streeter Aldrich
9. *The Farm* by Louis Bromfield
10. *Little Man, What Now?* by Hans Fallada

1934

1. *Anthony Adverse* by Hervey Allen
2. *Lamb in His Bosom* by Caroline Miller
3. *So Red the Rose* by Stark Young
4. *Good-Bye, Mr. Chips* by James Hilton
5. *Within This Present* by Margaret Ayer Barnes
6. *Work of Art* by Sinclair Lewis
7. *Private Worlds* by Phyllis Bottome
8. *Mary Peters* by Mary Ellen Chase
9. *Oil for the Lamps of China* by Alice Tisdale Hobart
10. *Seven Gothic Tales* by Isak Dinesen

1935

1. *Green Light* by Lloyd C. Douglas
2. *Vein of Iron* by Ellen Glasgow
3. *Of Time and the River* by Thomas Wolfe
4. *Time Out of Mind* by Rachel Field
5. *Good-Bye, Mr. Chips* by James Hilton
6. *The Forty Days of Musa Dagh* by Franz Werfel
7. *Heaven's My Destination* by Thornton Wilder
8. *Lost Horizon* by James Hilton
9. *Come and Get It* by Edna Ferber
10. *Europa* by Robert Briffault

1936

1. *Gone with the Wind* by Margaret Mitchell
2. *The Last Puritan* by George Santayana
3. *Sparkenbroke* by Charles Morgan
4. *Drums Along the Mohawk* by Walter Edmonds
5. *It Can't Happen Here* by Sinclair Lewis
6. *White Banners* by Lloyd C. Douglas
7. *The Hurricane* by Charles Nordhoff and James Norman Hall
8. *The Thinking Reed* by Rebecca West
9. *The Doctor* by Mary Roberts Rinehart
10. *Eyeless in Gaza* by Aldous Huxley

1937

1. *Gone with the Wind* by Margaret Mitchell
2. *Northwest Passage* by Kenneth Roberts
3. *The Citadel* by A. J. Cronin
4. *And So-Victoria* by Vaughan Wilkins
5. *Drums Along the Mohawk* by Walter Edmonds
6. *The Years* by Virginia Woolf
7. *Theatre* by W. Somerset Maugham
8. *Of Mice and Men* by John Steinbeck
9. *The Rains Came* by Louis Bromfield
10. *We Are Not Alone* by James Hilton

1938

1. *The Yearling* by Marjorie Kinnan Rawlings
2. *The Citadel* by A. J. Cronin
3. *My Son, My Son!* by Howard Spring
4. *Rebecca* by Daphne du Maurier
5. *Northwest Passage* by Kenneth Roberts
6. *All This, and Heaven Too* by Rachel Field
7. *And Tell of Time* by Laura Krey
8. *The Rains Came* by Louis Bromfield
9. *The Mortal Storm* by Phyllis Bottome
10. *Action at Aquila* by Hervey Allen

1939

1. *The Grapes of Wrath* by John Steinbeck
2. *All This, and Heaven Too* by Rachel Field
3. *Rebecca* by Daphne du Maurier
4. *Wickford Point* by J. P. Marquand
5. *Escape* by Ethel Vance
6. *Disputed Passage* by Lloyd C. Douglas
7. *The Yearling* by Marjorie Kinnan Rawlings
8. *The Tree of Liberty* by Elizabeth Page
9. *The Nazarene* by Sholem Asch
10. *Kitty Foyle* by Christopher Morley

BESTSELLERS, 1930–1939

General Nonfiction

1930

1. *The Story of San Michele* by Axel Munthe
2. *The Strange Death of President Harding* by Gaston B. Means and May Dixon Thacker
3. *Byron* by André Maurois
4. *The Adams Family* by James Truslow Adams
5. *Lone Cowboy* by Will James
6. *Lincoln* by Emil Ludwig
7. *The Story of Philosophy* by Will Durant
8. *The Outline of History* by H. G. Wells
9. *The Art of Thinking* by Ernest Dimnet
10. *The Rise of American Civilization* by Charles A. and Mary R. Beard

1931

1. *Education of a Princess* by Grand Duchess Marie
2. *The Story of San Michele* by Axel Munthe
3. *Washington Merry-Go-Round*, anonymous (Drew Pearson and Robert S. Allen)
4. *Boners: Being a Collection of Schoolboy Wisdom, or Knowledge as It Is Sometimes Written* compiled by Alexander Abingdon and illustrated by Dr. Seuss
5. *Culbertson's Summary* by Ely Culbertson
6. *Contract Bridge Blue Book* by Ely Culbertson
7. *Fatal Interview* by Edna St. Vincent Millay
8. *The Epic of America* by James Truslow Adams
9. *Mexico* by Stuart Chase
10. *New Russia's Primer* by Mikhail Ilin

1932

1. *The Epic of America* by James Truslow Adams
2. *Only Yesterday* by Frederick Lewis Allen
3. *A Fortune to Share* by Vash Young
4. *Culbertson's Summary* by Ely Culbertson
5. *Van Loon's Geography* by Hendrik Willem Van Loon
6. *What We Live By* by Ernest Dimnet
7. *The March of Democracy* by James Truslow Adams
8. *Washington Merry-Go-Round*, anonymous (Drew Pearson and Robert S. Allen)
9. *The Story of My Life* by Clarence Darrow
10. *More Merry-Go-Round*, anonymous (Drew Pearson and Robert S. Allen)

1933

1. *Life Begins at Forty* by Walter B. Pitkin
2. *Marie Antoinette* by Stefan Zweig
3. *British Agent* by R. H. Bruce Lockhart
4. *100,000,000 Guinea Pigs* by Arthur Kallet and F. J. Schlink
5. *The House of Exile* by Nora Waln
6. *Van Loon's Geography* by Hendrik Willem Van Loon
7. *Looking Forward* by Franklin D. Roosevelt
8. *Contract Bridge Blue Book of 1933* by Ely Culbertson
9. *The Archers of the Years* by Halliday Sutherland
10. *The March of Democracy, Vol. II* by James Truslow Adams

1934

1. *While Rome Burns* by Alexander Woollcott
2. *Life Begins at Forty* by Walter B. Pitkin
3. *Nijinsky* by Romola Nijinsky
4. *100,000,000 Guinea Pigs* by Arthur Kallet and F. J. Schlink
5. *The Native's Return* by Louis Adamic
6. *Stars Fell on Alabama* by Carl Carmer
7. *Brazilian Adventure* by Peter Fleming

8. *Forty-two Years in the White House* by Ike Hoover
9. *You Must Relax* by Edmund Jacobson
10. *The Life of Our Lord* by Charles Dickens

1935

1. *North to the Orient* by Anne Morrow Lindbergh
2. *While Rome Burns* by Alexander Woollcott
3. *Life with Father* by Clarence Day
4. *Personal History* by Vincent Sheen
5. *Seven Pillars of Wisdom* by T. E. Lawrence
6. *Francis the First* by Francis Hackett
7. *Mary Queen of Scotland and the Isles* by Stefan Zweig
8. *Rats, Lice, and History* by Hans Zinsser
9. *R. E. Lee* by Douglas Southall Freeman
10. *Skin Deep* by M. C. Phillips

1936

1. *Man the Unknown* by Alexis Carrel
2. *Wake Up and Live!* by Dorothea Brandle
3. *The Way of a Transgressor* by Negley Farson
4. *Around the World in Eleven Years* by Patience Abbe, Richard Abbe, and Johnny Abbe
5. *North to the Orient* by Anne Morrow Lindbergh
6. *An American Doctor's Odyssey* by Victor Heiser
7. *Inside Europe* by John Gunther
8. *Live Alone and Like It* by Marjorie Hillis
9. *Life with Father* by Clarence Day
10. *I Write as I Please* by Walter Duranty

1937

1. *How to Win Friends and Influence People* by Dale Carnegie
2. *An American Doctor's Odyssey* by Victor Heiser
3. *The Return to Religion* by Henry C. Link
4. *The Arts* by Hendrik Willem Van Loon
5. *Orchids on Your Budget* by Marjorie Hillis
6. *Present Indicative* by Noel Coward
7. *Mathematics for the Million* by Lancelot Hogben
8. *Life with Mother* by Clarence Day
9. *The Nile* by Emil Ludwig
10. *The Flowering of New England* by Van Wyck Brooks

1938

1. *The Importance of Living* by Lin Yutang
2. *With Malice Toward Some* by Margaret Halsey
3. *Madame Curie* by Eve Curie
4. *Listen! The Wind* by Anne Morrow Lindbergh
5. *The Horse and Buggy Doctor* by Arthur E. Hertzler
6. *How to Win Friends and Influence People* by Dale Carnegie
7. *Benjamin Franklin* by Carl Van Doren
8. *I'm a Stranger Here Myself* by Ogden Nash
9. *Alone* by Richard E. Byrd
10. *Fanny Kemble* by Margaret Armstrong

1939

1. *Days of Our Years* by Pierre van Paassen
2. *Reaching for the Stars* by Nora Waln
3. *Inside Asia* by John Gunther
4. *Autobiography with Letters* by William Lyon Phelps
5. *County Lawyer* by Bellamy Partridge
6. *Wind, Sand, and Stars* by Antoine de St.-Exupéry
7. *Mein Kampf* by Adolf Hitler
8. *A Peculiar Treasure* by Edna Ferber
9. *Not Peace but a Sword* by Vincent Sheen
10. *Listen! The Wind* by Anne Morrow Lindbergh

AWARDS AND PRIZES, 1930–1939

Pulitzer Prizes

1930
Fiction: *Laughing Boy* by Oliver La Farge
Poetry: *Selected Poems* by Conrad Aiken
Drama: *The Green Pastures* by Marc Connelly
History: *The War of Independence* by Claude H. Van Tyne
Biography/Autobiography: *The Raven (Sam Houston)* by Marquis James

1931
Fiction: *Years of Grace* by Margaret Ayers Barnes
Poetry: *Collected Poems* by Robert Frost
Drama: *Alison's House* by Susan Glaspell
History: *The Coming of the War, 1914* by Bernadotte E. Schmitt
Biography/Autobiography: *Charles W. Eliot* by Henry James (1879–1947)

1932
Fiction: *The Good Earth* by Pearl S. Buck
Poetry: *The Flowering Stone* by George Dillon
Drama: *Of Thee I Sing* by George S. Kaufman, Morrie Ryskind, and Ira Gershwin
History: *My Experiences in the World War* by Gen. John J. Pershing
Biography/Autobiography: *Theodore Roosevelt* by Henry F. Pringle

1933
Fiction: *The Store* by T. S. Stribling
Poetry: *Conquistador* by Archibald MacLeish
Drama: *Both Your Houses* by Maxwell Anderson
History: *The Significance of Sections in American History* by Charles M. Andrews
Biography/Autobiography: *Grover Cleveland* by Allan Nevins

1934
Fiction: *Lamb in His Bosom* by Caroline Miller
Poetry: *Collected Verses* by Robert Hillyer
Drama: *Men in White* by Sidney Kingsley
History: *The People's Choice* by Herbert Agar
Biography/Autobiography: *John Hay* by Tyler Dennett

1935
Fiction: *Now in November* by Josephine W. Johnson
Poetry: *Bright Ambush* by Audrey Wurdemann
Drama: *The Old Maid* by Zoë Akins
History: *The Colonial Period of American History* by Andrew C. McLaughlin

Biography/Autobiography: *R. E. Lee* by Douglas Southall Freeman

1936
Fiction: *Honey in the Horn* by Harold L. Davis
Poetry: *Strange Holiness* by Robert P. Tristram Coffin
Drama: *Idiot's Delight* by Robert Sherwood
History: *A Constitutional Period of American History* by Andrew C. McLaughlin
Biography/Autobiography: *The Thought and Character of William James* by Ralph B. Perry

1937
Fiction: *Gone with the Wind* by Margaret Mitchell
Poetry: *A Further Range* by Robert Frost
Drama: *You Can't Take It with You* by Moss Hart and George S. Kaufman
History: *The Flowering of New England* by Van Wyck Brooks
Biography/Autobiography: *Hamilton Fish: The Inner History of the Grant Administration* by Allan Nevins

1938
Fiction: *The Late George Apley* by J. P. Marquand
Poetry: *Cold Morning Sky* by Marya Zaturenska
Drama: *Our Town* by Thornton Wilder
History: *The Road to Reunion, 1865–1900* by Paul H. Buck
Biography/Autobiography: *Pedlar's Progress* by Odell Shepard and *Andrew Jackson* by Marquis James

1939
Fiction: *The Yearling* by Marjorie Kinnan Rawlings
Poetry: *Selected Poems* by John Gould Fletcher
Drama: *Abe Lincoln in Illinois* by Robert E. Sherwood
History: *A History of American Magazines* by Frank L. Mott
Biography/Autobiography: *Benjamin Franklin* by Carl Van Doren

Noble Prizes in Literature

1930
Sinclair Lewis

1936
Eugene O'Neill

1938
Pearl S. Buck

PAUL OSBORN (1901–1988): *The Vinegar Tree.* Osborn's first Broadway success considers the subject of free love from the perspective of a middle-aged married woman.

MORRIE RYSKIND (1895–1985) AND GEORGE S. KAUFMAN: *Strike Up the Band.* Originally produced in 1927 but withdrawn after its tryout, this war satire with biting lyrics by Ira Gershwin had been deemed too offensive. Ryskind, who worked with Kaufman on *Animal Crackers* (1928), softened Kaufman's original book, and the play is remounted in 1930.

ROBERT E. SHERWOOD: *Waterloo Bridge* and *This Is New York.* The playwright manages only moderate success with this pair of dramas. The first is a melodrama concerning an English chorus girl who becomes a prostitute during World War I. The second is a comedy about a North Dakota senator's daughter who gets involved with a New York playboy. The play is a defense of New York written in reaction to the anti–New York sentiment provoked by Al Smith's presidential campaign.

JOHN WEXLEY (1907–1985): *The Last Mile*. Wexley's best-known play is a taut drama about death-row inmates, noteworthy for launching Spencer Tracy's acting career. Theater historian Burns Mantle called it "a tragedy so tense, so stripped of theatrical artificialities and emotionally so moving that even callous reviewers of plays were frank to admit its disturbing and unsettling effect upon the nerves." Wexley's other full-length plays were *Steel* (1931), about labor agitation, and *They Shall Not Die* (1934), a dramatization of the Scottsboro case.

Fiction

SHOLEM ASCH (1880–1957): *The Mother*. The first of the Polish-born writer's books translated into English follows a Jewish immigrant family in New York. His other novels — all on Jewish themes — written during the decade are *Three Cities* (1933), *Salvation* (1934), *The War Goes On* (1936), and *Three Novels* (1938).

MARGARET AYER BARNES: *Years of Grace*. Barnes's novel about a Chicago matron's long life wins the Pulitzer Prize. Her other novels during the decade — *Westward Passage* (1931), *Within This Present* (1933), *Edna His Wife* (1935), and *Wisdom's Gate* (1938) — would all be popular but would not achieve the same degree of critical acclaim.

KAY BOYLE (1902–1992): *Wedding Day and Other Stories*. The Minnesota-born expatriate's first short story collection shows evidence of her association with the experimental Parisian literary monthly *transition*. Critic Katherine Anne Porter's review notes "a fighting spirit, freshness of feeling, curiosity, the courage of her own attitude and idiom, a violently dedicated search for the meanings and methods of art."

MAX BRAND (FREDERICK FAUST): *Destry Rides Again*. Brand publishes his best-known western, the story of Harry Destry's revenge on the men who sent him to prison under false pretenses.

JOHN DOS PASSOS: *42nd Parallel*. The first volume of the U.S.A. trilogy interweaves the stories of five characters along the west-to-east storm track of the forty-second parallel. The novel extends the experimental methods of *Manhattan Transfer* (1925), including the narrative innovations of the "Newsreel" (documentary materials), the "Camera Eye" (stream-of-consciousness personal commentary on his subjects), and brief biographies of important historical figures, such as Eugene Debs, Thomas Edison, Andrew Carnegie, and Bill Haywood. The trilogy is Dos Passos's masterwork, a panoramic portrait of the first three decades of the twentieth century in America.

WILLIAM FAULKNER: *As I Lay Dying*. Faulkner's most experimentally daring novel, written over a six-week period when Faulkner was working the night shift at a powerhouse, is a multivocal stream-of-consciousness account of the poor white Bundren family's journey to bury their mother, Addie, in her native town, Jefferson, Mississippi. The book combines horror, comedy, and a profound meditation on the nature of being.

EDNA FERBER: *Cimarron*. Ferber's popular novel capturing life in Oklahoma during the 1899 land rush, the discovery of oil, and more modern history continues the author's documentation of American history and its regions.

DASHIELL HAMMETT: *The Maltese Falcon*. Hammett's third novel introduces archetypal hard-boiled private eye Sam Spade in a grittily realistic, morally ambiguous mystery that is considered by many the standard by which subsequent American mysteries must be judged.

LANGSTON HUGHES: *Not Without Laughter*. The first of Hughes's two novels concerns a black family in Kansas. The book is praised for Hughes's ability to capture the complexity and believable humanity of African American characters.

CAROLYN KEENE: *The Secret of the Old Clock*. The novel marks the debut of teenage sleuth and enduring female juvenile icon Nancy Drew. In her sporty blue roadster, Nancy transforms the accepted image of passive femininity into that of an active problem solver; by 1933 the series would outsell popular boys' series, such as the Hardy Boys, by nearly two to one. "Carolyn Keene" is a pseudonym for the many contract authors of the Stratemeyer Syndicate, created by Edward Stratemeyer (1863–1930), which produced a number of popular juvenile fiction series. Many of the Nancy Drew mysteries were written, or were based on outlines prepared by, Stratemeyer's daughter Harriet Adams (1894–1982), who also wrote several Hardy Boys stories.

DOROTHY PARKER: *Laments for the Living*. The first of three volumes of short story collections published during the decade displays, like Parker's poetry, a dissecting wit and sardonic tone. It includes perhaps her finest story, "Big Blonde." Subsequent collections are *After Such Pleasures* (1932) and *Here Lies* (1939).

S. J. PERELMAN: *Parlor, Bedlam and Bath*. Perelman's second collection, a collaboration with reporter and foreign correspondent Quentin Reynolds (1902–1965), treats the comic misadventures of Charles Tattersall in a style that one reviewer describes as "up-to-the-minute, allusive, intelligent, urbane—and above all, mad."

KATHERINE ANNE PORTER (1890–1980): *Flowering Judas*. Porter's initial short story collection establishes her reputation among fellow writers as a formidable stylist and a master of the form. The title story (reissued with added stories as *Flowering Judas and Other Stories* in 1935) concerns the relationship of an American resident of Mexico with revolutionaries. Porter was born in a Texas log cabin and was largely self-educated, living in Mexico, Germany, and France.

ELMER RICE: *The Voyage to Purilia*. Rice's first novel is a satirical fantasy based on his experiences in Hollywood, describing a planet where inhabitants (without reproductive organs) conform to a narrow range of emotional types, to the sounds of a continual sweet soundtrack and under the direction of an all-powerful narrator called The Presence.

ELIZABETH MADOX ROBERTS: *The Great Meadow*. Roberts's historical novel of pioneer life in the author's native Kentucky wins praise for both its epic grandeur and its poetic style.

KENNETH ROBERTS (1885–1957): *Arundel*. The first in a series of best-selling, critically acclaimed historical novels centered on the southern Maine community of the title. Set during the Revolutionary War, the plot describes Benedict Arnold's unsuccessful expedition against Quebec. Several sequels would follow: *The Lively Lady* (1931), *Rabble in Arms* (1933), and *Captain Caution* (1934). Born in Maine, Roberts had been a journalist before becoming a fiction writer.

UPTON SINCLAIR: *Mountain City*. The novel treats the evils of money in the story of a westerner's drive to become a tycoon. It is, in the words of one reviewer, "exactly the kind of novel Horatio Alger might have written if he had possessed a social conscience."

GERTRUDE STEIN: *Lucy Church, Amiably*. Described on its title page as a "Novel of Romantic beauty and nature and which Looks Like an Engraving," the book is an extended meditation on a landscape. Its merits have divided Stein's critics, called "banal" and "lackadaisical" by some and "the purest and best pastoral romance we have had in this century" by another.

RUTH SUCKOW: *The Kramer Girls*. The novel looks at the relationship among three sisters. Suckow's other novel during the 1930s, *The Folks* (1934), is a similar quietly realistic study of a middle-class family.

CARL VAN VECHTEN: *Parties*. Van Vechten continues his satirical documentation of New York City high life during the 1920s in this story of a wealthy husband and wife in an endless pursuit of stimulation.

EDITH WHARTON: *Certain People*. Although Wharton would complete only one novel during the decade (*The Gods Arrive* in 1932, a sequel to *Hudson River Bracketed*), she publishes this and three additional collections of short stories with contemporary and nineteenth-century settings. Subsequent volumes are *Human Nature* (1933), *The World Over* (1936), and *Ghosts* (1937).

THORNTON WILDER: *The Woman of Andros*. Based on the Latin comedy *Andria* by Terence, Wilder's third novel presents a philosophical fable about the emptiness of the classical world on the brink of profound changes ushered in by the birth of Christ.

Literary Criticism and Scholarship

The Encyclopedia of the Social Sciences. This seminal reference source begins publication, edited by E.R.A. Seligman (1861–1939) and Alvin Johnson (1874–1971). With articles on source materials by prominent scholars, the *Encyclopedia* would reach fifteen volumes by 1935.

Nonfiction

JAMES TRUSLOW ADAMS: *The Adams Family*. This is the first of the historian's two books on the Adamses. Here he surveys four generations of the family. His biography of Henry Adams would appear in 1933.

JANE ADDAMS: *The Second Twenty Years at Hull-House*. This continuation of the author's *Twenty Years at Hull-House* (1910) chronicles the Chicago settlement's history from 1909 to 1929, along with Addams's reflections on world affairs during the period.

MARGARET C. ANDERSON (1893–1973): *My Thirty Years' War*. The founder and editor of the *Little Review* (1914–1929) supplies an account of her life and association with the most important figures in modern literature, including James Joyce, Ernest Hemingway, Ezra Pound, and Gertrude Stein. A second volume, *The Fiery Fountains*, would appear in 1950, and a third, *The Strange Necessity*, in 1970.

ROBERT BENCHLEY: *The Treasurer's Report, and Other Aspects of Community Singing*. Benchley's collection of humorous essays targets Sundays, exercise at sea, bathrooms, American sports, and other topics.

FRANK BUCK (1884–1950): *Bring 'Em Back Alive.* Written in collaboration with Edward Anthony (1895–1971), this lively account of Buck's adventures in the wilds, collecting animals for zoos and circuses, becomes a bestseller and establishes the popular heroic image of the intrepid big-game hunter. A sequel, *Wild Cargo*, would appear in 1932.

RICHARD E. BYRD: *Little America.* Admiral Byrd supplies an account of his recent exploration of Antarctica and his flight over the South Pole. The title refers to his base camp on the Ross Ice Shelf.

MICHAEL GOLD (IRWIN GRANICH): *Jews Without Money.* Gold coins the term *proletarian realism* in 1930 and uses it in his most acclaimed work, an autobiographical, gritty depiction of Jewish tenement life on New York's Lower East Side.

JAMES WELDON JOHNSON: *Black Manhattan.* Johnson supplies one of the first cultural studies of black life in New York City from colonial times to the present.

H. L. MENCKEN: *Treatise on the Gods.* Mencken's comparative study of religions illustrates his thesis that "all religions, at bottom, are pretty much alike. Go beneath, and one finds invariably the sense of helplessness before the cosmic mysteries, and the same pathetic attempt to resolve it by appealing to higher powers."

SAMUEL ELIOT MORISON (1887–1976) AND HENRY STEELE COMMAGER (1902–1998): *The Growth of the American Republic.* Morison, appointed the first Harmsworth Professor of American History at Oxford University in 1922, had produced *The Oxford History of the United States, 1783–1917* in 1927, mainly directed to English students. Morison revised the book with Commager for American students as this textbook, which would serve college students for the next fifty years.

JOHN CROWE RANSOM: *God Without Thunder: An Unorthodox Defense of Orthodoxy.* Ransom's true target in this polemic is not religion but modern science, which he accuses of destroying transcendent truths and spirituality. Ransom would resume his attack in *The World's Body* (1938).

Poetry

CONRAD AIKEN: *John Deth, a Metaphysical Legend, and Other Poems.* After winning the 1930 Pulitzer Prize, Aiken publishes the first in a series of highly abstract philosophical works. The title poem is a dramatic fantasy on the theme of the triumph of death over life.

HART CRANE: *The Bridge.* One of the singular American poetic achievements in the twentieth century, Crane's symphonic sequence uses the Brooklyn Bridge as a symbolic locus for a summation of American experience. As Crane asserted in a letter, "What I am really handling, you see, is the Myth of America."

BABETTE DEUTSCH: *Fire for the Night.* Deutsch's first of three poetry collections published during the 1930s displays her virtuosity in capturing what Louis Untermeyer identifies as her "inner poignancies," lyrical reflections on art, nature, and emotional states. Subsequent collections are *Epistle to Prometheus* (1931) and *One Part Love* (1939).

RICHARD EBERHART (b. 1904): *A Bravery of Earth.* Eberhart's lyrical mastery is first displayed in this initial collection based on his experiences as a student at Cambridge and during a world tour by freighter. His other collection published during the decade is *Reading the Spirit* (1937).

T. S. ELIOT: *Ash Wednesday.* Based on his Anglican conversion, Eliot's poetic sequence asserts his religious faith. Many take it as the poet's attempt to answer the spiritual despair of *The Waste Land* (1922). It employs a similar highly allusive multivocal style, interweaving elements from Dante's *Divine Comedy* and a sermon by the seventeenth-century Anglican bishop Lancelot Andrewes.

ROBERT FROST: *Collected Poems.* Poems from Frost's five previous volumes are collected here along with several previously unpublished works. It wins the poet his second of four Pulitzer Prizes. A new edition would be issued in 1939.

HORACE GREGORY (1898–1982): *Chelsea Rooming House.* Gregory's first volume is a series of free-verse dramatic monologues capturing New York's misfits and down-and-out population. It is praised as "one of the most impressive first books by any modern American poet," based mainly on Gregory's ability to capture convincingly the world of his characters. Gregory would alternate between publishing translations and original verse in the volumes *No Retreat* (1933) and *Chorus of Survival* (1935).

STANLEY KUNITZ (b. 1905): *Intellectual Things.* Kunitz's first collection establishes his reputation as an intellectual writer indebted to the seventeenth-century metaphysical poets. In his review, Granville Hicks detects a major talent and "a mind determined to probe beneath surfaces and ill-content until it states with precision what it finds."

ARCHIBALD MACLEISH: *New Found Land.* Reflecting the poet's return to the United States to live, this collection shifts from international to American themes. The volume includes two of his most admired works, "You, Andrew Marvell" and "Immortal Autumn."

EDWIN ARLINGTON ROBINSON: *The Glory of the Nightingale.* Robinson's blank-verse narrative poem dramatizes two friends' love for the same woman.

YVOR WINTERS: *The Proof.* The first of Winters's three poetry collections published during the decade — to be followed by *The Journey* (1931) and *Before Disaster* (1934). *The Proof* reflects his critical principles of classical restraint and moral seriousness.

Publications and Events

I'll Take My Stand. This anthology by twelve Southern writers, including John Gould Fletcher, John Crowe Ransom, Allen Tate, and Robert Penn Warren, articulates their so-called Agrarian Manifesto supporting Southern regionalism and opposing capitalism.

1931
Drama and Theater

PHILIP BARRY: *Tomorrow and Tomorrow.* Barry's sophisticated problem play poses the question of whether a woman should leave her husband for her former lover if he is the father of her child.

S. N. BEHRMAN: *Brief Moment.* This comedy about a young patrician's desire to marry a nightclub singer features a specially written role for dramatic critic and essayist Alexander Woollcott as a wisecracking onlooker, a possible source of inspiration for the comedy *The Man Who Came to Dinner* (1939), by Kaufman and Hart.

RACHEL CROTHERS: *As Husbands Go.* Crothers's sophisticated comedy describes two women from Dubuque who have flings in Europe that cause them to contemplate divorce and remarriage when they return home.

PAUL GREEN: *The House of Connelly.* The first production of the Group Theatre concerns the proletarian redemption of the heir of a declining aristocratic Southern family, through the love of a poor girl.

GEORGE S. KAUFMAN, MORRIE RYSKIND, AND GEORGE GERSHWIN: *Of Thee I Sing.* In the first musical to win a Pulitzer Prize and one of the first to tackle serious issues, George Gershwin's music, Ira Gershwin's lyrics, and a book by George S. Kaufman and Morrie Ryskind combine to create a satire on American politics as presidential candidate John P. Wintergreen agrees to marry the winner of a beauty contest as part of his campaign.

EUGENE O'NEILL: *Mourning Becomes Electra.* O'Neill's dramatic trilogy — *Homecoming*, *The Hunted*, and *The Haunted* — updates with clear Freudian overtones the

Oresteia by Aeschylus, focusing on a New England family during the Civil War. The five-hour play is performed nightly with a dinner break.

CHANNING POLLOCK: *The House Beautiful.* Pollock's final play is a preachy allegory on the idealism of a young married couple living in the suburbs. It prompts a classic, pithy review by Dorothy Parker: "*The House Beautiful* is the play lousy."

LYNN RIGGS (1899–1954): *Green Grow the Lilacs.* Riggs's folk drama set in Oklahoma's Indian Territory in 1900 is constructed "to recapture in a kind of nostalgic glow . . . the great range of mood which characterized the old folk songs and ballads." It would be adapted by Richard Rodgers and Oscar Hammerstein II into the landmark musical *Oklahoma!* in 1943. Riggs's other plays include *The Cherokee Night* (1932) and *Russet Mantle* (1936).

ROBERT E. SHERWOOD: *Reunion in Vienna.* In Sherwood's comedy, an exiled Austrian prince reunites with a former lover; her husband hopes that the meeting will break the nobleman's spell over his wife.

THORNTON WILDER: *The Long Christmas Dinner and Other Plays in One Act.* Wilder's second collection gathers his first major dramas, including the title play, *Pullman Car Hiawatha*, and *The Happy Journey to Trenton and Camden*, showing the experimental techniques with which he would be associated.

Fiction

JOHN PEALE BISHOP: *Many Thousands Gone.* Bishop's story cycle, generally regarded as his best fiction, is set in an imaginary version of his native Charleston, West Virginia, covering the period of 1850 to the turn of the century. The title story wins the *Scribner's Magazine* Prize. Bishop was the former managing editor of *Vanity Fair* and was an expatriate in Paris during the 1920s.

ARNA BONTEMPS (1902–1973): *God Sends Sunday.* Bontemps's first novel tells the story of a black jockey whose luck deserts him. The author would collaborate with Countee Cullen on a dramatic adaptation, *St. Louis Woman* (1946).

KAY BOYLE: *Plagued by the Nightingale.* The writer's first novel concerns the marriage of an American girl to an upper-class Frenchman. The couple must decide whether to have a child and ensure an inheritance, which also entails the risk of passing on a deadly hereditary disease.

PEARL S. BUCK (1892–1973): *The Good Earth.* This novel of Chinese peasant life, centered on the career of Wang Lung and his descendants, is the first volume of The House of Earth trilogy, which includes *Sons* (1932) and

A House Divided (1935). It wins both the Pulitzer Prize and the William Dean Howells Medal for the most distinguished work of American fiction published between 1930 and 1935. The child of missionaries in China, Buck used her firsthand experiences to bring an unprecedented authenticity to her depiction of Chinese life, infused by a mythic, universalized tonality that produces what critic Malcolm Cowley describes as "a parable of the life of man, in his relation to the soil that sustains him."

ERSKINE CALDWELL (1903–1987): *American Earth.* Critics view Caldwell's first story collection as case studies of American primitives and its author as "another pupil in the Hemingway branch of the Sherwood Anderson school." Born in Georgia, Caldwell worked as a reporter on the *Atlanta Journal*, as a Hollywood screenwriter, and from 1938 to 1941 as a foreign correspondent.

ROBERT CANTWELL (1908–1978): *Laugh and Lie Down.* The proletarian novelist's first book concerns the aimless lives of inhabitants of a Washington mill town. Cantwell grew up in Washington and worked for a time in a lumber mill. He would become an editor for *Time* and *Newsweek*.

WILLA CATHER: *Shadows on the Rocks.* Increasingly drawn to the past for the heroism and ideals she wishes to celebrate and finds lacking in the present, Cather dramatizes a year in the lives of a widowed apothecary and his twelve-year-old daughter in late-seventeenth-century Quebec.

JAMES GOULD COZZENS: *S.S. San Pedro.* Considered the first instance of the writer's mature work, in which Cozzens abandons his earlier romanticism for a detached, objective style, this novella is based on the actual mysterious sinking of the S.S. *Vestris* in 1929.

FLOYD DELL: *Love Without Money.* Dell looks at a couple who manage without either money or marriage while portraying a wide range of sexual expression, including free love and homosexuality.

WILLIAM FAULKNER: *Sanctuary.* Failing to reach the public with his previous novels, Faulkner set out to write a potboiler — "the most horrific tale I could imagine" — to make money. Composed in three weeks (but substantially reworked by a shocked Faulkner when he received the galleys), the story of Temple Drake's rape and torture by the sadistic psychopath Popeye becomes Faulkner's only bestseller. Also published in 1931 is the story collection *These 13*, including some of his greatest stories, such as "Victory," "Red Leaves," and "A Rose for Emily."

JESSIE REDMON FAUSET: *The Chinaberry Tree.* Fauset's novel about a black middle-class family draws criticism that the author presents an idealized projection of blacks conforming to white standards.

CAROLINE GORDON (1895–1981): *Penhally.* Gordon's first novel traces the lives of a Kentucky family through four generations, introducing her characteristic Southern setting, traditional fictional method, and psychological skill in characterization. Gordon was born in Kentucky and married poet and critic Allen Tate in 1924.

FANNIE HURST: *Back Street.* The novelist who specialized in portraying the plight of women dramatizes the conflicts of a married man's longtime mistress. Her other popular novels published during the decade are *Imitation of Life* (1933), *Anitra's Dream* (1934), and *Great Laughter* (1936).

YOUNGHILL KANG (1903–1972): *The Grass Roof.* The pioneering work by the first successful Korean American writer offers a fictionalized autobiography of his life in Korea, which culminates in his immigrating to the United States in 1922. Kang, whose friendship with Thomas Wolfe while both were teachers at New York University led to a publishing contract through Wolfe's editor Maxwell Perkins at Scribner's, would publish a sequel, *East Goes West*, in 1937.

MEYER LEVIN (1905–1981): *Yehuda.* Based on the author's firsthand experiences, the novel provides the first fictional treatment of life on a kibbutz in modern Palestine. Levin, born in Chicago, had worked for the *Chicago Daily News* and drew on his experiences there for his first two novels, *Reporter* (1929) and *Frankie and Johnny* (1930).

O. E. RÖLVAAG: *Their Fathers' God.* The novel concludes Rölvaag's epic trilogy on the Norwegian immigrants in America that had begun with *Giants in the Earth* (1927) and continued with *Peder Victorious* (1929). It concerns the marriage of Per Holm to an Irish Catholic girl and focuses on religious differences.

GEORGE S. SCHUYLER (1895–1977): *Black No More.* Concerning the discovery of a cream that allows blacks to become white, the novel is considered the first full-length satire written by an African American. Schuyler, a journalist, was born in Rhode Island.

UPTON SINCLAIR: *The Wet Parade.* Sinclair presents a tractlike fictional defense of prohibition, which, according to the writer, has failed not because it is wrong but because it has never really been tried, since enforcement is hampered by politics. Preaching to the choir, the book is praised by prohibition advocates as a new *Uncle Tom's Cabin* and derided by opponents as the worst kind of propaganda.

T. S. STRIBLING: *The Forge.* This is the Tennessee writer's initial installment of a highly acclaimed Civil War trilogy treating an Alabama family's rise from poverty to wealth before, during, and after the war. It would be followed by *The Store* (1932), a Pulitzer Prize winner, and *Unfinished Cathedral* (1934).

RUTH SUCKOW: *Children and Older People.* Suckow's short story collection offers characteristic glimpses of small-town Iowa life and skillful use of local color and psychological penetration.

NATHANAEL WEST (1903–1940): *The Dream Life of Balso Snell.* West's first novel is a surrealistic fantasy issued in an edition of five hundred copies, with West's blurb announcing the book's "use of the violently dissociated, the dehumanized marvelous, the deliberately criminal and imbecilic."

Literary Criticism and Scholarship

KENNETH BURKE (1897–1993): *Counter-Statement.* Burke's first volume of criticism employs his characteristic dialectical methods of isolating commonplace truths and considering alternative approaches. The volume includes important essays such as "Psychology and Form" and "The Poetic Process." Burke was born in Pittsburgh and worked as the music critic for the *Dial* (1927–1929) and *The Nation* (1934–1936).

HENRY SEIDEL CANBY (1878–1961): *Classic Americans: A Study of Eminent American Writers from Irving to Whitman.* Canby's first important literary history evaluates the major figures of the nineteenth century. As an indicator of future changes in literary reputation, Canby devotes thirty pages to Irving but only six to Melville. Canby helped found and became the first editor of the *Saturday Review of Literature* in 1924 and became the editorial board chairman for the Book-of-the-Month Club in 1926.

CONSTANCE ROURKE: *American Humor: A Study of the National Character.* One of the foundation texts of American studies, Rourke's literary and cultural analysis looks at American archetypes such as the Yankee and the backwoodsman to define an indigenous American sense of humor and what it tells us about the American personality.

EDMUND WILSON: *Axel's Castle: A Study in Imaginative Literature of 1870–1930.* Wilson's first collection of critical essays is one of the seminal texts on literary modernism. Wilson links writers such as William Butler Yeats, Paul Valéry, Marcel Proust, James Joyce, Gertrude Stein, and Arthur Rimbaud through their connection to the Symbolist movement. Critic Sherman Paul would write that the book "established the writers of the avant garde in the consciousness of the general reader."

LOUIS ZUKOFSKY (1904–1978): "Program 'Objectivists.'" Zukofsky sets out the principles of a new poetic movement in his notes to a special "Objectivists" issue of *Poetry*, which he edits. Inspired by the work of William Carlos Williams, Zukofsky expresses the group's intention to make a poem "an inclusive object," devoid of abstraction and commentary and relying on a direct appreciation of concrete reality. In 1932 Zukofsky would publish *An "Objectivist" Anthology*, collecting the work of the poets associated with the movement — Williams, George Oppen, Charles Reznikoff, Carl Rakosi, and others.

Nonfiction

LOUIS ADAMIC (1899–1951): *Dynamite: The Story of Class Violence in America.* Adamic chronicles the history of American labor as reflected by important strikes and violent clashes from the 1830s riots, through the Molly Maguires, the Haymarket Riot, and the Sacco-Vanzetti case. Adamic was born in Yugoslavia and describes his immigrant experience in *Laughing in the Jungle* (1932).

JAMES TRUSLOW ADAMS: *The Epic of America.* Adams combines a one-volume popular history with an analysis of the American character, which he defines optimistically as the collective "dream for a better, richer, and happier life for all our citizens of every rank."

FREDERICK LEWIS ALLEN (1890–1954): *Only Yesterday: An Informal History of the Nineteen-Twenties.* Allen offers a popular overview of the past decade's politics, morals, fashions, and art. Allen served on the editorial staff of the *Atlantic Monthly* (1914–1916), *Century* magazine (1916–1917), and *Harper's Magazine* (1923–1953).

SHERWOOD ANDERSON: *Perhaps Women.* The writer's curious amalgam of poetry, narrative, and opinion mounts an attack on modern life and posits that perhaps the solution to modern problems will come when women are in charge.

EDGAR LEE MASTERS: *Lincoln the Man.* This intemperate and hostile interpretation belittles Lincoln's character and denigrates his achievements. Reviewers are puzzled by it and speculate that the book would harm its author's reputation more than its subject's.

JOHN J. PERSHING (1860–1948): *My Experiences in the World War.* The commander of the American Expeditionary Force in World War I wins the Pulitzer Prize for this memoir based on his wartime diary and later reflections.

HENRY F. PRINGLE (1897–1958): *Theodore Roosevelt.* Pringle shocks his readers with this iconoclastic, highly critical reassessment, which initiates a less flattering view

George S. Schuyler

of Roosevelt to be further developed by many future historians.

MARGARET SANGER (1883–1966): *My Fight for Birth Control.* The leader of the birth control movement in America supplies her account of her crusade to disseminate birth control information and her imprisonment after opening the first birth control clinic in Brooklyn, New York, in 1916. Her autobiography, *Margaret Sanger,* would appear in 1938.

GEORGE SANTAYANA: *The Genteel Tradition at Bay.* The philosopher critiques the New Humanism by comparing its tenets with Renaissance humanism and suggesting that the ideas of Irving Babbitt and Paul Elmer More are an attempt to reimpose the rigid, morally absolutist views of the genteel tradition.

GEORGE S. SCHUYLER: *Slaves Today: A Story of Liberia.* The first African American to serve as a foreign correspondent on a major metropolitan newspaper, Schuyler reports on the Liberian slave trade for the *New York Evening Post.* This volume reflects his experiences there.

LINCOLN STEFFENS: *Autobiography.* The muckraking journalist's extensive account of his career and his development as a reformer is significant not only for its

insights into this important figure but in its depiction of his era and the various activist movements with which he was associated.

JAMES THURBER: *The Owl in the Attic and Other Perplexities.* The first in nearly annual collections of Thurber's humorous sketches, drawings, and reflections, taken mainly from *The New Yorker.* Subsequent volumes are *The Seal in the Bedroom and Other Predicaments* (1932), *My Life and Hard Times* (1933), and *The Middle-Aged Man on the Flying Trapeze* (1935).

Poetry

CONRAD AIKEN: *The Coming Forth of Osiris Jones* and *Preludes for Memnon.* Both volumes express Aiken's increasing metaphysical interests. The first deals with the progress of a soul from life to death; the second presents the night thoughts of consciousness.

E. E. CUMMINGS: *ViVa.* Cummings is at his most experimentally daring in this collection of seventy poems showing his characteristic scrambling of syntax, diction, and typography. It includes the much-anthologized "somewhere I have never travelled, gladly beyond," Cummings's impassioned defense of love, nature, and the individual.

GEORGE DILLON (1906–1968): *The Flowering Stone.* The editor of *Poetry* magazine wins the Pulitzer Prize for his second collection of verses, following *Boy in the Wind* (1927).

LANGSTON HUGHES: "Christ in Alabama." Hughes's protest poem dealing with the trial of the Scottsboro Boys equates the silence of black colleges over the verdict to the bystanders at Christ's crucifixion. When Hughes reads the poem, with the lines "Christ is a Nigger / Beaten and black" — at the University of North Carolina, a near riot ensues.

ROBINSON JEFFERS: *Descent to the Dead.* This is a series of elegies inspired by a trip to England and Ireland in which the poet repeats his contention that the individual must break through the bonds of humanity to achieve transcendence over time and nature.

FRANCIS SCOTT KEY: "The Star-Spangled Banner." Key's poem becomes the U.S. national anthem by an act of Congress.

EDNA ST. VINCENT MILLAY: *Fatal Interview.* The poet shows her mastery of the sonnet form in this cycle, in the Elizabethan manner, on the vagaries of love.

OGDEN NASH (1902–1971): *Free Wheeling* and *Hard Lines.* Nash's first solo collections of his humorous verses display the characteristic whimsy that would make him America's most popular and most quoted contemporary poet. Similar collections, *Happy Days* (1933) and *The Primrose Path* (1935), would follow.

DOROTHY PARKER: *Death and Taxes.* Parker's third collection of devilishly ironic verses causes prominent critic Henry Seidel Canby to enthuse, "This belle dame sans merci has the ruthlessness of the great tragic lyricist whose work was allegorized in the fable of the nightingale singing with her breast against a thorn. It is disillusion recollected in tranquility."

EDWIN ARLINGTON ROBINSON: *Matthias at the Door.* One of the poet's most powerful blank-verse narrative poems traces how the suicides of his neighbor and his wife shatter a man's shallow complacency and indifference to others.

MARK VAN DOREN: *Jonathan Gentry.* Van Doren's narrative poem follows five generations of an American family through the nineteenth century.

Publications and Events

The Group Theatre is formed by Harold Clurman (1901–1980), Cheryl Crawford (1902–1986), and Lee Strasburg (1901–1982), former associates of the Theatre Guild who wanted to create an acting and production company to present more politically and socially relevant works. Their first production is Paul Green's *The House of Connelly;* their first major success is Sidney Kingsley's *Men in White* (1933). The company produced all of the plays of Clifford Odets, a former actor in the company. The Group Theatre disbanded in 1941.

Story. The first periodical devoted exclusively to the short story is founded by Whit Burnett (1899–1973) and Martha Foley (c. 1897–1977) in Vienna to provide a forum for unknown writers and controversial subject matter. The publication moved to New York in 1933, where it continued until 1953.

1932

Drama and Theater

MAXWELL ANDERSON: *Night Over Taos.* Anderson's historical drama about Spanish resistance to the American incursion in nineteenth-century New Mexico, the third Group Theatre production, closes in its second week.

PHILIP BARRY: *The Animal Kingdom.* Barry's comedy shows a man divided between his wife and his mistress, with the witty conclusion that the faithfulness of a relationship is not confined to matrimony.

S. N. BEHRMAN: *Biography.* Regarded as the playwright's best comedy, the drama concerns the various loves of a fashionable portrait painter whose decision to write her memoir causes consternation among her present and former liaisons. The sophisticated comedy of manners bristles with the author's brilliant dialogue.

RACHEL CROTHERS: *When Ladies Meet.* In Crothers's comedy, a woman writer falls in love with her married publisher and meets his wife to discover what they have in common.

BEN HECHT AND CHARLES MacARTHUR: *Twentieth Century.* Broadway and Hollywood are the targets in this comedy about monomaniacal producer Oscar Jaffe, who tries to repair his fading fortunes by wooing his former discovery, movie star Lily Garland (formerly Mildred Plotka), while aboard the Twentieth Century Limited train.

LANGSTON HUGHES: *Scottsboro Limited.* First published in the *New Masses* and first performed at a mass rally to protest the Scottsboro verdict, Hughes's one-act protest play in verse uses a chorus as well as a bare stage with a single white man to represent the forces of oppression. It ends with black characters smashing an electric chair while the audience is encouraged to shout "Fight, fight, fight," and a red flag is symbolically raised. The play marks the beginning of Hughes's association with leftist politics.

GEORGE S. KAUFMAN AND EDNA FERBER: *Dinner at Eight.* Dinner guests at turning points in their lives interact in this literate social comedy.

ELMER RICE: *We, the People.* The first in a series of upbeat message plays trumpeting democratic values under threat would be followed by *Judgment Day* (1934), *Between Two Worlds* (1934), and *American Landscape* (1938). None succeed with critics or at the box office.

Fiction

SHERWOOD ANDERSON: *Beyond Desire.* In his first novel in seven years, Anderson shifts his setting from the Midwest to a Southern mill town but continues his exploration of a youth's search for meaning and fulfillment and a community's dislocation due to industrial change.

PEARL S. BUCK: *Sons.* The sequel to *The Good Earth* (1931) and the second of The House of Earth trilogy follows the careers of Wang Lung's three sons and the further disruption of traditional Chinese society by modern forces.

KENNETH BURKE: *Towards a Better Life.* Burke's experimental fiction takes the form of a series of epistles or declamations from a man who withdraws from society and degenerates into delusion and helpless isolation.

ERSKINE CALDWELL: *Tobacco Road.* Caldwell's first major success, and the first of a series of novels that the author would refer to as "a cyclorama of Southern life," concerns a squalid sharecropper family in Georgia. Caldwell's frank depiction of sexuality and physicality prompts bans and condemnation, particularly from Southerners, but the book becomes a bestseller. Adapted for the stage by Jack Kirkland in 1933, it would set a record, running on Broadway for eight years.

WILLA CATHER: *Obscure Destinies.* Cather's three long stories are linked by western rural settings and by dealing with protagonists who contend with the challenges of their environments. The book is warmly received as a return to the author's strengths.

COUNTEE CULLEN: *One Way to Heaven.* Cullen's only novel is commonly grouped with Wallace Thurman's *Infants of the Spring* (1932) and George S. Schuyler's *Black No More* (1931) as the most important fictional treatments of the Harlem Renaissance.

EDWARD DAHLBERG: *From Flushing to Cavalry.* Dahlberg's second novel continues to draw on his early experiences living in the Flushing section of Queens, New York. His socially realistic style earns him repute as one of the leading proletarian novelists of the decade.

JOHN DOS PASSOS: *1919.* The second volume in Dos Passos's monumental U.S.A. trilogy chronicles American life through the war years, from the vantage point of five central figures — a sailor, a minister's daughter, a Texas girl, a Jewish radical, and a young poet. It is interspersed with short biographies of historical figures such as John Reed, Theodore Roosevelt, Joe Hill, and J. P. Morgan. It had been preceded by *The 42nd Parallel* (1930) and would be followed by *The Big Money* (1936).

JAMES T. FARRELL (1904–79): *Young Lonigan: A Boyhood in Chicago Streets.* The first novel in the Studs Lonigan trilogy, one of the decade's great fictional achievements, introduces the Irish Catholic protagonist growing up on Chicago's South Side. Rendered in a stream-of-consciousness style, Farrell's meticulously documented naturalistic novel traces the connection between environment and the hero's choices, which determine his downfall. Farrell, a Chicago native, drew on his experiences on the south side of Chicago for his fictional work, which had first appeared in *This Quarter* in 1930.

WILLIAM FAULKNER: *Light in August.* One of Faulkner's greatest novels concerns the tragic ramifications of the purportedly mixed-blood heritage of the outcast Joe Christmas and the rigidity and alienation of a large cast of memorable characters, including New England liberal Joanna Burden, disgraced minister Gail Hightower, and seduced-and-abandoned country girl Lena Grove.

RUDOLPH FISHER: *The Conjure-Man Dies.* Fisher's second and final novel is a mystery set in Harlem, which is considered the first to employ black sleuths. Intending to write additional mysteries featuring his detective duo of a policeman and a physician, Fisher manages only a short story, "John Archer's Nose," published posthumously in 1935.

VARDIS FISHER (1895–1968): *In Tragic Life.* The first volume of an autobiographical tetralogy detailing Vridar Hunter's life in the West. The character was first introduced in Fisher's second novel, *Dark Bridewell* (1931). His story is continued in *I See No Sin* (1934), *Passions Spin the Plot* (1934), *We Are Betrayed* (1935), and *No Villain Need Be* (1936). Fisher was an Idaho native, and much of his work draws on aspects of the region and its history. Besides historical novels, Fisher is best known for his *Testament of Man*, a twelve-novel cycle tracing human development from prehistory.

ZELDA FITZGERALD (1900–1948): *Save Me the Waltz.* The only novel by the wife of F. Scott Fitzgerald is chiefly significant for providing her perspective on their relationship in a closely autobiographical account of a Southern belle who marries a prominent young artist.

ELLEN GLASGOW: *The Sheltered Life.* One of the author's most representative and finest novels concerns the destructive relationships of two declining extended families in Virginia — the Archibalds and the Birdsongs — who struggle to preserve old social traditions in the face of modern changes.

DASHIELL HAMMETT: *The Thin Man.* Hammett's last novel introduces the husband-and-wife sleuths Nick and Nora Charles (based on Hammett himself and Lillian Hellman), in what proves to be the writer's biggest-selling work. The book makes Hammett a celebrity and a fortune, but he would write no other novels or stories. Hammett would later state that "nobody ever invented a more insufferably smug pair of characters." His readers, however, find them irresistible, and the 1934 film, starring William Powell and Myrna Loy, was so popular that five sequels followed.

ROBERT HERRICK: *The End of Desire.* Herrick's novel concerns a middle-aged love affair that reverses expected sexual roles, with the woman casual in her sexual desires and the man longing for commitment.

GRACE LUMPKIN (c. 1892–1980): *To Make My Bread.* The Georgia-born proletarian novelist's first book concerns a family of Southern mountaineers. Forced off the land to work in a mill, they join in a strike. The book wins the Maxim Gorky Prize for best labor novel and would be dramatized in 1936 by Albert Bein as *Let Freedom Ring.* Her subsequent novels would be *A Sign for Cain* (1935), *The Wedding* (1939), and *Full Circle* (1962).

CHARLES BERNARD NORDHOFF (1887–1947) AND JAMES HALL (1887–1951): *Mutiny on the Bounty.* The first of a trilogy of novels dramatizing the infamous *Bounty* mutiny. *Men Against the Sea* and *Pitcairn's Island* would follow in 1934. The writers met while serving in the Lafayette Flying Corps. in World War I and lived for a number of years in Tahiti during the 1920s, researching the *Bounty* history.

CLAUDE McKAY: *Gingertown.* In this short story collection, half the stories are set in Harlem and half in the West Indies and North Africa. They share a theme of the exploitation and humiliation of blacks in white society.

ELIZABETH MADOX ROBERTS: *The Haunted Mirror.* This collection of short stories details the way of life among Kentucky hill people.

DAMON RUNYON (1884–1946): *Guys and Dolls.* The journalist and sportswriter produces his first collection of stories treating underworld figures, athletes, and Broadway denizens, all characterized in a slangy vibrancy. It would inspire the 1950 Broadway musical of the same name by Abe Burrows and others.

JOHN STEINBECK: *The Pastures of Heaven.* Steinbeck's second publication is a story collection linked by the setting of a California farming community. It introduces Steinbeck's characteristic subject of the common man's relationship with the land.

WALLACE THURMAN: *Infants of the Spring.* The second of Thurman's three novels is the only work by a participant of the Harlem Renaissance that attacks the movement, with fictionalized characters easily identified as Langston Hughes, Zora Neale Hurston, Countee Cullen, and others. Thurman accuses them of wasting their talent in decadent lifestyles and proclaiming intellectual and artistic freedom while courting white approval.

LAURA INGALLS WILDER (1897–1957): *Little House in the Big Woods.* The first book in Wilder's autobiographical series recounting her pioneer life becomes a bestseller and an instant children's classic. It would be followed by *Farmer Boy* (1933), *Little House on the Prairie* (1935), *On the Banks of Plum Creek* (1937), *By the Shores of Silver Lake* (1939), *The Long Winter* (1940), *Little Town on the Prairie* (1941), and *These Happy Golden Years* (1943). The series is unique in that its style "ages" as its narrator grows up.

WILLIAM CARLOS WILLIAMS: *The Knife of the Times, and Other Stories.* Williams's first story collection is a series of objectively rendered commonplace episodes.

THOMAS WOLFE: *A Portrait of Bascom Hawke.* Wolfe's novella, first appearing in *Scribner's,* is a unified and masterful portrait of an aging man's regrets over the futility of his life. It would be later incorporated into *Of Time and the River.*

ANZIA YEZIERSKA: *All I Could Never Be.* The novel is the author's fullest examination of her relationship with educator and philosopher John Dewey in the doomed romance between a young immigrant woman and an established American.

Literary Criticism and Scholarship

IRVING BABBITT: *On Being Creative, and Other Essays.* In addition to critical essays on William Wordsworth, Samuel Taylor Coleridge, and Johann Schiller, Babbitt reflects on the creative process and "The Critic and American Life."

V. F. CALVERTON: *The Liberation of American Literature.* This is generally considered the first comprehensive literary history of America from a Marxist perspective.

BERNARD DeVOTO (1897–1955): *Mark Twain's America.* DeVoto challenges Van Wyck Brooks's contention in *The Ordeal of Mark Twain* (1920) that the writer was a frustrated, limited figure. The Idaho-born professor at Northwestern (1922–1927) and Harvard (1929–1936) asserts Twain's achievement as a frontier humorist who opened up American life for literature.

T. S. ELIOT: *Selected Essays, 1917–1932.* This gathering of many of Eliot's most significant literary and cultural essays, including "The Metaphysical Poets," "Hamlet and His Problems," and "Tradition and the Individual Talent," solidifies Eliot's reputation as one of the era's most formidable and influential critics.

LUDWIG LEWISOHN: *Expression in America.* A critical analysis of the American spirit as expressed in literature, employing Freudian ideas to clarify American preoccupations and traits.

Nonfiction

LOUIS ADAMIC: *Laughter in the Jungle: The Autobiography of an Immigrant in America.* Adamic details his Yugoslavian childhood and life in America beginning in 1913. To explain his title, Adamic states that the

United States "is more a jungle than a civilization" in which "by far the most precious possession a sensitive and intelligent person can have is an active sense of humor."

JAMES TRUSLOW ADAMS: *The March of Democracy.* The first installment in a two-volume history of America covers the discovery and settlement to 1860. In 1933 the second volume would be published, detailing the Civil War and the evolution of industrial America.

ERNEST HEMINGWAY: *Death in the Afternoon.* Bullfighting as existential and artistic metaphor is Hemingway's subject in this discourse, which interweaves the history and practices of bullfighting with observations on death, modern literature, and the art of living. The book is an essential source for understanding Hemingway's philosophy of combat and "grace under pressure."

MABEL DODGE LUHAN (1879–1962): *Lorenzo in Taos.* Responsible for bringing D. H. Lawrence to Taos, New Mexico, the art patron and salon hostess in Italy and New York City describes Lawrence's residence there and includes several of the writer's letters, in print for the first time.

JOHN JOSEPH MATHEWS (c. 1894–1979): *Wah-Kon-Tah: The Osage and the White Man's Road.* Mathews's account of reservation life becomes a Book-of-the-Month Club selection, the first by a Native American. Mathews was an Osage, born in Oklahoma. His other significant work, *Talking to the Moon* (1945), is a Thoreau-like celebration of nature from the vantage point of a secluded retreat.

H. L. MENCKEN: *Making a President.* This work collects Mencken's reporting on the 1932 Republican and Democratic presidential conventions.

JOHN G. NEIHARDT: *Black Elk Speaks.* Neihardt converts his interviews with the Sioux holy man Black Elk (1863–1950) into a first-person autobiographical account, praised by Carl Jung for its mysticism and psychological insights. It has been called "a North American bible of all tribes." Black Elk survived the battles of Little Big Horn and Wounded Knee. His account of Sioux religious rites appears in *The Sacred Pipe* (1953).

ALLAN NEVINS (1890–1971): *Grover Cleveland: A Study in Courage.* Nevins, a former journalist and Columbia history professor, wins the first of his two Pulitzer Prizes for this sympathetic treatment of Cleveland's career and character, which remains the fullest portrait available. His second prize-winning book is *Hamilton Fish: The Inner History of the Grant Administration* (1936).

CARL SANDBURG: *Mary Lincoln, Wife and Widow.* Sandburg provides a biographical account of the married life of Mary Todd and Abraham Lincoln, as well as her years alone. It includes primary documents edited by Lincoln scholar Paul M. Angle (1900–1975).

UPTON SINCLAIR: *American Outpost: A Book of Reminiscences.* The writer supplies an account of his life and his artistic development.

DOROTHY THOMPSON: *"I Saw Hitler!"* The journalist and columnist admits taking only "five-sixth of a minute" in her interview with Hitler "to measure the startling insignificance of this man who has set the world agog."

FREDERICK JACKSON TURNER: *The Significance of Sections in American History.* Turner is posthumously awarded the Pulitzer Prize for this collection of articles on sectionalism. His long-anticipated but incomplete study, *The United States, 1830–1850: The Nation and Its Sections*, would appear in 1935.

CARL VAN VECHTEN: *Sacred and Profane Memories.* Before giving up writing for photography, Van Vechten collects this volume of autobiographical reflections and impressions.

EDMUND WILSON: *The American Jitters: A Year of the Slump.* Economic, political, and social events of 1931 are reviewed in this collection of articles praised by reviewer John Chamberlain as "probably the best that the period of the depression has brought forth."

Poetry

STERLING BROWN (1901–1989): *Southern Road.* Although Brown's initial poetry collection, one of the first to exploit black folk themes and dialect, is praised at the time and later recognized as one of the greatest achievements of the decade, the poet would be unable to find a publisher for his second volume; he would publish no new poetry until 1975. Brown was a professor of English at Howard University from 1929 to 1969 whose students included Amiri Baraka and Toni Morrison.

ROBERT P. TRISTRAM COFFIN (1892–1955): *Ballads of Square-Toed Americans.* The Maine poet's collection features a retelling of the *Aeneid* as an American quest narrative. It would be followed by the collection *Strange Holiness* (1935), a winner of the Pulitzer Prize.

LANGSTON HUGHES: *The Dream Keeper* and *Scottsboro Limited: Four Poems and a Play in Verse.* The first is a selection of the poet's works for young people; the second is a series of poems and a one-act play on the Scottsboro case.

ROBINSON JEFFERS: *Thurso's Landing, and Other Poems.* The narrative title poem dramatizes a destructive triangle as a California farmer vies with a rival for his wife's love. This domestic tragedy explores the dangers of passion when individuals lack a moral center.

ARCHIBALD MacLEISH: *Conquistador.* MacLeish's epic poem about the conquest of Mexico by Hernán Cortés is hailed as the poet's masterpiece; it wins the Pulitzer Prize in 1933.

EDWIN ARLINGTON ROBINSON: *Nicodemus.* Four of the ten poems in this collection have biblical subjects; three have a West Indies setting; all share a tone of tragic awareness.

ALLEN TATE (1899–1979): *Poems, 1928–1931.* Tate's third collection is well received for its stately, sensuous evocations of Southern experience.

Publications and Events

The *American Scholar.* This quarterly journal of the United Chapters of Phi Beta Kappa, edited by Hiram Hayden until his death in 1973, begins publication. Its title and mission are drawn from Ralph Waldo Emerson's 1837 lecture.

Common Sense. This liberal review of political, economic, and social affairs debuts, to include contributors such as John Dos Passos, Archibald MacLeish, Upton Sinclair, Norman Thomas, Louis Adamic, John Dewey, and Max Eastman. The magazine was absorbed by the *American Mercury* in 1946.

Folger Shakespeare Memorial Library. A gift from oil magnate Henry Clay Folger (1857–1930) and his wife, this research library in Washington, D.C., opens to the public. Administered by Folger's alma mater, Amherst, it contains the greatest collection of Shakespeareana in the United States, including seventy-nine copies of the First Folio, as well as much material relating to English history and literature of the sixteenth and seventeenth centuries.

1933

Drama and Theater

MAXWELL ANDERSON: *Both Your Houses.* The playwright's political satire on self- and special-interest politics wins the Pulitzer Prize. Anderson's other drama during the year is *Mary of Scotland,* a blank-verse tragedy that critic John Mason Brown praises as "the best historical drama that has been written by an American."

JOHN DOS PASSOS: *Fortune Heights.* The play traces the rise and fall of a real estate development. It would be collected in *Three Plays* (1934).

MOSS HART: *As Thousands Cheer.* This innovative revue, with sketches by Hart and music by Irving Berlin, takes the form of dramatized newspaper headlines.

Although mainly lighthearted, it features a segment on a lynching, featuring Ethel Waters singing "Supper Time."

SIDNEY HOWARD: *Alien Corn.* Katherine Cornell stars as a young pianist trapped in a dreary Midwestern college town in Howard's melodrama featuring a somewhat subdued, psychological honesty and an impressive star turn by Cornell.

SIDNEY KINGSLEY (1906–1995): *Men in White.* Kingsley's first Broadway production concerns the ethical conflict of a young intern forced to choose between a comfortable personal life and service to his profession. It wins the Pulitzer Prize and represents the first major success for the Group Theatre, establishing its reputation for offering realistic, socially relevant dramas. Kingsley was born in Philadelphia and began writing plays while a student at Cornell.

JACK KIRKLAND (1902–1969): *Tobacco Road.* The adaptation of Erskine Caldwell's 1932 novel about a shiftless sharecropper family is assailed by the critics as "repulsive," "ridiculously inept," and "an ugly wallowing sort of drama." It is, however, a box office phenomenon, running for a record 3,182 performances over eight years. Kirkland's only other Broadway success was *I Must Love Someone* (1939), an account of the Florodora girls.

EUGENE O'NEILL: *Ah, Wilderness!* The playwright's only comedy is an affectionate recollection of O'Neill's adolescence in New London, Connecticut. Its warmhearted treatment of his family life contrasts sharply with the lacerating portrait he would create in a *Long Day's Journey into Night.* Critic George Jean Nathan calls the play "the tenderest and most amusing comedy of boyhood in the American Drama."

Fiction

CONRAD AIKEN: *Great Circle.* Aiken's second novel is a highly psychological stream-of-consciousness story of a man who learns that his wife has betrayed him. It is said that Sigmund Freud so admired the book that he kept a copy permanently on his desk.

HERVEY ALLEN: *Anthony Adverse.* One of the decade's biggest sellers is this picaresque historical romance set during the Napoleonic era. The title character travels throughout Europe, Africa, and America in a series of adventures and encounters with historical figures such as Napoleon, Jean Lafitte, and Aaron Burr. A latter-day Childe Harold, Adverse is a brooding, reflective adventurer more suited to contemporary postwar tastes.

SHERWOOD ANDERSON: *Death in the Woods and Other Stories.* Arguably Anderson's strongest collection, the volume includes the title work, which Anderson considered his best, and the masterful "Brother Death." The bankruptcy of the book's publisher, Liveright, prevents wide distribution, and the volume has never received the attention it deserves.

KAY BOYLE: *Gentlemen, I Address You Privately.* Boyle's daring study of sexuality features two homosexuals, three lesbians, a brothel keeper, and a seduction in a generally sympathetic treatment of what standards at the time regard as sexual perversity. Boyle also publishes a story collection, *First Lover, and Other Stories*, which includes the admired "Rest Cure."

PEARL S. BUCK: *First Wife and Other Stories.* Buck's first and best story collection concerns China and features "Wang Lung," the story that introduces her protagonist and the central incident of *The Good Earth*. Other stories depict the Communist revolution, the contrast between traditional Chinese values and Western ideas, and incidents from the tragic Yangtze flood of 1931.

ERSKINE CALDWELL: *God's Little Acre.* The writer continues his controversial documentation of Southern lowlife in the story of Georgian Ty Ty Waldon's search for gold on his run-down farm. Considered by some to be Caldwell's masterpiece, the book is banned throughout the United States and excoriated in the South for its unflattering portrait of Southern degeneration. After publishing an initial, unsuccessful story collection, *American Earth* (1931), Caldwell also issues what is regarded as some of his strongest fiction in this second collection, *We Are the Living*.

RAYMOND CHANDLER (1888–1959): "Blackmailers Don't Shoot." Chandler's first detective story is published in the December issue of *Black Mask*. Born in Chicago, raised in Europe, Chandler served in World War I and worked in the oil business before beginning his writing career.

JAMES GOULD COZZENS: *The Last Adam.* Cozzens offers his first examination of a professional (here, a doctor) in conflict with community standards.

JAMES T. FARRELL: *Gas-House McGinty.* Farrell's novel about the interrelationships of the employees of a Chicago express company introduces the character of Danny O'Neill, who would become the protagonist in a series of novels beginning with *A World I Never Made* (1936).

ERLE STANLEY GARDNER (1889–1970): *The Case of the Velvet Claws.* The first case for defense attorney–sleuth Perry Mason, whose career would continue in nearly eighty books until the author's death. Mason becomes the most famous lawyer in fiction and makes his creator, called "the Henry Ford of detective novelists," one of the most successful writers in history, with sales during his lifetime in excess of 100 million copies.

ALBERT HALPER (1904–1984): *Union Square.* The Chicago-born proletarian writer's first book is a collective novel about how a cross-section of inhabitants around New York City's Union Square are shaped by their surroundings. His other realistic novels during the decade are *The Foundry* (1934), about a Chicago factory, and *The Chute* (1937), concerning workers in a mail-order company.

ERNEST HEMINGWAY: *Winner Take Nothing.* This short story collection includes important works such as "A Clean, Well-Lighted Place," "A Way You'll Never Be," "Homage to Switzerland," and "A Natural History of the Dead."

JOSEPHINE HERBST: *Pity Is Not Enough.* This is the first volume in a family saga trilogy, and the writer's most important work, concerning the fate of the Trexler family from the 1890s through the 1930s. Subsequent volumes are *The Executioner Waits* (1934) and *Rope of Gold* (1939).

ZORA NEALE HURSTON: "The Gilded Six-Bits." What is regarded by many as Hurston's finest short story appears in *Story*. It gains Hurston critical attention, which would help lead to the publication of her first novel, *Jonah's Gourd Vine* (1934).

JAMES JOYCE (1882–1941): *Ulysses.* In a landmark ruling, district court judge John M. Woolsey declares that "in spite of unusual frankness, I do not detect anywhere the leer of the sensualist" in the book; it thereby fails to meet his definition of pornography. The ruling lifts the ban on the 1922 novel and opens the way for American publication, while setting a precedent for future obscenity cases.

SINCLAIR LEWIS: *Ann Vickers.* Lewis, criticized for his treatment of his women characters, undertakes a novel with a female protagonist, an idealistic social worker. The novel features an acknowledgment of lesbianism and a moral justification for extramarital relationships.

WILLIAM MARCH (1893–1954): *Company K.* The Alabama-born writer's first book reflects his combat experiences during World War I as each member of an infantry company gives his perspective. Granville Hicks observes that the book "takes its place with the two or three first-rate American novels about the World War."

CLAUDE MCKAY: *Banana Bottom.* McKay's third novel, generally regarded as his most accomplished, concerns a black Jamaican peasant girl's conflict between her racial heritage and her education at the hands of white missionaries. The book underscores the writer's principal theme of the quest of the black individual for a cultural identity in a white society. Seen at the time as mainly valuable for its exotic setting, the novel is now regarded as a classic in establishing underlying racial and cultural tensions.

JOHN M. OSKISON (1874–1947): *Brothers Three*. The best work by one of the earliest Native American novelists is set in the Oklahoma Territory after the turn of the century and features major Indian characters for the first time in his fiction. Oskison was born in Oklahoma to a part-Cherokee mother and a white father. His short story "Only the Master Shall Praise" won a prize in 1899 from *Century* magazine, and it led to his work appearing in newspapers and magazines.

MARJORIE KINNAN RAWLINGS (1896–1953): *South Moon Under*. Rawlings's first novel is the story of a family of Florida moonshiners in the hummock country of Florida. Born in Washington, D.C., Rawlings was a reporter who settled in Cross Creek, Florida, in 1928.

JOHN STEINBECK: *To a God Unknown*. Steinbeck's second novel (but his third to be published) is a highly symbolic story of a California farmer's self-sacrifice as part of a fertility ritual. The novel is noteworthy for working out Steinbeck's philosophy of man's relationship with nature, a theme reflected in his future works.

NATHANAEL WEST: *Miss Lonelyhearts*. Introduced by his brother-in-law S. J. Perelman to an advice columnist for the *Brooklyn Eagle*, who showed him a sample of the pathetic letters she received, West conceives his bitterly ironic tale of a newspaperman who dispenses advice to the lovelorn and becomes tragically involved in his readers' desperate lives. Despite positive reviews, sales falter when the book's publisher, Horace Liveright, goes bankrupt. It is now considered one of the classics of the era.

EDITH WHARTON: *Human Nature*. Wharton's ninth story collection contains "Her Son," "The Day of the Funeral," "A Glimpse," "Diagnosis," and "Joy in the House."

Literary Criticism and Scholarship

T. S. ELIOT: *The Use of Poetry and the Use of Criticism*. Eliot's lecture series at Harvard includes discussions of Elizabethan poetry and drama; considerations of John Dryden, Samuel Taylor Coleridge, Percy Bysshe Shelley, John Keats, and Matthew Arnold; and an articulation of Eliot's increasing social and cultural conservatism.

GRANVILLE HICKS (1901–1982): *The Great Tradition*. Hicks's first volume of literary criticism is a Marxist interpretation of American literature since the Civil War. It is regarded as one of the first systematic analyses of the literary history of the period and establishes Hicks's reputation as a major critic. Hicks served on the editorial

board of *New Masses* and would resign from the Communist Party in 1939, becoming a vocal opponent of Soviet policies thereafter.

Nonfiction

HERBERT AGAR (1897–1980): *The People's Choice*. Agar's highly critical study of the American presidency wins the Pulitzer Prize. Agar was associated with the Agrarians and edited, with Allen Tate, *Who Owns America?* (1936).

E. E. CUMMINGS: *Eimi*. One of Cummings's strongest works is this account of his travels in Russia, which celebrates the power of the individual in the face of the regimentation and repression of Soviet life.

JAMES WELDON JOHNSON: *Along This Way*. Johnson's influential and acclaimed autobiography traces his career in the wider context of his times and the struggle for civil rights.

ALAIN LOCKE: *The Negro in America*. The first in a series of Locke's sociological and cultural studies of black life in America. It would be followed by *The Negro and His Music* (1936), *Negro Art — Past and Present* (1936), and *The Negro in Art* (1940).

MABEL DODGE LUHAN: *Background*. The socialite and saloniste offers the first installment of her four-volume autobiography, *Intimate Memories*, recording her association with a veritable who's who of international artists and writers. Subsequent volumes are *Europe Experiences* (1935), *Movers and Shakers* (1936), and *Edge of Taos Desert* (1937).

EZRA POUND: *ABC of Economics*. Pound's increasingly obsessive preoccupation with economics is evident in this reinterpretation of cultural history as a struggle between producers and usurers that creates, in Pound's mind, a new pantheon of heroes, including Thomas Jefferson and Benito Mussolini, based on their fiscal policies. In *Jefferson and/or Mussolini* (1935) Pound would attempt to demonstrate that the two have a great deal in common and that the Fascist revolution in Italy is the logical outcome of the American Revolution.

GERTRUDE STEIN: *The Autobiography of Alice B. Toklas*. Stein's only bestseller is this account of her life in Paris, written from the perspective of her secretary and companion. The book's popularity prompts the author's highly publicized lecture tour of the United States in 1934.

JAMES THURBER: *My Life and Hard Times*. Ernest Hemingway praises Thurber's witty recollections of the trials and tribulations in his life as "far superior to the autobiography of Henry Adams."

E. B. WHITE: *Alice Through the Cellophane*. White critiques the petty annoyances and disturbing trends of modern life in this collection.

Poetry

HART CRANE: *Collected Poems*. Published after his suicide in 1932, this work includes Crane's highly influential corpus of two previous volumes and a number of unpublished poems and West Indies sketches. Despite his short career and relatively small production, critics regard Crane as one of the pivotal figures in modern American literature. Allen Tate called him "one of those men whom every age seems to select as the spokesman of its spiritual life; they give the age away."

WILLIAM FAULKNER: *A Green Bough*. The writer, who would regard himself as a "failed poet," publishes his second and last poetry collection.

ROBERT HILLYER (1895–1961): *Collected Verse*. The poet best known for his use of the heroic couplet would receive the Pulitzer Prize for this collection. He also publishes a critical study, *Some Roots of English Poetry*. Hillyer, who taught at Harvard and Trinity, would publish his *Collected Poems* in 1961.

ROBINSON JEFFERS: *Give Your Heart to the Hawks, and Other Poems*. The volume's title poem tells the story of a man who kills his brother and who, in the words of the author, "having shaken off the code of humanity by murder, is forbidden to reenter the human world."

ARCHIBALD MACLEISH: *Frescoes for Mr. Rockefeller's City*. Intended as a "replacement" for the removed murals by Diego Rivera commissioned for New York's Rockefeller Center, MacLeish's sequence celebrates the American land and labor despite the excesses of both capitalists and radicals. MacLeish's "public speech" style and declamatory stance are also evident in his other 1933 collection, *Poems, 1924–1933*, particularly in "Elpenor," MacLeish's partisan version of the modern underworld.

EZRA POUND: *A Draft of XXX Cantos*. The first of three segments of Pound's massive poetic sequence to be published during the decade. *Eleven New Cantos, XXXI–XLI* would follow in 1934 and *The Fifth Decade of Cantos* in 1937.

EDWIN ARLINGTON ROBINSON: *Talifer*. Robinson attempts a dramatic narrative comedy featuring two men and two women who change partners. It is described as "the happiest of all Robinson's longer poems" and features Robinson's version of the modern independent woman.

SARA TEASDALE: *Strange Victory*. Published after the poet's suicide, the collection contains a series of farewells to her life and experiences. Her *Collected Poems* would be issued in 1937, solidifying Teasdale's reputation as one of the most popular American poets of the pre–World War II era, going through more than twenty printings before being reissued in paperback in 1966.

Publications and Events

The *American Review*. After the demise of the *Bookman*, its editor, Seward Collins (1899–1952), creates this journal to critique contemporary life. It would be published until 1937.

Esquire. The magazine begins publication as a glossy men's magazine whose racy illustrations of scantily clad women make it notorious. It also published serious work by leading writers, including Ernest Hemingway's *Green Hills of Africa*.

1934

Drama and Theater

MAXWELL ANDERSON: *Valley Forge*. Supposedly shamed into an American theme by his critics, Anderson fails to bring alive the struggle of George Washington and the American army during the Revolution, and the play manages only fifty-eight performances.

S. N. BEHRMAN: *Rain from Heaven*. The playwright tackles current events in this drama about a love affair between an English aristocrat and a Jewish refugee from the Nazis. Behrman's characteristic witty brilliance is lacking, replaced by a preachy high-mindedness.

MARC CONNELLY: *The Farmer Takes a Wife*. Cowritten with Frank B. Elser, this comedy, based on Walter B. Edmonds's novel *Rome Haul* (1929), is Connelly's last successful play, noteworthy for launching actor Henry Fonda's career.

T. S. ELIOT: *The Rock*. Eliot's initial attempt at poetic drama is this pageant play written on behalf of the Anglican diocese of London, which dramatizes the history of Christianity.

PAUL GREEN: *Roll, Sweet Chariot*. This "symphonic play of the Negro people" dramatizes the downfall of the black shantytown Potter's Field.

LILLIAN HELLMAN (1905–1984): *The Children's Hour*. The playwright's first production creates a sensation due to its subject of two private school teachers falsely accused of lesbianism. The play establishes Hellman as a major dramatic talent, and the controversy over its failure to win the Pulitzer Prize helps prompt the creation of the New York Drama Critics Circle Award.

SIDNEY HOWARD AND PAUL DE KRUIF: *Yellow Jack*. Howard teams with bacteriologist and popularizer of science de Kruif to create this documentary drama on the conquering of yellow fever. It would be made into a film in 1938.

SIDNEY HOWARD AND SINCLAIR LEWIS: *Dodsworth*. This successful adaptation of Lewis's 1929 novel owes much to the performance of Walter Huston in the title role, reprised in the 1936 film version.

JOHN HOWARD LAWSON: *The Pure of Heart* and *Gentlewoman*. Opening on Broadway within three days of each other, both plays have a strong social message. In the first, a small-town girl comes to New York and falls in love with a gunman; in the second, a rich woman tries to resolve her materialism with her sympathy for the poor.

EUGENE O'NEILL: *Days Without End*. The failure of the playwright's "modern miracle play," in which a divided character (played by two different actors) is redeemed by religious faith, contributes to O'Neill's retirement from the Broadway stage for twelve years, until the opening of *The Iceman Cometh* in 1946.

COLE PORTER (1891–1964): *Anything Goes*. Described as the "quintessential musical comedy of the thirties," the smash hit features one of Porter's greatest scores, with standards such as the title song, "I Get a Kick out of You," and "You're the Top." The story, written by Guy Bolton and P. G. Wodehouse (1881–1975), about a group of shipwrecked passengers, had to be changed during rehearsals when a cruise liner burned, killing 125.

GERTRUDE STEIN: *Four Saints in Three Acts*. The opera with music by Virgil Thomson actually comprises four acts and tells the story of as many as sixteen saints, including Saint Theresa and her male alter ego. It is first performed with an all-black cast, and the libretto features two of Stein's most famous lines: "Pigeons on the grass alas" and "When this you see remember me."

JOHN WEXLEY: *They Shall Not Die*. Wexley dramatizes the 1931 court case in Scottsboro, Alabama, in which nine black youths were charged with raping two white schoolgirls.

Fiction

CONRAD AIKEN: *Among the Lost People*. Aiken's story collection includes "Mr. Arcularis," which the author would adapt as a play published in 1957, about a lonely man's liberating mental journey while physically confined to an operating table.

JAMES M. CAIN (1892–1977): *The Postman Always Rings Twice*. The forty-two-year-old former journalist's first novel is his most enduring achievement, establishing his reputation as a master of hard-boiled realism. The novel about a drifter who conspires with his lover to murder her husband, the owner of a roadside sandwich stand, has been filmed three times and adapted as an opera.

ROBERT CANTWELL: *The Land of Plenty*. Cantwell's second novel is a powerful proletarian social drama concerning the impact of a strike at a Pacific Northwest lumber mill.

MARY ELLEN CHASE (1887–1973): *Mary Peters*. Chase's novel describes the life of a Maine ship captain's daughter. Chase, who was raised in Maine and taught at Smith College, was one of the leading regional writers of the period. Her other books include *Mary Christmas* (1926), *Uplands* (1927), *Gay Highway* (1933), and *Silas Crockett* (1935).

JAMES GOULD COZZENS: *Castaway*. In a departure into moral fantasy, Cozzens offers a "semi-symbolic, semi-allegorical fictional demonstration that the principle of living adds up to self-killing." The story tells of the plight of the sole survivor of a destroyed New York City, living amid the bounty of a great department store. The novel illustrates Cozzens's conviction regarding the necessity of social order.

EDWARD DAHLBERG: *Those Who Perish*. Dahlberg's third novel is one of the earliest to treat the impact of Nazism on American Jews. It was inspired when Dahlberg was beaten up by uniformed Nazis in a Berlin bar.

JAMES T. FARRELL: *The Young Manhood of Studs Lonigan*. The second volume of the Studs Lonigan trilogy follows the Chicago youth's career from 1917 to 1919 as a gang member and street tough, isolated in a debilitating life that results from what the author diagnoses as the falsity of the American dream. Farrell also publishes *Calico Shoes, and Other Stories*, vignettes of South Side Chicago street scenes that parallel the setting and themes of his novel.

WILLIAM FAULKNER: *Doctor Martino, and Other Stories*. Faulkner's story collection includes "Fox Hunt," "Smoke," "Mountain Victory," and "Honor."

JESSIE REDMON FAUSET: *Comedy, American Style*. Fauset's final novel is generally considered her most direct statement on the impact of racial discrimination. Her female protagonist, Olivia Carey, hates being black, and her futile desire to be white threatens to destroy her, while her husband and son are redeemed by embracing their black heritage.

F. SCOTT FITZGERALD: *Tender Is the Night*. Fitzgerald's fourth and final novel to be published during his lifetime is his most ambitious, an attempt to summarize the collapse of American values through the deterioration of expatriate psychiatrist Dick Diver, who marries his troubled patient, Nicole. Although praised by some as Fitzgerald's masterpiece, the novel mainly provokes disappointment and accusations that Fitzgerald is simply repeating himself. In 1938, convinced that the true beginning of the novel was buried in its middle, Fitzgerald would reorganize the book chronologically in a revised version, published in 1951.

DANIEL FUCHS (1909–1993): *Summer in Williamsburg.* The first in a trilogy of realistic novels by the New York writer portraying life in the Jewish section of Brooklyn. It would be followed by *Homage to Blenholt* (1936) and *Low Company* (1937).

MARTHA GELLHORN (1908–1997): *What Mad Pursuit.* Gellhorn's first novel follows the adventures of three women who, after graduating from college, undertake a restless search for fulfillment amid fashionable and bohemian society in the United States and Europe. Gellhorn would become a war correspondent for *Collier's* from 1938 to 1945, meeting Hemingway while covering the Spanish Civil War and marrying him in 1940.

CAROLINE GORDON: *Aleck Maury, Sportsman.* Gordon's novel about a retired Southern classics professor who devotes himself to his outdoor passions prompts comparison with Ernest Hemingway's hunting and fishing descriptions. Additional episodes involving Aleck Maury would be included in Gordon's 1945 story collection, *The Forest of the South.*

LANGSTON HUGHES: *The Ways of White Folks.* Hughes's first story collection deals with race relations from what at the time was considered a unique African American perspective.

ZORA NEALE HURSTON: *Jonah's Gourd Vine.* Hurston's first novel concerns a black preacher who is unable to stay faithful to his wife. It features elements from the author's fieldwork in black oral tradition and folklore.

JOSEPHINE W. JOHNSON (1910–1990): *Now in November.* This realistic first novel by the Missouri-born writer about a Midwestern farm family contending with drought, debt, and madness prompts comparisons with Willa Cather's books and would win the 1935 Pulitzer Prize.

MACKINLAY KANTOR (1904–1977): *Long Remember.* Until Michael Shaara's *The Killer Angels* (1974), Kantor's first major novel is considered the best fictionalized account of the Battle of Gettysburg. Kantor was an Iowa-born newspaperman whose first novel, *Diversey*, about the Chicago underworld, appeared in 1928.

SINCLAIR LEWIS: *Work of Art.* Reviewers detect a less angry author in this account of the travails of a hotel manager driven to create the perfect inn.

VICTORIA LINCOLN (1904–1981): *February Hill.* The popular novelist and short story writer's best-known work is this novel about family life set in her hometown of Fall River, Massachusetts. It would be adapted for the stage by George Abbott as *The Primrose Path* (1939).

JOHN JOSEPH MATHEWS: *Sundown.* One of the first Native American novels is a largely autobiographical work on the struggles of assimilation by a mixed-blood protagonist.

WILLIAM MAXWELL (1908–2000): *Bright Center of Heaven.* Maxwell's first novel concerns a group of people living in a Wisconsin farm boardinghouse. The book helps land him a position at *The New Yorker* in 1936, where he would work, mainly as a fiction editor, until 1976.

CAROLINE MILLER (1903–1992): *Lamb in His Bosum.* The first of the Georgia author's two published novels (the other is *Lebanon*, 1944) is a realistic historical novel set in antebellum Georgia; it wins the Pulitzer Prize.

HENRY MILLER (1891–1980): *Tropic of Cancer.* Miller's first book, published in France, proves to be his most famous, a fictionalized autobiographical account of Miller's Paris days, emphasizing the seamier side of bohemian life. Its frank depiction of sex causes the book to be banned in the United States until 1961. Subsequent installments of Miller's autobiographical reflections published in the 1930s are *Black Spring* (1936) and *Tropic of Capricorn* (1939).

JOHN O'HARA (1905–1970): *Appointment in Samarra.* O'Hara's first novel is based on the social conflict between Irish Catholics and the Protestant elite in his Pennsylvania hometown. A bestseller, the book shocks readers by its frank depiction of sexuality and social manners. O'Hara, a successful journalist who worked for *Newsweek, Time,* and *The New Yorker,* was able to devote his time to fiction because of the book's success.

KATHERINE ANNE PORTER: *Hacienda.* First published in the *Virginia Quarterly* in 1932, Porter's long story reflects her experiences on the set of Soviet film director Sergei Eisenstein in Mexico.

HENRY ROTH (1906–1995): *Call It Sleep.* Roth's stream-of-consciousness novel about the boyhood of a New York City Jew is likened to James Joyce's *A Portrait of the Artist as a Young Man* "but with a wider scope, a richer emotion, a deeper realism," according to critic Alfred Hayes. After going through two printings (four thousand copies), the book would disappear from view until being reissued in the 1960s and then hailed as a neglected masterpiece, ranked by Irving Howe as "one of the few genuinely distinguished novels written by a 20th-century American." Roth would not publish another novel until *Mercy of a Rude Stream* (1994).

DAMON RUNYON: *Blue Plate Specials.* Runyon's second collection of Broadway tales includes "Little Miss Marker," described as Runyon's "most representative story" with its blend of sentiment and biting satire.

WILLIAM SAROYAN (1908–1991): *The Daring Young Man on the Flying Trapeze and Other Stories.* Saroyan's first publication marks his initial success as a short story writer (in 1939 he would direct his energies toward playwriting and in 1943 toward novels). The title story, which wins the 1934 O. Henry Award, concerns an unemployed writer struggling to find work in the midst of the Depression. Born in Fresno, California, and raised in an orphanage, Saroyan left school at the age of twelve to work as a telegraph messenger.

TESS SLESINGER (1905–1945): *The Unpossessed.* The author's only novel concerns the contemporary New York intellectual scene. Reviewer John Chamberlain calls it "quite simply and dogmatically the best novel of contemporary New York City that we have read." It would be followed by her only short story collection, *Time: The Present* (1935). Slesinger worked in Hollywood during the late 1930s as a screenwriter.

IRVING STONE (1903–1989): *Lust for Life.* The California writer produces the first of his popular fictionalized biographies, treating the life of painter Vincent van Gogh.

REX STOUT (1886–1975): *Fer-de-Lance.* The Indiana-born writer introduces the cerebral, corpulent crime-solver Nero Wolfe, who rarely leaves his apartment, relegating the fieldwork to his partner, Archie Godwin. Stout would go on to produce nearly eighty Wolfe mysteries, which have sold more than sixty million copies.

RUTH SUCKOW: *The Folks.* Hailed as the "great Midwestern novel," the book documents life in a small Iowa town.

B. TRAVEN (c. 1890–1969): *Death Ship.* The secretive, elusive writer's first book, published in Germany in 1926, concerns an American sailor who is trapped on a doomed ship to be sunk for its insurance money. It is believed that the author was born Berick Traven Torsvan in Chicago and lived in Germany and Mexico from the 1920s to his death.

NATHANAEL WEST: *A Cool Million.* West's *Candide*-like picaresque satire is a bitter attack on the Horatio Alger myth of American success, told through the successive "dismantling" of the protagonist, Lemuel Pitkin.

STARK YOUNG (1881–1963): *So Red the Rose.* The Mississippi-born writer's most acclaimed novel deals with life in Mississippi before and during the Civil War. It is praised by novelist Ellen Glasgow as "the best and most completely realized novel of the Deep South in the Civil War that has yet been written." Young was the drama critic for the *New Republic* during the 1920s; his drama criticism was collected in *The Flower in Drama* (1923).

Literary Criticism and Scholarship

MALCOLM COWLEY: *Exile's Return: A Narrative of Ideas.* Cowley analyzes the postwar literary scene organized by autobiographical reflections on his own upbringing, war service, and acquaintance in Paris and New York with virtually all of the significant writers of the period. The book establishes Cowley's critical reputation and is one of the most important literary-historical accounts of the 1920s.

T. S. ELIOT: *After Strange Gods: A Primer of Modern Heresy.* In a series of lectures delivered at the University of Virginia, Eliot defines the tradition in modern English literature and discusses the effect on a writer who is not brought up in an "environment of a central and living tradition."

JOHN AVERY LOMAX (1872–1948) AND ALAN LOMAX (1915–2002): *American Ballads and Folk Songs.* Father-and-son folk musicologists collect nearly three hundred examples of indigenous American music, the largest such collection up to its time.

LEWIS MUMFORD: *Technics and Civilization.* The first of the four-volume Renewal of Life series — the author's major scholarly work and one of the classic texts in urban studies — traces urban development from the tenth century. Subsequent volumes studying the relationship between civilization and city life are *The Culture of Cities* (1938), *The Condition of Man* (1944), and *The Conduct of Life* (1951).

EZRA POUND: *ABC of Reading.* In an elaboration of his 1931 essay "How to Read," Pound offers practical suggestions for literary appreciation as well as lists of worthy writers and works. Pound also publishes *Make It New*, a defense of contemporary writing and its imperatives based on Pound's reviews and literary essays written over the previous twenty years.

EDITH WHARTON: *A Backward Glance.* The writer's autobiography includes observations about social life in New York, London, and Paris during the 1870s and 1880s, her relationship with Henry James and other writers, and statements about her artistic processes.

Nonfiction

ROBERT BENCHLEY: *From Bed to Worse; or, Comforting Thoughts About the Bison.* Benchley's miscellaneous collection features a darker, more biting tone than his previous volumes and includes two extended parodies, "How Seamus Coomora Met the Banshee," poking fun at Yeatsian folklore, and "Love Among the Thinkers," sending up prominent intellectual ideas of the day.

RUTH BENEDICT (1887–1948): *Patterns of Culture.* This groundbreaking comparative study by the Columbia anthropologist describing cultural patterns of three different primitive peoples — the Zuni of New Mexico, the Dobu of Melanesia, and the Kwakiutl of Vancouver

Island — shows how custom and tradition influence behavior. It would be followed by *Race, Science, and Politics* (1940).

JOHN DEWEY: *Art as Experience* and *A Common Faith*. The first work is an aesthetic treatise intended "to restore continuity between the refined and intensified forms of experience that are works of art and the everyday events, doings, and sufferings that are universally recognized to constitute experience." The second is an expression of the philosopher's nonsectarian faith.

JOHN DOS PASSOS: *In All Countries*. Dos Passos provides accounts of his travels in Russia, Mexico, Spain, and the United States, including reflections on the Sacco-Vanzetti case and the 1932 presidential conventions.

DOUGLAS SOUTHALL FREEMAN (1886–1953): *R. E. Lee*. The result of nearly twenty years of research, the first two volumes of Freeman's monumental four-volume biography are published. The concluding volumes would follow in 1935 and receive the Pulitzer Prize. Freeman's partisanship on behalf of his subject is a limitation, but the biography remains the most comprehensive study available. Freeman was the editor of Richmond's *News Leader* and a broadcaster.

JAMES WELDON JOHNSON: *Negro Americans, What Now?* The author's lectures delivered at Fisk University consider the future for African Americans in the United States, calling for integration.

MATTHEW JOSEPHSON (1899–1978): *The Robber Barons*. Regarded as a classic and Josephson's best-known book, this is an analysis of American industrialists such as Jay Gould, Cornelius Vanderbilt, J. P. Morgan, Andrew Carnegie, and John D. Rockefeller.

RING LARDNER: *First and Last*. This posthumously published collection gathers the author's initial sports page columns as well as his most recent writings for *The New Yorker*.

H. L. MENCKEN: *Treatise on Right and Wrong*. In a companion to *Treatise on the Gods* (1930), Mencken provides a study of ethical ideas.

GERTRUDE STEIN: *Portraits and Prayers*. Stein supplies experimental verbal portraits of members of her artistic circle, written since 1909.

E. B. WHITE: *Every Day Is Saturday*. A collection of the writer's "Notes and Comment" columns in *The New Yorker*, reflecting politics, fashion, and cultural trends since 1928.

Poetry

JAMES AGEE (1909–1955): *Permit Me Voyage*. Agee's first publication is a collection of lyrics, sonnets, and a narrative poem, "Ann Garner." Selected for the Yale Younger Poets series, Agee is greeted by reviewers as a writer to watch.

CONRAD AIKEN: *Landscape West of Eden*. A long, philosophical meditation on the soul's search for meaning.

PAUL ENGLE (1908–1991): *American Song*. The Iowan poet's first collection prompts comparisons with Walt Whitman in its exuberant energy and affirmation of American experience. The title poem wins the 1933 Century of Progress Prize sponsored by *Poetry*.

EDNA ST. VINCENT MILLAY: *Wine from These Grapes*. Millay's collection includes "In the Grave No Flower" and the sonnet sequence "Epitaph for the Race of Man," which though conceived as a "heartfelt tribute to the magnificence of man," predicts the eventual extinction of mankind.

GEORGE OPPEN (1908–1984): *Discrete Series*. One of the leaders of the objectivist school of poetry issues his first collection. He would abandon writing for politics as a Communist Party organizer and would not issue another volume until 1962.

EDWIN ARLINGTON ROBINSON: *Amaranth*. Robinson's blank-verse narrative poem looks at a group of individuals who chose the wrong lifework, ignoring their artistic passions to focus on the practical.

JESSE STUART (1907–1984): *Man with a Bull-Tongued Plow*. Stuart's first publication, a sonnet sequence about his native Kentucky mountain community, brings the regionalist writer national attention. The work wins the Jeannette Sewal Davis Prize from *Poetry* magazine.

WILLIAM CARLOS WILLIAMS: *Collected Poems, 1921–1931*. Some of the poet's greatest works are collected in this edition issued by the Objectivist Press with a preface by Wallace Stevens, who calls his friend the "Diogenes of modern poetry."

AUDREY WURDEMANN (1911–1960): *Bright Ambush*. The Seattle-born Wurdemann becomes the youngest poet ever to receive a Pulitzer Prize for her second collection, following *The House of Silk* (1926). The poems are graceful lyrics celebrating nature. She would publish three subsequent collections during the decade: *The Seven Sins* (1935), *Splendour in the Grass* (1936), and a sonnet sequence, *Testament of Love* (1938).

Publications and Events

Challenge. Dorothy West (1907–1998) creates this literary quarterly (*New Challenge* in 1937) as an outlet for the best black literature of the time, including that of Langston Hughes, Arna Bontemps, and Zora Neale Hurston. It was criticized by Richard Wright and others for ignoring younger writers and for being nonpolitical.

Partisan Review. Beginning as a quarterly in support of the Communist Party under the editorship of Philip Rahv, in 1938 it would be reconstituted as an independent publication with an emphasis on literary, intellectual, and cultural topics, publishing the first work of Delmore Schwartz (an editor) and Saul Bellow, as well as avant-garde literature and criticism by writers such as Dwight MacDonald and Lionel Trilling.

1935

Drama and Theater

ZOË AKINS: *The Old Maid.* Akins's sentimental dramatization of Edith Wharton's 1924 novella wins the Pulitzer Prize and helps prompt dismayed drama critics to form the New York Drama Critics Circle to present its own annual drama awards.

MAXWELL ANDERSON: *Winterset.* In the playwright's second attempt, following *Gods of the Lightning* (1928), to deal with the Sacco-Vanzetti case, Anderson dramatizes a son's investigation of the execution of his anarchist father in this blank-verse tragedy. It wins the first New York Drama Critics Circle Award for best American play.

T. S. ELIOT: *Murder in the Cathedral.* Eliot's verse drama of the martyrdom of Thomas à Becket is first performed in America at Yale University; the Federal Theatre Project would bring it to Broadway in 1936.

GEORGE GERSHWIN: *Porgy and Bess.* Gershwin's "folk opera," based on DuBose Heyward's 1925 novel and 1927 play about black life in Charleston's waterfront Catfish Row, initially fails at the box office, with only 124 performances. It would be subsequently recognized as a landmark in the history of the American musical theater and Gershwin's masterpiece, his last major work for the musical stage.

JOHN CECIL HOLM (1904–1981) AND GEORGE ABBOTT: *Three Men on a Horse.* In this farce, a mild-mannered greeting-card writer gets mixed up with gamblers because of his uncanny skill in picking winning horses. The play runs for two years on Broadway, is the basis for the musicals *Banjo Eyes* (1941) and *Let It Ride!* (1961), and is considered one of the best modern American comedies. Holm was an actor, director, and playwright whose other Broadway success was the book for the musical *Best Foot Forward* (1941).

LANGSTON HUGHES: *Mulatto.* Hughes achieves his only substantial dramatic success in this play about the biracial children of a white Georgia plantation owner and his black housekeeper. The Broadway run of 375 performances is the longest to date for any play with a racial theme and a predominantly black cast.

SIDNEY KINGSLEY: *Dead End.* This gritty melodrama about New York City slum and gang life shocks audiences with its street language. It would be adapted by Lillian Hellman into a successful film in 1937, which launched the Dead End Kids in subsequent films.

ARCHIBALD MACLEISH: *Panic.* In two special Broadway performances, Orson Welles stars in MacLeish's verse drama as a banker who is certain that he knows how to solve the problems of the Depression and is done in by selfishness. The play announces the author's shift of attention to pressing social issues.

CLIFFORD ODETS (1906–1963): *Waiting for Lefty.* After acting with the Theatre Guild and helping to found the Group Theatre, the playwright's electrifying theatrical debut is based on the 1934 New York City cab strike, as union members (seated in the audience) come forward to debate a strike vote. When word comes that the union's militant representative has been killed, the workers join together chanting "Strike! Strike! Strike!" One of the most powerful protest dramas of the era, it establishes Odets's reputation. The play moves from a downtown theater to Broadway on March 26 as part of a double bill with another one-act play by Odets, *Till the Day I Die,* concerning the anti-Nazi underground. After the success of *Waiting for Lefty,* Odets reworks an earlier play, *I Got the Blues,* into *Awake and Sing!* — a social drama of a lower-middle-class Jewish family in the Bronx and the conversion of the son, Ralph Berger, from social isolation to activism. It is produced by the Group Theatre. Odets's fourth drama to be performed on Broadway in 1935 — *Paradise Lost,* a scattershot attack on American middle-class life — is a failure. He departs for Hollywood to be a screenwriter, prompting accusations that he has abandoned his proletarian ideals for money.

AYN RAND (1905–1982): *Night of January 16.* The first of Rand's two Broadway plays (*The Unconquered* would follow in 1940) is a courtroom drama that uses the gimmick of employing members of the audience as jurors whose verdict determines which of the play's two conclusions would be performed nightly. Rand was born in Russia and came to the United States in 1926. She would be best known for her objectivist philosophy of "rational self-interest" and individualism.

DAMON RUNYON AND HOWARD LINDSAY (1889–1968): *A Slight Case of Murder.* Runyon's only drama is this farce about a reformed bootlegger who discovers the bodies of four armored-truck robbers in his new house and must arrange things to claim the reward for their capture. Lindsay was an actor, director, producer, and playwright involved in plays such as *Anything Goes* (1934), *Life with Father* (1939), and *State of the Union* (1945).

ROBERT E. SHERWOOD: *The Petrified Forest.* In a play that captures the anomie of the time, inspired by Adolf Hitler's unchecked rise to power, Sherwood presents a world-weary idealist's encounter with the outlaw Duke Mantee and his gang at the Black Mesa Bar-B-Q in the Arizona desert. A moral and philosophical allegory, the play pits Mantee's amoral violence against an ineffectual romantic idealism. Both Leslie Howard and Humphrey Bogart would re-create their stage performances in the popular 1936 film version.

SAMUEL SPEWACK (1899–1971) AND BELLA SPEWACK (1899–1990): *Boy Meets Girl.* The husband-and-wife playwrights' biggest success is this uproarious spoof on Hollywood in which screenwriters (patterned on Ben Hecht and Charles MacArthur) try to salvage a fading cowboy star's career by teaming him with a baby co-star. The pair produced a dozen plays that reached Broadway, including *Leave It to Me!* (1938), *Kiss Me, Kate* (1948), and *My Three Angels* (1953).

Fiction

LOUIS ADAMIC: *Grandsons: A Story of American Lives.* The first of the Yugoslavian-born writer's two novels (*Cradle of Life: The Story of One Man's Beginnings* would follow in 1936) dramatizes the assimilation process among a Slovenian extended family.

CONRAD AIKEN: *King Coffin.* A psychological thriller about the mental deterioration of an intellectual who becomes obsessed with the concept of the perfect crime.

NELSON ALGREN (1909–1981): *Somebody in Boots.* The first of the writer's published works concerning the misadventures of a youthful hobo in Texas draws on Algren's own experiences, including run-ins with the law, and introduces his characteristic social protest themes through gritty realism involving the dispossessed. Born in Detroit, Algren grew up in the slums of Chicago's west side, a locale for many of his novels and stories.

MARGARET AYER BARNES: *Edna His Wife.* The novel depicts the unhappiness of a simple, unsophisticated woman who gains every material advantage but fails to find happiness as a wife and mother.

JOHN PEALE BISHOP: *Act of Darkness.* Bishop's only published novel is a semi-autobiographical depiction of life in a small West Virginia community in the early years of the century. It concerns a protagonist attempting to reconcile his artistic and sexual impulses. Bishop also publishes his third volume of poetry, *Minute Particulars.*

PEARL S. BUCK: *A House Divided.* The concluding volume of the author's House of Earth trilogy, which had begun with *The Good Earth* (1931) and *Sons* (1932), chronicles the impact of modern Chinese history on the house of Wang. Neither sequel lives up to expectations generated by *The Good Earth.*

ERSKINE CALDWELL: *Journeyman.* The author continues what he calls his "cyclorama of Southern life" with an emphasis on Southern grotesque in the story of a Georgia community that comes under the sway of a lecherous, gun-toting, itinerant preacher. He also publishes *Kneel to the Rising Sun, and Other Stories*, a collection of character sketches and incidents in the lives of rural poor Southerners.

WILLA CATHER: *Lucy Gayheart.* Cather's novel about a pianist's unhappy affair with a married concert singer displays the author's characteristic interest in the artistic temperament, but critics divide over the book's achievement. Some praise the honesty of the love relationship; others complain about the novel's predictability and sentimentality.

MARY ELLEN CHASE: *Silas Crockett.* Chase's second novel is the story of four generations of a Maine seagoing family, told with the writer's distinctive skill in characterization and regional details.

H. L. DAVIS (1896–1960): *Honey in the Horn.* Davis's first novel is set in the Oregon Territory during the homesteading period and wins the Harper Prize and the Pulitzer Prize. Born in Oregon, Davis had worked on a cattle ranch and as a sheriff.

JAMES T. FARRELL: *Guillotine Party, and Other Stories.* Farrell's short stories echo the settings and themes of his Studs Lonigan trilogy. While some reviewers find the collection drab and dull, another proclaims Farrell unrivaled in the "post-Hemingway 'tough' school." Farrell also publishes *Judgment Day*, the concluding volume of the Studs Lonigan trilogy. It follows the continuing downward spiral of Lonigan through the Depression years to his death at age twenty-nine, a pitiable figure whose former bravado has collapsed under the weight of his misguided dream of success and fulfillment.

WILLIAM FAULKNER: *Pylon.* Between the masterful *Light in August* (1934) and *Absalom, Absalom!* (1936), Faulkner publishes what is generally regarded as a minor work about aviators during a Mardi Gras celebration.

F. SCOTT FITZGERALD: *Taps at Reveille.* The last of the author's short story collections published during his lifetime gathers work written since 1926. Reviewers find the stories more quaint than relevant, evidence that Fitzgerald has, in the words of one critic, "become the prisoner of his own past, a literary Peter Pan who refused to grow up with the feverish, glamorous youth he immortalized."

ELLEN GLASGOW: *Vein of Iron*. After a series of satirical novels of manners, Glasgow returns to the subject of rural Virginia life and the survival qualities needed there. Glasgow would regard the novel the last of her best work.

PAUL GREEN: *This Body the Earth*. Green's problem novel dramatizes the futility of a young man's attempt to escape the desolate fate of a sharecropper.

SINCLAIR LEWIS: *It Can't Happen Here*. Lewis projects present-day Germany into America's future in this social satire describing the rise to power of an American dictator. The author would collaborate with John C. Moffitt in a 1936 dramatization simultaneously performed by all units of the Federal Theatre Project. Also published in 1935 is Lewis's *Selected Short Stories*.

HORACE MCCOY (1897–1955): *They Shoot Horses, Don't They?* McCoy's first novel describes the tawdriness and brutality of a dance marathon. It would be adapted as a film in 1969. McCoy was born in Tennessee and worked as a newspaperman, sportswriter, and screenwriter. His other novels are *No Pockets in a Shroud* (1937), *I Should Have Stayed Home* (1938), *Kiss Tomorrow Goodbye* (1948), and *Scalped* (1952).

JOHN O'HARA: *Butterfield 8*. O'Hara's second novel continues his frank depiction of sexuality and social manners in the story of a promiscuous woman unable to shed her loose reputation. O'Hara also publishes his first story collection, *The Doctor's Son*. It displays his mastery of what has been called the "sensibility" story depicting a character confronting a hidden and often unpleasant truth about himself. Similar collections — *Files on Parade* (1939), *Pipe Night* (1945), and *Hellbox* (1947) — would follow.

MARJORIE KINNAN RAWLINGS: *Golden Apples*. The writer's second novel continues her documentation of Florida's rural community in the tale of the struggle of two orphans to survive on their own.

ELIZABETH MADOX ROBERTS: *He Sent Forth a Raven*. Roberts tells the story of a wealthy Kentucky farmer who, after the death of his wife, vows never to set foot on the earth again, managing his farm from his balcony.

GEORGE SANTAYANA: *The Last Puritan*. The philosopher's only novel offers a fictionalized treatment of Santayana's own background and many of his central ideas.

MARK SCHORER (1908–1977): *A House Too Old*. Schorer's first novel tells the story of a Wisconsin town from its founding to its contemporary condition one hundred years later. Born in Wisconsin, Schorer was a

critic and biographer as well as novelist who taught at Dartmouth, Harvard, and the University of California.

ISAAC BASHEVIS SINGER (1904–1991): *Satan in Goray*. Singer's first major work about the impact of a seventeenth-century pogrom is published in Warsaw (translated from Yiddish in 1955). Also in 1935 the writer immigrates from Poland to the United States, joining the staff of the *Jewish Daily Forward*, where he would work until his death.

JOHN STEINBECK: *Tortilla Flat*. Steinbeck's fourth novel becomes his first popular success. Treating the ethnically mixed "paisanos" of Monterey, California, it would be dramatized by Jack Kirkland in 1937.

B. TRAVEN: *The Treasure of the Sierra Madre*. Traven's best-known work is a study of the effects of greed on a trio of Americans in Mexico who discover a lost gold mine. In 1948 John Huston would direct a memorable film version starring Humphrey Bogart.

THORNTON WILDER: *Heaven's My Destination*. First published in England in 1934, Wilder's picaresque satire covers the misadventures of an idealistic dreamer who tries to live in the Midwest during the Depression according to the philosophies of Leo Tolstoy and Mahatma Gandhi. It is regarded by many as the writer's finest achievement in fiction.

THOMAS WOLFE: *From Death to Morning*. Wolfe's first story collection is the last of his fiction that he personally prepares for publication. It contains some of his finest work, including "Death the Proud Brother," "Only the Dead Know Brooklyn," "Circus at Dawn," and the novella *The Web of Earth*, a remarkable portrait of Eugene Gant's mother, Eliza. Wolfe also publishes *Of Time and the River*. Wolfe's editor, Maxwell Perkins, submitted the author's ever-evolving, massive manuscript to the typesetter without Wolfe's knowledge, judging it to be as complete as it would get. The result is a sprawling, episodic sequel to *Look Homeward, Angel*, in which Wolfe's surrogate, Eugene Gant, retraces the writer's own steps from 1920 to 1925 through schooling at Harvard, teaching in New York, and European travel.

Literary Criticism and Scholarship

R. P. BLACKMUR (1904–1965): *The Double Agent: Essays in Craft and Elucidation*. The poet and critic's first volume of essays considers Henry James, T. S. Eliot, Marianne Moore, and others. Blackmur, who never attended college, served as an editor of the little magazine *Hound and Horn*.

ZORA NEALE HURSTON: *Mules and Men*. Considered the first collection of African American folklore compiled by an African American, this is the first and the more important of the author's two folklore collections. *Tell My Horse*, a collection of Caribbean folktales that includes the first published transcripts of Haitian Creole, would follow in 1938.

F. O. MATTHIESSEN (1902–1950): *The Achievement of T. S. Eliot: An Essay on the Nature of Poetry.* The first of the literary critic's major works is an influential defense of Eliot's artistry and importance. Rejecting the prevailing historical approach to literary criticism for an emphasis on the poems' language and structure, Matthiessen helps define the principles of the New Criticism. Born in California, Matthiessen was a longtime professor at Harvard who served as the editor of the *New England Quarterly* from 1938 to 1940.

GERTRUDE STEIN: *Lectures in America.* Delivered during the writer's triumphant American tour following publication of *The Autobiography of Alice B. Toklas*, Stein's lectures present her theories of artistic composition.

Nonfiction

HERBERT AGAR: *Land of the Free.* Agar looks at current economic conditions and suggests a third alternative to Fascism and Communism, in a return to the republican ideals of America's founders.

FREDERICK LEWIS ALLEN: *The Lords of Creation.* Allen traces the American economic expansion from the 1890s, mixing analysis and biographical portraits of the leading financiers.

SHERWOOD ANDERSON: *Puzzled America.* The writer surveys the state of the nation in a series of sketches of miners, textile workers, and farmers. Irving Howe would observe that the work "is one of the few books that convey a sense of what it meant to live in depression America."

KENNETH BURKE: *Permanence and Change.* A study of the evolution of ethical ideas. Burke's analysis, like *Attitudes Toward History* (1937), which would follow it, is noteworthy in formulating the theoretical principles that would underlie his later literary and social views.

ERSKINE CALDWELL: *Some American People.* In addition to publishing a novel and a short story collection in this year, Caldwell issues this series of character sketches and vignettes from his travels across America, surveying the desolation caused by the Depression. The work helps solidify Caldwell's reputation as a proletarian writer.

CLARENCE DAY: *Life with Father.* The longtime contributor to *The New Yorker* has his greatest success with this affectionate series of recollections of his New York City childhood and his dominating father. The bestseller would be adapted into a long-running play in 1939 by Howard Lindsay and Russel Crouse and a film in 1947. Day's other autobiographical works include *God and My Father* (1932), *Life with Mother* (1937), and *Father and I* (1940).

JOHN DEWEY: *Liberalism and Social Action.* In a series of lectures, the philosopher attempts to define liberalism and apply its principles to current circumstances.

W.E.B. DU BOIS: *Black Reconstruction: An Essay Toward a History of the Part Which Black Folk Played in the Attempt to Reconstruct Democracy in America, 1860–1880.* Du Bois chronicles the role of African Americans during the Civil War and Reconstruction in a groundbreaking reevaluation of American history.

WILL DURANT: *Our Oriental Heritage.* The first of the author's ten-volume popular cultural history, *The Story of Civilization*, appears. It would be followed by *The Life of Greece* (1939), *Caesar and Christ* (1944), *The Age of Faith* (1950), *The Renaissance* (1953), *The Reformation* (1957), and, with his wife Ariel Durant (1898–1981), *The Age of Reason Begins* (1961), *The Age of Louis XIV* (1963), *The Age of Voltaire* (1965), and *Rousseau and Revolution* (1967).

ERNEST HEMINGWAY: *Green Hills of Africa.* Hemingway's account of an African safari is, in the author's words, an attempt "to write an absolutely true book to see whether the shape of a country and the pattern of a month's action can, if truly presented, compete with a work of the imagination." Most reviewers decide that he failed, but the work retains its major significance today as a repository for Hemingway's reflections on his art and literature.

ANNE MORROW LINDBERGH (1906–2001): *North to the Orient.* The first of the author's books is an account of her flight with her husband, Charles Lindbergh, from New York to China and Japan in 1931. It is enthusiastically received and praised for its stylish prose and lyricism.

RALPH BARTON PERRY (1876–1957): *The Thought and Character of William James.* James's former pupil produces an acclaimed study of his mentor that wins the Pulitzer Prize. Perry, a professor at Harvard, wrote works of philosophy such as *The New Realism* (1912) and *A Defense of Philosophy* (1931).

ELEANOR ROOSEVELT (1884–1962): "My Day." The First Lady's syndicated column begins. The six-day-a-week forum for Roosevelt's wide-ranging views would continue until 1962, interrupted only for four days at the time of President Roosevelt's death.

MARI SANDOZ (1896–1966): *Old Jules.* The Nebraska-born writer's first book and the first of her Great Plains series is a biography of her Swiss immigrant father who

Countee Cullen

settled in Nebraska in the 1880s. The book is praised as "a powerful, distinctly American history of a man, a region and an epoch."

JAMES THURBER: *The Middle-Aged Man on the Flying Trapeze.* A collection of humorous sketches previously printed in *The New Yorker,* including "If Grant Had Been Drinking at Appomattox" and "How to See a Bad Play."

HANS ZINSSER (1878–1940): *Rats, Lice, and History.* The leading bacteriologist and immunologist in the United States during the first half of the twentieth century publishes this history of typhus, which becomes both a popular and critical success.

Poetry

ROBERT P. TRISTRAM COFFIN: *Strange Holiness.* This collection of pastoral verse, most with a Maine setting, wins the Maine poet and essayist a Pulitzer Prize.

COUNTEE CULLEN: *The Medea and Some Poems.* Included with the first major translation of a classical work by a twentieth-century African American writer is the poem "Scottsboro Too, Is Worth Its Song," an accusation against poets who championed Sacco and Vanzetti but ignored the plight of the nine black youths charged with rape in 1931.

E. E. CUMMINGS. *No Thanks.* The title and dedication of Cummings's collection refer to the fourteen publishers who rejected this collection of unconventional and experimental poems, bound not on the left but at the top, like a stenographer's pad.

KENNETH FEARING: *Poems.* The poet's second collection is a bitter attack on middle-class life.

JOHN GOULD FLETCHER: *XXIV Elegies.* In this volume Fletcher ranges widely over subjects as diverse as Thomas Edison, Napoleon, a Civil War cemetery, the Russian Revolution, and the Last Judgment.

HORACE GREGORY: *Chorus for Survival.* The poet's fourth collection calls for spiritual regeneration in the face of the harsh conditions of existence.

ROBINSON JEFFERS: *Solstice and Other Poems.* The title poem retells the story of Medea. Included as well is "At the Birth of an Age," a poetic drama based on the Teutonic legend about a destructive quarrel among three brothers.

JAMES WELDON JOHNSON: *Saint Peter Relates an Incident: Selected Poems.* Johnson's last major collection includes the satirical narrative title poem, first published in 1930, in which a veterans' group discovers that the soldier in the Tomb of the Unknown is black. It is inspired by the author's outrage at the discrimination experienced by widows of African Americans killed in battle.

EDGAR LEE MASTERS: *Invisible Landscapes.* A collection of reflective, descriptive observations in marked contrast to the dramatic epigrammatic style of *Spoon River Anthology.* Masters also publishes the critical biography *Vachel Lindsay.*

MARIANNE MOORE: *Selected Poems.* After a decade's hiatus, Moore issues this collection of previously published and new poetry with an introduction by T. S. Eliot, who asserts that her poems "form part of the small body of durable poetry written in our time." Including such enduring work as "The Monkey Puzzle," "The Steeple Jack," and "The Jerboa," the volume fails to find an audience, selling only 864 copies by 1942.

EDWIN ARLINGTON ROBINSON: *King Jasper.* Robinson's final philosophical statement is contained in this long narrative allegory concerning an industrialist's downfall. Robert Frost memorializes Robinson in his introduction, stating that "Robinson stayed content with the old-fashioned ways to be new."

MURIEL RUKEYSER (1913–1980): *Theory of Flight.* Winner of the Yale Younger Poets Prize, Rukeyser's first volume is praised for its energy, experimental technique, and powerful social conscience, which, for a woman at the time, was considered unique.

WALLACE STEVENS: *Ideas of Order.* Stevens describes his collection "as essentially a book of pure poetry. I believe that in any society the poet should be the exponent of the imagination of that society. *Ideas of Order* attempts to illustrate the role of the imagination in life." The volume includes one of Stevens's greatest works, "The Idea of Order in Key West," containing the poet's imaginative and artistic credo.

ROBERT PENN WARREN (1905–1989): *Thirty-Six Poems.* Warren's first collection combines folk narratives drawn from his native Kentucky as well as verses influenced by the seventeenth-century metaphysical poets, examining the relation between humanity and nature. Warren was born in Kentucky and while a student at Vanderbilt was associated with the group of writers who called themselves the Fugitives.

WILLIAM CARLOS WILLIAMS: *An Early Martyr, and Other Poems.* Williams's collection includes one of his most anthologized poems, "The Yachts."

Publications and Events

American Prefaces. This literary magazine, sponsored by the University of Iowa, debuts and goes on to feature the work of figures such as T. S. Eliot, Muriel Rukeyser, Robert Frost, and Eudora Welty. It ceased publication in 1943.

Federal Writers' Project. Established for the relief of unemployed writers, editors, and researchers, under the direction of Henry G. Alsberg until it was abolished in 1939, the project employed more than sixty-six hundred on endeavors such as the American Guide series, documenting American life and cultural and ethnological history.

New York Drama Critics Circle. Formed by reviewers who, dissatisfied with recent Pulitzer Prize drama selections, begin their own annual selection of the best American play or musical. Maxwell Anderson's *Winterset* is the first winner.

The *Southern Review.* Edited successively by C. W. Pipkin, Cleanth Brooks, and Robert Penn Warren, until 1942, the literary quarterly would become one of the leading publications to promulgate the New Criticism.

1936
Drama and Theater

MAXWELL ANDERSON: *The Wingless Victory.* The playwright treats interracial marriage in this blank-verse tragedy of an eighteenth-century New England ship captain who returns home with a Malaysian wife.

ARTHUR ARENT (1904–1972): *Triple-A Plowed Under.* The first of the playwright's "Living Newspaper" productions, dramatizing timely social and political issues, looks at the lot of farmers during the Depression. It would be

followed by *Power* (1937), a plea for affordable energy for the poor. Arent contributed to the labor revue *Pins and Needles* (1937) and would subsequently write and adapt plays for radio and television.

S. N. BEHRMAN: *End of Summer.* Behrman's sophisticated social comedy dramatizes the impact on a rich matriarch when her daughter accepts a young radical suitor.

LILLIAN HELLMAN: *Days to Come.* Hellman's second Broadway production depicts a strike's effect on a Midwestern family. A failure with the critics and at the box office, the play closes after a week.

LANGSTON HUGHES AND ARNA BONTEMPS: *When the Jack Hollers.* The writers collaborate on a "Negro folk drama," set in the Mississippi Delta and concerning black sharecroppers. Hughes also writes *Little Ham*, a celebration of everyday Harlem life that anticipates his Simple stories.

GEORGE S. KAUFMAN AND EDNA FERBER: *Stage Door.* Although less critically acclaimed than the collaborators' previous plays, this drama about a group of aspiring actresses boarding together at the Footlights Club proves a popular success and includes identifiable portraits of contemporary theatrical figures such as Clifford Odets.

GEORGE S. KAUFMAN AND MOSS HART: *You Can't Take It with You.* The playwrights achieve their longest-running success and second Pulitzer Prize for this comedy about the eccentric New York Vanderhof family, who resists the forces of conformity and underscores the theme that money is not everything. One of the most enduring American comedies, the play is frequently revived and a staple of amateur and summer stock companies.

GEORGE KELLY: *Reflected Glory.* The former Pulitzer Prize–winning playwright has only a modest success after a five-year layoff from the stage with this drama. In it an actress struggles between the conflicting demands of her career and a desire for marriage and family.

SIDNEY KINGSLEY: *Ten Million Ghosts.* Kingsley's antiwar drama is a strident attack on munitions manufacturers.

CLARE BOOTHE LUCE (1903–1987): *The Women.* One of the biggest comedy hits of the decade concerns a group of wives who gather in Reno to gain divorces. Reviewer Brooks Atkinson calls the play "strikingly detailed pictures of some of the most odious harpies ever collected in one play." Luce was a former child actress who served as the managing editor of *Vanity Fair.* Her subsequent plays include *Kiss the Boys Goodbye* (1938) and *Margin for Error* (1939).

LYNN RIGGS: *The Cherokee Night.* In Riggs's only play to deal specifically with Native American life, he treats the lot of mixed-blood Cherokees who are bereft of their cultural past and unable to fit comfortably into white society. The play marks a significant change in the ways in which Native Americans are portrayed on stage.

RICHARD RODGERS (1902–1979), LORENZ HART (1895–1943), AND GEORGE ABBOTT: *On Your Toes.* In this innovative musical a dancer gets involved with both a Russian ballet company and gangsters. It features choreography by George Balanchine (1904–1983) and his celebrated ballet-within-the-play, "Slaughter on Tenth Avenue," set in a sleazy West Side bar.

IRWIN SHAW (1913–1984): *Bury the Dead.* Set in the "Second Year of War That Is to Begin Tomorrow," the dead on a battlefield refuse burial and enlist the living to resist the generals in this harrowing antiwar drama. The Brooklyn-born writer of socially aware dramas would shift to the novel with *The Young Lions* (1948).

ROBERT E. SHERWOOD: *Idiot's Delight.* The playwright's Pulitzer Prize–winning comedy is set in an Italian hotel at the outbreak of the next European war as an American song-and-dance man encounters a former flame posing as a Russian countess. Hailed as Sherwood's "best written and best acted play," the drama entertainingly presents a strong pacifist and anti-Fascist message. Sherwood also writes *Tovarich*, an adaptation of the French comedy by Jacques Deval concerning Russian nobility forced to work as servants in Paris after the Russian Revolution. It becomes a smash hit on Broadway.

Fiction

SHERWOOD ANDERSON: *Kit Brandon.* Anderson's final novel concerns a Virginia mountain girl who struggles as a mill worker, shop girl, and finally a moonshine runner. Written in an attempt to be "more objective," the novel is considered the best constructed of any of Anderson's longer works.

SHOLEM ASCH: *The War Goes On.* One of the first fictional treatments of life for Jews in Nazi Germany, the novel also deals with the conditions that made Hitler's rise to power possible.

DJUNA BARNES: *Nightwood.* Considered a modernist masterpiece and called by Dylan Thomas "one of the three great prose books ever written by a woman," Barnes's experimental stream-of-consciousness second novel concerns the sexual and psychological agonies of a group of expatriates in Paris and Berlin during the 1920s. The novel features a groundbreaking frank treatment of lesbianism.

ARNA BONTEMPS: *Black Thunder.* Concerning the aborted 1800 slave revolt led by Gabriel Prosser in Vir-

ginia, Bontemps's book has been called one of the best African American novels ever written.

KAY BOYLE: *Death of a Man.* Boyle's novel concerns the relationship between an American woman and a Nazi doctor. Also published is *The White Horses of Vienna and Other Stories.* The title story of this collection, set in Austria in the mid-1930s and dealing with anti-Semitism and the Nazis' destruction of moral values, is one of Boyle's most anthologized stories and regarded as one of her best.

JAMES M. CAIN: *Double Indemnity.* Cain continues his study of sexuality and betrayal in this tale of an insurance agent seduced by a woman into killing her husband to collect his life insurance. It would be made into a film noir classic starring Fred MacMurray and Barbara Stanwyck in 1944.

ERSKINE CALDWELL: *The Sacrilege of Alan Kent.* Caldwell's most experimental fiction is a fictionalized autobiography that critic Malcolm Cowley calls a "prose poem that corresponds on a lower scale to Walt Whitman's 'Song of Myself.'"

JAMES GOULD COZZENS: *Men and Brethren.* The first of Cozzens's novels to explore his characteristic theme of the duty owed by a man of responsibilities and intelligence, the story is a psychological portrait of the internal struggles of Episcopal minister Ernest Cudlipp.

JOHN DOS PASSOS: *The Big Money.* In the final novel of the writer's U.S.A. trilogy (collected 1938), preceded by *The 42nd Parallel* (1930) and *1919* (1932), Dos Passos concludes his epic social documentation of America in the first three decades of the twentieth century with the boom times of the 1920s.

WALTER D. EDMONDS: *Drums Along the Mohawk.* One of the classic fictional treatments of the American Revolution, Edmonds's most popular and acclaimed historical novel chronicles life in New York's Mohawk Valley from 1776 to 1784. The writer's authenticity and realism set a new standard for the historical novel.

JAMES T. FARRELL: *A World I Never Made.* The first of a series of naturalistic novels concerning the Studs Lonigan–type Danny O'Neill from the Irish slums of Chicago. Later volumes are *No Star Is Lost* (1938), *Father and Son* (1940), *My Days of Anger* (1943), and *The Face of Time* (1953).

WILLIAM FAULKNER: *Absalom, Absalom!* Regarded by many as the writer's masterpiece, this complex, multivocal novel depicts the fall of the house of Mississippi's Thomas Sutpen and reflects American and Southern history before, during, and after the Civil War.

MARTHA GELLHORN: *The Trouble I've Seen.* Based on the author's experience with the Federal Emergency

Relief, this collection of stories concerns the desperate struggles of the unemployed on relief and is praised for its hard-edged realism and empathy.

MUNRO LEAF (1905–1976): *The Story of Ferdinand.* Leaf's children's story of a Spanish bull with a gentle nature and a passion for flowers becomes a phenomenal success. Within thirteen months, eight editions are published, a Ferdinand balloon is featured in the Macy's Thanksgiving Day Parade, and a Ferdinand song becomes a hit. In 1938, *The Story of Ferdinand* for a time kept *Gone with the Wind* from the top spot on the best-seller list. Leaf was an English teacher who wrote and illustrated *Grammar Can Be Fun* (1934), *Manners Can Be Fun* (1936), and *Safety Can Be Fun* (1938).

H. P. LOVECRAFT (1890–1937): *The Shadow over Innsmouth.* Having published exclusively in pulp magazines, the master of supernatural horror publishes his single collection during his lifetime. Born in Providence, Rhode Island, Lovecraft was a recluse whose achievements as a master of tales of terror and fantasy would be recognized through posthumously published collections such as *The Outsider and Others* (1939) and *Beyond the Wall of Sleep* (1943).

ANDREW LYTLE (1902–1995): *The Long Night.* The Tennessee writer's first novel concerns a southern family's campaign of vengeance against an outlaw gang. It includes a convincing account of the Battle of Shiloh. Lytle, who contributed to *I'll Take My Stand* (1930), was an editor of the *Sewanee Review* in 1941.

D'ARCY MCNICKLE (1904–1977): *The Surrounded.* Called by one critic "the most significant novel by an American Indian written before World War II," McNickle's story of a mixed-blood protagonist's estrangement from both white and Indian culture is a pioneering and influential work in Native American literary history. McNickle grew up on the Flathead Indian reservation in Montana and directed the Newberry Library Center for the History of American Indians and was a cofounder of the National Congress of American Indians.

HENRY MILLER: *Black Spring.* Miller continues his autobiographical reflections begun in *Tropic of Cancer*, combining reflections of his childhood in Brooklyn with surrealistic passages from his dreambook. Included is the admired passage "The Angel Is My Watermark," describing the author painting a watercolor. The work is first published in Paris; an American edition would not be issued until 1963.

MARGARET MITCHELL (1900–1949): *Gone with the Wind.* Selling a record-breaking one million copies in its first six months, Mitchell's only novel became the largest-selling book in history behind the Bible and an American

Margaret Mitchell

cultural phenomenon. Mitchell's 1,307-page opus of the struggles of headstrong Southern belle Scarlett O'Hara before, during, and after the Civil War had been written from 1926 to 1934 and drew on the writer's childhood memories of stories of the South uprooted by history. Winner of the Pulitzer Prize and adapted in 1939 into one of the most popular films of all time, the novel achieved an unprecedented place in American cultural consciousness.

ANAÏS NIN (1903–1977): *The House of Incest.* After publishing her first book, a critical work entitled *D. H. Lawrence: An Unprofessional Study* (1932), Nin presents her initial creative work, an extended prose poem that is a dreamlike rendering of psychological states of an unnamed woman. The work's originality and intensity have caused many to regard the work as Nin's greatest fictional achievement. Nin was born in Paris and came to the United States as a teenager. She would be best known for her seven-volume *The Diary of Anaïs Nin* (1966–1980).

AYN RAND: *We the Living.* Written in response to a promise Rand made to a friend at a farewell party before she emigrated from Russia, her first novel is a searing indictment of life under the Communist regime, in which collectivism destroys individualism, a dominant theme in Rand's subsequent work.

CONRAD RICHTER (1890–1968): *Early Americana and Other Stories.* Richter's first major publication is a collection of nine stories of pioneer life in the Southwest. The writer's artistry and realism mark a new way of handling western subjects. Born in Pennsylvania, Richter worked as a reporter and moved to New Mexico in 1928 where he became fascinated by the region's history.

WILLIAM SAROYAN: *Inhale and Exhale.* The writer's second story collection continues his conversational, unconventional narrative approach, mixing character sketches, incidents, and opinions on diverse topics. He also publishes *Three Times Three*, a collection that includes "The Man with the Heart in the Highlands," which he would adapt as his first successful play in 1939.

JOHN STEINBECK: *In Dubious Battle.* The first of the writer's novels to take up the subject of California's migratory farm laborers, the story concerns the tragic impact of a fruit pickers' strike on a group of radical union organizers.

JESSE STUART (1907–1984): *Head o' W-Hollows.* The Appalachian regionalist's first story collection provides glimpses of life in the eastern Kentucky mountain community of W-Hollow, where he lived most of his life.

EDITH WHARTON: *The World Over.* A short story collection that includes "Confession," adapted from the author's incomplete and unpublished play *Kate Spain*, which deals with two Americans who meet at a European hotel and the secret of one. The story echoes the notorious Lizzie Borden murder case, and critics have suggested that the story is an attempt to exorcise Wharton's own childhood traumas.

RICHARD WRIGHT (1908–1969): "Big Boy Leaves Home." First published in the anthology *New Caravan* and later in his collection *Uncle Tom's Children* (1938), this harrowing story tells of a black adolescent who is forced to shoot a white man in self-defense after he watches his friend being lynched, burned alive, and mutilated. It is the first of Wright's works to receive wide critical attention. Wright was born in rural Mississippi, raised in Memphis, and migrated to Chicago at the age of nineteen.

Literary Criticism and Scholarship

VAN WYCK BROOKS: *The Flowering of New England, 1815–1865.* The first of the author's Makers and Finders series of literary and cultural histories of the United States wins the Pulitzer Prize. It looks at the social, political, and religious context of the careers of writers such as Longfellow, Emerson, Hawthorne, and Thoreau.

WILLA CATHER: *Not Under Forty.* The writer explains her theory of fiction and influences with interpretive essays on writers such as Sarah Orne Jewett, Katherine Mansfield, and Thomas Mann. The title refers to the author's contention that her book will be of interest only to those age forty or older.

T. S. ELIOT: *Essays, Ancient and Modern.* In an expansion of his previous critical volume, *For Lancelot Andrewes* (1928), Eliot considers moral, political, psychological, and theological topics as well as literary critiques of Alfred Tennyson and Blaise Pascal.

JAMES T. FARRELL: *A Note on Literary Criticism.* Literary historian Walter B. Rideout has described this volume as the "only extended discussion of Marxist aesthetics written from a Marxist standpoint in the United States during the thirties." The furor created by Farrell's diagnosis of the limitations of Marxist critical standards would be identified by the *New Masses* as "The Farrell Controversy."

GEORGE SANTAYANA: *Obiter Scripta.* A miscellany of the philosopher's essays, lectures, and reviews on both philosophical and literary subjects.

GERTRUDE STEIN: *The Geographical History of America; or, The Relation of Human Nature to the Human Mind.* Stein supplies a discursive meditation on literary masterpieces as well as a justification for her own departures from conventional literary forms.

ALLEN TATE: *Reactionary Essays on Poetry and Ideas.* Tate's first volume of critical essays includes studies of English and American poets and meditations on Southern culture.

THOMAS WOLFE: *The Story of a Novel.* Wolfe recounts his experience of writing *Look Homeward, Angel*, the impact following its publication, and his artistic theories.

Nonfiction

ROBERT BENCHLEY: *My Ten Years in a Quandary, and How They Grew.* The humorist's essays cover topics such as Pullman cars, white suits, smoking, and telephoning techniques.

DALE CARNEGIE (1888–1955): *How to Win Friends and Influence People.* Regarded as the first modern self-help book, Carnegie's advice in dealing with others, summarized by one reviewer as "Smile, be friendly, never argue or find fault, or tell a person he is wrong," would become one of the biggest-selling books of the century, with more than five million copies sold during Carnegie's lifetime.

MAX EASTMAN (1883–1969): *Enjoyment of Laughter.* The radical social critic offers a descriptive study of the psychology of humor, illustrated by examples from various American humorists.

JOHN GUNTHER (1901–1970): *Inside Europe.* The first of the journalist's best-selling sociopolitical regional surveys includes portraits of Adolf Hitler, Benito Mussolini, and Joseph Stalin, and analysis of current European affairs. Subsequent volumes are *Inside Asia* (1939), *Inside Latin America* (1941), *Inside U.S.A.* (1947), *Inside Africa* (1955), *Inside Russia Today* (1957), and *Inside Europe Today* (1961).

EDGAR LEE MASTERS: *Across Spoon River.* Masters supplies a frank autobiographical account of his Midwestern boyhood, his years as a struggling lawyer, and his writing career up to 1917.

EDMUND WILSON: *Travels in Two Democracies.* Combining a memoir with a travelogue, Wilson contrasts his observations about Depression-era America with life in the Soviet Union.

Poetry

CONRAD AIKEN: *Time in the Rock: Preludes to Definition.* Intended as the second half of the long philosophical poem *Preludes for Memnon* (1931); they collectively form a continuous self-examination in verse.

EMILY DICKINSON: *Unpublished Poems.* Edited by Martha Dickinson Bianchi (Dickinson's niece) and Alfred Leete Hamilton, the volume makes available poems and fragments discovered when Bianchi was gathering material for her book *Emily Dickinson: Face to Face* (1932).

T. S. ELIOT: *Collected Poems, 1909–1935.* Eliot's collected work includes his major poetic achievement of the 1930s, "Burnt Norton," originally conceived as an independent work but later incorporated as the first section of *Four Quartets.*

PAUL ENGLE: *Break the Heart's Anger.* Written while Engle was a Rhodes scholar, the poems take to task American materialism and pettiness with a style that is described by one reviewer as the "full long breath of a Whitman, and hard-hitting fist of a Sandburg."

ROBERT FROST: *A Further Range.* Frost's sixth volume of poems wins him his third Pulitzer Prize. Organized into two groups of poems—"Taken Doubly" and "Taken Simply"—the volume of humorous, satirical, and philosophical observations includes "Two Tramps in Mud Time," in which itinerant lumbermen are used to illustrate the connection between work and play, and important poems such as "Design," "Departmental," and "Desert Places."

ARCHIBALD MacLEISH: *Public Speech.* As its title indicates, the volume announces the poet's intention to use his verse to address important social and political issues, a stance that would dominate MacLeish's work thereafter.

EDGAR LEE MASTERS: *Poems of People.* Masters's character studies and verse portraits of fifty men and women fails to achieve the success of *Spoon River Anthology* (1915).

MARIANNE MOORE: *The Pangolin and Other Verse.* The volume shows the poet's penchant for employing animals as subjects and her abandonment of free verse for stanzas and rhyme patterns expressive of a more controlled mastery.

DOROTHY PARKER: *Not So Deep as a Well.* Parker's collection brings together all her earlier volumes and more recent work, enhancing her reputation as the master of light verse, combining acerbic wit, self-mockery, and clever satirical raillery.

KENNETH PATCHEN (1911–1972): *Before the Brave.* The poet's debut volume shows the influence of W. H. Auden and Kenneth Fearing but also an original, experimental style derived in part from techniques traceable from his work as an abstract expressionist painter.

LIZETTE WOODWORTH REESE: *The Old House in the Country.* Unfinished at the time of the poet's death, this long poem tenderly recalls Reese's childhood and life in the country.

CARL SANDBURG: *The People, Yes.* In the Whitman mode, Sandburg supplies a panoramic celebration of American working-class life in a vernacular collection of folklore, legends, and tall tales.

WALLACE STEVENS: *Owl's Clover.* This series of blank-verse meditations on the nature of art and the role of the artist is chiefly significant for Stevens's aesthetic ideas and for providing elements that he would rework more successfully in *The Man with the Blue Guitar* (1937).

ALLEN TATE: *The Mediterranean and Other Poems.* The title poem is a lament for the passing of the classical tradition. The other standout poem in this collection is "To the Lacedemonians," on the tragedy of the Civil War.

JOHN HALL WHEELOCK: *Poems, 1911–1936.* The longtime Scribner's editor provides this selection of the best of his traditional verses from his previous collections.

WILLIAM CARLOS WILLIAMS: *Adam & Eve & The City.* Besides the three title poems, the volume includes one of the poet's best lyrics of the period, "The Crimson Cyclamen."

Publications and Events

Federal Theatre Project. Established by Congress to assist theatrical professionals put out of work by the

Depression, the project at its height employed thirteen thousand people who helped mount twelve hundred productions attended by more than twelve million people. FTP productions included the Broadway premieres of T. S. Eliot's *Murder in the Cathedral* and Sinclair Lewis's *It Can't Happen Here.*

The Ford Foundation. Henry Ford and his son, Edsel, create this organization, which, after their deaths, would become the world's largest philanthropic endowment, with assets of more than $6 billion. The foundation has supported diverse programs in fields such as world law and peace, advancement of basic democratic principles, improvement of the world's economic conditions, and education.

Life. The weekly photo-news periodical is issued on November 23 by the publishers of *Time.* The large-format magazine continued as a ubiquitous presence on America's coffee tables until 1972.

New Directions. James Laughlin (1914–1997) receives his inheritance after graduating from college and begins an annual as an outlet for experimental works ignored by the commercial literary market. Contributors include Ezra Pound, Gertrude Stein, E. E. Cummings, and William Carlos Williams. Selling copies to bookstores out of his car, Laughlin eventually expanded his operation to create the most important avant-garde publishing house in the United States.

1937
Drama and Theater

MAXWELL ANDERSON: *High Tor.* One of Anderson's best and most successful plays, winning him his second New York Drama Critics Circle Award, is a dramatic fantasy in which a man who resists selling his mountain property along the Hudson to developers spends the night there and is visited by the ghosts of Dutch mariners, including the spirit of the Dutch captain's daughter, with whom he falls in love. Anderson also produces *The Star Wagon*, which imagines a married couple transported back in time to their youth to reaffirm their love.

STEPHEN VINCENT BENÉT: *The Headless Horseman.* An adaptation of Washington Irving's "The Legend of Sleepy Hollow," this is the first of Benét's two one-act folk operas. It would be followed by *The Devil and Daniel Webster* (1939).

RACHEL CROTHERS: *Susan and God.* Crothers's final play records the religious conversion of a vain, selfish woman.

PAUL GREEN: *Johnny Johnson.* An antiwar fantasy with music by Kurt Weill (1900–1950) in his first American musical, the play depicts a pacifist in World War I who

George S. Kaufman (*left*) and Moss Hart

sprays the Allied High Command with laughing gas, is sent to a mental asylum, and organizes the patients into a League of World Republicans. In the same year *The Lost Colony*, the first and most successful of the playwright's symphonic outdoor dramas, is presented with a cast of 150 on Roanoke Island, North Carolina, where it would continue to be staged annually.

SIDNEY HOWARD: *The Ghost of Yankee Doodle.* Howard's final play is set "eighteen months after the next world war" has begun and deals with the impact of war propaganda on a number of characters.

GEORGE S. KAUFMAN AND MOSS HART: *I'd Rather Be Right.* The first drama to depict an incumbent president in a lead role, this musical satire on the New Deal and the Roosevelt administration features George M. Cohan in his last dramatic role as FDR (a man the actor detested) surrounded by almost all of the important political figures of the day.

ARTHUR KOBER (1900–1975): *Having a Wonderful Time.* The Ukrainian-born playwright's only successful drama is this comedy of contemporary Jewish American life set in a Berkshires summer camp. Kober would adapt the play into the musical *Wish You Were Here* in 1952.

JOHN HOWARD LAWSON: *Marching Song.* The controversial radical playwright's final drama pits strikers against strikebreakers in the final production by the Theatre Union, a group formed in 1932 to mount dramas of social significance.

ARCHIBALD MacLEISH: *The Fall of the City.* MacLeish's attack on totalitarianism takes the form of the first American play in verse written for the radio. It is performed on April 11 by Orson Welles and Burgess Meredith.

CLIFFORD ODETS: *Golden Boy.* After a screenwriting foray in Hollywood, Odets returns to Broadway with this drama of an Italian slum dweller who abandons the violin for a prizefighting career. It is one of the playwright's least explicitly political dramas but his most popular. It would be revised in 1964 as an all-black musical starring Sammy Davis Jr.

HAROLD ROME (1908–1993): *Pins and Needles.* Rome had written his first Broadway score for this propagandistic union revue produced by the International Ladies Garment Workers' Union, which features a cast entirely made up of rank and file union members. For a time the revue would hold the record for the longest run for a Broadway musical (1,108 performances). Musical numbers such as "Sing Me a Song with Social Significance" and "It's Better with a Union Man" indicate the play's earnestness.

IRWIN SHAW: *Siege.* Shaw's Spanish Civil War drama tells the story of a group of Loyalists trapped in a surrounded redoubt.

JOHN STEINBECK: *Of Mice and Men.* Having written his 1937 novel "as a play," Steinbeck quickly adapts it for the stage. It wins the New York Drama Critics Circle Award.

EDMUND WILSON: *This Room and This Gin and These Sandwiches.* Wilson's three experimental dramas — *The Crime in the Whistler Room, A Winter in Beech Street,* and *Beppo and Beth* — are satiric portraits of American life. Critics generally complain that the art of the dramatist is lacking in these intelligent but talky exercises in social criticism.

Fiction

STEPHEN VINCENT BENÉT: "The Devil and Daniel Webster." Benét's short story about a New Hampshire farmer who sells his soul to the devil and is defended by Daniel Webster is published in the *Saturday Evening Post.* The author would adapt it in 1939 into a folk opera with music by Douglas Moore.

JAMES M. CAIN: *Serenade.* Cain's third novel continues his hard-boiled style in a tragic story about a famous opera singer.

JAMES T. FARRELL: *Can All This Grandeur Perish? and Other Stories.* Farrell's story collection echoes the naturalistic themes of his novels in various of slice-of-life looks at modern urban life. Several similar collections would follow, including *$1,000 a Week* (1942), *To Whom It May Concern* (1944), *When Boyhood Dreams Come True* (1946), and *The Life Adventurous* (1947).

DANIEL FUCHS: *Low Company.* In the final volume of a trilogy that includes *Summer in Williamsburg* (1934) and *Homage to Blenholt* (1936), Fuchs completes the documentation of his boyhood Jewish community in Brooklyn with the story of gambler Moe Karby. Disappointed by his books' commercial failure, Fuchs then turned to screenwriting. His series was rediscovered in 1961 when reissued as a single volume; Fuchs was belatedly recognized as a significant chronicler of modern urban life.

THEODOR SEUSS GEISEL (1904–1991): *And to Think That I Saw It on Mulberry Street.* Under the pseudonym "Dr. Seuss," Geisel publishes his first illustrated children's book, composed as a nonsense poem set to the rhythm of the ship's engine to amuse himself on his return from Europe in 1936. The fantasy of a boy on his way home from school is considered by many his best work. His other children's stories of the decade are *The 500 Hats of Bartholomew Cubbins* (1938), *The Seven Lady Godivas* (1939), and *The King's Stilts* (1939).

CAROLINE GORDON: *None Shall Look Back.* Gordon's ambitious Civil War–era novel is modeled on Tolstoy's *War and Peace,* alternating family scenes with battle action and appearances by historical figures, most notably General Nathan Bedford Forrest, an embodiment of heroic values. The novel is criticized as an apology for the old Southern way of life, turning a blind eye to the injustices of slavery. Gordon also publishes *The Garden of Adonis,* which treats contemporary Southern life through the interrelationships of several families of varying social backgrounds.

ERNEST HEMINGWAY: *To Have and Have Not.* Hemingway's only novel of the 1930s is the often cynically brutal story of Key West "conch" Harry Morgan, who is forced by economic necessity into illegal activities. His realization on the point of death that "One man alone ain't got . . . no chance" demonstrates Hemingway's increasing social concerns and his acknowledgment of the need for collective action, both derived from the writer's experiences in Spain. Reviewers, although impressed by some of the novel's passages and episodes, generally see in the novel signs of Hemingway's decline.

ZORA NEALE HURSTON: *Their Eyes Were Watching God.* Hurston's masterpiece about the liberation of black woman Janie Crawford to a wider concept of her identity and engagement with the world through three marriages is widely considered the first black feminist novel of the twentieth century.

JOSEPHINE W. JOHNSON: *Jordanstown.* Johnson's second novel looks as the effects of the Depression on a small

Midwestern town where an idealistic journalist takes up the cause of the oppressed in editorials in the local newspaper. Johnson also publishes her only collection of poetry, *Year's End.*

YOUNGHILL KANG: *East Goes West.* The sequel to *The Grass Roof,* the first book-length work in English by a Korean immigrant, treats Kang's experiences in America in a fictionalized autobiography that the author would regard as his finest work.

OLIVER LA FARGE: *The Enemy Gods.* The era's recognized authority on Native American culture, the anthropologist and director of the National Association of Indian Affairs, continues his documentation of Navajo life in this novel concerning the cultural conflict experienced by a young Indian's difficult progress to manhood.

MEYER LEVIN: *The Old Bunch.* Levin examines Jewish assimilation in the stories of a dozen second-generation Jews in Chicago, from their high school graduation in 1922 to 1934. Generally regarded as Levin's best novel, it has been described by critic Philip Rahv as "the classic American story of defeat and frustration."

J. P. MARQUAND (1893–1960): *The Late George Apley.* Marquand wins the Pulitzer Prize for this "novel in the form of a memoir," detailing the life story of a member of an old Boston family, which expertly presents a portrait of an age, a class, and a locality. The author would collaborate with George S. Kaufman in a dramatization in 1944. Marquand was raised in Newburyport, Massachusetts, the locale of many of his works, and was a journalist and advertising copywriter. His previous works included *The Unspeakable Gentleman* (1922), *The Black Congo* (1925), and *Warning Hill* (1930).

EDGAR LEE MASTERS: *The Tide of Time.* A chronicle of an Illinois town from its founding in 1822. Readers acknowledge the book's epic ambitions but mainly resist it as overly heavy going and dull.

WILLIAM MAXWELL: *They Came Like Swallows.* One of the most highly praised of the author's books, the novel dramatizes the impact of the Spanish influenza epidemic on a close-knit family.

ELMER RICE: *Imperial City.* Rice offers a panoramic social view of New York City in this novel about the lives of a diverse group of city dwellers.

CONRAD RICHTER: *The Sea of Grass.* Richter's first novel deepens the genre of the western in a depiction of cattle ranching in the Southwest.

KENNETH ROBERTS: *Northwest Passage.* In one of the most popular and acclaimed historical novels, Roberts chronicles the adventures of Major Robert Rogers and his rangers during the French and Indian War.

LEO ROSTEN (1908–1997): *The Education of H*Y*-M*A*N K*A*P*L*A*N.* Written under the pseudonym "Leonard Q. Ross," Rosten's most popular work is a collection of sketches, previously serialized in *The New Yorker,* about an immigrant's linguistic misadventures in an English-language night school for adults. Two sequels would follow: *The Return of H*Y*M*A*N K*A*P*L*A*N* (1959) and *O K*A*P*L*A*N! My K*A*P*-L*A*N!* (1976). Rosten is best remembered for *The Joys of Yiddish* (1968).

MARI SANDOZ: *Slogum House.* The Nebraska author's first novel looks at the darker side of the frontier ethic in a tale of a ruthless woman's drive for power. The book is banned by several Nebraska libraries.

WILLIAM SAROYAN: *Little Children.* In this volume of short stories about children or childish adults, reviewers note a more subdued writer with his characteristic bluster diminished.

DELMORE SCHWARTZ (1913–1966): "In Dreams Begin Responsibility." Schwartz's short story appears in the inaugural issue of the reconstituted *Partisan Review* and is immediately hailed as a masterpiece. It would provide the title for the writer's first volume of poetry, prose, and a dramatic work in 1938.

UPTON SINCLAIR: *The Flivver King: A Story of Ford-America.* Sinclair provides a fictionalized portrait of Henry Ford and his company as seen from the perspective of three generations of Ford's laborers. The United Auto Workers distributes 200,000 copies to union members.

WALLACE STEGNER (1909–1993): *Remembering Laughter.* Prompted by a writing contest sponsored by the publisher Little, Brown, Stegner attempted his first work of fiction, a realistic tale of a triangular relationship on an Iowa farm. It is selected as the best from thirteen hundred entries. Born in Iowa and educated in Utah, Stegner would gain recognition as one of the major modern chroniclers of the American West.

JOHN STEINBECK: *Of Mice and Men.* In Steinbeck's short novel the dreams of two itinerant laborers, George and Lennie, about a place of their own collapses when the simple-minded Lennie accidentally breaks the neck of another man's wife. Steinbeck weaves social themes around concepts of evolutionary biology and the survival of the fittest.

WATERS TURPIN (1910–1968): *These Low Grounds.* Turpin's first novel traces the lives of four generations of a black family living on the eastern shore of Maryland and earns him the title of "the progenitor of the Afro-American saga" and thus the forerunner of Alex Haley's method in *Roots* (1976). Turpin's mother had been the cook of writer Edna Ferber, who became his literary mentor. His other novels are *O Canaan!* (1939) and *The Rootless* (1957).

JEROME WEIDMAN (1913–1998): *I Can Get It for You Wholesale.* Written a chapter a night in thirty days while Weidman attended school, this first novel by the New York writer takes an unflattering look at the fortunes of unscrupulous Harry Bogen in New York's garment district. A sequel, *What's in It for Me?* would follow in 1938.

EDITH WHARTON: *Ghosts.* This supernatural story collection is issued posthumously, with a preface in which Wharton discusses the writing of ghost stories and worries that the "ghost instinct" is being destroyed by the wireless and the cinema, "enemies of the imagination," in the writer's view.

WILLIAM CARLOS WILLIAMS: *White Mule.* The first novel of a trilogy concerns the adjustment of an immigrant family, based on the author's in-laws, to life in America. Subsequent volumes are *In the Money* (1940) and *The Build-Up* (1952).

Literary Criticism and Scholarship

WALTER BLAIR (1900–1992): *Native American Humor, 1800–1900.* Blair, who taught at the University of Chicago, becomes one of the first academics to study American humor, and this work remains one of the authoritative books in the field. It would be revised in 1960. His other works include *Horse Sense in American Humor* (1942) and *Davy Crockett: Truth and Legend* (1955).

STERLING BROWN: *The Negro in American Fiction* and *Negro Poetry and Drama.* Brown's two critical volumes are generally regarded as the foundation texts for the study of African American literary history. As scholar Darwin T. Turner observed, "All trails led, at some point, to Sterling Brown" who "wrote the Bible for the study of Afro-American literature."

EDGAR LEE MASTERS: *Whitman.* Masters's critical biography attempts to deal with both the poet's private, emotional life and his wider cultural significance.

YVOR WINTERS: *Primitivism and Decadence: A Study of American Experimental Poetry.* The critic demonstrates what is wrong with modern poetry with what poet Hayden Carruth would later call his "magnificent wrath," able to prove that "our favorite poets are idiots, and in the process show us just why we like them so much."

Nonfiction

LUDWIG BEMELMANS (1898–1962): *My War with the United States.* The first adult book by the Austrian émigré writer-illustrator and future creator of the children's clas-

sic *Madeline* (1939) is a humorous depiction of his service with the American army during World War I.

KENNETH BURKE: *Attitudes Toward History.* The philosopher supplies a psychological interpretation of historical events and figures in this two-volume study.

ERSKINE CALDWELL AND MARGARET BOURKE-WHITE (1904–1971): *You Have Seen Their Faces.* This first of four volumes of photo-essays looks at Southern sharecroppers. Subsequent volumes are *North to the Danube* (1939) about Czechoslovakia, *Say, Is This the U.S.A.?* (1941), and *Russia at War* (1942). Bourke-White was one of the best-known photographers of the era.

ROBERT P. TRISTRAM COFFIN: *The Kennebec.* The Maine poet and essayist initiates the Rivers of America series, which would be followed by volumes by Struther Burt (1882–1954; *Powder River*, 1938) and Carl Carmer (1893–1976; *The Hudson*, 1939).

JOHN GOULD FLETCHER: *Life Is My Song.* The leader of the Agrarians, a group of writers that includes Allen Tate, John Crowe Ransom, and Robert Penn Warren who promoted the values of the agrarian South over twentieth-century industrialism, offers his autobiographical account of his involvement with the imagist poets before the war.

CLAUDE McKAY: *A Long Way from Home.* One of the key figures of the Harlem Renaissance provides his autobiographical reflections on his native Jamaica, life in Harlem, and his travels abroad, emphasizing the dominant theme of his books: the search for a viable cultural identity for a black in a white-dominated society.

ELLIOT PAUL (1891–1958): *The Life and Death of a Spanish Town.* The expatriate journalist documents the impact of the Spanish Civil War on a community in the Balearic islands. It is considered at the time one of the best treatments of the Spanish conflict. Paul's most popular work is his memoir, *The Last Time I Saw Paris* (1942).

S. J. PERELMAN: *Strictly from Hunger.* The writer's second book but the first of his mature work is a collection of deft sketches and reflections that had previously appeared in *The New Yorker* and other periodicals.

ELEANOR ROOSEVELT: *This Is My Story.* The First Lady's autobiography covers the years from her childhood to the Democratic convention of 1924 and her husband's election as governor of New York. Candid about herself, Roosevelt is discreet on the details of her marriage.

ODELL SHEPARD (1884–1967): *Pedlar's Progress.* This biography of Bronson Alcott, the father of writer Louisa May Alcott and one of the foremost Transcendentalists, wins the Pulitzer Prize and is praised for resurrecting the reputation of an important American figure and for skillfully capturing his era. A professor of English at Trinity

College from 1917 to 1946, Shepard edited the works of Thoreau, Alcott, and Longfellow, produced college literature textbooks, and cowrote with his son Willard two historical novels, *Holdfast Gaines* (1946) and *Jenkins' Ear* (1951).

HAROLD STEARNS: *America: A Reappraisal.* After an extended residence abroad, cultural critic Stearns returns to the United States and supplies this generally favorable assessment of the changes he found.

GERTRUDE STEIN: *Everybody's Autobiography.* In a sequel to *The Autobiography of Alice B. Toklas* (1933), Stein reflects on her six-month lecture tour of America in 1934–1935.

JAMES THURBER: *Let Your Mind Alone! and Other More or Less Inspirational Pieces.* The humorist takes satirical aim at inspirational books, popular psychology, intellectual critics, and the art of autobiography in this collection, most of which had previously appeared in *The New Yorker.*

Poetry

R. P. BLACKMUR: *From Jordan's Delight.* The literary critic's first volume of poetry is a collection of meticulously crafted lyrics with a coastal Maine setting.

LOUISE BOGAN: *The Sleeping Fury.* The poet's third collection solidifies her reputation as one of the major voices of the era that rejects the experimentation of Ezra Pound, T. S. Eliot, and others and embraces traditional poetic forms, echoing writers such as John Donne, George Herbert, and Henry Vaughan.

RICHARD EBERHART: *Reading the Spirit.* Eberhart's second collection contains his best-known poem, "The Groundhog," whose themes of life and death, man and nature, mind and body would recur throughout the poet's career.

ROBERT HILLYER: *A Letter to Robert Frost and Others.* Witty letters in heroic couplets to figures such as Robert Frost, Harvard professor Charles Townsend Copeland, Bernard De Voto, and Queen Nefertiti.

ROBINSON JEFFERS: *Such Counsels You Gave Me, and Other Poems.* The long narrative title poem is a modern adaptation of the Scottish ballad "Edward, Edward," concerning the collapse of a family in which the son poisons his father and must reject the incestuous passion of his mother. According to one reviewer, Jeffers "evokes a sense of personal tragedy against a background of universal terror."

EDGAR LEE MASTERS: *The New World.* This long epic poem presents the history of America before Columbus to the end of the Great War. Displaying a shift in style from the condensed portraiture of *Spoon River Anthology*, the author heaps scorn on the materialism that he sees dissolving American freedom and morality in a long-winded and often ponderous work.

EDNA ST. VINCENT MILLAY: *Conversation at Midnight.* In a departure from her characteristic lyricism, Millay attempts a narrative poem of ideas, recording the after-dinner conversation of seven men from diverse backgrounds on a number of topics. Critics are divided. Some read it as a "remarkable poetic indictment of modern life," while others find it prosy and pretentious.

MAY SARTON (1912–1995): *Encounter in April.* The writer's first collection of lyrics is well received. As one reviewer rhapsodized, the poems are "the fragile, brittle, irridescent work of a New England girl for whom the cruder passions are refined into the fleeting shadows of angel wings." Sarton was born in Belgium and came to the United States at the age of four. In addition to her poetry, she would write a number of novels and several volumes of autobiographical reflections.

WALLACE STEVENS: *The Man with the Blue Guitar, and Other Poems.* The poet's defense against charges that his work ignores social concerns takes the form of variations on the theme of the poet's transformative role of the imagination as the prime explicator of thought and feeling. As he writes in the title poem, "They said, 'You have a blue guitar, / You do not play things as they are.' / The man replied, 'Things as they are / Are changed upon the blue guitar.'" The work is crucial in Stevens's canon, articulating his concept of the poet's responsibility while renewing his faith in the power of his art.

ALLEN TATE: *Selected Poems.* Tate's collection includes what most agree is his finest poem, "Ode to the Confederate Dead."

Publications and Events

New Challenge. A reconstituted version of *Challenge* (1934) debuts, with Dorothy West and Martin Minus as coeditors and Richard Wright as associate editor. The inaugural and only issue features Wright's influential manifesto, "Blueprint for Negro Writing," and Ralph Ellison's first published piece, a review of Waters Turpin's *These Low Grounds* (1937). The short story "Hymie Bull," which Ellison wrote for the magazine, launches his fiction career.

1938
Drama and Theater

MAXWELL ANDERSON: *Knickerbocker Holiday.* As Washington Irving writes his history of New York, he is

431 · THE BIRTH OF MODERNISM

transported back to seventeenth-century New Amsterdam in this musical fantasy that indirectly satirizes the New Deal with music, including the popular "September Song" by Kurt Weill. Also, the playwright's prefaces to his plays and thoughts on the theater and his dramatic method are collected in *The Essence of Tragedy*, the first detailed theory of tragedy by an American playwright.

ARTHUR ARENT: *One Third of a Nation.* The most successful of the "Living Newspaper" productions of the Federal Theatre Project—theatrical documentaries using newspaper articles and other printed evidence for their text—illustrates the assertion made by President Roosevelt that a third of the nation was ill-housed, ill-clad, and ill-nourished.

PHILIP BARRY: *Here Come the Clowns.* Barry's most experimental play is an often preachy, symbolic drama depicting a group of vaudeville performers confronting the reality of their lives. The play baffles the critics and audiences.

S. N. BEHRMAN: *Wine of Choice.* Behrman's social comedy concerns a women courted by several men, including a young left-wing writer.

MARC BLITZSTEIN (1904–1964): *The Cradle Will Rock.* Blitzstein's anti-capitalist operetta about the effort to unionize steelworkers is opposed by the U.S. government and Actors Equity. Its New York premiere at the Mercury Theatre is stopped by injunction, and to circumvent this difficulty, John Houseman (1902–1988) and Orson Welles lead the cast and audience to another empty theater, where the cast perform from their seats as paying customers. Houseman became a director in 1935 with the Negro Theatre Project and with Welles founded the Mercury Theatre Company in 1937.

CLARE BOOTHE LUCE: *Kiss the Boys Goodbye.* The playwright's successful comedy dramatizes the Hollywood search for an actress to play Velvet O'Toole in a Civil War film. Although playgoers enjoy the presumed spoof on *Gone with the Wind*, Luce claims that she intended the play as an attack on "Southernism"—the "inspiration or forerunner of Fascism."

CLIFFORD ODETS: *Rocket to the Moon.* Many critics date the decline in the playwright's dramatic ability to this Group Theatre production, concerning a young dentist's unhappy marriage and affair. It is Odets's final play to evoke comparisons with his earlier Marxist works.

OLE OLSEN (1892–1963) AND CHICK JOHNSON (1891–1962): *Hellzapoppin.* The vaudeville team's zany revue would run until 1941, and its 1,404 performances prove to be the third longest in Broadway history (behind *Tobacco Road* and *Abie's Irish Rose*) up to that time.

PAUL OSBORN: *On Borrowed Time.* Based on Lawrence Edward Watkin's novel (1937), this dramatic fantasy concerns an aging curmudgeon who holds off the Angel of Death by chasing him up an apple tree until his grandson falls to his death from the same tree. The play establishes the reputation of its young director, Joshua Logan (1908–1988).

ELMER RICE: *American Landscape.* Rice continues his series of patriotic works with this drama of a man contemplating selling his estate to a pro-Nazi German American Bund. He is urged to resist by the spirits of Moll Flanders, Harriet Beecher Stowe, a Revolutionary War soldier, and the man's son killed in World War I.

RICHARD RODGERS AND LORENZ HART: *The Boys from Syracuse.* Considered the first musical based on a classic, this Rodgers and Hart collaboration, with book by George Abbott, is derived from Shakespeare's *The Comedy of Errors.*

ROBERT E. SHERWOOD: *Abe Lincoln in Illinois.* Sherwood wins his second Pulitzer Prize for this biographical drama of Lincoln's pre-presidential years. It is the first production of the Playwrights' Company and features a highly praised interpretation of Lincoln by Raymond Massey.

THEODORE WARD (1902–1983): *Big White Fog.* When the Chicago unit of the Federal Theatre Project performs this play—about a middle-class black family's encounter with racism and the political alternatives available to them in capitalism, black nationalism, and socialism—riot police stand on call on opening night to ward off an anticipated race riot. They would not be needed. The play would be performed in New York in 1940 as the first and last production of the Negro Playwrights Company. The Louisiana-born playwright has been called "the dean of black dramatists" for his contribution to African American drama. His other plays include *Our Lan'* (1947), *The Daubers* (1953), and *Candle in the Wind* (1967).

THORNTON WILDER: *Our Town.* Wilder's innovative depiction of small-town American life in Grover's Corners, New Hampshire, at the turn of the century uses a bare stage and employs a Stage Manager as narrator. Winner of the Pulitzer Prize, the play, one of the most popular and frequently performed American dramas, establishes Wilder as a distinctive voice in the American theater.

Fiction

DOROTHY BAKER (1907–1968): *Young Man with a Horn.* The Montana-born writer's first novel is inspired by the life of jazz musician Bix Beiderbecke in what is considered the first novel of consequence to document the jazz music scene. It would be dramatized in 1944. Her other books are *Our Gifted Son* (1948) and *Cassandra at the Wedding* (1962).

JAMES BRANCH CABELL: *The King Was in His Counting House.* Cabell publishes a satirical romance set in sixteenth-century Italy.

ERSKINE CALDWELL: *Southways.* Caldwell's fourth collection of short stories continues his documentation of life among poor blacks and whites in the South. One reviewer remarks, "The picture of the southland which is presented is about as far removed from the old atmosphere of moonlight and honey-suckle as could well be imagined."

JOHN DOS PASSOS: *U.S.A.* Dos Passos collects his trio of novels — *The 42nd Parallel* (1930), *1919* (1932), and *The Big Money* (1936) — to form a technically innovative social panorama of American life and history during the first three decades of the century.

WILLIAM FAULKNER: *The Unvanquished.* Faulkner groups previously published short stories into a narrative chronicling the Sartoris family of Mississippi during the Civil War and Reconstruction.

ERNEST HEMINGWAY: *The Fifth Column and the First Forty-nine Stories.* Hemingway's only play is combined with his collected stories, including recent ones such as "The Short Happy Life of Francis Macomber" and "The Snows of Kilimanjaro." *The Fifth Column*, set during the siege of Madrid during the Spanish Civil War, would be produced on Broadway in 1940.

SINCLAIR LEWIS: *The Prodigal Parents.* Lewis's novel describes the revolt of middle-aged parents from their two selfish and demanding offspring. Seen by many as second-rate Lewis, the novel draws fire from critic Malcolm Cowley, who charges that "From the first page to the last there wasn't a character that rises above the level of a good comic strip."

JOHN O'HARA: *Hope of Heaven.* Although a bestseller, this novel recording the unhappy affair between a Hollywood scenario writer and a bookshop clerk is a critical failure. O'Hara then turns his attention to the short story, not publishing another novel until 1949.

DAWN POWELL (1897–1965): *The Happy Island.* Powell's sardonic look at fashionable Manhattan life concentrates on café society from the perspective of a hard-boiled nightclub singer. Born in Ohio, Powell produced a number of satires on New York City life, including *Angels on Toast* (1940), *The Wicket Pavilion* (1954), and *The Golden Spur* (1962).

MARJORIE KINNAN RAWLINGS: *The Yearling.* Rawlings wins the Pulitzer Prize for this novel involving a boy's relationship with his pet fawn in northern Florida's hummock country. Although never intended as a children's book, *The Yearling* would become a children's classic.

ELIZABETH MADOX ROBERTS: *Black Is My Truelove's Hair.* The Kentucky regionalist's final novel is a ballad-like story of the betrayal of a simple village girl by a truck driver.

DAMON RUNYON: *Take It Easy.* This story collection dealing with Runyon's characteristic subject, Broadway life, features his specialty: capturing street patois.

WILLIAM SAROYAN: *Love, Here Is My Hat, and Other Short Romances* and *The Trouble with Tigers.* Two story collections display the author's characteristic exuberance and eccentricity, qualities that one reviewer labels "auto-intoxication" and that writer James T. Farrell calls an "exhibitionist act" that has "worn as thin as an old vaudeville gag."

MAY SARTON: *The Single Hound.* Sarton's first novel concerns a young English poet who seeks solace in the work and later the person of an elderly Belgian poet.

JOHN STEINBECK: *The Long Valley.* A short story collection mainly dealing with farming life in California's Salinas Valley. It includes highly regarded stories such as "The Snake," "Flight," "The Red Pony," the medieval parable "Saint Katy the Virgin," as well as "Chrysanthemums," widely regarded as Steinbeck's best story and one of the greatest American short stories of the twentieth century.

JESSE STUART: *Beyond Dark Hills.* This is the first of several autobiographical volumes by the Kentucky regionalist. Here he details his pioneer ancestry and his upbringing and education on a Kentucky hill farm.

ALLEN TATE: *The Fathers.* The poet and critic's only novel is set immediately before the outbreak of the Civil War and concerns the cultural conflict between traditional Southern society and contemporary forces.

B. TRAVEN: *The Bridge in the Jungle.* Traven's novel set in Central America concerns an explorer who gets involved in a village's tragedy when a boy drowns.

EDITH WHARTON: *The Buccaneers.* Wharton's last and unfinished novel concerns the attempt by socially ambitious American girls to enter English society. Although the novel breaks off before the moral climax, the book does provide the author's characteristically assured depictions of social manners and an accomplished portrait of Gilded Age society.

WILLIAM CARLOS WILLIAMS: *Life Along the Passaic River.* Williams's second short story collection includes highly regarded works such as "The Use of Force," "The Girl with the Pimply Face," and "Jean Beicke."

RICHARD WRIGHT: *Uncle Tom's Children*. Winner of the *Story* magazine prize for the best work from anyone connected with the Federal Writers' Project, Wright's first book of long short stories graphically details violent racial conflict in the South. Wright would expand the volume in 1940, adding the essay "The Ethics of Living Jim Crow," which helps contextualize the book's theme of the rejection of passive suffering.

Literary Criticism and Scholarship

CLEANTH BROOKS (1906–1994) AND ROBERT PENN WARREN: *Understanding Poetry*. The authors' textbook, applying the principles of the New Criticism to the interpretation of poetry, revolutionizes the teaching of literature on American campuses. Arranged by aesthetic categories rather than by author or chronology, with sample analyses and questions to prompt students' similar efforts, the book helps shift the emphasis to text-oriented criticism, which fosters close reading and structural analysis in literary assessment. Brooks was born in Kentucky, educated at Vanderbilt, Tulane, and Oxford, and was an English professor at Louisiana State University from 1932 to 1947.

EDGAR LEE MASTERS: *Mark Twain: A Portrait*. Masters's brief critical biography emphasizes Twain's troubled genius and divided nature as a social critic and one who yielded to his society's materialistic influences.

EZRA POUND: *Guide to Kultur*. Pound ranges widely over literary, political, and economic subjects in a series of polemical disquisitions, ranging from Benito Mussolini's Italy, to Dadaism, to T. S. Eliot's criticism, employing the same associative logic that operates in his poetry.

JOHN CROWE RANSOM: *The World's Body*. In this collection of critical essays, the writer articulates a theory of poetry that both bolsters the emerging tenets of the New Criticism and asserts verse's superiority to science in revealing reality.

EDMUND WILSON: *The Triple Thinkers: Ten Essays on Literature*. Wilson's collection explores the social and political conflict in writers such as Gustave Flaubert, Henry James, and George Bernard Shaw. It contains essays such as "Marxism and Literature" and "The Historical Interpretation of Literature," discussing the use of Marxist methodology to analyze literature.

YVOR WINTERS: *Maule's Curse: Seven Studies in the History of American Obscurantism*. In a study of nineteenth-century literature, Winters underscores the deficiencies of James Fenimore Cooper, Nathaniel Hawthorne, Edgar Allan Poe, Herman Melville, Ralph Waldo Emerson, Emily Dickinson, and Henry James in their refusal to confront fully shared human values. Their emphasis on private states of feeling leads, in Winters's view, to obscurity.

Nonfiction

ROBERT BENCHLEY: *After 1903—What?* A collection of the humorist's short pieces on topics such as parlor games, tea shops, and income tax forms, with illustrations by Gluyas Williams.

RICHARD E. BYRD: *Alone*. The polar explorer and aviator recounts his self-imposed isolation at a base camp in Antarctica in 1934.

JOHN DEWEY: *Experience and Education*. The philosopher assesses both traditional and progressive educational methods and points out the defects of both. His other important work published in 1938 is *Logic: The Theory of Inquiry*.

JOHN DOS PASSOS: *Journeys Between Wars*. The writer compiles extracts from his previous travel books with new accounts of the Spanish Civil War.

ERNEST HEMINGWAY: *The Spanish Earth*. Transcript of Hemingway's narration and commentary for the 1937 film documentary on the Spanish Civil War, produced and directed by Joris Ivens with a screenplay by Archibald MacLeish, John Dos Passos, and Lillian Hellman.

GRANVILLE HICKS: *I Like America*. In an autobiographical account, Hicks offers his defense as a Communist critic and what America stands to lose unless it chooses socialism. Hicks would resign from the Communist Party in 1939 in opposition to the German-Soviet nonagression pact and the American Communist Party's defense of Stalinism.

MARQUIS JAMES (1891–1955): *The Life of Andrew Jackson*. James wins his second Pulitzer Prize (the first was for his biography of Sam Houston, *The Raven*, in 1929) for this combination of his two previous volumes on Andrew Jackson's life and career—*Andrew Jackson, the Border Captain* (1933) and *Andrew Jackson: Portrait of a President* (1937). James was a journalist born in Oklahoma.

ANNE MORROW LINDBERGH: *Listen! The Wind*. Lindbergh's second book—an account of the 1933 survey flights made with her husband across the Atlantic, exploring possible commercial air routes—solidifies her reputation as an impressive prose stylist and writer of distinction, able to transform a technical account into literature.

RUTH MCKENNEY (1911–1972): *My Sister Eileen*. This book consists of humorous autobiographical sketches of the Indiana-born author's life in a Greenwich Village basement apartment with her sister (who would later

Anne Morrow Lindbergh in a photo taken by her husband, aviator Charles Lindbergh

marry novelist Nathanael West). It would be dramatized by Joseph A. Fields and Jerome Chodorov in 1940 as a play and in 1953 as the musical *Wonderful Town.*

ELEANOR ROOSEVELT: *This Troubled World.* The First Lady reflects on what is needed for world peace: brotherly love and the establishment of a strong United Nations–like organization to enforce it.

GERTRUDE STEIN: *Picasso.* Drawing on her longtime relationship with the painter, Stein offers a brief appreciatory study of Pablo Picasso's artistic development. Stein had written the work in French, and her companion Alice B. Toklas translated it to English.

CARL VAN DOREN: *Benjamin Franklin.* Van Doren's biography wins the Pulitzer Prize and would be long regarded as definitive and a classic of the biographer's art.

Poetry

E. E. CUMMINGS: *Collected Poems.* Cummings's most popular and most important work from his previous collections receives mixed reviews, with some critics praising the poet's innovations and others decrying his exhibitionism.

KENNETH FEARING: *Dead Reckoning.* Fearing's realistic and satirical poems of modern urban life help solidify his reputation as one of the most significant poets of the Depression.

JOHN GOULD FLETCHER: *Selected Poems.* Fletcher wins the Pulitzer Prize for this selection of published and previously unpublished works written since 1913.

ARCHIBALD MACLEISH: *Air Raid.* Described as a "verse play for the radio," the poem dramatizes the bombing of a city in a series of vignettes.

OGDEN NASH: *I'm a Stranger Here Myself.* This collection of the poet's winsome light verse, gently exposing human frailties and the absurdities of modern life, prompts contemporary reviewers to compare him with Mark Twain, G. K. Chesterton, P. J. Wodehouse, and Ring Lardner.

LAURA RIDING: *Collected Poems.* Riding collects her early poetry written since the 1920s about which writer Robert Fitzgerald would assert that "Of all the contemporary poems I know, these seem to me the furthest advanced, the most personal and the purest."

MURIEL RUKEYSER: *U.S. 1.* The poet's second collection explores working conditions along the East Coast highway and impressions of the war in Spain derived from Rukeyser's experience there as a journalist.

WILLIAM CARLOS WILLIAMS: *Complete Collected Poems, 1906–1938.* New Directions brings out the "definitive edition" of the poet's work up to this point.

Publications and Events

Broadcast of H. G. Wells's *War of the Worlds.* This play, adapted by Orson Welles and the Mercury Theatre, is broadcast on the radio the night before Halloween as if it were a news report, causing nationwide panic as listeners believe that what they hear is actually happening.

Dictionary of American English. The appearance of the first of the four volumes (completed in 1944) of the University of Chicago's project to collect distinctively

American words, phrases, and usages. It is edited by Sir William Craigie and James R. Hulbert.

The Playwrights' Company. Founded by Maxwell Anderson, S. N. Behrman, Sidney Howard, Elmer Rice, and Robert E. Sherwood as a production company for their works, the company continued until 1960.

Rocky Mountain Review. This quarterly regional magazine begins publication (it ceased in 1946). Contributors included important western writers such as Walter Van Tilburg Clark, Wallace Stegner, and Vardis Fisher.

Twice a Year. This semiannual "journal of literature, the arts, and civil liberties" begins publication. Contributors until its demise in 1948 included Muriel Rukeyser, Henry Miller, William Saroyan, and Kenneth Patchen.

1939

Drama and Theater

MAXWELL ANDERSON: *Key Largo.* Anderson's verse drama concerns an American Loyalist in the Spanish Civil War who deserts his comrades, returns to America, and is given the opportunity to expiate his crimes by confronting gangsters in a Florida hotel.

PHILIP BARRY: *The Philadelphia Story.* Barry's comedy about socialite Tracy Lord and her prominent Mainline

Orson Welles broadcasting on the radio in 1938

family on the eve of her remarriage had been written with actress Katharine Hepburn in mind and provides the playwright with his biggest commercial success. Hepburn would reprise her performance in the equally successful 1940 film.

S. N. BEHRMAN: *No Time for Comedy.* Considered by many the playwright's greatest achievement, the play concerns a popular author of light comedies (much like Behrman himself) who wishes to write about serious subjects.

RUSSEL CROUSE (1893–1966) AND HOWARD LINDSAY: *Life with Father.* Based on Clarence Day's autobiographical books, this drama about a domineering patriarch of a large New York City family in the 1880s set a record with 3,224 performances, becoming the longest-running non-musical play in Broadway history. A sequel, *Life with Mother,* appeared in 1948.

B. G. DE SYLVA (1895–1950): *Du Berry Was a Lady.* This Cole Porter musical about a washroom attendant who dreams that he is Louis XV and that the nightclub singer he loves is Madame Du Berry is one of the biggest hits of the season. De Sylva, a songwriter and librettist, worked with Gershwin, Jerome Kern, and others on several musicals and revues.

T. S. ELIOT: *The Family Reunion.* Eliot's verse drama attempts to re-create a modern Greek tragedy in an English country home.

BEN HECHT AND CHARLES MACARTHUR: *Ladies and Gentlemen.* A lone woman juror is able to convince her fellows of an alleged murderer's innocence in this star turn for MacArthur's wife, Helen Hayes.

LILLIAN HELLMAN: *The Little Foxes.* The playwright's most acclaimed work anatomizes the rapacious Hubbard clan of New Orleans at the turn of the century as they scramble for the means to prop up their declining fortunes, revealing rivalries and disloyalty in a lacerating power struggle. A "prequel," giving the Hubbards' earlier history, *Another Part of the Forest,* would appear in 1946.

DUBOSE HEYWARD AND DOROTHY HEYWARD: *Mamba's Daughters.* The authors of *Porgy* return to black life in Charleston, South Carolina, with this melodramatic adaptation of DuBose Heyward's 1929 novel.

GEORGE S. KAUFMAN AND MOSS HART: *The American Way.* The playwrights set aside their usual style of barbed comedy for an uplifting, patriotic spectacular, employing as many as 250 performers for crowd scenes illustrating American life from the 1890s. The duo also produce *The Man Who Came to Dinner,* one of the most popular American comedies. It concerns the acid-tongued celebrity (based on writer, actor, and radio commentator Alexander Woollcott) who recuperates from a fall in a middle-class Ohio household.

SIDNEY KINGSLEY: *The World We Make.* Based on Millen Brand's novel *The Outward Room* (1937), the play dramatizes a mentally disturbed woman who tries to live a normal life.

CLARE BOOTHE LUCE: *Margin for Error.* The playwright's comedy about a Jewish American policeman assigned to protect the Nazi consul in New York is called, by critic Burns Mantle, "the first successful anti-Nazi play to reach the stage."

PAUL OSBORN: *Morning's at Seven.* Osborn's most enduring original work is a comedy concerning the complex relationships among four sisters in a Midwestern town. Revived in 1980, it would be hailed by Harold Clurman as "one of the best American comedies."

WILLIAM SAROYAN: *My Heart's in the Highlands.* The success of Saroyan's odd-ball drama about a collection of eccentrics in Fresno, California, launches the short story writer's dramatic career. He also writes *The Time of Your Life.* Set in a San Francisco waterfront bar, Saroyan's most acclaimed play dramatizes the consequences when a wealthy drunk provides the means for the bar's denizens to indulge their fancies. The play is the first to win both the Pulitzer Prize and the New York Drama Critics Circle Award. Saroyan declines the Pulitzer, claiming that the businessmen who determine the award should not judge the arts.

IRWIN SHAW: *The Gentle People.* Shaw's play depicting Brooklyn life through two characters, a Jew and a Greek, who get mixed up with a racketeer is described by its author as "a fairy tale with a moral." Critics find it muddled and falling between the "two stools of allegory and simple realism."

TENNESSEE WILLIAMS (THOMAS LANIER WILLIAMS III, 1911–1983): *American Blues.* This group of related one-act plays wins a Group Theatre contest and brings the playwright his first national recognition. The plays would be published in 1948. Born in Mississippi, Williams attended the University of Missouri and Washington University before winning a Theatre Guild contest and enrolling in the playwriting program at the University of Iowa.

Fiction

SHOLEM ASCH: *The Nazarene.* The first in a series of Asch's novels on religious figures chronicles the life of Jesus from a variety of perspectives. *The Apostle* (1943), *Mary* (1949), and *The Prophet* (1953) would follow.

WILLIAM ATTAWAY (1911–1986): *Let Me Breathe Thunder.* The first of the African American writer's two novels about two hoboes who befriend a Mexican boy during the Depression evokes comparisons to Steinbeck's *Of Mice and Men* and to Hemingway for the novel's minimalist style. His second novel, *Blood on the Forge* (1941), tells about Southern blacks who compete with whites for steel-mill jobs in Pennsylvania.

ARNA BONTEMPS: *Drums at Dusk.* The author's final novel concerns the slave revolt in Haiti and the leadership of Toussaint L'Ouverture.

RAYMOND CHANDLER: *The Big Sleep.* Chandler's first novel introduces his hard-boiled Los Angeles private eye Philip Marlowe, in a dark, complex urban intrigue that in the words of one reviewer "makes Dashiell Hammett seem as innocuous as Winnie-the-Pooh."

PIETRO DI DONATO (1911–1992): *Christ in Concrete.* The former bricklayer's first novel is an autobiographical work documenting the life of Italian laborers in New York City. The book is considered by many a classic of the American immigrant experience. A less highly regarded sequel, *Three Circles of Light*, would appear in 1960.

JOHN DOS PASSOS: *Adventures of a Young Man.* In the first volume of a family saga trilogy that would be followed by *Number One* (1943) and *The Grand Design* (1949), Dos Passos dramatizes the story of an idealistic Communist betrayed by the party. Critic Philip Rahv would call the novel "perhaps the most thoughtful and realistic portrait of the radical movement that has so far been produced by an American writer."

JAMES T. FARRELL: *Tommy Gallagher's Crusade.* Farrell's novella describes a youth selling Fascist newspapers who is beaten up by Communist sympathizers. It features a thinly disguised portrait of Father Charles Coughlin, the popular, radical radio host.

WILLIAM FAULKNER: *The Wild Palms.* Two stories centered on the precariousness of love juxtapose a New Orleans doctor's tragic affair with a married woman and a convict's relationship with a pregnant hill woman during a flood.

KENNETH FEARING: *The Hospital.* Fearing's first novel treats events in a large metropolitan hospital from multiple perspectives. It would be followed by his first attempt at a thriller, *Dagger of the Mind* (1941), and *Clark Gifford's Body* (1942), the story of a modern-day John Brown who attacks a radio station.

VARDIS FISHER: *Children of God.* Fisher's most famous and acclaimed work chronicles the history of the Mormons from John Smith through the western migration and the settlement of Utah. Clifton Fadiman rates the novel as "one of the most extraordinarily interesting stories I have ever read and . . . I have rarely encountered a book whose faults one is more eager and easily able to condone."

ZORA NEALE HURSTON: *Moses: Man of the Mountain.* This is a retelling of the Exodus story and the myth of Moses as a version of African American experience, which Hurston biographer Robert Hemenway describes as a "noble failure."

CHRISTOPHER ISHERWOOD (1904–1986): *Goodbye to Berlin.* Published in the same year that Isherwood immigrates to the United States (he would become a naturalized citizen in 1946), this collection of autobiographical sketches of Berlin life in the years immediately preceding Hitler's coming to power would be adapted by John Van Druten as *I Am a Camera* (1951), which in turn became the basis for the musical *Cabaret* (1966).

H. P. LOVECRAFT: *The Outsiders and Others.* Lovecraft's friends and fellow writers August Derleth and Donald Wandrei set up the publishing firm of Arkham to bring out, posthumously, Lovecraft's horror fiction in book form; this is the first of several volumes.

J. P. MARQUAND: *Wickford Point.* The novelist widens the focus of Boston Brahmin life in *The Late George Apley* (1937), a chronicle of the well-to-do Brill family and their Massachusetts community.

HENRY MILLER: *The Cosmological Eye.* Miller's first U.S. publication is a miscellany of stories, essays, and excerpts that serves as an introduction to the writer's ideas and methods. *Tropic of Capricorn,* Miller's assortment of metaphysical speculations, surrealistic comedy, and sexually explicit scenes, is also published in Paris. It would be first published in the United States in 1962.

CHRISTOPHER MORLEY: *Kitty Foyle.* Morley's bestselling novel describes the life of a working-class Irish American and her affair with the son of a prominent Philadelphia family.

ANAÏS NIN: *The Winter of Artifice.* Nin's second volume of fiction contains three novellas; one of them, "Djuna," reflects the author's relationship with Henry Miller and his wife, June.

KATHERINE ANNE PORTER: *Pale Horse, Pale Rider.* Three short novels — the title story about a girl's love affair with a World War I veteran; "Old Mortality," about a Southern belle; and "Noon Wine," about a Swedish hired man on a Texas dairy farm — make up this acclaimed collection.

WILLIAM SAROYAN: *Peace, It's Wonderful.* The author's final important short story collection — his eighth since 1934 — before turning his attention to drama and the novel.

IRWIN SHAW: *Sailor Off the Bremen.* A collection of stories, many of which were first published in *The New Yorker,* demonstrates the writer's skill as capturing, in the words of one reviewer, "City College smarties, taxi drivers, hooligans, and fighting wives."

JOHN STEINBECK: *The Grapes of Wrath.* The only social protest novel of the 1930s to reach a mass audience, Steinbeck's dust-bowl saga of the Joad family's forced exodus from Oklahoma to California would be banned, burned, and acclaimed as the decade's defining masterpiece. Winner of the 1940 Pulitzer Prize, the book is regarded as an American classic, Steinbeck's most enduring work, and the summation of the author's artistic and moral vision.

JAMES THURBER: *The Last Flower.* Inspired by the Spanish Civil War and the Nazi and Soviet invasion of Poland, Thurber presents a parable of the folly of war in which the only survivors of World War XII are a man, a woman, and a flower. From these three love emerges, leading to family, tribe, civilization, and inevitably, another war.

DALTON TRUMBO (1905–1976): *Johnny Got His Gun.* Trumbo's searing antiwar novel is a stream-of-consciousness account of a soldier without arms, legs, face, sight, and hearing, whose desire to become a physical exhibit on the cruelty and futility of war is prevented by the powerful. Born in Colorado, Trumbo was a screenwriter, novelist, and essayist who would be blacklisted during the 1950s for refusing to testify before the House Committee on Un-American Activities.

WATERS TURPIN: *O Canaan!* Turpin's second novel, part of an uncompleted series of novels chronicling the black experience in America, documents the great migration of Southern farm laborers to Chicago during the Depression.

ROBERT PENN WARREN: *Night Rider.* Warren's first novel concerns the Kentucky Tobacco Wars of the early twentieth century, which took place between the growers and the manufacturers.

NATHANAEL WEST: *The Day of the Locust.* West's final and most ambitious novel looks at the unglamorous side of Hollywood — its losers and frustrated hangers-on for whom illusion leads to a sense of betrayal and finally apocalyptic violence. Praised in literary circles and called the best Hollywood novel ever written, the book is ignored by the public.

THOMAS WOLFE: *The Web and the Rock.* Despite the author's contention that this story of George Webber's Southern upbringing, schooling, and travels represents "the most objective novel I have written," reviewer Alfred Kazin and others find only an echo of Wolfe's autobiography already illustrated by Eugene Gant in *Look Homeward, Angel:* "It is the same Gant career . . . and always the same Wolfe." A sequel, *You Can't Go Home Again,* would be posthumously published in 1940.

Literary Criticism and Scholarship

CLEANTH BROOKS: *Modern Poetry and the Tradition.* Brooks's debut solo collection of critical essays, along with *Understanding Poetry* (1938), establishes his reputation as one of the leading practitioners and theorists of the New Criticism.

HENRY SEIDEL CANBY: *Thoreau.* The first truly scholarly biography of the writer would remain the standard work until the 1960s. Literary historian Robert Spiller has observed that the book is not only "the sanest biography of Thoreau, but it is one of the sanest I have read of anyone."

J. SAUNDERS REDDING (1906–1988): *To Make a Poet Black.* One of the earliest important works of African American literary criticism, Redding's study attempts to establish the canon of African American literature, traces the historical development of a black aesthetic, and identifies the major figures who contributed to its development. Redding became a faculty member at Brown University in 1949, the first African American professor at an Ivy League University.

Nonfiction

SAMUEL HOPKINS ADAMS: *Incredible Era.* Adams combines a biographical portrait of Warren G. Harding with a popular assessment of American culture and politics from World War I to Harding's death.

W.E.B. DU BOIS: *Black Folk: Then and Now.* Subtitled "An Essay in the History and Sociology of the Negro Race," Du Bois's outline history of blacks in Africa and America underscores racial kinship and the sources of pride in a black heritage.

CAREY MCWILLIAMS (1905–1980): *Factories in the Field.* Published in the same year as Steinbeck's *The Grapes of Wrath,* McWilliams's factual study of migratory fieldworkers in California helps substantiate the novel's portrait of widespread exploitation of labor. McWilliams was a California lawyer and sociologist.

Carl Sandburg standing next to the "Rail Splitter" statue of Abraham Lincoln at the Carl Sandburg National Historic Site in Flat Rock, North Carolina

CARL SANDBURG: *Abraham Lincoln: The War Years.* Completing one of the monumental works of the century, Sandburg's four-volume account of the Lincoln presidency picks up where his *Abraham Lincoln: The Prairie Years* (1926) left off. Historian Allan Nevins calls the book "unlike any other biography or history in the language." Prohibited by rules from awarding the biography prize for any work on Washington or Lincoln, the Pulitzer Prize committee gives the book the award for history.

DOROTHY THOMPSON: *Let the Record Speak*. A compilation of the outspoken foreign correspondent's syndicated column, "On the Record," dealing with politics and foreign affairs from 1936 to 1939.

E. B. WHITE: *Quo Vadimus? or, The Case of the Bicycle*. Stories and sketches illustrating regrettable developments in modern life. The humorist takes aim at radio broadcasts, long-distance plane flights, advertising, and cellophane.

Poetry

T. S. ELIOT: *Old Possum's Book of Practical Cats*. Eliot's collection of Edward Lear–like poems about fanciful felines such as Growltiger, Mistoffelees, and Macavity the Mystery Cat displays a playful side of the poet and critic. Andrew Lloyd Webber would adapt the poems into the long-running musical *Cats* in 1981.

PAUL ENGLE: *Corn*. The poet celebrates his native Iowa in this collection. As critic Selden Rodman observes, compared to his earlier work, the collection is "less pretentious, more honest, quieter, it quickens our hope that the Whitman tradition may still give the Wallace Stevenses and Delmore Schwartzes competition."

ROBERT FROST: *Collected Poems*. This new edition of Frost's collected verse includes the introductory essay "The Figure a Poet Makes," which asserts Frost's poetic principles, including "sound is the gold in the ore" and that a poem must be about things that matter: "It begins in delight and ends in wisdom."

ARCHIBALD MACLEISH: *America Was Promises*. A poetic call to action to save democracy. Fellow poet Louise Bogan complains that the work shows an essentially private poet being misled by assuming a public, prophetic role.

EDNA ST. VINCENT MILLAY: *Huntsman, What Quarry?* A collection of lyrics and sonnets recording the poet's feelings on the wars in Czechoslovakia, China, and Spain, as well as her tribute to poet Elinor Wylie. It sells sixty thousand copies within a month.

KENNETH PATCHEN: *First Will and Testament*. Patchen's second collection is self-described as "the legacy of a poet who speaks for a generation which was born in one war and seems destined to perish in another."

MURIEL RUKEYSER: *A Turning Wind*. The poet's third collection continues her social evaluation in a series of highly symbolic New England portraits. The volume prompts reviewer T. C. Wilson to declare that the poet "could be the most abundant of the younger American poets."

MAY SARTON: *Inner Landscape*. Sarton's second volume of introspective meditations evokes comparisons with Elinor Wylie and Edna St. Vincent Millay.

EDWARD TAYLOR: *Poetical Verse*. Discovered in manuscripts at Yale in 1937 by Thomas H. Johnson, the Puritan minister's poetry is published for the first time, establishing Taylor as seventeenth-century America's greatest poet.

MARK VAN DOREN: *Collected Poems, 1922–1938*. Van Doren's compilation from his six previous volumes and additional new poems wins the Pulitzer Prize.

Publications and Events

End of Federal Theatre Project. The project is abolished by Congress after conservatives repeatedly charge that the New Deal program, established in 1935 to provide work for theatrical professionals affected by the Depression, promulgates left-wing propaganda.

Kenyon Review. The literary quarterly is founded and edited until 1959 by John Crowe Ransom as a vehicle for writers such as Robert Penn Warren and Allen Tate, as well as a forum for the methods of the textual analysis of poetry that would become known as the New Criticism.

Scribner's Commentator. Scribner's Magazine is purchased by the *Commentator* and becomes *Scribner's Commentator*. The magazine abandons literary content to advance a political policy, and in 1942 its publisher would be prosecuted for accepting subsidies from Japan for publishing propaganda for the Japanese government.

1940
Drama and Theater

MAXWELL ANDERSON: *Journey to Jerusalem*. This blank-verse drama portrays Jesus Christ as a young man. Critic Joseph Wood Krutch complains that the playwright "has sometimes in the past been annoyingly showy; he has never, it seems to me, been so flat and tame [as here]."

LORENZ HART AND RICHARD RODGERS: *Pal Joey*. A musical about Joey Evans, a shabby nightclub performer, and the women he uses to further his career. John O'Hara wrote the libretto, based on his 1940 novel of the same name. The musical is considered a landmark because it features an unsympathetic main character while treating serious, realistic themes.

GEORGE S. KAUFMAN AND EDNA FERBER: *The Land Is Bright*. This multigenerational family saga, tracing the evolution of a social conscience, is only a moderate success, with one reviewer calling the play's uplifting

BIRTHS AND DEATHS, 1940–1949

Births

1940 Russell Banks, novelist
Thomas Harris, novelist
Robert Pinsky, poet and critic
David Rabe, playwright
James Welch, poet and novelist
Edmund White, novelist

1941 Anne Rice, novelist
Anne Tyler, novelist
John Edgar Wideman, novelist

1942 Michael Crichton, novelist
Robert Hass, poet
Erica Jong, poet and novelist
John Irving, novelist
William Matthews (d. 1997), poet
Sharon Olds, poet

1943 Louise Glück, poet
Doris Kearns Goodwin, historian
Sam Shepard, playwright and actor
Peter Straub, novelist
James Tate, poet

1944 Richard Ford, novelist
Alice Walker, novelist

1945 Robert Olen Butler, novelist and short story
writer
Pat Conroy, novelist
Annie Dillard, essayist and critic
August Wilson, playwright

1946 Michelle Cliff, poet
Michael Cristofer, playwright
Larry Shue (d. 1985), playwright

1947 Paul Auster, novelist
Ann Beattie, novelist and short story writer
Tom Clancy, novelist
Mark Helprin, novelist and short story writer
Jane Kenyon (d. 1995), poet
Stephen King, novelist
David Mamet, playwright, novelist, and film director
Marsha Norman, playwright
Camille Paglia, essayist and critic
Miguel Piñero (d. 1988), playwright

1948 T. Coraghessan Boyle, novelist and short story writer
James Ellroy, novelist
Charles Johnson, novelist
Leslie Marmon Silko, novelist, poet, and playwright

Dave Smith, poet
Timothy Steele, poet

1949 Jane Smiley, novelist
Scott Turow, novelist

Deaths

1940 F. Scott Fitzgerald (b. 1896), novelist
Hamlin Garland (b. 1860), novelist and short story writer
Edwin Markham (b. 1852), poet and editor
Nathaniel West (b. 1903), novelist

1941 Sherwood Anderson (b. 1876), novelist
Elizabeth Madox Roberts (b. 1881), novelist, short story
writer, and poet

1942 Alice Hegan Rice (b. 1870), novelist
Edwin Milton Royle (b. 1862), playwright

1943 Stephen Vincent Benét (b. 1898), poet and short story writer

1944 George Ade (b. 1866), short story writer
James Boyd (b. 1888), novelist
Max Brand (Frederick Faust) (b. 1892), western novelist
Ida Tarbell (b. 1857), journalist, historian, and biographer
William Allen White (b. 1868), novelist
Harold Bell Wright (b. 1872), novelist

1945 Robert Benchley (b. 1889), humorist
Margaret Deland (b. 1857), novelist
Theodore Dreiser (b. 1871), novelist
Ellen Glasgow (b. 1873), novelist
William Gilbert Patten (Burt L. Standish) (b. 1866),
novelist and short story writer
Amelie Rives (b. 1863), novelist

1946 Thomas Dixon (b. 1864), novelist
Countee Cullen (b. 1903), poet and novelist
Damon Runyon (b. 1884), journalist and short story writer
Gertrude Stein (b. 1874), literary writer and critic
Booth Tarkington (b. 1869), novelist

1947 Willa Cather (b. 1873), novelist and short story writer
Winston Churchill (b. 1871), novelist

1948 Gertrude Atherton (b. 1857), novelist
Susan Glaspell (b. 1876), playwright and novelist
Claude McKay (b. 1889), poet

1949 James Truslow Adams (b. 1878), historian
Hervey Allen (b. 1889), novelist, biographer, and poet
Philip Barry (b. 1896), playwright
Rex Beach (b. 1877), novelist and short story writer
S. S. McClure (b. 1857), editor and publisher
Margaret Mitchell (b. 1900), novelist

---

social theme "a sort of grease paint message of the new national ego."

GEORGE S. KAUFMAN AND MOSS HART: *George Washington Slept Here.* The failure of this comedy about country life leads Kaufman and Hart to dissolve their writing partnership.

GEORGE JEAN NATHAN: *Encyclopaedia of Drama.* A collection of the theater critic's reviews and pronouncements on theatrical matters, arranged alphabetically. Nathan was the leading drama critic of his day, who

collected his reviews in *The Theater Books of the Year* (1943–1951).

CLIFFORD ODETS: *Night Music.* The last of Odets's plays produced by the Group Theatre is a New York romance described by producer Harold Clurman as a "lyric improvisation . . . on the basic homelessness of the little man in the big city." It fails to win an audience.

EUGENE O'NEILL: *Long Day's Journey into Night.* Widely regarded as O'Neill's greatest achievement and arguably America's most impressive drama, the play is

BESTSELLERS, 1940–1949

Fiction

1940
1. *How Green Was My Valley* by Richard Llewellyn
2. *Kitty Foyle* by Christopher Morley
3. *Mrs. Miniver* by Jan Struther
4. *For Whom the Bell Tolls* by Ernest Hemingway
5. *The Nazarene* by Sholem Asch
6. *Stars on the Sea* by F. van Wyck Mason
7. *Oliver Wiswell* by Kenneth Roberts
8. *The Grapes of Wrath* by John Steinbeck
9. *Night in Bombay* by Louis Bromfield
10. *The Family* by Nina Fedorova

1941
1. *The Keys of the Kingdom* by A. J. Cronin
2. *Random Harvest* by James Hilton
3. *This Above All* by Eric Knight
4. *The Sun Is My Undoing* by Marguerite Steen
5. *For Whom the Bell Tolls* by Ernest Hemingway
6. *Oliver Wiswell* by Kenneth Roberts
7. *H. M. Pulham, Esquire* by J. P. Marquand
8. *Mr. and Mrs. Cugat* by Isabel Scott Rorick
9. *Saratoga Trunk* by Edna Ferber
10. *Windswept* by Mary Ellen Chase

1942
1. *The Song of Bernadette* by Franz Werfel
2. *The Moon Is Down* by John Steinbeck
3. *Dragon Seed* by Pearl S. Buck
4. *And Now Tomorrow* by Rachel Field
5. *Drivin' Woman* by Elizabeth Pickett
6. *Windswept* by Mary Ellen Chase
7. *The Robe* by Lloyd C. Douglas
8. *The Sun Is My Undoing* by Marguerite Steen
9. *Kings Row* by Henry Bellamann
10. *The Keys to the Kingdom* by A. J. Cronin

1943
1. *The Robe* by Lloyd C. Douglas
2. *The Valley of Decision* by Marcia Davenport
3. *So Little Time* by J. P. Marquand
4. *A Tree Grows in Brooklyn* by Betty Smith
5. *The Human Comedy* by William Saroyan
6. *Mrs. Parkington* by Louis Bromfield
7. *The Apostle* by Sholem Asch
8. *Hungry Hill* by Daphne du Maurier
9. *The Forest and the Fort* by Hervey Allen
10. *The Song of Bernadette* by Franz Werfel

1944
1. *Strange Fruit* by Lillian Smith
2. *The Robe* by Lloyd C. Douglas
3. *A Tree Grows in Brooklyn* by Betty Smith
4. *Forever Amber* by Kathleen Winsor
5. *The Razor's Edge* by W. Somerset Maugham
6. *The Green Years* by A. J. Cronin
7. *Leave Her to Heaven* by Ben Ames Williams
8. *Green Dolphin Street* by Elizabeth Goudge
9. *A Bell for Adano* by John Hersey
10. *The Apostle* by Sholem Asch

1945
1. *Forever Amber* by Kathleen Winsor
2. *The Robe* by Lloyd C. Douglas
3. *The Black Rose* by Thomas B. Costain
4. *The White Tower* by James Ramsey Ullman
5. *Cass Timberlane* by Sinclair Lewis
6. *A Lion Is in the Streets* by Aria Locke Langley
7. *So Well Remembered* by James Hilton
8. *Captain from Castile* by Samuel Shellabarger
9. *Earth and High Heaven* by Gwethalyn Graham
10. *Immortal Wife* by Irving Stone

1946
1. *The King's General* by Daphne du Maurier
2. *This Side of Innocence* by Taylor Caldwell
3. *The River Road* by Frances Parkinson Keyes
4. *The Miracle of the Bells* by Russell Janney
5. *The Hucksters* by Frederic Wakeman
6. *The Foxes of Harrow* by Frank Yerby
7. *Arch of Triumph* by Erich Maria Remarque
8. *The Black Rose* by Thomas B. Costain
9. *B. F.'s Daughter* by J. P. Marquand
10. *The Snake Pit* by Mary Jane Ward

1947
1. *The Miracle of the Bells* by Russell Janney
2. *The Moneyman* by Thomas Costain
3. *Gentleman's Agreement* by Laura Z. Hobson
4. *Lydia Bailey* by Kenneth Roberts
5. *The Vixens* by Frank Yerby
6. *The Wayward Bus* by John Steinbeck
7. *House Divided* by Ben Ames Williams
8. *Kingsblood Royal* by Sinclair Lewis
9. *East Side, West Side* by Marcia Davenport
10. *Prince of Foxes* by Samuel Shellabarger

1948
1. *The Big Fisherman* by Lloyd C. Douglas
2. *The Naked and the Dead* by Norman Mailer
3. *Dinner at Antoine's* by Frances Parkinson Keyes
4. *The Bishop's Mantle* by Agnes Sligh Turnbull
5. *Tomorrow Will Be Better* by Betty Smith
6. *The Golden Hawk* by Frank Yerby
7. *Raintree County* by Ross Lockridge Jr.
8. *Shannon's Way* by A. J. Cronin
9. *Pilgrim's Inn* by Elizabeth Goudge
10. *The Young Lions* by Irwin Shaw

1949
1. *The Egyptian* by Mika Waltari
2. *The Big Fisherman* by Lloyd C. Douglas
3. *Mary* by Sholem Asch
4. *A Rage to Live* by John O'Hara
5. *Point of No Return* by J. P. Marquand
6. *Dinner at Antoine's* by Frances Parkinson Keyes
7. *High Towers* by Thomas B. Costain
8. *Cutlass Empire* by Van Wyck Mason
9. *Pride's Castle* by Frank Yerby
10. *Father of the Bride* by Edward Streeter

BESTSELLERS, 1940–1949

General Nonfiction

1940

1. *I Married Adventure* by Osa Johnson
2. *How to Read a Book* by Mortimer Adler
3. *A Smattering of Ignorance* by Oscar Levant
4. *Country Squire in the White House* by John T. Flynn
5. *Land Below the Wind* by Agnes Newton Keith
6. *American White Paper* by Joseph W. Alsop Jr. and Robert Kintnor
7. *New England: Indian Summer* by Van Wyck Brooks
8. *As I Remember Him* by Hans Zinsser
9. *Days of Our Years* by Pierre van Paassen
10. *Bet It's a Boy* by Betty B. Blunt

1941

1. *Berlin Diary* by William L. Shirer
2. *The White Cliffs* by Alice Duer Miller
3. *Out of the Night* by Jan Valtin
4. *Inside Latin America* by John Gunther
5. *Blood, Sweat, and Tears* by Winston S. Churchill
6. *You Can't Do Business with Hitler* by Douglas Miller
7. *Reading I've Liked* edited by Clifton Fadiman
8. *Reveille in Washington* by Margaret Leech
9. *Exit Laughing* by Irving S. Cobb
10. *My Sister and I* by Dirk van der Heide

1942

1. *See Here, Private Hargrove* by Marion Hargrove
2. *Mission to Moscow* by Joseph E. Davis
3. *The Last Time I Saw Paris* by Elliot Paul
4. *Cross Creek* by Marjorie Kinnan Rawlings
5. *Victory Through Air Power* by Major Alexander P. de Seversky
6. *Past Imperfect* by Ilka Chase
7. *They Were Expendable* by William L. White
8. *Flight to Arras* by Antoine de St.-Exupéry
9. *Washington Is Like That* by W. M. Kiplinger
10. *Inside Latin America* by John Gunther

1943

1. *Under Cover* by John Roy Carlson
2. *One World* by Wendell Willkie
3. *Journey Among Warriors* by Eve Curie
4. *On Being a Real Person* by Harry Emerson Fosdick
5. *Guadalcanal Diary* by Richard Tregaskis
6. *Burma Surgeon* by Lt. Col. Gordon Seagrave
7. *Our Hearts Were Young and Gay* by Cornelia Otis Skinner and Emily Kimbrough
8. *U.S. Foreign Policy* by Walter Lippmann
9. *Here Is Your War* by Ernie Pyle
10. *See Here, Private Hargrove* by Marion Hargrove

1944

1. *I Never Left Home* by Bob Hope
2. *Brave Men* by Ernie Pyle
3. *Good Night, Sweet Prince* by Gene Fowler
4. *Under Cover* by John Roy Carlson
5. *Yankee from Olympus* by Catherine Drinker Bowen
6. *The Time for Decisions* by Sumner Welles
7. *Here Is Your War* by Ernie Pyle
8. *Anna and the King of Siam* by Margaret Landon
9. *The Curtain Rises* by Quentin Reynolds
10. *Ten Years in Japan* by Joseph C. Grew

1945

1. *Brave Men* by Ernie Pyle
2. *Dear Sir* by Juliet Lowell
3. *Up Front* by Bill Mauldin
4. *Black Boy* by Richard Wright
5. *Try and Stop Me* by Bennett Cerf
6. *Anything Can Happen* by George and Helen Papashvily
7. *General Marshall's Report* by the U.S. War Department General Staff
8. *The Egg and I* by Betty MacDonald
9. *The Thurber Carnival* by James Thurber
10. *Pleasant Valley* by Louis Bromfield

1946

1. *The Egg and I* by Betty MacDonald
2. *Peace of Mind* by Joshua L. Liebman
3. *As He Saw It* by Elliott Roosevelt
4. *The Roosevelt I Knew* by Elliott Roosevelt
5. *Last Chapter* by Ernie Pyle
6. *Starling of the White House* by Thomas Sugrue and Col. Edmund Starling
7. *I Chose Freedom* by Victor Kravchenko
8. *The Anatomy of Peace* by Emery Reves
9. *Top Secret* by Ralph Ingersoll
10. *A Solo in Tom-Toms* by Gene Fowler

1947

1. *Peace of Mind* by Joshua L. Liebman
2. *Information Please Almanac, 1947* edited by Jane Kieran
3. *Inside U.S.A.* by John Gunther
4. *A Study of History* by Arnold J. Toynbee
5. *Speaking Frankly* by James F. Byrnes
6. *Human Destiny* by Pierre Lecomte du Noüy
7. *The Egg and I* by Betty MacDonald
8. *The American Past* by Roger Butterfield
9. *The Fireside Book of Fold Songs* edited by Margaret B. Boni
10. *Together* by Katherine T. Marshall

1948

1. *Crusade in Europe* by Dwight D. Eisenhower
2. *How to Stop Worrying and Start Living* by Dale Carnegie
3. *Peace of Mind* by Joshua L. Liebman
4. *Sexual Behavior in the Human Male* by Alfred Kinsey et al.
5. *Wine, Women, and Words* by Billy Rose
6. *The Life and Times of the Shmoo* by Al Capp
7. *The Gathering Storm* by Winston Churchill
8. *Roosevelt and Hopkins* by Robert E. Sherwood
9. *A Guide to Confident Living* by Norman Vincent Peale
10. *The Plague and I* by Betty MacDonald

1949

1. *White Collar Zoo* by Clare Barnes Jr.
2. *How to Win at Canasta* by Oswald Jacoby
3. *The Seven Storey Mountain* by Thomas Merton
4. *Home Sweet Zoo* by Clare Barnes Jr.
5. *Cheaper by the Dozen* by Frank B. Gilbreth Jr. and Ernestine Gilbreth Carey
6. *The Greatest Story Ever Told* by Fulton Oursler
7. *Canasta, the Argentine Rummy Game* by Ottilie H. Reilly
8. *Canasta* by Josephine Artayeta de Viel and Ralph Michael
9. *Peace of Soul* by Fulton J. Sheen
10. *A Guide to Confident Living* by Norman Vincent Peale

AWARDS AND PRIZES, 1940–1949

Pulitzer Prizes

1940
Fiction: *The Grapes of Wrath* by John Steinbeck
Poetry: *Collected Poems* by Mark Van Doren
Drama: *The Time of Your Life* by William Saroyan (prize declined)
History: *Abraham Lincoln: The War Years* by Carl Sandburg
Biography/Autobiography: *Woodrow Wilson, Life and Letters* by Ray S. Baker

1941
Fiction: No Prize Awarded
Poetry: *Sunderland Capture* by Leonard Bacon
Drama: *There Shall Be No Night* by Robert E. Sherwood
History: *The Atlantic Migration, 1607–1860* by Marcus L. Hansen
Biography/Autobiography: *Jonathan Edwards* by Ola E. Winslow

1942
Fiction: *In This Our Life* by Ellen Glasgow
Poetry: *The Dust Which Is God* by William Rose Benét
Drama: No Prize Awarded
History: *Reveille in Washington* by Margaret Leech
Biography/Autobiography: *Crusader in Crinoline* by Forrest Wilson

1943
Fiction: *Dragon's Teeth* by Upton Sinclair
Poetry: *A Witness Tree* by Robert Frost
Drama: *The Skin of Our Teeth* by Thornton Wilder
History: *Paul Revere and the World He Lived In* by Esther Forbes
Biography/Autobiography: *Admiral of the Ocean Sea* by Samuel E. Morison

1944
Fiction: *Journey in the Dark* by Martin Flavin
Poetry: *Western Star* by Stephen Vincent Benét
Drama: No Prize Awarded
History: *The Growth of American Thought* by Merle Curti
Biography/Autobiography: *The American Leonardo: The Life of Samuel F. B. Morse* by Charleton Mabee

1945
Fiction: *A Bell for Adano* by John Hersey
Poetry: *V-Letter and Other Poems* by Karl Shapiro
Drama: *Harvey* by Mary Chase
History: *Unfinished Business* by Stephen Bonsal
Biography/Autobiography: *George Bancroft: Brahmin Rebel* by Russell B. Nye

1946
Fiction: No Prize Awarded
Poetry: No Prize Awarded

Drama: *State of the Union* by Russel Crouse and Howard Lindsay
History: *The Age of Jackson* by Arthur M. Schlesinger Jr.
Biography/Autobiography: *Son of the Wilderness* by Linnie M. Wolfe

1947
Fiction: *All the King's Men* by Robert Penn Warren
Poetry: *Lord Weary's Castle* by Robert Lowell
Drama: No Prize Awarded
History: *Scientists Against Time* by James P. Baxter III
Biography/Autobiography: *The Autobiography of William Allen White* by William A. White

1948
Fiction: *Tales of the South Pacific* by James A. Michener
Poetry: *The Age of Anxiety* by W. H. Auden
Drama: *A Streetcar Named Desire* by Tennessee Williams
History: *Across the Wide Missouri* by Bernard De Voto
Biography/Autobiography: *Forgotten First Citizen: John Bigelow* by Margaret Clapp

1949
Fiction: *Guard of Honor* by James Gould Cozzens
Poetry: *Terror and Decorum* by Peter Viereck
Drama: *Death of a Salesman* by Arthur Miller
History: *The Disruption of American Democracy* by Roy F. Nicholas
Biography/Autobiography: *Roosevelt and Hopkins* by Robert E. Sherwood

Noble Prizes in Literature

1948
T. S. Eliot (born in the United States; a British citizen at the time he was awarded the Nobel Prize)

1949
William Faulkner

Bancroft Prize (American History, Diplomacy, or Biography)

1948
Across the Wide Missouri by Bernard De Voto
Ordeal of the Union by Allan Nevins

1949
The Rising Sun in the Pacific by Samuel Eliot Morison
Roosevelt and Hopkins by Robert Sherwood

Bollingen Prize (Poetry)

1949
Ezra Pound

Eugene O'Neill

based on the conflicts in the playwright's mutually de-structive family. It was so intensely personal that O'Neill sealed the manuscript and stipulated that it not be pub-lished until twenty-five years after his death. His widow contravened this order, and the play was performed on Broadway in 1956.

ELMER RICE: *Flight to the West.* Rice takes up wartime issues in this debate-filled drama, set aboard the *Clipper* from Lisbon to New York as a mixed group of passen-gers discusses current events. Rice also writes *Two on an Island*, a romantic comedy depicting the difficult times of a playwright and his aspiring actress girlfriend as they try to achieve success on Broadway. To re-create a sense of modern city life, Rice filled the stage with recognizable big-city types.

ROBERT E. SHERWOOD: *There Shall Be No Night.* Sher-wood's war drama deals with Russia's invasion of Fin-land. It wins the 1941 Pulitzer Prize, but in December 1941, when the United States becomes allied with Rus-sia in the war against Germany, the playwright insists on closing it. He would restage it with a Greek setting, casting the Germans as villains.

JAMES THURBER AND ELLIOTT NUGENT (1899–1980): *The Male Animal.* In this comic satire about a Midwestern college dominated by football frenzy, a mild-mannered

English professor is castigated for being a Red when he seems to defend the Italian anarchists Sacco and Vanzetti. Nugent was an actor, director, and producer whose other works are *Kempy* (1922) and *Of Cheat and Charmer* (1962).

TENNESSEE WILLIAMS: *Battle of Angels.* Williams's first commercial production fails in Boston. The play-wright would later revise the play as *Orpheus Descending* (1945).

Fiction

CONRAD AIKEN: *Conversation; or, Pilgrims' Progress.* The novel records days in the lives of an artist, his wife, and their daughter on Cape Cod, narrated in stream-of-consciousness style.

KAY BOYLE: *The Crazy Hunter and Other Stories.* The collection, set in England and Italy, helps solidify Boyle's reputation, in the words of one reviewer, as "one of the best short-story writers in America."

JAMES BRANCH CABELL: *Hamlet Had an Uncle.* This playful farce shifts interest at Elsinore from Prince Ham-let to his uncle Wiglerus.

ERSKINE CALDWELL: *Jackpot: Short Stories of Erskine Caldwell.* This collection of seventy-five stories docu-ments the lives of poor Southern whites and the region's corrosive racial conflict.

WILLA CATHER: *Sapphira and the Slave Girl.* Cather's last novel, a story set in Virginia during the 1850s and concerning the persecution of a beautiful mulatto slave by a jealous white woman, receives mixed reviews and proves less enduring than her previous works.

RAYMOND CHANDLER: *Farewell, My Lovely.* A classic in the school of hard-boiled detective fiction, Chandler's second novel features the cynical, case-hardened private eye Philip Marlowe. Critics and the author himself con-sider the book Chandler's best.

WALTER VAN TILBURG CLARK (1909–1971): *The Ox-Bow Incident.* This is the first novel by the Maine-born writer who was raised in Nevada. It is a tense, moving morality drama about vigilantism on the western frontier, which attacks many of the assumptions, such as frontier justice, that had been constants in the western novel.

JAMES GOULD COZZENS: *Ask Me Tomorrow.* Cozzens's most autobiographical novel concerns a struggling young American writer in Europe who is forced to become a traveling tutor. It embodies many key philosophical po-sitions that would be repeated throughout the writer's career.

PETER DE VRIES (1910–1993): *But Who Wakes the Bu-gler?* Humorist De Vries would attempt to disown this work, his first novel, along with the two others he publishes in the 1940s — *The Handsome Heart* (1943) and *Angels Can't Do Better* (1944) — stating, "For a while I tried to buy up extant copies and burn them, but now it costs too much." Born in Chicago, De Vries was a radio actor in the 1930s and was an editor for *Poetry* magazine from 1938 to 1944.

WALTER D. EDMONDS: *Chad Hanna.* Edmonds continues his reconstruction of the history of upstate New York's Mohawk Valley in a story set in the 1830s, in which a stable boy runs away to join a traveling circus.

WILLIAM FAULKNER: *The Hamlet.* The first of a trilogy that includes *The Town* (1957) and *The Mansion* (1960), the novel covers the rise to power of the grasping, corrupt Flem Snopes and his kin in Faulkner's imagined county in Mississippi.

MARTHA GELLHORN: *The Stricken Field.* Gellhorn's first novel dramatizes the experiences of Mary Douglas, an American war correspondent in Prague who is exposed to the sufferings of two German refugees. It is based on her firsthand observations of Nazi atrocities in Czechoslovakia in 1938.

SUSAN GLASPELL: *The Morning Is Near Us.* The first of three novels that conclude Glaspell's career; they all focus on a woman's attempt to resolve past and present conflicts. *Norma Ashe* would follow in 1942, and *Judd Rankin's Daughter* in 1945.

ERNEST HEMINGWAY: *For Whom the Bell Tolls.* Hemingway's novel of the Spanish Civil War, arguably his most ambitious work, tells the story of Robert Jordan's mission to blow up a bridge vital to an upcoming Republican offensive. Written in a burst of creative energy, it counters the notion that Hemingway is a spent force. "Hemingway the artist is with us again," declares critic Edmund Wilson, "and it is like having an old friend back."

PAUL HORGAN (1903–1995): *Figures in a Landscape.* A short story collection dealing with the Southwest. Horgan was born in Buffalo, New York, but much of his work would deal with New Mexico and the American Southwest. He won the Harper Novel Prize in 1933 for *The Fault of Angels.*

SINCLAIR LEWIS: *Bethel Merriday.* The novel traces a young actress's theatrical career from high school dramatics, through summer stock and a touring company, to her first Broadway appearance.

CARSON McCULLERS (1917–1967): *The Heart Is a Lonely Hunter.* The Georgia-born writer's highly acclaimed first novel centers on a deaf-mute and establishes her principal themes of loneliness, isolation, and a search for love and faith.

ROBERT NATHAN (1894–1985): *Portrait of Jennie.* Nathan spins a characteristic gentle fantasy about a struggling young artist inspired by a young girl. It would be made into a film by David O. Selznick in 1948. Nathan was a New York City–born poet and novelist. His other books include *The Puppet Master* (1923), *The Fiddler in Barley* (1926), and *The Bishop's Wife* (1928).

DAWN POWELL: *Angels on Toast.* This witty satire concerns the lives and loves of two businessmen on the make.

MARJORIE KINNAN RAWLINGS: *When the Whippoorwill.* Rawlings continues her documentation of rural Florida in a series of stories, including one of her most popular, "Gal Young Un."

CONRAD RICHTER: *The Trees.* The first of a trilogy, to be named The Awakening Land, about pioneer life in the Ohio Valley. It follows successive generations of a family, beginning in the 1790s. The story would be continued in *The Fields* (1946), set during the 1820s, and conclude with *The Town* (1950), as the former wilderness is urbanized.

KENNETH ROBERTS: *Oliver Wiswell.* Roberts continues his vivid and accurate historical fiction with a chronicle of a Loyalist during the American Revolution. It is a rare sympathetic look at the losing side.

DAMON RUNYON: *My Wife Ethel.* Written in rich Brooklynese, this is a collection of stories about the travails of Joe and Ethel Turp. Runyon also publishes *Runyon à la Carte*, a notable collection that includes "Little Pinks" and "Your Highness."

UPTON SINCLAIR: *World's End.* The first of an eventual sequence of eleven novels tracing the course of twentieth-century history from 1913 through World War II from the perspective of Lanny Budd, the illegitimate son of a munitions manufacturer and a famous beauty. The author's most ambitious work, the novel cycle is an interesting measure of how Sinclair's radical Marxist interpretation of modern history gives way to conventional patriotic sentiment during the course of the war. Other titles in the series are *Between Two Worlds* (1941), *Dragon's Teeth* (1942), *Wide Is the Gate* (1943), *Presidential Agent* (1944), *Dragon Harvest* (1945), *A World to Win* (1946), *Presidential Mission* (1945), *One Clear Call* (1948), *O Shepherd Speak!* (1949), and *The Return of Lanny Budd* (1953).

WALLACE STEGNER: *On a Darkling Plain.* The novel tells the story of a Canadian World War I casualty who seeks solitude and purpose on the western Canadian prairie.

JESSE STUART: *Trees of Heaven.* Appalachian regional writer Stuart provides another chapter from his native Kentucky in the story of a backwoodsman forced to become civilized.

JAMES THURBER: *Fables of Our Time, and Famous Poems Illustrated*. Thurber provides a collection of witty fables in the manner of Aesop, such as "The Fairly Intelligent Fly" and "The Rabbits Who Caused All the Trouble." *Further Fables for Our Time* would appear in 1956.

GLENWAY WESCOTT: *The Pilgrim Hawk*. A widely acclaimed autobiographical novel, set in a French provincial town during the 1920s, provides lessons about love, marriage, and jealousy.

WILLIAM CARLOS WILLIAMS: *In the Money*. In the sequel to *White Mule* (1937), Williams continues the story of the Stecher family, particularly their two young daughters, as the former immigrants rise in prosperity and enter the American middle class. Williams would continue the story of their assimilation in *The Build-Up* (1952).

THOMAS WOLFE: *You Can't Go Home Again*. The posthumously published sequel to *The Web and the Rock* (1939) continues the story of George Webber from the late 1920s to the early 1930s, including his travels to England and Germany during the early years of the Nazi regime.

RICHARD WRIGHT: *Native Son*. Wright's groundbreaking and controversial depiction of the African American experience features the self-destructive Bigger Thomas, whose murder of a white woman is depicted as an act of liberation in the dehumanized, segregated Chicago of the 1930s. The first book by an African American writer selected as a Book-of-the-Month-Club Main Selection, it sells more than 200,000 copies in its first few weeks. James Baldwin would later declare that "no American Negro exists who does not have his private Bigger Thomas living in his skull."

Literary Criticism and Scholarship

JAMES TRUSLOW ADAMS: *The Dictionary of American History*. The completion of the monumental six-volume reference work, begun in 1936, edited by Adams and written by as many as one thousand historians. Companion volumes, *Atlas of American History* (1943) and *Album of American History* (six volumes, 1944–1961), would follow.

MORTIMER ADLER (1902–2001): *How to Read a Book*. Adler's self-improvement guidebook in defense of literacy and the humanities provides the philosophical foundation for the nationwide Great Books Program that Adler would establish in 1946. Alder taught philosophy at the University of Chicago from 1930 to 1952.

R. P. BLACKMUR: *The Expense of Greatness*. One of the important texts of the New Criticism, which dissects literary works in a close analysis of form, diction, style, and structure.

VAN WYCK BROOKS: *New England Indian Summer: 1865–1915*. The second of the author's Makers and Finders series on American culture is an anecdotally rich, impressionistic view of the American literary scene in the postbellum period. Brooks's clarity and vivid style help produce one of the rarest of successes: literary criticism on the bestseller list.

EZRA POUND: *Polite Essays*. First published in England in 1937, this is a collection of Pound's reviews and critical essays written during the 1920s and 1930s.

EDMUND WILSON: *To the Finland Station*. Wilson examines European revolutionary and socialist traditions from Jules Michelet to Vladimir Lenin and Leon Trotsky, combining character studies with intellectual history.

Nonfiction

FREDERICK LEWIS ALLEN: *Since Yesterday*. Allen supplies a popular social retrospective of the 1930s written in a chatty style.

SHERWOOD ANDERSON: *Home Town*. Anderson publishes a collection of autobiographical essays and portraits in pictures and text of small-town American life. Reviews note a mellowing of the author, and one describes him as a "cheerful Chekhov."

W.E.B. DU BOIS: *Dusk of Dawn: An Essay Toward an Autobiography of a Race Concept*. Du Bois's memoir attempts to connect his development with the history of African Americans.

T. S. ELIOT: *The Idea of a Christian Society*. In a series of lectures Eliot defines "the essential conditions which must obtain in any future society which is to be compatible with freedom for the Christian community within it to live the Christian life."

JANET FLANNER (1892–1978): *An American in Paris*. Having been forced out of Paris by the Nazis, the longtime author of *The New Yorker*'s "Letter from Paris" column supplies a collection of her letters and profiles.

ERICH FROMM (1900–1980): *Escape from Freedom*. The German American psychoanalyst and social philosopher explores what motivates human beings to accept tyranny. Fromm would continue exploring this theme in *Man for Himself* (1947).

MARCUS LEE HANSEN (1892–1938): *The Atlantic Migration, 1607–1860* and *The Immigrant in American History*. The most important work of the historian and sociologist are published posthumously. The first is awarded the Pulitzer Prize.

LANGSTON HUGHES: *The Big Sea*. This autobiographical account of the writer's life up to the age of twenty-seven includes his trip on a freighter to Africa, struggles in Paris during the 1920s, college experience, and early successes as a poet.

JOHN F. KENNEDY (1917–1963): *Why England Slept.* The twenty-four-year-old son of the U.S. ambassador to England assesses the reasons why Britain failed to rearm during the 1930s and its implications for the United States.

ANNE MORROW LINDBERGH: *The Wave of the Future.* An argument for democratic reforms and for America to stay out of the European war. Praised for its lyrical style, the book is condemned by some as a plea to appease the totalitarian powers.

ARCHIBALD MacLEISH: *The Irresponsibles.* MacLeish's attack on American academics and authors for not taking a firmer stand on the side of democracy causes critics such as Edmund Wilson and Morton D. Zabel to accuse the writer of succumbing to the role of propagandist.

H. L. MENCKEN: *Happy Days.* Mencken begins his multivolume memoirs with a nostalgic and whimsical account of his Baltimore childhood from his birth in 1880 to 1892.

S. J. PERELMAN: *Look Who's Talking.* A collection of humorous articles and parodies, many of which originally appeared in the *The New Yorker.*

ELEANOR ROOSEVELT: *The Moral Basis of Democracy.* The First Lady argues for a moral awakening to rectify inequity based on a "true sense of brotherhood."

GEORGE SANTAYANA: *The Realm of Spirit.* The philosopher examines skepticism and faith in the fourth and final volume of his ambitious series, which defines his philosophical system.

GERTRUDE STEIN: *Paris France.* Published on the day that Paris falls to the Germans, this is an affectionate tribute to the French capital and French civilization by the longtime resident.

MARY CHURCH TERRELL (1863–1954): *A Colored Woman in the White World.* The suffragist and racial activist provides a groundbreaking contribution to the record of black women in America in this autobiographical account of her struggles against racial and sexual discrimination.

Poetry

W. H. AUDEN (1907–1973): *Another Time.* The poet's first published work since taking up residence in the United States. It includes memorial poems on Sigmund Freud and William Butler Yeats.

LEONARD BACON (1887–1954): *Sutherland Capture.* Bacon's satirical lyrics win the Pulitzer Prize for poetry. Bacon, a professor of English at the University of California from 1910 to 1923, previously published volumes such as *Ulug Beg* (1923), *Ph.D.'s* (1925), and *Rhyme and Punishment* (1936).

STEPHEN VINCENT BENÉT: "Nightmare at Noon." Benét's stirring poem urges the United States to meet the Fascist challenge.

WITTER BYNNER: *Against the Cold.* This series of lyrics, fantasies, sonnets, and satirical poems is described by critic John Holmes as "a sort of quiet, pure, and confident poetry we get too little of."

JOHN CIARDI (1916–1986): *Homeward to America.* Ciardi's first book of poems offers reflections on his family's immigrant background and the nature of an American identity. The Boston-born teacher and translator would serve as the poetry editor of the *Saturday Review* from 1956 to 1972.

E. E. CUMMINGS: *50 Poems.* Cummings's collection is greeted as more of the same by reviewer Louise Bogan, who describes the poet as "irrevocably stuck in the past."

T. S. ELIOT: "East Coker." The second in the cycle of poems collected in 1943 as *Four Quartets.* The poem, like the larger sequence, is a meditation on the power of memory and experience to evoke a kind of transcendence.

KENNETH FEARING: *Collected Poems.* The collection reflects Fearing's leftist and satirical critique of America's preoccupation with wealth and success.

ROBERT HAYDEN (1913–1980): *Heart-Shape in the Dust.* The debut collection by the Detroit-born African American poet includes a long protest poem, "These Are My People," which describes the lot of blacks during the Depression, based on the author's observations while a researcher for the Federal Writers' Project.

STANLEY KUNITZ: *Passport to the War.* This volume includes selections from the poet's earlier volume, *Intellectual Things* (1930), and more recent works. Described as "intricate, personal, and difficult," Kunitz's poems are admired for their masterful craftsmanship and modern echoing of the English metaphysical poets.

CHRISTOPHER LA FARGE (1897–1956): *Poems and Portraits.* The author of two previous verse novels — *Hoxsie Sells His Acres* (1934) and *Each to the Other* (1939) — offers a collection of lyrics, mostly with pastoral themes. La Farge was the brother of writer and anthropologist Oliver La Farge.

EDNA ST. VINCENT MILLAY: *Make Bright the Arrows.* The poet's 1940 notebook is a collection of poems and fragments reflecting the former pacifist's view on the war in Europe, including her impassioned "There Are No Islands," urging solidarity with France and England. Millay would later characterize her propaganda verse as "acres of bad poetry."

OGDEN NASH: *The Face Is Familiar.* A collection of previously published works as well as thirty-one poems never before collected in book form.

EZRA POUND: *Cantos LII–LXXI.* This installment of the poet's massive poetic sequence features reflections on the history of China and the life of American founding father John Adams.

KENNETH REXROTH (1905–1982): *In What Hour.* The Indiana-born poet's first volume uses experimental techniques to reflect political topics such as the Spanish Civil War and the execution of Sacco and Vanzetti. Rexroth was a longtime San Francisco resident and would be associated with the Beat movement in the 1950s.

Publications and Events

Accent. This eclectic literary magazine, published on the campus of the University of Illinois, makes its first appearance. Until its demise in 1960 it published fiction, poetry, and critical pieces by contributors such as Thomas Mann, Katherine Anne Porter, Kay Boyle, John Crowe Ransom, Wallace Stevens, and E. E. Cummings.

Common Ground. The Common Council for American Unity founds this quarterly to further an appreciation of contributions to U.S. culture by diverse ethnic, religious, and national groups. Edited by Louis Adamic for its first two years, the magazine was published until 1949.

PM. This New York City tabloid daily newspaper, noted for its liberal, pro-labor policies, debuts, edited by former *Time* magazine publisher Ralph Ingersoll. Contributors included Ben Hecht and Margaret Bourke-White, and from 1945 until it ceased publication in 1948, it was owned by Marshall Field.

1941
Drama and Theater

MAXWELL ANDERSON: *Candle in the Wind.* This is a preachy melodrama about an American actress who remains in occupied Paris to be with the man she loves, an anti-Nazi journalist who is imprisoned.

S. N. BEHRMAN: *The Talley Method.* A social problem comedy concerning a talented surgeon's lack of humanity.

ROSE FRANKEN (1895–1988): *Claudia.* Franken's comedy, her first since *Another Language* in 1932, about an immature woman with a mother fixation, is called by one reviewer "the best new American play of the season." The Texas-born playwright followed it with the less successful *Outrageous Fortune* (1943) and *Soldier's Wife* (1944).

MOSS HART: *The Lady in the Dark.* Hart's first solo effort, a musical comedy with lyrics by Ira Gershwin and music by Kurt Weill, features an expressionistic method as a restless fashion editor explores her life through flashbacks and dreams shared with her therapist.

LILLIAN HELLMAN: *Watch on the Rhine.* Of the eleven war plays on Broadway during the 1940–1941 season, Hellman's anti-Nazi play set in Washington, D.C., along with Sherwood's *There Shall Be No Night*, are the two successes.

JOSEPH KESSERLING (1902–1967): *Arsenic and Old Lace.* The comedy centers on two sisters who murder their lonely male lodgers with poisoned elderberry wine. It is believed that Kesserling's originally serious thriller was turned into an uproarious comedy by the play's producers, Howard Lindsay and Russel Crouse. Kesserling was a New York–born actor and teacher.

CLIFFORD ODETS: *Clash By Night.* Written at the time that Odets's marriage fell apart, this play portrays two characters, Mae and Jerry Wilenski, in the midst of a sordid love triangle.

WILLIAM SAROYAN: *Three Plays.* These plays include *The Beautiful People, Sweeney in the Trees*, and *Across the Board on Tomorrow Morning.* All show the playwright's characteristic blend of unconventionality and optimism. As Saroyan writes in his foreword, "The comedy, tragedy, absurdity and nobility of these plays come from people whom the writer regards as beautiful." *The Beautiful People* opens on Broadway in 1941, financed by the playwright when no other backers could be found. It proves to be his last popular stage success.

DELMORE SCHWARTZ: *Shenandoah.* In this verse play on the birth and naming of a Jewish child in the Bronx, a ghostly projection of the man whom the child is to become takes part as a figure in the chorus.

RICHARD WRIGHT AND PAUL GREEN: *Native Son.* Although considered powerful, groundbreaking theater, the dramatic adaptation of Wright's novel, directed by Orson Welles, fails to attract an audience and closes after only 114 performances.

Fiction

WILLIAM ATTAWAY: *Blood on the Forge.* The author's second and last novel establishes Attaway's reputation as the chronicler of the great migration of blacks from the South to the industrial North. The novel dramatizes the tragic fate of three Kentucky sharecroppers who try to build new lives as they work in a Pennsylvania steel mill.

SALLY BENSON (1900–1972): *Junior Miss.* A collection of Benson's popular *New Yorker* stories about the misadventures of an awkward twelve-year-old New York City schoolgirl, Judy Graves. Dramatized by Jerome Chodorov and Joseph Fields also in 1941, they would subsequently be adapted as a popular radio drama, a movie, and a television musical. The Missouri-born writer also published collections of satirical short stories, *People Are Fascinating* (1936), *Emily* (1938), and *Stories of the Gods and Heroes* (1940).

JAMES CAIN: *Mildred Pierce.* Cain tells the story of sex, money, and snobbery in a divorcée's business, love, and family life. A reviewer remarks that Cain's hard-boiled social realism resembles an "iron-fist in a silk stocking."

MARY ELLEN CHASE: *Windswept.* The novelist delivers a characteristically muted but convincing portrait of family life along the Maine coast.

PAUL ENGLE: *Always the Land.* The poet's first novel takes an intimate look at Iowa farm life.

JAMES T. FARRELL: *Ellen Rogers.* Thomas Mann calls this story of blighted love set in Chicago in the 1920s "one of the best love-stories I know, of unusual truthfulness and simplicity."

HOWARD FAST (1914–2003): *The Last Frontier.* Complementing Walter Van Tilburg Clark's reassessment of frontier justice in *The Ox-Bow Incident* (1940), Fast describes a group of Cheyenne Indians in 1878 who, trying to escape to their homeland after deprivation and betrayal on a reservation, are relentlessly pursued by a powerful army unit. The novel is an important indicator of a paradigm shift in the myth of the American frontier. Fast, the author of many historical novels, was a member of the Communist Party between 1943 and 1956.

EDNA FERBER: *Saratoga Trunk.* Ferber's historical novel is set during the 1880s in Saratoga Springs, New York, and New Orleans.

F. SCOTT FITZGERALD: *The Last Tycoon.* Although only half completed before Fitzgerald's death, his satirical novel about Hollywood is praised as equal in quality to *The Great Gatsby*, enhancing the author's posthumous reputation.

MARTHA GELLHORN: *The Heart of Another.* Gellhorn's collection of short stories is based on her experiences during the Spanish Civil War.

ELLEN GLASGOW: *In This Our Life.* Glasgow's last novel traces the decline of the aristocratic Timberlake family of Virginia and concludes her series of novels (begun in 1897) treating the social history of the antebellum South.

MARCUS GOODRICH (1897–1991): *Delilah.* This sea novel set in 1916–1917 on a destroyer based in the Philippines is praised by James Michener as equal to "Joseph Conrad's *Youth* or the best of Herman Melville." Goodrich, a newspaperman and screenwriter, as well as a novelist, served on a destroyer in the Pacific during World War II.

CAROLINE GORDON: *The Green Centuries.* Gordon produces a historical novel set on the Kentucky frontier during the American Revolution.

J. P. MARQUAND: *H. M. Pulham, Esquire.* Marquand's bestseller is a wry satire on the Boston Brahmin class. It offers the autobiographical reflections of the title character, who is preparing for his twenty-fifth reunion at Harvard. His modest successes are deemed empty compared to the promise of his college years.

CARSON McCULLERS: *Reflections in a Golden Eye.* McCullers's dark novel addresses homosexuality on an army base in the South. The scandalous subject matter disappoints many after the success of *The Heart Is a Lonely Hunter.* The novel's bleak tone reflects the turbulence in McCullers's life at the time and the failure of her marriage.

ROBERT NATHAN: *They Went On Together.* The novel, in a shift from Nathan's characteristic gentle fantasy to realism, concerns wartime evacuees seen through the eyes of two homeless children.

KENNETH PATCHEN: *The Journal of Albion Moonlight.* Patchen's first novel is a powerful, stream-of-consciousness antiwar drama that would later serve the Beats as a manifesto for rebellion and social protest.

ELIZABETH MADOX ROBERTS: *Not by Strange Gods.* Roberts's last book is a collection of stories set in the Kentucky backwoods.

MARK SCHORER: *The Hermit Place.* Schorer's second novel is a psychological study of two sisters who fall in love with a mysterious aviator who then dies.

BUDD SCHULBERG (b. 1914): *What Makes Sammy Run?* The writer's first novel is a satiric critique of America's obsession with fame and fortune. The grasping Sammy Glick rises to the top in Hollywood by double-crossing his friends. The book is regarded as a notorious roman à clef. Born in New York, Schulberg was the son of a film producer. He wrote the screenplay for the acclaimed film *On the Waterfront* (1954).

ANYA SETON (1916–1990): *My Theodosia.* The first of the writer's popular historical novels concerns the daughter of Aaron Burr. Born in New York City, Seton was the daughter of Canadian naturalist Ernest Thompson Seton.

IRWIN SHAW: *Welcome to the City.* Shaw's collection of short stories set in New York is described by a reviewer as "minor crises in the lives of minor people."

WALLACE STEGNER: *Fire and Ice.* A college student flirts with Communism in Stegner's novel, which ultimately makes the case that any ideology is insufficient to explicate the range of human experience.

GERTRUDE STEIN: *Ida.* Stein's first novel in eleven years is a character sketch of a woman.

GEORGE R. STEWART (1895–1980): *Storm.* Stewart, a Pennsylvania-born professor of English at the University of California, chronicles the twelve-day history of a hypothetical Pacific storm. His previous novels were *East of the Giants* (1938) and *Doctor's Oral* (1939).

JESSE STUART: *Men of the Mountains.* The Appalachian regionalist's story collection deals with Kentucky hill farmers and their daily routines.

BOOTH TARKINGTON: *The Heritage of Hatcher Ide.* Tarkington continues his documentation of Midwestern life during the Depression. In the story, the title character returns from college, confident that a position is waiting for him in the family business, only to discover that the firm has collapsed. He must then adjust to a life of diminished prospects.

EUDORA WELTY (1909–2001): *A Curtain of Green, and Other Stories.* Welty's first published work features an appreciative foreword by Katherine Anne Porter and mainly concerns extraordinary occurrences that affect ordinary people. Welty was born in Jackson, Mississippi, the locale for much of her fiction.

THOMAS WOLFE: *The Hills Beyond.* Published three years after Wolfe's death, the miscellany includes parts of an incomplete novel on the Joyner clan of North Carolina and a number of short character studies.

Literary Criticism and Scholarship

VAN WYCK BROOKS: *On Literature Today.* Brooks delivers a harsh assessment of the perceived cynicism of writers such as John Dos Passos, Ernest Hemingway, and Thomas Wolfe, calling for a literature of affirmation rooted in "health, will, courage, and faith in human nature." The same themes are sounded in the author's other 1941 volume of criticism, *Opinions of Oliver Allston.*

KENNETH BURKE: *The Philosophy of Literary Form.* Burke justifies literary analysis through a variety of methods, including psychological, social, and structural. The work is seen as a synthesis of the aesthetic emphasis of the 1920s and the social emphasis of the 1930s. W. H. Auden calls Burke "unquestionably the most brilliant and suggestive critic now writing in America."

EDWARD DAHLBERG: *Do These Bones Live?* A volume of literary essays displaying the author's rhapsodic and aphoristic style. It includes criticism of Edgar Allan Poe

Edmund Wilson

and Walt Whitman as well as literary modernists such as Ezra Pound and T. S. Eliot. It supports a mythical kind of writing to redeem everyday life. The work would be later revived as *Sing O Barren* (1947) and *Can These Bones Live?* (1960).

F. O. MATTHIESSEN: *The American Renaissance.* A seminal critical study of the flowering of American literature in the nineteenth century, with examination of figures such as Ralph Waldo Emerson, Henry David Thoreau, Herman Melville, and Walt Whitman.

JOHN CROWE RANSOM: *The New Criticism.* An explication of the leading tenets of the New Criticism, which would dominate the interpretation of literature throughout the 1940s. Ransom primarily explains what the New Criticism is not, defined largely by the critical error of straying too far from the text itself for extraneous psychological and moral judgments.

ALLEN TATE: *Reason in Madness.* A collection of reviews, addresses, and critical essays asserting the claims of literature over science as the only true measure of human knowledge.

EDMUND WILSON: *The Wound and the Bow.* This collection of important critical essays on writers such as Ernest Hemingway, Henry James, and Edith Wharton includes an examination of Freudian literary theory and the relationship between Marxism and historical interpretation as regards literature. Wilson also publishes

The Boys in the Back Room: Notes on California Novelists, a critical assessment of writers who lived in and wrote about California, such as James Cain, John O'Hara, William Saroyan, and John Steinbeck, along with notes on Nathanael West and F. Scott Fitzgerald.

Nonfiction

LOUIS ADAMIC: *Two-Way Passage.* An account of the impact of the war on foreign nationals in the United States and reactions to the war abroad, with a proposal that at war's end, immigrants should return to their homelands to become ambassadors of democracy and help found a United States of Europe. Despite reactions that Adamic is overly naive in his proposal, he would actually meet with President Roosevelt and Prime Minister Churchill, later describing the encounter in *Dinner at the White House* (1946).

JAMES AGEE: *Let Us Now Praise Famous Men.* Agee's poignant account of the lives of Southern sharecroppers during the Depression, illustrated by the photographs of Walker Evans (1903–1975), is generally regarded as Agee's greatest achievement. Employing experimental narrative techniques to depict his subjects, the work demonstrates "Agee's extraordinary participation in the narrative," according to critic William Stott, which "set the book apart from other documentary writing of the thirties."

RACHEL CARSON (1907–1964): *Under the Sea Wind.* The marine biologist's first book is a series of descriptive narratives on natural life on shore, in the open ocean, and at the sea bottom.

WILBUR J. CASH (1900–1941): *The Mind of the South.* This is an analysis of the feelings, prejudices, and values of Southerners. Praised for its candor, the book is regarded by one reviewer as "one of the most revealing books we have yet had on any region in America." Cash commits suicide in Mexico City on July 1.

JOHN DOS PASSOS: *The Ground We Stand On.* In a series of biographical portraits of figures such as Roger Williams, Benjamin Franklin, and Thomas Jefferson, Dos Passos attempts to document the human impact of the pursuit of liberty.

THEODORE DREISER: *America Is Worth Saving.* Dreiser's polemic makes a case for American isolationism by arguing that there is no obvious choice as to which regime deserves support: Nazi Germany or Britain, with its history of imperialism, colonial tyranny, and disguised fascism.

EUGENE LYONS (1898–1985): *The Red Decade: The Stalinist Penetration of America.* On October 26 Columbia philosophy professor Corliss Lamont (1902–1995) sues publisher Bobbs Merrill, claiming that Lyons's book on radicalism in the 1930s portrays him as a Communist. Lyons served as the U.S. correspondent for the Soviet news agency Tass from 1923 to 1927, and as the United Press correspondent in Moscow.

ARCHIBALD MacLEISH: *The American Cause* and *A Time to Speak.* These collections of speeches include many on the meaning of democracy and the artist's responsibility in its defense. Another collection, *A Time to Act*, would appear in 1943.

H. L. MENCKEN: *Newspaper Days.* Mencken continues his reminiscences in an account of the years 1899 to 1906, when he worked as a reporter, dramatic critic, and editor on the *Baltimore Herald.* Mencken claims truthfulness, "with occasional stretchers."

HENRY MILLER: *Colossus of Maroussi; or, The Spirit of Greece.* After leaving Paris in 1939, Miller traveled to Greece, and his impressions are collected here, judged by both the author and others as one of Miller's finest works.

REINHOLD NIEBUHR (1894–1962): *The Nature and Destiny of Man.* The Missouri-born theologian provides his philosophical view of the supernatural characteristics of mankind. Niebuhr was a professor at Union Theological Seminary from 1928 to 1960.

ERNIE PYLE (1900–1945): *Ernie Pyle in England.* A collection of the war correspondent's dispatches from December 1940 to March 1941.

WILLIAM SHIRER (1904–1993): *Berlin Diary.* This is a compilation of Shirer's observations as a CBS radio correspondent in the years leading up to World War II. Shirer would publish a sequel, *End of a Berlin Diary* (1947), recording his return to Berlin after the war.

JOHN STEINBECK: *Sea of Cortez.* Written with marine biologist Edward F. Ricketts (1896–1948), this is a journal of the writer's travels and research in the Gulf of California. It is an important source document on the author's philosophy.

E. B. WHITE AND KATHARINE WHITE: *A Subtreasury of American Humor.* The Whites compile an anthology of humorists, from Benjamin Franklin to Alexander Woollcott, arranged in categories such as "Parodies and Burlesques," "Nonsense," and "The Critic at Work."

WILLIAM L. WHITE (1900–1973): *Journey for Margaret.* The war correspondent describes the London blitz and how he brought a three-year-old English orphan back to America.

RICHARD WRIGHT: *Twelve Million Black Voices: A Folk History of the Negro in the United States.* Wright provides text and a Marxist commentary on African American experience, with photographs by Edwin Rosskam.

Poetry

W. H. AUDEN: *The Double Man.* The collection includes a long poem in the form of a New Year's letter to a friend about the implications of current events, along with short poems, anecdotes, essays, and quotations related to the long poem. It also features a sonnet sequence about the search for a meaningful personal and social life.

WILLIAM ROSE BENÉT: *The Dust Which Is God.* This autobiographical novel in verse reflects social history and private experience from 1900 to the present. Maurice Swan of the *New York Times* predicts that if Americans "would suspend their distaste for poetry for just one book," Benét's earnest, impressionistic reflections "would go through the country like prairie fire." The elder brother of Stephen Vincent Benét, William Rose Benét wrote earlier volumes such as *Merchants from Cathay* (1913), *Moons of Grandeur* (1920), and *Golden Fleece* (1935).

LOUISE BOGAN: *Poems and New Poems.* A collection of intensely personal poems taken from her earlier books, with sixteen new poems written since 1937. Marianne Moore describes Bogan's art as "compactness compacted."

PAUL ENGLE: *West of Midnight.* Engle affirms American light in opposition to the darkness descending on Europe in a series of Whitmanesque celebrations of American values.

ROBINSON JEFFERS: *Be Angry at the Sun.* Jeffers's collection includes a long narrative poem, a dramatic dialogue, and shorter lyrics on current themes, all vehicles for the poet's pessimistic philosophical meditations on man's response to an indifferent universe.

NAOMI LONG MADGETT (b. 1923): *Songs to a Phantom Nightingale.* Accepted for publication in 1938, when its author was only fifteen, this is the African American poet's first collection. Born in Virginia, Madgett was a high school teacher in Detroit and a professor of English at Eastern Michigan University. Her best-known poem, "Midway," on the civil rights movement, is included in her 1965 collection *Star by Star.*

EDGAR LEE MASTERS: *Illinois Poems.* The poet continues his celebration of country and small-town life.

EDNA ST. VINCENT MILLAY: *Collected Sonnets.* A collection of 161 sonnets, all but two from the author's earlier volumes.

MARIANNE MOORE: *The Arctic Ox* and *What Are Years?* Moore's subjects in these two collections include the fall

of France in World War II, the celebration of human freedom, and sharply delivered perceptions of animals, birds, insects, and flowers.

THEODORE ROETHKE (1908–1963): *Open House.* Roethke's first published volume heralds the arrival of an impressive new poetic voice, in verse that is tightly constructed, spare, but capable of delivering effective meditations on the self, death, and nature.

MARK VAN DOREN: *The Mayfield Deer.* This long blank-verse narrative retells an American frontier legend of the feud that ensues when a boy shoots a lonely hunter's pet deer.

WILLIAM CARLOS WILLIAMS: *The Broken Span.* Williams's collection of imagist poems rooted in commonplace experience is the last book his publisher, New Directions, brings out before a five-year hiatus in publishing, due to drastic wartime paper shortages.

LOUIS ZUKOFSKY: *55 Poems.* One reviewer likens this collection of experimental verse to "sitting in a smoker at which Cummings, Williams, Crane, the editor of *Transition*, G. M. Hopkins, Marianne Moore, and Zukofsky toss ideas at each other."

1942
Drama and Theater

MAXWELL ANDERSON: *The Eve of St. Mark.* Anderson's contribution to the war effort, the only success of the twelve war plays on Broadway during the 1942–1943 season, dramatizes in heroic and at times maudlin terms the sacrifice of an American farm boy, who dies at Bataan.

IRVING BERLIN: *This Is the Army.* Berlin's patriotic army revue, an update of his World War I all-soldier show, *Yip Yip Yaphank* (1918), opens on Broadway on July 4 and includes three hundred soldiers in its cast.

JOSEPH FIELDS (1895–1966): *The Doughgirls.* Fields's comedy about women cohabitating with men in overcrowded wartime Washington is decried by some as immoral, but it proves to be one of the season's biggest hits. Fields, the son of popular performer Lew Fields (1867–1941), collaborated with Jerome Chodorov to write *My Sister Eileen* (1940), *Junior Miss* (1941), and *Wonderful Town* (1953).

WILLIAM SAROYAN: *Razzle-Dazzle.* Short plays, ballets, and vaudeville acts are interspersed with introductory essays on their composition — all evidence of the playwright's eccentric vitality and his attempt to fashion a popular art form.

THORNTON WILDER: *The Skin of Our Teeth.* For his allegorical drama reflecting the history of mankind in the experiences of the Antrobus family of Excelsior, New

Jersey, Wilder draws on traditional domestic comedy, movie slapstick, and James Joyce's *Finnegans Wake* for inspiration. Winner of the Pulitzer Prize for drama, the play has established itself as one of the most popular, innovative, and acclaimed American dramas.

Fiction

SAMUEL HOPKINS ADAMS: *The Harvey Girls.* This historical novel set in the 1890s concerns the Fred Harvey chain of restaurants and the girls who worked in them.

NELSON ALGREN: *Never Come Morning.* Algren documents crime and poverty on Chicago's West Side in the story of aspiring boxer Bruno Bicek. The novel solidifies Algren's reputation as a "Chicago novelist" and an exponent of the style known as native American realism.

GERTRUDE ATHERTON: *The Horn of Life.* Adding to her fictional chronicle of San Francisco, Atherton paints a portrait of a distinguished family in decline against the backdrop of the city during the 1920s.

SALLY BENSON: *Meet Me in St. Louis.* Episodes from the life of the Smith family of St. Louis from 1903 to 1904. Benson's novel would be adapted as a movie musical in 1944.

KAY BOYLE: *Primer for Combat.* A novel in diary form of life in France under German occupation.

PEARL S. BUCK: *Dragon Seed.* Buck's propaganda novel concerns a small group of Chinese farmers near Nanking who try to hold on to their land in the face of the advancing Japanese troops. Family solidarity and devotion are tested by the horrors of modern warfare.

JAMES M. CAIN: *Love's Lovely Counterfeit.* Described by one reviewer as "the dingdong daddy of the what-terrible-people school of novelists," Cain dramatizes a series of double-crosses in a Midwestern city, solidifying his reputation as America's most literary pulp writer.

JAMES GOULD COZZENS: *The Just and the Unjust.* Cozzens's dramatization of a Connecticut murder trial and its interlocking web of community relationships is praised for its accomplished objectivity and is cited as evidence of a superior novelist's coming of age.

LLOYD C. DOUGLAS (1877–1951): *The Robe.* Based on the imagined life of the Roman soldier in charge of Christ's crucifixion, Douglas's religious epic is one of the decade's biggest sellers. It spawns a host of subsequent "New Testament" novels. Douglas was an Indiana-born clergyman whose first book, *The Magnificent Obsession* (1929), appeared when he was more than fifty. His other popular historical novel, set during the time of Christ, is *The Big Fisherman* (1948).

Pearl S. Buck

HOWARD FAST: *The Unvanquished.* Fast's historical novel depicts another era in which American's resolve was tested under adversity — the bleak winter of 1776–1777 — from the perspective of George Washington's command. Washington grows in leadership ability despite continual setbacks, eventually prevailing by defeating the Hessians at Trenton. The novelist's ability to depict a heroic though human Washington is widely praised.

WILLIAM FAULKNER: *Go Down, Moses and Other Stories.* Faulkner's short story collection deals with the McCaslin clan and includes one of his most admired works, "The Bear." Reviewers alternately recognize evidence of Faulkner's maturity and greatness as a writer and express their irritation at the "hopelessly tangled skeins" of his sentences, creating opaqueness rather than lucidity.

KENNETH FEARING: *Clark Gifford's Body.* Fearing's experimental novel is a modern echoing of John Brown's raid and concerns the abortive seizure of a radio station.

ERNEST HEMINGWAY: *Men at War: The Best War Stories of All Time.* Hemingway supplies an introduction for this compilation of factual and fictional war stories he selected together with William Kozlenko.

MACKINLAY KANTOR: *Happy Land.* A novella about a young sailor killed in the Pacific and the recollections of

William Faulkner

his father, a Midwestern pharmacist, about the principal events in their lives. As Robert Van Gelder observes in his review, "The story is as sentimental as any Currier & Ives print, but it is effective and it fits its time."

MARY McCARTHY (1912–1989): *The Company She Keeps.* Described as "A Portrait of the Intellectual as a Young Woman," McCarthy's first novel is a sexually frank, satiric portrait of pretty, neurotic, bohemian Margaret Sargent and her misadventures among the New York City intelligentsia. McCarthy was born in Seattle, orphaned at the age of six, and educated at Vassar College. She was a book reviewer for *The Nation* and the *New Republic* and the drama critic for the *Partisan Review.*

WRIGHT MORRIS (1910–1998): *My Uncle Dudley.* Morris's first novel is a picaresque story of a Californian who returns home to Chicago. Morris was a Nebraska native who would draw on his Midwestern background for many of his works.

DAWN POWELL: *A Time to Be Born.* A satire on Manhattan high life, Powell's novel follows the career of a ruthlessly successful woman novelist.

UPTON SINCLAIR: *Dragon's Teeth.* Awarded the Pulitzer Prize, the third volume in the author's Lanny Budd series

covers the years between 1930 and 1934, including Budd's experiences in Germany and his attempt to free a Jewish friend from Dachau.

JOHN STEINBECK: *The Moon Is Down.* Steinbeck's attempt to show German soldiers in human rather than monstrous terms draws strong condemnation. Steinbeck's dramatic adaptation opens on Broadway on April 7.

JAMES THURBER: *My World— and Welcome to It.* Essays, stories, and drawings that originally had appeared in *The New Yorker.* The book includes Thurber's most famous story, "The Secret Life of Walter Mitty."

EUDORA WELTY: *The Robber Bridegroom.* Welty's first novel relocates this Grimms's folktale to the Natchez Trace area of Mississippi at the end of the eighteenth century.

Literary Criticism and Scholarship

ALFRED KAZIN (1915–1998): *On Native Grounds.* Kazin's debut critical volume provides a masterly interpretation of American prose writers and culture between 1890 and 1940. Lionel Trilling concludes that, based on Kazin's dispassionate and erudite judgment, "our literature of the last forty years seems far from adequate — seems, indeed, almost to have failed." The Brooklyn-born Kazin became an editor at the *New Republic* the same week that *On Native Grounds* was published.

Nonfiction

HERBERT AGAR: *A Time for Greatness.* The historian, critic, and editor of the *Louisville Courier-Journal* assesses U.S. responsibility for the war and its outcome.

SHERWOOD ANDERSON: *Memoirs.* One of the author's most impressive achievements is this blend of fact and fiction that traces the stages of his artistic development.

ESTHER FORBES: *Paul Revere and the World He Lived In.* Historical novelist Forbes publishes a best-selling biography of the Boston silversmith and Revolutionary War hero that features a remarkable reconstruction of the period. It is still regarded as one of the classic popular accounts of the Revolutionary War and its era.

DOUGLAS SOUTHALL FREEMAN: *Lee's Lieutenants: A Study in Command.* The first of three volumes (concluded in 1944) of biographical portraits of those who served under Lee in the Army of Northern Virginia. It is one of the seminal works of Civil War scholarship.

MARION HARGROVE (b. 1919): *See Here, Private Hargrove.* Hargrove, a former newspaperman, captures the lighter side of military life in this comic account of the author's military experiences at Fort Bragg, North Carolina. One reviewer recommends it as "an antidote for those who worry about their boys in our army camps."

JOHN HERSEY (1914–1993): *Men on Bataan*. Although the fate of U.S. soldiers is still not fully known, Hersey reconstructs the story of the fall of the Philippines from available news dispatches and interviews with friends of General Douglas MacArthur and soldiers' families. Hersey was born in China, served as a secretary to Sinclair Lewis, and worked as a magazine writer and war correspondent.

ZORA NEALE HURSTON: *Dust Tracks on a Road*. This autobiography of the writer, folklorist, and anthropologist traces her career from childhood in an all-black Florida community through her schooling and literary success. The book's factual reliability has been questioned by subsequent biographers.

MARGARET LEECH (1893–1974): *Reveille in Washington*. One of the year's standout historical works is this lively account of life in the capital during the Civil War. Critic Clifton Fadiman praises the work as evidence that the author is "among the foremost contemporary historians of America." Leech was a novelist, biographer, and historian whose other books include *The Back of the Book* (1924), *Tin Wedding* (1926), and *Roundsman of the Lord* (1927).

CAREY McWILLIAMS: *Ill Fares the Land: Migrants and Migratory Labor in the United States*. McWilliams documents the shift to large-scale industrialized farming in the United States and the subsequent dislocation of agricultural workers.

SAMUEL ELIOT MORISON: *Admiral of the Ocean Sea: A Life of Christopher Columbus*. To research his massive two-volume Pulitzer Prize–winning biography, Morison made voyages to the West Indies and across the Atlantic in the same types of vessels used by Columbus. Such firsthand experience sets Morison's biography apart from the many others that have tried to capture the explorer and his times.

ELLIOT PAUL: *The Last Time I Saw Paris*. Wartime nostalgia for pre-occupation Paris no doubt is responsible for the popularity of this whimsical and wistful evocation of the city and its residents, based on the author's eighteen-year residence there (1923–1940). It spawns a popular song and movie.

MARJORIE KINNAN RAWLINGS: *Cross Creek*. In an autobiographical memoir by the author of *The Yearling*, Kinnan details her thirteen years in a remote rural Florida community in what is regarded by many as a classic of regional portraiture.

J. SAUNDERS REDDING: *No Day of Triumph*. Commissioned by the University of North Carolina and the Rockefeller Foundation to report on black life in the South, the literary critic combines autobiographical reflections with a detailed portrait that writer Wallace Stegner commends as "perhaps the sanest and most eloquent study of the Negro American that has appeared."

LOUISE DICKINSON RICH (1903–1991): *We Took to the Woods*. Rich's account of her six years living in the Maine wilderness becomes a bestseller. *My Neck of the Woods* would follow in 1950. The Massachusetts-born writer's other books include *Happy the Land* (1946), *The Start of the Trail* (1949), and *Travel to the North* (1952).

E. B. WHITE: *One Man's Meat*. An essay collection that contrasts the complexity of modern urban life with the more essential lessons learned on the author's Maine farm, further justification of one reviewer's claim that White is "among the best writers of the familiar essay in English."

WILLIAM L. WHITE: *They Were Expendable*. The disastrous defeat of U.S. forces in the Philippines is chronicled from the perspective of a patrol torpedo boat squadron responsible for transporting General Douglas MacArthur safely to Australia. White takes a convincing documentary approach, based on interviews with four young naval officers.

PHILIP WYLIE (1902–1971): *Generation of Vipers*. Evidence that not all that is published in 1942 is staunchly patriotic, Wylie provocatively castigates American values, beliefs, and policies that he asserts have led the country into war and, unless corrected, threaten defeat. His chapter "Common Women" added the term *Momism* to the lexicon. The book becomes a sensation and compulsory reading on many campuses. Wylie was a prolific writer of short stories, articles, radio programs, and syndicated newspaper columns.

Poetry

CONRAD AIKEN: *Brownstone Eclogues, and Other Poems*. Aiken's poetic sequence deals with city life.

JOHN BERRYMAN (1914–1972): *Poems*. Selections from work done in 1939 and 1940 establishes Berryman's reputation as one of the leading young poets of his generation. Berryman's first publication in book form was in the anthology *Five Young American Poets* (1940).

R. P. BLACKMUR: *Second World*. The literary critic's second volume of poetry is a carefully wrought, highly allusive, somber, and at times declamatory meditation on the human condition.

J. V. CUNNINGHAM (1911–1985): *The Helmsman.* This is the poet's first collection of spare, satirical verse in traditional forms. Cunningham was raised in Montana and taught at Brandeis University. His *Collected Poems and Epigrams of J. V. Cunningham* would appear in 1971.

ROBERT FROST: *A Witness Tree.* This Pulitzer Prize–winning collection, Frost's seventh, includes important works such as "Come In," "The Gift Outright," and "The Subverted Flower."

LANGSTON HUGHES: *Shakespeare in Harlem and Other Poems.* The poet describes this volume as "a book of light verse. Afro-Americana in the blues mood."

RANDALL JARRELL (1914–1965): *Blood for a Stranger.* Jarrell's first published volume is an impressive debut of witty, sardonic, and technically accomplished verse, establishing him as a significant new poetic voice. Born in Nashville, Jarrell was influenced by John Crowe Ransom while a student at Vanderbilt. He served in the Air Force during the war.

EDNA ST. VINCENT MILLAY: *The Murder of Lidice.* Written at the request of the Writers' War Board for radio broadcast, Millay's contribution to the war effort is a trite ballad indicting Nazi atrocities committed against a village in Czechoslovakia.

KENNETH PATCHEN: *The Dark Kingdom* and *The Teeth of the Lion.* Patchen's two volumes are filled with private symbols, mixing eroticism, spirituality, and social criticism. They cause *New York Times* reviewer P. M. Jack to declare Patchen "one of the poets whom historians will turn to for intelligence about the year 1942."

KARL SHAPIRO (1913–2000): *Person, Place, and Thing.* Preceded by two privately printed collections — *Poems* (1935) and *The Place of Love* (1942) — this is the first major collection by the winner of the Levinson Prize for poetry. Shapiro's intensity and highly polished style mark him as a poet to watch.

WALLACE STEVENS: *Notes Toward a Supreme Fiction.* Stevens's philosophical poetic sequence is a meditation on the nature of reality, the imagination, and poetry. Stevens also publishes a new collection, *Parts of the World,* which includes "The Poems of Our Climate," "The Well Dressed Man with a Beard," "Examination of the Hero in a Time of War," and others exploring Stevens's conception of poetry.

JOSÉ GARCIA VILLA (1904–1997): *Have Come, Am Here.* Villa's first collection and the first volume of Filipino poetry published in the United States is highly praised and technically innovative. It introduces a new method of rhyming that the author terms "reversed consonance."

MARGARET WALKER (1915–1998): *For My People.* The first African American to be included in the Yale Series of Younger Poets, Walker's debut volume portrays the African American experience in dialect-rich free-verse ballads drawing on black folk tradition as well as conventional sonnets.

ROBERT PENN WARREN: *Eleven Poems on the Same Theme.* The collection traces a progress toward self-knowledge and contains one of Warren's finest poems, "End of Season."

EDMUND WILSON: *Note-Books of Night.* A miscellany of verses, satires, travel writings, and reminiscences. As poet Louise Bogan observes, the collection demonstrates that "America's most capable critic is not, at his creative lightest, a buffoon, or, at his most serious, a pendant."

Publications and Events

Langston Hughes's "Here to Yonder" column debuts. Published in the *Chicago Defender,* Hughes's column will continue for twenty years. In it he introduced his most beloved creation, the common man from Harlem, Jesse B. Semple, later called Jesse B. Simple, whose comments on life and race would be collected in five volumes and form the basis for Hughes's musical play *Simply Heavenly* (1959).

Seventeen. The first style and fashion magazine for teenage girls begins publication, signaling the emergent youth culture.

Stars and Stripes. The newspaper of the U.S. armed forces, created during World War I, is revived to distribute war news to American troops and to the occupation forces after the war.

Yank. This weekly magazine, written by and published for army soldiers, debuts and becomes the most widely circulated service periodical during World War II. It featured cartoons such as George Baker's popular "Sad Sack," pinups of girls, letters from soldiers, and stories, poems, and editorials by contributors such as Marion Hargrove, William Saroyan, and Irwin Shaw.

1943
Drama and Theater

EDWARD CHODOROV (1904–1988): *Those Enduring Young Charms.* A caddish flyer sets out to seduce a New York shop girl while on leave but then falls in love with her, in a play that attempts to capture the spirit of the times. The playwright-director was the brother of playwright Jerome Chodorov. His biggest hit was the comedy *Oh, Men! Oh, Women!* (1953).

JAMES GOW (1907–1952) AND ARNAUD D'USSEAU (1916–1990): *Tomorrow the World.* This propagandistic drama tells the story of a boy raised by the Nazis who comes to live in America. Gow and d'Usseau were mainly film-writers whose other stage success was the equally propagandistic *Deep Are the Roots* (1945).

OSCAR HAMMERSTEIN II: *Carmen Jones.* This update of Bizet's opera, with an all-black cast, features an army corporal who falls for the femme fatale, who is more interested in boxer Husky Miller. It would be made into a film starring Dorothy Dandridge and Harry Belafonte in 1954.

MOSS HART: *Winged Victory.* Based on the training and flight experience of a group of American aviators, Hart's drama features performances by actual soldiers.

AL HIRSCHFELD (1903–2003): Caricatures of Theater Personalities. The caricature artist for the *New York Times* begins incorporating the name of his newborn daughter, Nina, into his drawings, initiating a puzzle search that would continue for more than fifty years.

SIDNEY KINGSLEY: *The Patriots.* The playwright's most controversial play dramatizes the struggle between Thomas Jefferson and Alexander Hamilton to arrive at the best definition of good government during the formative years of the American republic. Though critics and audiences argue over the play's historical accuracy and dramatic merit, it earns the New York Drama Critics Circle Award.

S. J. PERELMAN AND OGDEN NASH: *One Touch of Venus.* A musical comedy with songs by Kurt Weill concerns a statue of Venus that comes to life in Manhattan. It is the first musical to repeat the ballet method popularized by Agnes De Mille in *Oklahoma!*

RICHARD RODGERS AND OSCAR HAMMERSTEIN II: *Oklahoma!* The landmark musical, based on the folk comedy *Green Grow the Lilacs* (1931) by Lynn Riggs, with choreography by Agnes De Mille, opens on Broadway. It wins a special Pulitzer Prize and is consistently cited for transforming the American musical by successfully blending music and dance into its plot.

IRWIN SHAW: *Sons and Soldiers.* A dramatization of the reflections of a young woman as she contemplates her unborn baby son during wartime.

JOHN VAN DRUTEN (1901–1975): *The Voice of the Turtle.* A popular comedy set in wartime New York, involving a soldier on leave and two women. The three-character play in a single setting would be much copied by other cost-conscious Broadway productions. The London-born playwright's other dramas include *Young Woodley* (1925), *There's Always Juliet* (1932), and *The Distaff Side* (1934).

Fiction

HERVEY ALLEN: *The Forest and the Fort.* The first book in a trilogy concerning eighteenth-century frontiersman Salathiel Albine, who is captured and raised by the Shawnee before rejoining the world of the settlers in the 1760s. Later volumes are *Bedford Village* (1944) and *Toward the Morning* (1948).

JANE BOWLES (1917–1973): *Two Serious Ladies.* Bowles's only novel is an experimental study of two women who gradually lose their inhibitions in a series of bizarre experiences. The book gains Bowles an underground, avant-garde reputation and the admiration of writers such as Truman Capote, James Purdy, and John Ashbery. The New York–born novelist and playwright married writer Paul Bowles in 1938.

TAYLOR CALDWELL (1900–1985): *The Arm and the Darkness.* A best-selling novel about the religious conflict between Catholics and Huguenots during the reign of the French king Louis XIII. The English-born novelist would produce a string of best-selling historical novels, such as *This Side of Innocence* (1946), *Dear and Glorious Physician* (1959), and *A Pillar of Iron* (1965).

RAYMOND CHANDLER: *The Lady in the Lake.* Chandler's continuing exploration of America's seamy and secret life finds a subject in an ambitious and amoral social climber who assumes a variety of identities to ensnare others in her schemes. The novel shows Chandler transforming the detective story into a striking critique of moral and social values.

JOHN CHEEVER (1912–1982): *The Way Some People Live.* Cheever's first collection of stories, many of which had first appeared in *The New Yorker*, establishes his reputation as a master of the form and displays his characteristic subject matter: life in the newly emergent American suburbia.

JOHN DOS PASSOS: *Number One.* Second in a trilogy following *Adventures of a Young Man* (1939), the novel concerns a Huey Long–like Southern politician and demagogue ruthless in his political ambitions and destructive to those who help him on his way up. Contemporaries view the novel either as vintage Dos Passos or as evidence of a slackening of his powers.

HOWARD FAST: *Citizen Tom Paine.* Fast continues his remarkable string of yearly historical novels with a fictional biography of the eighteenth-century writer and revolutionary. The book is praised for including Paine's blemishes in its portrait.

VARDIS FISHER: *Darkness and Deep.* The initial novel in Fisher's magnum opus, The Testament of Man, a twelve-novel sequence tracing human development from primitive humanity through the rise of Christianity and the Middle Ages to the present. Subsequent volumes are *The Golden Rooms* (1944), *Intimations of Eve* (1946), *Adam and the Serpent* (1947), *The Divine Passion* (1948), *The Valley of Vision* (1951), *The Island of the Innocent* (1952), *A Goat for Azazel* (1956), *Jesus Came Again* (1956), *Peace Like a River* (1957), *My Holy Satan* (1958), and *Orphans in Gethsemane* (1960). The series is largely ignored, and in retrospect Fisher would admit that "it was too big for me."

MARTIN FLAVIN (1883–1967): *Journey in the Dark.* The San Francisco–born playwright and novelist wins the Pulitzer Prize for this novel describing the ultimately unsatisfying rise to prominence of small-town Sam Braden as a Chicago businessman. The novel uses Braden's experiences to represent America's development from the 1880s to the 1940s.

ESTHER FORBES: *Johnny Tremain.* The author of the Pulitzer Prize–winning biography *Paul Revere and the World He Lived In* (1942) trades on her expertise on Revolutionary Boston to create this Newbery Medal–winning juvenile classic about a young apprentice who finds himself at the center of action at the outbreak of the Revolution.

SINCLAIR LEWIS: *Gideon Planish.* Lewis's satirical attack on philanthropic scam-artists is generally greeted as a retread of previous themes he had visited in *Babbitt* and *Elmer Gantry.*

H. P. LOVECRAFT: *Beyond the Wall of Sleep.* The second of the horror and fantasy writer's posthumously published collections of "weird tales," mixing dream imagery, gothic terror, and mythology.

J. P. MARQUAND: *So Little Time.* This novel concerns a successful dramatist's second thoughts about the direction of his life, set against the backdrop of the outbreak of war. Marquand's characteristic deft satiric touches and comedy of manners earn him the sobriquet "Martini-Age Victorian" by critic Charles A. Brady.

AYN RAND: *The Fountainhead.* Rand embodies her philosophy of individualism, egoism, and "rational self-interest" in this story of an independent crusading architect, Howard Roark, who defies the "collectivism of the soul" of conformity. Rand's novel attains cult status, and its creator would be eventually transformed from a popular writer of romances to an exponent of the philosophy

William Saroyan

of objectivism. Later adherents would refer to themselves as the "Class of '43" in reference to their first exposure to Rand's teachings in *The Fountainhead.*

WILLIAM SAROYAN: *The Human Comedy.* Saroyan's first novel, set in a small California town and concerning family life, presents the consoling message of the power of love and brotherhood and strikes a responsive chord in wartime America.

BETTY SMITH (1904–1972): *A Tree Grows in Brooklyn.* Smith's nostalgic treatment of tenement life in the Williamsburg section of New York City at the beginning of the century is a popular success. The author, with George Abbott, would adapt it as a musical in 1951. Smith was the author of many one-act plays. Her other novels include *Tomorrow Will Be Better* (1948), *Maggie-Now* (1958), and *Joy in the Morning* (1964).

WALLACE STEGNER: *The Big Rock Candy Mountain.* Stegner achieves his first popular and critical success with this novel concerning the itinerant Bo Mason and his family. Their quest for an elusive fortune takes them across the American and Canadian West.

JESSE STUART: *Taps for Private Tassie.* Stuart's comic novel looks at what happens to a poor white mountain family when they receive government insurance money after one of their own is killed in the war.

BOOTH TARKINGTON: *Kate Fennigate.* This novel, a comedy of manners, looks at the complications that arise when the heroine tries to control those around her.

ARTHUR TRAIN (1875–1945): *Yankee Lawyer: The Autobiography of Ephraim Tutt.* Train supplies a full biography for his best-known creation, the irascible Vermont lawyer. The New York lawyer collected his many Tutt stories in *Tutt and Mr. Tutt* (1920), *The Adventures of Ephraim Tutt* (1930), *Mr. Tutt's Case Book* (1936), and *Mr. Tutt Finds a Way* (1945).

ROBERT PENN WARREN: *At Heaven's Gate.* Warren's second novel concerns a shady Southern financier who gains great power within his state but loses his daughter.

EUDORA WELTY: *The Wide Net, and Other Stories.* Welty's second story collection continues her exploration of the interrelationship between myth and details of everyday life in Mississippi. The title story, about a domestic quarrel that suggests an ancient fertility myth, had won the 1942 O. Henry Award.

IRA WOLFERT (1908–1997): *Tucker's People.* The war correspondent's first novel is a realistic depiction of the numbers racket in Harlem during the 1920s. Wolfert also publishes *The Battle for the Solomons*, an eyewitness account, and *Torpedo 8*, the story of an American bomber squadron in the Pacific.

Literary Criticism and Scholarship

CLEANTH BROOKS AND ROBERT PENN WARREN: *Understanding Fiction.* The authors' companion volume to *Understanding Poetry* (1938) applies to prose works the principles of the New Criticism — eschewing biographical and historical approaches for a close analysis of language and structure.

HENRY SEIDEL CANBY: *Walt Whitman, an American: A Study in Biography.* Though it breaks no new ground, Canby's intellectual biography, concentrating on Whitman's internal conflicts and the American historical and cultural forces that shaped them, serves to make Whitman's poetry more accessible to a wider audience, enhancing the poet's reputation.

ELLEN GLASGOW: *A Certain Measure: An Interpretation of Prose Fiction.* This collection of the writer's prefaces to her novels offers both her theories on the art of fiction and insights into her development as a writer.

EDMUND WILSON: *The Shock of Recognition.* Wilson edits this innovative anthology of writings on American writers by their peers, from James Russell Lowell on Edgar Allan Poe to a collection of letters from Sherwood Anderson to Van Wyck Brooks.

YVOR WINTERS: *The Anatomy of Nonsense.* Winters's critical essays on Henry Adams, Wallace Stevens, T. S. Eliot, and John Crowe Ransom support his advocacy of literary classicism and moral seriousness, which he expresses in his own 1943 poetry collection, *The Giant Weapon.*

Nonfiction

CARLOS BULOSAN (1903–1956): *America Is in the Heart.* The Filipino American's memoir detailing his life as a migrant worker in the United States is declared by *Look* magazine to be one of the fifty most important American books ever published.

BERNARD DEVOTO: *The Year of Decision: 1846.* The first of an eventual trilogy on the western experience and American culture. Subsequent volumes are *Across the Wide Missouri* (1947) and *The Course of Empire* (1952).

JOHN HERSEY: *Into the Valley: A Skirmish of the Marines.* Hersey describes jungle combat on Guadalcanal from the perspective of a Marine company. *New York Times* reviewer S. T. Williamson declares, "It might be held up alongside Stephen Crane's *Red Badge of Courage* without too much inflation."

TED W. LAWSON (b. 1917): *Thirty Seconds over Tokyo.* One of the pilots who had participated in the Doolittle Raid on Tokyo in 1942 supplies his account of preliminary training, the mission, and its aftermath. The book would be adapted for the screen in 1944, with a script by Dalton Trumbo.

PARDEE LOWE (b. 1904): *Father and Glorious Descendant.* This autobiographical account of growing up in San Francisco's Chinatown during the early years of the century is widely regarded as a pioneering work of Asian American literature. It has also been charged with promulgating popular stereotypes of Chinese Americans and uncritically accepting the necessity of assimilation.

CAREY MCWILLIAMS: *Brothers Under the Skin.* A wide-ranging survey of racial affairs as well as a call for unified action against racial injustice.

H. L. MENCKEN: *Heathen Days.* Mencken offers a third volume of his autobiographical reflections — humorous anecdotes ranging over his experiences between 1890 and 1936.

S. J. PERELMAN: *The Dream Department.* A collection of the humorist's *New Yorker* articles on topics such as dentistry, underwear, taxes, and other annoyances of modern life.

ERNIE PYLE: *Here Is Your War.* Pyle's celebrated "worm's-eye view" of the North African campaign. One reviewer reflects the consensus view that "Few others reporting the war have his eye for the detail that counts. . . . None of the others have his balance between detached observation and personal narrative."

CARL SANDBURG: *Home Front Memo.* Sandburg weighs in with his reflections on the war in a miscellany of speeches, broadcasts, columns, and verses.

ROBERT LEE SCOTT (b. 1908): *God Is My Co-Pilot.* An aviator describes his prewar life and combat experience against the Japanese in Burma and China in the famous Twenty-third Fighter Group, the "Flying Tigers." Despite a title that embarrasses or annoys several reviewers, the book is a popular success, causing writer Sterling North to declare that it contains "the best writing to come from any flier with the exception of St.-Exupéry."

RICHARD W. TREGASKIS (1916–1973): *Guadalcanal Diary.* One of only two war correspondents who initially accompanied the marines during the invasion of Guadalcanal, Tregaskis records what he and others experienced there, in a day-to-day account from July to September 1942. What the book lacks in polish it makes up for in immediacy and is considered a classic of war journalism.

WILLIAM L. WHITE: *Queens Die Poorly.* White's follow-up to *They Were Expendable* (1942) is an oral documentary of the U.S. Army Air Corps in the Pacific. The "Queens" of the title refer to B-17 bombers, and the book tells their story through the words and experiences of a member of a bomber crew.

WENDELL WILLKIE (1892–1944): *One World.* The 1940 Republican presidential candidate describes his 1942 world tour while making a plea for global unity and understanding. The book sells more than one million copies in two months.

Poetry

LEONARD BACON: *Day of Fire.* The poet shifts from the satirical mode of the Pulitzer Prize–winning *Sunderland Capture* (1940) to a more reflective meditation on the origin of the war and its cost.

STEPHEN VINCENT BENÉT: *Western Star.* Benét lives long enough to complete only this one section (on the settlement of Jamestown and Plymouth) of a projected epic poem on America's colonization and western expansion. It wins the Pulitzer Prize.

T. S. ELIOT: *The Four Quartets.* Eliot's poetic sequence, previously published in parts in 1935 and 1940–1942, is published in full. The last of his major poetic works, it offers Eliot's philosophical and spiritual meditation on temporality and eternity. Many view it as his most accomplished achievement in poetry.

KENNETH FEARING: *Afternoon of a Pawnbroker and Other Poems.* The poet takes aim at modern urban society in a series of sharply realized portraits. As critic Dudley Fitts observes, "It is a frightening poetry, thank God, a poetry of angry conviction, few manners and no winsome graces."

ROBERT FITZGERALD (1910–1985): *A Wreath for the Sea.* A collection by the classical scholar and translator that, in the words of Louise Bogan, transports the reader to that "humane region where the gravity of learning and the seriousness of art function, never out of sight of life."

LANGSTON HUGHES: *Freedom's Plow.* Hughes's long "prose poem" concerns how blacks and whites jointly contributed to the building of America. Hughes also publishes a pamphlet of twenty-three poems, *Jim Crow's Last Stand*, a scathing attack on racial injustice.

WELDON KEES (1914–1955): *The Last Man.* The Nebraskan-born poet's first collection establishes his characteristic restrained and formalist style. His other collection of the decade is *The Fall of the Magicians* (1947). Kees's posthumous reputation would be enhanced with the publication of *Collected Poems* in 1960.

HOWARD MOSS (1922–1987): *The Wound and the Weather.* Moss, the future poetry editor of *The New Yorker* (1948–1987), publishes his first volume of calm and graceful observations.

KENNETH PATCHEN: *Cloth of the Tempest.* Patchen's poetic reflections on the atrocities of war help make him one of the most popular poets on college campuses during World War II. His other volumes of the decade are *An Astonished Eye Looks Out of the Air* (1945), *Sleepers Awake* (1946), *Panels for the Walls of Heaven* (1947), *Red Wine and Yellow Hair*, and *If You Love Someone* (1949).

DELMORE SCHWARTZ: *Genesis: Book One.* Schwartz explores Jewish American identity from the perspective of a young man who recalls his New York childhood, with interpretation given by a chorus of "ghosts."

ELINOR WYLIE: *Last Poems.* This collection contains unpublished lyrics from various stages of the poet's career.

1944
Drama and Theater

MAXWELL ANDERSON: *Storm Operation.* Anderson's war drama depicts U.S. soldiers in combat in North Africa. It fails with both the critics and the public.

S. N. BEHRMAN: *Jacobowsky and the Colonel.* Behrman has a popular success adapting Franz Werfel's comedy about a Jew and an anti-Semitic Polish officer during the fall of France.

MARY COYLE CHASE (1907–1981): *Harvey.* Chase's amiable comedy about alcoholic Elwood P. Dowd and his imaginary six-foot rabbit companion is the surprise winner of the Pulitzer Prize. Conceived by the playwright as wartime escapism, it has a run of 1,775 performances and would be adapted as a 1950 film starring James Stewart.

EDWARD CHODOROV: *Decision.* Chodorov sparks controversy with this play on race relations.

BETTY COMDEN (b. 1919) AND ADOLPH GREEN (1915– 2002): *On the Town.* Based on the Leonard Bernstein–Jerome Robbins ballet *Fancy Free,* this musical comedy tells the story of three sailors on a twenty-four-hour leave in New York City. The successful production establishes its authors, as well as Bernstein and Robbins, as significant forces in musical theater. Comden and Green began their careers as nightclub performers.

OSSIE DAVIS (b. 1917): *Goldbrickers of 1944.* African American actor, playwright, and producer Davis writes and directs this play based on his army experiences. It is first performed in Liberia, West Africa, where Davis is stationed.

JAMES GOW AND ARNAUD D'USSEAU: *Deep Are the Roots.* This effective social drama looks at what a black war hero faces when he returns to his Southern hometown. The romantic relationship between the black protagonist and the white daughter of a senator adds to the controversy stirred by the play.

LILLIAN HELLMAN: *The Searching Wind.* Hellman's play concerns an American ambassador and his family. Set in wartime Washington, it flashes back to the family's prewar life in Rome, Berlin, and Paris.

GEORGE S. KAUFMAN AND J. P. MARQUAND: *The Late George Apley.* The two writers collaborate on a dramatic version of Marquand's Pulitzer Prize–winning novel of 1937.

ARTHUR MILLER (b. 1915): *The Man Who Had All the Luck.* Miller's playwriting debut concerns an auto mechanic's uncanny success in marriage and business. It is dismissed as "incredibly turbid in its writing and stuttering in its execution" and folds after only four performances. Raised in Brooklyn, Miller attended the University of Michigan and intended to work as a journalist before winning an Avery Hopwood Prize for his first dramatic script.

IRWIN SHAW: *The Assassin.* This wartime drama is set in Algiers in 1942, during the invasion of North Africa.

It is based on the actual assassination of the traitorous French admiral Jean-Louis Darlan.

JOHN VAN DRUTEN: *I Remember Mama.* The playwright scores a major hit with this adaptation of nostalgic autobiographical sketches by Kathryn Forbes, based on her childhood in San Francisco during the early years of the century (*Mama's Bank Account,* 1943). A film adaptation of the stage play would be produced in 1948, followed by a television series.

TENNESSEE WILLIAMS: *The Glass Menagerie.* Williams's first Broadway success, based on the author's short story "Portrait of a Girl in Glass," dramatizes the enclosed world of the Wingfields: mother Amanda who dreams of success for her son, Tom, and a suitor for the crippled and withdrawn Laura, who retreats to a private fantasy world populated by her collection of glass animals. Their circumstances, relationships, and natures are clarified with the arrival of a purported "gentleman caller" for Laura. The play establishes Williams as one of the founders of the "New Drama," marked by poetic intensity and technical innovation.

PHILIP YORDAN (1914–2003): *Anna Lucasta.* Yordan's drama of a daughter of a working-class black family who becomes a prostitute is the first play, since *The Green Pastures* (1930), performed by an all-black cast to run for more than five hundred performances. It is also noteworthy as the first Off-Broadway production to receive major critical attention. Yordan, a Chicago-born writer, would achieve success as a Hollywood scriptwriter and producer.

Fiction

SAUL BELLOW (b. 1915): *Dangling Man.* Bellow's first novel uses the netherworld between civilian and military life to explore modern alienation and existential freedom. It focuses on a young man who quits his job and waits to be drafted. With overtones of Kafka and Dostoyevsky, the novel turns the wartime home front into an occasion for serious moral and philosophical meditation.

HARRY BROWN (1917–1986): *A Walk in the Sun.* The writer of humorous sketches in *Yank* about a Brooklyn G.I. (collected in *Artie Greengroin, Pfc.,* 1945) offers a more serious depiction of war in this realistic story of an American army platoon during the invasion of Italy. Brown would win an Academy Award for his screenplay for the 1945 film version.

ERSKINE CALDWELL: *Tragic Ground.* This book recounts how a Georgia backwoodsman is stranded in a wartime boomtown when a munitions factory closes. Obscenity charges are brought against a Boston book dealer for selling the novel, but twelve days later, all charges are dismissed when Boston judge Elijah Adlow rules that the book is not obscene.

HOWARD FAST: *Freedom Road*. Fast's moralistic, polemical novel is a searing indictment of the inhumanity of the post-Reconstruction period, as dramatized by the career of black leader Gideon Jackson. He becomes a Southern congressman following the Civil War but is brought down when Northern troops withdraw from the South.

CAROLINE GORDON: *The Women on the Porch*. A psychological novel about a woman who returns to her native Tennessee after her marriage fails.

JOHN HERSEY: *A Bell for Adano*. Hersey's first novel presents the moral ambiguity of war, viewed through the American military occupation of a Sicilian village. A U.S. major helps replace the village's ancient bell, winning the respect of the inhabitants but the wrath of the commanding general. The novel would win the Pulitzer Prize in 1945 and be dramatized by Paul Osborn.

CHARLES JACKSON (1903–1968): *The Lost Weekend*. A groundbreaking, realistic treatment of alcoholism, Jackson's novel documents a harrowing five-day binge by a writer whose desperate pursuit of the next drink alternates with explorations of the psychological causes of his addiction. It would be made into a memorable film in 1945, starring Ray Milland. Jackson was a newspaperman and radio writer.

ANNE MORROW LINDBERGH: *Steep Ascent*. Lindbergh's introspective first novel has a strong autobiographical basis and concerns a perilous flight over the Alps made by an American woman and her British husband, a pilot.

FREDERICK MANFRED (FREDERICK FEIKEMA, 1912–1994): *The Golden Bowl*. Writing under the pen name "Frederick Manfred," the regional novelist publishes his first book, concerning conflict on a South Dakota farm. Born in Iowa, Manfred would chronicle the region along the Minnesota and South Dakota border that he called Siouxland.

ANAÏS NIN: *Under a Glass Bell*. Edmund Wilson's praise of this story collection — he describes Nin's work as "half short stories, half dreams," mixing "exquisite poetry with a homely realistic observation" — would lead to Nin's finding a commercial publisher for her works in the United States.

JOSEPH STANLEY PENNELL (1908–1963): *The History of Rome Hanks*. The Kansas journalist presents a panoramic novel of the Civil War and small-town life, which he would continue in *The History of Nora Beckham* (1948).

KATHERINE ANNE PORTER: *The Leaning Tower, and Other Stories*. Porter's story collection studies how changes in the South affect various individuals. The volume solidifies her reputation as one of the masters of the genre.

DAWN POWELL: *My Home Is Far Away*. Powell departs from her characteristic milieu of fashionable New York City to chronicle small-town Midwestern life during the early years of the century.

LILLIAN SMITH (1897–1966): *Strange Fruit*. Miscegenation and lynching are dramatized in this first novel by a social worker in Georgia. It describes what happens when a mulatto woman falls in love with a white man in the Deep South. The book is banned in Boston and Detroit and from the mails; in 1945, the Massachusetts Supreme Court would support the obscenity conviction of a book dealer charged with owning and intending to sell it.

JEAN STAFFORD (1915–1979): *Boston Adventure*. Stafford's first novel concerns the relationship between a foreign-born companion and a wealthy Boston woman. Stafford, born in California and raised in Colorado, was married to poet Robert Lowell from 1940 to 1948.

IRVING STONE: *Immortal Wife*. Called the "most magisterial of all the popular novelists," Stone supplies another of his highly popular, well-researched, and fully documented fictional biographies, this one about Jessie Benton Frémont, wife of the explorer, military figure, and politician John C. Frémont.

KATHLEEN WINSOR (1919–2003): *Forever Amber*. One of the era's biggest sellers, with more than one million copies sold in less than a year, this novel tells the story of amorous adventuress Amber St. Clare in the court and bedroom of Charles II. The novel is banned in Boston (and throughout Massachusetts), and the controversy over its purported indecency stimulates sales. The book's popularity is further aided by the film version directed by Otto Preminger in 1947. The Minnesota-born writer would subsequently publish *Star Money* (1950), *The Lovers* (1952), *Wanders Eastward, Wanders West* (1965), *Calais* (1979), and *Robert and Arabella* (1986).

Literary Criticism and Scholarship

VAN WYCK BROOKS: *The World of Washington Irving*. A continuation of the author's masterly Makers and Finders series on American literary history. This volume covers the nation beyond New England in the period 1800 to 1840.

BERNARD DEVOTO: *The Literary Fallacy.* The critic and scholar takes aim at the literature of the 1920s, condemning writers such as Sinclair Lewis, Ernest Hemingway, John Dos Passos, and William Faulkner for ignoring common life, "the experience that alone gives life and validity to literature."

Nonfiction

CATHERINE DRINKER BOWEN (1897–1973): *Yankee from Olympus: Justice Holmes and His Family.* A popular biography and family chronicle of the Supreme Court justice. Bowen began her career writing about music and composers in *Beloved Friend* (1937) and *Free Artist* (1939).

MERLE CURTI (1897–1996): *The Growth of American Thought.* This interdisciplinary analysis of American intellectual history wins the Pulitzer Prize for history and is regarded as the first attempt at a comprehensive history of American thought. Curti, a longtime professor of history at the University of Wisconsin, would subsequently publish *The Roots of American Loyalty* (1946), *The Making of an American Community* (1959), and *Human Nature in American Thought* (1980).

JOHN DOS PASSOS: *State of the Nation.* Based on magazine articles written during a tour of America in 1943, the book impressionistically reports on the nation during wartime.

ROBERT DUNCAN (1919–1988): "The Homosexual in Society." Duncan's groundbreaking essay, published in *Politics*, calls for open-minded acceptance of homosexuality and sexual freedom. Born in Oakland, and long associated with the Bay Area literary scene, Duncan would publish his first volume of poetry, *Heavenly City, Earthly City*, in 1947.

DASHIELL HAMMETT: *The Battle of the Aleutians.* This pictorial booklet, written with Robert Colodny, describes military tactics on the Alaskan islands during 1942–1943.

CARLETON MABEE (b. 1914): *The American Leonardo: The Life of Samuel F. B. Morse.* This book wins the 1944 Pulitzer Prize in biography. Born in China, Mabee was a professor at Clarkson College from 1949 to 1961. His other major book was *Black Freedom: The Nonviolent Abolitionist from 1830 Through the Civil War* (1970).

CAREY MCWILLIAMS: *Prejudice: Japanese-Americans, Symbol of Racial Intolerance.* McWilliams places the treatment of Japanese Americans following the attack on Pearl Harbor in the wider context of racism in America.

ARTHUR MILLER: *Situation Normal.* Hired by the producer of the film *G.I. Joe* (1945) to gather research material for an honest, un-Hollywood depiction of military life,

George Santayana

the twenty-nine-year-old playwright toured army camps and publishes his field notes in this collection, documenting the process of turning civilians into soldiers. Miller would later cowrite the screenplay.

HENRY MILLER: *Sunday After the War.* A miscellany of essays, critical opinions, observations, and autobiographical sketches that introduce the author's literary processes and philosophy.

GUNNAR MYRDAL (1898–1987): *An American Dilemma: The Negro Problem and American Democracy.* The Swedish social scientist (winner of the 1974 Nobel Prize in economics) produces a landmark interdisciplinary, two-volume study of American race relations. Concluding that white America has betrayed its ideals in its treatment of race, the book is instrumental in the development of legal arguments against government-sanctioned discrimination.

ERNIE PYLE: *Brave Men.* Solidifying his reputation as America's favorite war correspondent, Pyle gathers his dispatches from the European front from the landing in Sicily in June 1943 to the liberation of Paris in August 1944.

GEORGE SANTAYANA: *Persons and Places.* The initial installment of the philosopher's three-volume memoirs (*The Background of My Life*), to be followed by *The Middle*

Span (1945) and *My Host the World* (1953). In the first volume Santayana traces his mixed Spanish and Boston Brahmin heritage, upbringing, and education, ending with his graduation from Harvard. One reviewer calls it "the most tranquil book of this stormy year."

Poetry

E. E. CUMMINGS: *1 × 1*. The poet's eleventh collection ranges in style from his characteristic linguistic and typographical experiments to sonnets with themes of the tawdriness of the age and the sustenance of the individual human identity. Fellow poet Marianne Moore proclaims the collection Cummings's "book of masterpieces."

BABETTE DEUTSCH: *Take Them, Stranger.* Deutsch reflects on the war and its personal cost as a mother with a son on the front lines. The series of reveries and lyrics contrasts the reliability of the past and memory with unexpected future circumstances.

H.D. (HILDA DOOLITTLE): *The Walls Do Not Fall.* In the first volume of a trilogy, to be followed by *Tribute to Angels* (1945) and *Flowering of the Rod* (1946), the poet uses Egyptian symbolism and the imagist method to depict bombed London.

ROBERT LOWELL (1917–1977): *Land of Unlikeness.* Lowell's first volume is a brooding, rebellious meditation on the corruption of modern life and the search for faith, informed by the author's conversion to Catholicism. Lowell prepared the volume while in jail, serving time because he had been refused conscientious objector status.

MARIANNE MOORE: *Nevertheless.* A collection of six poems, including "In Distrust of Merits," called by Oscar Williams of the *New Republic* "one of the finest war poems we have had by a first-line poet."

KENNETH REXROTH: *The Phoenix and the Tortoise.* Rexroth's second collection shows a shift of method from his objectivist roots to a more classical style, evident as well in his third volume of the decade, *The Signature of All Things* (1949).

MURIEL RUKEYSER: *Beast in View.* This collection, judged by many as one of her strongest, includes the poet's reflection on war and on her Jewish identity in the much-admired and anthologized "To Be a Jew in the Twentieth Century."

KARL SHAPIRO: *V-Letter, and Other Poems.* Shapiro wins the Pulitzer Prize for this collection, written while he was serving in the South Pacific. Insisting that he not be regarded as a war poet, Shapiro emphasizes his interest in "the spiritual progress or retrogression of the man in war, the increase or decrease in his knowledge of beauty, government and religion."

ALLEN TATE: *Winter Sea.* This collection includes the acclaimed sequence "Seasons of the Soul," a meditation on time and history and the spiritual collapse caused by the war.

MELVIN B. TOLSON (1898–1966): *Rendezvous with America.* The first collection by the African American poet includes "Dark Symphony," celebrating the contributions of black Americans, as well as meditations on the war's destruction and possibilities in creating a "new democracy of nations." Tolson would be named poet laureate of Liberia in 1947.

MARK VAN DOREN: *The Seven Sleepers, and Other Poems.* This collection features the group of war poems entitled "Our Lady Peace," as well as meditations on humanity's fate.

ROBERT PENN WARREN: *Selected Poems, 1923–1943.* Warren's selections from his poetry of the past two decades show his development from an early intricate, metaphysical style to simpler narrative and regional idioms, as well as growth in subtle intelligence, emotional precision, and skilled craftsmanship.

WILLIAM CARLOS WILLIAMS: *The Wedge.* Williams's most important volume since *Complete Collected Poems* (1938) shows both his imagist background and his characteristic method of suffusing ordinary life and details with emotional intensity.

Publications and Events

Sewanee Review. Allen Tate assumes the editorship of the literary journal started in 1892, beginning a shift in its focus to modern literature. It becomes an important outlet for writers such as John Crowe Ransom, Cleanth Brooks, Robert Penn Warren, and Randall Jarrell. Tate would serve as editor until 1946.

1945
Drama and Theater

S. N. BEHRMAN: *Dunnigan's Daughter.* Behrman's departure from a string of social comedies is a drama about a ruthless businessman in Mexico whose true identity is finally revealed to his wife.

RUSSEL CROUSE AND HOWARD LINDSAY: *State of the Union.* This Pulitzer Prize–winning political satire is so timely that new topical lines are added to it daily. It concerns a presidential candidate with a strong resemblance to Wendell Willkie. Spencer Tracy and Katharine Hepburn would star in the 1948 film adaptation.

ROBERT FROST: *A Masque of Reason.* This blank-verse play concerns Job's asking God for an explanation of the troubles inflicted upon him. Though it marks a playful departure for the poet, many readers are left unsure of Frost's intentions.

ARTHUR LAURENTS (b. 1918): *Home of the Brave.* Former radio dramatist Laurents's first Broadway play looks at the prejudice faced by a young Jewish soldier who has been shell-shocked. Winner of the Sidney Howard Memorial Award, it is praised as the best drama yet about World War II.

JOHN PATRICK (1905–1995): *The Hasty Heart.* The Louisville-born playwright's first success is based on his war experiences and concerns patients in an army hospital on the Burma front who attempt to cheer up a Scottish soldier who does not know that he is soon to die.

ELMER RICE: *Dream Girl.* Written for his wife, the actress Betty Field, who plays the title character, Rice's uncharacteristic venture into light romantic comedy concerns a woman whose discovery of love leads her to abandon her daydreaming.

RICHARD RODGERS AND OSCAR HAMMERSTEIN II: *Carousel.* The writing team follows the exuberant *Oklahoma!* with a more somber musical drama based on Hungarian playwright Ferenc Molnár's *Liliom* (1909). Relocated in Maine, it concerns the tragic consequence of a young girl's love for a carnival roustabout. Agnes De Mille choreographs the production.

TENNESSEE WILLIAMS: *You Touched Me!* Written with Williams's lover, Donald Windham (b. 1920), the play is based on D. H. Lawrence's short story of the same name, about a retired sea captain and his sadistic sister.

Fiction

WALTER VAN TILBURG CLARK: *The City of Trembling Leaves.* Clark's second novel is an autobiographical account of the adolescence of a sensitive boy from Reno who longs to become a composer.

CAROLINE GORDON: *The Forest of the South.* Gordon's first short story collection ranges widely through Southern life. Robert Penn Warren would place her alongside Eudora Welty, Flannery O'Connor, and Katherine Anne Porter as writers "who have been enriching our literature uniquely in this century."

ELIZABETH HARDWICK (b. 1916): *The Ghostly Lover.* Hardwick's first novel about a middle-class Kentucky family prompts Philip Rahv, editor of the *Partisan Review*, to invite her to contribute, beginning Hardwick's long association with the magazine as a social and literary critic.

CHESTER B. HIMES (1909–1984): *If He Hollers Let Him Go.* Having begun writing while serving a prison sentence for armed robbery, Himes converts his experiences working in California war factories into his first novel, a bitter indictment of racial intolerance.

MACKINLAY KANTOR: *Glory for Me.* This novel in verse depicts the reception received by three discharged American servicemen who return to the same hometown. It would become the basis for the acclaimed 1946 film *The Best Years of Our Lives*, with a screenplay by Robert E. Sherwood.

SINCLAIR LEWIS: *Cass Timberlane.* Subtitled "A Novel of Husbands and Wives," Lewis's book satirizes American marriage in a portrait of a Minnesota judge's second marriage to a woman half his age, along with side-glances at others' marital and extramarital relations. Critics generally regard this novel as the best of the author's books written after receiving the Nobel Prize in 1930.

FREDERICK MANFRED (FREDERICK FEIKEMA): *Boy Almighty.* This autobiographical novel depicts two years spent by a sensitive young writer in a Midwestern tuberculosis sanatorium.

J. P. MARQUAND: *Repent in Haste.* Marquand's novel concerns a war marriage gone bad, told with the author's characteristic deft touch of social comedy and strong character development.

WILLIAM MAXWELL: *The Folded Leaf.* The most acclaimed novel by the longtime *New Yorker* editor is a sensitive treatment of a friendship between two youths from high school through college, set in the Midwest during the 1920s.

ARTHUR MILLER: *Focus.* Miller's only adult novel deals with anti-Semitism, as an American named Newman begins to wear glasses and is mistaken for a Jew, becoming the target of prejudice and persecution.

WRIGHT MORRIS: *The Man Who Was There.* Morris's second novel reinterprets America's frontier myth from the perspective of protagonist Agee Ward, whose travels put the American heartland into a wider context.

JOSEFINA NIGGLI (1910–1983): *Mexican Village.* The playwright and writer's best-known work and the first book by a Mexican American to attract a wide audience, *Mexican Village* is a vivid depiction of life in a small northern Mexico village. Folktales and social customs enhance the account.

ANAÏS NIN: *This Hunger.* Self-published in a limited edition, the volume contains three related stories describing women's unconsciousness and sexual repression.

KENNETH PATCHEN: *The Memoirs of a Shy Pornographer.* This experimental, satirical novel traces the rise of a sensitive young writer whose risqué book, ironically, becomes a notorious sensation.

SAMUEL SHELLABARGER (1888–1954): *Captain from Castile*. Action-packed historical romance set during Cortés's conquest of the Aztecs. The novel would be made into a film in 1947, starring Tryone Power as Spanish nobleman Pedro De Vargas. Shellabarger was a historian who taught at Princeton from 1914 to 1923 before he became a full-time writer of popular historical romances, including *Prince of Foxes* (1947) and *The King's Cavalier* (1950).

JOHN STEINBECK: *Cannery Row*. In a return to the Monterey lowlife setting of *Tortilla Flat* (1935), Steinbeck offers a whimsical tale of what happens when a surprise party for a marine biologist goes awry. Many are charmed by Steinbeck's efforts here; others are disappointed, finding the novel overly sentimental.

BOOTH TARKINGTON: *The Image of Josephine*. Tarkington's portrait of the modern woman shows a self-centered snob challenged to reform by a shell-shocked war veteran.

JAMES THURBER: *The Thurber Carnival*. Thurber's collection of previously published and new work includes two of his best stories—"The Catbird Seat" and "The Cane in the Corridor." It is the first of Thurber's books to attract a mass audience, selling 375,000 copies through the Book-of-the-Month Club alone.

GLENWAY WESCOTT: *Apartment in Athens*. An attempt by the formerly romantic and lyrical novelist to write realistic fiction, this story portrays how the Nazi occupation of Greece affects a middle-class family. It is a popular success but a critical disappointment. Wescott would write no more novels.

JESSAMYN WEST (1907–1984): *The Friendly Persuasion*. The Indiana-born author's debut is a series of affectionate and humorous sketches recalling her ancestors, a Quaker farming family during the second half of the nineteenth century. The story would be adapted as a film, starring Gary Cooper, in 1956.

E. B. WHITE: *Stuart Little*. Inspired by a vivid dream, essayist White creates the first of his two children's classics, concerning a mouse born into an American family. It is illustrated by Garth Williams. Prior to the book's publication, Anne Carroll Moore, head of children's literature at the New York Public Library and the most influential person in juvenile publishing at the time, criticized the story as nonaffirmative, inconclusive, and unfit for children.

Literary Criticism and Scholarship

CLEANTH BROOKS AND ROBERT HEILMAN (b. 1906): *Understanding Drama*. The authors apply the principles of the New Criticism to dramatic works. Heilman was a professor of English at the University of Washington and the author of a number of critical works on drama and fiction.

KENNETH BURKE: *A Grammar of Motives*. Burke uses literary and linguistic analysis to interpret human motives.

RICHARD EBERHART AND SELDEN RODMAN (1909–2002): *War and the Poet: An Anthology of Poetry Expressing Man's Attitudes to War from Ancient Times to the Present*. Claiming to be "the first collection of the great war poems of the world," the editors include the works of 112 poets to document the continuity of human reaction to war over the centuries.

H. L. MENCKEN: *American Language, Supplement 1*. Having previously revised his 1919 study of the development of American English in numerous expanded editions, Mencken issues the first of two supplementary volumes of examples of the American dialect, as well as the author's unique view of the American character.

KARL SHAPIRO: *Essay on Rime*. This verse critique on the theories and practices of modern poetry is written while the author is on active duty in the Pacific. Despite the book's provocative assessment of poetry, one reviewer questions "in this age of the atomic bomb" whether "even the recipient of the Pulitzer Prize for poetry will receive more than scant attention from the general public."

Nonfiction

NORMAN COUSINS (1915–1990): *Modern Man Is Obsolete*. The editor of the *Saturday Review* expands a much-discussed editorial into a wide-ranging consideration of the social and political implications of the atomic bomb and atomic energy.

F. SCOTT FITZGERALD: *The Crack-Up*. Edited by Edmund Wilson, this miscellany of essays, letters, and excerpts from literary notebooks contributes to Fitzgerald's enhanced posthumous reputation as an artist and a fascinating personality.

BETTY MacDONALD (1908–1958): *The Egg and I*. The author's lighthearted, humorous account of her life on a remote, run-down chicken ranch in Washington's Olympia Mountains becomes a bestseller. It would be made into a 1947 film and inspire the popular Ma and Pa Kettle film series. MacDonald would go on to write other autobiographical books as well as the Piggle-Wiggle series for children.

BILL MAULDIN (1921–2003): *Up Front*. A collection of the Willie and Joe cartoons that had previously appeared in *Stars and Stripes*, with commentary by the artist.

Mauldin, who took part in the Italian invasion and drew on his firsthand view of the war to produce some of the most readily identifiable images of World War II. A second collection of war cartoons, *Back Home*, appeared in 1946.

HENRY MILLER: *The Air-Conditioned Nightmare.* The longtime Paris expatriate records his disappointing reacquaintance with his native country after his return to the United States in 1941. Miller would continue his caustic reflections on the American scene in *Remember to Remember* (1947).

SANTHA RAMA RAU (b. 1923): *Home to India.* The Indian-born writer's first book is an autobiographical account of a young woman's return to her paternal grandmother's home after education in the West.

ARTHUR M. SCHLESINGER JR. (b. 1917): *The Age of Jackson.* The historian's controversial reevaluation of the Jackson presidency wins the Pulitzer Prize in history. Schlesinger breaks with prevailing notions, claiming that Jacksonian democracy was not a frontier or regional phenomenom but a class struggle that paved the way for a strong central government, which Schlesinger compares to Roosevelt's philosophy and New Deal practices. Fellow historian Richard Hofstadter calls the book "a major contribution to American historiography."

GERTRUDE STEIN: *Wars I Have Seen.* Stein publishes the journal she had kept during the German occupation of France from the vantage point of her residence near the Swiss border. Readers find her account surprisingly lucid and intimate, though some are maddened by the suggestion that the war was largely a personal affront and inconvenience for the writer.

WALTER WHITE: *A Rising Wind.* White's essay collection describes the experiences of African American soldiers in Europe during World War II. He argues that combat situations brought down racial barriers and that black veterans "will not be content to return to the old way of life in the post-war era."

RICHARD WRIGHT: *Black Boy.* Wright's autobiography of his Southern childhood and youth up to the age of nineteen, when he went north, is one of the landmark memoirs of life in Jim Crow America, a brutally honest look at a climate of oppression and persecution. It also portrays the author's liberation as an individual and as an artist.

Poetry

W. H. AUDEN: *For the Time Being.* A volume containing two long poems: the title work, a Christmas oratorio that puts the contemporary world in a religious context, and

Richard Wright

"The Sea and the Mirror," a reflection on the relationship between art and society, stimulated by a consideration of Shakespeare's *The Tempest.*

GWENDOLYN BROOKS (1917–2000): *A Street in Bronzeville.* Brooks's debut is a passionate and authentic treatment of the lives of the black urban poor, people who, in the poet's words, "[scrape] life with a fine-tooth comb." Brooks, born in Topeka, Kansas, and a longtime Chicago resident, is named one of the ten women of the year in 1945 by *Mademoiselle* magazine.

EMILY DICKINSON: *Bolts of Melody.* Edited by Mabel Loomis Todd and Millicent Todd Bingham, this selection of more than 660 previously unpublished poems allows readers for the first time to appreciate the full range of the nineteenth-century poet's masterful achievement.

RICHARD EBERHART: *Poems, New and Selected.* Composed and compiled while the poet was on duty in the naval reserve, the volume includes some of Eberhart's most famous war poems, including "Dam Neck, Virginia," "World War," and "The Fury of Aerial Bombardment." Eberhart's other important collections of the decade are *Burr Oaks* (1947) and *Brotherhood of Men* (1949).

RANDALL JARRELL: *Little Friend, Little Friend.* Critics detect a new depth and directness in contrast to the poet's earlier witty, acerbic style and attribute the change to the poet's participation in the war, serving in the U.S. Army Air Corps. The volume includes Jarrell's most anthologized poem, "The Death of the Ball Turret Gunner."

OGDEN NASH: *Many Long Years Ago.* America's best-known and beloved contemporary poet collects his work from five previous volumes, as well as several previously uncollected poems.

JOHN CROWE RANSOM: *Selected Poems.* The poet's choices among twenty-five years of work show, in the words of one reviewer, "evidence necessary to define the author as one of the most accomplished poets of the period."

Publications and Events

Commentary. The journal founded by the American Jewish Committee "to promote Jewish cultural interests and creative achievement in America" begins publication. It was edited until 1959 by Elliot Cohen, to be succeeded by Norman Podhoretz.

1946
Drama and Theater

IRVING BERLIN: *Annie Get Your Gun.* Brought in at the last moment due to the death of Jerome Kern, Berlin composes what most regard as his greatest score for this Rodgers and Hammerstein production, with book by Herbert and Dorothy Fields. The smash hit includes standards such as "I Got the Sun in the Morning," "Anything You Can Do (I Can Do Better)," and "There's No Business Like Show Business."

ARNA BONTEMPS AND COUNTEE CULLEN: *St. Louis Woman.* A musical version of Bontemps's first novel, *God Sends Sunday* (1931), opens on Broadway with an all-black cast.

MOSS HART: *Christopher Blake.* Continuing his juxtaposition of drama and fantasy introduced in *Lady in the Dark*, Hart dramatizes the traumas suffered by a twelve-year-old boy because of his parents' divorce. Scenes alternate between the courthouse, where a custody battle ensues, and fantasies inside the boy's head.

LILLIAN HELLMAN: *Another Part of the Forest.* In a "prequel" to *The Little Foxes* (1939), Hellman looks at the Hubbard clan twenty years before the action of the previous drama. Reception is mixed; some reviewers find it too melodramatic and strident.

ROBINSON JEFFERS: *Medea.* Based on the Greek tragedy by Euripides, Jeffers's adaptation stars Judith Anderson and John Gielgud and runs for 214 performances.

Lillian Hellman

GARSON KANIN (1912–1999): *Born Yesterday.* Kanin's first and most successful Broadway play is a satirical comedy set in wartime Washington, D.C., involving a junk magnate, his chorus-girl mistress, and a writer from the *New Republic* who falls in love with her. It features a star-making performance by Judy Holliday, a relative unknown hired at the last minute when the original star, Jean Arthur, quit during the tryout. Kanin, an actor, director, and filmwriter, won an Academy Award in 1945 for his direction of the war documentary *The True Glory.*

ANITA LOOS: *Happy Birthday.* Set in a New Jersey cocktail lounge, this successful comedy provides a star turn for Helen Hayes as a timid Newark librarian who loosens up.

EUGENE O'NEILL: *The Iceman Cometh.* O'Neill's first Broadway play in twelve years (and the last during his lifetime) is set in Harry Hope's Bowery saloon; there, the "pipe dreams" of its shattered denizens are challenged by the annual arrival of traveling salesman Hickey. Written in 1940, the play anticipates many of the themes of the later existentialists and is regarded as one of O'Neill's greatest stage achievements.

GERTRUDE STEIN: *Yes Is for a Very Young Man.* Stein adapts material from her memoir, *Wars I Have Seen*, for this dramatization of life in occupied France.

TENNESSEE WILLIAMS: *27 Wagons Full of Cotton and Other One-Act Plays.* Williams's collection of eleven one-act plays displays the full range of his Southern gothic themes, including incest, murder, adultery, and nymphomania. One reviewer observes that the playwright seems to be "a sad young man, at times, wandering amid life in ruins to discover his wistful poetry."

Fiction

KAY BOYLE: *Thirty Stories.* Boyle's collection of short fiction establishes her as one of the form's masters.

PEARL S. BUCK: *Pavilion of Women.* The novel concerns a Chinese lady who withdraws from married life and finds happiness in experiencing a spiritual love for an Italian priest. It is Buck's first attempt to document upper-class Chinese life.

JAMES M. CAIN: *Past All Dishonor.* The novelist departs from hard-boiled detective stories and takes up historical fiction in this melodramatic western tale set in Virginia City during the Civil War.

ERSKINE CALDWELL: *A House in the Uplands.* Another of the author's tales of Southern collapse, this time describing the demise of a decadent aristocratic family.

TAYLOR CALDWELL: *This Side of Innocence.* The novelist scores another popular success in this family saga set in an upstate New York town during the latter half of the nineteenth century. Critics laud Caldwell's storytelling and historical accuracy but complain about the book's lack of literary style and subtlety.

FANNIE COOK (1893–1949): *Mrs. Palmer's Honey.* The Missouri-born teacher, social activist, and writer's novel about a St. Louis black woman's progress from faithful servant to social reformer wins the first George Washington Carver Memorial Award. *Storm Against the Wall* appeared in 1948.

THEODORE DREISER: *The Bulwark.* Dreiser's last completed novel, published posthumously, asserts the importance of spirituality in modern life as dramatized in the travails of a staunch Quaker and his wife. Critic F. O. Matthiessen calls it "as bare as a parable," and most agree that the novel is a sad end for the pioneer of unflinching realism in American fiction.

HOWARD FAST: *The American.* The fictional biography of liberal politician John Peter Altgeld renders a partisan account. Its passionate advocacy attracts admirers, but others object to its ideological oversimplifications and distortions.

WILLIAM FAULKNER: *The Portable Faulkner.* This selection and arrangement of Faulkner's work, edited by Malcolm Cowley, is widely credited with reviving interest in the writer, most of whose books were out of print by 1946.

KENNETH FEARING: *The Big Clock.* The poet and novelist's best-known work is a murder mystery featuring the detective as the one framed for the crime. It would be adapted as a film in 1948 and again in 1987, as *No Way Out.*

MARK HARRIS (b. 1922): *Trumpet to the World.* Harris's first novel concerns a young black soldier married to a white woman. He is put on trial for striking a white officer, who had struck him first. Harris, born in Mount Vernon, New York, would be best known for his novels featuring Henry W. Wiggen, such as *Bang the Drum Slowly* (1956) and *A Ticket for a Seamstitch* (1957).

ALFRED HAYES (1911–1985): *All Thy Conquests.* Hayes's first Hemingwayesque novel is set in wartime Rome and concerns the rise and fall of a petty gangster during the American liberation in World War II. It avoids typical idealized treatments of the conquered and the conquerors. During the war, Hayes served in Italy and worked with director Roberto Rossellini on the movie *Paisan* (1946).

THOMAS HEGGEN (1919–1949): *Mister Roberts.* Based on the author's own naval service, this entertaining and popular account of life aboard a cargo ship in the Pacific involves a martinet captain, an oddball, rowdy crew, and a beloved cargo officer. Heggen would collaborate with Joshua Logan on the 1948 dramatic adaptation; actor Henry Fonda would play the title character both on Broadway and in the successful 1955 film adaptation. The Iowa-born Heggen worked for *Reader's Digest* before and after sea duty in the Pacific.

ERIC HODGINS (1899–1971): *Mr. Blandings Builds His Dream House.* The editor of *Fortune* fictionalizes his tribulations when buying and restoring an old farmhouse in Connecticut. Although he loses money on the eventual sale of the farmhouse, both the book sales and a subsequent movie are moneymakers. It is one of the first works to depict urbanites fleeing to the suburbs.

CHARLES JACKSON: *The Fall of Valor.* The author of *The Lost Weekend* (1944) follows that success with a treatment of a married man's discovery of his homosexuality. Edmund Wilson writes that Jackson "made homosexuality middle-class and thereby removed it from the privileged level at which Gide and Proust had set it."

CHRISTOPHER LA FARGE: *The Sudden Guest.* The writer uses a New England spinster's disregard for her neighbors during the hurricanes of 1938 and 1944 as an oblique allegory on U.S. foreign relations during the same periods.

J. P. MARQUAND: *B.F.'s Daughter*. The novelist continues his documentation of American social manners in the story of a domineering daughter of a wealthy industrialist.

CARSON McCULLERS: *The Member of the Wedding*. A study in child psychology, McCullers's novel presents twelve-year-old Frankie Adams's confused expectations over being asked to participate in her brother's wedding. The author would produce a dramatized version in 1950.

WRIGHT MORRIS: *The Inhabitants*. The first of a projected series of photo-text books, commissioned by Charles Scribner's Sons, is based on a tour of the United States undertaken by the author in 1940–1941. *The Home Place* would follow in 1948, and *The World in the Attic* (without photographs) would conclude the series in 1949.

ANAÏS NIN: *Ladders to Fire*. Nin's novel about a "woman's struggle to understand her own nature" initiates a five-volume "continuous novel," *Cities of the Interior*. The continuations that follow are *Children of the Albatross* (1947), *The Four-Chambered Heart* (1950), *A Spy in the House of Love* (1954), and *Solar Barque* (1959).

ANN PETRY (1908–1997): *The Street*. In her first novel, the Connecticut-born Petry becomes the first African American woman to address in fiction the plight of black women coping with ghetto life. Set in Harlem, the novel follows the efforts of a young black woman to protect herself and her young son from the troubled life outside their tiny apartment.

AYN RAND: *The Anthem*. First published in England in 1938, Rand's novella is a dystopian parable about a collectivized world that suffers due to the suppression of individualism. Frequently reprinted, the book becomes a perennial favorite among high school students.

WILLIAM SAROYAN: *The Adventures of Wesley Jackson*. In what has been described as the first antiwar novel of World War II, Saroyan chronicles the experiences of an army private.

MAY SARTON: *The Bridge of Years*. Sarton's second novel traces the period between the wars in the life of a Belgian family.

GERTRUDE STEIN: *Brewsie and Willie*. Stein's "conversation piece" uses the talk of two American soldiers in Europe during the war as mouthpieces for the author's critique of American life.

GORE VIDAL (b. 1925): *Williwaw*. Vidal's first novel, written at age nineteen, is an uncharacteristically spare and restrained story about the effects of an Arctic squall (a "williwaw") on the crew of an army transport ship in the Bering Sea. Drawing on his own wartime service as a transport ship officer, Vidal announces his arrival as a writer to watch from the war generation.

MARY JANE WARD (b. 1905): *The Snake Pit*. A harrowing description of life in an insane asylum as a young woman suffers a mental blackout and awakens to find herself a patient in a mental hospital. The novel chronicles her year-long struggle to regain her sanity and her freedom. Ward, an Indiana native, also wrote *The Tree Has Roots* (1937), *The Wax Apple* (1938), *The Professor's Umbrella* (1948), and *A Little Night Music* (1951).

ROBERT PENN WARREN: *All the King's Men*. Warren's most popular work and one of the enduring American political novels tells the story of a Huey Long–like Southern demagogue, Willie Stark, who features a complex blend of strengths and weaknesses and is corrupted by power.

EUDORA WELTY: *Delta Wedding*. The author's first novel shows a noticeable shift in technique from a mythic, dreamlike rendering of Southern experience to a more realistic portrait, this time of an extended Mississippi Delta family that comes together for a wedding. Critics note Welty's mature mastery of place and character.

EDMUND WILSON: *Memoirs of Hecate County*. Wilson's satirical stories about affluent New York suburbia are notorious for their frank sexuality, sparking protests and calls for the book's suppression. In 1948, the U.S. Supreme Court would uphold a New York court's conviction of the book's publisher (Doubleday) on obscenity charges.

FRANK YERBY (1916–1991): *The Foxes of Harrow*. This is the first in a string of best-selling historical romances that would make Yerby the era's most popular black novelist. Set in the antebellum South (and mainly avoiding racial issues), it concerns the rise from poverty to prominence of adventurer Stephen Fox. One of the decade's biggest successes, the book sells more than two million copies. Yerby would later confess that the novel includes "every romantic cliché in history." The Georgia-born writer's subsequent novels would include *The Vixens* (1947), *Pride's Castle* (1949), *The Dahomean* (1971), and *McKenzie's Hundred* (1985).

Nonfiction

MARY R. BEARD: *Woman as a Force in History*. Beard makes a groundbreaking attempt to rectify past historians' neglect of women's role in shaping history.

RUTH BENEDICT: *The Chrysanthemum and the Sword*. The anthropologist publishes a nonfiction classic on

Japanese culture that helps Americans better understand their former enemy.

JOHN DOS PASSOS: *Tour of Duty.* The author views events from December 1945 to December 1946, from different vantage points in Europe and the Pacific. While some critics note a diminishment of a former powerful writing talent, others praise Dos Passos's reportorial skills.

JOHN HERSEY: *Hiroshima.* The entire August 31 issue of *The New Yorker* is devoted to Hersey's reporting on the effects of the atomic bombing on half a dozen people. Published in book form, this report is the author's most enduring work, instantly recognized as one of the classics of the war.

S. J. PERELMAN: *Keep It Crisp.* Perelman takes aim at advertising, movies, radio, magazines, and other subjects in this collection of humorous essays.

ERNIE PYLE: *Last Chapter.* Killed by a machine-gun bullet on Iwo Jima in 1945, Pyle is mourned as a national hero. Collected here are his final dispatches from the Pacific, regarded by most as testimony to his status as America's favorite war correspondent. In the words of one reviewer, Pyle "understood the nameless men who fought and swore and scratched and died and won a war."

ELEANOR ROOSEVELT: *If You Ask Me.* Eleanor Roosevelt responds to questions on a variety of topics submitted to the *Ladies Home Journal.*

BENJAMIN SPOCK (1903–1998): *The Common Sense Book of Baby and Child Care.* As the opening event of a publishing and cultural phenomenon, Dr. Spock's book provides a practical approach to child rearing, which fills a need as the postwar baby boom begins. It sells nearly one million copies annually and becomes the top-selling nonfiction book of all time. Spock was a pediatrician in private practice in New York and in 1947 became a consultant in psychiatry at the Mayo Clinic and a professor of child development at the University of Pittsburgh and Western Reserve University.

ERA BELL THOMPSON (1906–1986): *American Daughter.* One of the first black women in American journalism, Thompson supplies an autobiographical account from her girlhood on a North Dakota farm through her education and successful career.

E. B. WHITE: *The Wild Flag.* A collection of editorials first published in *The New Yorker.* In the author's words, they were "written in anger and always in haste" and make a case for the creation of a true world government "as distinct from the sort of international league which is now functioning under the name 'United Nations.'"

WILLIAM ALLEN WHITE: *Autobiography.* A Pulitzer Prize–winning, posthumously published memoir by the Kansas newspaper editor, writer, and Progressive and Republican leader. As one reviewer ruefully observes, White's lucid account of his life up to 1923 shows "the spiritual climate of an age which now seems far away."

Poetry

ELIZABETH BISHOP (1911–1979): *North and South.* Chosen from among 843 manuscripts for the Houghton Mifflin Poetry Award in 1945, Bishop's debut volume displays a distinctive and powerful new poetic voice of intense feeling and accurate observation. While a student at Vassar College, Bishop met Marianne Moore, who became her mentor and wrote an introduction to Bishop's first published poems in the anthology *Trial Balances* (1935).

JOHN GOULD FLETCHER: *The Burning Mountain.* Fletcher's final collection of poems written after his Pulitzer Prize–winning volume *Selected Poems* (1938).

ROBERT LOWELL: *Lord Weary's Castle.* Lowell wins the Pulitzer Prize for this collection, which includes major works such as "The Quaker Graveyard in Nantucket," "Mr. Edwards and the Spider," and "Christmas Eve Under Hooker's Statue." Selden Rodman declares, "One would have to go back as far as 1914 the year that saw the publication of Robert Frost's 'North of Boston' or to T. S. Eliot's 'The Love Song of J. Alfred Prufrock' to find a poet whose first public speech has had the invention and authority of Robert Lowell's."

MARK VAN DOREN: *The Country New Year.* In a seeming intentional contrast to the contemporary scene, the poet offers the assurance of natural permanence and continuity in this collection of pastoral lyrics arranged by season.

REED WHITTEMORE (b. 1919): *Heroes and Heroines.* This is the first collection of the Connecticut-born Whittemore's popular witty verses. Subsequent volumes include *An American Takes a Walk* (1956), *Self-Made Man* (1959), and *The Boy from Iowa* (1962). Whittemore taught at Carleton College, where he revived *Furioso*, a literary magazine he had helped establish while a student at Yale. It became in 1960 the *Carleton Miscellany.*

WILLIAM CARLOS WILLIAMS: *Paterson.* Book one of the poet's magnum opus — Williams's *Leaves of Grass* — is an immense free-verse poetic sequence, incorporating historical documents, newspaper clippings, and personal letters, in order to capture Paterson, New Jersey, in its historical, personal, and mythic dimensions. Subsequent books would be published in 1948, 1949, 1951, and 1958, with a fragmentary sixth book appearing posthumously in 1963.

1947
Drama and Theater

MAXWELL ANDERSON: *Joan of Lorraine.* The first of the playwright's three successive historical dramas looks at the character of Joan of Arc in a play-within-a-play, as a theatrical company rehearses a drama about the French saint. Ingrid Bergman stars in the title role and would reprise her performance in the 1948 film version.

ROBERT FROST: *A Masque of Mercy.* The poet's second blank-verse play after *A Masque of Reason* (1945) similarly involves biblical characters in a discussion of God's justice and relations with mankind.

RUTH GOETZ (1908–2001) AND AUGUSTUS GOETZ (1901–1957): *The Heiress.* Based on Henry James's *Washington Square*, the play concerns a fortune-hunter's courtship of a woman with a dominating, unloving father. After several producers reject the unhappy ending that is faithful to James's original, the writers supply an acceptable happy ending. The husband-and-wife playwriting team were also responsible for *One Man Show* (1945), *The Immoralist* (1954), based on André Gide's novel, and *The Hidden River* (1957).

WILLIAM WISTER HAINES (1908–1989): *Command Decision.* This military drama about the attempt to destroy German jet production is first written as a play but is then turned into a best-selling novel. Clark Gable would star in the film adaptation (1948). The Iowa-born writer achieves his greatest success as a Hollywood screenwriter.

E. Y. HARBURG (1896–1981): *Finian's Rainbow.* This popular musical fantasy about an Irishman who comes to America to plant a crock of gold has a strong social component: in it, a racist Southerner is turned black to realize his errors. The musical is also noteworthy for its integrated cast, a mute character who expresses himself solely through dance, and a less-than-comic ending. Harburg was a popular lyricist and librettist who worked on productions such as *Hooray for What!* (1937), *Bloomer Girls* (1944), *Flahooley* (1951), and *The Happiest Girl in the World* (1961).

ALAN JAY LERNER (1918–1986) AND FREDERICK LOEWE (1904–1988): *Brigadoon.* The duo's first successful collaboration on a Broadway musical concerns a Scottish village that comes to life once every hundred years. It is the season's biggest hit and establishes Lerner and Loewe as leading figures in American musical theater. Lerner, a member of a wealthy New York family, worked as a radio scriptwriter before teaming up with the German-born composer Loewe. Together they would be responsible for musical hits such as *My Fair Lady* (1956) and *Gigi* (1973).

ARTHUR MILLER: *All My Sons.* Wartime corruption, family secrets, and moral accountability are the themes of Miller's drama about a manufacturer who knowingly sells defective parts to the military, causing planes to crash in battle. He is made to see the truth about his actions by his idealistic young son. The play establishes Miller as one of the most promising playwrights of his generation.

EUGENE O'NEILL: *A Moon for the Misbegotten.* The out-of-town failure of this play effectively ends O'Neill's active participation in the theater. Published in 1952 and premiered on Broadway in 1957, the play forms a kind of lyrical coda to the Tyrone family saga, as Jamie finds comfort in the arms of the hulking Irish American farm girl Josie Hogan.

ELMER RICE: *Street Scene.* The playwright adapts his 1929 drama of realistic city life into a musical, with lyrics by Langston Hughes and music by Kurt Weill. Although unsuccessful on Broadway, this innovative production would subsequently enter the repertory of several opera companies.

VIRGIL THOMSON AND GERTRUDE STEIN: *The Mother of Us All.* Thomson's opera, with a libretto by Gertrude Stein, is a tribute to women's rights activist Susan B. Anthony and is widely considered the composer's greatest achievement, called by music critic Harold C. Schonberg "one of the few examples of Americana on the lyric stage."

TENNESSEE WILLIAMS: *A Streetcar Named Desire.* Williams's New Orleans masterpiece dramatizes the explosive confrontation between ethereal and delusional Blanche DuBois and the earthy Stanley Kowalski. It wins the playwright the first of his two Pulitzers and is universally regarded as a landmark of modern American theater. Marlon Brando plays Kowalski on the stage and in the 1951 film.

Fiction

NELSON ALGREN: *The Neon Wilderness.* Called by scholar Chester E. Eisinger "the poet of the jail and the whorehouse," Algren looks at the seamy side of Chicago in this story collection.

LOUIS AUCHINCLOSS (b. 1917): *The Indifferent Children.* Published under the pseudonym "Andrew Lee," Auchincloss's first novel introduces his characteristic subject, upper-class New York life, in a comedy of manners set during the war.

SAUL BELLOW: *The Victim.* Bellow's second novel combines existential themes with anti-Semitism in a story of a Jew who inadvertently causes a Gentile to lose his job, prompting recriminations, persecution, and a painful reassessment of how a good man should live.

Nelson Algren

VANCE BOURJAILY (b. 1922): *The End of My Life.* Based on the author's wartime service, this first novel concerns a group of American ambulance drivers with the British armies in Syria and Sicily. The Ohio-born novelist would subsequently publish books such as *The Hound of Earth* (1955), *The Violated* (1958), *Confessions of a Spent Youth* (1960), and *The Man Who Knew Kennedy* (1967).

MARGARET WISE BROWN (1910–1952): *Goodnight Moon.* In one of the most beloved children's bedtime stories, a rabbit bids good night to various objects in its cozy room. Brown was the author of more than one hundred children's books, who critic Barbara Bader called "the first author of picturebooks to be recognized in her own right," and the first "to make the writing of picturebooks an art."

JOHN HORNE BURNS (1916–1953): *The Gallery.* One of the most acclaimed fictional treatments of the war consists of a series of portraits of Americans and Italians who meet in the arcade, Galleria Umberto, in Naples in 1944. Burns's perspective is distinguished from others by his harsh assessment of the American conquerors. The Massachusetts-born writer became a teacher in a prep school following his wartime service, the locale of his second novel, *Lucifer with a Book* (1949).

JAMES M. CAIN: *The Butterfly.* Cain tackles the theme of incest, portraying a father's passionate desire for his grown daughter in a novel that many view as one of the writer's strongest efforts.

THEODORE DREISER: *The Stoic.* The final volume of Dreiser's Cowperwood trilogy finally appears, thirty-three years after *The Titan* (1914). The novel shifts emphasis from the material to the spiritual and is generally viewed as evidence of Dreiser's decline.

A. B. GUTHRIE (1901–1991): *The Big Sky.* Montana-raised Guthrie produces a novel that is the first in a series of classic western tales. It concerns mountain man Boone Caudill's life as an explorer, guide, and trapper during the 1830s and 1840s. Guthrie's sequel, *Fair Land, Fair Land* (1982), shows how the West had changed since Caudill's time.

ALFRED HAYES: *Shadow of Heaven.* Hayes's second novel is the study of an aging, embittered labor organizer.

CHESTER HIMES: *Lonely Crusade.* Himes's second novel concerns a black labor organizer in an airplane factory during the war. He contends with union agitators, Communists, and racism.

LAURA Z. HOBSON (1900–1986): *Gentleman's Agreement.* Hobson's novel focuses on the anti-Semitism that a non-Jewish journalist experiences when he poses as a Jew. It sells two million copies, and the film adaptation, starring Gregory Peck, would win the Academy Award for best picture in 1947.

SINCLAIR LEWIS: *Kingsblood Royal.* Lewis takes up the theme of racial intolerance in this problem novel about a Midwestern banker who learns that he is biracial. *Ebony* magazine recognizes Lewis's efforts to dispel racial preconceptions with an award. Some find the book a heavy-handed tract; others applaud the perceived renewed power of one of America's most controversial novelists.

FREDERICK MANFRED (FREDERICK FEIKEMA): *This Is the Year.* A realistic account of the daily battles of an embittered Frisian farmer in Iowa.

JAMES A. MICHENER (1907–1997): *Tales of the South Pacific.* Serving as a naval historian in the Pacific during the war, Michener had visited some fifty islands and later converted his observations about island-hopping warfare and the activities of nurses, Seabees (naval construction battalions), and the Marines into the eighteen related sketches collected in this book. His first fictional work, it wins the Pulitzer Prize in 1948 and would be adapted by Rodgers and Hammerstein as the musical comedy *South Pacific* in 1949.

WILLARD MOTLEY (1912–1965): *Knock on Any Door.* Motley's first novel is a naturalistic account of Chicago ghetto life and the transformation of an altar boy into a hardened killer. The African American author defends his decision to deal with a white protagonist by declaring, "My race is the human race." A sequel, *Let No Man Write My Epitaph*, would appear in 1958. The Chicago-born writer is considered one of the last American naturalists.

VLADIMIR NABOKOV (1899–1977): *Bend Sinister.* Nabokov's first novel written after he had immigrated to the United States in 1940 concerns a university professor living in an unnamed totalitarian state who struggles to maintain personal integrity in the face of defeat, madness, and finally death. Nabokov, who left Russia after the revolution, attended Cambridge University and wrote his first novels and stories in Russian while living in Berlin. He would teach literature at Cornell University from 1948 to 1959.

ANN PETRY: *Country Place.* Petry's second novel shifts its setting from black urban life to a New England village, where a returning soldier learns that gossip about his wife's infidelity is true.

J. F. POWERS (1917–1999): *Prince of Darkness and Other Stories.* The Illinois-born writer's debut collection introduces his characteristic subject — the Catholic clergy in the Midwest — and the theme of the conflict between the spiritual and the secular.

MARK SCHORER: *The State of Mind.* A collection of short stories, most of which had appeared first in *The New Yorker.*

BUDD SCHULBERG: *The Harder They Fall.* Schulberg's second novel turns to the corruption of professional boxing for his theme in a story about an unscrupulous fight promoter.

SAMUEL SHELLABARGER: *Prince of Foxes.* One of the decade's bestsellers is this historical romance set during the Renaissance and concerning the treachery of Cesare Borgia.

MICKEY SPILLANE (FRANK MORRISON, b. 1918): *I, the Jury.* Spillane debuts as a writer of hard-boiled detective stories. Written in three weeks, the book introduces tough-guy private eye Mike Hammer. Spillane would parlay his combination of violence, sex, and crime to become one of the all-time best-selling writers. As the author points out, "I have no fans. You know what I got? Customers."

JEAN STAFFORD: *The Mountain Lion.* Stafford's second novel concerns the relationship between a brother and a sister in rural Colorado, in a deftly constructed work with psychological and symbolic implications.

JOHN STEINBECK: *The Wayward Bus.* Steinbeck uses a microcosmic group of passengers stranded overnight in a California gas station to explore and criticize contemporary American values.

LIONEL TRILLING (1905–1975): *The Middle of the Journey.* The literary and social critic's only novel concerns John Laskell's recuperation from a near-fatal illness in rural Connecticut. There he is confronted with differing assertions of values, beliefs, and moral responsibility through the death of a friend's young daughter. A novel of ideas, the book is important for its depiction of the moral and political climate of the 1930s and 1940s. Trilling, who joined the faculty at Columbia in 1931, previously published two critical studies, *Matthew Arnold* (1939) and *E. M. Forster* (1943).

GORE VIDAL: *In a Yellow Wood.* Vidal's second novel dramatizes contemporary manners in the postwar world, as a young veteran struggles to decide what to do with his life. It features close observations of life in a New York brokerage firm, at a fashionable cocktail party, and in a Greenwich Village club.

ROBERT PENN WARREN: *Circus in the Attic, and Other Stories.* This collection of stories with rural and small-town settings demonstrates Warren's skill in detailed observation and the rendering of the rhythms and idiom of Southern speech. It includes his first published story, "Prime Leaf" (1930), and what many consider his best, "Blackberry Winter," a tale of lost innocence.

HERMAN WOUK (b. 1915): *Aurora Dawn.* Wouk's first novel takes a satirical look at the radio and advertising businesses. Born in New York City, Wouk wrote for comedian Fred Allen in the 1930s and served in the navy during World War II.

Literary Criticism and Scholarship

CLEANTH BROOKS: *The Well-Wrought Urn.* In an influential application of the methods of the New Criticism, Brooks establishes his reputation as one of the leading critical voices of the period.

VAN WYCK BROOKS: *The Time of Melville and Whitman.* The fourth of the critic's Makers and Finders series on writers in America covers the period from the 1840s to the 1880s.

HENRY JAMES: *Notebooks.* Edited by F. O. Matthiessen and Kenneth B. Murdock (1895–1975), James's working notebooks shed considerable light on the writer's creative methods and the art of fiction.

YVOR WINTERS: *In Defense of Reason.* This collection of critical writings includes the earlier volumes *Primitivism and Decadence, Maule's Curse,* and *The Anatomy of Non-sense,* as well as a new essay on Hart Crane's *The Bridge.*

Nonfiction

CLEVELAND AMORY (1917–1998): *The Proper Bostonians.* The self-styled curmudgeon's first book is an anecdotally rich, sardonic portrait of Boston society and its prominent families from colonial times to the present. The Massachusetts-born writer began his career in the 1930s as a journalist and satirist of American high society.

HENRY SEIDEL CANBY: *American Memoir.* Professor of literature and the cofounder and first editor of the *Saturday Review of Literature,* Canby revises and condenses the first two volumes of his autobiography — *The Age of Confidence* (1934) and *Alma Mater* (1936) — and continues the story of his life, offering a wide view of the literary scene during the first half of the twentieth century.

BERNARD DEVOTO: *Across the Wide Missouri.* The second of the author's studies on the impact of the West on American culture chronicles the Rocky Mountain fur trade during the 1830s. It wins the Pulitzer Prize in history.

OTTO EISENSCHIML (1880–1963) AND RALPH G. NEWMAN (1911–1998): *The American Iliad.* The team prepares a massive oral history of the Civil War based on the perspectives of hundreds of eyewitnesses. Eisenschiml was a Vienna-born chemist and popular lecturer on Lincoln, the Civil War, and criminology. Newman was a Civil War specialist who helped found the Civil War Round Table discussion group in 1940 and was the owner of Chicago's Abraham Lincoln Book Shop.

G. M. GILBERT (1911–1977): *Nuremberg Diary.* The prison psychologist at the Nuremberg trial records his daily contacts with the principal Nazi war criminals, allowing them to speak for themselves in a chilling record of Nazism and self-justification.

JOHN GUNTHER: *Inside U.S.A.* The journalist turns his attention to America in this massive, best-selling sociopolitical survey and geographical guidebook. It would be adapted as a Broadway revue in 1948.

WALTER LIPPMANN: *The Cold War.* Lippmann assesses and criticizes U.S. foreign policy toward the Soviet Union, the concept of containment, and the so-called Truman Doctrine.

FERDINAND LUNDBERG (1905–1995) AND MARYNIA F. FARNHAM (1900–1979): *Modern Woman: The Lost Sex.* This polemical antifeminist bestseller claims that modern American women have abandoned their traditional roles as wives and mothers to the detriment of society and their own happiness. Lundberg was an economist, educator, and journalist.

ALLAN NEVINS: *Ordeal of the Union.* Nevins publishes the first two books of a six-volume series on nineteenth-century American history from the 1850s through the Civil War. Determined to broaden the consideration of the Civil War beyond the perspective of military history, to include the political, social, economic, and cultural aspects of the period, Nevins is awarded the Scribner Centenary Prize and the Bancroft Prize.

MARY WHITE OVINGTON (1865–1951): *The Walls Come Tumbling Down.* The author, one of the founders of the NAACP, supplies an important historical record on racial affairs in her autobiography.

GEORGE S. PATTON JR. (1885–1945): *War as I Knew It.* The U.S. general's war memoirs are a compilation of "open" letters to his wife written during the African and Sicilian campaigns, a technical summary of the movement of the Third Army across Europe taken from his diary, and diverse observations and maxims on the art of war and generalship.

GERTRUDE STEIN: *Four in America.* Posthumously published essays on George Washington, Ulysses S. Grant, the Wright brothers, and Henry James, with a critical introduction by Thornton Wilder.

Poetry

CONRAD AIKEN: *The Kid.* This ambitious poetic sequence uses the seventeenth-century New Englander William Blackstone to define the "prototypical American"; his traits are glimpsed in later figures such as John James Audubon, Johnny Appleseed, Kit Carson, Billy the Kid, Herman Melville, Walt Whitman, Henry Adams, and Emily Dickinson.

JOHN CIARDI: *Other Skies.* Reflecting the poet's war experience as a B-29 gunner in the Pacific, Ciardi's collection is hailed as some of the strongest war poetry of his generation.

ROBERT DUNCAN: *Heavenly City, Earthly City.* Duncan's debut collection would embarrass the poet later in life. Seen as overly derivative and declamatory, the volume causes Duncan to observe that "I couldn't read it aloud any longer, and I never republished it until I came to admit . . . that it is part of the whole."

ROBERT FROST: *Steeple Bush.* Critics are divided about this collection of lyrics. Some find clear evidence of the poet's decline and age; others, such as Randall Jarrell, consider the volume to be evidence of the mature mastery of "one of the subtlest and saddest of poets."

ROBERT HILLYER: *Poems for Music.* The 1934 Pulitzer Prize winner (for *Collected Verse*) makes this selection of what he considers his best lyrics.

LANGSTON HUGHES: *Fields of Wonder.* Hughes publishes his only collection of lyrics on nonracial themes.

HOWARD NEMEROV (1920–1991): *The Image and the Law.* Nemerov's first collection presents the conflict between the "poetry of the eye" and the "poetry of the mind." Nemerov, a New York City native, was a pilot during World War II, and would teach at Bennington, Brandeis, and Washington University.

KARL SHAPIRO: *Trial of a Poet, and Other Poems.* Shapiro's collection includes a defense in dramatic form of the poet and his mission versus materialistic society and religion.

WALLACE STEVENS: *Transport to Summer.* Stevens's collection includes the long poem "Esthetique du Mal," which asserts the utility of evil in service of the imagination. Critic Harold Bloom would declare that the poem is the poet's "major humanistic polemic" of the mid-1940s.

RICHARD WILBUR (b. 1921): *The Beautiful Changes and Other Poems.* Wilbur's first collection incorporates his experiences as an infantry soldier in Europe and establishes a common theme of the search for order amid chaos and destruction.

Publications and Events

The Actors Studio. A workshop for professional actors is founded by Cheryl Crawford (1902–1986), Elia Kazan (1909–2003), and Robert Lewis (b. 1909). In 1948 Lee Strasberg (1901–1982) joined the group and popularized the "method" school of acting, which encourages actors to tap into their feelings in performance. Both the Actors Studio and the acting style it encouraged would become major forces in contemporary American theater.

The Living Theatre Company. The experimental company is founded by Julian Beck (1925–1985) and his wife, Judith Malina (b. 1926). It became the leading avant-garde repertory company in America.

The Tony Awards. These awards are established by the American Theatre Wing to honor distinguished achievement in the theater. Named after actress and chairman of the board and secretary of the American Theatre Wing, Antoinette Perry (1888–1946), the Tonys have been awarded annually since 1947 and are considered, along with the Pulitzer Prize and the New York Drama Critics Circle Award, the most respected of all American theatrical honors.

1948
Drama and Theater

MAXWELL ANDERSON: *Anne of the Thousand Days.* After *Joan of Lorraine* (1947), the playwright takes up the subject of the relationship between Anne Boleyn and Henry VIII.

MOSS HART: *Light Up the Sky.* Hart's lighthearted comedy, about a new play's Boston tryout, recalls his past triumphs with George S. Kaufman. It is Hart's last success; his final play, *The Climate of Eden* (1952), would close after only twenty performances.

CLIFFORD ODETS: *The Big Knife.* The playwright tackles Hollywood in this drama about a movie star who struggles to retain his integrity.

COLE PORTER: *Kiss Me, Kate.* Porter supplies the songs for this successful musical version of Shakespeare's *Taming of the Shrew.* The score, with tunes such as "Another Op'nin', Another Show," "Too Darn Hot," and "Wunderbar," is generally viewed as Porter's masterwork.

TENNESSEE WILLIAMS: *Summer and Smoke.* Alma Winemiller, a prim minister's daughter, is awakened to her sexuality in this drama of sexual repression set in a small Southern town. Williams would revise the play in 1964 under a new title: *The Eccentricities of a Nightingale.*

THOMAS WOLFE: *Mannerhouse.* Probably written in 1926 and posthumously published, Wolfe's allegorical tragedy about the South during the Civil War has been called "virtually his sole use of non-autobiographical material."

Fiction

PEARL S. BUCK: *Peony.* Buck's novel deals with racial conflict experienced by a Jewish family living in China.

JAMES M. CAIN: *The Moth.* The novelist's ambitious attempt at a social chronicle depicting the various adventures of his protagonist, Jack Dillon, is a critical and popular failure.

ERSKINE CALDWELL: *This Very Earth.* Caldwell continues to dramatize the violent, seamy side of Southern life in the story of a poor white farmer who sells his homestead and moves his family to town.

TRUMAN CAPOTE (1924–1984): *Other Voices, Other Rooms.* Capote's provocative debut concerns an adolescent's maturation on a Louisiana plantation and the discovery of his homosexuality. Shocking in its subject matter at the time and impressive in its luxuriant style, the book begins the process of turning the writer into a celebrity. Capote was born in New Orleans and began his literary career working at *The New Yorker.*

WILLA CATHER: *The Old Beauty and Others.* The last three short stories written by the author are published to a mixed reception. Some view them as a fitting valediction for a beloved writer; others believe they add little to her stature.

JOHN GOULD COZZENS: *Guard of Honor.* Cozzens's most acclaimed novel is a tightly plotted look at a U.S. Army Air Force base in Florida in 1943. Characters deal with charges of segregation and accidental death in a story illustrating the complexity of human actions and relationships. The book wins the Pulitzer Prize in 1949.

WILLIAM FAULKNER: *Intruder in the Dust.* In a working out of Faulkner's response to the South's "Negro Problem" (as it was called at the time), Lucas Beaucamp, a black Mississippi farmer, is charged with the murder of a white man. He is eventually cleared by black and white teenagers and a spinster from an old Southern family.

MARTHA GELLHORN: *The Wine of Astonishment.* This story about men in combat, one of the few by a woman, occurs during the last winter of the war and focuses on prejudice existing between Jews and Gentiles.

ZORA NEALE HURSTON: *Seraph on the Suwanee.* Hurston's last novel is a melodramatic treatment of a rural Florida family at the beginning of the century. By breaking what she calls "that old silly rule about Negroes not writing about white people," Hurston faces charges that she is abandoning her race. When the book is published, Hurston is falsely accused of molesting a ten-year-old boy. The scandal contributes to Hurston's abandonment of writing and her rapid descent into obscurity.

CHARLES JACKSON: *The Outer Edge.* Jackson continues his studies of human pathology in the story of a brutal murder of two young girls by a teenager and its consequences for various members of a suburban community.

SHIRLEY JACKSON (1919–1965): *The Road Through the Wall.* The San Francisco–born writer's first novel looks at the violence beneath the surface of middle-class small-town life from the vantage point of disturbed adolescents. Jackson also publishes "The Lottery," her most famous short story. It appears in *The New Yorker* on June 26. The magazine then receives an unprecedented 450 letters from twenty-five states, most expressing their outrage at Jackson's dark, moral allegory of humankind's evil. The story establishes Jackson as a master of contemporary gothic horror.

LUDWIG LEWISOHN: *Anniversary.* Narrated in stream-of-consciousness style, the novel concerns a rich, spoiled young woman who finally finds Mr. Right after two unsuccessful marriages. Despite the novel's modernist techniques, reviewers finds its themes dated; one observes that "the conception of middle-class morality as a drag on the free-ranging human spirit may seem irrelevant these days."

ROSS LOCKRIDGE (1914–1948): *Raintree County.* The events of a single day (July 4, 1892) in the life of an Indiana high school principal occasion an impressive animation of a region and an era in the author's first and only novel. In the midst of the acclaim that greets the book, Lockridge commits suicide.

NORMAN MAILER (b. 1923): *The Naked and the Dead.* Drawing on his combat experiences in the Pacific, Mailer's naturalistic first novel about an American platoon's involvement in an invasion and occupation of a Japanese-held island is acclaimed as the most ambitious and powerful novel so far based on the war. The book tops the *New York Times* bestseller list for eleven consecutive weeks, and the twenty-five-year-old writer emerges as a literary celebrity of whom much is expected.

WILLIAM MAXWELL: *Time Will Darken It.* The fiction editor of *The New Yorker* sets this novel in a small Illinois town in 1912, chronicling how a family is affected by a visit from relatives from Mississippi.

HORACE MCCOY: *Kiss Tomorrow Good-Bye.* McCoy's intentionally shocking novel about a highly educated criminal prompts a strong negative reaction. One reviewer calls it "one of the nastiest novels ever published in this country."

HENRY MILLER: *The Smile at the Foot of the Ladder.* Miller's parable-like story concerns a clown's search for ultimate happiness.

KENNETH PATCHEN: *See You in the Morning.* Patchen's novel concerns a love affair between a maid at a summer resort and a dying man.

DAWN POWELL: *Locusts Have No Kings.* Powell looks at postwar Greenwich Village in a satire on New York's social and literary scene.

J. D. SALINGER (b. 1919): "A Perfect Day for Bananafish." The crucial story in Salinger's evolving Glass family saga details the suicide of Seymour Glass while on his honeymoon with "Miss Spiritual Tramp of 1948." The story had first appeared in *The New Yorker.* Salinger, a native New Yorker who served as a counterintelligence officer in France during World War II, began publishing his stories in 1940 in *Collier's,* the *Saturday Evening Post, Story,* and *The New Yorker.*

CARL SANDBURG: *Remembrance Rock.* Sandburg's first work of fiction is a patriotic celebration of American history, connecting the establishment of Plymouth, Massachusetts, the American Revolution, and the Civil War.

DELMORE SCHWARTZ: *The World Is a Wedding*. A collection of short stories, many concerning middle-class Jewish families during the Depression.

IRWIN SHAW: *The Young Lions*. Shaw's first novel follows the prewar and combat lives of three men: a Jew, a Christian, and a Nazi, who eventually meet in a Bavarian forest. A popular and critical success, the novel is regarded as one of the best fictional treatments of the war.

B. F. SKINNER (1904–1990): *Walden Two*. The behavioral psychologist presents a utopian community in which positive and negative reinforcements are built into the social structure. The book stirs controversy over the implications of Skinner's vision.

WILLIAM GARDNER SMITH (1926–1974): *Last of the Conquerors*. One of the few fictional depictions of African American soldiers during the war, the novel concerns a black G.I. in occupied Germany who falls in love with a German girl. The African American writer was born in Philadelphia and served as a clerk-typist in occupied Berlin. His other novels would include *Anger at Innocence* (1950), *South Street* (1954), and *The Stone Face* (1963).

ELIZABETH SPENCER (b. 1921): *Fire in the Morning*. The Mississippi-born novelist's first book is a sensitive depiction of her native region involving the impact of a family feud. Her subsequent books include *This Crooked Way* (1952), *The Voice at the Back Door* (1956), and *The Snare* (1972).

JOHN STEINBECK: *The Pearl*. In a retelling of a Mexican folktale, Steinbeck relates how a great pearl found by a Mexican fisherman brings only misfortune.

GEORGE RIPPEY STEWART: *Fire*. Stewart chronicles the life cycle of a forest fire, from a lightning strike through the fire's eventual defeat.

PETER TAYLOR (1917–1994): *A Long Fourth, and Other Stories*. The Tennessee writer's first collection, dealing with urban middle-class life in the modern South, establishes the author's reputation as a master of the short story. His first novel, *A Woman of Means*, would appear in 1950.

GORE VIDAL: *The City and the Pillar*. Vidal's third novel explicitly takes up the subject of homosexuality. As he would later recall, "I wanted to take risks, to try something no American had done before." Vidal innovatively presents his homosexual protagonist, Jim Willard, as an all-American boy-next-door. A controversial bestseller, the book is panned by the *New York Times*, which refuses to take advertising for it, and subsequently either would not review or would harshly treat Vidal's next five books,

forcing him to write under the pseudonym "Edgar Box" to get a hearing of his work.

DOROTHY WEST (1907–1998): *The Living Is Easy*. West's first novel is an influential work in the black women's literary tradition, offering an unusual look at the world of upwardly mobile blacks. The novel's central figure is the predatory Cleo Judson, who destroys her sisters' marriages. West, a member of a prominent black Boston family, published her first work in the *Boston Post* at age fourteen. A significant figure during the Harlem Renaissance, she founded *Challenge* (1934) and *New Challenge* (1937).

THORNTON WILDER: *The Ides of March*. In an experimental approach, Wilder depicts the events leading up to Julius Caesar's assassination in a series of imaginary documents and perspectives.

TENNESSEE WILLIAMS: *One Arm, and Other Stories*. Williams's first collection of short stories includes the controversial "Desire and the Black Masseur," dealing with homosexuality and sadomasochism, and "The Night of the Iguana," which Williams would adapt into a play in 1962.

LIN YUTANG (1895–1976): *A Chinatown Family*. The prolific writer, editor, and lexicographer's only novel about the Chinese American experience traces the rise to prosperity of the Fong family during the 1930s and the conflict between assimilation and upholding traditional values.

Literary Criticism and Scholarship

JOSEPH CAMPBELL (1904–1987): *The Hero with a Thousand Faces*. Campbell traces the archetypal myth of a hero's departure, initiation, and return in various cultures' folklore to uncover a "monomyth." The work is a bravura performance of applied principles derived from Freud, Jung, and Campbell's own mysticism. Campbell, a member of the literature department at Sarah Lawrence College since 1934, published his first study of mythology, *Where the Two Come to Their Father: A Navaho War Ceremony*, in 1943. His four-volume study, *Mask of God*, would be published in 1969.

ALEXANDER COWIE (1896–1978): *The Rise of the American Novel*. This groundbreaking critical history of the American novel proceeds comparatively, with chapters on the leading figures of the nineteenth century. Born in Minnesota, Cowie was a longtime professor of English at Wesleyan University.

STANLEY EDGAR HYMAN (1919–1970): *The Armed Vision: A Study in the Methods of Modern Literary Criticism*. The literary critic of *The New Yorker* widens the reach of

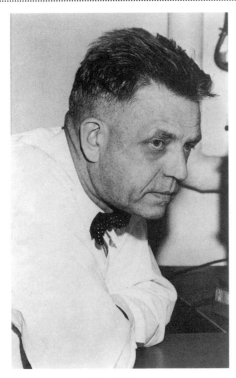

Alfred Kinsey

DWIGHT D. EISENHOWER (1890–1969): *Crusade in Europe.* The former Supreme Allied Commander in Europe provides his personal narrative of the war, with thoughtful assessments of the events and his fellow commanders. The book is greeted as one of the most important of war memoirs.

DOUGLAS SOUTHALL FREEMAN: *George Washington.* The first two volumes of the author's monumental six-volume biography is published (completed in 1954). Freeman's meticulous research, narrative skill, and balanced approach establish him in the minds of many as America's most eminent biographer and military historian.

ALFRED KINSEY (1894–1956) **AND OTHERS:** *Sexual Behavior in the Human Male.* The first part of what would become known as the Kinsey Report, a groundbreaking survey of American sexuality, is published. *Sexual Behavior in the Human Female* would follow in 1953. Kinsey, who taught biology at Indiana University, headed the study of human sexual behavior sponsered by the Institute of Sex Research at Indiana, beginning in 1938.

FIORELLO LA GUARDIA (1882–1947): *The Making of an Insurgent: An Autobiography, 1882–1919.* The former progressive mayor of New York chronicles his first thirty-seven years and his political development in this posthumously published memoir.

CHARLES LINDBERGH: *Of Flight and Life.* The aviator's reflections on the postwar world include a savage attack on "scientific materialism," the faith in technological progress to which Lindbergh had once subscribed.

DUMAS MALONE (1892–1986): *Jefferson and His Time.* Malone publishes the first volume of his massive six-volume biography, which would be completed in 1981. Malone, a professor of history at Columbia, worked as an editor of the *Dictionary of American Biography.*

CAREY McWILLIAMS: *A Mask for Privilege.* A historical and sociological study of anti-Semitism in America. McWilliams locates its modern origin in attitudes among the upper classes following the Civil War.

THOMAS MERTON (1915–1969): *The Seven Storey Mountain.* Merton's best-selling autobiography recounts his undisciplined youth, conversion to Catholicism, and entry into a Trappist monastery in Kentucky in 1941. Clare Boothe Luce declares that "It is to a book like this that men will turn a hundred years from now to find out what went on in the heart of men in this cruel century."

S. J. PERELMAN: *Westward Ha! or, Around the World in Eighty Clichés.* The humorist's first volume devoted entirely to travel chronicles an around-the-world trip Perelman untook with caricaturist Al Hirschfeld.

the New Criticism by justifying the use of nonliterary techniques from mythography, psychology, anthropology, and rhetoric to provide insights into literature.

ROBERT E. SPILLER (1896–1988) **AND OTHERS:** *Literary History of the United States.* Spiller, along with fifty-five contributors, supplies the most comprehensive general presentation of American literary history since the publication of the *Cambridge History of American Literature* (1917–1921). Spiller, who was a professor of English at the University of Pennsylvania, is regarded as one of the most distinguished scholars in the field of American studies.

ALLEN TATE: *On the Limits of Poetry: Selected Essays, 1928–1948.* Essays from earlier volumes, with new pieces, show the author's precise analysis of poetic method that helps define the procedures of the New Criticism.

Nonfiction

CHARLES A. BEARD: *President Roosevelt and the Coming of The War.* Beard makes the controversial charge that the Japanese were intentionally maneuvered by Franklin Roosevelt into assaulting the United States in World War II.

ARNA BONTEMPS: *The Story of the Negro.* A chronicle of black history from 1700 B.C. to the present, written for children.

PAUL SAMUELSON (b. 1915): *Economics: An Introductory Analysis.* Samuelson's introduction to economics becomes one of the most widely read college textbooks, selling in multiple editions more than four million copies.

ROBERT E. SHERWOOD: *Roosevelt and Hopkins: An Intimate History.* The dramatist who served as a speechwriter in the Roosevelt administration receives a Pulitzer Prize for this study of the relationship between FDR and his principal adviser, Harry Hopkins, in a behind-the-scenes look at the New Deal.

JOHN STEINBECK: *Russian Journal.* An impressionistic account of the author's brief tour of Russia, with photographs by Robert Capa (1913–1954).

JAMES THURBER: *The Beast in Me and Other Animals.* These short pieces and drawings represent Thurber's reporting days, working on *The New Yorker*'s "Talk of the Town" column.

WALTER WHITE: *A Man Called White.* White's autobiography is an important record of the activities of the NAACP, with which he was associated for more than thirty years, including undercover work passing as a white reporter to investigate lynchings.

NORBERT WIENER (1894–1964): *Cybernetics.* The Missouri-born mathematician's pioneering study of information technology features his title coinage from the Greek word for *helmsman*. The work helps earn Wiener the title "the father of automation."

Poetry

W. H. AUDEN: *The Age of Anxiety: A Baroque Eclogue.* Auden wins the Pulitzer Prize for this long, dramatic poem set in a wartime New York bar as four protagonists — projections of fractured psychic states — search for integration.

JOHN BERRYMAN: *The Dispossessed.* Berryman's volume is praised for its craft and penetration, and the poet is identified as someone "to be followed by those interested in America's current poetic trend."

JOHN PEALE BISHOP: *Collected Poems.* Selected and arranged by Allen Tate, with a personal reminiscence of his close friend, this collection is drawn from the poet's four books of verse and includes several unpublished works. Bishop's *Collected Essays* are also published, edited by Edmund Wilson.

RANDALL JARRELL: *Losses.* The poet's third collection is an impassioned response to the war in poems such as "Burning the Letters," "The Dead Wingman," and "Eighth Air Force."

ROBINSON JEFFERS: *The Double Axe and Other Poems.* In a long narrative poem and shorter lyrics, the poet

Ezra Pound

declares his intention "to present a certain philosophical attitude, which might be called Inhumanism, a shifting of emphasis and significance from man to not-man; the rejection of human solipsism and recognition of the trans-human magnificence."

ARCHIBALD MacLEISH: *Active and Other Poems.* The title work is a dramatic poem in which MacLeish imagines a totally destructive war and laments the collapse of humanity and heroism.

WILLIAM MEREDITH (b. 1919): *Ships and Other Figures.* Following the publication in 1944 of his first volume of poems, *Love Letter from an Impossible Land*, in the Yale Series of Younger Poets, Meredith draws on his service as a navy aviator for this second collection.

EZRA POUND: *The Pisan Cantos.* These poems were written while Pound was a prisoner at the end of World War II, charged by U.S. military authorities with treason for the pro-Fascist and anti-Semitic broadcasts he made for the Italian government. The sequence supplies the emotional core of Pound's massive volume in which, as fellow poet Louise Bogan observes, "imprisonment in Pisa seems to have brought him back to art and to life." It would be awarded the first Bollingen Prize in Poetry in 1949, sparking a major controversy.

THEODORE ROETHKE: *The Lost Son, and Other Poems.* Roethke discovers his distinctive voice in this collection of introspective verses, including frequently anthologized poems such as "My Papa's Waltz" and "Dolor," probing his background in dreamlike images.

MURIEL RUKEYSER: *The Green Wave.* These lyrics and translations show the poet's characteristic social overtones.

MAY SARTON: *The Lion and the Rose.* A collection of lyrics written during the decade since her first volume, *Encounter in April* (1937), touching on some of the same themes of an optimistic faith derived from nature and love.

ALLEN TATE: *Poems, 1922–1947.* The poet's selection of his most important work.

MARK VAN DOREN: *New Poems.* A collection of over one hundred poems on a wide range of subjects and styles, from philosophical meditations to lullabies.

PETER VIERECK (b. 1916): *Terror and Decorum.* Viereck's first volume of poetry, mostly reflecting war experience, wins the Teitjens Prize and the Pulitzer Prize and alerts readers and critics alike to a writer to watch. He previously published a study of Nazism, *Metapolitics* (1941), and his novella, *Who Killed the Universe?* appeared in 1948. His subsequent collections would include *Strike Through the Mask!* (1950), *The First Morning* (1952), and *The Persimmon Tree* (1956).

Publications and Events

Books in Print. An annual listing of books published in and available in the United States begins publication.

The *Hudson Review.* After graduating from Princeton, Frederick Morgan (b. 1922) launches and edits this literary quarterly, which helps promulgate the New Criticism.

1949

Drama and Theater

MAXWELL ANDERSON: *Lost in the Stars.* Anderson adapts Alan Paton's novel *Cry, the Beloved Country* (1948) about apartheid in South Africa into a musical, with songs by Kurt Weill.

MARC BLITZSTEIN: *Regina.* This opera is based on Lillian Hellman's play *The Little Foxes.*

OSCAR HAMMERSTEIN II, JOSHUA LOGAN (1908–1988), AND RICHARD RODGERS: *South Pacific.* The team adapts two of James A. Michener's stories from *Tales of the South Pacific* to create a classic American musical, the second to be awarded a Pulitzer Prize. The story of navy nurse Nellie Forbush's relationship with a French planter who has fathered children with a native woman

adds a social component to the drama that — like *Oklahoma!* — incorporates realistic situations and believable dialogue into a musical.

SIDNEY KINGSLEY: *Detective Story.* Kingsley's gritty melodrama set in a New York police precinct house concerns a disillusioned and ethically compromised detective. It would be adapted as a movie, starring Kirk Douglas, in 1951.

ARTHUR MILLER: *Death of a Salesman.* Willy Loman, an aging salesman "riding on a smile and a shoe shine," confronts the consequences of his career on the road in the decade's most acclaimed play. A lacerating portrait of a man, his family, and the concept of the American Dream, Miller's play wins the Pulitzer Prize and is widely regarded as one of the most significant accomplishments of the American theater.

GERTRUDE STEIN: *Last Operas and Plays.* A collection of nineteen dramatic works written by Stein between 1917 and 1945.

Fiction

NELSON ALGREN: *The Man with the Golden Arm.* Winner of the first National Book Award, Algren's gritty novel, set in Chicago's Polish community, concerns card dealer and morphine addict Frankie Machine. A bestseller despite its strong theme, the novel is the first serious treatment of drug addiction in American literature and would be turned into a successful 1955 film directed by Otto Preminger and starring Frank Sinatra.

PAUL BOWLES (1910–1999): *The Sheltering Sky.* Bowles's first novel traces the disintegration of an American couple who travel into the North African desert. Regarded as a cult classic of existentialism, it is one of the defining novels of the postwar period. Bowles, who studied with Aaron Copland and Virgil Thompson, was a composer who produced the opera *The Wind Remains* (1943). Bowles met Gertrude Stein in the 1930s, and she suggested that he explore Morocco, where he would live for much of the rest of his life.

KAY BOYLE: *His Human Majesty.* In this novel, a multinational ski troop trains in Colorado for action against the Nazis in 1944.

FREDERICK BUECHNER (b. 1926): *A Long Day's Dying.* Buechner's ambitious, Jamesian first novel concerns a widow who conceals her affair with her son's teacher by alleging a homosexual relationship between her son and the teacher.

W. R. BURNETT: *The Asphalt Jungle.* The first volume of the author's City trilogy portrays the "corruption of a whole city in three stages: status quo, imbalance, and anarchy." It follows the effect of a jewel heist on a gang of criminals in an unnamed Midwestern city. It would be followed by *Little Men, Big World* (1951) and *Vanity Row* (1952).

JOHN HORNE BURNS: *Lucifer with a Book.* Burns's second novel examines the postwar world from the perspective of new faculty, an ex-WAC, and a disfigured infantry veteran at a private boys' school.

ERSKINE CALDWELL: *A Place Called Estherville.* In this installment of what the author describes as his "cyclorama of Southern life," Caldwell takes up the subject of racial conflict in a small Southern town.

TRUMAN CAPOTE: *Tree of Life, and Other Stories.* Capote's collection is described by one critic as exposing "a sinister underwater universe populated by monstrous children, expressionistic automata, and zombie adults."

MARY ELLEN CHASE: *The Plum Tree.* Set in a home for aged women, the novel concerns a day when three old ladies are to be transferred to an asylum.

WALTER VAN TILBURG CLARK: *The Track of the Cat.* Clark's final novel is a symbolic depiction of the struggle between good and evil as revealed in a panther hunt on a remote Nevada ranch.

JOHN DOS PASSOS: *The Grand Design.* In the conclusion of his trilogy on the Spottswood family, Dos Passos chronicles the New Deal years and the failures of the Roosevelt administration. Despite praise for the novel's vivid evocation of Washington during the Depression and World War II, critics detect a conservative shift in Dos Passos's views and a reduction of his former daring experimental methods to the simplifications of a propagandist.

WILLIAM FAULKNER: *Knight's Gambit.* A story collection featuring country attorney Gavin Stephens in Faulkner's version of the detective genre. According to critic Malcolm Cowley, the work is "the slightest . . . and the pleasantest of all the books that Faulkner has published."

SHELBY FOOTE (b. 1916): *Tournament.* Foote's debut novel begins his exploration of his native Mississippi Delta community through the plight of a farmer during the post–Civil War period.

A. B. GUTHRIE: *The Way West.* Guthrie wins the Pulitzer Prize for this chronicle of an overland trek by wagon train along the Oregon Trail in 1846.

JOHN HAWKES (1925–1998): *The Cannibal.* Hawkes's first novel is a nightmarish vision of occupied Germany as a plot is hatched to assassinate the lone American overseer. Hawkes said, "I began to write fiction on the assumption that the true enemies of the novel were plot, character, setting, and theme." In this, his first fictional experiment, he replaces what he abandoned with "totality of vision" and "structure — verbal and psychological coherence."

ALFRED HAYES: *The Girl on Via Flaminia.* Hayes's story of an American G.I.'s relationship with an Italian girl is a moody portrait of cultural difference separating the conqueror and the conquered. Critic Siegfried Mandel observes, "With more substance and intensity, . . . [it] conceivably could have been this war's *A Farewell to Arms.*"

SINCLAIR LEWIS: *The God-Seeker.* Lewis's penultimate novel is a historical story set in Minnesota in the 1850s. Intended as part of a projected series that Lewis never completed, it is mainly noteworthy for exposing the decline of Lewis's skills, evident as well in his final novel, *World So Wide* (1951), about an American in Europe, which would be published posthumously.

ROSS MacDONALD (1915–1983): *The Moving Target.* MacDonald (a pseudonym for Kenneth Miller) introduces Southern California private detective Lew Archer in the first of a popular series of psychologically oriented mysteries.

FREDERICK MANFRED (FREDERICK FEIKEMA): *The Primitive.* The first volume in the author's World Wanderer trilogy follows the career of a Siouxland farm boy to college. His story would continue in *The Brother* (1950) and *The Giant* (1951).

J. P. MARQUAND: *Point of No Return.* As a banker awaits news of a promotion, he returns to his Massachusetts home to review his life.

MARY McCARTHY: *The Oasis.* The writer takes satirical aim at the contemporary intellectual elite in this novel describing an attempt to establish a utopian society on a New England mountaintop.

JAMES A. MICHENER: *The Fires of Spring.* Michener's follow-up to *Tales of the South Pacific* is an autobiographical character study of a Pennsylvania youth who eventually discovers his vocation as a writer.

TOSHIO MORI (1910–1980): *Yokohama, California.* Scheduled for publication in 1942, this story collection dealing with the West Coast Japanese American community was delayed when its author was interned during the war. His subsequent collections are *Woman from Hiroshima* (1979) and *The Chauvinist and Other Stories* (1979).

HOWARD NEMEROV: *The Melodramatists.* Nemerov's first novel is a satiric portrait of a Boston family's frustrated search for meaning in their lives.

JOHN O'HARA: *A Rage to Live.* O'Hara breaks a long silence with his most ambitious work, about the destruction of a marriage by an unfaithful wife. The writer would later observe that his "earlier books were special books about specialized people; but this is the big one, the overall one." An unfavorable review in *The New Yorker* prompts O'Hara to break relations with the magazine for eleven years.

ELMER RICE: *The Show Must Go On.* Rice supplies an insider's view of the theatrical world in a novel about the travails of a young playwright's Broadway debut.

JACK SCHAEFER (1907–1991): *Shane.* Schaefer's first and best-known novel is a western classic about a young boy's relationship with a former gunfighter who comes to work on his family's farm and gets involved in the violent clash between the farmers and cattlemen. *Shane* would be followed by other significant contributions to the western genre, including *The Canyon* (1953), *Company of Cowards* (1957), *Old Ramon* (1960), and *Monte Walsh* (1963).

GEORGE RIPPEY STEWART: *Earth Abides.* The author's third treatment of a natural disaster looks at the aftermath of a worldwide viral epidemic, which leaves only a handful of survivors. The book is regarded as a science fiction classic.

GORE VIDAL: *The Season of Comfort.* A young painter growing up between the wars in a prominent Washington family struggles to escape the domination of his selfish mother and the pressure to conform.

EUDORA WELTY: *The Golden Apples.* This short story sequence chronicles life in a small Mississippi town, employing mythical echoings and a displacement of conventional gender boundaries.

Literary Criticism and Scholarship

T. S. ELIOT: *Notes Towards the Definition of Culture.* Eliot takes up Matthew Arnold's role as cultural critic in this consideration of the concept of culture and its social impact.

LANGSTON HUGHES AND ARNA BONTEMPS: *Poetry of the Negro, 1746–1949.* A groundbreaking anthology of poetry from African American and Caribbean writers.

PHILIP RAHV (1908–1973): *Image and Idea.* Rahv's critical collection includes the paradigm-creating essay "Paleface and Redskin," which identifies a dichotomy between experience and consciousness among American writers. Rahv, who came to the United States as a child from Russia, cofounded the *Partisan Reivew* in 1933.

AUSTIN WARREN (1899–1986) AND RENÉ WELLEK (1903–1989): *Theory of Literature.* In one of the most influential and comprehensive analyses of the New Criticism, the

Eleanor Roosevelt

authors compare the "extrinsic approach" to literature, which emphasizes biography and history, with the "intrinsic approach" of the New Criticism, which concentrates on the work itself. Granting the importance of knowing the conditions out of which literary works emerged, they argue that such knowledge cannot take the place of "description, analysis, and evaluation" of the work itself.

Nonfiction

JOHN GUNTHER: *Death Be Not Proud.* The journalist provides a moving tribute to his seventeen-year-old son, who died of a brain tumor in 1947.

MARGARET MEAD: *Male and Female: A Study of the Sexes in a Changing World.* Applying insights derived from studying Pacific Islanders, Mead considers gender differences, similarities, traits, and problems.

THOMAS MERTON: *The Waters of Siloe* and *Seeds of Contemplation.* The former is a history of the Trappist order; the latter, reflections on prayer and the spiritual life. Both are bestsellers.

HENRY MILLER: *Sexus.* Published in Paris, this is the first volume of the author's trilogy The Rosy Crucifixion, a memoir of Miller's life prior to his departure for Europe in 1930. It would be followed by *Plexus* (1953) and

Nexus (1960) and published in America by Grove Press in 1965.

AUDIE MURPHY (1924–1971): *To Hell and Back.* The most decorated American soldier in World War II offers a diary account of his combat experience. Murphy would later play himself in a 1955 film version of the story.

S. J. PERELMAN: *Listen to the Mocking Bird.* A collection of the humorist's sketches for *The New Yorker*, including "Cloudland Revisted," a reevaluation of the bestsellers of the 1920s.

ELEANOR ROOSEVELT: *This I Remember.* In a continuation of her previous autobiographical volume, *This Is My Story* (1937), Roosevelt covers the years 1924 to 1945 in what is regarded as the best memoir produced by a First Lady.

LILLIAN SMITH: *Killers of the Dream.* The author of *Strange Fruit* (1944) applies a Freudian method to understand Southern race relations.

E. B. WHITE: *Here Is New York.* White celebrates New York City in this essay collection.

Poetry

CONRAD AIKEN: *Divine Pilgrim* and *Skylight One.* The first volume is a series of "philosophical symphonies" on the problem of identity and consciousness; the second is a collection of love poems and observations on the American scene.

GWENDOLYN BROOKS: *Annie Allen.* The poet's second volume is a coming-of-age verse narrative of a black girl's development and struggles with poverty and racial identity. For her achievement, Brooks becomes the first black author to win the Pulitzer Prize.

JOHN CIARDI: *Live Another Day.* Ciardi's third volume includes an introductory essay on the nature of poetry and the responsibilities of the reader and the poet.

KENNETH FEARING: *Stranger at Coney Island and Other Poems.* Criticism of this volume of urban scenes suggests that the poet's best work is behind him, a sentiment that contributes to Fearing's abandonment of poetry for fiction until 1955.

LANGSTON HUGHES: *One-Way Ticket.* The poet returns to black urban themes and features one of his most endearing creations, Alberta K. Johnson, in the poem "Madam to You."

MURIEL RUKEYSER: *Orpheus.* This long poem turns the Orpheus myth into an allegory of the fate of the artist.

LOUIS SIMPSON (b. 1923): *The Arrivistes: Poems, 1940–49.* The poet's first collection shows promise in the use of conventional verse forms to consider a wide range of social and cultural issues, many reflecting Simpson's combat experience. Simpson was born in Jamaica, saw combat in Europe as a paratrooper, and would earn his reputation chronicling wartime experience and the contradictions of the American Dream.

Publication and Events

American Heritage. Founded by the American Association for State and Local History, the magazine was expanded into a hardbound journal of American history for a general audience in 1954.

American Quarterly. This scholarly journal devoted to American studies begins publication at the University of Minnesota.

The Bollingen Prize in Poetry. Ezra Pound is the first recipient of this award, for the *Pisan Cantos*, prompting widespread protest. Acting on a congressional recommendation, the U.S. Library of Congress halts all awards given for art, literature, and music. The Bollingen Prize was reinstated in 1950, administered by the Yale University Library.

V

Modernism and Postmodernism

1950–1999

THE LAST FIVE decades of the twentieth century are the most perplexing and contradictory in American history. The United States ended the century triumphant, the last superpower left standing after a protracted ideological struggle with the Soviet Union. During the period, the standard of living, freedom, and opportunity Americans enjoyed became the envy of the world. The nation's scientific prowess put men on the moon and pioneered a computer revolution comparable in its impact to the invention of the printing press. American ideas and innovations had achieved an unrivaled dominant position in political, economic, and cultural affairs worldwide by the century's end.

Yet the period 1950–1999 is also one of the most socially disruptive eras in American history. Losing the first war in U.S. history traumatized the American psyche, as did the assassinations of John F. Kennedy, Martin Luther King Jr., and Robert Kennedy. The struggles for racial justice, gender equality, and sexual freedom fractured the nation. Despite great technological advances and apparent plenty, America seemed increasingly a frustratingly dangerous and threatening place. If one dominant theme of the period was liberation — the redefinition of traditional concepts of gender, race, and class — a countertheme was the dissolution of long-esteemed sources of order and authority, necessitating an anxious search for sustaining values. In a society that increasingly seemed to lack coherence and consensus, the writers of the period became preoccupied with defining who Americans were. They reveled in an unprecedented freedom of expression but were as beset by the same underlying tensions, uncertainties, and paradoxes that their readers faced.

In retrospect, the 1950s represents a benchmark of stability against which to measure the changes to come. The decade, at least as we nostalgically recall it, seemed the calm before the storm, an era of material prosperity, contentment, and conformity. The postwar economy supported a growing middle class who redefined the American Dream as owning a home, fitted with the latest labor-saving appliances, in burgeoning suburban America. Large families, stay-at-home mothers, and "Father Knows Best" were the norm for the culturally dominant white middle class. Despite a war in Korea, anxiety over nuclear annihilation, and anti-Communist hysteria fomented by Senator Joseph McCarthy and others, Americans during the 1950s were determined to enjoy their prosperity and their dominance in the world. Much of the serious writing during the decade challenged that complacency. The ruling aesthetic was still that of the pre-war literary modernists, including Ernest Hemingway, William Faulkner, T. S. Eliot, Ezra Pound, and Eugene O'Neill, whose final significant works appeared during the 1950s. New directions and divergent points of view began to appear from Southerners, such as Flannery O'Connor (*A Good Man Is Hard to Find*, 1955), who blended regional, grotesque, and spiritual elements into darkly comic existential works that helped revitalize the American short story. Jewish American writers such as Saul Bellow, Bernard Malamud, Isaac Bashevis Singer, and Philip Roth provided an alternative to the WASP norm. African American writers such as Ralph Ellison, James Baldwin, and Lorraine Hansberry produced innovative and searing works on America's racial divide.

If these writers challenged the narrow and smug perspective of many Americans during the decade, more direct and extensive critiques of their values and limitations came from a number of provocative sociological and cultural studies. David Riesman's *The Lonely Crowd* (1950) anatomized American conformity, the subject also of Sloan Wilson's novel *The Man in the Gray Flannel Suit* (1955). C. Wright Mills's *White Collar* (1951) assessed the American middle class, while his *The Power Elite* (1956) suggested that the control of America rested in a powerful corporate, military, and political cadre. Paul Goodman's *Growing Up Absurd* (1959) analyzed the contradictions faced by the young in a materially oriented but spiritually empty society. Youthful angst and alienation in a world dominated by adult "phoniness" were the subjects of J. D. Salinger's iconic 1950s novel *The Catcher in the Rye* (1951). Rebellion and protest over accepted American values and conventional literary methods formed the agenda of the Beats, a collection of New York and San Francisco writers including Jack Kerouac, Allen Ginsberg, Lawrence Ferlinghetti, and Gary Snyder, who became the precursors of the counterculture of the 1960s. Ginsberg's *Howl* (1956) and Kerouac's *On the Road* (1957) were milestone works of dissent from accepted societal norms that also expressed an experimental aesthetic of spontaneity and personal intensity in opposition to the detached formalism of the literary modernists. By decade's end, a spirit of opposition, new viewpoints, and experimental modes of expression were coalescing to produce the cultural revolution of the 1960s.

Bounded by the presidential elections of John F. Kennedy and Richard M. Nixon, dominated by the civil rights movement, opposition to the war in Vietnam, and a youth culture that challenged social norms with drug use and sexual experimentation, the 1960s were among the most expressive and experimental years in American literary history. In 1959, Grove Press's publication of D. H. Lawrence's *Lady Chatterley's Lover* effectively ended censorship in America, a harbinger of the subsequent decade's assault on traditional values. While some novelists such as John Cheever and John Updike relied on realistic methods to survey the social and personal dislocations of the period, others pursued a more radical approach. Joseph Heller's *Catch-22* (1961) and Kurt Vonnegut's *Slaughterhouse-Five* (1969) reimagined World War II as absurdist comedy, while Ken Kesey's *One Flew over the Cuckoo's Nest* (1962) inverted accepted views of madness and sanity and celebrated the heroism of the nonconformist rebel. Others, such as John Barth, John Hawkes, Robert Coover, Thomas Pynchon, and Donald Barthelme, destabilized novelistic conventions with a self-reflective, ironic antirealism that established the basic outlines of postmodernism. Still others undermined the distinction between the novel and nonfiction, between subjective and objective representation, in works such as Truman Capote's *In Cold Blood* (1966), Norman Mailer's *Armies of the Night* (1968), and the so-called New Journalism practiced by Tom Wolfe (*The Kandy-Kolored Tangerine-Flake Streamline Baby*, 1965; *The Electric Kool-Aid Acid Test*, 1968).

In poetry, Robert Lowell's intensely personal *Life Studies* (1959) challenged modernist detachment and initiated a new introspective, intimately autobiographical mode of expression of the so-called confessional poets, who included W. D. Snodgrass, Anne Sexton, John Berryman, and Sylvia Plath. Other poets, such as Gwendolyn Brooks, Denise Levertov, and Adrienne Rich, emphasized public rather than private themes, confronting the major political, gender, and racial issues of the period.

In drama Edward Albee became the most prominent of a new generation of playwrights, who created one of the most experimental periods in American theater history. Strongly influenced by European drama, particularly the theater of the absurd, Albee and playwrights such as Jack Gelber and Arthur Kopit challenged audiences with both strong social and psychological content and symbolic, nonrepresentational techniques. The creative energy of American drama shifted during the decade from Broadway to off-Broadway and off-off-Broadway venues and to experimental and regional companies that served as launch pads for the careers of playwrights such as LeRoi Jones (Amiri Baraka), Ed Bullins, Sam Shepard, and Lanford Wilson.

If the 1960s saw an explosion of creative energy released by new modes of expression and imaginative responses to the crisis and contradictions of American experience, the 1970s were years of consolidation of energies and a transition to the more socially conservative, self-centered 1980s and 1990s, as once-radical ideas joined with, but became diluted in, the main current of American thought. Increasingly, the writer as college faculty member came to dominate American literary culture. Subsidized by a teaching salary, American writers of so-called serious literature relied far less on reaching a wide popular audience. The effect was to widen the gap between highbrow and lowbrow writing, with the bestseller list dominated by less demanding formulaic entertainment. Movies and television, rather than books, increasingly became the principal means to reach a mass audience.

Among the noteworthy achievements during the 1970s were the first major imaginative assessments of the Vietnam experience and its personal and national costs, including Robert Stone's *Dog Soldiers* (1974), David Rabe's *Sticks and Bones* (1972) and *Streamers* (1976), Michael Herr's *Dispatches* (1977), Philip Caputo's *A Rumor of War* (1977), and Tim O'Brien's *Going After Cacciato* (1978). Other fictional accomplishments of the period included Thomas Pynchon's encyclopedic rendering of World War II and its aftermath in forming modern consciousness (*Gravity's Rainbow*, 1973), E. L. Doctorow's remarkable fictional reanimation of American history at the turn of the century (*Ragtime*, 1975), and the first novels of Toni Morrison, who would become one of the few challenging literary authors to claim a wide popular audience. The major poets of the period include James Merrill and John Ashbery. In drama several important American playwrights, including David Mamet, Charles Durang, and Beth Henley, achieved their initial successes.

During the 1980s and 1990s important work continued to appear from authors who remained productive throughout the entire five decades, such as Saul Bellow, Norman Mailer, Philip Roth, John Updike, and Gore Vidal. One of the most important trends was the emergence of stripped-down realism used to portray everyday American life. Labeled minimalism, it was most often associated with the short fiction of Raymond Carver. The postmodernist fabulists, such as John Barth, Thomas Pynchon, and Don DeLillo, along with the neo-realists, such as Carver, Bobbie Anne Mason, and Richard Ford, set in motion an oscillation between the centrifugal and the centripetal, between writers who tried to encompass all of the protean American experience in their works and others who sought to strip its often baffling complexities down to essentials — polarities that characterize much of the writing of the period.

American writing during the final years of the twentieth century lacked a dominating synthesizing presence of the magnitude of William Faulkner, Ernest Hemingway, or T. S. Eliot. In compensation, the diversity of ethnic and racial perspectives broadened the concept of what constitutes American experience. Toni Morrison, who in 1993 became the first American writer of color to be awarded the Nobel Prize in literature, headed the distinguished list of successful and acclaimed African American fiction writers of the period, which included Alice Walker, Ernest Gaines, John Edgar Wideman, Charles Johnson, and Terry McMillan. African American poets of note included Maya Angelou (selected to read a poem at President Bill Clinton's inauguration in 1993), Michael Harper, Audre Lord, and Rita Dove, chosen as Poet Laureate in 1993. Prominent Asian American writers included Maxine Hong Kingston, Amy Tan, David Henry Hwang, Frank Chin, Cathy Song, Garrett Hongo, and Chang-Rae Lee. Among the leading Hispanic writers were Rolando Hinojosa, Oscar Hijuelos, Lorna Dee Cisneros, Sandra Cisneros, Julia Alvarez, and Denise Chavez. Native American writers of note included N. Scott Momaday, Leslie Marmon Silko, James Welch, and Louise Erdrich.

At the end of the millennium American writers continued to struggle with America's destiny and identity, issues that have dominated the national debate since the nation's founding. What differed markedly was the unprecedented diversity of opinion and imaginative expression that emerged out of the social and cultural upheavals that characterized one of the most dynamic periods in American history.

1950

Drama and Theater

ABE BURROWS (1910–1985) AND FRANK LOESSER (1910–1969): *Guys and Dolls.* Based on Damon Runyon's short stories about Broadway gamblers and showgirls, the musical features a double romance concerning crap-game operator Nathan Detroit and his long-suffering girlfriend, Adelaide, and gambler Sky Masterson's relationship with the Salvation Army's Sister Sarah, whom he courts on a bet. Its exuberant use of street slang and cohesion of song and story have made it one of the most popular and influential American musicals. Burrows was a former radio and television writer whose later hits would include *Can-Can* (1953), *Silk Stockings* (1955), and *How to Succeed in Business Without Really Trying* (1961).

T. S. ELIOT: *The Cocktail Party.* Eliot's play employs a standard dramatic device — an uninvited outsider — to address the issue of religious faith. Written in blank verse that is almost conversational in effect, the play baffles the critics but has a nearly year-long run on Broadway.

WILLIAM INGE (1913–1973): *Come Back, Little Sheba.* Inge's first Broadway success is generally considered his best play — a psychologically realistic portrait of a childless married couple who deal with their disappointments through alcohol and wish-fulfilling delusions. Inge was born in Kansas and worked as the drama critic for the *St. Louis Star-Times* from 1943 until his first play, *Farther off from Heaven*, was produced in Dallas in 1947.

CARSON McCULLERS: *The Member of the Wedding.* The author adapts her 1946 novel about an adolescent's response to her brother's wedding plans. Despite critical skepticism that a play so lacking in dramatic action could work, it is a popular success, noteworthy for touching on race relations in a Southern town in the 1940s.

CLIFFORD ODETS: *The Country Girl.* Odets would later dismiss this backstage drama, about an alcoholic actor trying for a comeback and his protective, abused wife, as lacking his characteristic social critique and written solely for money. However, after *Golden Boy*, it is Odets's biggest success.

BIRTHS AND DEATHS, 1950–1959

Births

1950　Carolyn Forché, poet
　　　Edward Hirsch, poet
　　　Gloria Naylor, novelist
　　　Alex D. Pate, novelist
　　　Wendy Wasserstein, playwright

1951　Jorie Graham, poet
　　　Terry McMillan, novelist

1952　William Boyd, novelist
　　　Christopher Bram, novelist
　　　Michael Cunningham, novelist
　　　Andrew Delbanco, author
　　　Rita Dove, poet
　　　Walter Mosley, novelist
　　　Amy Tan, novelist

1953　Brad Leithauser, poet
　　　Alice McDermott, novelist
　　　Cornell West, writer and social critic

1954　Louise Erdrich, novelist and poet
　　　Harvey Fierstein, playwright and actor

1955　John Grisham, novelist
　　　Barbara Kingsolver, novelist
　　　Jay McInerney, novelist

1956　Patricia Cornwell, novelist
　　　David Guterson, novelist
　　　Tony Kushner, playwright

1957　Madison Smartt Bell, novelist
　　　David Henry Hwang, novelist
　　　Richard Powers, novelist

Deaths

1950　Irving Bacheller (b. 1859), novelist
　　　William Rose Benét (b. 1886), poet, author, and editor
　　　Edgar Rice Burroughs (b. 1875), novelist and science fiction author

　　　James Gould Fletcher (b. 1886), poet
　　　Edgar Lee Masters (b. 1868), poet and biographer
　　　Edna St. Vincent Millay (b. 1892), poet and playwright
　　　Ernest Poole (b. 1880), novelist and journalist
　　　Agnes Repplier (b. 1858), author and critic
　　　Carl Van Doren (b. 1885), historian, editor, and critic

1951　Louis Adamic (b. 1899), novelist and journalist
　　　Lloyd C. Douglas (b. 1877), novelist
　　　Sinclair Lewis (b. 1885), novelist

1952　George Santayana (b. 1863), philosopher, poet, novelist, and critic

1953　Douglas Southall Freeman (b. 1886), historian
　　　Eugene O'Neill (b. 1888), playwright
　　　Marjorie Kinnan Rawlings (b. 1896), novelist

1954　Frederick Lewis Allen (b. 1890), historian and editor
　　　Leonard Bacon (b. 1887), poet and critic
　　　Maxwell Bodenheim (b. 1893), poet, playwright, and novelist
　　　Samuel Shellabarger (b. 1888), novelist

1955　James Agee (b. 1909), poet, novelist, screenwriter, and critic
　　　Bernard De Voto (b. 1897), historian and novelist
　　　Weldon Kees, (b. 1914), poet and short story writer
　　　Robert E. Sherwood (b. 1896), playwright
　　　Wallace Stevens (b. 1879), poet
　　　Robert P. Tristram Coffin (b. 1892), poet

1956　Michael Arlen (b. 1895), novelist and short story writer
　　　H. L. Mencken (b. 1880), journalist, editor, and critic

1958　Eleanor Hallowell Abbott (b. 1872), novelist and short story writer
　　　Zoë Akins (b. 1886), playwright and poet
　　　James Branch Cabell (b. 1879), novelist
　　　Dorothy Canfield Fisher (b. 1879), novelist
　　　Mary Roberts Rinehart (b. 1876), mystery writer

1959　Maxwell Anderson (b. 1888), playwright
　　　Raymond Chandler (b. 1888), mystery writer

JOHN STEINBECK: *Burning Bright.* The only work Steinbeck wrote initially for the stage is his last dramatic work, closing after only thirteen performances. Conceived as a modern morality play about a man's acceptance of a child fathered by another, it employs expressionistic techniques, with universalized characters and symbolic settings, elements of what Steinbeck calls "this new form—the play-novelette."

JOHN VAN DRUTEN: *Bell, Book, and Candle.* Van Druten's urbane comedy concerns a modern witch who decides to forgo her supernatural powers when she falls in love with an ordinary man. It would be adapted into a successful film in 1958, starring Kim Novak and James Stewart.

EDMUND WILSON: *The Little Blue Light.* Wilson's futuristic fantasy of totalitarian control baffles the critics, one of whom writes that if the play "is a joke, it is no laughing matter."

Fiction

ISAAC ASIMOV (1920–1992): *I, Robot.* Asimov's first book is a groundbreaking short story collection describing a future society in which humans coexist with nearly sentient robots. The work earns literary credibility for the genre of science fiction and furthers its development, particularly the realistic aspects of the story line. Asimov would write about robots in two subsequent novels, *The Caves of Steel* (1954) and *The Naked Sun* (1957). Born in Russia, Asimov earned a Ph.D. from Columbia in 1947 and taught biochemistry at the Boston University School of Medicine.

PAUL BOWLES: *The Delicate Prey and Other Stories.* Bowles presents disturbing images and existential themes in exotic locales in this story collection, which prompts critic Leslie Fiedler to call the author "the pornographer of terror." It includes the frequently anthologized story "A Distant Episode," in which an American professor is

BESTSELLERS, 1950–1959

Fiction

1950

1. *The Cardinal* by Henry Morton Robinson
2. *Joy Street* by Frances Parkinson Keyes
3. *Across the River and into the Trees* by Ernest Hemingway
4. *The Wall* by John Hersey
5. *Star Money* by Kathleen Winsor
6. *The Parasites* by Daphne du Maurier
7. *Floodtide* by Frank Yerby
8. *Jubilee Trail* by Gwen Bristow
9. *The Adventurer* by Mika Waltari
10. *The Disenchanted* by Budd Schulberg

1951

1. *From Here to Eternity* by James Jones
2. *The Caine Mutiny* by Herman Wouk
3. *Moses* by Sholem Asch
4. *The Cardinal* by Henry Morton Robinson
5. *A Woman Called Fancy* by Frank Yerby
6. *The Cruel Sea* by Nicholas Monsarrat
7. *Melville Goodwin, U.S.A.* by J. P. Marquand
8. *Return to Paradise* by James A. Michener
9. *The Foundling* by Cardinal Spellman
10. *The Wanderer* by Mike Waltari

1952

1. *The Silver Chalice* by Thomas B. Costain
2. *The Caine Mutiny* by Herman Wouk
3. *East of Eden* by John Steinbeck
4. *My Cousin Rachel* by Daphne du Maurier
5. *Steamboat Gothic* by Frances Parkinson Keyes
6. *Giant* by Edna Ferber
7. *The Old Man and the Sea* by Ernest Hemingway
8. *The Gown of Glory* by Agnes Sligh Turnbull
9. *The Saracen Blade* by Frank Yerby
10. *The Houses in Between* by Howard Spring

1953

1. *The Robe* by Lloyd C. Douglas
2. *The Silver Chalice* by Thomas B. Costain
3. *Désirée* by Annemarie Selinko
4. *Battle Cry* by Leon Uris
5. *From Here to Eternity* by James Jones
6. *The High and the Mighty* by Ernest K. Gann
7. *Beyond This Place* by A. J. Cronin
8. *Time and Time Again* by James Hilton
9. *Lord Vanity* by Samuel Shellabarger
10. *The Unconquered* by Ben Ames Williams

1954

1. *Not as a Stranger* by Morton Thompson
2. *Mary Anne* by Daphne du Maurier
3. *Love Is Eternal* by Irving Stone
4. *The Royal Box* by Frances Parkinson Keyes
5. *The Egyptian* by Mika Waltari
6. *No Time for Sergeants* by Mac Hyman
7. *Sweet Thursday* by John Steinbeck
8. *The View from Pompey's Head* by Hamilton Basso
9. *Never Victorious, Never Defeated* by Taylor Caldwell
10. *Benton's Row* by Frank Yerby

1955

1. *Marjorie Morningstar* by Herman Wouk
2. *Auntie Mame* by Patrick Dennis
3. *Andersonville* by MacKinlay Kantor
4. *Bonjour Tristesse* by Françoise Sagan
5. *The Man in the Gray Flannel Suit* by Sloan Wilson
6. *Something of Value* by Robert Ruark
7. *Not as a Stranger* by Morton Thompson
8. *No Time for Sergeants* by Mac Hyman
9. *The Tontine* by Thomas B. Costain
10. *Ten North Frederick* by John O'Hara

1956

1. *Don't Go Near the Water* by William Brinkley
2. *The Last Hurrah* by Edwin O'Connor
3. *Peyton Place* by Grace Metalious
4. *Auntie Mame* by Patrick Dennis
5. *Eloise* by Kay Thompson
6. *Andersonville* by MacKinlay Kantor
7. *A Certain Smile* by Françoise Sagan
8. *The Tribe That Lost Its Head* Nicholas Monsarrat
9. *The Mandarins* by Simone de Beauvoir
10. *Boon Island* by Kenneth Roberts

1957

1. *By Love Possessed* by James Gould Cozzens
2. *Peyton Place* by Grace Metalious
3. *Compulsion* by Meyer Levin
4. *Rally 'Round the Flag, Boys!* by Max Schulman
5. *Blue Camellia* by Frances Parkinson Keyes
6. *Eloise in Paris* by Kay Thompson
7. *The Scapegoat* by Daphne du Maurier
8. *On the Beach* by Nevil Shute
9. *Below the Salt* by Thomas B. Costain
10. *Atlas Shrugged* by Ayn Rand

1958

1. *Doctor Zhivago* by Boris Pasternak
2. *Anatomy of a Murder* by Robert Traver
3. *Lolita* by Vladimir Nabokov
4. *Around the World with Auntie Mame* by Patrick Dennis
5. *From the Terrace* by John O'Hara
6. *Eloise at Christmastime* by Kay Thompson
7. *Ice Palace* by Edna Ferber
8. *The Winthrop Woman* by Anya Seton
9. *The Enemy Camp* by Jerome Weidman
10. *Victorian* by Frances Parkinson Keyes

1959

1. *Exodus* by Leon Uris
2. *Doctor Zhivago* by Boris Pasternak
3. *Hawaii* by James A. Michener
4. *Advise and Consent* by Allen Drury
5. *Lady Chatterley's Lover* by D. H. Lawrence
6. *The Ugly American* by William J. Lederer and Eugene L. Burdick
7. *Dear and Glorious Physician* by Taylor Caldwell
8. *Lolita* by Vladimir Nabokov
9. *Mrs. 'Arris Goes to Paris* by Paul Gallico
10. *Poor No More* by Robert Ruark

BESTSELLERS, 1950–1959

Nonfiction

1950

1. *Betty Crocker's Picture Cook Book*
2. *The Baby* (Picture book published by Simon & Schuster)
3. *Look Younger, Live Longer* by Gaylord Hauser
4. *How I Raised Myself from Failure to Success in Selling* by Frank Bettger
5. *Kon-Tiki* by Thor Heyerdahl
6. *Mr. Jones, Meet the Master* by Peter Marshall
7. *Your Dream Home* by Hubbard Cobb
8. *The Mature Mind* by H. A. Overstreet
9. *Campus Zoo* by Clare Barnes Jr.
10. *Belles on Their Toes* by Frank Gilbreth Jr. and Ernestine Gilbreth

1951

1. *Look Younger, Live Longer* by Gaylord Hauser
2. *Betty Crocker's Picture Cook Book*
3. *Washington Confidential* by Jack Lait and Lee Mortimer
4. *Better Homes and Gardens Garden Book*
5. *Better Homes and Gardens Handyman's Book*
6. *The Sea Around Us* by Rachel L. Carson
7. *Thorndike-Barnhart Comprehensive Desk Dictionary* edited by Clarence L. Barnhart
8. *Pogo* by Walt Kelly
9. *Kon-Tiki* by Thor Heyerdahl
10. *The New Yorker Twenty-Fifth Anniversary Album*

1952

1. *The Holy Bible: Revised Standard Version*
2. *A Man Called Peter* by Catherine Marshall
3. *U.S.A. Confidential* by Jack Lait and Lee Mortimer
4. *The Sea Around Us* by Rachel L. Carson
5. *Tallulah* by Tallulah Bankhead
6. *The Power of Positive Thinking* by Norman Vincent Peale
7. *This I Believe* edited by Edward P. Morgan with a foreword by Edward R. Murrow
8. *This Is Ike* edited by Wilson Hicks
9. *Witness* by Whittaker Chambers
10. *Mr. President* by William Hillman

1953

1. *The Holy Bible: Revised Standard Version*
2. *The Power of Positive Thinking* by Norman Vincent Peale
3. *Sexual Behavior in the Human Female* by Alfred C. Kinsey
4. *Angel Unaware* by Dale Evans Rogers
5. *Life Is Worth Living* by Fulton J. Sheen
6. *A Man Called Peter* by Catherine Marshall
7. *This I Believe* edited by Edward P. Morgan with a foreword by Edward R. Murrow
8. *The Greatest Faith Ever Known* by Fulton Oursler and G.A.O. Armstrong
9. *How to Play Your Best Golf* by Tommy Armour
10. *A House Is Not a Home* by Polly Adler

1954

1. *The Holy Bible: Revised Standard Version*
2. *The Power of Positive Thinking* by Norman Vincent Peale
3. *Better Homes and Gardens New Cook Book*
4. *Betty Crocker's Good and Easy Cook Book*
5. *The Tumult and the Shouting* by Grantland Rice
6. *I'll Cry Tomorrow* by Lillian Roth, Gerold Frank, and Mike Connolly
7. *The Prayers of Peter Marshall* edited by Catherine Marshall
8. *This I Believe, 2* edited by Raymond Swing

9. *But We Were Born Free* by Elmer Davis
10. *The Saturday Evening Post Treasury* edited by Roger Butterfield

1955

1. *Gift from the Sea* by Anne Morrow Lindbergh
2. *The Power of Positive Thinking* by Norman Vincent Peale
3. *The Family of Man* by Edward Steichen
4. *A Man Called Peter* by Catherine Marshall
5. *How to Live 365 Days a Year* by John A. Schindler
6. *Better Homes and Gardens Diet Book*
7. *The Secret of Happiness* by Billy Graham
8. *Why Johnny Can't Read* by Rudolf Flesch
9. *Inside Africa* by John Gunther
10. *Year of Decisions* by Harry S. Truman

1956

1. *Arthritis and Common Sense, Revised Edition* by Dan Dale Alexander
2. *Webster's New World Dictionary of the American Language, Concise Edition* edited by David B. Guralnik
3. *Betty Crocker's Picture Cook Book, Second Edition*
4. *Etiquette* by Frances Benton
5. *Better Homes and Gardens Barbecue Book*
6. *The Search for Bridey Murphy* by Morey Bernstein
7. *Love or Perish* by Smiley Blanton, M.D.
8. *Better Homes and Gardens Decorating Book*
9. *How to Live 365 Days a Year* by John A. Schindler
10. *The Nun's Story* by Kathryn Hulme

1957

1. *Kids Say the Darndest Things!* by Art Linkletter
2. *The FBI Story* by Don Whitehead
3. *Stay Alive All Your Life* by Norman Vincent Peale
4. *To Live Again* by Catherine Marshall
5. *Better Homes and Gardens Flower Arranging*
6. *Where Did You Go? Out. What Did You Do? Nothing.* by Robert Paul
7. *Baruch: My Own Story* by Bernard M. Baruch
8. *Please Don't Eat the Daisies* by Jean Kerr
9. *The American Heritage Book of Great Historic Places*
10. *The Day Christ Died* by Jim Bishop

1958

1. *Kids Say the Darndest Things!* by Art Linkletter
2. *'Twixt Twelve and Twenty* by Pat Boone
3. *Only in America* by Harry Golden
4. *Masters of Deceit* by J. Edgar Hoover
5. *Please Don't Eat the Daisies* by Jean Kerr
6. *Better Homes and Gardens Salad Book*
7. *The New Testament in Modern English* translated by J. P. Phillips
8. *Aku-Aku* by Thor Heyerdahl
9. *Dear Abby* by Abigail Van Buren
10. *Inside Russia Today* by John Gunther

1959

1. *'Twixt Twelve and Twenty* by Pat Boone
2. *Folk Medicine* by D. C. Jarvis
3. *For 2¢ Plain* by Harry Golden
4. *The Status Seekers* by Vance Packard
5. *Act One* by Moss Hart
6. *Charley Weaver's Letters from Mamma* by Cliff Arquette
7. *The Elements of Style* by William Strunk Jr. and E. B. White
8. *The General Foods Kitchens Cookbook*
9. *Only in America* by Harry Golden
10. *Mine Enemy Grows Older* by Alexander King

AWARDS AND PRIZES, 1950–1959

Bancroft Prize (American History, Diplomacy, or Biography)

1950 *The Great War for the Empire, Vol. III: The Victorious Years 1758–1760*, by Lawrence H. Gipson
Coronado by Herbert E. Bolton

1951 *Our More Perfect Union* by Arthur N. Holcombe
Virgin Land by Henry N. Smith

1952 *Charles Evans Hughes* by Merlo J. Pusey
Origins of the New South by C. Vann Woodward

1953 *The Era of Good Feelings* by George Dangerfield
Rendezvous with Destiny by Eric F. Goldman

1954 *Seedtime of the Republic* by Clinton Rossiter
The Undeclared War by William Langer and S. Everett Gleason

1955 *Great River, the Rio Grande* by Paul Horgan
The Jacksonians by Leonard D. White

1956 *Henry Adams* by Elizabeth Stevenson
Last Full Measure: Lincoln the President by J. G. Randall and Richard N. Current

1957 *Russia Leaves the War* by George F. Kennan
The New Freedom by Arthur S. Link

1958 *The Crisis of the Old Order* by Arthur M. Schlesinger Jr.
A History of American Magazines, Vol. IV by Frank Luther Mott

1959 *Henry Adams, the Middle Years* by Ernest Samuels
The Americans: The Colonial Experience by Daniel J. Boorstin

Bollingen Prize (Poetry)

1950 Wallace Stevens
1951 John Crowe Ransom
1952 Marianne Moore
1953 Archibald MacLeish
William Carlos Williams
1954 W. H. Auden
1955 Léonie Adams
Louise Bogan
1956 Conrad Aiken
1957 Allen Tate
1958 E. E. Cummings
1959 Theodore Roethke

National Book Awards

1950
Fiction: *The Man with the Golden Arm* by Nelson Algren
Nonfiction: *Ralph Waldo Emerson* by Ralph L. Rusk

Poetry: *Paterson III and Selected Poems* by William Carlos Williams

1951
Fiction: *The Collected Stories of William Faulkner* by William Faulkner
Nonfiction: *Herman Melville* by Newton Arvin
Poetry: *The Auroras of Autumn* by Wallace Stevens

1952
Fiction: *From Here to Eternity* by James Jones
Nonfiction: *The Sea Around Us* by Rachel L. Carson
Poetry: *Collected Poems* by Marianne Moore

1953
Fiction: *Invisible Man* by Ralph Ellison
Nonfiction: *The Course of Empire* by Bernard De Voto
Poetry: *Collected Poems: 1917–1952* by Archibald MacLeish

1954
Fiction: *The Adventures of Augie March* by Saul Bellow
Nonfiction: *A Stillness at Appomattox* by Bruce Catton
Poetry: *Collected Poems* by Conrad Aiken

1955
Fiction: *A Fable* by William Faulkner
Nonfiction: *The Measure of Man* by Joseph Wood Krutch
Poetry: *Collected Poems* by Wallace Stevens

1956
Fiction: *Ten North Frederick* by John O'Hara
Nonfiction: *American in Italy* by Herbert Kubly
Poetry: *The Shield of Achilles* by W. H. Auden

1957
Fiction: *The Field of Vision* by Wright Morris
Nonfiction: *Russia Leaves the War* by George F. Kennan
Poetry: *Things of This World* by Richard Wilbur

1958
Fiction: *The Wapshot Chronicle* by John Cheever
Nonfiction: *The Lion and the Throne* by Catherine Drinker Bowen
Poetry: *Promises: Poems, 1954–1956* by Robert Penn Warren

1959
Fiction: *The Magic Barrel* by Bernard Malamud
Nonfiction: *Mistress to an Age: A Life of Madame de Stael* by J. Christopher Herold
Poetry: *Words for the Wind* by Theodore Roethke

---

seized by nomads, mutilated, and turned into a dancing pet. Tennessee Williams would regard the story as "a true masterpiece of short fiction."

RAY BRADBURY (b. 1920): *The Martian Chronicles.* Bradbury's masterpiece is a series of linked stories about the colonization of Mars. With this work, Bradbury, along with Isaac Asimov, helps gain increased respect for the genre of science fiction. Born in Illinois and educated in Los Angeles, Bradbury began his writing career, which would include short stories,

AWARDS AND PRIZES, 1950–1959

Pulitzer Prizes

1950
Fiction: *The Way West* by A. B. Guthrie
Poetry: *Annie Allen* by Gwendolyn Brooks
Drama: *South Pacific* by Richard Rodgers, Oscar Hammerstein II, and Joshua Logan
History: *Art and Life in America* by O. W. Larkin
Biography/Autobiography: *John Quincy Adams and the Foundations of American Foreign Policy* by Samuel F. Bemis

1951
Fiction: *The Town* by Conrad Richter
Poetry: *Complete Poems* by Carl Sandburg
Drama: No Prize Awarded
History: *The Old Northwest: Pioneer Period, 1815–1840* by R. Carlyle Buley
Biography/Autobiography: *John C. Calhoun: American Portrait* by Margaret L. Coit

1952
Fiction: *The Cain Mutiny* by Herman Wouk
Poetry: *Collected Poems* by Marianne Moore
Drama: *The Shrike* by Joseph Kramm
History: *The Uprooted* by Oscar Handlin
Biography/Autobiography: *Charles Evans Hughes* by Merlo J. Pusey

1953
Fiction: *The Old Man and the Sea* by Ernest Hemingway
Poetry: *Collected Poems, 1917–1952* by Archibald MacLeish
Drama: *Picnic* by William Inge
History: *The Era of Good Feelings* by George Dangerfield
Biography/Autobiography: *Edmund Pendleton, 1721–1803* by David J. Mays

1954
Fiction: No Prize Awarded
Poetry: *The Waking* by Theodore Roethke
Drama: *The Teahouse of the August Moon* by John Patrick
History: *A Stillness at Appomattox* by Bruce Catton
Biography/Autobiography: *The Spirit of St. Louis* by Charles A. Lindbergh

1955
Fiction: *A Fable* by William Faulkner
Poetry: *Collected Poems* by Wallace Stevens

Drama: *Cat on a Hot Tin Roof* by Tennessee Williams
History: *Great River: The Rio Grande in North American History* by Paul Horgan
Biography/Autobiography: *The Taft Story* by William S. White

1956
Fiction: *Andersonville* by MacKinlay Kantor
Poetry: *Poems, North and South* by Elizabeth Bishop
Drama: *The Diary of Anne Frank* by Albert Hackett and Frances Goodrich
History: *The Age of Reform* by Richard Hofstadter
Biography/Autobiography: *Benjamin Henry Latribe* by Talbot F. Hamlin

1957
Fiction: No Prize Awarded
Poetry: *Things of This World* by Richard Wilbur
Drama: *Long Day's Journey into Night* by Eugene O'Neill
History: *Russia Leaves the War* by George F. Kennan
Biography/Autobiography: *Profiles in Courage* by John F. Kennedy

1958
Fiction: *A Death in the Family* by James Agee
Poetry: *Promises: Poems 1954–1956* by Robert Penn Warren
Drama: *Look Homeward, Angel* by Ketti Frings
History: *Banks and Politics in America—from the Revolution to the Civil War* by Bray Hammond
Biography/Autobiography: *George Washington, Vols. I–VI* by Douglas S. Freeman and *George Washington, Vol. VII* by John A. Carroll and Mary W. Ashworth

1959
Fiction: *The Travels of Jaimie McPheeters* by Robert Lewis Taylor
Poetry: *Selected Poems, 1928–1958* by Stanley Kunitz
Drama: *J.B.* by Archibald MacLeish
History: *The Republican Era: 1869–1901* by Leonard D. White and Jean Schneider
Biography/Autobiography: *Woodrow Wilson: American Prophet* by Arthur Walworth

Nobel Prizes for Literature

1954   Ernest Hemingway

novels, plays, and film, radio, and television scripts, in 1943.

WALTER VAN TILBURG CLARK: *The Watchful Gods and Other Stories.* Clark's last book features a young boy's initiation in the title novella and the frequently anthologized story "The Portable Phonograph."

WILLIAM DEMBY (b. 1922): *Battlecreek.* The African American writer's first novel treats race relations in West Virginia. Rejecting a characterization of the book as naturalistic, Demby would suggest instead that it be described as existentialist "because black experience is itself and has been historically in this country existentialist, that is precarious, tied to the moment, history-conscious." His later novels include *The Catacombs* (1965), *Love Story Black* (1978), and *Blueboy* (1979). Demby was born in Pittsburgh and lived for a long period in Italy, where he wrote scripts for Italian films.

WILLIAM FAULKNER: *Collected Stories.* These forty-two stories represent what, according to Faulkner, constitutes his achievement as a short story writer. The stories are arranged with care into six thematic units that provide a key to the author's intentions. The collection is universally praised and receives the National Book Award.

WILLIAM GOYEN (1915–1983): *The House of Breath.* Goyen's first novel, an autobiographical family chronicle, is widely and favorably reviewed. Katherine Anne Porter writes that it contains "long passages of the best writing, the fullest and richest and most expressive, that I have read in a very long time." Born in Texas, Goyen was an editor for McGraw-Hill.

ERNEST HEMINGWAY: *Across the River and into the Trees.* Hemingway's first novel in a decade concerns aging army colonel Robert Cantwell's trip to revisit the place where he was wounded in World War I. Generally regarded as one of Hemingway's weakest books, it is viewed as the bitter work of a defeated man whose writing skills have failed him.

JOHN HERSEY: *The Wall.* Hersey's ambitious novel chronicles the destruction of the Warsaw Ghetto by the Nazis as reflected in the fictional diary of a Jewish scholar.

PATRICIA HIGHSMITH (1921–1995): *Strangers on a Train.* Highsmith's first suspense novel concerns a conspiracy between two strangers who agree to kill each other's intended victims; without an apparent motive for murder, each hopes to escape detection. Alfred Hitchcock would make the story into a memorable film in 1951. Born in Texas and raised in New York City, Highsmith lived most of her life abroad.

JACK KEROUAC (1922–1969): *The Town and the City.* Kerouac's first published novel is an autobiographical depiction of the disintegration and dispersal of a family in Lowell, Massachusetts, modeled on the novels of Thomas Wolfe. Kerouac would later dismiss the work as written by the rules taught him at Columbia University: "But . . . the novel's dead. Then I broke loose from all that and wrote picaresque narratives. That's what my books are."

MARY McCARTHY: *Cast a Cold Eye.* McCarthy's story collection includes two of her most admired works, "The Weeds" and "The Cicerone." The second half of the volume presents autobiographical sketches, including "Yon-

Isaac Bashevis Singer

der Peasant, Who Is He?" and "The Tin Butterfly," which would be later included in *Memories of a Catholic Girlhood* (1957).

J. D. SALINGER: "For Esmé—with Love and Squalor." One of Salinger's most admired stories concerns an encounter between an American soldier in England and a self-possessed young girl; it appears in *The New Yorker.*

MARY SARTON: *Shadow of a Man.* Sarton's lyrical novel follows the development of a young man in France who is suffering grief over his mother's death; friendship gradually rejuvenates him.

BUDD SCHULBERG: *The Disenchanted.* Schulberg's novel concerns dissolute, doomed Manley Halliday, a once-famous novelist (based on F. Scott Fitzgerald, with whom Schulberg once collaborated in Hollywood). Schulberg would later adapt the novel for Broadway, where it premiered in 1958.

ISAAC BASHEVIS SINGER: *The Family Moskat.* Singer's second novel, a family saga tracing the destruction of the Jewish community in Poland from the turn of the century to World War II, had been serialized in Yiddish from 1945 to 1948 and becomes Singer's first book to appear in English.

WALLACE STEGNER: *The Preacher and the Slave.* Stegner offers a fictionalized treatment of the life of labor radical Joe Hill. It marks Stegner's first use of historical material in his fiction, which would be the source for his masterpiece, *Angle of Repose* (1971). *The Preacher and the Slave* would be republished as *Joe Hill: A Biographical Novel* in 1969. Stegner also publishes *The Woman in the Wall,* a collection of previously published stories written between 1940 and 1949.

GORE VIDAL: *Dark Green, Bright Red* and *A Search for a King.* The first is a novel of intrigue inspired by the author's residence in Guatemala, which echoes the work of Graham Greene and Joseph Conrad. The second is Vidal's first attempt at a historical novel, detailing the search for Richard the Lion-Hearted by the troubadour Blondel in the twelfth century. Reviewer Edward Wagenknecht presciently observes, "One wishes he might do more in this field, for he is just the man to redeem the historical novel from the lushness and bad taste into which it is always in danger of falling."

ROBERT PENN WARREN: *World Enough and Time.* Warren's most ambitious novel is a fictionalized version of the sensational nineteenth-century Beauchamp-Sharp murder case in Kentucky, in which a modern researcher probes the evidence for the key to understanding the complex tragedy.

TENNESSEE WILLIAMS: *The Roman Spring of Mrs. Stone.* The first and generally recognized as the better of Williams's two novels (the other is *Moise and the World of Reason,* 1975) concerns an aging actress's tawdry affair with an Italian gigolo in postwar Rome. Carson McCullers praises the novel as standing "as a work of art with *Daisy Miller* and *Death in Venice.* There is in the book the hallmark of the masterpiece."

WILLIAM CARLOS WILLIAMS: *Make Light of It.* To his two previous story collections Williams adds new works, grouped as "Beer and Cold Cuts." His final collection, *The Farmers' Daughters: The Collected Stories,* would appear in 1961.

ANZIA YEZIERSKA: *Red Ribbon on a White Horse.* The author's last important work is a fictionalized autobiographical treatment of a writer's struggles during the Depression and her work with the WPA Federal Writers Project.

Literary Criticism and Scholarship

JOHN BERRYMAN: *Stephen Crane.* Berryman's pioneering critical biography offers a psychological interpretation of Crane's development and genius.

KENNETH BURKE: *A Rhetoric of Motives.* In a sequel to the linguistic analysis of *Grammar of Motives* (1946), Burke demonstrates how rhetorical interpretation can be applied to literary texts and human relationships.

ARCHIBALD MacLEISH: *Poetry and Opinions.* MacLeish comes to the defense of Ezra Pound over the controversy surrounding the latter being awarded the Bollingen Prize for *The Pisan Cantos* in 1949. MacLeish argues that a poem's "bad opinions" do not necessarily make a poem bad.

CHARLES OLSON (1910–1970): "Projective Verse." Olson's influential essay defining an open poetic form, written to follow no preconceived pattern but in response to the sound and rhythm of the human voice, is published in *Poetry.* Its concepts are derived from the works and ideas of Walt Whitman, William Carlos Williams, E. E. Cummings, and others. The essay would be reprinted in *The New American Poetry: 1945–1960* (1960) and collected in *Olson's Selected Writings* (1966). Born in Worcester, Massachusetts, Olson spent summers at Gloucester, which would become the setting for his *Maximus Poems,* a sequence of three hundred poems that Olson collected from 1945 to his death.

HENRY NASH SMITH (1906–1986): *Virgin Land: The American West as Symbol and Myth.* In one of the seminal works in the evolving academic discipline of American studies, Smith examines, through analysis of the literature of the period, how the West in the nineteenth century shaped American ideas and society.

LIONEL TRILLING: *The Liberal Imagination.* Trilling's first collection of essays mingles literary criticism with analyses of culture, politics, and history. It brings Trilling immediate national attention as a literary critic of the first order, ranking alongside F. R. Leavis and Edmund Wilson.

EDMUND WILSON: *Classics and Commercials.* Wilson's essay collection critiques both popular writing and modernist masterpieces. In the essay "Thoughts on Being Bibliographed" Wilson attacks contemporary intellectuals, the publishing scene, and what he perceives as "the drop of a trajectory in modern literature."

Nonfiction

TRUMAN CAPOTE: *Local Color.* Capote's first nonfiction work is a series of travel sketches and portraits reflecting the author's journeys in America and abroad. It is the first instance of Capote's characteristic blending of objective and subjective viewpoints.

HENRY STEELE COMMAGER: *The American Mind: An Interpretation of American Thought and Character Since the 1880s.* Commager's assessment of the American character is regarded as the most serious and comprehensive attempt to supply a history of American thought since Parrington.

CAREY McWILLIAMS: *Witch-Hunt: The Revival of Heresy*. Published as Senator Joseph McCarthy launches his anti-Communist crusade, McWilliams reports on the growing threat to American civil liberties.

DAVID RIESMAN (1909–2002): *The Lonely Crowd: A Study of the Changing American Character*. In his influential sociological study, Riesman describes three social types—"tradition-directed," "inner-directed," and "other-directed"—and uses the categories to explain the conformity of the era. *Faces in the Crowd* (1952), a companion volume, would later provide character portraits supporting his assertions. Riesman was professor of social sciences at the University of Chicago from 1949 to 1958 and at Harvard from 1958 to 1980.

JADE SNOW WONG (b. 1922): *Fifth Chinese Daughter*. In the first installment of her autobiography, Wong relates the tension—between passivity and acceptance and inner rage at social and familial inequities—that lies at the heart of many Asian American women's lives. Wong would continue her story in *No Chinese Stranger* (1976).

Poetry

E. E. CUMMINGS: *Xaipe: Seventy-One Poems*. Taking its title from the Greek word for "rejoice," Cummings's collection of lyrics celebrates "the great advantage of being alive," and, as one reviewer observes, his technical and typographical dislocations are strategies "by which he surprises us into awareness."

ROBERT DUNCAN: *Medieval Scenes*. Duncan's third collection features the poet's version of the "serial poem," a series of verses on a common subject presented in the manner of an improvisation. Duncan regards the long title sequence as "the first poem in which I knew what I had to do."

HOWARD NEMEROV: *Guide to the Ruins*. Nemerov's second collection is praised by reviewer Milton Crane as the "work of an original and sensitive mind, alive to the thousand anxieties and agonies of our age."

CARL SANDBURG: *Complete Poems*. Sandburg is awarded the Pulitzer Prize for this compilation of his verse written between 1910 and 1950, with personal descriptions of how many of his poems came to be written.

WALLACE STEVENS: *The Auroras of Autumn*. Stevens's last major collection of new works includes poems such as "Large Red Man Reading," "The Ultimate Poem Is Abstract," and the long poem "An Ordinary Evening in New Haven," about which Stevens declared his intention "to get as close to the ordinary, the commonplace and the ugly as it is possible for a poet to get. It is not a question of grim reality but of plain reality. The object

is of course to purge oneself of the false." The volume earns the National Book Award.

RICHARD WILBUR: *Ceremony and Other Poems*. Wilbur's second collection celebrates the power of nature and the search for order. It includes one of his most anthologized poems, "The Death of a Toad," in which a representative of primal life is destroyed by an instrument of modern humanity, the lawn mower.

Publications and Events

The National Book Awards. These awards are established by the American Book Publishers Council, the American Booksellers Association, and the Book Manufacturers Institute. In 1976, sponsorship changed to an entity called the National Book Committee, which awarded prizes in the areas of arts and letters, children's literature, contemporary affairs, fiction, history, biography, and poetry until 1979. That year the National Book Awards were replaced with the American Book Awards of the Association of American Booksellers. Then, beginning in 1985, the prizes—once again called the National Book Awards—began to be administered by the National Book Foundation, which limits itself to the areas of fiction, nonfiction, and poetry, also giving out a National Medal for Literature.

Peanuts. Charles M. Schulz (1922–2000) debuts the most popular comic strip of all time in eight newspapers. Charlie Brown, his dog Snoopy, and their friends reflected both childhood pleasures and adult anxieties for the next fifty years. By 1969 the comic strip appeared in one thousand newspapers in the United States and Canada and more than one hundred worldwide.

1951
Drama and Theater

MAXWELL ANDERSON: *Barefoot in Athens*. Anderson's last major dramatic work concerns the final months in the life of Socrates. A talky polemic on democracy, the play has a Cold War edge, with the Spartans made to resemble the Communists. It fails with both the critics and the public, and Anderson would follow it with his final three plays—*The Bad Seed* (1954), *The Day the Money Stopped* (1958), and *The Golden Six* (1958)—which he would regard as potboilers written to pay off his debts.

DONALD BEVAN (b. 1920) AND EDMUND TRZCINSKI (b. 1921): *Stalag 17*. This comedy-melodrama about American prisoners of war in a German camp is the work of two former prisoners of war. It would be made into a successful film in 1953, directed by Billy Wilder, and also inspired the television series *Hogan's Heroes*.

LOUIS COXE (1918–1993): *Billy Budd*. Coxe adapts Melville's symbolic drama of good versus evil, which concerns the persecution of the innocent sailor Billy Budd by the malevolent master-at-arms John Claggart. Born in New Hampshire, Coxe was also a poet and a professor at the University of Minnesota and at Bowdoin College.

LILLIAN HELLMAN: *The Autumn Garden*. Hellman produces a play about a group assembled at a summer resort who confront the reality of their lives. The drama is praised for its lifelike characterizations; one reviewer notes that Hellman has few peers in presenting "meanness, loneliness, or frustration" on stage.

SIDNEY KINGSLEY: *Darkness at Noon*. The playwright's last significant work is an adaptation of Arthur Koestler's 1941 novel about Communist repression during the Stalin era. It wins the New York Drama Critics Circle Award for best play.

PAUL OSBORN: *Point of No Return*. Osborn adapts J. P. Marquand's novel about a businessman who regains his integrity by revisiting his hometown and reviewing his past.

RICHARD RODGERS AND OSCAR HAMMERSTEIN II: *The King and I*. The musical, based on Margaret Landon's novel *Anna and the King of Siam* (1943), transports its audience to nineteenth-century Siam, where a Welsh schoolteacher attempts to instruct the children of the imperious king. It is the final role for actress Gertrude Lawrence, who died during its run, and the star-making role for Yul Brynner, who would continue to perform the role of the king until his death in 1985. The popular musical features a lengthy Siamese ballet version of *Uncle Tom's Cabin*, choreographed by Jerome Robbins.

JOHN VAN DRUTEN: *I Am a Camera*. Van Druten adapts Christopher Isherwood's *Goodbye to Berlin* (1939) in a New York Drama Critics Circle Award–winning production featuring Julie Harris as Sally Bowles. The play would in turn be adapted as the musical *Cabaret* (1966).

TENNESSEE WILLIAMS: *The Rose Tattoo*. Williams's play, set in a Sicilian Gulf Coast community, concerns a widow's illusions about her husband and her restoration to the passions of life by another man.

Fiction

JAMES AGEE: *The Morning Watch*. The first of Agee's two novels tells the story of a young student at a religious school whose doubts lead to both alienation and self-awareness.

ISAAC ASIMOV: *Foundation*. Asimov pioneers the science fiction genre of "future history" in the first volume of his Foundation trilogy, to be followed by *Foundation and Empire* (1952) and *Second Foundation* (1953). His account of the entire history of a galactic empire, inspired by Gibbons's *Decline and Fall of the Roman Empire*, is regarded as one of the most influential works of modern science fiction.

RAY BRADBURY: *The Illustrated Man*. Bradbury's story collection explores issues such as the atom bomb and racial intolerance in a series of deftly plotted fantasies linked as the illustrated images on a tattooed man.

HORTENSE CALISHER (b. 1911): *In the Absence of Angels*. Calisher's first book is a story collection that includes the first of her Hester works, autobiographically based coming-of-age stories, as well as the critically acclaimed story "In Greenwich There Are Many Graveled Walks." A New York City native, Calisher would publish short stories (*Collected Stories*, 1975), novellas (*The Novellas of Hortense Calisher*, 1997), and novels.

TRUMAN CAPOTE: *The Grass Harp*. Capote's charming, lyrical second novel concerns a group of youthful outcasts who retreat to a tree fort to oppose the adult world of responsibility and limitation.

WILLIAM FAULKNER: *Requiem for a Nun*. This sequel to *Sanctuary* is yet another of Faulkner's experiments with novelistic form. Three prose sections providing historical background are interspersed with three others constituting a three-act play. The story concerns the fate of Nancy Mannigoe, a black nurse accused of murdering a white child.

HERBERT GOLD (b. 1924): *Birth of a Hero*. Gold's first novel treats a successful lawyer's midlife crisis. His attempts to live a more heroic life backfire. It is the first of the Cleveland-born writer's skillful portraits of American life and modern angst.

JOHN HAWKES: *The Beetle Leg*. Hawkes's intensely surrealistic second novel concerns a construction worker buried alive during the building of an irrigation dam in the West. According to the reviewer of the *Saturday Review*, "The avant garde has now taken over the western story and I'm afraid it will never be quite the same again."

SHIRLEY JACKSON: *The Hangsaman*. Jackson's second novel concerns a college girl whose friend may or may not be a figment of her imagination. The book shows Jackson's increasing interest in abnormal psychological states.

JAMES JONES (1921–1977): *From Here to Eternity*. Based on Jones's experiences in the Pacific with the U.S. Army during World War II, the novel provides a realistic account of army life in Hawaii on the eve of Pearl Harbor. Readers drawn both to the story and to Jones's liberal

T. S. Eliot

use of profane dialogue make the book an immediate bestseller.

NORMAN MAILER: *Barbary Shore.* Mailer's second novel deals with the inhabitants of a Brooklyn boardinghouse. This novel of ideas mixes political and existential themes with realistic and surrealistic methods, reminding reviewers of the works of both Franz Kafka and James A. Cain.

J. P. MARQUAND: *Melville Godwin, U.S.A.* Marquand's satire concerns the effort to turn a professional soldier into a national hero. His ironic portrait of contemporary American life, skillfully delivered by an unreliable narrator, is mainly misread by reviewers, who see the book as an affirmation of American values.

CARSON MCCULLERS: *The Ballad of the Sad Café.* In a collection of stories and a novella, the title work, which would be dramatized in 1963 by playwright Edward Albee, concerns an almost unnaturally tall, strong woman who falls in love with a hateful dwarf, who teams up with the woman's husband to destroy her. Later criticism would link this plot to McCullers's bisexuality and tortured relationship with her own—also bisexual—husband.

WRIGHT MORRIS: *Man and Boy.* Morris provides a satirical character study of a selfish, controlling woman.

WILLARD MOTLEY: *We Fished All Night.* Motley's second novel treats the social disruptions of postwar America through the experiences of three veterans. It is widely viewed as a disappointing follow-up to *Knock on Any Door* (1948).

J. D. SALINGER: *The Catcher in the Rye.* Narrated in the first person by disaffected adolescent Holden Caulfield, Salinger's novel conveys modern youth's alienation from adult society. The novel continues to speak to the imagination of contemporary readers and retains its status as one of the classics of the postwar era.

WILLIAM SAROYAN: *Rock Wagram.* This is the first in a series of novels indirectly exploring Saroyan's failed marriage. It would be followed by *The Laughing Matter* (1953), *Boys and Girls Together* (1963), and *One Day in the Afternoon* (1964). Saroyan also publishes *Tracy's Tiger*, a short fable on love.

WILLIAM STYRON (b. 1925): *Lie Down in Darkness.* Styron's first novel is published to critical acclaim. The plot, revolving around a family funeral in Tidewater, Virginia, is strongly reminiscent of William Faulkner's *As I Lay Dying*, which also makes use of interior monologue. The Virginia-born writer served in the Marine Corps before graduating from Duke University in 1947.

HERMAN WOUK: *The Caine Mutiny.* Wouk's novel about life in the U.S. Navy during World War II introduces the reading public to the unforgettable Captain Queeg, who quickly becomes a symbol of autocracy. The novel wins a Pulitzer Prize and would sell more than two million copies by 1953. Wouk would adapt his novel as a play, *The Caine Mutiny Court-Martial*, in 1953, to be followed by a film version of *The Caine Mutiny*, starring Humphrey Bogart as Captain Queeg (1954).

Literary Criticism and Scholarship

T. S. ELIOT: *Poetry and Drama.* Eliot discusses his own plays and dramatic aims and methods in this published version of a lecture delivered at Harvard in 1950.

WALLACE STEVENS: *The Necessary Angel.* Stevens's essay collection, drawn from his addresses, discusses the relationship between the imagination and reality and includes the poet's conception of "supreme fictions" and the transformative power of art.

Nonfiction

NELSON ALGREN: *Chicago: City on the Make.* Algren takes the reader on an impressionistic verbal tour of Chicago's backstreets. The work is largely ignored in 1951, but ten years later Jean-Paul Sartre's translation would

Hannah Arendt

become a European bestseller, leading to its being reissued in the United States in 1962.

HANNAH ARENDT (1906–1975): *Origins of Totalitarianism.* Arendt's first major work is an analysis of the historical circumstances, including nineteenth-century anti-Semitism and imperialism, that contributed to Hitler's rise to power and the development of Fascism. Born in Germany, Arendt came to the United States in 1941 and taught at Princeton, the University of Chicago, and the New School.

RACHEL CARSON: *The Sea Around Us.* Carson issues a clear-eyed, conservation-minded account of the formation of the world's oceans and their importance to the planet. After eighty-six weeks on the bestseller list, the book would be translated into more than thirty languages, permitting Carson to resign her job as an administrator for the U.S. Fish and Wildlife Service and devote herself full-time to writing.

BRUCE CATTON (1899–1978): *Mr. Lincoln's Army.* The first volume of the author's popular Civil War trilogy concerns the establishment of the Union Army of the Potomac under General George McClellan. It would be followed by *Glory Road* (1952) and *A Stillness at Appomattox*

(1953), a winner of the Pulitzer Prize. Catton was a Michigan-born journalist and historian who served during the war as Director of Information for the War Production Board.

ALFRED KAZIN: *A Walker in the City.* The first of Kazin's three acclaimed autobiographical works details his Brooklyn childhood. *Starting Out in the Thirties* (1965) and *New York Jew* (1978) would follow.

C. WRIGHT MILLS (1916–1962): *White Collar.* Mills's first important sociological study of the postwar American middle class helps define central targets of social criticism, especially the conformity and materialism of the era.

VLADIMIR NABOKOV: *Conclusive Evidence.* Nabokov's first attempt at an autobiography is a series of sketches dealing with his Russian background and artistic development. It would be revised and expanded as *Speak, Memory* in 1966.

J. SAUNDERS REDDING: *On Being a Negro in America.* Redding's meditation on the psychological and social conflicts experienced by African Americans is praised as "one of the most effective statements . . . of the constant conflict experienced by the Negro between his reactions as a normal human being and those which life in America requires of him."

PAUL TILLICH (1886–1965): *Systematic Theology.* The first volume of Tillich's masterwork attempts to reconcile theology with contemporary scientific and social ideas. It would be followed by additional volumes in 1957 and 1963.

WILLIAM CARLOS WILLIAMS: *Autobiography.* Although filled with many factual mistakes, Williams's memoir is still an important reflection of his writing life.

Poetry

W. H. AUDEN: *Nones.* Auden's collection includes one of his most anthologized poems and his favorite among all his work, "In Praise of Limestone." It also features the first elements of the brilliant sequence "Horae Canonicae," which would appear in *The Shield of Achilles* (1955). Auden also produces in 1951 a volume of literary criticism, *The Enchafèd Flood*, and completes the libretto for the opera version of *The Rake's Progress.*

JOHN CIARDI: *From Time to Time.* Ciardi's collection treats time and the daily concerns of life. Noteworthy is his admired poem "My Father's Watch."

LANGSTON HUGHES: *Montage of a Dream Deferred.* Hughes incorporates musical rhythms into a series of vibrant images that depict modern urban black life. "Harlem"—with the line "What happens to a dream deferred?" — becomes one of Hughes's best-known and admired poems.

RANDALL JARRELL: *The Seven-League Crutches.* Jarrell's collection, which includes his first translations, is enthusiastically praised by Robert Lowell, who declares Jarrell to be "our most talented poet under 40."

ROBERT LOWELL: *The Mills of the Kavanaughs.* Lowell shifts his method to predominantly dramatic monologues in his third collection. The title poem, Lowell's longest work, takes the form of a Maine widow's lament for her husband. Other poems are "Mother Marie Therese," about a nun who drowned in 1912, and "Falling Asleep over the Aeneid," about an old man reading Virgil who recalls his uncle, a young officer in the Civil War. The poem is generally regarded as one of the poet's greatest achievements.

JAMES MERRILL (1926–1995): *First Poems.* Merrill's first major collection is an eloquent and witty group of poems written in the style of the metaphysical poets. Praised for its formal precision, the collection is also criticized by some for a lack of emotional intensity.

MARIANNE MOORE: *Collected Poems.* Replete with the surprising metaphors and exotic subject matter that are the poet's trademark, Moore's collected poems appear to almost universal acclaim, garnering four literary prizes over the next two years.

ADRIENNE RICH (b. 1929): *A Change of World.* Rich's first volume is selected by W. H. Auden for the Yale Series of Younger Poets. Auden states that her verses "speak quietly but do not mumble, respect their elders but are not cowed by them, and do not tell fibs."

THEODORE ROETHKE: *Praise to the End!* Borrowing its title from William Wordsworth's *The Prelude*, the volume consists of thirteen long poems exploring a child's sensibility and the development of consciousness. It employs surreal images and nongrammatical language to celebrate the preverbal world of childhood, self-discovery, and the union of body and spirit.

1952

Drama and Theater

GEORGE AXELROD (b. 1922): *The Seven Year Itch.* The season's biggest hit is a comedy exploring the Walter Mitty–ish libidinal fantasies of a married man, left on his own for the summer and tempted by his young neighbor. One critic calls it "a grand and goofy comedy, and it will relieve the dolors of even a [Adlai] Stevenson voter." Tom Ewell would reprise his stage performance in the 1955 Billy Wilder film, co-starring Marilyn Monroe. The New York–born writer would have one subsequent success, a Hollywood spoof, *Will Success Spoil Rock Hunter?* (1955).

ALICE CHILDRESS (1920–1994): *Gold Through the Trees.* After writing a debut drama, *Florence* (1949), set in a segregated railroad waiting room, Childress becomes the first black woman to have a play professionally produced on the American stage. This revue treats the oppression of African people throughout history. Childress began her theater career as an actress and director with the American Negro Theatre. She would gain notoriety with her young adult novel *A Hero Ain't Nothin' but a Sandwich* (1973).

MOSS HART: *The Climate of Eden.* The playwright's last work is an adaptation of Guyanese writer Edgar Mittelholzer's novel *Shadows Move Among Them* (1951), about the confrontation that occurs when a missionary and his daughter encounter a mentally unstable young man.

JOSEPH KRAMM (b. 1907): *The Shrike.* Kramm's only successful play is a gripping melodrama about a man who is committed to a psychiatric ward after a suicide attempt; he is manipulated by his vicious, estranged wife. The play wins the Pulitzer Prize. Kramm was a Philadelphian who worked as a journalist before becoming a playwright and director.

ARTHUR LAURENTS: *The Time of the Cuckoo.* Laurents's drama concerns an American spinster who travels to Venice in search of romance, only to be disillusioned in an affair with a married Italian businessman. A 1955 film version, *Summertime*, would star Katharine Hepburn, and the playwright would later team with Richard Rodgers and Stephen Sondheim for a musical adaptation, *Do I Hear a Waltz?* (1965).

JOHN STEINBECK: *Viva Zapata!* Steinbeck writes the film script for Elia Kazan's popular film on the Mexican revolutionary, starring Marlon Brando. The script's characterizations and themes recall Steinbeck's best work from the 1930s.

Fiction

PAUL BOWLES: *Let It Come Down.* Bowles's second novel details the dislocation and self-destruction of a New York bank clerk who travels to Tangiers, entering a tangled world of drugs, violence, and betrayal. William S. Burroughs considered the novel's ghastly ending among his favorite passages in contemporary literature.

JOHN HORNE BURNS: *A Cry of Children.* Burns's final novel concerns a wealthy concert pianist who marries a poor Catholic woman in Boston. An exploration of various forms of gender conflict, the book disappoints critics.

RALPH ELLISON (1914–1994): *Invisible Man.* Ellison's remarkable novel debut presents a nameless black protagonist's quest for identity, from his high school graduation through college and in Harlem in a series of surrealistic scenes. With a rich verbal texture, the novel incorporates vernacular elements from black folklore and music as well as modernist techniques derived from James Joyce, William Faulkner, and T. S. Eliot. The novel wins the National Book Award and is considered one of the most ambitious fictional treatments of the African American experience, as well as one of the greatest postwar American novels. Ellison would spend the rest of his life wrestling with his unfinished second novel, posthumously assembled from draft material by John F. Callahan as *Juneteenth*, in 1999.

HOWARD FAST: *Spartacus.* Fast's historical novel, chronicling the first-century B.C. Roman slave revolt led by the gladiator Spartacus, reverberates with references to America under the threat of McCarthyism.

EDNA FERBER: *Giant.* Ferber's last major work tells the story of Texas rancher Bick Benedict and the Virginia girl he marries and introduces to Texas life. The novel stirs regional resentment at the perceived unflattering portrait of Texas. A 1956 film version, featuring the last screen appearance by James Dean, would help popularize the novel.

SHELBY FOOTE: *Shiloh.* After three previous novels drawing on his native Mississippi — *Tournament* (1949), *Follow Me Down* (1950), and *Love in a Dry Season* (1951) — Foote gains his first popular success with his innovative treatment of the Civil War battle. The book's monologues, delivered by both fictional and historical participants, include a memorable portrait of Confederate cavalry officer Nathan Bedford Forrest.

WILLIAM GOYEN: *Ghost and Flesh: Stories and Tales.* Goyen's first story collection includes two of his most anthologized and admired works, "The White Rooster" and "The Grasshopper's Burden."

ERNEST HEMINGWAY: *The Old Man and the Sea.* Hemingway's moving parable about humanity's struggle to survive in a hostile world helps the writer recapture critical approval. Some regard this novella, about an aged Cuban fisherman's futile attempts to save his catch of a giant marlin from preying sharks, as Hemingway's greatest work. *The Old Man and the Sea* is mentioned prominently when Hemingway is awarded the Nobel Prize two years later.

PATRICIA HIGHSMITH: *The Price of Salt.* One of the best-selling lesbian novels of all time, the work concerns a woman who loses custody of her child because of the woman's sexual identity. Published under the name "Claire Morgan" after the book was initially rejected, the novel would be reissued in 1993 as *Carol.*

CHESTER HIMES: *Cast the First Stone.* Drawing on his own prison experiences but employing a white protagonist, Himes provides a naturalistic account of penitentiary life that features a frank and daring depiction of homosexual relations among the inmates.

JOHN CLELLON HOLMES (1926–1988): *Go.* Holmes, who had met Jack Kerouac and Allen Ginsberg as a student at Columbia in the 1940s, gains distinction as the first novelist to portray major figures of the Beat generation such as Kerouac, Ginsberg, and Neal Cassady in this roman à clef depicting bohemian life in New York City in 1950. *The Horn*, a novel about jazz, would follow in 1958, and *Get Home Free*, depicting the later fate of two characters from *Go*, would appear in 1964.

LANGSTON HUGHES: *Laughing to Keep from Crying.* A collection of stories composed in the 1930s and 1940s, treating the conflicts experienced by African Americans. Hughes's final collection, *Something in Common*, would appear in 1963.

BERNARD MALAMUD (1914–1986): *The Natural.* Malamud's first novel is a mythopoetic treatment of baseball and heroism as reflected in the career of Roy Hobbs. Although it contains no Jewish characters, the novel's theme of suffering and redemption foreshadows Malamud's future work. Malamud was the son of Russian Jewish immigrants, born in Brooklyn, and educated at New York's City College.

MARY MCCARTHY: *The Groves of Academe.* McCarthy's witty and satirical academic novel, set in a liberal women's college, concerns an incompetent faculty member whose dismissal turns him into a martyr because of his Communist past and his alleged political persecution.

WRIGHT MORRIS: *The Works of Love.* Dedicated to Sherwood Anderson, Morris's novel offers a life story of an Anderson-like "grotesque," Will Brady of Nebraska, a victim of his environment and needs, which force him into a progressively more desperate search for love and relief. It is generally considered the most personal of Morris's books, with the protagonist based on the author's father.

FLANNERY O'CONNOR (1925–1964): *Wise Blood.* The first of O'Connor's two novels concerns a zealot who founds the Church of Christ Without Christ, then blinds and tortures himself after killing a false prophet of his church. O'Connor nonetheless refers to her work as a "comic novel." A Georgia native, O'Connor began her writing career publishing short stories, most of which were completed as part of her master's thesis at the University of Iowa.

JEAN STAFFORD: *The Catherine Wheel.* Stafford's third and final novel traces the emotional paralysis of a female protagonist who is in love with the man who marries her cousin. Her most ambitious and technically challenging work, the novel gains only mixed reviews.

JOHN STEINBECK: *East of Eden.* Steinbeck's most ambitious work explores both social history and his home region, the Salinas Valley of California, by following three generations of the Trask family. Loosely structured by the biblical story of Cain and Abel, the novel revolves around free will and the capacity to forgive. A popular 1954 movie version would star James Dean.

GORE VIDAL: *The Judgment of Paris.* In this modernization of the Paris and Helen myth, an American in Europe must decide among three women and what they represent. The book is chiefly noteworthy for the skill Vidal shows in rendering his secondary characters and anecdotal situations that will become the hallmark of his later books.

KURT VONNEGUT JR. (b. 1922): *Player Piano.* Vonnegut's first novel converts the author's experience working in public relations for General Electric from 1947 to 1951 into a futuristic fantasy in which managers and engineers run a machine world. Vonnegut was born in Indianapolis, served in the army, and witnessed the firebombing of Dresden during the war.

E. B. WHITE: *Charlotte's Web.* White's second children's book, about the runty pig Wilbur who is saved from slaughter by a spider who weaves the words "Some Pig" above his pen, is described by critic Roger Sale as "probably the classic American children's book of the last thirty years." White would observe that it is "a story of friendship, life, death, salvation." The death of the title character is an unusual departure for a children's story.

Literary Criticism and Scholarship

R. P. BLACKMUR: *Language as Gesture.* Blackmur treats modern poetry in an essay collection that, as reviewer Milton Rugoff observes, offers "a demonstration of poetic dissection by a master anatomist."

VAN WYCK BROOKS: *The Confident Years.* In the final volume of his masterful Makers and Finders series of American cultural and literary history, Brooks treats the period 1885–1915, completing his one-hundred-year survey.

F. O. MATTHIESSEN: *Responsibilities of the Critic.* This posthumously published volume of uncollected essays and reviews displays the critic's major preoccupations

with the American past, modern poetry, and the state of criticism.

KATHERINE ANNE PORTER: *The Days Before: Collected Essays and Occasional Writings.* Porter's collection of personal essays and reviews offers analysis of the works of Henry James, Willa Cather, Gertrude Stein, and others, as well as insights into her writing process and methods, particularly evident in her introduction to the second edition of *Flowering Judas* (1940).

EDMUND WILSON: *The Shores of Light: A Literary Chronicle of the Twenties and Thirties.* Wilson's miscellany of reworked reviews and essays on literature helps present and explain the work of modernist authors, such as William Faulkner, E. E. Cummings, and Wallace Stevens, to a general audience. It also offers strong assessments of several American writers, including Robert Frost ("excessively dull"), Sinclair Lewis ("flat and unoriginal"), and Willa Cather ("feminine melodrama").

Nonfiction

CONRAD AIKEN: *Ushant: An Essay.* Aiken's most admired prose work is a fictionalized autobiography dealing with his development and featuring portraits of literary figures such as Ezra Pound, T. S. Eliot, and Malcolm Lowry.

WHITTAKER CHAMBERS (1901–1961): *Witness.* In what is considered by some a classic of confessional literature and by others the work of a pathological liar, the magazine editor Chambers offers his account — one of the most famous anti-Communist documents of the century — of his own involvement with the Communist Party, his accusations against Alger Hiss, and the wave of anti-Communist hysteria those accusations stirred.

BERNARD DeVOTO: *The Course of Empire.* The last installment of DeVoto's trilogy about the significance of the American West addresses westward exploration from the sixteenth through the nineteenth centuries. The first volume, *The Year of Decision* (1947), concerns the Mexican War. The second, *Across the Wide Missouri* (1947), an examination of the fur trade, won a Pulitzer Prize. DeVoto would consider the trilogy his most significant accomplishment.

RUTH KRAUSS (1911–1993) AND MAURICE SENDAK (b. 1928): *A Hole Is to Dig: A First Book of First Definitions.* Illustrator Sendak has his first major success with his humorous and unsentimentalized drawings for Krauss's collection of children's definitions, such as "The world is so you have something to stand on." Krauss was a distinguished children's book author, credited with being one of the first to use the words and ideas of young people in her works. Sendak, who has been called by critic John Rowe Townsend "the greatest creator of picture books in the hundred-odd years' history of the form," became the first American to win a Hans Christian Andersen International Medal in 1970.

REINHOLD NIEBUHR: *The Irony of History.* The Protestant theologian's application of his ideas to history suggests that the United States had been established by "children of light" intent on creating a virtuous society, and he traces the implications of this intention for American culture and politics. The book raises a controversy by suggesting that American moral innocence ill-equipped the country for exercising authority in the world as a superpower.

PAUL TILLICH: *The Courage to Be.* The philosopher's most widely read book shows his attempt to integrate existentialism and religion.

Poetry

ARCHIBALD MacLEISH: *Collected Poems, 1917–1952.* MacLeish wins his second Pulitzer Prize for this compilation spanning more than thirty-five years. It prompts a reevaluation and renewed critical acclaim. According to poet Richard Eberhart, "There is something basically lithe, wiry, direct and clear-seeing about his talent. We feel him as distinctly American."

W. S. MERWIN (b. 1927): *A Mask for Janus.* Merwin's first collection, issued in the Yale Series of Younger Poets, shows his characteristic use of traditional form, symbolism, and mythical motifs. His theme of the universal cycle of birth, death, and rebirth is echoed in the two volumes that would follow — *The Dancing Bear* (1954) and *Green with Beasts* (1956).

KENNETH REXROTH: *The Dragon and the Unicorn.* Rexroth's verse journal of his European travels is praised by poet Richard Eberhart for its mastery in lines that are "hard and clear, precise and lean, with continuous tensile strength and nothing fuzzy."

Publications and Events

New World Writing. This eclectic paperback anthology of world fiction, drama, essays, and poetry debuts. Until its demise in 1959, it featured the kind of writing usually found in little magazines or literary quarterlies. Contributors included established authors such as W. H. Auden, Robinson Jeffers, and Dylan Thomas, as well as the newer writers James Baldwin and Jack Kerouac.

1953
Drama and Theater

ROBERT ANDERSON (b. 1917): *Tea and Sympathy.* Anderson achieves his greatest success for this drama set in a New England prep school. It deals with a sensitive adolescent who is shunned as a homosexual and then befriended and sexually initiated by the wife of the school's headmaster. Anderson served as a naval intelligence officer in the Pacific during the war and wrote his first play, *Come Marching Home* (1945), aboard ship. His other works include *The Eden Rose* (1948) and *All Summer Long* (1951).

PADDY CHAYEFSKY (1923–1981): *Marty.* Chayefsky's live television drama about a shy Bronx butcher and his tentative courtship of a spinster schoolteacher features realistic dialogue and a concentration on ordinary life. It launches Chayefsky's career as a screenwriter and playwright and is considered a classic of early television drama. Adapted as a film in 1955, it would become the first transfer from television to win the Academy Award for best picture.

JEROME CHODOROV AND JOSEPH FIELDS: *Wonderful Town.* In a musical version of Ruth McKenney's *My Sister Eileen*, two sisters from Ohio try to make it in New York City. The play reunites the *On the Town* (1944) team of Leonard Bernstein (music), Betty Comden and Adolph Green (lyrics), and George Abbott (direction).

T. S. ELIOT: *The Confidential Clerk.* Inspired by Euripides' *Ion*, Eliot's verse comedy deals with a financier's clerk who is suspected of being the businessman's illegitimate son. Although dealing with some of Eliot's major themes, such as sin, redemption, and the search for identity and vocation, the play receives contradictory critical assessments, with some considering it the worst of Eliot's dramas and others, the best.

WILLIAM INGE: *Picnic.* The playwright's second Broadway production deals with the impact a virile vagabond makes on a group of repressed women in a small Kansas town. The play wins both the Pulitzer Prize and the New York Drama Critics Circle Award.

GEORGE S. KAUFMAN AND HOWARD TEICHMANN (1916–1987): *The Solid Gold Cadillac.* Kaufman's last produced play is a comedy about a sweet old lady who manages to take over a huge, corrupt corporation. Teichmann, who began his theater career with the Mercury Theatre, would write biographies of Kaufman and Alexander Woollcott.

ARTHUR MILLER: *The Crucible.* The parallels between the Salem witchcraft trials and the McCarthy hearings are inescapable in Miller's drama about John Proctor's decision whether to make a false confession and save

Arthur Miller

himself or maintain his integrity. Running for only 197 performances on Broadway, the play would become one of Miller's most admired and frequently revived, filmed, and televised dramas.

JOHN PATRICK: *The Teahouse of the August Moon.* Patrick's comedy about Japanese reaction to the attempt to bring democracy to an Okinawa village becomes a surprise winner of both the Pulitzer Prize and the New York Drama Critics Circle Award for best play.

LOUIS PETERSON (1922–1998): *Take a Giant Step.* The seventh play by an African American playwright to reach Broadway explores the conflicts of a young middle-class black youth growing up in a predominantly white neighborhood. Peterson wrote *Take a Giant Step* while touring as an actor and stage manager in a production of Carson McCullers's *The Member of the Wedding.* He would go on to write scripts for films and television.

TENNESSEE WILLIAMS: *Camino Real.* Williams's surrealistic fantasy is an expansion of his one-act play *Ten Blocks on the Camino Real.* Mixing invented lowlife and historical figures, including Byron and Casanova, the play celebrates romantic idealism, baffles critics, and fails with audiences, closing after only thirty performances. Williams would later declare it to be his favorite play, but most critics have judged it one of his weakest.

Fiction

JAMES BALDWIN (1924–1987): *Go Tell It on the Mountain.* Baldwin's first novel, about a day in the life of congregation members of Harlem's storefront Temple of Fire Baptised, incorporates, through flashbacks, several generations in the struggles of African Americans. The book establishes Baldwin as one of the most significant black novelists since Richard Wright. Baldwin was born in Harlem. His stepfather was a storefront Pentecostal preacher, and the writer himself preached for a time in various Harlem churches.

SAUL BELLOW: *The Adventures of Augie March.* This picaresque novel about a young Chicago Jew allows Bellow to express his views on American immigrant life while at the same time inventing an expansive, multivocal narrative style that is new to American fiction in the 1950s.

RAY BRADBURY: *Fahrenheit 451.* Bradbury's best-known novel concerns a futuristic dystopia in which books are destroyed as a threat to a populace lulled into conformity by material comforts. The novel echoes the censorship and persecution of the McCarthy era, as well as the period's consumerism and media domination. Bradbury also publishes *The Golden Apples of the Sun,* his first story collection involving non–science fiction subjects.

GWENDOLYN BROOKS: *Maud Martha.* Brooks's only adult novel traces the maturation of a young black woman in Chicago during the 1930s and 1940s. Noteworthy as one of the first and best characterizations of a black woman in fiction, it transcends stereotypes for a complex, multidimensional portrait.

WILLIAM S. BURROUGHS (1914–1997): *Junkie.* Burroughs's first novel, an autobiographically based, graphic account of heroin addiction, is published under the pseudonym "William Lee." It is Burroughs's most conventional narrative — ironically, his only book written while under the influence of heroin. It is one of the first fictional treatments of the drug subculture in postwar America.

JOHN CHEEVER: *The Enormous Radio, and Other Stories.* This collection includes two of Cheever's best-known and most admired stories, the title work, in which a couple's radio broadcasts their neighbor's private quarrels and becomes a catalyst in their own breakup, and

"Torch Song," a Kafkaesque story about a woman vampire.

MARK HARRIS: *The Southpaw.* Harris initiates a novel sequence involving baseball pitcher Henry Wiggen of the New York Mammoths. The series, considered one of the greatest fictional depictions of the sport, would be continued in *Bang the Drum Slowly* (1956), *A Ticket for a Seamstitch* (1957), and *It Looked Like for Ever* (1979).

JOHN HERSEY: *The Marmot Drive.* The first of Hersey's series of novels treating the inadequacies of modern life is an allegory about the conflict among residents of a small New England town, which echoes Nathaniel Hawthorne's *The Scarlet Letter.* It would be followed by *A Single Pebble* (1956), about a young American engineer whose experiences in China force him to reconsider his Western assumptions.

LOUIS L'AMOUR (1908–1988): *Hondo.* L'Amour's first popular success (and what many regard as his best novel and a western classic) is the novelization of a screenplay based on his earlier short story "The Gift of Cochise." It features all the elements — the tough nomadic gunman, the damsel in distress, and authentic period touches — that would make L'Amour the most widely read western writer and one of the best-selling authors of all time. The writer, born Louis LaMoore in North Dakota, worked as a manual laborer after leaving school at fifteen and was a tank corps officer during the war.

JAMES A. MICHENER: *The Bridges of Toko-Ri.* The first of Michener's two novels treating the Korean War, and one of the first novels to do so, deals with a bombing mission by American jet pilots. Michener would follow it with *Sayonara* (1954), an interracial love story between an American soldier and a Japanese woman.

WRIGHT MORRIS: *The Deep Sleep.* Morris's novel details the life and character of a judge as viewed by those who knew him. Set in the affluent Main Line of Philadelphia, the novel anatomizes the lack of fulfillment among those who have achieved the American dream of material success.

ANN PETRY: *The Narrows.* Petry's last adult novel treats an interracial love affair in a Connecticut community. She would publish a collection of short stories, *Miss Muriel and Other Stories*, in 1971.

J. D. SALINGER: *Nine Stories.* Of the thirty stories Salinger published between 1940 and 1953, he selects these nine, including "A Perfect Day for Banana Fish," "For Esmé — with Love and Squalor," "Down at the Dinghy," and "Uncle Wiggly in Connecticut," for his only published collection. The stories show chapters in the Glass family saga and other stories all connected by a common theme of alienation, psychic damage, and spiritual malaise.

ISAAC BASHEVIS SINGER: "Gimpel the Fool." Saul Bellow's translation of Singer's short story appears in the *Partisan Review* and brings its author his first major recognition beyond his Yiddish-speaking audience. It would be followed by an English translation of Singer's first novel, *Satan in Goray*, in 1955 and stand as the title story of Singer's first short story collection in 1957.

JEAN STAFFORD: *Children Are Bored on Sunday.* Stafford's first story collection helps establish her as one of the modern masters of the short form. It would be followed by one other volume — *Bad Characters* (1966) — before her *Collected Stories* (1969).

JESSAMYN WEST: *Cress Delahanty.* One of West's most popular and best works is this series of episodes in the title character's development from ages twelve to sixteen.

RICHARD WRIGHT: *The Outsider.* Published while Wright was living in Paris, the book employs elements of autobiography and concerns an African American man in Chicago whose mistaken identity and falsely reported death permit him to take up a new life in New York. After joining the Communist Party there, he is manipulated into performing a murder before he himself is killed by the party. Granville Hicks calls the work "one of the first consciously existentialist novels to be written by an American."

Literary Criticism and Scholarship

M. H. ABRAMS (b. 1912): *The Mirror and the Lamp: Romantic Theory and the Critical Tradition.* Abrams's paradigm-setting evaluation of the Romantic poets elaborates a shift from the mimetic to the expressive in the works of the English Romantics. It is consistently cited as one of the fundamental studies on the subject. Abrams is a longtime professor of English at Cornell University whose students included Harold Bloom and Thomas Pynchon.

ERIC BENTLEY (b. 1916): *In Search of Theater.* This collection of essays written between 1947 and 1952 reveals Bentley's preference for what he calls the "heroic failure," drama that is more personal than marketable. Bentley makes it clear that minority art trumps mass art in nearly every case, arguing that George Bernard Shaw and Shakespeare were popular in spite of their greatness, not because of it. The English-born writer, translator, and editor was the drama critic for the *New Republic* from 1952 to 1956 and was a professor at Columbia from 1953 to 1969.

VAN WYCK BROOKS: *The Writer in America*. Brooks responds to criticism that his literary histories fail to discriminate between important and lesser writers on the basis of literary skill. He argues that "The main interest of American literature resides in other aspects than the purely aesthetic" and that "biography and social analysis are an indispensable part of literary history."

LEON EDEL (1907–1997): *Henry James: The Untried Years*. The first installment of Edel's magisterial five-volume biography covers James's early years from 1843 to 1870. Completed in 1972, the biography is considered one of the greatest ever on a literary figure. The longtime professor at New York University was the primary editor of James's works. His other critical books include *James Joyce* (1947), *The Modern Psychological Novel* (1955), and *Literary Biography* (1957).

RANDALL JARRELL: *Poetry and the Age*. Jarrell's first book of criticism includes general essays on the state of modern poetry and criticism, as well as important evaluations of poets such as Walt Whitman, Marianne Moore, Robert Frost, Wallace Stevens, and Robert Lowell.

Nonfiction

DANIEL J. BOORSTIN (b. 1914): *The Genius of American Politics*. In a series of lectures Boorstin summarizes American political history from the Puritans through the American Revolution and the Civil War, outlining the major philosophical views that will buttress his popular historical series, The Americans (1958–1973). Born in Georgia and raised in Oklahoma, Boorstin graduated from Harvard and Oxford and taught at the University of Chicago from 1944 to 1969 when he became the director of the National Museum of History and Technology of the Smithsonian Institution.

BRUCE CATTON: *A Stillness at Appomattox*. This classic of Civil War history, the third volume of Catton's trilogy that had begun with *Mr. Lincoln's Army* (1951) and *Glory Road* (1952), wins a Pulitzer Prize and National Book Award, recognized for both its literary power and its historical insight.

NORMAN COUSINS: *Who Speaks for Man?* Cousins mounts a plea for world federation and nuclear non-proliferation.

ALFRED KINSEY, AND OTHERS: *Sexual Behavior in the Human Female*. The companion study to *Sexual Behavior in the Human Male* (1948) appears. Kinsey and his team of researchers present their findings on preadolescent sexual development and premarital and extramarital sexual relations among women, prompting an open discussion of sex. The work establishes an important benchmark for subsequent research on sexual behavior and has been cited as a predictor of both the sexual revolution and the women's movement to come.

CHARLES A. LINDBERGH: *The Spirit of St. Louis*. Never satisfied with the quickly written memoir *We* (1927), recounting his early flying career and famous transatlantic flight, Lindbergh labored for fifteen years on this revision of his autobiography, which is awarded the Pulitzer Prize. The work does much to restore the luster of Lindbergh's heroic image, which had been tarnished by his pro-Nazi sympathies.

PERRY MILLER (1905–1963): *The New England Mind: From Colony to Province*. In the sequel to *The New England Mind: The Seventeenth Century* (1939), Miller provides an influential intellectual history, from Richard Mather's farewell sermon in 1657 to Jonathan Edwards's Harvard lectures in 1731, to document the process by which the Puritans became Americans.

FULTON J. SHEEN (1895–1979): *Life Is Worth Living*. The first volume of transcripts from Bishop Sheen's popular inspirational weekly television program, which attracted thirty million viewers, appears. It would be followed by best-selling annual volumes until 1957.

MONICA SONE (b. 1919): *Nisei Daughter*. This autobiographical bildungsroman is set during World War II and addresses the racism directed toward Japanese Americans during the period, including their internment. It is considered one of the seminal works of Asian American literature.

Poetry

RICHARD EBERHART: *Undercliff: Poems, 1946–1953*. Eberhart's collection includes his striking social commentary in "Fragment of New York, 1929."

KENNETH KOCH (1925–2002): *Poems*. Koch becomes the first of the so-called New York school of poets, including Frank O'Hara and John Ashbery, to achieve notoriety, chiefly because this slim volume of six poems and a short play draws the ire of critic Harry Roskolenko in *Poetry*, sparking a war of words with Frank O'Hara, who replies in Koch's defense. Koch defines the values of the New York school of poets as "anti-traditional, opposed to the heavy use of irony and symbolism."

CHARLES OLSON: *In Cold Hell, in Thicket*. Olson's first major collection shows the first examples of his poems written to the formula outlined in his influential manifesto, "Projective Verse," published in *Poetry* in 1950: an open poetic form, not controlled by a preconceived pattern but by sound and breathing pattern. Olson also publishes his initial installment of what would become his masterpiece, *The Maximus Poems*, a poetic sequence treating the history and development of Gloucester, Massachusetts, as representative of American experience.

THEODORE ROETHKE: *The Waking*. The Pulitzer Prize–winning collection marks a return to traditional poetic forms, which Roethke had abandoned for surreal mysticism in his two preceding poetry collections, *The Lost Son* (1948) and *Praise to the End!* (1952). It includes admired poems such as the title work, regarded by some as the best poem Roethke ever wrote, "Elegy for Jane," and "Four for Sir John Davies."

KARL SHAPIRO: *Poems: 1940–1953*. Shapiro supplies selections from his three previous collections along with uncollected works. He also publishes a book-length critical essay, *Beyond Criticism*, arguing the poet's primary responsibility to his craft.

MELVIN B. TOLSON: *Libretto for the Republic of Liberia*. Named poet laureate of Liberia in 1947, Tolson produces this complex, allusive poem, incorporating a view of African history, to celebrate the nation's centennial. In his introduction, the poet Allen Tate observes, "For the first time, it seems to me, a Negro poet has assimilated completely the full poetic language of his time and, by implication, the language of the Anglo-American poetic tradition."

ROBERT PENN WARREN: *Brother to Dragons: A Tale in Verse and Voices*. Based on an actual incident, Warren's ambitious narrative poem treats the murder of a slave in 1811 by Thomas Jefferson's nephews. In it Jefferson deals with disillusion with his humanistic idealism and confronts his attitudes toward slavery. Robert Lowell considers the poem "superior to any of the longer works of Browning," and Randall Jarrell calls it "an event, a great one."

Publications and Events

Discovery. This literary paperback journal, edited by John W. Aldrich and Vance Bourjaily, appears. It was discontinued in 1955, after just six issues, and featured the work of some of the best younger writers of the period, including Norman Mailer, Hortense Calisher, William Styron, and others.

The *Paris Review*. This quarterly devoted to contemporary writing debuts. Founded and edited by George Plimpton (1927–2003) and other expatriates living in Paris, the first issue featured what would become the journal's trademark, a long interview with a contemporary writer (in this case, E. M. Forster) on the craft of writing.

Playboy. Hugh Hefner (b. 1926), sensing the era's new sexual permissiveness, launches a men's magazine featuring nude photographs (Marilyn Monroe appeared on the initial cover and in a pictorial), along with general articles, advice, and reviews, like those of other mainstream magazines. Selling seventy thousand copies of its first issue, the magazine evolved a hedonistic "Playboy Philosophy" and featured interviews with and contributions by prominent writers, such as John Steinbeck, Ray Bradbury, Saul Bellow, Kurt Vonnegut, and others, allowing readers to justify purchases "for the articles."

1954
Drama and Theater

GEORGE ABBOTT: *Pajama Game*. Based on Richard Bissell's novel *7½ Cents* (1953), the musical is set during a threatened strike at a pajama factory. It presents the Broadway choreography debut of Bob Fosse (1927–1987) and his signature number, "Steam Heat," and features the songs of songwriting team Richard Adler (b. 1921) and Jerry Ross (1926–1955). It wins the Tony Award for best musical and would be filmed in 1957.

MAXWELL ANDERSON: *The Bad Seed*. Anderson's last play is a dramatization of the novel of the same name written by William March (1893–1954), a psychological study of an apparently innately evil child. It would be made into a popular motion picture in 1956.

TRUMAN CAPOTE: *House of Flowers*. Capote's second theatrical venture is a romantic musical about the conflict between two Haitian brothels. Critics admire Harold Arlen's music rather than Capote's story, but the play manages a Broadway run of nearly five months.

JEROME CHODOROV AND JOSEPH FIELDS: *Anniversary Waltz*. The comedy develops when a married couple reveal to their children that they had premarital sex. Called by a reviewer "the season's high in tasteless hackwork," the play is chiefly noteworthy as an indicator of the growing sexual openness on stage.

N. RICHARD NASH (1913–2000): *The Rainmaker*. Nash's romantic comedy about a con man who brings rain to a drought-stricken land while bringing love to a spinster is extremely popular, winning the Karl Gosse Award and inspiring a musical adaptation, *110 in the Shade* (1963). *The Rainmaker* would be the Philadelphia-born playwright's only success.

CLIFFORD ODETS: *The Flowering Peach*. Odets's final play recounts the biblical story of Noah in which the patriarch and his family attempt to cope with the disastrous flood. The Columbia Faculty Committee votes to award the play the Pulitzer Prize, but their decision is overruled by the trustees, who grant it to Tennessee Williams's *Cat on a Hot Tin Roof* (1955).

Chester Himes

THORNTON WILDER: *The Matchmaker.* Wilder's comedy is a revision of his 1938 play *The Merchant of Yonkers,* treating the marital machinations of Dolly Levi. It would be the basis for the 1962 smash musical *Hello, Dolly!*

Fiction

HARRIETTE ARNOW (1908–1986): *The Dollmaker.* Its title having been changed by the publisher from *Dissolution,* the third installment of Arnow's Kentucky trilogy (preceded by *Mountain Path,* 1936, and *Hunter's Horn,* 1949), is a bestseller and generally considered her greatest achievement. In what Joyce Carol Oates calls "our most unpretentious masterpiece," Arnow follows the career of an Appalachian woman who, as part of the great migration northward, tries but fails to transplant her talents and values to the inhospitable landscape of Detroit. The novel is edged out by William Faulkner's *A Fable* for the Pulitzer Prize.

HAMILTON BASSO (1904–1964): *The View from Pompey's Head.* Basso's novel about a New York lawyer who returns to his Southern hometown to investigate a murder is the writer's best-known and most critical admired work, featuring a subtle portrait of Southern social distinctions. The New Orleans–born journalist was a frequent contributor to *The New Yorker.* His other books include *Sun in Capricorn* (1942), *The Light Infantry Ball* (1959), and *A Touch of the Dragon* (1964).

RAYMOND CHANDLER: *The Long Goodbye.* Chandler's last major novel is his most ambitious work, showing both a more vulnerable side to private eye Philip Marlowe and an extended range of psychological portraiture and social commentary. Chandler would state, "I didn't care whether the mystery was fairly obvious but I cared about the people, about the strange corrupt world we live in, and how any man who tried to be honest looks in the end either sentimental or plain foolish."

PETER DE VRIES: *Tunnel of Love.* De Vries's fourth novel (the first that he would acknowledge) introduces his preferred topic of marital relationship and his typical pun-addicted characters. His other novels of the decade are *Comfort Me with Apples* (1956), *The Mackerel Plaza* (1958), and *The Tents of Wickedness* (1959).

WILLIAM FAULKNER: *A Fable.* Faulkner's novel is a long parable about the passion of Christ, set during World War I. Faulkner had labored for years over the novel and considered it his masterwork. Although it wins the Pulitzer Prize, later critics would deem it one of his weakest books.

JOHN HAWKES: *The Goose and the Grave* and *The Owl.* Called by one reviewer "perhaps the only militant surrealist writer in America," Hawkes publishes two short novels, both set in a dream version of Italy.

CHESTER HIMES: *Third Generation.* Based on a narrative history written by Himes's mother, the novel is a multigenerational saga of a mixed-race black family dealing with intraracial conflict due to color differences.

CHRISTOPHER ISHERWOOD: *The World in the Evening.* The first of Isherwood's books with an American setting shows the struggles faced by a homosexual in a homophobic society. A popular success but a critical failure, the book marks a decline in Isherwood's reputation but would later be recognized as an important precursor work for the gay liberation movement.

SHIRLEY JACKSON: *The Bird's Nest.* Jackson's third novel, regarded by many as her finest, is a psychological study of a woman with multiple personalities. It would be followed by *The Sundial* (1958), a satire on a family's preparation for doomsday, that mixes, as one reviewer points out, "Gothic horror and suburban fun."

RANDALL JARRELL: *Pictures from an Institution.* Jarrell's satirical novel anatomizes incivility, complacency, and provincialism in a progressive women's college. Robert Lowell calls it "a unique and serious jokebook," and others regard it as a clever portrait of the intellectual life of the period.

JOHN OLIVER KILLENS (1916–1987): *Youngblood.* Killens's first novel is a black family saga set in rural Georgia. It explores what life was like for African Americans living in the South during the first third of the twentieth century. Killens was born in Georgia and founded the Harlem Writers Guild in 1952.

PETER MATTHIESSEN (b. 1927): *Race Rock.* The writer's first novel concerns a group of young people in New England. It would be followed by two other apprentice works, *Partisans* (1955) and *Raditzer* (1960). Matthiessen, a native New Yorker, was one of the founders of the *Paris Review* and worked for several years as a commercial fisherman.

WRIGHT MORRIS: *The Huge Season.* Morris's treatment of the 1920s and the American Dream in this novel has been described as his most "literary" work, with allusions to F. Scott Fitzgerald, Ernest Hemingway, T. S. Eliot, and James Joyce.

HOWARD NEMEROV: *Federigo; or, the Power of Love.* Nemerov's second novel concerns a bored husband who creates an alter ego and inadvertently makes his fantasies a disturbing reality.

JOHN STEINBECK: *Sweet Thursday.* Steinbeck brings back characters from *Cannery Row* in a comedy set on the Monterey waterfront during the postwar period, concerning Doc's marriage to the prostitute Suzy. It would be turned into the musical *Pipe Dream* by Rodgers and Hammerstein in 1955.

GORE VIDAL: *Messiah.* After publishing three mysteries under the pseudonym "Edgar Box" — *Death in the Fifth Position* (1952), *Death Before Bedtime* (1953), and *Death Likes It Hot* (1954) — Vidal adopts what will become his characteristic device of a fictional memoir in this satire of a messianic cult promulgated by the mass media.

EUDORA WELTY: *The Ponder Heart.* Welty's novella is a dramatic monologue told by Southerner Edna Ponder, recollecting her eccentric uncle who accidentally tickles his wife to death and is then put on trial for her murder. Featuring a masterful use of Southern dialect, the book earns the William Dean Howells Medal as the most distinguished work of American fiction between 1950 and 1955.

TENNESSEE WILLIAMS: *Hard Candy.* The second volume of Williams's underappreciated short stories would be followed by several additional collections: *Three Players of a Summer Game* (1960), *The Knightly Quest* (1966), *Eight Mortal Ladies Possessed* (1974), *It Happened the Day the Sun Rose* (1982), and *Collected Stories* (1985).

RICHARD WRIGHT: *Savage Holiday.* Wright's psychological thriller treats the violent explosion of a repressed white insurance salesman, a symbol of modern alienation. Forgoing racial themes, Wright attempts to embody existential and Freudian ideas in what most consider his least effective work.

Literary Criticism and Scholarship

BABETTE DEUTSCH: *Poetry in Our Time.* Deutsch produces an admired critical survey of modern poetry emphasizing the interrelationships between poetry and politics. Deutsch would also produce an alphabetical lexicon, *Poetry Handbook: A Dictionary of Terms*, in 1957.

EZRA POUND: *The Literary Essays.* This selection of Pound's literary criticism includes essays from earlier books and previously uncollected articles. In his introduction, T. S. Eliot asserts that Pound's works represent "the least dispensable body of critical writing in our time."

Nonfiction

ELLEN GLASGOW: *The Woman Within.* Published nine years after her death, Glasgow's autobiography is a candid portrait of the writer's private tragedies and personal challenges faced over her long writing career.

BEN HECHT: *A Child of the Century.* In what is generally regarded as one of the finest American autobiographies of the century, Hecht provides a detailed and candid summary of his life and career.

GRANVILLE HICKS: *When We Came Out.* The critic discusses his involvement with the Communist Party and his gradual disillusionment with it.

PAUL HORGAN: *Great River: The Rio Grande in North American History.* Horgan wins the Pulitzer Prize in history for this work. As critic Jonathan Yardley observes, "His is not the West of Zane Grey and Louis L'Amour but that of Willa Cather: a West of pioneers and settlers, of priests and ranchers, of ordinary people set down in an extraordinary landscape."

JOSEPH WOOD KRUTCH: *The Measure of Man.* Returning to the themes of his classic social analysis, *The Modern Temper* (1929), Krutch refutes his earlier mechanistic conclusions, asserting the attributes of what he calls "Minimal Man," capable of reason and choice. "If we do not resolve now to think rather than merely contrive," he writes, "and to will rather than merely to submit to 'the logic of evolutionary technology,' we may never think again."

ALICE B. TOKLAS (1877–1967): *The Alice B. Toklas Cookbook.* A collection of recipes and reminiscences donated by friends of Toklas and her late companion, the writer Gertrude Stein. Owing in part to its recipe for marijuana brownies, the cookbook would become a favorite of the youth counterculture in the 1960s and 1970s.

HARRY S. TRUMAN (1884–1972): *The Year of Decision.* The initial volume of Truman's memoirs deals with his first year as president. *Years of Trial and Hope* (1956) would cover the remainder of his presidential years.

Alice B. Toklas

Truman's recollections have been called the most candid self-assessment ever made by a U.S. president.

RICHARD WRIGHT: *Black Power.* Wright records his impressions of a tour of Africa's Gold Coast (later Ghana) and his analysis of what must be done for the emerging African nations to survive. Despite overgeneralizations and a simplistic solution, the book contains some of Wright's finest nonfiction writing.

Poetry

LOUISE BOGAN: *Collected Poems, 1923–1953.* The publication of Bogan's collected works prompts a positive reassessment. John Ciardi writes that Bogan "began in beauty, but she has aged to magnificence." The book includes one of her finest poems, "Song for the Last Act," and wins Bogan the Bollingen Prize (shared with Léonie Adams).

E. E. CUMMINGS: *Poems, 1923–1954.* Bringing together all the work of Cummings's previous ten collections, the volume prompts reviewer David Burns to assert that "it should now be apparent that Cummings is one of the finest lyric poets and social satirists America has yet produced."

ANTHONY HECHT (b. 1923): *A Summoning of Stones.* Hecht's first collection is marked by technical mastery and an ornate, even baroque style. Included is Hecht's elegy "Upon the Death of George Santayana." The New York–born poet would subsequently publish collections such as *The Seven Deadly Sins* (1958), *A Bestiary* (1960), and *The Hard Hours* (1967).

DANIEL HOFFMAN (b. 1923): *An Armada of Thirty Whales.* Hoffman's debut collection, part of the Yale Series of Younger Poets, is commended by W. H. Auden in his introduction as providing a new direction for nature poetry in the post-Wordsworthian world.

ROBINSON JEFFERS: *Hungerfield and Other Poems.* Jeffers's last major volume published during his lifetime wins the Pulitzer Prize. The title work deals indirectly and movingly with the poet's reaction to his wife's death.

HOWARD MOSS: *The Toy Fair.* After his debut collection, *The Wound and the Weather* (1946), Moss gains a reputation as one of the leading contemporary poets for this second volume, which Howard Nemerov calls "one of the most accomplished collections of lyric poetry to appear since the war."

WALLACE STEVENS: *The Collected Poems.* Published to celebrate the poet's seventy-fifth birthday, this final collection published during Stevens's lifetime features twenty-five poems written since *The Auroras of Autumn* in a section titled "The Rock." They include some of his finest poems, such as "To an Old Philosopher in Rome," his homage to George Santayana, "St. Armorer's Church from the Outside," and "Prologues to What Is Possible."

MAY SWENSON (1927–1989): *Another Animal.* Swenson's debut collection, like her second, *A Cage of Spines* (1958), is critically praised for technical mastery, verbal ingenuity, and exploration of nature and perception.

WILLIAM CARLOS WILLIAMS: *The Desert Music and Other Poems.* In his first collection since his stroke in 1952, Williams shows a renewed celebration of humanity and the rediscovery of poetic inspiration. Williams also publishes his *Selected Essays.*

Publications and Events

The Black Mountain Review. Edited by Robert Creeley, the journal of the experimental liberal arts college in Asheville, North Carolina, is first issued. It became an important vehicle for the writers associated with the college, including Charles Olson, Robert Duncan, and others who came to be known as the Black Mountain poets, advocates of Olson's ideas of "open" or "projective" verse.

The National Medal for Literature. This annual award honoring the achievements and career of an American literary figure is established by the National Book Committee and would be later sponsored by the National Institute of Arts and Letters (1975–1977), The American Book Awards (1979–1983), and the New York Public Library (1978, 1984–1985). Awarded until 1985, the medal was bestowed on writers such as Thornton Wilder (1965), Vladimir Nabokov (1973), and Mary McCarthy (1984).

The New York Shakespeare Festival. The festival is founded by Joseph Papp (1921–1991) to "encourage and cultivate interest in poetic drama, with emphasis on the works of William Shakespeare and his Elizabethan contemporaries, and to establish an annual summer Shakespeare Festival" performing at various locations around the city. The Festival gained a permanent base in Central Park in 1957 and an off-Broadway location in Greenwich Village in 1967, where it became an important sponsor of new dramas and experimental revival of the classics.

1955
Drama and Theater

GEORGE ABBOTT: *Damn Yankees*. Based on Douglas Wallop's novel *The Year the Yankees Lost the Pennant* (1954), this clever musical concerns a frustrated Washington Senators fan who sells his soul to the devil to become a star player and lead his team in trouncing the hated Yankees. It is the second and last Broadway success for the songwriting team of Richard Adler and Jerry Ross, the composers of *Pajama Game* (1954).

S. N. BEHRMAN AND JOSHUA LOGAN: *Fanny*. The season's biggest hit is this musical about a Marseille café owner whose son leaves a young woman pregnant and unwed.

ALICE CHILDRESS: *Trouble in Mind*. Childress becomes the first black woman to win an Obie Award for best original drama for this work. It depicts a group of mostly black actors rehearsing a play about a lynching, which reveals the black stereotypes held by its white writer, director, and producer.

FRANCIS GOODRICH (1891–1984) AND ALBERT HACKETT (1900–1995): *The Diary of Anne Frank*. The husband-and-wife team adapts the worldwide postwar bestseller *Anne Frank: The Diary of a Young Girl*. This compelling drama wins the Pulitzer Prize, the New York Drama Critics Circle Award, and Tony Award for best play. The husband-and-wife playwrights were first performers and later screenwriters.

WILLIAM INGE: *Bus Stop*. One of Inge's most popular plays concerns the miscellaneous passengers discharged by a snowbound long-distance bus and focuses on the romance that develops between a cheap, world-weary showgirl, Cherie, and Bo, an innocent but aggressive cowboy. Marilyn Monroe would star as Cherie in a successful 1956 film version.

JEROME LAWRENCE (b. 1915) AND ROBERT E. LEE (1918–1994): *Inherit the Wind*. In this fictionalized version of the 1925 Scopes "monkey trial," Matthew Harrison Brady (based on William Jennings Bryan) defends a literal interpretation of the Bible against lawyer Henry Drummond (based on Clarence Darrow). Both playwrights were Ohio natives who would have their biggest hit with *Auntie Mame* (1956) and its musical adaptation, *Mame* (1966).

IRA LEVIN (b. 1929): *No Time for Sergeants*. Based on Mac Hyman's 1954 novel, Levin's comedy concerns the misadventures of a hillbilly drafted into the air force. The play launches the acting career of Andy Griffith. Levin would gain a reputation as a master of suspense in works such as *Rosemary's Baby* (1967), *The Stepford Wives* (1972), *The Boys from Brazil* (1976), and *Deathtrap* (1978).

ARTHUR MILLER: *A View from the Bridge*. Miller's drama about romance and revenge among Italian longshoremen premieres on Broadway as half of a double bill with *A Memory of Two Mondays* (1955). Miller would subsequently revise and expand the play, to be successfully presented off-Broadway in 1965 and revived on several occasions.

COLE PORTER: *Silk Stockings*. Porter's last musical is an adaptation of the 1939 film *Ninotchka*, about a female Russian commissar who falls in love with an American agent. Cold War relations between the United States and the Soviet Union give the play's theme of a stern socialist yielding to capitalism a heightened relevance.

TENNESSEE WILLIAMS: *Cat on a Hot Tin Roof*. Williams's treatment of mendacity in a rich Mississippi planter's family wins both the Pulitzer Prize and the New York Drama Critics Circle Award for best play. The relationship between the ex–football player Brick and his wife, Maggie, turns on Brick's facing his homosexual attraction to his closest friend. The family's partriarch, Big Daddy, also must confront his disappointments and mortality.

Fiction

PAUL BOWLES: *The Spider's House*. Bowles's most conventional novel is the story of an expatriate American writer living in Morocco, who tries to bridge the cultural gap between the Western and the Muslim worlds. In the characterization of the young Moroccan, Amar, Bowles delivers one of the most convincing portraits of an Arab by a Western writer.

Tennessee Williams

EILEEN CHANG (ZHANG AILING, 1921–1995): *The Rice Sprout Song.* The first book published after this highly praised Chinese author immigrates to the United States probes the ironies of life under the Communists. Chang's inspiration for the novel is a newspaper article about a party member who finds himself questioning orders to shoot peasants who are raiding a granary during a famine. His potential victims, he realizes, are the very ones responsible for filling the granary.

J. P. DONLEAVY (b. 1926): *The Ginger Man.* Published in France by Maurice Girodias's Olympia Press, Donleavy's first novel chronicles the bawdy picaresque adventures of the likable, amoral Sebastian Dangerfield, who helps define the archetype of the romantic rebel for the era. The book becomes a cult hit and college favorite, published in an expurgated edition in the United States in 1958 and an unexpurgated edition in 1965. Born in Brooklyn, Donleavy was educated at Trinity College, Dublin, and became an Irish citizen in 1967.

WILLIAM FAULKNER: *Big Woods.* Faulkner's collection brings together his previously printed hunting stories — "The Bear," "The Old People," and "A Bear Hunt" — with a new story, "Ride at Morning," as well as the author's explanatory comments.

JACK FINNEY (1911–1995): *The Body Snatchers.* Finney's science fiction thriller about alien invaders who take over the bodies of their human victims would inspire three

film adaptations as *Invasion of the Body Snatchers* and be interpreted as a social and political satire on the conformity of the era. The Milwaukee-born writer would win acclaim for his time travel fantasy *Time and Again* (1970).

WILLIAM GADDIS (1922–1998): *The Recognitions.* Gaddis's dense, allusive, encyclopedic first novel concerns the search by artist Wyatt Gwyon for artistic and spiritual truth amid a corrupt modern world characterized by forgery and falsehood. Described by critic Richard Toney as "956 pages of linguistic pyrotechnics and multilingual erudition unmatched by any American writer in the century — perhaps in any century," the novel mainly baffles contemporary readers but slowly gains a cult and critical following as one of the most ambitious and accomplished works of fiction of the period. Gaddis was born in New York City, was president of the *Harvard Lampoon*, and traveled widely in Central America and Europe, experiences reflected in his first novel.

WILLIAM GOYEN: *In a Farther Country.* Goyen's novel is a romantic fantasy about a Spanish American woman's retreat into a dream world in the face of the dehumanizing industrial culture that surrounds her.

PATRICIA HIGHSMITH: *The Talented Mr. Ripley.* The first in the author's acclaimed series of novels featuring a charming, guilt-free, opportunistic murderer who is never brought to justice. Other books in the series are *Ripley Under Ground* (1970), *Ripley's Game* (1974), *The Boy Who Followed Ripley* (1980), *The Mysterious Mr. Ripley* (1985), and *Ripley Under Water* (1992).

CHESTER HIMES: *The Primitive.* Himes's last naturalistic protest novel is an autobiographically based story of a black writer's relationship with his white mistress. The author would regard the novel as his favorite among his works.

MACKINLAY KANTOR: *Andersonville.* Kantor's documentary novel treating the desperate conditions in the notorious Confederate prison earns the Pulitzer Prize. Historian Bruce Catton called it "the best Civil War novel I have ever read."

NORMAN MAILER: *The Deer Park.* Mailer's third novel, set in a California desert community controlled by Hollywood, employs the film industry as a metaphor for America. The critics are unkind, calling the book self-indulgent and underdeveloped, and Mailer abandons his plan to make the novel part of a much larger cycle.

J. P. MARQUAND: *Sincerely, Willis Wayde.* Marquand continues his ironic portrayal of American life in the story of an industrialist's rise to success. It is Marquand's harshest social portrait, employing his most contemptible protagonist.

MARY McCARTHY: *A Charmed Life*. McCarthy turns her satirical eye on inhabitants of a Cape Cod–like artist-and-writer colony of irresponsible egotists. The heroine faces a moral dilemma when she becomes pregnant by her estranged first husband.

VLADIMIR NABOKOV: *Lolita*. Nabokov's darkly comic novel about an older man's relationship with a twelve-year-old girl garners critical plaudits and controversy. The book, rejected by four publishers in the United States, is first published in France by Maurice Girodias's Olympia Press, better known for pornographic publications, and was subsequently banned in France. Copies of it surface in the United States, where U.S. Customs agents deem it objectionable. The publicity would eventually lead to *Lolita*'s 1958 publication by Putnam in the United States and the surrounding controversy, which the author subsequently described as "hurricane *Lolita*," making Nabokov a much-debated, internationally known figure.

FLANNERY O'CONNOR: *A Good Man Is Hard to Find, and Other Stories*. The first of O'Connor's two story collections, which help redefine the short story in the postwar period, includes acclaimed works such as "Good Country People," "The Artificial Nigger," "The Displaced Person," and the title story, perhaps her most famous and notorious work, concerning the encounter between an insufferable Southern family and a homicidal psychopath named The Misfit, who becomes an agent of spiritual redemption.

JOHN O'HARA: *Ten North Frederick*. O'Hara's novel is an innovative character study of the "first citizen" of a Pennsylvania town, which shows the ironic contrast between the public man and the private. It wins the National Book Award.

ROBERT PENN WARREN: *Band of Angels*. Warren's complex Civil War–era exploration of race and personal identity concerns the pampered daughter of a Kentucky plantation owner who learns that her mother was a slave and who is herself sold to a man in New Orleans, beginning a struggle for freedom that is finally realized after years of marriage to a Union captain.

EUDORA WELTY: *The Bride of Innisfallen, and Other Stories*. Welty's fourth story collection features a more experimental, allusive style and a wider geographical range, with three stories — the title work, "Circe," and "Going to Naples" — set in Europe. Also included is "The Burning," her only Civil War story, which earns Welty her second O. Henry Prize.

SLOAN WILSON (1920–2003): *The Man in the Gray Flannel Suit*. Wilson's best-known novel, about the daily routine of a typical New York commuter, would help name and characterize the conformity of the era and is called by one critic "one of the great artifacts of popular culture in the fifties." Wilson, born in Connecticut and educated at Harvard, worked as a journalist and in public relations.

HERMAN WOUK: *Marjorie Morningstar*. Wouk's novel dramatizes a young Jewish woman's rebellion from the values of her hardworking parents through several affairs until she settles down as a conventional housewife. The book's advocacy of chastity before marriage, anti-bohemianism, and suggestion that a woman's happiness lies in the home prompt one reviewer to call Wouk "Sinclair Lewis in reverse." Critic Leslie A. Fiedler would later declare the novel "the first fictional celebration of the mid-twentieth-century détente between the Jews and middle-class America."

Literary Criticism and Scholarship

R. P. BLACKMUR: *The Lion and the Honeycomb*. Blackmur's essay collection addresses the relationship between literature and society, attacks the narrowness of the New Criticism, and considers writers such as Herman Melville and Henry James.

LESLIE A. FIEDLER (1917–2003): *An End to Innocence: Essays on Culture and Politics*. Fiedler's debut volume of criticism includes essays on Whittaker Chambers, Alger Hiss, and Joseph McCarthy. The controversial literary essay "Come Back to the Raft Again, Huck Honey!" detects a homoerotic pattern in the works of James Fenimore Cooper, Nathaniel Hawthorne, Mark Twain, and other American writers, a view that would be expanded in Fiedler's seminal *Love and Death in the American Novel* (1959).

R.W.B. LEWIS (1917–2002): *The American Adam: Innocence, Tragedy, and Tradition in the Nineteenth Century*. Lewis's first major critical work is an influential intellectual and literary study of nineteenth-century America, which traces the Edenic myth in the works of American writers. Lewis would win the Pulitzer Prize for *Edith Wharton: A Biography* (1975).

LIONEL TRILLING: *The Opposing Self: Nine Essays in Criticism*. Trilling combines literary and social criticism, dealing with the state of the individual in modern society through analysis of the works of Jane Austen, William Dean Howells, Henry James, Charles Dickens, and others. Trilling also publishes *Freud and the Crisis of Our Culture*.

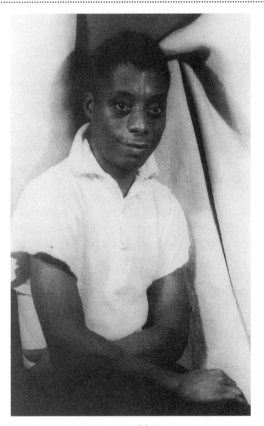

James Baldwin

EDMUND WILSON: *The Scrolls from the Dead Sea*. Wilson supplies an account of the origin, discovery, and implications of the Dead Sea Scrolls, discovered in 1947. He would revive his essay as *The Dead Sea Scrolls, 1947–1969* (1969), incorporating new findings.

Nonfiction

JAMES BALDWIN: *Notes of a Native Son*. Baldwin's essay collection supplies an account of his boyhood in Harlem, his assessment of black intellectuals, and a harsh critique of Richard Wright. A second volume of reflections, *Nobody Knows My Name: More Notes of a Native Son*, would appear in 1961.

JIM BISHOP (1907–1987): *The Day Lincoln Was Shot*. The first of the journalist and columnist's "day in the life" popular histories is a best-selling account of the Lincoln assassination conspiracy. It would be followed by the even more popular *The Day Christ Died* (1957), *The Day Christ Was Born* (1960), and *The Day Kennedy Was Shot* (1968).

RACHEL CARSON: *The Edge of the Sea*. Carson treats the seashore in a naturalist study that ranges along the East

Coast from Maine to Key West. As the *Time* reviewer observes, "Again author Carson has shown her remarkable talent for catching the breath of science on the still glass of poetry."

RUDOLF FLESCH (1911–1986): *Why Johnny Can't Read*. Flesch's controversial bestseller critiques the inadequacy of American education to improve literacy among the young. The sequels *Teaching Johnny to Read* (1956) and *Why Johnny Still Can't Read* (1981) would follow. Born in Vienna, Flesch immigrated to the United States in 1938; he was a literacy and writing expert who advocated a phonetic approach to teaching reading.

LOUIS HARTZ (1919–1986): *The Liberal Tradition in America*. The Harvard government professor provides an analysis of American political thought since the Revolution. His best-known work, it is awarded the Woodrow Wilson Prize and the Lippincott Prize for its fresh insights into American history.

WILL HERBERG (1909–1977): *Protestant-Caltholic-Jew*. Herberg offers a sociological analysis of contemporary religious practices and their historical contexts. Herberg was a professor of Judaic studies and philosophy at Drew University.

RICHARD HOFSTADTER (1916–1970): *The Age of Reform: From Bryan to F.D.R.* Hofstadter's account of the 1890s through the New Deal earns the Pulitzer Prize. The book prompts criticism among liberals who feel that Hofstadter is too critical of the progressive era. Hofstadter was a distinguished historian at Columbia, whose other works include *Social Darwinism in American Thought* (1944), *The American Political Tradition* (1948), and *The Development of Academic Freedom in the U.S.* (1955).

ANNE MORROW LINDBERGH: *Gift from the Sea*. Lindbergh's series of personal essays on love and marriage is considered an important early feminist work that challenges the concept of women defined solely by their role as wives and mothers. Lindbergh would continue her meditations in her only volume of poetry, *The Unicorn* (1956).

WALTER LIPPMANN: *Essays in Public Philosophy*. Lippmann diagnoses a decline in the "traditions of civility" and a disintegration in responsible authority.

HERBERT MARCUSE (1888–1979): *Eros and Civilization*. The sociologist and political philosopher attempts to relate sexual repression to political and social repression. Advocating more sexual freedom and openness, the book is considered one of the theoretical sources for the sexual revolution of the 1960s. Marcuse immigrated to the United States from Germany in 1934. He taught at Columbia, Harvard, Brandeis, and the University of California at San Diego.

NORMAN VINCENT PEALE (1898–1993): *The Power of Positive Thinking*. One of the best-selling books of the decade, remaining on the bestseller list for a record three years, Peale's "applied Christianity," stressing the cultivation of a positive attitude as the key to happiness, would become the model for many future self-help books. The Protestant clergyman would author forty books and publish the inspirational magazine *Guideposts*.

C. VANN WOODWARD (1908–1999): *The Strange Case of Jim Crow*. Woodward's analysis of the development of Southern segregation debunks the popularly held belief that Jim Crow laws in the South were enacted when federal troops were withdrawn in 1877, asserting instead that segregation laws did not become widespread until the late 1890s. Woodward's legal study is misunderstood for presumably suggesting the existence of racial harmony in the South prior to the 1890s and criticized for ignoring the human cost of segregation. Born in Arkansas, Woodward taught at Johns Hopkins and Yale and was regarded as the leading historian of the post–Civil War South.

Poetry

A. R. AMMONS (1926–2001): *Ommateum with Doxology*. Ammons's first collection displays his characteristic interest in humanity's relationship to nature and the multiple ways of viewing the world. Born in North Carolina, Ammons began writing poetry while serving on a destroyer escort in World War II. After attending Wake Forest and teaching in a small school in New Jersey, Ammons worked as a business executive from 1952 to 1964.

W. H. AUDEN: *The Shield of Achilles*. Auden's National Book Award–winning collection, regarded by many as his best, includes two major poetic sequences, "Horae Canonicae" and "Bucolics." The title poem and "Memorial for the City" were inspired by Auden's experience of viewing the devastation of Europe following World War II.

ELIZABETH BISHOP: *Poems: North & South—A Cold Spring*. Bishop's second collection combines her first with nineteen new poems, including important works such as "The Fish," "At the Fishhouses," "Cape Breton," and "The Prodigal," her only poem dealing with alcoholism. The volume is awarded the Pulitzer Prize.

JOHN CIARDI: *As If: Poems New and Selected*. Organized by sections on love, war, and family life, Ciardi's collection underscores the poet's view that "As if strikes me as the enduring mode of poetry. . . . Poetry AS IF's reality." He would follow it with two subsequent collection

during the decade: *I Marry You: A Sheaf of Love Poems* (1958) and *Thirty-nine Poems* (1959).

EMILY DICKINSON: *The Complete Poems*. The scholarly complete edition of Dickinson's poetry is edited by Thomas H. Johnson (1902–1985), who restores the poet's original texts. As Robert Hillyer declares in his review, this "is not only a major work of scholarship; it is a monument in American literature."

LAWRENCE FERLINGHETTI (b. 1919): *Pictures of the Gone World*. Ferlinghetti's first collection is the initial work in his Pocket Poet series, issued from the San Francisco City Lights bookstore, which he co-owned. The fourth volume in the series, Allen Ginsberg's landmark *Howl and Other Poems* (1956), would prompt Ferlinghetti's arrest in 1957 on charges of obscenity, gaining national notoriety for the Beat movement.

DONALD HALL (b. 1928): *Exiles and Marriages*. Hall's first collection of tightly structured verses earns him early acclaim. Included is the poem "Exiles," the first work by an American to win England's Newdigate Prize. A second volume of similar poems, *The Dark Houses*, would appear in 1958. The Connecticut-born poet was the poetry editor of the *Paris Review* and was a literature professor at the University of Michigan from 1957 to 1977.

ROBERT HAYDEN: *Figure of Time*. Hayden's only publication during the decade is this pamphlet containing new and previously published work treating human suffering. It is noteworthy as the first of Hayden's works to show his religious beliefs after his conversion to the Baha'i faith.

RANDALL JARRELL: *Selected Poems*. Jarrell compiles selections from his previous volumes, many revised, in addition to two new works, along with an introduction that explains the background and intent of some of his poems.

HOWARD NEMEROV: *The Salt Garden*. Many critics regard this volume as the first of Nemerov's poetic maturity, establishing his characteristic lyrical meditations on nature and the transience of existence, in acclaimed works such as "The Goose Fish," "The Lives of Gulls and Children," "Elegy of Last Resort," and "Fables of the Moscow Subway."

ADRIENNE RICH: *The Diamond Cutters*. Although critically praised, Rich's second collection would be later dismissed by its author: "By the time that book came out I was already dissatisfied with those poems, which seemed to me more exercises for poems I hadn't written."

LOUIS SIMPSON: *Good News of Death and Other Poems*. Simpson's volume features war poems, such as "The Battle" and "The Ash and the Oak," love poems, such as "A Woman Too Well Remembered," and his initial poetic examinations of contemporary American life, in "West" and other poems.

WILLIAM CARLOS WILLIAMS: *Journey to Love.* Williams's collection features one of his most important later poems, "Asphodel, That Greeny Flower," a long meditative love poem addressed to Williams's wife, which Auden calls "one of the most beautiful poems in the language."

Publications and Events

Daedalus. The American Academy of Arts and Sciences publishes the first issue of its quarterly, containing, in each issue, scholarly and critical articles on a single topic, such as mass culture and mass media, excellence and leadership in a democracy, and perspectives on the novel.

The Village Voice. The Greenwich Village–based alternative weekly, cofounded by Daniel Wolf, Edwin Fancher, and Norman Mailer, who supplied its name, begins publication. Mailer was featured as a columnist in 1956, and the publication quickly established itself as one of the major platforms for the avant-garde of the 1950s and 1960s.

1956

Drama and Theater

PADDY CHAYEFSKY: *The Middle of the Night.* Chayefsky's first Broadway production is a transfer from television concerning the romance between an aging widower and his newly divorced receptionist.

LILLIAN HELLMAN: *Candide.* In one of the most notorious initial failures in Broadway history, this musical treatment of Voltaire's novel features remarkable artistic credentials, including Hellman's book, lyrics by poet Richard Wilbur, music by Leonard Bernstein, and direction by Tyrone Guthrie. Yet the play fails with audiences, lasting for only seventy-three performances. It would finally succeed in 1974, in Harold Prince's radically revised version.

JEROME LAWRENCE AND ROBERT E. LEE: *Auntie Mame.* The playwrights adapt Patrick Dennis's 1953 autobiographical novel about the flamboyant, eccentric Mame, who provides an unconventional upbringing for her orphaned nephew. Rosalind Russell stars on stage and would reprise the title role in the 1958 film version. Lawrence and Lee would convert the play into the successful musical *Mame* in 1966.

ALAN JAY LERNER AND FREDERICK LOEWE: *My Fair Lady.* The musical version of George Bernard Shaw's *Pygmalion* is considered by many as the greatest of all American musicals, featuring a brilliant score, a clever story, and masterful staging. Its 2,717 performances set a new record for a musical.

FRANK LOESSER: *The Most Happy Fella.* Loesser writes the book and the music for this version of Sidney Howard's play *They Knew What They Wanted* (1924), about an aging Italian wine grower who proposes by mail to a San Francisco waitress, sending her a photo of his hired hand. Almost entirely sung, the musical is considered Loesser's masterpiece, and it has entered the repertory of many opera companies.

EUGENE O'NEILL: *Long Day's Journey into Night.* Written in 1940, O'Neill's masterpiece finally opens on Broadway. Its production countermands O'Neill's express wish that the play not be produced until twenty-five years after his death.

Fiction

NELSON ALGREN: *A Walk on the Wild Side.* Algren rewrites his autobiographical novel, *Somebody in Boots* (1935), about a poor white youth from Texas who gets involved with prostitutes, pimps, and derelicts in the French Quarter of New Orleans. The book is viewed as part of an underground movement against the conformity and regimentation of the era.

JAMES BALDWIN: *Giovanni's Room.* Baldwin's second novel presents a young white man in Paris who is conflicted over his homosexuality. The novel represents a considerable breakthrough in treating the formerly taboo subject and is praised by critic Stanley Macebuh as "one of the few novels in America in which the homosexual sensibility is treated with some measure of creative seriousness."

JOHN BARTH (b. 1930): *The Floating Opera.* Barth's debut novel deals with a middle-aged lawyer in Tidewater, Maryland, who recalls his decision not to commit suicide based on the recognition that if there is no absolute reason to go on living, there is also no imperative for self-destruction. Anxious for publication, Barth agrees to a more affirmative conclusion than originally planned. Although recognized for its originality as a modern echoing of Laurence Sterne's *Tristram Shandy*, the book initially sells only 1,682 copies.

SAUL BELLOW: *Seize the Day.* The volume combines the title novella with three short stories and a one-act play. The title work, about Tommy Wilhelm's existential crisis, is a brilliantly crafted synthesis of Bellow's dominant themes. Many consider it his masterpiece.

WILLIAM BRINKLEY (1917–1993): *Don't Go Near the Water.* Brinkley's best-known book is this comic novel set in the South Pacific during World War II. It would be made into a successful 1957 film. Born in Oklahoma, Brinkley worked as a journalist for the *Washington Post* and *Life*.

PEARL S. BUCK: *Imperial Woman.* Buck's most accomplished later novel is this biographical reconstruction of the life of Tzu Hsi, the last empress of China.

DIANA CHANG (b. 1934): *The Frontiers of Love.* Chang's first novel treats a group of Eurasians searching for love and identity in Shanghai during the last days of the Japanese occupation. The work continues to draw high praise as one of the key works of the evolving canon of Asian American literature.

HERBERT GOLD: *The Man Who Was Not with It.* Gold's third novel, following two realistic depictions of Midwestern life, *Birth of a Hero* (1951) and *The Prospect Before Us* (1954), is considered by many his best. It concerns a carnival worker who is a morphine addict.

MARK HARRIS: *Bang the Drum Slowly.* Most consider this second of Harris's baseball novels concerning New York Mammoths pitcher Henry Wiggens his finest. It concerns a catcher dying of Hodgkin's disease and his relationship with his teammates.

MEYER LEVIN: *Compulsion.* Levin's greatest popular and critical success is this novel treating the Leopold-Loeb murder case. Evoking comparisons with Theodore Dreiser's *An American Tragedy*, the novel considers the killers' background, their psychological makeup, their trial, and the community's reaction. The novel would be dramatized by the author in 1957; a film version would follow in 1959.

GRACE METALIOUS (1924–1964): *Peyton Place.* Metalious publishes a notorious bestseller about the sexual goings-on in a small New England community. As one reviewer notes, "Sex is never long out of the town's mind; anyway it seldom is out of hers . . . and her love scenes are as explicit as love scenes can get without the use of diagrams and tape recorders." Another reviewer ruefully observes that "More Americans . . . have purchased *Peyton Place* than the works of Fitzgerald, Hemingway, Melville, Dreiser, or James Joyce." Metalious would publish a sequel, *Return to Peyton Place*, in 1959.

WRIGHT MORRIS: *The Field of Vision.* Morris wins the National Book Award for this innovative novel, which looks at the lives of a group of Nebraskan tourists at a Mexican bullfight. It is Morris's most complex and successful work.

EDWIN O'CONNOR (1918–1968): *The Last Hurrah.* O'Connor's bestseller shows an Irish American big-city political machine at work in a portrait of Mayor Frank Skeffington, who resembles Boston's James Michael Curley. Despite efforts by Curley to halt production, the novel would be adapted as a successful 1958 film, starring Spencer Tracy. Born in Rhode Island, O'Connor became a radio announcer after graduating from college, an experience that provided the subject for his first novel, *The Oracle* (1951).

J. F. POWERS: *The Presence of Grace.* Powers's collection includes both secular stories — "The Poor Thing" and "Blue Island" — and ecclesiastical ones about Roman Catholic clergymen in the Midwest.

MARY LEE SETTLE (b. 1918): *O Beulah Land.* The first of the author's Beulah Quintet traces the development of American culture and history over three hundred years, from the perspectives of three fictional West Virginia families. It would be followed by *Know Nothing* (1960), *Prisons* (1973), *The Scapegoat* (1980), and *The Killing Ground* (1982).

WALLACE STEGNER: *The City of the Living and Other Stories.* Joe Allston, a character who appears in three of Stegner's major works, debuts in the story "Field Guide to the Western Birds."

WILLIAM STYRON: *The Long March.* Called to active service in the Marine Corps during the Korean War, Styron bases this novel on his actual experience of a punishing forced march at Camp Lejeune, North Carolina. The story had been published in the first issue of *Discovery* in 1953.

GORE VIDAL: *A Thirsty Evil.* Vidal's short story collection, his first and only (up to this point), contains works treating childhood ("The Robin" and "A Moment of Green Laurel"), the theme of appearance and reality ("The Ladies in the Library" and "Erlinda and Mr. Coffin"), as well as three dealing with homosexuality ("Three Strategems," "The Zenner Trophy," and "Pages from an Abandoned Journal").

Literary Criticism and Scholarship

MURRAY KRIEGER (1923–2000): *The New Apologists for Poetry.* Krieger critiques the current state of criticism in what René Wellek describes as "the best discussion of the New Criticism in existence." Krieger solidified his reputation as an influential literary critic and theoretician with *The Tragic Vision* (1960). He became the first American chaired professor in literary criticism at the University of Iowa in 1963.

MARY McCARTHY: *Sights and Spectacles: Theatre Chronicles, 1937–1956.* The volume collects McCarthy's drama reviews and profiles of playwrights and actors.

Senator John F. Kennedy signing a copy of *Profiles in Courage* in 1956

She also publishes the first of her two Italian city portraits, *Venice Observed*. The second, *The Stones of Florence*, would follow in 1959.

Nonfiction

MOREY BERNSTEIN (1919–1999): *The Search for Bridey Murphy*. Bernstein's best-selling book concerns housewife Virginia Tighe's hypnotic regression, revealing a past life as an Irish woman in the nineteenth century. The book produces a hypnosis craze and an interest in reincarnation until it is revealed that Tighe had simply recast childhood memories into an intriguing narrative.

TRUMAN CAPOTE: *The Muses Are Heard*. Capote continues to develop his nonfictional portraiture method in this witty account of his trip to Russia with the all-black cast of a road company production of *Porgy and Bess*.

LANGSTON HUGHES: *I Wonder as I Wander: An Autobiographical Journey*. In the second installment of Hughes's autobiographical recollections following *The Big Sea* (1940), the writer continues his account of his life up to 1938.

GEORGE F. KENNAN (b. 1904): *Russia Leaves the War*. The diplomat and historian wins the National Book Award,

the Bancroft Prize, and the Pulitzer Prize for the first of two volumes treating Soviet-American relations from 1917 to 1920. *The Decision to Intervene* would follow in 1958.

JOHN F. KENNEDY: *Profiles in Courage*. Kennedy's testimonial on behalf of eight political leaders' tests of conscience earns the Pulitzer Prize as well as attention for the budding politician and future president. Later reports indicates that Kennedy's friend and adviser Theodore Sorensen is the book's actual author.

C. WRIGHT MILLS: *The Power Elite*. Mills attempts to determine who makes the crucial decisions in contemporary America, and why, in this influential sociological study.

ROBERT PENN WARREN: *Segregation: The Inner Conflict in the South*. Warren presents a survey of Southern opinion on the issue. *Who Speaks for the Negro?* would follow in 1965, based on Warren's interviews with prominent black leaders.

WILLIAM H. WHYTE (1917–1999): *The Organization Man*. In one of the defining theoretical works of the period, Whyte studies the cost to the individual of the institutionalization of modern life and the proliferation of bureaucracies and conformity. Whyte was a journalist and editor of *Fortune* magazine.

RICHARD WRIGHT: *The Color Curtain*. Wright reports on the Asian-African Bandung Conference in Indonesia, expanding his thesis, presented in *Black Power* (1954), concerning the exploitation of nonwhites.

Poetry

JOHN ASHBERY (b. 1927): *Some Trees*. The poet's first commercially published collection, selected by W. H. Auden for the Yale Series of Younger Poets, is made up of verses dealing with the problematic nature of poetic expression. It includes some of his best poems, including "Instruction Manual" and "Illustration." Born in Rochester, New York, and educated at Harvard, Columbia, and New York University, Ashbery lived in France from 1955 to 1966 and was the art critic for the *Herald Tribune* and *Art News*.

JOHN BERRYMAN: *Homage to Mistress Bradstreet*. Berryman's lengthy ode on the personal and spiritual life of the American colonial poet Anne Bradstreet appears in book form. With its fractured syntax and dreamy images, the poem introduces Berryman's new, more personal style.

EDGAR BOWERS (1924–2000): *The Form of Loss*. Bowers's first collection wins the Swallow Press New Poetry Series Award and features his distinctive compact and intense style in admired poems such as "Dark Earth and Summer" and "The Prince." Born in Georgia, Bowers earned a Ph.D. from Stanford and taught at the University of California at Santa Barbara.

ALLEN GINSBERG (1926–1997): *Howl and Other Poems*. Publication of Ginsberg's Whitmanesque, rhapsodic, gritty portrait of contemporary America by San Francisco poet and bookshop owner Lawrence Ferlinghetti occasions the latter's trial and acquittal on obscenity charges. The trial catapults Ginsberg into the spotlight, making him a spokesperson for the Beat movement. Ginsberg's poetic method, so contrary to the formality of his peers, helps reshape modern poetry. Besides the title work, the collection includes well-known poems such as "A Supermarket in California" and "Sunflower Sutra."

W. S. MERWIN: *Green with Beasts*. Merwin's third collection displays a noticeable shift from narrative to lyric and from the mythological to the personal in poems such as "Leviathan," "The Annunciation," and "The Prodigal Son." Poet Richard Howard notes the difference between Merwin's previous recounting of experience and this volume's dwelling inside experience.

MARIANNE MOORE: *Like a Bulwark*. Moore's first new poems since 1944 follow nine years devoted to translation, resulting in *The Fables of La Fontaine* (1954); during those years she had also published *Predilections* (1955), a volume of essays and reviews. Another volume of new work, *O to Be a Dragon*, would appear in 1959.

EZRA POUND: *Section, Rock-Drill, 85–95 de los Cantores*. The first of the two final major sections of *The Cantos* appears. It would be followed by *Thrones; 96–109 de los Cantores* in 1959.

RICHARD WILBUR: *Things of This World*. Wilbur's third collection is generally regarded as his best, containing acclaimed works such as "Love Calls Us to the Things of This World," "A Baroque Wall-Fountain in the Villa Sciarra," and "For the New Railway Station in Rome." The book wins the Pulitzer Prize, the National Book Award, and the Edna St. Vincent Millay Memorial Award. Wilbur would follow his success with *Poems 1943–1956* in the following year.

1957
Drama and Theater

JEROME CHODOROV AND JOSEPH FIELDS: *The Ponder Heart*. The veteran playwrights base their play on Eudora Welty's 1954 comic fantasy, about life in a small Mississippi town. Despite an engaging story revolving around a bride's suspected murder by her husband, it receives mixed reviews and a short run on the New York stage.

KETTI FRINGS (1910–1981): *Look Homeward, Angel*. Frings's adaptation of Thomas Wolfe's 1929 novel earns the Pulitzer Prize and the New York Drama Critics Circle Award. It is her only drama success. Frings was a Hollywood screenwriter who wrote the film adaptation of William Inge's *Come Back, Little Sheba* in 1952.

WILLIAM INGE: *The Dark at the Top of the Stairs*. Inge's somber drama presents a lower-middle-class Midwestern family during the 1920s, torn apart by economic forces, sexual trauma, and violence. The play is characteristic of the playwright's ability to endow presumably simple small-town American characters with psychological and emotional depth.

ARTHUR LAURENTS: *West Side Story*. This musical update of Shakespeare's *Romeo and Juliet*, set in New York's tenements and reflecting gang conflict between whites and Puerto Ricans, is a landmark work in the history of the American musical. It features music by Leonard Bernstein, lyrics by Stephen Sondheim, and choreography by Jerome Robbins. Some initial reviewers complain that the play's violence and realism are inappropriate for a musical, while others praise these innovations.

CARSON McCULLERS: *The Square Root of Wonderful.* McCullers's final play reflects her attempt to cope with the suicide of her husband and death of her mother. The play closes after only forty-five performances, and its failure prompts McCullers to abandon drama.

EUGENE O'NEILL: *A Moon for the Misbegotten.* Having failed in its out-of-town tryout in 1947, O'Neill's drama finally reaches Broadway for a disappointingly short run of sixty-eight performances. The play would be subsequently hailed as one of O'Neill's masterpieces in more successful productions in 1968 and 1973.

WILLIAM SAROYAN: *The Cave Dwellers.* Saroyan's last play to appear on Broadway is an allegorical fantasy about several refugees "from the obvious" who take shelter in an abandoned theater slated for demolition. Showing clearly the influence of postwar French drama, particularly the works of Samuel Beckett, the play prompts critic Harold Clurman to label it "sugared existentialism."

GORE VIDAL: *Visit to a Small Planet.* Vidal's first stage success, originally a television drama broadcast in 1955, is a whimsical satire about an extraterrestrial's perspective on modern life on earth.

TENNESSEE WILLIAMS: *Orpheus Descending.* Williams reworks and retitles his earlier play, *Battle of Angels* (1940), about lust and hatred in a small Southern town.

MEREDITH WILLSON (1902–1984): *The Music Man.* Drawing on the former band leader and composer's memories of boyhood in Iowa, the musical presents the machinations of a con man who convinces the inhabitants of River City to outfit a town band. The nostalgic celebration of small-town American life wins both the New York Drama Critics Circle Award and the Tony Award for best musical, edging out *West Side Story.*

Fiction

JAMES AGEE: *A Death in the Family.* Agee's unfinished novel details how the sudden death of Jay Follett in an auto accident plunges his once-happy family into chaos. Based on Agee's own experience following his father's death, the novel concentrates on six-year-old Rufus, who is thrust prematurely into an understanding of matters such as existence and faith. The work wins the Pulitzer Prize, and in 1960 Tad Mosel (b. 1922) would adapt it for the stage as *All the Way Home,* another Pulitzer Prize winner.

ANN BANNON (b. 1937): *Odd Girl Out.* The first of a series of lesbian "pulps," paperback original novels featuring a rotating set of female characters and their romantic entanglements. "Ann Bannon" is the pseudonym of Ann Weldy, an author widely credited with creating a sense of community among lesbians in the 1950s and early 1960s, when lesbian life was covert and plagued by prejudice. *Odd Girl Out* proves enormously popular, as would its sequels, and the entire series would be reissued in the 1970s and again in the 1980s.

HAROLD BRODKEY (1930–1996): *First Love and Other Stories.* Brodkey's first collection is a linked sequence on the progression of youthful love and its many compromises. The stories are widely praised for their control and perceptiveness. Brodkey's subsequent collections include *Women and Angels* (1985) and *Stories in an Almost Classical Mode* (1988). Born in Illinois, Brodkey worked as a staff writer for *The New Yorker* beginning in 1953 when it published his first short story, "State of Grace."

JOHN CHEEVER: *The Wapshot Chronicle.* Cheever's first novel follows the fortunes of a New England family, loosely based on Cheever's own, skillfully contrasting happy family rituals with darker portraits of modern American life. It wins Cheever a National Book Award; a sequel, *The Wapshot Scandal,* would follow in 1964.

JAMES GOULD COZZENS: *By Love Possessed.* Cozzens's novel about a conservative, middle-aged lawyer's recollections of his love life becomes a bestseller, employing as narrator a mature professional man capable of dispassionately assessing society's foibles while at the same time acquiescing to them.

W.E.B. DU BOIS: *The Ordeal of Mansart.* Volume one of Du Bois's The Black Flame trilogy offers his version of American history from Reconstruction to the present. It would be followed by *Mansart Builds a School* (1959) and *Worlds of Color* (1961).

WILLIAM FAULKNER: *The Town.* The second installment of Faulkner's Snopes trilogy appears seventeen years after the first volume, *The Hamlet* (1940). The novel focuses on an outsider, the lawyer Gavin Stevens, and his naive longing for two of the Snopes women. Narration by another outsider, the itinerant sewing machine salesman V. K. Ratliff, integrates *The Town* with its predecessor in the trilogy. The set would be completed with the 1960 publication of *The Mansion.*

CHESTER HIMES: *For Love of Imabelle.* The first of the nine detective novels Himes would write up to 1969. They feature the black police detectives Coffin Ed Johnson and Gravedigger Jones in a violent, almost surrealistic Harlem setting. Other novels in the series include *The Real Cool Killers* (1959), *Cotton Comes to Harlem* (1965), and *Blind Man with a Pistol* (1969).

JAMES JONES: *Some Came Running.* Jones's second novel is a nonmilitary follow-up to *From Here to Eternity,* concerning postwar life in a small Midwestern town.

The book is a commercial success but a critical failure; reviewers object to its long-winded philosophizing. One reviewer calls it "a 1,200 page orgy of sex, self-pity, and sloppy prose."

JACK KEROUAC: *On the Road.* Kerouac's first-person roman à clef, written in 1951 and frequently revised, finally appears, transforming its author into the chief chronicler of the Beat generation. Initially produced by "spontaneous writing" on a roll of teletype, the book is, Kerouac asserts, intended as a jazz composition. It tells the story of the friendship between two men and their cross-country journeys. *On the Road* becomes a best-selling cult classic.

C. Y. LEE (b. 1917): *The Flower Drum Song.* Lee's novel about generational conflict within an Asian American family over an arranged marriage in San Francisco's Chinatown would be adapted into a musical by Rodgers and Hammerstein in 1958. Born in China, Lee came to the United States in 1942. His other books include *Lover's Point* (1958), *Madame Goldenflower* (1960), *The Second Son of Heaven* (1990), and *Gate of Rage* (1991).

BERNARD MALAMUD: *The Assistant.* Set in the Brooklyn grocery of a struggling Jewish immigrant, the novel mirrors Malamud's own background. Many regard its story of reverse assimilation, in which a grocer's assistant takes up both his employer's position and his religion after the older man's death, as Malamud's most significant work.

WRIGHT MORRIS: *Love Among the Cannibals.* Two Hollywood songwriters pick up two young women and take them to Acapulco for an encounter with the primitive. A departure for Morris, the novel employs a cynical first-person narrator to focus on contemporary life.

VLADIMIR NABOKOV: *Pnin.* Drawing on his own college teaching experience, Nabokov presents a satirical look at American higher education and campus social mores from the perspective of an émigré Russian professor at an upstate New York college. Some consider the protagonist one of the most endearing characters in modern fiction.

HOWARD NEMEROV: *The Homecoming Game.* Nemerov's third and final novel is a comedy about a professor who fails a star football player on the eve of an important game. The writer's most conventional work and biggest success, it would be dramatized by Howard Lindsay and Russel Crouse as *Tall Story* in 1959.

JOHN OKADA (1923–1971): *No-No Boy.* Okada's only published work, and the first Japanese American novel published in the United States, depicts a Nisei (person born of Japanese immigrants to America) who resists the draft during World War II and the racism experienced by Japanese Americans during and after the war. The novel rejects the image of the docile "model minority," recording the self-hatred, uncertainty, and divisions within the Japanese American community. Largely ignored at the time, it would be subsequently recognized as a classic work of Asian American literature.

AYN RAND: *Atlas Shrugged.* Rand dramatizes the efforts of five heroic figures to save America from socialism. Dismissed by critics as a "polemic inadequately disguised as a novel," the book becomes a bestseller and contributes to Rand's cult status.

JAMES SALTER (b. 1925): *The Hunters.* Salter's first novel deals with the author's experiences as a fighter pilot in Korea. When reissued in 1997, it would prompt the *Times Literary Supplement* reviewer to describe it as a "brisk, controlled novel, written on titanic lines. As other books of its era have fallen away, this one turns out to be a classic." Salter graduated from West Point and pursued an air force career until 1957.

JOHN STEINBECK: *The Short Reign of Pippin IV.* Steinbeck's unusual departure is a limp satire on French politics, which imagines the restoration of the monarchy in the twentieth century.

Literary Criticism and Scholarship

RICHARD CHASE (1914–1962): *The American Novel and Its Tradition.* Chase's analysis has long served as a paradigm-making critique of the American novel, distinguishing it from European fiction by its preference for romance over realism.

T. S. ELIOT: *On Poetry and Poets.* The volume collects Eliot's major criticism from the 1940s and 1950s, including "The Music of Poetry," a central document for the New Criticism, and "Poetry and Drama," which supplies Eliot's definition of and justification for his poetic drama.

IRVING HOWE (1920–1993): *Politics and the Novel.* Having published a critical biography of Sherwood Anderson (1951) and a critical study of William Faulkner (1952), Howe contributes an important summary work on American literature, with chapters on Henry James, Nathaniel Hawthorne, and Henry Adams, and an influential general study, "Some American Novelists: The Politics of Isolation." Howe, a professor of English at Hunter College from 1963 to 1986, frequently contributed literary and social essays to the *Partisan Review*. He is best known for his social history of New York Jewish life, *World of Our Fathers* (1976).

YVOR WINTERS: *The Function of Criticism: Problems and Exercises.* The essay collection includes important assessments of Gerard Manley Hopkins and Robert Frost.

Nonfiction

NOAM CHOMSKY (b. 1928): *Syntactic Structures.* The scholar at the Massachusetts Institute of Technology introduces ideas about language that transform the study of linguistics, human language, and communication. Several important works, expanding his views, would follow; they include *Current Issues in Linguistic Theory* (1964), *Aspects of the Theory of Syntax* (1965), *Topics in the Theory of Generative Grammar* (1966), and *Sound Patterns in English* (1968). Chomsky's concept of "transformational grammar," that it was possible to predict sentence combinations in a language and to describe their structure, in the words of critic John Lyons, "revolutionized the scientific study of language."

LEON FESTINGER (1919–1989): *A Theory of Cognitive Dissonance.* The psychologist's most famous work presents his influential assertion that contradictory beliefs, held simultaneously, result in irrational behavior.

JEAN KERR (1923–2003): *Please Don't Eat the Daisies.* This is the first and the best of Kerr's whimsical accounts of "suburban housewifery" of the period. *The Snake Has All the Lines* (1960) and *How I Got to Be Perfect* (1978) would follow. Kerr was the wife of drama critic Walter Kerr (1913–1996), with whom she collaborated in an adaptation of Franz Werfel's *The Song of Bernadette* (1946) and the musical comedy *Goldilocks* (1948).

ART LINKLETTER (b. 1912): *Kids Say the Darndest Things!* The first of the popular television personality's best-selling collections of amusing comments made by children, whom he interviewed on his television program.

DWIGHT MacDONALD (1906–1982): *Memoirs of a Revolutionist.* The volume collects MacDonald's political criticism, which modulates widely across the political spectrum, from pacifism to Trotskyism to anti-Communism. MacDonald describes his personal ideology as "conservative anarchist." After founding the journal *Politics* (1944–1949) as a platform for his anarchist and pacifist views, MacDonald became a staff writer for *The New Yorker* in 1952.

NORMAN MAILER: "The White Negro." Mailer's essay attempts to trace the source of the "destructive, the liberating, the creative nihilism of the Hip" to African American experience, defining how the "psychic outlaw" opposes social and political repression. Regarded as one of the significant cultural documents of the period, it

Mary McCarthy

appears in *Dissent*, which Mailer edits, and would later be included in *Advertisements for Myself* (1959).

MARY McCARTHY: *Memories of a Catholic Girlhood.* One of McCarthy's most admired works, this series of autobiographical sketches depicts her upbringing by two sets of grandparents from different religious backgrounds after her parents died in the influenza epidemic of 1918. She would continue her recollections in *How I Grew* (1987).

HENRY MILLER: *Big Sur and the Oranges of Hieronymus Bosch.* Miller treats his years living on the California coast as a sage of human liberation, expressed in a combination of anecdotes and ruminations. The most sustained narrative of the book, describing a visit by an eccentric astrologer, had been previously published as *A Devil in Paradise* in 1956.

VANCE PACKARD (1914–1996): *The Hidden Persuaders.* The first of Packard's best-selling popular sociological studies of contemporary American business practices deals with advertising and its reliance on research and subliminal messages to reach consumers. Its sequels are *The Status Seekers* (1959) and *The Waste Makers* (1960).

Packard was a staff writer and editor for *American* magazine from 1942 to 1956 and has been described as "our most popular popularizer of sociology," and by William Barrett as "a blend of amateur sociologist and crusading journalist."

RICHARD WRIGHT: *Pagan Spain* and *White Man, Listen!* The first of Wright's two prose works of 1957 is a bitter series of impressions he gathered while touring Spain, then under the dictatorship of General Francisco Franco. The second, Wright's last book of nonfiction, consists of lectures delivered between 1950 and 1956 throughout Europe, recapitulating his ideas about race. Included is "The Literature of the Negro in the United States," a survey of African American writing.

Poetry

DONALD HALL, ROBERT PACK (b. 1929), AND LOUIS SIMPSON, EDITORS: *The New Poets of England and America.* With an introduction by Robert Frost, this influential anthology introduces the public to many of the most significant contemporary poets. A second edition would appear in 1962.

DENISE LEVERTOV (1923–1997): *Here and Now.* Having published her first collection, *The Double Image* (1946), in England before immigrating to America in 1948, Levertov issues her second collection with the clear intention to be regarded as an American poet. The work, like the two that would immediately follow it — *Five Poems* (1958) and *Overland the Islands* (1958) — shows the influences of William Carlos Williams and methods derived from the Black Mountain poets, such as Charles Olson, Robert Duncan, and Robert Creeley.

HOWARD MOSS: *A Swimmer in the Air.* Moss's third collection contains one of his most admired poems, "A Summer Gone," concerning the passing of time, death, and change. Other poems, such as "Horror Movie," show the poet's witty wordplay.

FRANK O'HARA (1926–1966): *Meditations in an Emergency.* After two of his earlier collections — *A City Winter and Other Poems* (1952) and *Oranges* (1953) — had been published by a New York City art gallery, O'Hara's third collection reaches a wider audience and establishes him as one of the leading exponents of the New York school of poetry. Born in Baltimore, O'Hara was a member of the staff of the Museum of Modern Art from 1951 until his death; from 1953 to 1956 he was an editor, reviewer, and writer for *Art News*.

KENNETH PATCHEN: *Hurrah for Anything.* Jazz influence is evident in this collection of poems, with each verse forming a kind of jazz riff, accompanied by a drawing by the author. Patchen also publishes an enlarged edition of his *Selected Poems* and a volume of prose poems, *Here Together.*

WALLACE STEVENS: *Opus Posthumous.* This posthumously published miscellany includes plays, essays, notebook entries, and some previously uncollected and unpublished poems, including "Adagia," a collection of aphorisms on poetry and the imagination.

ROBERT PENN WARREN: *Promises: Poems 1954–1956.* Warren's collection, which marks a shift in style from narrative to personal introspection, receives both the National Book Award and the Pulitzer Prize. It includes the powerful sequence "Ballad of a Sweet Dream of Peace."

JAMES WRIGHT (1927–1980): *The Green Wall.* Wright's first collection, selected by W. H. Auden as part of the Yale Series of Younger Poets, shows the influence of Robert Frost and Edwin Arlington Robinson as well as his characteristic fascination with outcast figures, including mental patients, prostitutes, and lesbians. One of the major works is "A Poem About George Doty in the Death House." Wright was born in Ohio, a Kenyon College graduate who received his Ph.D. from the University of Washington, and taught at the University of Minnesota, Macalester College, and Hunter College.

Publications and Events

Evergreen Review. This influential literary magazine, published until 1973, featured avant-garde American and world fiction, poetry, drama, criticism, interviews, and photographs. During the 1970s it focused on liberal politics, civil liberties, and the counterculture. Contributors included Jean-Paul Sartre, Albert Camus, Alain Robbe-Grillet, Henry Miller, Jack Kerouac, Allen Ginsberg, and Denise Levertov.

1958
Drama and Theater

S. N. BEHRMAN: *The Cold Wind and the Warm.* Behrman's drama is an autobiographical work about Jewish life in a small town at the turn of the century.

T. S. ELIOT: *The Elder Statesman.* Eliot's final poetic drama is a romantic comedy dealing with the moral rebirth of a man who, after a long life of public success, finally acknowledges his private failures. It is noteworthy as one of Eliot's most sympathetic treatments of humanity.

WILLIAM GIBSON (b. 1914): *Two for the Seesaw.* The New York City native's Broadway debut is a two-person drama concerning the relationship between a married man and a bohemian Jewish girl. It would be adapted as the musical *Seesaw* in 1973.

ARCHIBALD MACLEISH: *J.B.* MacLeish's verse drama recounts the trials of the biblical Job in a modern setting and becomes a surprise Broadway hit, playing for 364 performances and earning both a Pulitzer Prize and a Tony Award.

EUGENE O'NEILL: *A Touch of the Poet.* This is the only completed play in a projected dramatic cycle to be entitled *Tale of Possessors Self-Dispossessed*, which O'Neill abandoned. It concerns an Irish American pub owner whose aristocratic pretensions are dealt a blow when a rich New Englander snubs his daughter.

DORE SCHARY (1905–1980): *Sunrise at Campobello.* Schary's biographical drama treats Franklin Roosevelt's polio from his first being stricken in 1921 to his reemergence in the public eye at the 1924 Democratic Convention. The play wins five Tony Awards. Schary was an actor and director whose screenplay for the film *Boys Town* (1938) won an Academy Award.

SAMUEL TAYLOR (1912–2000) AND CORNELIA OTIS SKINNER (1901–1979): *The Pleasure of His Company.* This sophisticated social comedy treats the disruption caused by the arrival of a bride's philandering father at her wedding. Taylor wrote for radio and is the author of the successful comedy *The Happy Time* (1950). Skinner was an actress who in 1937 played all the parts in an adaptation of Margaret Ayer Barnes's novel *Edna, His Wife.*

TENNESSEE WILLIAMS: *Suddenly Last Summer.* One of Williams's most gothic explorations of the nature of evil concerns a homosexual's sacrificial slaying and cannibalistic consumption. It is produced, together with *Something Unspoken* (1958), as *Garden District* and would be adapted for the screen the following year in a film starring Katharine Hepburn, Elizabeth Taylor, and Montgomery Clift.

Fiction

JOHN BARTH: *The End of the Road.* Conceived as a "nihilistic tragedy" companion to his nihilistic comedy *The Floating Opera*, Barth's second novel concerns Jack Horner's psychological paralysis, his therapy at a "Remobilization Farm," and his tragic relationship with a faculty colleague and his wife. When the wife becomes pregnant, Horner arranges an illegal abortion from which she dies, causing him to revert to his paralyzed state.

THOMAS BERGER (b. 1924): *Crazy in Berlin.* Berger's first novel is a comic picaresque tale introducing Carlo Reinhart, an American G.I. in postwar Berlin who gradually sheds his optimism in a corrupt world of threat and betrayal. Reinhart's career would continue in *Reinhart in Love* (1962), *Vital Parts* (1970), and *Reinhart's Women* (1981). Born in Cincinnati, Berger graduated from the University of Cincinnati after wartime service and worked as a librarian at the Rand School of Social Science, as a staff writer for the *New York Times Index*, and as an associate editor of *Popular Science.*

TRUMAN CAPOTE: *Breakfast at Tiffany's: A Short Novel and Three Stories.* Capote's collection includes one of his most admired works, the novella portraying free spirit Holly Golightly, inspired by Christopher Isherwood's Sally Bowles. The work is the first that displays Capote's fascination with wealth, parties, and the Manhattan elite, as well as the discrepancy between its perceived glamour and its reality.

JOHN CHEEVER: *The Housebreaker of Shady Hills.* Cheever's story collection records the often desperate and frustrated lives of the suburban affluent in works such as the title story, "O Youth and Beauty!" and "The Country Husband."

WILLIAM FAULKNER: *New Orleans Sketches.* This book collects Faulkner's experimental prose pieces written in 1925, marking his transition from poetry to fiction.

SHIRLEY ANN GRAU (b. 1929): *The Hard Blue Sky.* Grau's first novel depicts the lives of descendants of Louisiana's French-Spanish pioneers, who inhabit a coastal island in the mouth of the Mississippi. It helps establish the New Orleans–born writer as an anthropologist, via fiction, of the American South.

LANGSTON HUGHES: *Tambourines to Glory.* Hughes's second novel treats the goings-on in a black storefront church in a comic morality play. Begun as a gospel musical, Hughes converted the story into fiction; he would restore it as a musical in 1963.

SHIRLEY JACKSON: *The Sundial.* Jackson's novel concerns a group awaiting the end of the world.

JACK KEROUAC: *The Dharma Bums.* Kerouac's follow-up to *On the Road* is another quasi-autobiographical quest novel, here derived from the search for Zen Buddhist enlightenment. The main character, Japhy Ryder, is based on Beat poet Gary Snyder. Kerouac also publishes *The Subterraneans*, a confessional account of a writer's failed relationship with a black woman, written in a three-night, benzedrine-assisted composition marathon. The novels are Kerouac's last popular successes.

WILLIAM J. LEDERER (b. 1912) AND EUGENE BURDICK (1918–1965): *The Ugly American.* In one of the first fictional works to address American involvement in Southeast Asia, the novel, about the inept handling of a U.S. aid program in the fictional country of Sarkhan, is denounced on the Senate floor and reportedly causes President Eisenhower to appoint a committee to review American foreign aid policies. It aditionally contributes the term *ugly American* to the lexicon. Lederer was a career naval officer who served during World War II with the Pacific fleet. Burdick was an Iowan who also created a sensation with his novel about a nuclear war by accident, *Fail-Safe* (1962).

BERNARD MALAMUD: *The Magic Barrel.* Malamud's first story collection wins the National Book Award. The volume depicts a search for hope and meaning in naturalistic urban settings, illuminated by elements derived from Yiddish folktales and mythology. Included are some of Malamud's best stories, including the title work, "The First Seven Years," "The Last Mohican," and "Angel Levine."

VLADIMIR NABOKOV: *Lolita.* Nabokov's darkly comic novel of pedophilia, in which Humbert Humbert records his obsession with teenager Dolores Haze, that first appeared in Paris in 1955 is finally published in the United States, provoking a storm of controversy. The book's popularity allowed Nabokov to retire from teaching to devote himself to his writing. He would, as he declared, be "kept by a girl named Lolita."

JOHN O'HARA: *From the Terrace.* The writer would consider this social chronicle, depicting Pennsylvanian Alfred Eaton's drive for success from 1897 to 1946, as his greatest achievement. The novel sells more than 2.5 million copies in paperback, one of the highest book sales figures of the decade.

ROBERT LEWIS TAYLOR (1912–1998): *The Travels of Jamie McPheeters.* This picaresque adventure story of a boy and his father's trip to California during the 1840s has been called a classic of western Americana. It wins the Pulitzer Prize. Taylor would follow it with a historical picaresque companion volume, *A Journey to Matecumbe* (1961), about a journey from Illinois to the Florida Keys. Born in Illinois, Taylor was a St. Louis newspaperman before working from 1938 to 1948 as a profile writer for *The New Yorker.*

ROBERT TRAVERS (1903–1991): *Anatomy of a Murder.* "Robert Travers" is a pseudonym for Michigan attorney, prosecutor, and judge John D. Voelker. His best-selling novel is based on an actual murder case in which Voelker had served as the defense attorney.

LEON URIS (1924–2003): *Exodus.* Having published two previous novels — *Battle Cry* (1953), based on his war experiences as a Marine, and *The Angry Hills* (1955), about a Jewish unit of British soldiers fighting in Greece — Uris publishes a best-selling novelization of the creation of the modern state of Israel. His characteristic extensive documentary method, based on interviews with more than twelve hundred eyewitnesses, joins the fictional story to historical events.

RICHARD WRIGHT: *The Long Dream.* Wright's final novel issued during his lifetime is the only completed volume of a projected trilogy set in the Jim Crow South of Wright's boyhood. It concerns the liberation of a young black man from the control of his corrupt father and racist repression. Critics are hostile, complaining that the book is crudely conceived and shows that Wright is out of touch with contemporary African American experience.

Literary Criticism and Scholarship

JOHN CROWE RANSOM, DELMORE SCHWARTZ, AND JOHN HALL WHEELOCK: *American Poetry at Mid-Century.* Based on a series of lectures delivered at the Library of Congress, the book is considered an important position statement about the current state of the art.

Nonfiction

JAMES AGEE: *Agee on Film.* A posthumous collection of Agee's much-admired film reviews. *Agee on Film II* (1960) reprinted his film scripts, including his adaptations of Stephen Crane's "The Bride Comes to Yellow Sky" and "The Blue Hotel."

HANNAH ARENDT: *The Human Condition.* Arendt diagnoses the causes of modern alienation in an influential study that asserts the triumph of the active over the contemplative life and the modern loss of a sense of publicly significant action.

WILLIAM BARRETT (1913–1992): *Irrational Man: A Study in Existential Philosophy.* In one of the classic commentaries on the modern intellectual scene, Barrett argues that a "deranged rationality" has corrupted Western society. This popular and well-received study, reprinted many times in paperback, remains a classic often taught in college. Barrett was the associate editor of *Partisan Review* from 1943 to 1953 and a professor of philosophy at New York University.

DANIEL BOORSTIN: *The Americans: The Colonial Experience.* Boorstin begins his survey of American history by dealing not with the major figures and events but with the cultural shifts that establish the American character and shape the American nation. The book would be followed by *The National Experience* (1965) and *The Democratic Experience* (1973).

F. SCOTT FITZGERALD: *Afternoon of an Author.* This volume collects Fitzgerald's nonfiction magazine work published during his last fifteen years, including "Princeton," "How to Live on $36,000 a Year," and "Author's House."

SHELBY FOOTE: *The Civil War: A Narrative*. The first volume of Foote's acclaimed trilogy on the Civil War appears. A second volume would appear in 1968, and the last, in 1973.

JOHN KENNETH GALBRAITH (b. 1908): *The Affluent Society*. Galbraith's best-known work is an influential assessment of the U.S. economy during the 1950s boom. A sequel, *The New Industrial State*, about the threat to individualism, would follow in 1967. The son of a Canadian politician and farmer, Galbraith, who became a U.S. citizen in 1937, is widely regarded as one of the foremost and influential modern economists.

MARTIN LUTHER KING JR. (1929–1968): *Stride Toward Freedom: The Montgomery Story*. King's first book is an account of the Montgomery bus boycott of 1956 and his philosophy of nonviolent confrontation.

J. SAUNDERS REDDING: *The Lonesome Road: The Story of the Negro's Part in America*. Redding memorializes the military contributions of African Americans and the achievements of figures such as Frederick Douglass, Sojourner Truth, Booker T. Washington, W.E.B. Du Bois, and Thurgood Marshall.

JOHN STEINBECK: *Once There Was a War*. The volume collects Steinbeck's 1943 war dispatches from England, Africa, and Italy.

EDMUND WILSON: *The American Earthquake*. This miscellany of Wilson's nonliterary articles from the 1920s and 1930s includes film and drama reviews, social critiques, and several short fictions.

Poetry

GREGORY CORSO (1930–2001): *Gasoline* and *Bomb*. Corso's first major collections deal with aspects of death and destruction in jazz-influenced poems such as "Don't Shoot the Warthog" and "Bomb," which treats both the threat of nuclear annihilation and the need for a radical restructuring of American values. Corso, one of the significant members of the Beat movement, had served prison sentences for theft before meeting in a Greenwich Village bar in 1950 Allen Ginsberg, who encouraged Corso's exuberant, Whitmanesque style.

E. E. CUMMINGS: *95 Poems*. This is the last collection of new poems published during Cummings's lifetime. Cummings also publishes *E. E. Cummings: A Miscellany*, a collection of prose pieces.

ROBERT DUNCAN: *Letters Poems*. With this collection Duncan declares his intention to enter "the process which sets self-creation and self-consciousness in constant interplay."

LAWRENCE FERLINGHETTI: *A Coney Island of the Mind*. Ferlinghetti's second collection, following *Pictures of the Gone World* (1955), is his most popular work, one of the key books of the Beat period. Selling more than one million copies, it also becomes one of the biggest-selling contemporary poetry collections of all time.

JOHN HOLLANDER (b. 1929): *A Crackling of Thorns*. W. H. Auden selected Hollander's first collection for the Yale Series of Younger Poets. Hollander's controlled reflections of literary and mythological subjects include admired works such as "Icarus Before Knossus," "Susanna's Song," and "Enter Machiavel, Waving His Tail." Born in New York City, Hollander graduated from Columbia and received a Ph.D. from Indiana University. He has been a faculty member at Connecticut College, Hunter College, and Yale.

STANLEY KUNITZ: *Selected Poems: 1928–1958*. Because Kunitz's last book had been published in 1944 and was long out of print, several publishers balked at bringing out this selection from Kunitz's two previous volumes, along with a handful of new works. It wins the Pulitzer Prize and establishes Kunitz as one of the leading contemporary poets.

HOWARD NEMEROV: *Mirrors and Windows*. Nemerov's fourth collection continues his emphasis on nature first evident in *The Salt Garden* (1955).

THEODORE ROETHKE: *Words for the Wind*. Containing poems such as "The Dying Man" and "I Knew a Woman," the volume is generally considered Roethke's best and earns both the National Book Award and the Bollingen Prize.

MURIEL RUKEYSER: *Body of Waking*. Rukeyser's collection includes the long narrative poem "Suite for Lord Timothy Dexter" as well as translations of the work of Mexican poet Octavio Paz.

KARL SHAPIRO: *Poems of a Jew*. Shapiro combines previous and new works to form "documents of an obsession"—of being Jewish. Included is one of his strongest poems, "The Messias," in which a middle-class Jewish boy confronts his heritage.

JOHN UPDIKE (b. 1932): *The Carpentered Hen and Other Tame Creatures*. Updike's first book is a collection of light verse in the manner of Ogden Nash. Several volumes of poetry would follow—*Telephone Poles* (1963), *Midpoint* (1969), *Tossing and Turning* (1977), and *Collected Poems: 1953–1993* (1993)—which together reflect a progressively darkening and serious personal tone.

Publications and Events

Tri-Quarterly. This little magazine is founded as a publication of Northwestern University and by 1964 was directed to the general public. It devoted special issues, or subsections of its regular issues, to in-depth analyses of particular subjects, such as contemporary American fiction, a modern literary movement, or an American or foreign author.

1959
Drama and Theater

EDWARD ALBEE (b. 1928): *The Zoo Story.* This short one-act drama, Albee's debut, is first performed in Berlin and would appear in New York in 1960. It focuses on an encounter between a complacent middle-class man, sitting on a bench in New York City's Central Park, and an alienated young man who goads him into violence. Like much of Albee's early work, it challenges confidence in conventional American values. Albee was born in Virginia and grew up in a wealthy household in Larchmont, New York. He wrote his first play while working as an office boy, record salesman, and Western Union delivery boy.

PADDY CHAYEFSKY: *The Tenth Man.* Chayefsky's drama concerns an exorcism at an orthodox synagogue; the participants enlist a passerby to make up the quorum of ten specified by Jewish law. The outsider proves as disturbed as the troubled woman the intervention is meant to help.

JACK GELBER (1932–2003): *The Connection.* This Living Theatre production by the Chicago-born playwright features a group of heroin addicts awaiting their fix. In a play-within-a-play, the characters and the playwright address the audience directly. The drama's controversial subject anticipates the social problem plays of the 1960s.

WILLIAM GIBSON: *The Miracle Worker.* This popular and critically acclaimed play dramatizes the relationship between Helen Keller and her teacher, Annie Sullivan. Critics praise the sheer physical vitality and intensity these two women share, as well as the moving story of Keller's emergence from a world of total isolation to one in which she is able to articulate her dreams and desires. A continuation of the Keller-Sullivan story, *Morning After the Miracle*, would appear in 1982.

LORRAINE HANSBERRY (1930–1965): *A Raisin in the Sun.* The first play written by an African American woman to reach Broadway, Hansberry's drama concerns a black family in which a widow wants to use her husband's life insurance to move the family to the suburbs. Her son loses a portion of the money investing in a liquor store, and he is tempted to make up the loss by accepting money from a representative of the white suburban neighborhood, offered to prevent them from moving there. The play wins the New York Drama Critics Circle Award, making Hansberry not only the first African

Paddy Chayefsky

American and the first woman to win the award, but also the youngest person to do so.

ARTHUR LAURENTS: *Gypsy.* Based on stripper Gypsy Rose Lee's autobiography, this musical, with lyrics by Stephen Sondheim and music by Jule Styne, concerns a domineering stage mother who pushes her daughter to become a burlesque queen. The play features a realistic look at the world of vaudeville and burlesque in the 1920s and proves to be the last major stage role for Ethel Merman as the indomitable mother, Rose.

HOWARD LINDSAY AND RUSSEL CROUSE: *The Sound of Music.* This musical about the Austrian Von Trapp family is the last collaboration between Rodgers and Hammerstein. Criticized as overly sentimental, the play nevertheless becomes a major popular success, running for 1,443 performances and achieving cult status in the wake of the 1965 film version.

JEROME WEIDMAN AND GEORGE ABBOTT: *Fiorello!* This musical biography, chronicling the early career of Fiorello La Guardia, wins the Pulitzer Prize, the New York Drama Critics Circle Award, and two Tony Awards.

TENNESSEE WILLIAMS: *Sweet Bird of Youth.* Williams expands his 1956 one-act play into a drama about an aging Hollywood actress and a young gigolo in a small Gulf Coast town, where the local political boss seeks vengeance for the gigolo's treatment of his daughter. Reviewer Walter Kerr observes that the play is "a succession of fuses, deliberately—and for the most part magnificently—lighted."

Fiction

SAUL BELLOW: *Henderson the Rain King.* Bellow's novel about a Connecticut millionaire's symbolic journey into Africa marks a departure for its author, who declares he "had to tame and restrain the style I developed in *Augie March.*" Although a powerfully comic tale, the protagonist's adventures and hijinks are interwoven with a thread of spirituality. Henderson confronts death in the jungle and emerges reborn.

WILLIAM S. BURROUGHS: *The Naked Lunch.* Published in Paris and later issued as *Naked Lunch* in the United States in 1962, Burroughs's experimental, hallucinatory story of a junkie's adventures is described by the author as "necessarily brutal, obscene, and disgusting." It lacks a consistent narrative point of view or progression and had been assembled in part with the help of Allen Ginsberg and Jack Kerouac from pages dropped at random on the floor as they emerged from Burroughs's typewriter. Kerouac supplied the title, which, according to Burroughs, indicates "a frozen moment when everyone sees what is at the end of every fork."

RICHARD CONDON (1915–1996): *The Manchurian Candidate.* Called by critic Charles McCarthy "arguably the best thriller ever written," Condon's novel depicts an American soldier brainwashed by the Chinese during the Korean War and turned into a controlled assassin. The novel reflects American politics during the McCarthy era. It would be adapted as a controversial film in 1962, starring Frank Sinatra. Condon was a film publicist before publishing his first novel, *The Oldest Confession* (1958).

EVAN S. CONNELL JR. (b. 1924): *Mrs. Bridge.* The Kansas City–born writer's first novel, about a bored upper-class Midwestern matron, features what has been called the most fully developed character portrait in the post–World II American novel. A companion novel, *Mr. Bridge,* would appear in 1969.

PETER DE VRIES: *The Tents of Wickedness.* De Vries continues the story of writer Chick Swallow, introduced in *Comfort Me with Apples* (1956), in a series of amusing parodies of Faulkner, Wolfe, Hemingway, and Fitzgerald.

ALLEN DRURY (1918–1998): *Advise and Consent.* Based on more than twenty years of covering politics in Washington as a journalist, Drury's first novel is a behind-the-scenes look at American politics and politicians during a confirmation hearing for a controversial choice for secretary of state. Drury's best-known book, it would be described by critic Richard L. Neuberger as "one of the finest and most gripping political novels of our era."

WILLIAM FAULKNER: *The Mansion.* Faulkner concludes his trilogy on the Snopes family, begun with *The Hamlet* (1940) and continued in *The Town* (1957). The novel shows a prosperous Flem Snopes and the vengeance of his cousin Mink, which ends Flem's career.

HERBERT GOLD: *The Optimist.* Gold's novel about an idealist's pursuit of the American dream shows the writer's shift from realism to a more symbolic, allegorical approach.

JOHN HERSEY: *The War Lover.* Having previously published two smaller studies of the confrontation between the individual and the challenges of modern life in *The Marmot Drive* (1953) and *The Single Pebble* (1956), Hersey publishes one of his most ambitious works, an exploration of the persistent human attraction to war from the perspective of a bomber crew during World War II.

SHIRLEY JACKSON: *The Haunting of Hill House.* Jackson's novel deals with an experimental psychic investigation of a gothic mansion presumed to be haunted. It would be filmed as *The Haunting* in 1963.

JAMES JONES: *The Pistol.* Jones describes the book as "an experiment in writing a deliberately symbolic little novella." This return to a Pearl Harbor setting concerns an infantryman whose pistol becomes a symbol for his survival and others' envy.

JACK KEROUAC: *Doctor Sax* and *Maggie Cassidy.* Kerouac's popularity prompts him to issue works written between 1951 and 1957. The first is a fictionalized treatment of the author's childhood in the character of Jack Duluoz; the second continues Duluoz's story into adolescence. In hopes of establishing himself as a poet, Kerouac also publishes the collection *Mexico City Blues*, but it is savaged by the critics.

PAULE MARSHALL (b. 1929): *Brown Girl, Brownstones.* Marshall's first novel draws on her background as the child of Barbadian immigrants. With its accurate renditions of West Indian speech, the novel marks the first time since Claude McKay's fiction of the 1920s and 1930s that a literary connection was made between African Americans and their West Indian counterparts.

JAMES A. MICHENER: *Hawaii.* Michener publishes the first of his signature encyclopedic, semi-documentary, panoramic novels, depicting the history and culture of the newest U.S. state. A number of best-selling, heavily researched books connecting fictional stories with the history of a region would follow, including *The Source* (1965), about Israel; *Centennial* (1974), about Colorado; *Chesapeake* (1980), about the eastern shore of Maryland;

The Covenant (1980), about South Africa; *Poland* (1983); *Texas* (1985); and *Caribbean* (1989).

HOWARD NEMEROV: *A Commodity of Dreams*. Nemerov's only story collection prompts critical praise, including Warren Beck's comment that "This volume presents further evidence that Nemerov is one of the most gifted writers of his generation, with strong poetic imagination, a searching view of human behavior, and a way of storytelling that is at once rich, deliberate, urbane, and subtle."

GRACE PALEY (b. 1922): *The Little Disturbances of Man: Stories of Men and Women at Love*. Based in part on Paley's experiences in an army camp during the World War II, the collection marks the appearance of a major new literary talent, with wit, clarity of vision, and the ability to capture the voices of urbanites like her fellow New Yorkers.

JAMES PURDY (b. 1923): *Malcolm*. After publishing his first major collection of stories, *The Color of Darkness* (1956), the Ohio-born writer produces his first novel, a picaresque tale of a teenage boy's search for his lost father and a key to understanding the world. It would be dramatized by Edward Albee in 1965.

PHILIP ROTH (b. 1933): *Goodbye, Columbus and Five Short Stories*. This volume introduces Roth to the reading public and earns a National Book Award. Roth's comic take on middle-class Jewish life in America in the middle of the twentieth century alienates many Jewish readers, a portent of things to come.

PETER TAYLOR: *Happy Families Are All Alike*. Taylor's third story collection is hailed by the *New York Times* reviewer as "a literary event of the first importance." It is a study in family dynamics, employing Taylor's characteristic unreliable narrator. Included is one of his most anthologized works, "Venus, Cupid, Folly and Time," which wins the 1959 O. Henry Award.

JOHN UPDIKE: *The Poorhouse Fair*. Updike's first novel is set in an imagined world of the 1970s and concerns a revolt by the elderly in an old folk's home against an administration that denies their human needs. Updike also publishes his first story collection, *The Same Door*, which includes his earliest published work for *The New Yorker*, several set in Ollinger, a fictional version of his Pennsylvania hometown.

JOSÉ ANTONIO VILLARREAL (b. 1924): *Pocho*. The first novel by a Mexican American brought out by a major U.S. publisher is a bildungsroman reflecting the Mexican immigrant experience in America and an identity crisis of the protagonist, who is caught between two cultures. Later, the book would receive renewed attention as one of the precursor works of Chicano literature. Villarreal was born in Los Angeles, the son of migrant laborers. His other books are *The Fifth Horseman* (1974) and *Clemente Chacón* (1984).

KURT VONNEGUT JR.: *The Sirens of Titan*. Written for the paperback science fiction market, Vonnegut's second novel tells the story of playboy millionaire Malachi Constant, who becomes a space traveler, experiencing different societies on various planets. Called by critic Peter Reed "Existential Science Fiction," the novel follows science fiction formula more than any other of Vonnegut's novels but also addresses his characteristic theme of the struggle of the individual in the face of the absurdity of existence. Many regard the book as Vonnegut's finest.

ROBERT PENN WARREN: *The Cave*. Based on an actual incident, the novel uses the plight of a young Tennessee hillbilly who becomes trapped in a cave to study the reaction of his rescuers and their community. The novel is unusual in that the object of the rescue is never shown.

Nonfiction

JACQUES BARZUN (b. 1907): *The House of Intellect*. Barzun critiques American intellectual life, identifying muddy thinking, pedantry, and pretentiousness. Meant to provoke, the book is praised by critic Perry Miller, who calls it "about the most intelligent discussion of the modern intellect we have had in this nation for a long time."

NORMAN O. BROWN (1913–2002): *Life Against Death: A Psychoanalytic Meaning of History*. Brown draws on Freudian concepts to construct a history of the human race in this influential and provocative study. A graduate of Oxford University who received a Ph.D. from the University of Wisconsin, Brown was a professor of languages, classics, and comparative literature at Wesleyan University, the University of Rochester, and the University of California at Santa Cruz.

MARTHA GELLHORN: *The Face of War*. This collection of the correspondent's war reporting covers conflicts in Spain, Finland, and China, as well as in Europe during World War II. It has been praised as some of the finest journalism of the period.

MOSS HART: *Act One*. Hart's autobiography is described by both S. N. Behrman and Walter Kerr as the best book on the theater written in the twentieth century.

JOSEPH WOOD KRUTCH: *Human Nature and the Human Condition*. Krutch's assessment of modern life suggests that scientific knowledge is not enough to ensure humanity's survival and argues for humanistic values to offset an increasingly mechanized and depersonalized society.

MARGARET LEECH: *In the Days of McKinley.* Leech wins the Bancroft Prize and her second Pulitzer Prize (following *Reveille in Washington,* 1941) for this biography of William McKinley, noteworthy for its reassessment of the twenty-fifth president's administration and character.

NORMAN MAILER: *Advertisements for Myself.* Mailer's brawling miscellany includes important essays such as "The White Negro" and "Reflections on Hip"; poetry, plays, and short fiction, including "The Man Who Studied Yoga" and "The Time of Her Time"; and a running assessment of the writer's personal obsessions and professional career. By placing himself at the center of his work, Mailer anticipates his subsequent nonfictional efforts and the style of the so-called New Journalism.

SAMUEL ELIOT MORISON: *John Paul Jones: A Sailor's Biography.* Morison wins the Pulitzer Prize for the first of two biographies of American naval heroes, to be followed by *Old Bruin: Commodore Matthew C. Perry, 1794–1858* (1967).

WILLIAM STRUNK JR. (1869–1946) **AND E. B. WHITE:** *The Elements of Style.* One of the all-time best-selling writing handbooks is a revision by White of Strunk's "little book," first published in 1920. It advocates simple, lucid, and vigorous prose. White had been one of Strunk's students at Cornell.

Poetry

HAYDEN CARRUTH (b. 1921): *The Crow and the Heart.* Carruth's first collection of poems, written before, during, and after his 1953–1954 stay in a psychiatric hospital, features the important poetic sequence "Asylum," which connects his experiences with modern life.

DENISE LEVERTOV: *With Eyes at the Back of Our Head.* The volume, her first issued by New Directions, shows the poet's assimilation of American influences through William Carlos Williams and the Black Mountain poets and the emergence of her own original voice. She explores gender stereotypes and identity in works such as "The Goddess" and "Lie Castle."

ROBERT LOWELL: *Life Studies.* This four-part collection of poetry and prose takes its title from the last section, devoted to the author's deeply personal recollections of his family and childhood, his marriage, and his mental breakdown. The volume's confessional nature helps revolutionize American poetry, freeing it from depersonalized modernism and influencing poets such as Anne Sexton and John Berryman.

JAMES MERRILL: *The Country of a Thousand Years of Peace and Other Poems.* Having explored drama in *The Bait* (1953) and *The Immortal Husband* (1958) and fiction in the novel *The Seraglio* (1957), Merrill returns to poetry in his last volume written in the formal style of the seventeenth-century metaphysical poets.

DELMORE SCHWARTZ: *Summer Knowledge.* Schwartz receives the Bollingen Prize and the Shelley Memorial Award for this collection of works from his earlier volumes and new works, including one of his most acclaimed poems, "Seurat's Sunday Afternoon Along the Seine."

LOUIS SIMPSON: *A Dream of Governors.* Half of the poems in Simpson's collection are war poems, including the impressive narrative poem "The Runner," featuring scenes from the Battle of the Bulge. The other half explores contemporary American life. The volume is also noteworthy as the beginning of Simpson's shift from traditional verse forms to free verse.

W. D. SNODGRASS (b. 1926): *Heart's Needle.* The poet's first collection is influenced by Snodgrass's association with his former teacher Robert Lowell. Taking its title from an autobiographical poem about a father's longing for a much-loved but frequently absent daughter, the volume is confessional in tone but still universal in implication. It wins the Pulitzer Prize.

GARY SNYDER (b. 1930): *Riprap.* Having achieved notoriety before he published anything as the inspiration for the character Japhy Ryder in Jack Kerouac's *The Dharma Bums* (1958), Snyder issues his first collection of poems, treating his experiences in the forest service, as a tanker seaman, and in Japan. It features some of his best poems, including the title work, "A Stone Garden," and "Praise for Sick Women."

MONA VAN DUYN (b. 1921): *Valentines to the Wide World.* The writer's first collection gives evidence of what would become her long-standing preoccupation with the power of love. The volume's final poem, "Toward a Definition of Marriage," addresses both matrimony's strength and its indescribable quality.

JAMES WRIGHT: *Saint Judas.* Wright's second collection deals with various kinds of human suffering in poems such as "In Shame and Humiliation," "Old Man Drunk," and "At the Executed Murderer's Grave." Compared to those in his first volume, the poems are less formally structured and far more pessimistic.

LOUIS ZUKOFSKY: *A 1–12.* Zukofsky publishes the first installment of his long poetic sequence, one of the great longer poetic works of the century. Additional sections would appear in 1969 and 1979. Concerned with the

Births

1962 David Foster Wallace, novelist and short story writer
1964 Michael Chabon, novelist
1965 Andrea Barrett, novelist and short story writer
1966 Sherman Alexie, novelist and short story writer

Deaths

1960 Harold L. Davis (b. 1894), novelist
      Zora Neale Hurston (b. 1901), novelist
      J. P. Marquand (b. 1893), novelist
      Richard Wright (b. 1908), novelist
1961 Dashiell Hammett (b. 1894), mystery writer
      Ernest Hemingway (b. 1899), novelist
      Robert Hillyer (b. 1895), poet and critic
      George S. Kaufman (b. 1889), playwright and Broadway
         director
      James Thurber (b. 1894), humorist, novelist, and
         playwright
1962 E. E. Cummings (b. 1894), poet and novelist
      William Faulkner (b. 1897), novelist
      Robinson Jeffers (b. 1887), poet
1963 Van Wyck Brooks (b. 1886), author and critic
      W.E.B. Du Bois (b. 1868), historian, educator, and
         reformer
      Robert Frost (b. 1874), poet
      Oliver La Farge (b. 1901), novelist and short story writer
      Clifford Odets (b. 1906), playwright
      Sylvia Plath (b. 1932), poet
      Theodore Roethke (b. 1908), poet
      William Carlos Williams (b. 1883), poet, novelist, and
         playwright
1964 Hamilton Basso (b. 1904), novelist and journalist
      Rachel Carson (b. 1907), environmental writer
      Ben Hecht (b. 1894), novelist, playwright, and journalist
      Flannery O'Connor (b. 1925), novelist and short story
         writer
      Carl Van Vechten (b. 1880), novelist and critic

1965 R. P. Blackmur (b. 1904), poet and critic
      T. S. Eliot (b. 1888), poet, critic, and playwright
      Lorraine Hansberry (b. 1930), playwright
      Randall Jarrell (b. 1914), poet
      Shirley Jackson (b. 1919), short story writer and novelist
      Arthur M. Schlesinger (b. 1888), historian
      T. S. Stribling (b. 1881), novelist
1966 Kathleen Norris (b. 1880), novelist
      Delmore Schwartz (b. 1913), poet
      Lillian Smith (b. 1897), novelist and social critic
      Melvin B. Tolson (b. 1898), poet
1967 Margaret Ayer Barnes (b. 1886), novelist and short story
         writer
      Martin Flavin (b. 1883), novelist
      Esther Forbes (b. 1891), novelist and historian
      Langston Hughes (b. 1902), poet, novelist, and playwright
      Carson McCullers (b. 1917), novelist and playwright
      Dorothy Parker (b. 1893), short story writer, poet, and
         dramatist
      Elmer Rice (b. 1892), playwright and novelist
      Carl Sandburg (b. 1878), poet
1968 Dorothy Dodds Baker (b. 1907), novelist
      George Dillon (b. 1906), poet and editor
      Edna Ferber (b. 1885), novelist, short story writer, and
         dramatist
      Fannie Hurst (b. 1889), novelist and short story writer
      Conrad Richter (b. 1890), novelist
      Upton Sinclair (b. 1878), novelist and social reformer
      John Steinbeck (b. 1902), novelist, short story writer, and
         dramatist
      Waters Turpin (b. 1910), novelist
      Yvor Winters (b. 1900), poet and critic
1969 Floyd James Dell (b. 1887), novelist, poet, editor, and social
         critic
      Max Eastman (b. 1883), writer and critic
      Jack Kerouac (b. 1922), novelist and poet
      John Kennedy Toole (b. 1937), novelist

search for order, the sequence alternates autobiographical and historical elements, presenting a tour of many of the century's key events.

1960

Drama and Theater

EDWARD ALBEE: *The Sandbox.* The play is an excoriating attack on the contemporary American family, represented by cartoonlike characters (Mommy, Daddy, and Grandma). Grandma is relegated to a sandbox, infantilized by her family, but still protesting her fate in remarkably graphic language.

LILLIAN HELLMAN: *Toys in the Attic.* Hellman's last theatrical success is a family drama about two spinster sisters' domination over their brother, whose proposed marriage tears the family apart in jealousy and repressed

desire. The play earns the New York Drama Critics Circle Award.

TOM JONES (b. 1928) AND HARVEY SCHMIDT (b. 1929): *The Fantasticks.* The musical version of Edmond Rostand's *Les Romanesques* opens in the tiny 150-seat Sullivan Street Playhouse. Despite initial mixed reviews, it becomes the longest-running play in New York theater history; it would finally close forty-two years later in 2002, after 17,162 performances. Librettist Jones and composer Schmidt were Texans who began collaborating while students at the University of Texas. They would be responsible for *110 in the Shade* (1963) and *I Do! I Do!* (1966).

ARTHUR KOPIT (b. 1937): *Oh Dad, Poor Dad, Mamma's Hung You in the Closet and I'm Feelin' So Bad.* Kopit's first produced play treats a dominating woman who travels with her husband's stuffed corpse and her timid son. Called "a pseudo-tragifarce," the play becomes an

BESTSELLERS, 1960–1969

Fiction

1960

1. *Advise and Consent* by Allen Drury
2. *Hawaii* by James A. Michener
3. *The Leopard* by Giuseppe di Lampedusa
4. *The Chapman Report* by Irving Wallace
5. *Ourselves to Know* by John O'Hara
6. *The Constant Image* by Marcia Davenport
7. *The Lovely Ambition* by Mary Ellen Chase
8. *The Listener* by Taylor Caldwell
9. *Trustee from the Toolroom* by Nevil Shute
10. *Sermons and Soda-Water* by John O'Hara

1961

1. *The Agony and the Ecstasy* by Irving Stone
2. *Franny and Zooey* by J. D. Salinger
3. *To Kill a Mockingbird* by Harper Lee
4. *Mila 18* by Leon Uris
5. *The Carpetbaggers* by Harold Robbins
6. *Tropic of Cancer* by Henry Miller
7. *Winnie Ille Pu* translated by Alexander Lenard
8. *Daughter of Silence* by Morris West
9. *The Edge of Sadness* by Edwin O'Connor
10. *The Winter of Our Discontent* by John Steinbeck

1962

1. *Ship of Fools* by Katherine Anne Porter
2. *Dearly Beloved* by Anne Morrow Lindbergh
3. *A Shade of Difference* by Allen Drury
4. *Youngblood Hawke* by Herman Wouk
5. *Franny and Zooey* by J. D. Salinger
6. *Fail-Safe* by Eugene Burdick and Harvey Wheeler
7. *Seven Days in May* by Fletcher Knebel and Charles W. Bailey II
8. *The Prize* by Irving Wallace
9. *The Agony and the Ecstasy* by Irving Stone
10. *The Reivers* by William Faulkner

1963

1. *The Shoes of the Fisherman* by Morris L. West
2. *The Group* by Mary McCarthy
3. *Raise High the Roof-Beam, Carpenters; and Seymour—an Introduction* by J. D. Salinger
4. *Caravans* by James A. Michener
5. *Elizabeth Appleton* by John O'Hara
6. *Grandmother and the Priests* by Taylor Caldwell
7. *City of Night* by John Rechy
8. *The Glass-Blowers* by Daphne du Maurier
9. *The Sand Pebbles* by Richard McKenna
10. *The Battle of the Villa Fiorita* by Rumer Godden

1964

1. *The Spy Who Came in from the Cold* by John Le Carré
2. *Candy* by Terry Southern and Mason Hoffenberg
3. *Herzog* by Saul Bellow
4. *Armageddon* by Leon Uris
5. *The Man* by Irving Wallace
6. *The Rector of Justin* by Louis Auchincloss
7. *The Martyred* by Richard E. Kim
8. *You Only Live Twice* by Ian Fleming
9. *This Rough Magic* by Mary Stewart
10. *Convention* by Fletcher Knebel and Charles W. Bailey II

1965

1. *The Source* by James A. Michener
2. *Up the Down Staircase* by Bel Kaufman
3. *Herzog* by Saul Bellow
4. *The Looking Glass War* by John Le Carré
5. *The Green Berets* by Robin Moore
6. *Those Who Love* by Irving Stone
7. *The Man with the Golden Gun* by Ian Fleming
8. *Hotel* by Arthur Hailey
9. *The Ambassador* by Morris West
10. *Don't Stop the Carnival* by Herman Wouk

1966

1. *Valley of the Dolls* by Jacqueline Susann
2. *The Adventurers* by Harold Robbins
3. *The Secret of Santa Vittoria* by Robert Crichton
4. *Capable of Honor* by Allen Drury
5. *The Double Image* by Helen MacInnes
6. *The Fixer* by Bernard Malamud
7. *Tell No Man* by Adela Rogers St. Johns
8. *Tai-Pan* by James Clavell
9. *The Embezzler* by Louis Auchincloss
10. *All in the Family* by Edwin O'Connor

1967

1. *The Arrangement* by Elia Kazan
2. *The Confessions of Nat Turner* by William Styron (tie)
3. *The Chosen* by Chaim Potok (tie)
4. *Topaz* by Leon Uris
5. *Christy* by Catherine Marshall
6. *The Eighth Day* by Thornton Wilder
7. *Rosemary's Baby* by Ira Levin
8. *The Plot* by Irving Wallace
9. *The Gabriel Hounds* by Mary Stewart
10. *The Exhibitionist* by Henry Sutton

1968

1. *Airport* by Arthur Hailey
2. *Couples* by John Updike
3. *The Salzburg Connection* by Helen MacInnes
4. *A Small Town in Germany* by John Le Carré
5. *Testimony of Two Men* by Taylor Caldwell
6. *Preserve and Protect* by Allen Drury
7. *Myra Breckinridge* by Gore Vidal
8. *Vanished* by Fletcher Knebel
9. *Christy* by Catherine Marshall
10. *The Tower of Babel* by Morris L. West

1969

1. *Portnoy's Complaint* by Philip Roth
2. *The Godfather* by Mario Puzo
3. *The Love Machine* by Jacqueline Susann
4. *The Inheritors* by Harold Robbins
5. *The Andromeda Strain* by Michael Crichton
6. *The Seven Minutes* by Irving Wallace
7. *Naked Came the Stranger* by Penelope Ashe
8. *The Promise* by Chaim Potok
9. *The Pretenders* by Gwen Davis
10. *The House on the Strand* by Daphne du Maurier

BESTSELLERS, 1960–1969

Nonfiction

1960

1. *Folk Medicine* by D. C. Jarvis
2. *Better Homes and Gardens First Aid for Your Family*
3. *The General Foods Kitchens Cookbook*
4. *May This House Be Safe from Tigers* by Alexander King
5. *Better Homes and Gardens Dessert Book*
6. *Better Homes and Gardens Decorating Ideas*
7. *The Rise and Fall of the Third Reich* by William Shirer
8. *The Conscience of a Conservative* by Barry Goldwater
9. *I Kid You Not* by Jack Paar
10. *Between You, Me, and the Gatepost* by Pat Boone

1961

1. *The New English Bible: The New Testament*
2. *The Rise and Fall of the Third Reich* by William Shirer
3. *Better Homes and Gardens Sewing Book*
4. *Casserole Cook Book*
5. *A Nation of Sheep* by William Lederer
6. *Better Homes and Gardens Nutrition for Your Family*
7. *The Making of the President, 1960* by Theodore H. White
8. *Calories Don't Count* by Dr. Herman Taller
9. *Betty Crocker's New Picture Cook Book: New Edition*
10. *Ring of Bright Water* by Gavin Maxwell

1962

1. *Calories Don't Count* by Dr. Herman Taller
2. *The New English Bible: The New Testament*
3. *Better Homes and Gardens Cook: New Edition*
4. *O Ye Jigs and Juleps!* by Virginia Cary Hudson
5. *Happiness Is a Warm Puppy* by Charles M. Schulz
6. *The Joy of Cooking: New Edition* by Irma S. Rombauer and Marion Rombauer Becker
7. *My Life in Court* by Louis Nizer
8. *The Rothschilds* by Frederic Morton
9. *Sex and the Single Girl* by Helen Gurley Brown
10. *Travels with Charley* by John Steinbeck

1963

1. *Happiness Is a Warm Puppy* by Charles M. Schulz
2. *Security Is a Thumb and a Blanket* by Charles M. Schulz
3. *J.F.K.: The Man and the Myth* by Victor Lasky
4. *Profiles in Courage: Inaugural Edition* by John F. Kennedy
5. *O Ye Jigs and Juleps!* by Virginia Cary Hudson
6. *Better Homes and Gardens Bread Cook Book*
7. *The Pillsbury Family Cookbook*
8. *I Owe Russia $1200* by Bob Hope
9. *Heloise's Housekeeping Hints*
10. *Better Homes and Gardens Baby Book*

1964

1. *Four Days* by American Heritage and United Press International
2. *I Need All the Friends I Can Get* by Charles M. Schulz
3. *Profiles in Courage: Memorial Edition* by John F. Kennedy
4. *In His Own Write* by John Lennon
5. *Christmas Is Together-Time* by Charles M. Schulz
6. *A Day in the Life of President Kennedy* by Jim Bishop
7. *The Kennedy Wit* compiled by Bill Adler
8. *A Moveable Feast* by Ernest Hemingway
9. *Reminiscences* by General Douglas MacArthur
10. *The John F. Kennedys* by Mark Shaw

1965

1. *How to Be a Jewish Mother* by Dan Greenburg
2. *A Gift of Prophecy* by Ruth Montgomery
3. *Games People Play* by Eric Berne, M.D.
4. *World Aflame* by Billy Graham
5. *Happiness Is a Dry Martini* by Johnny Carson
6. *Markings* by Dag Hammarskjöld
7. *A Thousand Days* by Arthur M. Schlesinger Jr.
8. *My Shadow Ran Fast* by Bill Sands
9. *Kennedy* by Theodore C. Sorensen
10. *The Making of the President, 1964* by Theodore H. White

1966

1. *How to Avoid Probate* by Norman F. Dacey
2. *Human Sexual Response* by William H. Masters and Virginia E. Johnson
3. *In Cold Blood* by Truman Capote
4. *Games People Play* by Eric Berne, M.D.
5. *A Thousand Days* by Arthur M. Schlesinger Jr.
6. *Everything but Money* by Sam Levenson
7. *The Random House Dictionary of the English Language*
8. *Rush to Judgment* by Mark Lane
9. *The Last Battle* by Cornelius Ryan
10. *Phyllis Diller's Housekeeping Hints* by Phyllis Diller

1967

1. *Death of a President* by William Manchester
2. *Misery Is a Blind Date* by Johnny Carson
3. *Games People Play* by Eric Berne, M.D.
4. *Stanyan Street and Other Sorrows* by Rod McKuen
5. *A Modern Priest Looks at His Outdated Church* by Father James Kavanaugh
6. *Everything but Money* by Sam Levenson
7. *Our Crowd* by Stephen Birmingham
8. *Edgar Cayce—the Sleeping Prophet* by Jess Stearn (tie)
9. *Better Homes and Gardens Favorite Ways with Chicken* (tie)
10. *Phyllis Diller's Housekeeping Hints* by Phyllis Diller (tie)

1968

1. *Better Homes and Gardens New Cook Book*
2. *The Random House Dictionary of the English Language: College Edition* edited by Laurence Urdang
3. *Listen to the Warm* by Rod McKuen
4. *Between Parent and Child* by Haim G. Ginott
5. *Lonesome Cities* by Rod McKuen
6. *The Doctor's Quick Weight Loss Diet* by Erwin M. Stillman and Samm Sinclair Baker
7. *The Money Game* by Adam Smith
8. *Stanyan Street and Other Sorrows* by Rod McKuen
9. *The Weight Watcher's Cook Book* by Jean Nidetch
10. *Better Homes and Gardens Eat and Stay Slim*

1969

1. *American Heritage Dictionary of the English Language* edited by William Morris
2. *In Someone's Shadow* by Rod McKuen
3. *The Peter Principle* by Laurence J. Peter and Raymond Hull
4. *Between Parent and Teenager* by Dr. Haim G. Ginott
5. *The Graham Kerr Cookbook* by the Galloping Gourmet
6. *The Selling of the President, 1968* by Joe McGinniss
7. *Miss Craig's 21-Day Shape-Up Program for Men and Women* by Marjorie Craig
8. *My Life and Prophecies* by Jean Dixon and René Noorbergen
9. *Linda Goodman's Sun Signs* by Linda Goodman
10. *Twelve Years of Christmas* by Rod McKuen

AWARDS AND PRIZES, 1960–1969

Bancroft Prize (American History, Diplomacy, or Biography)

1960 *The Age of the Democratic Revolution: A Political History of Europe and America, 1760–1800* by R. R. Palmer
In the Days of McKinley by Margaret Leech

1961 *The Jefferson Image in the American Mind* by Merrill D. Peterson
The Struggle for Neutrality, 1914–1915 by Arthur S. Link

1962 *The Transformation of the School* by Lawrence A. Cremin
To the Farewell Address: Ideas of Early American Foreign Policy by Felix Gilbert
Charles Francis Adams, 1807–1866 by Martin B. Duberman

1963 *John Adams* by Page Smith
Pearl Harbor: Warning and Decision by Roberta Wohlstetter
The Might of Nations: World Politics in Our Time by John G. Stoessinger

1964 *Franklin D. Roosevelt and the New Deal, 1932–1940* by William E. Leuchtenburg
The Liberator: William Lloyd Garrison by John L. Thomas
The Foreign Policy of the United States of America by Paul Seabury

1965 *Castlereagh and Adams: England and the United States, 1812–1823* by Bradford Perkins
Portrait of a General: Sir Henry Clinton in the War of Independence by William B. Wilcox
The United States and the Far Eastern Crisis of 1933–1938 by Dorothy Borg

1966 *The Peacemakers: The Great Powers and American Independence* by Richard B. Morris
Between Two Empires: The Ordeal of the Philippines by Theodore W. Friend III

1967 *Prelude to Civil War: The Nullification Controversy in South Carolina, 1816–1836* by William W. Freehling
James K. Polk, Continentalist, 1843–1846, Vol. II by Charles Sellers
The Washington Community, 1800–1828 by James Sterling Young

1968 *The History of Negro Education in the South from 1619 to the Present* by Henry Allan Bullock
From Puritan to Yankee: Character and Social Order in Connecticut, 1690–1765 by Richard L. Bushman
The Ideological Origins of the American Revolution by Bernard Bailyn

1969 *White over Black: American Attitudes Toward the Negro, 1550–1812* by Winthrop D. Jordan
Woodrow Wilson and World Politics: America's Response to War and Revolution by N. Gordon Levin Jr.
The Brains Trust by Rexford Guy Tugwell

Bollingen Prize (Poetry)

1960 Delmore Schwartz
1961 Yvor Winters
1962 John Hall Wheelock
        Richard Eberhart
1963 Robert Frost
1965 Horace Gregory
1967 Robert Penn Warren
1969 John Berryman
        Karl Shapiro

off-Broadway sensation and would transfer to Broadway for a brief run in 1963.

ALAN JAY LERNER AND FREDERICK LOEWE: *Camelot.* Opening a month after Kennedy's election victory, the musical based on T. H. White's popular Arthurian novel, *The Once and Future King,* becomes synonymous with the Kennedy administration, naming its idealistic era and, following Kennedy's assassination, echoing its "one brief shining moment." It is Lerner and Loewe's last collaboration.

JACK RICHARDSON (b. 1935): *The Prodigal.* Richardson's first production is a version of the Orestes-Agamemnon story turned into a modern existential drama. George Wellwarth praises it as "undoubtedly the most brilliantly written new American play to come out since the end of World War II," and it wins the Obie Award. Richardson's follow-up would be his last theatrical success, *Gallows Humor* (1961), contrasting a condemned man's acceptance of his execution with his hangman's dissatisfaction with life.

MICHAEL STEWART (b. 1929): *Bye Bye Birdie.* In the first musical to treat the phenomenon of rock 'n' roll and 1950s youth culture, the drafting of the Elvis Presleyesque character Conrad Birdie prompts a send-off in Sweet Apple, Ohio, to be broadcast on the *Ed Sullivan* television program.

GORE VIDAL: *The Best Man.* Vidal's taut, knowing political drama concerns the scramble for a presidential nomination. Audiences can easily see resemblances between the characters and political figures such as Harry S. Truman, Adlai Stevenson, and Joseph McCarthy.

TENNESSEE WILLIAMS: *Period of Adjustment.* Williams's attempt at domestic comedy looks at married life among distraught honeymooners and an estranged married couple. Subtitled "A Serious Comedy," the play is full of psychologizing and portentous declamations. It closes after only 132 performances.

Fiction

JOHN BARTH: *The Sot-Weed Factor.* Barth's exuberant comic novel depicting the American colonial experience chronicles the life and career of Ebenezer Cooke, the poet laureate of Maryland. The book is an accomplished pastiche of the eighteenth-century novel, which blends fact

AWARDS AND PRIZES, 1960–1969

National Book Awards

1960
Fiction: *Goodbye, Columbus* by Philip Roth
Nonfiction: *James Joyce* by Richard Ellmann
Poetry: *Life Studies* by Robert Lowell

1961
Fiction: *The Waters of Kronos* by Conrad Richter
Nonfiction: *The Rise and Fall of the Third Reich* by William Shirer
Poetry: *The Woman at the Washington Zoo* by Randall Jarrell

1962
Fiction: *The Moviegoer* by Walker Percy
Nonfiction: *The City in History* by Lewis Mumford
Poetry: *Poems* by Alan Dugan

1963
Fiction: *Morte D'Urban* by J. F. Powers
Nonfiction: *Henry James: Vol. II: The Conquest of London, 1870–1881; Vol. III: The Middle Years, 1881–1895* by Leon Edel
Poetry: *Traveling Through the Dark* by William Stafford

1964
Fiction: *The Centaur* by John Updike
Arts and Letters: *John Keats: The Making of a Poet* by Aileen Ward
History and Biography: *The Rise of the West* by William H. McNeill
Science, Philosophy, and Religion: *Man-Made America: Chaos or Control?* by Christopher Tunnard and Boris Pushkarev
Poetry: *Selected Poems* by John Crowe Ransom

1965
Fiction: *Herzog* by Saul Bellow
Arts and Letters: *The Oysters of Locmariaquer* by Eleanor Clark
History and Biography: *The Life of Lenin* by Louis Fischer
Science, Philosophy, and Religion: *God and Golem, Inc.* by Norbert Wiener
Poetry: *The Far Field* by Theodore Roethke

1966
Fiction: *Collected Stories of Katherine Anne Porter* by Katherine Anne Porter
Arts and Letters: *Paris Journal (1944–1965)* by Janet Flanner (Genet)
History and Biography: *A Thousand Days* by Arthur M. Schlesinger Jr.
Science, Philosophy, and Religion: No Award
Poetry: *Buckdancers Choice* by James Dickey

1967
Fiction: *The Fixer* by Bernard Malamud
Arts and Letters: *Mr. Clemens and Mark Twain* by Justin Kaplan
History and Biography: *The Enlightenment* by Peter Gay
Science, Philosophy, and Religion: *La Vida* by Oscar Lewis
Poetry: *Nights and Days* by James Merrill

1968
Fiction: *The Eighth Day* by Thornton Wilder
Arts and Letters: *Selected Essays* by William Troy
History and Biography: *Memoirs (1925–1950)* by George F. Kennan
Science, Philosophy, and Religion: *Death at an Early Age* by Jonathan Kozol
Poetry: *The Light Around the Body* by Robert Bly

1969
Fiction: *Steps* by Jerzy Kosinski
Arts and Letters: *The Armies of the Night* by Norman Mailer
History and Biography: *White over Black: American Attitudes Toward the Negro, 1550–1812* by Winthrop D. Jordan
Science, Philosophy, and Religion: *Death in Life: Survivors of Hiroshima* by Robert Jay Lifton
Children's Literature: *Journey from Peppermint Street* by Meindert DeJong
Poetry: *His Toy, His Dream, His Rest* by John Berryman

---

and fiction into a dizzying meditation on the relationship between history, imagination, and the nature of storytelling.

E. L. DOCTOROW (b. 1931): *Welcome to Hard Times.* Reacting to the movie scripts he had encountered as a reader at Columbia Pictures in the late 1950s, Doctorow radically reinterprets the western in his first novel, which shows a psychopathic killer's destruction of a frontier town. It challenges many western myths in a dark moral parable on the persistence of evil and the difficulty of resisting destruction.

JOHN HERSEY: *The Child Buyer.* Hersey's satiric novel imagines a society in which gifted children are purchased and "engineered" to become thinking machines.

JACK KEROUAC: *Tristessa.* Kerouac's novel treats the narrator's relationship with a morphine-addicted Mexican prostitute. Kerouac also publishes *Lonesome Traveler*, a collection of travel sketches that includes an important autobiographical introduction. It would be followed by *Book of Dreams* (1961), a series of stream-of-consciousness fantasies.

JOHN KNOWLES (1926–2001): *A Separate Peace.* Set at a New Hampshire prep school during World War II, Knowles's first novel concerns the relationship between the introvert Gene and the athletic Finney. The Virginia-born writer would later say that the book is a study "of how adolescent personality develops, identifying with an admired person, then repudiating that

AWARDS AND PRIZES, 1960–1969

Pulitzer Prizes

1960

Fiction: *Advise and Consent* by Allen Drury

Poetry: *Heart's Needle* by W. D. Snodgrass

Drama: *Fiorello!* book by Jerome Weidman and George Abbott, music by Jerry Block, and lyrics by Sheldon Harnick

History: *In the Days of McKinley* by Margaret Leech

Biography/Autobiography: *John Paul Jones* by Samuel Eliot Morison

1961

Fiction: *To Kill a Mockingbird* by Harper Lee

Poetry: *Times Three: Selected Verses from Three Decades* by Phillis McGinley

Drama: *All the Way Home* by Tad Mosel

History: *Between War and Peace: The Potsdam Conference* by Herbert Feis

Biography/Autobiography: *Charles Sumner and the Coming of the Civil War* by David Donald

1962

Fiction: *The Edge of Sadness* by Edwin O'Connor

Poetry: *Poems* by Alan Dugan

Drama: *How to Succeed in Business Without Really Trying* by Frank Loesser and Abe Burrows

History: *The Triumphant Empire: Thunderclouds Gather in the West* by Lawrence H. Gipson

General Nonfiction: *The Making of the President, 1960* by Theodore H. White

Biography/Autobiography: No Prize Awarded

1963

Fiction: *The Reivers* by William Faulkner

Poetry: *Pictures from Brueghel* by William Carlos Williams

Drama: No Prize Awarded

History: *Washington: Village and Capital, 1800–1878* by Constance Green

General Nonfiction: *The Guns of August* by Barbara Tuchman

Biography/Autobiography: *Henry James: Vol. II: The Conquest of London, 1870–1881; Vol. III: The Middle Years, 1881–1895* by Leon Edel

1964

Fiction: No Prize Awarded

Poetry: *At the End of the Open Road* by Louis Simpson

Drama: No Prize Awarded

History: *Puritan Village: The Formation of a New England Town* by Sumner C. Powell

General Nonfiction: *Anti-intellectualism in American Life* by Richard Hofstadter

Biography/Autobiography: *John Keats* by Walter Jackson Bate

1965

Fiction: *The Keepers of the House* by Shirley Ann Grau

Poetry: *77 Dream Songs* by John Berryman

Drama: *The Subject Was Roses* by Frank D. Gilroy

History: *The Greenback Era* by Irwin Unger

General Nonfiction: *O Strange New World* by Howard Mumford Jones

Biography/Autobiography: *Henry Adams* by Ernest Samuels

1966

Fiction: *Collected Stories of Katherine Anne Porter* by Katherine Anne Porter

Poetry: *Selected Poems* by Richard Eberhart

Drama: No Prize Awarded

History: *Life of the Mind in America* by Perry Miller

General Nonfiction: *Wandering Through Winter* by Edwin Way Teale

Biography/Autobiography: *A Thousand Days* by Arthur M. Schlesinger Jr.

1967

Fiction: *The Fixer* by Bernard Malamud

Poetry: *Live or Die* by Anne Sexton

Drama: *A Delicate Balance* by Edward Albee

History: *Exploration and Empire: The Explorer and Scientist in the Winning of the American West* by William H. Goetzmann

General Nonfiction: *The Problem of Slavery in Western Culture* by David Brion Davis

Biography/Autobiography: *Mr. Clemens and Mark Twain* by Justin Kaplan

1968

Fiction: *Confessions of Nat Turner* by William Styron

Poetry: *The Hard Hours* by Anthony Hecht

Drama: No Prize Awarded

History: *The Ideological Origins of the American Revolution* by Bernard Bailyn

General Nonfiction: *Rousseau and Revolution* by Will Durant and Ariel Durant

Biography/Autobiography: *Memoirs (1925–1950)* by George F. Kennan

1969

Fiction: *House Made of Dawn* by N. Scott Momaday

Poetry: *Of Being Numerous* by George Oppen

Drama: *The Great White Hope* by Howard Sackler

History: *Origins of the Fifth Amendment* by Leonard W. Levy

General Nonfiction: *So Human an Animal: How We Are Shaped by Surroundings and Events* by René Dubos

Biography/Autobiography: *The Man from New York* by B. L. Reid

Nobel Prize for Literature

1962   John Steinbeck

Harper Lee

person." The novel wins the Rosenthal Award and the William Faulkner Award. A sequel, *Peace Breaks Out*, would follow in 1980.

LOUIS L'AMOUR: *The Daybreakers*. This is the first of L'Amour's massive twenty-five-volume family saga, The Sacketts, following the extended family from England through the settlement of America.

HARPER LEE (b. 1926): *To Kill a Mockingbird*. Lee's autobiographical account of the trial of an Alabama black man accused of raping a white woman is seen through the perspective of Scout, the young daughter of defense attorney Atticus Finch. Lee's first and (as of 2003) only novel wins the Pulitzer Prize, sells more than five million copies, and would be made into an award-winning film in 1962.

WALTER M. MILLER JR. (1923–1996): *A Canticle for Leibowitz*. Miller's postnuclear holocaust tale, in which a group of monks struggles to salvage human civilization, sells more than two million copies, making it one of the most popular science fiction books and helping to establish science fiction as a significant modern literary form. Born in Florida, Miller served in the army air corps during World War II and participated in the bombing of Cassino.

WRIGHT MORRIS: *Ceremony in Lone Tree*. Revisiting characters from *The Field of Vision* (1956), Morris dramatizes the ninetieth birthday celebration of Tom Scanlon, the last resident of a Nebraska ghost town. The novel is generally regarded as one of Morris's best.

FLANNERY O'CONNOR: *The Violent Bear It Away*. O'Connor's second and final novel concerns the efforts of a backwoods prophet, Francis Marion Tarwater, to escape his calling. The book is an elaborate, symbolic treatment of the soul's tortuous struggle for faith, drawing on the author's characteristic Southern grotesque elements.

JOHN O'HARA: *Ourselves to Know*. O'Hara provides a character study of a man who kills his wife. Also appearing is *Sermons and Soda-Water*, a collection of three novellas.

JAMES PURDY: *The Nephew*. Purdy follows up his highly acclaimed *Malcolm* with the first in a series of controversial novels dealing with homosexuality and sexual deviance. Here, a conventionally minded woman discovers her nephew's homosexuality. It would be followed by *Cabot Wright Begins* (1964), about a rapist, and *Eustace Chisholm and the Works* (1967), about a homosexual affair.

CONRAD RICHTER: *The Waters of Kronos*. Richter wins the Pulitzer Prize for this autobiographically derived novel about an aging writer's imagined return to his Pennsylvania hometown, which has been submerged beneath the waters of the dammed-up Kronos River. A prequel, concerning the writer's father, *A Simple Honorable Man*, would appear in 1962.

ISAAC BASHEVIS SINGER: *The Magician of Lublin*. Written in 1958 and serialized in the *Jewish Daily Forward* in 1959, Singer's novel is set in nineteenth-century Poland and concerns a master magician whose powers are insufficient for him to escape his self-imposed prisons.

WILLIAM STYRON: *Set This House on Fire*. Styron's second novel concerns a murder that becomes a redemptive act for a painter. One of the writer's most ambitious and complex works, the novel is faulted as collapsing under the weight of its allusions and portentousness.

JOHN UPDIKE: *Rabbit, Run*. The novel introduces readers to Updike's most memorable character, Harry "Rabbit" Angstrom, an immature former high school athlete who hungers for lost glory and flees responsibility by deserting his wife and child. The book makes Updike one of the most celebrated writers of his generation and would spawn three sequels. Together, the "Rabbit chronicles" reflect the successive decades of the 1950s through the 1980s.

Literary Criticism and Scholarship

LESLIE A. FIEDLER: *Love and Death in the American Novel.* In his groundbreaking controversial study of American fiction, Fiedler argues that male American novelists are obsessed with death and also incapable of portraying rounded female characters, managing instead "monsters of virtues or bitchery, symbols of the rejection or fear of sexuality."

Nonfiction

DANIEL BELL (b. 1919): *The End of Ideology: On the Exhaustion of Political Ideas in the Fifties.* Bell considers the social and political changes in the United States since World War II. Regarding the book's title, Bell would assert that "Marxism and other traditional idea-systems have proved unable either to explain or to guide new patterns of social behavior."

DAVID H. DONALD (b. 1920): *Charles Sumner and the Coming of the Civil War.* Donald is awarded the Pulitzer Prize for this biography of the radical New England abolitionist. The book is praised by critic John McCardell for "subtly interweaving social and psychological insights . . . graphically depicting a man of many facets who achieved national political prominence despite, rather than because of, his personal traits." Donald, born in Mississippi, has been a professor of history at Columbia, Princeton, Johns Hopkins, and Harvard.

HERBERT FEIS (1893–1972): *Between War and Peace: The Potsdam Conference.* Feis, who was a consultant to the secretary of war from 1944 to 1946, wins the Pulitzer Prize for the fourth of his five-volume diplomatic history of World War II, which had been preceded by *The Road to Pearl Harbor* (1950), *The China Tangle* (1953), and *Churchill, Roosevelt, Stalin* (1957); it would conclude with *Japan Subdued* (1961).

PAUL GOODMAN (1911–1972): *Growing Up Absurd.* One of the major philosophical justifications of the youth rebellion of the 1960s is this critique of modern American culture. Subtitled "Problems of Youth in an Organized Society," the book treats the threat to the individual in America and advocates nonconformity and rebellion against societal strictures. Born in New York City, Goodman gained a Ph.D. in English at the University of Chicago. He was the author of poetry, fiction, and drama as well as works of social criticism.

W. W. ROSTOW (b. 1916): *Stages of Economic Growth.* Rostow's best-known work is an influential economic study that attempts to articulate a non-Marxist model to interpret economic development in emerging countries. It provides the theoretical underpinning for U.S. foreign policy in Asian, Africa, and Latin America during the decade.

Poetry

W. H. AUDEN: *Homage to Clio.* Auden's collection of new works includes light verse and "academic graffiti," sketches of literary figures, as well as "On Installing an American Kitchen in Austria," the initial poem in the evolving sequence "Thanksgiving for a Habitat," which would appear in its entirety in *About the House* in 1965.

GWENDOLYN BROOKS: *The Bean Eaters.* Some of Brooks's finest poems show her shift from personal themes to social concerns in portraits of the frustrations, alienation, and despair of African Americans in the 1950s. Included are "We Real Cool," capturing the defiance of black denizens of a pool hall, and "Ballad of Rudolph Reed," showing the tragic result of a black family's move to a white neighborhood.

CHARLES BUKOWSKI (1920–1994): *Flower, Fist, and Bestial Wail.* The first of Bukowski's more than sixty books establishes in aggressively unsettling verses his characteristic themes of desolation among society's misfits and outcasts and the absurdity of life. Nearly annual volumes would follow, published during the decade by small presses to a small, appreciative coterie. Born in Germany and raised in Los Angeles, Bukowski endured a nearly decade-long alcoholic binge before beginning his professional writing career at age thirty-five.

GREGORY CORSO: *The Happy Birthday of Death.* Poems such as "Police" and "1953" present an American police state, while others deal with the threat of nuclear annihilation. Balancing the volume's pessimism is "Marriage," one of Corso's finest comic poems, a humorous parody of T. S. Eliot's "The Love Song of J. Alfred Prufrock."

JAMES DICKEY (1923–1997): *Into the Stone and Other Poems.* Dickey's first collection, like the two that would follow — *Drowning with Others* (1962) and *Helmets* (1964) — deals with the poet's guilt over his role as a fighter pilot in World War II and Korea, the death of his older brother, and his Southern heritage.

ROBERT DUNCAN: *The Opening of the Field.* As its title indicates, Duncan's collection indicates a new direction in his verse, resulting in some of his best work, such as "Often I Am Permitted to Return to the Meadow," "The Dance," "Poetry, a Natural Thing," "Poem Beginning with a Line by Pindar," and his best-known poem, "My Mother Would Be a Falconess."

RANDALL JARRELL: *The Woman at the Washington Zoo.* Published to critical acclaim and winning a National Book Award, the collection contains some of Jarrell's finest verse, including the title work, a confessional poem disguised as a monologue delivered by a fictitious speaker. This technique becomes one of Jarrell's hallmarks.

GALWAY KINNELL (b. 1927): *What a Kingdom It Was.* Kinnell's first published work is viewed by critic Ralph Mills as "one of those volumes signaling decisive changes in the mood and character of American poetry, as it departed from the witty, pseudo-mythic verse . . . of the 1950's to arrive at the authentic, liberated work of the 1960's." Born in Rhode Island, Kinnell cultivated his interest in poetry at Princeton, where poet W. S. Merwin introduced him to the works of William Carlos Williams.

KENNETH KOCH: *Ko; or, a Season on Earth.* Koch's first commercially published collection is a long comic poem modeled on Byron. A companion volume, *The Duplications*, would appear in 1977, and the work establishes Koch's reputation as "the funniest serious poet we have," according to critic David Lehman.

PHYLLIS MCGINLEY (1905–1978): *Times Three: Selected Verse for Three Decades.* Having published numerous collections of urbane light verse since her first book, *On the Contrary* (1934), McGinley earns critical acclaim for her selected works, including an appreciative introduction by W. H. Auden and the Pulitzer Prize.

W. S. MERWIN: *The Drunk in the Furnace.* This is the first of Merwin's collections to show a shift of style, incorporating more colloquial language and metrical irregularities as well as more personal subjects.

HOWARD MOSS: *A Winter Come, A Summer Gone: Poems, 1946–1960.* Moss selects works from his first three collections around the theme of love. The poems display characteristics of his work identified by critic Karl Malkoff as tracing the "connections between the human universe and the cosmos as a whole" through "wit and intellect."

FRANK O'HARA: *Second Avenue.* The title work of O'Hara's collection is a long succession of juxtaposed images, approximating the poet's conception of verbal abstract expressionism. Kenneth Koch calls the work "among the wonders of contemporary poetry." Included as well are some of O'Hara's finest short poems, including "Easter" and "In Memory of My Feelings." *Lunch Poems* (1964) would follow, the first of O'Hara's volumes to gain a wide audience.

SYLVIA PLATH (1932–1963): *The Colossus and Other Poems.* The only poetry volume published during Plath's lifetime appears in Britain. The poems display both Plath's technical mastery and her harrowing self-examination and torment. It would be published in the United States in 1962.

ANNE SEXTON (1928–1974): *To Bedlam and Part Way Back.* Sexton's first volume of poetry, concerning her experience of mental instability, had been written with the encouragement of Robert Lowell; it reflects Lowell's confessional style and poetic treatment of his own mental illness. While Sexton's subsequent works would take on other themes, all are informed by the instability of what she refers to as her "dwarf heart."

ROBERT PENN WARREN: *You, Emperors, and Others: Poems, 1957–1960.* The collection contains Warren's moving sequence "Mortmain," about the death of his father.

YVOR WINTERS: *Collected Poems.* Winters declares that this collection represents "a kind of definition by example of the style which I have been trying to address for a matter of thirty years." It wins the Bollingen Prize.

Publications and Events

Noble Savage. Described as "a magazine for writers, edited by writers," this semiannual paperback literary collection is founded by Saul Bellow and others. It included contributions from Ralph Ellison, Arthur Miller, Harvey Swados, as well as an "Ancestors" section featuring reprints of past authors such as Samuel Butler and D. H. Lawrence. The magazine ceased publication in 1962.

1961
Drama and Theater

EDWARD ALBEE: *An American Dream.* Albee's surrealistic one-act play brings back the characters from *The Sandbox* — the dominating Mommy and hen-pecked Daddy — to present a grotesque version of the American family. The parents kill their son when he fails to meet their expectations. It is presented with the playwright's *The Death of Bessie Smith*, winner of the Berlin Festival Award and chosen as best play of the 1960–1961 season by the Foreign Press Association. It is a dramatization of the singer's end when she is refused treatment at a whites-only hospital.

ABE BURROWS, JACK WEINSTOCK (d. 1969), AND WILLIE GILBERT (1916–1980): *How to Succeed in Business Without Really Trying.* Based on the 1952 book by Shepherd Mead (b. 1914), with music and lyrics by Frank Loesser, this satire of American business follows the career of a caddish opportunist on his climb from window washer to chairman of the board. Loesser's final work becomes the fourth musical to win the Pulitzer Prize.

PADDY CHAYEFSKY: *Gideon.* In a dramatization of the biblical story of Gideon, Chayefsky arranges a philosophical debate between the reluctant Gideon and God over issues of free will, obedience, and self-sacrifice. Despite critical coolness, the play manages a respectable 236 performances.

OSSIE DAVIS: *Purlie Victorious.* Davis's comedy satirizes Southern race relations as an ambitious black man returns to his Georgia hometown hoping to integrate a black church. The author would adapt the play as the musical *Purlie* in 1970.

LANGSTON HUGHES: *Black Nativity.* Hughes's celebration of the birth of Christ with gospel music, spirituals, dance, and drama proves to be his most successful musical play.

JEAN KERR: *Mary, Mary.* Kerr's comedy treats a divorced couple's verbal combat in one of the era's biggest successes, managing 1,572 performances and becoming the fifth-longest-running play in Broadway history.

ARTHUR MILLER: *The Misfits.* Miller writes the screenplay for the John Huston film about a woman who comes to Nevada for a divorce and gets involved with cowboys herding horses for slaughter. It provides the last screen roles for Miller's then-wife Marilyn Monroe and film legend Clark Gable. The short story upon which Miller's screenplay is based would be published in his story collection *I Don't Need You Anymore* (1967).

TAD MOSEL (b. 1922): *All the Way Home.* The Ohio-born dramatist's adaptation of James Agee's *A Death in the Family* (1957) wins both the Pulitzer Prize and the New York Drama Critics Circle Award for best play. Both awards stayed separate closing notices, and the resuscitation has been described as "the miracle on Forty-fourth Street."

NEIL SIMON (b. 1927): *Come Blow Your Horn.* The playwright's first full-length play concerns a Jewish businessman's relationship with his rebellious sons. It is the first in an unprecedented string of dramatic successes that would make Simon the most popular playwright of his era.

Fiction

WILLIAM S. BURROUGHS: *The Soft Machine.* The initial volume of a trilogy displays Burroughs's montage technique of assembling manuscript pages in random order, first employed in *The Naked Lunch* (1959). It would be followed by *The Ticket That Exploded* (1962) and *Nova Express* (1964).

JOHN CHEEVER: *Some People, Places, and Things That Will Not Appear in My Next Novel.* Cheever's story collection features several works with an Italian setting, as well as his more characteristic suburban locales, including one of Cheever's favorite stories, "The Death of Justina."

LOUIS CHU (1915–1970): *Eat a Bowl of Tea.* Chu's only publication is a realistic novel depicting life in New York's

Chinatown during the 1940s. Initially ignored, the book would be rediscovered in the 1970s and is now considered one of the key works of Asian American literature. Born in Canton, Chu came to the United States in 1922. He served in the army during World War II and owned a record store and was a disc jockey in New York City.

JOHN DOS PASSOS: *Midcentury.* Dos Passos's final novel shows his return to the broad-canvas techniques of the U.S.A. trilogy, tracing the decline and fall of the labor movement and celebrating American capitalism. Although sporadically showing signs of his former power, particularly in his brilliant biographical profile of actor James Dean, the work is mainly noteworthy for demonstrating Dos Passos's increasingly conservative views, expressed in previous novels such as *Chosen Country* (1951), *Most Likely to Succeed* (1954), and *The Great Days* (1958), as well as in nonfiction works such as *The Theme Is Freedom* (1956) and *Occasions and Protests* (1964).

SHIRLEY ANN GRAU: *The House on Coliseum Street.* Grau's second novel is set in the author's native New Orleans and concerns the impact of an abortion and a failed loved affair on a young woman.

JOHN HAWKES: *The Lime Twig.* Most critics consider this the first novel of Hawkes's major phase and one of the novels, along with Barth's *Sot-Weed Factor*, Nabokov's *Pale Fire*, and Pynchon's *V.*, that helped expand the possibilities of American fiction and usher in literary postmodernism. Set in wartime and postwar Britain, it concerns an attempt to steal a famous racehorse and run it under a false name. Flannery O'Connor writes, "You suffer *The Lime Twig* like a dream. It seems to be something that is happening to you, that you want to escape from but can't."

ROBERT HEINLEIN (1907–1988): *Stranger in a Strange Land.* Heinlein's utopian fantasy and science fiction novel is about a human raised by Martians who is brought back to Earth. It sells nearly five million copies and becomes a cult classic. Heinlein, born in Missouri and educated at Annapolis and UCLA, began publishing science fiction stories in 1939.

JOSEPH HELLER (1923–1999): *Catch-22.* In Heller's black comedy about military life during World War II, flyer Yossarian tries to survive the dehumanizing military bureaucracy. The book's attitudes toward war and the military would resonate in later protests over U.S. involvement in Vietnam. The novel draws on the Brooklyn-born writer's own service in the air force during World War II. The book's title also enters the lexicon, to indicate an unresolvable contradictory situation.

ELMORE LEONARD (b. 1925): *Hombre.* The best known of Leonard's western stories features a characteristic

Bernard Malamud

unheroic protagonist and unconventional treatment of conventional western elements. It would be voted one of the twenty-five best western novels of all time by *Western Writer of America* and made into a successful 1967 film, starring Paul Newman. The New Orleans–born writer would be most celebrated for his crime novels such as *Stick* (1983), *Glitz* (1985), and *Get Shorty* (1990).

BERNARD MALAMUD: *A New Life*. Based on the author's experience teaching at Oregon State University, where he was allowed to teach only composition, Malamud provides what he would call his "American" novel in the story of a New York Jew—a recovering alcoholic who tries to make a fresh start at an Oregon "cow college." Academic satire is combined with Malamud's characteristic interest in the search for sustaining values and the often destructive nature of desire.

PAULE MARSHALL: *Soul Clap Hands and Sing*. Marshall's novella collection about four aging men's reevaluations of their lives is noteworthy for showing an expansion of her range to consider Caribbean and South American perspectives as well as the growth of political themes that would become central in her work.

CARSON MCCULLERS: *Clock Without Hands*. McCullers's final novel deals with the last months in the life of a small-town Georgia druggist and the explosion of his community into racial violence. A commercial rather than a critical success, the novel shows a final shift in McCullers's work from female to male protagonists and from personal to social concerns.

LARRY MCMURTRY (b. 1936): *Horseman Pass By*. McMurtry's first novel, which would be turned into the critically acclaimed film *Hud* in 1963, is the first of what has been called his Thalia trilogy, about Texas ranching and small-town life. It would be followed by *Leaving Cheyenne* (1963) and *The Last Picture Show* (1966).

WALKER PERCY (1916–1990): *The Moviegoer*. Percy's first novel, about an adrift New Orleans man who compensates for the disappointments in his life through films, surprisingly wins the 1962 National Book Award for the previously unknown Alabama-born writer and resident of Louisiana. Percy earned a medical degree but stopped practicing due to his own ill health from tuberculosis.

HAROLD ROBBINS (1916–1997): *The Carpetbaggers*. The most popular of Robbins's unprecedented string of bestsellers, which had begun with *Never Love a Stranger* (1948), uses a formula of page-turning action, glamorous settings, and plenty of sex and violence to sell more than eight million copies. Born Francis Kane, Robbins became a millionaire in the food industry at age twenty and began his writing career with Universal Pictures.

J. D. SALINGER: *Franny and Zooey*. Salinger continues his Glass family saga, combining stories originally published in *The New Yorker* in 1955 and 1957. In the first, Franny, a college senior, breaks down over the emptiness and hypocrisy of life during a football weekend; in the second, her brother Zooey attempts to talk her out of her despair by reminding her of their brother Seymour's advice, during their radio whiz-kid days, to "do their best for the Fat Lady in the listening audience."

ISAAC BASHEVIS SINGER: *The Spinoza of Market Street and Other Stories*. Singer's second story collection features the title work about a Jewish scholar who finds happiness in marriage rather than philosophy. Two additional collections would be published during the decade, *Short Fridays* (1964) and *The Seance* (1968).

JOHN STEINBECK: *The Winter of Our Discontent*. Steinbeck's final novel is a bleak portrait of a materialistic American wasteland dramatized through the financial and moral collapse of a member of an old New England family.

LEON URIS: *Mila 18*. Despite critical complaints that he has turned a tragedy into a melodrama, Uris's follow-up to *Exodus* is another bestseller, dramatizing the revolt in the Warsaw ghetto against the Nazis.

KURT VONNEGUT JR.: *Mother Night*. Vonnegut's third novel uses first-person narration and the author himself as a character to offer commentary on an American playwright who spies in Nazi Germany, under cover as a pro-Nazi propagandist. Characteristically, Vonnegut is concerned with the ambiguous role of the artist. "We are what we pretend to be," Vonnegut would declare in his introduction to the 1966 edition, "so we must be careful about what we pretend to be."

EDWARD LEWIS WALLANT (1926–1962): *The Pawnbroker*. Wallant achieves his greatest success in this grim novel about a Holocaust survivor working as a Harlem pawnbroker. It is one of the first fictional explorations of the impact of the Holocaust by an American survivor and makes a controversial link between Jewish suffering and that of African Americans.

ROBERT PENN WARREN: *Wilderness: A Tale of the Civil War*. Warren's novel follows the career of a Bavarian Jew who joins the Union army during the Civil War. Warren also publishes a volume of essays, *The Legacy of the Civil War*, in which he asserts that the Civil War "holds in suspension the great unresolved issues of our society — justice, tolerance, true brotherhood, understanding, and charity."

RICHARD WRIGHT: *Eight Men*. Wright's posthumously published collection offers a series of portraits of black men attempting to cope with living in a white world. Included are "The Man Who Was Almost a Man" (written in the 1930s), "The Man Who Went to Chicago" (from the 1940s), and what many consider Wright's most artistically accomplished work, "The Man Who Lived Underground."

RICHARD YATES (1926–1992): *Revolutionary Road*. Yates's first novel, the story of a suburban salesman with a disintegrating marriage, demonstrates his talent for portraying the lives of ordinary people in starkly honest terms. For reviewer James Atlas the book is "one of the few novels I know that could be called flawless." Kurt Vonnegut called the novel "*The Great Gatsby* of [his] time." Born in Yonkers, New York, Yates served as an infantryman during World War II and later worked as a rewriter for United Press and as a publicity writer and ghostwriter.

Literary Criticism and Scholarship

DANIEL AARON (b. 1912): *Writers on the Left*. Aaron, a Harvard English professor, provides a important social chronicle of leftist writers from 1912 to the early 1940s. Irving Howe calls it "indispensable, a testimonial to what is best in American liberal scholarship."

WAYNE C. BOOTH (b. 1921): *The Rhetoric of Fiction*. Booth's study of narrative technique establishes the concept of the implied audience and narrative reliability in one of the foundation texts for the study of narrative art. Born in Utah, Booth earned a Ph.D. from the University of Chicago, where he would teach from 1962 to 1992.

Nonfiction

JAMES BALDWIN: *Nobody Knows My Name*. The title work of Baldwin's collection is an essay inspired by Baldwin's trip to the South after returning to the United States from his self-imposed exile in Paris. The collection deals at length with the struggle for civil rights but also includes deeply personal meditations on the artist's relationship with society, with his fellow writers, and his homosexuality.

LAWRENCE A. CREMIN (1925–1990): *The Transformation of the School*. Cremin, a professor at Teachers College of Columbia University, wins the Bancroft Prize and solidifies his reputation as one of the foremost historians of American education with this broad survey of American pedagogical changes. He would go on to produce the definitive three-volume *American Education*, made up of *The Colonial Experience* (1970), *The National Experience* (1980), and *The Metropolitan Experience* (1988).

LAWRENCE H. GIPSON (1880–1971): *The Triumphant Empire*. Gipson's tenth installment in his thirteen-volume history of the British Empire before the American Revolution wins the Pulitzer Prize. The series has been described by critic C. F. Mullett as "the greatest single author multi-volume project of this generation." Gipson was a professor of history at Lehigh University.

JANE JACOBS (b. 1916): *The Death and Life of Great American Cities*. Jacobs's study of the architecture of American cities and city planning has had a significant impact on contemporary literature about the city, influencing many writers in criticism and the creative arts.

MARY McCARTHY: *On the Contrary*. This essay collection is divided into three sections — "Politics and the Social Scene," "Woman," and "Literature and the Arts." The latter includes assessments of Arthur Miller and Hannah Arendt as well as McCarthy's statements about the art of fiction.

LEWIS MUMFORD: *The City in History: Its Origin, Its Transformations, and Its Prospects*. Many regard this study of the roles played by cities in civilization from ancient to modern times as Mumford's masterwork. It wins the National Book Award.

WILLIAM SHIRER: *The Rise and Fall of the Third Reich*. Blacklisted during the 1950s, Shirer used the time when he was unemployable to research his massive 1,245-page history of Nazi Germany. The book wins a National Book Award for its synthesis of a vast amount of data into a compelling narrative.

THEODORE H. WHITE: *The Making of the President, 1960.* The first of White's insider looks at presidential campaigns would be followed by similar treatments of the 1964, 1968, and 1972 campaigns, with an overview, *America in Search of Itself: The Making of the President, 1956–1980,* appearing in 1982.

Poetry

ALAN DUGAN (b. 1923): *Poems.* Dugan's first collection of concise, colloquial, ironic, and unsentimental observations of commonplace life wins the Pulitzer Prize, the National Book Award, and the Prix de Rome from the American Academy of Arts and Letters. It would be followed during the decade by *Poems 2* (1963) and *Poems 3* (1968).

ALLEN GINSBERG: *Kaddish and Other Poems, 1958–1960.* Standing next to *Howl* as the poet's finest work, the volume includes Ginsberg's moving confessional lament for his deceased mother. Ginsberg also publishes *Empty Mirror: Early Poems.*

LANGSTON HUGHES: *Ask Your Mama: 12 Moods for Jazz.* Many consider this work Hughes's masterpiece, a fusion of poetry and jazz, history and myth. Inspired by the riot of white youths at the Newport Jazz Festival in 1960, the sequence is structured by the African American verbal insult game, the "dozen," and anticipates the escalation of confrontation and violence that would mark American racial history during the decade.

LEROI JONES (AMIRI BARAKA, b. 1934): *Preface to a Twenty-Volume Suicide Note.* Jones's first collection explores modern alienation outside of the context of racial identity with which Jones would be later associated. Born Everett LeRoy Jones in Newark, New Jersey, the writer attended Howard University and, after a dishonorable discharge from the air force, moved to Greenwich Village in 1957, where he founded and edited the avant-garde magazines *Yugen* (1958–1962) and *Floating Bear* (1961–1969).

CAROLYN KIZER (b. 1925): *The Ungrateful Garden.* Kizer's first major collection treats various responses to nature in verse that employs highly charged, often grotesque imagery. It contains one of her most admired poems, "The Great Blue Heron." Born in Spokane, Washington, Kizer studied in China, worked for the State Department in Pakistan, and became the first director for literature of the National Endowment for the Arts (1966–1970).

MAXINE KUMIN (b. 1925): *Halfway.* Kumin's first collection explores characteristic themes of religious and cultural identity, loss, and the relationship between humanity and nature. It contains admired works such as "One Dead Friend" and "400-Meter Free Style." *The Privilege* would follow in 1965, exploring Kumin's Jewish background and including the poem "Pawnbroker," about her father's death. Born and raised in Philadelphia, Kumin began her career as a poet after enrolling in a poetry workshop conducted by John Clellon Holmes, where she met poet Anne Sexton.

DENISE LEVERTOV: *The Jacob's Ladder.* Levertov's collection explores the role of the poet and the proper language for poetry in major works such as the title poem, "Matins," and "Six Variations." On the basis of this volume, James Wright calls her "one of the best living poets in America."

ROBERT LOWELL: *Imitations.* Lowell's controversial "repoetizations" of works by poets such as Homer, Sappho, Rilke, Villon, and Baudelaire attempt versions of their work based on "what my authors might have done if they were writing poems now and in America." Lowell also publishes his translation of Jean Racine's *Phèdre.*

RICHARD WILBUR: *Advice to a Prophet, and Other Poems.* Wilbur's fourth collection includes translations and "Pangloss's Song" from his adaptation of Voltaire's *Candide,* as well as admired poems such as "Junk" and "Grasshopper," which Donald Hall calls "a minor masterpiece." Although praised for its technical mastery, the work is also criticized for its perceived aesthetic detachment and absence of topicality.

Publications and Events

Floating Bear. This mimeographed magazine and newsletter published by Diane di Prima and LeRoi Jones (Amiri Baraka) debuts in New York City and includes contributions from Robert Creeley, Robert Duncan, and William S. Burroughs. It ceased publication in 1969.

1962
Drama and Theater

EDWARD ALBEE: *Who's Afraid of Virginia Woolf?* Generally regarded as Albee's most thoroughly realized play, the realistic and allegorical drama concerns a middle-aged married couple, George and Martha, who in the course of one drunken evening engage in a sadistic catfight before an unwilling younger couple obliged by social niceties to stay and watch. The struggle ends only when George symbolically murders his and Martha's nonexistent son and the couple, in Albee's words, fulfill the need to "try to claw [their] way into compassion."

RICHARD EBERHART: *Collected Verse Plays.* Bringing together Eberhart's dramatic work produced regionally in the 1950s and 1960s, the volume contains *The Apparition, The Visionary Farms, Triptych, The Mad Musicians,* and *Devils and Angels.*

FRANK D. GILROY (b. 1925): *Who'll Save the Plowboy?* Gilroy's initial drama success concerns a veteran, haunted by the trauma of his war experiences, in a reunion with the man who saved his life. Produced off-Broadway, it wins the Obie Award.

ADRIENNE KENNEDY (b. 1931): *Funnyhouse of a Negro.* While the work of other black playwrights such as LeRoi Jones and Ed Bullins features realism, Kennedy establishes herself as one of the major figures of the avant-garde theater of the period in this expressionistic dream play, in which a young black woman is tormented by her identity. The play receives the Obie Award in 1964.

THORNTON WILDER: *Plays for Bleecker Street.* Wilder collects three one-act plays, part of an unfinished fourteen-play cycle on the Seven Ages of Man and the Seven Deadly Sins.

TENNESSEE WILLIAMS: *The Night of the Iguana.* Concerning a defrocked priest-turned-Mexican tour director who is drawn to two women representing spiritual and sensual opposites, Williams's drama wins the New York Drama Critics Circle Award. It is his final commercial and critical success.

Fiction

LOUIS AUCHINCLOSS: *Portrait in Brownstone.* One of Auchincloss's strongest novels traces the lives of a prominent New York society family during the first half of the twentieth century. The powerful psychological profile of Ida Trask as a dominating matriarch is an elegy to New York's lost elegance.

JAMES BALDWIN: *Another Country.* Baldwin's third novel depicts a series of interracial and bisexual couplings in New York City during the 1950s, using the suicide of an angry jazz musician as a catalyst. It prompts obscenity charges, efforts to ban the work, and mixed reviews.

THOMAS BERGER: *Reinhart in Love.* The second novel in the Reinhart series shows Reinhart out of the army and trying to cope with civilian life. He falls into the clutches of employer Claude Humbold, a real estate agent/con man, and into the arms of a scheming woman, whom he marries. Critics admire Berger's exuberant comic genius.

HORTENSE CALISHER: *Tales from the Mirror.* After publishing a first novel, *False Entry* (1961), Calisher issues her second story collection, which includes her most anthologized work, "The Scream on Fifty-Seventh Street." It is followed by her most conventional novel, *Textures of Life* (1963), about newlyweds adjusting to the routine of everyday life.

WILLIAM FAULKNER: *The Reivers: A Reminiscence.* Published one month before his death, Faulkner's final novel is a nostalgic last look at Yoknapatawpha County in a comic tale set in 1905. It wins Faulkner a second Pulitzer Prize.

F. SCOTT FITZGERALD: *The Pat Hobby Stories.* Published in *Esquire* in 1940 and 1941, the stories collected in this volume concern a Hollywood hack writer down on his luck; it features some of Fitzgerald's bitterest portraits of the movie business.

BRUCE JAY FRIEDMAN (b. 1930): *Stern.* The New York City native's first novel introduces his characteristic black humor in looking at the lives of American Jews. It would be followed by his first story collection, *Far from the City of Class* (1963), as well as *A Mother's Kiss* (1964) and *The Dick* (1970).

SHIRLEY JACKSON: *We Have Always Lived in the Castle.* Jackson's final book, judged by many to be her greatest achievement as a novelist, is a masterful psychological study of two sisters persecuted by their small New England community for allegedly murdering the rest of their family.

JAMES JONES: *The Thin Red Line.* Jones provides an unglamorous look at warfare in a tale of Company C on Guadalcanal, where the author had fought and was wounded. Norman Mailer calls Jones's treatment of combat "so broad and true . . . that it could be used as a textbook at the Infantry School."

JACK KEROUAC: *Big Sur.* Kerouac reflects on his celebrity as a leader of the Beat generation in a fictional account of his life after the publication of *On the Road.* He flees to a cabin on the California coast for a more direct, authentic life but is wrecked by alcoholism.

KEN KESEY (1935–2001): *One Flew over the Cuckoo's Nest.* Kesey's first novel, set in an Oregon mental hospital, pits the rebellious McMurphy against the sadistic, authoritarian Nurse Ratched. It becomes one of the iconic counterculture works of the 1960s, celebrating both the need for rebellion in a dehumanized society and its cost. Kesey was born in Colorado, educated at the University of Oregon, and in 1961 volunteered for a government-sponsored experimental drug program. He also worked as a night attendant in a psychiatric ward.

JOHN OLIVER KILLENS: *And Then We Heard the Thunder.* Killens's best-known novel, his second, deals with segregation and racism in the military during World War II. It would be followed by *'Sippi* (1967), a fictional treatment of the civil rights struggle, and *The Cotillion* (1971), exposing the cultural shallowness of the members of a black women's club in Brooklyn.

MADELEINE L'ENGLE (b. 1918): *A Wrinkle in Time.* L'Engle's best-known work and a children's classic is the first of her Time Fantasy series, combining time travel, science fiction, and family themes as Meg Murray attempts to rescue her captive father by learning the meaning of love. The book had been earlier rejected by twenty-six publishers who found it too difficult to classify. Born Madeleine L'Engle Camp in New York City, she has written adult novels, plays, poetry, and essays.

ALISON LURIE (b. 1926): *Love and Friendship.* This is the first of the author's witty, satirical accounts of academic and literary life. It would be followed by *The Nowhere City* (1965), *Imaginary Friends* (1967), and *Real People* (1969).

VLADIMIR NABOKOV: *Pale Fire.* Nabokov's complex tour de force about the nature of literature consists of a 999-line poem and a critical commentary. Readers of this sly but difficult work soon discover that it has more to do with its editor's fantasy life than with an exegesis of the poem itself. Mary McCarthy describes the book as "a Jack-in-the-box, a Fabergé gem, a clockwork toy, a trap to catch reviewers, a cat-and-mouse game, a do-it-yourself novel." It has been subsequently judged as one of the great modernist masterpieces and arguably Nabokov's supreme achievement.

JOHN O'HARA: *The Big Laugh.* O'Hara's treatment of Hollywood during the Depression is centered on an amoral actor, one of the most villainous characters O'Hara would ever create. He also issues the first in a series of story collections, *The Cape Cod Lighter,* to be followed by *The Hat on the Bed* (1963) and *The Horse Knows the Way* (1964).

TILLIE OLSEN (b. 1913): *Tell Me a Riddle: A Collection.* Olsen's story collection is published to critical acclaim. The title work concerns an elderly couple who are forced to reassess their lives, and the collection contains one of her most frequently anthologized stories, "I Stand Here Ironing," about a mother's guilt. Born in Omaha, Nebraska, Olsen developed her vocation as a writer inspired by Rebecca Harding Davis's "Life in the Iron Mills" (1861).

KATHERINE ANNE PORTER: *Ship of Fools.* Porter's long-awaited first (and only) novel is a moral allegory set on board a passenger freighter on the eve of Hitler's rise to power. It illustrates her principle that "evil is always done

with the collusion of good." Long known as a "writer's writer" based on her finely crafted short stories, Porter finally gained a wider audience with the book, and its subsequent adaptation for the big screen in 1965.

J. F. POWERS: *Morte d'Urban.* Powers's National Book Award–winning first novel treats a worldly priest who is sent to a remote monastery in Minnesota and whose efforts to improve conditions there lead to his spiritual collapse.

REYNOLDS PRICE (b. 1933): *A Long and Happy Life.* Price, born in North Carolina and educated at Duke and Oxford, receives high praise for his first novel, set in rural North Carolina and dealing with the romantic aspirations and disappointments of Rosacoke Mustian. Price's second novel, *A Generous Man* (1966), treats Rosacoke's older brother Milo, and Rosacoke returns in the novel *Good Hearts* (1988).

PHILIP ROTH: *Letting Go.* Roth's ambitious novel concerns a group of young Jewish intellectuals at the University of Chicago and in New York City during the 1950s. Its exploration of the nuances of relationships evokes comparisons to Henry James, encouraged by numerous allusions in the text.

ISAAC BASHEVIS SINGER: *The Slave.* Regarded by many as Singer's finest novel, the story is set in seventeenth-century Poland and concerns a Jewish scholar and teacher who is sold into slavery by the invading Cossacks. He falls in love with a Ukrainian peasant's daughter, and when the couple are forbidden to marry by Polish and Jewish law, they become outcasts. The novel presents multiple forms of enslavement to God, religion, and conscience in a powerful love story.

MARK TWAIN (SAMUEL LANGHORNE CLEMENS): *Letters from the Earth.* Written in 1909, his last major work, Twain's treatise on humanity and religion is finally published after the death of his daughter Clara, who had blocked its release. Expressing Twain's frank opinion on morals and sexuality, the work, which becomes a bestseller, sparks renewed interest in Twain's ideas and previously overlooked serious side.

JOHN UPDIKE: *Pigeon Feathers and Other Stories.* Updike's second story collection includes some of his most admired and anthologized works, including "A&P," "Wife-Wooing," "The Doctor's Wife," and "Should Wizard Hit Mommy?" Arthur Mizener praises the collection as a "demonstration of how the most gifted writer of his generation is coming to maturity."

HERMAN WOUK: *Youngblood Hawke.* Wouk's bestselling novel chronicles the career of an ambitious novelist for whom success entails compromise.

Rachel Carson conducting research work along the Florida Keys in the 1950s. Robert W. Hines works alongside her.

Literary Criticism and Scholarship

W. H. AUDEN: *The Dyer's Hand.* Auden's essay collection contains some of his most important statements on poetry and art. It would be followed by *Secondary Worlds* (1968), about the relationship between artistic creation and common experience.

ALFRED KAZIN: *Contemporaries.* Kazin collects essays written from the 1950s, sounding a frequent complaint about contemporary novelists creating "subjective fantasies" as an inadequate substitute for "public belief." Edmund Wilson calls the book Kazin's best, but others rank it as his worst.

GORE VIDAL: *Rocking the Boat.* This collection of essays displays Vidal's characteristic contrarianism on politics, the theater, and literature, including assessments of John Dos Passos, Norman Mailer, Carson McCullers, Robert Penn Warren, and others.

EDMUND WILSON: *Patriotic Gore: Studies in the Literature of the American Civil War.* Essays devoted to the writings of diverse authors such as soldiers, women diarists, and statesmen, in addition to novelists such as Ambrose Bierce and Albion W. Tourgée. The reevaluation of writings nearly a century old brings fresh insight to and renews interest in some forgotten writers.

Nonfiction

HELEN GURLEY BROWN (b. 1922): *Sex and the Single Girl.* Brown creates a stir in this account of the lifestyle of single career women by suggesting that sex is an attractive option outside of marriage. She would follow it with *Sex in the Office* (1964) and in 1965 would relaunch the venerable magazine *Cosmopolitan*, serving as its editor-in-chief until 1997, to address the concerns of the "Cosmo girl" not treated by other women's magazines.

RACHEL CARSON: *Silent Spring.* Carson's best-known work details the dangers of insecticide. It is roundly denounced by the chemical industry, but President John F. Kennedy appoints a landmark investigative committee in response to the book. Afterward, the first anti-pesticide bills would become law, marking the advent of the modern environmentalist movement.

LEON EDEL: *Henry James: The Conquest of London* and *Henry James: The Middle Years.* Edel wins both the National Book Award and the Pulitzer Prize for the second and third volumes of his magisterial five-volume biography. Critic James Atlas calls it "one of the greatest achievements in modern biography," and essayist Joseph Epstein describes it as "the single greatest work of biography produced in our century."

CONSTANCE GREEN (1897–1975): *Washington: Village and Capital, 1800–1878.* Green, who directed the Washington history project for American University from 1954 to 1960, wins the Pulitzer Prize for this cultural urban history that would be continued in *Washington: Capital City, 1879–1950* (1963).

MICHAEL HARRINGTON (1928–1989): *The Other America.* Harrington's widely discussed study documents a poor underclass beneath the surface of American affluence. Called by reviewer A. H. Raskin "a scream of rage, a call to conscience," the book prompts President Kennedy to support increased federal assistance and would provide an impetus for Lyndon Johnson's War on Poverty in 1964. Harrington would revise his book in 1970 and issue another study, *The New American Poverty,* in 1984. Born in St. Louis, Harrington was the editor of *New America* (1961–1962) and a prominent advocate for democratic socialism.

LANGSTON HUGHES: *Fight for Freedom: The Story of the NAACP.* Hughes commemorates the accomplishments of the NAACP and its leaders over half a century, including a defense of contemporary activities in the South.

THOMAS KUHN (1922–1996): *The Structure of Scientific Revolutions.* The historian and philosopher of science's best-known book advances a new theory, suggesting that scientific change depends on psychological and social causes.

RICHARD M. NIXON (1913–1994): *Six Crises.* Nixon provides his perspective on six important chapters in his political life, including the Alger Hiss case, his encounter with Nikita Khrushchev, and the 1960 presidential campaign. As reviewer Tom Wicker notes, "It offers no answer at all to the question that has hung from the beginning over his head: what kind of man is he?"

WILLIAM SAROYAN: *Here Comes, There Goes, You Know.* This is the first of a series of autobiographical reflections, to be followed by *Not Dying* (1963) and *Short Drive, Sweet Chariot* (1966).

UPTON SINCLAIR: *Autobiography.* Sinclair adds several chapters to his previous memoir, *American Outpost* (1932), providing both an important self-assessment and a record of the progressive era.

PAGE SMITH (1917–1995): *John Adams.* Smith wins the Kenneth Roberts Memorial Award and the Bancroft Prize for this biography. He is among the first to make use of the extensive Adams papers to chronicle comprehensively Adams's long career, complex character, and ideas in the context of his times.

JOHN STEINBECK: *Travels with Charley: In Search of America.* Steinbeck's odyssey to "rediscover" America,

John Steinbeck holding a copy of his 1962 nonfiction book, *Travels with Charley*

accompanied by his pet poodle in a converted truck named Rocinante, offers an often bitter reaction to contemporary American life and includes a frank self-assessment of Steinbeck's career and capabilities.

BARBARA TUCHMAN (1912–1989): *The Guns of August.* Tuchman's popular history of the first month of World War I wins a Pulitzer Prize and turns this unaffiliated scholar into a literary celebrity. She would follow it with a more expansive review of the years leading up to August 1914, *The Proud Tower* (1966).

E. B. WHITE: *The Points of My Compass.* White's essays treat diverse topics such as the United Nations, television, living in Maine, automobiles, and hurricanes. Included is his appreciation of William Strunk, his former teacher at Cornell and the original author of *The Elements of Style,* which White had revised.

Poetry

JOHN ASHBERY: *The Tennis Court Oath.* Ashbery departs from his previous witty style to produce a series of disjunctive, illogical images. He claims he has used words "as an abstract painter uses paint."

ROBERT BLY (b. 1926): *Silence in the Snowy Fields.* Bly's first collection depicts his native Minnesota's harsh landscape, probed for revelations. It includes two of his best-known works, "Driving Toward the Lac Qui Parle River" and "Poem in Three Parts."

ROBERT CREELEY (b. 1926): *For Love: Poems, 1950–1960.* Collecting Creeley's early epigrammatic works dealing with marital themes, the volume includes poems such as "The Whip," "A Marriage," "Ballad of the Despairing Husband," and the long poem "The Door," a meditation on female sexuality. *Words* (1967) and *Pieces* (1968), volumes of experimental verses, mainly of two- and three-syllable lines dealing with love, friendship, and marital relations, would follow. The Massachusetts-born writer taught briefly at Black Mountain College, helped found the *Black Mountain Review*, and was an associate of Charles Olson and Robert Duncan.

ROBERT FROST: *In the Clearing.* Frost's last collection of new poems, issued on his eighty-eighth birthday, contains the long poem "Kitty Hawk" and a final meditation, "In the Winter in the Woods," considering the relationship between humanity and nature.

ROBERT HAYDEN: *A Ballad of Remembrance.* Hayden's collection shows the poet's shift from predominantly black subjects to a wider range of interest, which will dominate his subsequent publications. It wins the grand prize at the first World Festival of Negro Arts in Dakar, Senegal.

JOHN HOLLANDER: *Movie-Going and Other Poems.* Hollander's collection takes a nostalgic look at the movie houses of the poet's youth and the redemptive nature of illusions. A similar evocation of the poet's boyhood in New York City would follow in *Visions from the Ramble*, published in 1965.

NORMAN MAILER: *Death for the Ladies and Other Disasters.* Mailer issues a series of short, mainly comic poems called by one reviewer "topographical trickery" and another "private silliness."

JAMES MERRILL: *Water Street.* Merrill's collection celebrates his residence in Stonington, Connecticut, in a series of poems exploring his life, travels, and past with an increased candor and intimacy.

GEORGE OPPEN: *The Materials.* Having published his first collection, *Discrete Series*, in 1934, Oppen produces his second twenty-eight years later, a collection of verse reflecting his experiences as a political activist and exile during the McCarthy era. He would follow it with a third volume, *This in Which*, a celebration of ordinary life.

CHARLES REZNIKOFF (1894–1976): *By the Waters of Manhattan.* Associated with the objectivist poets of the 1920s, Reznikoff gains critical recognition for his artistry in treating New York City scenes and reflections on being a Jew in this collection of his selected poems. Allen Ginsberg would later cite Reznikoff as one of his chief influences.

MURIEL RUKEYSER: *Waterlily Fire: Poems, 1935–1962.* Rukeyser's selection of new and older works prompts poet Richard Eberhart to praise her "primordial and torrential" verses that "pour out excitements of a large emotional force, taking in a great deal of life and giving out profound realizations of the significance of being."

ANNE SEXTON: *All My Pretty Ones.* Many regard this second collection, with poems such as "Letter Written on a Ferry While Crossing Long Island Sound," "In the Deep Museum," "The Truth the Dead Know," and "The Abortion," as the poet's finest. The poems dwell on loss, Sexton's ambivalent feelings for her parents, and her reactions to their deaths.

WILLIAM STAFFORD (1914–1993): *Traveling Through the Dark.* Stafford's second collection, following *West of Your City* (1960), wins the 1963 National Book Award and is praised for its sensitive reflections on the poet's Kansas upbringing and his Oregon home. Equally acclaimed collections would follow, including *The Rescued Year* (1966), *Allegiances* (1970), *Sunday, Maybe* (1973), and *Stories That Could Be True: New and Collected Poems* (1977).

WILLIAM CARLOS WILLIAMS: *Pictures from Brueghel and Other Poems.* Williams's final collection of his later work, including "The Desert Music" and "Journey to Love," earn the Pulitzer Prize.

Publications and Events

La MaMa Experimental Theatre Club. Founded by Ellen Stewart (b. 1920), the experimental company presents its first production, an adaptation of Tennessee Williams's short story "One Arm," in its downtown New York basement theater. It became the leading avant-garde theater in the United States, introducing and supporting important playwrights such as Sam Shepard, Harvey Fierstein, Lanford Wilson, and Adrienne Kennedy.

1963
Drama and Theater

EDWARD ALBEE: *The Ballad of the Sad Café.* Critics commend Albee's adaptation of Carson McCullers's story, but it manages only a fifteen-week engagement.

KENNETH BROWN (b. 1936): *The Brig.* Brown's searing antimilitary drama documenting the brutal routine in a Marine Corps prison in Japan is produced by the Living Theatre. It is the final New York production of the company, whose theater had been closed by the IRS. For the final performance, audience members enter the padlocked theater through windows. Born in Brooklyn, Brown served in the Marine Corps and described *The Brig* as an experiment confirming "Meyerhold's Constructivist Theory and Artaud's Theatre of Cruelty."

MARTIN DUBERMAN (b. 1931): *In White America.* Duberman arranges various powerful statements on American race relations, including those of a doctor aboard an eighteenth-century slave ship, Thomas Jefferson's views, and the thoughts of a young black girl attempting to enter an all-white high school in 1957. Duberman, a Harvard Ph.D., is also the author of biographies of Charles Francis Adams, James Russell Cowell, and Paul Robeson, as well as the study of the gay rights movement in America *Stonewall* (1993).

LILLIAN HELLMAN: *My Mother, My Father, and Me.* The final play in Hellman's career is an adaptation of Burt Blechman's novel *How Much?* (1961), a comedy about a beatnik. It is universally panned by reviewers, one of whom calls it "dismally dull."

NEIL SIMON: *Barefoot in the Park.* Simon's second Broadway hit is a comedy about honeymooners coping with married life in their tiny sixth-floor Greenwich Village walk-up. Actor Robert Redford plays his first major role as the buttoned-down husband who learns to cut loose.

TENNESSEE WILLIAMS: *The Milk Train Doesn't Stop Here Anymore.* The terminally ill, drug-addicted, many-times-widowed Flora Goforth dictates her memoirs and is visited by a young poet known as the Angel of Death. Williams's heavily freighted symbolic drama is unenthusiastically received and manages a run of only sixty-nine performances.

LANFORD WILSON (b. 1937): *So Long at the Fair.* The Missouri-born playwright's first production, described by Wilson as a "silly comedy" he wrote in one day, concerns a country boy's big-city experiences. It opens at Caffe Cino, a small coffeehouse in New York's Greenwich Village.

Fiction

JOAN DIDION (b. 1934): *Run River.* The first of the California writer's novels introduces her characteristic subject of California life. The protagonist, Lily McClellan, registers the impact of social, economic, and personal changes in the postwar Sacramento Valley. After graduating from the University of California at Berkeley, Didion worked as a writer for *Vogue* magazine. In 1964 she married writer John Gregory Dunne, and the couple returned to California to work as freelance journalists.

J. P. DONLEAVY: *A Singular Man.* Donleavy's second novel treats the obsession of the wealthy George Smith to construct a grand mausoleum, suggesting the dead end associated with dreams of material success. The book gets bad reviews, and Donleavy does additional damage to his reputation by following the novel with one of his weakest books, the story collection *Meet My Maker the Mad Molecule* (1964).

JAMES T. FARRELL: *The Silence of History.* Farrell initiates his final novel cycle with the intellectual history of an aspiring writer, Eddie Ryan, in Chicago during the 1920s. It would be followed by several volumes that form a personal and social history: *Lonely for the Future* (1966), *New Year's Eve, 1929* (1967), *A Brand New Life* (1968), and *Judith* (1969).

WILLIAM GOYEN: *The Fair Sister.* In what many consider Goyen's most accomplished novel, the religious fanatic Ruby Drew tries to save her sister's soul.

JACK KEROUAC: *Visions of Gerard.* Chronologically the first in the autobiographical narrative cycle called "The Legend of Duluoz," which would eventually incorporate all of Kerouac's works, the book describes the writer's childhood in Lowell, Massachusetts, and the central trauma of his early life, the death of his older brother.

BERNARD MALAMUD: *Idiots First.* Malamud's second story collection includes several of his Italian stories, which would be subsequently incorporated into *Pictures of Fidelman* (1969), as well as stories in the manner of *The Magic Barrel*, including "The Jewbird," "Take Pity," and "The German Refugee."

MARY MCCARTHY: *The Group.* McCarthy's most famous book follows the careers of eight Vassar graduates of the class of 1933 over thirty years. Filled with trenchant social observation, the book generates controversy for its frank sexual content; Vassar alumnae lobby to have their alma mater rescind McCarthy's degree.

JOHN O'HARA: *Elizabeth Appleton.* O'Hara's academic novel depicts the marriage of an ambitious society woman and a modest history professor at a small, less-than-prestigious Pennsylvania college. O'Hara also publishes a story collection, *The Hat on the Bed.*

JOYCE CAROL OATES (b. 1938): *By the North Gate.* Oates's first book is a story collection, beginning a nearly uninterrupted string of yearly publications. It would be followed by her first novel, *With Shuddering Fall* (1964), and a second story collection, *Upon the Sweeping Flood and Other Stories* (1966). Oates, born and raised in rural upstate New York, studied at Syracuse, the University of Wisconsin, and the University of Texas, and began her teaching career at the University of Detroit.

SYLVIA PLATH: *The Bell Jar.* Plath's autobiographical novel appears under the pseudonym "Victoria Lucas." The novel revisits Plath's own breakdown and suicide attempt and would be later regarded as a classic feminist text.

THOMAS PYNCHON (b. 1937): *V.* Pynchon's first novel introduces readers to the writer's complex encyclopedic style, absurdist comedy, and penchant for paranoia. It takes the form of a quest for an illusive figure who is in turns a woman, a construction, and a force across major portions of nineteenth- and twentieth-century history. It has been described as a black comic odyssey into the bizarre anxieties of the modern world. Born on Long Island, New York, Pynchon served in the navy and graduated from Cornell, where one of his professors was Vladimir Nabokov.

JOHN RECHY (b. 1934): *City of Night.* Rechy's first novel, a story about homosexuality and male prostitution, is published to mixed reviews but becomes an international bestseller. General speculation about the autobiographical nature of the work, impatience with Rechy's chaotic technique, and disapproval of his explicit sexual scenes are balanced by admiration for the candor evinced by a writer venturing into new, previously off-limits terrain. Rechy, the son of Mexican immigrants, was born in Texas and got involved with the gay subculture of New York City after serving in the army in Germany.

J. D. SALINGER: *Raise High the Roof-Beam, Carpenters; and Seymour— an Introduction.* Salinger continues the story of the Glass family in Buddy's recollections of his brother Seymour's wedding and suicide.

WILLIAM SAROYAN: *Boys and Girls Together.* The first of two novels dealing with writers with marital problems. It would be followed by *One Day in the Afternoon* (1964).

MAURICE SENDAK: *Where the Wild Things Are.* Sendak achieves his greatest success with this Caldecott Medal– winning picture book about a boy banished to his bedroom without his supper. He deals with his anger by imagining himself king of an island filled with enormous, frightening monsters. Critically acclaimed and controversial, Sendak is one of the first children's writers to deal frankly with the fears and anxieties of childhood. *Where the Wild Things Are* is the first in a trilogy, to be followed by *In the Night Kitchen* (1970) and *Outside over There* (1981), which, in Sendak's words, are "all variations on the same theme: how children master various feelings — anger, boredom, fear, frustration, jealousy — and manage to come to grips with the realities of their lives."

SUSAN SONTAG (b. 1933): *The Benefactor.* Sontag's first book is a novel set in Paris, an introspective roman à clef depicting French writers Antonin Artaud and Jean Genet. Regarded as an experiment in producing a "European novel," the book assimilates modernist elements through an introspective narrative strategy that replaces surface action with the workings of consciousness itself.

JOHN UPDIKE: *The Centaur.* Updike pays homage to his father, a schoolteacher who, like the hero of the book, made quiet sacrifices for his son. Like other characters in the book, father and son are presented as creatures out of Greek mythology, respectively, the pedagogical centaur Chiron and the hero Prometheus. The novel wins the National Book Award.

KURT VONNEGUT JR.: *Cat's Cradle.* Vonnegut's black comedy deals with the destructive capacity of technology as shown by the invention of "ice-nine," a substance capable of freezing all the water on earth. Vonnegut contrasts science with a religion called Bokononism, based on the ultimate absurdity of life.

RICHARD WRIGHT: *Lawd Today.* Written before *Native Son* (1940), this posthumously published novel records a day in the life of a desperate black postal worker in Chicago during the Depression. One of Wright's most naturalistic works, the novel features an unsympathetic black protagonist who has been called a black George Babbitt.

Literary Criticism and Scholarship

WALTER JACKSON BATE (1918–1999): *John Keats.* In a significant year for Keats scholarship, Bate wins the Pulitzer Prize for his meticulously researched and comprehensive biography; Aileen Ward (b. 1919) receives the National Book Award for her psychological study of Keats's development, *John Keats: The Making of a Poet.*

IRVING HOWE: *Politics and the Novel.* Howe's critical collection seeks to show "how the passions of ideology twist themselves about, yet also liberate creative energies." Included is a discussion of Henry James and a long section on nineteenth-century American fiction.

WALTER KERR (1913–1996): *The Theater in Spite of Itself.* Winner of a George Jean Nathan Award for drama criticism, this review collection helps establish Kerr as one of the most respected critics of Broadway and mainstream theater. His previous books included *How Not to Write a Play* (1955), *Criticism and Censorship* (1956), *Pieces of Eight* (1957), and *The Decline of Pleasure* (1962).

HOWARD NEMEROV: *Poetry and Fiction: Essays.* The first collection of Nemerov's well-respected critical essays would be followed by *Figures of Thought* (1978) and *New and Selected Essays* (1985).

Nonfiction

JAMES BALDWIN: *The Fire Next Time.* Baldwin's essay collection on racial matters includes an autobiographical portrait of his youth and a critique of the Black Muslim

Betty Friedan

movement, in which he voices his admiration of Malcolm X but also his opposition to the call for racial separation.

BETTY FRIEDAN (b. 1921): *The Feminine Mystique*. Debunking the widely held belief that white middle-class American women's roles in society are limited to wife and mother, Friedan's influential polemic immediately finds an audience, sparking the modern women's movement. Friedan, born in Illinois, sacrificed an academic career for marriage and was fired from a journalism position after requesting a second maternity leave. Her interviews with housewives form the basis for *The Feminine Mystique*.

NATHAN GLAZER (b. 1923) AND **DANIEL PATRICK MOYNIHAN** (1927–2003): *Beyond the Melting Pot*. Moynihan's first book is an ethnographic study of New York City, which, according to critic Andrew Hacker, initiated "the so-called 'ethnic revival'" of books treating ethnicity and assimilation issues. Moynihan would follow it with *The Negro Family: The Case for National Action* (1965), which highlights the breakdown of the traditional black family. Glazer, a sociologist, taught at the University of California at Berkeley. Moynihan was a professor of urban politics and education at Harvard and would serve as U.S. ambassador to India (1973–1975) and as a U.S. Senator from New York (1977–2000).

RICHARD HOFSTADTER: *Anti-Intellectualism in American Life*. Hofstadter's cultural analysis, "conceived in response to the political and intellectual conditions of the 1950s," earns the historian his second Pulitzer Prize, following *The Age of Reform* (1956). The work examines the threat to intellectual life in America.

LEROI JONES (AMIRI BARAKA): *Blues People: Negro Music in White America*. Jones's important cultural study treats the black experience in America as reflected in the development of the blues and jazz, underscoring the music's social, economic, and psychological roots.

MARTIN LUTHER KING JR.: "Letter from the Birmingham Jail." King responds to critics of his confrontational methods in what biographer Stephen Oates has called "a classic in protest literature, the most elegant and learned expression of the goals and philosophy of the nonviolent movement ever written." King would deliver his famous "I Have a Dream" speech on August 28 at the March on Washington.

DWIGHT MACDONALD: *Against the American Grain*. MacDonald's essay collection includes his influential cultural analysis "Masscult and Midcult."

NORMAN MAILER: *The Presidential Papers*. Employing the same devices of introductions and commentary in *Advertisements for Myself*, Mailer collects a number of essays and interviews purportedly to help instruct President Kennedy in "existential styles of political thought." Kennedy's death shortly after its publication dampens the book's reception. Included are some of Mailer's best journalistic pieces, such as "Superman Comes to the Supermarket," on the 1960 Democratic National Convention, and "Ten Thousand Words a Minute," on prizefighting.

JESSICA MITFORD (1917–1996): *The American Way of Death*. English muckraking author Mitford creates a furor over her exposé of the American funeral industry.

SUMNER C. POWELL (b. 1924): *Puritan Village: The Formation of a New England Town*. Powell wins the Pulitzer Prize for his study of Sudbury, Massachusetts, from 1638 to 1657. He traces the settlers' background and the social organization they created.

Poetry

E. E. CUMMINGS: *73 Poems*. The posthumously published collection of verse draws appreciation from reviewers such as Lionel Abel, who states that the work shows Cummings at "his most unfoolish and poetical best" in which "there is more ecstasy and less argumentation for ecstasy than in most of his earlier books."

ALLEN GINSBERG: *Reality Sandwiches*. Ginsberg's collection of poems written from 1953 to 1960 are mainly

Dr. Martin Luther King Jr.

of interest for their autobiographical revelations and the view they provide of the Beat lifestyle and sensibility.

ROBINSON JEFFERS: *The Beginning and the End.* Jeffers's last collection of new works is issued posthumously to mixed reviews. It would be followed by several additional posthumous compilations, including *The Alpine Christ* (1973), *Brides of the South Wind* (1974), and *Granite and Cypress* (1975).

PHILIP LEVINE (b. 1928): *On the Edge.* As the title of Levine's debut collection suggests, his work characteristically deals with marginal characters, often in working-class environments, and with the struggles of ordinary life. Similar volumes — *Silence in America* (1965) and *Not This Pig* (1968) — would follow. Levine was born in Detroit and educated at Wayne State University and the University of Iowa.

W. S. MERWIN: *The Moving Target.* Merwin's collection of increasingly personal poems contemplate self-alienation and show a loosening of previous formal conventions, including discordant rhythms, informal diction, and a lack of punctuation.

JOHN CROWE RANSOM: *Selected Poems.* Ransom wins the National Book Award for this second edition of

Selected Poems (1945), which adds new stanzas and revises lines. A final *Selected Poems* would appear in 1969.

ADRIENNE RICH: *Snapshots of a Daughter-in-Law.* Rich's collection marks a shift to free verse and an emphasis on women's roles and a feminist-oriented consciousness.

CARL SANDBURG: *Honey and Salt.* The poet's final collection is an uneven mix of sentimental echoes of his earlier work and powerful original verses, such as the title poem and "Foxgloves."

LOUIS SIMPSON: *At the End of the Open Road.* Simpson's Pulitzer Prize–winning collection is a stylistic departure from traditional poetic forms to unrhymed free verse and colloquial language. Poems include "The Marriage of Pocahontas," "Walt Whitman at Bear Mountain," "In the Suburbs," and "My Father in the Night Commanding No."

Publications and Events

The New York Review of Books is founded by editor Jason Epstein, novelist Elizabeth Hardwick, and others to take the place of absent newspaper book reviews during a printers' strike. The journal's success leads to regular biweekly issues of a liberal publication addressing not only literary criticism but also sociopolitical concerns in lengthy essays written by some of the world's most influential writers and thinkers.

1964
Drama and Theater

EDWARD ALBEE: *Tiny Alice.* Albee's play concerns the world's richest woman, whose $2 billion donation to the Catholic Church involves seducing and murdering the lay brother whom she invites to pick up the money. Audiences find the play baffling, and critics are divided concerning its merits.

JAMES BALDWIN: *Blues for Mister Charlie.* Baldwin's drama is inspired by the murder of Emmett Till, a black teenager killed in Mississippi in 1955 for allegedly flirting with a white woman. Baldwin uses the case and the acquittal of the murderers as a potent indictment of American race relations. Baldwin's earlier play, *The Amen Corner*, first produced at Howard University in 1954, about a black clergywoman who tries to turn her son against his father, would reach Broadway in 1965.

SAUL BELLOW: *The Last Analysis.* Bellow's farce concerns a comedian whose career is jeopardized by his growing seriousness. He seeks a cure for his "humanitis" by acting out the main events of his life. Despite critic John Simon's contention that it is the most substantial comic drama of the season, the play closes quickly. Bellow would publish the play in 1965 after substantial revision.

PADDY CHAYEFSKY: *The Passion of Josef D.* This biographical drama on the life of Stalin fails on Broadway. When Chayefsky's next play, *The Latent Heterosexual* (1968), fails even to reach Broadway, the playwright abandons the stage for film work.

FRANK D. GILROY: *The Subject Was Roses.* Gilroy's subtle portrait of the postwar American family deals with parents competing for the affection of a son who has returned home after his army service. It wins both the Pulitzer Prize and the New York Drama Critics Circle Award.

WILLIAM HANLEY (b. 1931): *Slow Dance on the Killing Ground.* Three characters meet and interact in a late-night candy store in New York City in this naturalistic drama by the Ohio-born dramatist and novelist whose books would include *Blue Dreams* (1971), *Mixed Feelings* (1977), and *Leaving Mount Venus* (1977).

LORRAINE HANSBERRY: *The Sign in Sidney Brustein's Window.* Hansberry's second produced play concerns a white intellectual in Greenwich Village. It fails with audiences. She also writes the captions for a group of photographs documenting the civil rights struggle, *The Movement.*

LEROI JONES (AMIRI BARAKA): *Dutchman.* Initiating black revolutionary drama of the 1960s and 1970s, Jones causes a sensation with his play about a black man taunted and eventually murdered by a white woman on a New York City subway. It wins the Obie Award for best play. His next plays are *The Toilet*, about a white homosexual beaten by a gang of blacks, and *The Slave*, in which a black revolutionary leader converses with his white former wife. The latter is, in Jones's words, "the last play where I tried to balance and talk to blacks and whites."

ISOBEL LENNART (1915–1971): *Funny Girl.* Barbra Streisand's greatest Broadway success comes in this musical based on the life of Ziegfeld performer Fanny Brice. The Brooklyn-born Lennart was a successful Hollywood screenwriter from 1942 to 1968.

ROBERT LOWELL: *The Old Glory.* First intending to write an opera libretto based on Melville's "Benito Cereno," Lowell adapts the story as a play, adding dramatizations of two Hawthorne stories ("My Kinsman, Major Molineux" and "Endicott and the Red Cross") to form a trilogy. The title, in Lowell's words, "refers both to the flag and also to the glory with which the Republic of America started."

TERRENCE McNALLY (b. 1939): *And Things That Go Bump in the Night.* McNally's first produced play opens at Minnesota's Guthrie Theater and in New York in 1965. It dramatizes a family who shut themselves into a bomb shelter in the cellar.

ARTHUR MILLER: *After the Fall.* Miller's drama depicts a middle-aged lawyer trying to make sense of his life and his relationships with his mother, his first wife, and his prospective third wife. The drama has been viewed as an autobiographical probing of the playwright's failed marriage to actress Marilyn Monroe. Also produced is *Incident at Vichy*, about a group of Frenchmen arrested by the Nazis in 1942.

EUGENE O'NEILL: *Hughie.* O'Neill's drama, written in 1941, finally reaches Broadway after being produced in Stockholm in 1958 and published in 1959. Set in a run-down New York hotel lobby, it concerns the characters' fantasy lives. It is the only completed play in a projected series of dramatic monologues to be delivered to a life-size dummy meant to represent the "Good Listener."

MURRAY SCHISGAL (b. 1926): *Luv.* Having gained his first recognition for the off-Broadway double bill of *The Typist* and *The Tiger* (1963), Schisgal's greatest success is this offbeat comedy about a husband who succeeds in matching his wife with his best friend so he can marry another. The Brooklyn-born playwright had his first theatrical success in London with *The Typist, The Postman,* and *A Simple Kind of Love Story* (1960).

SAM SHEPARD (b. 1943): *Cowboy* and *The Rock Garden.* The first of Shepard's plays to be produced are largely ignored by critics but generate a cult following for the playwright's disjointed dramatic structure, often explicit language, and explorations of character through lengthy monologues. Born on an Illinois army base and raised in southern California and on a succession of army bases, Shepard began his career as an actor and writer after arriving in Greenwich Village in 1963.

JOSEPH STEIN (b. 1912): *Fiddler on the Roof.* Based on Shalom Aleichem's *Tevye's Daughters* (1949), the musical, set in a Jewish shtetl in czarist Russia in 1905, concerns a pious milkman's attempt to arrange marriages for his independent-minded daughters. The play shows the dissolution of the Jewish community as a pogrom threatens.

MICHAEL STEWART: *Hello, Dolly!* In the musical adaptation of Thornton Wilder's *The Matchmaker* (1954), Carol Channing stars in the role of Dolly Levi. The musical's 2,844-performance run establishes a new record.

LANFORD WILSON: *Home Free* and *Madness of Lady Bright.* The playwright gains his first major success and acclaim for these one-act plays, produced off-off-

Louis Auchincloss

Broadway. The first dramatizes an incestuous union; the second concerns a fading transvestite homosexual performer. *Balm in Gilead*, Wilson's first full-length play, also appears. It involves thirty-two characters, including junkies, prostitutes, homosexuals, lesbians, and various hustlers interacting in an all-night New York coffee shop.

Fiction

LOUIS AUCHINCLOSS: *The Rector of Justin.* Auchincloss's most popular work, and one of his most acclaimed, is this character study of a deceased headmaster of a New England private school, presented from the various perspectives of those who knew him.

DONALD BARTHELME (1931–1989): *Come Back, Dr. Caligari.* Barthelme's first story collection, featuring his characteristic disjointed, illogical, and absurdist narratives, appears to enthusiastic critical reviews. Barthelme was raised in Houston, where he was the director of the Museum of Contemporary Art. He moved to New York City in the 1960s and began publishing his stories in *The New Yorker*.

SAUL BELLOW: *Herzog.* Bellow wins the National Book Award for this novel. It presents the intellectual and academic Moses Herzog, whose life is spinning out of control, forcing him to reassess his Jewish heritage and responsibilities in a series of meditations and letters to friends, family, and the famous.

THOMAS BERGER: *Little Big Man.* Jack Crabb, a 111-year-old survivor of Custer's Last Stand, narrates his mock-heroic, picaresque adventures. This western pastiche explodes many of the cherished legends about the Old West and portrays several of its most famous figures. A sequel, *The Return of Little Big Man*, would appear in 1999.

RICHARD BRAUTIGAN (1935–1984): *A Confederate General from Big Sur.* Having published a number of poetry collections, Brautigan issues his first novel, which playfully combines a portrait of hippie life in California with the musings of a man who thinks he is a Confederate officer planning the siege of Oakland.

JOHN CHEEVER: *The Wapshot Scandal.* Cheever continues to chronicle the decline of the New England Wapshot family, begun in *The Wapshot Chronicle* (1957). The title refers to the discovery that Aunt Honoria has never paid her income taxes, a fact that seals the family's fate. Cheever also publishes the story collection *The Brigadier and the Golf Widow*, which includes one of his most famous stories, "The Swimmer."

STANLEY ELKIN (1930–1995): *Boswell: A Modern Comedy.* Elkin's first novel, recounting the misadventures of a man parasitically living off celebrities, is greeted enthusiastically as evidence of a new major fictional talent. Born in New York City and raised in Chicago, Elkin became an English professor at Washington University in 1960.

ERNEST J. GAINES (b. 1933): *Catherine Carmier.* Set in the author's native Louisiana, Gaines's first novel, like his second, *Love and Dust* (1967), looks at racial conflict among whites, blacks, Cajuns, and Creoles. It would be followed by *Bloodline* (1968), a story collection celebrating the power of folk culture.

SHIRLEY ANN GRAU: *The Keepers of the House.* In a Pulitzer Prize–winning novel about Southern racism and miscegenation, Grau chronicles three generations of the Howland family, prompting comparisons with Faulkner.

JOHN HAWKES: *Second Skin.* Regarded by many as Hawkes's masterpiece, the novel chronicles the rebirth and regeneration from violence and despair of a middle-aged former naval officer, Papa Cue Ball.

CAROLYN HEILBRUN (1926–2003): *In the Last Analysis.* Published under the pseudonym "Amanda Cross," this is the first in a series of mysteries featuring Kate Fansler, literary scholar, devoted feminist, and amateur sleuth. Other titles include *The James Joyce Murder* (1967), *Poetic Justice* (1970), and *Death in a Tenured Position* (1981). The books impress readers as a parody of Dorothy L. Sayers's mysteries of manners, and Kate Fansler becomes a hero for a feminist age. Heilbrun conceals her authorship until she receives tenure at Columbia University, for fear she would jeopardize her scholarly reputation.

PAUL HORGAN: *Things as They Are.* This is the first of a trilogy of autobiographically based novels treating a young boy's maturation. It would be followed by *Everything to Live For* (1968) and *Thin Mountain Air* (1977).

CHRISTOPHER ISHERWOOD: *A Single Man.* Isherwood's novel, considered by many his masterpiece, treats a day in the life of an expatriate British professor in Los Angeles in the 1960s, mourning the death of his longtime lover.

KEN KESEY: *Sometimes a Great Notion.* Kesey's ambitious second novel concerns a fiercely independent logging family in Oregon under attack by the local union.

RICHARD E. KIM (b. 1932): *The Martyred.* Kim's first novel is a critically acclaimed bestseller about the Korean War, which would be made into a play, an opera, and a film. It was followed by *The Innocent* (1968), about politics in postwar South Korea, and *Lost Names: Scenes from a Korean Boyhood* (1970), a collection of autobiographical stories. Kim, born in Korea, attended universities in the United States and would become a naturalized citizen in 1964.

JOHN D. MacDONALD (1916–1986): *The Deep Blue Good-By.* This book introduces MacDonald's Florida-based private eye, Travis McGee, in the initial installment of a popular and critically acclaimed mystery series. Originally named Dallas McGee, the name of MacDonald's hero was changed after President Kennedy's assassination. Other titles in the rainbow-hued series include *Nightmare in Pink* (1964), *The Dead Lemon Sky* (1975), *The Green Ripper* (1979), *Free Fall in Crimson* (1981), and *The Lonely Silver Rain* (1985). MacDonald was born in Pennsylvania, gained a degree from the Harvard Graduate School of Business, and began his writing career in 1948 writing science fiction stories.

WALLACE MARKFIELD (1926–2002): *To an Early Grave.* The Brooklyn-born writer's first novel treats a group of Jewish intellectuals in Brooklyn who attend the funeral of a friend. The methods and themes of the book echo James Joyce's *Ulysses.*

KATHERINE ANNE PORTER: *Collected Stories.* Winner of the National Book Award and the Pulitzer Prize, this volume contains all the stories from Porter's previous collections, including major works such as "The Old Order," "The Downward Path to Wisdom," "Flowering Judas," "The Circus," and "The Leaning Tower," as well as three previously uncollected stories — "The Fig Tree," "Virgin Violeta," and "The Martyr."

JANE RULE (b. 1931): *Desert of the Heart.* Rule's first novel is a story about two women who meet and fall in love in Reno, Nevada. The book breaks with convention by presenting its female lovers in a positive light, eschewing the psychologizing that characterizes most lesbian literature that had preceded it. No American publisher would bring out the book, so it is published in Canada; Rule had immigrated there in the 1950s.

HUBERT SELBY JR. (b. 1928): *Last Exit to Brooklyn.* The Brooklyn writer's first novel provides a graphic treatment of squalid urban street life. The subject of an obscenity trial in Britain and banned in Italy for its shocking scenes of rape and homosexual acts, it becomes a notorious bestseller in the United States. Subsequent novels would be *The Room* (1971), *The Demon* (1976), *Requiem for a Dream* (1978), and *The Willow Tree* (1998).

TERRY SOUTHERN (1924–2000): *Candy.* Originally published in Paris in 1958 and written with Mason Hoffenberg (1922–1986), this sexual parody of Voltaire's *Candide* and conventional pornography is attacked as obscene but avidly read more for its titillation than its satire. Born in Texas, Southern is also known for his screenplays *Dr. Strangelove* (1964) and *Easy Rider* (1969).

GORE VIDAL: *Julian.* Vidal's historical novel, treating the reign of Julian the Apostate, the fourth-century Roman emperor who abandoned Christianity and tried to restore paganism, marks the novelist's discovery of his fictional specialty: animation of the past with provocative commentary on politics and power.

ROBERT PENN WARREN: *Flood: A Romance of Our Times.* Warren's novel is a group portrait of residents of a small Tennessee community that is to be flooded when a dam is completed.

Literary Criticism and Scholarship

ERIC BENTLEY: *The Life of the Drama.* Bentley's attempt to formulate a comprehensive theory of theater is hailed as the drama critic's finest work. Clancy Segal calls it "the best general book on theater I have read bar none."

RALPH ELLISON: *Shadow and Act.* Ellison's collection of essays, reviews, and interviews deals with, in its author's words, "literature and folklore, with Negro musical expression — especially jazz and the blues — and with the complex relationship between the Negro American subculture and North American culture as a whole." In it, Ellison answers critic Irving Howe on the responsibility of the black writer, contests the nature of black folklore presented by Stanley Edgar Hyman, and criticizes LeRoi Jones on his interpretation of the blues.

LESLIE A. FIEDLER: *Waiting for the End.* Fiedler's second major study of American fiction, begun in *Love and Death in the American Novel* (1960), looks at more recent novelists from Ernest Hemingway to James Baldwin, detecting in them an apocalyptic consciousness driven by a desire for a return to a state of innocence. *The Return of the Vanishing American* would follow in 1968, examining the myth of the Indian and its revival in the literature of the 1960s.

LEO MARX (b. 1919): *The Machine in the Garden: Technology and the Pastoral Ideal in America.* Marx's seminal critical work on the relationship between culture and technology appears to widespread critical acclaim. Marx was a professor of English and American studies at Amherst College from 1958 to 1977.

Nonfiction

ELEANOR CLARK (1913–1996): *The Oysters of Locmariaquer.* The New England novelist and essayist wins the National Book Award for her depiction of a fishing community in Brittany. It would be followed by her two major novels, both dealing with small-town New England life, *Baldur's Gate* (1970) and *Gloria Mundi* (1979).

ERNEST HEMINGWAY: *A Moveable Feast.* A posthumously published collection of sketches about the writer's life and acquaintances in Paris during the early 1920s. Together with a nostalgia for the past and the city, Hemingway shows a mean-spirited attitude toward his rival and sometime friend, F. Scott Fitzgerald.

HOWARD MUMFORD JONES (1892–1980): *O Strange New World: American Culture — The Formative Years.* Jones, a Harvard professor of English, wins the Pulitzer Prize for this first volume in a series of books on American culture that would include *Belief and Disbelief in American Literature* (1967) and *The Age of Energy* (1971).

MARTIN LUTHER KING JR.: *Why We Can't Wait.* In the year that King is named the first African American "Man of the Year" by *Time* and receives the Nobel Peace Prize, he provides an account of the Birmingham demonstrations of 1963 and the March on Washington.

HERBERT MARCUSE: *One-Dimensional Man.* Marcuse provides an influential study of modern consumer culture and of "today's man who finds that even as his life fills with gadgetry and convenience, it is emptied of meaning and fulfillment."

ERNEST SAMUELS (1903–1996): *Henry Adams: The Major Phase.* Samuels, a professor of English at Northwestern, receives the Pulitzer Prize for this final volume of his biographical trilogy, which had begun with *The Young Henry Adams* (1948) and continued with *Henry Adams: The Middle Years* (1958) — winner of the Bancroft Prize and the Francis Parkman Prize.

IRWIN UNGER (b. 1927): *The Greenback Era.* Unger's economic study of America from 1865 to 1879 wins the Pulitzer Prize in history. It is praised by critic R. P. Sharkey as "the most thorough, fair-minded, and balanced appraisal of the money question . . . which has yet been produced." Born in Brooklyn, Unger, a historian, taught at the University of California at Davis and New York University.

Poetry

JOHN BERRYMAN: *77 Dream Songs.* Berryman issues the first in a sequence that would eventually number 385, collected in his 1969 masterwork, *The Dream Songs.*

ROBERT DUNCAN: *Roots and Branches.* Duncan's collection includes the autobiographical "Sequence of Poems for H.D.'s Birthday" and other important works, such as "Apprehensions," "The Dance," and "The Continent." *Bending the Bow* would follow in 1968, continuing his open series of poems, "Structures of Rime," and beginning a new sequence, "Passages."

RICHARD EBERHART: *The Quarry: New Poems.* The collection includes elegies, meditations, lyrics, letters in verse addressed to W. H. Auden and William Carlos Williams, dramatic monologues, character sketches, and dialogues.

LEROI JONES (AMIRI BARAKA): *The Dead Lecturer.* Jones's second collection shows his increased racial consciousness, a break with Western literary conventions, and angry protest directed at white society.

GALWAY KINNELL: *Flower Herding on Mount Monadnock.* Kinnell's second collection features rough, conversational free verse depicting the physical world in poems such as "Tillamook Journal," "On Hardscrabble Mountain," "Middle of the Way," and the title sequence.

DENISE LEVERTOV: *O Taste and See.* Levertov's collection of new works written since 1962 includes her first published short story, "Say the Word." It would be followed in 1965 by the publication of the important essay "Some Notes on Organic Form," which discusses her poetic method.

ROBERT LOWELL: *For the Union Dead.* The title poem of Lowell's collection is widely regarded as the poet's greatest work. It is a meditation on the unheroic reality of modern life typified by the construction of a car park under Boston Common, which displaces a monument to Colonel Robert Gould Shaw and his African American

Civil War regiment, heroes who suffered great casualties at the Battle of Fort Wagner.

WILLIAM MEREDITH: *The Wreck of the Thresher and Other Poems.* The title work commemorates the loss at sea of the U.S. submarine in 1963. Reviewer S. F. Morse declares that the poem "may well come to stand as a model of the elegy in our time."

THEODORE ROETHKE: *The Far Field.* Roethke's posthumously published collection wins the National Book Award. It contains two highly acclaimed poetic sequences, "Sequence, Sometimes Metaphysical" and "North American Sequence."

MARK STRAND (b. 1934): *Sleeping with One Eye Open.* Strand's first collection introduces his characteristic dark meditations on modern alienation. Similar volumes — *Reasons for Mercy* (1968) and *Darker* (1970) — would follow. Born on Prince Edward Island and raised in the United States, Strand would produce translations, short stories, and children's books.

1965

Drama and Theater

WILLIAM ALFRED (1922–1999): *Hogan's Goat.* Alfred's blank-verse drama concerns a mayoral contest between Irish Americans in Brooklyn in 1890, in which a candidate's all-consuming ambition leads to his wife's death. It is the playwright's only theatrical success. He would adapt it as a musical, *Cry for All of Us,* in 1970. Alfred was born and raised in Brooklyn, and his play was inspired by the stories of his great-grandmother, an Irish immigrant.

ED BULLINS (b. 1935): *Clara's Ole Man.* Bullins, the former Black Panther Minister of Culture, establishes his dramatic reputation with this play, produced by San Francisco's Firehouse Repertory Theatre (and in New York in 1968). It is the story of a young man's encounter with a woman whose roommate, Big Girl, turns out to be her dominating lover. Bullins also produces black propagandistic consciousness-raising dramas such as *How Do You Do?* and *Dialect Determinism.*

ABE BURROWS: *Cactus Flower.* Burrows's adaptation of the French comedy *Fleur de Cactus,* by Pierre Barillet and Jean-Pierre Grédy, about a dentist's relationship with his nurse manages a run of 1,234 performances, a record for a foreign play on Broadway.

MARIA IRENE FORNES (b. 1930): *Promenade.* Having received some attention from her earlier play, *Tango Palace* (1964), the Cuban-born playwright composes her first full-length production, a musical play about two prisoners released back into the world. It is noteworthy for its use of innovative cinematic techniques and zany humor to treat serious problems. It would be followed by *The Successful Life of Three* (1965) and *Dr. Kheal* (1968).

MICHAEL McCLURE (b. 1932): *The Beard.* McClure's experimental drama depicts Billy the Kid confronting the actress Jean Harlow in the afterlife, in an exploration of American attitudes on sex and violence. *Newsweek* declares that the play's language is "without question the filthiest ever heard on a commercial stage in the English speaking nations." Because of the play's simulated sex act, cast members in a Los Angeles production in 1968 would be arrested and jailed after each performance for fourteen consecutive nights.

SAM SHEPARD: *Icarus's Mother.* The playwright wins his second Obie Award for this drama about a group of picnickers who, prompted by the sight of a passing jet, discuss their obsessions.

NEIL SIMON: *The Odd Couple.* The most enduring of Simon's early plays was inspired to answer the question "What's funny about divorce?" Simon's response is to create mismatched divorced roommates, the obsessively clean Felix and slovenly Oscar, whose interactions display the very characteristics that had led to their marital breakups. The play would be successfully adapted for film and television. Simon also writes one of his few missteps, *The Star-Spangled Girl,* about two struggling radicals in San Francisco.

LANFORD WILSON: *This Is the Rill Speaking.* Wilson produces his first work set in his native Ozarks. Wilson's first Broadway production, *The Gingham Dog,* about the failure of an interracial marriage, would draw critical praise but close after only five performances in 1969.

Fiction

JAMES BALDWIN: *Going to Meet the Man.* Having produced a photographic essay, *Nothing Personal,* with Richard Avedon in 1964, Baldwin issues a story collection that includes one of his most acclaimed works, "Sonny's Blues," about a young man's struggle for identity and self-expression.

HORTENSE CALISHER: *Journal from Ellipsia.* Calisher departs from her characteristic realistic examination of commonplace life with a science fiction fantasy about life in a perfect world that has dispensed with feelings and gender differences.

JACK KEROUAC: *Desolation Angels.* The first section of Kerouac's ongoing fictional autobiography treats time spent as a fire lookout on a mountain in Washington; the second half describes his travels in Mexico and Morocco and across the United States.

JERZY KOSINSKI (1933–1991): *The Painted Bird*. Kosinski's first novel is partly based on his own experience during World War II. In graphic and surrealistic scenes, the novelist portrays the nightmarish world of a child who wanders through remote country villages and confronts the hostility and cruelty of Polish peasants.

MAXINE KUMIN: *Through Dooms of Love*. Kumin's first novel is an autobiographically based story of the relationship between a radical Radcliffe student and her pawnbroker father. It would be followed by *The Passions of Uxport* (1968), about suburban life near Boston.

NORMAN MAILER: *An American Dream*. Stephen Rojack, the protagonist of Mailer's novel, murders his wife, sexually abuses his maid, and evades police prosecution. The book draws the ire of feminists, most notably Kate Millett, who in *Sexual Politics* (1970) describes the novel as "an exercise in how to kill your wife and live happily ever after." Others defend the book as one of Mailer's most powerful evocations of violence and madness in American society.

PETER MATTHIESSEN: *At Play in the Fields of the Lord*. Matthiessen's breakthrough novel concerns a group of naive American missionaries in the Amazon. They attempt to convert a primitive tribe but are manipulated by local authorities intent on destroying the tribe. The book prompts one reviewer to proclaim Matthiessen "our most eccentric major writer."

CORMAC McCARTHY (b. 1933): *The Orchard Keeper*. McCarthy's first novel concerns violence in the mountains of his native Tennessee. It is the first in a series of intense, dark Southern gothic novels—followed by *Outer Dark* (1968), *Child of God* (1974), and *Suttree* (1979)—that prompt comparisons with William Faulkner, Flannery O'Connor, and Carson McCullers.

WRIGHT MORRIS: *One Day*. Morris juxtaposes the discovery of an unwanted baby with the backdrop of the Kennedy assassination to form a group character study of a San Francisco community.

HUGH NISSENSON (b. 1933): *A Pile of Stones*. Nissenson's first story collection is highly praised for its depiction of Jewish history and myth. Cynthia Ozick describes the stories as "meticulous . . . perfected . . . polished" and "often radiant."

FLANNERY O'CONNOR: *Everything That Rises Must Converge*. O'Connor's second, posthumously published story collection contains two of her greatest stories, "Judgment Day" and "Parker's Back." Her *Complete Stories* would be issued in 1971.

J. D. SALINGER: "Hapworth 16, 1924." Salinger's last (as of 2003) published work appears in *The New Yorker*. In it Seymour Glass, age seven, writes a letter home describing his experiences at summer camp and his thoughts on the nature of human existence.

MAY SARTON: *Mrs. Stevens Hears the Mermaids Singing*. Referred to as her "coming out" book, the novel concerns a modern woman's attempt to find her place in society as an artist and a lesbian. It marks a turning point in Sarton's literary career. Her work would subsequently be taken up by numerous women's studies programs in universities across the country.

STEPHEN SCHNECK (1933–1996): *The Nightclerk*. Schneck's surrealistic first novel about a six-hundred-pound hotel clerk, described by one reviewer as "the fattest man in American literature," becomes an international counterculture favorite. Schneck would follow it with another novel, *Nocturnal Vaudeville* (1971), before devoting himself to writing cat-care books and television situation comedies.

ANNE TYLER (b. 1941): *If Morning Ever Comes*. Tyler's first novel introduces her characteristic subject of family life and characters trapped in prescribed roles. Three similar books would follow: *The Tin Can Tree* (1965), *A Slipping-Down Life* (1970), and *The Clock Winder* (1973).

JOHN UPDIKE: *Of the Farm*. Updike's fourth novel dramatizes a son's visit to his widowed mother on her Pennsylvania farm. The woman, Mrs. Robinson, is one of the writer's most complex and vivid characterizations. He also publishes *Assorted Prose*, a collection of parodies, humorous sketches, and reviews.

KURT VONNEGUT JR.: *God Bless You, Mr. Rosewater*. Responding to his motto, "God damn it, you've got to be kind," a shell-shocked philanthropist tries to use his inherited fortune to better humankind in this satirical novel about how money-obsessed society views altruism as madness.

MARGARET WALKER: *Jubilee*. Walker's only novel is a groundbreaking historical saga about a slave family during and after the Civil War. It pioneers the depiction of American history from a black perspective and an insider's view of the daily life and customs of the slave community.

MARGUERITE YOUNG (1909–1995): *Miss MacIntosh, My Darling*. Young's novel, almost twelve hundred pages in length, is set at the New England seaside. It explores the nature of dreams and reality through the relationship between Vera Cartright and the seemingly prosaic Miss MacIntosh and is the result of nearly eighteen years of labor. It is hailed by writer William Goyen as "a mammoth epic, a massive fable, a picaresque journey, a Faustian quest and a work of stunning magnitude and beauty."

Born in Indianapolis, Young published her first book, a volume of poetry, *Prismatic Ground*, in 1937. A second collection *Moderate Fable*, appeared in 1945.

Literary Criticism and Scholarship

ROBERT BRUSTEIN (b. 1927): *The Theatre of Revolt: An Approach to Modern Drama.* The outspoken drama critic is a proponent of experimental and avant-garde theater as well as a severe critic of established figures such as Arthur Miller.

T. S. ELIOT: *To Criticize the Critic and Other Writings.* Eliot's final critical collection brings together essays mostly from the 1950s along with some of his earliest pieces, including "Ezra Pound: His Metric and Poetry" and "Reflections on 'Vers Libre,'" both from 1917. The title essay is a candid review of Eliot's critical career, including his confessions about errors of judgment.

WILLIAM FAULKNER: *Essays, Speeches, and Public Letters.* This collection includes Faulkner's review of Ernest Hemingway's *The Old Man and the Sea*, lectures, introductions, essays on various writers including Sherwood Anderson and Albert Camus, impressions of Japan and New England, and comments about social issues such as race relations.

PHILIP RAHV: *The Myth and the Powerhouse.* The title essay, first published in 1953, attacks the prevalence of myth-criticism popularized by Northrup Frye, which, in Rahv's view, detaches works of art from their historical context.

LIONEL TRILLING: *Beyond Culture: Essays on Literature and Learning.* Trilling's essay collection includes a sequel to his essays on literature and psychoanalysis in *The Liberal Imagination* (1950), as well as an analysis of the cultural crisis produced by the turmoil of the era.

Nonfiction

CLAUDE BROWN (1937–2002): *Manchild in the Promised Land.* Brown achieves notoriety and acclaim for these autobiographical reflections of his youth in Harlem. Many consider it one of the groundbreaking works of the decade to portray inner-city black culture. Brown would follow it with *The Children of Ham* (1976), a short story sequence about Harlem residents coping with poverty, crime, and drugs.

HARVEY COX (b. 1929): *The Secular City.* The theologian's popular work attempts to make Christianity relevant and understandable in the context of modern secularization and urbanization.

JANET FLANNER: *Paris Journal, 1944–1965.* Flanner wins the National Book Award for this collection of her postwar "Letters from Paris," previously appearing in *The New Yorker.* A second volume, covering 1965 to 1971, would be published in 1971, and excerpts from prewar letters would be collected in *Paris Was Yesterday* (1972) and *London Was Yesterday* (1975).

DAVID HALBERSTAM (b. 1934): *The Making of a Quagmire: America and Vietnam During the Kennedy Era.* The Pulitzer Prize–winning war correspondent examines America's deepening involvement in Southeast Asia.

ALEX HALEY (1921–1992): *The Autobiography of Malcolm X.* Haley ghostwrites this memoir of the black nationalist leader, born Malcolm Little (1926–1965). The book becomes one of the most influential African American autobiographies of the twentieth century.

ALFRED KAZIN: *Starting Out in the Thirties.* In the second installment of his memoirs, begun in *A Walker in the City* (1951), Kazin treats his political and critical coming of age during the 1930s and includes sketches of several prominent figures he met during the period. *New York Jew* (1978) would continue his story from 1942 to 1970.

PERRY MILLER: *Life of the Mind in America: From the Revolution to the Civil War.* Miller posthumously receives the Pulitzer Prize for his unfinished third volume of *The New England Mind*, his intellectual history that had begun with *The Seventeenth Century* (1939) and *From Colony to Province* (1953). The volume comprises three sections — "The Evangelical Basis," "The Legal Mentality," and "Science: Theoretical and Applied." Left incomplete were intended sections on education, politics, philosophy, and theology.

JOSEPH MITCHELL (1908–1996): *Joe Gould's Secret.* The *New Yorker* writer's last original work treats the life of a derelict well known in Greenwich Village from the 1920s to the 1940s. Joe Gould was purportedly writing a massive oral history, which Mitchell exposes as a fabrication. The work includes Mitchell's own reflections on the writing life.

RICHARD B. MORRIS (1904–1989): *The Peacemakers: The Great Powers and American Independence.* Morris's study of the diplomatic maneuvering from 1779 to 1783 that ended the American Revolution wins the Bancroft Prize and is praised as the most comprehensive account of this aspect of the Revolution ever attempted. Morris taught American history at Columbia University from 1949 to 1973.

RALPH NADER (b. 1934): *Unsafe at Any Speed: The Designed-in Dangers of the American Automobile.* Nader's first book on the safety defects of American cars establishes his reputation as a crusading consumer advocate.

Arthur M. Schlesinger Jr. at the White House
with President John F. Kennedy in July 1962

ARTHUR M. SCHLESINGER JR.: *A Thousand Days: John F. Kennedy in the White House.* Schlesinger wins the 1966 National Book Award for history and biography and the Pulitzer Prize for biography for his account of the Kennedy administration.

EDWIN WAY TEALE (1899–1980): *Wandering through Winter.* Teale's naturalist observations become the first nature book to win the Pulitzer Prize in general nonfiction. It completes his seasonal studies begun with *North with Spring* (1951), *Autumn Across America* (1956), and *Journey into Summer* (1960). Born in Illinois, Teale was a staff writer for *Popular Science* magazine and the author of nearly thirty books of travel and nature studies.

TOM WOLFE (b. 1931): *The Kandy-Kolored Tangerine-Flake Streamline Baby.* Wolfe's first important collection of articles on "pop society," written in the innovative style and approach that would be described as the New Journalism, stems from his taking an assignment from *Esquire* to report on California's car customizers. When he had trouble with the story, his editor suggested that he type up his notes for another to finish. The result was forty-nine pages of impressionistic scenes and characterizations that were published as written, incorporating the novelistic elements that characterize Wolfe's distinctive style.

Poetry

A. R. AMMONS: *Corsons Inlet* and *Tape for the Turn of the Year.* The first collection includes the title work, one of Ammons's best-known poems, and the important sequence "Hymn." The second is a 205-page verse diary composed on an adding machine, which uses the narrow width of the paper to determine line length.

W. H. AUDEN: *About the House.* Auden's collection is made up of the sequence "Thanksgiving for a Habitat," poems on every room of his country home in Austria. Auden considers the verse collection his happiest and the first to offer a candid and frank treatment of his private life.

ELIZABETH BISHOP: *Questions of Travel.* Having moved to Brazil in 1951, where she would reside until 1973, Bishop explores the move and her growing understanding of Brazilian culture in this collection, which also includes reflections on the Nova Scotia of her childhood and a prose poem memoir, "In the Village." Bishop's *Complete Poems* would appear in 1969, winning the National Book Award.

EDGAR BOWERS: *The Astronomers.* This collection contains the sequence "Autumn Shade," an exploration of identity that critic Helen P. Trimpi states is "like little else in modern poetry . . . simultaneously, profoundly intellectual and profoundly emotional."

JAMES DICKEY: *Buckdancer's Choice.* Dickey's collection is awarded both the National Book Award and the Melville Cane Award. It opens with "The Firebombing," a poem based on Dickey's own experiences as a fighter pilot. In its contemplation of what happens to a man forced to destroy, it is, claims Joyce Carol Oates, the central poem of Dickey's work.

RICHARD EBERHART: *Selected Poems, 1930–1965.* Eberhart's second collection of his selected works (the first had appeared in 1951) is awarded the Pulitzer Prize. Eberhart would win the National Book Award for his *Collected Poems, 1930–1976* (1976) and would later issue *New and Selected Poems, 1930–1990* (1990).

RANDALL JARRELL: *The Lost World.* Jarrell's final collection of new works includes an appreciatory introduction by Robert Lowell. The poems continue the style and autobiographical method of *The Woman at the Washington Zoo* (1960).

CAROLYN KIZER: *Knock upon Silence.* Kizer's collection contains perhaps her best-known work, a satire on women's liberation, "Pro Femina," in hexameters derived from Juvenal's satires.

HOWARD MOSS: *Finding Them Lost and Other Poems.* Moss's most highly praised collection offers various treatments of loss, including "The Pruned Tree" and "September Elegy," as well as the sequence "Lifelines."

GARY SNYDER: *Six Sections from Mountains and Rivers Without End.* This is the initial installment of what would prove to be the poet's magnum opus, described as the "great long poem of the West." It would be enlarged in 1970 and completed in 1996.

MELVIN B. TOLSON: *Harlem Gallery: Book I, the Curator.* Tolson completes only this initial section of a planned five-book epic of Harlem life to reflect a history of black life in America. Here, an art gallery owner meditates on the scene outside his shop and the place of the black artist in white America. It is Tolson's final collection and includes poet Karl Shapiro's controversial introductory statement that Tolson "writes and thinks in Negro."

JEAN VALENTINE (b. 1934): *Dream Barker and Other Poems.* After a decade of rejection of her work, Valentine issues her first collection as part of the Yale Series of Younger Poets. It introduces her characteristic stripped-down, intense depictions of personal experiences in a series of vivid images. Subsequent volumes are *Pilgrims* (1969), *Ordinary Things* (1974), *The Messenger* (1979), *Home, Deep, Blue* (1988), *The River at Wolf* (1992), and *Growing Light* (1997).

LOUIS ZUKOFSKY: *All: The Collected Short Poems, 1923–1958.* The first volume of Zukofsky's collected poems not included in the multipart poetic sequence *A*. *All: The Collected Short Poems, 1956–1964* would followed in 1966, and *Prepositions: The Collected Critical Essays* in 1967.

Publications and Events

Salmagundi. This little magazine concentrating on the humanities and social sciences debuts. Beginning in 1969, Skidmore College sponsored it. Essentially a literary journal, it devoted one issue a year to a single subject, such as contemporary poetry or a particular author.

1966
Drama and Theater

EDWARD ALBEE: *A Delicate Balance.* Despite generally negative reviews and a modest run of only 132 performances, Albee's metaphysical drawing-room drama exploring the connection between sanity and madness is awarded the Pulitzer Prize.

JOE MASTEROFF (b. 1919): *Cabaret.* This musical version of John Van Druten's *I Am a Camera*, based on Christopher Isherwood's *Berlin Stories*, features lyrics by Fred Ebb and music by John Kander. In it the decadent master of ceremonies at the Kit Kat Club provides a unifying link between the musical numbers and the play's theme: the retreat into a world of unreality that ignores the coming of the Nazis. The Philadelphia-born librettist had his first Broadway success with *She Loves Me* (1963). He would later produce the libretto for the opera *Desire Under the Elms* (1989).

RONALD RIBMAN (b. 1932): *The Journey of the Fifth Horse.* Having gained initial attention with his play *Harry, Noon and Night* (1965), Ribman wins the Obie Award for best play for this adaptation of a short story by Ivan Turgenev. The subsequent works by the New York City–born playwright would include *The Poison Tree* (1973) and *Cold Storage* (1977).

NEIL SIMON: *Sweet Charity.* Based on the Federico Fellini film *Nights of Cabiria* (1957), the musical concerns a dance hall hostess's search for love and a relationship; it showcases the dynamic choreography of Bob Fosse.

MEGAN TERRY (b. 1932): *Viet Rock.* Terry's best-known play, dramatizing episodes in an American soldier's experience at home and in Vietnam, is generally regarded as the first rock musical and the first protest play about the Vietnam War. Terry was a leading figure with the Open Theatre whose other works include *The People vs. Ranchman* (1967), *Approaching Simone* (1970), and *Hot House* (1974).

JEAN-CLAUDE VAN ITALLIE (b. 1936): *America Hurrah.* The Belgian-born playwright's collection of three short plays employs various expressionistic devices to satirize American business and protest U.S. involvement in Vietnam.

TENNESSEE WILLIAMS: *Slapstick Tragedy.* Williams's double bill of one-act plays consists of *The Gnadiges Fraulein*, a parable of the artist's struggle that is set in a seedy Key West boardinghouse, and *The Mutilated*, about the rivalry between two New Orleans prostitutes. It is, in the words of the playwright, "vaudeville, burlesque, and slapstick, with a dash of pop art." Critics and audiences are unenthusiastic, and the production lasts for only seven performances.

LANFORD WILSON: *The Rimers of Eldritch.* Wilson's second full-length play employs another large cast to portray inhabitants of a decaying Midwestern town who reveal their true natures, prompted by the murder of the town's hermit.

Fiction

JOHN BARTH: *Giles Goat Boy.* Barth's "gigantistic," satirical allegory presents the modern world as an academic campus and treats the progress of the first programmed man, the son of a computer who is reared by a herd of goats. The novel, parodying mythic archetypes, solidifies Barth's reputation as an exponent of self-reflective "metafiction," which comments on the artifice of storytelling.

EVAN S. CONNELL JR.: *The Diary of a Rapist.* Connell's anatomy of the mind of a psychopath is called by one reviewer "a triumph of art over case history."

ROBERT COOVER (b. 1932): *The Origin of the Brunists.* The Iowa-born writer's first novel is his most conventional, about a survivor of a coal-mine disaster who founds a cult to help him explain his experiences. The novel, which wins the Faulkner Award for best new novel, shows Coover's characteristic theme of the need to create myth to give meaning to the world.

E. L. DOCTOROW: *Big as Life.* Doctorow's unusual second novel imagines the impact of the arrival of a pair of nearly motionless nude giants in New York Harbor. According to Doctorow, "Unquestionably, it is the worst I've done."

J. P. DONLEAVY: *The Saddest Summer of Samuel S.* Donleavy's novel treats a man trapped in his isolation, prevented from positive relationships by excessive self-analysis.

STANLEY ELKIN: *Criers and Kibitzers, Kibitzers and Criers.* Elkin's first story collection shows a darker side to his imagination, presenting a series of stories that reflect the fragility of life and the human capacity for suffering.

RICHARD FARINA (1936–1966): *Been Down So Long It Looks Like Up to Me.* A contemporary of Thomas Pynchon at Cornell University, folksinger and writer Farina dies in a motorcycle accident two days after publication of this first novel, a comic picaresque story of Gnossos Pappadoupoulis, which takes place in the American West, in Cuba during the revolution, and at an upstate New York university. Pynchon, who would dedicate *Gravity's Rainbow* (1973) to his friend, described the book as "coming on like the Hallelujah Chorus done by 200 kazoo players with perfect pitch."

WILLIAM H. GASS (b. 1924): *Omensetter's Luck.* Gass's first novel, set in Ohio during the 1890s, concerns newcomer Brackett Omensetter, whose luck gives out when his experience deepens. His nemesis is the Reverend Jethro Ferber, and their duel typifies basic philosophical conflicts between mind and body, reason and feeling. Critics greet the work as the arrival of an important writing talent. Born in North Dakota, Gass became a professor of English and philosophy at Washington University.

JOHN HERSEY: *Too Far to Walk.* Hersey looks at the contemporary campus scene, depicting undergraduates who pursue intense sensory experience by using LSD.

JOHN KNOWLES: *Indian Summer.* Having ventured to the French Riviera for his flawed second novel, *Morning in Antibes* (1962), Knowles returns to the American scene with this novel about the relationship between a former flyer and his friend's family. Critics find the book a somewhat ponderous allegorical meditation on the makeup of the American character. It would be followed in 1968 by *Phineas*, a story collection.

BERNARD MALAMUD: *The Fixer.* Malamud's story of a Jew falsely accused of murder in czarist Russia in 1912 ends with the declaration that there is "no such thing as an unpolitical man." Taken as commentary on the civil rights movement, the book achieves popular as well as critical success and would be made into a 1968 film after winning both the National Book Award and the Pulitzer Prize.

CYNTHIA OZICK (b. 1928): *Trust.* Ozick's dense, Jamesian first novel concerns a young woman's search for identity. After a less-than-enthusiastic critical response and limited commercial success, Ozick would turn to short fiction to establish her literary reputation.

WALKER PERCY: *The Last Gentleman.* Percy's second novel is about a Southerner, Will Barrett, who suffers from bouts of amnesia and searches to answer the question of how to live. Barrett would resume his quest in *The Second Coming* (1980).

THOMAS PYNCHON: *The Crying of Lot 49.* Pynchon's second novel concerns Oedipa Maas's search to uncover a vast underground conspiracy. Pynchon's shortest and most accessible novel would be later dismissed by its author as a "story . . . which was marketed as a 'novel,' and in which I seem to have forgotten most of what I thought I'd learned up till then." Critics have generally disagreed, finding in the work most of Pynchon's major themes.

ISAAC BASHEVIS SINGER: *Zlateh the Goat and Other Stories.* Singer's first collection of children's stories is illustrated by Maurice Sendak.

JACQUELINE SUSANN (1921–1974): *Valley of the Dolls.* The actress-turned-writer sexually escalates the romance genre in this depiction of a collection of glamorous women who indulge in various excesses and pay the price. Through relentless self-promotion, Susann would make the book, and the two guilty pleasures that followed — *The Love Machine* (1969) and *Once Is Not Enough* (1973) — bestsellers, despite universal critical scorn.

Susan Sontag

JOHN UPDIKE: *The Music School.* Updike's third story collection shows his shift of subject to middle-aged characters in a suburban setting, documenting the marital discord, infidelity, and confusion that results from a search for an unattainable romantic ideal. Standouts include "Leaves" and "Giving Blood," featuring the recurring Maples family.

Literary Criticism and Scholarship

KENNETH BURKE: *Language as Symbolic Action.* Burke's final book of criticism attempts "to define and track down the implication of the term symbolic action" and to demonstrate its operation in a number of literary works, including texts by Shakespeare, Ralph Walso Emerson, Theodore Roethke, William Carlos Williams, and Djuna Barnes.

RICHARD POIRIER (b. 1925): *A World Elsewhere: The Place of Style in American Literature.* Poirier's critical volume on American writers suggests that out of distaste for social systems, they attempt to create "verbal consciousness of freedom." The book helps establish Poirier as one of America's foremost literary critics.

SUSAN SONTAG: *Against Interpretation.* Sontag's collection of critical essays establishes her as one of the most controversial, daring, and provocative modern critics.

The essay "Notes on 'Camp,'" her first important work (published in 1964), helps define postmodern attitudes. Other influential essays include the title work and "On Style."

Nonfiction

TRUMAN CAPOTE: *In Cold Blood.* Capote's in-depth, harrowing account of a notorious multiple murder in Kansas, committed by two psychopaths who are later executed, inaugurates the era of the "nonfiction novel."

WILLIAM H. GOETZMANN (b. 1930): *Exploration and Empire: The Explorer and Scientist in the Winning of the American West.* Goetzmann wins the Pulitzer Prize and the Francis Parkman Award for this study chronicling the expeditions and travels of the early nineteenth century that opened up the territory beyond the Missouri River. Goetzmann taught American studies at Yale and the University of Texas.

LEROI JONES (AMIRI BARAKA): *Home: Social Essays.* Jones's first collection of sociopolitical essays includes the important "Cuba Libre," tracing the raising of Jones's political and racial consciousness, and "The Legacy of Malcolm X, and the Coming of the Black Nation."

JACK KEROUAC: *Satori in Paris.* Kerouac describes his travels in France to research his lineage as a comic search for various forms of illumination. It is among the best of Kerouac's later work.

MARK LANE (b. 1927): *Rush to Judgment.* An early best-seller of the many books dealing with the Kennedy assassination. Lane disputes the Warren Commission's conclusion that Lee Harvey Oswald was guilty by presenting discrepancies among the evidence. He would follow it with *Executive Action* (1973), a novel positing a conspiracy by right-wing Texas oilmen to kill Kennedy. Lane was a New York attorney hired by the family of Lee Harvey Oswald to represent their interests before the Warren Commission.

OSCAR LEWIS (1914–1970): *La Vida.* The anthropologist wins the National Book Award for this account of the lives of a Puerto Rican mother and her children in San Juan and New York. Lewis was an anthropology professor at the University of Illinois. His other notable books include *Five Families* (1957) and *Children of Sanchez* (1961).

NORMAN MAILER: *Cannibals and Christians.* Mailer's third miscellany of political, social, and literary writings from 1960 includes his reports on the 1964 presidential conventions and profiles of the nominees, Barry Goldwater and Lyndon Johnson.

WILLIAM H. MASTERS (1915–2001) AND VIRGINIA E. JOHNSON (b. 1925): *Human Sexual Response.* The husband-and-wife researchers establish their reputation as the leading experts on sexuality during the era. The book proves to be a controversial bestseller and would be followed by *Human Sexual Inadequacy* (1970).

VLADIMIR NABOKOV: *Speak, Memory.* Regarded by many as one of the greatest autobiographies in English, Nabokov's revision of his earlier memoir, *Conclusive Evidence* (1951), treats his boyhood in prerevolutionary Russia and his first forty-one years in vividly recalled incidents and a meditation on memory.

ANAÏS NIN: *Diary.* The first of six volumes of Nin's diary is published (completed in 1976). The sexually frank and revealing diaries help make Nin a spokesperson for the liberated woman of the period.

GEORGE PLIMPTON (1927–2003): *Paper Lion.* Plimpton's best-selling account of his experiences as a backup quarterback for the Detroit Lions is described by reviewer Hal Higdon as "the best book written about pro football — maybe about any sport — because he captured with absolute fidelity how the average fan might feel given the opportunity to try out for a professional football team."

ISAAC BASHEVIS SINGER: *In My Father's Court.* The first volume of Singer's memoirs. Subsequent volumes are *A Little Boy's Search for God* (1976), *A Young Man's Search for Love* (1978), *Lost in America* (1981), and *Love and Exile* (1984).

JOHN STEINBECK: *America and Americans.* Steinbeck's final book published during his lifetime is a reflective essay accompanying a book of photographs in which he meditates on the American character and his own American odyssey.

Poetry

A. R. AMMONS: *Northfield Poems.* Ammons demonstrates a more imagistic style in this collection inspired by nature, which includes works such as "Saliences" and "Discoverer."

JOHN ASHBERY: *Rivers and Mountains.* Reviewer Stephen Koch cites the poem "The Skaters" from this collection as "the most successful long poem written by an American since Berryman and Lowell wrote theirs."

ROD MCKUEN (b. 1933): *Stanyan Street and Other Sorrows.* McKuen's best-selling poetry collection of earnest and sensitive verses helps make him one of the most popular poets of the decade. The equally popular *Listen to the Warm* would appear in 1967.

JAMES MERRILL: *Nights and Days.* In Merrill's National Book Award–winning collection, the poet continues his exploration of personal experience begun in *Water Street* (1962), most notably in poems such as "The Broken Home" and "Matinees." A similar collection, *The Fire Screen*, containing the long verse narrative "The Summer People," would follow in 1969.

MARIANNE MOORE: *Tell Me, Tell Me: Granite, Steel, and Other Topics.* Moore's last major collection before her death prompts poet John Ashbery to comment that "Reading her, one has the illusion that one could somehow manage without the other great modern poets if one had to." Moore's *Complete Poems* would follow in 1967, expanded in 1981.

SYLVIA PLATH: *Ariel.* This collection of poems written in the months leading up to her suicide contains some of Plath's most famous and enduring works, including "Lady Lazarus" and "Daddy."

ADRIENNE RICH: *Necessities of Life: Poems, 1962–1965.* Rich's collection of new works and translations of several modern Dutch poets is generally viewed as marking a transition in her work to a more confrontational tone, exploring her personal and political beliefs, experimental methods, and growing feminist consciousness.

ANNE SEXTON: *Live or Die.* Sexton wins the Pulitzer Prize for this collection examining the author's many breakdowns and suicide attempts. The frequent connection in the volume between madness and sexuality would lead to later speculation that Sexton was a victim of childhood sexual abuse.

DIANE WAKOSKI (b. 1937): *Discrepancies and Apparitions.* After an initial small press collection, *Coins and Coffins* (1961), Wakoski's first major volume features her characteristic "personal narrative" style of vividly delivered intimate moments of recognition. Born in California, Wakoski has since 1967 been a teacher at Michigan State University.

1967
Drama and Theater

ROBERT ANDERSON: *You Know I Can't Hear You When the Water's Running.* Anderson gains his biggest commercial success with this collection of one-act dramas exploring topics such as gender assumptions, marital relationships, and the connection between memory and experience. It would be followed by a second collection of one-act plays, *Solitaire/Double Solitaire:* the first shows life in a dystopian future; the second presents relationships among three married couples.

JULES FEIFFER (b. 1929): *Little Murders.* Feiffer's first full-length play is an absurdist comedy about an eccentric family forced to deal with the violence of city life. Successfully produced in London, the play initially fails on Broadway but would be successfully revived off-Broadway in 1969. Since 1956 Feiffer's sardonic cartoons have appeared in the *Village Voice.*

BARBARA GARSON (b. 1942): *MacBird!* This outrageous pastiche of *Macbeth*, one of the most controversial dramas of the decade, takes aim at Lyndon Johnson, who is accused of being responsible for the assassination of John F. Kennedy. When Lady MacBird goes mad, she sprays deodorant to mask the stench of her husband with the words "Out, damned odor." The play offends many, but it is an off-Broadway success. Born in Brooklyn, Garson would win an Obie Award for her children's play *The Dinosaur Door* (1976).

JOSEPH HELLER: *We Bombed in New Haven.* The first of Heller's two plays is a Pirandello-influenced drama about a group of actors rehearsing a play about airmen dispatched on a bombing mission to Minnesota. His other drama is *Clevinger's Trial* (1974).

AMIRI BARAKA (LEROI JONES): *Slave Ship.* The play is a searing historical pantomime dramatizing the experiences of Africans on a slave ship to America.

EUGENE O'NEILL: *More Stately Mansions.* O'Neill's unfinished drama in his projected work *Tale of Possessors Self-Dispossessed* reaches Broadway after its debut in Stockholm in 1962. The play continues the family saga introduced in *A Touch of the Poet* and dwells on the destruction of idealism in the pursuit of material success.

ROCHELLE OWENS (b. 1936): *Futz.* First performed at the Tyrone Guthrie Workshop in 1965, Owens's initial dramatic success is a controversial experimental drama that wins the Obie Award. One of the era's most outrageous, it concerns the sexual relationship between a man and his pig. Born and raised in Brooklyn, Owens would continue to shock, exploring themes of perversity, violence, and repression in works such as *Belch* (1967), *Kontraption* (1970), and *The Karl Marx Play* (1973).

GEROME RAGNI (1942–1991) AND JAMES RADO (b. 1939): *Hair.* Subtitled an "American Tribal Love-Rock Musical," the groundbreaking, iconic 1960s musical displays hippie life in New York's East Village. First produced at New York's Public Theater, it would be transferred to Broadway in 1968. The first major musical to employ a rock music score, it includes the 1960s anthem "Aquarius/Let the Sunshine In" and features a notorious nude scene, the first in a commercial musical production.

SAM SHEPARD: *La Turista.* Shepard's first full-length play is a surrealistic comedy depicting a couple suffering from dysentery on a vacation to Mexico. In act one they are treated by a Mexican doctor's voodoo cure; in act two, the couple prepares for their trip by being treated by a doctor dressed in a Civil War uniform.

Fiction

DONALD BARTHELME: *Snow White.* Barthelme's first novel is a modernist repossession of the fairy tale, featuring a succession of incongruous, absurdist episodes, a cast of priapic dwarfs, a prince obsessed with hot baths, and a liberated Snow White.

THOMAS BERGER: *Killing Time.* Berger's most ambitious novel sheds his characteristic comic satire for a dark exploration of a mass murderer and the prevalence of violence in modern American life. A similar serious treatment of American life is evident in *Sneaky People* (1975), about a man who schemes to murder his wife.

RICHARD BRAUTIGAN: *Trout Fishing in America.* This loosely organized, comic work about the search for the perfect trout stream becomes a best-selling cult classic of the youth counterculture. It would be followed by the equally popular *In Watermelon Sugar* in 1968.

ALLAN W. ECKERT (b. 1931): *The Frontiersmen.* The first in the seven-volume Winning of America series tells the stories of Simon Kenton, who opened the Northwest, and Tecumseh, the Shawnee chief who tried to stop the white man's westward expansion. The series of historical novels combines scholarship and historical fiction by employing authentic dialogue taken from diaries and other historical sources. Born in Buffalo, New York, Eckert was the outdoor and nature editor of the *Dayton Journal-Herald.*

STANLEY ELKIN: *A Bad Man.* A department-store owner willingly goes to prison in this novel exploring the protagonist's search for existential authenticity through suffering.

HERBERT GOLD: *Fathers: A Novel in the Form of a Memoir.* Weaving together fact and fiction, Gold treats his background and his relationship with his parents in the first of two novels. *Family* would follow in 1981.

SHIRLEY HAZZARD (b. 1931): *People in Glass Houses.* Hazzard's collection of interrelated stories wittily describe an unnamed organization that is clearly the United Nations. Hazzard was born in Australia and settled in the United States after working for the United Nations in New York City.

S. E. HINTON (b. 1948): *The Outsiders.* Hinton's first novel, begun when she was a high school sophomore, deals with teenage gang violence and has been described as "one of the most successful, and the most emulated, young adult books of all time." Credited with revolutionizing the young adult novel genre by portraying teenagers realistically, Hinton would follow her first success with novels such as *That Was Then, This Is Now* (1971), *Rumble Fish* (1975), *Tex* (1979), and *Taming the Star Runner* (1988).

JAMES JONES: *Go to the Widow-Maker.* A successful playwright tests his manhood by learning to skin-dive and hunt sharks in this novel about masculinity, which mixes sex and undersea adventure with Freudian analysis. Jones's friend, William Styron, characterizes it as "a chaotic novel of immeasurable length, filled with plywood characters, implausible dialogue, and thick wedges of plain atrocious writing." It would be followed by *The Merry Month of May* (1971), in which an American family is torn apart by the 1968 Paris riots, and *A Touch of Danger* (1973), a detective story set on a Greek island.

IRA LEVIN: *Rosemary's Baby.* Levin updates the gothic thriller in a bestseller about a woman on New York's West Side who conceives Satan's child. The work initiates a rage for novels of contemporary supernatural horror. The book is the basis of Roman Polanski's first American film in 1968, starring Mia Farrow.

NORMAN MAILER: *Why Are We in Vietnam?* Mailer provides an answer in the grotesque details of a bear hunt in Alaska. The story is narrated by a Dallas teenager, D.J., in a pastiche of contemporary American vernacular.

WRIGHT MORRIS: *In Orbit.* Morris offers a meditation on contemporary American life across the generational divide in this novel about a high school dropout and draft dodger on a crime spree in a small Indiana town, which is also hit by a tornado.

JOYCE CAROL OATES: *A Garden of Earthly Delights.* Oates's second novel initiates a series dealing with the "social and economic facts of life in America." Here she treats the world of the migrant farm laborer. The book would be followed by *Expensive People* (1968), set in affluent suburbia, and *them* (1969), about an inner-city family.

CHAIM POTOK (1929–2002): *The Chosen.* Set in an orthodox Jewish community, the novel covers the conflict between secular and spiritual life in the story of a young man's relationship with his rabbi father. The story would be continued in *The Promise* (1969). Born in New York City, Potok trained as a rabbi and served as an army chaplain.

JOHN RECHY: *Numbers.* Set around Griffith Park in Los Angeles, Rechy's novel about a hustler's quest to pick up thirty sex partners as quickly as possible provokes a strong reaction. Rechy defends the book as not pornographic but "a book about a nightmare, about someone trying to avoid death." Death and nightmare also figure prominently in his next novel, *The Day's Death* (1969), connecting the death of the protagonist's mother and a trial on a sex-perversion charge.

ISHMAEL REED (b. 1938): *The Free-Lance Pallbearers.* Reed's first novel parodies the black novel of identity crisis and search for selfhood in the surrealistic career of Bukka Doopeyduk, whose earnest attempt to fit in and get on leads to his crucifixion beneath a giant ball of human excrement. Reed was born in Chattanooga, Tennessee, and grew up in Buffalo.

PHILIP ROTH: *When She Was Good.* Roth's second novel, about an imperious housewife, is his only book to feature a female protagonist, a noncharacteristic Midwestern setting, and a Protestant cast of characters.

JAMES SALTER: *A Sport and a Pastime.* Salter's third novel tells the story of a Yale dropout who has an affair in Paris with a young shop girl. It prompts reviewer Reynolds Price to declare it "as nearly perfect as any American fiction I know."

THOMAS SAVAGE (b. 1915): *The Power of the Dog.* Depicting the conflict between two ranch-owning brothers, Savage's novel is praised by reviewer Roger Sale as "the finest single novel I know about the modern west." Raised in Montana, Savage depicted the region in *The Pass* (1944), *Lona Hanson* (1948), *The Liar* (1969), and *The Corner of Rife and Pacific* (1988).

ISAAC BASHEVIS SINGER: *The Manor.* Set between the Polish insurrection of 1863 and the end of the nineteenth century, Singer's panoramic social chronicle documents the transition of Polish and Jewish communities into the modern world. Written between 1953 and 1965 and first serialized in the *Daily Forward*, the saga would be concluded in *The Estate* (1969).

SUSAN SONTAG: *Death Kit.* Sontag's second novel explores a passive protagonist's disintegration and retreat into death. Maureen Howard, in a positive review, declares that the novel "is about the endless and insane demands put upon us to choose coherence and life over chaos and death."

WALLACE STEGNER: *All the Little Live Things.* Stegner comments satirically on the youth culture of the period from the vantage point of one of his recurring characters, Joe Allston.

ROBERT STONE (b. 1937): *A Hall of Mirrors.* Stone's first novel is set in New Orleans during Mardi Gras. Portrayed with a nightmarish quality, it mixes race riots, narcotics, and various forms of self-destructive behavior. The novel wins the William Faulkner Award for best first novel and would be adapted as the film *WUSA* in 1970. A Brooklyn native, Stone served as a radio man on an attack troop carrier during the Suez Crisis of 1956 and lived for a time in New Orleans before receiving a Wallace Stegner fellowship at Stanford.

WILLIAM STYRON: *The Confessions of Nat Turner.* A first-person account of an actual 1931 slave rebellion in Virginia—told from the perspective of its leader—proves both successful and highly controversial. The novel wins a Pulitzer Prize but is criticized by black writers who complain that Styron had played on stereotypes in his portrayal of Turner and other slaves.

GORE VIDAL: *Washington, D.C.* Vidal introduces the fictional Sanford family in a depiction of American politics from 1937 to 1952, which involves appearances by historical figures such as FDR and Joseph McCarthy. The novel is the first in Vidal's Narrative of Empire series, depicting American history from its beginnings.

JOHN EDGAR WIDEMAN (b. 1941): *A Glance Away.* Wideman's first novel, describing a day in the life of a rehabilitated drug addict who struggles to stay clean, is enthusiastically received. It reveals many of the themes that Wideman would continue to explore in his second novel, *Hurry Home* (1968), including personal and collective liberty and responsibility, isolation, and the importance of family and community. The novel evokes comparisons with European modernist writers. Wideman, educated at the University of Pennsylvania and at Oxford as a Rhodes scholar, was raised in Homewood, the African American section of Pittsburgh and the setting of many of his works.

THORNTON WILDER: *The Eighth Day.* In his first novel since 1948, Wilder attempts his longest and most complex narrative, the story of two early-twentieth-century Illinois families animated by a murder trial. The novel wins the National Book Award.

JOHN A. WILLIAMS (1925–1994): *The Man Who Cried I Am.* Williams's fourth novel, which many regard as his greatest achievement, is the first of a trilogy, to be follow by *Sons of Darkness, Sons of Light* (1969) and *Captain Blackman* (1972). In these "armageddon novels," racial conflict escalates into destructive violence. Earlier Williams had published another trilogy, dealing with the problems faced by blacks in white society—*The Angry Ones* (1960), *Night Song* (1961), and *Sissie* (1963).

Literary Criticism and Scholarship

JOHN BARTH: "The Literature of Exhaustion." Barth's influential essay assessing the state of contemporary fiction appears in the *Atlantic Monthly.* Defining *exhaustion* as "used-upness of certain possibilities," most notably those from the realistic tradition, Barth defines the postmodernist writer as one who "confronts an intellectual dead end and employs it against itself to accomplish new human work."

R. P. BLACKMUR: *A Primer of Ignorance.* This posthumously published collection of essays considers "the economy of the American writer" and includes some important critical foundation statements such as a definition of the intellectual.

E. D. HIRSCH JR. (b. 1928): *Validity in Interpretation.* Hirsch, an English professor at the University of Virginia, examines the origins and development of literary criticism, asserting that "the will of the author is the determiner of textual meaning." He would continue to explore this theme in *The Aims of Interpretation* (1977), in which he argues that authorial intention is stable and knowable and that "critics have an ethical obligation to acknowledge and respect it when determining the significance of a text."

WILLIAM TROY (1903–1961): *Selected Essays.* Troy, who has been described as one of the most neglected critics of his generation, wins the Pulitzer Prize for this posthumously published collection of his literary essays on writers such as Henry James, Gertrude Stein, D. H. Lawrence, and Shakespeare.

Nonfiction

BERNARD BAILYN (b. 1922): *The Ideological Origins of the American Revolution.* Bailyn, a professor of history at Harvard, wins the Bancroft Prize and the Pulitzer Prize for this study, helping to earn him accolades from Robert V. Remini as "the foremost historian of the American Revolution." He would later win a National Book Award for *The Ordeal of Thomas Hutchinson* (1974) and a second Pulitzer Prize for *Voyagers to the West* (1986).

ERIC BERNE (1910–1970): *Games People Play.* Berne's popular psychological study of human interactions had first been published in 1964. It reaches the bestseller list three years later, largely through word of mouth, selling more than 2.5 million copies and remaining on the bestseller list longer than any other nonfiction book in the previous ten years. Born in Canada, Berne was a consultant to the surgeon general in psychology and a lecturer at the Stanford–Palo Alto Psychiatric Clinic.

FRANK CONROY (b. 1936): *Stop-Time.* Conroy's first book, a memoir, deals only with the first eighteen years of his life but marks, in the view of many, a literary breakthrough in the portrayal of the transformation from childhood to adolescence. Critic Charles Bronze in *Commonweal* writes that the book "resists categorization. Autobiography, yes, closet novel, yes, nonfiction chronicle, yes—but more important, it is art." Born in New York City, Conroy has been a writing teacher, editor, and author of works such as *Midair* (1985) and *Body & Soul* (1994).

DAVID BRION DAVIS (b. 1927): *The Problem of Slavery in Western Culture.* Called by reviewer J. H. Plumb "one of the most scholarly and penetrating studies of slavery," Davis's study wins the Pulitzer Prize. It would be followed by *The Problem of Slavery in the Age of Revolution* (1975), *Slavery and Human Progress* (1984), and *From Homicide to Slavery* (1986). Davis has been a professor of history at Cornell and Yale.

WILL DURANT AND ARIEL DURANT: *Rousseau and Revolution.* This tenth volume of the Durants' Story of Civilization series wins the Pulitzer Prize. The series would be completed with *The Age of Napoleon* (1975).

JUSTIN KAPLAN (b. 1925): *Mr. Clemens and Mark Twain.* A Pulitzer Prize and National Book Award winner, Kaplan's literary biography traces Twain's career from 1866 and the split between the man and his mask. Kaplan, born in New York City, was a senior editor at Simon & Schuster.

GEORGE F. KENNAN: *Memoirs, 1925–1950.* The diplomat and historian wins the Pulitzer Prize and the National Book Award for this first volume of his recollections. It would be followed by *Memoirs, 1950–1963* (1972).

JONATHAN KOZOL (b. 1936): *Death at an Early Age: The Destruction of the Hearts and Minds of Negro Children in the Boston Public Schools.* Kozol's account of his experience teaching in Roxbury before school integration in Boston, which indicts repressive teaching methods and segregational policies, wins the 1968 National Book Award.

WILLIAM MANCHESTER (b. 1922): *Death of a President.* Jacqueline Kennedy had asked Manchester to write this account of the Kennedy assassination, granting him exclusive interviews with family members. However, she withdrew her permission prior to publication for fear that the book would harm Robert Kennedy's presidential bid. The book goes forward nevertheless, and the controversy helps generate major sales. Manchester would be best known for his biographies of Douglas MacArthur, *American Caesar* (1978), and Winston Churchill, *The Lost Lion* (1983, 1987).

MARY McCARTHY: *Vietnam.* The first collection of McCarthy's views on the war reflects her visit to Saigon and her contention that the war is a corruption of American values. She states, "The worst thing that could happen to our country would be to win this war." She would follow it with *Hanoi* (1968), an account of her visit to North Vietnam, and *Medina* (1972), about the My Lai massacre. All three works are collected in *The Seventeenth Degree* (1974).

WILLIE MORRIS (1934–1999): *North Toward Home.* Morris's autobiography is an ambitious attempt to link his personal history with American experience from the 1940s through the 1960s. Born in Jackson, Mississippi, Morris was the editor in chief of *Harper's* from 1967 to 1971.

NORMAN PODHORETZ (b. 1930): *Making It.* The book recounts in an engaging, self-deprecating manner the author's successful attempt to break into the ranks of the New York intellectual elite. The editor of *Commentary* alienates many in the literary world with this frank and unflattering depiction, and he would continue his account of the rift and his conservative conversion in *Breaking Ranks* (1979).

PIRI THOMAS (b. 1928): *Down These Mean Streets.* Written in prison, Thomas's poetic and admired autobiography treats the challenge of his mixed Puerto Rican and black heritage. It is the first of three volumes of memoirs, to be followed by *Savior, Savior, Hold My Hand* (1972) and *Seven Long Times* (1974).

Poetry

DANIEL BERRIGAN (b. 1921): *Time Without Number.* This book reflects Berrigan's experience as a Roman Catholic priest, activist, antiwar protestor, and poet. Critics cite his adept use of alliteration, rhyme, and typography, and Fred Moramarco notes that in Berrigan's poetry "artiface makes way for feeling."

JOHN BERRYMAN: *Berryman's Sonnets.* The poet publishes a sonnet sequence about a love affair. Written in 1947, the work anticipates the use of disrupted syntax and the probing of his own experiences that Berryman would employ in *Homage to Mistress Bradstreet* and *Dream Songs. Short Poems,* a gathering of his lyrics, is also published; it includes "Formal Elegy," on the death of John F. Kennedy.

PAUL BLACKBURN (1926–1971): *The Cities.* This collection prompts critic M. L. Rosenthal to declare that Blackburn is "probably our finest poet of city life since Kenneth Fearing." Born in Vermont, Blackburn was associated with the Black Mountain College Poets. His earlier books include *The Dissolving Fabric* (1955) and *Brooklyn-Manhattan Transit* (1960).

ROBERT BLY: *The Light Around the Body.* Bly's second collection, which wins the National Book Award, shows a shift of emphasis to political and social themes as well as a more surrealistic style, juxtaposing the familiar with the bizarre, in works such as "A Dream of Suffocation" and "War and Silence."

ANTHONY HECHT: *The Hard Hours.* Hecht's Pulitzer Prize–winning collection of new and previously published works includes his best-known poems, such as

"Behold the Lilies of the Field," "The Dover Bitch," and "More Light! More Light!"

LANGSTON HUGHES: *The Panther and the Lash: Poems of Our Times.* Hughes's last collection is noteworthy for its rising tone of militancy, particularly in "Words on Fire."

DENISE LEVERTOV: *The Sorrow Dance.* Levertov's collection features the sequence "Olga Poems," an elegy for the poet's sister, as well as Levertov's first protest poems, including "Life at War," reflecting her antiwar activism.

ROBERT LOWELL: *Near the Ocean.* Lowell's collection includes new works celebrating the Maine coast and New York City, an elegy to Theodore Roethke, and translations of Horace, Juvenal, and Dante.

W. S. MERWIN: *The Lice.* Merwin's most highly acclaimed collection, and one of the most admired works of the postwar period, is a series of surrealistic lyrics that capture the spirit of the age. They include "The Gods," "The Finding of Reasons," "The Last One," and perhaps Merwin's most famous poem, "For the Anniversary of My Death."

HOWARD NEMEROV: *The Blue Swallows.* Nemerov wins the first Theodore Roethke Memorial Award for this collection. The poet's increasing interest in nature evokes comparisons with Robert Frost.

JAMES TATE (b. 1943): *The Lost Pilot.* At the age of twenty-three, Tate becomes the youngest poet to win the prestigious Yale Younger Poets Award for this collection concerning the death of Tate's father, reported missing over Germany during World War II.

DIANE WAKOSKI: *The George Washington Poems.* Wakoski treats Washington as a central symbol of the male mystique in a series of witty, acerbic verses addressed to the founding father from a variety of female perspectives.

Publications and Events

Negro Ensemble Company. The company is founded by Douglas Turner Ward (b. 1930), Robert Hooks (b. 1937), and Gerald Krone to train black actors and produce works of relevance to the black community. Among its notable productions are *The River Niger* (1973) and *A Soldier's Play* (1981).

Rolling Stone. Founded and edited by Jann Wenner (b. 1946), the magazine debuts to cover the rock music scene and more — it is "not just about music, but also the things and attitudes that the music embraces." By 1971 it had become the leading rock music and counterculture publication, with a circulation of 600,000. It featured writers such as Jon Landau, Joe Eszterhas, and Hunter S. Thompson.

1968
Drama and Theater

EDWARD ALBEE: *Box* and *Quotations from Chairman Mao Tse-Tung.* Albee's interrelated one-act plays show his intention to apply "musical form to dramatic structure." In the first play, an offstage voice comments on the decline of Western civilization while a large cube is illuminated on stage. In the second, the cube becomes the deck of a cruise ship where Mao recites from his "Little Red Book," an elderly woman recites doggerel, and another woman offers a personal anecdote.

ROBERT ANDERSON: *I Never Sang for My Father.* Anderson's autobiographical drama depicting a son's struggle to become reconciled with his dying father manages only a modest run of 124 performances. Anderson, however, would win an Academy Award for his screenplay for the 1976 film adaptation.

MART CROWLEY (b. 1935): *The Boys in the Band.* Reviewer Clive Barnes calls this play the "finest treatment of homosexuality I have ever seen on stage." It is one of the first plays to avoid many of the conventional gay stereotypes for a more complex psychological treatment of the play's various gay characters, brought together for a birthday party. Born in Vicksburg, Mississippi, Crowley became a television screenwriter.

BRUCE JAY FRIEDMAN: *Scuba Duba.* Friedman's first produced play wins the Obie Award for its comic deflation of a Jewish liberal intellectual whose wife is having an affair. It would be followed in 1970 by *Steambath*, in which God is portrayed by a Puerto Rican steamroom attendant.

ISRAEL HOROVITZ (b. 1939): *The Indian Wants the Bronx.* The playwright gains his first critical acclaim with this one-act play depicting senseless urban violence as a street tough (played by Al Pacino) torments a man from India on a Bronx street. Horovitz had been the resident playwright with the Royal Shakespeare Company in 1965. In 1979 he would found the Gloucester Stage Company in Massachusetts, where most of his subsequent plays, such as *A Rosen by Any Other Name* (1987) and *The Chopin Playoffs* (1988), would premier.

TERRENCE MCNALLY: *Sweet Eros.* McNally's play about a man who kidnaps a woman and ties her to a chair to tell her his maladjusted life story features a performance by Sally Kirkland as the captive; she becomes the first New York actress to appear nude throughout an entire play.

ARTHUR MILLER: *The Price.* Miller achieves a popular stage success in this powerful family drama depicting two brothers disposing of the family's possessions.

HOWARD SACKLER (1929–1982): *The Great White Hope.* Sackler's blank-verse drama portrays scenes in the life of the first black champion prizefighter, Jack Johnson, whose arrogance, assertiveness, and marriage to a white woman prompt a desire for a white champion to topple him. The play, featuring a powerful performance by James Earl Jones, wins both the Pulitzer Prize and the New York Drama Critics Circle Award. Born in New York, Sackler worked as a record director and screenwriter.

NEIL SIMON: *Plaza Suite*. Simon's comedy links three one-act plays centered on the various goings-on in Suite 719 of New York's Plaza Hotel. They include a middle-aged couple's doomed second honeymoon, a producer's attempt to seduce his high school girlfriend, and the bickering of parents of a bride on her wedding day. Simon also supplies the book for the musical *Promises, Promises*, based on the film *The Apartment*.

TENNESSEE WILLIAMS: *The Seven Descents of Myrtle*. Adapted from his short story "Kingdom of Earth," Williams's play about a white Mississippi farmer, his new wife, and his half-black half-brother manages only a brief New York run.

Fiction

JAMES BALDWIN: *Tell Me How Long the Train's Been Gone*. In Baldwin's novel a successful black actor stricken by a heart attack surveys his youth in Harlem, his family, an affair with a white actress, and his current relationship with his black male lover.

JOHN BARTH: *Lost in the Funhouse: Fiction for Print, Tape, Live Voice*. This collection of experimental short fiction shows Barth's search for alternatives to conventional writing and various exercises in literary self-reflexiveness, which explore the issues of a writer writing. Despite its unconventionality, the book sells twenty thousand copies in hardcover and is nominated for a National Book Award.

DONALD BARTHELME: *Unspeakable Practices, Unnatural Acts*. Barthelme's second story collection contains some of his best-known work, including "The Indian Uprising," in which Comanches conquer a modern city, and "The President," about a forty-eight-inch-tall chief executive.

SAUL BELLOW: *Mosby's Memoirs, and Other Stories*. The story collection brings together Bellow's short fiction from the 1950s and newer works, including the title story, about a diplomat's reflections on his life and career.

ROBERT COOVER: *The Universal Baseball Association, Inc., J. Henry Waugh, Prop.* Coover's inventive second novel treats an accountant's fantasy baseball league, which assumes a disturbing reality. The novel, like most of Coover's work, explores the relationship between myth and reality and the implications of creation and artifice.

JAMES GOULD COZZENS: *Morning, Noon, and Night*. Cozzens's last novel, his first to employ a first-person point of view, contains the reflections of an upper-class man, representative of both his class and times, who tries to come to terms with his experiences and values.

J. P. DONLEAVY: *The Beastly Beatitudes of Balthazar B.* This novel of education follows the career of a young French nobleman with Irish ancestry from innocence to experience. Many consider it one of Donleavy's finest efforts, mixing serious themes with his characteristic manic inventiveness. It would be followed by one of Donleavy's weakest efforts, *The Onion Eaters* (1971), a surrealistic fantasy featuring a hero with "three glands."

FREDERICK EXLEY (1929–1992): *A Fan's Notes*. Rejected by fourteen publishers, Exley's "fictional memoir" of the desperate life of a man living vicariously through his love for the New York Giants and their star player, Frank Gifford, wins critical praise and the Faulkner Award for best novel of 1968. Born in Watertown, New York, Exley would follow it with two more autobiographically derived books featuring relentless self-examination, including his alcoholism and stays in mental hospitals, and reflections on contemporary American life: *Pages from a Cold Island* (1975) and *Last Notes from Home* (1988).

WILLIAM H. GASS: *In the Heart of the Heart of the Country*. Gass's short fiction collection explores small-town Midwestern life among isolated and alienated characters who often retreat into a fantasy world.

JACK KEROUAC: *The Vanity of Duluoz*. Kerouac continues his ongoing autobiographical saga with an account of his surrogate's coming of age in the 1930s and 1940s.

JERZY KOSINSKI: *Steps*. The sequel to *The Painted Bird* (1965) shows the unnamed boy of the earlier novel becoming an adult; his youthful suffering makes him unable to conform to accepted social norms. The novel wins the National Book Award.

URSULA K. LE GUIN (b. 1929): *A Wizard of Earthsea*. Le Guin launches her best-known fantasy series, following the life of Ged, who rises from goatherd to become a great wizard, fusing fantasy and magic with commonplace concerns. It would be followed by *The Tombs of Atuan* (1971), *The Farthest Shore* (1972), and *Tehanu* (1990). The daughter of the eminent anthropologist Alfred Louis Kroeber, Le Guin graduated from Radcliffe and lived for a time in France before settling in Portland, Oregon, where she began her career as a science fiction and fantasy writer.

REYNOLDS PRICE: *Love and Work*. Price's highly regarded novel is a portrait of a writer and teacher struggling to cope with the death of his mother and assorted responsibilities.

LEE SMITH (b. 1944): *The Day the Dogbushes Bloomed.* The Virginia-born writer's first novel is a first-person narrative of Susan Toby, about the summer when she was nine. Its skill in rendering the language and preoccupations of preadolescence evokes comparison with Carson McCullers's *The Member of the Wedding* (1946). *Fancy Strut* (1973) and *Black Mountain Breakdown* (1980) would follow.

RONALD SUKENICK (b. 1932): *Up.* Sukenick's first novel, a treatment of a young man's growing up in Brooklyn, is the initial work in a series of experimental fictions designed to challenge conventional forms. Later books include *The Death of the Novel and Other Stories* (1969), *Out* (1973), and *98.6* (1975). Born in Brooklyn, Sukenick was educated at Cornell and Brandeis.

JOHN UPDIKE: *Couples.* The novel stakes out classic Updike territory and times: affluent New England suburbs in the latter half of the twentieth century. Treating the theme of marital infidelity, Updike connects the novel's sexual and moral disruptions with American values in the 1960s. The book remains on the bestseller lists for thirty-six weeks.

GORE VIDAL: *Myra Breckinridge.* Vidal's satire about the campy escapades of a transsexual in Hollywood predictably creates a scandal and becomes a bestseller. A companion volume, *Myron*, would follow in 1974.

KURT VONNEGUT JR.: *Welcome to the Monkey House.* In the revision of his earlier book, *Canary in a Cathouse* (1962), Vonnegut collects stories and sketches written between 1950 and 1968.

Nonfiction

EDWARD ABBEY (1927–1989): *Desert Solitaire: A Season in the Wilderness.* Abbey's account of his work as road inspector for the Forest Service and as a ranger for the National Parks Service has been cited as a key source of inspiration for the modern environmentalist movement and by critic Grace Lichtenstein as "among the towering works of American nature writing."

ELDRIDGE CLEAVER (1935–1998): *Soul on Ice.* This collection of essays, written during Cleaver's nine-year imprisonment for rape and drug dealing, recounts his involvement with Malcolm X and the Black Panther Party. Inspired by writers such as Thomas Paine, Karl Marx, and James Baldwin, Cleaver's work expresses "the profound alienation from America which black nationalists feel and the extreme political and cultural view of its future which they take," according to reviewer Jervis Anderson.

JOAN DIDION: *Slouching Towards Bethlehem.* Didion borrows a phrase from "The Second Coming" by William Butler Yeats for the title of this volume of essays exploring a decadent modern world. The collection contains perhaps her most well known work, the title essay about hippie culture.

RENÉ DUBOS (1901–1982): *So Human an Animal.* The French-born microbiologist receives the Pulitzer Prize in science for this popular study of human development, which argues for careful environmental planning to support humanity's basic biological needs.

JOHN HERSEY: *The Algiers Motel Incident.* Hersey reports on the killing of three African Americans in a gunfight with the police during the 1967 Detroit riots. In the author's view, the incident is symptomatic of America's racial divide.

WINTHROP D. JORDAN (b. 1931): *White over Black: American Attitudes Toward the Negro, 1550–1812.* Jordan's study wins the Ralph Waldo Emerson Prize, the Francis Parkman Prize, the Bancroft Prize, and the National Book Award. Jordan has been a professor of history at the University of California at Berkeley.

LEONARD W. LEVY (b. 1923): *Origins of the Fifth Amendment.* Levy, a professor of American constitutional history at Brandeis University, wins the Pulitzer Prize in history for this account of the roots of the U.S. Constitution's protection against self-incrimination.

ROBERT JAY LIFTON (b. 1926): *Death in Life: Survivors of Hiroshima.* Lifton, a Yale professor of psychiatry, wins the National Book Award for his study of psychoses and behavior patterns among Hiroshima survivors; it reports common feelings of guilt and a desire for death.

NORMAN MAILER: *The Armies of the Night.* Mailer's recollections of his participation in the October 1967 antiwar march on the Pentagon showcase his mastery of the "nonfiction novel." The book wins the Pulitzer Prize. Mailer receives the National Book Award for his other 1968 publication, *Miami and the Siege of Chicago*, his account of the Republican and Democratic presidential conventions.

ANNE MOODY (b. 1940): *Coming of Age in Mississippi.* The civil rights activist supplies an important account of life for a black woman in the South from the end of World War II through the civil rights struggles.

B. L. REID (1918–1990): *The Man from New York: John Quinn and His Friends.* Reid, an English professor at Mount Holyoke and Amherst, wins the Pulitzer Prize for his biography of the American attorney and patron of the arts who supported important artistic and literary figures during the 1920s, including T. S. Eliot and Ezra Pound.

LEO ROSTEN: *The Joys of Yiddish.* Rosten's witty lexicon of Yiddish words and phrases becomes a bestseller, helping to popularize a wide assortment of Yiddish expressions.

REXFORD GUY TUGWELL (1891–1979): *The Brains Trust.* An original member of Roosevelt's "Brains Trust" wins the Bancroft Prize for his account of the group's role in formulating New Deal policies.

TOM WOLFE: *The Electric Kool-Aid Acid Test.* Wolfe's first full-length book chronicles the counterculture moment through the antics of novelist Ken Kesey and his band of stoned-out mischief makers, the Merry Pranksters. Wolfe also publishes his second collection of articles, *The Pump House Gang*, dealing with various forms of American status seekers, including California surfers, topless dancers, pop art collectors, and Hugh Hefner.

Poetry

JOHN BERRYMAN: *His Toy, His Dream, His Rest.* The volume continues Berryman's ambitious sequence begun with *77 Dream Songs* (1964) and completed the following year with *The Dream Songs.* The collection provides additional incidents in the progress of the middle-aged character Henry, who reflects on his life and losses as well as on contemporary history.

GWENDOLYN BROOKS: *In the Mecca.* The long title work describes a mother's search for her lost child, which leads her to an understanding of the tragic lives of her tenement neighbors. The collection marks a transition in Brooks's career to the more overtly political tone of her subsequent work. Included are poems commemorating Medgar Evers and Malcolm X.

ALLEN GINSBERG: *Planet News: 1961–1967.* Ginsberg's most important work during the 1960s is collected in this volume, including impressionistic portraits of the era and the poet's reflections on his own aging and grief at the deaths of Neal Cassady and Jack Kerouac.

NIKKI GIOVANNI (b. 1943): *Black Feeling, Black Talk.* In Giovanni's self-published first book, the militancy of poems such as "The True Import of Present Dialogue, Black v. Negro," which asks "Nigger / Can you kill?" makes her a central, controversial figure of the black liberation movement. Subsequent works, however, would have a less strident tone, employing the language of blues and jazz and eventually focusing on her own domestic life.

DAVID IGNATOW (1914–1997): *Rescue the Dead.* Many consider this collection Ignatow's finest. He explores various searches for meaning and personal redemption in poems such as "Walk There" and "The Inheritance." Ignatow, whose mentor was William Carlos Williams, became the coeditor of the literary journal *Chelsea* in 1967.

GALWAY KINNELL: *Body Rags.* Kinnell's third collection, according to its author, "focuses on our painful attachment to the minimal shreds of our mortality, our 'body rags.' In our last moments and even in those instants when we have intuitions of harmony, peace, or transcendence, we are involved with decaying and desiring body."

ETHERIDGE KNIGHT (1931–1991): *Poems from Prison.* Wounded in Korea, addicted to drugs and alcohol, and imprisoned for armed robbery in 1960, Knight is encouraged in his writing by a chance meeting with Gwendolyn Brooks in prison and produces this collection of explosive free verse.

HOWARD MOSS: *Second Nature.* Moss's collection displays a noticeable shift in approach in a series of conversational poems approximating free verse.

GEORGE OPPEN: *Of Being Numerous.* Oppen's Pulitzer Prize–winning collection contains two of his longest and most highly regarded poems, the title work, a meditation on city life, individuality, and community, and "Route," a contemplation of man's essential isolation.

W. D. SNODGRASS: *After Experience.* Snodgrass's second major collection continues to mine the poet's memories and personal experiences in typical works such as "Mementos 1" and "Mementos 2." Included as well are several satirical portraits of figures such as John Foster Dulles and Richard Nixon in "Exorcism."

GARY SNYDER: *The Back Country.* One of Snyder's best collections depicts various untamed regions of the West and Asia, associating them with the unconscious mind.

JUDITH VIORST (b. 1931): *It's Hard to Be Hip over Thirty and Other Tragedies of Married Life.* Viorst initiates a popular series of witty, light verses on the vicissitudes of aging, to be followed by *How Did I Get to Be Forty?* (1976), *When Did I Stop Being Twenty?* (1987), *Forever Fifty* (1989), and *Suddenly Sixty* (2000).

DIANE WAKOSKI: *Greed.* Wakoski publishes the first two parts of an evolving sequence, with a subject that the poet defines as the failure to choose, the obstinate desire to "have it all." Wakoski writes in an immediate, personal, highly idiosyncratic style to meditate on what critic Alicia Ostriker calls the "All or Nothing syndrome in female romantic fantasies." *The Collected Greed* would be published in 1984.

ROBERT PENN WARREN: *Incarnations: Poems, 1966–1968*. The collection shows the poet's experiments with typography and poetic diction. The following year he would produce the verse ballad *Audubon: A Vision* (1969), chronicling the life of the ornithologist and painter John James Audubon.

1969
Drama and Theater

ED BULLINS: *Goin' a Buffalo*. Written in 1966 but staged in New York in 1969, Bullins's play is about a group of ex-convicts and hookers planning one final drug deal before jumping bail in Los Angeles and attempting to start over in Buffalo.

LONNE ELDER (1931–1996): *Ceremonies in Dark Old Men*. Elder's highly acclaimed drama concerns a Harlem barber and his family's efforts to cope with the impact of racism on their lives. Elder became the director of the Negro Ensemble Company's Playwrights' Unit before moving to Hollywood to write screenplays, including *Sounder* (1972).

LEONARD GERSHE (1923–2002): *Butterflies Are Free*. Gershe's only successful play concerns a blind man's attempt to escape from his dominating mother and his relationship with an actress who fears commitment.

CHARLES GORDONE (1925–1995): *No Place to Be Somebody*. The first off-Broadway play to win the Pulitzer Prize, and the first by a black playwright, concerns a black bar owner's losing struggle against the Mafia. The Cleveland-born Gordone had been a barroom waiter while struggling as a New York actor. His other works would include *Gordone is a Mutha* (1970) and *The Last Chord* (1976).

LORRAINE HANSBERRY: *To Be Young, Gifted, and Black*. Robert Nemiroff, Hansberry's ex-husband, assembles the late playwright's unfinished works, letters, and diary entries for the first of two dramatic collections. The other is *Les Blancs* (1970).

ADRIENNE KENNEDY: *A Rat's Mass*. Kennedy's drama performed off-Broadway at La Mama concerns the relationship between a black brother and sister and the white girl next door. Also in 1969, the New York Shakespeare Festival produces Kennedy's *The Owl's Answer*, a symbolic drama in which a New York subway door opens into the Tower of London where Chaucer, Shakespeare, Anne Boleyn, and the Virgin Mary appear.

ARTHUR KOPIT: *Indians*. One of the groundbreaking dramas of the decade is this depiction of American hypocrisy and violence during the nineteenth century, as scenes from the lives of Sitting Bull and Buffalo Bill Cody are juxtaposed in a scathing, symbolic attack on American genocide. The play had first been produced by the Royal Shakespeare Company in London in 1968.

ANNE SEXTON: *45 Mercy Street*. Sexton's only play is produced. Concerned with incest, the drama lends credence to Sexton's claims that she herself had been sexually molested by relatives when she was a young child.

NEIL SIMON: *The Last of the Red Hot Lovers*. Simon's comedy concerns a middle-aged married restaurant owner's bungled attempt to join the sexual revolution.

KENNETH TYNAN (1927–1980): *Oh! Calcutta!* The British drama critic assembles an erotic revue featuring contributions by Jules Feiffer, Bruce Jay Friedman, Sam Shepard, and others. Its extensive nudity and blatant sexual content prompt a national debate on censorship. After an initial run of 610 performances, the play would be revived in 1970. When it finally closed in 1989 after 5,959 performances, it was the second-longest-running musical in Broadway history.

JEAN-CLAUDE VAN ITALLIE: *The Serpent*. This Open Theatre production, first performed in Italy in 1968, is an amalgam of period theatrical innovation; an ensemble cast mimes the Kennedy assassination and scenes set in the Garden of Eden. The play wins the Obie Award and would be viewed as a kind of high-water mark for American experimental theater of the decade.

TENNESSEE WILLIAMS: *In the Bar of a Tokyo Hotel*. One of Williams's most intensely personal plays concerns an artist facing the disintegration of his talent. The play manages only a short off-Broadway run, with critics viewing the play as evidence of the playwright's own collapse.

Fiction

PENELOPE ASHE: *Naked Came the Stranger*. Conceived by *Newsday* columnist Mike McGrady, this novel, written under a pseudonym, parodies the works of Harold Robbins and Jacqueline Susann. It is jointly produced by McGrady and his colleagues, based on an "unremitting emphasis on sex." The hoax reaches number four on the *New York Times* bestseller list, the seventh-biggest-selling novel of 1969.

JUDY BLUME (b. 1938): *The One in the Middle Is the Green Kangaroo*. The first of Blume's juvenile novels draws praise and criticism for treating adolescence realistically. Dealing with the traumas of a middle child who claims the attention of his parents when he is cast as a green kangaroo in the school play, the novel would be followed by *Iggie's House* (1970), treating racial prejudice;

Are You There, God? It's Me, Margaret (1970), about a twelve-year-old whose father is Jewish and mother is Christian; *It's Not the End of the World* (1972), about divorce; *Deenie* (1973), dealing with a girl suffering from scoliosis; and *Blubber* (1974), treating adolescent obesity.

JIMMY BRESLIN (b. 1930): *The Gang That Couldn't Shoot Straight.* The New York journalist and columnist's first novel is a comic depiction of inept New York underworld figures. *World Without End, Amen* (1973), *Table Money* (1987), and *He Got Hungry and Forgot His Manners* (1987) would follow, all dealing with various aspects of New York City from a working-class perspective.

HORTENSE CALISHER: *The New Yorkers.* One of Calisher's major works gives the background of her recurring character Ruth Mannix. The book is praised for its knowing look at New York City life.

JOHN CHEEVER: *Bullet Park.* Cheever's third novel concerns a suburban family and a madman's attempt to disrupt their complacency. Called by Wilfrid Sheed "a brutal vivisection of American life," it is the least optimistic and most caustic of Cheever's books.

ROBERT COOVER: *Pricksongs and Descants.* Coover's collection of short fiction is one of the major examples of innovative "metafictions," works ultimately about themselves. Included are intriguing works such as "The Babysitter," "The Elevator," and "The Sentient Lens."

MICHAEL CRICHTON (b. 1942): *The Andromeda Strain.* The first of Crichton's best-selling thrillers (concerning a deadly microorganism from outer space that threatens life on earth) that would make him one of the most successful writers in America. Many of his novels — *The Terminal Man* (1972), *Congo* (1980), *Jurassic Park* (1990), and *The Lost World* (1995) — would be adapted into blockbuster films.

NICHOLAS DELBANCO (b. 1942): *Consider Sappho Burning.* Following his first novel, *The Martlet's Tale* (1966), based on the biblical story of the prodigal son, Delbanco produces one of his best-known works, an experimental novel about a lesbian poet. Born in London and educated at Harvard and Columbia, Delbanco has been a teacher of creative writing at the University of Michigan and elsewhere.

JOHN HAWKES: *Lunar Landscapes.* This collection includes short stories, the novella *Charivari*, and two short novels, *The Goose on the Grave* and *The Owl*.

URSULA K. LE GUIN: *The Left Hand of Darkness.* Le Guin's much-admired, controversial science fiction novel is set on a distant, frozen planet populated by hermaphrodites. Widely considered her most significant book, it looks at gender relations from a unique Taoist perspective.

ELMORE LEONARD: *The Big Bounce.* The first of Leonard's crime novels had been rejected eighty-four times before being sold as a film story and appearing as a paperback original. It features the writer's characteristic offbeat realism and stripped-down prose style, reminiscent of the works of Ernest Hemingway and James M. Cain. It would be followed by a number of contemporary crime thrillers that solidified Leonard's reputation.

BERNARD MALAMUD: *Pictures of Fidelman: An Exhibition.* This volume collects episodes in the career of a middle-aged man from the Bronx who journeys to Italy to become an artist.

PAULE MARSHALL: *The Chosen Place, the Timeless People.* Marshall's most political novel concerns an American research group on a Caribbean island and an exploration of identity shaped by history, race, class, and culture.

THOMAS MCGUANE (b. 1939): *The Sporting Club.* McGuane's well-received debut, a comedy set at a fashionable Midwestern gun club, shows the author's characteristic manic humor. McGuane would employ the same black comic style in his second novel, *The Bushwacked Piano* (1971), about a young man's break from his conventional lifestyle.

JAMES ALAN MCPHERSON (b. 1943): *Hue and Cry.* McPherson's first acclaimed story collection treats ordinary working-class characters, described by one reviewer as "mostly desperate, mostly black, and mostly lost figures in the urban nightmare of violence, rage, and bewilderment that is currently America." Ralph Ellison, in praising McPherson's achievement and potential, declares that as a writer McPherson will never be "an embarrassment to such people of excellence as Willie Mays, Duke Ellington, Leontyne Price — or, for that matter, Stephen Crane or F. Scott Fitzgerald."

LEONARD MICHAELS (1933–2003): *Going Places.* Michaels's first story collection establishes his reputation as one of the masters of the short story. A second collection, *I Would Have Saved Them If I Could*, would follow in 1975. Michaels, the son of immigrant Polish Jews, grew up on New York's Lower East Side and spoke only Yiddish until he was six years old.

N. SCOTT MOMADAY (b. 1934): *House Made of Dawn.* After publishing his first book, *Journey of Tai-me* (1968), a nonfiction recounting of Kiowa folktales and myths, Momaday produces his first novel. It traces the career of a young Native American unable to find a home in either white or Indian society. The book wins accolades — as well as a Pulitzer Prize — for Momaday, who is seen as the herald of a new generation of Native American writers that would include Leslie Marmon Silko, James Welch, and Louise Erdrich.

VLADIMIR NABOKOV: *Ada or Ardor: A Family Chronicle.* The memoir of Van Veen, describing his lifelong love for his half-sister, is one of Nabokov's most ambitious works and his most exuberant celebration of language, artifice, and love. While granting the novel's genius, critics are divided over whether this is Nabokov's masterpiece or a self-indulgent exercise in literary exhibitionism.

JOYCE CAROL OATES: *them.* Oates's chronicle of a blue-collar Detroit family from the Depression through the Detroit race riots wins the National Book Award.

MARIO PUZO (1920–1999): *The Godfather.* After two previous critically acclaimed but unpopular novels, Puzo produces what has been described as the fastest-selling novel in American history. The story of Don Vito Corleone's career as a Mafia don remains number one on the bestseller list for sixty-seven weeks and sells eight million paperback copies. Puzo would share the Academy Award with Francis Ford Coppola for their screenplays for *The Godfather* (1972) and *The Godfather, Part II* (1974), the first two films based on the novel. Puzo would follow up his success with other popular novels about organized crime: *The Sicilian* (1984), *The Last Don* (1996), and *Omerta* (2000).

ISHMAEL REED: *Yellow Back Radio Broke-Down.* Reed's zany fantasy has been described as an African American postmodern western. Set in a time warp, it portrays the Loop Garoo Kid, a black cowboy against an evil rancher, and introduces the concept of HooDoo, Reed's version of primitive forces of life pitted against the white Christian tradition.

PHILIP ROTH: *Portnoy's Complaint.* Alexander Portnoy's autobiography—"as told to" his psychiatrist—records his "complaint" that he can find relief from the guilt inflicted by his archetypally possessive Jewish mother only through compulsive masturbation. The comic style and, at the time, scandalous subject matter bring Roth a multitude of readers and a notorious reputation.

ISAAC BASHEVIS SINGER: *A Day of Pleasure: Stories of a Boy Growing Up in Warsaw.* Singer wins the second National Book Award ever given in children's literature (the first had been won by Meindert Dejong [1906–1991] for *Journey from Peppermint Street,* 1968) for this collection of scenes of Jewish ghetto life in Poland in the 1930s.

JEAN STAFFORD: *Collected Stories.* Stafford's story collection wins the Pulitzer Prize and prompts a recognition of the writer as one of the modern masters of the short story form.

KURT VONNEGUT JR.: *Slaughterhouse-Five; or, The Children's Crusade: A Duty-Dance with Death.* Billy Pilgrim is a shell-shocked prisoner of war in Germany who witnesses the firebombing of Dresden while also "time-tripping" to the distant planet of Tralfamadore, where he is put in a zoo and mated with a movie star. Blending dark comedy, farce, and philosophical speculation, the novel is widely considered Vonnegut's masterpiece.

LARRY WOIWODE (b. 1941): *What I Am Going to Do, I Think.* The North Dakota native's first novel, an intense character study of two newlyweds adjusting to each other and an unwanted pregnancy, wins the William Faulkner Foundation Award. A sequel, *Indian Affairs,* would appear in 1992.

Literary Criticism and Scholarship

IRVING HOWE: *The Decline of the New.* Howe's harsh assessment of literary modernism and contemporary writing in America includes one of his most important essays, "The New York Intellectual."

FLANNERY O'CONNOR: *Mystery and Manners.* This posthumously published collection of lectures and essays contains O'Connor's fullest explication of her works, creative process, and artistic vision.

PHILIP RAHV: *Literature and the Sixth Sense.* This collection of critical and political essays is united by an awareness of the historical, which Rahv defines as the sixth sense.

Nonfiction

DEAN ACHESON (1893–1971): *Present at the Creation: My Years in the State Department.* Acheson covers his long political career and his role in U.S. foreign relations from 1941 to 1953. According to reviewer Wallace Carroll, "As autobiography, this book is enthralling, as history indispensable, as a manual for government and diplomacy invaluable."

H. RAP BROWN (b. 1943): *Die, Nigger, Die.* The black militant and former chair of the Student Nonviolent Coordinating Committee provides a polemical autobiography of his Louisiana childhood and the development of his racial and political ideas. As Jamil Addullah Al-Amin, he would be sentenced in 2002 to life in prison for killing a police officer in Georgia.

NOAM CHOMSKY: *American Power and the New Mandarins.* The linguistic scholar enters the political arena with this scathing attack on the failure of liberal intellectuals to prevent America's war policies. Chomsky would continue his attack in *At War with Asia* (1970).

ERIK ERIKSON (1902–1994): *Gandhi's Truth: On the Origin of Militant Nonviolence.* The German-born psychoanalyst wins both the National Book Award and the Pulitzer Prize for his study of Gandhi, noteworthy for its application of psychoanalytic theory to an understanding of Gandhi's ideas and development.

THOMAS HARRIS (1910–1995): *I'm OK, You're OK.* Harris, a psychiatrist and supporter of the methods of Dr. Eric Berne, supplies a popular practical guide to transactional analysis, a psychoanalytical method focused not on the past but on interactions among individuals.

LILLIAN HELLMAN: *An Unfinished Woman.* The first volume of Hellman's memoirs appears and is instantly taken up by the women's movement. Later, many would question the veracity of Hellman's account.

ABBIE HOFFMAN (1936–1989): *Revolution for the Hell of It.* Written under the pseudonym "Free," this is the first of Hoffman's polemical works asserting his Yippie philosophy of counterculture activism. It would be followed by *Woodstock Nation* (1970) and *Steal This Book* (1971). Born in Worcester, Massachusetts, a graduate of Brandeis, Hoffman was the cofounder in 1968 of the Youth International Party (Yippies) and described himself as "the super salesman of radical ideas."

ELIZABETH KÜBLER-ROSS (b. 1926): *On Death and Dying.* Based on interviews with dozens of dying hospital patients, Kübler-Ross's first book becomes a bestseller and a standard reference tool for physicians, patients, and families, outlining the five stages of dying: denial, anger, bargaining, depression, and acceptance. It would be followed by *Questions and Answers About Death and Dying* (1972), *Death: The Final Stage* (1974), *Living with Death and Dying* (1981), *On Children and Death* (1983), *AIDS: The Ultimate Challenge* (1987), and *The Wheel of Life: A Memoir of Death and Dying* (1997).

JOE McGINNISS (b. 1942): *The Selling of the President, 1968.* McGinniss's first book is a critically praised and best-selling analysis of the effort by the Nixon team to recast the image of their candidate by using modern marketing techniques and television. McGinniss was a Philadelphia-based reporter and a freelance writer whose subsequent books would include *Heroes* (1976), *Fatal Vision* (1983), and *Blind Faith* (1988).

N. SCOTT MOMADAY: *The Way to Rainy Mountain.* Momaday connects the Kiowa myths he learned from his grandmother and collected in his initial book, *The Journey of Tai-me* (1967), with autobiographical reflec-

tions, in an innovative blending of myth, history, and personal experience.

DAVID REUBEN (b. 1933): *Everything You Wanted to Know About Sex (But Were Afraid to Ask).* Psychiatrist Reuben's folksy, demystifying approach to human sexuality becomes one of the decade's most popular books, selling more than eight million copies in two years.

THEODORE ROSZAK (b. 1933): *The Making of a Counter Culture.* Coining the term that described the youth movement of the late 1960s, Roszak, a professor of history, traces its sources among intellectuals such as Allen Ginsberg, Timothy Leary, and Paul Goodman, as well as its implications. One reviewer describes it as "the best guide yet published to the meaning . . . of youthful dissent."

CHARLES COLEMAN SELLERS (1903–1980): *Charles Willson Peale.* Sellers, a librarian at Dickinson College, wins the Bancroft Prize for his biography of his great-great-grandfather, the early American painter and naturalist who established the first popular museum of natural history in America in 1786.

GARY SNYDER: *Earth House Hold.* Snyder's essay collection contains comments on the environment, helping establish him as a cult figure of the ecology movement.

SUSAN SONTAG: *Styles of Radical Will.* Sontag's provocative essay collection includes her account of a trip to North Vietnam, film reviews, and influential essays such as "The Aesthetic of Silence" and "The Pornographic Imagination," in which she argues for the legitimacy of pornography as a literary genre.

GAY TALESE (b. 1932): *The Kingdom and the Power.* Talese's behind-the-scenes look at the *New York Times,* employing the novelistic techniques of the New Journalism, is his first bestseller. Talese began at the *Times* as a copy boy and became a reporter.

GORE VIDAL: *Reflections on a Sinking Ship.* Vidal's second essay collection considers pornography, the Kennedys, Nixon, and the future of liberalism.

T. HARRY WILLIAMS (1909–1979): *Huey Long.* Williams wins both the National Book Award and the Pulitzer Prize for his massive biography of the Louisiana politician, based on extensive interviews with Long's friends and associates. It has been frequently cited as one of the best justifications for the oral history method in biographical research.

GORDON S. WOOD (b. 1933): *The Creation of the Amerian Revolution.* Wood's first book on the American Revolution wins the Bancroft Prize. Several respected volumes on the Revolution would follow, including the Pulitzer Prize–winning *Radicalism of the American Revolution*

(1992). Wood has been a history professor at the College of William and Mary, Harvard, the University of Michigan, and Brown University.

Poetry

JOHN BERRYMAN: *The Dream Songs.* Berryman completes 385 eighteen-line poems that trace the progress of his protagonist, Henry; his experiences provide a mirror on the era. Additional poems from the sequence would be published posthumously in *Harry's Fate and Other Poems, 1967–1972* (1977).

GWENDOLYN BROOKS: *Riot.* The first in a series of small volumes intended to inspire black pride and activism. It would be followed by *Family Pictures* (1970), *Aloneness* (1971), and *Beckonings* (1975), all intended to reach a wide popular audience by using ordinary language, "story poems," and "loose rhythms."

RICHARD HOWARD (b. 1929): *Untitled Subjects.* This Pulitzer Prize–winning collection is made up of fifteen dramatic monologues of actual and imaginary nineteenth-century writers, artists, and composers, causing some to call Howard the successor to Robert Browning. It would be followed by additional collections featuring dramatic monologues, including *Findings* (1971), *Two-Part Inventions* (1974), *Fellow Feelings* (1976), and *Misgivings* (1979). Born in Cleveland and educated at Columbia and the Sorbonne, Howard has been the poetry editor of the *Paris Review.*

ROBERT LOWELL: *Notebook, 1967–1968.* Combining personal and public concerns, this sequence of irregular and unrhymed sonnets is one of Lowell's most ambitious attempts to treat a wide range of issues. An expanded edition would be issued in 1970. Lowell also publishes a prose "re-creation" of Aeschylus's *Prometheus Bound.*

JAMES MERRILL: *The Fire Screen.* Merrill's collection includes the long poem "The Summer People," "Matinees," and a sonnet sequence.

ROBERT PACK: *Home from the Cemetery.* Pack's fourth collection, following *The Irony of Joy* (1955), *A Stranger's Privilege* (1959), and *Guarded by Women* (1963), contains "The Last Will and Testament of Art Evergreen," called by Anne Sexton "one of the great American poems."

ADRIENNE RICH: *Leaflets.* Rich's collection shows her increasing concern for social issues, including the Vietnam War, student unrest, and racial violence. Her approach divides critics, some of whom see a decline in her art, others a powerful new forcefulness.

ANNE SEXTON: *Love Poems.* Sexton's frank depiction of female sexuality in an extramarital affair and a lesbian relationship proves to be her most popular work,

DEATHS, 1970–1979

Deaths

1970 Louise Bogan (b. 1897), poet
John Dos Passos (b. 1896), novelist
John O'Hara (b. 1905), novelist

1971 Ogden Nash (b. 1902), poet
Allan Nevins (b. 1890), historian and editor
Mark Van Doren (b. 1894), poet, novelist, and critic

1972 John Berryman (b. 1914), poet
Marianne Moore (b. 1887), poet
Ezra Pound (b. 1885), poet
Edmund Wilson (b. 1895), critic and novelist

1973 Conrad Aiken (b. 1889), poet, novelist, and critic
W. H. Auden (b. 1907), poet
S. N. Behrman (b. 1893), playwright
Jane Bowles (b. 1917), short story writer, novelist, and playwright
Pearl S. Buck (b. 1892), novelist
William Inge (b. 1913), playwright and novelist
John Neihardt (b. 1881), poet
Margaret Wilson (b. 1882), novelist

1974 George Kelly (b. 1887), playwright
Walter Lippmann (b. 1889), journalist, editor, and author
Olive Prouty (b. 1882), novelist
John Crowe Ransom (b. 1888), poet and critic
Anne Sexton (b. 1928), poet

1975 Thornton Wilder (b. 1897), playwright and novelist

1976 Samuel Eliot Morison (b. 1887), historian

1977 James M. Cain (b. 1892), novelist
James Jones (b. 1921), novelist
MacKinlay Kantor (b. 1904), novelist
Robert Lowell (b. 1917), poet
Vladimir Nabokov (b. 1899), novelist

1978 James Gould Cozzens (b. 1903), novelist
John Hall Wheelock (b. 1886), poet and editor
Margaret Widdemer (b. 1884), novelist and poet

1979 Elizabeth Bishop (b. 1911), poet
James T. Farrell (b. 1904), novelist
S. J. Perelman (b. 1904), humorist
Jean Stafford (b. 1915), novelist and short story writer
Alan Tate (b. 1899), poet and critic

selling more than fourteen thousand copies in eighteen months.

RICHARD WILBUR: *Walking to Sleep: New Poems and Translations.* Wilbur is awarded the Bollingen Prize for this collection of thematically linked poems meditating on how to live. It includes "The Lilacs," "Playboy," and "Running," one of his most personal poems.

1970
Drama and Theater

DANIEL BERRIGAN: *The Trial of the Catonsville Nine.* Berrigan provides a free-verse dramatization based on the actual records of the trial in which he and other

BESTSELLERS, 1970–1979

Fiction

1970

1. *Love Story* by Erich Segal
2. *The French Lieutenant's Woman* by John Fowles
3. *Islands in the Stream* by Ernest Hemingway
4. *The Crystal Cave* by Mary Stewart
5. *Great Lion of God* by Taylor Caldwell
6. *QB VII* by Leon Uris
7. *The Gang That Couldn't Shoot Straight* by Jimmy Breslin
8. *The Secret Woman* by Victoria Holt
9. *Travels with My Aunt* by Graham Greene
10. *Rich Man, Poor Man* by Irwin Shaw

1971

1. *Wheels* by Arthur Hailey
2. *The Exorcist* by William Peter Blatty
3. *The Passions of the Mind* by Irving Stone
4. *The Day of the Jackal* by Frederick Forsyth
5. *The Betsy* by Harold Robbins
6. *Message from Malaga* by Helen MacInnes
7. *The Winds of War* by Herman Wouk
8. *The Drifters* by James A. Michener
9. *The Other* by Thomas Tryon
10. *Rabbit Redux* by John Updike

1972

1. *Jonathan Livingston Seagull* by Richard Bach
2. *August 1914* by Alexandr Solzhenitsyn
3. *The Odessa File* by Frederick Forsyth
4. *The Day of the Jackal* by Frederick Forsyth
5. *The Word* by Irving Wallace
6. *The Winds of War* by Herman Wouk
7. *Captains and the Kings* by Taylor Caldwell
8. *Two from Galilee* by Marjories Holmes
9. *My Name Is Asher Lev* by Chaim Potok
10. *Semi-Tough* by Dan Jenkins

1973

1. *Jonathan Livingston Seagull* by Richard Bach
2. *Once Is Not Enough* by Jacqueline Susann
3. *Breakfast of Champions* by Kurt Vonnegut Jr.
4. *The Odessa File* by Frederick Forsyth
5. *Burr* by Gore Vidal
6. *The Hollow Hills* by Mary Stewart
7. *Evening in Byzantium* by Irwin Shaw
8. *The Matlock Paper* by Robert Ludlum
9. *The Billion Dollar Sure Thing* by Paul E. Erdman
10. *The Honorary Consul* by Graham Greene

1974

1. *Centennial* by James A. Michener
2. *Watership Down* by Richard Adams
3. *Jaws* by Peter Benchley
4. *Tinker, Tailor, Soldier, Spy* by John Le Carré
5. *Something Happened* by Joseph Heller
6. *The Dogs of War* by Frederick Forsyth
7. *The Pirate* by Harold Robbins
8. *I Heard the Owl Call My Name* by Margaret Craven
9. *The Seven-Per-Cent Solution* edited by John H. Watson, M.D., and Nicholas Meyer
10. *The Fan Club* by Irving Wallace

1975

1. *Ragtime* by E. L. Doctorow
2. *The Moneychanger* by Arthur Hailey
3. *Curtain* by Agatha Christie
4. *Looking for Mister Goodbar* by Judith Rossner
5. *The Choirboys* by Joseph Wambaugh
6. *The Eagle Has Landed* by Jack Higgins
7. *The Greek Treasure: A Biographical Novel of Henry and Sophia Schliemann* by Irving Stone
8. *The Great Train Robbery* by Michael Crichton
9. *Shogun* by James Clavell
10. *Humboldt's Gift* by Saul Bellow

1976

1. *Trinity* by Leon Uris
2. *Sleeping Murder* by Agatha Christie
3. *Dolores* by Jacqueline Susann
4. *Storm Warning* by Jack Higgins
5. *The Deep* by Peter Benchley
6. *1876* by Gore Vidal
7. *Slapstick: or, Lonesome No More!* by Kurt Vonnegut Jr.
8. *The Lonely Lady* by Harold Robbins
9. *Touch Not the Cat* by Mary Stewart
10. *A Stranger in the Mirror* by Sidney Sheldon

1977

1. *The Silmarillion* by J.R.R. Tolkien and Christopher Tolkien
2. *The Thorn Birds* by Colleen McCullough
3. *Illusions: The Adventures of a Reluctant Messiah* by Richard Bach
4. *The Honourable Schoolboy* by John Le Carré
5. *Oliver's Story* by Erich Segal
6. *Dreams Die First* by Harold Robbins
7. *Beggarman, Thief* by Irwin Shaw
8. *How to Save Your Own Life* by Erica Jong
9. *Delta of Venus: Erotica* by Anaïs Nin
10. *Daniel Martin* by John Fowles

1978

1. *Chesapeake* by James A. Michener
2. *War and Remembrance* by Herman Wouk
3. *Fools Die* by Mario Puzo
4. *Bloodlines* by Sidney Sheldon
5. *Scruples* by Judith Krantz
6. *Evergreen* by Belva Plain
7. *Illusions: The Adventures of a Reluctant Messiah* by Richard Bach
8. *The Holcroft Covenant* by Robert Ludlum
9. *Second Generation* by Robert Ludlum
10. *Eye of the Needle* by Ken Follett

1979

1. *The Matarese Circle* by Robert Ludlum
2. *Sophie's Choice* by William Styron
3. *Overload* by Arthur Hailey
4. *Memories of Another Day* by Harold Robbins
5. *Jailbird* by Kurt Vonnegut Jr.
6. *The Dead Zone* by Stephen King
7. *The Last Enchantment* by Mary Stewart
8. *The Establishment* by Howard Fast
9. *The Third World War: August 1985* by General Sir John Hackett et al.
10. *Smiley's People* by John Le Carré

BESTSELLERS, 1970–1979

Nonfiction

1970
1. *Everything You Always Wanted to Know About Sex (but Were Afraid to Ask)* by David Reuben, M.D.
2. *The New English Bible*
3. *The Sensuous Woman* by "J"
4. *Better Homes and Gardens Fondue and Tabletop Cooking*
5. *Up the Organization* by Robert Townsend
6. *Ball Four* by Jim Bouton
7. *American Heritage Dictionary of the English Language* by William Morris
8. *Body Language* by Julius Fast
9. *In Someone's Shadow* by Rod McKuen
10. *Caught in the Quiet* by Rod McKuen

1971
1. *The Sensuous Man* by "M"
2. *Bury My Heart at Wounded Knee* by Dee Brown
3. *Better Homes and Gardens Blender Cook Book*
4. *I'm O.K., You're O.K.* by Thomas Harris
5. *Any Woman Can!* by David Reuben, M.D.
6. *Inside the Third Reich* by Albert Speer
7. *Eleanor and Franklin* by Joseph P. Lash
8. *Wunnerful, Wunnerful!* by Lawrence Welk
9. *Honor Thy Father* by Gay Talese
10. *Fields of Wonder* by Rod McKuen

1972
1. *The Living Bible* by Kenneth Taylor
2. *I'm O.K., You're O.K.* by Thomas Harris
3. *Open Marriage* by Nena and George O'Neill
4. *Harry S. Truman* by Margaret Truman

5. *Dr. Atkins' Diet Revolution* by Robert C. Atkins
6. *Better Homes and Gardens Menu Cook Book*
7. *The Peter Prescription* by Laurence J. Peter
8. *A World Beyond* by Ruth Montgomery
9. *A Journey to Ixtlan* by Carlos Castaneda
10. *Better Homes and Gardens Low-Calorie Desserts*

1973
1. *The Living Bible* by Kenneth Taylor
2. *Dr. Atkins' Diet Revolution* by Robert C. Atkins
3. *I'm O.K., You're O.K.* by Thomas Harris
4. *The Joy of Sex* by Alex Comfort
5. *Weight Watchers Program Cookbook* by Jean Nidetch
6. *How to Be Your Own Best Friend* by Mildred Newman et al.
7. *The Art of Walt Disney* by Christopher Finch
8. *Better Homes and Gardens Home Canning Cookbook*
9. *Alistair Cooke's America* by Alistair Cooke
10. *Sybil* by Flora R. Schreiber

1974
1. *The Total Woman* by Marabel Morgan
2. *All the President's Men* by Carl Bernstein and Bob Woodward
3. *Plain Speaking: An Oral Biography of Harry S. Truman* by Merle Miller
4. *More Joy: A Lovemaking Companion to The Joy of Sex* by Alex Comfort
5. *Alistair Cooke's America* by Alistair Cooke
6. *Tales of Power* by Carlos Castaneda
7. *You Can Profit from a Monetary Crisis* by Harry Browne
8. *All Things Bright and Beautiful* by James Herriot
9. *The Bermuda Triangle* by Charles Berlitz with J. Manson Valentine
10. *The Memory Book* by Harry Lorayne and Jerry Lucas

Catholic priests were convicted for the 1968 burning of selective service files as a protest against U.S. involvement in the war in Vietnam. It is produced in Los Angeles in 1970 and on Broadway in 1971.

LEE BREUER (b. 1937): *The Red Horse Animation.* This is the first work of the playwright's experimental Animation trilogy, ritualistic theater productions based on stream-of-consciousness successions of images. It would be followed by *The B. Beaver Animation* (1974) and *The Shaggy Dog Animation* (1978). Breuer was one of the founders of the avant-garde theater company Mabou Mines in San Francisco in 1970.

ED BULLINS: *The Duplex.* The third play of Bullins's Twentieth Century cycle is set in a Los Angeles rooming house and concerns a tenant's love affair with his abused landlady and his violent confrontation with her husband.

JULES FEIFFER: *The White House Murder Case.* Feiffer wins the Outer Circle Critics Award for this political satire that imagines the United States at war with Brazil. The president's wife, who is against the war, is murdered by someone in the cabinet.

SAM SHEPARD: *Operation Sidewinder.* Shepard's first major production is a satire on the social and political turmoil of the 1960s. In it, various representatives of American society compete to appropriate an experimental computer designed in the form of rattlesnake.

STEPHEN SONDHEIM: *Company.* Sondheim's musical shows a young bachelor celebrating his birthday as his married friends reveal their discontents. The musical employs songs not to advance the plot but "in a Brechtian way, as comment and counterpoint." It wins the New York Drama Critics Circle Award and the Tony Award for best musical.

MEGAN TERRY: *Approaching Simone.* Considered a landmark in American feminist drama, Terry's play treats the life of French philosopher Simone Weil, who died as a result of a hunger strike to protest the conditions faced by soldiers in World War II. It wins the Obie Award for best play.

BESTSELLERS, 1970–1979

1975
1. *Angels: God's Secret Agents* by Billy Graham
2. *Winning Through Intimidation* by Robert Ringer
3. *TM: Discovering Energy and Overcoming Stress* by Harold H. Bloomfield
4. *The Ascent of Man* by Jacob Bronowski
5. *Sylvia Porter's Money Book* by Sylvia Porter
6. *Total Fitness in Thirty Minutes a Week* by Laurence E. Morehouse and Leonard Gross
7. *The Bermuda Triangle* by Charles Berlitz with J. Manson Valentine
8. *The Save-Your-Life Diet* by David Reuben, M.D.
9. *Bring on the Empty Horses* by David Niven
10. *Breach of Faith: The Fall of Richard Nixon* by Theodore H. White

1976
1. *The Final Days* by Bob Woodward and Carl Bernstein
2. *Roots* by Alex Haley
3. *Your Erroneous Zones* by Dr. Wayne W. Dyer
4. *Passages: The Predictable Crises of Adult Life* by Gail Sheehy
5. *Born Again* by Charles W. Colson
6. *The Grass Is Always Greener over the Septic Tank* by Erma Bombeck
7. *Angels: God's Secret Agents* by Billy Graham
8. *Blind Ambition: The White House Years* by John Dean
9. *The Hite Report: A Nationwide Study of Female Sexuality* by Shere Hite
10. *The Right and the Power: The Prosecution of Watergate* by Leon Jaworski

1977
1. *Roots* by Alex Haley
2. *Looking Out for Number One* by Robert Ringer
3. *All Things Wise and Wonderful* by James Herriot
4. *Your Erroneous Zones* by Dr. Wayne W. Dyer
5. *The Book of Lists* by David Wallechinsky, Irving Wallace, and Amy Wallace

6. *The Possible Dream: A Candid Look at Amway* by Charles Paul Conn
7. *The Dragons of Eden: Speculations on the Evolution of Human Intelligence* by Carl Sagan
8. *The Second Ring of Power* by Carlos Castaneda
9. *The Grass Is Always Greener over the Septic Tank* by Erma Bombeck
10. *The Amityville Horror* by Jay Anson

1978
1. *If Life Is a Bowl of Cherries — What Am I Doing in the Pits?* by Erma Bombeck
2. *Gnomes* by Will Huygen and Rien Poortvliet
3. *The Complete Book of Running* by James Fixx
4. *Mommie Dearest* by Christina Crawford
5. *Pulling Your Own Strings* by Dr. Wayne W. Dyer
6. *RN: The Memoirs of Richard Nixon* by Richard Nixon
7. *A Distant Mirror: The Calamitous Fourteenth Century* by Barbara Tuchman
8. *Faeries* by Brian Froud and Alan Lee
9. *In Search of History: A Personal Adventure* by Theodore H. White
10. *The Muppet Show Book* by the Muppet People

1979
1. *Aunt Erma's Cape Book* by Erma Bombeck
2. *The Complete Scarsdale Medical Diet* by Herman Tarnower, M.D., and Samm Sinclair Baker
3. *How to Prosper During the Bad Years* by Howard J. Ruff
4. *Cruel Shoes* by Steve Martin
5. *The Pritikin Program for Diet and Exercise* by Nathan Pritikin and Patrick McGrady Jr.
6. *White House Years* by Henry Kissinger
7. *Lauren Bacall: By Myself* by Lauren Bacall
8. *The Brethren: Inside the Supreme Court* by Bob Woodward and Scott Armstrong
9. *Restoring the American Dream* by Robert Ringer
10. *The Winner's Circle* by Charles Paul Conn

KURT VONNEGUT JR.: *Happy Birthday, Wanda June.* Vonnegut imagines the afterlife of two American military men who dropped the atom bomb on Nagasaki. He would write the screenplay for the 1971 film version.

TENNESSEE WILLIAMS: *Small Craft Warnings.* In this drama about a group of outcasts in a California oceanside bar, Williams writes candidly for the first time about his own homosexuality, creating a self-hating gay artist who expresses disdain for the "deadening coarseness" of the lives of most homosexuals.

LANFORD WILSON: *Lemon Sky.* Written and initially performed in 1968, Wilson's highly autobiographical play opens in Buffalo and New York City. It traces a college student's futile attempts to be reconciled with his estranged father. Wilson also produces *Serenading Louie*, a drama concerning suburban couples disappointed by their lives and marriages.

PAUL ZINDEL (b. 1936): *The Effect of Gamma Rays on Man-in-the-Moon Marigolds.* First produced in Houston in 1965, the drama concerns a widowed housewife's tyrannical rule over her two daughters. It becomes the second off-Broadway play to win the Pulitzer Prize. Zindel was a former high school chemistry teacher who would subsequently write television plays and novels for young adults.

Fiction

POUL ANDERSON (1926–2001): *Tau Zero.* Critic Michael McClintock has suggested Anderson is one of the five or six most important science fiction novelists since World War II, singling out this novel about a spaceship

AWARDS AND PRIZES, 1970–1979

Bancroft Prize (American History, Diplomacy, or Biography)

1970   *Charles Willson Peale* by Charles Coleman Sellers
The Creation of the American Republic, 1776–1787 by Gordon S. Wood
Scottsboro: A Tragedy of the American South by Dan T. Carter

1971   *The Image Empire: A History of Broadcasting in the United States, Vol. III* by Erik Barnouw
Birth Control in America: The Career of Margaret Sanger by David M. Kennedy
Andrew Carnegie by Joseph Frazier Wall

1972   *Neither Black nor White* by Carl N. Degler
The Mathers: Three Generations of Puritan Intellectuals, 1696–1728 by Robert Middlekauff
The European Discovery of America: The Northern Voyages by Samuel Eliot Morison

1973   *Fire in the Lake: The Vietnamese and the Americans in Vietnam* by Frances FitzGerald
The United States and the Origins of the Cold War by John Lewis Gaddis
Booker T. Washington by Louis R. Harlan

1974   *Frederick Jackson Turner: Historian, Scholar, Teacher* by Ray Allen Billington
The Devil and John Foster Dulles by Townsend Hoopes
The Other Bostonians: Poverty and Progress in the American Metropolis, 1880–1970 by Stephen Thernstrom

1975   *Time on the Cross: The Economics of American Negro Slavery* and *Time on the Cross: Evidence and Methods — a Supplement* by Robert W. Fogel and Stanley L. Engerman
Deterrence in American Foreign Policy: Theory and Practice by Alexander L. George and Richard Smoke
Roll, Jordan, Roll by Eugene Genovese

1976   *The Problem of Slavery in the Age of Revolution: 1770–1823* by David B. Davis
Edith Wharton by R.W.B. Lewis

1977   *Clash and Community: The Industrial Revolution* by Alan Dawley
The Minutemen and Their World by Robert A. Gross
Slave Population and the Economy in Jamaica, 1807–1834 by Barry W. Higman

1978   *The Visible Hand* by Alfred Chandler Jr.
The Transformation of American Law by Morton Horwitz

1979   *Allies of a Kind* by Christopher Thorne
Rockdale by Anthony Wallace

Bollingen Prize (Poetry)

1971   Richard Wilbur
Mona Van Duyn

1973   James Merrill

1975   A. R. Ammons

1977   David Ignatow

1979   W. S. Merwin

---

caught in an uncontrollable acceleration. Anderson's grasp of science makes his plots seem particularly authentic. Raised in Texas and Denmark, Anderson was trained as a physicist. He published his first science fiction story in 1947 while still an undergraduate at the University of Minnesota.

DONALD BARTHELME: *City Life.* Barthelme's story collection characteristically mixes the mundane and the fantastic in stories such as "Views of My Father Weeping," "At the Tolstoy Museum," and "Paraguay." It would be followed by his fourth collection, *Sadness* (1972).

SAUL BELLOW: *Mr. Sammler's Planet.* A seventy-year-old Holocaust survivor contemplates life's meaning on the streets of New York's Upper West Side. Appalled by scenes of moral disorder and decay, he is prevented from attaining the disengagement he desires by an encounter with a black pickpocket. The book is one of Bellow's most blistering critiques of modern American life.

BARBARA CHASE-RIBOUD (b. 1939): *Sally Hemings.* Encouraged by Jackie Kennedy Onassis, Chase-Riboud publishes this controversial novel focused on the young slave girl whom Thomas Jefferson owned and with whom he is alleged to have had children. A sequel, *The President's Daughter,* about Harriet Hemings, purportedly Jefferson's daughter, would appear in 1994. Born in Philadelphia, Chase-Riboud was an internationally recognized sculptor before becoming a writer.

JAMES DICKEY: *Deliverance.* Dickey's first novel concerns the disaster that strikes a group of Southern businessmen on a back-to-nature canoe trip. Dickey also publishes the poetry collection *The Eye-Beaters, Blood, Victory, Madness, Buckhead and Mercy,* which includes major poems such as "The Cancer Match" and "Victory."

JOAN DIDION: *Play It as It Lays.* Didion's novel follows the disintegration of a former film actress in Southern California as she drives aimlessly on Los Angeles freeways in search of relief from her existential pain. She embodies the fate of the author's native California, where, in Didion's view, the American dream has been lost in a fruitless search for instant gratification.

JACK FINNEY: *Time and Again.* Finney's best-known science fiction work depicts Simon Morley's time travel adventures in New York City during the 1880s. A sequel, *From Time to Time,* would appear in 1995.

JOHN GARDNER (1933–1982): *The Wreckage of Agathon.* Gardner follows his first novel, *The Resurrection* (1966),

AWARDS AND PRIZES, 1970–1979

National Book Awards

1970

Fiction: *Them* by Joyce Carol Oates

Arts and Letters: *An Unfinished Woman* by Lillian Hellman

History and Biography: *Huey Long* by T. Harry Williams

Science, Philosophy, and Religion: *Gandhi's Truth: On the Origins of Militant Nonviolence* by Erik H. Erikson

Children's Literature: *A Day of Pleasure: Stories of a Boy Growing Up in Warsaw* by Isaac Bashevis Singer

Poetry: *The Complete Poems* by Elizabeth Bishop

1971

Fiction: *Mr. Sammler's Planet* by Saul Bellow

Arts and Letters: *Cocteau* by Francis Steegmuller

History and Biography: *Roosevelt: The Soldier of Freedom* by James MacGregor Burns

The Sciences: *Science in the British Colonies of America* by Raymond Phineas Stearns

Children's Literature: *The Marvelous Misadventures of Sebastian* by Lloyd Alexander

Poetry: *To See, To Take* by Mona Van Duyn

1972

Fiction: *Flannery O'Connor: The Complete Stories* by Flannery O'Connor

Arts and Letters: *The Classical Style: Haydn, Mozart, Beethoven* by Charles Rosen

Biography: *Eleanor and Franklin* by Joseph P. Lash

History: Ordeal of the Union Series — Vol. 3, *The War for the Union: The Organized War, 1863–1864*; Vol. 4, *The War for the Union: The Organized War to Victory, 1864–1865* by Allan Nevins

The Sciences: *The Blue Whale* by George L. Small

Philosophy and Religion: *Righteous Empire: The Protestant Experience in America* by Martin E. Marty

Children's Literature: *The Slightly Irregular Fire Engine or the Hithering Thithering Djinn* by Donald Barthelme

Poetry: *Selected Poems* by Howard Moss and *The Collected Poems* by Frank O'Hara

1973

Fiction: *Chimera* by John Barth and *Augustus* by John Williams

Arts and Letters: *Diderot* by Arthur M. Wilson

Biography: *George Washington: Anguish and Farewell, 1793–1799* by James Thomas Flexner

History: *The Children of Pride* by Robert Manson Myers and *Judenrat* by Isaiah Trunk

The Sciences: *The Serengeti Lion: A Study of Predator-Prey Relations* by George B. Schaller

Philosophy and Religion: *A Religious History of the American People* by Sydney E. Ahlstrom

Children's Literature: *The Farthest Shore* by Ursula K. Le Guin

Poetry: *Collected Poems: 1951–1971* by A. R. Ammons

1974

Fiction: *A Crown of Feathers and Other Stories* by Isaac Bashevis Singer and *Gravity's Rainbow* by Thomas Pynchon

Arts and Letters: *Deeper into Movies* by Pauline Kael

Biography: *Malcolm Lowry* by Douglas Day

History: *Macauley: The Shapping of the Historian* by John Clive

The Sciences: *Life: The Unfinished Experiment* by S. E. Luria

Philosophy and Religion: *Edmund Husserl: Philosopher of Infinite Tasks* by Maurice Nathanson

Children's Literature: *The Court of the Stone Children* by Eleanor Cameron

Poetry: *The Fall of America: Poems of These States, 1965–1971* by Allen Ginsberg and *Diving into the Wreck: Poems 1971–1972* by Adrienne Rich

1975

Fiction: *Dog Soldiers* by Robert Stone and *The Hair of Harold Roux* by Thomas Williams

Arts and Letters: *Marcel Proust* by Roger Shattuck and *The Lives of a Cell: Notes of a Biology Watcher* by Lewis Thomas

Biography: *The Life of Emily Dickinson* by Richard Sewall

History: *The Ordeal of Thomas Hutchinson* by Bernard Bailyn

The Sciences: *Interpretation of Schizophrenia* by Silvano Arieti

Philosophy and Religion: *Anarchy, State, and Utopia* by Robert Nozick

Children's Literature: *M. C. Higgins the Great* by Virginia Hamilton

Poetry: *Presentation Piece* by Marilyn Hacker

1976

Fiction: *JR* by William Gaddis

Arts and Letters: *The Great War and Modern Memory* by Paul Fussell

History: *The Problem of Slavery in the Age of Revolution: 1770–1823* by David B. Davis

Children's Literature: *Bert Breen's Barn* by Walter D. Edmonds

Poetry: *Self-Portrait in a Convex Mirror* by John Ashbery

1977

Fiction: *The Spectator Bird* by Wallace Stegner

Biography and Autobiography: *Norman Thomas: The Last Idealist* by W. A. Swanberg

History: *World of Our Fathers* by Irving Howe

Children's Literature: *The Master Puppeteer* by Katherine Paterson

Poetry: *Collected Poems: 1930–1976* by Richard Eberhart

1978

Fiction: *Blood Tie* by Mary Lee Settle

Biography and Autobiography: *Samuel Johnson* by Walter Jackson Bate

History: *The Path Between the Seas: The Creation of the Panama Canal* by David McCullough

Children's Literature: *The View from the Oak* by Judith Kohl and Herbert Kohl

Poetry: *The Collected Poems of Howard Nemerov* by Howard Nemerov

1979

Fiction: *Going After Cacciato* by Tim O'Brien

Biography and Autobiography: *Robert Kennedy and His Times* by Arthur M. Schlesinger Jr.

Children's Literature: *The Great Gilly Hopkins* by Katherine Paterson

History: *Intellectual Life in the Colonial South, 1585–1763* by Richard Beale Davis

Poetry: *Mirabell: Books of Number* by James Merrill

AWARDS AND PRIZES, 1970–1979

Pulitzer Prizes

1970
Fiction: *Collected Stories* by Jean Stafford
Poetry: *Untitled Subjects* by Richard Howard
Drama: *No Place to Be Somebody* by Charles Gordone
History: *Present at the Creation: My Years in the State Department* by Dean Acheson
General Nonfiction: *Gandhi's Truth* by Erik H. Erikson
Biography/Autobiography: *Huey Long* by T. Harry Williams

1971
Fiction: No Prize Awarded
Poetry: *The Carrier of Ladders* by W. S. Merwin
Drama: *The Effect of Gamma Rays on Man-in-the-Moon Marigolds* by Paul Zindel
History: *Roosevelt: The Soldier of Freedom* by James M. Burns
General Nonfiction: *The Rising Sun* by John Toland
Biography/Autobiography: *Robert Frost: The Years of Triumph, 1915–1938* by Lawrance Thompson

1972
Fiction: *Angle of Repose* by Wallace Stegner
Poetry: *Collected Poems* by James Wright
Drama: No Prize Awarded
History: *Neither Black nor White* by Carl N. Degler
General Nonfiction: *Stilwell and the American Experience in China, 1911–1945* by Barbara W. Tuchman
Biography/Autobiography: *Eleanor and Franklin* by Joseph P. Lash

1973
Fiction: *The Optimist's Daughter* by Eudora Welty
Poetry: *Up Country* by Maxine Kumin
Drama: *That Championship Season* by Jason Miller
History: *People of Paradox: An Inquiry Concerning the Origin of American Civilization* by Michael Kammen
General Nonfiction: *Fire in the Lake* by Frances FitzGerald and *Children of Crisis* by Robert Coles
Biography/Autobiography: *Luce and His Empire* by W. A. Swanberg

1974
Fiction: No Prize Awarded
Poetry: *The Dolphin* by Robert Lowell
Drama: No Prize Awarded
History: *The Americans: The Democratic Experience* by Daniel J. Boorstin
General Nonfiction: *The Denial of Death* by Ernest Becker
Biography/Autobiography: *O'Neill, Son and Artist* by Louis Sheaffer

1975
Fiction: *The Killer Angels* by Michael Shaara
Poetry: *Turtle Island* by Gary Snyder
Drama: *Seascape* by Edward Albee
History: *Jefferson and His Time* by Dumas Malone
General Nonfiction: *Pilgrim at Tinker Creek* by Annie Dillard
Biography/Autobiography: *The Power Broker: Robert Moses and the Fall of New York* by Robert A. Caro

1976
Fiction: *Humboldt's Gift* by Saul Bellow
Poetry: *Self-Portrait in a Convex Mirror* by John Ashbery
Drama: *A Chorus Line* by James Kirkwood and Nicholas Dante
History: *Lamy of Santa Fe* by Paul Horgan
General Nonfiction: *Why Survive? Being Old in America* by Robert N. Butler
Biography/Autobiography: *Edith Wharton: A Biography* by R.W.B. Lewis

1977
Fiction: No Prize Awarded
Poetry: *Divine Comedies: Poems* by James Merrill
Drama: *The Shadow Box* by Michael Cristofer
History: *The Impending Crisis: 1841–1861* by David M. Potter
General Nonfiction: *Beautiful Summers* by William W. Warner
Biography/Autobiography: *A Prince of Our Disorder: The Life of T. E. Lawrence* by John E. Mack

1978
Fiction: *Elbow Room* by James Alan McPherson
Poetry: *The Collected Poems* by Howard Nemerov
Drama: *The Gin Game* by Donald L. Coburn
History: *The Visible Hand: The Managerial Revolution in American Business* by Alfred D. Chandler Jr.
General Nonfiction: *The Dragons of Eden* by Carl Sagan
Biography/Autobiography: *Samuel Johnson* by Walter Jackson Bate

1979
Fiction: *The Stories of John Cheever* by John Cheever
Poetry: *Now and Then: Poems, 1976–78* by Robert Penn Warren
Drama: *Buried Child* by Sam Shepard
History: *The Dred Scott Case: Its Significance in American Law and Politics* by Don E. Fehrenbacher
General Nonfiction: *On Human Nature* by Edward O. Wilson
Biography/Autobiography: *Days of Sorrow and Pain: Leo Baeck and the Berlin Jews* by Leonard Baker

Nobel Prizes for Literature

1976   Saul Bellow
1978   Isaac Bashevis Singer

about a philosophy professor dying of cancer, with a metaphysical and social dialogue between an ancient philosopher and his disciple, who are both imprisoned in Sparta. Born in Batavia, New York, Gardner earned a Ph.D. from the University of Iowa and taught literature at various universities.

GAIL GODWIN (b. 1937): *The Perfectionists.* Godwin's first novel depicts the disintegration of a "perfect but unhappy marriage." It introduces the writer's characteristic focus on women's reevaluation of their lives when faced with adversity, a theme that would be fully developed in her second novel, *Glass People* (1972). Born in Alabama, Godwin worked at the U.S. embassy in London from 1962 to 1965 before returning to do graduate work at the University of Iowa.

ERNEST HEMINGWAY: *Islands in the Stream.* Hemingway's posthumously published novel features the recollections of a lonely painter who much resembles Hemingway himself. It is the first of several discarded or abandoned Hemingway fragments to appear. John Updike calls it "a gallant wreck of a novel" being "paraded as the real thing."

TONY HILLERMAN (b. 1925): *The Blessing.* This is the first of Hillerman's popular and critically acclaimed mysteries set on Navajo Land and featuring Joe Leaphorn of the Navajo Tribal Police Force, who uses his knowledge of Native American traditions and history to solve crimes. After two subsequent Leaphorn novels — *Dance Hall of the Dead* (1973) and *Listening Woman* (1978) — Hillerman would feature a new Navajo detective, Jim Chee, in *People of Darkness* (1980), *The Dark Wind* (1982), and *The Ghostway* (1984), before pairing Leaphorn and Chee in novels beginning with *Skinwalkers* (1986).

WALLACE MARKFIELD: *Teitlebaum's Widow.* Markfield's best-known work follows the development of Simon Sloan from the age of eight in 1932 to his first year at Brooklyn College and the attack on Pearl Harbor, evoking comparisons to Joyce's *A Portrait of the Artist as a Young Man.* Markfield's later novels are *You Could Live if They Let You* (1974), *Multiple Orgasms* (1977), and *Radical Surgery* (1991).

TONI MORRISON (b. 1931): *The Bluest Eye.* Morrison's first novel concerns a poor and abused black girl who imagines that her life would improve if only she could possess blue eyes, a white-derived standard for beauty. The novel introduces the writer's characteristic subject of black women's search for meaning and identity. Born in Ohio and educated at Howard University, Morrison taught English and worked as an editor at Random House.

JOYCE CAROL OATES: *The Wheel of Love.* This is the first in a series of short story collections dealing with the vagaries of love. It would be followed by *Marriage and Infidelities* (1972), *The Seduction* (1975), and *Crossing the Border* (1976).

REYNOLDS PRICE: *Permanent Errors.* Price's story collection dramatizes the perspective of a blocked writer contending with his mother's death and his wife's suicide.

JAMES PURDY: *Jeremy's Version.* The first volume of Purdy's Sleepers in Moon-Crowded Valleys trilogy, about a dysfunctional Midwestern family, is published. It would be followed by *The House of the Solitary Maggot* (1974) and *Mourners Below* (1981).

ERICH SEGAL (b. 1937): *Love Story.* The Yale classics professor combines a mismatched college romance between the Harvard WASP Oliver Barrett and the working-class Radcliffe student Jennifer Cavilleri, a fatal illness, and the line "Love means not ever having to say you're sorry" to create one of the best-selling novels of the decade, with sales in excess of nine million copies. A sequel, *Oliver's Story*, would follow in 1977.

IRWIN SHAW: *Rich Man, Poor Man.* Shaw achieves his greatest popular success in this family saga reflecting the American social scene from the 1940s to the 1960s. It sells more than six million copies and would be adapted as the first television mini-series. A sequel, *Beggarman, Thief,* would follow in 1977.

ISAAC BASHEVIS SINGER: *Enemies: A Love Story.* Singer's first novel set in the United States deals with the complications that arise when a Polish Jew marries the woman who had helped him escape the Nazis; he wrongly assumes that his first wife had been killed in the war. Singer also issues *A Friend of Kafka, and Other Stories,* a collection treating Jewish immigrants in America, Israel, and Argentina.

JOHN UPDIKE: *Bech: A Book.* Updike reflects on the literary scene through the experiences of a formerly successful but now blocked writer, the Jewish American Henry Bech. Two sequels would follow: *Bech Is Back* (1982) and *Bech at Bay* (1998).

GORE VIDAL: *Two Sisters.* Vidal's tripartite novel takes the form of a screenwriter's diary, excerpts from his screenplay about two sisters in Ephesus in the third century B.C., and a memoir written years later by the screenwriter's old friend, Gore Vidal.

ALICE WALKER (b. 1944): *The Third Life of Grange Copeland.* Having previously published a collection of poems, *Once* (1968), Walker produces her first novel, a realistic family saga detailing struggles against racial, class, and gender obstacles. It is noteworthy for examining the African American experience in a broad psychological, moral, and sexual context. Born in Georgia, Walker was educated at Spelman College and Sarah Lawrence.

EUDORA WELTY: *Losing Battles.* The novel, one of Welty's most ambitious and accomplished and her first to reach the bestseller list, depicts two days in the 1930s in the life of the Banner family of Mississippi, who meet to celebrate the matriarch's ninetieth birthday and attend a funeral.

AL YOUNG (b. 1939): *Snakes.* Young's first novel concerns an African American jazz musician. Critic Douglass Bolling praises it for seeking "to reach out for the universals in human experience rather than to restrict itself to Black Protest or Black aesthetic considerations." *Who Is Angelina?* (1975) and *Sitting Pretty* (1976) would follow. Born in Mississippi, Young is a poet as well as a novelist, whose collections include *Dancing* (1969), *The Song Turning Back into Itself* (1971), and *Geography of the Near Past* (1976).

Literary Criticism and Scholarship

WILLIAM H. GASS: *Fiction and the Figures of Life.* In a collection of literary and philosophical essays, Gass treats his characteristic subject, the relationship between language and experience, asserting that the artist's task is not to reproduce reality but to create a self-governing artifice, which must be appreciated on its own terms.

GEOFFREY H. HARTMAN (b. 1929): *Beyond Formalism: Literary Essays 1958–1970.* Hartman's collection establishes his reputation as one of America's major critic-theorists and represents, in the words of fellow critic J. Hillis Miller, "a broadening of literary criticism in America." Hartman has been since 1967 a professor of English at Yale. His other books would include *The Fate of Reading* (1975), *Criticism in the Wilderness* (1980), and *A Critic's Journey* (1999).

MARY McCARTHY: *The Writing on the Wall.* McCarthy's literary essays cover writers Vladimir Nabokov, J. D. Salinger, Hannah Arendt, William S. Burroughs, and others, as well as general topics including "Communism in Literature."

KATE MILLETT (b. 1934): *Sexual Politics.* This version of Millett's Columbia University doctoral dissertation takes aim at the male dominance of the literary canon. Among the first works of literary criticism written from a feminist perspective, the book sells eighty thousand copies within six months of publication and prompts Norman Mailer to respond with *The Prisoner of Sex* (1971).

Nonfiction

MAYA ANGELOU (b. 1928): *I Know Why the Caged Bird Sings.* The actor, playwright, and writer achieves her first major literary and popular success with this autobiographical account of her life in rural Arkansas and St. Louis. It details her rape at age seven, after which she became mute, and ends with the birth of a son when she is sixteen. Additional volumes of her memoirs are *Gather Together in My Name* (1974), *Singin' and Swingin' and Gettin' Merry Like Christmas* (1976), *The Heart of a Woman* (1981), and *All God's Children Need Traveling Shoes* (1987).

ERIK BARNOUW (1908–2001): *The Image Empire: A History of Broadcasting in America.* Barnouw receives the Bancroft Prize for his third and final volume tracing the history of radio and television in America up to 1953; it had been preceded by *A Tower of Babel* (1966) and *The Golden Web* (1968). An immigrant from Holland, Barnouw founded the division of film, radio, and television at Columbia, which he chaired until 1973.

DEE BROWN (1908–2002): *Bury My Heart at Wounded Knee.* Western writer Brown produces his best-known work, the history of the settlement of the American West from the Native American perspective, based on eyewitness accounts. The book tops the bestseller lists and sells in excess of a million copies.

JAMES MacGREGOR BURNS (b. 1918): *Roosevelt: The Soldier of Freedom.* Burns's sequel to *Roosevelt: The Lion and the Fox* (1956) wins both the National Book Award and the Pulitzer Prize. Despite respect for Roosevelt's accomplishments, Burns is often harshly critical of him, documenting the many contradictions of a deeply divided man. Burns was a professor of politics at Williams College.

VINE DELORIA JR. (b. 1933): *Custer Died for Your Sins.* This is the most popular and the initial work of the Native American activist attorney and social historian. Subtitled "An Indian Manifesto," the book excoriates white America's treatment of Native Americans and explores the strengths and weaknesses of tribalism, which fosters a sense of community but also a sense of isolation from other Americans. The work prompts social scientists to reassess their study of tribal peoples and various institutions to return human remains and artifacts to the tribes from which they had been taken.

NORA EPHRON (b. 1941): *Wallflower at the Orgy.* The first of two collections of Ephron's articles commenting on contemporary mores, which had originally appeared in the *New York Post* and *Esquire.* The second is *Crazy Salad* (1975). Born in New York City, Ephron graduated from Wellesley College. She would become a successful screenwriter of films such as *When Harry Met Sally . . .* (1989) and *Sleepless in Seattle* (1993).

NORMAN MAILER: *Of a Fire on the Moon.* Adopting his nom de plume "Aquarius," Mailer contemplates the moon landing and the role of technology in modern society.

MARTIN E. MARTY (b. 1928): *Righteous Empire: The Protestant Experience in America.* The theologian and historian's study of Protestant sects in America and their influences on national values and politics wins the National Book Award.

NANCY MILFORD (b. 1938): *Zelda.* This sympathetic biography of F. Scott Fitzgerald's gifted, frustrated, and finally mad wife tells the story of the golden couple from the wife's point of view. Critic Carolyn Heilbrun has declared that contemporary women's biography began with Milford's groundbreaking book.

ROBIN MORGAN (b. 1941): *Sisterhood Is Powerful: An Anthology of Writing from the Women's Liberation Movement.* Morgan edits this groundbreaking collection, which includes both historic documents such as the Bill of Rights and modern position pieces such as Pat Mainardi's "The Politics of Housework." The volume becomes a kind of bible for late-twentieth-century feminists, who adopt its cover art — a clenched fist inside the universal symbol for female — as their emblem. Morgan was a contributing editor of *Ms.* magazine beginning in 1977 and its editor in chief from 1989 to 1993.

ALBERT MURRAY (b. 1916): *The Omni-Americans: New Perspectives on Black Experience and American Culture.* Murray's essay collection explores the uniqueness of African American experience and identity. Countering the views of black nationalists, Murray contends that African Americans are "uncontestably mulatto," synthesizing cultural and racial elements, which is the source of black and American greatness. Born in Alabama and educated at Tuskegee, Murray joined the air force in 1943 and retired as a major in 1962. His correspondence with his friend Ralph Ellison would be collected in *Trading Twelves* (2000).

CHARLES A. REICH (b. 1928): *The Greening of America.* The Yale Law School professor creates a stir in his analysis of contemporary social change, identifying the evolution of what he labels "Consciousness III" in the current youth culture.

STUDS TERKEL (b. 1912): *Hard Times: An Oral History of the Depression.* The Chicago radio and television commentator achieves his first major success, using his characteristic interviewing technique. He would follow it with a succession of well-regarded oral histories, including *Working* (1974), *Talking to Myself* (1977), and *The Good War* (1984).

LAWRANCE THOMPSON (1906–1973): *Robert Frost: The Years of Triumph, 1915–1938.* Volume two of Thompson's Frost biography receives a Pulitzer Prize despite the controversy raised by Thompson's less-than-sympathetic portrait of this American literary giant. The final volume would appear in 1976.

JOHN TOLAND (b. 1912): *The Rising Sun: The Decline and Fall of the Japanese Empire, 1936–1945.* Toland wins the Pulitzer Prize for his narrative history, which employs the skills of the investigative reporter, uncovering new information and crafting a suspenseful, popular account. He would use a similar approach in equally popular studies such as *Adolf Hitler* (1976), *No Man's Land: 1918* (1980), *Infamy: Pearl Harbor and Its Aftermath* (1982), and *Gods of War* (1985).

IDA B. WELLS-BARNETT: *Crusade for Justice: The Autobiography of Ida B. Wells.* The posthumously published memoir of the anti-lynching activist, reporter, and feminist.

TOM WOLFE: *Radical Chic and Mau-Mauing the Flak Catchers.* In his dissection of a party hosted by Leonard Bernstein for the Black Panthers, Wolfe coins a new term for the phenomenon of liberals embracing fashionable radical causes. A second essay treats the hypocritical scramble for government money by militant black groups in San Francisco.

Poetry

A. R. AMMONS: *Uplands.* Called by critic Harold Bloom the beginning of Ammons's "major phase," the collection features shorter lyrics dealing with the nature of external reality. It includes praised works such as "Snow Log" and "Mountain Talk."

JOHN ASHBERY: *The Double Dream of Spring.* Ashbery meditates on his art in works such as "Fragment," "Soonest Mended," "Definition of Blue," and "Young Man with a Letter."

W. H. AUDEN: *City Without Walls.* Auden's penultimate collection appearing during his lifetime contains "The Horatians," Auden's version of the Horatian ode. Other poems treat both private and public events. His final collection, *Epistle to a Godson and Other Poems,* would follow in 1972.

JOHN BERRYMAN: *Love and Fate.* In the final collection published before Berryman's suicide, the poet autobiographically explores his background and Catholic faith. *Delusions, Etc.,* a posthumous gathering of late poems, would appear in 1972, and *Henry's Fate*, a collection of previously unpublished segments from *The Dream Songs*, would follow in 1977.

RICHARD BRAUTIGAN: *Rommel Drives Deep into Egypt.* Brautigan's poetry is described by one reviewer as "an amalgam of Zen Buddhism, William Carlos Williams, and the stoned comic strips of R. Crumb."

GWENDOLYN BROOKS: *Family Pictures.* This collection contains "The Life of Lincoln West," a free-verse ballad about a young black boy denigrated by a white man. The boy draws consolation from his being described as "the real thing."

NIKKI GIOVANNI: *Re: Creation.* The poet's third collection of black revolutionary verse includes "Ego Tripping," a celebration of the African American woman as the creator of the universe. Giovanni also edits *Night Comes Softly: An Anthology of Black Female Voices.*

ROBERT HAYDEN: *Words in the Mourning Times.* Hayden's collection features meditations on the assassinations of Martin Luther King Jr., Robert Kennedy, and the war in Vietnam. It is the first of three volumes that show an expansion of his range to consider metaphysical and spiritual as well as racial issues; the others are *The Night-Blooming Cereus* (1972) and *Angle of Ascent* (1975).

CAROLYN KIZER: *Midnight Was My Cry.* Kizer adds to poems previously appearing in *The Ungrateful Garden* (1961) and *Knock upon Silence* (1965). Her new works show a shift of attention from nature to contemporary social and political problems. For example, "Poem, Small and Delible" deals with civil rights protest, "The First of June Again" describes American marines in Saigon, and "Seasons of Lovers and Assassins" treats the murder of Robert Kennedy.

DENISE LEVERTOV: *Relearning the Alphabet.* Levertov's collection attempts to recast poetic expression to match her shift from personal to political concerns, including war resistance, women's rights, poverty, and Third World oppression. It contains two long sequences: "The Cold Spring" and "Embroideries."

WILLIAM MEREDITH: *Earth Walk: New and Selected Poems.* Some of Meredith's best work is on display in this collection, which shows a shift from a formal to a conversational style in observing nature and personal experience.

W. S. MERWIN: *The Carrier of Ladders.* Merwin receives the Pulitzer Prize for this collection, which contains important poems such as "Midnight in Early Spring" and "Lemuel's Blessing." The volume also contains a sequence on the westward expansion of the United States. Merwin also publishes *The Miner's Pale Children*, a collection of prose pieces.

STANLEY PLUMLY (b. 1939): *In the Outer Dark.* The Ohio-born poet's first collection, which wins the Delmore Schwartz Memorial Award, deals extensively with the implications of the early death of the Plumly's father due to alcoholism. Two other collections would follow during the decade: *Giraffe* (1973), which treats the artistic process and the poet's relationship with his father, and *Out-of-the-Body Travel* (1977).

EZRA POUND: *The Cantos of Ezra Pound.* The poet's esoteric but highly influential kaleidoscopic poetic sequence is finally, definitively collected and published. An epic project begun in 1915, *The Cantos* are filled with both brilliant insights and discredited social theories in an ambitious attempt to sum up civilization in poetic form.

LUIS OMAR SALINAS (b. 1937): *Crazy Gypsy.* The Chicano poet achieves a commercial and critical success with his first collection, exploring themes of alienation and loneliness experienced by Mexican Americans in a series of surrealistic images. The collection contains several frequently anthologized works, including the title poem, "Nights and Days," "Aztec Angel," "Mexico, Age Four," and "Sunday . . . Dig the Empty Sounds." Subsequent volumes are *Afternoon of the Unreal* (1980), *Prelude to Darkness* (1981), *Darkness Under the Trees/Walking Behind the Spanish* (1982), and *The Sadness of Days* (1987).

SONIA SANCHEZ (b. 1934): *We a BaddDDD People.* The book introduces readers to Sanchez's experimentation with language, typography, and punctuation. Influenced by African American leaders such as Malcolm X, Sanchez attempts to reproduce on the page the chanting rhythms of the black tradition of oratory and to empower her people by demonstrating the poetry of their speech. The book would be followed by *A Blues Book for Blue Black Magical Women* and *Love Poems* (both 1973) and *I've Been a Woman: New and Selected Poems* (1978).

GARY SNYDER: *Regarding Wave.* In one of Snyder's best works, he chronicles both his domestic life and his growing reaction to environmental abuses.

MAY SWENSON: *Iconographs.* Swenson's fifth collection is her most experimental, made up of "shape poems," constructed in typographic forms associated with each poem's subject.

JAMES TATE: *The Oblivion Ha-Ha.* Tate's second major collection contains some of his finest works, including "The Blue Booby," "It's Not the Heat So Much as the Humidity," and "The Wheelchair Butterfly." It would be followed by *Hints to Pilgrims* (1971), *Absences* (1972), and *Viper Jazz* (1976).

MONA VAN DUYN: *To See, to Take.* The poet's third collection earns the National Book Award. It features some of her best work, including "The Voyeur," "The Creation," and poems written in response to William Butler Yeats's "Leda and the Swan." It would be followed by *Bedtime Stories* (1972), dialect narrative poems, and *Merciful Disguises* (1973), mainly selections from her previous volumes.

MARGARET WALKER: *Prophets for a New Day.* Walker's second collection reflects on the civil rights movement. The title poem compares black leaders with biblical prophets. *October Journey* (1973), with tributes to Mary McLeod Bethune, Paul Laurence Dunbar, Gwendolyn Brooks, and Harriet Tubman, and *This Is My Century* (1989), would follow.

Publications and Events

Aion. The first Asian American literary journal is founded by writer Janice Mirikitani, treating political, cultural, and literary topics, with contributions by Toshio Mori, Frank Chin, Alex Hung, and others.

The Black Woman. This first anthology of the works of black women writers is edited by Toni Cade Bambara. Contributors include Nikki Giovanni, Audre Lorde, Alice Walker, Paule Marshall, and others.

The Feminist Press. The press is founded by Florence Howe (b. 1929) to reprint important nineteenth- and twentieth-century books by women writers.

"The Woman-Identified Woman." Radical lesbians submit this position paper to the second Congress to Unite Women. A year later, the paper was anthologized and widely disseminated in *Notes from the Third Year: Women's Liberation.* It quickly becomes a manifesto, then a catalyst for feminist theoreticians such as Adrienne Rich, who expanded the concept of the woman-identified woman beyond sexual orientation to include all women who identify themselves as feminists.

1971
Drama and Theater

EDWARD ALBEE: *All Over.* Albee's drama treats the deathbed wrangling of friends and relatives while awaiting a man's passing. The playwright's most extensive examination of death and dying, it fails with both critics and audiences.

ED BULLINS: *The Fabulous Miss Marie.* Bullins's drama is his first to treat the black middle class. Along with his other 1971 production, *In New England Winter*, it gains Bullins an Obie Award for distinguished playwriting.

JOHN GUARE (b. 1938): *The House of Blue Leaves.* Guare's initial major success comes with his first full-length play, about an eccentric collection of characters:

a middle-aged zookeeper who aspires to be a Hollywood songwriter; his wife, Bananas, who aspires to be a dog; and a woman who agrees to pre- and extramarital sex but will not cook for a man before marriage. The play is set in Queens, New York, in 1965, during Pope Paul VI's visit. Born in New York City, Guare attended Georgetown University and the Yale Drama School. His first play, *Muzeeka*, was produced in 1967 and won an Obie Award.

ARCHIBALD MACLEISH: *Scratch.* Disappointed by the social unrest of the period, MacLeish responds with his only prose play, inspired by Stephen Vincent Benét's "The Devil and Daniel Webster," arguing for personal liberty and social order. Closing after only four performances, it is called by one reviewer "too arbitrary for a drama, too ambiguous for a history, and too shallow for a biography." MacLeish would follow it with his final dramatic effort, *The Great American Fourth of July Parade* (1975), dramatizing the philosophical battle between John Adams and Thomas Jefferson.

TERRENCE MCNALLY: *Where Has Tommy Flowers Gone?* Many consider this play about a young man's development and the conflicts that he faces in the 1960s as one of McNally's greatest achievements.

DAVID RABE (b. 1940): *The Basic Training of Pavlo Hummel* and *Sticks and Bones.* Rabe launches his theatrical career with the initial plays of his Vietnam trilogy. The first follows a soldier from boot camp to his death in a Saigon brothel; the second, a Tony Award winner, depicts a fictional version of TV's Nelson family coping with a son's return from the war. A Dubuque, Iowa, native, Rabe served in Vietnam, an experience that would have an impact on much of his work.

NEIL SIMON: *The Prisoner of Second Avenue.* After an unsuccessful departure from comedy, *The Gingerbread Lady* (1970), about a failed singer dealing with alcoholism, Simon returns to form with this dark comedy about a New Yorker's mental breakdown under the stress of modern urban life and eventual recovery.

STEPHEN SONDHEIM: *Follies.* This innovative musical, suggested by the demolition of the Ziegfeld Theatre, features the reunion of former performers of a Ziegfeld-like revue whose past is juxtaposed with their present. It wins the New York Drama Critics Circle Award.

JOHN-MICHAEL TEBELAK (1949–1985): *Godspell.* This religious rock musical adapts the Gospel of Matthew into a celebration of hippiedom. It runs for 2,924 performances off-Broadway and 527 on Broadway, competing with two other biblical dramas, *Two by Two* and *Jesus Christ Superstar.* Tebelak wrote *Godspell* as a master's thesis at Carnegie-Mellon University. He was the drama director at New York's Cathedral Church of St. John the Divine.

MELVIN VAN PEEBLES (b. 1932): *Ain't Supposed to Die a Natural Death.* Van Peebles's musical treats black ghetto life during the 1960s in a series of vignettes. Born in Chicago, Van Peebles has been an actor, composer, and film director, as well as a novelist, short story writer, and essayist.

MICHAEL WELLER (b. 1942): *Moonchildren.* Weller's most popular play depicts a group of college seniors sharing an apartment in the mid-1960s. It has been described as "an epitaph for its time," and "one of the better plays written about American youth." A New York–born playwright educated at Brandeis and Mancester Universities, Weller presented the first version of *Moonchildren*, entitled *Cancer*, at London's Royal Court in 1970.

PAUL ZINDEL: *And Miss Reardon Drinks a Little.* Zindel's second play treats the relationship among three sisters over the question whether one should be institutionalized. The play receives mixed reviews, as would Zindel's follow-ups, *The Secret Affairs of Mildred Wild* (1972) and *Ladies at the Alamo* (1977).

Fiction

WILLIAM PETER BLATTY (b. 1928): *The Exorcist.* The biggest-selling novel published during the decade is this thriller about demonic possession, based on an actual exorcism in 1949. The novel remains on the bestseller list for fifty-five weeks and sells nearly twelve million copies, inspiring the blockbuster 1973 film adaptation and several sequels. The son of Lebanese immigrants, Blatty graduated from Georgetown University and previously published the novels *Which Way to Mecca, Jack* (1960), *John Goldfarb, Please Come Home!* (1963), *I, Billy Shakespeare!* (1965), and *Twinkle, Twinkle, "Killer" Kane* (1967).

RICHARD BRAUTIGAN: *The Abortion: An Historical Romance 1966.* The last of Brautigan's popular successes and the first of a series of parodies of various fictional forms, including *The Hawkline Monster: A Gothic Western* (1974), *Willard and His Bowling Trophies: A Perverse Mystery* (1975), *Sombrero Fallout: A Japanese Novel* (1976), and *Dreaming of Babylon: A Private Eye Novel 1942* (1977). All would fail to duplicate his successes of the 1960s.

WILLIAM S. BURROUGHS: *The Wild Boys: A Book of the Dead.* The only one of Burroughs's works following *The Naked Lunch* to receive comparable critical attention, the novel blends elements of science fiction, westerns, and juvenile fiction in a montage structure. It imagines a future world in which a group of militant homosexuals battles the forces of totalitarianism. It is the first in a novel

cycle that includes *The Exterminator!* and *Port of Saints* (1973), combining themes of space travel and biological mutation.

HORTENSE CALISHER: *Queenie.* Described as a female Portnoy, the novel's protagonist narrates adventures that reflect the social disruptions of the 1960s. *Eagle Eye* (1973) serves as a kind of companion novel, viewing the decade from the perspective of a computer whiz.

DON DE LILLO (b. 1936): *Americana.* De Lillo's first novel deals with a TV executive on a cross-country car trip and spiritual quest for renewal. He meets a number of grotesque projections of American character types and obsessions. Born in New York City, De Lillo attended Fordham University and worked as an advertising copywriter.

PETER DE VRIES: *Into Your Tent I'll Creep.* Borrowing its title from a popular song about a mythical seductive sheik, De Vries's comic novel satirizes women's liberation in the context of modern marriage. *I Hear America Swinging* (1976) comments comically on the sexual revolution.

E. L. DOCTOROW: *The Book of Daniel.* Doctorow's third novel is a fictional biography of a young man whose parents have been executed during the Cold War, suggestive of the fates of convicted spies Julius and Ethel Rosenberg. The novel thoughtfully explores America of the 1950s and 1960s, mixing fact and fiction in a fashion that would become a Doctorow trademark.

STANLEY ELKIN: *The Dick Gibson Show.* Elkin chronicles the comic adventures of a radio personality. Reviewer Joseph McElroy declares it "a funny, melancholy, frightening, scabrous, absolutely American compendium that may turn out to be our classic about radio."

ERNEST J. GAINES: *The Autobiography of Miss Jane Pittman.* Called a "folk autobiography," the novel traces the history of a 110-year-old black Southern woman, from slavery through the civil rights movement. A bestseller, the novel is eagerly read by white Americans for insights into the black experience.

JOHN GARDNER: *Grendel.* Gardner's breakout novel is a tour de force retelling the story of Beowulf from the perspective of the monster. It features a masterful animation of the Anglo-Saxon world while anticipating Gardner's argument in *On Moral Fiction* (1978), in which Grendel's nihilism is contrasted with the affirmation of art.

GEORGE GARRETT (b. 1929): *Death of the Fox.* Garrett makes his most acclaimed literary contribution in this account of the execution of Sir Walter Ralegh, bringing sophistication, subtlety, and authenticity to the genre. It is the first in an Elizabethan trilogy that includes *The Succession* (1984) and *Entered from the Sun* (1990). Garrett was born in Florida and educated at Princeton. His previous novels included *The Finished Man* (1959), *Which Ones Are the Enemy?* (1961), and *Do, Lord, Remember Me* (1965).

WILLIAM H. GASS: *Willie Masters' Lonesome Wife.* First published in *TriQuarterly* in 1968, Gass's experimental novella suggests that the book the reader holds is in fact the title character and that the act of reading is a sexual encounter with words as sensuous objects.

JOHN HAWKES: *The Blood Oranges.* Hawkes's novel about the breaking down of sexual conventions concerns two American couples on a Greek island who swap partners. It is the first in a series of novels employing an unreliable narrator.

JACK KEROUAC: *Pic.* The first of Kerouac's posthumously published works is a novel about a black musician traveling from the South to Harlem. *Scattered Poems* is also published.

JERZY KOSINSKI: *Being There.* Kosinski's satire on American popular culture follows the career of a simpleminded gardener named Chance who assumes the persona of those he watches on television and whose simple statements about gardening are taken as sage wisdom by the powerful. Kosinski would also write the screenplay for the much-praised 1979 film version starring Peter Sellers and Shirley MacLaine.

BERNARD MALAMUD: *The Tenants.* An African American writer and a Jewish writer living in a condemned East Side New York apartment building battle each other and their landlord in this novel. The story reflects both social and artistic issues, contrasting the discipline and control of the white writer, whose abilities are fading, with the erratic vitality of the black writer.

MARY McCARTHY: *Birds of America.* McCarthy treats the generational divide in a domestic novel about a mother's strained relationship with her son.

WRIGHT MORRIS: *Fire Sermon.* Morris continues his examination of the contemporary social scene in this novel about a hippie couple's encounter with an old man and a boy. A sequel, *A Life*, would appear in 1973.

JOYCE CAROL OATES: *Wonderland.* Oates begins a series of novels dealing with various professions, starting here with medicine. It would be followed by *Do with Me What You Will* (1973), on law; *Assassins* (1975), on politics; and *Son of the Morning* (1978), on religious vocations.

FLANNERY O'CONNOR: *Complete Stories.* The volume adds to O'Connor's previously collected works her first published story, "The Geranium," and several other early works. It receives the National Book Award and substantiates O'Connor's reputation as one of the American masters of short fiction.

JOHN JAY OSBORN JR. (b. 1945): *The Paper Chase.* Osborn becomes one of the first of the popular modern lawyers-turned-writers producing this fictional treatment of his days as a student at Harvard Law School. Film and television versions would follow.

CYNTHIA OZICK: *The Pagan Rabbi, and Other Stories.* Ozick's first collection of stories depicts various attempts at self-realization by characters faced with irreconcilable demands. The title story, one of her finest, explores the implications of a rabbi's suicide and the clash between secularism and Judaism.

WALKER PERCY: *Love in the Ruins.* Percy's satire, set "at the end of the Auto age," shows a scientist's struggle to maintain order and harmony among the residents of Paradise Estates.

TOM ROBBINS (b. 1936): *Another Roadside Attraction.* Robbins's first novel, about the discovery of the mummified body of Christ used to decorate a hot dog stand outside Seattle, introduces the writer's characteristic bizarre plots and eccentric cast of characters. It makes little impression until being issued in paperback in 1973, thereafter becoming a counterculture favorite. Born in North Carolina and raised in Virginia, Robbins was expelled from high school and dropped out of college, hitchhiking cross-country until settling in Greenwich Village in 1956. After military service, Robbins moved to Seattle, where he worked as a reviewer and art critic for *Seattle Magazine* and as a disc jockey.

PHILIP ROTH: *Our Gang.* Roth offers an over-the-top send-up of the Nixon administration, featuring President Trick E. Dixon, Vice President What's-his-Name, Defense Secretary Lard, and others. Dwight MacDonald calls the book "far-fetched, unfair, tasteless, disturbing, logical, coarse, and very funny."

HUBERT SELBY JR.: *The Room.* Selby's violent stream-of-consciousness narrative about an incarcerated criminal is described by one reviewer as "an exquisite, meticulous execution of the curious piteous lust between oppressor and oppressed." Two less successful novels, *The Demon* (1976) and *Requiem for a Dream* (1978), would follow.

WALLACE STEGNER: *Angle of Repose.* Some consider this fictionalized treatment of the life of western realist novelist Mary Hallock Foote (1847–1938) Stegner's masterpiece.

JOHN UPDIKE: *Rabbit Redux.* Set in the summer of 1969, the second volume of Updike's Rabbit Angstrom saga shows the thirty-six-year-old attempting to cope with the 1960s in one of the most accomplished satirical treatments of the period.

ROBERT PENN WARREN: *Meet Me in the Green Glen.* Warren's novel depicts a domestic tragedy surrounding a young Sicilian man's affair with a Tennessee farm wife.

HERMAN WOUK: *The Winds of War.* Wouk completes the first half of his most ambitious project: a two-volume fictional history of World War II and its aftermath, embodied in the adventures of indomitable naval officer Pug Henry. Called "the American *War and Peace,*" the story would be made into a successful television miniseries (1983). The second volume, *War and Remembrance,* would follow in 1978.

Literary Criticism and Scholarship

PAUL DE MAN (1919–1983): *Blindness and Insight: Essays in the Rhetoric of Contemporary Criticism.* De Man's first book establishes his reputation as an important critic, helps stimulate interest in European criticism in America, and contributes to the development of poststructuralist psychoanalytic criticism. Born in Antwerp, de Man came to the United States in 1947, earning his Ph.D. from Harvard. He taught at Yale from 1970 until his death.

ADDISON GAYLE JR. (1932–1991): *The Black Aesthetic.* This work collects and comments on a broad range of African American literature and criticism to espouse the view that the standards set by white society and its critics do not apply to black writers and artists. What matters, Gayle argues, is how a work of art transforms the lives of African Americans, not how the African American artist can be assimilated into the white mainstream. Gayle's book is frequently cited as a controversial and landmark study in the history of African American criticism. Gayle taught English at the City University of New York's City College and at Bernard M. Baruch College for more than twenty-five years.

EDMUND WILSON: *Upstate.* Wilson combines reflections on his northern New York summer home with literary comments about his career and the writers he has known.

Nonfiction

ROBERT COLES (b. 1929): *Children of Crisis: A Study in Courage and Fear.* Coles wins the Pulitzer Prize for the second and third volumes of his admired five-book series on childhood development. Begun in 1967, the series would conclude in 1978. Coles, a trained psychiatrist, was inspired to become a physician by William Carlos Williams, the pediatrician and poet whom Coles met while writing a thesis on *Paterson* at Harvard.

CARL N. DEGLER (b. 1921): *Neither Black nor White: Slavery and Race Relations in Brazil and the United States.* Degler, a professor of history at Stanford, wins the Bancroft Prize and the Pulitzer Prize for his comparative study of the two largest slave-holding nations in the Western world. The book attempts to answer the question of why Brazil never developed a segregationist society following the abolition of slavery, as did the United States.

ERNESTO GALARZA (1905–1984): *Barrio Boy.* The Mexican American leader of a farmworkers's union issues one of the most admired and widely reprinted Chicano autobiographies, chronicling Galarza's own migration from Mexico and acculturation in California.

NIKKI GIOVANNI: *Gemini: An Extended Autobiographical Statement of My First Twenty-Five Years of Being a Black Poet.* Giovanni's unconventional autobiographical reflections treat social, personal, and literary influences and positions. She also publishes *Spin a Soft Black Song,* her first volume of children's verse.

AMIRI BARAKA (LEROI JONES): *Raise, Race, Rays, Raze: Essays Since 1965.* This collection of writing on black nationalism and the black theater includes the essay "7 Principles of US: Maulana Karenga & the Need for a Black Value System," showing the influence of black nationalist Ron Karenga (b. 1941).

JOSEPH P. LASH (1909–1987): *Eleanor and Franklin.* The popular biography by the political activist, journalist, and editor draws on his twenty-year relationship with Eleanor Roosevelt to create a winning portrait of an unhappy marriage that still produced a powerful political partnership. Lash's portrayal of Eleanor Roosevelt's metamorphosis from private person to public icon proves compelling to readers and reviewers alike. It wins the Pulitzer Prize and the National Book Award.

NORMAN MAILER: *The Prisoner of Sex.* Mailer responds to Kate Millett's *Sexual Politics* (1970), offering his interpretation of sexual matters in literature, women's liberation, and homosexuality. Mailer attacks feminists' "dull assumption that the sexual force for a man was the luck of his birth, rather than his finest moral product" and accuses feminism of being "artfully designed to advance the fortunes of the oncoming technology of the state." First published in *Harper's* magazine, it prompts the largest sales for any issue in the magazine's history and the dismissal of editor Willie Morris over the piece's language, which the owners deemed offensive.

ROBERT MIDDLEKAUFF (b. 1929): *The Mathers: Three Generations of Puritan Intellectuals, 1696–1728.* The Yale history professor's study of the changes in English Puritanism after its transplantation in America focuses on the Mather family. It wins the Bancroft Prize.

SAMUEL ELIOT MORISON: *The European Discovery of America: The Northern Voyages.* Morison wins the Bancroft Prize for this first of two volumes chronicling the voyages of American discovery. *The Southern Voyages* would appear in 1974. Both books achieve a vivid immediacy based on Morison's firsthand exploration of the landfalls of the first European explorers.

ALLAN NEVINS: *The War for the Union, Volume 3: The Organized War, 1863–1864* and *Volume 4: The Organized War to Victory, 1864–1865.* Nevins's final two volumes of his tetralogy on the Civil War, published posthumously, receive the National Book Award.

GAY TALESE: *Honor Thy Father.* Talese's insider's portrait of the life and career of Mafia figure Bill Bonanno sells more than 300,000 copies in its first four months.

Poetry

JOHN HOLLANDER: *The Night Mirror.* Hollander's collection is noteworthy for demonstrating a more direct poetic voice, treating emotional experiences in poems such as "Under Cancer."

GALWAY KINNELL: *The Book of Nightmares.* One of Kinnell's most acclaimed books is a sequence described by a reviewer as "the attempt of the lonely soul, existing in a world where communication has broken down, to reforge connections."

STANLEY KUNITZ: *The Testing-Tree.* Kunitz's collection marks a departure to a more conversational style; in it he comments, "I've learned to depend on simplicity that seems almost nonpoetic on the surface but has reverberations within that keep it intense and alive." The collection explores personal traumas, particularly the poet's feelings about the suicide of his father before his birth.

DENISE LEVERTOV: *To Stay Alive.* Levertov's war poetry is meant to be read, in the poet's words, "not as mere 'confessional' autobiography, but as a document of some historical value, to record one person's inner/outer experiences in America during the '60's and the beginning of the '70's." She would follow it with collections of more private concerns — *Footprints* (1972), *The Freeing of the Dust* (1974), and *Life in the Forest* (1978).

HOWARD MOSS: *Selected Poems.* This compilation of the poet's best work from the 1960s, with several new poems, wins the National Book Award. *New Selected Poems* would appear in 1985.

SYLVIA PLATH: *Crossing the Water.* Plath's second posthumously published collection is made up of poems written in 1960 and 1961, after *The Colossus*, her first collection, had been published. The poems are described by one reviewer as Plath's work between her "strange precocity and full maturity." An additional collection, *Winter Trees*, would appear in 1972, and a collection of prose, *Johnny Panic and the Bible of Dreams*, in 1977.

ADRIENNE RICH: *The Will to Change.* Thematically, the poems in this collection treat breaks in relationships and in previous conceptions of self.

ANNE SEXTON: *Transformations.* Sexton produces a series of poems based on the tales of the brothers Grimm, a sometimes comic and decidedly feminist reinterpretation of traditional fairy stories.

CHARLES SIMIC (b. 1938): *Dismantling the Silence.* Poet Richard Howard praises this collection of works from Simic's earlier volumes — *What the Grass Says* (1967) and *Somewhere Among Us a Stone Is Taking Notes* (1969) — for expressing what "has been absent from recent American verse — a gnomic utterance, convinced accent, collective in reference, original in impulse." Born in Belgrade, Simic settled in Chicago in 1954 and attended the University of Chicago and New York University.

LOUIS SIMPSON: *Adventures of the Letter I.* The collection treats subjects of identity and contains a major section on the poet's exploration of his Russian ancestry as well as several poems continuing his criticism of American imperialism and consumer culture.

WALLACE STEVENS: *The Palm at the End of the Mind.* This selection of previously uncollected works includes the first complete version of Stevens's play, *Bowl, Cat, and Broomstick.*

DIANE WAKOSKI: *The Motorcyle Betrayal Poems.* This collection confirms Wakoski's reputation as one of the finest of contemporary confessional poets. She mounts a ferocious but also comic attack on all the men who have betrayed her, while excoriating a world where women take second place to men.

JAMES WRIGHT: *Collected Poems.* The book contains most of Wright's first collection, *The Green Wall* (1957), and all of his next ones, *Saint Judas* (1959), *The Branch Will Not Break* (1963), and *Shall We Gather at the River?* (1968), along with translations and previously unpublished works. The volume wins the Pulitzer Prize and establishes Wright's reputation.

JAY WRIGHT (b. 1935): *The Homecoming Singer.* Wright's first major collection draws on the poet's autobiography to reflect a process of artistic and spiritual development and an evolving conception of African American culture. Included are poems dealing with Crispus Attucks and W.E.B. Du Bois.

Publications and Events

Our Bodies, Ourselves. Produced by the Boston Women's Health Collective, this compilation of information on women's health and sexuality is one of the first to treat women's health issues from a female perspective. The book would sell more than four million copies.

The Pentagon Papers. Documents supplied by Defense Department official Daniel Ellsberg (b. 1931) are printed in the *New York Times*. They reveal that the Pentagon had consistently lied about details of U.S. involvement in Vietnam. Ellsberg is indicted on criminal charges of conspiracy, theft, and violations of the Espionage Act, but the case would be dismissed in 1973.

1972

Drama and Theater

FRANK CHIN (b. 1940): *The Chickencoop Chinaman.* The first play by an Asian American playwright to be produced on a mainstream New York stage is Chin's debut, about an Asian American loner's search for a sustaining heritage and identity.

PAUL CARTER HARRISON (b. 1936): *The Great MacDaddy.* The winner of the Obie Award for best off-Broadway play concerns the spiritual quest of the title character, set in Depression-era America, an environment inhospitable to African Americans. Considered Harrison's masterpiece, the play combines African American folklore and street talk with African music and myth. Harrison is a professor of theater and African American literature and the author of *The Drama of Nommo: Black Theater in the African Continuum* (1974).

JIM JACOBS (b. 1942) AND WARREN CASEY (1935–1988): *Grease.* This musical, exploiting the popular nostalgic craze for 1950s popular culture, becomes for a time the longest-running show on Broadway, with 3,388 performances. Jacobs is a Chicago-born actor; Casey, born in New York City, appeared in local productions before *Grease.* He would originate the role of Bernie Litko in David Mamet's *Sexual Perversity in Chicago* (1974).

DAVID MAMET (b. 1947): *Duck Variations.* The Chicago playwright gains his first attention for this play about two old men who are sitting on a park bench and musing about their lives and the habits of ducks. The play showcases Mamet's characteristic sparse plot and convincing dialogue.

ARTHUR MILLER: *The Creation of the World and Other Business.* Miller's dramatic treatment of the Book of Genesis fails with both critics and audiences and closes quickly.

JASON MILLER (1939–2001): *That Championship Season.* The actor-playwright's only Broadway success

Neil Simon

depicts the reunion of members of a former championship basketball team with their old coach. The former triumph is contextualized by the characters' current failings.

SAM SHEPARD: *The Tooth of Crime.* Regarded by many as Shepard's best play, the drama takes the form of a duel between competing rock stars, reflecting contemporary American values and myths.

NEIL SIMON: *The Sunshine Boys.* Simon revives the themes of *The Odd Couple* in the relationship of two retired vaudeville performers who try to set aside their differences for a reunion performance. The play would be followed by two failures, *The Good Doctor* (1973), an adaptation of short stories by Anton Chekhov, and *God's Favorite* (1976), a retelling of the Job story.

JOSEPH A. WALKER (1935–2003): *The River Niger.* This production by the Negro Ensemble Company deals with a black house-painter and failed poet who tries to make sense of his life. It would reach Broadway in 1973 and win the Pulitzer Prize, the New York Drama Critics Circle Award, and the Tony Award for best play.

Fiction

OSCAR ZETA ACOSTA (1935–?): *The Autobiography of a Brown Buffalo.* Acosta, who is depicted as "Dr. Gonzo" in Hunter S. Thompson's *Fear and Loathing in Las Vegas,* offers a fictionalized version of his autobiography as a Chicano's odyssey of self-discovery. A sequel, *The Revolt of the Cockroach People*, would appear in 1973; the next year Acosta disappeared in Mexico.

RUDOLFO ANAYA (b. 1937): *Bless Me, Ultima.* Anaya's first novel, and the first of his New Mexico trilogy, chronicles how the atomic blast at White Sands, New Mexico, affects a Mexican American, who tries to forge a new identity from Spanish, Indian, and Anglo elements. The book establishes Anaya as a leading Chicano writer. Anaya was born in New Mexico and taught in the Albuquerque public schools, at the University of Albuquerque, and at the University of New Mexico.

RICHARD BACH (b. 1936): *Jonathan Livingston Seagull.* Bach's inspirational fable about a seagull who discovers the joy of flight becomes a surprising bestseller, eclipsing the hardcover record set by *Gone with the Wind*, with more than three million copies sold. Bach had worked as a charter pilot and barnstormer throughout the Midwest.

TONI CADE BAMBARA (1939–1995): *Gorilla, My Love.* Following her editing one of the first important anthologies of black women writers, *The Black Woman* (1970), Bambara produces her best-known work, a story collection called by one reviewer "among the best portraits of black life to have appeared in some time."

JOHN BARTH: *Chimera.* Barth's short fiction collection revisits well-known tales such as those of the legendary storyteller Scheherazade while reflexively addressing the composition difficulties of the author — Barth himself — thus making the act of writing a part of the volume's theme. It wins the National Book Award.

DON DE LILLO: *End Zone.* De Lillo gains his first major critical attention in this second novel, which conflates football and nuclear warfare in the experiences of a West Texas college running back. It would be followed by *Great Jones Street* (1973), an exploration of the rock 'n' roll and drug culture.

JOHN GARDNER: *The Sunlight Dialogues.* Gardner's philosophical novel, set in his native Batavia, New York, pits the concept of freedom, represented by a free-spirited magician, against law and order, represented by the town's police chief.

BARRY HANNAH (b. 1942): *Geronimo Rex.* The first novel by the Mississippi-born writer depicts the picaresque adventures of an aspiring writer who draws inspiration from the Apache warrior. A sequel, *Nightwatchman*, would follow in 1973.

JOHN HERSEY: *The Conspiracy.* Hersey's epistolary historical novel dramatizes the plot in A.D. 64 to kill Emperor Nero, drawing correspondences between political corruption and civil liberty in ancient Rome and the contemporary scene.

IRA LEVIN: *The Stepford Wives.* Levin adapts issues from the women's movement into a best-selling thriller in which suburban women are modified as automatons to serve their husbands.

STEVEN MILLHAUSER (b. 1943): *Edwin Mulhouse: The Life and Death of an American Writer, 1943–1954, by Jeffrey Cartwright.* Millhauser's inventive first novel treats the eleven-year life of a precocious writer, recounted by his best friend. As one reviewer observes, "It is at once a satire of literary biography, an evocation of childhood and an exploration of the creative mind." Millhauser would continue his examination of childhood with *Portrait of a Romantic* (1977), an autobiography of the narrator's life from age eleven to fifteen.

VLADIMIR NABOKOV: *Transparent Things.* Nabokov's novella, dealing with Hugh Person's memories of several visits to Switzerland, serves as the writer's valediction, his final important meditation on the relationship between experience and the imagination and the persistence of memory.

JAMES PURDY: *I Am Elijah Thrush.* This exotic fable treats the pursuit of freedom and artistic independence in a series of surrealistic and allegorical scenes and characterizations.

ISHMAEL REED: *Mumbo Jumbo.* Reed's novel, set in New Orleans in the 1920s, is a different kind of African American detective novel, combining diverse elements such as film noir, jazz, and the occult in a kind of "gumbo," or cross-cultural mélange, appropriate to the Crescent City. A sequel, *Last Days of Louisiana Red*, would follow in 1974.

PHILIP ROTH: *The Breast.* Roth constructs a Kafka-like fable in which an academic awakes to find that he has metamorphosed into a giant female breast. Roth would bring this character back in *The Professor of Desire* (1977).

ALIX KATES SHULMAN (b. 1932): *Memoirs of an Ex–Prom Queen.* Regarded as the first important novel to come out of the women's movement, this work tells the coming-of-age story of a white middle-class girl in the Midwest during the 1950s. A bestseller, the novel is nominated for the National Book Award. Shulman's next novel, *Burning Questions* (1978), deals with the formative years of the modern women's movement and the changes it produced in women's lives. Shulman was born in Cleveland. Her subsequent novels are *Burning Questions* (1978), *On the Stroll* (1981), *In Every Woman's Life . . .* (1987), and *Drinking the Rain* (1995).

JOHN UPDIKE: *Museums and Women.* Several of the stories in this collection deal with the Maples, Updike's representative distressed American family. As one reviewer observes, "There is not a writer around today who is better able to capture people, their marriages, children, affairs — really their lives — and wry emotion from what others consider sterile suburbia."

EUDORA WELTY: *The Optimist's Daughter.* Welty's novel follows a young professional woman's attempt to reinterpret her parents' marriage. It is Welty's most autobiographical work and considered her best by reviewer Howard Moss, a "long goodbye in a very short space not only to the dead but to delusion and to sentiment as well."

KATHLEEN E. WOODIWISS (b. 1939): *The Flame and the Flower.* Woodiwiss's first novel is generally credited with creating the genre known as the erotic historical romance, featuring detailed sexual content. The novel would go through more than eighty printings and sell more than four million copies. A sequel, *The Elusive Flame*, would appear in 1998.

HELEN YGLESIAS (b. 1915): *How She Died.* The author's first novel focuses on Mary Moody Schwartz, daughter of a Communist convicted of spying for the Soviets in the 1930s. Critics praise the author for rendering the history of American radicalism with imaginative specificity and passion that is remarkably free of cliché. She would follow it with the novel *Family Feeling* (1976) and the memoir *Starting: Early, Anew, Over, and Late* (1978), describing her decision to leave her position as literary editor of the *Nation* and pursue a writing career.

Literary Criticism and Scholarship

HOWARD NEMEROV: *Reflections on Poetry and Poetics.* Nemerov provides technical analysis of the poetical works of William Butler Yeats, T. S. Eliot, James Dickey, and others, as well as reflections on the critical process and the state of modern poetry.

PETER PRESCOTT (b. 1935): *Soundings: Encounters with Contemporary Books.* In a selection of his reviews for *Look, Newsweek,* and other magazines, Prescott not only evaluates works by significant writers such as Saul Bellow and Joyce Carol Oates, but he also examines the role of the book critic in a way that other reviewers find shrewd and practical. Prescott was a book editor and has been the book critic for *Newsweek* since 1971.

LIONEL TRILLING: *Sincerity and Authenticity.* The collection of lectures Trilling had delivered at Harvard form, according to reviewer Anatole Broyard, "a brilliant study of our moral life in process of revising itself." The lectures address the evolution of literature and society, from the sincerity that dominated the work of writers until the Romantic era, when the conception of selfhood began to emphasize authenticity.

SHERLEY ANNE WILLIAMS (1944–1999): *Give Birth to Brightness: A Thematic Study of Neo-Black Literature.* This groundbreaking work places the black aesthetic writers of the 1960s squarely in the context of African American folk culture. For Williams, such writers are heroes whose work dignifies the black experience. A poet and novelist, Williams grew up in Fresno, California. Her other books would include *The Peacock Poems* (1975), *Some One Sweet Angel Chile* (1982), and *Dessa Rose* (1986).

Nonfiction

SYDNEY E. AHLSTROM (1919–1984): *A Religious History of the American People. Christian Century* magazine in 1979 would declare this National Book Award–winning study by the professor of relgious history at Yale the most outstanding book on religion published during the 1970s.

JAMES BALDWIN: *No Name in the Street.* This work collects autobiographical fragments and statements on the author's positions on racial matters, along with a recollection of Martin Luther King Jr. In it Baldwin states that "as social and moral and political and sexual entities, white Americans are probably the sickest and certainly the most dangerous people of any color, to be found in the world today."

GWENDOLYN BROOKS: *Report from Part One.* Brooks provides an autobiographical account of her background, her personal and family history, and the evolution of her political and racial consciousness.

FRANCES FITZGERALD (b. 1940): *Fire in the Lake: The Vietnamese and Americans in Vietnam.* The journalist wins the Bancroft Prize and the Pulitzer Prize for this essay collection, exploring American involvement in Vietnam from the perspective of the South Vietnamese people and demonstrating how Vietnamese traditions conflict with American notions of progress and technology. Fitzgerald's subsequent books would be *American Revised* (1979), *Cities on a Hill* (1986), and *Way Out There in the Blue* (2000).

JAMES THOMAS FLEXNER (1908–2003): *George Washington: Anguish and Farewell, 1793–1799.* Flexner, a biographer and art historian, wins the National Book Award and receives a special Pulitzer Prize citation for his final volume of what is generally considered the definitive biography of George Washington. Earlier volumes are *The Forge of Experience* (1965), *George Washington in the American Revolution* (1968), and *George Washington and the New Nation* (1970). The entire series has been described by critic John L. Gignilliat as "one of the monumental American biographies."

JOHN LEWIS GADDIS (b. 1941): *The United States and the Origins of the Cold War: 1941–1947.* Gaddis, a history professor at Ohio University, establishes his reputation as the leading authority on the Cold War with this Bancroft Prize–winning study. The first and most influential of the so-called postrevisionist studies of American-Soviet relations, it attempts an impartial assessment.

DAVID HALBERSTAM: *The Best and the Brightest.* Halberstam's National Book Award–nominated work about America's entry into the Vietnam War is a bestseller. Its title contributes a catchphrase to the national debate about this controversial conflict.

LOUIS R. HARLAN (b. 1922): *Booker T. Washington: The Making of a Black Leader, 1856–1901.* Harlan, a history professor at the University of Maryland, wins the Bancroft Prize for the first of his two-volume definitive biography. The second volume, *The Wizard of Tuskegee, 1901–1915* (1983), would also earn the Bancroft Prize as well as the Pulitzer Prize.

NORMAN MAILER: *Existential Errands.* Mailer collects a miscellany of essays, speeches, letters, a one-act play, and translations. He also publishes *St. George and the Godfather,* his reporting on the 1972 presidential conventions.

ROBERT MANSON MYERS (b. 1921): *The Children of Pride.* Myers, an English professor at the University of Maryland, receives the National Book Award for this collection of letters from a prominent Georgia family written between 1854 and 1868. Reviewer Reynolds Price calls it "the best book known to me which is concerned with the daily lives and minds of upper- and middle-class white Southerners during the war." Additional volumes would appear in 1977 and 1978; Myers would adapt the letters to form several dramas, published as *Quintet: A Five-Play Cycle Drawn from The Children of Pride* (1991).

W. A. SWANBERG (1907–1992): *Luce and His Empire.* Swanberg's biography of Henry R. Luce, cofounder of Time, Inc., wins the Pulitzer Prize. It is one of the Minnesota-born freelance writer's several biographical studies of American tycoons, including *Jim Fisk* (1959), *Citizen Hearst* (1961), and *Pulitzer* (1967). Swanberg would win the National Book Award for his final biography, *Norman Thomas: The Last Idealist* (1976).

HUNTER S. THOMPSON (b. 1937): *Fear and Loathing in Las Vegas.* Thompson displays his irreverent brand of "Gonzo journalism" in this account of a drug-filled tour of Las Vegas. Thompson would later describe the book as "a vile epitaph for the Drug Culture of the Sixties," while Tom Wolfe ranked it as the "Best Book of the Dope Decade." Thompson's follow-up is *Fear and Loathing on the Campaign Trail '72* (1973), and his magazine articles are collected in *The Great Shark Hunt: Strange Tales from a Strange Time* (1979).

BARBARA TUCHMAN: *Stilwell and the American Experience in China, 1911–1945.* Tuchman wins her second Pulitzer Prize for this historical study treating American relations with China and its emergence as a modern country. She publishes additional reflections on China in *Notes from China.*

Poetry

A. R. AMMONS: *Collected Poems 1951–1971.* This National Book Award–winning collection brings together works from Ammons's first six volumes as well as new works, including the long poems "Extreme Moderations," "Hibernaculum," and "Essay on Poetics."

JOHN ASHBERY: *Three Poems.* Considered by many a turning point in Ashbery's career, the collection shows him abandoning the verse line for long prose paragraphs, attempting to revitalize ordinary language while establishing the poet's philosophy of life and writing.

NIKKI GIOVANNI: *My House.* The collection marks a transition to more personal subjects and a more lyrical, introspective method. Divided into two sections — "The Rooms Inside" and "The Rooms Outside" — the arrangement suggests a dialogue between two sides of the poet's nature. Giovanni's next collection, *The Women and the Men* (1975), shows a similar method and concerns.

MAXINE KUMIN: *Up Country.* Kumin's collection of unsentimental meditations and observations about her life in rural New England wins the Pulitzer Prize. The collection invites comparisons with Thoreau, but as Joyce Carol Oates has observed, Kumin's work provides "a sharp-edged, unflinching and occasionally nightmarish subjectivity exasperatingly absent in Thoreau."

DENISE LEVERTOV: *Footprints.* The first in a series of collections, followed by *The Freeing of the Dust* (1975) and *Life in the Forest* (1978), that shows the modulation of the poet's public stances into explorations of private thoughts and experiences.

PHILIP LEVINE: *They Feed the Lion.* This collection establishes Levine as one of the major American poets and links him with Walt Whitman and William Carlos Williams in celebrating common humanity. It includes the admired sequence "Thistles."

JAMES MERRILL: *Braving the Elements.* Merrill earns the Bollingen Prize for this collection thematically linked by different survival responses to existential, natural, and interpersonal crises in works such as "After the Fire" and "Days of 1935."

ANNE SEXTON: *The Book of Folly.* The collection marks a return to the confessional mode in works such as "The Death of the Fathers" and "Angels of the Love Affair." Included as well is the sequence "The Jesus Papers,"

Gloria Steinem

anticipating the religious themes that would dominate Sexton's final collections.

Publications and Events

The American Indian Theatre Ensemble. The first all-Indian repertory company (later renamed the Native American Theatre Ensemble) is founded by Hanay Geiogamah (b. 1945). Its first production is Geiogamah's drama *Body Indian*.

Ms. Cofounded by Gloria Steinem (b. 1934) to celebrate the women's movement and provide a forum for women's issues ignored by mainstream periodicals, *Ms.* first appears as a preview supplement in *New York* magazine in December 1971. Its first issue of 300,000 copies sells out in eight days. *Ms.* helped introduce to a wide readership writers such as Alice Walker, Erica Jong, and Mary Gordon while helping to set the agenda for women's concerns during the period.

1973
Drama and Theater

MARK MEDOFF (b. 1940): *When You Comin' Back, Red Ryder?* Set in a New Mexico diner, this suspense drama depicts a group victimized by an ominous, mysterious figure. Medoff, born in Illinois, has been an actor, director, and playwright and has taught English at New Mexico

State University. His other major success would be *Children of a Lesser God* (1980).

ROBERT PATRICK (b. 1937): *Kennedy's Children.* Set in a downtown New York bar, the play focuses on a representative group who discuss their shattered dreams in the aftermath of John F. Kennedy's assassination and the end of the idealism he represented. Born in Texas, Patrick would become the author of more than seventy off-Broadway plays, produced at La MaMa and elsewhere, including *My Cup Runneth Over* (1979) and *Blue Is for Boys* (1987).

MIGUEL PINERO (1947–1988): *Short Eyes.* The Puerto Rican playwright's greatest success is a gritty look at prison life, acted mostly by former prisoners. It wins the New York Drama Critics Circle Award and two Obie Awards.

STEPHEN SONDHEIM: *A Little Night Music.* Sondheim creates a musical adaptation of Ingmar Bergman's film *Smiles of a Summer Night* (1955), the story of a romantic tangle set in turn-of-the-century Sweden. Winning the New York Drama Critics Circle and a Tony Award, the musical features Sondheim's signature song "Send in the Clowns."

LANFORD WILSON: *The Hot l Baltimore.* Wilson's drama is set in a seedy hotel inhabited by prostitutes, hustlers, and indigents. It wins the New York Drama Critics Circle Award.

ROBERT M. WILSON (b. 1944): *The Life and Times of Joseph Stalin.* The experimental playwright, director, and stage designer mounts a twelve-hour, seven-act drama with multiple scenes from Stalin's life and times performed simultaneously on different sets.

Fiction

THOMAS BERGER: *Regiment of Women.* Berger imagines the world controlled by women in the year 2125, in a heavy-handed satire of women's liberation pushed to extremes.

RITA MAE BROWN (b. 1944): *Rubyfruit Jungle.* One of the first mainstream American novels to frankly celebrate lesbian sexuality is a popular success and quickly becomes a standard text in women's studies courses. Brown would follow it with *In Her Day* (1974) and *Six of One* (1977).

WILLIAM S. BURROUGHS: *Exterminator!* Burroughs's collection of stories and poems dealing with various forms of death through sinister forces. It is regarded as Burroughs's most self-reflexive work, treating the writer and his creations.

JOHN CHEEVER: *The World of Apples.* Cheever's story collection treats the disruption of married life by a loss of love and miscommunication. As one reviewer observed, all of Cheever's main elements are here: "marriage as theater of the absurd, New England as a land of eccentrics, and Italy as a refuge for those who no longer can cope with their lives on this side of the Atlantic."

ALICE CHILDRESS: *A Hero Ain't Nothin' but a Sandwich.* Childress's groundbreaking juvenile novel tells the story of a thirteen-year-old black heroin addict from a variety of perspectives. The book is both widely praised for its gritty realism and honesty and banned by libraries and schools throughout the country.

STANLEY ELKIN: *Searches and Seizures.* Elkin's short fiction collection combines three novellas, including an undisputed masterwork, "The Bailbondsman." Reviewer Thomas R. Edward observes that "No American novelist tells us more about where we are and what we're doing to ourselves."

PAULA FOX (b. 1923): *The Slave Dancer.* Fox's children's novel about a boy kidnapped to serve on a slave ship in the 1840s wins the Newbery Medal and has been called one of the finest achievements in American children's literature, despite some protests against its portrayal of black characters. Born in New York City of Irish and Spanish heritage, Fox was raised in Cuba.

JOHN GARDNER: *Nickel Mountain.* Gardner's novel is set in the Catskills and concerns the relationship between the overweight owner of a diner and a young waitress left pregnant by a rich man's son. Their married life together is threatened by a variety of forces. Gardner also publishes *Jason and Medeia*, a poetic version of the voyage of the *Argo* in the quest for the Golden Fleece and Medeia's revenge on her husband, Jason.

ERICA JONG (b. 1942): *Fear of Flying.* Jong's first novel portrays exuberant female sexuality with a frankness and humor previously reserved for male writers. The bawdy autobiographical bildungsroman of Isadora Wing creates a loud stir. It would be followed by the sequels *How to Save Your Own Life* (1977) and *Parachutes and Kisses* (1984).

JACK KEROUAC: *Visions of Cody.* Published posthumously, this revision of the material previously treated in *On the Road* is a prolonged meditation on Neal Cassady in Kerouac's spontaneous prose style.

BERNARD MALAMUD: *Rembrandt's Hat.* Malamud's third story collection is noteworthy for its consistently pessimistic tone and theme of failed communication in stories such as "My Son the Murderer," "The Silver Crown," and "The Letter."

THOMAS McGUANE: *Ninety-two in the Shade.* Set in Key West, among the fishing guide community, the novel shows an escalation of violence prompted by male competition.

NICHOLASA MOHR (b. 1935): *Nilda.* Mohr's semi-autobiographical first novel introduces readers to the world of "Nuyoricans," marginalized New Yorkers of Puerto Rican descent. A graphic artist, Mohr also illustrated this tale of people caught between two worlds, neither of which embraces them. She would follow it with several well-received story collections — *El Bronx Remembered* (1975), *In Nueva York* (1977), and *Rituals of Survival* (1985) — and the juvenile novels *Felita* (1979) and *Going Home* (1986).

TONI MORRISON: *Sula.* Morrison's second novel, a complex tale of the relationship between two black women and life in an Ohio black community, brings her first major public recognition.

MARGE PIERCY (b. 1936): *Small Changes.* Piercy's novel about various forms of female subjugation is described by its author as an attempt to "produce in fiction the equivalent of a full experience in a consciousness-raising group for many women who would never go through that experience."

THOMAS PYNCHON: *Gravity's Rainbow.* Set during the waning days of World War II, the encyclopedic novel leads readers through plot and stylistic twists so labyrinthine that reality can no longer be differentiated from extravagant fantasy. The book becomes one of the most widely discussed of its day and wins the National Book Award. Pynchon's masterwork has prompted comparisons with James Joyce's *Ulysses* and other modernist classics.

PHILIP ROTH: *The Great American Novel.* Roth uses the collapse of a minor league baseball team in the 1940s as a comic allegory on destructively competitive American life.

ISAAC BASHEVIS SINGER: *A Crown of Feathers and Other Stories.* Singer's collection shares the National Book Award for fiction with Thomas Pynchon's *Gravity's Rainbow.* It is noteworthy for its depiction of life in America.

PAUL THEROUX (b. 1941): *Saint Jack.* After three previous novels, *Fong with the Indians* (1968), *Girls at Play* (1969), and *Jungle Covers* (1971) set in Africa, Theroux receives his first critical and popular success with this dramatization of an American expatriate's life in Singapore. It is described by one reviewer as an "amusing, withering account of prostitution in the once glamorous East." A movie version would appear in 1979.

GORE VIDAL: *Burr.* Vidal offers a revisionist view of the founding fathers and the early years of the Republic from the perspective of an irascible and self-justifying Aaron Burr.

KURT VONNEGUT JR.: *Breakfast of Champions; or, Goodbye Blue Monday!* The novel marks Vonnegut's return to fiction after several years of experimenting with other forms. It is also a return to Tralfamadore, the comic-fictitious planet he had created in *Slaughterhouse Five* (1969) as a metaphor for the arbitrariness of human existence.

ALICE WALKER: *In Love and Trouble: Stories of Black Women.* Walker's collection wins the American Academy and Institute of Arts and Letters Rosenthal Award. She also publishes her third book of poetry, *Revolutionary Petunias and Other Poems*, as well as two children's books, *Langston Hughes, American Poet* and *The Life of Thomas Hodge.*

JOHN EDGAR WIDEMAN: *The Lynchers.* Wideman's third novel concerns a black intellectual who responds to the violence of his heritage by plotting a ritualized lynching of a white policeman.

THORNTON WILDER: *Theophilus North.* Wilder's final book portrays a tutor in Newport, Rhode Island, during the 1920s. He explores various career paths that eventually lead to his becoming a writer.

Literary Criticism and Scholarship

HAROLD BLOOM (b. 1930): *The Anxiety of Influence.* The Yale professor and literary critic's controversial study of poetic influence suggests that poets compete not with their contemporaries but with their predecessors by misreading the works of those who influenced them. He would apply his thesis in *A Map of Misreading* (1974).

MALCOLM COWLEY: *A Second Flowering: Works and Days of the Lost Generation.* Cowley treats the representative American writers born between 1894 and 1900 — F. Scott Fitzgerald, Ernest Hemingway, John Dos Passos, E. E. Cummings, Thornton Wilder, William Faulkner, Thomas Wolfe, and Hart Crane — figures who produced, in his view, a second literary renaissance rivaling the achievements of the 1850s.

CAROLYN HEILBRUN: *Toward a Recognition of Androgyny: Aspects of Male and Female in Literature.* In the first of her explorations of gender issues through an analysis of literary texts, Heilbrun recommends abandoning fixed gender roles for a new conception that combines the best of both male and female characteristics. She would follow this work with *Reinventing Womanhood* (1979).

IRVING HOWE: *The Critical Point.* Howe's collection includes appreciations of Edwin Arlington Robinson and Émile Zola and well-known attacks on feminist critic Kate Millett, the fascism of Ezra Pound, and Philip Roth's *Portnoy's Complaint. Celebrations and Attacks*, a companion volume of short pieces written between 1950 and 1973, would appear in 1979.

ALFRED KAZIN: *Bright Book of Life.* Kazin provides an equally accomplished and masterly continuation of his literary history *On Native Grounds* (1942), treating American fiction from the 1940s to 1971.

VLADIMIR NABOKOV: *Strong Opinions.* Nabokov addresses journalists' questions about his life, his works, and his views on various topics.

RICHARD SLOTKIN (b. 1942): *Regeneration Through Violence: The Mythology of the American Frontier, 1600–1860.* In one of the groundbreaking works of American studies, Slotkin, a professor at Wesleyan University, demonstrates how national attitudes and traditions evolved from the myth of the hunter-hero and the frontier. The book forms the first of a trilogy, to be followed by *The Fatal Environment* (1985) and *Gunfighter Nation* (1992).

TOM WOLFE: *The New Journalism.* Wolfe provides samples from his fictionalized nonfiction, including commentary on his own work and that of others such as Norman Mailer and Gay Talese. In Wolfe's view, the New Journalism, blending objective reporting with personal experience and opinion, has taken on the responsibilities of the abandoned novel of social realism.

Nonfiction

ERNEST BECKER (1925–1975): *The Denial of Death: A Perspective in Psychiatry and Anthropology.* The psychoanalyst wins the Pulitzer Prize for this study, which asserts that knowledge of mortality is the basis for a human's "primary repression," not sexuality, as Freud insisted.

DANIEL BOORSTIN: *The Americans: The Democratic Experience.* Boorstin receives the Pulitzer Prize for this concluding volume of his historical trilogy covering modern America from the end of the Civil War to the *Apollo* moon landing.

W.E.B. DU BOIS: *Correspondence.* The first volume of a three-volume set of Du Bois's letters appears, edited by the Marxist historian Herbert Aptheker. Subsequent volumes would appear in 1976 and 1978.

LILLIAN HELLMAN: *Pentimento.* The second volume of Hellman's memoirs consists largely of recollections of interesting persons Hellman had encountered. One of them, a woman Hellman calls Julia, seems to be a fictional creation drawn from the biography of the psychoanalyst Muriel Gardiner, who would later accuse Hellman of appropriating her life. This part of *Pentimento* is the source for the 1977 film *Julia.*

EDWARD HOAGLAND (b. 1932): *Walking the Dead Diamond River.* This is one of the most admired of the author's essay collections using nature to reflect on human life and modern times. Born in Connecticut, Hoagland began as a novelist. His books include *Cat Man* (1956), *The Circle Home* (1960), and *The Peacock's Tail* (1965).

TOWNSEND HOOPES (b. 1922): *The Devil and John Foster Dulles: The Diplomacy of the Eisenhower Era.* Hoopes's biography and assessment of the Eisenhower-Dulles foreign policy wins the Bancroft Prize and is described by Bernard Brodie as "a brilliant book, marvelously readable, insightful and enlightening." Hoopes had been a senior adviser in the Defense Department and the undersecretary of the air force from 1967 to 1969.

JOHN D. HOUSTON (b. 1933) AND JEANNE WAKATSUKI HOUSTON (b. 1934): *Farewell to Manzanar: A True Story of Japanese American Experience During and After the World War II Internment.* Husband and wife together produce this moving account based on the experiences of Jeanne Wakatsuki Houston's family. It is praised by one reviewer as "a dramatic, telling account of one of the most reprehensible events in the history of America's treatments of its minorities."

PAULINE KAEL (1919–2001): *Deeper into Movies.* Kael's third collection of film reviews receives a National Book Award, an acknowledgment of both Kael's eminence and the significance of film as an artistic medium. According to Kael's introduction, the reviews constitute "a record of the interaction of movies and our national life during a time when three decades seem to have been compressed into three years and I wrote happily—like a maniac—to keep up with what I thought was going on in movies—which is to say, in our national theatre."

ANNE MORROW LINDBERGH: *Hour of Gold, Hour of Lead.* The second volume of Lindbergh's diaries and letters recounts the most highly publicized incidents of her life: marriage to celebrated aviation pioneer Charles Lindbergh and the abduction and murder of their infant son. Lindbergh's writing skill, coupled with the drama of her story, produces a bestseller.

NORMAN MAILER: *Marilyn.* The first of Mailer's two works dealing with film icon Marilyn Monroe takes a speculative biographical approach. *Of Women and Their Elegance* (1980) attempts an "imaginary memoir" from Monroe's perspective.

JOYCE MAYNARD (b. 1953): *Looking Back: A Chronicle of Growing Old in the Sixties.* Using herself as "a looking glass," Maynard chronicles her world-weary youth at age nineteen, describing her generation as bored, tired, and old before its time due to permissiveness, conformity, and television. The book is an elaboration of a much-discussed article, "An Eighteen-Year-Old Looks Back on Life," that Maynard had published in 1972.

TIM O'BRIEN (b. 1946): *If I Die in a Combat Zone.* O'Brien's first book reflects his Vietnam service in a genre described as "autofiction," combining autobiographical material with fictional techniques. He would follow the book with a novel, *Northern Lights* (1975). Born in Minnesota, O'Brien was wounded near My Lai.

LOUIS SHEAFFER (1912–1993): *O'Neill, Son and Artist.* Sheaffer wins the Pulitzer Prize for the second volume of his biography of the playwright, begun with *O'Neill: Son and Playwright* (1968). Meticulously researched and detailed, Sheaffer's biography is widely accepted as the definitive life. He had worked as the drama and film critic for the *Brooklyn Eagle* and as the theatrical press agent for New York's Circle in the Square Theater.

Poetry

FRANK BIDART (b. 1939): *Golden State.* This debut collection by the California poet introduces a new master of the dramatic monologue, delivered by characters such as the narrator of "Herbert White," a psychopathic child killer and necrophiliac. Reviewer Sharon Mayer Libera notes that Bidart's gift is to make characters like Herbert White all too human and understandable. *The Book of the Body* would follow in 1977.

ROBERT BLY: *Sleepers Joining Hands.* The volume includes two long poems, "The Teeth Mother Naked at Last," an invective against the Vietnam War, and the title poem, along with a prose section in which Bly discusses the reawakening of a "Mother culture."

EDGAR BOWERS: *Living Together.* Critic Paul Ramsey declares that Bowers's works collected here are "among the best American poems," including major works such as the title poem, "Insomnia," "An Elegy: December 1970," and "Autumn Shade."

ALLEN GINSBERG: *The Fall of America: Poems of These States.* Ginsberg is finally granted formal recognition by the literary establishment when his collection receives a National Book Award, granted despite the inclusion of poems like "Done, Finished with the Big Cock" and "Elegy: Che Guevara," the likes of which had previously kept Ginsberg—however much admired—on the margins of literary society.

ROBERT HASS (b. 1942): *Field Guide.* Selected for the Yale Series of Younger Poets, Hass's first collection features descriptive and meditative poems evoking the poet's native California. A second, equally admired collection, *Praise*, would follow in 1979. Born in San Francisco, Hass served as U.S. Poet Laureate from 1995 to 1997.

ETHERIDGE KNIGHT: *Belly Song and Other Poems.* Knight's collection contains some of his finest work, including "He Sees Through Stone," "Idea of Ancestry," and "Ila, the Talking Drum," which Robert Bly considers one of the best poems of the past fifty years because of its original and intense rhythm.

ROBERT LOWELL: *The Dolphin.* Lowell's last sonnet cycle explores the later stages of his life and acts as a sort of aesthetic summation. Lowell also publishes selections from his notebook, *For Lizzie and Harriet*, dealing with his relationship with his wife and daughter, and *History*, treating contemporary political and social issues.

W. S. MERWIN: *Writings to an Unfinished Accompaniment.* Merwin's collection treats the theme of humanity's relationship to time and history.

FRANK O'HARA: *Selected Poems.* O'Hara is posthumously awarded the National Book Award for this 590-page collection, which displays the poet's remarkable range and mastery. A collection of essays, *Standing Still and Walking in New York*, would appear in 1975.

ADRIENNE RICH: *Diving into the Wreck.* Rich's collection of overtly feminist, frequently angry poems wins the National Book Award. Rich accepts the award on behalf of all women and insists on sharing it with fellow nominees Alice Walker and Audre Lorde.

MARK STRAND: *The Story of Our Lives.* Strand's series of extended poetic narratives wins the Edgar Allan Poe Award of the Academy of American Poets. His other major collection during the decade is *The Late Hour* (1978).

JAMES WRIGHT: *Two Citizens.* Wright's collection of verse written between 1970 and 1973 is, in the poet's words, "an expression of my patriotism, of my love and discovery of my native place."

1974

Drama and Theater

FRANK CHIN: *The Year of the Dragon.* Chin's drama concerns the disintegration of a Chinese American family.

DAVID MAMET: *Sexual Perversity in Chicago.* Mamet receives his first critical success in this Chicago production of a drama about a budding romance jeopardized by the sexual hostility of the lovers' best friends. The play would reach New York in 1975, to be followed by a film version, *About Last Night* (1985).

TERRENCE McNALLY: *Bad Habits.* This double bill of the complementary one-act plays *Ravenswood* and *Dune Lawn*, both set in sanatoriums and describing contrary

treatments of mental illness, had been initially produced off-Broadway in 1971 before reaching Broadway.

DAVID RABE: *The Boom Boom Room.* For his fourth play, Rabe departs from dealing with the Vietnam War for a character study of the disintegration of a young go-go dancer in a tawdry Philadelphia bar. Despite mixed reviews, it is nominated for a Tony Award for best play. It is revised in 1974 off-Broadway as *In the Boom Boom Room*.

JOHN UPDIKE: *Buchanan Dying.* Updike's biographical drama concerns a fellow Pennsylvanian and neglected figure of American history, President James Buchanan, a subject Updike would return to in *Memories of the Ford Administration* (1992).

Fiction

WALTER ABISH (b. 1931): *Alphabetical Africa.* Abish's first novel follows the adventures of two jewel thieves across Africa in search of an abducted lover. In a linguistic tour de force, its first chapter consists of words beginning with the letter *A*, the next incorporates words beginning with *B*, and so on, through the alphabet to *Z*, at which point the order is reversed. Abish was born in Vienna and raised in China and became a U.S. citizen in 1960.

JAMES BALDWIN: *If Beale Street Could Talk.* The novel concerns the effort to clear the name of a black man falsely accused of raping a Puerto Rican woman. Critics are divided over the book's achievement, with many finding it contrived and sentimental and others impressed by Baldwin's first extensive treatment of an artist protagonist.

DONALD BARTHELME: *Guilty Pleasures.* This work collects Barthelme's experimental prose pieces, parodies, and pastiches, including his initial submissions to *The New Yorker*.

PETER BENCHLEY (b. 1940): *Jaws.* Benchley's novel about an East Coast beach community terrorized by a giant shark becomes the most successful first novel in American publishing history, remaining on the bestseller list for more than forty weeks and selling in excess of nine million copies. The 1975 movie adaptation by Steven Spielberg ushers in the era of the escapist blockbuster film and would spawn numerous sequels. Benchley's other sea-oriented thrillers include *The Deep* (1976) and *The Island* (1979). Benchley is the son of humorist Nathaniel Benchley (1915–1981) and grandson of Robert Benchley.

RICHARD CONDON: *Winter Kills.* Condon gains a critical and commercial success with this taut thriller about a CIA-influenced presidential assassination with clear Kennedy echoes.

EVAN S. CONNELL JR.: *The Connoisseur.* Connell's novel charts the aesthetic progress of an insurance executive who after buying a Mayan figurine becomes obsessed with pre-Columbian art.

GUY DAVENPORT (b. 1927): *Tatlin!* The South Carolina–born scholar and critic's first story collection is described by reviewer Richard Wertine as "tales full of engaging, imaginative renditions of historical facts, revolving meditations on the philosophic problems that have vexed our century." Similar volumes — *Da Vinci's Bicycle* (1979), *Eclogues* (1981), *Trois Caprices* (1982), *The Jules Verne Steam Balloon* (1987), *A Table of Green Fields* (1993), *The Cardiff Team* (1996), and *Twelve Stories* (1997) — would follow.

JOHN GARDNER: *The King's Indian: Stories and Tales.* Gardner's first collection of short fiction includes "The Warden," an echoing of Franz Kafka's *The Trial*, the title novella, a nautical adventure combining philosophy, fantasy, and parody, and other admired stories such as "John Napper Sailing Through the Universe" and "Pastoral Care." A second collection, *The Art of Living*, would follow in 1981.

GAIL GODWIN: *The Odd Woman.* Godwin's acclaimed third novel uses the affair between a literature professor and a married man as an occasion to reflect on women's roles. A collection of stories, *Dream Children* (1976), and a novel about the relationship between an artist and her vocation, *Violet Clay* (1978), would follow.

WILLIAM GOYEN: *Come the Restorer.* Goyen would regard his fourth novel, about a West Texas community's search for a savior, as his "biggest accomplishment."

JOHN HAWKES: *Death, Sleep, and the Traveler.* The narrator describes his relationship with his wife and her lover in a novel that reviewer Calvin Benedict asserts is "likely to endure as a small classic."

JOSEPH HELLER: *Something Happened.* Heller's long-awaited second novel records the many setbacks and disappointments of an ordinary businessman, Bob Slocum, described as one of the dreariest protagonists in American literature. The book is an unrelenting critique of American values, and Kurt Vonnegut would praise its author as "the first major American writer to deal with unrelieved misery at novel length."

JOHN JAKES (b. 1932): *The Bastard.* The first in Jakes's popular multivolume American Bicentennial series of historical novels about the Kent family is noted for its wealth of accurate historical detail and memorable characters. The series includes ten books, which would eventually be adapted into a successful television miniseries. Jakes was an advertising copywriter who began his writing career with mysteries, science fiction, and adventure novels.

CHARLES JOHNSON (b. 1948): *Faith and the Good Thing.* Johnson's first novel, written with the guidance and encouragement of John Gardner, is a folk-influenced story of a Southern black girl's questing journey to Chicago. It receives wide critical acclaim as the work of an important new African American writer. Born in Illinois and a professor at the University of Washington, Johnson previously published two collections of cartoons, *Black Humor* (1970) and *Half-Past Nation Time* (1972).

STEPHEN KING (b. 1947): *Carrie.* The Maine-born writer's first novel, about a put-upon high school girl who gains her revenge through her telekinetic powers, initiates an unprecedented string of best-selling horror and suspense novels that would make King the best-selling American author during the final quarter of the twentieth century. *The Shining* (1977), *The Stand* (1978), *Cujo* (1981), *Misery* (1987), and other popular books would follow.

JOHN KNOWLES: *Spreading Fires.* Knowles's psychological thriller, set in a villa in the south of France, explores the conflict between sexuality and repression.

URSULA K. LE GUIN: *The Dispossessed: An Ambiguous Utopia.* One of Le Guin's best-known and admired science fiction novels concerns a physicist trying to reconcile the cultural conflicts between his home planet and the one he is exploring. The novel wins the Hugo Award, the Nebula Award, and the Jupiter Award for best novel.

ALISON LURIE (b. 1926): *The War Between the Tates.* Lurie's novel chronicles the breakdown of a marriage, which she employs as a metaphor for the decline of U.S. fortunes during the war in Vietnam. She would revisit many of the same themes in *Only Children* (1979). Born in Chicago and educated at Radcliffe, Lurie taught English at Cornell University after 1968.

CORMAC McCARTHY: *Child of God.* McCarthy's third novel is set, like its predecessors, in eastern Tennessee and centers on a demented backwoodsman who is, among others things, a murderer and a necrophiliac. McCarthy's treatment prompts comparison with the work of the ancient Greek playwrights for its deep religious feeling and stubborn insistence on the mystery of existence.

ALBERT MURRAY: *Train Whistle Guitar.* Murray's first novel is the initial volume of an autobiographically based trilogy depicting an African American's boyhood in the South, in college, and during his career as a jazz musician. *The Spyglass Tree* (1991) and *The Seven League Boots* (1996) complete the trilogy.

VLADIMIR NABOKOV: *Look at the Harlequins!* Nabokov creates an alter ego and an alternative fictional memoir in this story of a Russian émigré who, as a successful American novelist, writes a controversial book about a nymphet.

JOHN NICHOLS (b. 1940): *The Milagro Beanfield War.* The first volume of the California-born novelist's New Mexico trilogy traces the transformation of a small New Mexico town by modern commercialism. Critics see Nichols as a kind of throwback, a "proletarian" writer who wants his work to change the system. He would follow the novel with *The Magic Journey* (1978) and *The Nirvana Blues* (1981).

TILLIE OLSEN: *Yonnondio.* Olsen's family chronicle treats life during the Great Depression. Olsen had begun writing the book in the 1930s, publishing a chapter in the *Partisan Review* in 1934. After devoting decades to raising her four children and working as a secretary, she finally completed the novel nearly forty years later.

GRACE PALEY: *Enormous Changes at the Last Minute.* Paley's acclaimed second story collection contains her most frequently anthologized story, "A Conversation with My Father," as well as one of her most ambitious works, "The Long-Distance Runner."

ROBERT B. PARKER (b. 1932): *The Godwulf Manuscript.* Parker introduces his Boston private detective Spenser in the first of his series of popular and critically acclaimed mysteries, described by critic Anne Ponder as "the best American hard-boiled detective fiction since Ross MacDonald and Raymond Chandler." Parker earned a Ph.D. from Boston University in 1970, writing his thesis on detective masters Chandler, Hammett, and MacDonald.

PHILIP ROTH: *My Life as a Man.* Roth shifts from broad comedy and satire to confession in this autobiographical treatment of writer Peter Tarnopol, who is in turn writing about novelist Nathan Zuckerman. Zuckerman returns in a series of subsequent novels beginning with *The Ghost Writer* (1979).

MICHAEL SHAARA (1929–1988): *The Killer Angels.* Many regard this Pulitzer Prize–winning novel on the Battle of Gettysburg as one of the greatest American historical novels and among the finest fictional treatments of the Civil War. Born in New Jersey, Shaara had been a paratrooper and merchant seaman.

ROBERT STONE: *Dog Soldiers.* Stone wins the National Book Award for his second novel, set in Vietnam and the United States. It concerns a drug deal that goes violently awry. The novel establishes its author as a major chronicler of the contemporary scene.

ANNE TYLER: *Celestial Navigation.* Tyler receives her first major critical attention for this novel about an agoraphobic artist's marriage to a self-sufficient woman. John Updike would give her next novel, *Searching for Caleb* (1976), a positive review, helping to establish Tyler in the front ranks of contemporary writers.

JAMES WELCH (b. 1940): *Winter in the Blood.* After a first book of poetry, *Riding the Earthboy 40* (1971), Welch issues his first novel about reservation life as a young man tries to come to terms with his Indian heritage. The book is greeted as the arrival of a major writer reflecting the Native American experience. Welch was born in Montana, of mixed Blackfoot and Gros Ventre heritage.

Literary Criticism and Scholarship

WAYNE C. BOOTH: *The Rhetoric of Irony.* Booth enhances his critical reputation for this study of literary irony, which critic Denis Donoghue declares "a grammar of communication."

RICHARD KOSTELANETZ (b. 1940): *The End of Intelligent Writing: Literary Politics in America.* Experimental novelist, poet, and editor Kostelanetz generates controversy in this polemical attack on an alleged New York literary conspiracy among major publishers, book reviewers, and East Coast academics who neglect younger and innovative writers.

Nonfiction

MAYA ANGELOU: *Gather Together in My Garden.* Angelou's second volume of memoirs continues the story of her life from age sixteen through a variety of jobs during the postwar period.

CARL BERNSTEIN (b. 1944) AND BOB WOODWARD (b. 1943): *All the President's Men.* The *Washington Post* reporters who broke the Watergate scandal deliver their account of following the story from the break-in through the cover-up that toppled the Nixon administration.

ROBERT A. CARO (b. 1935): *The Power Broker: Robert Moses and the Fall of New York.* Caro's first book on the career of New York State's longtime public works commissioner receives the Pulitzer Prize. As a study of political power and urban development the book has become a standard college text. Caro worked as an investigative reporter for Long Island's *Newsday* from 1959 to 1966.

ANGELA DAVIS (b. 1944): *Autobiography.* The black activist reviews her childhood, family, education, and political development, including her 1972 trial for murder, kidnapping, and conspiracy charges.

ANNIE DILLARD (b. 1945): *Pilgrim at Tinker Creek.* Dillard wins the Pulitzer Prize for this essay collection, a record of the seasons in Virginia and meditations by a writer who describes herself as "a poet and a walker with a background in theology and a penchant for quirky facts."

ROBERT W. FOGEL (b. 1926) AND STANLEY L. ENGERMAN (b. 1936): *Time on the Cross: The Economics of American Negro Slavery* and *Time on the Cross: Evidence and Methods—a Supplement.* The authors receive the Bancroft Prize and generate a storm of controversy for their economic study of slavery, which asserts that on average slaves fared slightly better than comparable laborers in the North. Walter Clemons, in his review, declares that the book reworks popular conceptions of slavery "so drastically . . . that 'revisionist' is a feeble description of its thrust." Fogel was an economics professor at the University of Chicago; Engerman was a professor of economics and history at the University of Rochester.

EUGENE GENOVESE (b. 1930): *Roll, Jordan, Roll: The World the Slaves Made.* The Marxist critic presents a massively detailed account of slave life in America, which explores what he terms a paternalistic dynamic that restrained slaveholders and forced recognition of slaves' humanity.

DUMAS MALONE: *Jefferson and His Time.* Malone's fourth volume dealing with the second Jefferson administration receives the Pulitzer Prize. Begun in 1948 and completed in 1981, Malone's massive six-volume biography has been called the greatest biography ever written by an American.

WILLIAM MANCHESTER: *The Glory and the Dream: A Narrative History of America, 1932–1972.* Manchester provides a popular history from the perspective of the generation who grew up during the Depression.

MARY MCCARTHY: *The Mask of State: Watergate Portraits.* McCarthy portrays the major Watergate figures, including John Mitchell, John Ehrlichman, H. D. Haldeman, G. Gordon Liddy, Frank McCord, and John Dean, as well as the members of the Senate Investigating Committee.

KATE MILLETT: *Flying.* The first of two autobiographical works recording Millett's life after the publication of *Sexual Politics* (1970) includes her marriage and lesbian affairs. It would be followed by *Sita* (1977), about her mental breakdown.

MARABEL MORGAN (b. 1937): *The Total Woman.* Countering the prevailing notions of the women's liberation movement, Morgan, a Miami housewife, makes a case for submission to male desires as the key to improving married life. Despite scathing reviews, the book becomes the number one bestseller for 1974. Her other books would include *Total Joy* (1976), *The Total Woman Cookbook* (1980), and *The Electric Woman* (1985).

ROBERT M. PIRSIG (b. 1928): *Zen and the Art of Motorcycle Maintenance.* Pirsig's musings during a cross-country motorcycle trip becomes a popular philosophical self-help manual. Born in Minnesota, Pirsig had worked as a technical writer for electronics firms.

RICHARD B. SEWALL (1908–2003): *The Life of Emily Dickinson.* The work of twenty years of research, the Yale English professor's two-volume National Book Award–winning biography uncovers new information about the poet's life and challenges the myth that Dickinson was a neurotic recluse who turned to poetry as a solace for an unhappy life. Sewall shows Dickinson as far from a hermit who deliberately chose poetry as her vocation early in life.

LEWIS THOMAS (1913–1993): *The Lives of a Cell.* Thomas's collection of some of his "Notes of a Biology Watcher" from the *New England Journal of Medicine* is a surprise bestseller and wins critical acclaim for its style and the theme of the interconnection of all living things. It wins the National Book Award and would be followed by the collections *The Medusa and the Snail* (1979) and *The Youngest Science: Notes of a Medicine Watcher* (1983). Trained as a neurologist and a researcher in immunology and microbiology, Thomas became the dean of New York University Medical School and the Yale School of Medicine, and the president of the Sloan-Kettering Institute.

Poetry

A. R. AMMONS: *Sphere: The Form of a Motion.* Ammons's book-length poem, considered by many his finest long poem, is a diverse meditation organized by the concept of the sphere and the search for unity and wholeness.

W. H. AUDEN: *Thank You, Fog.* Auden's last lyrics are collected in this volume, which the poet was working on when he died.

WILLIAM EVERSON (1912–1994): *Man-Fate: The Swan Song of Brother Antoninus.* After leaving the Dominican order—to which he had belonged for twenty years, during which he produced poetry under the name Brother Antoninus—Everson publishes a poetry collection mostly devoted to explaining why he renounced his religious vows to marry the woman he loved and the difficulties he experienced adjusting to a secular life.

MARILYN HACKER (b. 1942): *Presentation Piece.* Hacker's first major collection receives the National Book Award and critical acclaim for her exploration of feminist themes using traditional verse forms. Similar themes and methods are employed in the subsequent volumes *Separations* (1976) and *Taking Notice* (1980). Born in New York City, Hacker worked as an antiquarian book dealer in London from 1971 to 1976.

GALWAY KINNELL: *The Avenue Bearing the Initial of Christ into the New World.* The title work is a Whitmanesque meditation on life along New York City's shabby Avenue C and its struggling inhabitants.

ANNE SEXTON: *The Death Notebooks.* Like her final volume published after her suicide, *The Awful Rowing Toward God* (1975), Sexton's poems collected here enact her fighting despair with a search for spiritual meaning. It contains three of her finest sequences, "The Death Baby," "The Furies," and "O Ye Tongues."

GARY SNYDER: *Turtle Island.* Taking its title from a Native American name for the North American continent, Snyder's collection, judged by some critics as his finest, wins the Pulitzer Prize. Snyder remarks in his preface, "The poems speak of places and the energy pathways that sustain life."

ROBERT PENN WARREN: *Or Else — Poem/Poems, 1968–1974.* Warren's collection of new works examines the private and public life of the narrator, identified as "R.P.W." Included as well is verse dealing with writers: "Homage to Theodore Dreiser" and "Flaubert in Egypt."

Publications and Events

Aiiieeeee!: An Anthology of Asian-American Writing. Edited by Frank Chin and others, this popular anthology helps popularize Asian American writers such as Carlos Bulosan and Diana Chang.

The Black Book. A scrapbook record of African American life, compiled by the authority on black history M. A. Harris (1908–1977), is conceived and edited by Toni Morrison as a celebration of black cultural history. The material collected, including newspaper clippings, photographs, songs, and advertisements, would provide Morrison with the historical incident that inspired her novel *Beloved* (1987).

People. The magazine begins publication, launched by Time, Inc., to recoup circulation lost when *Life* magazine ceased publication in 1972.

1975

Drama and Theater

EDWARD ALBEE: *Seascape.* The playwright wins his second Pulitzer Prize for this expressionistic fantasy play depicting the confrontation on a beach between a couple and two humanoid figures.

ED BULLINS: *The Taking of Miss Janie.* One of Bullins's most acclaimed and controversial plays is this drama treating the relationship between a black revolutionary and a white liberal woman whose rape becomes the play's central metaphor. The play receives an Obie Award and the New York Drama Critics Circle Award but also strong feminist condemnation.

FRED EBB (b. 1933) AND BOB FOSSE (1927–1987): *Chicago.* This "concept" musical treats the 1920s in a series of vaudeville acts. It is based on a 1926 comedy by Maurine Watkins (1901–1969) about a married woman who shoots her lover and whose trial transforms her into a celebrity.

JAMES KIRKWOOD (1930–1989) AND NICHOLAS DANTE (1941–1991): *A Chorus Line.* The Pulitzer Prize–winning musical about the experiences of a group of chorus dancers begins its fifteen-year Broadway run, closing in 1990 after 6,137 performances. The idea for the musical had come from its choreographer, Michael Bennet (1943–1987), who had interviewed hundreds of Broadway "gypsies" during his career. Kirkwood was an actor and novelist of works such as *P.S. Your Cat Is Dead* (1972) and *Some Kind of Hero* (1975). Dante, born Conrado Morales in New York City, was a dancer who drew on his own experiences for *A Chorus Line.*

DAVID MAMET: *American Buffalo.* Premiering in Chicago, Mamet's drama about a bungled heist of a valuable coin collection would reach Broadway in 1977, winning the New York Drama Critics Circle Award and praise for its symbolic naturalism.

TERRENCE MCNALLY: *The Ritz.* McNally's greatest popular success is this farce, set at a steambath catering to homosexuals; a man fleeing from his murderous brother-in-law goes there to hide.

LANFORD WILSON: *The Mound Builders.* Wilson juxtaposes different attitudes about the land and life in the values of archaeologists excavating an Indian burial site and a realtor who wants to develop the area.

Fiction

EDWARD ABBEY: *The Monkey Wrench Gang.* Abbey's novel about the misadventures of a group of eco-terrorists becomes an underground classic, selling half a million copies. It is believed that the book inspired the formation of the underground environmentalist group Earth First! *Fool's Progress* (1981) would continue the adventures of the Monkey Wrench Gang.

DONALD BARTHELME: *The Dead Father.* Barthelme's second novel depicts the fantastical journey of a monumental carcass—a father being hauled by nineteen of his children, in an absurdist Freudian fable.

SAUL BELLOW: *Humboldt's Gift.* Bellow revisits his relationship with the writer Delmore Schwartz (1913–1966), whose fictitious counterpart, a visionary poet named Von Humboldt Fleischer, suffers the same neglect and premature death. Bellow's surrogate, a writer named Charlie Citrine, and Humboldt embody the fate of artists destroyed by America's materialistic culture—until, that is, Charlie is saved by the success of a comedy about cannibalism that the two friends had written years before Humboldt's death. The ironic revival of Charlie's career is thus "Humboldt's gift."

JUDY BLUME: *Forever....* Opening with the words "Sybil Davison has a genius I.Q. and has been laid by at least six different guys," Blume's juvenile novel radically challenges former depictions of sexuality in adolescent literature. As Blume explains, she "set out to write a book that didn't equate sex with punishment." Banned and attacked in editorials as too explicit, it would be followed by the semiautobiographical *Starring Sally J. Freedman as Herself* (1977) and *Tiger Eye* (1981), about coping with a parent's murder.

E. L. DOCTOROW: *Ragtime.* Doctorow rewrites the rules of the historical novel in his inventive story, set at the turn of the twentieth century and incorporating real events and actual personages, such as Harry Houdini, Emma Goldman, J. Pierpont Morgan, and Henry Ford, in imaginary scenes and relationships. The novel's success would lead to a screen adaptation and a Broadway musical version.

ANDRE DUBUS (1936–1999): *Separate Flights.* Dubus's debut collection deal with the ramifications of infidelity in stories such as "The Doctor" and "We Don't Live Here Anymore." The theme would be continued in his second volume, *Adultery and Other Choices* (1977). Born in Louisiana, Dubus taught at Bradford College in Massachusetts until his injury in an automobile accident in 1986.

WILLIAM GADDIS: *JR.* Gaddis's remarkable second novel is a tour de force made up almost exclusively of dialogue. It depicts an eleven-year-old's rise to become the master of a financial empire. The novel explores the theme of the emptiness of modern American life, dominated by a money ethic that erodes all relationships. The book wins the National Book Award.

WILLIAM GOYEN: *Collected Stories.* Goyen's stories exhibit an extraordinary range and universality and gain their author renewed critical respect. Goyen states in his introduction to the volume, "I've not been interested in simply reproducing a big section of life off the streets or from the Stock Exchange or Congress. I've cared most about the world in one person's head."

GAYL JONES (b. 1949): *Corregidora.* Jones's first novel, written while she was still a graduate student at Brown University, treats Ursa Corregidora, a blues singer and the subject of domestic abuse so brutal that it replicates the experience of her maternal forebears at the hands of Brazilian slave masters.

WILLIAM KENNEDY (b. 1928): *Legs.* This is the first in a series of novels set in the author's hometown of Albany, New York. It concerns gangster "Legs" Diamond and would be followed by additional chapters of Kennedy's evolving Albany cycle: *Billy Phelan's Greatest Game* (1978), about the kidnapping of a political boss during the Depression, and *Ironweed* (1983), about an alcoholic ex–baseball player.

JERZY KOSINSKI: *Cockpit.* After publishing a business satire, *The Devil Tree* (1973), Kosinski produces his first novel featuring a character who attempts to control his own destiny in the story of a former government agent who creates alternative identities for himself. *Blind Date* (1977), *Passion Play* (1979), and *Pinball* (1982) would follow, failing to generate much commercial or critical enthusiasm.

PETER MATTHIESSEN: *Far Tortuga.* The writer's innovative treatment of a turtle-hunting voyage in the Caribbean employs a stripped-down, objective style that aspires, in Matthiessen's words, to "a musical score." Reviewer Terence Des Pres calls it "an outright masterpiece," and William Kennedy hails it as "a virtuoso novel."

LARRY McMURTRY: *Terms of Endearment.* McMurtry achieves a popular success with this story of feisty widow Aurora Greenwood, her many suitors, and her daughter's terminal cancer. The story would be made into a popular film in 1983.

MILTON MURAYAMA (b. 1923): *All I Asking for Is My Body.* Murayama's first book deals with the lives of Japanese Americans living and working on Hawaiian sugar plantations during World War II. Only modestly received initially, when reissued in 1980 it would win the American Book Award and be recognized as one of the significant works of Hawaiian American literature.

J. F. POWERS: *Look How the Fish Live.* Powers's third and final story collection contains both secular stories set in Ireland and clerical stories, including one of his finest, "Farewell," about a Minnesota bishop's retirement.

REYNOLDS PRICE: *The Surface of the Earth.* This generational family saga set in rural North Carolina chronicles the period 1903 to 1944. It features a Victorianesque accretion of details, building up a group portrait of a regional community.

JAMES PURDY: *In a Shallow Grave.* Purdy's novel about obsession and alienation concerns a horribly disfigured war veteran's search for his childhood sweetheart. One reviewer calls it "a modern Book of Revelations" due to its "prophecies, vision, and demonic landscapes."

JUDITH ROSSNER (b. 1935): *Looking for Mr. Goodbar.* The New York City writer treats the dark underside of sexual liberation in this best-selling novel based on the 1973 murder of a schoolteacher by a man she had picked up at a Manhattan singles bar.

JOANNA RUSS (b. 1937): *The Female Man.* The best-known of the author's feminist science fiction works presents multiple heroines from different times and places who represent contrasting possibilities for women in society. It becomes an underground classic and wins a Hugo Award. Russ previously published the essay "What Can a Heroine Do? Or Why Women Can't Write" (1972) and the novels *Picnic on Paradise* (1968), *And Chaos Died* (1970), and *Alyx* (1976).

ISAAC BASHEVIS SINGER: *Passions and Other Stories.* Singer's story collection treats various occurrences of passion gone astray in works such as "Old Love" and "The Admirer." It would be followed by Singer's eighth story collection, *Old Love* (1979).

JOHN UPDIKE: *A Month of Sundays.* Updike's novel chronicles the sexual indiscretions of an errant minister during a month's stay at a rest home. He also publishes *Picked-Up Pieces,* a collection of book reviews.

LARRY WOIWODE: *Beyond the Bedroom Wall.* Woiwode's novel is set in the author's boyhood home of North Dakota and dramatizes the fortunes of a family much like Woiwode's own. This acclaimed family chronicle is described as "a collage of preserved sensations," in which geographical detail matters as much as character development.

Literary Criticism and Scholarship

JONATHAN CULLER (b. 1944): *Structuralist Poetics.* Winning the James Russell Lowell Prize from the Modern Language Association, the Cornell professor's guide is the first full-length study of structuralism and attempts to demonstrate the value of linguistic approaches to the study of literature and to reconcile structuralist semiotics with the practices of the New Criticism. Culler's other critical volumes include *The Pursuit of Signs* (1981) and *On Deconstruction* (1982).

PAUL FUSSELL (b. 1924): *The Great War and Modern Memory.* Fussell, a professor of English at the University of Pennsylvania, wins the National Book Award for this critical study of the literary responses to World War I and its persistence in modern consciousness. He would follow it with a similar consideration of World War II, in *Wartime: Understanding and Behavior in the Second World War* (1989).

GEOFFREY HARTMAN: *The Fate of Reading, and Other Essays.* Hartman deals with the relationship between literary analysis and psychoanalysis, the nature of literary history, and the role and status of literary criticism.

HUGH KENNER (b. 1923): *A Homemade World: The American Modernist Writers.* Kenner, professor of English at Johns Hopkins and author of *The Pound Era* (1971), treats the differences between European and American modernism in the works of writers such as William Faulkner, Wallace Stevens, William Carlos Williams, Marianne Moore, Ernest Hemingway, and F. Scott Fitzgerald.

ANNETTE KOLODNY (b. 1941): *Lay of the Land: Metaphor as Experience and History in American Life and Letters.* Having published in 1975 the influential essay "Some Notes on Defining a 'Feminist' Literary Criticism," Kolodny, a professor of English and women's studies at the University of New Hampshire, applies her theories in one of the first feminist critiques of American literature and culture. A companion volume, *The Land Before Her,* about women writers on the West, would follow in 1984.

R.W.B. LEWIS: *Edith Wharton.* Lewis wins the Bancroft Prize, the National Book Critics Circle Award, and the Pulitzer Prize for this biography, which uncovers new material on the writer and challenges conventional views of Wharton as genteel. Mark Royden Winchell declares the book "one of the very best we have on an American writer."

PHILIP ROTH: *Reading Myself and Others.* This work collects interviews, essays, and articles on literary issues and Roth's own and others' works. Included are the significant essays "Imagining Jews" and "Looking at Kafka."

KARL SHAPIRO: *The Poetry Wreck: Selected Essays, 1950–1970.* Shapiro's contrarian views are on display in this collection of essays, which debunk the elevation of T. S. Eliot, Ezra Pound, and William Butler Yeats to the poetic pantheon and criticize the tendency to equate "semi-literates and rock singers" with genuine poets.

LOUIS SIMPSON: *Three on a Tower.* Simpson supplies biographical portraits and an assessment of Pound, Eliot, and Williams.

PATRICIA MEYER SPACKS (b. 1929): *The Female Imagination.* One of the seminal texts in feminist criticism is this interpretive study of patterns revealed by women writers from the seventeenth century to the present. Spacks, born in San Francisco and educated at Rollins College, Yale, and the University of California, is a professor of English at Wellesley College.

Nonfiction

SUSAN BROWNMILLER (b. 1935): *Against Our Will: Men, Women, and Rape.* Brownmiller's provocative and influential study of the history, cultural significance, and psychology of sexual assault helps alter conceptions of rape, defining it not as a sexual act but as an expression of power and control. "My purpose in the book," Brownmiller observed, "has been to give rape its history. Now we must deny its future."

DAVID BRION DAVIS: *The Problem of Slavery in the Age of Revolution: 1770–1823.* Davis continues his analysis of slavery, begun in the Pulitzer Prize–winning *The Problem of Slavery in Western Civilization* (1967), with this study of the growth and development of the antislavery movement in America. It wins the Bancroft Prize and the National Book Award.

ROBERT N. BUTLER (b. 1927): *Why Survive? Being Old in America.* Butler, director of the National Institute on Aging, wins the Pulitzer Prize for this study, which questions the value of long life for its own sake. Modern medicine, in the author's view, has ironically created "a huge group of people for whom survival is possible but satisfaction in living elusive." The book proposes reforms for what Butler calls the "tragedy of old age in America."

PAUL HORGAN: *Lamy of Santa Fe.* Winner of the Pulitzer Prize in history, the book explores the life of the archbishop of Santa Fe and has been compared favorably to Willa Cather's classic novel *Death Comes for the Archbishop.* Horgan dramatizes Lamy's opposition to slavery and his relationships with Indians in vivid passages that go well beyond, but do not contradict, the historical record.

JAMES JONES: *WW II.* In the last book the writer lived to complete, Jones supplies the text for a collection of 160 sketches and paintings of the war, describing combat from the viewpoint of the "evolution of a soldier." One of Jones's most effective works, it summarizes many of the themes of his novels.

MICHAEL KORDA (b. 1933): *Power! How to Get It, How to Use It.* Korda, editor in chief of Simon & Schuster, produces a best-selling guidebook on office politics for the "Me Decade." *Success! How Every Man and Woman Can Achieve It* (1977) would follow.

NORMAN MAILER: *The Fight.* Mailer provides his perspective on Muhammad Ali's recapture of the heavyweight boxing title from George Foreman in their bout in Kinshasa, Zaire.

PAUL THEROUX: *The Great Railway Bazaar.* This is the first of Theroux's popular travel books with an emphasis on train travel, here an account of a trip through Asia. Similar books include *The Old Patagonian Express* (1979) and *Riding the Iron Rooster* (1988).

TOM WICKER (b. 1926): *A Time to Die.* The *New York Times* columnist recounts his experience of being asked by rebelling inmates to observe and mediate their negotiations during the insurrection at New York's Attica Prison in 1971. This soul-searching insider's account combines journalism with autobiographical elements.

TENNESSEE WILLIAMS: *Memoirs.* The writer reflects on the influences that shaped his career. Equally confessional and autobiographical is *Moise and the World of Reason*, a novel about a disappointed, failed homosexual writer.

EDMUND WILSON: *The Twenties.* Leon Edel edits this compilation of extracts from Wilson's notebooks of the period, providing insights into the critic's life and ideas.

TOM WOLFE: *The Painted Word.* Wolfe tackles the world of contemporary art in a contentious assessment, which asserts that modern art has become a parody of itself, as academic and staid as the salon paintings its first practitioners rebelled against.

Poetry

JOHN ASHBERY: *Self-Portrait in a Convex Mirror.* Ashbery's best-known collection is praised by one reviewer for its "breathtaking freshness and adventure in which dazzling orchestrations of language open up whole areas of consciousness no other American poet has even begun to explore." The collection sweeps the Pulitzer Prize, the National Book Award, and the National Book Critics Circle Award.

TURNER CASSITY (b. 1929): *Yellow for Peril, Black for Beautiful.* This collection, derived from the Mississippi-born poet's surrealistic meditations on scenes from his world travels, contains the verse drama "Men of the Great Man," about the death of Cecil Rhodes.

EDWARD DORN (1929–1999): *The Slinger.* This work collects the various books of Dorn's major poetic achievement, *Gunslinger* (1968–1972), an epic, picaresque narrative reflection of contemporary American life. Also published is *The Collected Poems: 1956–1974.* Born in Illinois, Dorn attended Black Mountain College and was influenced by the poet Charles Olson.

LOUISE GLÜCK (b. 1943): *The House on Marshland.* Glück's second collection, following *Firstborn* (1968), deals with the pain of love and loss in works such as "Pomegranate," "Here Are My Black Clothes," and "Love

Poem." Born in New York City, Glück suffered from an eating disorder as a teenager, an experience that figures prominently in her work. She would win a Pulitzer Prize in 1993 for *Wild Iris*.

JOY HARJO (b. 1951): *The Last Song.* The collection introduces readers to the mixture of feminism, Native American mythology, and current events that is the continuing subject matter of this Creek poet and screenwriter. Seeking "another way of seeing language and another way of using it that wasn't white European male," Harjo concentrates on depicting the world of contemporary Native American women while celebrating both their spirituality and their sexuality. *The Last Song* would be followed by the collections *What Moon Drove Me to This?* (1979), *She Had Some Horses* (1983), and *Secrets from the Center of the World* (1989).

JOHN HOLLANDER: *Tales Told of the Father.* The collection contains the long poem "The Head of the Bed," which has been interpreted as a despairing commentary on the state of modern poetry.

MAXINE KUMIN: *House, Bridge, Fountain, Gate.* Kumin's collection of verse written between 1971 and 1975 offers a reexamination of her life, family connections, childhood, and motherhood.

WILLIAM MEREDITH: *Hazard the Painter.* Meredith treats the life of an artist as an opportunity for reflection on art and the artistic process.

HOWARD MOSS: *Buried City.* Moss's collection offers various reflections of New York City life and contains admired works such as "Tattoo," "Chekhov," and the title poem.

ROBERT PINSKY (b. 1940): *Sadness and Happiness.* Pinsky's first collection receives praise and comparison with the works of Rilke, James Wright, and Robert Lowell. Reviewer Louis L. Martz declares that the volume suggests that "somehow, American poetry has entered a new era of confidence."

ADRIENNE RICH: *Poems: Selected and New.* Rich's collection is described by the poet as "the graph of a process still going on," tracing her evolving gender ideas and the evolution of her poetical technique from more formal structures to a looser, more personal style.

ANNE SEXTON: *The Awful Rowing Toward God.* The first volume of poetry to appear after Sexton's death reveals a more religious and mystical side to this confessional poet. *45 Mercy Street* (1976) and *Word for Dr. Y* (1978) would follow.

DIANE WAKOSKI: *Virtuoso Literature for Two and Four Hands.* The poet describes in a preface her intention to explore in this collection "the images of fantasy and my past. My keyboard now is the typewriter." Poems include "Winter Sequence" and "Driving Gloves."

ROBERT PENN WARREN: *Or Else-Poem.* Warren explores the private and public life of the persona identified as "R.P.W." He also publishes *Democracy and Poetry*, offering a survey of his career and poetics.

1976
Drama and Theater

D. L. COBURN (b. 1938): *The Gin Game.* The first play produced by this former advertising writer makes its debut at a small Los Angeles theater. It would appear on Broadway the next year, in 1978 becoming the first two-character play ever to receive a Pulitzer Prize. The play centers on Weller and Fonsia, an elderly man and woman who play a series of gin rummy games. During the games, each examines the many issues of their lives.

CHARLES FULLER (b. 1939): *The Brownsville Raid.* Fuller's drama is based on an actual incident in Brownsville, Texas, in which 167 black soldiers were dishonorably discharged in response to a shooting by an unknown assailant in a nearby town. Fuller was born in Philadelphia and was from 1967 to 1971 the director of Philadelphia's Afro-American Arts Theatre.

JOHN GUARE: *Rich and Famous.* Guare's black comedy chronicles the experiences of Bing Ringling, a young playwright in a desperate pursuit of fame and fortune.

PRESTON JONES (1936–1979): *A Texas Trilogy.* Jones's major theatrical achievements are these three plays, set in a mythical West Texas town and employing idiosyncratic language and characters. The play manages only a brief run on Broadway but does well in a number of regional productions. Jones was born in New Mexico and was for most of his career associated with the Dallas Theatre Center as an actor and director.

DAVID RABE: *Streamers.* Rabe's final drama in his Vietnam trilogy, set in an army barracks in 1965, creates a microcosm of American society and attitudes of the time and explodes into murderous rage. It would be adapted as a film in 1983, directed by Robert Altman.

RONALD RIBMAN: *The Poison Tree.* Ribman's realistic prison drama sets black convicts against their white guards. It would be followed by the Dramatists Guild Award–winning black comedy about death, *Cold Storage* (1977).

NTOZAKE SHANGE (PAULETTE WILLIAMS, b. 1948): *for colored girls who have considered suicide / when the rainbow is enuf.* One of the most critically acclaimed African American dramas is described by its author as a "choreopoem" in which seven black women dressed in different colors treat various aspects of their lives in poetry, music, and dance. Shange graduated from Barnard College and received an M.A. in American Studies from the University of Southern California. She has taught playwrighting and creative writing at the University of Houston.

NEIL SIMON: *California Suite*. The playwright rebounds from infrequent previous failures by relocating the method of *Plaza Suite* (1968) to a California setting.

STEPHEN SONDHEIM: *Pacific Overtures*. Sondheim's innovative musical dramatizes the opening of Japan to the West. Performed by an all-Asian cast, this highly stylized production, employing Japanese stage elements borrowed from Kabuki and Noh dramas, fails with audiences but wins the New York Drama Critics Circle Award for best musical.

Fiction

RENATA ADLER (b. 1938): *Speedboat*. Adler's controversial first novel is a series of vignettes told from the perspective of a woman journalist. Defying most novelistic conventions, the narrative proceeds by the juxtaposition of unrelated incidents, collectively presenting a disturbing portrait of contemporary urban life. The similarly unconventional *Pitch Dark* (1983) would follow. Adler was born in Italy and was an acclaimed film reviewer for the *New York Times* and a frequent contributor to *The New Yorker*.

LISA ALTHER (b. 1944): *Kinflicks*. The Tennessee writer's first novel draws praise for her depiction of a woman's struggle for self-realization in her Tennessee hometown. Some readers view the protagonist, Ginny Babcock, as a female Holden Caulfield. *Original Sins* (1981), *Other Women* (1985), and *Bedrock* (1990) would follow.

RUDOLFO ANAYA: *Heart of Aztlan*. Anaya's second novel in his New Mexico trilogy studies the conflict and challenge that occur when a Mexican family moves to Albuquerque and must adjust to urban American life. The trilogy, depicting growing up in New Mexico, concludes with *Tortuga* (1980), the story of a sixteen-year-old boy's recovery from a paralyzing accident.

DONALD BARTHELME: *Amateurs*. The collection features stories constructed almost exclusively from dialogue, such as "You Are as Brave as Vincent Van Gogh" and "The Captured Woman."

ANN BEATTIE (b. 1947): *Distortions* and *Chilly Scenes of Winter*. Beattie's first story collection and novel are released. She specializes in spare, still-life snapshots in the lives of the generation who came of age in the 1960s and find themselves lost and adrift in the 1970s. Along with Raymond Carver, Beattie contributes to the revival of interest in the short story during the 1970s and 1980s. Her second collection, *Secrets and Surprises*, would follow in 1978.

RAYMOND CARVER (1938–1988): *Will You Please Be Quiet, Please?* Carver's first major story collection establishes his characteristic subject — the desperate lives of ordinary blue-collar and lower-middle-class characters — in stories such as "Nobody Said Anything" and "Neighbors." Another collection, *Furious Seasons and Other Stories*, would follow in 1977. His breakout collection, *What We Talk About When We Talk About Love* (1981), would reshape the modern short story by introducing the methods of fictional minimalism.

DON DE LILLO: *Ratner's Star*. De Lillo's most ambitious early novel is this surrealistic work concerning a fourteen-year-old mathematics whiz charged with decoding a radio message from a distant star. The novel is as abstruse as it is ingenious in presenting the world of science and technology. It would be followed by two more-compact satires of contemporary urban life, *Players* (1977) and *Running Dog* (1978).

STANLEY ELKIN: *The Franchiser*. Elkin's comic novel about a traveling businessman who lives to acquire franchises and is stricken with multiple sclerosis solidifies the writer's reputation as one of the leading contemporary chroniclers of American life.

JOHN GARDNER: *October Light*. Gardner wins the National Book Critics Circle Award for this novel presenting a philosophical debate between an elderly Vermont farmer and his older sister. The novel includes a long parody of a contemporary novel of existential alienation.

GAEL GREENE (b. 1935): *Blue Skies, No Candy*. Restaurant reviewer and food critic Greene's best-selling novel concerns the extramarital adventures of a female scriptwriter. The book is a succès de scandale, owing to Greene's application of the same sensual language she uses in her food writing to the portrayal of female sexual response. She would follow it with a similar novel, *Doctor Love* (1982), told from the male perspective and called the "male fantasy of the 1980s."

JOHN HAWKES: *Travesty*. The novel takes the form of a monologue by a French poet who explains why he intends to crash his car, killing himself, his daughter, and her friend. It is the final installment of a series of three novels, begun with *The Blood Oranges* and continued with *Death, Sleep, and the Traveler*, which uses unreliable narrators reflecting on the connection between love and the imagination.

GAYL JONES: *Eva's Man*. Jones's powerful second novel explores the sexual victimization of African American

Marge Piercy

women based on the reflections of a woman who has poisoned and dismembered her abusive lover. Jones would follow the novel with a story collection treating similar themes of sexual violence and racial identity, *White Rat and Other Stories* (1977).

MAXINE HONG KINGSTON (b. 1940): *The Woman Warrior: Memoir of a Girlhood Among Ghosts.* Kingston's autobiographical novel is infused with Chinese legend and history but delivered in a distinctly modern Chinese American voice. It creates a sensation among both critics and readers and becomes a frequently taught college text. Born in Stockton, California, and a graduate of the University of California at Berkeley, Kingston was a longtime resident of Hawaii, teaching English as a Second Language at a private school and literature courses at the University of Hawaii.

CYNTHIA OZICK: *Bloodshed and Three Novellas.* Ozick's acclaimed second collection of short fiction includes "Usurpation," the O. Henry contest winner for 1975.

MARGE PIERCY: *Woman on the Edge of Time.* This science fiction novel presents a feminist utopia in which woman are free of reproductive responsibilities, property does not exist, and the concept of gender is moot.

ISHMAEL REED: *Flight to Canada.* Reed's inventive novel treats the American Civil War and slavery and uses

deliberate anachronisms, suggesting the connection between past and present in a mixture of satire, allegory, and farce. It lampoons slave narratives and earnest works such as Harriet Beecher Stowe's *Uncle Tom's Cabin.* Edmund White calls it "the best work of black fiction since *Invisible Man.*"

ANNE RICE (b. 1941): *Interview with the Vampire.* The first of the New Orleans–raised author's best-selling modern-day vampire novels emphasizes eroticism and horror. A sequel, *The Vampire Lestat,* would appear in 1985.

TOM ROBBINS: *Even Cowgirls Get the Blues.* Having gained a cult following for his first novel, *Another Roadside Attraction* (1971), Robbins achieves his biggest popular success with this picaresque novel featuring a compulsive hitchhiker with a nine-inch thumb, who winds up at a health ranch taken over by alienated feminist cowgirls. Reviewer Ann Cameron calls its zany humor "a brilliant affirmation of private visions and private wishes and the power to transform life and death."

WALLACE STEGNER: *The Spectator Bird.* Stegner's National Book Award–winning novel brings back the character Joe Allston of *All the Live Things* (1967), who recalls a trip to Denmark twenty years before.

GORE VIDAL: *1876.* Vidal's contribution to the bicentennial is an account of the centennial, as Charles Schuyler returns to Washington at the height of the corrupt Grant administration.

JOHN UPDIKE: *Marry Me.* Updike's treatment of an adulterous affair contains one of his strongest female portraits in Ruth Conant, the betrayed wife.

KURT VONNEGUT JR.: *Slapstick; or, Lonesome No More!* Vonnegut's absurdist fantasy shows a former U.S. president who suffers from Tourette's syndrome and lives on the Island of Death with his twin sister.

ALICE WALKER: *Meridian.* Walker's second novel concerns a black woman and civil rights activist who returns to her Southern home to deal with the gap between her political ideals and the realities she finds. The work establishes one of Walker's dominant themes: the racism and sexism experienced by black women.

Literary Criticism and Scholarship

E. D. HIRSCH JR.: *Aims of Interpretation.* Hirsch attacks the New Criticism and argues for a renewed multidisciplinary, humanistic approach to literary criticism.

ELLEN MOERS (1929–1979): *Literary Women: The Great Writers.* In this groundbreaking feminist interpretation, Moers, a professor of English at Barnard College, helps revise the literary canon, stimulating scholarly attention

Alex Haley presenting Clifford Alexander Jr., the secretary of the army, an album from *Roots*, while visiting the Pentagon on April 4, 1977

to previously forgotten women writers. The work coins the terms *heroinism* and *literary feminism*. Moers's final work is *Harriet Beecher Stowe and American Literature* (1978).

Nonfiction

MAYA ANGELOU: *Singin' and Swingin' and Gettin' Merry Like Christmas.* Angelou's third volume of memoirs covers her unsuccessful marriage and her theatrical career.

JAMES BALDWIN: *The Devil Finds Work.* Baldwin's essay collection concerns the history of blacks in films.

SAUL BELLOW: *To Jerusalem and Back.* Based on his 1975 extended visit to Israel, Bellow addresses the question of Jewish identity in the twentieth century.

WILLIAM H. GASS: *On Being Blue.* Gass employs what Susan Sontag calls the "erotics of art" in this fanciful meditation on the meaning of blue, ranging from thoughts on the Platonic conception of blue to the importance of so-called blue movies.

ALEX HALEY: *Roots.* Haley's search in Gambia, West Africa, and twelve years of research result in a work that combines the fruits of his highly personal labor with a number of imaginative embellishments to tell the generational story of his ancestors in Africa and America. It remains on the bestseller list for nine months, is awarded a special Pulitzer Prize, and would become a phenomenon when adapted into a twelve-hour TV miniseries in 1977, launching a genealogy craze.

LILLIAN HELLMAN: *Scoundrel Time.* The third installment of Hellman's memoirs recounts the playwright's experiences with the House Un-American Activities Committee. Hellman's opposition to the Communist witch hunts of the 1950s mark her as a cultural hero, despite revelations by others of her support for Soviet dictator Joseph Stalin.

SHERE HITE (b. 1942): *The Hite Report: A Nationwide Study of Female Sexuality.* Based on surveys of 1,844 women, Hite, the director of the Feminist Sexuality Project (1972–1978), hypothesizes on the current state of sexuality for women in a best-selling, though controversial, study; many fault her methodology and conclusions. The volume would be followed by the additional studies *The Hite Report on Male Sexuality* (1981), *Women and Love* (1987), and *The Hite Report on the Family* (1995).

IRVING HOWE: *World of Our Fathers.* Howe's history of Eastern European Jewish immigrants in America is a bestseller and wins the National Book Award. It is described by the reviewer Jacob Neusner as an "elegant, monumental work" and "the finest work of historical literature ever written on American Jews."

CHRISTOPHER ISHERWOOD: *Christopher and His Kind.* Isherwood's autobiography deals frankly with the writer's homosexual experiences between 1929 and 1939, from his arrival in Berlin to his immigration to the United States. The book helps fuel the American gay liberation movement of the period.

RON KOVIC (b. 1946): *Born on the Fourth of July.* The memoir of a Vietnam veteran turned anti-war activist is widely praised as an honest and powerful account of an all-American boy's maturation based on the lessons of the war. Kovic would collaborate with director Oliver Stone on a movie adaptation in 1989.

N. SCOTT MOMADAY: *The Names.* Described as "a portrait of the artist as a young Indian," Momaday offers an autobiographical account of his childhood, adolescence, and the evolution of his artistic development.

DAVID MORRIS POTTER (1910–1971): *The Impending Crisis, 1848–1861.* Potter, a Stanford University historian, receives the National Book Award and the Pulitzer Prize posthumously for his final study of the origins of the Civil War. It is described by reviewer Eric Foner as "history in the grand tradition." His other books include *Lincoln and His Party in the Secession Crisis* (1942), *The Background* *of the Civil War* (1961), and *The South and the Sectional Conflict* (1968).

ADRIENNE RICH: *Of Woman Born: Motherhood as Experience and Institution.* Rich surveys motherhood from personal, anthropological, and political perspectives to demonstrate her thesis that the social institution of motherhood is a male construct designed to keep women under control.

GAIL SHEEHY (b. 1937): *Passages: Predictable Crises of Adult Life.* In one of the most popular of modern self-help books, Sheehy puts a positive slant on the aging process by identifying the "natural" stages each individual must negotiate. She would follow it with other pop psychology bestsellers: *The Silent Passage: Menopause* (1992), *New Passages: Mapping Your Life Across Time* (1995), and *Understanding Men's Passages* (1998). Sheehy was a contributing editor of *New York Magazine* from 1968 to 1977.

WILLIAM W. WARNER (b. 1920): *Beautiful Swimmers: Watermen, Crabs, and the Chesapeake Bay.* Based on a year spent living and working with crab fishermen on the Chesapeake, Warner's first book receives the Pulitzer Prize. It would be followed by *Distant Water: The Fate of the North Atlantic Fisherman* (1983) and *Into the Porcupine and Other Odysseys* (1999).

THEODORE H. WHITE: *In Search of History.* White provides an account of his life and career in what has been called "a minor classic of American biography" and the writer's most accomplished work.

TOM WOLFE: *Mauve Gloves and Madmen, Clutter and Vine.* This work collects fiction and essays written between 1967 and 1976, covering diverse topics such as computers, pornography, private-school accents, and getting a cab in New York City.

Poetry

ELIZABETH BISHOP: *Geography III.* Bishop's final collection contains some of her greatest works, including "In the Waiting Room," "The Moose," and "Crusoe in England." The volume wins the National Book Critics Circle Award.

RICHARD EBERHART: *Collected Poems: 1930–1976.* Eberhart wins the National Book Award and increased recognition as one of the most important living poets for this collection of more than three hundred poems, fifty previously unpublished in book form.

WILLIAM EVERSON: *River-Root.* This long poem, composed in 1957 but unpublished due to the poet's religious vocation as a Dominican monk, about sexual love is notable for its explicitly erotic imagery. It has been compared with the verse of his most significant influence, Robinson Jeffers.

JOHN HOLLANDER: *Reflecting on Espionage.* Ostensibly a book-length poem about espionage, the volume is actually a witty commentary on art and artists.

AUDRE LORDE (1934–1992): *Coal.* Lorde's first collection issued by a major publisher combines poems from her first two books — *The First Cities* (1968) and *Cables to Rage* (1970) — the latter containing "Martha," in which Lorde confirms her lesbianism. Lorde, of West Indian heritage, was born and raised in New York City.

JAMES MERRILL: *Divine Comedies.* The first installment of a trilogy ultimately published in 1982 as *The Changing Light at Sandover* wins the Pulitzer Prize. The trilogy gains notoriety because Merrill's lover, David Jackson, appears in it as a co-medium with whom the poet recalls dead spirits while using a Ouija board.

SIMON J. ORTIZ (b. 1941): *Going for the Rain.* Ortiz's first major collection contributes to his reputation as one of the finest contemporary Native American poets and short story writers. A companion volume of poems reflecting Pueblo Indian myth and oral traditions, *A Good Journey*, would follow in 1977, and his first story collection, *Howbah Indians*, would be published in 1978. Ortiz, born in Albuquerque, is an Acoma Pueblo Indian.

KARL SHAPIRO: *Adult Bookstore.* This volume contains some of the poet's finest work, including "My Father's Funeral," "Garage Sale," "Girls Working in Banks," and "The Rape of Philomel."

LOUIS SIMPSON: *Searching for the Ox.* This autobiographically based collection is organized by a search for the means of uniting the sensual and the intellectual.

RICHARD WILBUR: *The Mind-Reader.* Critics praise Wilbur's sixth volume of new works and translations for its craftsmanship. It includes "Cottage Street, 1953," about Wilbur's meeting with the young Sylvia Plath, and his response to the Kent State shootings and subsequent student protests, "For the Student Strikers."

JAY WRIGHT: *Soothsayers and Omens* and *Dimensions of History.* Wright's collections place African American development in a wider context of ritual, history, and culture. According to E. Ethelbert Miller, the first volume builds "bridges healing the wounds that exist within the souls of black Americans"; Harold Bloom declares that the second is "the year's best book of poems from a small press" — it had been published by Kayak in Santa Cruz, California.

BERNICE ZAMORA (b. 1938): *Restless Serpents.* Zamora, the daughter of a Colorado coal miner and farmer, treats issues of Chicano cultural tradition and gender in what many regarded as a landmark work in the history of Chicano literature.

1977

Drama and Theater

EDWARD ALBEE: *Counting the Ways*. Albee's one-act play, subtitled "A Vaudeville," explores various responses to love. It is performed with *Listening*, an expressionistic drama dealing with mental illness.

ED BULLINS: *Daddy!* The sixth play of Bullins's Twentieth Century cycle shows Michael Brown trying to reunite with his wife and children, whom he had abandoned, and explores the meaning of fatherhood in the context of African American family life.

MICHAEL CRISTOFER (b. 1946): *The Shadow Box*. Cristofer's drama about three terminally ill patients in a hospice wins the Pulitzer Prize and the Tony Award for best play. Cristofer would observe that the play "says something about the fact that life is not meaningless, that relationships are important, that people can communicate, that things like love and hope and trust and faith are possible in a real sense."

MARIA IRENE FORNES: *Fefu and Her Friends*. Considered one of the foundation works of modern feminist drama, the play treats aspects of women's oppression and possibilities for opposition. The audience is divided into groups, and each experiences different locations around a New England country house and the evocative monologues of the play's all-female cast.

JOHN GUARE: *Landscape of the Body*. Guare's absurdist drama concerns a Maine woman's experiences in New York City. "The play is about a decapitation," Guare explains, "about people living without any reflective powers, without their reason, without their imagination."

ALBERT INNAURATO (b. 1948): *Gemini*. The Philadelphia playwright's most successful drama presents a Harvard student's reaction to his working-class background and confused sexual orientation, prompted by the unexpected visit by two upper-class friends on the eve of his twenty-first birthday. It runs for more than four years on Broadway.

DAVID MAMET: *A Life in the Theater*. Mamet's drama contrasts attitudes toward acting and the theater from the perspectives of established and younger actors. Critics praise it as a witty encapsulation of the twentieth-century stage. *The Water Engine*, a play about the business world, in which an inventor is murdered after refusing to sell his creation, is also produced.

ARTHUR MILLER: *The Archbishop's Ceiling*. Performed at Washington's Kennedy Center, Miller's play is a response to Soviet treatment of dissident writers in which a prominent novelist must decide whether to choose exile or a treason trial.

MARSHA NORMAN (b. 1947): *Getting Out*. The Kentucky-born dramatist's first play explores a woman's reentry into society from prison. Co-winner of the Great American Play Contest, it also wins the Oppenheimer Award, the John Gassner Playwrighting Medallion, and the American Theatre Critics Association Citation. It would be followed in 1978 by *Third and Oak*, two one-act plays that would both be made into films, *The Laundromat* (1985) and *The Pool Hall* (1989).

SAM SHEPARD: *Curse of the Starving Class*. Shepard dramatizes the disintegration of a family in southern California as a metaphor for the demise of the western frontier and American society.

NEIL SIMON: *Chapter Two*. Drawing on his own experience of remarriage following the death of his first wife, Simon treats a novelist's relationship with a divorced actress. Many view the play as Simon's best.

WENDY WASSERSTEIN (b. 1950): *Uncommon Women and Others*. Wasserstein's first full-length play depicts the reunion of five women graduates from Mount Holyoke College who share recollections of their college days. It wins an Obie Award.

TENNESSEE WILLIAMS: *Vieux Carré*. In a drama that recalls *The Glass Menagerie*, Williams's play, set in a boardinghouse in the French Quarter of New Orleans, considers various forms of dying. It manages only five performances on Broadway, dismissed by critic Clive Barnes as "the murmurings of genius, not a major statement."

Fiction

TONI CADE BAMBARA: *The Sea Birds Are Still Alive*. Bambara's second collection shows a widening of range, a reflection of her travels to Cuba and Vietnam and her community activism. Two stories, "Medley" and "Witchbird," have been cited as excellent depictions of contemporary African American women.

THOMAS BERGER: *Who Is Teddy Villanova?* The first of two parodies and send-ups of fictional genres, here, the detective novel. It would be followed by *Arthur Rex* (1978), Berger's version of the Arthurian legend.

HORTENSE CALISHER: *On Keeping Women*. In Calisher's novel, a thirty-seven-year-old mother of four ponders her identity as a woman in a novel selected by the *New York Times* as one of the most noteworthy titles of 1977, described as "always skillful and brilliant in its effects."

JOHN CHEEVER: *Falconer.* Many regard this novel about a university professor sent to a Connecticut prison for murder to be Cheever's greatest achievement as a novelist. The novel is also Cheever's first attempt to deal explicitly with homosexuality.

ROBIN COOK (b. 1940): *Coma.* Cook, a surgeon and clinical instructor at Harvard Medical School, helps create the genre of the medical thriller in his first novel, depicting a black market for human organs. The novel was adapted as a film in 1978.

ROBERT COOVER: *The Public Burning.* One of the most controversial novels of the decade uses the execution of the Rosenbergs in 1953 to encapsulate American moral values. Richard Nixon appears as a narrator, along with other historical figures. The novel had been refused by nearly every major U.S. publisher for fear of libel suits. Critics are split on the book's merits.

NICHOLAS DELBANCO: *Possession.* This is the first volume of the author's Sherbrooke trilogy, the history of a Vermont family in decline. *Sherbrookes* (1978) and *Stillness* (1980) complete the series. "Without anyone's much noticing," John Gardner would observe, Delbanco "has turned into one of the country's best novelists."

JOAN DIDION: *A Book of Common Prayer.* Didion's third novel, set in an imagined Central American country, mirrors the fragmentation of American society and culture in the experiences of a complacent woman's search for her revolutionary daughter.

J. P. DONLEAVY: *The Destinies of Darcy Dancer.* Launching what has been called his greatest sustained achievement as a novelist, Donleavy presents a modern version of the eighteenth-century picaresque novel in the career of a rogue hero, set in Ireland. Two sequels would follow: *Leila* (1983) and *That Darcy, That Dancer, That Gentleman* (1990).

JOHN GREGORY DUNNE (b. 1932): *True Confessions.* The longtime California resident's first bestseller is a hard-boiled police novel written in the manner of Raymond Chandler. It is praised for both its humor and its sharply observed depiction of Los Angeles in the 1940s and Irish-Catholic family dynamics. Dunne collaborated with his wife, Joan Didion, on screenplays such as *Panic in Needle Park* (1971), *Play It as It Lays* (1972), and the adaptation of *True Confessions* (1981).

MARILYN FRENCH (b. 1929): *The Women's Room.* French's controversial bestseller tells a composite story of middle-class women betrayed by their men and their society. Some critics complain about the book's relentless accumulation of injustices, but the emotion of French's novel plainly appeals to a large segment of women readers. A New York City native, French received a grad-uate degree from Harvard and published a scholarly examination of James Joyce's *Ulysses* in 1976.

JUDITH GUEST (b. 1936): *Ordinary People.* This best-selling novel is a sensitive story of a suicidal adolescent and his confused parents. The book would be adapted into an Academy Award–winning film in 1980. The Detroit-born novelist's other books would include *Second Heaven* (1982), *The Mythic Family* (1988), and *Errands* (1997).

JAMES ALAN McPHERSON: *Elbow Room.* The Georgia-born writer becomes only the second African American to receive the Pulitzer Prize, and the first in fiction, for his second short story collection, preceded by *Hue and Cry* (1977). His stories, such as "Why I Like Country Music," "The Story of a Scar," and "A Sense of the Story," deal with ordinary people in desperate situations, reflecting black experience and universal human conditions.

TONI MORRISON: *Song of Solomon.* Morrison's break-through novel mixes naturalistic elements, myth, fantasy, and folklore as Milkman Dead tries to find a missing treasure and come to terms with his identity and black heritage. It is the first novel by an African American chosen as a Book-of-the-Month Club main selection since Richard Wright's *Native Son* (1940).

MARCIA MULLER (b. 1944): *Edwin of the Iron Shoes.* The Detroit-born crime writer introduces the character of Sharon McCone, the first contemporary female hard-boiled private eye, in the initial installment of a mystery series.

WALKER PERCY: *Lancelot.* Percy's darkest novel is a monologue of a New Orleans man who discovers that his wife has been unfaithful. He murders her and her lover, is confined to a mental institution, and is finally released to a lonely isolated future.

PHILIP ROTH: *The Professor of Desire.* Roth brings back literature professor David Kapesh from *The Breast* (1972) for a series of angst-inducing entanglements with women.

THOMAS SAVAGE: *I Hear My Sister Speak My Name.* Savage's greatest success is this semiautobiographical account of a woman's search for her birth mother, who had given her up for adoption as an infant. The story is narrated by the woman's discovered brother and describes her attempt to establish connections with her new family.

MARY LEE SETTLE: *Blood Ties.* Settle's novel about a group of expatriates living in Turkey is the surprise winner of the National Book Award.

LESLIE MARMON SILKO (b. 1948): *Ceremony.* Silko's first novel shows a dispossessed mixed-blood veteran of World War II who restores his own balance and that of the Indian community through the use of Native American myths and rituals. Reviewer Frank McShane declares Silko "the most accomplished Indian writer of her generation." Silko was raised on New Mexico's Laguna Pueblo Reservation and lived during the 1970s in a remote Inuit village in Alaska.

PETER TAYLOR: *In the Miro District and Other Stories.* Taylor's collection of prose and verse stories is widely praised for innovative techniques and masterful depiction of characters and situations. Included are the admired title story, about an elderly Civil War veteran's relationship with his grandson, "The Captain's Son," and "The Hand of Emmagene."

ANNE TYLER: *Earthly Possessions.* Tyler's novel depicts a woman, on the verge of leaving her husband, who is taken hostage by a bank robber. Together they form a kind of ad hoc family. Tyler would comment that the novel has been misunderstood as "another Unhappy Housewife Leaves Home book, which was the last thing in my mind."

ROBERT PENN WARREN: *A Place to Come To.* In Warren's final novel a sixty-year-old classics scholar from Alabama reflects on his life and times.

Literary Criticism and Scholarship

ANN DOUGLAS (b. 1942): *The Feminization of American Culture.* The Columbia English professor's study examines popular culture in nineteenth-century America and demonstrates how an alliance between women and the clergy fostered a sentimental society and gave birth to modern mass culture.

ROBERT PINSKY: *The Situation of Poetry.* Pinsky considers the modernist and Romantic roots of contemporary poetry.

ELAINE SHOWALTER (b. 1941): *A Literature of Their Own.* In writing one of the foundation texts of feminist scholarship, Showalter becomes one of the first literary scholars to identify a separate tradition of women's fiction in England. Showalter, a professor of English at Rutgers University, edited the anthology *Women's Liberation and Literature* (1971) and would publish "Toward a Feminist Politics" in 1979.

BARBARA SMITH (b. 1946): *Toward a Black Feminist Criticism.* Smith, a professor at the University of Massachusetts, is the first scholar to approach the study of black women writers and the fictional depiction of black women from a feminist perspective. She would edit *Home Girls: A Black Feminist Anthology* in 1983.

Nonfiction

WALTER JACKSON BATE: *Samuel Johnson.* Bate wins the National Book Award, the Pulitzer Prize, and the Nation Book Critics Circle Award for his biography, which joins Johnson's career, character, and work into an interpretive whole that stresses Johnson's modernity.

PHILIP CAPUTO (b. 1941): *A Rumor of War.* Caputo, a former Marine officer in Vietnam, recollects his experiences in an account praised by *New York Times Book Review* critic Peter Andrews as "the finest memoir of men at arms in our generation."

ALFRED D. CHANDLER JR. (b. 1918): *The Visible Hand: The Managerial Revolution in America.* The Harvard Business School professor's study of American economic history and the evolution of managerial practices in the 1840s wins the Bancroft Prize and the Pulitzer Prize and is considered one of the most influential works on the American corporation.

SARA DAVIDSON (b. 1943): *Loose Change: Three Women of the Sixties.* Davidson, a California-born journalist, reports on the formative college years and subsequent careers of three Berkeley women in a work that is described as "an astonishingly vivid social history of the Sixties." It becomes a bestseller and is adapted as a popular TV mini-series.

MICHAEL HERR (b. 1940): *Dispatches.* After reporting on the war in Vietnam for *Esquire* magazine in 1967 and 1968, Herr powerfully recasts his personal experiences into one of the best-regarded treatments of the war. Novelist Robert Stone calls it "the best personal journalism about war, any war, that any writer has ever accomplished."

DAVID McCULLOUGH (b. 1933): *The Path Between the Sea: The Creation of the Panama Canal.* Having written a narrative history on the building of the Brooklyn Bridge in *The Great Bridge* (1972), McCullough turns his attention to the monumental construction project of the Panama Canal in this National Book Award–winning history. Born in Pittsburgh, McCullough had been an editor and writer for *Time*, the U.S. Information Agency, and the American Heritage Publishing Company.

JOHN McPHEE (b. 1931): *Coming into the Country.* McPhee's depiction of Alaskan life establishes his reputation as one of America's finest nature and personal essay writers. Born in New Jersey and educated at Princeton, McPhee had been an editor for *Time* magazine and a staff writer for *The New Yorker.* His previous books included *Oranges* (1967), *The Pine Barrens* (1968), *The Curve of Binding Engergy* (1974), and *The Survival of the Bark Canoe* (1975).

S. J. PERELMAN: *Eastward, Ha!* The humorist's last collection before his death treats his final round-the-world trip. A posthumously published collection, *The Last Laugh* (1981), includes previously uncollected *New*

Yorker pieces and chapters from an unfinished autobiography.

CARL SAGAN (1934–1996): *The Dragons of Eden: Speculation on the Evolution of Human Intelligence.* The Cornell University astronomer gains his first bestseller with this popularization of scientific ideas of evolution. It would be followed by the equally popular *Broca's Brain: Reflections on the Romance of Science* (1979).

SUSAN SONTAG: *On Photography.* Sontag explores the social and aesthetic implications of photography in a series of essays diagnosing how the medium encourages an "acquisitive relation to the world" that promotes "emotional detachment." The writer's provocative inquiry into the nature of the art raises profound questions about morality and aestheticism.

W. A. SWANBERG: *Norman Thomas: The Last Idealist.* This National Book Award–winning biography tells the story of the American socialist once imprisoned by President Wilson. Swanberg presents Thomas's story in its full human scale, showing his subject's strengths and weaknesses.

DIANA TRILLING (1905–1996): *We Must March, My Darlings.* Trilling's essay collection grew out of her return to her alma mater, Radcliffe College, where she found a generation of students lacking the impulse toward social reform that had characterized her own college years. Even before being published, the book stirs up controversy concerning Trilling's negative references to Lillian Hellman's account of the McCarthy years.

RICHARD WRIGHT: *American Hunger.* This posthumously published memoir continues Wright's account of his life begun in *Black Boy* (1945), describing the period 1927 to 1937 in Chicago as he struggles as a writer and as a member of the Communist Party.

Poetry

A. R. AMMONS: *The Snow Poems.* Ammons's collection, a long sequence in the form of a poetic diary, details daily life and the poet's wrestling with his craft.

JOHN ASHBERY: *Houseboat Days.* This work contains some of Ashbery's best short poems, including "Street Musicians," "Wet Casements," "The Other Tradition," and "What Is Poetry."

ANTHONY HECHT: *Millions of Strange Shadows.* Hecht's third collection contains some of his finest work, including "Apprehensions," a long evocation of the poet's childhood.

ROBERT LOWELL: *Day by Day.* For his final collection, Lowell abandons the sonnet for free verse and returns to the confessional subjects of *Life Studies* in this "verse autobiography."

W. S. MERWIN: *The Compass Flower.* The first of a series of collections showing the influence of classical Chinese poetry, including *Feathers from a Hill* (1978) and *Finding the Islands* (1982).

HOWARD NEMEROV: *Collected Poems.* Nemerov wins both the National Book Award and the Pulitzer Prize for this retrospective volume, which prompts reviewer Victor Howes to declare that "Here he is with all his runes about him. Nemerov at full length, an important contemporary poet."

W. D. SNODGRASS: *The Fuhrer Bunker.* Snodgrass's collection is made up of dramatic monologues by the Nazi leadership, including Adolf Hitler, Albert Speer, Joseph Goebbels, Martin Bormann, and lesser figures, during the regime's final days. A play based on the work would be produced in 1982, and additional poems would be added in 1983 and 1985, with the complete cycle published in 1995.

GARY SOTO (b. 1952): *The Elements of San Joaquin.* The Fresno, California–born writer's first collection records the experience of a Chicano in California's Central Valley. It receives the United States Award of the International Poetry Forum and would be followed by *The Tale of Sunlight* (1978), *Where Sparrows Work Hard* (1981), and *Who Will Know Us?* (1990), collections that establish Soto's reputation as one of America's best Chicano writers. Some compare the bleakness of his poems to T. S. Eliot's *The Waste Land.*

GERALD STERN (b. 1925): *Lucky Life.* Stern's third collection, following *The Naming of the Beasts* (1973) and *Rejoicings* (1973), earns the Lamont Poetry Selection award and brings the poet his first national attention. Critics praise its portrayal of the ordinary details of American life, suffused with elements from the Pittsburgh-born poet's Jewish heritage.

DIANE WAKOSKI: *Waiting for the King of Spain.* The collection contains "To the Thin and Elegant Woman Who Resides Inside of Alix Nelson," one of her most characteristic and accomplished poems. *The Man Who Shook Hands* (1978) would follow; it includes an essay on music and poetry, which Wakoski has said provide a key "to where my philosophies and meditations are leading me."

C. K. WILLIAMS (b. 1936): *With Ignorance.* After two previous volumes of topical protest poems — *Lies* (1969) and *I Am a Bitter Name* (1972) — the New Jersey–born Williams discovers his distinctive voice and style in Whitmanesque narratives exploring the American sensibility. The poems employ such long lines that the book is published in a wide-page format.

JAMES WRIGHT: *To a Blossoming Pear Tree.* The final volume published in Wright's lifetime includes the frequently anthologized poems "With the Shell of a Hermit Crab" and "Beautiful Ohio."

1978
Drama and Theater

E. L. DOCTOROW: *Drinks Before Dinner*. Doctorow's attempt at drama is a purposely talky play of ideas, featuring a main character, who, at gunpoint, harangues a gathering on the collapse of modern civilization. Doctorow credits Gertrude Stein and Mao Zedong for inspiring the "rhythm of repetition" in the play's language.

CHRISTOPHER DURANG (b. 1949): *A History of the American Film*. Durang's first major success of the decade presents a parody of numerous films, illustrating the evolution of movie stereotypes in American culture. Durang was born in New Jersey and educated at Harvard and Yale.

IRA LEVIN: *Deathtrap*. Levin's popular thriller about a double-dealing mystery writer's relationship with his wife and a younger writer becomes the longest-running mystery play by an American playwright in Broadway history, with 1,809 performances.

SAM SHEPARD: *Buried Child*. Shepard continues his depiction of the American family in one of his most conventionally structured, naturalistic dramas, about a Midwestern farm family beset by incest and infanticide. The play wins the Pulitzer Prize.

LUIS VALDEZ (b. 1940): *Zoot Suit*. The first Hispanic American play to reach Broadway dramatizes gang conflict in Los Angeles during World War II. Valdez, who was a member of the San Francisco Mime Troupe in the 1960s, used bilingual performances to help César Chávez organize migrant workers and formed El Teatro Campesino (The Farmworkers' Theater), which inspired the formation of other Chicano theater groups.

LANFORD WILSON: *The Fifth of July*. The first of Wilson's plays treating the Talley family depicts the return home of a paraplegic Vietnam War veteran.

Fiction

ALICE ADAMS (1926–1999): *Listening to Billie*. Adams's well-received third novel, following *Careless Love* (1966) and *Families and Survivors* (1974), concerns a woman haunted by hearing Billie Holiday singing in the 1950s as she searches for a meaningful life. It would be followed by Adams's first story collection, *Beautiful Girls* (1979).

RAYMOND ANDREWS (1934–1991): *Appalachee Red*. Andrews's novel, which wins the first James Baldwin Prize for fiction, tells the story of a young black woman who has a child by a white man while her husband is in jail. The child, Appalachee Red, is sent north for his education, but he returns home to confront his father and his hometown. Critics praise Andrews's depiction of a small community of sharecroppers in rural Georgia who have to contend with interracial tensions. The Georgia-born writer's subsequent novels would be *Rosiebelle Lee Wildcat Tennessee* (1979) and *Baby Sweet's* (1983).

LAURIE COLWIN (1944–1992): *Happy All the Time*. After a well-received initial story collection, *Passion and Affect* (1974), and a first novel, *Shine On, Bright and Dangerous Object* (1975), Colwin, a New York City native, achieves her greatest critical and popular success with this "Manhattan pastoral," about the courtship dilemmas of two upper-class New York cousins. The work invites comparisons with Jane Austen, John Cheever, and John Updike. Colwin's third novel, *Family Happiness*, would appear in 1982, and a final story collection, *Another Marvelous Thing*, in 1986.

ERNEST J. GAINES: *In My Father's House*. A black minister and civil rights leader contends with the surprise appearance of his illegitimate son, who has returned to kill him for having wronged his mother.

MARY GORDON (b. 1949): *Final Payments*. Gordon's acclaimed debut novel treats a disillusioned Catholic woman who leaves home for the first time after spending eleven years caring for her invalid father. Gordon, born on Long Island, has specialized in depicting the experiences of Irish American Catholics.

JOHN IRVING (b. 1942): *The World According to Garp*. After three modestly successful novels — *Setting Free the Bears* (1968), *The Water-Method Man* (1972), and *The 158-Pound Marriage* (1974) — Irving breaks through with a fanciful tale about a writer murdered by a disapproving reader. The story interweaves the writer's characteristic fascinations with marital infidelity, Vienna, wrestling, and violent death. It sells over three million copies and establishes Irving in the front rank of literary novelists. Born in New Hampshire, Irving attended Phillips Exeter Academy, the model for the Steering School in *The World According to Garp*.

JAMES JONES: *Whistle*. Jones's final novel (completed by Willie Morris) is the final volume of the author's World War II trilogy. It concerns infantry soldiers in a Tennessee army hospital and how the war has crippled them physically and psychologically.

LARRY KRAMER (b. 1935): *Faggots*. Kramer's first novel about the gay community on New York's Fire Island receives a poor initial reception. However, when re-released in 1987, it would become a bestseller, hailed as a work of historic importance for its unsparingly honest portrayal of the gay community. Kramer had worked as a screenwriter and received an Academy Award nomination for his adaptation of D. H. Lawrence's *Women in Love* in 1969.

JUDITH KRANTZ (b. 1927): *Scruples.* The former fashion editor of *Good Housekeeping* produces one of the decade's biggest sellers, an escapist romance set in the world of fashion and the movie business. Its reliance on a popular formula of sex, wealth, beauty, and power keeps the book on the bestseller list for nearly a year and gains its author the biggest payment for paperback rights up to that time ($3,208,875) for her next book, *Princess Daisy* (1979).

THOMAS MCGUANE: *Panama.* Considered McGuane's most autobiographical work, the novel concerns a rock star who disintegrates because of his dissolute lifestyle. Reviewer Jonathan Yardley calls it "a drearily self-indulgent book, a contemplation of the price of celebrity that was, in point of fact, merely an exploitation of the author's new notoriety."

D'ARCY MCNICKLE: *Wind from an Enemy Sky.* McNickle's second and final adult novel treating misguided federal policy toward American Indians and how it affects the fictional Little Elk People is published posthumously. A collection of McNickle's short fiction, *The Hawk Is Hungry, and Other Stories,* would appear in 1992.

TIM O'BRIEN: *Going After Cacciato.* O'Brien wins the National Book Award for his second novel, which connects a Vietnam War soldier's combat experiences to his imagined pursuit of the deserter, Cacciato. The book is widely praised as one of the finest fictional treatments of the Vietnam experience.

JAMES PURDY: *Narrow Rooms.* One of Purdy's darkest and most graphic novels concerns a group of young men in a West Virginia community who destroy their lives because they are unable to come to terms with their desires for one another.

ISAAC BASHEVIS SINGER: *Shosha.* After more contemporary stories, Singer returns to ghetto life in Poland before World War II in this novel about a young journalist/budding novelist who chooses a quiet backward woman for his bride. Singer also publishes *A Young Man in Search of Love,* a memoir treating his struggles to become a writer.

SUSAN SONTAG: *I, etcetera.* A collection of stories depicting characters grappling with crises of conscience and identity.

DANIELLE STEEL (b. 1947): *The Promise.* Steel gains her first best-selling success establishing the formula of romantic complications among the rich and famous that would lead her to have by 1986 at least one of her books on the *New York Times* bestseller list for 225 consecutive

weeks. Other titles include *Changes* (1983), *Jewels* (1992), and *Malice* (1996).

GORE VIDAL: *Kalki.* Vidal's satirical novel tackles feminism and Eastern mysticism in a story about a Vietnam War veteran who proclaims himself the Hindu god Kalki, intent on destroying the world.

WILLIAM WHARTON (b. 1925): *Birdy.* One of the decade's surprise bestsellers is this first novel about a war victim who aspires to be a bird. The Philadelphia-born writer trained as a painter at UCLA. His other books would include *Dad* (1981), *A Midnight Clear* (1982), and *Pride* (1985).

EDMUND WHITE (b. 1940): *Nocturnes from the King of Naples.* After a well-received first novel, *Forgetting Elena* (1973), a social satire that can be read as a allegory of gay life, White's second novel deals explicitly with homosexuality as the narrator reviews his relationship with his lover.

HERMAN WOUK: *War and Remembrance.* Despite criticism for employing ludicrous plotting and cardboard characters, Wouk's sequel to *The Winds of War* (1971) is nominated for an American Book Award.

Literary Criticism and Scholarship

NINA BAYM (b. 1936): *Women's Fiction: A Guide to Novels by and About Women in America, 1820–1870.* Baym's study helps promote a reconception of the canon of nineteenth-century American literature. Born in New Jersey and educated at Cornell and Harvard, Baym has been a professor of English at the University of Illinois at Urbana-Champaign.

MALCOLM COWLEY: *And I Worked at the Writer's Trade.* Cowley surveys American literature in the twentieth century as well as his long and distinguished career as a critic and editor.

JOHN GARDNER: *On Moral Fiction.* Gardner's essay attacks contemporary literature's dearth of moral content. This involves him in a war of words with other writers and critics that would dominate the rest of his life. In Gardner's view, moral fiction "attempts to test human values, not for the purpose of preaching or peddling a particular ideology, but in a truly honest and open-minded effort to find out which best promotes human fulfillment."

WILLIAM H. GASS: *The World Within the Word.* This work collects Gass's literary essays on writers such as Samuel Beckett, Gertrude Stein, and Marcel Proust, as well as his reflections on topics such as suicide, art and order, and the grammar of sentences.

EDWARD W. SAID (1935–2003): *Orientalism.* Said, a Jerusalem-born professor of comparative literature at Columbia, examines European and American views of the Middle East, arguing that their negative stereotypes have been used to justify economic and political domination of the region. Despite objections to his conclusions by Islamic and Arabic specialists, the book becomes a standard text in courses on literary theory and cultural studies, praised by critic Scott Sherman as "among the most influential works of critical theory in the postwar period."

DIANA TRILLING: *Reviewing the Forties.* This is a selection of the reviews written during Trilling's years as book critic for the *Nation.* Elizabeth Janeway notes, "To the extent that America has an intellectual conscience, Diana Trilling is part of it."

EUDORA WELTY: *The Eye of the Story.* This selection from Welty's essays and reviews contains some of her most important statements about literature and her writing practices.

Nonfiction

NANCY CHODOROW (b. 1944): *The Reproduction of Mothering: Psychoanalysis and the Sociology of Gender.* Chodorow's groundbreaking study challenges the traditional view that women are biologically predisposed toward nurturing infants and explores the psychological basis of mothering. A trained psychoanalyst, Chodorow has taught sociology at the University of California at Santa Cruz and at Berkeley.

ELDRIDGE CLEAVER: *Soul on Fire.* Cleaver supplies his memoirs after returning from an eight-year exile during which he lived in Cuba, Algeria, and France to escape capture by the FBI. It recounts the former Black Panthers leader's disillusionment with radical politics and his embrace of evangelical Christianity. The religious conversion described in the book helps Cleaver win a plea-bargain with the government and renews his celebrity in the United States, where he would later run for Congress as an independent conservative.

MARY DALY (b. 1928): *Gyn/Ecology: The Metaethics of Radical Feminism.* Daly, a professor of theology at Boston College, declares patriarchy the primary cause of female oppression in many cultures and attempts to define a female understanding of theology. Part of that definition is an index of nearly two hundred new words Daly coins as a tool for reformulating language from a feminist perspective.

RICHARD BEALE DAVIS (1907–1981): *Intellectual Life in the Colonial South, 1585–1763.* Davis, a professor of English at the University of Tennessee, Knoxville, wins the National Book Award for his three-volume intellectual and literary history of the Southern colonists. He contends that they had as much, if not more, a part in shaping American culture as the New England colonists.

DON E. FEHRENBACHER (1920–1997): *The Dred Scott Case: Its Significance in American Law and Politics.* Fehrenbacher, a distinguished Lincoln scholar and authority on the Civil War, wins the Pulitzer Prize for what is considered the most thorough study of the Supreme Court decision that upheld slavery.

ALFRED KAZIN: *New York Jew.* Kazin traces literary and political history from 1939 into the 1970s, while also delivering a third installment of the critic's personal history. The book gives profiles of figures such as Ezra Pound, T. S. Eliot, Robert Frost, and Robert Lowell.

FRAN LEBOWITZ (b. 1951): *Metropolitan Life.* Lebowitz's collection of satirical essays becomes a bestseller and a critical success, owing to what reviewer Richard Locke calls Lebowitz's skillful evocation of "the 70's New York know-it-all fashion-magazine/artistic world." Lebowitz captures a unique moment in a unique place with a "firm didactic statement or a desperate Basic English sneer," a style that many find irresistible.

PETER MATTHIESSEN: *The Snow Leopard.* This winner of the National Book Award and the American Book Award is a memoir linking an account of the author's Himalayan trek with a spiritual autobiography in which he, in the words of one reviewer, "travels to the limits of the world and the inner limits of the self."

RICHARD M. NIXON: *RN: The Memoirs of Richard Nixon.* Like the man, the ex-president's account of his administration divides the critics. Some call it a fascinating self-portrait, others, a selective self-defense.

JOHN RECHY: *The Sexual Outlaw.* A documentary account of the gay underworld of Los Angeles and exhibitionist subculture.

ARTHUR M. SCHLESINGER JR.: *Robert Kennedy and His Times.* Schlesinger's admittedly partisan biography is a bestseller and earns the writer his second National Book Award.

SUSAN SONTAG: *Illness as Metaphor.* Written in the wake of the author's own treatment for cancer, the book aims to demystify the disease by considering the metaphors commonly employed to describe illness, which serve, in the author's view, only to distort reality. Sontag would continue her "reading" of illness in *AIDS and Its Metaphors* (1989).

BARBARA TUCHMAN: *A Distant Mirror.* Tuchman's historical work about Europe in the fourteenth century draws parallels with the modern world. Tuchman's accessible style helps make the book a bestseller.

ANTHONY F. C. WALLACE (b. 1923): *Rockdale: The Growth of an American Village in the Early Industrial Revolution.* Wallace, a professor of anthropology, wins the Bancroft Prize for his detailed reconstruction of life in a Pennsylvania mill town during the first half of the nineteenth century. Reviewer Alan Trachtenberg calls it "a powerful interpretive reading that reconceives the very basis for the study of American industrialization."

GARRY WILLS (b. 1934): *Inventing America: Jefferson's Declaration of Independence.* Wills, a professor of humanities at Johns Hopkins University, provides a close reading and interpretation of the document that established crucial assumptions about American ideals and their origin.

EDWARD O. WILSON (b. 1929): *On Human Nature.* The Harvard entomologist who helped pioneer the field of sociobiology, contending in *Sociobiology: The New Synthesis* (1975) that all behavior is genetically based, wins the Pulitzer Prize for this study, which tries to reconcile humanism and science.

Poetry

NIKKI GIOVANNI: *Cotton Candy on a Rainy Day.* Giovanni's introspective collection treats loneliness and isolation and the aftermath of the loss of 1960s idealism.

ROBERT HAYDEN: *American Journal.* Hayden's final collection continues his exploration of the achievements of African Americans, with poems about Phillis Wheatley, Paul Laurence Dunbar, and Matthew Hensen, the black explorer who accompanied Robert Peary to the North Pole.

JOHN HOLLANDER: *Spectral Emanations: New and Selected Poems.* The title poem of this collection is a demanding sequence concerning the attempt to combine lessons of color into the "white light of truth." Hollander would offer similar exploratory meditations in his next collection, *Blue Wine and Other Poems* (1979).

JANE KENYON (1947–1995): *From Room to Room.* Kenyon's impressive debut collection is a poetic diary of a young wife's relationship with her new husband. The poems evoke comparisons with Robert Frost, Emily Dickinson, and Anne Sexton. Before her early death, Kenyon would solidify her reputation with three more poetry collections, *The Little Boat* (1986), *Let Evening Come* (1990), and *Constance* (1993).

AUDRE LORDE: *The Black Unicorn.* Considered by many Lorde's masterpiece, the volume contains a sequence surveying the black diaspora.

JAMES MERRILL: *Mirabell: Books of Number.* Merrill's National Book Award–winning collection continues the poetic narrative begun two years earlier in "The Book of Ephraim," a poem described as "Merrill's supreme fiction, a self-mythologizing within an epic program."

ADRIENNE RICH: *The Dream of a Common Language.* The collection affirms women's power and place in history in poems treating various historical figures, including Marie Curie and the mountaineer Elvira Shatayev.

L. E. SISSMAN (1928–1976): *Hello, Darkness.* Sissman's posthumously published collected works win the National Book Critics Circle Award and prompt a recognition of the poet's masterful use of traditional poetic forms. The work includes his original explorations of ordinary experience and his moving meditations on his own impending death from Hodgkin's disease.

MAY SWENSON: *New and Selected Things Taking Place.* The poems in this collection are markedly more introspective, with a more personal voice emerging from the poet's characteristic verbal display.

ROBERT PENN WARREN: *Now and Then: Poems, 1976–1978.* Warren wins his third Pulitzer Prize for this collection treating his Kentucky boyhood and later experiences.

1979
Drama and Theater

CHRISTOPHER DURANG: *Sister Mary Ignatius Explains It All for You.* Durang gains a popular success in this witty satire on the hypocrisies of the Catholic Church as an elderly nun offers her peculiar interpretation of church dogma.

JOHN GUARE: *Bosoms and Neglect.* Guare explores the relationship between a mother and her son in this witty, darkly comic psychoanalytic satire. It is the sparest and most naturalistic of Guare's full-length plays and manages only four performances on Broadway. However, when restaged in Boston, it is hailed as "brilliant" and too "fiercely uncompromising" for Broadway.

ARTHUR KOPIT: *Wings.* Originally written as a radio play and first produced at the Yale Repertory Theatre in 1978, Kopit's drama about the recovery of a stroke victim employs innovative staging techniques to replicate the healing process.

BERNARD POMERANCE (b. 1940): *The Elephant Man.* The New York City–born playwright who immigrated to London in the 1970s achieves his greatest success with this play based on the true story of Englishman John Merrick, afflicted with a deforming genetic disorder.

STEPHEN SONDHEIM: *Sweeney Todd.* Sondheim's controversial musical, derived from an 1847 melodrama about a London barber who kills his customers and converts them into pie ingredients, divides critics because of its sordid and violent subject matter. However, it wins the New York Drama Critics Circle Award and serveral Tony Awards; it would subsequently enter the opera repertoire.

ERNEST THOMPSON (b. 1949): *On Golden Pond.* Thompson's first full-length play dramatizes crotchety former college professor Norman Thayer's coming to terms with his mortality and his recognition of the power of love and family at the Thayers' summer cottage. Thompson wins the Best Play Award from the Broadway Drama Guild and would later receive an Academy Award for his screenplay of the popular 1981 film adaptation. The Vermont-born Thompson had been an actor and screenwriter. His play *The West Side Waltz* would reach Broadway in 1981.

MICHAEL WELLER: *Loose Ends.* Serving as a kind of 1970s complement to *Moonchildren* (1972), his drama about the 1960s, Weller treats former youthful idealists who must adjust to the demands of marriage, careers, and families. The play captures with skill the changing zeitgeist.

TENNESSEE WILLIAMS: *A Lovely Sunday for Crève Coeur.* Williams's drama is set in St. Louis during the Depression and concerns a spinster teacher's reaction to the engagement of the man with whom she has been conducting a flirtation. Combining slapstick comedy and pathos, as well as recycling old themes, the play lasts less than a month in its New York run.

LANFORD WILSON: *Talley's Folly.* The second of the playwright's dramas about the Talley family treats the courtship of Sally Talley by a Jewish accountant. Like other plays in the series, it brilliantly conflates the conflicts in individuals' lives with family histories and the social manners and mores of the times. The play wins the Pulitzer Prize and would also claim the New York Drama Critics Circle Award after transferring from off-Broadway to Broadway in 1980.

Fiction

JAMES BALDWIN: *Just Above My Head.* Baldwin's final novel treats a homosexual gospel singer from Harlem and his family relationships. The book displays a calmer, more accepting perspective, and Baldwin, following publication, would remark that he had come "full circle," that "From *Go Tell It on the Mountain* to *Just Above My Head* sums up something of my experience . . . that sets me free to go someplace else".

JOHN BARTH: *Letters.* Barth's experiment in epistolary fiction traces the history of the novel while at the same time recapitulating his own literary career by revisiting characters from his previous novels. The final letter in the volume is Barth's address to the reader, heralding the more naturalistic style of his subsequent novels.

DONALD BARTHELME: *Great Days.* Several of the stories in this collection, including the title work (adapted as a play in 1983), "The Crisis," "The Apology," and "The New Music," are composed entirely of undifferentiated dialogue.

FREDERICK BUECHNER: *The Book of Bebb.* Buechner's tetralogy brings together *Lion Country* (1971), *Open Heart* (1972), *Love Feast* (1974), and *Treasure Hunt* (1977), chronicling the activities of Leo Bebb, former Bible salesman, founder of the Church of Holy Love, Inc., and president of the Gospel Faith College, a religious diploma mill. Many believe Buechner's comic satire on the business of religion in America to be his finest work.

OCTAVIA E. BUTLER (b. 1947): *Kindred.* The California writer's most widely read fantasy novel concerns a contemporary African American woman who is transported to antebellum Maryland, contrasting contemporary racial attitudes with those held during slavery.

JOHN CHEEVER: *The Stories of John Cheever.* A comprehensive collection of one of the century's masters of the short story. Praised by Joan Didion and others, Cheever's stories explore the gap between his characters' expectations and the reality of their lives. He sees absurdity in his characters and in everyday life, yet he never loses respect or affection for them or their predicaments.

STANLEY ELKIN: *The Living End.* Elkin's fantasy triptych connects three versions of the afterlife. Elkin's greatest commercial success as well as his most controversial work, it unsettles many readers' beliefs about God, heaven, and hell.

JIM HARRISON (b. 1937): *Legends of the Fall.* Harrison, a Michigan-born poet and novelist, receives his first major popular success and critical acclaim for this collection of novellas, described by reviewer Jerome Klinkowitz as "three short novels about revenge, redemption, and sorrow." The title work, about a Montana farmer who goes mad after his brother is killed in World War I, would be adapted as a film in 1995. His other novels include *Warlock* (1981), *Dalva* (1988), and *The Road Home* (1998).

JOHN HAWKES: *The Passion Artist.* Having admitted to being "tired of being called America's best unknown writer," Hawkes makes a bid for a wider readership by reducing his customary demands on his readers. The story concerns protagonist Konrad Vost's relationships with various women.

JOSEPH HELLER: *Good as Gold.* Heller follows the unrelentingly depressing *Something Happened* with a freewheeling, and often belabored, comedy that combines a Philip Roth–like Jewish family farce with a satire on academic life and contemporary politics.

JOHN KNOWLES: *A Vein of Riches.* In a narrative and stylistic departure, Knowles produces a novel set in his native West Virginia in the early years of the twentieth century to depict the corrupting influences of capitalism.

NORMAN MAILER: *The Executioner's Song.* Mailer's Pulitzer Prize–winning "true-life" novel about Gary Gilmore, the first person to be executed (in 1977) in the United States for more than a decade, shows the author skillfully mining the territory of the "nonfiction novel" and the contemporary American cultural landscape.

BERNARD MALAMUD: *Dubin's Lives.* Malamud depicts the life of a prominent American biographer caught between his passion and his honesty in a love affair with a younger woman. Malamud calls the book his "attempt at bigness, at summing up what he . . . learned over the long haul."

MARY McCARTHY: *Cannibals and Missionaries.* In one of the first novels to treat modern terrorism, McCarthy depicts a group of prominent liberals and art collectors who fly to Iran and become hostages of the PLO.

MARY MORRIS (b. 1947): *Vanishing Animals and Other Stories.* This volume, winner of the Rome Prize in Literature, concentrates on the childhood and adolescent reminiscences of its characters. Anne Tyler, among others, expresses admiration for Morris's exploration of the ambiguous relationships among her characters and the author's tactful, precise use of language. The Chicago-born writer's other books include the novels *Crossroads* (1983), *The Waiting Room* (1989), and *A Mother's Love* (1993).

JAYNE ANNE PHILLIPS (b. 1952): *Black Tickets.* The West Virginia–born writer's third story collection, preceded by *Sweethearts* (1976) and *Counting* (1978), establishes her as one of the finest chroniclers of the generation that came of age in the 1970s. A fourth collection, *Fast Lanes*, would appear in 1984.

MARY ROBISON (b. 1949): *Days.* Robison's first story collection treating the mundane lives of unexceptional characters in a stripped-down, deadpan style connects her with the so-called minimalist school of writers, which includes Ann Beattie and Raymond Carver. It would be followed by two collections — *An Amateur's Guide to the Night* (1983) and *Believe Them* (1988) — and the novels *Oh!* (1981) and *Subtraction* (1991). Born in Washington, D.C., Robison was a student of writer John Barth at Johns Hopkins.

PHILIP ROTH: *The Ghost Writer.* Roth's novel treats writer Nathan Zuckerman's relationship with a famous Jewish writer and his alleged affair with a younger woman whom Zuckerman imagines to be Anne Frank. Subsequent Zuckerman novels would follow — *Zuckerman Unbound* (1981) and *The Anatomy Lesson* (1983) — collected with *The Ghostwriter* and an epilogue, "The Prague Orgy," as *Zuckerman Bound* (1985).

GILBERT SORRENTINO (b. 1929): *Mulligan Stew.* A tour de force that is, according to John Leonard, "literally a synthesis of almost everything Sorrentino had read and written in the past twenty-five years," Sorrentino's comic novel takes the form of a literary thriller written by a pretentious, untalented writer whose characters rebel and take their revenge. The Brooklyn-born writer's other books include *Steelwork* (1970), *Imaginative Qualities of Actual Things* (1971), and *Aberrations of Starlight* (1980).

SCOTT SPENCER (b. 1945): *Endless Love.* Spencer's third novel treating a teenager's obsessive sexual relationship gains its author both critical acclaim and popularity. His subsequent novels include *Waking the Dead* (1986), *Secret Anniversaries* (1990), and *Men in Black* (1995).

WALLACE STEGNER: *Recapitulations.* Stegner returns to the character of Bruce Mason from *The Big Rock Candy Mountain*, showing him as a former American diplomat returning to the Utah of his childhood to face his past.

WILLIAM STYRON: *Sophie's Choice.* Styron draws praise and criticism for his novel about a young writer's involvement with a damaged concentration camp survivor. Connecting the Holocaust with slavery in America, Styron is both accused of misappropriating a subject for fictional effect and applauded for being one of the first American writers to deal with the moral and psychological consequences of the Holocaust.

JOHN UPDIKE: *Problems and Other Stories* and *Too Far to Go.* The first of Updike's 1978 story collections treats various adversities of middle age; the second gathers the stories dealing with the marital relationship between Joan and Richard Maple, Updike's representative American couple. Updike also publishes *The Coup*, a freewheeling satire that concerns government mismanagement in the fictional African nation of Kush, as well as America's compulsion to dispense its largesse.

KURT VONNEGUT JR.: *Jailbird.* Vonnegut covers the Watergate scandal in this satirical novel about a fictional conspirator trying to rebuild his life.

JAMES WELCH: *The Death of Jim Loney.* Welch's second novel is about the self-destruction of an alienated, alcoholic mixed-blood protagonist in Montana, who is unable to exist comfortably in either the white or the Indian world.

Literary Criticism and Scholarship

SANDRA M. GILBERT (b. 1936) **AND SUSAN GUBAR** (b. 1944): *The Madwoman in the Attic.* The scholars' first collaboration is a groundbreaking work of feminist criticism that examines the methods nineteenth-century women writers employed to cope with restrictions imposed by a male-dominated society. Gilbert, an English professor at the University of California at Davis, and Gubar, a professor of English at Indiana University, would continue their collaboration with *The Norton Anthology of Literature by Women* (1985) and *No Man's Land: The Place of the Woman Writer in the Twentieth Century* (1988–1994).

Nonfiction

LAUREN BACALL (b. 1924): *Lauren Bacall: By Myself.* The actress (born Betty Joan Perske) wins the National Book Award for this best-selling autobiography, which deals intimately with her relationship with Humphrey Bogart and her years since his death.

ROBERT DALLEK (b. 1934): *Franklin D. Roosevelt and American Foreign Policy, 1932–1945.* Dallek's Bancroft Prize–winning study is hailed by reviewer Basil Rauch as "much the most detailed, thoughtful, and objective study of Roosevelt as a maker of foreign policy that we are likely to have in our time." The historian would subsequently publish biographies of Lyndon Johnson (*The Lone Star Rising*, 1991) and John F. Kennedy (*An Unfinished Life*, 2003).

JOAN DIDION: *The White Album.* This essay collection devoted to the author's native California takes its name from the title of the popular Beatles album. One track on the album, "Helter Skelter," provides a theme for the demonic La Bianca–Tate murders in Los Angeles in 1969, which Didion in turn uses as a kind of leitmotif in the collection.

DAVID HALBERSTAM: *The Powers That Be.* The second volume of a trio of books dealing with power in America, which had begun with *The Best and the Brightest* and continued with *The Reckoning* (1986), on the auto industry, examines the ways in which media giants such as CBS, the *Washington Post, Time,* and the *Los Angeles Times* shape American politics and society.

DOUGLAS R. HOFSTADTER (b. 1945): *Gödel, Escher, Bach: An Eternal Golden Braid.* The professor of computer science at Indiana University explores human consciousness and the connections among mathematician Kurt Gödel's Incomplete Theorem, the art of M. C. Escher, and the music of Johann Sebastian Bach. Despite its complex subject, it wins the Pulitzer Prize and sells more than 100,000 copies in the year following its publication.

ZORA NEALE HURSTON: *I Love Myself When I Am Laughing, and Then Again When I Am Looking Mean and Impressive.* This collection of selections from Hurston's autobiographical works, folklore, essays, and stories, edited by Alice Walker, stimulates interest in Hurston and her works.

HENRY A. KISSINGER (b. 1923): *The White House Years.* Kissinger wins the National Book Award for his account of his various roles in the Nixon administration. It would be followed by *Years of Upheaval* (1982), treating the last years of the Nixon presidency, and *Years of Renewal* (1994), describing the Ford administration.

CHRISTOPHER LASCH (1932–1994): *The Culture of Narcissism: American Life in an Age of Diminishing Expectations.* Lasch, a professor of history at the University of Rochester, considers the family, education, sex and mores, and sports to present a thesis that contemporary Americans have retreated into a disengaged self-absorption. Winner of the American Book Award, the book would be followed by a sequel applying his theories, *The Minimal Self* (1984).

LEON F. LITWACK (b. 1929): *Been in the Storm So Long.* The University of Wisconsin history professor's study of the end of slavery in the American South wins both the Pulitzer Prize and the National Book Award. It is the first comprehensive history of slavery that makes use of the thousands of slave narratives collected by interviewers from the Federal Writers Project during the New Deal.

CATHARINE A. MACKINNON (b. 1946): *Sexual Harassment of Working Women.* MacKinnon, a legal scholar and law professor, breaks new legal ground by arguing that sexual harassment of women in the workplace is a violation of existing civil rights statutes.

EDMUND MORRIS (b. 1940): *The Rise of Theodore Roosevelt.* Morris, who was born in Kenya and was an advertising copywriter in London before coming to the United States in 1968, receives both the Pulitzer Prize and the National Book Award for the first volume of his masterful biography (*Theodore Rex* would appear in 2001). The book impresses Ronald Reagan so much that he grants Morris unprecedented access, which Morris would use to produce *Dutch: A Memoir of Ronald Reagan* (1999).

ADRIENNE RICH: *On Lies, Secrets, and Silence: Selected Prose, 1966–1978.* This work collects Rich's essays and speeches dealing with feminism and literature. It includes "Vesuvius at Home: The Poetry of Emily Dickinson" and "When We Dead Awaken," urging female self-determination.

TELFORD TAYLOR (1908–1998): *Munich: The Price of Peace.* Drawn from the author's experiences as chief prosecution counsel at the Nuremberg war crimes trials, the book analyzes the diplomatic failure of the Munich Conference, where Adolf Hitler and British prime minister Neville Chamberlain met in 1938. The book is described as a "masterful synthesis and an original contribution" and wins the National Book Critics Circle Award.

TOM WOLFE: *The Right Stuff.* Wolfe's biggest-selling nonfiction book covers the background, selection, and training of the first seven U.S. astronauts and the fraternity of test pilots. The book makes a cultural hero out of Chuck Yeager, the first pilot to break the sound barrier, and adds the phrases *the right stuff* and *pushing the envelope* to the popular lexicon.

DONALD E. WORSTER (b. 1941): *Dust Bowl.* Worster, a professor of American studies at the University of Hawaii, wins the Bancroft Prize for his study, which identifies aggressive capitalistic greed as the root cause of the problems faced by Plains farmers during the 1930s.

Poetry

JOHN ASHBERY: *As We Know.* In one of Ashbery's most experimental collections, the verse alternates between several two-line poems and the long poem "Litany," printed in double columns and "meant to be read as simultaneous but independent monologues."

ROBERT BLY: *This Tree Will Be There for a Thousand Years.* Bly returns to the pastoral scene of his first collection, *Silence in the Snowy Fields* (1963), in a collection of meditations on the duality of consciousness: the poet's consciousness, "which is insecure, anxious, massive, earth bound, persistent, cunning, hopeful; and a second consciousness which is none of these things."

JAMES DICKEY: *The Strength of Fields.* The title work is written for and delivered at President Jimmy Carter's inaugural. It and other poems in the collection feature a renewed faith in humanity and an acceptance of pain and death.

ANTHONY HECHT: *The Venetian Vespers.* Hecht's most ambitious poem is the title work of this collection, a long meditation of an American who has come to Venice to reassess his life and times.

DONALD JUSTICE (b. 1924): *Selected Poems.* The Florida-born poet wins the Pulitzer Prize for this collection, made up of works from this three previous collections — *The Summer Anniversaries* (1961), *Night Light* (1967), and *Departures* (1973) — along with new and previously uncollected works.

PHILIP LEVINE: *Seven Years from Somewhere* and *Ashes.* Levine's two collections show a shift in subject and method from portraits and narratives to lyrical retrospectives on the poet's early life, evident in poems such as "Here and Now" and "The Life Ahead." *Ashes* wins the National Book Award.

ROBERT PINSKY: *An Explanation of America.* Pinsky's second volume is a book-length poem, which ranges over the history of America. Critic Michael Hamburger remarks that it "seems to defy not only all the dominant trends in contemporary poetry but all the dominant notions — both American and non-American — of what is expected of an American poet."

TIMOTHY STEELE (b. 1948): *Uncertainties and Rest.* Steele's first collection shows his use of traditional meter and rhyme, which will establish his reputation as one of the leading proponents of what critics label the New Formalism. The Vermont-born poet's other books would include *Sapphics Against Anger and Other Poems* (1986), *Sapphics and Uncertainties: Poems, 1970–1986* (1995), and *Missing Measures: Modern Poetry and the Revolt Against Meter* (1990).

LOUIS ZUKOFSKY: *A.* The great poem Zukofsky had started in 1927 appears in its final form posthumously. Hugh Kenner calls it "the most hermetic poem in the language, which they will still be elucidating in the 22nd century." Ranging widely over personal and historical events, many of the poem's sections are regarded as masterpieces.

1980
Drama and Theater

CHARLES FULLER: *Zooman and the Sign.* Fuller wins the Obie Award for best playwright for this Negro Ensemble Company production exploring community reaction when a black teenager accidentally kills a black girl.

DAVID HENRY HWANG (b. 1957): *FOB.* Hwang's Obie Award–winning first play, the title of which stands for "fresh off the boat," is about a young Chinese immigrant's encounter with two Chinese American students; together they explore the cost of assimilation. Hwang is the son of Chinese immigrants who was educated at Stanford and Yale Drama School.

WILLIAM MASTROSIMONE (b. 1947): *The Woolgatherers.* The New Jersey–born playwright's first produced work explores the relationship between a truck driver and a manipulative salesgirl who collects wool sweaters as trophies from her various lovers.

MICHAEL MCCLURE: *Josephine the Mouse Singer.* McClure wins an Obie Award for this adaptation of a story by Franz Kafka, in which all the characters are mice. The title character defends artistic freedom in modern society.

MARK MEDOFF: *Children of a Lesser God.* Medoff questions assumptions about disabilities and communication in this drama about a speech therapist's relationship with a deaf woman who refuses to learn to read lips or try to speak. The couple fall in love and marry, but the relationship falls apart when they are unable to resolve the issues that divide them. As reviewer Jack Kroll observes, the play's major theme is that "we are all hard of hearing."

ARTHUR MILLER: *The American Clock.* Set in Miller's familiar territory of 1930s Depression-era America, the play features documentary-style montages and vignettes that are meant to capture the spirit of the times in much the same way that Studs Terkel did in *Hard Times.* The play has no single plot line but rather is a collage of scenes, reminiscent of John Dos Passos's *U.S.A.*

SAM SHEPARD: *True West.* Set in the contemporary West, Shepard's play concerns two brothers — one a professional screenwriter and the other a scruffy drifter/cowboy. The latter proves to have the greater imagination and energy as the two wrangle over an improbable cliché-ridden screenplay. The plot becomes as much about their conflicts and the desire to get ahead as it is about the ostensible story they are developing.

Fiction

WALTER ABISH: *How German Is It.* Abish's novel about an American writer's visit to the "New Germany" receives the PEN/Faulkner Award and prompts recognition for Abish as a significant contemporary fiction writer.

TONI CADE BAMBARA: *The Salt Eaters.* This novel focuses on an African American activist who attempts suicide out of frustration over the seeming futility of creating consensus in the black community.

ANN BEATTIE: *Falling in Place.* This contemporary novel of manners combines two love stories, that of John Knapp and his mistress, Nina, and that of Cynthia Forrest and her lover, Peter Spangle. The events occur during the summer of 1978, when the *Skylab* space station is falling to earth, making the characters feel fragile. Critics admire Beattie's careful craftsmanship and her profound understanding of her characters. The novel would be followed by *Love Always* (1985), a satire on show business and publishing, and *Picturing Will* (1989), a psychological portrait of parenthood.

THOMAS BERGER: *Neighbors.* Berger's novel is about Earl Keese, who lives on a dead-end street and feels he has also reached an impasse. Two new neighbors, Harry and Romana, are free spirits who destroy Earl's stasis. Critics cite the novel as a fine example of Berger's wordplay and energizing language.

KAY BOYLE: *Fifty Stories.* This collection of short fiction written over Boyle's forty-year career helps establish her reputation as one of the modern masters of the short story.

T. CORAGHESSAN BOYLE (b. 1948): *Water Music.* Boyle's first book announces a writer of great promise. His novel

BESTSELLERS, 1980–1989

Fiction

1980
1. *The Covenant* by James A. Michener
2. *The Bourne Identity* by Robert Ludlum
3. *Rage of Angels* by Sidney Sheldon
4. *Princess Daisy* by Judith Krantz
5. *Firestarter* by Stephen King
6. *The Key to Rebecca* by Ken Follett
7. *Random Winds* by Belva Plain
8. *The Devil's Alternative* by Frederick Forsyth
9. *The Fifth Horseman* by Larry Collins and Dominique Lapierre
10. *The Spike* by Arnaud de Borchgrave and Robert Moss

1981
1. *Noble House* by James Clavell
2. *The Hotel New Hampshire* by John Irving
3. *Cujo* by Stephen King
4. *An Indecent Obsession* by Colleen McCullough
5. *Gorky Park* by Martin Cruz Smith
6. *Masquerade* by Kit Williams
7. *Goodbye, Janette* by Harold Robbins
8. *The Third Deadly Sin* by Lawrence Sanders
9. *The Glitter Dome* by Joseph Wambaugh
10. *No Time for Tears* by Cynthia Freeman

1982
1. *E.T. the Extra-Terrestrial Storybook* by William Kotzwinkle
2. *Space* by James A. Michener
3. *The Parsifal Mosaic* by Robert Ludlum
4. *Master of the Game* by Sidney Sheldon

5. *Mistral's Daughter* by Judith Krantz
6. *The Valley of Horses* by Jean M. Auel
7. *Different Seasons* by Stephen King
8. *North and South* by John Jakes
9. *2010: Odyssey Two* by Arthur C. Clarke
10. *The Man from St. Petersburg* by Ken Follett

1983
1. *Return of the Jedi Storybook* adapted by Joan D. Vinge
2. *Poland* by James A. Michener
3. *Pet Sematary* by Stephen King
4. *The Little Drummer Girl* by John Le Carré
5. *Christine* by Stephen King
6. *Changes* by Danielle Steel
7. *The Name of the Rose* by Umberto Eco
8. *White Gold Wielder: Book Three of the Second Chronicles of Thomas Covenant* by Stephen R. Donaldson
9. *Hollywood Wives* by Jackie Collins
10. *The Lonesome Gods* by Louis L'Amour

1984
1. *The Talisman* by Stephen King and Peter Straub
2. *The Aquitaine Progression* by Robert Ludlum
3. *The Sicilian* by Mario Puzo
4. *Love and War* by John Jakes
5. *The Butter Battle Book* by Dr. Seuss
6. *. . . And Ladies of the Club* by Helen Hooven Santmyer
7. *The Fourth Protocol* by Frederick Forsyth
8. *Full Circle* by Danielle Steel
9. *The Life and Hard Times of Heidi Abramowitz* by Joan Rivers
10. *Lincoln: A Novel* by Gore Vidal

tells the story of Scottish explorer Mungo Park and a London criminal, Ned Rise, who converge on each other in Africa. Critics are so impressed with the verve and black humor of this novel that they compare it with contemporary classics such as *The Sot-Weed Factor* and *Little Big Man*. Born in Peekskill, New York, Boyle earned a Ph.D. from the University of Iowa and published his first story collection, *Descent of Man*, in 1979.

TRUMAN CAPOTE: *Music for Chameleons.* This collection includes short stories, a true murder tale, recollections of the author's childhood, and "Conversation Portraits" describing time spent with Marilyn Monroe and a New York City cleaning woman.

PHILIP CAPUTO: *Horn of Africa.* Caputo's first novel treats the civil war in Ethiopia, as a trio of American mercenaries attempt to deliver weapons to Muslim rebels in the desert. Caputo would continue his study of war in *DelCorso's Gallery* (1983), set in Vietnam and Lebanon, and *Indian Country* (1987), about troubled Vietnam War veterans.

E. L. DOCTOROW: *Loon Lake.* Set in the 1930s, this novel traces the journeys of a young man during the Great Depression. He leaves Paterson, New Jersey, to seek his fortune and finds himself entrapped in the world of Loon Lake, a cold and remote setting in the Adirondack Mountains, where he confronts the tyranny of wealth and power. The book is thus a vehicle for Doctorow's indictments of American capitalism.

ANDRE DUBUS: *Finding a Girl in America.* Dubus's third collection contains his O. Henry Award–winning story "The Pitcher" as well as "The Killings" and the title work, part of the Linhart-Allison trilogy. It would be followed by *The Times Are Never So Bad* (1983) and *Voices from the Moon* (1984).

MARILYN FRENCH: *The Bleeding Heart.* The novel centers on Dolores, a divorced feminist, and Victor, a married executive, whose illicit relationship reveals much about themselves and the society they live in. Dolores realizes how much women are expected to bear suffering. Victor realizes that he is the one who is expected to express anger and wield power. Although it does not receive the accolades equal to those greeting *The Women's Room*, it furthers French's reputation as a feminist novelist.

BESTSELLERS, 1980–1989

1985
1. *The Mammoth Hunters* by Jean M. Auel
2. *Texas* by James A. Michener
3. *Lake Wobegon Days* by Garrison Keillor
4. *If Tomorrow Comes* by Sidney Sheldon
5. *Skeleton Crew* by Stephen King
6. *Secrets* by Danielle Steel
7. *Contact* by Carl Sagan
8. *Lucky* by Jackie Collins
9. *Family Album* by Danielle Steel
10. *Jubal Sackett* by Louis L'Amour

1986
1. *It* by Stephen King
2. *Red Storm Rising* by Tom Clancy
3. *Whirlwind* by James Clavell
4. *The Bourne Supremacy* by Robert Ludlum
5. *Hollywood Husbands* by Jackie Collins
6. *Wanderlust* by Danielle Steel
7. *I'll Take Manhattan* by Judith Krantz
8. *Last of the Breed* by Louis L'Amour
9. *The Prince of Tides* by Pat Conroy
10. *A Perfect Spy* by John Le Carré

1987
1. *The Tommyknockers* by Stephen King
2. *Patriot Games* by Tom Clancy
3. *Kaleidoscope* by Danielle Steel
4. *Misery* by Stephen King
5. *Leaving Home: A Collection of Lake Wobegon Stories* by Garrison Keillor

6. *Windmills of the Gods* by Sidney Sheldon
7. *Presumed Innocent* by Scott Turow
8. *Fine Things* by Danielle Steele
9. *Heaven and Hell* by John Jakes
10. *The Eyes of the Dragon* by Stephen King

1988
1. *The Cardinal of the Kremlin* by Tom Clancy
2. *The Sands of Time* by Sidney Sheldon
3. *Zoya* by Danielle Steel
4. *The Icarus Agenda* by Robert Ludlum
5. *Alaska* by James A. Michener
6. *Till We Meet Again* by Judith Krantz
7. *The Queen of the Damned* by Anne Rice
8. *To Be the Best* by Barbara Taylor Bradford
9. *One: A Novel* by Richard Bach
10. *Mitla Pass* by Leon Uris

1989
1. *Clear and Present Danger* by Tom Clancy
2. *The Dark Half* by Stephen King
3. *Daddy* by Danielle Steel
4. *Star* by Danielle Steel
5. *Caribbean* by James A. Michener
6. *The Satanic Verses* by Salman Rushdie
7. *The Russia House* by John Le Carré
8. *The Pillars of the Earth* by Ken Follet
9. *California Gold* by John Jakes
10. *While My Pretty One Sleeps* by Mary Higgins Clark

JOHN GARDNER: *Freddy's Book.* This work contains a novel-within-a-novel, a historical tale set in sixteenth-century Sweden. Reviews are mixed. Some critics find it good, reflexive fun in the manner of John Barth and Vladimir Nabokov; others consider it fiction "too much in the service of ideas."

HERBERT GOLD: *He/She.* This novel is about a marriage breakup and the difference between male and female perceptions of the world. Critics admire Gold's sympathetic portrait of a woman who does not love her husband and tries to face that fact squarely. Each phase of this couple's estrangement is charted with perception and humor—a hallmark of Gold's best fiction.

SHIRLEY HAZZARD: *The Transit of Venus.* Hazzard gains her greatest critical and popular success for this novel, about Australian sisters who immigrate to England and America. As one reviewer notes, "Character and circumstance unite to illumine the irony that one may be not only redeemed but also destroyed by the truth."

ROBERT A. HEINLEIN: *The Number of the Beast.* Heinlein's last major work, for which he was paid a then-record advance of half a million dollars, chronicles the experiences of space travelers to alternative universes. It can be described as a meta–science fiction in which the fictional space travelers end up at a conference attended by the author and science fiction luminaries such as Isaac Asimov. The novel thereby questions the nature of reality while suggesting that we all live within a fiction.

ERICA JONG: *Fanny, Being the True History of the Adventures of Fanny Hackabout Jones.* This rollicking parody of an eighteenth-century novel features a female picaresque hero whose adventures rival those of Fielding's character Tom Jones. It is one of Jong's best efforts to combine her comic vision and her feminism. Fanny's exploits include participation in a witch's coven and in a brothel, and she encounters famous figures such as Jonathan Swift and Alexander Pope.

JOHN KNOWLES: *Peace Breaks Out.* In a continuation of his most famous book, *A Separate Peace*, Knowles returns to Devon Academy in the year World War II ends. Already America is beginning to experience the fears that will culminate in the Cold War, and the school becomes a focal point for what is happening in society at large.

BESTSELLERS, 1980–1989

Nonfiction

1980

1. *Crisis Investing: Opportunities and Profits in the Coming Great Depression* by Douglas R. Casey
2. *Cosmos* by Carl Sagan
3. *Free to Choose: A Personal Statement* by Milton and Rose Friedman
4. *Anatomy of an Illness as Perceived by the Patient* by Norman Cousins
5. *Thy Neighbor's Wife* by Gay Talese
6. *The Sky's the Limit* by Dr. Wayne W. Dyer
7. *The Third Wave* by Alvin Toffler
8. *Craig Claiborne's Gourmet Diet* by Craig Claiborne and Peter Franey
9. *Nothing Down* by Robert Allen
10. *Shelley: Also Known as Shirley* by Shelley Winters

1981

1. *The Beverly Hills Diet* by Judy Mazel
2. *The Lord God Made Them All* by James Herriot
3. *Richard Simmons' Never-Say-Diet Book* by Richard Simmons
4. *A Light in the Attic* by Shel Silverstein
5. *Cosmos* by Carl Sagan
6. *Better Homes and Gardens New Cook Book*
7. *Miss Piggy's Guide to Life* by Miss Piggy as told to Henry Beard
8. *Weight Watchers 365-Day Menu Cookbook*
9. *You Can Negotiate Anything* by Herb Cohen
10. *A Few Minutes with Andy Rooney* by Andy Rooney

1982

1. *Jane Fonda's Workout Book* by Jane Fonda
2. *Living, Loving, and Learning* by Leo Buscaglia
3. *And More by Andy Rooney* by Andy Rooney
4. *Better Homes and Gardens New Cookbook*
5. *Life Extension: Adding Years to Your Life and Life to Your Years — a Practical Scientific Approach* by Durk Pearson and Sandy Shaw

6. *When Bad Things Happen to Good People* by Harold S. Kushner
7. *A Few Minutes with Andy Rooney* by Andy Rooney
8. *The Weight Watchers Food Plan Diet Cookbook* by Jean Nidetch
9. *Richard Simmons' Never-Say-Diet Cookbook* by Richard Simmons
10. *No Bad Dogs: The Woodhouse Way* by Barbara Woodhouse

1983

1. *In Search of Excellence: Lessons from America's Best-Run Companies* by Thomas J. Peters and Robert H. Waterman Jr.
2. *Megatrends: Ten New Directions Transforming Our Lives* by John Naisbitt
3. *Motherhood: The Second Oldest Profession* by Erma Bombeck
4. *The One Minute Manager* by Kenneth Blanchard and Spencer Johnson
5. *Jane Fonda's Workout Book* by Jane Fonda
6. *The Best of James Herriot* by James Herriot
7. *The Mary Kay Guide to Beauty: Discovering Your Special Look*
8. *On Wings of Eagles* by Ken Follett
9. *Creating Wealth* by Robert G. Allen
10. *The Body Principal: The Exercise Program for Life* by Victoria Principal

1984

1. *Iacocca: An Autobiography* by Lee Iacocca and William Novak
2. *Loving Each Other* by Leo Buscaglia
3. *Eat to Win: The Sports Nutrition Bible* by Robert Haas, M.D.
4. *Pieces of My Mind* by Andy Rooney
5. *Weight Watchers Fast and Fabulous Cookbook*
6. *What They Don't Teach You at Harvard Business School: Notes from a Street-Smart Executive* by Mark H. McCormack
7. *Women Coming of Age* by Jane Fonda and Mignon McCarthy
8. *Moses the Kitten* by James Herriot
9. *The One Minute Salesperson* by Spencer Johnson, M.D., and Larry Wilson
10. *Weight Watchers Quick Start Program Cookbook* by Jean Nidetch

Critics call the work a worthy successor to Knowles's signature work.

DEAN KOONTZ (b. 1945): *Whispers.* The author of several previous science fiction and suspense novels achieves his breakout popular success with this thriller about a stalker. It would be followed by a string of bestsellers, making Koontz one of the biggest-selling authors of the 1980s and 1990s.

WRIGHT MORRIS: *Plains Song, for Female Voices.* Winner of the American Book Award and hailed as the "best feminist novel by an American" — a remarkable accolade for an author otherwise attacked for not doing women justice in his fiction — the novel is a panoramic exploration of several generations of women in Nebraska.

JOYCE CAROL OATES: *Bellefleur.* Oates's modern take on the gothic novel concerns a family of psychics living in the Adirondack Mountains, where time seems variable — stretching back thousands of years and giving a sense of elemental forces that shape human life. Critics point to Oates's mesmerizing scenes and her ability to evoke the uncanny in this revival of the gothic genre.

WALKER PERCY: *The Second Coming.* A critical and popular success, the novel is one of Percy's most optimistic works. He returns to the main character of his earlier successful novel, *The Last Gentleman*, Will Barrett, who is now a widower. In astonishingly comic fashion, he finds both love and salvation. Percy conveys his theological concerns in supple, playful prose.

MARGE PIERCY: *Vida.* Reflecting the author's involvement with Students for a Democratic Society, the novel concerns a former activist in the 1960s forced to live un-

BESTSELLERS, 1980–1989

1985

1. *Iacocca: An Autobiography* by Lee Iacocca and William Novak
2. *Yeager: An Autobiography* by Chuck Yeager and Leo Janos
3. *Elvis and Me* by Priscilla Beaulieu Presley with Sandra Harmon
4. *Fit for Life* by Harvey and Marilyn Diamond
5. *The Be-Happy Attitudes* by Robert Schuller
6. *Dancing in the Light* by Shirley MacLaine
7. *A Passion for Excellence: The Leadership Difference* by Thomas J. Peters and Nancy K. Austin
8. *The Frugal Gourmet* by Jeff Smith
9. *I Never Played the Game* by Howard Cosell with Peter Bonventre
10. *Dr. Berger's Immune Power Diet* by Stuart M. Berger, M.D.

1986

1. *Fatherhood* by Bill Cosby
2. *Fit for Life* by Harvey and Marilyn Diamond
3. *His Way: The Unauthorized Biography of Frank Sinatra* by Kitty Kelley
4. *The Rotation Diet* by Martin Katahn
5. *You're Only Old Once* by Dr. Seuss
6. *Callanetics: Ten Years Younger in Ten Hours* by Callan Pinckney
7. *The Frugal Gourmet Cooks with Wine* by Jeff Smith
8. *Be Happy — You Are Loved!* by Robert H. Schuller
9. *Word for Word* by Andy Rooney
10. *James Herriot's Dog Stories* by James Herriot

1987

1. *Time Flies* by Bill Cosby
2. *Spycatcher: The Candid Autobiography of a Senior Intelligence Officer* by Peter Wright with Paul Greengrass
3. *Family: The Ties That Bind . . . and Gag!* by Erma Bombeck
4. *Veil: The Secret Wars of the CIA, 1981–1987* by Bob Woodward
5. *A Day in the Life of America* by Rick Smolan and David Cohen
6. *The Great Depression of 1990* by Ravi Batra

7. *It's All in the Playing* by Shirley MacLaine
8. *Man of the House: The Life and Political Memoirs of Speaker Tip O'Neill* by Thomas P. O'Neill Jr. with William Novak
9. *The Frugal Gourmet Cooks American* by Jeff Smith
10. *The Closing of the American Mind* by Allan Bloom

1988

1. *The 8-Week Cholesterol Cure* by Robert E. Kowalski
2. *Talking Straight* by Lee Iacocca with Sonny Kleinfeld
3. *A Brief History of Time: From the Big Bang to Black Holes* by Steven W. Hawking
4. *Trump: The Art of the Deal* by Donald J. Trump with Tony Schwartz
5. *Gracie: A Love Story* by George Burns
6. *Elizabeth Takes Off* by Elizabeth Taylor
7. *Swim with the Sharks Without Being Eaten Alive* by Harvey MacKay
8. *Christmas in America* by David Cohen
9. *Weight Watchers Quick Success Program Book* by Jean Nidetch
10. *Moonwalk* by Michael Jackson

1989

1. *All I Really Needed to Know I Learned in Kindergarten: Uncommon Thoughts on Common Things* by Robert Fulghum
2. *Wealth Without Risk: How to Develop a Personal Fortune Without Going Out on a Limb* by Charles J. Givens
3. *A Woman Named Jackie* by C. David Heymann
4. *It Was on Fire When I Lay Down on It* by Robert Fulghum
5. *Better Homes and Gardens New Cook Book*
6. *The Way Things Work* by David Macaulay
7. *It's Always Something* by Gilda Radner
8. *Roseanne: My Life as a Woman* by Roseanne Barr
9. *The Frugal Gourmet Cooks Three Ancient Cuisines: China, Greece, and Rome* by Jeff Smith
10. *My Turn: The Memoirs of Nancy Reagan* by Nancy Reagan with William Novak

derground. Through flashbacks, the book chronicles the rise and fall of the militant anti-war movement, along with its personal costs.

TOM ROBBINS: *Still Life with Woodpecker*. Robbins's extravaganza depicts the daughter of an exiled king in Seattle and her activist outlaw lover, known as the Woodpecker. He deciphers messages contained in the illustrations on a cigarette package. *Jitterbug Perfume*, about a Seattle waitress's attempt to invent the ultimate perfume and the search for a mysterious blue bottle, would follow in 1984.

MARY LEE SETTLE: *The Scapegoat*. The action of the novel, the first of Settle's Beulah quintet, takes place on a single day in 1912 and recounts the armed clash between West Virginia mine workers and the thugs the mine owner has hired. One of the owner's idealistic daughters, Lilly Ellen Lacy, makes matters worse when her friendship with a young striker becomes public knowledge and

angers both sides. The novel is praised by Anne Tyler as "a great masterpeice."

JANE SMILEY (b. 1949): *Barn Blind*. Smiley's debut novel treats the Karlson family of rural Illinois and its demanding mother. It would be followed by other skilled portraits of family and American life: *At Paradise Gate* (1981), *Duplicate Keys* (1984), and *The Age of Grief* (1987). Born in Los Angeles, Smiley earned a Ph.D. from the University of Iowa.

JOHN KENNEDY TOOLE (1937–1969): *A Confederacy of Dunces*. The New Orleans writer's comic novel, written during the 1960s, is rediscovered by novelist Walker Percy, who hails it as a work of genius. It concerns the career of Ignatius Reilly, a larger-than-life slovenly figure who is also a medieval scholar, in a vividly portrayed New Orleans. The novel explores the ambiguity of both the character's sexuality and his Catholicism. Karl Miller speaks for many critics in calling the book a classic of black humor. A second novel, *The Neon Bible*, written when Toole was a teenager, would appear in 1989.

ANNE TYLER: *Morgan's Passing.* Morgan Gower is a forty-two-year-old hardware store manager, a good example of what one critic calls Tyler's "oddball" characters. These extroverts and eccentrics resemble Eudora Welty's creations — she is one of the formative influences on Tyler's work. The underlying seriousness of Tyler's humor — even in the presentation of Morgan — is revealed in her treatment of families in which individual members feel isolated from one another.

EUDORA WELTY: *Complete Stories.* Including all of Welty's stories from her previous volumes and uncollected works from the 1960s, the collection helps solidify her reputation as one of the most important contemporary American writers.

PAUL WEST (b. 1930): *The Very Rich Hours of Count Von Stauffenberg.* West achieves his first substantial popular and critical success for his imaginative exploration of the German plot to assassinate Adolf Hitler. It is the first in a series of admired animations of history and historical figures, including *Rat Man of Paris* (1986), *Lord Byron's Doctor* (1989), *The Women of Whitechapel and Jack the Ripper* (1992), *The Tent of Orange Mist* (1995), and *Sporting with Amaryllis* (1997). The British-born West became a U.S. citizen in 1971.

Literary Criticism and Scholarship

LAWRENCE FERLINGHETTI: *Literary San Francisco.* In a collaboration with Nancy J. Peters, Ferlinghetti provides a pictorial history of the San Francisco literary scene, which includes the poet's prose portraits of some major figures of the Beat movement.

STANLEY FISH (b. 1938): *Is There a Text in This Class?* The Johns Hopkins English professor's influential volume of reader-response criticism argues that texts do not exist in isolation, independent from their readers. Rather, texts are constituted by an "interpretive community" to which the academic interpreter belongs. Fish's argument is groundbreaking in that he shifts the idea of text interpretation away from the original individual creator and toward readers/interpreters who collectively determine the meaning of works of literature.

PAUL FUSSELL: *Abroad: Literary Traveling Between the Wars.* This compelling study of travel books deals with those written by major writers such as Rebecca West, Evelyn Waugh, and D. H. Lawrence but also with neglected but important books by Robert Byron and others. Fussell explores these works as a literary genre, not just as a history of ideas.

GEOFFREY HARTMAN: *Criticism in the Wilderness.* Continuing his argument begun in *The Fate of Reading*, Hartman attacks the separation made between literature, philosophy, and history by academics in the United States and Britain. Hartman, part of the Yale school of critics, contends that the European model as represented by Jacques Derrida and earlier by Hegel should be more fully represented in Anglo-American academia.

ANNETTE KOLODNY: "Dancing Through the Minefield." Kolodny's essay, appearing in *Feminist Studies* and collected in *Dancing Through the Minefield: Theory, Method, and Politics in Feminist Literary Criticism* in 1983, has been described by Anne Goodwyn Jones as "a landmark essay in feminist thought." Kolodny surveys the previous decade in feminist literary inquiry and identifies the challenges ahead.

AWARDS AND PRIZES, 1980–1989

National Book Awards

1980*

Fiction (Hardcover): *Sophie's Choice* by William Styron

Autobiography (Hardcover): *Lauren Bacall: By Myself* by Lauren Bacall

Biography (Hardcover): *The Rise of Theodore Roosevelt* by Edmund Morris

Children's Books (Hardcover): *A Gathering of Days: A New England Girl's Journal* by Joan W. Blois

General Nonfiction (Hardcover): *The Right Stuff* by Thomas Wolfe

History (Hardcover): *The White House Years* by Henry A. Kissinger

Mystery (Hardcover): *The Green Ripper* by John D. MacDonald

Poetry: *Ashes* by Philip Levine

Science (Hardcover): *Gödel, Escher, Bach: An Eternal Golden Braid* by Douglas Hofstadter

Science Fiction (Hardcover): *Jem* by Frederik Pohl

Western: *Bendigo Shafter* by Louis L'Amour

1981

Fiction (Hardcover): *Plains Song* by Wright Morris

Autobiography/Biography (Hardcover): *Walt Whitman* by Justin Kaplan

Children's Book, Fiction (Hardcover): *The Night Swimmers* by Betsy Byars

Children's Book, Nonfiction (Hardcover): *Mali— Oh, Boy! Babies* by Alison Cragin Herzig and Jane Lawrence

General Nonfiction (Hardcover): *China Men* by Maxine Hong Kingston

History (Hardcover): *Christianity, Social Tolerance, and Homosexuality* by John Boswell

Poetry: *The Need to Hold Still* by Lisel Mueller

Science (Hardcover): *The Panda's Thumb: More Reflections on Natural History* by Stephen Jay Gould

1982

Fiction (Hardcover): *Rabbit Is Rich* by John Updike

Autobiography/Biography (Hardcover): *Mornings on Horseback* by David McCullough

Children's Book, Fiction (Hardcover): *Westmark* by Lloyd Alexander

Children's Book, Nonfiction: *A Penguin Year* by Susan Bonners

General Nonfiction (Hardcover): *The Soul of a New Machine* by Tracy Kidder

History (Hardcover): *People of the Sacred Mountain* by Father Peter John Powell

Poetry: *Life Supports: New and Collected Poems* by William Bronk

Science (Hardcover): *Lucy: The Beginnings of Humankind* by Donald C. Johanson and Maitland A. Edey

1983

Fiction (Hardcover): *The Color Purple* by Alice Walker

Autobiography/Biography (Hardcover): *Isak Dinesen: The Life of a Storyteller* by Judith Thurman

Children's Book, Fiction (Hardcover): *Homesick: My Own Story* by Jean Fritz

Children's Book, Nonfiction: *Chimney Sweeps* by James Cross Giblin

General Nonfiction (Hardcover): *China: Alive in the Bitter Sea* by Fox Butterfield

History (Hardcover): *Voices of Protest: Huey Long, Father Coughlin, and the Great Depression* by Alan Brinkley

Poetry: *Selected Poems* by Galway Kinnell and *Country Music: Selected Early Poems* by Charles Wright

Science (Hardcover): *"Subtle Is the Lord...": The Science and Life of Albert Einstein* by Abraham Pais

1984

Fiction: *Victory over Japan: A Book of Stories* by Ellen Gilchrist

Nonfiction: *Andrew Jackson and the Course of American Democracy, 1833–1845* by Robert V. Remini

1985

Fiction: *White Noise* by Don De Lillo

Nonfiction: *Common Ground: A Turbulent Decade in the Lives of Three American Families* by J. Anthony Lukas

1986

Fiction: *World's Fair* by E. L. Doctorow

Nonfiction: *Arctic Dreams* by Barry Lopez

1987

Fiction: *Paco's Story* by Larry Heinemann

Nonfiction: *The Making of the Atom Bomb* by Richard Rhodes

1988

Fiction: *Paris Trout* by Pete Dexter

Nonfiction: *A Bright Shining Lie: John Paul Vann and America in Vietnam* by Neil Sheehan

1989

Fiction: *Spartina* by John Casey

Nonfiction: *From Beirut to Jerusalem* by Thomas L. Friedman

* From 1980 to 1983, the National Book Awards were expanded to over twenty categories. For these years, we are including only the major hardcover awards.

AWARDS AND PRIZES, 1980–1989

Pulitzer Prizes

1980

Fiction: *The Executioner's Song* by Norman Mailer

Poetry: *Selected Poems* by Donald Justice

Drama: *Talley's Folly* by Lanford Wilson

History: *Been in the Storm So Long* by Leon F. Litwack

General Nonfiction: *Gödel, Escher, Bach: An Eternal Golden Braid* by Douglas R. Hofstadter

Biography/Autobiography: *The Rise of Theodore Roosevelt* by Edmund Morris

1981

Fiction: *A Confederacy of Dunces* by John Kennedy Toole

Poetry: *The Morning of the Poem* by James Schuyler

Drama: *Crimes of the Heart* by Beth Henley

History: *American Education: The National Experience, 1783–1876* by Lawrence A. Cremin

General Nonfiction: *Fin-de-Siècle Vienna: Politics and Culture* by Carl E. Schorske

Biography/Autobiography: *Peter the Great: His Life and World* by Robert K. Massie

1982

Fiction: *Rabbit Is Rich* by John Updike

Poetry: *The Collected Poems* by Sylvia Plath (posthumous)

Drama: *A Soldier's Play* by Charles Fuller

History: *Mary Chesnut's Civil War* by C. Vann Woodward

General Nonfiction: *The Soul of a New Machine* by Tracy Kidder

Biography/Autobiography: *Grant: A Biography* by William S. McFeely

1983

Fiction: *The Color Purple* by Alice Walker

Poetry: *Selected Poems* by Galway Kinnell

Drama: *'Night, Mother* by Marsha Norman

History: *The Transformation of Virginia, 1740–1790* by Rhys L. Issac

General Nonfiction: *Is There No Place on Earth for Me?* by Susan Sheehan

Biography/Autobiography: *Growing Up* by Russell Baker

1984

Fiction: *Ironweed* by William Kennedy

Poetry: *American Primitive* by Mary Oliver

Drama: *Glengarry Glen Ross* by David Mamet

History: No Prize Awarded

General Nonfiction: *The Social Transformation of American Medicine* by Paul Starr

Biography/Autobiography: *Booker T. Washington* by Louis R. Harlan

1985

Fiction: *Foreign Affairs* by Alison Lurie

Poetry: *Yin* by Carolyn Kizer

Drama: *Sunday in the Park with George* by Stephen Sondheim and James Lapine

History: *The Prophets of Regulation* by Thomas K. McCraw

General Nonfiction: *The Good War: An Oral History of World War Two* by Studs Terkel

Biography/Autobiography: *The Life and Times of Cotton Mather* by Kenneth Silverman

---

FRANK LENTRICCHIA (b. 1940): *After the New Criticism.* In what critics call an authoritative and engrossing work, Lentricchia, an English professor at the University of California at Irvine, surveys the work of important twentieth-century critics such as Northrop Frye, Frank Kermode, Jacques Derrida, Roland Barthes, Murray Krieger, E. D. Hirsch Jr., Paul de Man, and Harold Bloom. What their different theories—from structuralism to existentialism to deconstruction—have in common, Lentricchia argues, is a severing of literature from its social and historical context, making literary criticism esoteric. He then offers his own recipe for a more open and accessible study of literature.

HARRY LEVIN (1912–1994): *Memories of the Moderns.* This volume by the respected modernist scholar and Harvard professor of comparative literature collects reviews, essays, lectures, and introductions on figures such as Ezra Pound, T. S. Eliot, James Joyce, and Ernest Hemingway. Included as well are reminiscences of W. H. Auden and Delmore Schwartz.

MARY McCARTHY: *Ideas and the Novel.* McCarthy offers a negative assessment of the modern novel, charging that the genre has become overly aestheticized, losing its sense of audience and place and its purpose: to explore complex, important ideas about human existence.

VLADIMIR NABOKOV: *Lectures on Literature.* These lectures presented to Cornell students range across a spectrum of great works, including *Bleak House*, *Madame Bovary*, and *Mansfield Park*. Nabokov reiterates his view that literature has no instructive or moral purpose, although he argues that understanding the "textures" of literary works does strengthen, inspire, and make the mind more precise.

WILLIAM H. PRITCHARD (b. 1932): *Lives of the Modern Poets.* Pritchard's aim is not merely to provide biographical essays on nine poets (including William Butler Yeats, T. S. Eliot, Wallace Stevens, and Robert Frost) but to take issue with contemporary literary criticism. Echoing the approach of Samuel Johnson, Pritchard, a professor of English at Amherst College, addresses the intelligent,

AWARDS AND PRIZES, 1980–1989

1986

Fiction: *Lonesome Dove* by Larry McMurtry

Poetry: *The Flying Change* by Henry Taylor

Drama: No Prize Awarded

History: *. . . The Heavens and the Earth* by Walter A. McDougall

General Nonfiction: *Common Ground: A Turbulent Decade in the Lives of Three American Families* by J. Anthony Lukas and *Move Your Shadow: South Africa, Black and White* by Joseph Lelyveld

Biography/Autobiography: *Louise Bogan: A Portrait* by Elizabeth Frank

1987

Fiction: *A Summons to Memphis* by Peter Taylor

Poetry: *Thomas and Beulah* by Rita Dove

Drama: *Fences* by August Wilson

History: *Voyagers to the West* by Bernard Bailyn

General Nonfiction: *Arab and Jew: Wounded Spirits in a Promised Land* by David K. Shipler

Biography/Autobiography: *Bearing the Cross: Martin Luther King Jr. and the Southern Christian Leadership Conference* by David J. Garrow

1988

Fiction: *Beloved* by Toni Morrison

Poetry: *Partial Accounts: New and Selected Poems* by William Meredith

Drama: *Driving Miss Daisy* by Alfred Uhry

History: *The Launching of Modern American Science, 1846–1876* by Robert V. Bruce

General Nonfiction: *The Making of the Atomic Bomb* by Richard Rhodes

Biography/Autobiography: *Look Homeward: A Life of Thomas Wolfe* by David Herbert Donald

1989

Fiction: *Breathing Lessons* by Anne Tyler

Poetry: *New and Collected Poems* by Richard Wilbur

Drama: *The Heidi Chronicles* by Wendy Wasserstein

History: *Parting the Waters: America in the King Years, 1954–1963* by Taylor Branch and *Battle Cry of Freedom: The Civil War Era* by James M. McPherson

General Nonfiction: *A Bright Shining Lie: John Paul Vann and America in Vietnam* by Neil Sheehan

Biography/Autobiography: *Oscar Wilde* by Richard Ellmann

Nobel Prizes for Literature

1980   Czeslaw Milosz (Polish-born U.S. citizen)

1987   Joseph Brodsky (Russian-born U.S. citizen)

PEN/Faulkner Award for Fiction

1981   *How German Is It* by Walter Abish

1982   *The Chaneysville Incident* by David Bradley

1983   *Seaview* by Toby Olson

1984   *Sent for You Yesterday* by John Edgar Wideman

1985   *The Barracks Thief* by Tobias Wolff

1986   *The Old Forest* by Peter Taylor

1987   *Soldiers in Hiding* by Richard Wiley

1988   *World's End* by T. Coraghessan Boyle

1989   *Dusk* by James Salter

---

general reader — not the academic specialist. In lucid and engaging prose, Pritchard raises important issues about the use of history and biography in criticism and writes, many critics agree, in a style that is both accessible and erudite.

LIONEL TRILLING: *Speaking of Literature and Society*. The twelfth and final volume in the uniform edition of this important critic's works. These fifty-eight pieces had been written between 1924 and 1968 and mainly consist of book reviews demonstrating Trilling's extraordinary care in considering different points of view. Also published is *The Last Decade: Essays and Reviews, 1965–1975*, demonstrating Trilling's impressive critical range in pieces such as "What Is Criticism?" and a review of the Freud-Jung letters, as well as studies of Jane Austen, William Morris, and James Joyce.

Nonfiction

JOHN BOSWELL (1947–1994): *Christianity, Social Tolerance, and Homosexuality: Gay People in Western Europe* *from the Beginning of the Christian Era to the Fourteenth Century*. Reviewer Martin B. Duberman hails Boswell's American Book Award–winning study of the origins of Christian intolerance toward homosexuality as "one of the most profound, explosive works of scholarship to appear within recent memory." Boswell was a history professor at Yale who helped establish its Center for Lesbian and Gay Studies.

MALCOLM COWLEY: *The Dream of the Golden Mountains: Remembering the 1930s*. Cowley's memoir deals with his years as book editor and reviewer at the *New Republic*, his involvement with Communist politics and the anti-Fascist cause, his gradual disillusionment with leftist activism, and his withdrawal to a more exclusively literary career.

STEPHEN JAY GOULD (1941–2002): *The Panda's Thumb: More Reflections on Natural History*. Having issued his first collection of popular reflections on natural history, *Ever Since Darwin* (1977), Gould, a professor of geology and zoology at Harvard, receives the National Book

Award for this collection of essays. It would be followed by the equally popular *Hen's Teeth and Horse's Toes* (1983) and *The Flamingo's Smile* (1985).

LILLIAN HELLMAN: *Maybe.* The fourth in Hellman's series of memoirs in many ways resembles a novel, and its title suggests its speculative mode. The account presents Sarah Cameron, Hellman's friend, a character who assumes many guises that indicate the ambiguity in storytelling, memory, and the lives people create for themselves. Hellman includes conflicting reports of Sarah's whereabouts and events in her life; she reveals her vulnerability and feminism when she speaks of her "feminine hurts and feminine humiliations."

JUSTIN KAPLAN: *Walt Whitman: A Life.* Kaplan wins the National Book Award for this richly detailed, acutely psychological profile of the writer, which avoids both undue adulation and denigration.

MAXINE HONG KINGSTON: *China Men.* Kingston recalls the men in her family, using the technique of drawing on myth, folktales, and memories that distinguished *Woman Warrior.* She tells of the exploitation of male Chinese laborers in America, their loneliness and anguish, the toll that violence and racism took on their families, and the way their freedom of movement was restricted.

NORMAN MAILER: *Of Women and Their Elegance.* Accompanied by Milton Greene's stylish photographs of Marilyn Monroe, this "autobiography" of the actress assumes her voice and comments on aspects of her private life that she did not address in her own published autobiography. As in *Marilyn* (1973), his earlier biography, the book explores questions of identity, her attraction to acting, and the nature of her sexuality.

ROBERT K. MASSIE (b. 1929): *Peter the Great.* Massie's Pulitzer Prize–winning biography is considered the new standard biography of the architect of modern Russia. Though not a scholarly work, Massie's work is cited as a "model for what scholarly writing ought to be" because it brings its subject vibrantly to life. Massie, a journalist, became interested in Russian history and the family history of Nicholas II after his son was diagnosed with hemophilia, the same disease that affected Nicholas's heir Alexei. Massie produced his first biography, *Nicholas and Alexandra*, in 1967.

SUSAN SONTAG: *Under the Sign of Saturn.* Sontag explores the lives and works of several important writers, including Paul Goodman, Elias Canetti, and Walter Benjamin, as well as avant-garde drama theoretician Antonin Artaud and filmmaker Leni Riefenstahl, confirming Sontag's place as one of the best American interpreters of European culture.

RONALD STEEL (b. 1931): *Walter Lippmann and the American Century.* Anthony Lewis praises this Bancroft Prize–winning biography by the scholar on American foreign policy and author of *Pax Americana* (1967) as "a fascinating book: on journalism, on America in the world, on a mysterious human being."

JEAN STROUSE (b. 1945): *Alice James: A Biography.* An acclaimed biography of the sister of Henry and William James. Critics hail Strouse's compassionate handling of her subject's life and of the family dynamics that made it difficult for Alice James to find her own voice. Strouse was a book critic for *Newsweek* from 1979 to 1983.

EDMUND WILSON: *The Thirties: From the Notebooks and Diaries of the Period.* Edited by Leon Edel, this collection records Wilson's own intellectual growth as he comments on the social and literary developments of the decade.

Poetry

RITA DOVE (b. 1952): *The Yellow House on the Corner.* Dove's first major collection is praised for its historical and personal vision. The African American was born in Akron, Ohio, and would be named American Poet Laureate in 1993.

LOUISE GLÜCK: *Descending Figure.* The descending in the title refers to various forms of falling and destruction, including drowned children, a child focusing on her dead sister's prostrate figure, and other allusions to disintegrating and destroyed civilizations—such as the biblical city of Jerusalem.

GALWAY KINNELL: *Mortal Acts, Mortal Words.* The poet explores his personal and family history, along with vivid images of nature and evocations of distinctive voices. Critics praise the poet's handling of many different kinds of love—a theme that unifies this collection.

LISEL MUELLER (b. 1924): *The Need to Hold Still.* Having received the Lamont Poetry Prize of the Academy of American Poets for her first major collection, *The Private Life* (1976), Mueller wins the National Book Award and further acclaim for this collection, which includes "Talking to Helen," a poem addressed to Helen Keller, and the long sequence "The Triumph of Life: Mary Shelley." Born in Germany, Mueller came to the United States in 1939. Her subsequent volumes would include *Second Language* (1986), *Waving from the Shore* (1989), and *Alive Together* (1996).

SHARON OLDS (b. 1942): *Satan Says.* The poet's first volume, which wins the inaugural San Francisco Poetry Center Award, features intensely personal probing of family life and child abuse. It would be followed by *The*

Gold Cell in 1987. Born in San Fransisco, Olds earned a Ph.D. from Columbia.

JAMES SCHUYLER (1923–1991): *The Morning of the Poem.* The Chicago-born poet, playwright, and novelist wins the Pulitzer Prize for this collection, whose long title work, a meditation on the breakdown of mind and body and the means of recovery, is considered a masterpiece and among the best long poems written by an American in the second half of the twentieth century.

LOUIS SIMPSON: *Caviare at the Funeral.* Simpson's poetic treatment of childhood, family, and American life contains poems such as "Why Do You Write About Russia?"; "Chocolates," an account of an incident from Chekhov's life; and "American Classic," about a broken-down car.

ROBERT PENN WARREN: *Being Here: Poetry, 1977–1980.* This collection reflects Warren's strong grasp of narrative and his desire to involve the reader's reactions directly in his poems. The result is a remarkable immediacy in the treatment of topics such as the making of poetry in old age ("Fear and Trembling"), the nature of the world ("August Moon)," and the nature of time ("Speleology").

JAY WRIGHT: *The Double Invention of Komo.* Wright's poetic sequence depicting the Komo initiation rites of the African Bambara people is considered the poet's most ambitious work, his intellectual biography, and, in the words of John Hollander, "a considerable achievement of a major imagination." Wright's *Selected Poems* would appear in 1987.

1981

Drama and Theater

HARVEY FIERSTEIN (b. 1954): *Torch Song Trilogy.* These three one-act plays explore the lives of gay men with wit and compassion. Fierstein, an actor and playwright, wins high praise from critics for his sensitive, hilarious, and wide-ranging exploration of gay life. His play wins the Tony Award for best play, and he earns a Tony Award for his starring performance.

CHARLES FULLER: *A Soldier's Play.* When a black sergeant is murdered at a Louisiana army base, a black officer is sent to investigate and confronts the hostility of his white fellow officers. Critics praise the play for its probing, complex development of the social, political, and psychological ramifications of white-black relationships as well as its searing look at the tensions experienced by its protagonist.

AMLIN GRAY (b. 1946): *How I Got That Story.* Gray wins the Obie Award for this innovative drama about the Vietnam War, in which a war correspondent's experiences are refracted through encounters with another actor playing multiple roles. It is described by Edith Oliver as "one of the most original and powerful plays ever to be done off-Broadway." Gray served in the medical corps in Vietnam. He has been since 1977 the playwright in residence at the Milwaukee Repertory Theatre.

BETH HENLEY (b. 1952): *Crimes of the Heart.* First performed in Louisville, Kentucky, in 1979, the Mississippi-born dramatist's Chekhovian play about a day in the life of three unsettled Mississippi sisters premieres on Broadway. It would be adapted for the screen five years later. Henley's style, sometimes called "Southern gothic," combines dark humor with a decidedly regional idiom. The combination proves popular with audiences and critics, prompting Frank Rich to write in the *New York Times:* "Be grateful that we have a new writer from hurricane country who gives her characters room to spin and spin and spin."

VELINA HASU HOUSTON (b. 1957): *Asa Ga Kimashita (Morning Has Broken).* This winner of the Lorraine Hansberry Playwriting Award and the David Library Playwriting Award for American Freedom is the first part of a trilogy dealing with a family's experiences in Japan, New York, and Kansas. Critics praise Houston for doing justice both to her Japanese milieu (depicting Japanese characters who fear American hegemony) and the speech rhythms and actions of her American characters. It would be followed by *American Dreams* (1984) and *Tea* (1987). Houston, a poet as well as a playwright, is of mixed Japanese, African American, and Native American heritage.

DAVID HENRY HWANG: *The Dance and the Railroad* and *Family Devotions.* The first of Hwang's 1981 dramas focuses on Chinese workmen on the transcontinental railroad during a 1867 strike; the second examines the destructive influence of Christianity on Asian cultural traditions from the vantage point of a well-to-do Chinese American family.

EMILY MANN (b. 1952): *Still Life.* First performed in Chicago in 1980 before transferring to New York, this documentary drama is built on interviews with three people in Minnesota — a Vietnam War vet, his battered wife, and his mistress — exploring the domestic side of the Vietnam legacy. Mann, born in Chicago, was inspired for her first play (*Annulla Allen: Autobiography of a Survivor,* 1977) by the oral histories collected by her father of concentration camp survivors.

LANFORD WILSON: *A Tale Told.* This is the third installment in the Talley family saga, to be retitled *Talley and Son* in 1985. It is set on the same night in 1944 as *Talley's*

Folly and depicts the family's quarrel over their garment business.

Fiction

DONALD BARTHELME: *Sixty Stories.* Barthelme wins the PEN/Faulkner Award for this retrospective collection, which confirms his status as one of the most innovative masters of the modern short story. It would be followed by a second retrospective collection, *Forty Stories,* in 1987.

THOMAS BERGER: *Reinhart's Women.* In the fourth of Berger's novels dealing with the unheroic Carlo Reinhart, the protagonist is now in his fifties and dealing with America in the late 1970s.

DAVID BRADLEY (b. 1950): *The Chaneysville Incident.* Bradley wins the PEN/Faulkner Award for this novel about a Pennsylvania community that had been a stop on the Underground Railroad. It is praised by reviewer Art Seidenbaum as "the most significant work by a new male black author since James Baldwin" and by Bruce Allen as "the best novel about the black experience in America since Ellison's *Invisible Man* nearly 30 years ago." Bradley's first novel, *South Street* (1975), explored the lives of the denizens of the Philadelphia ghetto.

WILLIAM S. BURROUGHS: *Cities of the Red Night.* The novel concerns a group of homosexual pirates and a private detective who travel to several cities, including one that is suffering an epidemic of a sexual virus with many characteristics of AIDS. Like much of Burroughs's other fiction, this novel features not only eccentric characters but a flamboyant style that reflects the author's rejection of conventional realism.

ROBERT OLEN BUTLER (b. 1945): *The Alleys of Eden.* Butler's first novel is the initial volume of a Vietnam War trilogy focusing on noncombat aspects of the war from the perspective of several U.S. soldiers. Here, a deserter falls in love with a Vietnamese prostitute. It would be followed by *Sun Dogs* (1982) and *On Distant Grounds* (1985). Butler served in army intelligence in Vietnam.

RAYMOND CARVER: *What We Talk About When We Talk of Love.* Critics praise this story collection, citing Carver's spare language and minimalism, which are compared to Hemingway's work. Carver's characters are reticent, and the events of the stories vary from violent to mundane. Their themes often center on the tenuous relationships between men and women, who are often on the verge of separation, already alienated from each other.

ROBERT COOVER: *Spanking the Maid.* Coover's novella parodies nineteenth-century pornography while explor-

ing the conflict between self and other and the various permutations of converting desire into an object.

PETER DE VRIES: *Sauce for the Goose.* De Vries wittily enters the gender wars with this novel in which a feminist journalist goes undercover to provoke male chauvinism in a magazine publisher with whom she falls in love.

ANDREA DWORKIN (b. 1946): *Pornography.* The feminist activist examines pornography as an instrument of male domination of women. She would join forces with law professor Catharine MacKinnon to campaign for antipornography legislation, and the pair would collaborate on *Pornography and Civil Rights* (1988).

JOHN GARDNER: *The Art of Living.* In this story collection Gardner applies his philosophy, outlined in *On Moral Fiction,* offering several examples of the value of art as a life-affirming moral force. Anne Tyler declares, "These are miracles of stories — fully-realized, far-reaching, greater than the sum of their parts." Others are less enthusiastic, finding them self-indulgent and strident.

ELLEN GILCHRIST (b. 1935): *In the Land of Dreamy Dreams.* This first collection of short stories gains immediate approval from critics, who welcome a new Southern writer who can depict childhood and adolescence with considerable freshness and humor. Born in Mississippi, Gilchrist worked as a journalist and a radio commentator.

CAROLINE GORDON: *The Collected Stories.* Although Gordon regarded herself as preeminently a novelist, her critical reputation rests today mainly on her achievement as a short story writer. In his introduction, Robert Penn Warren groups Gordon with Eudora Welty, Flannery O'Connor, and Katherine Anne Porter as Southern writers "who have been enriching our literature uniquely in this century."

MARY GORDON: *The Company of Women.* The novel is composed of monologues by Father Cyprian and the women attracted to his magnetic personality, especially Felicitas Taylor, a young woman grappling with issues such as abortion and social activism. Like her acclaimed first novel, *Final Payments,* Gordon demonstrates a subtle and sure grasp of contemporary Catholic life.

MARK HELPRIN (b. 1947): *Ellis Island and Other Stories.* Helprin's collection ranges widely in subject matter and style, from the epistolary "Letters from the Samantha" to the highly praised "Ellis Island," an immigrant's account of his arrival in the foggy, strange environment of the New World. Born in New York City, a Harvard graduate, Helprin served in the Israeli Air Force. His previous books were *A Dove of the East and Other Stories* (1975) and *Refiner's Fire* (1977).

JOHN IRVING: *The Hotel New Hampshire.* Irving treats three decades of the troubled Berry family, proprietors of hotels in New Hampshire, Vienna, and Maine, with a plot that blends violent and grotesque situations. The book generally disappoints critics as a retread of characteristics better handled in *The World According to Garp.*

LEONARD MICHAELS: *The Men's Club.* Michaels's novel about a group of men who assemble to tell their life stories, sexual conquests, and marital frustrations is controversial: some critics see it as antifeminist, but others consider it a direct assault on male fantasies.

TONI MORRISON: *Tar Baby.* Morrison's novel portrays a love affair between a black upper-middle-class woman (Jadine Childs) and a white French art historian. Jadine, a model who claims no affinity with the African American heritage, opts for a cosmopolitanism that isolates her from her people and her history. In her story, Morrison deftly explores the meaning of blackness and creates considerable tension between characters who represent cultural tradition in its clash with modernity and mobility.

DAVID PLANTE (b. 1940): *The Country.* Critics consider this the best novel in Plante's trilogy on the Francoeur family, headed by Catholic, French Canadian parents. There is little plot in the novel, which is taken up with the relationships among the nine members of the family, each of them struggling to come to terms with the themes of time and death. The other titles by the Rhode Island–born writer are *The Family* (1978) and *The Woods* (1982).

REYNOLDS PRICE: *The Source of Light.* Part of the Kendal-Mayfield saga, Price's family history has been compared, in its scope and artistic achievement, with Faulkner's creation of the Compson clan.

MARILYNNE ROBINSON (b. 1944): *Housekeeping.* Robinson's first novel is acclaimed for its lyrical prose in telling the story of a nonconformist woman who raises important issues about the role of women and the social and cultural myths that inform people's lives. Born in Idaho, Robinson earned a Ph.D. in English from the University of Washington.

PHILIP ROTH: *Zuckerman Unbound.* Roth continues the series begun with *The Ghost Writer.* Roth's fictional surrogate, Nathan Zuckerman, recounts the perils that await a writer upon publication of a popular but controversial novel, which bears a close resemblance to Roth's own 1969 succès de scandale, *Portnoy's Complaint.*

LESLIE MARMON SILKO: *Storyteller.* This collection includes short fiction and poetry, some of which is autobiographical, and deals with the lives of Native Americans, such as a Navajo woman who has suffered from personal and cultural losses. The theme of the Native American's bond with the earth — how every aspect of the individual's life is bound up in this relationship with nature — pervades each piece.

MARTIN CRUZ SMITH (b. 1942): *Gorky Park.* Smith produces a best-selling thriller featuring Soviet homicide detective Arkady Renko, who would return in *Polar Star* (1989), *Red Square* (1992), and *Havana Bay* (1999). Of Pueblo Indian heritage, Smith imagined an alternate Native American history in his first novel, *Indians War* (1970).

ROBERT STONE: *A Flag for Sunrise.* The novel concerns a former CIA operative who teaches in a Central American country. A hardened veteran, he is bemused by Americans who think they can master and modernize another country. Reviewers are impressed with Stone's probing of foreign involvements reminiscent of America's morass in Vietnam.

JOHN UPDIKE: *Rabbit Is Rich.* In this third Rabbit novel, Rabbit Angstrom gets in the swing of the 1970s by jogging and enjoying prosperity from his successful Toyota dealership. Though now an upstanding member of the consumer economy, his earlier restless period — including the drowning of a child and marital discord — is never far from his thoughts. Nelson, Rabbit's son, also becomes a problem, threatening to resurrect the kind of chaos Rabbit himself experienced. Critics admire Updike's social commentary on the 1970s and his ability to place Rabbit in new and persuasive contexts.

GORE VIDAL: *Creation.* Set in the fifth century, the novel re-creates the world of the kings Darius and Xerxes of ancient Persia, the China of Confucius, the life of Buddha, and the Greece of Socrates. Vidal's vision of different cultures is panoramic and provocative, challenging conventional judgments of history, gender, and individual identity.

ALICE WALKER: *You Can't Keep a Good Woman Down.* Walker's second story collection treats a number of issues raised by feminists in the 1970s, including abortion, pornography, and rape.

JOHN EDGAR WIDEMAN: *Hiding Place* and *Damballah.* Wideman issues the first two volumes of his Homewood trilogy, set in the black section of Pittsburgh and exploring African American history, a community, and an extended family. The final book in the series, *Sent for You Yesterday,* would appear in 1983.

TOBIAS WOLFF (b. 1945): *In the Garden of the North American Martyrs.* Wolff's first collection of stories receives positive reviews and the St. Lawrence Award for Fiction. He employs a "taut lyricism," one critic observes, to explore the "underside" of American life. Wolff served in Vietnam, worked as a journalist for the *Washington Post*, and became the writer in residence at Syracuse University.

Literary Criticism and Scholarship

BELL HOOKS (b. 1952): *Ain't I a Woman: Black Women and Feminism*. This is the first in a series of critical studies tracing the connections between black women and feminism. It would be followed by *Feminist Theory: From Margin to Center* (1984) and *Talking Black: Thinking Feminist, Thinking Black* (1988). Born Gloria Jean Watkins in Kentucky, she took the name of her maternal great-grandmother. She uses the lowercase spelling "to get away from the ego attachment we have to a name."

VLADIMIR NABOKOV: *Lectures on Russian Literature*. The second volume of Nabokov's college lectures provides insights into the writer's view on the great figures of Russian literature, including Nikolay Gogol, Ivan Turgenev, Fyodor Dostoyevsky, Leo Tolstoy, and Anton Chekhov. Included as well is the lecture "The Art of Translation."

JOYCE CAROL OATES: *Contraries*. This collection of literary essays provides Oates's response to works such as Oscar Wilde's *The Picture of Dorian Gray*, Fyodor Dostoyevsky's *The Possessed*, and D. H. Lawrence's *Women in Love*. A second collection, *The Profane Art: Essays and Reviews*, would follow in 1983.

C. VANN WOODWARD: *Mary Chesnut's Civil War*. Woodward wins the Pulitzer Prize for his editing of the complete scholarly edition of the diaries of Mary Chesnut, one of the greatest firsthand accounts of the Civil War.

Nonfiction

JACK HENRY ABBOTT (1944–2002): *In the Belly of the Beast*. This harrowing account of life in prison is written by an inmate who had spent most of his life behind bars. Critics praise its authenticity. Abbott had come to Norman Mailer's attention while Mailer was writing *The Executioner's Song*. Abbott and Mailer then corresponded, and Mailer encouraged him to develop his letters into a book. Largely on the strength of it, Abbott was paroled. Almost immediately he stabbed and killed a man and was sent back to prison, where he committed suicide.

MAYA ANGELOU: *The Heart of a Woman*. In the fourth volume of this poet and performer's autobiography, Angelou describes with characteristic warmth, candor, and eloquence her transition from nightclub singer and dancer to writer and political activist.

ANDREA DWORKIN: *Pornography and Civil Rights: A New Day for Women's Equality*. Coauthored with law professor Catharine A. MacKinnon, the work defines pornography as sexual subordination of women in images and writings. Five years earlier the two women had introduced legislation making pornography legally actionable as sex discrimination. Although the legislation was deemed unconstitutional, it sparked a national debate on pornography.

STEPHEN JAY GOULD: *The Mismeasure of Man*. In this National Book Critics Circle Award winner, Gould debunks "scientific" attempts to quantify human intelligence by means such as cranial measurement. The resulting work is a piece of natural history with all the narrative interest of a novel. Gould revives the ghosts of once-estimable scientists whose true aim was to perpetuate unscientific notions such as racial purity.

ERNEST HEMINGWAY: *Selected Letters, 1917–1961*. Edited by Carlos Baker, this volume offers a representative sampling of Hemingway's correspondence. Both his noble, sensitive side and his crass, bullying side are displayed. Baker includes the writer's letters to his parents and to famous writers such as F. Scott Fitzgerald, William Faulkner, and John Dos Passos.

DONALD C. JOHANSON (b. 1943) AND MAITLAND A. EDEY (1910–1992): *Lucy: The Beginnings of Humankind*. This duo wins the American Book Award for this account of Johanson's discovery in Ethiopia in 1974 of the oldest, most complete human skeleton and the implications of the find. The skeleton was named Lucy after the Beatles' song "Lucy in the Sky with Diamonds," which was played frequently at the dig site.

TRACY KIDDER (b. 1945): *The Soul of a New Machine*. Kidder's chronicle of an eighteen-month struggle by engineers at the Data General Corporation to create a supercomputer receives the American Book Award and the Pulitzer Prize. It is the first of Kidder's insider views of aspects of American life, to be followed by *House* (1985) and *Among Schoolchildren* (1989). Born in New York City and a graduate of Harvard, Kidder served as a lieutenant in Vietnam and earned an M.F.A. from the University of Iowa.

PHILLIP LOPATE (b. 1943): *Bachelorhood: Tales of the Metropolis*. Considered one of the leading contemporary essayists, Lopate delves into his life as a bachelor in New York City. His strong narrative sense turns some of the essays into stories — as in his evocation of "Willy," the bachelor-lover of Lopate's mother who remains for Lopate a shadowy figure. Critics admire Lopate's feel for New York City streets and his wistful but never sentimental evocation of urban experience. Lopate's subsequent books would include *Against Joie de Vivre* (1989) and *Portrait of My Body* (1996).

DAVID McCULLOUGH: *Mornings on Horseback.* McCullough supplies a biographical profile of Theodore Roosevelt's life from age ten to age twenty-eight, with an emphasis on his family and the social background that helps explain Roosevelt's later values. The book receives the American Book Award.

WILLIAM S. McFEELY (b. 1930): *Grant: A Biography.* This Pulitzer Prize–winning biography by the professor of history at Mount Holyoke College presents, in one critic's words, the "first full-scale treatment of all aspects of Grant's life," a sympathetic but by no means uncritical view.

WRIGHT MORRIS: *Will's Boy.* Morris provides an innovative memoir of his first twenty years, with passages from his novels, short stories, and essays included to emphasize how fused his life and work have been. The book is thus the product of his imagination and a sourcebook that relates events in his life that went into the making of his fiction.

S. J. PERELMAN: *The Last Laugh.* This posthumously published collection of sketches and memoirs demonstrates Perelman's eclectic range of targets — a newspaper item, a fad, an odd person or event — reduced to absurdity in comic dialogues.

CARL SAGAN: *Cosmos.* This is the companion volume for the astronomer's PBS series on the universe. The highest-rated public television program to date, it reached a worldwide audience of 400 million viewers (to be surpassed in 1990 by Ken Burns's *The Civil War*) and made Sagan a celebrity and his catchphrase, "billions and billions," common parlance. The book remains on the bestseller list for seventy weeks.

ISAAC BASHEVIS SINGER: *Lost in America.* Singer's third autobiographical volume is described as "fiction set against a background of truth." Singer remains a storyteller, omitting, distorting, and adding details that make a good story but not necessarily an entirely factual record of his life.

DIANA TRILLING: *Mrs. Harris: The Death of the Scarsdale Diet Doctor.* Trilling's Pulitzer Prize–nominated book is part true crime story, part biography, part courtroom drama. It tells the sordid tale of prep school headmistress Jean Harris's affair with and murder of diet doctor Herman Tarnower, carefully examining the moneyed world they inhabited. It is Trilling's first critically and financially successful book.

BARBARA TUCHMAN: *Practicing History.* Tuchman's essay collection is arranged in three parts: "The Craft," "The Yield," and "Learning from History." Within these categories she explores topics such as the role of accident in history, the writing of military history, the role of the biographer, and the nature of contemporary history.

KURT VONNEGUT JR.: *Palm Sunday: An Autobiographical Collage.* This collection of Vonnegut's speeches, letters, short fiction, and reminiscences forms a kind of record of his life and imagination. Critics admire the way Vonnegut expresses his opinions with humor, in contrast with the usual pomposity that characterizes many such collections.

TOM WOLFE: *From Bauhaus to Our House.* Wolfe takes aim at modern architecture, particularly the Bauhaus school, which, with its emphasis on function over form, the writer finds a lamentable departure from indigenous American architecture.

Poetry

A. R. AMMONS: *A Coast of Trees.* Ammons's collection includes poems such as "Getting Through," "Eventually Is Soon Enough," "Density," and "Vehicle," dealing with the poet's observations during his walks, periods of observation, and writing. Critics admire his deft linking of personal and everyday experience with the rhythms of nature.

JOHN ASHBERY: *Shadow Train.* This collection of poems, each in a sixteen-line, four-quatrain form, explores the distance between language and experience. Notable poems include "The Pursuit of Happiness," "Punishing the Myth," and "Paradoxes and Oxymorons."

JARED CARTER (b. 1939): *Work, for the Night Is Coming.* Winner of the Walt Whitman Award for a first book of poems, this collection by the Indiana-born poet shows a remarkable mastery of its Midwestern settings. Included are "Turning the Brick," which deals with the Depression years, and "The Undertaker," an evocative poem about the burial of the dead and the continuity of life.

LORNA DEE CERVANTES (b. 1954): *Emplumada.* This first collection by the San Francisco–born Chicana poet features bilingual free verse, employing simple diction to describe the social realities of Cervantes's background and heritage. It wins the American Book Award.

FRED CHAPPELL (b. 1936): *Midquest.* The North Carolina–born poet's most acclaimed work is this compilation of his four previous volumes — *River* (1975), *Bloodfire* (1978), *Wind Mountain* (1979), and *Earthsleep* (1979) — forming a poetic autobiography. Subsequent volumes include *Castle Tzingal* (1984), *First and Last Words* (1989), *C: Poems* (1993), and *Spring Garden* (1995). Chappell would receive the Bollingen Prize in 1985.

CAROLYN FORCHÉ: *The Country Between Us.* Forché's second collection, winner of the Lamont Prize, reflects her activities with Amnesty International in El Salvador, most notably in the powerful poem "The Colonel."

SIMON J. ORTIZ: *From Sand Creek.* Ortiz's Pushcart Prize–winning collection explores the 1864 massacre of 133 Cheyenne and Arapaho at Sand Creek, Colorado, by U.S. cavalry as the basis for the poet's "analysis of myself as an American." Ortiz had written the work while being treated for alcoholism at a veterans hospital.

LINDA PASTAN (b. 1932): *Waiting for My Life.* Pastan's fourth collection establishes her reputation for finding engaging insights and pleasures in everyday experiences. Her topics include "Dreams," sending a child off to school ("Helen Bids Farewell to Her Daughter Hermione"), "Letter to a Son at Exam Time," "By the Mailbox," "Meditation by the Stove," and "Weather Forecast." Subsequent collections by the New York City–born poet would include *PM/AM* (1983), *A Fraction of Darkness* (1985), and *Imperfect Paradise* (1988).

SYLVIA PLATH: *The Collected Poems.* Plath's collected verse, arranged and edited by her husband, Ted Hughes, earns the Pulitzer Prize. Also published is the first edition of *The Journals of Sylvia Plath.*

ADRIENNE RICH: *A Wild Patience Has Taken Me This Far: Poems, 1978–1981.* The predominating themes in this volume are anger and love. Critics single out Rich's best poems — such as "For Julia in Nebraska" (a tribute to writer Willa Cather) — for their matter-of-fact but penetrating style.

ALAN SHAPIRO (b. 1952): *After the Digging.* Shapiro's first collection challenges the predominant free verse of most contemporary American poetry with formal verse narratives, one devoted to the Irish potato famine, the other to seventeenth-century American Puritans. The next collections by the Boston-born poet who became a professor of English at the University of North Carolina — *The Courtesy* (1983) and *The Happy Hour* (1987) — deal with contemporary problems of family and spiritual values.

ROBERT PENN WARREN: *Rumor Verified: Poems, 1979–1980.* This collection, evidence of Warren's prolific last period, includes poems such as "Rumor at Twilight," "Vermont Ballad: Change of Season," and "Glimpses of Seasons," which demonstrate his continuing mastery of verse at once grounded in natural imagery, metaphysical speculation, and a sense of place and history.

1982
Drama and Theater

HOWARD ASHMAN (1950–1991) AND ALAN MENKEN: *Little Shop of Horrors.* This fantasy play is about Seymour, who brings a small plant into Mushnik's florist shop, and the ensuing mayhem the plant causes by growing and growing, feeding off Mushnik, and forming designs to take over the world. The play's zany quality — which includes a huge puppet who plays the plant (called Audrey II after Seymour's girlfriend) — appeals to audiences in several countries. Ashman would become the lyricist for Disney films such as *The Little Mermaid* (1989), *Beauty and the Beast* (1991), and *Aladdin* (1992).

A. R. GURNEY JR. (b. 1930): *The Dining Room.* Gurney covers the decline in the WASP governing class. Several generations of privileged people bemoan their waning authority over a changing culture in a dining room that is itself a relic of that world — an emblem of the characters' irrelevance and nostalgia for the good old days. Born in Buffalo, New York, Gurney has been a professor of humanities and literature at MIT. His earlier plays include *The Middle Ages* (1977) and *The Golden Age* (1981).

DAVID MAMET: *Edmond.* Mamet's play shows a middle-class New Yorker's descent into the city's seamy, criminal subculture, depicting, in the words of one reviewer, how "we become part of our destructive surroundings."

WILLIAM MASTROSIMONE: *Extremities.* This controversial drama depicts the violent revenge of an intended rape victim. It wins the Outer Critics Circle Award and would be adapted by the playwright as a 1986 film starring Farrah Fawcett.

MARSHA NORMAN: *'Night, Mother.* Jessie, an overweight epileptic girl who lives with her divorced mother, announces her intention to commit suicide in this Pulitzer Prize–winning play. It receives high praise for its unflinching portrayal of Jessie's deliberate choice to destroy herself in the face of her mother's mounting terror.

JOHN PIELMEIER (b. 1949): *Agnes of God.* A psychiatrist tries to determine how a twenty-one-year-old nun came to murder her newborn child. The play raises provocative questions about the nature of religious belief and the limitations of a secular view of the world. Pielmeier's next Broadway shows would be *The Boys of Winter* (1985), about the My Lai massacre, and *Sleight of Hand* (1987), a thriller.

LANFORD WILSON: *Angels Fall.* A group of travelers seek refuge in a New Mexico mission during a nuclear accident, developing a degree of cooperation that is unusual in Wilson's plays.

Fiction

JOHN BARTH: *Sabbatical: A Romance.* In Barth's novel, Fenwick Scott Key Turner, a former CIA operative and a novelist who is married to an academic and literary critic, embarks on a sea journey. Critics note a literary self-reflexiveness that shows Barth's customary wit, mischief, and portrayal of fiction itself as a source for intrigue, philosophy, and coincidence.

ANN BEATTIE: *The Burning House.* This collection features characters somewhat older than those of Beattie's previous volumes. Time is beginning to pass them by, and they want to grasp the opportunities that come along, although, like typical Beattie characters, they have a strong sense of irony and a feeling that they are doomed to be disappointed. Critics admire Beattie's spare prose, which they compare with Raymond Carver's.

SAUL BELLOW: *The Dean's December.* Bellow's first novel in seven years is set both in his native Chicago and in Bucharest, Rumania. The narrator compares the anarchy of the West with the state control of the eastern bloc countries and finds both systems lacking, contributing to the destruction of culture that seems to encompass the globe in the waning days of the twentieth century.

RITA MAE BROWN: *Southern Discomfort.* Although Brown rejects the label "Southern writer," she provides critically praised evocations of the South — in this case, Montgomery, Alabama. The story is about an interracial and intergenerational love affair between a white matron and a black teenager, which provokes a scandal in segregated society. Brown would follow it with *High Hearts* (1986), a historical novel set during the Civil War.

JOHN CHEEVER: *Oh What a Paradise It Seems.* Cheever's last important work, this novella concerns an older man who regains his energy in a love affair and sets out to save the land where he grew up. Cheever eloquently combines the man's desire for renewal with his need to protect the environment from encroaching developers.

RICHARD CONDON: *Prizzi's Honor.* Condon's black comedy depicts a mob hit man who falls in love with his contract — also a hired killer. Condon would cowrite the screenplay for a successful 1985 film version.

DON DE LILLO: *The Names.* James and Kathryn become involved with Owen Brademas, an archaeologist investigating a cult of hammer killers driven by a belief in the hidden names of God. As the couple's marriage dissolves, so does their belief in an ordered world, with Brademas symbolizing the future quest for absolute truth.

JOHN GREGORY DUNNE: *Dutch Shea, Jr.* Dutch is an attorney who specializes in defending lowlife characters whom no one else wishes to represent. The plot turns on the killing of Shea's daughter in a London terrorist attack by the Irish Republican Army; it leads to Dutch's own collapse as he become enmeshed in his own embezzlement scheme. Critics consider Dunne a successor to the great hard-boiled detective novelists Dashiell Hammett and Raymond Chandler, with a profound and affectionate grasp of Irish American life.

STANLEY ELKIN: *George Mills.* A working-class man feels he has been betrayed by God. Elkin achieves impressive effects by treating his humble subjects with considerable wit and energy.

JOHN GARDNER: *Michelsson's Ghosts.* Gardner treats a philosophy professor who is haunted by various ghosts, including that of the founder of Mormonism, Joseph Smith. The novel is called a "highbrow potboiler" that explores a number of ethical dilemmas.

GAIL GODWIN: *A Mother and Two Daughters.* As the title suggests, this carefully integrated novel is about three women, each of whom is striking out in new directions — the mother recovering from her husband's death and taking a new lover, her two daughters trying to balance a sense of independence while becoming involved with new men. Critics are impressed with Godwin's sensitive and compassionate portrayal of contemporary women.

SUE GRAFTON (b. 1940): *A is for Alibi.* The first of Grafton's popular "alphabetical" mysteries features woman detective Kinsey Millhone. Born in Kentucky, Grafton began writing crime novels aided by her father, C. W. Grafton, an attorney.

JOHN HAWKES: *Virginie: Her Two Lives.* Hawkes employs his first female narrator, recording her existence in 1740 and 1945 in a parody of the pornographic novel. The book makes fun of the various erotic fantasies men have constructed.

ROLANDO HINOJOSA (b. 1929): *Rites and Witnesses.* The first English translation of a novel from the Texas-born writer's sequence, "Klail City Death Trip," set in a fictional Texas town in the lower Rio Grande Valley. This novel, like the others in the series — *The Valley* (1983), *Dear Rafe* (1985), and *Klail City* (1987) — wins praise for Hinojosa's deft deployment of character, theme, and multiple narration.

CHARLES JOHNSON: *Oxherding Tales.* Johnson's second novel concerns a slave with a black father and white mother, set in the antebellum South. It would be followed by a short story collection, *The Sorcerer's Apprentice* (1986), combining realistic and fantasy elements derived from black voodoo practices.

BERNARD MALAMUD: *God's Grace.* Typifying Malamud's gift for fable and allegory, the novel tells the story of a nuclear holocaust survivor who must, in biblical fashion, begin the world anew — this time among apes.

Reviewers call the novel a prophetic text exploring the dreams and failures of humanity.

BOBBIE ANN MASON (b. 1940): *Shiloh and Other Stories.* The collection includes what would become Mason's most anthologized short story, "Shiloh," which, like much of her work, explores the urbanization of once-rural Kentucky and the tensions between the Southern past and modern progress. Born and raised in western Kentucky, Mason taught at Mansfield State College in Pennsylvania. Her first books were *Nabokov's Garden: A Guide to Ada* (1974) and *The Girl Sleuth* (1975).

THOMAS MCGUANE: *Nobody's Angel.* Set in Deadrock, Montana, the novel concerns Patrick Fitzpatrick, a hard drinker and ex-soldier who has returned to his family ranch. Critics praise the novel as a fine contribution to the author's continuing exploration of how the people and institutions of the West adapt to contemporary life.

GLORIA NAYLOR (b. 1950): *The Women of Brewster Place.* This novel by the New York City writer comprises seven connected stories, describing seven black women in an urban ghetto and their struggle to revitalize their dead-end community. A sequel, *Men of Brewster Place*, would appear in 1998.

JOYCE CAROL OATES: *The Bloodsmoor Romance.* Described by its author as "the other side of *Little Women*," this parody of the nineteenth-century romance treats the experiences of five daughters of an eccentric inventor. It includes an appearance by a dandy named Mark Twain.

TOBY OLSON (b. 1937): *Seaview.* Olson's novel about a professional golf hustler and his wife who is dying of cancer receives the PEN/Faulkner Award and is praised by reviewer Ronald De Feo as "unlike any other recent American novel in the freshness of its approach and vision." The Illinois-born writer is also the author of several volumes of "talk poems," conversational meditations on multiple subjects.

CYNTHIA OZICK: *Levitation: Five Fictions.* The title work of this collection, regarded as one of Ozick's greatest achievements, treats the dilemmas faced by a Jewish-Christian married couple. The collection continues Ozick's examination of the difficulty of being Jewish in modern Western society.

SARA PARETSKY (b. 1947): *Indemnity Only.* This is the debut mystery featuring woman detective V. I. Warshawski and bringing a feminist perspective to the hard-boiled detective genre previously dominated by male writers. Born in Iowa, Paretsky earned an MBA from the University of Chicago and gave up in a career in business after conceiving her Chicago sleuth.

MARGE PIERCY: *Braided Lives.* In one of Piercy's most admired and autobiographical works, an aspiring writer in Detroit struggles against gender and class assumptions while her friends succumb to conventional roles as wives and mothers.

ISHMAEL REED: *The Terrible Twos.* Reed's novel depicts President Dean Clift (resembling Ronald Reagan), who had previously worked as a model. He is the dupe of corporate forces who have exiled Santa Claus, and it is up to Nane Saturday, an African American detective, to liberate Santa. The novel reflects Reed's characteristic combination of outlandish satire and an extraordinary gift for language.

NTOZAKE SHANGE: *Sassafras, Cypress, and Indigo.* Shange's first full-length novel deals with three sisters and their relationships with men and one another. It features a style described as "narrative potpourri," mixing together story episodes with recipes and poetry. Shange's next work, *Betsy Brown* (1985), is an account of a middle-class adolescent's coming of age in St. Louis in the 1950s.

ISAAC BASHEVIS SINGER: *Collected Stories.* This volume contains forty-seven stories, considered the best work by this Nobel Prize winner because they so deftly portray the human spirit ensnared in a world of powerful, callous, and sometimes hostile forces.

PAUL THEROUX: *The Mosquito Coast.* The novel concerns Ally Fox, a Yankee inventor who arduously tries to bring an ice machine to the natives of a Central American jungle village. His efforts are portrayed as mad, a misguided effort to transform an environment alien to his values. Theroux impresses critics with the verve of his narrative, probing the extremes of individualism and modern civilization against the backdrop of cultures resistant to change.

ANNE TYLER: *Dinner at the Homesick Restaurant.* Tyler's novel focuses on the long, unhappy life of a deserted wife, made worse by an interfering mother. Many critics consider this novel — Tyler's eleventh — her best. In John Updike's words, she attains a "new level of power," primarily because she treats her familiar theme of the family with so many complex improvisations.

JOHN UPDIKE: *Bech Is Back.* This is Updike's second collection of stories about Bech, a successful Jewish novelist who struggles with his usual enemies: travel, the problems of fame, and his relationships with women.

KURT VONNEGUT JR.: *Deadeye Dick.* Rudy Waltz, known as "Deadeye Dick" for accidentally shooting a pregnant woman, writes his memoirs, detailing other deaths and the explosion of a neutron bomb in Midland,

Ohio. Vonnegut's novel expresses his persistent theme of finding ways to cope with the accidental, irrational, and the fatal.

ALICE WALKER: *The Color Purple.* Walker's novel concerns the oppression of a black woman by both white and black society. The book violates many taboos with its considerations of black-on-black violence, incest, and lesbian love. A bestseller, it earns Walker both a Pulitzer Prize and a National Book Award. In 1988, the novel would be adapted for the screen by director Stephen Spielberg.

EDMUND WHITE: *A Boy's Own Story.* The great success of this autobiographical novel establishes its author as a key figure in gay literature. The novel's importance lies in its use of the conventions of the bildungsroman to tell the story of a boy's discovery of his gay orientation. It is as much a story about growing up as it is specifically about gay life.

JOHN A. WILLIAMS: *!Click Song.* Set mainly in the post–World War II world of publishing in New York, the novel describes the struggles of a black novelist.

Literary Criticism and Scholarship

LEON EDEL: *Stuff of Sleep and Dreams: Experiment in Literary Psychology.* The noted biographer and literary critic here explores how psychology and psychoanalytic concepts enhance the study of literature. Even critics who are dubious about psychology's claims find Edel's writing graceful and thoughtful — a work of literature itself.

LESLIE A. FIEDLER: *What Was Literature? Class Culture and Mass Society.* Fiedler stimulates controversy by contending that academic critics have made too rigid a distinction between "high culture" and "low culture." Works of genius — such as *Uncle Tom's Cabin* and *Gone with the Wind* — in Fiedler's view deserve far more recognition. He says literature itself suffers when it is divided into works for the elite and for the masses.

Nonfiction

EDWARD ABBEY: *Down the River.* Considered one of the foremost commentators on the American environment, Abbey presents excerpts from his journals in a style and manner reminiscent of Henry David Thoreau.

NINA AUERBACH (b. 1943): *Woman and the Demon: The Life of a Victorian Myth.* Auerbach, a professor of English at the University of Pennsylvania, contends that the stereotype of the repressed Victorian woman obscures a countermyth of the dangerous, demonic woman. Critic George Levine finds Auerbach's scholarship impressive and persuasive, noting that she had culled her argument

from an impressive array of evidence: poems, paintings, popular and serious fiction, biographies, essays, and psychological studies.

RUSSELL BAKER (b. 1925): *Growing Up.* Baker's memoir of his childhood wins a Pulitzer Prize. A Virginia-born jounalist for the *Baltimore Sun*, Baker began writing the nationally syndicated "Observer" column for the *New York Times* in 1962. A second volume of memoirs, *The Good Times*, would follow in 1989.

WILLIAM BARRETT (1913–1992): *The Truants: Adventures Among the Intellectuals.* A key figure in the group of New York intellectuals who wrote for the influential *Partisan Review*, Barrett provides vivid portraits of Philip Rahv and William Phillips (the journal's editors) and of contributors such as Clement Greenberg and Dwight MacDonald. Reviewer Christopher Lehmann-Haupt calls Barrett's description of poet and critic Delmore Schwartz as good as Saul Bellow's in his novel *Humboldt's Gift.*

MARSHALL BERMAN (b. 1940): *All That Is Solid Melts into Air: The Experience of Modernity.* In this highly praised, searching examination of the idea of progress, Berman, a professor of political science at New York's City College, examines the writings of Johann Goethe, Fyodor Dostoyevski, and others and explores the ramifications of modern architecture to reveal how modernism has fostered and responded to change. The title of his book refers to the prospect of nihilism and the denial of universal values, which seem to be inherent in modernism.

FOX BUTTERFIELD (b. 1939): *China: Alive in the Bitter Sea.* In 1979 Butterfield had become the first correspondent for the *New York Times* based in Beijing in thirty years. This American Book Award–winning volume records his experiences and the views of ordinary Chinese citizens.

ANGELA DAVIS: *Women, Race, and Class.* Davis's essay collection explores the connections between the black liberation and the women's rights movements.

ANNIE DILLARD: *Teaching a Stone to Talk: Expeditions and Encounters.* In this volume of essays, Dillard often begins with an observation of the natural world, which she then proceeds to explore. The subjects include weasels, a total eclipse — anything that will lead her in the direction of philosophical or metaphysical speculation. Underpinning this technique is a broad background in anthropology, biology, history, culture, and geography.

BETTY FRIEDAN: *The Second Stage.* In a book that helps launch the postfeminist era, Friedan addresses the "feminist mystique" of the superwoman who is expected to juggle effortlessly career, marriage, and motherhood.

She also targets for criticism radical feminists who have co-opted the movement with an anti-male, anti-family orientation that Friedan finds counterproductive.

PAUL FUSSELL: *The Boy Scout Handbook and Other Observations.* Fussell's keen perceptions of American life rest on his experience in World War II, the subject of one of this volume's most memorable essays. War taught him a sense of irony and skepticism that he applies in shrewd and astringent assessments of the American ideals evident in a handbook for Boy Scouts, the fiction about World War II, and the American academy's handling of literature.

IRVING HOWE: *A Margin of Hope.* In his autobiography, Howe, an important American critic and one of the writers affiliated with the *Partisan Review*, describes his political and literary journey from his early days as a Trotskyist to his evolving sense of democratic socialism and his writing about Yiddish and American culture, literature, and politics.

NORMAN MAILER: *Pieces and Pontifications.* In this collection of Mailer's essays from the 1970s, the most important is "A Harlot High and Low," a long and probing examination of the CIA and the psychology of the spy. It would prepare the ground for his CIA novel, *Harlot's Ghost* (1991).

RICHARD RODRIGUEZ (b. 1947): *Hunger of Memory.* The book details Rodriguez's evolution from a Mexican American schoolchild who knew only fifty words of English to a literary scholar and nationally acclaimed memoirist. His memoir also describes his gradual alienation from his cultural roots as his assimilation into mainstream culture deprives him of his native tongue and his connection to his past. The book achieves popularity at a time when multiculturalism is becoming a force in American education. Two subsequent volumes of autobiographically based reflections on American life — *Days of Obligation* (1992) and *Brown: The Last Discovery of America* (2002) — would follow.

JONATHAN SCHELL (b. 1943): *The Fate of the Earth.* Schell's best-selling study is described by reviewer Richard Rhodes as "the first accurate, honest, full-scale examination of the certain and probable consequences of nuclear war." Schell was a contributing editor for *The New Yorker* from 1967 to 1987.

SUSAN SHEEHAN (b. 1937): *Is There No Place on Earth for Me?* Winner of a Pulitzer Prize, this book portrays a woman's decline into mental illness and the institutions that attempt to cure her. Critics are impressed with the authenticity and sensitivity of the Vienna-born journalist's work, which had appeared initially in *The New Yorker;* several reviewers call it one of the best reports on life within mental institutions ever written.

KATE SIMON (1912–1990): *Bronx Primitive.* Simon's National Book Critics Circle Award–winning memoir is praised for its lucid and unidealized portrayal of the author's childhood as the eldest daughter of an immigrant Polish shoemaker. Two other autobiographical volumes, *A Wider World* (1986) and *Etchings in an Hourglass* (1990), would follow.

WALLACE STEGNER: *One Way to Spell Man.* Part autobiography, part a collection of essays, this volume includes the distinguished writer's work from the 1950s to the early 1980s. Some essays focus on individual writers such as Owen Wister, Walter van Tilburg Clark, and A. B. Guthrie who influenced Stegner's view of the American West. Other essays promote the importance of the American West and the idea of the wilderness.

GORE VIDAL: *The Second American Revolution and Other Essays: 1976–1982.* Vidal's essay collection wins the National Book Critics Circle Award for criticism. Included is "Notes on Abraham Lincoln," Vidal's working notes for *Lincoln* (1984).

Poetry

WILLIAM BRONK (1918–1999): *Life Supports.* Bronk wins the American Book Award and his first widespread attention for his meditative verse. "His poetry of statement," reviewer Robert D. Spector observes, "impresses with its clarity and precision of language; it manages to make metaphysics a subject of human emotion rather than a grand abstraction." Bronk ran a family business until he retired in 1970. His other volumes include *Vectors and Smoothable Curves* (1983), *Selected Poems* (1995), and *The Cage of Age* (1996).

DENIS JOHNSON (b. 1949): *The Incognito Lounge and Other Poems.* Johnson's third collection was selected by Mark Strand for the National Poetry Series. The poems give voice to marginalized Americans — denizens of the street, diners, seedy lounges, and buses. "The person who really can't say anything for himself," Johnson has observed, "is often the one who fascinates me." *The Veil* (1987) and *The Throne of the Third Heaven of the Nation's Millennium General Assembly* (1995), his collected poems, would follow. Johnson was born in Germany and lived during his childhood and adolescence in Tokyo and Manila. His first book of poetry, *The Man Among the Seals* (1969), was published while he was still an undergraduate at the University of Iowa.

MAURICE KENNY (b. 1929): *Blackrobe: Isaac Jogues, b. March 11, 1607, d. October 18, 1646: Poems.* Kenny's poetic account of the early encounters between Jesuit missionaries and the Mohawks is nominated for a Pulitzer Prize. Born in Watertown, New York, of Mohawk ancestors, Kenny would win the American Book Award for *The Mama Poems* (1984).

GALWAY KINNELL: *Selected Poems.* Kinnell's collection, which wins the Pulitzer Prize and the American Book Award, is hailed by reviewer Morris Dickstein as a "full scale dossier" of "one of the true master poets of his generation." The volume contains poems written over three decades, including Kinnell's nature poetry from the 1960s and many of the death-defying, Whitmanesque poems in *The Book of Nightmares* (1971) and *Mortal Acts, Mortal Wounds* (1980).

BRAD LEITHAUSER (b. 1953): *Hundreds of Fireflies.* Compared by critics with Elizabeth Bishop's poetry, Leithauser's verse is highly formal and usually rhymed. As the collection's title suggests, his work is suffused with a concern to portray light as points of perception. Reviews find the range of his poems impressive — from "An Expanded Want Ad," a lush evocation and expansion of an advertisement for a summer cottage in Michigan, to "Alternate Landscape," in which the poet watches the earthly landscape vanish into the clouds seen from a jet plane, to "Miniature," an exquisite description of an anthill. Born in Detroit, Leithauser graduated from Harvard and lived for several years in Japan.

WILLIAM MATTHEWS (1942–1997): *Flood.* Several critics cite this volume as evidence of the Ohio-born writer's emergence as a major poet. The collection has a strong retrospective cast, suffused with marine metaphors. His vivid evocations of nature have been compared with Robert Frost's and his economical poetic line with William Carlos Williams's. He would win the National Book Critics Circle Award for *Time & Money: New Poems* (1995).

JAMES MERRILL: *The Changing Light at Sandover.* Critics praise this collection as a "sacred epic in a postreligious age." It combines parts of three previous books, *Divine Comedies* (1976), *Mirabell: Books of Number* (1978), and *Scripts for the Pageant* (1980). This trilogy, plus a new coda, "The Higher Keys," reflects Merrill's ambitious poetic program — akin to Dante's and Milton's — to portray the spiritual dimension of the world in verse.

MARGE PIERCY: *Circle on the Water: Selected Poems.* This collection is culled from the poet's seven previous volumes published from 1963 to 1982. The poems reflect her upbringing as a poor white in Detroit's black slums, and the subjects include class discrimination, racism, sexism, but also her intense enjoyment of life's simple pleasures and the bond that is possible between people and nature.

KATHA POLLITT (b. 1949): *Antarctic Traveller.* Winner of the National Book Critics Circle Award, the collection shows its author as a keen observer and writer of free verse. Pollitt's subjects range from "Ballet Blanc" (exploring the imagination of a member of the audience) to "Archeology" (treating life like an archaeological dig). Born in New York City, Pollitt has been an editor of *The Nation* since 1982.

CATHY SONG (b. 1955): *Picture Bride.* Selected for the Yale Series of Younger Poets, Song's first collection captures the experiences of the author's grandmother, who journeyed from Korea to Hawaii to be married after being selected by her husband based on her photograph. A second volume, *Frameless Windows, Squares of Light*, would follow in 1988.

MONA VAN DUYN: *Letters from a Father and Other Poems.* The title work describes the physical decline of the poet's aging parents. Robert Hass observes that despite the potential for sentimentality, the sequence "gets at an area of human experience that literature — outside of Samuel Beckett — has hardly touched."

CHARLES WRIGHT: *Country Music.* Winner of the National Book Award, this is the first of Wright's anthology collections. It includes his previous volumes *Hard Freight* (1973), *Bloodlines* (1975), and *China Trace* (1977), which constitute chapters in Wright's spiritual autobiography. It would be followed by *The World of Ten Thousand Things* (1997) and *Negative Blue* (2000), similarly composed of three previous collections.

Publications and Events

The Library of America. Originally proposed by critic Edmund Wilson in 1968, the nonprofit Library of America begins to publish authoritative texts of major American literary works. Appearing with an introductory essay by a recognized scholar and a chronology, the volumes are aimed at the general reading public.

USA Today. The national daily newspaper debuts. With its short news items, color photos, and eye-catching graphics, it is quickly labeled "McPaper," the journalistic equivalent of fast food. However, it proves successful, and its style is widely imitated in newspapers across the country.

1983
Drama and Theater

MARIA IRENE FORNES: *Mud.* The playwright has acknowledged her debt to Samuel Beckett, and *Mud*, one of her frequently produced plays, echoes his terse, elliptical style. The drama centers on a woman who struggles to express herself and throw off the burden of the men in her life. The setting is reminiscent of John Steinbeck's *The Grapes of Wrath*, wherein the struggle to be free is not just political but elemental and biological.

TINA HOWE (b. 1937): *Painting Churches*. In Howe's play, a daughter helps her aging parents move out of their house while struggling to remain focused on her work as a painter. She does so by painting a portrait of her parents, depicting their decline but also preserving a part of her past. Howe calls it her "deepest play," and critic Gerald Bordman singles it out as one of her most memorable, distinguished by her fundamental humanity and insight into human character. The New York City playwright's previous plays include *The Nest* (1969), *Museum* (1976), and *The Art of Dining* (1979).

DAVID MAMET: *Glengarry Glen Ross*. Mamet's ensemble play features several male characters in a real estate office, vying to obtain sales from the same list of prospects. As much a comedy as a drama, Mamet explores not only the salesmen's mentality but the different ages of man, as they desperately confront the demand to get ahead. Notable critics such as Robert Brustein call the play a classic—as good or better than Arthur Miller's *Death of a Salesman*.

SAM SHEPARD: *Fool for Love*. Shepard's three-character play about a love-hate relationship between a half-brother and a half-sister opens at the Circle Repertory Company in New York, where it runs for one thousand performances. A play about sometimes violent, nearly inarticulate people nonetheless makes for good drama, winning four Obie Awards and going on to many revivals with regional theater companies.

NEIL SIMON: *Brighton Beach Memoirs*. Set in the Brighton Beach section of Brooklyn, the play centers on Eugene Jerome, a young Jewish boy who dreams of becoming a writer. Critics consider this comedy-drama one of Simon's best, largely because his humor seems more deeply imbedded in the fabric of the family life he depicts with such authenticity and compassion.

Fiction

RENATA ADLER: *Pitch Dark*. Adler's second novel, about a woman journalist's affair with a married man, is one of the most widely discussed books of the year because of its mixture of narrative elements and a "meditation on writing a novel."

PAULA GUNN ALLEN (b. 1939): *The Woman Who Owned the Shadows*. In this novel, Allen, part Sioux and Lebanese American, integrates tribal songs, rituals, and legends into the story of a mixed-blood woman whose survival depends, in part, on the strength she derives from Spider Grandmother, a powerful figure in ancient tribal mythology. Allen's achievement has been compared to that of Leslie Marmon Silko and Louise Erdrich, who also explore the role of women and family in Native American culture.

DONALD BARTHELME: *Overnight to Many Distant Cities*. Although employing his characteristic dreamlike monologue technique, this collection shows Barthelme dealing more directly with human emotions and allowing some hope to creep into his assessment of contemporary life.

FREDERICK BARTHELME (b. 1943): *Moon Deluxe*. After two experimental books — *Rangoon* (1970), a story collection, and *War and War* (1971), a novel — Barthelme, the younger brother of Donald Barthelme, receives his first extensive critical response with this collection of spare and cryptic stories dealing with middle-aged men's failed marriages, dissolving relationships, and frustrations. Reviewer Richard Eder calls the volume "a nearly perfect minimalist work." Similar themes and treatment are in evidence in his second novel, *Second Marriage* (1984), about a triangular relationship among a man, his wife, and his ex-wife.

THOMAS BERGER: *The Feud*. Berger receives a Pulitzer Prize nomination for this black comedy of proliferating disasters that begin when a hardware store owner asks a customer to put away his unlit cigar.

MARION ZIMMER BRADLEY (1930–1999): *The Mists of Avalon*. The fantasy writer achieves her greatest popular success with this retelling of the Arthurian legend from a feminist perspective. Bradley began publishing science fiction stories in the 1950s. She is the author of the Darkover science fiction series that began with *The Sword of Aldones* (1962).

RAYMOND CARVER: *Cathedral*. Critics find this collection of stories less austere than Carver's earlier work but just as accomplished in its contribution to the development of the American short story. Its more hopeful attitude toward life contrasts with the spareness of his earlier work. *Cathedral* is more explicit and outgoing, and more discursive, with characters talking about their emotions and seeking to explain themselves. His subject remains the same—the complex tensions between men and women—but the movement in these stories is toward reconciliation and renewal.

ANDRE DUBUS: *The Times Are Never So Bad*. This story collection is noteworthy for its keen and ruminative use of psychology to explore people and places. In "The Pretty Girl," for example, Dubus portrays several points of view of Polly, a barmaid, who shoots Ray, her ex-husband. Extensive use of flashback highlights the connection between past and present and Polly's motivations.

ERNEST J. GAINES: *A Gathering of Old Men.* To investigate a murder on a Louisiana plantation, the sheriff must listen to the individual stories of a group of aging black men, who each confesses to a murder. As one reviewer observes, their "individual stories coalesce into a single powerful tale of subjugation, exploitation, and humiliation at the hands of landowners."

MARK HELPRIN: *Winter's Tale.* The novel concerns Peter Lake, a murderer whose talent is operating machines that run the city. Part fantasy, part historical novel, Helprin's book establishes his reputation as an important and ambitious contemporary novelist.

RACHEL INGALLS (b. 1940): *Mrs. Caliban.* Ingalls, an American writer living in London, would be little known until 1986, when the British Book Marketing Council would name her 1983 novella one of the twenty best novels written by living American writers who had come of age after World War II. It is the improbable story about a depressed California housewife's passionate affair with her own fantasy, a six-foot-seven creature known as "Aquarius the Monsterman," whom she calls Larry. The work is both a parable of modern life and an utterly realistic portrait of derangement.

WILLIAM KENNEDY: *Ironweed.* Set in Kennedy's hometown of Albany, and part of a series of novels about upstate New York, the novel centers on Francis Phelan, a former major league pitcher, now retired. In the midst of the Great Depression, Phelan struggles with the burdens of the past as well as his lover's alcoholism. His moving, fitful efforts to redeem his life and to prevail, set against Kennedy's profound understanding of the region and its people, wins high praise from critics, and the book receives both the National Book Award and the Pulitzer Prize.

NORMAN MAILER: *Ancient Evenings.* Mailer's mammoth book, set in Egypt during the years 1320–1121 B.C., concerns reincarnation, sexuality, and the correspondences between the age of Ramses II and modern America.

PAULE MARSHALL: *Praisesong for the Widow.* Marshall presents Avey Johnson, a black New Yorker with middle-class (white) attitudes. On a Caribbean vacation she is stimulated by watching how black women dance, and she begins to realize that she has a black spirit that needs liberating. What makes her story persuasive is Marshall's grasp of Barbadian idiom and her vivid characterizations.

CYNTHIA OZICK: *The Cannibal Galaxy.* This novel is about Joseph Brill, a Jewish child hidden in a French convent during the Holocaust. Although he aspires to be an astronomer, his later career in the United States is a failure. Critics single out Ozick's deft handling of what would become her signature theme: how to remain a Jew in a secular, assimilationist world.

PHILIP ROTH: *The Anatomy Lesson.* In the third volume of the novelist's portrayal of his writerly alter ego, Zuckerman is now forty, in broken health, balding, and suffering a crisis of confidence in his career. As usual, Roth treats his subject with remarkable humor, and critics praise his profound examination of his character's self-doubt in the context of larger twentieth-century concerns about the fate of humanity.

THOMAS SAVAGE: *For Mary, with Love.* This novel is narrated by Mary Skoning, a schemer who comes to grief, losing both her money and her social prestige. Savage presents his character with sensitivity, preserving the ambiguity of her actions in a well-paced narrative that provokes several critics to call him one of the best novelists of the past three decades.

ISAAC BASHEVIS SINGER: *The Penitent.* Singer's novel concerns Joseph Shapiro, "the penitent," who tells his story to Singer at the Wailing Wall in Jerusalem in 1969. A Polish Jew who had escaped the Holocaust and settled in New York City and then in Israel recounts his search for a code of life and a place in the world. This search entails the abandonment of Orthodox Judaism and any kind of religious orientation. Through Shapiro's narrative, Singer relentlessly explores the troubling consequences of a world that forsakes traditional forms of belief and culture.

LEE SMITH: *Oral History.* Smith's multigenerational saga of the Southern Cantrell family, told through several points of view, wins the Sir Walter Raleigh Award for fiction and the North Carolina Award. Reviewer David Bradley praises the book, stating, "you could make comparisons to Faulkner and Carson McCullers, to *The Sound and the Fury*, *As I Lay Dying*, and *Wuthering Heights*." Smith's subsequent novels include *Family Linen* (1985), *Saving Grace* (1995), and *Fair and Tender Ladies* (1998).

STEVE STERN (b. 1947): *Isaac and the Undertaker's Daughter.* This collection of stories is set in the South and concerns Jewish American life. Stern's characters delve into the occult, believe in ghosts, and are devotees of mystical texts. Critic Morris Dickstein notes that Jewish American writers rarely explore this magical vein of Jewish lore, and he compares Stern's deft handling of his subject matter with the accomplished work of Stanley Elkin and Bernard Malamud. Subsequent books by the Memphis-born writer would include *The Moon and Ruben Shein* (1984), *Lazar Malkin Enters Heaven* (1986), and *Harry Kaplan's Adventures Underground* (1991).

GORE VIDAL: *Duluth*. Vidal offers a Swiftian satire on American life, emphasizing the excesses of American mass culture from the perspective of a typical American town.

JOHN EDGAR WIDEMAN: *Sent for You Yesterday*. Wideman's PEN/Faulkner Award–winning autobiographical novel is the third set in Homewood, the Pittsburgh ghetto where he was raised. The first person narrator is, like Wideman, a young black writer who has moved far away, returning to Homewood only for reactions and inspiration. Reviewer Alan Cheuse declares that the book "establishes a mythological link between character and landscape," which shows Wideman at the height of his considerable powers.

Literary Criticism and Scholarship

WENDELL BERRY (b. 1934): *Standing by Words: Essays*. In this collection the Kentucky poet, novelist, and essayist is dismayed at the decline of language skills in contemporary culture. Critics compare this work with George Orwell's stance in "Politics and the English Language," which critiques modern vocabulary for its debasement of direct simple language in favor of jargon. Berry anchors his insights in his experience as a farmer and his direct contact with nature.

NOEL RILEY FITCH (b. 1937): *Sylvia Beach and the Lost Generation: A History of Literary Paris in the Twenties and Thirties*. Beach, the proprietor of the Shakespeare and Company Bookshop in Paris, helped foster and publish some of the century's greatest authors, including James Joyce and Ernest Hemingway. Critics praise the California literature professor's handling of literary history.

JOHN GARDNER: *On Becoming a Novelist*. Part memoir, part guide to aspiring writers of fiction, this book is also a sensitive introduction to why novels matter, how novels should be read, and, as one critic observes, a lively inquiry into the creative process itself.

CYNTHIA OZICK: *Art and Ardor*. In this highly praised collection of essays, Ozick explores the demands of religious belief and artistic creation. Critics admire her passion for her subject and her moral subtlety. Ozick's own dilemma, as she eloquently shows, is how to maintain her Jewish identity while remaining a thoroughly modern writer.

JOANNA RUSS: *How to Suppress Women's Writing*. Russ tackles head-on the reasons why few women are included in the literary canon. She looks at the way men establish the profession of teaching and writing about literature, concluding that they have engaged in various ploys to relegate women to the status of minor authors.

EDWARD W. SAID: *The World, the Text, and the Critic*. Said's essay collection wins the René Wellek Award in literary criticism. The volume outlines Said's conception of "antithetical thinking," arguing that literary criticism should take oppositional stands to established views and be an investigative activity.

JOHN UPDIKE: *Hugging the Shore: Essays in Criticism*. Updike's collection of essays and reviews wins the National Book Critics Circle Award for criticism. A second collection, *Odd Jobs*, would appear in 1991.

ALICE WALKER: *In Search of Our Mothers' Gardens: Womanist Prose*. Regarded as an important feminist critic of both African American and white American male writers, Walker discusses the important influences on her and on the women and men she believes should be included in her womanist perspective. Walker's criticism is distinctive, combining literary analysis with an autobiographical and narrative structure.

EDMUND WILSON: *The Forties: From Notebooks and Diaries of the Period*. Wilson writes about ideas for his important books such as *The Wound and the Bow*, about his travels throughout North America, South America, and Europe, and about literary figures such as Edna St. Vincent Millay and John Dos Passos.

Nonfiction

JACQUES BARZUN: *A Stroll with William James*. In this volume, Barzun delves into James's biography to discuss the founder of American psychology. He finds in James a model thinker and participant in his own times.

PETER BRAZEAU (b. 1942): *Parts of a World: Wallace Stevens Remembered*. This oral biography, based on more than 150 interviews with the friends and the family of this distinguished poet, offers some insight into an elusive figure. Although certain critics wish for more information about the private and inner life of the artist, they recognize Brazeau's effort to document what Stevens meant to his family, friends, and associates.

FREDERICK BUECHNER: *Now and Then*. This second volume of Buechner's autobiography covers 1950 to the early 1980s. Besides providing deft and compact portraits of the important figures in his life, he explores the way he believes God has been at work in his life as a contemporary novelist.

JOAN DIDION: *Salvador.* Didion supplies a probing study of U.S. policy in El Salvador during the period of terror that made the country one of the most dangerous places in the world. Critics praise her for bringing to this heart of darkness a sensibility worthy of Joseph Conrad.

WILLIAM LEAST HEAT-MOON (b. 1939): *Blue Highways: A Journey into America.* The writer's account of his thirteen-thousand-mile transcontinental journey along America's two-lane roads provokes comparisons with Alexis de Tocqueville, Mark Twain, Jack Kerouac, and John Steinbeck. Heat-Moon took a leave from teaching at Stephens College in Missouri to undertake his road odyssey.

SEYMOUR M. HERSH (b. 1937): *The Price of Power: Henry Kissinger in the Nixon White House.* Hersh, a former *New York Times* reporter, continues his controversial critique of American power in a profile that portrays Kissinger as conniving, ambitious, and devious. His previous books included *My Lai Four* (1970) and *Cover-Up* (1972).

JOYCE JOHNSON (b. 1935): *Minor Characters: A Young Woman's Coming-of-Age in the Beat Orbit of Jack Kerouac.* Johnson's National Book Critics Circle Award–winning memoir details her associations with members of the Beat movement in Greenwich Village in the 1950s and her two-year romantic involvement with Jack Kerouac. The book is praised not only for its portraits of famous writers but also for its sensitive treatment of young women like Johnson, "minor characters" in the larger drama being played out around them.

STANLEY KARNOW (b. 1925): *Vietnam: A History.* The Asian correspondent for *Time*, the *Washington Post*, and NBC News received Emmy, Peabody, and Dupont Awards for his script for the PBS documentary series, the basis for this companion volume. It features extensive interviews with participants, most notably several North Vietnamese military leaders.

ARCHIBALD MACLEISH: *Letters of Archibald MacLeish, 1907–1982.* Much of the politics and literature of the modern period is reflected in these wide-ranging letters. MacLeish's correspondents include Ernest Hemingway, Ezra Pound, Dean Acheson, and John Peale Bishop.

WALKER PERCY: *Lost in the Cosmos: The Last Self-Help Book.* Percy's collection of essays — as its subtitle signals — is a parody. There is no help for existential man bereft of absolute beliefs in a secular world. He finds in the nature of language itself a supple way of dealing with an ambiguous world, which modern science attempts to rationalize and contemporary culture tries to simplify or ignore. The work claims that only a renewed sense of the religious impulse can retrieve humankind from the chaos of its own inventions.

PAUL STARR (b. 1949): *The Social Transformation of American Medicine.* Critics hail the Harvard sociologist's study, winner of the Bancroft Prize and the Pulitzer Prize, as the definitive history of the medical profession in America.

GLORIA STEINEM (b. 1934): *Outrageous Acts and Everyday Rebellions.* This work collects essays and articles, including "I Was a Playboy Bunny" and portraits of Marilyn Monroe, Linda Lovelace, and Jacqueline Onassis.

MICHAEL WALZER (b. 1935): *Spheres of Justice: A Defense of Pluralism and Equality.* Walzer advances a widely debated argument that all people are not created equal. Since not everyone possesses equal talent and intelligence, simple egalitarianism (keeping everyone as equal as possible) is not feasible. Instead, he argues that a "complex" equality must evolve to acknowledge individual differences.

Poetry

MAYA ANGELOU: *Shaker, Why Don't You Sing?* Critics praise Angelou's verse for its light but deft lyrical quality. As in her autobiographies, her poetry gracefully deals with somber subjects such as racial tensions and the poet's melancholy sensibility. Included are "Family Affairs" and "Caged Bird."

FRANK BIDART: *The Sacrifice.* Bidart receives critical acclaim for this collection of verse exploring the theme of guilt, most notably in the long poem "The War of Vaslav Nijinsky."

AMY CLAMPITT (1920–1994): *The Kingfisher.* The first major collection by the sixty-three-year-old poet is called by reviewer Edmund White "one of the most brilliant debuts in recent American history." Clampitt treats with mastery scenes of growing up in rural Iowa, observations along the Maine coast, and appreciations of John Keats. Two additional acclaimed collections would appear during the decade — *What the Light Was Like* (1985) and *Archaic Figure* (1987).

RITA DOVE: *The Museum.* The poet widens her focus in this powerful collection. An example is the poem "Parsley," describing the order of Dominican Republic dictator Rafael Trujillo to have twenty thousand blacks killed because they could not pronounce the letter *r* in *perejil*, the Spanish word for *parsley*.

NORMAN DUBIE (b. 1945): *Selected and New Poems.* The Maine-born poet's twelfth collection consolidates his reputation as a major contemporary poet with an impressive range of subject matter, including both Asian and European history, culture, and art.

JORIE GRAHAM (b. 1951): *Erosion.* This collection is admired for its meditative quality. Critics such as Helen Vendler praise the poet's supple exploration of metaphysical and religious questions — clearly announced in the titles of poems such as "In What Manner the Body Is United with the Soule," "At the Exhumed Body of Santa Chiara, Assisi," and "At Luca Signorelli's Resurrection of the Body." The New York City–born poet would win the Pulitzer Prize for *The Dream of the Unified Field* (1995).

MARY OLIVER (b. 1935): *American Primitive.* This volume of poems dedicated to Oliver's observation of the natural world earns the Pulitzer Prize. It presents a new kind of Romanticism that refuses to acknowledge boundaries between nature and the observing self. Born in Ohio, Oliver has been a longtime resident of Cape Cod and Vermont as a teacher at Bennington College. Her previous volumes include *No Voyage, and Other Poems* (1963), *The River Styx, Ohio* (1972), and *Twelve Moons* (1978).

DAVE SMITH (b. 1948): *In the House of the Judge.* The poet's seventh collection, considered his best by several critics, evokes a strong sense of place (tidewater Virginia, Salt Lake City, New York City) in four highly structured sequences of poems. The title poem is a sensitive exploration of how human character is tied to place or the "house" people make of their lives. The Ohio-born poet's other volumes include *The Fisherman's Whore* (1974), *Goshawk, Antelope* (1979), and *Dream Flights* (1981).

GARY SNYDER: *Axe Handles.* This collection includes brief lyrics, riddles, and free-verse narratives inspired by the poet's deep immersion in Asian languages and cultures. Understatement, vivid imagery, and highly crafted spare syntax are evident in the title poem, which suggests poetry should be like a fine hand-crafted tool, the language sharp and incisive, cutting through the clutter of thought.

DAVID WAGONER (b. 1926): *First Light.* Wagoner's thirteenth book is considered by many his best. Especially impressive is his range of topics, including family history ("The Bad Uncle"), national myth ("The Author of American Ornithology Sketches a Bird, Now Extinct"), nature ("Backtracking"), animal behavior ("Loons Mating"), and portraits of individuals ("A Woman Standing in the Surf"). The previous collections by the Ohio-born poet who teaches at the University of Washinton include *Dry Sun, Dry Wind* (1953), *The Nesting Ground* (1963), *Staying Alive* (1966), and *Collected Poems* (1976).

ROBERT PENN WARREN: *Chief Joseph of the Nez Perce.* Warren's penultimate poetry collection is a book-length narrative poem chronicling Chief Joseph's heroic resistance to relocation efforts before defeat by U.S. army troops. Warren's final collection, *New and Selected Poems*, would appear in 1985.

C. K. WILLIAMS: *Tar.* In poems such as "One of the Muses," Williams explores the role of the poet who seems unable to have an impact on his environment. Evident are the poet's verve, deft use of Whitmanesque long lines, and dedication to poetry itself as a redeeming feature of life.

Publications and Events

Vanity Fair. Condé Nast Publications issues a new version of the magazine forty-six years after its last issue. In 1984, British editor Tina Brown (b. 1953) would be brought in to edit the magazine.

1984
Drama and Theater

BETH HENLEY: *The Miss Firecracker Contest.* Henley explores Southern manners and the mother-daughter relationship in this play. A young woman named Carnelle is determined to win the Miss Firecracker Contest as a way of getting back at provincial townspeople and her rival. But fame turns out not to be so desirable when it means engaging in rather fierce competition. Henley's comic characters are juxtaposed against the rituals of Southern life.

ARTHUR KOPIT: *End of the World.* Like much of Kopit's other work, this play explores the corrupting forces in American life. A playwright becomes a private investigator and exposes the parties responsible for nuclear proliferation. Kopit uses black humor to explore this troubling subject and shows how easily even his good characters are caught up in the momentum toward destruction.

MARSHA NORMAN: *Traveler in the Dark.* Norman's play features a surgeon coping with the death of his childhood friend, on whom he has unsuccessfully operated.

DAVID RABE: *Hurlyburly.* Set in a bungalow in the Hollywood Hills, Rabe's play chronicles the lives of four men, separated or divorced, who confront their disappointments in love and in their careers in the movie and television industries. Critics find Rabe's presentation of a world in moral chaos powerful, if sometimes painful to watch. *Those the River Keeps* (1994) is a prequel, exploring earlier details in the lives of some of the protagonists.

LARRY SHUE (1946–1985): *The Foreigner.* An extremely shy Englishman disrupts a Georgia fishing lodge when he feigns an inability to speak English in this drama by the New Orleans–born playwright and actor. Critics find the play remarkably effective in presenting the "oddball" visitor who suddenly overturns the customary way of seeing things. His other Broadway success would be *The Nerd* (1987).

STEPHEN SONDHEIM: *Sunday in the Park with George.* This musical, based on the life of painter Georges Seurat, is an elaborate and playful reconstruction of the process by which he constructed his great painting *A Sunday Afternoon on the Island of La Grande Jatte.*

AUGUST WILSON (b. 1945): *Ma Rainey's Black Bottom.* Set in the 1920s, the play centers on a lively jazz singer and her group who decide whether to pursue their art or cave in to commercial considerations. The play establishes Wilson's theme of the African American response to the demands of assimilation, which erodes black identity and corrupts the individual artist.

Fiction

SAUL BELLOW: *Him with His Foot in His Mouth and Other Stories.* Bellow's collection deals with ordinary people and intellectuals struggling to maintain their personal dignity and manage some form of affirmation. Along with the title work, it includes "Cousins," "A Silver Dish," "What Kind of a Day Did You Have?" and "Zetland: By a Character Witness."

T. CORAGHESSAN BOYLE: *Budding Prospects: A Pastoral.* Boyle's well-received adventure novel focuses on the inept Felix Nasmyth, who tries to seize the day by growing a marijuana crop in northern California. Critics delight in this novel's characters and praise Boyle for his deft skewering of the myth of American enterprise.

SANDRA CISNEROS (b. 1954): *The House on Mango Street.* The Chicago-born author's first novel is her most critically acclaimed work. In subsequent works Cisneros would continue to use the simple, almost childlike narrative voice developed here to tell the story of a young Chicana writer. *Woman Hollering Creek and Other Stories* would follow in 1991.

TOM CLANCY (b. 1947): *The Hunt for Red October.* The first of Clancy's techno-thrillers, first published by the scholarly Naval Institute Press, becomes a bestseller. Its story of a Soviet submarine commander's attempt to defect with his state-of-the-art vessel introduces Jack Ryan, CIA consultant and scholar. Other thrillers would follow — *Red Storm Rising* (1986), *Patriot Games* (1987), and *Clear and Present Danger* (1989) — making Clancy one of the biggest-selling authors of the 1980s and 1990s. The Baltimore native worked as an insurance agent before beginning his writing career.

JOAN DIDION: *Democracy.* Set in Southeast Asia, this novel exemplifies Didion's grasp of international politics and the American character. The novel's protagonist is Inez Christian Victor, the wife of a liberal California senator. She is obsessed with the mysterious Jack Lovett, a political operative working in Vietnam, where Inez goes to collect the body of her daughter, a heroin addict. Inez and her author soon find themselves on the shifting ground of fiction and fact, with Didion injecting herself into the narrative as an author trying to make sense of characters caught in the ambiguity of history.

E. L. DOCTOROW: *Lives of the Poets.* Doctorow's story collection contains the admired work "The Hunter," the title novella, and "The Waterworks," a brief sketch of what would become his 1994 novel, *The Waterworks.*

HARRIET DOERR (1910–2002): *Stones for Ibarra.* Doerr's first novel concerns an idealistic American couple's move to a small Mexican village where they are the only foreigners. The novel receives glowing reviews and the American Book Award for first work of fiction. A second novel, *Consider This, Señora*, would follow in 1995.

ANDRE DUBUS: *We Don't Live Here Anymore.* This volume collects *Adultery, Finding a Girl in America*, and the title work, which together form a trilogy detailing the marital difficulties of two couples with academic careers.

LOUISE ERDRICH (b. 1954): *Love Medicine.* The first volume of a tetralogy draws on the North Dakota–raised writer's Chippewa–German American background. The novel, which consists of fourteen related stories told by seven members of three generations of two Chippewa families, borrows at least some of its form from William Faulkner. Erdrich was married to Native American scholar and writer Michael Dorris (1946–1997).

WILLIAM GIBSON (b. 1948): *Neuromancer.* Gibson's first novel, about the near-future urbanized world of "the Sprawl," pioneers the science fiction genre of cyberpunk, combining futurism and a hard-boiled detective style. It wins the Nebula Award, the Hugo Award, and the Philip K. Dick Memorial Award. The South Carolina–born science fiction writer's other novels would include *Count Zero* (1986), *The Difference Engine* (1990), and *Virtual Light* (1993).

ELLEN GILCHRIST: *Victory Over Japan: A Book of Stories.* The stories in this critically acclaimed, American Book Award–winning volume treat the lives of several eccentric women, many of whom would appear in Gilchrist's subsequent work.

GAIL GODWIN: *The Finishing School.* Justin Stokes, a forty-year-old actress, recalls the summer she turned fourteen and came under the influence of Ursula DeVane, who showed her that a life can be composed like a work of art. Critics regard this novel as another high achievement in Godwin's continuing exploration of how women can learn to thrive independently.

KENT HARUF (b. 1943): *The Tie That Binds.* Haruf's first novel chronicling the hard life of Edith Goodnough through the twentieth century wins a special citation from the PEN/Hemingway Foundation and wins the American Library Notable Books Award. Born in Colorado, Haruf served in the Peace Corps in Turkey and has taught English in high schools and at Nebraska Wesleyan University and Southern Illinois University.

JOSEPH HELLER: *God Knows.* King David of Israel looks back from old age on his life and recounts the "real" story of his battle with Goliath, his affair with Bathsheba, and his other domestic troubles. At the same time, David is also aware of later developments — such as Michelangelo's statue of him (to which he objects). The novel, like Heller's other work, elicits critical praise for its comic inventiveness and its telling indictment of the myths people live by.

JOSEPHINE HUMPHREYS (b. 1945): *Dreams of Sleep.* Humphreys's Hemingway Prize–winning debut novel concerns a highly dysfunctional marriage. It is praised for its characterization and for its evocation of the author's native Charleston, South Carolina. Her subsequent novels would be *Rich in Love* (1987), *The Fireman's Fair* (1991), and *Nowhere Else on Earth* (2000).

JAMAICA KINCAID (b. 1949): *At the Bottom of the River.* These seven stories represent many of Kincaid's repeated concerns: mother-daughter tensions; the restraints put on a young, intelligent, attractive black woman; youthful disaffection with home and community; and a writer's quest to create a world that blends the actual and the imaginary. Critics praise Kincaid's lyrical prose and her powerful ability to endow ordinary events with magical resonance. Born on Antigua, Kincaid came to New York as a teenager. She began writing for *The New Yorker* in 1975.

ALISON LURIE: *Foreign Affairs.* Lurie's story takes place on a college campus and in London and exemplifies her satiric approach to academic life and her Henry James–like observations of contemporary manners. The novel wins the Pulitzer Prize.

NORMAN MAILER: *Tough Guys Don't Dance.* Mailer adapted this crime thriller into a film that he directed in 1987.

DONALD MCCAIG (b. 1940): *Nop's Trials.* The novelist, poet, and sheep farmer who had previously labored in obscurity gains sudden fame and fortune with the publication of his classic man-and-dog tale. Expecting a mawkish story, reviewers are surprised by the delicate balance McCaig achieves between gritty details of animal laboratory experiments and the understated relationship between a Border collie and his master. Nop is a talking dog, but McCaig translates his ritualized body language into a highly stylized form of English that reviewers find novel and winning.

THOMAS MCGUANE: *Something to Be Desired.* In this novel, McGuane focuses on Lucien Taylor, a romantic who thinks nothing of destroying his marriage and seeking other women, who are viewed through an intensely masculine lens. Yet the masculine view is found wanting, and the novel resolves itself in Lucien's efforts to rebuild his family. Critics admire the way McGaune brings his protagonist through self-absorption to a recognition of the larger forces of life.

JAY MCINERNEY (b. 1955): *Bright Lights, Big City.* McInerney's first novel, concerning a young man thrust into the heady environs of New York City, gains widespread critical praise and popularity. Contributing to the novel's immediacy is its present-tense, second-person narration as the protagonist, Jamie, plunges into the drug-laden club scene, loses his job and his wife, exploits his friends, and winds up, in a sense, where he started, according to the novel's last line: "You will have to learn everything all over again." The Hartford-born writer's other books would include *Ransom* (1985), *The Story of My Life* (1988), and *Brightness Falls* (1992).

JOYCE CAROL OATES: *Mysteries of Winthurn.* Oates adapts the gothic mystery genre to feminist concerns in this novel, which shows the plight of nineteenth-century women. Characters include domineering and sadistic males such as Erasmus Kilgarven, who commits incest with his daughter Georgina; she becomes the novel's heroine when she publishes her poetry and stands up to her father's bullying violence.

MARGE PIERCY: *Fly Away Home.* Piercy's novel deals with a woman trying to rebuild her life after a divorce. Despite this well-traveled topic, one reviewer commends the author for achieving "something new and appealing: a romance with a vision of domestic life that only a feminist could imagine."

THOMAS PYNCHON: *Slow Learner.* Breaking a long silence since the publication of *Gravity's Rainbow* (1973), Pynchon collects his early short stories and provides in an introduction the fullest self-revelations available about his works.

HELEN HOOVEN SANTMYER (1895–1986): *. . . And Ladies of the Club.* The eighty-eight-year-old author's first novel in more than fifty years depicts four generations of ordinary life in a fictional small town in Ohio between the Civil War and the Great Depression. The novel invites comparisons with Sinclair Lewis's work. Novelist Vance Bourjaily praises the Victorian amplitude of Santmyer's work, and critic Paul Galloway compares her social observations with those of Jane Austen. The book stays on the bestseller list for eight months. Her previous novels were *Herbs and Apples* (1925) and *The Fierce Dispute* (1929).

JOHN UPDIKE: *The Witches of Eastwick.* Updike's novel continues the writer's fascination with spiritual questions, although this comic novel treats the potentially somber subject matter with considerable humor and whimsy. It concerns three Rhode Island witches, vibrant uninhibited women who have been cut loose from their husbands and revel in their recently discovered supernatural powers. Naturally they rebel against the satanic figure who tries to control them.

GORE VIDAL: *Lincoln.* Known previously for his debunking approach to historical figures, Vidal treats Lincoln with uncharacteristic respect. The novelist does not blink at Lincoln's ruthless bending of the Constitution, but he makes it clear that no other man was up to the job of saving the Union. Many critics consider the novel Vidal's greatest work.

TOM WICKER: *Unto This Hour.* Steeped in the history of the Civil War, the author re-creates the second battle of Bull Run, winning praise from critics for his handling of both fictional and historical figures.

TOBIAS WOLFF: *The Barracks Thief.* Wolff's PEN/ Faulkner Award–winning novella follows a character through basic training prior to service in Vietnam.

Literary Criticism and Scholarship

HOUSTON A. BAKER JR. (b. 1943): *Blues, Ideology, and Afro-American Literature: A Vernacular Theory.* In Baker's influential study he articulates a theoretical framework for analyzing African American literature by using the paradigm of blues music, which he shows to be a means for understanding American culture as a whole. Born in Kentucky and a graduate of Harvard University, Baker earned a Ph.D. from UCLA and has taught at the University of Virginia and the University of Pennsylvania.

ROBERT HASS: *Twentieth Century Pleasures: Prose on Poetry.* These collected essays and reviews treat the works of Robert Lowell, James Wright, Stanley Kunitz, and others. This winner of the National Book Critics Circle Award for criticism also includes an analysis of prosody, rhythm, and image, focusing on the haiku and its use by contemporary American poets.

ALFRED KAZIN: *An American Procession.* Kazin provides a survey of American literature from the 1830s to the 1930s.

Nonfiction

LEE IACOCCA (b. 1924): *Iacocca.* The memoirs of the automobile executive who saved Chrysler from bankruptcy sell more than two million copies within a year, setting a record for general-interest nonfiction in hardcover. It remains number one on the nonfiction bestseller list for 1984 and 1985.

AMIRI BARAKA (LEROI JONES): *The Autobiography of LeRoi Jones.* Written while the writer was serving a sentence in a Harlem halfway house for a domestic dispute, this memoir chronicles Jones's developing political ideas, from his Newark boyhood through his black nationalist period.

SUZANNE LEBSOCK (b. 1949): *The Free Women of Petersburg: Status and Culture in a Southern Town, 1784– 1860.* The Rutgers history professor's study of the lives of women in a slaveholding town between the American Revolution and the Civil War wins the Bancroft Prize.

THOMAS K. MCCRAW (b. 1940): *Prophets of Regulation.* McCraw, a professor of business at Harvard, wins the Pulitzer Prize for his study of four men — Charles Francis Adams, Louis D. Brandeis, James M. Landis, and Alfred E. Kahn — who helped establish economic regulatory policy in the United States.

REYNOLDS PRICE: *Clear Pictures: First Loves, First Guides.* Novelist Price explores how he recovered many early memories of family life through hypnosis, a therapy recommended as part of a program to relieve intense pain from spinal surgery that had left him a paraplegic in 1984. The book evokes his family history in such lush and intense detail that it has been compared with James Joyce's classic *A Portrait of the Artist as a Young Man* and Eugene O'Neill's *Long Day's Journey into Night.*

ROBERT V. REMINI (b. 1921): *Andrew Jackson and the Course of American Democracy, 1833–1845.* Remini, a professor of American history at the University of Illinois at Chicago Circle, wins the Pulitzer Prize for his final volume of what many consider the definitive Jackson biography. It had been preceded by *Andrew Jackson and the Course of American Empire* (1977) and *Andrew Jackson and the Course of American Freedom* (1981).

KENNETH SILVERMAN (b. 1936): *The Life and Times of Cotton Mather.* Silverman, a professor of English at New York University, receives the Bancroft Prize and the Pulitzer Prize for the first full-length analytical biography of the American Puritan, which is acclaimed as masterful and definitive.

STUDS TERKEL: *The Good War: An Oral History of World War II.* Terkel weaves together the testimony of many witnesses to, and participants in, World War II to

Studs Terkel speaking at one of his book tours

Eudora Welty

create a kind of collective first-person account of an event that defined a generation. It wins the Pulitzer Prize.

EUDORA WELTY: *One Writer's Beginnings.* Welty's memoirs are based on lectures delivered at Harvard, exploring her development as a writer. It is divided into three sections: "Listening," "Learning to See," and "Finding a Voice."

JOHN EDGAR WIDEMAN: *Brothers and Keepers.* Wideman's first nonfiction work — "a personal essay about my brother and myself" — meditates on the fate of his younger brother, who is serving a life sentence in a Pennsylvania prison.

Poetry

JOHN ASHBERY: *The Wave.* Ashbery wins the Bollingen Prize for this collection, which includes some of his most important later works exploring art, change, and perspective with a "calculated recklessness." Critic Helen Vendler describes the experience of reading Ashbery's poems "like playing hide-and-seek in a sprawling mansion designed by M. C. Escher." Ashbery would follow the volume with *Selected Poems* (1985) and *April Galleons* (1987).

ROBERT DUNCAN: *Ground Work: Before the War.* Duncan's last major work is a Whitmanesque experiment

in an open form, wherein "theoretically everything can co-exist." A continuation, *Ground Work II: In the Dark* (1987), would be issued two months before the poet's death and would win the first National Poetry Award.

LOUISE ERDRICH: *Jacklight.* Erdrich's first published book of poetry contains works centering around "jacklight," the term for an illegal light used to lure game when hunting. The poet sets her work in the Turtle Mountain Chippewa reservation in North Dakota, but her characters range from Chippewa to Cree, French, English, Scottish, and German — all of whom interact with Native Americans. While many of her characters seem degraded by their sordid lives, they are resilient and remarkably free of self-pity.

ALLEN GINSBERG: *Collected Poems, 1947–1980.* This volume collects verse from ten previous volumes and includes an important preface and notes. The poetry also reflects Ginsberg's immersion in Zen Buddhism, jazz, and the drug scene and counterculture of the 1950s and 1960s. As both a record of cultural history and of this poet's accomplishment, this book is a significant contribution to American literature.

MICHAEL S. HARPER (b. 1938): *Healing Song for the Inner Ear.* Harper's collection continues his exploration of the lives and significance of folk heroes, musicians, poets, family, and friends. Notable poems include "Chronicles," "The Hawk Tradition," "In Hayden's Collage," and "The View of Mount Saint Helens." The Brooklyn-born poet is the author of *Dear John, Dear Coltrane* (1970), *Nightmare Begins Responsibility* (1974), and *Images of Kin* (1977).

CAROLYN KIZER: *Yin.* This Pulitzer Prize–winning collection reflects Kizer's strong affinity for Chinese poetry. In "A Muse" Kizer admires her mother's spirited nature, although she admits this talented woman suffered from self-doubt. Her character portrait suggests that Kizer's mother is the inspiration of all her poetry, although she also pays tribute to her father's voice, which "throbbed with feeling."

SHARON OLDS: *The Dead and Living.* Olds's second, award-winning collection lives up to its title, including verse devoted to the death of Marilyn Monroe and to a mother's experience with her own children. Olds's work once again focuses on the physical body, directly connecting sexual abuse with political repression.

ROBERT PINSKY: *History of My Heart.* Pinsky combines an autobiographical impulse with poems about political, social, and philosophical issues. His dreams of becoming a musician also figure in his many references to music and musicians such as Fats Waller. Sensitive evocations of his childhood shift abruptly to his recollection, for example, of visiting a concentration camp. Such "tonal shifts," as one critic puts it, reflect a much-admired versatility in his work.

KENNETH REXROTH: *Selected Poems.* This collection spans sixty years of writing by this radical San Francisco poet often associated with the Beat movement. Rexroth's main topics include a philosophical questioning of life's meaning, an exploration of nature as a source of human identity, an active engagement with the political and social issues of his time, and a considerable range of commentary on the nature of love. These poems also reflect Rexroth's career as a translator, which endows his poetry with a sophisticated grasp of different cultural attitudes.

ADRIENNE RICH: *The Fact of a Doorframe: Poems Selected and New, 1950–1984.* Rich's collection explores perception and the forces of history. The same themes are present in her next collection, *Your Native Land, Your Life* (1986).

ALICE WALKER: *Horses Make a Landscape Look More Beautiful.* Walker's collection deals with racial oppression and personal fulfillment in poems such as "Well," "Family Of," "Killers," and "The Dreams of Liz's Bosom."

CHARLES WRIGHT: *The Other Side of the River.* Wright continues his autobiographical explorations, employing

the long lines he debuted in *The Southern Cross* (1981). Wright's "retrospective authority" and "visionary gift" prompt reviewer David Kalstone to declare him "one of our best middle-generation poets, writing at the peak of his form."

1985
Drama and Theater

CHRISTOPHER DURANG: *The Marriage of Bette and Boo.* This black comic play, first produced in a shorter version at Yale in 1973, treats a dysfunctional American family. The narrator (originally played by the author) examines his life and guides the audience through a series of tragicomic family disasters.

HERB GARDNER (1934–2003): *I'm Not Rappaport.* Two octogenarians — one white, one black — meet in Central Park every day. This odd couple, Nat and Midge, argue about politics and their views of life. Winner of three Tony Awards, the play has been frequently revived because of its good humor and affection for its characters. The Brooklyn-born playwright is the author of *A Thousand Clowns* (1962), *The Goodbye People* (1968), and *Conversations with My Father* (1991).

SPALDING GRAY (b. 1942): *Swimming to Cambodia.* Gray's monologue performance recounts his experiences in Thailand while filming *The Killing Fields* and other deadpan observations about modern life. Gray acted with the experimental Performance Group in the 1970s and cofounded New York's Wooster Group. He is the author of the trilogy *Three Places in Rhode Island* (1975–1978).

WILLIAM M. HOFFMAN (b. 1939): *As Is.* Hoffman's drama treating the AIDS epidemic wins the Obie Award and three Tony nominations. The New York City–born poet, editor, and playwright is the author of *Luna* (1970) and *Gilles de Rais* (1975).

LARRY KRAMER: *The Normal Heart.* Kramer's two-act play about the AIDS epidemic opens off-Broadway. The play is one of the first stage productions to deal with the issue, going on to win numerous awards and to be produced around the world.

SAM SHEPARD: *A Lie of the Mind.* The play centers on Jake, who has beaten his wife, Beth, and run away. Jakes's brother intervenes and attempts to reconcile Jake and Beth. This bleak play probes family tensions and violence, though Shepard's tenderness and sympathy for his characters have been compared to that of Tennessee Williams, especially evident in *The Glass Menagerie*.

NEIL SIMON: *Biloxi Blues.* In a continuation of *Brighton Beach Memoirs*, Eugene Jerome's dream of becoming a writer is temporarily deferred when he is drafted into the army. The play captures his army experiences and a comic effort to lose his virginity. Lighter in tone than the first play in Simon's autobiographical trilogy, it nevertheless portrays youthful ambition in shrewdly playful terms.

Fiction

PAUL AUSTER (b. 1947): *City of Glass.* The first part of Auster's acclaimed New York trilogy plays with the conventions of the detective story, posing questions about human identity that are intensified in the ambiguous arena of New York City. *Ghosts* (1986) and *The Locked Room* (1987) would follow, variations on Auster's version of the postmodern detective novel.

RUSSELL BANKS: *Continental Drift.* Banks's acclaimed novel juxtaposes a Haitian woman's attempt to escape oppression with an American man's relocation of his family from New Hampshire to Florida. It would be followed by the story collection *Success Stories* (1986), which continues the theme of the relationship between the First World and the Third World.

T. CORAGHESSAN BOYLE: *Greasy Lake and Other Stories.* Boyle's second story collection (following *Descent of Man*, 1979) prompts one reviewer to declare that the writer should be included in "the select cadre of great American humorists" for his comic inventiveness; for example, in "Ike and Nina," President Eisenhower falls in love with Mrs. Khrushchev. A third collection, *If the River Was Whiskey*, would appear in 1989, to be followed by *Collected Stories* in 1993.

CAROLYN CHUTE (b. 1947): *The Beans of Egypt, Maine.* The Maine native's first novel, about the down-and-out backwoods Bean clan, is a popular and critical success, prompting comparisons with the works of William Faulkner and Erskine Caldwell. The novels *Letourneau's Used Auto Parts* (1988) and *Merry Men* (1994) would follow.

DON DE LILLO: *White Noise.* De Lillo publishes what many consider his finest novel, which uses minimalist language to tell the story of a professor of Hitler studies who plumbs American culture as manifested in the supermarket. This National Book Award–winning novel uses effects at once weird and realistic to articulate De Lillo's career-long exploration into the sense of apocalypse that haunts contemporary life.

E. L. DOCTOROW: *World's Fair.* Set during the 1938 World's Fair, the novel focuses on a young boy growing up in the Bronx and a world still coming out of the Depression, poised on the eve of World War II. It includes a loving picture of home life, a sense of secure domestic-

ity that is relatively rare in the annals of great American fiction.

BRET EASTON ELLIS (b. 1964): *Less Than Zero.* Ellis's first novel is a controversial debut, depicting a world-weary college student's return to his L.A. neighborhood and its preoccupation with sex, drugs, and violence. Ellis was born in Los Angeles and attended Bennington College.

WILLIAM GADDIS: *Carpenter's Gothic.* Gaddis's third novel is an uncharacteristically short work that continues his assessment of contemporary American society as inauthentic and corrupted by greed. In a Victorian mansion on the Hudson River, a Vietnam War veteran tries to invest his wife's inheritance with the help of an evangelist and a right-wing politician. According to Cynthia Ozick, this is "an unholy landmark of a novel — an extra turret added to the ample, ingenious, audacious Gothic mansion William Gaddis has been slowly building in American letters."

MOLLY GILES (b. 1942): *Rough Translations.* Giles's first story collection announces a major new talent, and the book receives the Flannery O'Connor Award, the Boston Globe Award, and the Bay Area Book Reviewers Award for Fiction. The collection invokes comparisons with Grace Paley's "voice-driven stories." A second collection from the California witer, *Creek Walk* (1996), would follow, and her first novel, *Iron Shoes*, would appear in 2000.

MARY GORDON: *Men and Angels.* This novel is about Anne Foster, an art historian with a troubled relationship with her son. But young women gravitate to Anne, seeing her as the "perfect mother." A complex weave of plot and characters turns on the issue of mothering even as it explores Gordon's much-praised probing of moral and religious issues.

JOHN HAWKES: *Adventures in the Alaskan Skin Trade.* Hawkes echoes Jack London in this novel narrated by the proprietor of an Alaskan brothel who is haunted by the adventures and mysterious death of her father. A section of the novel, *Innocent in Extremis*, is published separately.

JOHN HERSEY: *The Call.* Hersey's novel treats the career of an American missionary in China through the first half of the twentieth century. It is considered one of the novelist's strongest works — in the words of reviewer Jonathan D. Spence, "the capstone to a writing career of enviable range and originality."

JOHN IRVING: *The Cider House Rules.* The novel recounts the career of Dr. Wilbur Larch, an obstetrician between the 1890s and the mid–twentieth century, whose Maine orphanage doubles as a clinic for safe, illegal abortions. Irving would win an Academy Award for the 1999 film screenplay.

DENIS JOHNSON: *Fiskadoro.* After his first novel, *Angels* (1983), about a desperate couple's descent into crime, Johnson continues to explore the theme of survival in this futuristic novel about life following a nuclear holocaust. The novels *The Stars at Noon* (1986) and *Resuscitation of a Hanged Man* (1991) would follow.

GARRISON KEILLOR (b. 1942): *Lake Wobegon Days.* By the host of *A Prairie Home Companion* on National Public Radio, Keillor's series of linked stories based on his monologues from his radio show evokes a tender and wry vision of American small-town life. It draws on the author's upbringing in Minnesota, his Lutheran community, and a range of characters with Midwestern folkways, which Keillor both respects and satirizes. Critics compare his sensitive and comic tales to those of Mark Twain, James Thurber, and Sherwood Anderson.

JAMAICA KINCAID: *Annie John.* This story collection, named after its reappearing character, explores her efforts to escape a repressive culture and a domineering mother. Annie clearly has budding talent, which heightens the conflict with her mother but also spurs Annie to come to terms with her and develop an understanding of her womanhood. Critics praise Kincaid for brilliantly applying the conventions of the bildungsroman.

BOBBIE ANN MASON: *In Country.* This short novel is about Sam(antha) Hughes, a seventeen-year-old living in western rural Kentucky. Her father, killed in Vietnam before her birth, is the focus of her search for family history and the meaning of that conflict. Critics admire the way Mason deftly integrates her knowledge of popular culture through allusions to singers and song lyrics. The book would be followed by *Spence + Lila* (1988), a moving portrait of a long-married Kentucky couple battling with the implications of the wife's breast cancer.

CORMAC MCCARTHY: *Blood Meridian.* This story about a Tennessee boy traveling in Texas in the 1840s is based on actual events. The main character joins a band of irregulars to fight in Mexico and then falls in with a band of outlaws. Critics compare the book with American classics such as *Moby-Dick* and *The Confidence Man* in its unremitting look at the shady side of the American character.

LARRY MCMURTRY: *Lonesome Dove.* McMurtry's affinity for the western novel achieves a kind of apotheosis in this Pulitzer Prize–winning epic chronicle about an 1879 cattle drive from Texas to Montana. The relationship between two former Texas Rangers, McCrae and Call, and their implacable foe, the Indian known as Blue Duck,

makes for good reading. The book would be made into an acclaimed television mini-series and inspire a sequel, *Streets of Laredo* (1993), and the prequels *Dead Man's Walk* (1995) and *Comanche Moon* (1997).

STEVEN MILLHAUSER: *In the Penny Arcade.* The first of Millhauser's acclaimed short fiction collections explores the relationship between illusion and reality. *The Barnum Museum* (1990), *Little Kingdoms* (1993), *The Knife Thrower* (1998), and *Enchanted Night* (1999) would follow.

GLORIA NAYLOR: *Linden Hills.* Set in an affluent suburb, this novel deals with two poets who support themselves by doing odd jobs in a black middle-class neighborhood, which has lost touch with its roots. Naylor is noted for her searing portraits of abusive black males and the struggle of black women to surmount the double oppression perpetuated by their own male partners and the white majority.

HUGH NISSENSON: *The Tree of Life.* The writer's best-known work is this historical novel written in the form of a diary kept by a widower on the Ohio frontier in 1811. It dramatizes, in the words of reviewer Paul Gray, "the American dream and its attendant nightmare."

JOYCE CAROL OATES: *Solstice.* Oates's novel exploring the friendship between two women initiates a series of novels dealing with the lives of contemporary women in America, including *Marya: A Life* (1986) and *You Must Remember This* (1987).

GRACE PALEY: *Later the Same Day.* In her third story collection, Paley explores a range of human motivations and actions, including the nature of friendship, the trials of aging, and the reaction to change and loss. Critics commend Paley's succinct depictions of tough-minded characters, including survivors and seekers after success.

T. R. PEARSON (b. 1956): *A Short History of a Small Place.* Pearson's first novel, set in the mythical town of Neely, North Carolina, prompts comparisons with William Faulkner's Yoknapatawpha County. The North Carolina writer would continue the chronicle of everyday existence in the subsequent novels *Off for the Sweet Hereafter* (1986) and *The Last of How It Was* (1987).

PADGETT POWELL (b. 1952): *Edisto.* Powell's award-winning first novel — named for the predominantly African American undeveloped backwater near prosperous Hilton Head, South Carolina — is a coming-of-age story written in a style that conjures up comparisons with Mark Twain and Tennessee Williams. It is praised for its humorous but unsentimental take on the "new" South. A continuation, *Edisto Revisited*, would appear in 1996. Powell, a one-time day-laborer and roofer, read William

Faulkner in his spare time and eventually enrolled in the University of Houston's graduate writing program.

RICHARD POWERS (b. 1957): *Three Farmers on Their Way to a Dance.* Powers's multiple award–winning debut novel gives evidence of what is to come from this ambitious intellectual writer. Taking its title from a 1914 German photograph, the novel concerns the narrator's obsession with the picture, its discovery by a magazine editor, the horrors of World War I, and ultimately, the interconnectedness of all things. Powers's subsequent novels would include *The Gold Bug Variations* (1991), *Galatea 2.2* (1995), and *Gain* (1998).

CARL SAGAN: *Contact.* The popular astronomer publishes a science fiction thriller about scientist Eleanor Arroway, who receives a message from an alien civilization and is plunged into a media and political frenzy. A film version would appear in 1997.

ISAAC BASHEVIS SINGER: *The Image, and Other Stories.* While continuing to explore the comic and outrageous behavior of Polish Jews in their small villages, Singer also shrewdly depicts the lives of New World Jews, immigrants, and the tensions between religious and spiritual awareness and the desire for love, and the success and comfort of a materialistic life.

PETER TAYLOR: *The Old Forest and Other Stories.* Taylor's final retrospective collection, including two previously uncollected stories, the title work and "The Gift of the Prodigal," wins the PEN/Faulkner Award and prompts Anne Tyler's declaration that Taylor is "the undisputed master of the short story form."

ANNE TYLER: *The Accidental Tourist.* This story of a travel writer who rarely leaves home is peopled with the eccentric, somewhat sentimentally portrayed characters that are Tyler's trademark. These quirky characters would translate well to the big screen in the 1988 film adaptation.

KURT VONNEGUT JR.: *Galapagos.* Vonnegut turns to the world of a million years ago and the creation of the human race. This witty commentary on Charles Darwin's theory of evolution (the novel includes a cruise to the Galapagos Islands) weaves a fantasy that defies chronology, shifting from the past to the future and back again. It presents fascinating alternative views of humanity's origin.

Literary Criticism and Scholarship

JOHN BARTH: *The Friday Book.* Barth collects his critical writing, produced on the one day weekly not devoted to his fiction. The subjects vary widely, but most shed light on Barth's fictional ideas and methods.

ELIZABETH FRANK (b. 1945): *Louise Bogan: A Portrait.* The Bard College English professor's Pulitzer Prize–winning biography devotes as much space to reviewing Bogan's poetry as to reporting the details of her life.

TORIL MOI (b. 1953): *Sexual/Textual Politics: Feminist Literary Theory.* This controversial critic mounts a powerful argument against liberal individualism and feminist humanism. Discussion of literature, in her view, has been skewed to favor middle-class women's writing and has ignored the subversive, marginalized sensibilities of Third World, black, and lesbian writers. Born in Norway, Moi has been a faculty member at Duke University. Her subsequent books would include *Feminist Literary Theory and Simone de Beauvoir* (1990) and *What Is a Woman?: And Other Essays* (1999).

Nonfiction

JAMES BALDWIN: *The Evidence of Things Not Seen.* Baldwin's penultimate collection of essays memorializes his thoughts about the serial murders of African American children in Atlanta, Georgia, in 1980 and 1981. After conducting his own investigation, Baldwin interprets the case of the alleged murderer in light of his skeptical view of American racial justice.

GRETEL EHRLICH (b. 1946): *The Solace of Open Spaces.* Winner of the Harold D. Vursell Memorial Award, Erhlich's essay collection extols the Wyoming landscape and lifestyle in prose that evokes comparisons with the photography of Ansel Adams. Born in California, Ehrlich has worked as a ranch hand and sheepherder. Her subsequent books would include *Heart Mountain* (1988) and *A Blizzard Year* (1999).

DAVID J. GARROW (b. 1953): *Bearing the Cross: Martin Luther King Jr. and the Southern Christian Leadership Conference.* Garrow wins the Pulitzer Prize for this biographical study of King's leadership of the civil rights movement and the significant role his religious faith played in shaping ideas and strategies. The work draws on more than seven hundred interviews with King's associates and opponents, as well as FBI and CIA files recently made available.

ERNEST HEMINGWAY: *The Dangerous Summer.* This book reprints a long article commissioned by *Life* magazine in 1959, dealing with bullfighting and including Hemingway's reflections about the 1950s.

JACQUELINE JONES (b. 1948): *Labor of Love, Labor of Sorrow.* The Wellesley College historian's study of slaves and rural working-class women in the South from 1830 to 1915 and the factors that led to the black migration to the North wins the Bancroft Prize and praise from novelist Toni Morrison for exorcising "several malignant stereotypes and stubborn myths about black women and the black family."

JOSEPH LELYVELD (b. 1937): *Move Your Shadow: Africa Black and White.* Lelyveld, a journalist for the *New York Times*, wins the Pulitzer Prize for this collection of observations of South Africans recorded in 1965–1966 and 1980–1983. As reviewer Janet Devine observes, Lelyveld "does for South Africa today what Dickens did for nineteenth-century London.... His eye for the small, personal dramas of everyday South African life makes the inhumanity of apartheid society vivid and real."

J. ANTHONY LUKAS (1933–1997): *Common Ground: A Turbulent Decade in the Lives of Three American Families.* Lukas, a former *New York Times* correspondent who won a Pulitzer Prize in 1968 for local reporting, wins the National Book Award and the Pulitzer Prize for his chronicle of Boston families and the impact of court-ordered busing in the Boston public schools. Framing a wider consideration of American bigotry and race relations, the book prompts reviewer Robert B. Parker to observe that "To say that *Common Ground* is about busing in Boston is a bit like saying that *Moby-Dick* is about whaling in New Bedford, but it's a start."

WALTER A. McDOUGALL (b. 1946): *... the Heavens and Earth: A Political History of the Space Age.* The University of California at Berkeley history professor's chronicle of the space race between the United States and the Soviet Union wins the Pulitzer Prize.

GARY SOTO: *Living Up the Street: Narrative Recollections.* Soto's autobiography is full of vivid vignettes that reveal racial tensions as they register in his consciousness. Critics note his perceptive writing about everyday life and the balance he achieves in honoring his Hispanic heritage while also seeking experiences that transcend ethnic boundaries and allegiances.

Poetry

AMY CLAMPITT: *What the Light Was Like.* Critics praise the poet's luminous verse, which delicately focuses on moments of perception, suffused with sounds and images evoking the evanescent quality of experience. Her settings include the Maine coast, the Midwest, Europe, and California.

LOUISE GLÜCK: *The Triumph of Achilles.* Praised by critics for its spare style and deft handling of Glück's

familiar themes of pain, loss, and betrayal, this collection wins the National Book Critics Circle Award in poetry.

LANCE HENSON (b. 1944): *Selected Poems, 1970–1983.* For this retrospective volume, Henson, one of the few Native American poets who writes bilingual verse, is praised for his knowledge of Cheyenne language and culture. He would follow the book with *Another Song for America* (1987), a collection juxtaposing violence done to Native Americans with the anti-war protest at Kent State in 1970. Henson, raised on a farm in Oklahoma, was of mixed Cheyenne, Oglala, and French ancestry.

JAMES MERRILL: *Late Settings.* Merrill treats life as a comedy worthy of precise observation. His easygoing yet polished verse also reflects Merrill's affection for popular culture. He tends to eschew obviously profound subjects and instead focuses on elegant, disciplined observation of the commonplace.

HENRY TAYLOR (b. 1942): *The Flying Change.* The title of this Pulitzer Prize–winning collection refers to an equestrian term for a midair change of pace, and the collection deals with disruptions of otherwise predictable lives. In the poem "Landscape with Tractor," the narrator discovers a corpse in a field; in "At the Swings," a man swinging his son reflects on his mother's terminal illness. Born in Virginia, Taylor has taught at the University of Utah and at the American University in Washington, D.C.

1986
Drama and Theater

A. R. GURNEY JR.: *The Perfect Party.* This witty farce concerns a middle-aged college professor's futile efforts to host the perfect party. Critics see a parable about the theater itself, which tries to force a degree of spontaneity out of an artificial setting and is subject to the same kind of carping that the poor professor invites.

EMILY MANN: *Execution of Justice.* Mann's most ambitious drama deals with the trial of Dan White for the 1978 murder of San Francisco mayor George Moscone and gay city supervisor Harvey Milk. It portrays the uproar among San Francisco's gay community when White was sentenced to less than eight years in prison.

RICHARD NELSON (b. 1950): *Principia Scriptoriae.* Nelson's award-winning play concerns two young intellectuals who meet while imprisoned in a Latin American jail for distributing subversive literature. It features Nelson's characteristic concern with writers torn between personal beliefs and professional obligations. The Chicago-born playwright has been described as America's most prolific dramatist during the 1980s. His other works include *Vienna Notes* (1978), *Rip Van Winkle or "The Works"* (1981), *Between East and West* (1984), and *Americans Abroad* (1989).

NEIL SIMON: *Broadway Bound.* The last play in Simon's trilogy, preceded by *Brighton Beach Memoirs* and *Biloxi Blues*, concerns aspiring writer Eugene Jerome, who is now on the verge of fulfilling his ambition by writing for the radio—but his life is complicated by family and personal troubles. Simon's adept character development makes his hero's ambitions arise naturally from the fully depicted social context of the post–World War II years.

AUGUST WILSON: *Joe Turner's Come and Gone.* Set in a turn-of-the-century black boardinghouse in Pittsburgh, the play is one of a series that explores African American life decade by decade. In it Herald Loomis turns up, claiming he has escaped from forced labor, only to find that his wife is now a religious fanatic. The plot is less important than Wilson's provocative effort to render the feel of African American life and the conflicts, neuroses, and confused quests engendered in a world marked by paranoia.

ROBERT M. WILSON: *the CIVIL warS: a tree is best measured when it is down.* Wilson's multimedia stage epic is described by reviewer John Rockwell as "a sequence of dreamy stage-pictures without overt plot but interweaving a variety of world myths and historical personages." It is the unanimous choice of the Pulitzer Prize drama jury, but their decision is overturned by the Pulitzer board because of reluctance to give the award to a work so few had seen.

Fiction

KATHY ACKER (1948–1997): *Don Quixote.* Controversial because of her "plagiarism," Acker, who has been described as a "punk novelist," deliberately borrows from Cervantes, destabilizing his text by overlaying it with surrealism. Acker counters that "plagiarism became a strategy of originality." She also dismisses charges of pornography leveled by feminist critics: only by glorifying the taboo, Acker claims, can one create a "new myth" for empowering women. The writer's other books include *I Dreamt I Was a Nymphomaniac* (1974), *Great Expectations* (1982), *Blood and Guts in High School* (1984), and *Pussy, King of the Pirates* (1996).

PAUL AUSTER: *Ghosts.* The second novel in Auster's New York trilogy is another takeoff on the detective novel genre. Blue, a detective, is hired by White to follow Black. All three allegorical characters merge, as Blue spends years watching Black writing a book in a room across the street. Why? The answer is never clear, though critics

suggest that Auster's theme is precisely the unresolved nature of reality, which detective stories usually resolve with a closed plot and simplified characters.

DONALD BARTHELME: *Paradise.* Barthelme's novel shows a middle-aged architect living out a male fantasy with three lingerie models. According to one reviewer, "It is a disturbing book because it is a fantasy of freedom in a world where there is no freedom."

PAT CONROY (b. 1945): *The Prince of Tides.* Conroy achieves his greatest success with this saga of the dysfunctional Wingo family of South Carolina. Conroy would write the screenplay for the popular 1991 film version. His previous novels include *The Water Is Wide* (1972), *The Lords of Discipline* (1980), and *Beach Music* (1995).

ROBERT COOVER: *Gerald's Party.* Coover's surrealistic novel treats a fashionable party during which a celebrated actress is found murdered. One reviewer discerns a social satire "exposing the crude sensationalism which underlies the guests' cultural pretensions" and "the moral insensibility which binds them to all but pleasure."

ANDRE DUBUS: *The Last Worthless Enemy.* The collection draws its central theme from the conflict between religious belief and desire. Notable stories include "Land Where My Fathers Died," "Deaths at Sea," and "Rose." His *Selected Stories* would appear in 1988.

STANLEY ELKIN: *Stanley Elkin's The Magic Kingdom.* Elkin's darkly humorous novel explores human perseverance in the face of an absurd universe. Eddy Bale, having lost his own son to a terminal illness, takes a group of dying children to Disney World.

LOUISE ERDRICH: *The Beet Queen.* This novel is about a family who live in Argus, North Dakota, near an Indian reservation. Karl fathers a mixed-blood child named Dot, the beet queen of the title. She later marries Gerry Nanapush, making the worlds of the town and the reservation converge and confront each other. This novel is part of a tetralogy focusing on life near the same reservation.

RICHARD FORD (b. 1944): *The Sportswriter.* The book concerns Frank Bascombe, a man who has not been able to fulfill his dreams as a writer and is devastated by his young son's death. It wins the PEN/Faulkner Award for fiction. Critics note Ford's grasp of the lives of ordinary people, making their unremarkable trials the stuff of intensely imaginative prose. *Rock Springs*, a story collection, would follow in 1987, and a sequel to *The Sportswriter*, *Independence Day*, would appear in 1995. Born in Mississippi, Ford was educated at Michigan State University and the University of Michigan.

LARRY HEINEMANN (b. 1944): *Paco's Story.* Heinemann's novel about a wounded soldier's return home from Vietnam wins the National Book Award and confirms the writer's reputation, according to Duncan Spencer, as "the grunt's novelist of the Vietnam War." Heinemann was an infantry sergeant in Vietnam.

ERNEST HEMINGWAY: *The Garden of Eden.* At his death Hemingway left more than three thousand pages of manuscript, including novels he was still working on. This posthumous publication is autobiographical and concerns an author's first two marriages. The work is noteworthy for its exploration of the nature of sex and male-female relationships, demonstrating a less macho side of the author.

TAMA JANOWITZ (b. 1957) *Slaves of New York.* Janowitz loosely weaves together episodes from the quirky but rather mundane lives of Manhattanites living on the fringes of the art scene. Her apparently affectless prose style keeps the stories going despite the lethargy and randomness of her subjects' lives. The work would inspire a 1989 film in which Janowitz also appeared. *A Cannibal in Manhattan* (1987), *The Male Cross-Dresser Support Group* (1992), and *By the Shores of Gitchee Gumee* (1996) would follow.

DAVID LEAVITT (b. 1961): *The Lost Language of Cranes.* Leavitt's novel concerns a father who has concealed his homosexuality for twenty-seven years, his uncomprehending wife, and their gay son. Leavitt's abiding theme is the repercussions of gay identity for family and society. His sensitive but also provocative handling of this theme has attracted considerable critical controversy and respect. The Pittsburgh-born writer's first book, *Family Dancing* (1984), treats various domestic conflicts.

SUE MILLER (b. 1943): *The Good Mother.* Miller's debut novel concerns a divorced mother's attempt to retain custody of her daughter in the face of charges that she had negligently permitted her lover to have an "improper" relationship with the child. Much of the book is taken up with a courtroom battle, which Miller renders "dramatic and convincing," according to reviewer Robert Wilson. After spending six months atop the bestseller list, the novel would be made into a film in 1988.

SUSAN MINOT (b. 1956): *Monkeys.* Minot's highly praised first novel depicts the siblings of the Vincent family of suburban Boston. They are forced to cope with their father's alcoholism and their mother's death. The book prompts Anne Tyler to proclaim Minot as "one of the youngest and most impressive new arrivals on the literary scene." *Lust and Other Stories* would follow in 1989, and her second novel, *Folly,* about an upper-class Boston family between the two world wars, would be published in 1992.

REYNOLDS PRICE: *Kate Vaiden.* Kate's life is marred by her father's murder of her mother and his suicide when she is only eleven. She cannot break free from her past, though her efforts to confront it are remarkable, and Price eloquently evokes her memories.

ISHMAEL REED: *Reckless Eyeballing.* With his typical shotgun satire, Reed sprays many targets—especially New York women and Jews—for dominating the political and culture discourse of the 1980s. Reed's protagonist, Ian Ball, a struggling playwright, shamelessly fawns on the feminists to get his work produced. The book is attacked as anti-Semitic and misogynist by some critics, while others claims that Reed retains his preeminent position as an African American satirist whose target this time is the cultural establishment.

PHILIP ROTH: *The Counterlife.* This novel continues the story of Nathan Zuckerman, Roth's alter ego. Part of the novel is set in Israel and includes vibrant political discussions; another part shifts to London, where Nathan is married to an English woman and confronts anti-Semitism. Critics consider it one of Roth's most intellectually alive and masterfully written novels.

NORMAN RUSH (b. 1933): *Whites.* Rush receives high praise and a Pulitzer Prize nomination for this story collection, described by reviewer George Packer as exploring the "moral and spiritual quandaries of middle-class foreigners who happen to be stuck out in Botswana." Their experiences are based on the author's as codirector of the Peace Corps in Botswana.

MARY LEE SETTLE: *Celebration.* Settle authentically evokes widely different settings and characters—in this case, London, Kurdistan, Hong Kong, and Africa. Three characters face crises—the death of a husband and cancer surgery, a disastrous love affair, the betrayal and murder of innocent people—against a backdrop of the first moon landing in 1969.

MONA SIMPSON (b. 1957): *Anywhere But Here.* Simpson's acclaimed first novel treats a mother's attempt to make her daughter into a child star in Hollywood. The book is praised by Laura Shapiro in *Newsweek* as a "big, complex and masterfully written . . . achievement," which establishes Simpson as one of America's "best young novelists." *The Lost Father* (1991) is a sequel. Born in Wisconsin, Simpson was educated at the University of California at Berkeley and received an MFA from Columbia.

ART SPIEGELMAN (b. 1948): *Maus: A Survivor's Tale— My Father Bleeds History.* The first volume of Spiegelman's illustrated Holocaust tale substitutes mice and cats for the Jews and the Nazis. Derived from his family history and described as "a meditation on my awareness of myself as a Jew," Spiegelman's acclaimed "comic book" would be continued in *Maus II: A Survivor's Tale: And Here the Troubles Begin* (1991), a winner of the National Book Critics Circle Award that also prompts a special Pulitzer Prize for the series. Born in Sweden, where his parents lived after their release from Nazi concentration camps, Spiegelman created the underground comic anthology *Raw*.

ROBERT STONE: *Children of Light.* A screenwriter's wife deserts him and, looking for a way to recapture his youth, he becomes involved with an actress who is also attempting to regain her bearings after marital troubles. Critics admire Stone's penetrating portrayal of characters who attempt to recapture the spirit of the 1960s only to be corrupted by crass commercialism and careerism.

PETER TAYLOR: *A Summons to Memphis.* Taylor's novel is a Southern family drama in which a widower's decision to remarry at the age of eighty-one prompts his son to review the past, particularly the family's move from Nashville to Memphis in 1931. The book wins the Pulitzer Prize.

JOHN UPDIKE: *Roger's Version.* In this ingenious rewriting of *The Scarlet Letter*, theology professor Roger Lambert is Updike's version of Roger Chillingworth. Lambert suspects his wife of committing adultery but manages eventually to recover some of his compassion and spirituality, reflecting Updike's faith in human redemption and his mitigation of Nathaniel Hawthorne's dark vision.

DAVID FOSTER WALLACE (b. 1962): *The Broom of the System.* Wallace's debut novel, a quest told from multiple perspectives and through many subplots, provokes some critics to compare the work favorably with the novels of Thomas Pynchon and John Barth; others find it self-indulgent and derivative. Wallace would follow it with a story collection, *Girl with Curious Hair* (1989). Born in Ithaca, New York, Wallace attended Amherst College and the University of Arizona.

JAMES WELCH: *Fool's Crow.* Welch portrays the clash between indigenous Americans and white settlers in the Two Medicine territory of Montana in the 1870s. The book draws on both historical documentation and the author's own family stories in what historian Dee Brown has said is perhaps "the closest we will ever come in western literature to understanding what life is like for a western Indian."

RICHARD WILEY (b. 1944): *Soldiers in Hiding.* Wiley's PEN/Faulkner Award–winning first novel focuses on the dilemma of a young Japanese American trumpet player who is in Japan at the time of the Pearl Harbor attack and is subsequently forced to fight with the Japanese army. One reviewer describes the protagonist as "a remarkably apt symbol for the dislocation of World War II." The California-born writer had served in the Peace Corps in Korea and had been a language teacher in Japan. His subsequent novels would include *Fools' Gold* (1988), *Festival for Three Thousand Maidens* (1991), *Indigo* (1992), and *Ahmed's Revenge* (1998).

SHERLEY ANNE WILLIAMS: *Dessa Rose.* In what has been described as a "neo-slave narrative," Williams explores the relationship between a slave and the white plantation mistress who harbors her. Williams is also author of the critical volume *Give Birth to Brightness* (1972) and the poetry collections *The Peacock Poems* (1975) and *Some One Sweet Angel Chile* (1982).

RICHARD YATES: *Cold Spring Harbor.* Considered by critics as one of the finest contemporary writers on suburban America, Yates sets this novel in the period just before the attack on Pearl Harbor. Although his male protagonist's problems — a failing marriage, a divorce, alcoholism — make this work seem morbid, it is also praised for Yates's impressive integration of character and environment in a compelling narrative.

Literary Criticism and Scholarship

RALPH ELLISON: *Going to the Territory.* Ellison's second collection of essays, reviews, speeches, and interviews treats figures such as Erskine Caldwell, Richard Wright, and Duke Ellington while considering the question of American democracy and identity. His *Collected Essays* would be issued in 1995.

MARIANNE MOORE: *The Complete Prose.* This is a collection of four hundred essays, reviews, and short stories written between 1907 and 1968. Many deal with Moore's reflections on the art and craft of poetry.

ARNOLD RAMPERSAD (b. 1941): *The Life of Langston Hughes: Volume 1: 1902–1941: I, Too, Sing America.* This biography by the distinguished professor and literary critic, covering Hughes's childhood through the Harlem Renaissance, wins virtually universal praise. Reviewer David Nicholson calls it "the best biography of a black writer we have had." The second volume, *Dream a World*, would appear in 1988.

Nonfiction

RENATA ADLER: *Reckless Disregard: Westmoreland v. CBS, et al.; Sharon v. Time.* Adler examines the issues and the courtroom maneuvering in two famous 1984–1985 libel cases. Adler concludes that in both cases the press acted irresponsibly.

PAULA GUNN ALLEN: *The Sacred Hoop: Recovering the Feminine in American Indian Traditions.* Allen contends that there is no contradiction between being an American, a Native American, and a woman. A poet and novelist as well, with a Ph.D. in Native American studies, Allen is one of the most important scholars of Native American literature and history.

MAYA ANGELOU: *All God's Children Need Traveling Shoes.* The fifth installment of Angelou's memoirs describes her four-year residence in Ghana during the 1960s and African Americans' search for their African roots.

BERNARD BAILYN: *Voyagers to the West: A Passage in the Peopling of America at the Eve of the Revolution.* Bailyn wins his second Pulitzer Prize for this account of immigration to America, based on records kept by customs officials in England and Scotland from 1773 to 1776.

JOHN W. DOWER (b. 1938): *War Without Mercy: Race and Power in the Pacific War.* Dower, a professor of history and Japanese studies at the University of California at San Diego, wins the National Book Critics Circle Award for this exploration of racism in the Pacific theater of World War II and the ways in which both the Americans and the Japanese promoted demeaning ethnic stereotypes of each other.

BARRY HOLSTUN LOPEZ (b. 1945): *Arctic Dreams: Imagination and Desire in a Northern Landscape.* This is both a travel book and work of natural history in which natural phenomena symbolize larger philosophical concepts. Based on fifteen extended trips to the Canadian Yukon over the course of five years, the work wins a National Book Award. The natural history writer's other books include *Winter Count* (1981), *Field Notes* (1994), and *About This Life* (1998).

RICHARD RHODES (b. 1937): *The Making of the Atom Bomb.* Journalist Rhodes had devoted five years of research to this detailed account of the Manhattan Project, which wins the National Book Award, the National Book Critics Circle Award, and the Pulitzer Prize. *Dark Sun: The Making of the Hydrogen Bomb* would follow in 1995.

DAVID K. SHIPLER (b. 1942): *Arab and Jew: Wounded Spirits in a Promised Land.* Shipler, a *New York Times* correspondent and chief of the Jerusalem bureau from 1979 to 1984, is awarded the Pulitzer Prize for his account (to be updated and revised in 2002) of everyday life of ordinary people on both sides of the Arab-Israeli conflict.

GLORIA STEINEM: *Marilyn.* Written to accompany George Barris's photographs, Steinem supplies a biographical portrait of Marilyn Monroe in a feminist and archetypal context.

Poetry

TURNER CASSITY: *Hurricane Lamp.* This collection concerns travel, newspapers, books, and unusual items such as bar guides and annual reports. Turner's ingenuity is evident in the way he makes poetry out of material such as stock market reports. His major contribution to contemporary poetry is his insistence that no subject matter — if intensely and imaginatively explored — is unfit for poetry.

RITA DOVE: *Thomas and Beulah.* Composed of two sequences of poems in a novel-like structure, this book shifts between male and female viewpoints — those of a husband and wife based partly on the poet's grandparents. One of the main themes is how this couple shapes their private lives. This sensitive epic of family life, with its intimacies and solitude, established Dove's reputation and won her the Pulitzer Prize.

BRAD LEITHAUSER: *Cats of the Temple.* Leithauser's second collection is nominated for the National Book Critics Circle Award and prompts critic John Gross to declare Leithauser "one of the most gifted American poets to have come over the horizon in years." He would be recognized as one of the leading exponents of the so-called New Formalists. Subsequent collections are *The Mail from Anywhere* (1990) and *The Odd Last Thing She Did* (1998).

Publications and Events

Poet laureate of the United States. Robert Penn Warren is named the first official poet laureate of the United States.

1987
Drama and Theater

ROBERT HARLING (b. 1951): *Steel Magnolias.* Harling, who earned a law degree at Tulane University, had written his hit play, about a young woman stricken with an illness but determined to live life to the fullest, in a ten-day stretch while coping with the death of his sister from kidney failure in 1985. It is, by Harling's admission, the first thing he ever wrote. After opening off-Broadway, *Steel Magnolias* tours the United States and Europe before being adapted for the big screen in 1989. Harling would cowrite the screenplay for the comedy *Soapdish* (1991).

VELINA HASU HOUSTON: *Tea.* The third part of a well-received trilogy, this play concerns four Japanese war brides living on a military base in Kansas. The tea ceremony becomes their refuge in an alien culture. Much of their talk concerns a fifth war bride who committed suicide after killing her husband.

TINA HOWE: *Coastal Disturbances.* Howe specializes in American eccentrics — this time, a group at the beach in a time of late-summer romances. As in her other work, she enjoys conflating the ordinary, conventional scenes of American life with absurd, spontaneous, and irrational elements that mock accepted notions of reality.

TERRENCE McNALLY: *Frankie and Johnny in the Clair de Lune.* A middle-aged man and woman, wary of each other because of many disappointments, gradually explore the possibility of a life together. A comedy, it also has serious overtones expressing McNally's wry sensibility and compassion for his characters. Critics praise the play for honestly portraying its characters' valiant efforts to overcome their sense of injury.

ARTHUR MILLER: *Danger: Memory!* This work collects two one-act plays: *I Can't Remember Anything* and *Clara.* Each is performed at New York's Lincoln Center.

STEPHEN SONDHEIM: *Into the Woods.* In Sondheim's inventive musical, Cinderella, Jack (and the Beanstalk), Little Red Riding Hood, and other fairy tale figures encounter one another on the same day in the forest. This delightful fantasy pokes fun at the self-enclosed world of fairy tales and makes their characters not only react to one another but to the consequences of their actions.

ALFRED UHRY (b. 1937): *Driving Miss Daisy.* Uhry's first nonmusical drama opens off-Broadway, where it plays for 1,195 performances. The story revolves around the relationship between an elderly Jewish matron in Atlanta and her black driver, on whom she becomes increasingly dependent. Actress Jessica Tandy would earn an Oscar for her 1989 performance in the title role of the film version.

AUGUST WILSON: *Fences.* Wilson's play about a disappointed former Negro Baseball League veteran, ex-con, and garbage collector opens in New York, where it plays for 526 performances. It sets a record for nonmusical drama on Broadway by grossing $11 million in its first year while capturing the Pulitzer Prize, the Tony Award, and the New York Drama Critics Circle Award.

Fiction

PAUL AUSTER: *The Locked Room.* The final volume of Auster's New York trilogy, concerns Fanshawe, a brilliant writer who has disappeared and is presumed dead. Critics praise this novel as both the most accessible and brilliantly conceived in the trilogy because it fuses Auster's philosophical concerns with the creation of riveting characters and a suspenseful plot.

JOHN BARTH: *The Tidewater Tales.* Barth's novel concerns a case of writer's block as a writer and his wife sail around Chesapeake Bay.

SAUL BELLOW: *More Die of Heartbreak.* This comic novel is largely the monologue of Kenneth Trachtenberg, a Russian history expert who tells the story of his uncle, Benn Crader, a botanist. Though perhaps it is less ambitious than Bellow's greatest novels, critics nevertheless find in this work a continuation of Bellow's concern with the way the world of ideas crosses the world of human characters.

T. CORAGHESSAN BOYLE: *World's End.* Boyle's novel, set in the author's native Peekskill, New York, is a work of magic realism in which characters from the seventeenth and twentieth centuries interact. It is widely considered Boyle's most accomplished work to date, and its structure and scope mark a departure from his usual absurdist black humor.

TRUMAN CAPOTE: *Answered Prayers: The Unfinished Novel.* What had long been promised as Capote's magnum opus is finally published, consisting of stories previously appearing in *Esquire* in the 1970s. It is a roman à clef, anatomizing the New York social set in what many regard as a series of malicious character portraits but others defend as a disappointingly unfulfilled social satire that might well have become Capote's masterpiece.

ROBERT COOVER: *Whatever Happened to Gloomy Gus of the Chicago Bears?* The novella, first published in the *American Review* in 1975, recounts the title character's football career, off-the-field sexual exploits, and death during a steel strike. Dealing with myth and history, Coover turns, in the words of one reviewer, "a very amusing novel to a seriously funny one."

JAMES DICKEY: *Alnilam.* Dickey's second novel concerns a blind man's investigation of his flyer son's death. The writer declares that he "tried to do for the air what Melville did for the water." Critic Robert Towers calls it a "vast, intricate work distinguished not by its forward momentum but by its symbolic suggestiveness and its bravura passages, some of which rise to visionary heights."

MICHAEL DORRIS (1945–1997): *A Yellow Raft in Blue Water.* Dorris's best-selling and critically acclaimed first novel, treating the experiences of three generations of Native American women, establishes Dorris as a leading contemporary Native American writer. He would treat more fully the background of a part African American, part Native American character introduced here in his final novel, *Cloud Chamber* (1997). Dorris, of Modoc

Indian heritage, founded the Native American studies program at Dartmouth College in 1972. In 1981 he married novelist Louise Erdrich.

JOHN GREGORY DUNNE: *The Red White and Blue.* In this ambitious political novel, the plot centers on the Brodericks, a family that loosely resembles the Kennedys. Power games abound both in politics and in the Catholic Church—a subject that Dunne had also covered in *True Confessions* (1977). While *The Red White and Blue* lacks the intensity of Dunne's earlier fiction, critics admire the broad canvas of the novel and its shrewd judgments of American institutions.

STANLEY ELKIN: *The Rabbi of Lud.* This novel about a New Jersey rabbi reflects Elkin's characteristic obsession with mortality. Rabbi Jerry Goldkorn is beset with problems with his family and his spiritual vocation. In a typical Elkin move, Goldkorn travels to Alaska and becomes the rabbi of the Alaskan pipeline. Critics admire Elkin's unblinking portrayal of rather grim material, which he is able to energize and even make endearing.

BRET EASTON ELLIS: *The Rules of Attraction.* Ellis's second novel depicts the self-indulgent lifestyle of faculty and students at a small eastern liberal arts college who, in the words of reviewer Scott Spencer, "live in a world of conspicuous and compulsive consumption—consuming first one another, and then drugs, and then anything else they can lay their hands on."

RICHARD FORD: *Rock Spring.* Ford's first collection contains some of his most admired stories, set mainly in Montana, including "Children," "Great Falls," and the title work, which face the crisis moments in relationships and families.

KAYE GIBBONS (b. 1960): *Ellen Foster.* Gibbons's first novel treats an eleven-year-old girl's coping with the suicide of her mother as well as her abusive father. It introduces Gibbons's characteristic subject of Southern women trying to fashion satisfactory lives for themselves. The North Carolina–born writer's other works would include *A Virtuous Woman* (1989), *A Cure for Dreams* (1991), *Charms for the Easy Life* (1993), and *Sights Unseen* (1995).

ROLANDO HINOJOSA: *Klail City.* The second novel of the writer's "Klail City Death Trip" continues the story of Jehu Malacara and Rafe Buenrostro, characters introduced in the novelist's exploration of the borderland between Mexico and Texas, *The Valley* (1983). More than just a document of a period in American and Mexican history, these novels have been celebrated for their irony, satire, and stark realism.

JERZY KOSINSKI: *The Hermit of 69th Street.* Kosinski's final novel, an "autofiction," describes the travails of a burnt-out writer. It incorporates Kosinski's defense against charges of plagiarism leveled at him in 1982, when Geoffrey Stokes and Eliot Fremont-Smith suggested in a *Village Voice* article that certain passages of Kosinski's works had actually been written by editorial assistants.

JOSEPH MCELROY (b. 1930): *Women and Men.* This twelve-hundred-page novel is McElroy's most ambitious work. Set in the 1970s, the story focuses on James Mayn, a journalist, and Grace Kimball, a radical feminist. The way these characters view the world is influenced by their gender and also by an informed understanding of science. His previous novels include *A Smuggler's Bible* (1966), *Hind's Kidnap* (1969), and *Cookout Cartridge* (1974).

LARRY MCMURTRY: *Texasville.* McMurtry returns to Thalia, Texas, and to Sonny and Duane, the memorable characters from his highly praised *The Last Picture Show* (1966). The problems centering on the characters' love lives (and Duane's involvement in civic affairs) receive comic treatment in a work that critics praise as a fine farewell to the phase of McMurtry's closely observed works about northern Texas.

TONI MORRISON: *Beloved.* Morrison's harrowingly powerful novel deals with a black woman who must deal with the effect of murdering her own child rather than having the girl returned to slavery. The spirit of the murdered child returns to claim retribution. Suffused with realism and fantasy, the novel wins the Pulitzer Prize and is widely regarded as Morrison's masterpiece.

HOWARD NORMAN (b. 1949): *The Northern Lights.* This debut novel is a coming-of-age story inspired by the writer's life among the Cree Indians while working as a firefighter in Manitoba in the 1960s. It is nominated for a National Book Award.

CYNTHIA OZICK: *The Messiah of Stockholm.* Ozick's novel concerns Lars Andemening, a Polish refugee who takes a Swedish name but fantasizes that he is the son of Bruno Schulz, the famous Polish Jewish writer who wrote about and was a victim of the Holocaust. His fate poses yet another version of Ozick's much-praised quest for what it means to be a contemporary Jew.

WALKER PERCY: *The Thanatos Syndrome.* Dr. Thomas More, the protagonist of an earlier Percy novel, *Love in the Ruins* (1971), returns home from prison to find his former patients depressed and physically debilitated. As in Percy's other novels, the symptoms are as much spiritual as material. Like Flannery O'Connor, however, Percy is such a fine dramatist of human misery and sin that his

Walker Percy

theological vision does not detract from the development of character and plot but positively energizes it.

MARGE PIERCY: *Gone to Soldiers.* Piercy registers the impact of World War II on a large collection of characters in this novel, which draws praise for its sensitivity.

JANE SMILEY: *The Age of Grief: A Novella and Stories.* Nominated for a National Book Critics Circle Award, the volume includes stories about family life and marriage. Critics admire the psychological penetration of the title story, in which an apparently happy and attractive couple are devastated by infidelity.

SCOTT TUROW (b. 1949): *Presumed Innocent.* Turow's first novel, a legal thriller about a prosecuting attorney charged with the murder of his female colleague with whom he had been having an affair, was written while Turow was commuting from his job as a U.S. district attorney in Chicago. It spends more than forty-three weeks on the bestseller list and sells more than four million paperback copies.

GORE VIDAL: *Empire.* One of Vidal's most rousing and comprehensive historical novels features pithy portraits of Henry Adams, Henry James, William Randolph Hearst, John Hay, and Theodore Roosevelt. His fictional plot, concerning the newspaper dynasty of Caroline and Blaise Sanford and Congressman James Burden Day, provides a fascinating conjunction of government and media in the creation of modern America.

KURT VONNEGUT JR.: *Bluebeard.* Vonnegut brings back the painter Rabo Karabekian from *Breakfast of Champi-*

ons (1973) in this meditation on art and war, as Rabo composes both his autobiography and his daily diary.

TOM WOLFE: *The Bonfire of the Vanities.* Wolfe's first novel, about the downfall of a successful New York financial trader, captures a cultural moment and the public imagination. Illustrating the differences between life on Park Avenue and life in the outer borough projects of New York City during the "greedy 1980s," Wolfe's book is a bestseller and one of the era's defining reflections.

Literary Criticism and Scholarship

SVEN BIRKERTS (b. 1951): *An Artificial Wilderness: Essays on Twentieth-Century Literature.* This collection by the Michigan literary critic and lecturer in expository writing at Harvard reflects the critic's penchant for European literature. A foe of minimalism, Birkerts prefers writers such as Robert Musil, Thomas Bernhard, and Erich Heller, and Americans such as Susan Sontag, who carry on European traditions. Reviewer Donald Hall celebrates Birkerts as a critic worth arguing with, and he honors Birkerts's efforts to revive the importance of European literature in America, even if readers must absorb it in translation. His second book, *The Electric Life* (1989), would win the PEN Award for distinguished essays.

HAZEL V. CARBY (b. 1948): *Reconstructing Womanhood: The Rise of the Black Woman Novelist.* Carby, a British-born professor at Wesleyan University, sees the advent of black women novelists as an important corrective to black male writers, who have favored a romanticized view of black folk roots. Carby's strongly argued neo-Marxist view gains considerable influence in academic circles. *Race Men* would follow in 1998.

HENRY JAMES: *The Complete Notebooks of Henry James.* This is the most thorough edition of James's extant notebooks and pocket diaries — an extraordinary source for following the development of his stories, plays, and novels.

ROBERT LOWELL: *Collected Prose.* This collection consists of reviews, essays, eulogies, interviews, and memoirs. The work includes essays on Robert Frost, Wallace Stevens, William Carlos Williams, and other poets. Lowell's method is both critical and biographical. Included also are searching portraits of New England writers and a final section of commentary on his own work.

HELEN VENDLER (b. 1933): *Voices and Visions: The Poet in America.* One of America's most distinguished critics of poetry and a Harvard professor, Vendler edits a collection of essays on poets from Walt Whitman to Sylvia Plath, the companion volume of a 1988 PBS series. She notes the common focus of the essays: explorations of the poetic traditions that American writers inherited, modified, and later transformed into unique expressions of the American character. A highly integrated and comprehensive study, it includes the work of critics such as Calvin Bedient, Richard Sewall, Richard Poirier, and Helen McNeil.

Nonfiction

ALLAN BLOOM (1930–1992): *The Closing of the American Mind.* Bloom's scathing analysis of the shortcomings of modern higher education provokes a storm of controversy — and self-flagellation — in the academy. The book becomes a number one bestseller, attacks contemporary students for their spiritual decline and lack of intellectual curiosity, and blames universities for contributing to this decline. Born in Indianapolis, Bloom was educated at the University of Chicago, where he was professor of philosophy and political science.

JOAN DIDION: *Miami.* Didion explores the Cuban exile community and finds an insulated, solipsistic, and politically unstable environment. Her view of the exiles' fixation on Communist Cuba is scorching and forms part of her long-term study of displaced persons and alienated individuals, extending over several distinguished novels and works of nonfiction.

DONALD HERBERT DONALD: *Look Homeward: A Life of Thomas Wolfe.* Donald wins his second Pulitzer Prize for this biography of Thomas Wolfe, praised for its balance and thoroughness.

ANDREA DWORKIN: *Intercourse.* Dworkin's controversial polemic is a literary and cultural analysis that depicts heterosexual intercourse as the basis for women's oppression.

IAN FRAZIER (b. 1951): *Nobody Better, Better Than Nobody.* Frazier, an Ohio-born essayist and journalist, establishes his critical reputation as a meticulous observer of details that add up to a comic vision of modern life. His descriptions of people are memorable — the proprietor of a fishing-goods store who discourses on exotic flies, the writer of the "Hints from Heloise" columns, and two Russian immigrant artists.

JAMES GLEICK (b. 1954): *Chaos: Making a New Science.* Gleick, a science and technology reporter for the *New York Times,* is lauded for his skill in writing a popular book about science — particularly the complex and mysterious new field known as chaos theory.

DORIS KEARNS GOODWIN (b. 1943): *The Fitzgeralds and the Kennedys: An American Saga.* Goodwin chronicles three generations of the Irish American political dynasty, from John "Honey Fitz" Fitzgerald in 1863 to the inaugu-

ration of his grandson John F. Kennedy in 1961. Goodwin is the author of the biography *Lyndon Johnson and the American Dream* (1976) and *No Ordinary Time* (1994), a study of Franklin and Eleanor Roosevelt during wartime.

E. D. HIRSCH JR.: *Cultural Literacy: What Every American Needs to Know.* Literary critic Hirsch analyses the causes of the decline of literacy. Although he acknowledges the role of television and other media, which draw students away from reading, his main target is American educators. They have failed, in his view, to insist on basic cultural literacy. Although his thesis is controversial, Hirsch's ideas prompt many critics to call for an increase in the sheer quantity of literature and history that students must master in order to become "culturally literate."

MARY MCCARTHY: *How I Grew.* This is a continuation of McCarthy's celebrated *Memoirs of a Catholic Girlhood* (1957), moving beyond her childhood to cover her maturation. Though it is less evocative than her earlier volume, critics nevertheless find it a compelling account of the writer's adolescent reading, her years at Vassar, and her first marriage — a record of what life was like for a brilliant young woman in the 1920s.

ARTHUR MILLER: *Timebends.* This autobiography is a cinematically constructed work, roaming back and forth between Miller's life and works — rather like a film with flashbacks, montages, and fades. He deals with his controversial leftist politics and his marriage to Marilyn Monroe, analyzing the mistakes he made in public and in private.

RANDY SHILTS (1951–1994): *And the Band Played On: Politics, People, and the AIDS Epidemic.* Shilts, a staff reporter for the *San Francisco Chronicle,* wins numerous awards as well as plaudits for providing the most definitive study of the illness to date. Shilts tells his story by focusing on individuals both obscure and well known, and the book has the sweep and momentum of a well-constructed novel.

Poetry

A. R. AMMONS: *Sumerian Vistas.* This collection, inspired by various landscapes, includes the powerful lyrical sequence "Tombstones" and the Whitmanesque "The Ridge Farm."

LUCILLE CLIFTON (b. 1936): *Good Woman: Poems and a Memoir, 1969–1980.* This book collects works from Clifton's previous volumes — *Good Times* (1969), *Good News About the Earth* (1972), *An Ordinary Woman* (1974), and *Two-Headed Woman* (1984) — dealing with the struggles of African Americans, along with a collection of autobiographical pieces that had first appeared in *Generations* (1976). She also publishes *Next: New Poems*.

MARK DOTY (b. 1953): *Turtle, Swan*. Doty's first collection is praised by one reviewer for turning gay experience into "an example of how we live, how we suffer and transcend suffering." It would be followed by a similarly acclaimed second collection, *Bethlehem in Broad Daylight*, in 1991.

SUSAN HOWE (b. 1937): *Articulation of Sound Forms in Time*. One part of this collection by the Boston-born poet is about Hope Atherton, a sixteenth-century minister who fought against the Indians in Deerfield, Massachusetts. The other part concentrates on twentieth-century artists. In both parts, Howe employs unconventional punctuation and lines. Critics generally find Howe's experiments convincing and praise her radical effort to foster a "synchronic flow," which impels readers past the breaks or pauses of more traditional poetry.

WILLIAM MEREDITH: *Partial Accounts: New and Selected Poems*. This collection of works from Meredith's seven previous volumes, along with eleven new works, mainly reflects the poet's travels. It wins the Pulitzer Prize.

SHARON OLDS: *The Gold Cell: The Matter of This World*. Olds's third collection contains works, such as "The Quest," "What If God," and "I Go Back to May 1937," treating her family, the nature of her own body, scenes from urban life, and gruesome accounts of rapes and abandoned babies. *The Sign of Saturn: Poems, 1980–1987* would follow in 1991.

ELLEN BRYANT VOIGT (b. 1943): *The Lotus Flowers*. The Virginia-born poet's third collection, following *Claiming Kin* (1977) and *The Forces of Plenty* (1983), is praised for its skill in depicting the author's Virginia childhood and scenes of rural life in Vermont. Subsequent volumes would include *Two Trees* (1992), *Kyrie* (1995), and *Shadow of Heaven* (2002).

THEODORE WEISS (1916–2003): *From Princeton One Autumn Afternoon*. The volume provides selections and revisions from Weiss's previous volumes, including the long work "Gunsight," described by one reviewer as a "virtuoso performance." Included as well are several new works. Born in Reading, Pennsylvania, Weiss was a poet-in-residence and English professor at Princeton.

C. K. WILLIAMS: *Flesh and Blood*. Critics compare the prose effects of Williams's poetry to work by Walt Whitman and William Carlos Williams. Like them, Williams eschews rhyme and even conventional rhythm. Although his lines are long, his poems are short and intense, relying not on imagery but on rhetoric to explore ideas such as "Dignity," "Will," "Reading," "Suicide," "Love," and "Good Mother." The collection wins the National Book Critics Circle Award.

1988
Drama and Theater

DAVID HENRY HWANG: *M. Butterfly*. A French diplomat ruins his career because of his obsession with the actress Song Liling, who plays the part of Cio-Cio-San in Puccini's opera *Madama Butterfly*. She is his "feminine ideal." In fact, Song is a male and a spy. Hwang deftly explores the ambiguity of gender roles to reveal the unsatisfactory boundaries of societal conventions. It is the first play by an Asian American to win a Tony Award.

HOWARD KORDER (b. 1958): *Boys' Life*. Korder's first highly successful full-length play explores the lives of three men just out of college who spend much of their time carousing and chasing women. Yet Korder engages the audience's sympathies even as he exposes his characters and their milieu to biting social commentary. The New York–born playwright's works include *Middle Kingdom* (1985), *Fun* (1987), and *Wonderful Party!* (1989).

LARRY KRAMER: *Just Say No*. Kramer calls this play the most controversial he has written, "a farce about sexual hypocrisy in high places — about people who make the rules that they insist the rest of us live by, and they don't live by these rules themselves." Two of the characters — First Lady and her gay son — show unmistakable resemblances to Nancy Reagan and Ronald Reagan Jr.

DAVID MAMET: *Speed-the-Plow*. Mamet's trenchant dissection of Hollywood concerns a producer who is having an affair with his secretary. She persuades him to back a film adaptation of a literary work instead of his usual big-budget action films. The work wins the Tony Award for best play.

NEIL SIMON: *Rumors*. The playwright describes this play as an all-out farce that treats marriage in terms of the gossiping that goes on among friends who delight in rumors of marital discord. The exuberance and deliberate caricature of a society full of rumormongers receives admiring critical notices but fails with audiences.

WENDY WASSERSTEIN: *The Heidi Chronicles*. Wasserstein's drama concerning an educated young woman's attempt to reconcile career and family in the second half of the twentieth century is performed off-Broadway before transferring uptown in 1989. Attacked by some feminist critics as "antifeminist" in its portrayal of women and the feminist cause, it wins the Pulitzer Prize and the Tony Award for best play in 1989, making Wasserstein the first woman playwright to win the award in that category.

LANFORD WILSON: *Burn This.* Wilson's play concerns the accidental death of a dancer, which brings together his young brother and his male and female roommates. The drama's emotional intensity is praised by reviewer J. M. Ditsky, who states that "Nothing quite like it has been encountered since Tennessee Williams departed the American theatrical scene."

Fiction

PAUL AUSTER: *In the Country of Last Things.* Set in a devastated apocalyptic future, the novel depicts Anna Blume's search for her brother in a vast city. As details accumulate, it becomes clear that what seems at first to be a foreign setting in the future is actually the urban present, intensified and piercingly examined. Critics praise Auster for his melding of philosophical and aesthetic concerns with the creation of vivid settings and characters.

FREDERICK BARTHELME: *Two Against One.* Barthelme's novel presents Edward Lasko's meditations on his failed marriage and his life on his fortieth birthday. Francine Prose calls the novel "by far the most powerful, disturbing, and interior of [his] fictions, inviting us to be flies on the wall of a particularly shadowy and unwelcoming corner of its hero's psyche."

ELIZABETH BENEDICT (b. 1954): *The Beginner's Book of Dreams.* Benedict's second novel (following *Slow Dancing*, 1985) concerns an eight-year-old girl who has to contend with divorced parents (an alcoholic mother and an irresponsible father). Ann Tyler calls the book complex and "morbidly funny," adding that it is surprising that such a sad story is so pleasurable to read. The Hartford-born writer's subsequent books would include *The Joy of Writing Sex* (1996) and *Almost* (2001).

THOMAS BERGER: *The Houseguest.* Berger's black comedy concerns the perfect visitor to a summer house who gradually becomes sinister and violent. Reviewer Paul Gray observes, "At his best, as he is here, Thomas Berger can command attention solely as a lonely, insidious voice insisting in a stage whisper, that fiction can be stranger than truth."

ETHAN CANIN (b. 1960): *Emperor of the Air.* Canin's first book, a collection of short stories, becomes a surprising bestseller. It is commended for its craft and for dealing with major themes of aging, growing up, family relationships, and inner conflicts. Canin's first novel, *Blue River*, followed in 1991 and a second collection, *The Palace Thief*, in 1994. Canin began publishing stories at age nineteen and would become a practicing physician after graduating from Harvard Medical School in 1992.

RAYMOND CARVER: *Where I'm Calling From.* Carver's final major story collection is released shortly before his death. Dealing with characteristic subjects of alienation and failed relationships, the stories continue to show the more affirming tone of *Cathedral* (1984). It was nominated for both a Pulitzer Prize and a National Book Critics Circle Award.

FRANK CHIN: *The Chinaman Pacific and Frisco R.R. Co.* Critics regard Chin as in the vanguard of Asian American literature, and many stories in this collection had received awards. They are set in San Francisco's Chinatown where Chin's characters lead isolated lives — not only from whites but from the different generations of Chinese as well. It evokes themes of death and decay, for Chin's characters fail to break through to a larger society, which views them as stereotypes.

DON DE LILLO: *Libra.* De Lillo's novel connects Lee Harvey Oswald with characters from De Lillo's earlier work to form a national allegory. The novel, despite its complexity, is a popular success and transforms the writer from a cult figure to a mainstream author with a considerable literary reputation.

PETE DEXTER (b. 1943): *Paris Trout.* A hardware store owner and loan shark to the black community in Cotton Point, Georgia, goes to prison after he kills two people in an effort to collect an outstanding debt. He bribes his way out of prison and goes crazy, becoming, in reviewer Richard Eder's words, "primal evil, all will and no humanity." The novel wins the National Book Award. Dexter is known for his expert blend of violence and humor, evocative dialogue, and shrewd use of local color.

LOUISE ERDRICH: *Tracks.* As in Erdrich's other novels, in this book Native Americans strive to nurture traditions that erode in the confrontation with majority white culture. Catholicism represents a countertradition — and in this novel it captures the imagination of Pauline, a young Native American torn between loyalty to her people's beliefs and Catholic views.

THOMAS HARRIS (b. 1940): *The Silence of the Lambs.* Harris's thriller about the FBI's hunt for a serial killer features the diabolical Hannibal Lecter, who has been described as the "best literary villain since Iago." After a popular and critically acclaimed 1991 film adaptation, Harris would produce the sequel, *Hannibal*, in 1999. The Mississippi-born writer worked as a police reporter in Waco, Texas.

JOHN HAWKES: *Whistlejacket.* Hawkes's novel alternates between scenes from the life of nineteenth-century artist George Stubbs and the modern Van Fleet family, owners of Stubbs's portrait of the title figure. Patrick

McGrath calls it an "interesting and tantalizing book" that is "quite strong enough to maintain John Hawkes's position as the most consistently interesting writer, in terms of formal inventiveness, intelligence, and the sheer grace of the prose, at work in the United States today."

WILLIAM KENNEDY: *Quinn's Book.* Kennedy widens and deepens his exploration of Albany, New York, by chronicling the career of Irishman Daniel Quinn, who arrives in 1849. The novel is praised by critic J. K. Van Dover for adding a "crucial new dimension to Kennedy's portrayal of the paradigmatic Irish-American experience of America."

BARBARA KINGSOLVER (b. 1955): *The Bean Trees.* Kingsolver's impressive debut concentrates on the plight of women in contemporary society. The novel is narrated by Taylor Greer, a Kentucky native, who leaves homes to seek her fortune in the West, adopting along the way a Cherokee child, Turtle. Kingsolver, born in Annapolis, Maryland, and educated at DePauw University and the University of Arizona, is a master of describing places, both Kentucky and Arizona, and her novel grows in strength as her characters get to know one another.

JOSEPH MCELROY: *The Letter Left to Me.* The letter in question is from a father, recently deceased, to his son. It makes a profound impression — so much so that it eventually is distributed far and wide, including to the boy's New England college, where the freshman class is given it for analysis. Responding enthusiastically to McElroy's profound meditation on the significance of writing, critics place him in the tradition of great novelists who have critiqued the nature of their own work.

LARRY MCMURTRY: *Anything for Billy.* This novel, set on the nineteenth-century frontier, satirizes legends about Billy the Kid. His story is related by an easterner whose imagination has been distorted by dime novels about the Old West. Critics praise McMurtry's powerful evocation of violence laced with manic, surrealistic humor.

BHARATI MUKHERJEE (b. 1940): *The Middleman and Other Stories.* Winner of the National Book Critics Circle Award, this collection of stories treats immigrants from various lands who embrace their new lives in America with gusto. Born in Calcutta, Mukherjee came to the United States to study at the Iowa Writer's Workshop in 1963.

GLORIA NAYLOR: *Mama Day.* Naylor's novel, set in an all-black island community founded by a slave off the coast of South Carolina and Georgia, is one of the writer's most ambitious works, evoking comparisons with Toni Morrison's *Beloved* (1987) for likewise showing the haunted past of a family and community.

REYNOLDS PRICE: *Good Hearts.* The book revisits the characters Rosacoke Mustian and Wesley Beavers from Price's first novel, *A Long and Happy Life* (1962). After twenty-eight years of marriage, Wesley abandons Rosacoke, whose rape becomes a catalyst in reuniting her extended family. According to reviewer Jay Tolson, "Using the still powerful idiom of the rural South, Price has brilliantly inscribed the story of the modern-day Pilgrim's Progress. He is our age's Bunyan."

E. ANNIE PROULX (b. 1935): *Heart Songs and Other Stories.* Proulx's first book, a collection of stories dealing with backwoods communities in northern New England, receives little attention until reissued in 1994, when it would gain widespread critical acclaim for its power and stylistic mastery. Of French-Canadian descent, Proulx was born in Connecticut and did doctoral work in history at Concordia University in Montreal.

JAMES SALTER: *Dusk and Other Stories.* This collection of stories is populated by upper-middle-class characters in New York City, Long Island, and Europe who are coping with divorce, alcoholism, and career frustrations. The book wins the PEN/Faulkner Award and prompts several reviewers to proclaim Salter the most underrated of underrated writers.

THOMAS SAVAGE: *The Corner of Rife and Pacific.* This novel is set in the West, one of Savage's favorite locations, and deals with a family struggling to overcome one disaster after another. Critics note his poignant and compassionate treatment of these characters and the graceful, tightly constructed plot.

ISAAC BASHEVIS SINGER: *The Death of Methuselah, and Other Stories.* The last of Singer's story collections published during his lifetime deals with the danger of desire in stories set in eastern Europe, New York City, Florida, and ancient Babylon. Singer also publishes *The King of the Fields*, a novel set in prehistoric Poland, which deals with the conflict between farmers and hunter-gatherers in a parable of modern civilization.

JANE SMILEY: *The Greenlanders.* Smiley has called this massive historical novel, chronicling the destruction of the Norse settlements in Greenland in the tenth century, "the true masterpiece" among her works.

ANNE TYLER: *Breathing Lessons.* Tyler's Pulitzer Prize–winning novel relates the story of a marriage of twenty-eight years. Some critics complain that it is "formula" Tyler, filled with her customary parade of eccentric characters and odd events. Others, however, hail her treatment of marriage and middle age in a work that interweaves memory and nostalgia.

JOHN UPDIKE: *S.* Like his previous novel, *Roger's Version* (1986), *S.* continues Updike's exploration of the adulterous triangle—in the spiritual and sexual terms set out by *The Scarlet Letter*. Critics call this novel the capstone of Updike's brilliant trilogy of novels about modern marriage, sexuality, and spiritual striving, initiated by *A Month of Sundays* (1975).

EDMUND WHITE: *The Beautiful Room Is Empty*. In the sequel to *A Boy's Own Story*, White portrays his hero's college years and builds toward the climax of the novel—the Stonewall riots (1969), which initiated the gay rights movement and the development of gay literature as a separate area of study. White himself had been radicalized by this event (he was there when police raided the Stonewall Inn and brutally arrested homosexuals), and the novel reflects much of his own experience.

HISAYE YAMAMOTO (b. 1921): *Seventeen Syllables and Other Stories*. This work collects four decades of writing by this much-admired Japanese American author. Including essays as well as stories, it begins with her first major publication, an essay on sexual harassment that had appeared in *Partisan Review* in 1948. Yamamoto, who claims "my output is minimal," took twenty years to write "Educational Opportunities."

Literary Criticism and Scholarship

WAYNE C. BOOTH: *The Company We Keep: An Ethics for Fiction*. Booth calls for an ethical engagement with fiction in which criticism should be a conversation about "kinds of personal and social goods that fiction can serve or destroy."

HENRY LOUIS GATES JR. (b. 1950): *The Signifying Monkey: Toward a Theory of Afro-American Literary Criticism*. Gates, professor of English and African American studies at Cornell, argues that more critical attention should be paid to black writers' use of language rather than just their evocation of the black experience. Gates demonstrates his point by analyzing the linguistic patterns of African American texts, finding a form of signification—wordplay—that is unique in American writing, relying on the black vernacular as well as on traditional figures of speech such as metaphor, irony, understatement, and exaggeration.

SANDRA GILBERT AND SUSAN GUBAR: *No Man's Land: The Place of the Woman Writer in the Twentieth Century—Volume I: The War of the Words*. The authors publish the first volume of a trilogy exploring "the interactions in the twentieth century between male and female literary traditions and figures." It would be followed by *Sexchanges* (1989) and *Letters from the Front* (1994).

ALFRED KAZIN: *A Writer's America: Landscape in Literature*. Kazin organizes an approach to American literature through the impact of place on the literary imagi-

nation of writers such as Ralph Waldo Emerson, Henry David Thoreau, Walt Whitman, Henry James, Robert Frost, and Ernest Hemingway.

ROBERT PINSKY: *Poetry and the World*. Pinsky's second collection of criticism explores the impact of words on his life and the importance of the literary tradition. Reviewer Amy Edith Johnson praises its "jargon-free analyses" and commitment to larger issues, which confirm "the dignity and creative dimensions of . . . the function of criticism at the present time."

Nonfiction

TAYLOR BRANCH (b. 1947): *Parting the Waters: America in the King Years, 1954–1963*. Branch, a journalist for *Harper's* and *Esquire*, wins the National Book Critics Circle Award and the Pulitzer Prize for his biographical social history, which reviewer Jim Miller calls "a landmark achievement and a paradigm of the new American history at its best." *Pillar of Fire: America in the King Years, 1963–1965* would follow in 1997.

JAMES M. McPHERSON (b. 1936): *Battle Cry of Freedom: The Civil War Era*. Critics describe this Pulitzer Prize–winning sixth volume in *The Oxford History of the United States* as the best single-volume treatment of the Civil War available. McPherson is a professor of history at Princeton.

PAUL MONETTE (1945–1999): *Borrowed Time: An AIDS Memory*. The first volume of Monette's acclaimed memoirs describes his relationship with a longtime lover who died of AIDS. Monette's account of growing up gay, *Becoming a Man*, would follow in 1992.

ARNOLD RAMPERSAD: *The Life of Langston Hughes: I Dream a World, 1941–1967*. The second volume and conclusion of an authoritative biography of the great African American writer. Poet Rita Dove speaks for many reviewers when she calls Rampersad's book a "superlative study of . . . the most proment Afro-American poet of our century."

PHILIP ROTH: *The Facts*. While many of Roth's novels seem transparently autobiographical, with his writer/hero Zuckerman a stand-in for Roth himself, this book purports—as its title suggests—to provide a straightforward, no-frills account of the author's life. But Roth is cleverly selective, implying with his assessment of his character Zuckerman that fact and fiction are inextricably connected. Indeed, critics view the work as a brilliant logical extension of his mature exploration of storytelling and history.

NEIL SHEEHAN (b. 1936): *A Bright Shining Lie: John Paul Vann and America in Vietnam*. Sheehan spent nearly sixteen years researching this study of the Vietnam War, prompting his friends to call him the war's last casualty. The book looks at events from the perspective of a lieutenant colonel and top military adviser whose contradictions become representative of American involvement.

SUSAN SONTAG: *AIDS and Its Metaphors.* The book serves as a kind of coda to her earlier work, *Illness as Metaphor* (1978), showing Sontag's attempt to demystify—or, as she says, "dedramatize"—an apparently incurable disease. The work is criticized by AIDS activists, who decry Sontag's cool, reserved tone.

Poetry

JIMMY SANTIAGO BACA (1952–1987): *Martin and Meditations on the South Valley.* The winner of the American Book Award follows the adventures of an Apache man who travels across the United States. Baca began writing poetry after teaching himself to read while incarcerated in an Arizona prison on drug charges. His work is remarkable for its lack of bitterness, since, unlike many other prison poets, he does not write so much about human suffering as about joy and triumph.

JUDITH BAUMEL (b. 1956): *The Weight of Numbers.* Winner of the Walt Whitman Award, Baumel's collection is noteworthy for its impressive shifts between different kinds of diction and rhythm. "Speaking in Blizzards" begins with a matter-of-fact tone, then switches to a kind of grand formality associated with the early verse of Robert Lowell. Critics admire the New York–born poet's rigorous sense of composition and her "athletic intellect."

DONALD HALL: *The One Day.* Critics note the careful structure of this volume, which is built on a dialogue of male and female voices, mediated at times by an omniscient narrator—as in "Shrubs Burnt Away." Hall explores what a house means to a man and a woman in terms of the history of their relationship, with each room signifying an aspect of their personal history.

GARRETT HONGO (b. 1951): *The River of Heaven.* Hongo's second collection, following *Yellow Light* (1982), wins the Lamont Poetry Prize and receives a Pulitzer Prize nomination. The poems address the experiences of Asian Americans, mixing personal memory, cultural history, and narrative elements. Born in Hawaii of Japanese heritage, Hongo was the founder and director of the Seattle theater group Asian Exclusion Act (1975–1977).

RICHARD WILBUR: *New and Collected Poems.* Wilbur earns his second Pulitzer Prize for this collection, which includes a tribute to W. H. Auden and "On Freedom's Ground," the lyrics for a cantata by William Schuman to commemorate the refurbishing of the Statue of Liberty.

CHARLES WRIGHT: *Zone Journals.* Continuing his exploration of the poetic journal begun in *Five Journals* (1986), Wright, in the words of reviewer Helen Vendler, weaves "diverse thematic threads into a single autobiographical fabric."

1989
Drama and Theater

LARRY GELBART (b. 1923): *City of Angels.* In a witty takeoff on Hollywood detective films of the 1940s, this inventive musical by the Chicago-born writer for film and television features a writer at his typewriter, creating his detective. Critics find this examination of how Hollywood film has shaped our culture exhilarating and the staging spectacular—with film characters appearing on stage in black and white, simulating their celluloid existence. The play wins numerous awards, including the Tony Award for best musical. Gelbart's other theater credits include *Sly Fox* (1976), *Power Failure* (1990), and *Feats of Clay* (1991).

A. R. GURNEY: *Love Letters.* The format of the play is simple: two characters recite from their years of correspondence, beginning with the childhood valentines they wrote to each other. In a New York production, the two characters are played by different well-known actors each week. Gurney's play *The Cocktail Hour* is also produced. In it a playwright returns home to confront his past—a hectoring mother and an aging father. Gurney earns praise for his fluent dialogue—in this case, concerning the family's conflict over the son's script, entitled *The Cocktail Hour*, and obviously based on the son's relatives.

DAVID MARGULIES (b. 1954): *The Lomax Family Picnic.* Margulies's black comedy interweaves recollections of the playwright's own Brooklyn childhood and themes from Arthur Miller's *Death of a Salesman.* It treats a middle-class Jewish family's conflict over the oldest son's bar mitzvah.

TERRENCE MCNALLY: *Lisbon Traviata.* Concerned with the dynamics of gay life, this play centers on four men who argue the merits of the opera diva Maria Callas. The subtext is their own lives and concerns about fleeting relationships and betrayals. Critics admire McNally's wry sensibility and his ability to balance social criticism with character development.

Fiction

PAULA GUNN ALLEN: *Spider Woman's Granddaughters: Traditional Tales and Contemporary Writing by Native American Women.* In this landmark anthology, Allen extends her effort to demonstrate the continuity between past and present in Native American women's lives and literature. This work is a companion piece to Allen's influential critical work *The Sacred Hoop: Recovering the Feminine in American Indian Traditions* (1986).

PAUL AUSTER: *Moon Palace.* Auster, who often presents innovative versions of traditional genres, this time creates a picaresque novel with a hero's search for an inheritance on a cross-country drive. This bildungsroman contains the classic elements of an orphan questing to become a man and to establish an independent identity.

RUSSELL BANKS: *Affliction.* Banks's autobiographically based novel treats two adult sons as they deal with their alcoholic, abusive father. The author explains that he wrote the book "to understand my own life, and also my father's and grandfather's. I wanted to know what brought them to be the human beings they were, and why they inflicted so much suffering."

ANN BEATTIE: *Picturing Will.* Beattie's fourth novel is a study of family dynamics from the perspective of the child Will, whose father has abandoned him. His mother's second husband steps in to provide him with his only true parental figure. T. Coraghessan Boyle declares that this is Beattie's best novel since *Chilly Scenes of Winter* (1976); its "depth and movement are a revelation."

SAUL BELLOW: *The Theft.* Bellow's novella focuses on a fashion writer whose stability and assumptions about life are shattered when a ring is stolen, prompting a reassessment of her faith in the power of love. Bellow also publishes *The Bellarosa Connection*, a stylish novella that probes the nature of American identity and the place of Jews in American culture. The wealthy narrator reminisces about Greenwich Village life in the 1940s, when he was earning his intellectual credentials, feeling very young and callow, and confronting the awesome literary heights he wanted to scale.

JOHN CASEY (b. 1939): *Spartina.* The title of this National Book Award–winning novel refers to the boat Rhode Island fisherman Dick Pierce is building as he struggles to survive economically and emotionally. In the words of reviewer Susan Kenney, its "fearless romantic insistence on lyric, even mythic symbolism, coupled with the relentless salt-smack clarity of realistic detail" makes it "just possibly the best American novel about going fishing since *The Old Man in the Sea,* maybe even *Moby-Dick.*"

E. L. DOCTOROW: *Billy Bathgate.* Doctorow wins the PEN/Faulkner Award and the National Book Critics Circle Award for this novel about a Bronx youth who gets involved with the Dutch Schultz gang in Depression-era New York.

ALLAN GURGANUS (b. 1947): *Oldest Living Confederate Widow Tells All.* This critical and popular success by the North Carolina–born writer concerns Lily Marsden, who marries a Confederate veteran when she is only fifteen and later recalls his anguished and florid memories of the Civil War. Critics praise the sheer zest of Gurganus's work and his ability to inhabit the persona of the loquacious Lily, an ebullient voice able to imitate the voices of all the characters in her husband's stories as told to her.

OSCAR HIJUELOS (b. 1951): *The Mambo Kings Play Songs of Love.* This novel pivots between the Cuban music scene of the 1940s and 1950s and its transplantation to New York City. Two brothers—the Mambo Kings—swing from their quest for stardom to adventures in love. Flamboyant and macho, they leave a legacy to the generation of the 1980s in the form of Eugenio, who carries on their cultural and musical mission. The author's stunning command of both English and Spanish and his narrative perspective make this an ambitious and challenging work, which earns the Pulitzer Prize and would be made into a motion picture. Born in New York City, Hijuelos published his first novel, *Our House in the Last World* (1983), about the assimilation challenges faced by a Cuban American family.

JOHN IRVING: *A Prayer for Owen Meany.* In Irving's novel, the title character tries to prevent his friend Johnny (the narrator) from going to Vietnam. Seen as tragic, the war forms the backdrop to the novel's exploration of the era's significance. Irving's powerful storytelling, his gift for creating memorable characters, his humor, and his elemental emotional power stimulate critics to compare him to Charles Dickens.

BARBARA KINGSOLVER: *Homeland and Other Stories.* This story collection is linked by characters struggling to make homes for themselves. Critics praise the title story, concerned with an old Indian woman's effort to cope with the commercializing of her Cherokee homeland.

MAXINE HONG KINGSTON: *Tripmaster Monkey: His Fake Book.* This novel contains Kingston's characteristic blend of fact, fiction, legend, history, autobiography, and myth in an intensely poetic prose. The story of Wittman Ah Sing is bracketed by the story of the Monkey King, who brought the Buddhist scriptures from India to China.

NORMAN MACLEAN (1902–1990): *A River Runs Through It and Other Stories.* Rejected by several trade publishers, Maclean's collection is eventually published by the University of Chicago Press, its first fiction, and it becomes a bestseller. The title work deals with Maclean's youth and fly-fishing with his father and brother on Montana's Big Bigfoot River. Alfred Kazin can think of "No other 20th-century American work that is at all like [it] . . . there are passages here of physical rapture in the presence of unsullied primitive America that are as beautiful as anything in Thoreau and Hemingway." Born in Iowa and raised in Montana, Maclean taught English at the University of Chicago.

BERNARD MALAMUD: *The People, and Uncollected Stories.* The volume contains an unfinished novel about a Russian Jewish peddler in the American West who becomes a marshal and is kidnapped by Indians. It also includes fourteen stories written between 1943 and 1985.

THOMAS MCGUANE: *Keep the Change.* Set in McGuane's characteristic Montana landscape, this novel represents, through the characters Joe Starling and Billy Kelton, another study of male competition and the metaphor of sports as a counter to conventional, everyday life. Both men see the limitation of the masculine code — a code, critics note, that is increasingly devalued in McGuane's novels as he explores the need for a more satisfying and humanistic emotional life.

N. SCOTT MOMADAY: *The Ancient Child.* This novel is about a successful artist living in California and estranged from his Kiowa heritage. When he returns home for a funeral, he cannot avoid his bond with his people and his home. Like Momaday's other work, this novel suggests that what seems lost in the Native American culture can be recaptured through vivid memory and the imagination, leading to a reintegration of a self and a people.

BHARATI MUKHERJEE: *Jasmine.* The novel chronicles the life story of the title heroine, which takes her from India to America, where she assumes a variety of identities.

JOYCE CAROL OATES: *American Appetites.* Oates begins a series of novels treating different aspects of American society, in this case, affluence. It would be followed by *Because It Is Bitter and Because It Is My Heart* (1990), on racism; *I Lock the Door on Myself* (1990), about alienation; *The Rise of Life on Earth* (1991), dealing with poverty; *Heat* (1992), on class; and *Black Water* (1992), about gender politics.

CYNTHIA OZICK: *The Shawl.* The volume is made up of the harrowing title story, about Rosa Lubin's failed attempt to hide her baby in her shawl to keep it from concentration camp guards, and a novella revisiting Rosa's life three decades later, at a Miami hotel for retirees.

ISHMAEL REED: *The Terrible Threes.* In a sequel to *The Terrible Twos,* Reed imagines a neo-Nazi president of the United States who plots to expel all minorities, the poor, and the homeless, and to establish a fundamentalist Christian state.

MARY LEE SETTLE: *Charley Bland.* Settle's novel concerns a young novelist who resists her mother's effort to have her marry Charley Bland, a charming but rather stereotypical Southern male. She enjoys a romance with him, but it confirms her view that a stultifying society is alien to an imaginative mind. Settle's novel epitomizes, in several critics' views, the clash between the rich and the poor in the post–World War II South.

AMY TAN (b. 1952): *The Joy Luck Club.* The popular and critical success of this novel about the generational conflict between the protagonist, June, and three older Chinese women, members of a social club, establishes Tan's preeminence as the novelist of Chinese American women — immigrant mothers and their offspring — who see each other in terms of their struggles to achieve an identity in China and in America.

ALICE WALKER: *The Temple of My Familiar.* Walker's ambitious panoramic novel traces 500,000 years of human history and sexism through the various incarnations of Miss Lissie, an African goddess.

Literary Criticism and Scholarship

ROBERT B. ALTER (b. 1935): *The Pleasures of Reading: In an Ideological Age.* Alter, a professor of Hebrew and comparative literature at the University of California at Berkeley, challenges prevailing views fostered by structuralism and deconstruction with a defense of character in literature and other "discarded orthodoxies."

HAROLD BLOOM: *Ruin the Sacred Truths: Poetry and Belief from the Bible to the Present.* The noted critic publishes his Charles Eliot Norton Lectures delivered at Harvard. He argues for the central importance of the poetic imagination in the Old Testament, which contains a sublimity that pervades the greatest works of Western literature and continues to inform the best of contemporary writing.

WILLIAM MAXWELL: *The Outermost Dream.* A collection of essays and reviews concerning the works of figures such as Virginia Woolf and E. B. White.

Nonfiction

JILL KER CONWAY (b. 1934): *The Road from Coorain.* This much-praised autobiography portrays a young Australian woman who leaves her native land to pursue an academic career, eventually becoming the first female president of Smith College. The style as much as the subject matter impresses critics, who compare the work with novel-like autobiographies by Richard Wright and Lillian Hellman.

SEBASTIAN DE GRAZIA (1917–2000): *Machiavelli in Hell.* De Grazia, a professor of political philosophy at Rutgers University, wins the Pulitzer Prize for this intellectual biography of the Renaissance thinker, who, the author argues, should be evaluated in political rather than moral terms.

ANNIE DILLARD: *The Writing Life.* Dillard explores the complexities of literary creation, writing not for her fellow practitioners but for readers curious about the writer's habits and methods.

MICHAEL DORRIS: *The Broken Cord.* This is a moving account of a child with fetal alcohol syndrome adopted by Dorris and his wife, the writer Louise Erdrich. Dorris recounts the heartbreak and fear of dealing with a problem that is undiagnosed and powerfully disturbing. Critics find the account as riveting as Dorris's fiction. Complicating and enriching the book is the fact that it occurs within a Native American context, and the author wrestles with individual responsibility and the role society has to play in taking care of such children.

IAN FRAZIER: *Great Plains.* Describing himself as a refugee from New York City, Frazier drives to Montana to begin his research on the Great Plains. His book conveys history, topography, the history of the people of the Plains, and an argument against exploiting this great land. Critics call this travel writing in the grand tradition of Washington Irving, Mark Twain, and Francis Parkman.

THOMAS L. FRIEDMAN (b. 1953): *From Beirut to Jerusalem.* The Beirut and Jerusalem bureau chief for the *New York Times* wins the National Book Award for this account of his experiences in the Middle East and his transformation from being a staunch supporter of Israel to taking a more objective, critical position concerning both sides in the Arab-Israeli conflict.

STANLEY KARNOW: *In Our Image: America's Empire in the Philippines.* Karnow wins the Pulitzer Prize for what reviewer James Halsema describes as "the best popular history of America's nine-decade relationship with the Philippines."

LARRY KRAMER: *Reports from the Holocaust: The Making of an AIDS Activist.* Kramer collects his essays and speeches dealing with the AIDS crisis and his indictment of government indifference. It would be republished and updated in 1994.

DALE MAHARIDGE (b. 1956) AND MICHAEL WILLIAMSON: *And Their Children After Them: The Legacy of "Let Us Now Praise Famous Men," James Agee, Walker Evans, and the Rise and Fall of Cotton in the South.* The duo wins the Pulitzer Prize for this pictorial portrait of the descendants of cotton farmers depicted in Agee and Evans's classic documentary study of sharecroppers during the Depression.

STEVEN WOODWARD NAIFEH (b. 1952) AND GREGORY WHITE SMITH (b. 1951): *Jackson Pollock: An American Saga.* Despite winning the Pulitzer Prize, this biography of the painter, based on interviews with more than two thousand people, divides critics. It is hailed as the definitive biography of the greatest American painter of the twentieth century and criticized as minutiae linked with dubious psychological interpretations. Naifeh and Smith met as students at Harvard's School of Law.

JOHN UPDIKE: *Just Looking: Essays on Art.* Considered one of the most elegant and perceptive commentators on contemporary art, Updike includes essays on the work of many artists but reserves his highest praise for Cézanne and Matisse.

TOBIAS WOLFF: *This Boy's Life: A Memoir.* Wolff treats his teenage years when he and his mother moved from Florida to Utah and Washington to escape her abusive boyfriend; it also charts his difficult adjustment to his stepfather. *In Pharaoh's Army* (1994) would continue the account of Wolff's life during his army service.

Poetry

RITA DOVE: *Grace Notes.* This collection continues the poet's autobiographical exploration of family and generational relationships. The speaker of the poems reflects Dove's position as a kind of mediator, performing the roles of mother and daughter, black woman and poet, while seeking the universal cord that ties them all together.

ADRIENNE RICH: *Time's Power.* As the title of her collection suggests, Rich is concerned with history — especially in poems such as "Harpers Ferry" — and also in the individual personal sense of time in works such as "Living Memory." Critics note how she deftly swings from expressing her sense of political outrage to very personal lyrics in poems such as "Letters in the Family," "One Life," "Divisions of Labor," and "Turning."

MARY JO SALTER (b. 1954): *Unfinished Painting.* Salter's second collection, following *Henry Purcell in Japan* (1985), wins the Lamont Poetry Prize and recognition for the poet as one of the leading New Formalists, the group of contemporary American poets who eschew free verse and experimentalism for traditional verse forms. Subsequent volumes are *Sunday Skaters* (1994) and *A Kiss in Space* (1999).

CHARLES SIMIC: *The World Doesn't End.* Simic's collection of prose poems wins the Pulitzer Prize. Critic John

Ash calls the book "a beautifully designed box of verbal fireworks . . . a seamless fusion of wild jazz and delicate, moonstruck European chamber music."

1990

Drama and Theater

JOHN GUARE: *Six Degrees of Separation*. Based on an actual incident in which a young African American claimed to be actor Sidney Poitier's son, the play explores the American cult of celebrity. A well-off Manhattan couple invite the young man into their home and are taken in by his compelling stories. They want to believe him as much as he wants to fool them. In the play Guare satirizes liberal guilt and the isolation and dullness of modern urban life.

CRAIG LUCAS (b. 1951): *Prelude to a Kiss*. First performed in California in 1988, this romance-fantasy about a young woman who kisses and exchanges souls with an old man opens at New York's Circle Rep before transferring to Broadway. The woman's husband slowly realizes that his wife has become someone else, while the woman struggles with the debilitating consequences of old age. Although the play is very funny, it also raises important issues about sexual identity and the human experience of time. The Atlanta-born playwright's previous works are *Reckless* (1983), *Blue Window* (1984), and *Three Postcards* (1986).

AUGUST WILSON: *The Piano Lesson*. Wilson's play is set in 1936 and focuses on a dispute among African Americans about an heirloom piano. It explores connections between blacks and their past. The play, which had been written in 1986 and was previously presented at the O'Neill and Yale Repertory Theaters in Connecticut, is the first drama ever to win a Pulitzer Prize before opening in New York.

Fiction

PAUL AUSTER: *The Music of Chance*. The novel is about Jim Nashe, who sets out on travels meant to define himself. He falls in with Pozzi, a gambler, and the two men end up in debt. Gambling and traveling become Auster's metaphors for the role of chance and coincidence in individual lives. The novel impresses critics, who see in it an extension of his early philosophical speculations detailed in the New York trilogy.

NICOLSON BAKER (b. 1957): *Room Temperature*. This novel, which in format somewhat resembles an investigative report, concentrates on a father's life at home with his infant daughter. The day-to-day feeding of the child is reported in exquisite detail. The comedy and insight that arise out of making the subject matter of daily life into an epic of the imagination have been compared to Laurence Sterne's effort in the classic *Tristram Shandy*. Born in Rochester, New York, Baker worked as an oil analyst and stockbroker on Wall Street. His other books include *The Mezzanine* (1988), *Vox* (1992), and *Fermata* (1994).

DONALD BARTHELME: *The King*. Completed in the month before his death, Barthelme's novel is a version of the Arthurian legend set in England during World War II. Reviewer Alan R. Davis calls it "a playful lifeboat of a book" in which "we are in for a bit of fun, but we are constantly reminded that escape from self-consciousness is barely possible."

THOMAS BERGER: *Orrie's Story*. Berger's novel is a parodic version of Aeschylus's *Oresteia*, as a World War II war hero returns to his Midwestern hometown to find that his wife has taken a lover; the two conspire to murder him.

T. CORAGHESSAN BOYLE: *East Is East*. Cultural cross-purposes pervade this novel about Hiro Tanaka, a twenty-year-old cook aboard a Japanese ship who escapes to the Georgia coast, where he finds refuge in a community of artists. Critics like Boyle's satirical edge — which is aimed equally at everyone, including his fellow artists.

PATRICIA CORNWELL (b. 1956): *Postmortem*. Cornwell, a police reporter in Charlotte, North Carolina, from 1979 to 1981, publishes the first novel in her popular forensic mystery series, featuring medical examiner Kay Scarpetta. It is the only novel ever to win the Edgar Award, the Creasy Award, the Anthony Award, and the Macavity Award for best first crime or mystery novel.

MICHAEL CUNNINGHAM (b. 1952): *A Home at the End of the World*. This second novel (following *Golden States*, 1984) is about two boys growing up in the Midwest and then moving to Manhattan. Jonathan is gay and Bobby is straight, and they both become involved with a woman who bears a child by Bobby. This complication provides Cunningham with the opportunity to explore different kinds of love and contemporary mores in a thoughtful, subtle style, which lifts the novel above being a mere record of contemporary life. The Cincinnati-born writer would win the Pulitzer Prize for *The Hours* (1998).

RICHARD FORD: *Wild Life*. Ford's novel wins high praise for its stark realism and minimalist style, verging on the poetic. Joe, the novel's narrator, focuses on three days in the life of his parents, whose marriage is disintegrating. His mother has an affair, while his father

DEATHS, 1990–2000

Deaths

1990 Paul Bowles (b. 1910), novelist
Alex Haley (b. 1921), journalist and author
Josephine W. Johnson (b. 1910), novelist and short story writer
Lewis Mumford (b. 1895), author, historian, and social critic
Walker Percy (b. 1916), novelist

1991 Theodor Seuss Geisel (Dr. Seuss) (b. 1904), children's author
A. B. Guthrie Jr. (b. 1901), novelist
Jerzy Kosinski (b. 1933), novelist
Howard Nemerov (b. 1920), poet and novelist
Laura Riding (b. 1901), poet
James Schuyler (b. 1923), poet
Isaac Bashevis Singer (b. 1904), novelist and short story writer
Frank Yerby (b. 1916), novelist

1992 Isaac Asimov (b. 1920), novelist and short story writer

1993 Kay Boyle (b. 1903), novelist and short story writer
John Hersey (b. 1914), novelist
William Stafford (b. 1914), poet
Wallace Stegner (b. 1909), novelist

1994 Charles Bukowski (b. 1920), poet
Ralph Ellison (b. 1914), novelist

Peter Taylor (b. 1917), short story writer and novelist

1995 Stanley Elkin (b. 1930), novelist
Patricia Highsmith (b. 1921), novelist
Paul Horgan (b. 1903), novelist and historian
Jane Kenyon (b. 1947), poet
James Merrill (b. 1926), poet
Henry Roth (b. 1906), novelist

1996 Richard Condon (b. 1915), novelist
Carl Sagan (b. 1934), scientist and author

1997 William S. Burroughs (b. 1914), novelist
James Dickey (b. 1923), poet
Allen Ginsberg (b. 1926), poet
David Ignatow (b. 1914), poet
William Matthews (b. 1942), poet
James A. Michener (b. 1907), novelist
Harold Robbins (b. 1916), novelist

1998 Allen Drury (b. 1918), novelist
William Gaddis (b. 1922), novelist
Wright Morris (b. 1910), novelist

1999 William Bronk (b. 1918), poet
Joseph Heller (b. 1923), novelist
Mario Puzo (b. 1920), novelist
C. Vann Woodward (b. 1908), historian

2000 Gwendolyn Brooks (b. 1917), poet
Edgar Bowers (b. 1924), poet

becomes a firefighter in Grand Falls, Montana. The raging forest fires become a metaphor for the explosiveness of human passion.

PAULA FOX: *The God of Nightmares.* This novel is set in New Orleans just after the end of World War II and concerns a young woman's struggles to come to terms with herself — confronting first her mother's death and then her relationship with her husband. In both cases, she breaks free from rigid views of these intimates. Critics praise both the author's subtle exploration of character and fate and how human character interacts with environment.

JESSICA HAGEDORN (b. 1949): *Dogeaters.* The novel is set in the Philippines, Hagedorn's birthplace (she immigrated to the United States in the 1960s) and the inspiration for much of her work. The "dogs" are an extraordinary array of homeless delinquents and disaffected youths, and the novel reflects Hagedorn's impressive ability to dramatize a wide range of social types. A performance artist in New York during the 1970s, Hagedorn's books include *Dangerous Music* (1975), *Pet Food and Tropical Apparitions* (1981), and *The Gangster of Love* (1996).

SUE HARRISON (b. 1950): *Mother Earth, Father Sky.* Set in 7056 B.C., this ambitious first novel depicts prehis-

torical times and deals with a tribe's migration from the Aleutian Islands to northern Michigan. The novel focuses on the fate of a young woman, Chagak, who is raped after her people are massacred. The Michigan writer who worked in public relations researched her book for three years and shopped it to publishers for five years before Doubleday offered her half a million dollars for the publishing rights.

MICHAEL HERR: *Walter Winchell.* Herr adapts his biographical sketch of the famed newspaper columnist, presented in *The Big Room* (1987), first as a screenplay and then as this novel, which combines novelistic and cinematic devices.

LINDA HOGAN (b. 1947): *Mean Spirit.* The Native American poet and essayist's first novel chronicles the effects of the 1920s Oklahoma oil boom on two Indian families. A second novel, *Solar Storms*, would appear in 1995.

CHARLES JOHNSON: *Middle Passage.* Johnson's novel is about a recently emancipated slave who, to escape marriage, stows away on a slave ship. Critics laud both the authentic historical account of the infamous middle passage and Johnson's rousing account of sea adventures and vivid characters. Winner of a National Book Award, the book makes Johnson the first male African American

BESTSELLERS, 1990–2000

Fiction

1990
1. *The Plains of Passage* by Jean M. Auel
2. *Four Past Midnight* by Stephen King
3. *The Burden of Proof* by Scott Turow
4. *Memories of Midnight* by Sidney Sheldon
5. *Message from Nam* by Danielle Steel
6. *The Bourne Ultimatum* by Robert Ludlum
7. *The Stand: The Complete and Uncut Edition* by Stephen King
8. *Lady Boss* by Jackie Collins
9. *The Witching Hour* by Anne Rice
10. *September* by Rosamunde Pilcher

1991
1. *Scarlett: The Sequel to Margaret Mitchell's "Gone with the Wind"* by Alexandra Ripley
2. *The Sum of All Fears* by Tom Clancy
3. *Needful Things* by Stephen King
4. *No Greater Love* by Danielle Steel
5. *Heartbeat* by Danielle Steel
6. *The Doomsday Conspiracy* by Sidney Sheldon
7. *The Firm* by John Grisham
8. *Night over Water* by Ken Follett
9. *Remember* by Barbara Taylor Bradford
10. *Loves Music, Loves to Dance* by Mary Higgins Clark

1992
1. *Dolores Claiborne* by Stephen King
2. *The Pelican Brief* by John Grisham
3. *Gerald's Game* by Stephen King

4. *Mixed Blessings* by Danielle Steel
5. *Jewels* by Danielle Steel
6. *The Stars Shine Down* by Sidney Sheldon
7. *Tale of the Body Thief* by Anne Rice
8. *Mexico* by James A. Michener
9. *Waiting to Exhale* by Terry McMillan
10. *All Around the Town* by Mary Higgins Clark

1993
1. *The Bridges of Madison County* by Robert James Waller
2. *The Client* by John Grisham
3. *Slow Waltz at Cedar Bend* by Robert James Waller
4. *Without Remorse* by Tom Clancy
5. *Nightmare and Dreamscapes* by Stephen King
6. *Vanished* by Danielle Steel
7. *Lasher* by Anne Rice
8. *Pleading Guilty* by Scott Turow
9. *Like Water for Chocolate* by Laura Esquivel
10. *The Scorpio Illusion* by Robert Ludlum

1994
1. *The Chamber* by John Grisham
2. *Debt of Honor* by Tom Clancy
3. *The Celestine Prophecy* by James Redfield
4. *The Gift* by Danielle Steel
5. *Insomnia* by Stephen King
6. *Politically Correct Bedtime Stories* by James Finn Garner
7. *Wings* by Danielle Steel
8. *Accident* by Danielle Steel
9. *The Bridges of Madison County* by Robert James Waller
10. *Disclosure* by Michael Crichton

novelist to be so honored since Ralph Ellison in 1952, for *Invisible Man.*

ERICA JONG: *Any Woman's Blues.* Isadora Wing narrates this account of the sexual addiction of painter Leila Sand for a younger man; it also satirizes the era's self-help craze and the hedonistic lifestyle of the well-heeled and shallow.

BARBARA KINGSOLVER: *Animal Dreams.* Codi Noline is attempting to reorient her life in her Arizona hometown, which she had left fourteen years earlier. She becomes involved in political struggles, disputes over the polluted environment, and racism. While the novel contains Kingsolver's signature theme — the quest for a stable home — it brings a new, gripping political dimension to her work. Ursula K. Le Guin calls it "a new fiction of relationship, aesthetically rich and of great political and spiritual significance and power."

PETER MATTHIESSEN: *Killing Mr. Watson.* One of the few authors whose work has been nominated for the National Book Award in the categories of both fiction and nonfiction, Matthiessen brings his considerable gifts in both areas to bear on the story of Edgar J. Watson, a

real-life, turn-of-the-nineteenth-century outlaw in the Florida Everglades. Part history, part fiction, the book is the first in a trilogy about the national treasure once thought of as an abysmal swamp. It would be followed by *Lost Man's River* (1997) and *Bone by Bone* (1999).

SUE MILLER: *Family Pictures.* Miller's best-selling and National Book Award–nominated second novel, like her first, *The Good Mother* (1986), concentrates on the dynamics of a nontraditional family. It concerns an upper-middle-class Chicago family whose destiny hinges on the fate of an autistic son. Critic Christopher Lehmann-Haupt observes, "Miller is particularly good at dramatizing scenes of domestic chaos and the complex interplay of adults and children."

PAUL MONETTE: *Afterlife.* The novel treats the difficulty that a man diagnosed with AIDS experiences as he enters into another relationship. Monette's final novel before his death, *Halfway Home* (1991), would depict an AIDS-afflicted artist managing a fulfilling life despite having the disease.

WALTER MOSLEY (b. 1952): *Devil in a Blue Dress.* The Los Angeles–born writer's first detective novel introduces a

BESTSELLERS, 1990–2000

1995
1. *The Rainmaker* by John Grisham
2. *The Lost World* by Michael Crichton
3. *Five Days in Paris* by Danielle Steel
4. *The Christmas Box* by Richard Paul Evans
5. *Lightning* by Danielle Steel
6. *The Celestine Prophecy* by James Redfield
7. *Rose Madder* by Stephen King
8. *Silent Night* by Mary Higgins Clark
9. *Politically Correct Holiday Stories* by James Finn Garner
10. *The Horse Whisperer* by Nicholas Evans

1996
1. *The Runaway Jury* by John Grisham
2. *Executive Orders* by Tom Clancy
3. *Desperation* by Stephen King
4. *Airframe* by Michael Crichton
5. *The Regulators* by Richard Bachman
6. *Malice* by Danielle Steel
7. *Silent Honor* by Danielle Steel
8. *Primary Colors* by Anonymous
9. *Cause of Death* by Patricia Cornwell
10. *The Tenth Insight* by James Redfield

1997
1. *The Partner* by John Grisham
2. *Cold Mountain* by Charles Frazier
3. *The Ghost* by Danielle Steel
4. *The Ranch* by Danielle Steel
5. *Special Delivery* by Danielle Steel
6. *Unnatural Exposure* by Patricia Cornwell
7. *The Best Laid Plans* by Sidney Sheldon
8. *Pretend Your Don't See Her* by Mary Higgins Clark
9. *Cat and Mouse* by James Patterson
10. *Hornet's Nest* by Patricia Cornwell

1998
1. *The Street Lawyer* by John Grisham
2. *Rainbow Six* by Tom Clancy
3. *Bag of Bones* by Stephen King
4. *A Man in Full* by Tom Wolfe
5. *Mirror Images* by Danielle Steel
6. *The Long Road Home* by Danielle Steel
7. *The Klone and I* by Danielle Steel
8. *Point of Origin* by Patricia Cornwell
9. *Paradise* by Toni Morrison
10. *All Through the Night* by Mary Higgins Clark

1999
1. *The Testament* by John Grisham
2. *Hannibal* by Thomas Harris
3. *Assassins* by Jerry B. Jenkins and Tim LaHaye
4. *Star Wars: Episode 1, The Phantom Menace* by Terry Brooks
5. *Timeline* by Michael Crichton
6. *Hearts in Atlantis* by Stephen King
7. *Apollyon* by Jerry B. Jenkins and Tim LaHaye
8. *The Girl Who Loved Tom Gordon* by Stephen King
9. *Irresistible Forces* by Danielle Steel
10. *Tara Road* by Maeve Binchy

2000
1. *The Brethren* by John Grisham
2. *The Mark: The Beast Rules the World* by Jerry B. Jenkins and Tim LaHaye
3. *The Bear and the Dragon* by Tom Clancy
4. *The Indwelling: The Beast Takes Possession* by Jerry B. Jenkins and Tim LaHaye
5. *The Last Precinct* by Patricia Cornwell
6. *Journey* by Danielle Steel
7. *The Rescue* by Nicholas Sparks
8. *Roses Are Red* by James Patterson
9. *Cradle and All* by James Patterson
10. *The House on Hope Street* by Danielle Steel

new but archetypal hard-boiled hero, Easy Rollins, whose use of black slang and code words reminds reviewers of the Harlem detective stories of Chester Himes. Others find that Mosley provides "a sort of social history that doesn't exist in other detective fiction."

TIM O'BRIEN: *The Things They Carried*. O'Brien's story collection, including the frequently anthologized title work and "The Sweetheart of the Song Tra Bong," about an all-American girl's bizarre combat experiences, is widely acclaimed as one of the essential fictional works on the Vietnam War.

JOYCE CAROL OATES: *Because It Is Bitter and Because It Is My Heart*. Oates examines race relations and violence in America through the experiences of a black teenager and his white friend from 1956 to 1963.

REYNOLDS PRICE: *The Tongues of Angels*. The novel is about Bridge Boatner, a successful artist, who tells his son about his mentor, Raphael (Rafe) Noren, a man of enormous talents whose sudden death provides the traumatic source for much of Boatner's art. This characteristic fable about the way individuals' lives are marked by shocking events also becomes, in many critics' minds, a sensitive reflection about the sources and the content of art.

THOMAS PYNCHON: *Vineland*. Pynchon's novel juxtaposes the declining radicalism of the 1960s with the leftism of the 1930s and nineteenth-century progressivism. Unassimilated hippies Zoyd Wheeler, his wife, and their daughter, Prairie, are the focus of the plot, which deals with FBI agents, the ubiquitous mind control of television, and in general, the modern tendency for bureaucracy to stifle individuality. Like Pynchon's other fiction, this novel explores a broad social canvas with eccentric characters and a dominant strain of paranoia.

BESTSELLERS, 1990–2000

Nonfiction

1990

1. *A Life on the Road* by Charles Kuralt
2. *The Civil War* by Geoffrey C. Ward with Rick Burns and Ken Burns
3. *The Frugal Gourmet on Our Immigrant Heritage: Recipes You Should Have Gotten from Your Grandmother* by Jeff Smith
4. *Better Homes and Gardens New Cook Book*
5. *Financial Self-Defense: How to Win the Fight for Financial Freedom* by Charles J. Givens
6. *Homecoming: Reclaiming and Championing Your Inner Child* by John Bradshaw
7. *Wealth Without Risk: How to Develop a Personal Fortune Without Going Out on a Limb* by Charles J. Givens
8. *Bo Knows Bo* by Bo Jackson and Dick Schapp
9. *An American Life: An Autobiography* by Ronald Reagan
10. *Megatrends 2000: Ten New Directions for the 1990s* by John Naisbitt and Patricia Aburdene

1991

1. *Me: Stories of My Life* by Katherine Hepburn
2. *Nancy Reagan: The Unauthorized Biography* by Kitty Kelley
3. *Uh-Oh: Some Observations from Both Sides of the Refrigerator Door* by Robert Fulghum
4. *Under Fire: An American Story* by Oliver North with William Novak
5. *Final Exit: The Practicalities of Self-Deliverence and Assisted Suicide for the Dying* by Derek Humphry
6. *When You Look Like Your Passport Photo, It's Time to Go Home* by Erma Bombeck
7. *More Wealth Without Risk* by Charles J. Givens
8. *Den of Thieves* by James B. Stewart
9. *Childhood* by Bill Cosby
10. *Financial Self-Defense* by Charles J. Givens

1992

1. *The Way Things Ought to Be* by Rush Limbaugh
2. *It Doesn't Take a Hero: The Autobiography* by Gen. H. Norman Schwarzkopf
3. *How to Satisfy a Woman Every Time* by Naura Hayden
4. *Every Living Thing* by James Herriot
5. *A Return to Love* by Marianne Williamson
6. *Sam Walton: Made in America* by Sam Walton
7. *Diana: Her True Story* by Andrew Morton
8. *Truman* by David McCullough
9. *Silent Passage* by Gail Sheehy
10. *Sex* by Madonna

1993

1. *See, I Told You So* by Rush Limbaugh
2. *Private Parts* by Howard Stern
3. *Seinlanguage* by Jerry Seinfeld
4. *Embraced by the Light* by Betty J. Eadie with Curtis Taylor
5. *Ageless Body, Timeless Mind* by Deepak Chopra
6. *Stop the Insanity* by Susan Powter
7. *Women Who Run with the Wolves* by Clarissa Pinkola Estés
8. *Men Are from Mars, Women Are from Venus* by John Gray
9. *The Hidden Life of Dogs* by Elizabeth Marshall Thomas
10. *And If You Play Golf, You're My Friend* by Harvey Penick with Bud Shrake

1994

1. *In the Kitchen with Rosie* by Rosie Daley
2. *Men Are from Mars, Women Are from Venus* by John Gray
3. *Crossing the Threshold of Hope* by Pope John Paul II
4. *Magic Eye I* by N. E. Thing Enterprises
5. *The Book of Virtues* by William J. Bennett
6. *Magic Eye II* by N. E. Thing Enterprises
7. *Embraced by the Light* by Betty J. Eadie with Curtis Taylor
8. *Don't Stand Too Close to a Naked Man* by Tim Allen
9. *Couplehood* by Paul Reiser
10. *Magic Eye III* by N. E. Thing Enterprises

TOM ROBBINS: *Skinny Legs and All.* Robbins mixes the erotic exploits of a newly married couple in New York, Middle Eastern politics, and side glances at art, religion, sex, and money. While some reviewers greet the book as a welcome alternative to the current trend of minimalism in fiction, another suggests that Robbins "and we — are getting a bit old for comic books."

PHILIP ROTH: *Deception.* In a novel written completely in dialogue, a married middle-aged American named Philip has an affair with a married Englishwoman.

JOHN UPDIKE: *Rabbit at Rest.* The fourth installment in Updike's Rabbit Angstrom series completes it with reflections on the 1980s. Rabbit, now retired and somewhat reconciled to life with his wife, Janice, restricts his athleticism to the golf course. At the end of the book, he succumbs with uncharacteristic grace to a heart attack.

GORE VIDAL: *Hollywood.* Another of the novelist's bravura historical animations, set in the administrations of Woodrow Wilson and Warren Harding, is largely an extension of the work's predecessor, *Empire* (1987). Its title emphasizes that politics in the 1920s had become show business.

WILLIAM T. VOLLMANN (b. 1959): *The Ice-Shirt.* This is the first volume in the California-born writer's projected novel cycle *Seven Dreams: A Book of North American Landscapes*, attempting a "symbolic history" of the cultural conflict between Caucasians and native peoples. This novel deals with the Vikings' arrival in North America, mixing in Vollmann's travel observations, glossaries, chronologies, and bibliographies. Later volumes include *Fathers and Crows* (1992), which concerns the cultural clash between North American Indians and Jesuit missionaries, and *The Rifles* (1994), which juxtaposes

BESTSELLERS, 1990–2000

1995
1. *Men Are from Mars, Women Are from Venus* by John Gray
2. *My American Journey* by Colin Powell
3. *Miss America* by Howard Stern
4. *The Seven Spiritual Laws of Success* by Deepak Chopra
5. *The Road Ahead* by Bill Gates
6. *Charles Kuralt's America* by Charles Kuralt
7. *Mars and Venus in the Bedroom* by John Gray
8. *To Renew America* by Newt Gingrich
9. *My Point . . . and I Do Have One* by Ellen DeGeneres
10. *The Moral Compass* by William J. Bennett

1996
1. *Make the Connection* by Oprah Winfrey and Bob Greene
2. *Men Are from Mars, Women Are from Venus* by John Gray
3. *The Dilbert Principle* by Scott Adams
4. *Simple Abundance* by Sarah Ban Breathnach
5. *The Zone* by Barry Sears with Bill Lawren
6. *Bad As I Wanna Be* by Dennis Rodman
7. *In Contempt* by Christopher Darden
8. *A Reporter's Life* by Walter Cronkite
9. *Dogbert's Top Secret Management Handbook* by Scott Adams
10. *My Sergei: A Love Story* by Ekaterina Gordeeva with E. M. Swift

1997
1. *Angela's Ashes* by Franck McCourt
2. *Simple Abundance* by Sarah Ban Breathnach
3. *Midnight in the Garden of Good and Evil* by John Berendt
4. *The Royals* by Kitty Kelley
5. *Joy of Cooking* by Irma S. Rombauer, Marion Rombauer Becker, and Ethan Becker
6. *Diana: Her True Story* by Andrew Morton
7. *Into Thin Air* by John Krakauer
8. *Conversations with God, Book I* by Neale Donald Walsch
9. *Men Are from Mars, Women Are from Venus* by John Gray
10. *Eight Weeks to Optimum Health* by Andrew Weil

1998
1. *The Nine Steps to Financial Freedom* by Suze Orman
2. *The Greatest Generation* by Tom Brokaw
3. *Sugar Busters!* by H. Leighton Steward, Morrison C. Bethea, Sam S. Andrews, and Luis A. Balart
4. *Tuesdays with Morrie* by Mitch Albom
5. *The Guinness Book of Records 1999*
6. *Talking to Heaven* by James Van Praagh
7. *Something More: Excavating Your Authentic Self* by Sarah Ban Breathnach
8. *In the Meantime* by Iyanla Vanzant
9. *A Pirate Looks at Fifty* by Jimmy Buffett
10. *If Life Is a Game, These Are the Rules* by Cherie Carter-Scott, Ph.D.

1999
1. *Tuesdays with Morrie* by Mitch Albom
2. *The Greatest Generation* by Tom Brokaw
3. *Guinness World Records 2000: Millennium Edition*
4. *'Tis* by Frank McCourt
5. *Who Moved My Cheese?* by Spencer Johnson
6. *The Courage to Be Rich* by Suze Orman
7. *The Greatest Generation Speaks* by Tom Brokaw
8. *Sugar Busters!* by H. Leighton Steward, Morrison C. Bethea, Sam S. Andrews, and Luis A. Balart
9. *The Art of Happiness* by the Dalai Lama and Howard C. Cutler
10. *The Century* by Peter Jennings and Todd Brewster

2000
1. *Who Moved My Cheese?* by Spencer Johnson
2. *Guinness World Records 2001*
3. *Body for Life* by Bill Phillips
4. *Tuesdays with Morrie* by Rich Albom
5. *The Beatles Anthology* by the Beatles
6. *The O'Reilly Factor* by Bill O'Reilly
7. *Relationship Rescue* by Philip C. McGraw, Ph.D.
8. *The Millionaire Mind* by Thomas J. Stanley
9. *Ten Things I Wish I'd Known—Before I Went Out into the Real World* by Maria Shriver
10. *Eating Well for Optimum Health* by Andrew Weil, M.D.

the Canadian government's relocation of the Inuit with Sir John Franklin's 1845 expedition to find the Northwest Passage to the Pacific.

KURT VONNEGUT JR.: *Hocus Pocus*. Vonnegut treats the legacy of the Vietnam War from the perspective of Eugene Debs Hartke, reputedly the last American out of Vietnam.

JOHN EDGAR WIDEMAN: *Philadelphia Fire*. Wideman wins the PEN/Faulkner Award and the American Book Award for this novel, which blends fact and fiction. It connects two events: the black mayor Wilson Goode's order for police to bomb the headquarters of a protest group in Philadelphia, killing six adults and five children, and the author's relationship with his son, who received a life sentence for murder. Wideman is praised by reviewer Rosemary L. Bray for taking "his readers on a tour of urban America perched on the precipice of hell, a tour in which even his own personal tragedy is part of the view."

KAREN TEI YAMASHITA (b. 1951): *Through the Arc of the Rain Forest*. Yamashita, an American of Japanese heritage, had traveled to Brazil in 1975 to study Japanese immigration. She stayed there for nine years, and out of her experience wrote this fictional account. Called an "elaborate parable about the effects of Western culture on the Brazilian rain forest," it would be nominated for an American Book Award in 1991.

Literary Criticism and Scholarship

JUDITH BUTLER (b. 1956): *Gender Trouble: Feminism and the Subversion of Identity*. One of the defining and most influential theoretical studies of gender by the Johns

AWARDS AND PRIZES, 1990–2000

Bancroft Prize (American History, Diplomacy, or Biography)

1990   *Dark Journey* by Neil McMillen
       The Indian's New World by James Merrell

1991   *A Midwife's Tale* by Laurel Thatcher Ulrich

1993   *Margaret Fuller* by Charles Capper
       A Preponderance of Power by Melvyn Leffler

1994   *The Age of Federalism* by Stanley Eakins and Eric
          McKintrick
       Tumult and Silence at Second Creek by Winthrop
          Jordan
       W.E.B. Du Bois: Biography of a Race, 1868–1919 by David
          Levering Lewis

1995   *The Refiner's Fire* by John Brooke
       Local People by John Dittmer

1996   *Walt Whitman's America* by David Reynolds
       William Cooper's Town by Alan Taylor

1997   *Explicit and Authentic Acts* by David Kyvig
       Grand Expectations by James Patterson

1998   *Southern Cross* by Christine Leigh Heyrman
       The Clash by Walter Lafeber
       The Origins of the Urban Crisis by Thomas Sugrue

1999   *Many Thousands Gone* by Ira Berlin
       The Name of War by Jill Lepore
       Slave Counterpoint by Philip Morgan

2000   *Embracing Defeat: Japan in the Wake of World War II* by
          John Dower
       The Great Arizona Orphan Abduction by Linda Gordon
       Into the American Woods by James Merrell

Bollingen Prize (Poetry)

1991   Laura Riding Jackson
       Donald Justice

1993   Mark Strand

1995   Kenneth Koch

1997   Gary Snyder

1999   Robert Creeley

Hopkins humanities professor shows how gender categories are inherently unstable and should be understood as "performative," that is, "always a doing, though not a doing by a subject who might be said to preexist the deed." *Bodies That Matter: On the Discursive Limits of "Sex"* would follow in 1993.

HENRY LOUIS GATES JR.: *Reading Black, Reading Feminist*. Gates edits this anthology of essays on African American women writers including Phillis Wheatley, Gwendolyn Brooks, Octavia Butler, and Rita Dove.

ALISON LURIE: *Don't Tell the Grown-Ups: Subversive Children's Literature*. This collection of essays and reviews by the renowned novelist explores the nuances of children's literature. She deals with the Nancy Drew mysteries, the Oz books, *The Adventures of Tom Sawyer*, *Little Women*, *Peter Pan*, and other works that convey to children precisely the kind of knowledge about their world that their parents and guardians wish to withhold from them.

CAMILLE PAGLIA (b. 1947): *Sexual Personae: Art and Decadence from Nefertiti to Emily Dickinson*. This polemical tour de force, with a decidedly iconoclastic approach to received feminist wisdom, catapults Paglia to public attention and onto the lecture circuit. Paglia's unorthodox feminist views would be further displayed in *Sex, Art, and American Culture* (1992) and *Vamps & Tramps* (1994).

EVE KOSOFSKY SEDGWICK (b. 1950): *Epistemology of the Closet*. This groundbreaking book by the Duke professor of English exploring why writers and others prefer to remain in the closet — to hide gay or lesbian sexuality — combines astute reading of literary texts with Sedgwick's own autobiographical commentary, providing a rich amalgam of literary and cultural insights into the way sexual identity is revealed and concealed in literature and life.

Nonfiction

RON CHERNOW (b. 1949): *The House of Morgan: An American Banking Dynasty and the Rise of Modern Finance*. Chernow's massive banking history is hailed as a book that has "the movement and tension of an epic novel." Combining economics, biography, and high finance, the book wins a National Book Award for nonfiction. Chernow is a Brooklyn-born freelance book, magazine, and newspaper writer.

STANLEY CROUCH (b. 1945): *Notes of a Hanging Judge: Essays and Reviews, 1979–1989*. Crouch is one of the most important commentators on African American culture and its relationship with mainstream society, and this collection of essays reflects his interest in jazz, civil rights, and affirmative action — the last a concept that he finds problematic because, in his view, it resegregates African Americans by giving them preferential treatment.

JOHN GREGORY DUNNE: *Crooning*. A frequent contributor to the *New York Review of Books*, Dunne collects some of his best essay-reviews in this volume. His subjects are Hollywood, the American West, and politics. Critics consider Dunne one of the best commentators on contemporary West Coast sensibility.

RICHARD M. NIXON: *In the Arena: A Memoir of Victory, Defeat, and Renewal*. The ex-president supplies a series of

AWARDS AND PRIZES, 1990–2000

National Book Awards

1990

Fiction: *Middle Passage* by Charles Johnson

Nonfiction: *The House of Morgan: An American Banking Dynasty and the Rise of Modern Finance* by Ron Chernow

Poetry: *No Prize Awarded*

1991

Fiction: *Mating* by Norman Rush

Nonfiction: *Freedom* by Orlando Patterson

Poetry: *What Work Is* by Philip Levine

1992

Fiction: *All the Pretty Horses* by Cormac McCarthy

Nonfiction: *Becoming a Man: Half a Life Story* by Paul Monette

Poetry: *New and Selected Poems* by Mary Oliver

1993

Fiction: *The Shipping News* by E. Annie Proulx

Nonfiction: *United States: Essays, 1952–1992* by Gore Vidal

Poetry: *Garbage* by A. R. Ammons

1994

Fiction: *A Frolic of His Own* by William Gaddis

Nonfiction: *How We Die: Reflections on Life's Final Chapter* by Sherwin B. Nuland

Poetry: *A Worshipful Company of Fletchers* by James Tate

1995

Fiction: *Sabbath's Theater* by Philip Roth

Nonfiction: *The Haunted Land: Facing Europe's Ghosts After Communism* by Tina Rosenberg

Poetry: *Passing Through: The Later Poems* by Stanley Kunitz

1996

Fiction: *Ship Fever and Other Stories* by Andrea Barrett

Nonfiction: *An American Requiem: God, My Father, and the War That Came Between Us* by James Carroll

Poetry: *Scrambled Eggs and Whiskey* by Hayden Carruth

Young People's Literature: *Parrott in the Oven: MiVida* by Victor Martinez

1997

Fiction: *Cold Mountain* by Charles Frazier

Nonfiction: *American Sphinx: The Character of Thomas Jefferson* by Joseph J. Ellis

Poetry: *Effort at Speech: New and Selected Poems* by William Meredith

Young People's Literature: *Dancing on the Edge* by Han Nolan

1998

Fiction: *Charming Billy* by Alice McDermott

Nonfiction: *Slaves in the Family* by Edward Ball

Poetry: *This Time: New and Selected Poems* by Gerald Stern

Young People's Literature: *Holes* by Louis Sachar

1999

Fiction: *Waiting* by Ha Jin

Nonfiction: *Embracing Defeat: Japan in the Wake of World War II* by John W. Dower

Poetry: *Vice: New and Selected Poems* by Ai

Young People's Literature: *When Zachary Beaver Came to Town* by Kimberly Willis Holt

2000

Fiction: *In America* by Susan Sontag

Nonfiction: *In the Heart of the Sea: The Tragedy of the Whaleship Essex* by Nathaniel Philbrick

Poetry: *Blessing the Boats: New and Selected Poems, 1988–2000* by Lucille Clifton

Young People's Literature: *Homeless Bird* by Gloria Whelan

---

capsule reflections on various events in his long and controversial career. The book is both praised for its candor and criticized for its defensive posture.

GARY SOTO: *A Summer Life.* This prominent Chicano writer provides a vivid portrait of growing up in Fresno, California, in the 1950s and 1960s. Soto's title hints at the book's nostalgic evocation of childhood, but he does not discount the poverty of his surroundings, his adolescent angst, or the loss of innocence he felt as he grew up.

LAUREL THATCHER ULRICH (b. 1938): *A Midwife's Tale: The Life of Martha Ballard, Based on Her Diary, 1785–1812.* Ulrich wins the Bancroft Prize and the Pulitzer Prize for this account of a midwife's life in colonial Maine, based on a diary that Ulrich rescued from obscurity in a Maine archive. The book provides a remarkable firsthand

look at medical, social, and historical details of colonial American life.

EDWARD O. WILSON (b. 1929) AND BERT HOLLDOBLER (b. 1936): *The Ants.* Wilson considers this collection of all the known facts about ant life, cowritten with fellow Harvard scientist Holldobler, to be his magnum opus. The book receives the Pulitzer Prize and would be used as the basis for the computer game SimAnt in 1991. Wilson and Holldobler would return to the subject in *Journey to the Ants: A Story of Scientific Exploration* in 1994.

Poetry

AMY CLAMPITT: *Westward.* Clampitt's collection prompts reviewer Phoebe Pettingell to declare the poet "our new Virgil — guiding us through the middle of our

AWARDS AND PRIZES, 1990–2000

Pulitzer Prizes

1990

Fiction: *The Mambo Kings Play Songs of Love* by Oscar Hijuelos

Poetry: *The World Doesn't End* by Charles Simic

Drama: *The Piano Lesson* by August Wilson

History: *In Our Image: America's Empire in the Philippines* by Stanley Karnow

General Nonfiction: *And Their Children After Them* by Dale Maharidge and Michael Williamson

Biography/Autobiography: *Machiavelli in Hell* by Sebastian de Grazia

1991

Fiction: *Rabbit at Rest* by John Updike

Poetry: *Near Changes* by Mona Van Duyn

Drama: *Lost in Yonkers* by Neil Simon

History: *A Midwife's Tale* by Laurel Thatcher Ulrich

General Nonfiction: *The Ants* by Bert Holldobler and Edward O. Wilson

Biography/Autobiography: *Jackson Pollock* by Steven Naifeh and Gregory White Smith

1992

Fiction: *A Thousand Acres* by Jane Smiley

Poetry: *Selected Poems* by James Tate

Drama: *The Kentucky Cycle* by Robert Schenkkan

History: *The Fate of Liberty: Abraham Lincoln and Civil Liberties* by Mark E. Neely Jr.

General Nonfiction: *The Prize: The Epic Quest for Oil, Money, and Power* by Daniel Yergin

Biography/Autobiography: *Fortunate Son: The Autobiography of Lewis B. Puller Jr.* by Lewis B. Puller Jr.

1993

Fiction: *A Good Scent from a Strange Mountain* by Robert Olen Butler

Poetry: *The Wild Iris* by Louise Glück

Drama: *Angels in America: Millennium Approaches* by Tony Kushner

History: *The Radicalism of the American Revolution* by Gordon S. Wood

General Nonfiction: *Lincoln at Gettysburg: The Words That Remade America* by Garry Wills

Biography/Autobiography: *Truman* by David McCullough

1994

Fiction: *The Shipping News* by E. Annie Proulx

Poetry: *Neon Vernacular: New and Selected Poems* by Yusef Komunyakaa

Drama: *Three Tall Women* by Edward Albee

History: No Prize Awarded

General Nonfiction: *Lenin's Tomb: The Last Days of the Soviet Empire* by David Remnick

Biography/Autobiography: *W.E.B. Du Bois: Biography of a Race, 1868–1919* by David Levering Lewis

1995

Fiction: *The Stone Diaries* by Carol Shields

Poetry: *The Simple Truth* by Philip Levine

Drama: *The Young Man from Atlanta* by Horton Foote

History: *No Ordinary Time: Franklin and Eleanor Roosevelt; The Home Front in World War II* by Doris Kearns Goodwin

General Nonfiction: *The Beak of the Finch: A Story of Evolution in Our Time* by Jonathan Weiner

---

lives' journeys along the tortuous spiral tracks of our culture."

ROBERT FAGLES (b. 1933): *The Iliad.* Fagles's translation of Homer's epic is greeted with near-universal acclaim. His version of the ancient classic is nominated for a National Book Award and makes him, according to reviewer Oliver Taplin, "a son or nephew of [fabled translators] Lattimore and Fitzgerald." In 1996, Fagles would repeat his success with a best-selling translation of Homer's *The Odyssey.* Fagles, a Yale English Ph.D., was the founding chair of Princeton's department of comparative literature.

LOUISE GLÜCK: *Ararat.* This collection is quite different from Glück's earlier symbolic work. More realistic in tone, it concerns a child's growing separation from a parent and unavailing efforts to achieve reunion. While some critics find the poetry too flat, others admire the poet's frank effort to explore a theme without resort to her customary mythic vocabulary.

JOY HARJO: *In Mad Love and War.* Preceded by *What Moon Drove Me to This?* (1980), *She Had Some Horses* (1983), and *Secrets from the Center of the World* (1989), this is the best-known collection by the Creek Indian poet whose verse treats personal, gender, racial, and political themes in free verse and prose poem. The volume wins the William Carlos Williams Award, the Delmore Schwartz Memorial Prize, and the Josephine Miles Award.

ROBERT PINSKY: *The Want Bone.* "Visions of Daniel," one of the major poems in this collection, is representative of Pinksy's exploration of moral dilemmas in verse that is formal yet supple. Daniel as prophet metamorphoses into a twentieth-century poet who must speak out of his political, social, and philosophical concerns.

MONA VAN DUYN: *Near Changes.* In the poet's first collection in eight years, Van Duyn reflects on everyday life and experience. The volume is awarded the Pulitzer Prize.

AWARDS AND PRIZES, 1990–2000

1996
Fiction: *Independence Day* by Richard Ford
Poetry: *The Dream of the Unified Field* by Jorie Graham
Drama: *Rent* by Jonathan Larson
History: *William Cooper's Town* by Alan Taylor
General Nonfiction: *The Haunted Land: Facing Europe's Ghosts After Communism* by Tina Rosenberg
Biography/Autobiography: *God: A Biography* by Jack Miles

1997
Fiction: *Martin Dressler: The Tale of an American Dreamer* by Steven Millhauser
Poetry: *Alive Together: New and Selected Poems* by Lisel Mueller
Drama: No Prize Awarded
History: *Original Meanings: Politics and Ideas in the Making of the Constitution* by Jack N. Rakove
General Nonfiction: *Ashes to Ashes: America's Hundred-Year Cigarette War, the Public Health, and the Unabashed Triumph of Philip Morris* by Richard Kluger
Biography/Autobiography: *Angela's Ashes* by Frank McCourt

1998
Fiction: *American Pastoral* by Philip Roth
Poetry: *Black Zodiac* by Charles Wright
Drama: *How I Learned to Drive* by Paula Vogel
History: *Summer for the Gods: The Scopes Trial and America's Continuing Debate over Science and Religion* by Edward J. Larson
General Nonfiction: *Guns, Germs, and Steel: The Fates of Human Societies* by Jared Diamond
Biography/Autobiography: *Personal History* by Katherine Graham

1999
Fiction: *The Hours* by Michael Cunningham
Poetry: *Blizzard of One* by Mark Strand

Drama: *Wit* by Margaret Edson
History: *Gotham: A History of New York City to 1898* by Edwin G. Burrows and Mike Wallace
General Nonfiction: *Annals of the Former World* by John McPhee
Biography/Autobiography: *Lindbergh* by A. Scott Berg

2000
Fiction: *Interpreter of Maladies* by Jhumpa Lahiri
Poetry: *Repair* by C. K. Williams
Drama: *Dinner with Friends* by Donald Margulies
History: *Freedom from Fear: The American People in Depression and War, 1929–1945* by David M. Kennedy
General Nonfiction: *Embracing Defeat: Japan in the Wake of World War II* by John W. Dower
Biography/Autobiography: *Vera (Mrs. Vladimir Nabokov)* by Stacy Schiff

Nobel Prize for Literature

1993   Toni Morrison

PEN/Faulkner Award for Fiction

1990   *Billy Bathgate* by E. L. Doctorow
1991   *Philadelphia Fire* by John Edgar Wideman
1992   *Mao II* by Don De Lillo
1993   *Postcards* by E. Annie Proulx
1994   *Operation Shylock* by Philip Roth
1995   *Snow Falling on Cedars* by David Guterson
1996   *Independence Day* by Richard Ford
1997   *Women in Their Beds* by Gina Berriault
1998   *The Bear Comes Home* by Rafi Zabor
1999   *The Hours* by Michael Cunningham
2000   *Waiting* by Ha Jin

CHARLES WRIGHT: *The World of Ten Thousand Things: Poems 1980–1990.* Wright's collection of his poems from *Southern Cross* (1981), *The Other Side of the River* (1984), *Zone Journals* (1988), and *Xionia* (1990) enhances his reputation as a leading contemporary poet. "There is no poet of his generation whose career has unfolded with such genuine authority," reviewer J. D. McClatchy observes. ". . . There is no book published this year I could recommend more highly."

1991
Drama and Theater

A. R. GURNEY: *The Old Boy.* Gurney's drama dealing with the impact of AIDS focuses on an aspiring politician slated to deliver the commencement address at his prep

school, who learns that a former schoolmate has committed suicide after being diagnosed with AIDS. The news prompts the man's reassessment of his past behavior and assumptions about sexuality.

TONY KUSHNER (b. 1956): *Angels in America: A Gay Fantasia on National Themes, Part One: Millennium Approaches.* The winner of the Pulitzer Prize and the Tony Award for best play is a "political call to arms for the age of AIDS," according to Frank Rich in the *New York Times.* This radical new departure in the treatment of American politics uses camp humor and raw sexuality while exploring the public and private lives of historical figures such as Roy Cohn. The play's second part, *Perestroika,* would premiere in 1992.

DONALD MARGULIES (b. 1954): *Sight Unseen.* Margulies wins the Obie Award for best American play for this drama about an American Jewish painter whose reputation skyrockets and his works are bought unseen. The experience causes him to reevaluate the means by which self-worth can be found.

TERRENCE McNALLY: *Lips Together, Teeth Apart.* This drama takes place on July 4 at Fire Island, where Sally and Sam host his sister and her husband. Amid comic dialogue, the characters debate class differences, homophobia, and the dread of death. McNally's work wins considerable praise for dealing with tragic issues with brio.

MARSHA NORMAN: *The Secret Garden.* Norman wins the Tony Award and the Drama Desk Award for this musical version of Frances Hodgson Burnett's children's classic.

PAUL RUDNICK (b. 1957): *I Hate Hamlet.* Rudnick's inventive comedy brings back the ghost of legendary actor John Barrymore to help a television performer prepare to tackle the role of Shakespeare's Danish prince. The New Jersey–born writer would become the screenwriter of films such as *Sister Act* (1992), *Addams Family Values* (1993), and *In & Out* (1997).

ROBERT SCHENKKAN (b. 1953): *The Kentucky Cycle.* This Pulitzer Prize–winning six-hour epic by the North Carolina–born dramatist is composed of nine plays covering two hundred years. It ranges from the Indians wars, through the Revolutionary period, to the Civil War and the mining and ecological disasters of early-twentieth-century eastern Kentucky. Although some critics dislike its grim depiction of violence, others deem its revenge tragedy structure comparable to Eugene O'Neill's unfinished epic drama of American life.

SAM SHEPARD: *The States of Shock.* Shepard shifts between a battlefield scene and a coffee shop, making the point that the atrocities of war are ignored by characters preoccupied with their own trivial problems and conflicts. Although some critics call the play "glib," others are attracted to its provocative theme and intensive theatricality — with sound effects calling to mind the shattering impact of high-tech bombs.

NEIL SIMON: *Lost in Yonkers.* Simon's play is about young brothers who live in Yonkers with relatives so that their father can get on with his career. Winner of a Pulitzer Prize, the Tony Award for best play, and the Drama Desk Award, the play reflects Simon's most important period — eschewing light comedy and wisecracks, he pursues a more complex story line and a deeper critical probing of his characters.

STEPHEN SONDHEIM: *Assassins.* Sondheim's challenging musical treats the lives of assassins and would-be assassins of U.S. presidents, such as John Wilkes Booth and Lynette "Squeaky" Fromme. Despite its dark tone, its entire limited run at New York's Playwrights Horizons sells out.

Fiction

JULIA ALVAREZ (b. 1950): *How the Garcia Girls Lost Their Accents.* Alvarez was born in New York City and raised until the age of ten in the Dominican Republic, when she was forced to flee with her family due to her father's involvment in overthrowing dictator Rafael Trujillo. She achieves a critical and popular success with this collection of interrelated stories. They detail the lives of four sisters and their family before and after their exile from the Dominican Republic, as they adjust to their new life in New York City. Alvarez would continue the sisters' stories in *!Yo!* (1996).

RUSSELL BANKS: *The Sweet Hereafter.* Banks's novel is a harrowing account of a fatal school-bus accident, which destroys an upstate New York community. Donna Rifkind notes, "This catastrophe was villainless: it was a cruel whimsical event, beyond control. This fact, and Banks's subtle handling of it, are what lift the novel up out of ordinary gritty realism toward something approaching the sublime."

JOHN BARTH: *The Last Voyage of Somebody the Sailor.* Barth retells the stories of *The Arabian Nights* as a postmodernist, reflexive commentary on memory, reality, and the art of storytelling.

HAROLD BRODKEY: *The Runaway Soul.* After spending four decades publishing short fiction, Brodkey finally publishes his long-awaited first novel. Wildly uneven, this long autobiographical work about an adopted child raised in St. Louis in the 1930s satisfies many but frustrates other readers with its postmodern indefiniteness and frequent use of amorphic terms such as "stuff" and "things."

FRANK CHIN: *Donald Duk.* Chin's first novel depicts a young boy in San Francisco's Chinatown whose embarrassment about his Chinese heritage is overcome by dreaming about his ancestors' heroism in working to complete the transcontinental railroad. A second novel, *Gunga Din Highway*, would appear in 1994.

ROBERT COOVER: *Pinocchio in Venice.* In Coover's novel Pinocchio is an elderly professor of aesthetics who returns to Venice for inspiration to finish a book. Anthony Burgess remarks that "This book is about Venice and Pinocchio (the title does not lie), but only if these are taken as themes for fantastic variations. This book is about itself."

DON DE LILLO: *Mao II.* De Lillo's novel concerning CIA operatives in Greece is a follow-up to his breakthrough book, *Libra* (1988), about the assassination of John F. Kennedy. This later work, however, also concerns the writing life, as its protagonist is the world's most famous reclusive writer — forced out of his writer's block by convoluted conspiracies.

STANLEY ELKIN: *The MacGuffin.* Elkin's novel explores the consciousness of Robert Druff, the commissioner of streets in a Midwestern city. Paranoid, self-pitying, and prone to criminal activity, Druff reveals an extraordinary imagination, which Elkin comically details by following him through a few typical days of his life. Critics admire not only Elkin's verbal dexterity but his sharp report of life on the street.

BRET EASTON ELLIS: *American Psycho.* Ellis's third novel, following *Less Than Zero* (1985) and *The Rules of Attraction* (1987), traces random acts of violence against women by a twenty-six-year-old Wall Street investment banker. It prompts a national debate over whether the book is a satire or a work of exploitation that, in the words of reviewer Matthew Tyrnauer, made Ellis "the most reviled writer in America, the Salman Rushdie of too much, too soon."

LOUISE ERDRICH AND MICHAEL DORRIS: *The Crown of Columbus.* Husband and wife collaborate on this philosophical thriller exploring the significance of Columbus's arrival in the New World, particularly for Native Americans. Though the novel is a popular success, critical reviewers judge it inferior to the writers' solo efforts.

KAYE GIBBONS: *A Cure for Dreams.* Gibbons's third award-winning novel marks a new level of achievement for this acclaimed writer of Southern chronicles whose forte is her use of rural, idiomatic Southern speech. This tale of three generations of women uses oral family history handed down through everyday talk.

GAIL GODWIN: *Father Melancholy's Daughter.* The novel's protagonist is Margaret Gower, who has taken care of her father since she was six. Her mother had abandoned the family, and Margaret's sense of responsibility grows as her father ages. The novel shows Godwin's skill in portraying complex human beings wrestling with conflicted feelings.

JOHN GRISHAM (b. 1955): *The Firm.* The Mississippi lawyer's second novel, a legal thriller set in an upscale Memphis law firm, is promoted as *L. A. Law* meets *The Godfather.* The first in a string of Grisham's bestsellers, it remains on the bestseller list for forty-seven weeks, selling 600,000 copies in hardcover and 6.5 million in paperback.

Mark Helprin

MARK HELPRIN: *A Soldier of the Great War.* Helprin powerfully relates the often incredible adventures of Alessandro, an Italian officer on the Austro-Italian front in World War I. Told in flashbacks from the old veteran's point of view, it is a harrowing tale of his long march from the edge of Rome to his village. Critics note Helprin's gift for mesmerizing narrative scenes, in which Alessandro reveals both the horror and the romance of war.

GISH JEN (b. 1955): *Typical American.* Jen's first novel focuses on a brother and sister, Chinese immigrants eager to forsake their heritage for quick assimilation into American life — even when that entails the crudest forms of the American dream. The siblings treat each other shabbily, but Jen finds humor, wit, and great energy in their struggle. Critics admire the book's honesty and utter lack of sentimentality about the immigrant experience. Jen, a daughter of Chinese immigrants, graduated from Harvard and taught English in China before earning an MFA at the University of Iowa.

NORMAN MAILER: *Harlot's Ghost.* In this mammoth novel about the CIA, Mailer's protagonist, Harry Hubbard, travels to Berlin, Uruguay, Washington, D.C., Miami, and Cuba, becoming involved in Cold War spying and conspiracies that cover most of the important political events between 1955 and 1963. While some critics find the work turgid, others praised its drive and comprehensiveness.

PAULE MARSHALL: *Daughters.* Marshall's novel describes a young woman with an American mother and West Indian father as she tries to come to terms with the two worlds that have shaped her.

WHITNEY OTTO (b. 1955): *How to Make an American Quilt.* Like a quilt, this novel fuses different stories concerning a group of older women who sew together in a small California town. The narrator is a granddaughter who overhears them; she reports on and forges a unity out of these diverse lives in the story that closes the novel. Critics praise the work's structure, which mimics the idea of community explored in the stories. The California writer wrote the short story that she expanded when she was working on an MFA at the University of California at Irvine.

MARGE PIERCY: *He, She, and It.* Piercy wins the Arthur C. Clarke Award for Best Science Fiction Novel for this story, set in a twenty-first-century world ravaged by environmental disaster and war. It concerns a divorced woman's return to her childhood home, one of the few free Jewish towns, where she falls in love with a cyborg created to defend the town. The story echoes the Jewish legend of the Golem.

ALEXANDRA RIPLEY (b. 1934): *Scarlett: The Sequel to Margaret Mitchell's Gone with the Wind.* The estate of Margaret Mitchell selected romance writer Ripley to produce the long-anticipated sequel, which Mitchell had refused to write. The continuing adventures of Scarlett O'Hara in Georgia and Ireland sell nearly 2.5 million copies from September 25 to the end of the year, becoming the fastest-selling novel in history.

NORMAN RUSH: *Mating.* Rush's National Book Award–winning novel concerns a Ph.D. candidate in nutritional anthropology who has traveled to Botswana to do research. There she gets involved with a scientist and specialist in Third World rural development who is attempting to sustain a utopian community in the Kalahari Desert. An ambitious novel of ideas, the book is likened by reviewer David Kaufman to *Lost Horizon* "written by Mary McCarthy."

LESLIE MARMON SILKO: *Almanac of the Dead.* The almanac of the title is an ancient Mayan book of prophecy, which describes the invasion of white Europeans and the decline of Mayan culture. The novel, set in the near future, is about twins, Lecha and Zeta, mixed-blood Yaquis who piece together the story from the book and converge on Tucson to await apparently apocalyptic changes that are to occur after the novel ends. Critics praise both the sweep of Silko's canvas and her experimentation.

MONA SIMPSON: *The Lost Father.* In a sequel to *Anywhere but Here,* Simpson continues her exploration of Mayan Atassi, now seeking the father who had abandoned her family when she was ten. Her quest makes her increasingly monomaniacal, and the novel asks penetrating questions about the nature of the family. Critics admire Simpson's ability to portray her heroine's unflattering side without losing a basic sympathy for her throughout a long novel.

ISAAC BASHEVIS SINGER: *Scum.* Set in 1906, this posthumously published novel concerns a Jewish businessman who travels back to his roots in Warsaw, where he gets involved with a rabbi's daughter.

JANE SMILEY: *A Thousand Acres.* Smiley's best-selling novel, winner of the Pulitzer Prize and the National Book Award, has been called a feminist reworking of *King Lear.* Her deft handling of human character and her deep feeling for her rural setting elicit critical approval.

CHARLIE SMITH (b. 1947): *Crystal River.* Winner of the Aga Khan Prize of the *Paris Review,* Smith, a Georgia-born novelist and poet, is a notable stylist whose work is praised for its lyrical fluidity. His book contains three novellas — all of which turn on the relationships of a pair of males. Their close bonds of brotherly love are challenged by strong women who obey different codes of behavior. His other novels include *The Lives of the Dead* (1990), *Chimney Rock* (1993), and *Cheap Ticket to Heaven* (1996).

AMY TAN: *The Kitchen God's Wife.* Though a more traditional narrative than Tan's popular debut novel, *The Joy Luck Club* (1989), this book concerns one of the same themes: the difficulty of bridging a communication gap between a Chinese mother and a Chinese American daughter. This time, however, the narrative comes from the mother's perspective, skillfully presented in a unique patois.

Literary Criticism and Scholarship

STEVEN CASSEDY (b. 1952): *Flight from Eden: The Origins of Modern Literary Criticism and Theory.* Cassedy is specifically concerned with American literary criticism and theory, arguing that its most important inspiration has been taken from European poet and critics such as Paul Valéry and Rainer Maria Rilke rather than from French academic theorists such as Jacques Derrida and Roland Barthes. Critics admire Cassedy's wide-ranging references to phenomenologists, Russian futurists, and members of other literary movements, which together provide an impressive historical context for discussing recent developments in literary theory and criticism.

FREDERIC JAMESON (b. 1934): *Postmodernism*. This highly influential academic critic views postmodernism within the context of Marxist theory. The term itself, he argues, arises out of a new phase of capitalism — the multinational variety of capital expansion. Postmodernism is to this third phase of capitalism what realism is to the first phase of market capitalism and modernism is to the second phase — monopoly, or imperialistic capitalism.

WENDY LESSER (b. 1952): *His Other Half: Men Looking at Women Through Art.* Lesser, the founding editor of Berkeley's *Threepenny Review*, ranges over the works of Charles Dickens and D. H. Lawrence, the photography of Cecil Beaton, the poetry of Randall Jarrell, the paintings of Edgar Degas, the films of Alfred Hitchcock, and the careers of Marilyn Monroe and Barbara Stanwyck. She argues that there is no single category for male representations of women, yet it is impossible to deny that males have projected a distinctive view of women.

WALKER PERCY: *Signposts in a Strange Land.* Percy's subjects are language, literature, and the American South, which he canvasses in a series of book reviews, letters, addresses, essays, and interviews. Several essays deal with Percy's Catholicism and the role he believes it plays in his life and in the modern world. Critics note that Percy stands out among most of his fellow novelists because of the way he combines an interest in science and religion with a very sophisticated theory of language.

Nonfiction

ROBERT BLY: *Iron John: A Book About Men.* Bly's exploration of the positive image of masculinity becomes a surprise bestseller and prompts a national debate on the need for male support groups and the "releasing of the wild inner man."

SUSAN FALUDI (b. 1959): *Backlash: The Undeclared War Against American Women.* Faludi's National Book Critics Circle Award–winning essay collection brings her nationwide attention for her examination of the attacks endured by women in the wake of the women's liberation movement of the 1970s. Faludi won a Pulitzer Prize in 1991 for an article written for the *Wall Street Journal*.

WILLIAM LEAST HEAT-MOON: *PrairyErth (A Deep Map).* The book describes Chase County, Kansas, one of the last surviving areas of tall-grass prairie in the United States. Reviewer Paul Theroux observes that the author

"has succeeded in capturing a sense of the American grain that will give the book a permanent place in the literature of our country."

JONATHAN KOZOL: *Savage Inequalities: Children in America's Schools.* Kozol contrasts inner-city schools with those in America's affluent suburbs. *Publishers Weekly* devotes its September 27 cover to an open letter to President Bush, urging him to read Kozol's book and its "story of two nations that are separate and unequal in their educational facilities."

NICHOLAS LEMANN (b. 1954): *The Promised Land: The Great Black Migration and How It Changed America.* The managing and contributing editor of *Washington Monthly* publishes this best-selling narrative history. It is praised by reviewer Christopher Lehmann-Haupt for a structure that is "like a novel, or rather a series of short stories, which enable the reader to understand the lives of the characters in them."

MARK E. NEELY JR. (b. 1944): *The Fate of Liberty: Abraham Lincoln and Civil Liberties.* The compiler of the exhaustive *The Abraham Lincoln Encyclopedia* (1981), Neely, the director of the Louis A. Warren Lincoln Library and Museum in Fort Wayne, Indiana, wins the Pulitzer Prize for this account of Lincoln's relationship with the courts during the Civil War. *The Last Best Hope of Earth: Abraham Lincoln and the Promise of America* would follow in 1993.

P. J. O'ROURKE (b. 1947): *Parliament of Whores.* The writer for the *National Lampoon* and *Rolling Stone* supplies a humorous tour of the federal government. It stays on the bestseller list for nearly a year. "Every government is a parliament of whores," O'Rourke writes. "The only trouble is, in a democracy, the whores are us."

LEWIS B. PULLER JR. (1945–1994): *Fortunate Son: The Autobiography of Lewis B. Puller Jr.* Puller wins the Pulitzer Prize for this memoir of a Vietnam War veteran who had lost both his legs and several fingers from a Vietcong booby trap. Detailing a long and painful process of physical and psychic healing, the book is praised as one of the best accounts of the costs of the war. Puller would die of a self-inflicted gunshot wound in 1994.

PHILIP ROTH: *Patrimony.* Roth's award-winning memoir about his father's life and death is praised for its humor and tough-mindedness.

DANIEL H. YERGIN (b. 1947): *The Prize: The Epic Quest for Oil, Money, and Power.* Yergin, a business and government professor at Harvard, wins the Pulitzer Prize for this history of the oil industry, from the first well drilled in Pennsylvania in 1859 to the Iraqi invasion of Kuwait.

Poetry

JOHN ASHBERY: *Flow Chart.* Ashbery's book-length meditation in long verse lines prompts reviewer Frank Muratori to call it "as close to an epic poem as our postmodern, nonlinear, deconstructed sensibilities will allow." *Hotel Lautréamont* would follow in 1992.

LUCILLE CLIFTON: *Quilting: Poems, 1987–1990.* Organized in sections named for traditional quilting patterns, Clifton's admired collection explores themes of matriarchy, gender empowerment, and individuality. *The Book of Light* would follow in 1993.

BILLY COLLINS (b. 1941): *Questions About Angels.* Winner of the National Poetry Series Competition, the collection of witty observations drawn from the commonplace brings Collins his first widespread attention as an important American poet. The New York City native and professor of English at New York's Lehman College would be named poet laureate in 2001.

PHILIP LEVINE: *What Work Is.* The title of this National Book Award–winning collection aptly captures Levine's continuing devotion to a poetry that honors the lives of working men and women. The poems liberate the voices of workers too busy, too tired, too hemmed in to write the lives that emerge from his poems.

ADRIENNE RICH: *An Atlas of the Difficult World: Poems, 1988–1991.* The title poem in Rich's thirteenth collection is a sequence cataloguing contemporary America through images of survival, frustration, and marginality.

1992

Drama and Theater

PEARL CLEAGE (b. 1948): *Flyin' West.* Cleage's play concerns four African American women who migrate from the South to become Midwestern homesteaders. It becomes one of the most frequently produced plays during the early 1990s and launches Cleage's playwriting career. The playwright-in-residence at Atlanta's Spelman College, Cleage is the author of *Deals with the Devil: And Other Reasons to Riot* (1993).

WILLIAM FINN (b. 1952): *Falsettos.* Finn's musical play about families dealing with AIDS draws on two earlier versions produced off-Broadway. The drama centers on a New Yorker who leaves his wife for a male lover. Critics find the play both moving and funny, and the musical score earns a Tony Award.

HERB GARDNER: *Conversations with My Father.* This memory play concerns Eddie Ross, who owned a Manhattan bar for forty years. Hard at work making his immigrant life a success, Ross has little time for his son. The bar setting provides Gardner with a memorable cast of characters, and though the play deals specifically with Jewish American life, the father-son story and the immigrant milieu are comparable, critics point out, to the best work of Eugene O'Neill and Arthur Miller.

JOHN GUARE: *Four Baboons Adoring the Sun.* Guare's play concerns a married couple—academics who are working in Sicily and hosting their children from their previous marriages. The couple is happy; the children are disconcerted by having stepparents. Critics find that this tension between generations is explored with considerable sensitivity.

ADRIENNE KENNEDY: *The Alexander Plays.* This collection of one-act plays deals with the life of Suzanne Alexander, a fictionalized version of the playwright; it includes *The Ohio State Murders*, which many consider the best of Kennedy's plays.

LARRY KRAMER: *The Destiny of Me.* Kramer provides a sequel to *The Normal Heart* (1985), exploring Ned Weeks's family and history as he faces his imminent death from AIDS.

TONY KUSHNER: *Angels in America: A Gay Fantasia on National Themes, Part Two: Perestroika.* Kushner wins a second Tony Award for the second part of *Angels in America*, which records Roy Cohn's death from AIDS and the partners, Prior and Harper, adjusting to the changes in their lives that had occurred in the first half of the play.

DAVID MAMET: *Oleanna.* Mamet's two-character play explores the timely subject of sexual harassment through the interactions of a female student and her professor, whom she denounces as a sexist. The professor may be self-satisfied or worse, but the audience is left to decide for itself whether he deserves the denial of tenure and ruined career that result from what might be the work of a manipulative woman with a political agenda.

SCOTT McPHERSON (1959–1992): *Marvin's Room.* Produced shortly before McPherson's death from AIDS, this comedy deals with a woman who has devoted her life to the care of others and learns that she herself has leukemia.

ARTHUR MILLER: *The Ride Down Mount Morgan.* First produced in London in 1991, Miller's play concerns a prosperous charismatic businessman caught in a farcical relationship with a first wife (whom he has not divorced) and a second; both reflect his unquenchable appetite and feeling that the law does not apply to him. Critics feel that Miller gets considerable humor out of this manic character while also exploring the mayhem created by overweening egos.

NEIL SIMON: *Jake's Women.* The play depicts scenes in the life of a writer and the significant women he has known. Receiving mixed reviews, the play is praised for its expressionistic blend of realism and fantasy but criticized for its unsympathetic central protagonist, contrived happy ending, and tendency toward jargon-heavy psychologizing.

WENDY WASSERSTEIN: *The Sisters Rosensweig*. In Wasserstein's drama, three Jewish American sisters discuss their future. As in her other plays, women's issues are played off against a background of social and political change and how the individual copes with or evades her complicity in social customs and public controversies.

AUGUST WILSON: *Two Trains Running*. Continuing his play cycle treating African American experience during different eras, Wilson sets this play, first performed at Yale in 1990, on a single day in 1968 in a run-down Pittsburgh diner that is on the verge of closing. Its patrons reflect on their lives and community.

GEORGE C. WOLFE (b. 1955): *Jelly's Last Jam*. The Kentucky-born actor, playwright, and director's musical vividly re-creates the life of Jelly Roll Morton (1885–1941), the brilliant jazz composer and performer. His bragging, his womanizing, but also his artistic genius are celebrated in this affectionate but candid portrait, which wins virtually unanimous critical approval.

Fiction

DOROTHY E. ALLISON (b. 1949): *Bastard Out of Carolina*. Allison's autobiographical novel makes her a finalist for the National Book Award. Critics praise this story, about a poor girl growing up in South Carolina, for its humorous but unsentimental portraits of eccentrics, the "white trash" Allison declines to treat with condescension. Her other books include *Trash* (stories, 1988), *The Women Who Hate Me* (poetry, 1991), *Skin: Talking About Sex, Class & Literature* (essays, 1994), and a second novel, *Cavedweller* (1998).

DONALD BARTHELME: *The Teachings of Don B.* This posthumously published collection of Barthelme's unpublished, uncollected, or revised shorter works includes parodies of Michelangelo Antonioni, Carlos Castaneda, and Bret Easton Ellis, along with three plays. It also features an introduction by Thomas Pynchon.

ROSELLEN BROWN (b. 1939): *Before and After*. In this harrowing novel a family (mother, father, daughter) come to terms with the fact that their son and brother is a murderer. Family members reveal as much about themselves as about the murderer, and the novel becomes a story of how families struggle with issues that cannot be resolved, even when — in this case — the family remains intact. Critics admire the Philadelphia-born poet, short story writer, and novelist's subtle handling of family relationships and her refusal to come to a definitive conclusion.

ROBERT OLEN BUTLER: *A Good Scent from a Strange Mountain*. In Butler's Pulitzer Prize–winning collection, Vietnamese refugees living in Louisiana tell their own stories in first-person narratives. The vision that emerges combines Vietnamese folklore, American popular culture, and haunting memories of war.

RITA DOVE: *Through the Ivory Gate*. Dove's first novel is about a young African American woman frustrated by the restrictions of race. She is a brilliant student, musician, and actress who does not want to be bound by racial categories, but she finds she cannot ignore the demands of her community. Critics cite this novel as a good example of a new generation of African American writers, who attempt to go beyond the obsession with race found in earlier African American writing.

CRISTINA GARCIA (b. 1958): *Dreaming in Cuban*. This first novel by the Cuban American author, who immigraged to the United States in the 1960s, follows three generations of a Cuban family. A finalist for the National Book Award, it is praised for its humor, originality, and deft shifts from first-person to third-person narration as Garcia moves between the past and the present, between Havana and Brooklyn. A second novel, *The Aguero Sisters*, would follow in 1997.

OLIVIA GOLDSMITH (b. 1954): *The First Wives Club*. Critics call this debut novel fun and evocative of the spirit of the late 1980s as it concentrates on the lives of three wives who have been deserted by their husbands for younger women. The wives eventually thrive as the husbands fail in love and at work. Goldsmith was a management consultant for eleven years before beginning a writing career. Her subsequent novels would include *Flavor of the Month* (1993), *The Bestseller* (1996), and *Switcheroo* (1998).

ROBERT GRUDIN (b. 1938): *Book: A Novel*. This Pulitzer Prize nominee and *New York Times* Notable Book of the Year is a satire about literary scholars — their feuds and follies — in a plot following the career of Adam Snell, an English professor who has written a novel ridiculing his colleagues' ideas. Grudin is a professor of English at the University of Oregon.

MAUREEN HOWARD (b. 1930): *Natural History*. The subject of this highly praised experimental novel is Bridgeport, Connecticut, and an Irish American family's ambivalent place in it. Born in Bridgeport, Howard is the author of the autobiography *Facts of Life* (1978) and the novels *Before My Time* (1975) and *Grace Abounding* (1982).

DENIS JOHNSON: *Jesus' Son.* Johnson's collection of interrelated stories, narrated by an unnamed alcohol and heroine addict, treats the grim and often violent world of America's outcast in a hallucinatory, dreamlike style. One reviewer compares it with "reading ticker tape from the subconscious."

RANDALL KENAN (b. 1963): *Let the Dead Bury Their Dead.* Kenan is praised for his feel for his characters in Tims Creek, North Carolina, which is compared with William Faulkner's Yoknapatawpha County. The characters (preachers, lawyers, mill workers, farmers) are mostly black and poor, and though racism and violence mar their lives, the predominant mood is comic. Storytellers and mythmakers, the characters share similarities with those of Eudora Welty. Kenan, an editorial lecturer at Vassar and Columbia, is the author of the novel *A Visitation of Spirits* (1989).

CRIS MAZZA (b. 1956): *How to Leave a Country.* Mazza, a writer-in-residence at Allegheny College, wins the PEN/Nelson Algren Award for her first novel, concerning the relationship between two artists. It is described by reviewer Janet Byrne as "an experiment" in conveying "powerlessness, grief and raw rage, often in comic terms." Subsequent novels are *Exposed* (1994), *Your Name Here* (1995), and *Dog People* (1997).

CORMAC McCARTHY: *All the Pretty Horses.* Cole and Rawlins set off into nineteenth-century Mexico in this novel, which vividly re-creates the world of Mexican bandits and Texas ranchers. Part of McCarthy's Border trilogy, it wins the National Book Award and is praised by critics for endowing the genre of the western with literary grandeur while maintaining lucid and accessible prose.

THOMAS McGUANE: *Nothing but Blue Skies.* The novel is about Frank Copenhaver, another of McGuane's rugged male characters, who wrecks his family life and becomes a sexual predator. Critics note McGuane's continuing evolution as an eloquent interpreter of masculinity and his understanding of institutions such as the family.

TERRY McMILLAN (b. 1951): *Waiting to Exhale.* McMillan achieves her greatest success to date in this free-spirited novel about the friendships among four African American professional women living in Phoenix. It would be followed by *How Stella Got Her Groove Back* (1996). The Michigan-born writer's first books were *Mama* (1987) and *Disappearing Acts* (1989).

JOSEPH MITCHELL (1908–1996): *Up in the Old Hotel.* Critics extravagantly praise this collection of *New Yorker* stories, calling Mitchell the "Balzac of lowlife New York." Mitchell specializes in portraits of eccentrics, mis-fits, and brilliant urban oddballs, whom he seems to present transparently, without verbal tricks, contrived ironies, or self-consciousness. Born in North Carolina, Mitchell worked as a staff writer for *The New Yorker* since 1938.

TONI MORRISON: *Jazz.* Set in Harlem in the 1920s, Morrison's novel chronicles a triangle involving a middle-aged door-to-door salesman, his mentally unstable wife, and his eighteen-year-old girlfriend.

GLORIA NAYLOR: *Baily's Cafe.* Naylor's novel is about a woman who runs a Brooklyn café frequented by an all-black cast of characters, including Eve (a brothel owner), Sadie (an alcoholic and prostitute), Miss Maple (a transvestite), Jesse Bell (a lesbian), and of course, Baily herself, who provides asylum to these characters, who tell her their life stories. Naylor's sensitive narrative and gift for characterization have been compared with Sherwood Anderson's classic, *Winesburg, Ohio.*

BARBARA NEELY (b. 1941): *Blanche on the Lam.* Neely produces the first in her popular mystery series featuring black domestic servant Blanche White. *Blanche Among the Talented Tenth* (1994) and *Blanche Cleans Up* (1998) would follow.

DARRYL PINCKNEY (b. 1953): *High Cotton.* This exuberant satiric novel is about black identity, which the narrator would like to escape but cannot because he is fascinated with different shades of black skin, how black people dress, how they speak, and the manners they adopt. The self-deprecating sly narrator has been compared with that of Ralph Ellison's classic *Invisible Man.* Pinckney, born in Indianapolis, would write *Sold and Gone: African American Literature and U.S. Society* (2001).

E. ANNIE PROULX: *Postcards.* Proulx's first novel depicting the decline of a Vermont family wins the PEN/Faulkner Award. It is praised by fellow novelist Frederick Busch for "its furious action, its searing contemplations, its language born of fury . . . and the author's powerful sense of the gothic soul of New England."

ISAAC BASHEVIS SINGER: *The Certificate.* This translation of an early autobiographical novel by Singer had been serialized in the *Jewish Daily Forward* in 1967. It concerns an aspiring writer's return to Warsaw in the 1920s and is noteworthy for what it reveals about Singer's early artistic ideas.

SUSAN SONTAG: *The Volcano Lover.* In an artistic departure, Sontag takes on historical fiction with this exploration of the affair between Emma Hamilton and Horatio Nelson from the perspective of Hamilton's husband, Sir William Hamilton. This masterful portrait of society and culture in Naples from 1764 to 1780 has unmistakable correspondences with the contemporary.

DONNA TARTT (b. 1964): *The Secret History.* Tartt had begun writing her mystery novel while still an undergraduate at Bennington College. The story, about moral arrogance among undergraduates leading to murder, took her eight years to complete. Tartt eventually received an advance of $450,000, a record for a first novel. *The Secret History* is well received, but its advance publicity had threatened to overshadow the book itself. A second novel, *The Little Friend*, would follow in 2002.

JOHN UPDIKE: *Memories of the Ford Administration.* Historian Alfred Clayton writes his reflections on his life during the Ford administration while also working on a biography of President James Buchanan. The novel alternates between these two texts to contrast two periods of history.

GORE VIDAL: *Live from Golgotha.* Vidal's novel about a computer genius who is able to animate the past satirizes both television and religion. Networks compete to broadcast the Crucifixion during sweeps, and representatives from various religious denominations scramble to take charge of the media event.

ALICE WALKER: *Possessing the Secret of Joy.* Walker revisits the character of Tashi from *The Color Purple* in this novel dealing with the African ritual of genital mutilation, a topic Walker would return to in the nonfiction book *Warrior Marks* (1994).

ROBERT JAMES WALLER (b. 1939): *The Bridges of Madison County.* Waller's sentimental novella, the love story of a lonely Iowa farm wife and a footloose photographer, becomes a publishing phenomenon. Written in two weeks, the book is almost universally panned by critics but stays on the bestseller lists for well over a year, at first promoted by independent booksellers, then picked up by the major chain stores. It would be made into a popular 1995 film directed by Clint Eastwood. Waller was a professor of business at the University of Northern Iowa.

JOHN EDGAR WIDEMAN: *The Stories of John Edgar Wideman.* Set in Homewood, a black neighborhood in Pittsburgh, the stories in this collection are widely praised for their author's grasp of black vernacular. Wideman's handling of race and the black family has been compared favorably with James Baldwin's best work.

Literary Criticism and Scholarship

JOHN W. ALDRIDGE (b. 1922): *Classics and Contemporaries.* The volume collects essays written between 1968 and 1991, which provide thoughtful, insightful reconsiderations of literary heavyweights such as Henry James,

William Faulkner, and John Barth. The professor of English at the University of Michigan is the author of *After the Lost Generation* (1951) and *The American Novel and the Way We Live Now* (1983).

HENRY LOUIS GATES JR.: *Loose Canons: Notes on the Culture Wars.* This essay collection on literary and social topics focuses on questions of cultural pluralism, canon formation, and the legitimacy of African American studies.

MARY GORDON: *Good Boys and Dead Girls and Other Essays.* Noted novelist Gordon crafts provocative essays that reflect the same concerns evinced in her fiction, including meditations on what it means for a writer to grow up Catholic and how women react to the demands of religious institutions. These issues relate to what she sees as male dominance in American literature; women characters rarely achieve the autonomy and authority of their male counterparts.

CAMILLE PAGLIA: *Sex, Art, and American Culture.* In this essay collection, cultural critic Paglia takes on the academic vogue for French postexistentialist language theorists such as Jacques Derrida and Michel Foucault. Her critics in turn charge Paglia with showboating, citing her focus on popular culture.

HENRY TAYLOR: *Compulsory Figures: Essays on Recent American Poets.* The prize-winning poet and critic discusses here how poets develop, drawing examples from J. V. Cunningham, Anthony Hecht, Gwendolyn Brooks, May Sarton, George Garrett, and many other contemporaries. Critics are most impressed with Taylor's ability to empathize with a broad range of poets and definitions of what poetry is.

GARRY WILLS: *Lincoln at Gettysburg: The Words That Remade America.* Wills wins the Pulitzer Prize and the National Book Critics Circle Award for criticism for his close reading of Lincoln's "Gettysburg Address," placing the speech in its historical and cultural context.

Nonfiction

MARY CANTWELL (1930–2000): *American Girl: Scenes from a Small-Town Childhood.* Cantwell produces a widely admired account of growing up Irish Catholic in a Protestant town. She would continue the story, including her career as a journalist and her affair with the poet James Dickey, in *Manhattan, When I Was Young* (1995) and *Speaking with Strangers* (1998).

BLANCHE WIESEN COOKE (b. 1941): *Eleanor Roosevelt, 1884–1933.* Cook's reassessment of Roosevelt's private and public lives wins both praise and criticism for its feminist interpretation. A second volume, *The Defining Years,*

1933–1938, would appear in 1999. Cooke is a professor of history at John Jay College of Criminal Justice of the City University of New York.

JOAN DIDION: *After Henry*. This collection of essays continues Didion's meditation on her home state of California. She also focuses on Ronald Reagan, a California product she deems "all Hollywood." Critics praise the author as one of the finest of contemporary essayists, remarkable for her astringent take on American politics and culture.

STANLEY ELKIN: *Pieces of Soap*. This collection of thirty essays by one of the most highly regarded contemporary novelists reveals his eccentric and eclectic interest in American culture—from a piece on the world's largest purveyor of whoopee cushions and joy buzzers ("Recherche du Whoopee Cushion") to his report on attending a party for Ronald and Nancy Reagan.

AL GORE (b. 1948): *Earth in the Balance*. Soon to be vice president, Gore publishes a best-selling environmental treatise. It attracts attention not only because of its author's celebrity but also because of its radical proposals for environmental conservation, assailed by the political right as politically correct "psychobabble" and heralded by those on the left for "passionate authenticity."

JOHN GRAY (b. 1951): *Men Are from Mars, Women Are from Venus*. Gray, a former schoolteacher and protégé of the Maharishi Mahesh Yogi produces a major bestseller and a popular paradigm in this guide to marital and relationship problems based on distinct and pervasive gender differences.

DAVID McCULLOUGH: *Truman*. McCullough wins the Pulitzer Prize and praise for his considerable narrative skill in this biography of the Missourian president. "I wanted the book to unfold like David Copperfield and the old-style biographies," McCullough has observed, casting Truman as "an ordinary man faced with extraordinary problems. He is the part Jimmy Stewart plays in American movies."

PAUL MONETTE: *Becoming a Man: Half a Life Story*. Winner of the National Book Award for nonfiction, this is a blunt, angry account of growing up gay in a working-class, homophobic culture and the struggle to break out of the confining atmosphere of the closet.

GLORIA STEINEM: *Revolution from Within: A Book of Self-Esteem*. Steinem's best-selling self-help book provokes criticism and dismay among feminists such as Carol Sternhell, who asks, "How can it be after many years of trying to change the world that one of our best-known feminists is suddenly advising women to change ourselves instead?"

GORE VIDAL: *Screening History*. Vidal writes with humor and insight about the historical and biographical films he saw as a boy, his own experience viewing epics such as *Ben Hur* (1959) and *Caligula* (1980), and his notions about how history might be taught by using film as a medium. Vidal also publishes *United States: Essays, 1951–1991*, comprising two thirds of his published essays. This monumental collection is divided into three sections: "State of the Art," on literature, "State of the Union," on politics and public life, and "State of Being," made up of "personal responses to people and events."

GORDON S. WOOD (b. 1933): *The Radicalism of the American Revolution*. The Brown University history professor's analysis of the ideological underpinnings of the Revolution and its impact wins the Pulitzer Prize and is praised by reviewer Pauline Maier as "the most important study of the Revolution to appear in over 20 years . . . mandatory reading for anyone seriously interested in the American past." *Creation of the American Republic, 1776–1787* would follow in 1998.

Poetry

JOHN ASHBERY: *Hotel Lautréamont*. Although the poet is renowned for his difficult and brilliant verse, his later work has been characterized as more casual and accessible, dealing with the "most basic powers of survival," according to one critic. Reviewers note this volume's extraordinary shifts in tone from the highly serious to the whimsical in the "blinking of an eyelid."

HAYDEN CARRUTH: *Collected Shorter Poems, 1946–1991*. Winner of the National Book Critics Circle Award, this collection explores the destructive nature of the world ("Wreck of the Circus Train"), the power of nature and especially of birds to suggest a metaphysical realm of existence ("The Loon on Forrester's Pond"), and the yearning for an unfettered self, which is often revealed in evocations of farm life and rural environments ("John Spain's White Heifer").

TESS GALLAGHER (b. 1943): *Moon Crossing Bridge*. Gallagher's collection is made up of poems treating loss and grief at the death of her husband, Raymond Carver, in 1988. *My Black Horse* (1995) would collect her best work written between 1976 and 1992.

LOUISE GLÜCK: *The Wild Iris*. The poet describes a garden as it develops from early spring to the first frost in autumn in this collection. Each flower represents an aspect of human feeling related to the poet. This Elizabethan-like notion impresses critics. As reviewer Stephen Dobyns asserts, "No American poet writes better than Louise

Glück, perhaps none can lead us so deeply into our own nature."

GARRETT HONGO: *The Open Boat.* Hongo edits and supplies an introduction for this anthology of the work of thirty-one Asian American poets, including Cathy Song, David Mura, and Maxine Hong Kingston.

N. SCOTT MOMADAY: *In the Presence of the Sun.* Momaday collects poems, stories, and drawings, which include a sequence on Billy the Kid and depictions and narratives of Kiowa tribal shields.

MARY OLIVER: *New and Selected Poems.* Winner of the National Book Award, this collection reflects Oliver's terse style, using short lines and minute details as though she is putting life under the microscope. She writes many fine pastoral poems ("Being Country Bred"), as well as autobiographical, family-oriented works ("Ohio"). Her lyrical style has been compared with John Keats's.

JAMES TATE: *Selected Poems.* Tate receives the Pulitzer Prize for this retrospective collection of work from his previous nine books. John Ashbery writes that the volume "allows us finally to take the measure of his genius: passionate, humane, funny, tragic, and always surprising and mind-delighting."

MONA VAN DUYN: *Firefall.* The collection is a series of elegies and responses to poems by Yeats, Eliot, Auden, and Frost, along with Van Duyn's experimental minimalist sonnets. *If It Be Not I,* her collected works written between 1959 and 1982, would be issued in 1994.

1993
Drama and Theater

FRANK D. GILROY: *Any Given Day.* Gilroy revisits the family he dealt with in his most famous play, *The Subject Was Roses* (1964), in action predating the original, at the outbreak of World War II.

STEVE MARTIN (b. 1945): *Picasso at the Lapin Agile.* Pablo Picasso and Albert Einstein meet in a Paris bar in this witty comedy by the popular comedian and actor. The play has little plot, but critics find it provocative for its treatment of both men as young geniuses and for its depiction of life in the early twentieth century, full of optimism and a sense of being on the verge of great discoveries.

ARTHUR MILLER: *The Last Yankee.* This one-act play had debuted in 1991; revised and expanded, it runs at New York's Manhattan Theatre Club. Miller's drama is set in a mental hospital and deals with two woman suffering from clinical depression who are visited by their husbands.

PAUL RUDNICK: *Jeffrey.* Praised by critics as a master of light comedy, Rudnick presents the subject of AIDS in humorous and affirmative terms. His finely realized gay and straight characters are integrated into a complex view of sex, which abjures abstinence but also counsels caution. According to this play, sex is an eruptive force that simply cannot be denied.

NEIL SIMON: *Laughter on the 23rd Floor.* Simon's play hilariously re-creates the atmosphere of early 1950s television. The scene is the writers' room of the *Sid Caesar Show.* Simon, one of Caesar's writers and a mainstay of other comedy shows, writes with nostalgia and sensitivity about this era. In the play a group of writers compete against one another but also share the joy of participating in a new medium that can still be bent to their will.

ROBERT M. WILSON: *The Black Rider.* Wilson collaborates with singer-composer Tom Waits and William S. Burroughs for this reworking of Karl Maria von Weber's *Der Freischütz* (The Freeshooter, 1821), about an aspiring marksman's bargain with the devil. Considered Wilson's most accessible work, it is commended by reviewer Charles Michener for confirming that Wilson is "not only a high-minded mystifier but a real, low-down entertainer."

Fiction

WALTER ABISH: *Eclipse Fever.* Abish's third novel concerns a Mexican literary critic's suspicions that his wife is unfaithful. It is praised by critic Harold Bloom: "At once disturbing and wildly entertaining, this ironic novel may well be one of the handful of essential American works emanating from the decade preceding the end of the second millennium."

SHERMAN ALEXIE (b. 1966): *The Lone Ranger and Tonto Fist Fight in Heaven.* The Native American writer's first collection of stories treats, in the words of reviewer Brian Schneider, "the nation-within-a-nation status of American Indians and the contradictions such a status provides." The book wins the PEN/Hemingway Award for best first book of fiction. Born and raised on the Spokane Indian Reservation in Washington, Alexie is the author of the novel *Indian Killer* (1996).

FREDERICK BARTHELME: *The Brothers.* Barthelme's novel presents newly divorced Del Tribute's stay at his brother's house and his infatuation with his sister-in-law. Del's career would be continued in *Painted Desert* (1995).

PAUL BOWLES: *Too Far from Home.* This omnibus collection of Bowles's writings, including travel essays, parts of a memoir, letters, and journals, is most notable for its inclusion of several highly regarded short stories and the complete text of the 1949 novel that is Bowles's masterpiece, *The Sheltering Sky*.

T. CORAGHESSAN BOYLE: *The Road to Wellville*. The novel is a send-up of the nineteenth-century craze for physical and spiritual self-improvement. Set in Dr. John Kellogg's Battle Creek, Michigan, sanatorium, the story concerns inmates who are subjected to bizarre diet and physical regimens.

RITA MAE BROWN: *Venus Envy*. Brown's social satire looks at what happens when thirty-five-year-old Mary Armstrong, diagnosed with a terminal illness, writes letters to her family and friends, telling them what she thinks of them and informing them that she is a lesbian — only to learn that she will live after all.

FRANK CONROY: *Body & Soul*. Conroy's first novel concerns the transformation of a child piano prodigy into a mature and accomplished composer.

HARRIET DOERR: *Consider This, Señora*. The octogenarian author returns to the scene of her earlier success, *Stones for Ibarra* (1984), with a story of American expatriates in Mexico. The novel gains favorable notices, including that of *New York Times Book Review* critic Sandra Scofield, who writes that the novel "captures a time and place as surely as a jeweler sets a stone."

STANLEY ELKIN: *Van Gogh's Room at Arles*. The book contains three comic novellas: the title work, about a community-college professor's dealing with Vincent van Gogh's bedroom; *Her Sense of Timing*, about a wheelchair-bound professor whose wife leaves him; and *Town Crier Exclusive...*, which comically attacks the tabloid press and the fascination with British royalty.

JEFFREY EUGENIDES (b. 1960): *The Virgin Suicides*. Eugenides gains critical acclaim for his first novel, about five teenagers living in an affluent suburb in the 1970s who kill themselves. The Michigan-born writer would win the Pulitzer Prize for his novel *Middlesex* (2002).

ALBERT FRENCH (b. 1943): *Billy*. French's debut novel is a fictional re-creation of the accidental killing of a white girl and the resulting trial of a black boy that took place in rural Mississippi in 1937. Some reviewers state that French, a photographer by trade, has created a classic American tragedy out of this mix of death, racial tension, and injustice. French, a Vietnam veteran, is the author of a memoir, *Patches of Fire: A Story of War and Redemption* (1996), and the novels *Holly* (1995) and *I Can't Wait on God* (1998).

ERNEST J. GAINES: *A Lesson Before Dying*. Set in 1948 in the pre–civil rights South, this is the story of the edu-cation of an African American man unjustly condemned to die. His journal drives home the failure of democratic ideals in a place and time in which racism was the de facto law of the land.

JOHN HAWKES: *Sweet William: A Memoir of Old Horse*. Hawkes continues his equine theme begun in *Whistlejacket* (1988) with this autobiography of a racehorse.

OSCAR HIJUELOS: *The Fourteen Sisters of Emilio Montez O'Brien*. A succession of female narrators provides a wide-ranging history of an Irish Cuban family in Pennsylvania over the course of the twentieth century. It would be followed by *Mr. Ives' Christmas* (1995).

THOM JONES (b. 1945): *The Pugilist at Rest*. The stories in Jones's first collection focus primarily on the Vietnam War and its aftermath and constitute what critic Mary Park calls "the darkest, funniest, most urgent fictional debut in years." The Illinois-born writer was a boxer. The collections *Cold Snap* (1995) and *Sonny Liston Was a Friend of Mine* (1999) would follow.

BARBARA KINGSOLVER: *Pigs in Heaven*. Kingsolver returns to the characters and settings that made her first novel, *The Bean Trees* (1987), so memorable, putting her heroine, Taylor Greer, in the middle of a custody battle over a part-Cherokee child.

DAVID LEAVITT: *While England Sleeps*. Leavitt's historical novel is criticized for its unacknowledged use of English poet Stephen Spender's memoirs of the Spanish Civil War. The controversy brings Leavitt's book into the spotlight, however, as does his candid writing about homosexual love.

BOBBIE ANN MASON: *Feather Crown*. Set in 1900, Mason's novel describes the impact on a Kentucky family when a woman gives birth to quintuplets. As the author explains, "It's about being faced with a bewildering set of circumstances. She tries to make sense of it all and tries to rise above it and be herself, a survivor. I think that's also the challenge for us in this part of the twentieth century."

BHARATI MUKHERJEE: *The Holder of the World*. Mukherjee's novel connects the world of Puritan New England in the seventeenth century with India in an ingenious multicultural repossession of Hawthorne's *The Scarlet Letter*.

RICHARD POWERS: *Operation Wandering Soul*. Nominated for a National Book Award, Powers's novel concerns a pediatrics ward in inner-city modern Los Angeles.

E. ANNIE PROULX: *The Shipping News*. Proulx's Pulitzer Prize–winning novel, about a down-on-his-luck newspaperman who travels with his young daughters to his ancestral home in Newfoundland, is praised for its humor, eccentricity, and careful observation of the telling detail. Before writing it, Proulx had made several trips to the Newfoundland coast — a far-flung place she knew nothing of — simply to soak up the atmosphere.

JAMES REDFIELD (b. 1950): *The Celestine Prophecy.* Redfield's novel about the quest for enlightenment had been rejected by a number of publishers, and he initially self-published it. Its popularity among New Age devotees causes it to become a publishing marvel. As of 1996 it had sold 5.8 million copies and held the top spot on the *New York Times* bestseller list for 116 weeks. Redfield's best-selling follow-ups include *The Tenth Insight* (1996) and *The Secret of Shambhala* (1999). The Alabama writer worked previously as a counselor for abused children.

ISHMAEL REED: *Japanese by Spring.* An African American professor at a predominantly white liberal arts college suddenly becomes the academic dean, with the power to settle old scores. Reed critiques contemporary academic culture, political correctness, and multiculturalism as the story progresses.

PHILIP ROTH: *Operation Shylock: A Confession.* Roth formulates a new genre — the quasi-autobiographical novel — by inventing a novelist named Philip Roth who, in the midst of a breakdown, learns that an imposter using his name is promoting "Diasporism," Jewish resettlement in Europe as an antidote to Zionism. As Harold Bloom observes, "What fascinates about *Operation Shylock* is the degree of the author's experimentation in shifting the boundaries between his life and his work."

RICHARD RUSSO (b. 1949): *Nobody's Fool.* Like his previous two novels — *Mohawk* (1986) and *The Risk Pool* (1988) — Russo's novel treats blue-collar inhabitants of an upstate New York town. It gains the writer increased attention as well as praise from writer E. Annie Proulx as a "rude, comic, harsh, galloping story of four generations of small-town losers, the best literary portrait of the backwater burg since *Main Street.*" The Johnstown, New York, native would win the Pulitzer Prize in fiction for *Empire Falls* (2001).

CATHLEEN SCHINE (b. 1953): *Rameau's Niece.* The novel centers on a female writer who translates a response to the French Enlightenment philosopher Denis Diderot's 1805 work, *Rameau's Nephew.* Schine's frankly sexual reply to Diderot is inventive and decidedly postmodern, resulting in a satisfyingly moral tale that reviewers compare with the novels of Henry Fielding and Jane Austen. Schine's other books include *Alice in Bed* (1983), *The Love Letter* (1995), and *The Evolution of Jane* (1998).

BOB SHACOCHIS (b. 1951): *Swimming in the Volcano.* Nominated for the National Book Award, this is an ambitious first novel by an author known for his short fiction. The novel's mix of sexual intrigue, politics, and volcanoes invites comparisons with Susan Sontag's best-selling novel *The Volcano Lover.* Shacochis's other books include *Easy in the Islands* (1985), *The Next New World* (1989), and *The Immaculate Invasion* (1999).

Literary Criticism and Scholarship

ALLAN DAVID BLOOM: *Love and Friendship.* In his last published work Bloom attempts to dissect and destroy modern attitudes toward personal relationships with the same sharp scalpel he had used to carve up higher education in his controversial work *The Closing of the American Mind* (1987). He uses as his standard for comparison classic literary works by the likes of William Shakespeare and Jean Jacques Rousseau.

E. L. DOCTOROW: *Jack London, Hemingway, and the Constitution.* Doctorow's first essay collection consists of literary criticism, political insights, and historical meditations.

ADRIENNE RICH: *What Is Found There: Notebooks on Poetry and Politics.* Rich collects her literary criticism, devoted mainly to commentary on newer, mainly female writers.

Nonfiction

JAMES E. B. BRESLIN (1935–1996): *Mark Rothko.* Breslin, an English professor, is criticized for venturing outside of his field with this biography, the first full-length treatment of one of the twentieth century's most significant painters. The work also receives a full measure of praise, both for its analysis of Rothko and its presentation of the New York art scene at midcentury.

ANDREI CODRESCU (b. 1946): *Road Scholar.* Rumanian-born poet Codrescu recounts his participation in a quintessentially American adventure, the long road trip, wending his way from Greenwich Village (where he receives Allen Ginsberg's blessing before setting off to San Francisco) to the West. Along the way Codrescu's discerning eye discovers the offbeat contradictions essential to the form, but he also realizes that "paradoxically, the most materialistic country in the world is also the most spiritual."

SARAH DELANY (1889–1999) AND ELIZABETH DELANY (1891–1995): *Having Our Say: The Delany Sisters' First Hundred Years.* The African American sisters' view of their long lives becomes a bestseller and would be adapted as a play by Emily Mann in 1996.

MARTIN DUBERMAN: *Stonewall.* Duberman's groundbreaking study explores the history of the gay rights movement of the late 1960s and 1970s, sparked by the

1969 riot at New York's Stonewall Inn, a gay bar in which patrons protested police harassment.

BETTY FRIEDAN: *The Fountain of Age.* Friedan shifts her focus from feminism to gerontology, challenging the pervasive "age mystique" in American culture.

DONALD HALL: *Life Work.* Hall's memoir begins as a meditation on the writing life but changes directions halfway through when he discovers that he has life-threatening liver cancer. The work is praised by many critics, who see it as an enlightening look into the habits and work ethic of a distinguished American poet and author.

ERICA JONG: *The Devil at Large.* Jong's critical biography of Henry Miller, in part the product of a six-year friendship with Miller, is an unacademic look at an author long considered antifeminist.

DAVID LEVERING LEWIS (b. 1936): *W.E.B. Du Bois: Biography of a Race, 1868–1919.* The award-winning biography by the professor of history at Rutgers is quickly hailed as the standard reference source not only for the life of the civil rights leader but for the period of American social history covered by this first installment of a two-volume biography (completed in 2000).

ALAN LOMAX: *The Land Where the Blues Began.* Lomax, long a collector and popularizer of indigenous American music, publishes the fruits of his search "from the Brazos bottoms of Texas to the tidewater country of Virginia" for the roots of an American art form.

WILMA MANKILLER (b. 1945): *Mankiller: A Chief and Her People.* Both an autobiography and a history of the Cherokee people, Mankiller's book describes her grim childhood and youth in California and in Oklahoma, her years of poverty and struggle with racism, and her gradual overcoming of obstacles to obtain a college degree and eventually — through her work as a community development director — her selection as the first woman chief of her people.

JOHN MCPHEE: *Assembling California.* A geological history of a state notorious for earthquakes is the result of fifteen years of field research conducted with tectonicists and sedimentologists. McPhee assembles their arcane knowledge into readable and beautifully crafted prose.

DAVID REMNICK (b. 1958): *Lenin's Tomb: The Last Days of the Soviet Empire.* This Pulitzer Prize–winning book grew out of Remnick's coverage of the decline and fall of the Soviet Union for the *Washington Post.* The *Wall Street Journal* compares the fruit of Remnick's reportage with John Reed's influential eyewitness account of the formation of the Soviet Union, *Ten Days That Shook the World* (1919).

Wilma Mankiller

TINA ROSENBERG (b. 1960): *The Haunted Land: Facing Europe's Ghosts After Communism.* Rosenberg wins the National Book Award and the Pulitzer Prize for her study of Czechoslovakia, Poland, and the former East Germany. Reviewer David Rieff calls it the "definitive account of what the transition away from communism in Eastern Europe has meant in moral terms."

RICHARD SLOTKIN: *Gunfighter Nation: The Myth of the Frontier in Twentieth-Century America.* This volume completes Slotkin's highly acclaimed trilogy about the impact of the West on the American imagination, following *Regeneration Through Violence* (1973) and *The Fatal Environment: The Myth of the Frontier in the Age of Industrialization, 1800–1890* (1985).

PAGE SMITH (1917–1995): *Rediscovering Christianity: A History of Modern Democracy and the Christian Ethic.* Smith traces the relationship between Christianity and fundamental American notions of law and justice, putting the lie to sociologist Max Weber's notion of the "Protestant ethic," which equates democracy and Christianity with capitalism.

DIANA TRILLING: *The Beginning of the Journey: The Marriage of Diana and Lionel Trilling.* Diana Trilling's memoir bears witness to her contention, as she once told an interviewer, that the headline on her obituary would read as follows: "Diana Trilling Dies at 150. Widow of Distinguished Professor and Literary Critic Lionel Trilling." While distinguished in her own right as a social and literary critic, Diana Trilling is obliged to write not a personal memoir but a portrait of her marriage.

GORE VIDAL: *United States: Essays, 1952–1992.* This collection of essays ranges in subject matter from politics (Richard Nixon, Robert Kennedy) to sociology (feminism, American attitudes toward sex) to literature (Tennessee Williams, Thornton Wilder).

CORNEL WEST (b. 1953): *Race Matters.* West, a professor of religion and director of African American studies at Princeton, exhibits an impressive range in essays such as "Nihilism in Black America," "The Pitfalls of Racial Reasoning," "The Crisis of Black Leadership," "Demystifying the New Black Conservatism," "Beyond Affirmative Action: Equality and Identity," "On Black Jewish Relations," "Black Sexuality: The Taboo Subject," and "Malcolm X and Black Rage."

EDMUND WHITE: *Genet.* The novelist's lengthy biography of the French novelist and playwright Jean Genet (1910–1986) is deemed by more than one critic to be definitive—perhaps even exhaustive. Despite its length and surfeit of detail, the biography is widely reviewed and wins numerous awards, including the National Book Critics Circle Award for biography.

EDMUND WILSON: *The Sixties.* The final installment of Wilson's published journals ends with an entry written the day before he died. The volume is controversial for its candor about sexual matters and Wilson's misanthropy.

Poetry

A. R. AMMONS: *Garbage.* This National Book Award–winning collection is an eighteen-section, 2,200-line poem composed on adding machine tape and constituting a meditation on the implications of trash, that is, the remains of all life-forms.

MAYA ANGELOU: "On the Pulse of Morning." Angelou reads this poem at Bill Clinton's presidential inauguration. She is the first African American woman to be asked to compose and deliver an inaugural poem for a president.

MARK DOTY: *My Alexandra.* Doty becomes the first American to win the prestigious T. S. Eliot Prize, as well as the National Book Critics Circle Award, for this collection offering various responses to the AIDS crisis. *Atlantis* (1995) and *Sweet Machine* (1998) would follow.

CAROLYN FORCHÉ: *Against Forgetting: Twentieth-Century Poetry of Witness.* Forché edits this important collection of poems written by more than 140 poets from five continents, covering topics as diverse as human rights, genocide, war, and political repression. Selections include poems on the Armenian genocide, the Holocaust, and the Spanish Civil War. In the *New York Review of Books*, critic John Bayley calls the collection a "remarkable book. Not only in itself and for the poems it contains, but for the ideas that lie behind their selection."

DONALD HALL: *The Museum of Clear Ideas.* The title poem in Hall's collection is an imitation of Horace, but other verse is concerned with one of Hall's favorite topics, baseball.

DANIEL HALPERN (b. 1945) *Inferno.* Halpern, the editor in chief and cofounder of Ecco Press, edits a new version of Dante's poem in which twenty-one contemporary poets—ranging from Richard Howard to Amy Clampitt—produce their own distinctive versions of the classic cantos.

LINDA HOGAN: *The Book of Medicines.* Hogan's collection draws on Native American folklore and ritual to address the spiritual and moral failures of the modern world. It is praised by reviewer Robert L. Benner as "a significant step, indeed a great stride, in the development of a major American poet."

YUSEF KOMUNYAKAA (b. 1947): *Neon Vernacular.* Komunyakaa's Pulitzer Prize–winning collection concerns his life as an African American growing up in Louisiana and serving in the Vietnam War. The poems are written in simple language and short lines, which critics agree help to revive the moribund Deep Image poetry movement, which emphasizes psychological symbolism. Born in Louisiana, Komunyakaa teaches at Indiana University. His other books include *Copacetic* (1984), *Magic City* (1992), and *Thieves of Paradise* (1998).

SHARON OLDS: *The Father.* This collection, a great critical success, treats Olds's father's death from cancer and how she came to an understanding with him near the end of his life. Told with unsparing candor, the poetry penetrates the core of the writer's private life, her sense of grievance and her grieving, making her father come painfully alive so that the writing seems, as reviewers note, an act of atonement.

ROBERT PACK: *Fathering the Map: New and Selected Poems.* Pack brings together new works with selections from his previous five volumes—*The Irony of Joy* (1955), *A Stranger's Privilege* (1959), *Guarded by Women* (1963), *Home from the Cemetery* (1969), *Nothing but Light* (1972), and *Keeping Watch* (1976). Included is "Wild Turkey in Paradise," which has been called Pack's best single work.

MARK STRAND: *Dark Harbor.* This long poem in forty-five parts recounts an episodic journey into old age and a twilight land full of mystery and menace.

JOHN UPDIKE: *Collected Poems.* The volume collects 350 poems, many of them hitherto unpublished, in which

Updike tackles home life, sex, daily life, travel, and religion with the gusto, wit, and humor associated with his novels. Critics admire his deft handling of verse forms, especially the sonnet.

MONA VAN DUYN: *Firefall.* Van Duyn's collection of meditations, occasional poems, and "minimalist sonnets" prompts reviewer Ellen Kaufman to call the poet laureate "perhaps the most beloved American poet writing today."

Publications and Events

Poet laureate of the United States. Rita Dove becomes the first African American to be named poet laureate. She asserts that her appointment is significant "in terms of the message it sends about the diversity of our culture and our literature."

1994

Drama and Theater

EDWARD ALBEE: *Three Tall Women.* A powerful woman dominates this play, first as a young adult, then in middle age, and finally as an aging matriarch. Albee has confessed that the character is based on his rather difficult adoptive mother, a figure — like the character in the play — prone to great hatreds and paranoia. At the same time, though, she is impressive for her extraordinary self-confidence and stamina. The play also contains Albee's trademark absurdist humor. Critics consider it his finest work in thirty years.

RITA DOVE: *The Darker Face of the Earth.* Dove's first play, a verse drama, is a version of the Oedipus myth set during slavery, as the white wife of a plantation owner has a black son who is sold into slavery. He returns twenty years later for a fateful confrontation with his origins.

CORMAC MCCARTHY: *The Stonemason.* In a departure of genre and subject, the novelist offers a domestic drama examining the lives of four generations of a black family in Louisville during the 1970s.

TERRENCE MCNALLY: *Love! Valour! Compassion!* McNally, the master of ensemble performances, brings eight gay men together during summer holidays in the home of an aging choreographer and his young companion. They explore the nature of masculine love and friendship and the search for solidarity. A Tony Award winner, the play is considered one of McNally's major achievements.

ARTHUR MILLER: *Broken Glass.* Miller's first full-length play on Broadway since *The American Clock* (1984) explores the impact of the Holocaust from the perspective of the physical and sexual paralysis of a woman as a result of the persecution of Jews in Germany during and after Kristallnacht, the "night of broken glass," in November 1938.

ANNA DEAVERE SMITH (b. 1950): *Twilight: Los Angeles, 1992.* Smith's one-woman show depicts various viewpoints on the Rodney King case and the riots following the verdict, by which the policemen responsible for his beating were acquitted. Smith has been a director, an actress, and a teacher of acting at New York University and the University of Southern California.

STEPHEN SONDHEIM: *Passion.* Although critics are divided over the merits of what one calls a "chamber opera," others declare it a work of great distinction. *Passion* explores the nature of love — both its transcendent power and its destructiveness — as an army officer is ordered out of town and has to leave his lover. Even as he writes letters to her, sustaining their love, he is stalked by Fosca, a revolting, self-pitying woman who has fallen in love with him.

Fiction

SHERMAN ALEXIE: *Reservation Blues.* Alexie wins the American Book Award for his first novel, about the meteoric career of an Indian rock 'n' roll band. It would be followed by *Indian Killer* (1996), a murder mystery set in Seattle, depicting tensions between the white and Indian communities there.

JULIA ALVAREZ: *In the Time of Butterflies.* Alvarez's novel treats an incident in Dominican history in which three sisters who denounced dictator Rafael Trujillo are persecuted.

LOUIS AUCHINCLOSS: *The Collected Stories of Louis Auchincloss.* The author's fiftieth book collects nineteen stories published over the course of a long and accomplished career. The oldest, "Maud," had originally appeared forty years earlier, and the most recent are reprinted from Auchincloss's collection *Tales of Yesteryear* (1994).

JOHN BARTH: *Once upon a Time.* Barth sets sail yet again in this fictional memoir of a middle-aged writer's recollections during an autumnal cruise of Chesapeake Bay with his wife. It presents a vintage Barthian review of life and its many fictions.

THOMAS BERGER: *Robert Crews.* Berger updates Defoe's *Robinson Crusoe* for the 1990s, depicting the survival experiences of a middle-class man when the plane carrying his fishing party in the wilderness goes down. It would be followed by *Suspects* (1996), about a homicide investigation.

T. CORAGHESSAN BOYLE: *Without a Hero.* Boyle's fourth story collection is marked by the same black humor he brings to his longer fiction. Of special note is a parody of Ernest Hemingway's book about big-game hunting (*The Green Hills of Africa*, 1935) and "Filthy with Things," in which a wealthy California couple bring in a "specialist in aggregation disorders" to help them cope with their collectibles.

HAROLD BRODKEY: *Profane Friendship.* Brodkey's second (and final) novel dramatizes the affair of an American novelist and an Italian actor in Venice. As reviewer Guy Manne-Abbot observes, "Brodkey interrogates the limits of truth and love with great power."

ROBERT OLEN BUTLER: *They Whisper.* A Vietnam War veteran recounts the breakdown of his marriage and his search for sexual and religious fulfillment in Butler's follow-up to the Pulitzer Prize–winning *A Good Scent from a Strange Mountain* (1992).

CALEB CARR (b. 1955): *The Alienist.* Carr brings his talents as a military historian to bear on this best-selling mystery, the story of the hunt for a serial killer in New York City in 1896. Intermingling historical figures such as Jacob Riis and Theodore Roosevelt with fictional characters, the novel achieves some of its best effects through an accretion of historical detail, reminding many of E. L. Doctorow's *Ragtime.*

EDWIDGE DANTICAT (b. 1969): *Breath, Eye, Memory.* The Haitian-born writer's acclaimed first novel tells the story of a young woman who leaves her island community to be reunited with her mother, forcing her to confront her past and her mixed heritage.

E. L. DOCTOROW: *The Waterworks.* Set in New York City in 1871, the novel centers on Augustus Pemberton, a tycoon presumed to be dead until his son spots him one day on a Manhattan street. Doctorow grandly recreates the world of Boss Tweed and waterfront taverns, the era of robber barons and the mansions they erect in their capital of capitalism. The mystery is never quite solved, even though the novel's detective does penetrate the waterworks, the venue for the metropolis's conniving financiers.

BRET EASTON ELLIS: *The Informers.* Ellis's collection of loosely related stories, depicting the lifestyles of the young and feckless in Los Angeles, reflects the author's characteristic deadpan prose style, describing fashionable ennui that regularly explodes into graphic violence.

LOUISE ERDRICH: *The Bingo Palace.* The fourth in Erdrich's series of novels portraying contemporary life on a Chippewa reservation in North Dakota finds Lipsha Morrisey returning home to deal with his family, his heritage, and his romance with Shawnee Ray.

WILLIAM GADDIS: *A Frolic of His Own.* Gaddis's National Book Award–winning novel addresses the subject of law through the author's customary methods of indirect, nearly free association. The result is a pleasing, accessible story about a man who contrives to have his own car run him over, only to focus then on whom to sue for the accident.

WILLIAM H. GASS: *The Tunnel.* Narrated by William Frederick Kohler, a history professor at a Midwestern university and an expert on Nazi Germany, the novel portrays Kohler as a kind of fascist at home, contemptuously dominating his wife, family, and colleagues. Critics consider it a brilliant study in solipsism.

ELLEN GILCHRIST: *The Age of Miracles.* Gilchrist's story collection features Rhoda Manning, the child in *Victory over Japan* (1984) and the wife and mother in *Net of Jewels* (1992). She is now a divorced, middle-aged writer coping with aging and with failed relationships.

DAVID GUTERSON (b. 1956): *Snow Falling on Cedars.* Guterson's first novel concerns a murder and anti-Japanese prejudice on a small island in Puget Sound in the 1950s. The novel, a bestseller and a critical success, wins the PEN/Faulkner Award. Born in Seattle, Guterson taught high school English and was a contributing editor of *Harper's Magazine.*

JOSEPH HELLER: *Closing Time.* A sequel to Heller's 1961 classic *Catch-22*, the book resurrects the earlier novel's protagonist, Yossarian, now living alone in Manhattan. Twice divorced, he is facing his mortality. *Time* magazine reviewer Paul Gray finds the sequel "an alternately appealing and annoying bag of mostly old tricks."

JOHN IRVING: *A Son of the Circus.* Irving assembles his characteristic cast of eccentrics in a series of often bizarre situations, as an Indian-born orthopedic surgeon living in Canada returns to Bombay to study the genetics of dwarfism among Indian circus clowns. Bharati Mukherjee calls the novel Irving's "most daring and most vibrant" but also his "least satisfying" — he "India-surfs himself into exhaustion until the subcontinent becomes, for the reader as well as for one of his characters, neither symbol nor place but a blur of alarming images."

JONATHAN LETHEM (b. 1964): *Gun, with Occasional Music.* Lethem's debut novel combines science fiction with the conventions of hard-boiled detective stories. Chosen by *Publishers Weekly* as one of the best books of the year, this novel about what Lethem calls a "Private Inquisitor" is set in the twenty-first century and includes oddities such as a trench-coat-wearing kangaroo named Joey Castle and the abolition of both memory and questions. Born in New York City, Lethem would win the

National Book Critics Circle Award for his novel *Motherless Brooklyn* (1999).

BARRY LOPEZ: *Field Notes.* In this story collection, nature writer Lopez translates his close observation of natural phenomena into close observation of other observers, each of whom — like the anchorite in the story "Teal Creek" — has devoted himself or herself to a numinous location in the manner of Annie Dillard in *Pilgrim at Tinker Creek* (1974).

CORMAC McCARTHY: *The Crossing.* This second novel in the Border trilogy concerns Billy Parham, a young horseman dragging a trapped wolf from New Mexico to the Sierra Madre of Chihuahua, Mexico. On the way he encounters several characters, many of whom reflect on the nature of life in the West — a place of dazzling beauty and hope but also the territory of beasts and incredible violence. More discursive than *All the Pretty Horses*, the novel presents a sharp-eyed revision of the meaning of the West in the American consciousness.

HOWARD NORMAN: *The Bird Artist.* Ethnographer-turned-novelist Norman employs details of northern island life he learned while researching a remote Inuit whale-hunting community. This unconventional love story set in Newfoundland is a finalist for the 1994 National Book Award.

JOYCE CAROL OATES: *What I Lived For.* Oates's twenty-third novel concerns a middle-aged everyman named Corky Corcoran, who on Memorial Day 1992 discovers why he is so driven to consume food, sex, and drink and to demand attention and respect in an attempt to escape the past. *New York Times* reviewer James Carroll calls the novel's conclusion "a ringing affirmation of the most basic law of private and public morality and also of fiction: that character is destiny."

TIM O'BRIEN: *In the Lake of the Woods.* O'Brien's novel about a Vietnam War veteran charged with his wife's murder is called by *Time* magazine the best work of fiction in 1994. O'Brien's most wide-ranging and ambitious work, it blends fictional and nonfictional elements in the manner of John Dos Passos's *U.S.A.*

GRACE PALEY: *Collected Stories.* A National Book Award nominee and a Pulitzer Prize finalist, Paley's collected stories prompt renewed critical appreciation for her mastery of the short fiction form.

JAYNE ANNE PHILLIPS: *Shelter.* This initiation novel involves a drifter, two young sisters, a feral boy, and violence at a summer camp in West Virginia in 1963. Praised for its atmospherics, it is also condemned by some critics for being too self-consciously literary. Nonetheless, this second novel by the much-praised author of the story collection *Black Tickets* (1979) wins several awards.

TOM ROBBINS: *Half Asleep in Frog Pajamas.* Robbins's comic fantasy depicts Gwen, a stockbroker, torn between straitlaced Belford and his born-again monkey and Larry Diamond, who offers her a trip to Timbuktu. As reviewer Karen Karbo observes, "To love this book, the reader must be entranced and entertained by Diamond's pontificating about, for example, the visit by amphibian aliens to a village in sub-Saharan Africa, occasionally punctuated by Mr. Robbins's breathtakingly nonsensical metaphors."

HENRY ROTH: *Mercy of a Rude Stream: A Star Shines over Morris Park.* The first major work by Roth to appear since his highly influential novel *Call It Sleep* (1934) is an autobiographical bildungsroman about a Jewish writer in New York in the 1920s and 1930s. It is the first work in a projected six-volume cycle. A second volume, *A Diving Rock on the Hudson*, would be published in 1995; a third, *From Bondage* (1996), and a fourth, *Requiem for Harlem* (1998), would appear posthumously.

PETER TAYLOR: *In the Tennessee Country.* Taylor's last completed work is an expanded version of a short story, "Cousin Aubrey," which had appeared in 1993. Set in the Tennessee of 1916 and concerning the narrator's obsession with a lost cousin, the novel evokes the genteel South of a bygone era.

JOHN UPDIKE: *The After Life: And Other Stories.* Updike's eleventh short fiction collection contains stories about middle age and — like many of Updike's works — is highly autobiographical. Like one of his early collections, *Pigeon Feathers* (1962), many of the stories include a fictionalized version of Updike's own mother.

Literary Criticism and Scholarship

LOUIS AUCHINCLOSS: *The Style's the Man: Reflections on Proust, Fitzgerald, Wharton, Vidal, and Others.* Novelist Auchincloss writes entertainingly about literary fashion, discussing the once overlooked, now fashionable Edith Wharton and making a case for the seemingly superannuated Ivy Compton-Burnett (1892–1969).

HAROLD BLOOM: *The Western Canon: The Books and Schools of the Ages.* Bloom calls this defense of classic literary texts by "dead white men" a polemic against "the recent politics of multiculturalism." It predictably provokes the wrath of academics whom Bloom labels "the School of Resentment" — feminists, Marxists, New Historicists, deconstructionists, semioticians, and others.

GERALD EARLY (b. 1952): *The Culture of Bruising: Essays on Prizefighting, Literature, and Modern American Culture.* Early's collection takes a novel and notably eclectic approach to contemporary art and life, combining disparate elements in this engaging collection, which wins the 1994 National Book Critics Circle Award. Born in Philadelphia and educated at the University of Pennsylvania and Cornell, Early is a professor of English and African American studies at Washington University.

LOUISE GLÜCK: *Proofs and Theories.* This award-winning collection of essays on poetry examines the work of modernist masters such as T. S. Eliot and offers a tribute to Glück's teacher and mentor, Stanley Kunitz.

IRVING HOWE: *A Critic's Notebook.* This posthumously published collection of essays, edited by Howe's son, is notable both for its insights and for its argument against formalism. According to Howe, "If you are caught discussing a fictional character in the way that you might talk about a human being, you will probably be convicted of being a 'naive reader' by new formalist critics."

J. E. LIGHTER (b. 1949): *Historical Dictionary of American Slang.* The publication of the first of three volumes of Lighter's study is enthusiastically received by scholars on both sides of the Atlantic as a landmark book. The chief editor of the *Oxford English Dictionary* proclaims the work "one of those rare books which prompts the realization that you have never seen the subject in sharp focus before." Lighter is a professor of English at the University of Tennessee, Knoxville.

Nonfiction

SHARI BENSTOCK (b. 1944): *No Gifts from Chance.* Benstock's biography of the novelist Edith Wharton takes its title from a poem by Matthew Arnold, describing someone who "conquered fate." It is the first Wharton biography to draw on unpublished sources, which Benstock uses to buttress her thesis that the novelist underwent a "self-transformation" from her supposed destiny as a society matron. Benstock is a professor of English at the University of Miami.

JOHN BERENDT (b. 1939): *Midnight in the Garden of Good and Evil.* Berendt's portrait of Savannah, Georgia, including a murder case in which a respected antique dealer is accused of killing his young companion, proves to be breakout hit, remaining on the bestseller list for more than 186 weeks. Edmund White calls it "the best non-fiction novel since *In Cold Blood.*" Berendt had been an editor of *New York Magazine* (1977–1979) and a columnist at Esquire (1982–1994).

ELIZABETH BISHOP: *One Art: Letters.* Beginning with correspondence the poet wrote while still an undergraduate at Vassar and ending with a letter written the day she died, this collection constitutes a kind of autobiography, filled with personal revelations and insights into Bishop's work.

DAVID J. GARROW (b. 1953): *Liberty and Sexuality.* In his detailed study of the landmark U.S. Supreme Court abortion case, *Roe v. Wade*, Garrow, a professor of political science at Duke University, covers uncharted ground, interviewing minor players and coming up with telling details that breathe new life into this modern battleground of morality.

HENRY LOUIS GATES JR.: *Colored People: A Memoir.* Gates provides an account of his childhood and upbringing in a West Virginia mill town during the 1950s and 1960s. It is an authentic portrait of black life before integration and black liberation.

DAVID GELERNTER (b. 1955): *The Muse in the Machine: Computerizing the Poetry of Human Thought.* In 1993 the author had survived a mail-bomb attack by the antitechnology terrorist known as the "Unabomber." Gelernter spent the next year recuperating and finishing this book, which establishes operative principles for human consciousness. It identifies a high-focus mode of human thought for rational ideas and an opposite low-focus mode as the source of creative ideas.

DORIS KEARNS GOODWIN: *No Ordinary Time: Franklin and Eleanor Roosevelt; The Home Front in World War II.* Goodwin's Pulitzer Prize–winning joint biographical portrait during the war years offers an unprecedented glimpse inside the couple's marriage and the Roosevelt administration.

LUCY GREALY (1963–2002): *Autobiography of a Face.* Grealy memorably recounts the story of a childhood cancer that left her horribly disfigured. Some thirty reconstructive surgeries later, Grealy explores not only her own trauma but "the deep bottomless grief . . . called ugliness."

BELL HOOKS: *Teaching to Transgress: Education as the Practice of Freedom.* hooks argues for a participatory model of education, in which students are actively involved in the process and not seen merely as the recipients of knowledge. Her work wins praise for its impassioned intellectuality.

ERICA JONG: *Fear of Fifty.* The author supplies autobiographical reflections along with a consideration of aging. It is described by one reviewer as "funny, wise, candid, poignant, brash, painful, soul-baring, occasionally moralistic, but never dull." Jong would follow it with an essay collection, *What Do Women Want?: Bread, Roses, Sex, Power* (1998).

JUNE JORDAN (1936–2002): *Technical Difficulties: African American Notes on the State of the Union.* A self-confessed radical and part of the cultural left, the Harlem-born poet, novelist, and essayist sets out a program for state-supported family life and employment and attacks the record of the Reagan-Bush years. While critics take issue with her politics, they find her personal essays, reminiscences, and vivid re-creation of neighborhood life in Brooklyn compelling and supportive of her political opinions.

PAUL MONETTE: *Last Watch of the Night.* Monette's book is devoted to the state of the nation during the AIDS crisis as well as his own illness. Monette castigates institutions — such as the Catholic Church — that have failed him and others.

SHERWIN NULAND (b. 1930): *How We Die: Reflections on Life's Final Chapter.* Physician Nuland draws on personal and professional experience to demythologize death in his National Book Award–winning book. Nuland had been a surgeon at the Yale–New Haven Hospital before beginning a writing career. He is the author of *Doctors: The Biography of Medicine* (1988) and *How We Live* (1998).

REYNOLDS PRICE: *A Whole New Life.* Novelist Reynolds Price provides a chronological narrative of his being stricken with spinal cord cancer in 1984.

BRENT STAPLES (b. 1951): *Parallel Time: Growing Up in Black and White. New York Times* editorial writer Staples writes a coming-of-age memoir about his estrangement not only from his highly dysfunctional family but from the white world he had found so inviting. After the death of a younger brother involved in the drug trade, Staples raises the question that informs this memoir: where does the family end and the individual begin?

GLORIA STEINEM: *Moving Beyond Words.* Steinem's collection of essays treats the various ways in which gender distinctions operate in modern American society. Included are essays such as "The Masculinization of Wealth," "Sex, Lies, and Advertising," and "What If Freud Were Phyllis?"

JONATHAN WEINER (b. 1953): *The Beak of the Finch: A Story of Evolution in Our Time.* Weiner's profile of evolutionary biologists Peter and Rosemary Grant and their study of finches on the Galapagos Islands wins the Pulitzer Prize. Weiner, a senior editor of *The Sciences*, is the author of the column "Field Notes."

JAMES WELCH AND PAUL STEKLER: *Killing Custer: The Battle of the Little Big Horn and the Fate of the Plains Indians.* Blackfoot novelist Welch brings a different perspective to the Indian wars in this narrative of the Battle of Little Big Horn, tracing both the foreground and the aftereffects of the battle, along with Welch's family history.

JOHN EDGAR WIDEMAN: *Fatheralong.* Wideman provides "a meditation on fathers and sons, race and society." Combining autobiography with social commentary,

Wideman's book continues the memoir he had begun with *Brothers and Keepers* (1984).

EDWARD O. WILSON: *Naturalist.* Prominent biologist Wilson applies the principles of sociobiology to his own life, describing how a lonely nature-loving boy grew to become a world-class scientist. Reviewer Alan Lightman declares the book "one of the greatest scientific autobiographies ever written."

TOBIAS WOLFF: *In Pharaoh's Army.* Wolff continues the memoirs begun in 1989 with *This Boy's Life*, recalling his army service in Vietnam, where as a special forces soldier he was consigned to a muddy backwater with a great deal of time to meditate on the enemy and his own absurd experiences.

Poetry

JOHN ASHBERY: *And the Stars Were Shining.* In the title poem of his sixteenth volume Ashbery declares, "We sure live in a bizarre and furious / galaxy." The remainder of the collection's fifty-eight poems are briefer than this one but arrive at similar gnomic conclusions in a typical display of Ashbery's free association.

AMY CLAMPITT: *A Silence Opens.* Clampitt's fifth and final collection before her death shows the poet's characteristic wry and challenging meditations on the forces of history and life's odd juxtapositions. These are revealed in "Discovery," which connects the perspective of a manatee with the liftoff of a space shuttle.

CAROLYN FORCHÉ: *The Angel of History.* This *Los Angeles Times* Book Prize–winning poetic sequence reviews modern history, including the Holocaust, Hiroshima, the Soviet invasion of Czechoslovakia, the Chernobyl disaster, and genocide in El Salvador, meditating on the challenge of shaping language to deal with these events.

JOY HARJO: *The Woman Who Fell from the Sky.* This collection of prose poems is based on an Iroquois myth about the descent of a female creator and deals with the forces of creation and destruction in contemporary society.

EDWARD HIRSCH (b. 1950): *Earthly Measures.* This collection of poetic meditations on the manifestations of the divine in everyday life is one of only a handful of contemporary poetry volumes that critic Harold Bloom considered worthy enough to include in his controversial book *The Western Canon* (1994). Born in Chicago, Hirsch teaches English at the University of Houston.

RICHARD HOWARD: *Like Most Revelations.* The verse in this collection takes the form of dramatic monologue and alternates between elegies for friends who have recently succumbed to AIDS and other more mundane concerns, such as the wealthy foreign tourists summed up in "Centenary Peripeteia and Anagnoresis Beginning with a Line by Henry James." The review in *Poetry* calls the volume "limber, literate, jubilantly crafted, wry, and above all, densely populated."

GALWAY KINNELL: *Imperfect Thirst.* Kinnell's collection offers reflections on the past, relationships, music, language, sex, and mortality, containing works such as "My Mother's R & R," "The Night," "Rapture," and "The Cellist."

KENNETH KOCH: *One Train.* This collection of new verse is one of two volumes Koch publishes this year, the other being a selection of poems from the period 1950–1988. The first collection, which brings him the Bollingen Prize, includes the Chinese-influenced "One Step" and a series of short verse collectively called "On Aesthetics."

PHILIP LEVINE: *The Simple Truth.* The poet's fifteenth collection is elegiac but unsentimental. A fitting companion to his autobiographical essays, *The Bread of Time* (1994), the book is awarded the Pulitzer Prize.

W. S. MERWIN: *Travels.* Merwin's collection features narrative poems based on historical figures such as Arthur Rimbaud, David Douglas, and Manuel Cordova. Other poems include "The Hill of Evening," "A Distance," "Another Place," and "Immortelles."

CATHY SONG: *School Figures.* Song's collection treats the Hawaiian-American experience in poems on the poet's childhood and family, including such admired works as "The Grammar of Silk," "A Conservative View," "Sunworshippers," and "Journey."

JAMES TATE: *Worshipful Company of Fletchers.* Tate's National Book Award–winning poetry collection is full of his trademark inventiveness, which one critic declares, "solicits the reader with the familiar, then proceeds to act as trail guide to other worlds."

1995

Drama and Theater

HORTON FOOTE (b. 1916): *The Young Man from Atlanta.* A Pulitzer Prize winner, Foote's play is set in the east Texas of his boyhood. Willy Kidder, who has been compared with Willy Loman, is fired from his job by the son of his old boss. Willy's son commits suicide, and the play becomes a study in how Willy deals with this tragedy. The Texas-born writer is best known for his film work, including *To Kill a Mockingbird* (1962), *Tender Mercies* (1983), and *The Trip to Bountiful* (1985).

DAVID MAMET: *Cryptogram.* The playwright wins the Obie Award for best play for this drama set in Chicago during the 1950s, about a child's emotional abuse. Re-

viewer Vincent Canby calls it "a horror story that also appears to be one of Mr. Mamet's most personal plays."

DAVID MAMET, ELAINE MAY (b. 1932), AND WOODY ALLEN (b. 1935): *Death Defying Acts.* Three authors each write one one-act play: Mamet, *An Interview* (in which a lawyer is sent to hell); May, *Hotline* (in which a hooker tries to gain solace from a neophyte phone volunteer); and Allen, *Central Park West* (a comic attack on Manhattan's upper crust). The plays are unified by an astringent, hard-boiled, big-city attitude.

EMILY MANN: *Having Our Say. The Delany Sisters' First 100 years.* Mann's best-known and most highly praised drama is this adaptation of the best-selling 1993 memoir by Sarah and Elizabeth Delany, chronicling the lives of two elderly African American sisters.

DONALD MARGULIES: *The Model Apartment.* Margulies's play about two Holocaust survivors in Florida and their schizophrenic daughter wins the Obie Award for best drama.

TERRENCE MCNALLY: *Master Class.* McNally's play recreates a class taught by the opera diva Maria Callas as she reminisces about her great career. Critics find the play an extraordinary animation of the artist's biography and sensibility and a deeply romantic work about a suffering artist.

NEIL SIMON: *London Suite.* Essentially a deftly written farce, the play is about a famous actress who reconciles with her gay ex-husband. The plot becomes complicated when the ex throws his back out and remains immobile on the floor while all around him turns to chaos. Critics admire Simon's blending of sentiment and humor.

AUGUST WILSON: *Seven Guitars.* Wilson continues his chronicle of African American life, focusing on blues musician Floyd "Schoolboy" Barton, his musical colleagues, and their neighbors in Pittsburgh in 1948.

Fiction

MADISON SMARTT BELL (b. 1957): *All Souls' Rising.* Bell's novel about the Haitian revolution of 1791–1804 is told from a variety of perspectives and focuses on the second-generation slave leader of the rebellion, Toussaint L'Ouverture. It is the first of a projected trilogy devoted to the historical event. *Master of the Crossroads* would follow in 2000. The Tennessee-born writer's other novels include *The Washington Square Ensemble* (1983), *Soldier's Joy* (1989), and *Save Me, Joe Louis* (1993).

T. CORAGHESSAN BOYLE: *The Tortilla Curtain.* Boyle's novel concerns the clash between California nouveau riche and illegal Mexican immigrants, whose labor the wealthy exploit but whom they otherwise try—

literally — to wall out of their lives. It is a kind of latter-day version of John Steinbeck's *The Grapes of Wrath* (1939).

CHRISTOPHER BRAM (b. 1952): *Father of Frankenstein.* Bram's biographical novel re-creates the final days of horror film director James Whale. Told in the present tense, the book mimics a film script; like Billy Wilder's 1950 film *Sunset Boulevard*, it takes the discovery of Whale's body floating in a swimming pool as its jump-off point. The novel is also notable for its treatment of Whale's homosexuality, which in 1950s Hollywood was necessarily kept in the closet and perhaps contributed to his death. The book would be adapted as the film *Gods and Monsters* (1998).

MICHAEL CHABON (b. 1964): *The Wonder Boys.* Chabon's novel tells the tale of an English professor's search for an ending to his novel — eight years in the making and also called *The Wonder Boys.* Chabon's witty use of pop-culture vernacular is noted by Hollywood, which would adapt the popular and critically acclaimed book into a film in 2000. Born in Washington, D.C., Chabon graduated from the University of Pittsburgh and the University of California at Irvine. His first novel was *The Mysteries of Pittsburgh* (1988), and he would win the Pulitzer Prize for *The Amazing Adventures of Kavalier & Clay* (2000).

PAT CONROY: *Beach Music.* Conroy continues to mine personal and family traumas in this story of Jack McCall, who returns to South Carolina from his exile to Italy following his wife's suicide. He deals with his mother's impending death and the legacy of the past among his family and friends.

EDWIDGE DANTICAT: *Krik? Krak!* This Haitian American writer's collection of stories reflects, in its title, the call-and-response form of Haitian storytelling. Its subject matter — stories mostly relating to Haitian life — offer a unique perspective in modern American letters.

STANLEY ELKIN: *Mrs. Ted Bliss.* Elkin's final novel, winner of the National Book Critics Circle Award, presents his finest female portrait, the sweet-natured eighty-year-old Dorothy Bliss, a widow living in a Miami retirement community. Her sale of the family car tests her resourcefulness and humanity.

ROSARIO FERRÉ (b. 1938): *The House on the Lagoon.* Set in the author's native Puerto Rico, this is the first of Ferré's books composed in English. Flavored by magic realism, the novel presents a history of modern Puerto Rico from the vantage point of a woman writing a novel on her Puerto Rican family. *Eccentric Neighborhoods*, a family saga of linked stories capturing Puerto Rican social and political history, would follow in 1997.

RICHARD FORD: *Independence Day.* Ford's novel continues the story of Frank Bascombe, the main character of Ford's acclaimed *The Sportswriter* (1986). Bascombe seeks a reconciliation with his estranged and uncooperative son, which proves extremely difficult. Bascombe himself cannot quite overcome his fixation on the past or adjust to life in the suburbs. Ford is praised for subtle use of psychology and an acute sense of place.

MARK HELPRIN: *Memoir from Antproof Case.* Helprin's novel features an elderly American in hiding in Brazil, reviewing his life: his childhood in New York, his stay in a Swiss asylum, his involvement in World War II, his marriage, and the circumstances resulting in his aversion to coffee.

THOM JONES: *Cold Snap.* Jones's second collection shifts the focus on Vietnam found in *The Pugilist at Rest* (1993) to Africa, where several of the stories deal with characters associated with humanitarian aid to Rwanda. Joyce Carol Oates compares certain scenes with "the paintings of Bosch and Goya, the terrifying portraits of Frances Bacon."

JAMAICA KINCAID: *The Autobiography of My Mother.* Kincaid's shocking semi-autobiographical novel is about the casual cruelties of early-twentieth-century Caribbean life, related in the first person by a bitterly angry woman. Reviewer Michiko Kakutani observes that this woman is more than an absent mother; she "represents . . . a connection to earlier generations of women and blacks who endured the indignities of colonial and post-colonial oppression."

CHANG-RAE LEE (b. 1965): *Native Speaker.* The Korean-born writer's first novel explores modern Asian immigrant experiences. It wins more than six major literary prizes, including the PEN/Hemingway Award and the American Book Award.

BRUCE OLDS (b. 1951): *Raising Holy Hell.* Olds's first novel is a fictionalized account of the career of abolitionist John Brown. Named novel of the year by the American Library Association and nominated for a Pulitzer Prize, the novel features a collage technique made up of diaries, newspaper articles, songs, poems, internal monologues, and eyewitness recollections. Born in Wisconsin, Olds is the author of *Bucking the Tiger* (2001), about western gunfighter "Doc" Holliday.

PHILIP ROTH: *Sabbath's Theater.* Roth tells the story of a suicidal, priapic New Jersey puppeteer. The book wins a National Book Award but also inspires severe criticism for its deliberately offensive — some say pornographic — obsession with sex.

JANE SMILEY: *Moo*. Smiley's academic satire surveys a Midwestern agricultural "cow-college," filled with professional rivalries and pretenses.

AMY TAN: *The Hundred Secret Senses*. Tan's novel contrasts two Chinese half-sisters, one thoroughly Americanized, the other a mystic who can communicate with the spirit world.

ANNE TYLER: *Ladder of Years*. Tyler's novel describes the fate of middle-aged Delia Grinstead, who walks out on her obnoxious husband and uncaring teenage children to start a new life — only to be drawn back to her family for a reassessment of her identity and relationships.

EDMUND WHITE: *Skinned Alive*. This collection of tales about gay life at home and abroad is a series of what White has called "auto-fictions," which blur distinctions between autobiography and imagination.

Literary Criticism and Scholarship

KELLY CHERRY (b. 1940): *Writing the World*. This collection of essays and reviews explores what it means to be a writer and, more particularly, a Southern female writer. As poet and novelist Cherry concludes, "To be a writer in America is to be marginal."

ALFRED KAZIN: *Writing Was Everything*. Part memoir and part literary criticism, Kazin's collection gives thumbnail sketches of the literary and critical fashions Kazin had witnessed from the 1930s through the 1990s. The more recent decades come up short in his view. "Only in an age so fragmented," Kazin laments, "so ignorant of the unloseable past working in us, can presumably literate persons speak of Dante, Beethoven, or Tolstoy as 'dead white European males.'"

Nonfiction

BILL BRYSON (b. 1951): *Notes from a Small Island*. Bryson's humorous memories of two decades of residence in Britain, recalled during a return trip, is both a notable piece of travel writing and a kind of latter-day *The Innocents Abroad*. Born in Iowa, Bryson had moved to Britain in 1977, where he worked as a journalist and travel writer.

ANDREW DELBANCO (b. 1952): *The Death of Satan: How Americans Have Lost the Sense of Evil*. This prodigious work of intellectual history appears, to great notoriety. The book adds to Delbanco's growing reputation, culminating six years later when *Time* magazine would name him America's best social critic.

DAVID H. DONALD: *Lincoln*. Publishing the first full-length biography of Lincoln in a generation, Donald receives high praise for shedding new light on Lincoln's development, particularly on his legal career before his presidency.

DAVID GELERNTER: *1939: The Lost World of the Fair*. Gelernter chronicles the cultural significance of the 1939 World's Fair, dedicated to conceptions of the future, through a fictional composite character's tour of the exhibits.

STEPHEN JAY GOULD: *Dinosaur in a Haystack*. Gould's seventh collection of essays continues his fluent, eloquent writing about complex scientific concepts, turning natural history into an art form.

GARRETT HONGO: *Volcano*. Hongo returns to his roots in a little village named Volcano on the Big Island of Hawaii, using his poet's eye to describe not just the natural history of his birthplace but also the gritty details of Japanese American life in the twentieth century.

MARY KARR (b. 1965): *The Liars' Club*. This frank look at the author's Texas childhood tells of a father who hung out at the local American Legion "Liars' Club" and a mother who fancied herself a sort of "Bohemian Scarlett O'Hara." The book spends many weeks on the bestseller list and is generally credited with sparking a vogue for memoirs. A second volume, *Cherry*, would appear in 2000.

JONATHAN KOZOL: *Amazing Grace: The Lives of Children and the Conscience of a Nation*. Kozol supplies a sobering account of time spent in Mott Haven, an impoverished neighborhood in the South Bronx, and a meditation on poverty and race in America.

LI-YOUNG LEE (b. 1957): *The Winged Seed*. This memoir by a writer better known for his poetry recalls how his mother, a member of the former Chinese nobility, and his father, once physician to Mao Zedong, fled the country in the 1950s, only to be persecuted in Indonesia for their Christian faith. Reviewer Lisa Sack compares the effect of Lee's book with that of Maxine Hong Kingston's *The Woman Warrior* (1976), which two decades earlier had broken the code of silence governing filial piety among Chinese Americans.

LYLE LEVERICH (1920–1999): *Tom*. The first book of a projected two-volume authorized biography of Tennessee Williams is published after a long delay, owing to squabbles between the biographer and the Williams estate. Leverich would die before completing the second volume of his award-winning work.

NORMAN MAILER: *Oswald's Tale: An American Mystery*. Mailer's massive biography of Lee Harvey Oswald, accused assassin of John F. Kennedy, draws on formerly secret files of the Russian KGB in an attempt to discover

Oswald's true character and resolve the question of his guilt. Mailer also publishes *Portrait of Picasso as a Young Man*, a long-delayed biography of the painter, which receives mixed reviews. Many critics complain that the biography contains little that is new and that Mailer had missed an opportunity to bring something original to a subject with whom he had much in common.

JACK MILES (b. 1942): *God: A Biography.* Controversy ensues when the Pulitzer Prize in biography is awarded to Miles's book. Based on biblical interpretation, it treats God as a character in a work of literature, who has evident faults, internal contradictions, and a split personality yet nonetheless is able to develop and mature. Many critics regard the title of the book as not only audacious but a marketing ploy. Nevertheless, Miles, a former Jesuit and renegade biblical scholar, finds a wide popular audience for his biographical portrait.

ELAINE PAGELS (b. 1943): *The Origin of Satan.* This scholarly but still accessible work critiques the concept of evil and how it has changed over time. Pagels would become a recognized popularizer of theological history in 1997 with her award-winning *The Gnostic Gospels.*

ROBERT D. RICHARDSON JR. (b. 1934): *Emerson: The Mind on Fire.* Richardson's biography wins plaudits for breathing life into the seemingly stale biography of the "Sage of Concord," revealed here as a man of passionate personal attachments. Richardson, a former professor of English at the University of Denver, is the author of *Henry Thoreau: A Life of the Mind* (1986).

ALAN TAYLOR (b. 1955): *William Cooper's Town: Power and Persuasion on the Frontier of the Early American Republic.* Taylor, a professor of history at the University of California at Davis, wins the Bancroft Prize and the Pulitzer Prize for this combined biography of William Cooper, founder of Cooperstown and father of James Fenimore Cooper, and the social history of the settlement of upstate New York.

GORE VIDAL: *Palimpsest.* This gossipy memoir, which Vidal had once said would never appear in print, is published out of what reviewer Christopher Lehmann-Haupt calls "revenge." Others delight in the spectacle of a writer's mind sifting through the shards of memory.

TERRY TEMPEST WILLIAMS (b. 1955): *Desert Quartet: An Erotic Landscape.* The popular nature writer asks the rhetorical question "How might we make love to the land?" Her evocative writing about her native Utah would lead to a presidential invitation the next year to speak at the dedication of the Grand Staircase-Escalante National Monument.

AL YOUNG (b. 1939): *Drowning in a Sea of Love: Musical Memoirs.* The book collects the novelist and poet's previous memoirs, *Kinds of Blue* (1984), *Things Ain't What They Used to Be* (1987), and *Mingus/Mingus* (1989), in one volume, together with several new essays about his relationship with music. With his long history of writing about American music in fiction and poetry, Young's memoirs provide an especially welcome venue for his meditations on the visceral art of music.

Poetry

BILLY COLLINS: *The Art of Drowning.* Collins solidifies his reputation as both a critically acclaimed and popular poet with this collection of poems, which John Updike praises as "lovely in a way almost nobody's since Roethke's are. Limpid, gently and consistently startling, more serious than they seem, they describe all the worlds that are and were and some others besides."

RITA DOVE: *Mother Love.* The poet renders the myth of Demeter and Persephone in startlingly vivid and deeply personal terms. Critics admire the flexibility Dove shows in adapting the sonnet form to contemporary idiom, and overall the collection wins high marks for its unity and character.

JORIE GRAHAM: *The Dream of the Unified Field.* Graham's Pulitzer Prize–winning collection selects poems from five collections published over the past two decades, demonstrating, as one reviewer observes, that Graham's gifts range from a "great vision like Blake's" to "Dickinsonian philosophical introspection."

DONALD JUSTICE: *New and Selected Poems.* Justice's collection from three decades of work supersedes his Pulitzer Prize–winning *Selected Poems* (1979) and prompts reviewer Michael Hoffman to declare that Justice "probably has few peers when it comes to the musical arrangement of words in a line" and another to call the collection "probably the definitive Justice."

STANLEY KUNITZ: *Passing Through.* The National Book Award–winning collection is released to coincide with the poet's ninetieth birthday. It is a spare collection of some of the best of Kunitz's works from the three preceding decades, including the sequence "The Layers" (1979).

PHILIP LEVINE: *The Simple Truth.* Levine's fifteenth volume, awarded the Pulitzer Prize, is made up of elegies and meditations on the past, drawing on the poet's recollection of his life in Detroit.

JAMES MERRILL: *A Scattering of Salts.* Published posthumously, this is the last of Merrill's works. In it the poet meditates on his art in poems such as "Nine Lives," a work that assigns him only a small role in the great drama of life.

ADRIENNE RICH: *Dark Fields of the Republic.* Rich's collection combines lyrical celebrations of women with large, sweeping odes filled with the public voices of historical personages such as the political activist Rosa Luxemburg, the political philosopher Hannah Arendt, and Ethel Rosenberg, executed as a spy.

CHARLES WRIGHT: *Chickamauga.* Wright's collection uses the Civil War battle as the backdrop for meditations on the impact of history and the challenge to discover permanent values. Awarded the Lenore Marshall Prize from the Academy of American Poets, it would be followed by *Appalachia* (1998), Wright's revisiting of landscapes from his past.

1996
Drama and Theater

EVE ENSLER (b. 1953): *The Vagina Monologues.* Ensler's one-woman show, based on interviews with hundreds of women about their experiences with the vagina, debuts. It is performed throughout the country, with well-known actresses taking part; in 2002 it would inspire a movement called V-Day to stop violence against women. The New York City–born playwright is the author of the plays *Floating Rhoda and the Glue Man* (1995) and *Necessary Targets* (1996).

DAVID HENRY HWANG: *Golden Child.* Hwang's play about the viability and power of Asian cultural traditions shows a Chinese American about to become a father. He is visited by the ghost of his grandmother, who urges him to honor his ancestors and origins. The play would reach Broadway in 1998, receiving nominations for the Tony Award and the Outer Critics Circle Award.

JONATHAN LARSON (1961–1996): *Rent.* Winner of the Pulitzer Prize, this reworking of the opera *La Bohème* as a musical takes a high-energy, gritty look at contemporary society. The main character is Roger, a struggling songwriter whose friends are fellow artists. This world of heroin and AIDS has a powerful sentimental streak, as in *La Bohème*, and a dynamic faith in art as an antidote to death.

EMILY MANN: *Greensboro—A Requiem.* Described by the playwright as "theater of testimony," the play is based on the murders of five anti–Ku Klux Klan protesters in Greensboro, North Carolina, in 1979, using interviews, court transcripts, and personal testimony.

Fiction

SHERMAN ALEXIE: *Indian Killer.* The novel is indeed about a deranged Native American serial killer, an "Indian without a tribe." Showing the sardonic humor that had distinguished Alexie's earlier fiction, it is also filled with meditations on the nature of identity.

ANDREA BARRETT (b. 1954): *Ship Fever and Other Stories.* Barrett wins the National Book Award for her first story collection, which draws on science and history to present intimate portraits of family relationships. Born in Boston, Barrett grew up mainly on Cape Cod and received a degree in biology from Union College. Her other books include *Lucid Stars* (1988), *The Middle Kingdom* (1991), and *The Forms of Water* (1993).

JOHN BARTH: *On with the Story.* Barth's story collection contains typically self-reflexive, challenging fare such as the title story, in which two characters discuss a story they are reading—which is clearly another piece in *On with the Story.*

MADISON SMARTT BELL: *Ten Indians.* Bell treats black-white relations and the tension between altruism and urban violence in this novel about a white, middle-class children's therapist. He opens a tae kwan do school in inner-city Baltimore, which draws members of rival drug gangs.

THOMAS BERGER: *Suspects.* Berger's novel about crime and punishment includes characters taken straight out of the O. J. Simpson case. The *Times Literary Supplement* calls Berger "one of the 20th century's most important writers in the English-speaking world."

GINA BERRIAULT (1926–1999): *Women in Their Beds: New and Selected Stories.* Berriault wins the PEN/Faulkner Award and the National Book Critics Circle Award for her final collection, focused on ordinary people at moments of crisis. It is praised by Andre Dubus as "the best book of short stories by a living American." The California writer's previous works include *The Descent* (1962), *The Mistress* (1965), and *The Infinite Passion of Expectation* (1982).

ROBERT OLEN BUTLER: *Tabloid Dreams.* In his story collection Butler draws on hackneyed hype ("Every Man She Kisses Dies") for his inspiration. But as *New York Times* reviewer Thomas Mallon observes, Butler "transforms the material's coarseness—and a reader's anticipated guffaws—into lyricism and wonder."

ROBERT COOVER: *John's Wife* and *Briar Rose.* The first is a novel about a woman's fascination with the inhabitants of a Midwestern town. It is described by critic Michael Harris as "on one level a bawdy and deadly satire of good-ol'-boy mores; on another level a complex portrait of the townspeople . . . on still another, a philosophical inquiry into the relationship between life and art." The second is a retelling of the fairy tale "Sleeping Beauty," suffused with more sexuality than the traditional version and reflecting on the act of storytelling itself.

TOM DE HAVEN (b. 1949): *Derby Dugan's Depression Funnies.* Set in the New York newspaper world of the

1930s, the novel is cited as a *New York Times* Notable Book of the Year. Reviewer Bruce McCall finds the novel not just funny but also a "useful contribution to social history." A sequel by the New Jersey–born writer, *Dugan Under Ground*, would appear in 2001.

JUNOT DIAZ (b. 1968): *Drown.* Diaz's debut story collection reflects his experience as a Dominican born in the barrios of Santo Domingo who was later transplanted to the gritty environment of urban northern New Jersey. Some of these stories of absent fathers, aimless sex, and dreary housing projects had appeared earlier in august venues such as *The New Yorker* and *Story*, prompting critics to tout Diaz as a hot new talent. *Negocios* (1997) and *A Cheater's Guide to Love* (2000) would follow.

ANDRE DUBUS: *Dancing After Hours.* Dubus's first story collection in almost a decade includes works devoted to contemporary American life. The *New York Times* hails the volume as a Notable Book of the Year, calling Dubus "a genuine hero of the American short story." The *Village Voice* compares Dubus with Anton Chekhov.

RALPH ELLISON: *Flying Home.* A collection of Ellison's short fiction appears posthumously, including early pieces that foreshadow the writer's classic American novel, *Invisible Man.*

LOUISE ERDRICH: *Tales of Burning Love.* Erdrich's sixth novel, set in her customary North Dakota landscape, concerns the miraculous powers of love in the tale of four widows comparing notes at the funeral of the man they each had once married.

BRUCE JAY FRIEDMAN: *A Father's Kisses.* Friedman's story of a dim-witted widower who becomes a professional hit man is a witty and modern comic novel.

HA JIN (b. 1956): *Ocean of Words.* Ha Jin, who had immigrated to the United States in 1986, wins the PEN/Hemingway Award for first fiction for this collection of stories set on the Chinese-Russian border and based on the author's experiences in the Chinese army. It is described by reviewer Jocelyn Lieu as "a nearly flawless treasure." A second collection, winnner of the Flannery O'Connor Award and entitled *Under the Red Flag*, would appear in 1998.

GEORGE GARRETT: *The King of Babylon Shall Not Come Against You.* The *New York Times* calls Garrett's novel, the story of a murder that takes place in a small Southern town on the same day as Martin Luther King Jr.'s assassination, "a contemporary folk-art version of an early Renaissance altarpiece." While the foreground of the novel features the martyrdom of a saint, the background is taken up with cartoonish antics.

RON HANSEN (b. 1947): *Atticus.* Hansen's novel is nominated for the National Book Award and is at once a mystery and a tale about the bonds between a father and a son—told from both perspectives. The Nebraska-born novelist, short story writer, essayist, and screenwriter is the author of *Mariette in Ecstasy* (1991) and *Hitler's Niece* (1999).

JOHN HAWKES: *The Frog.* Hawkes's Kafkaesque novel depicts a French boy with a frog living in his stomach. It would be followed by his last fiction, *An Irish Eye* (1996), a monologue by a female foundling who falls in love with a World War I veteran.

GISH JEN: *Mona in the Promised Land.* Jen's second novel is a first-person account of Mona Chang, the daughter of Chinese immigrants, from 1968—when she is in the eighth grade—to adulthood. Living in affluent Westchester County, New York, Mona calls herself a "self-made mouth," who is Jewish by choice but Chinese by name. The result is an acclaimed multicultural tour of the American suburbs.

WILLIAM KENNEDY: *The Flaming Corsage.* The sixth installment in Kennedy's much-praised Albany cycle is set thirty years earlier than the other works in the series. It concerns the Daughertys, minor figures in the earlier works. The title is taken from a play that is the locus of the novel.

JOE KLEIN (b. 1946): *Primary Colors.* A roman à clef about the 1992 presidential race and a less-than-flattering view of Bill Clinton creates a sensation largely because its author, clearly an eyewitness to the events re-created in the book, initially published it anonymously. A frenzied guessing game ensues, with the *Washington Post* conducting handwriting analysis to compare the handwriting on a corrected manuscript to that of several possible authors. On July 17 Klein holds a press conference to admit to the book's authorship. Klein was the Washington, D.C., bureau chief and senior editor for *Newsweek* from the 1970s to 1996.

BETTE BAO LORD: (b. 1938): *The Middle Heart.* The highly acclaimed Chinese American writer provides a history of China itself, from the 1930s on. Named as a *New York Times* Notable Book of the Year, *The Middle Heart* pays tribute to the endurance of the Chinese people. Born in Shanghai, Lord immigrated to the United States in 1946; she is married to Winston Lord, former U.S. ambassador to China.

ELIZABETH MCCRACKEN (b. 1966): *The Giant's House.* Having received praise for her skill in creating a rich gallery of misfits in her first book of stories, *Here's Your Hat, What's Your Hurry* (1993), the Boston-born writer presents an odd pairing in her first novel, about the relationship between a spinster librarian living on Cape Cod in the 1950s and a schoolboy afflicted with gigantism.

JANE MENDELSOHN (b. 1965): *I Was Amelia Earhart.* Mendelsohn's best-selling evocation of the life of the famous aviator gains critical approval in part because of the book's ingenious structure. The first part follows the historical record very closely—Earhart's marriage to publisher G. P. Putnam and the plans for her historic around-the-world flight. The second part—a fantasy and speculation on what happened when Earhart crashed and was alone on a Pacific island with her navigator—provides the novelist with the opportunity to evoke the significance and mystery of Earhart's life poetically. A Yale graduate, Mendelsohn is the author of a second novel, *Innocence* (2000).

STEVEN MILLHAUSER: *Martin Dressler: The Tale of an American Dreamer.* Like Millhauser's earlier novel *Edwin Mullhouse* (1972), this is an American fable, the story of an early-twentieth-century bootstrap-capitalist who finds his apotheosis in building the Grand Cosmo hotel. The book wins the Pulitzer Prize.

RICK MOODY (b. 1961): *The Ring of Brightest Angels Around Heaven.* The novella that gives Moody's collection its title is a gritty urban piece that invites comparisons with Nelson Algren. Other stories in the collection are praised for their experimental form. Born in New York, Moody studied writing with Stanley Elkin at Brown University. His other works include *Garden State* (1991), *The Ice Storm* (1994), and *Purple America* (1997).

ANTONYA NELSON (b. 1961): *Talking in Bed.* After publishing three award-winning story collections, Nelson writes her first novel, a serious, understated story about romantic entanglements that disrupt the lives of two families. The story affords Nelson ample room to explore the messy business of middle age. Nelson was born in Wichita, Kansas, and was educated at the University of Kansas and the University of Arizona.

JOYCE CAROL OATES: *We Were the Mulvaneys.* Oates's twenty-sixth novel returns to familiar Oates territory: the dysfunctional family. This story about the unraveling of a perfect middle-class American family in the wake of a daughter's rape could have been, as critic Anita Urquhart remarks, "the stuff of a bad television movie." Instead, Oates's penchant for the dark side and profound grasp of the grotesque breathe life into this modern American tragedy.

E. ANNIE PROULX: *Accordion Crimes.* In a series of vignettes, Proulx's narrative follows a green, handmade accordion from its beginning in 1890 Sicily through a succession of owners of various ethnic backgrounds, to document the American immigrant experience. It wins the Dos Passos Prize for literature.

HENRY ROTH: *From Bondage.* The third installment of Roth's multivolume autobiographical novel, *Mercy of a Rude Stream*, appears posthumously. In the book, Roth's fictional counterpart struggles to escape the poverty of his childhood as a Jewish immigrant to New York. A final installment, Requiem for Harlem, would apper in 1998.

JOHN UPDIKE: *In the Beauty of the Lilies.* This story of a Presbyterian clergyman's loss of faith is heralded by some as the prolific writer's most ambitious book to date, in part because of the book's "underlying symphonic order," which employs several themes—religion and Hollywood, reality and illusion.

DAVID FOSTER WALLACE: *Infinite Jest.* Despite the marketing blitz that accompanies its publication and the enviable sales figures it generates, Wallace's novel about a future America ruled by advertisers is overlooked by the National Book Awards nominating committee. This oversight generates considerable controversy among literary insiders, who regard Wallace as the new Thomas Pynchon.

JOHN EDGAR WIDEMAN: *The Cattle Killing.* Wideman wins the James Fenimore Cooper Prize for this historical novel connecting the plight of African Americans in Philadelphia in the late eighteenth century with the story of the Xhosa tribe of South Africa.

TOBIAS WOLFF: *The Night in Question.* The stories of the writer's first collection in eleven years are praised by Christopher Lehmann-Haupt for "the power with which they seize your imagination."

Literary Criticism and Scholarship

CARLOS BAKER (1909–1987): *Emerson Among the Eccentrics: A Group Portrait.* The final work of the distinguished literary scholar and biographer appears posthumously. Although the book takes in the whole Transcendentalist movement, its main focus is Emerson, whose magnetism is nearly palpable.

DAVID DENBY (b. 1943): *Great Books.* Denby relates his experience as a middle-aged critic returning to Columbia University, where he reenrolled in two core humanities classes to reconsider the likes of Homer, Jean Jacques Rousseau, Virginia Woolf, and "other indestructible writers of the western world."

JOHN IRVING: *Trying to Save Piggy Sneed.* In a miscellaneous collection of short stories and essays, Irving offers homage to Günter Grass and Charles Dickens; in "An Imaginary Girlfriend," he treats his development as a writer.

CYNTHIA OZICK: *Fame and Folly.* Ozick describes the subject of this essay collection as "famous literary figures in our famously rotting century who have been associated with one sort of folly or another." Figures include Isaac Babel, H. G. Wells, and Henry James.

BOB PERELMAN (b. 1947): *The Marginalization of Poetry: Language Writings and Literary History.* Perelman supplies a history of the language poets, a group of loosely allied experimental writers of the late 1970s and the 1980s, such as Charles Bernstein, Lyn Hejinian, Leslie Scalapino, Ron Silliman, and Perelman himself, who set out to disrupt syntax, argument, and narrative in poetry.

GEORGE STEINER (b. 1929): *No Passion Spent: Essays 1978–1995.* The book collects seventeen years' worth of essays by the eminent critic, a professor of comparative literature at Oxford University. Steiner's collection pays particular attention to the relationship between literature and religion, as in the piece titled "Two Suppers," comparing Jesus' last supper and Socrates' symposium.

Nonfiction

STEPHEN AMBROSE (1936–2002): *Undaunted Courage: Meriwether Lewis, Thomas Jefferson, and the Opening of the American West.* Ambrose's highly readable account of the Lewis and Clark Expedition becomes a bestseller and inspires an equally popular 1997 television documentary produced by Ken Burns. Ambrose received his Ph.D. from the University of Wisconsin, taught at the University of New Orleans, and produced biographies of Dwight Eisenhower and Richard Nixon, as well as several histories of World War II.

NICHOLSON BAKER: *The Size of Thoughts.* Baker's essay collection includes notable meditations on diverse topics such as nail clippers and information retrieval, all composed by a writer whom the *New York Times* says is "one of those writers who almost cannot not give pleasure."

JIMMY BRESLIN: *I Want to Thank My Brain for Remembering Me.* A life-threatening bout with a brain aneurysm occasions this memoir, which, as reviewer Christopher Lehmann-Haupt observes, provides a "dizzying glimpse of great depths, both of his own brain under a microscope and of his gratitude to the medicine that saved his life." Breslin, a New York journalist and columnist, is the author of *The Gang That Couldn't Shoot Straight* (1969), *.44* (1978), and *Table Money* (1987).

HAROLD BRODKEY: *The Wild Darkness: The Story of My Death.* Brodkey's posthumously published collection of essays, journal entries, and notations take the reader right up to the time of the writer's death from AIDS. Critics such as Eva Hoffman admire Brodkey's tenacious talent, "wresting awareness from extinction until the very end."

JAMES P. CARROLL (b. 1943): *An American Requiem: God, My Father, and the War That Came Between Us.* The novelist and former priest wins the National Book Award for this account of his break with his father over the war in Vietnam.

JAMES ELLROY (b. 1948): *My Dark Places: An L.A. Crime Memoir.* True-crime author Ellroy, whose books have been described as "Chandler crossed with Tarantino, Hammett hybrid with Spillane," writes about his mother's 1958 murder. Reviewer Michiko Kakutani calls the book "an introduction for new readers to this gifted writer's disturbing oeuvre" and "a revealing map to the autobiographical sources of his fiction."

MARY GORDON: *The Shadow Man.* Gordon describes her search to find out more about her father, who had died when she was seven years old. The deceit uncovered by this Catholic writer includes the fact that her anti-Semitic father was himself Jewish. This discovery forces Gordon to question her own identity in a memoir that reviewer William H. Pritchard calls "a passionate and extravagant account."

BARBARA GRIZZUTI HARRISON (b. 1934): *An Accidental Autobiography.* Essayist Harrison's book, more like a scrapbook than an autobiography, is a *New York Times* Notable Book of the Year. *Times* reviewer Molly Haskell states that the book is "like a collage or a mosaic... closer to the visual arts than to conventional prose narrative."

MICHAEL KAMMEN (b. 1936): *The Lively Arts: Gilbert Seldes and the Transformation of Cultural Criticism in the United States.* Kammen's biography of Seldes paints an attractive portrait of the booster of lowbrow art. Kammen is a distinguished historian who has taught at Cornell University and won a Pulitzer Prize for *People of Paradox: An Inquiry Concerning the Origins of American Civilization* (1972).

ALFRED KAZIN: *A Lifetime Burning in Every Moment.* Kazin's journals form a memoir of this distinguished scholar of American literature, who ends his book with Henry James's last words: "The starting point of my life has been loneliness."

RICHARD KLUGER (b. 1934): *Ashes to Ashes: America's Hundred-Year Cigarette War, the Public Health, and the Unabashed Triumph of Philip Morris.* Kluger, a former editor at *Forbes* magazine, Simon & Schuster, and Atheneum, adds considerably to the charges against the tobacco industry with this Pulitzer Prize–winning history of business practices centered on cigarette giant Philip Morris.

JOHN RAKOVE (b. 1947): *Ordinary Meanings: Politics and Ideas in the Making of the Constitution.* Rakove wins the Pulitzer Prize for this narrative history of the ratification of the U.S. Constitution and an analysis of the concept of "originalism," an interpretation of the Constitution based on the assumption of the framers' original intentions.

ALAN SHAPIRO: *The Last Happy Occasion.* The poet produces the first volume of his acclaimed memoirs, treating his youth and development as a writer. It would be followed by *Vigil* (1997), recounting his relationship with his sister before her death from breast cancer.

Poetry

VIRGINIA ADAIR (b. 1913): *Ants on the Melon.* At age eighty-three, Adair publishes her first poetry collection; she had first begun publishing poems in the 1930s and 1940s. The collection is widely and favorably reviewed—greeted, as *New York Times* critic Brad Leithauser writes, "with fireworks."

JOSEPH BRODSKY: *So Forth.* A collection of work written during the Russian émigré poet's final decade appears posthumously. Reviewer John Bayley declares that the collection presents a man who "comes across as a complete and above all familiar human being."

HAYDEN CARRUTH: *Scrambled Eggs and Whiskey: Poems, 1991–1995.* Carruth wins both the National Book Award and the Pulitzer Prize for this collection of meditations on politics, history, aging, and relationships.

LOUISE GLÜCK: *Meadowlands.* The poet juxtaposes the story of a failing marriage against echoes of *The Odyssey;* the minute particulars of the contemporary are thus played off against the perennial and mythic story of love and loss. What makes this volume such a success is its superb craftsmanship and its absorption of its literary predecessors.

ROBERT HASS: *Sun Under Wood: New Poems.* The U.S. poet laureate (1995–1997) wins the National Book Critics Circle Award for this collection exploring family life, natural history, and literature. Its poems include "Our Lady of the Snows" and "Iowa City: Early April."

ANTHONY HECHT: *Flight Among the Tombs.* Hecht's collection takes death as its central theme and includes elegies to fellow poets Joseph Brodsky and James Merrill.

WILLIAM HEYEN: *Crazy Horse in Stillness.* Heyen wins the Fairchild Award and the Small Press Book Award for this exploration of the lives and significance of George Armstrong Custer and Crazy Horse.

CAROLYN KIZER: *Harping On: Poems, 1985–1995.* Kizer's retrospective collection alternates between political themes and, in the words of one reviewer, "those vividly recalling parents and friends in small masterpieces of verse narratives."

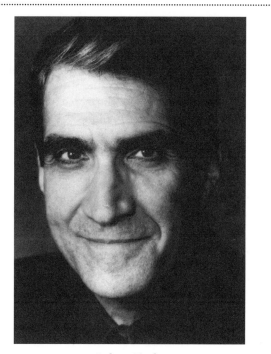

Robert Pinsky

LISEL MUELLER: *Alive Together: New and Selected Poems.* Mueller wins the Pulitzer Prize for this retrospective collection exploring a wide range of topics, including culture and family history, music, and language.

SHARON OLDS: *The Wellspring.* Olds's fifth volume deals with various aspects of creation in poems dealing with childbirth, the transition of children to adulthood, and love maturing into middle age.

ROBERT PINSKY: *The Figured Wheel.* Pinsky's volume contains new and collected poems dating from the past three decades. For reviewer Katha Pollitt, one of Pinsky's distinctions is "the way he recoups for poetry some of the pleasures of prose: storytelling, humor, the rich texture of a world filled with people and ideas."

1997
Drama and Theater

TINA HOWE: *Pride's Crossing.* Howe's play supplies a dramatic portrait of ninety-year-old Mabel Tiding Bigelow, the first woman to swim the English Channel the more difficult way—from England to France—as she reviews her life and times.

DAVID MAMET: *The Old Neighborhood.* Mamet's play is about Bobby, returning to his roots, rethinking what it has meant to grow up as a Jew. Critics find him an engaging character and are intrigued by Mamet's rare foray into his own Jewish background; they are also divided on how successfully this material is integrated into the play.

DONALD MARGULIES: *Collected Stories.* Margulies's play is based on the controversy surrounding novelist David Leavitt's borrowing of unattributed passages from Stephen Spender's memoir for his novel *While England Sleeps* (1993).

NEIL SIMON: *Proposals.* Set in 1953, as the Hines family vacations in the Poconos, Simon's play features an uncharacteristic outdoor setting and the playwright's first major African American character, the housekeeper Clemma Diggins, who serves as narrator. Receiving mixed reviews, the play manages only a two-month Broadway run.

ALFRED UHRY: *The Last Night of Ballyhoo.* Set in Atlanta in 1939, this drama is a witty exploration of Jewish experience in the South in the pre–World War II era. It centers on a Jewish family whose sharply intelligent daughter, Sunny, is scornful of assimilationist Jews who act like Episcopalians. However, Sunny is forced to reevaluate her stance when she meets Adolph, an unassimilated Brooklyn Jew. The play wins the Tony Award for best play.

PAULA VOGEL (b. 1951): *How I Learned to Drive.* In this play about child molestation, a country girl is abused by her uncle, who is not treated as a monster but as a man who is clearly in love with his niece. Critics point out that Vogel is writing as much about how human beings manipulate each other as she is about a sex crime. Her subtle, perfectly pitched dialogue wins her play the New York Drama Critics Circle Award, the Drama Desk Award, and the Pulitzer Prize. The Washington, D.C.–born playwright's previous works include *The Oldest Profession* (1990), *The Baltimore Waltz* (1992), and *Hot 'n' Throbbing* (1993).

WENDY WASSERSTEIN: *An American Daughter.* Wasserstein's comedy, with a serious political theme, is about Lyssa Dent Hughes, nominated to be the U.S. surgeon general. Then various trivial incidents in her past are magnified in the media, and she lashes out — prompting the president to withdraw her nomination. Critics admire the playwright's effort to explore the terrain of American political life, which still tends to limit what women can say and how they should behave.

Fiction

KIRSTEN BAKIS (b. 1968): *Lives of the Monster Dogs.* Bakis publishes an ingenious story of a race of doomed but superintelligent dogs, who become Manhattan celebrities in the year 2008. Critics compare this original work with Mary Shelley's *Frankenstein.* Born in Switzerland, Bakis attended the Iowa University Writers' Workshop.

FREDERICK BARTHELME: *Bob the Gambler.* Barthelme's novel describes the life of an architect living in Biloxi, Mississippi, whose life unravels because of gambling. The book is praised by reviewer Richard Bernstein as a "lovingly detailed focus on American life in the fast lane . . . a kind of updated American Gothic." The writer would later supply an account of his own gambling addiction in *Double Down: Reflections on Gambling and Loss* (1999).

DOUGLAS BAUER (b. 1945): *The Book of Famous Iowans.* The plot of Bauer's novel — bored Iowa farmwife meets charismatic drifter — is superficially similar to that of Robert James Waller's best-selling but critically panned novel *The Bridges of Madison County.* But as reviewer Michiko Kakutani observes, Bauer turns the hackneyed story to advantage through "insight into his characters' inner lives, his mastery of psychological detail, his control of narrative tension." Bauer was born in Wyoming and worked as an advertsising copywriter, journalist, and associate editor of *Playboy.* His other books include *Prairie City, Iowa* (1979), *Dexterity* (1989), and *The Very Air* (1993).

ANN BEATTIE: *My Life, Starring Dora Falcon.* Narrated by Jean Warner, Beattie's novel describes her fascination with the glamorous and mysterious Dora Falcon, who is eventually revealed as a manipulative, self-centered, pathological liar.

SAUL BELLOW: *The Actual.* Bellow's novella concerns a businessman's return to his Chicago hometown and new encounter with a former love in an elegiac portrait of the tenacity of first love and the search for the real.

FREDERICK BUSCH (b. 1941): *Girls.* A bereaved father attempts to assuage his grief over his own daughter's death by finding a missing girl. The *Washington Post* gives the book the "highest compliment a reader can pay a literary thriller . . . the claim that the book is nearly as intricate and mysterious as life itself." Busch, a professor of English at Colgate University, is the author of *The Mutual Friend* (1978), *Harry and Catherine* (1990), and *Closing Arguments* (1991).

PHILIP CAPUTO: *Exiles.* The three short novels in Caputo's collection are set, respectively, in Connecticut, Australia's Torres Straits, and the Vietnamese jungle — but all these settings resemble nothing so much as Flannery O'Connor's landscape of emotional alienation. The lead novella, *Standing In,* is singled out by *New York*

Times reviewer Christopher Lehmann-Haupt as Caputo's most engaging work of fiction.

PEARL CLEAGE: *What Looks Like Crazy on an Ordinary Day—*. The playwright's first novel brings attention to African American women's attitudes toward AIDS when her story, about the struggles of black women living with HIV, is made a book club selection by talk-show host Oprah Winfrey. It would stay on the bestseller list for ten weeks in 1998.

DON DE LILLO: *Underworld.* De Lillo offers a remarkable exploration of the American sensibility during the Cold War through the experiences of Nick Shay, who is trying to outrun his past, and the artist Klara Sax. The novel opens with a tour de force: an account of Bobby Thomson's 1951 home run in the National League pennant race, the "Shot Heard Round the World."

MICHAEL DORRIS: *Cloud Chamber.* In his first solo novel in nearly a decade, Dorris returns to the characters he had introduced in his acclaimed first novel, *A Yellow Raft in Blue Water* (1987), tracing five generations of a multicultural American family. The *Los Angeles Times* proclaims the book a confirmation that Dorris "is one of the true masters of voice, of character and of storytelling in contemporary American literature."

DOMINICK DUNNE: *Another City Not My Own: A Novel in the Form of a Memoir.* Dunne revisits the O. J. Simpson murder trial as his fictional alter ego, Gus Bailey, reflects on the courtroom scene and the impact of violence, race, and celebrity on contemporary America.

RICHARD FORD: *Women with Men.* Ford's second story collection (following *Rock Springs*, 1987) contains two stories about men pondering their relationships with women and a third about a boy's witnessing a barroom shooting in Montana. The title of the collection and the collection's theme and style invite comparison with Hemingway.

CHARLES FRAZIER (b. 1950): *Cold Mountain.* The North Carolina writer's National Book Award–winning debut novel echoes *The Odyssey* in a love story set in the American South at the end of the Civil War. It is one of those rare publishing events—a literary first novel that is both critically acclaimed and a major bestseller.

GEORGE V. HIGGINS (1939–1999): *A Change of Gravity.* Higgins's novel about the fortunes of a modestly corrupt Massachusetts politician, who faces changing social mores, unfolds through Higgins's characteristic use of overheard conversations. Higgins, a Boston journalist, lawyer, and former federal prosecuter, is the author of *The Friends of Eddie Coyle* (1971) and *The Patriot Game* (1982).

DENIS JOHNSON: *Already Dead.* Johnson calls his novel "A California Gothic." Others label it a contemporary noir. It is the tale of a failed son of fortune who manages to botch the drug-smuggling junket that is his last hope. The book alternates interior monologues with third-person narration.

DIANE JOHNSON (b. 1934): *Le Divorce.* Both a bestseller and a National Book Award finalist, Johnson's novel concerns the adventures of two California sisters in Paris. Critics hail it as a transatlantic novel of manners written in the style of Henry James and Edith Wharton.

ERICA JONG: *Inventing Memory: A Novel of Mothers and Daughters.* Jong provides a multigenerational family saga, treating the experiences of Jewish women and artists.

DAVID LEAVITT: *Arkansas: Three Novellas.* Leavitt interweaves autobiographical elements and considerations of love and loss. In *The Term Paper Artist*, a writer named David Leavitt writes school papers in exchange for sexual favors; in *Saturn Street*, a gay man who delivers lunches to homebound AIDS victims falls in love with one of his clients; and in *The Wooden Anniversary*, Nathan and Celia, characters from Leavitt's previous story collections, reunite after a five-year separation.

BERNARD MALAMUD: *The Complete Stories.* This collection consists of fifty-five works written over the course of Malamud's career. Richard Stern writes in the *Chicago Tribune* that it is "an essential American book." It includes stories from the award-winning *The Magic Barrel* (1959) as well as the forgotten early piece "Armistice" (1940).

THOMAS MALLON (b. 1951): *Dewey Defeats Truman.* Set in Thomas Dewey's hometown of Owasso, Michigan, on the eve of the 1948 presidential election, Mallon's novel tells the story of a local love triangle that parallels the national election. Just as the nation must choose between two candidates, a local belle must decide between two suitors with political ambitions. *New York Times* reviewer Jay Parini likens it to "one of Shakespeare's summery comedies." Born on Long Island, New York, Mallon was educated at Brown and Harvard. His other books include *Aurora Seven* (1991), *Henry and Clara* (1994), and *Two Moons* (2000).

DENNIS McFARLAND (b. 1950): *A Face at the Window.* McFarland's novel about a pair of American empty-nesters vacationing in London exhibits a rare combination of the literary and the supernatural, which reminds reviewers of both Henry James and Stephen King. McFarland is the author of *The Music Room* (1990), *School for the Blind* (1994), and *Singing Boy* (2001).

BHARATI MUKHERJEE: *Leave It to Me.* The novel treats a young woman abandoned as a girl by her hippie mother in India. She struggles to define her identity based on the conflicting claims of her multicultural background.

CYNTHIA OZICK: *Puttermesser Papers.* Ozick adds new and collects previously published stories dealing with the Jewish American attorney Ruth Puttermesser, whose vivid fantasy world springs into disturbing life, including the creation of a golem who helps Ruth transform New York City.

JAY PARINI (b. 1948): *Benjamin's Crossing.* This biographical novel is based on the life of social critic Walter Benjamin. Reviewer Robert Grudin declares that the book "has something important to tell us, not just about Benjamin but about the role of the intellectual in modern Western society."

THOMAS PYNCHON: *Mason & Dixon.* Pynchon's long-anticipated "big book" is a picaresque pastiche of the eighteenth-century novel, following British surveyors Charles Mason and Jeremiah Dixon as they establish the boundary between Pennsylvania and Maryland (and much else).

JOHN UPDIKE: *Toward the End of Time.* Set in 2020 after a nuclear war between the United States and China, Updike's novel takes the form of a survivor's journal of a year in his life.

KURT VONNEGUT JR.: *Timequake.* The writer's self-proclaimed final novel depicts a disruption in the space-time continuum, which forces everyone on earth to re-live the 1990s and presents Vonnegut's valediction on the state of Western civilization at the close of the twentieth century. Critics note the author's "familiar tone of weary bemusement," and reviewer Brad Stone calls the book Vonnegut's "funniest since *Breakfast of Champions.*" *Bagombo Snuff Box*, a collection of short fiction, would follow in 1999.

EDMUND WHITE: *The Farewell Symphony.* This is the third and final installment of the autobiographical trilogy White had begun in 1982 with *A Boy's Own Story* and continued in *The Beautiful Room Is Empty* (1988). In this novel — named for the work by Haydn in which the instrumentalists leave the stage one after another until only a single violin remains playing — the protagonist is left standing nearly alone in a world beset by AIDS.

RAFI ZABOR (b. 1946): *The Bear Comes Home.* The jazz musician's first novel, about a bear who performs jazz on the saxophone, wins the PEN/Faulkner Award and praise from a *Publishers Weekly* reviewer as a "hilarious, richly imagined, bear's eye view of love, music, alienated manhood and humanity."

Literary Criticism and Scholarship

MARK EDMUNDSON (b. 1949): *Nightmare on Main Street: Angels, Sadomasochism, and the Culture of Gothic.* A highly praised, wide-ranging, and searching investigation of the role of the gothic in American literature and culture. Edmundson deals with film (*A Nightmare on Elm Street*), drama (*Angels in America*), and novels by Toni Morrison and Ann Radcliffe; he also discusses Sigmund Freud and Mary Shelley. American writers, he notes, have been better at conveying a sense of gothic doom than a sense of renewal and a vision of the future.

JOHN M. ELLIS (b. 1936): *Literature Lost: Social Agendas and the Corruption of the Humanities.* In an articulate, controversial attack on college humanities departments, Ellis, a professor of German and dean of the graduate division at the University of California at Santa Cruz, deplores the devaluation of Western literature in favor of appeasing the call for political correctness. Critics argue about Ellis's thesis but recognize his passion for literature.

JOSEPH EPSTEIN (b. 1937): *Life Sentences: Literary Essays.* A widely read contemporary essayist on literary topics, Epstein ranges from Montaigne to F. Scott Fitzgerald to Elizabeth Bishop and John Dos Passos in these essays. Favoring an elegant, aphoristic style, Epstein, the editor from 1975 to 1997 of the quarterly journal *American Scholar*, also champions more loquacious writers, such as Theodore Dreiser, who wrestle with life's tragedies.

ALFRED KAZIN: *God and the American Writer.* Kazin conducts a literary, theological, and political analysis of writers who can neither accept traditional religion nor feel comfortable in their unbelief. Kazin focuses on Ralph Waldo Emerson, Herman Melville, Walt Whitman, Mark Twain, and William Faulkner — writers he spent a lifetime studying and writing about. Critics single out Kazin's searching examination of the impact of slavery on these writers' ideas of religion.

RICHARD WILBUR: *The Catbird's Song: Prose Pieces, 1963–1995.* In an important compilation, the master poet, critic, and translator collects some of his finest works — especially his critical essays on Edgar Allan Poe, the art of translation, and the nature and the central importance of poetry, in essays such as "The Persistence of Riddles."

Nonfiction

PAUL AUSTER: *Hand to Mouth: A Chronicle of Early Failure.* Auster writes about the period before his great success as a novelist, when he tried to live only by his pen and confronted considerable failure, almost relishing it as a sign of his seriousness. He reveals little about his personal life, except insofar as it impinges on his literary ambitions. Critics admire Auster's spare prose and stark, unflinching look at his own literary ambition.

JARED DIAMOND (b. 1937): *Guns, Germs, and Steel: The Fates of Human Societies*. The physiologist and ecologist wins the Pulitzer Prize for his controversial thesis that the people of Europe and Asia were able to conquer the indigenous peoples of America, Africa, and Australia not from any innate superiority but through an accident of geography, which allowed them to develop advanced weaponry, immunity to certain diseases, and complex social structures.

JOHN GREGORY DUNNE: *Monster: Living off the Big Screen*. Dunne, who had cowritten screenplays with his wife, Joan Didion, writes a funny, self-critical memoir of life in Hollywood. Not taking himself too seriously, he documents the stages by which a screenplay he and his wife had cowritten becomes a script for a Robert Redford vehicle, bearing virtually no resemblance to the original they had produced. Critics praise the authority and authenticity of Dunne's account.

JOSEPH J. ELLIS (b. 1943): *American Sphinx: The Character of Thomas Jefferson*. Having won acclaim for *The Passionate Sage: The Character and Legacy of John Adams* (1993), Ellis, a professor of history at Mount Holyoke College, turns to Adams's longtime nemesis in a study of key moments of Jefferson's life: writing the Declaration of Independence, his sojourn in Paris, his presidency, and his retirement. Ellis portrays a complex individual of great strengths and foibles. His book wins the National Book Award.

HENRY LOUIS GATES JR.: *Thirteen Ways of Looking at a Black Man*. Based on interviews with figures such as James Baldwin, Harry Belafonte, and Colin Powell, Gates collects various perspectives on the lot of the black man in American society. The book is praised by reviewer Michael A. Lutes as "a riveting commentary on race in America."

KATHERINE GRAHAM (1917–2001): *Personal History*. The newspaper and magazine publisher provides an intimate account of her life and, after the suicide of her husband in 1963, her transformation from society woman and housewife to business leader, who helped build the *Washington Post* into one of the country's most respected newspapers. The memoir wins the Pulitzer Prize.

CHRISTINE LEIGH HEYRMAN (b. 1950): *Southern Cross: The Beginnings of the Bible Belt*. The professor of history at the University of Delaware wins the Bancroft Prize for this account of the rise of Southern evangelicalism. The study is extravagantly praised by reviewer Curtis Wilkie

Jamaica Kincaid

as having "much of the beauty of the Psalms and the wisdom of the prophets."

SEBASTIAN JUNGER (b. 1962): *The Perfect Storm*. Junger, a Boston-born freelance writer, combines novelistic techniques with reporting and scientific research to record the impact of a fierce storm during October 1991. The narrative reconstructs the last moments of a doomed Gloucester fishing boat and the rescue at sea of other victims of the storm.

JAMAICA KINCAID: *My Brother*. Kincaid deals with the death of her youngest brother and his record of drug addiction and violence. A promiscuous homosexual, he had dreamed of becoming a famous singer. Kincaid does not try to resolve the dilemmas and tensions of family life and her own quest for a career. Rather, she kindles in her prose what she calls her "combustion of feelings."

JON KRAKAUER (b. 1954): *Into Thin Air*. Krakauer's harrowing account of a disastrous 1996 Mount Everest expedition becomes a bestseller and exposes the consequences of opening up Everest to inexperienced, paying thrill seekers.

EDWARD J. LARSON (b. 1953): *Summer for the Gods: The Scopes Trial and America's Continuing Debate over Science and Religion*. Larson's account of the celebrated trial of the Tennessee teacher prosecuted for teaching evolution and the case's continuing relevance is awarded the Pulitzer Prize and heralded as the definitive treatment of the case, based on new archival material.

FRANK McCOURT (b. 1931): *Angela's Ashes*. McCourt wins the Pulitzer Prize and achieves a remarkable popular and critical success with his debut work, a harrowing account of his poverty-stricken upbringing in the Depression-era slums of Limerick, Ireland.

PAUL METCALF (b. 1917): *Collected Works*. Critics find it difficult to categorize the work of this innovative and highly praised writer. To some extent he resembles Henry David Thoreau, but Metcalf digresses into geology, sociology, travel writing, and history as well, giving an account of westward expansion, the massacre of Indians, the consequences of slavery, and the fate of small-town America. He often centers on places — as in "I-57," his description of Illinois, which evokes a place in poetic detail reminiscent of William Carlos Williams's treatment of Paterson, New Jersey.

N. SCOTT MOMADAY: *The Man Made of Words: Essays, Stories, Passages*. Whether Momaday is discussing language, the oral tradition, or the land, he imbues his subjects with a Native American perspective. His interest in Native American sacred places extends to similar settings in Russia, Bavaria, and Spain. Critics praise not only the range of Momaday's subject matter but also his candor about his development as a writer.

JAMES SALTER: *Burning the Days: Recollection*. A highly regarded novelist and screenwriter, Salter explores his early days as a fighter pilot during the Korean War and relates that defining experience to the rest of his life. Presenting a memoir rather than an autobiography, Salter tends to concentrate only on moments or periods that seem to encapsulate his life. Critics praise the work as being elegant and as sensuously evocative as his novels.

DAVID FOSTER WALLACE: *A Supposedly Fun Thing I'll Never Do Again: Essays and Arguments*. Wallace's high-energy, profane wit is aimed at 1990s popular culture. Critics admire his Swiftian attacks on the world of young tennis professionals, the fraudulence of television, a weekend cruise in the Caribbean, and American food inventions such as the corn dog.

Poetry

AMY CLAMPITT: *Collected Poems*. Clampitt's work, which has been compared with Emily Dickinson's and Elizabeth Bishop's, vividly focuses on an object (such as a single seedling in "Fireweed") and endows it with both sensuous and metaphysical properties. Although a city poet in many respects ("Times Square Water Music" is representative), her subject matter ranges wide in poems such as "The Prairie" and "Grasmere" (a tribute to Wordsworth).

JORIE GRAHAM: *The Errancy*. This collection of lyrics develops the character of the quester or knight errant. A highly cerebral poet, Graham is interested in the clash

of worldviews — as in this collection's most important poem, "Flood," based on a passage in Ovid's *Metamorphoses*.

JUNE JORDAN: *Kissing God Goodbye: New Poems, 1991–1997*. Jordan's final collection intersperses love lyrics with poems on Bosnia, Africa, urban America, and the poet's battle with breast cancer.

JANE KENYON: *Otherwise: New and Selected Poems*. The collection adds twenty new poems to a selection from Kenyon's previously published volumes made shortly before her death. The subjects derive mainly from everyday life around her New Hampshire farm.

MAXINE KUMIN: *Selected Poems, 1960–1990*. This collection draws on nine separately published volumes, many of which focus on Kumin's New Hampshire farm, which is presented as a complete, unified world, with vivid descriptions of farm animals, crops, and the poet's family. Poems such as "The First Rain of Spring," "The Hermit Wakes to Bird Sounds," and "The Death of the Uncles" display Kumin's evocation of the cycle of the seasons, human life, and nature itself in vivid images and metaphors.

WILLIAM MEREDITH: *Effort at Speech: New and Selected Poems*. Meredith provides a distinguished retrospective of his unadorned formal verse, which reveals a remarkable honesty and clarity.

MARY OLIVER: *West Wind: Poems and Prose Poems*. Like *White Pine* (1994), which had preceded it, and *Winter Hours* (1999), which would follow it, Oliver's collection of sharply observed natural scenes prompts critical comparison with other great American lyric poets who celebrated the natural world, such as Edna St. Vincent Millay, Marianne Moore, and Elizabeth Bishop.

JAMES TATE: *Shroud of the Gnome*. Tate's collection, selected as a *New York Times* Notable Book of the Year, provides often comic, always revealing meditations on the luminous qualities of ordinary experience.

CHARLES WRIGHT: *Black Zodiac*. Winner of both the Pulitzer Prize and the National Book Critics Circle Award, Wright's collection continues his autobiographically based journal meditations and observations, offering in "Apologia Pro Vita Sua" his poetic credo: "Journal and landscape / — Discredited form, discredited subject matter — / I tried to resuscitate them both, breath and blood / making them whole again."

1998

Drama and Theater

MARGARET EDSON (b. 1961): *Wit*. This first play by an Atlanta schoolteacher receives rave reviews for its wry treatment of cancer. The plot centers on an English professor devoted to the work of John Donne who needs all of her learning, humor, and intelligence to cope with terminal ovarian cancer. In spite of the play's grim subject matter, critics call it a vivid, energizing portrait of a remarkable woman.

A. R. GURNEY: *Labor Day.* In a sequel to *The Cocktail Hour* (1989), Gurney shows his playwright protagonist composing a play about his wife and children, reflecting on his personal and professional life, and conducting lengthy discussions on the dramatic arts and American theater.

WARREN LEIGHT: *Side Man.* This eloquent play has been compared to *The Glass Menagerie* because Leight's narrator (Clifford) broods about his family in scenes that shift between past and present, as in Tennessee Williams's play. Clifford watches helplessly as his parents fumble through their marriage, taking the role of "adult" to sort out the problems of his often-unemployed jazz musician father and the tirades of his drunken mother. The play wins the 1999 Tony Award for best play.

DONALD MARGULIES: *Dinner with Friends.* First premiering in Louisville, Margulies's drama about two couples coping with divorce and the various pressures on modern marriage would win the Pulitzer Prize in 2000, following its New York opening.

TERRENCE MCNALLY: *Ragtime.* McNally provides a remarkably faithful adaptation of E. L. Doctorow's 1975 novel, working in fascinating vignettes of historical figures such as Harry Houdini, Booker T. Washington, J. P. Morgan, and Henry Ford.

ARTHUR MILLER: *Mr. Peters' Connections.* Written as the final play for New York's Signature Theater Company's 1997–1998 season, dedicated to Miller's work, the play takes place inside the protagonist's mind and concerns Mr. Peters's search for meaning in life.

PAUL RUDNICK: *The Most Fabulous Story Ever Told.* The play is about Adam and Steve and Jane and Mabel, gay couples in the Garden of Eden who meet two straight couples and are revolted to learn about heterosexual sex. This hilarious play undermines stereotypes but also probes the psychology of its characters. Critics generally agree that the play rises above its one-joke premise to expose cultural assumptions deftly.

Fiction

RUSSELL BANKS: *Cloudsplitter.* Banks's impressive novel about John Brown is narrated by Owen Brown, the only son of the abolitionist crusader who survived him. Critics note Banks's fresh way of retelling history by having Brown respond to the questions of a historical researcher.

ANDREA BARRETT: *The Voyage of the Narwhal.* Barrett's richly imagined historical novel follows a young botanist from Philadelphia on a polar expedition. Combining Barrett's interest in science and history, the novel manages to achieve a psychological intimacy in events that are usually reserved for adventure stories.

ANN BEATTIE: *Park City: New and Selected Stories.* Beattie adds eight previously unpublished works to this collection of thirty-six, culled from her previous collections and providing an interesting retrospective on the development of one of the most admired contemporary short-fiction writers.

T. CORAGHESSAN BOYLE: *Riven Rock.* Riven Rock is the family sanctuary in California, where Stanley McCormick, heir to the McCormick Reaper fortune, lives, a victim of schizophrenia. The novel's flashbacks suggest that McCormick's illness may be in part due to the pressures inherent in his inheritance. Critics note the conflation of history and biology and Boyle's panoramic view of society.

FREDERICK BUECHNER: *The Storm.* Critics call this novel's reworking of Shakespeare's *The Tempest* "dazzling." Set in a Florida resort, it features Kenzie Maxwell, an older writer who has escaped a sex scandal and become a kind of Prospero ruling over Plantation Island.

ROBERT OLEN BUTLER: *The Deep Green Sea.* In this novel an American veteran returns to Vietnam, where he reviews his past and falls in love with a Vietnamese woman.

MARTHA S. COOLEY (b. 1955): *The Archivist.* This much-praised first novel delves deeply into what it means to do research and how it can transform the researcher—in this case, a literary scholar and poet, Roberta, who is researching the life of T. S. Eliot.

ROBERT COOVER: *Ghost Town.* In a dazzling parody of the American western, Coover arranges a series of ribald dislocations for an unnamed cowboy who is overtaken by a seemingly deserted ghost town. The effect is something like "Zane Grey meets Samuel Beckett."

MICHAEL CUNNINGHAM: *The Hours.* In a brilliant repossession of Virginia Woolf's *Mrs. Dalloway*, Cunningham connects the stories of Woolf's suicide, a dissatisfied American housewife in 1949, and a modern-day Clarissa Dalloway in New York City who is giving a party for her friend, a writer dying of AIDS. The novel would be adapted into an award-winning film in 2002.

EDWIDGE DANTICAT: *The Farming of Bones.* Danticat's novel is a moving first-person account of an actual incident in 1937, in which an estimated twelve thousand to fifteen thousand Haitians in the Dominican Republic were murdered in an exercise in ethnic cleansing.

LOUISE ERDRICH: *The Antelope Wife.* The novel chronicles the lives of two Ojibwa families living in contemporary Minneapolis; it also circles back into the past in a series of magical, dreamlike sequences of mythical continuities and cultural dislocations. It is praised by reviewer Michiko Kakutani as "one of her most powerful and fully imagined novels yet."

WILLIAM H. GASS: *Cartesian Sonata and Other Novellas.* Gass's quartet of novellas mixes the ordinary and extraordinary in stories about a middle-aged clairvoyant, a traveling salesman who falls in love with his hotel room, and a spinster who literally loses herself in a line from a poem by Elizabeth Bishop. Reviewer Steven Moore declares Gass "the finest prose stylist in America" and states that "he is positively Shakespearean in his metaphor-making abilities and brings a jeweler's attention to every detail of his sentences."

ELLEN GILCHRIST: *Flights of Angels.* Gilchrist's story collection dealing with failed and successful relationships is praised in *Publishers Weekly* as "easily her best book in years," which "conveys the old-fashioned idea that clarity, compassion and good works can change the world."

ALLEGRA GOODMAN (b. 1967): *Kaaterskill Falls.* Goodman's novel is about several New York Jewish families who get together during the summer holidays. Critics praise the novelist's ear and eye for ethnic life in America and the epic nature of the interactions — usually resulting in comic results. Goodman, who grew up in Hawaii, was educated at Harvard and Stanford. She is the author of *Total Immersion* (1989), *The Family Markowitz* (1996), and *Paradise Park* (2001).

MARY GORDON: *Spending.* Like many of Gordon's novels, this one features an artist figure, Monica Szabo, who is surprised by a male admirer who promises to remedy her complaint that women do not have muses to look after them and pay the rent. This rich man is everything she dreams of, even when he suddenly loses all his money — a disaster solved when Monica finds a new (elderly female) patron. This witty parable about art and life lives up to its subtitle: "A Utopian Divertimento."

LINDA HOGAN: *Power.* Hogan's novel is a coming-of-age story of a young Indian girl who witnesses the hunting and killing of her tribe's sacred animal, the Florida panther, an act that forces her to come to terms with her Indian heritage.

MAUREEN HOWARD: *A Lover's Almanac.* This book concentrates on an artist and a computer graphics designer who reevaluate their relationship as the new millennium approaches. Critics suggest that Howard is at her best in portraying male-female relationships in contemporary America.

JOHN IRVING: *A Widow for One Year.* Irving's novel features his first female main character, writer Ruth Cole, who is shown at several stages of her life trying to cope with childhood trauma and adult relationship failures, all of which fuel her writing career.

CHARLES JOHNSON: *Dreamer.* The novel focuses on a drifting Korean War veteran who physically resembles Martin Luther King Jr. Johnson uses the character to explore King's life and career. Critics find this new expression of biography and racial issues an absorbing human drama and a penetrating interpretation of American history.

GAYL JONES: *The Healing.* In her first novel since *Eva's Woman* (1975), and the first original fiction published by Beacon Press in its 150-year history, Jones tells the story of Harlan Jane Eagleton's transformation from a rock star's manager to a traveling faith healer.

BARBARA KINGSOLVER: *The Poisonwood Bible.* A bestseller and a *New York Times Book Review* best books of 1998 selection, Kingsolver's novel chronicles the lives of a Baptist missionary and his family in the Congo, connecting three decades of violent African history with the domestic affairs of the family, seen from the multiple perspectives of different family members. It is praised by reviewer Michiko Kakutani as "an old-fashioned nineteenth-century novel, a Hawthornian tale of sin and redemption and the 'dark necessity' of history."

ALISON LURIE: *The Last Resort.* Highly praised for her novels about marriage and social manners, Lurie focuses in this novel on a middle-aged couple who decide to separate and explore romance in Key West.

CORMAC McCARTHY: *Cities of the Plain.* The novel concludes the writer's Border trilogy, bringing together John Grady Cole from *All the Pretty Horses* (1992) and Billy Parham from *The Crossing* (1994). Set in New Mexico in the 1950s, the novel shows both men working as horse wranglers and deals with Cole's doomed love for the Mexican prostitute Magdalena and the violent retribution following her death.

ALICE McDERMOTT (b. 1953): *Charming Billy.* McDermott's fourth novel, dealing with the life and loves of an Irish American who dies of alcoholism, is a surprise winner of the National Book Award, praised for its revealing, intimate portrait of Irish American culture. The Brooklyn-born McDermott's previous novels are *A Bigamist's Daughter* (1982), *That Night* (1987), and *At Weddings and Wakes* (1991).

SUSAN MINOT: *Evening.* Terminally ill, Ann Grant Lord relives a defining affair she had had forty years before in this novel, which writer Thomas McGuane calls "A wonderful, truthful, heartbreaking book" that "vindicates the wildest assertions any of us have made about Susan Minot's talent."

LORRIE MOORE (b. 1957): *Birds of America.* Considered one of the best short fiction collections of the year, Moore's stories focus on women in different stages of family life and romantic relationships. Her articulate, self-critical women — like the angry mother grieving over her dying child in "People Like That Are the Only People Here" — have much to say about the state of contemporary life. Born in Glens Falls, New York, Moore teaches writing at the University of Wisconsin. Her other books include *Self-Help* (1985), *Anagrams* (1986), and *Like Life* (1990).

TONI MORRISON: *Paradise.* Morrison bases her novel on a group of former slaves who establish a utopian community in the West. The novel opens in 1976, when the descendants of the slaves are caught in a bitter conflict linking past and present and demonstrating not merely the legacy of racism but the continuing tensions between black men and women, which Morrison has explored in many of her novels.

WALTER MOSLEY: *Always Outnumbered, Always Outgunned.* The creator of the Easy Rawlins mystery series introduces a new protagonist, ex-con Socrates Fortlow, trying to live a moral life in Watts in Los Angeles. Fortlow's existential dilemmas prompt comparisons with Ralph Ellison's *Invisible Man. Walkin' the Dog* (1999) would continue Fortlow's crises. In 1998, Mosley also ventures into science fiction with *Blue Light;* residents of San Francisco in the 1960s are struck by a mysterious blue light that gives them superpowers to combat evil.

GLORIA NAYLOR: *Men of Brewster Place.* Naylor adds to her portraits of women living in an urban housing project in *The Women of Brewster Place* (1982) a gallery of male profiles.

JOYCE CAROL OATES: *My Heart Laid Bare.* The novel portrays the history of a family of confidence artists in the nineteenth and early twentieth centuries, based on the memoir of the protagonist Abraham Licht. He takes a survival-of-the-fittest view of society, instructing his children to be loyal only to the family. But Licht's values lead him to a dead end when his own family betrays him and he loses his fortune in the 1929 stock market crash. Oates's novel prompts comparisons with Vladimir Nabokov's brilliant panorama of America in *Lolita.*

ANNA QUINDLEN (b. 1953): *Black and Blue.* Quindlen's novel is about the torments of a battered wife. *Time* mag-

Jane Smiley

azine suggests that it might be to domestic violence "what *Uncle Tom's Cabin* was to slavery — a morally crystallizing act of propaganda that works because it has the ring of truth." Quindlen, a reporter and columnist for the *New York Times,* is the author of *Living Out Loud* (1988), *Object Lessons* (1991), and *One True Thing* (1995).

PHILIP ROTH: *American Pastoral.* Roth's alter ego, Nathan Zuckerman, chronicles the life of his high school sports idol Seymour "Swede" Levov, whose perfect American dream life begins to unravel during the 1960s when his beloved daughter commits an act of political terrorism. The book wins the Pulitzer Prize. Roth also publishes *I Married a Communist,* a novel about Murray Ringold, a radio actor blacklisted during the McCarthy era and a hero to the novel's protagonist, again, writer Nathan Zuckerman. Ringold's wife, disgusted by his fame as a political martyr, publishes a tell-all book exposing her husband's slavish obedience to the Communist Party. Critics find Roth's re-creation of an era and its political controversies powerful, if conservative in its conclusions.

JANE SMILEY: *The All-True Adventures of Lidie Newton.* The novelist invents a female abolitionist active in the Kansas Territory. Critics admire the character's eloquence, the period setting, and Smiley's ability to meld an adventure story with a keen moral sensibility.

ROBERT STONE: *Damascus Gate*. Stone's novel treats several characters who come to Jerusalem, convinced that they are on a godly mission in the midst of the Middle East conflict. Several critics consider it Stone's best work and are impressed with the intricate thriller plot, dazzling imagery, and supple language.

ANNE TYLER: *A Patchwork Planet*. Tyler offers one of her richest galleries of characters in thirty-year-old Barnaby Gaitlin's account of his misspent youth and his regeneration by getting involved in the lives of the elderly and infirm.

JOHN UPDIKE: *Bech at Bay: A Quasi-Novel*. Updike's third book on his writer protagonist, who is now in his seventies, is, like others in the series, a linked set of stories—this time featuring the played-out writer on a gloomy book tour in Prague. One of the best stories, critics note, is Bech's fantasy of taking revenge on his critics. Surprisingly, Bech wins the Nobel Prize—or perhaps not so surprisingly, since Updike might be commenting on the Swedish academy's penchant for awarding the prize to writers who are past their prime.

ALICE WALKER: *By the Light of My Father's Smile*. Walker's novel describes a family's move to the remote sierras of Mexico amid a band of mixed-race blacks and Indians. Walker describes her book as "a celebration of sexuality, its absolute usefulness in the accessing of one's mature spirituality, and the father's role in assuring joy or sorrow in this arena for his female children."

DONALD E. WESTLAKE (b. 1933): *The Ax*. Westlake's novel, about a downsized middle manager whose quest to find a job turns him into a serial murderer, is "pretty much flawless, with a surprise ending that will unplug your expectations," declares reviewer D. Keith Mano. Mano also compares the novel's protagonist with notable predecessors such as George Babbitt and Holden Caulfield. The New York City native and prolific writer has been described as "the Neil Simon of the crime novel."

JOHN EDGAR WIDEMAN: *Two Cities*. The title refers to Pittsburgh and Philadelphia, both fraught with street violence. The characters are worn down by their losses, but at the center is the triumphant figure of Mallory, a black photographer who has recorded his people's suffering over many generations and who shows through his art a way to come to terms with a tragic world.

TOM WOLFE: *A Man in Full*. Set in Atlanta, Georgia, Wolfe's sprawling, ambitious second novel centers on Charlie Croker, famous ex–football hero and now a real estate tycoon. Like *The Bonfire of the Vanities*, this novel is as much a study of a city and an era as it is a portrayal of its characters.

Literary Criticism and Scholarship

HAROLD BLOOM: *Shakespeare: The Invention of the Human*. Reviewer Frank McConnell describes Bloom's study of Shakespeare's works "the book of a lifetime, the culmination of a career." In it Bloom argues that our sense of human psychology and consciousness originated with Shakespeare's unsurpassed explorations of the human character.

ROBERT PINSKY: *The Sounds of Poetry*. Pinsky considers sound as the building block of English-language verse. This practical book is addressed to poets and those interested in how sound is manipulated in different verse forms. Pinsky's style is informal and free of jargon, and he draws examples from canonical poems by William Wordsworth, Elizabeth Bishop, Robert Browning, Robert Frost, and others.

Nonfiction

MITCH ALBOM (b. 1958): *Tuesdays with Morrie*. Sportswriter Albom produces the top-selling nonfiction book of the year with this inspirational account of weekly encounters with his former Brandeis professor, who is dying of Lou Gehrig's disease. Albom shares the insights into life and death he gained from him.

JULIA ALVAREZ: *Something to Declare*. The poet and novelist writes essays about her move from the Dominican Republic to the United States and her emergence as a writer. She discusses her plight as a political refugee (her family opposed the dictator Rafael Trujillo), her painful adjustment to an American life marred by racism, and her awareness that she can never return to her roots.

EDWARD BALL (b. 1959): *Slaves in the Family*. Ball, a member of a socially prominent and well-established South Carolina family, wins the Pulitzer Prize for his genealogical investigation of his family's treatment of their slaves.

A. SCOTT BERG (b. 1949): *Lindbergh*. Berg wins the Pulitzer Prize for this biography of the aviator, based on unprecedented unrestricted access to Charles Lindbergh's papers and extensive interviews with family members and associates. Berg rebuts charges that Lindbergh was a Nazi or a traitor but does criticize his anti-Semitism. Reviewer Benjamin Schwartz calls it "one of the most important biographies of the decade." The Connecticut-born writer won the National Book Award for his biography *Max Perkins: Editor of Genius* (1978).

IRA BERLIN (b. 1941): *Many Thousands Gone: The First Two Centuries of Slavery in North America*. The University of Maryland history professor's Bancroft Prize–winning study is praised by critic Kenneth Maxwell for restoring the "historical depth and a human face to a field usually mired in . . . narrow qualifications."

TOM BROKAW (b. 1940): *The Greatest Generation.* News anchorman Brokaw achieves a popular success with this homage to the generation who came of age in the Great Depression, fought in World War II, and helped create modern America. The work is based on letters and interviews with the famous, such as Julia Child and George Bush, and ordinary individuals forced to respond to extraordinary times.

RON CHERNOW: *Titan: The Life of John D. Rockefeller.* Chernow supplies the first comprehensive biography of Rockefeller since Allan Nevins's *Study in Power* (1953) and the first to draw on the extensive materials now available to scholars at the Rockefeller Archive Center. The book, like Chernow's previous work, is admired for its synthesis, narrative force, and ability to set a life story in the wider context of American business practices and development.

JILL KER CONWAY: *When Memory Speaks: Reflections on Autobiography.* This thoughtful historical study by a distinguished autobiographer explores the cultural assumptions of autobiographers and the difference between the way men and women handle the genre. It concludes with an examination of issues such as homosexuality, gender, and sexual abuse, which dominate contemporary life narratives.

STANLEY CROUCH: *Always in Pursuit: Fresh American Perspectives, 1995–1997.* Crouch continues to argue for his integrationist view of American life and to oppose any definition of African American culture that segregates it from the mainstream. Always an independent voice, Crouch provides fresh perspectives on topics such as the O. J. Simpson trial and slavery in contemporary Africa as well as an inspired comparison between the film director John Ford and jazz greats Louis Armstrong and Duke Ellington.

ANDRE DUBUS: *Meditations from a Movable Chair.* The highly praised writer of short stories crafts a series of essays resembling the moral denouements of his fiction. Permanently confined to a wheelchair after a traffic accident, Dubus meditates not merely on his own plight but on the nature of evil and accident.

DAVID HALBERSTAM: *The Children.* Halberstam's study of the early days of the civil rights movement wins the Robert Kennedy Award. It is centered on the contribution of young activists such as Georgia representative John Lewis, former Washington, D.C., mayor Marion Barry, and particularly the Methodist minister James Lawson,

who learned nonviolent strategies directly from Gandhi while a missionary in India.

JILL LEPORE (b. 1966): *The Name of War: King Philip's War and the Origins of American Identity.* Lepore, a professor of American studies at Boston University, wins the Bancroft Prize for this chronicle of the conflict that has been called America's "first Civil War."

NORMAN MAILER: *The Time of Our Time.* To celebrate the fiftieth anniversary of the publication of *The Naked and the Dead,* Mailer delivers a massive retrospective of samples from his writing career, grouped by the historical eras they describe. Reviewer James Shapiro calls the book "a remarkable portrait of an artist and of the indelible mark he has left on American life and letters."

MALACHY MCCOURT (b. 1932): *A Monk Swimming.* The brother of celebrated autobiographer Frank McCourt details his life in America as an actor and bartender. Critics find some of his tales preposterous but agree that his accounts of Peter O'Toole, Richard Burton, Jack Paar, Robert Mitchum, and other celebrities are provocative. If less serious and profound than his brother's work, this memoir nevertheless earns high praise for its style and evocative portraits of Irish immigrant life.

JOHN MCPHEE: *Annals of the Former World.* McPhee collects his four previous volumes, describing his journeys across America with professional geologists — *Basin and Range* (1981), *In Suspect Terrain* (1983), *Rising from the Plains* (1986), and *Assembling California* (1993). He adds a fifth, *Crossing the Craton,* to create what one reviewer calls "the epic on the Earth's formation."

PHILIP D. MORGAN (b. 1949): *Slave Counterpoint: Black Culture in the Eighteenth-Century Chesapeake and Lowcountry.* Critic T. H. Breen describes Morgan's Bancroft Prize–winning study as "a massive reconstruction of life in the eighteenth-century American South." Morgan is a professor of history at the College of William and Mary.

GRACE PALEY: *Just As I Thought.* Poet and short story writer Paley collects pieces from the 1950s to the 1990s, which reflect her intense participation in cultural and political affairs. This impressive record of her times provides a consideration of race, war, and a multicultural society.

DAVID REMNICK: *King of the World: Muhammad Ali and the Rise of an American Hero.* Remnick's biographical profile and survey of the early career of the heavyweight champion receives high praise for its fresh approach, which places Ali's career in a wider cultural context. Writer David Halberstam praises Remnick as "one of the signature figures in a wonderful new generation of nonfiction writers."

Poetry

JOHN ASHBERY: *Wakefulness.* Ashbery is at his most brilliantly playful in this collection. Poems such as "Daffy Duck in Hollywood," "La Celestina," and "Of Rumford's Baking Powder" reflect a desire to write poetry that is both silly and sublime. Although his verse is highly structured, critics admire Ashbery's subversion of expectations for unity and closure in a poem.

FRANK BIDART: *Desire.* Bidart's poetry, which has been compared to Ezra Pound's for its use of other languages, translations, and allusions to world literature, includes a version of Tacitus's *Annals,* a poem out of a short story by Jorge Luis Borges, and "The Second Hour of the Night," a poetic version of Hector Berlioz's autobiography.

HAYDEN CARRUTH: *Reluctantly.* Carruth calls this collection a series of fragments torn from his life. Included is "Suicide," about Carruth's nearly successful attempt to end his life. Throughout he writes with an intensity and a mastery of painful detail that have been compared with the work of Albert Camus.

RAYMOND CARVER: *All of Us: The Collected Poems.* Best known for his short fiction, Carver had begun writing as a poet and continued writing verse throughout his career. His poetry, collected here, is described by his widow, the poet Tess Gallagher, as "the spiritual current out of which he moved to write the short stories."

BILLY COLLINS: *Picnic, Lightning.* Collins's wry, amusing observations drawn from various aspects of contemporary life prompt reviewer John Taylor to observe, "Rarely has anyone written poems that appear so transparent on the surface yet become so ambitious, thought-provoking, or simply wise once the reader has peered into the depths."

DONALD HALL: *Without.* Largely autobiographical, Hall's admired collection deals with harrowing subjects — including his wife's dying of cancer ("Her Long Illness"), which makes innovative use of the technical terminology used in treating disease and of the letter form to express his feelings to his dead wife.

KENNETH KOCH: *Straits.* Koch's fifteenth collection deals with themes of aging, change, and the "loss of the sacred in everyday life." Its strong autobiographical elements would recur in his final collection, *New Addresses* (2000), issued two years before his death.

CLARENCE MAJOR (b. 1936): *Configurations: New and Selected Poems 1958–1998.* Strongly influenced by Ezra Pound's method of melding historical and literary allusions, Major adapts this technique to African American concerns in poems such as "The Slave Trade: View from the Middle Passage." But Major takes on other traditional subjects as well — such as the biblical story of Solomon and the two mothers in "The Dispute." Born in Georgia, Major is the author of the essay collection *The Darkened Feeling: Black American Writers and Their Work* (1974) and the novel *My Amputations* (1986).

GERALD STERN: *This Time: New and Selected Poems.* Having published his first collection, *Rejoicings,* in 1973 when he was forty-eight, Stern, twenty-five years later, wins accolades and the National Book Award for this retrospective collection. A poet whose works are often compared with Walt Whitman's, Stern is praised by poet C. K. Williams as "one of those rare poetic souls who make it almost impossible to remember what our world was like before his poetry came to exalt it."

MARK STRAND: *Blizzard of One.* Strand's collection of distinctive spare, metaphysical verse is awarded the Pulitzer Prize. As reviewer Deborah Garrison observes, "There are a handful of contemporary poets whom we can consider only by gazing upward. . . . Mark Strand is undeniably one of these luminaries."

1999

Drama and Theater

A. R. GURNEY: *Ancestral Voices.* Returning to the concept of a play to be read rather than fully staged, which he had employed in *Love Letters* (1988), Gurney's autobiographical drama considers the decline of his grandparents and his native Buffalo, New York.

TERRENCE McNALLY: *Corpus Christi.* This controversial play, a retelling of the Christ story from a gay perspective and featuring a gay Jesus, is attacked as anti-Christian. Critics, however, find no mockery in the drama and instead are impressed with the way the playwright integrates his characters' moral and sexual natures.

ALFRED UHRY: *Parade.* Despite its downbeat subject matter for a musical, Uhry wins a Tony Award for best book, based on the true story of the trial of Leo Frank, a Jewish factory manager in Atlanta, charged with the rape and murder of a thirteen-year-old employee in 1913.

PAULA VOGEL: *And Baby Makes Seven.* Vogel takes gay and lesbian literature to a new level of comedy and melancholy in this play about a lesbian couple and a gay male who parent one actual child and indulge in the fantasy of raising three more. The real and fantasy children are emblematic of the characters' reactions to reality and their desire to dream of a world less prejudiced and more open to possibility than the one they inhabit.

Fiction

LOUIS AUCHINCLOSS: *The Anniversary and Other Stories.* Auchincloss continues his well-established and highly praised series of portraits of upper-class easterners. His characters include the head of a mammoth media corporation, a rich American married to a European aristocrat, and the hypocritical headmaster of a boarding school. Critics are especially impressed with his handling of period details from the Civil War through the late 1970s.

TONI CADE BAMBARA: *Those Bones Are Not My Child.* This posthumously published novel by one of the masters of the American short story is edited by Toni Morrison, who had lost and then found the author's manuscript. It is an ambitious work of fiction based on the child murders in Atlanta in the 1970s. Critics observe that the novel explores a cycle of fear, accusation, and acrimony with considerable sensitivity in an epic of contemporary culture.

MELISSA BANK (b. 1960): *The Girls' Guide to Hunting and Fishing.* This series of stories relates the escapades of Jane Rosenal, an independent young editor who takes readers on a tour of her lovers — young, old, and in between. Critics praise the high comedy of the novel and Bank's creation of a distinctive narrator who is interested in the variations of romantic love, not marriage.

THOMAS BERGER: *The Return of Little Big Man.* In a sequel to Berger's classic revisionist western, *Little Big Man* (1964), the 111-year-old Jack Crabb continues his memoirs with offbeat profiles of western legends such as Wyatt Earp, Doc Holliday, Annie Oakley, and Buffalo Bill, and the "real story" behind the shoot-out at the O.K. Corral.

BLISS BROYARD (b. 1966): *My Father, Dancing.* This first collection of stories by the young author explores relationships between fathers and daughters. Broyard's eight stories, some of them already anthologized, are clearly autobiographical, such as the title piece, about a daughter reflecting on life with her father (critic Anatole Broyard), who is dying of prostate cancer. "Mr. Sweetly Indecent" explores a daughter's awareness of her father's adultery. Other stories also explore sexuality and the way it impinges on father-daughter relationships.

PHILIP CAPUTO: *The Voyage.* Caputo's richly imagined novel connects a perilous voyage undertaken by three teenage boys in 1901, from Maine to the Florida Keys, with a family secret that explains the reason for the journey.

BRET EASTON ELLIS: *Glamorama.* Praised and sometimes attacked for his flashy style, Ellis finds the world of high fashion a fit for his mordant, comic sensibility. Critics praise his cast of characters, including a nightclub organizer, a supermodel, a supermodel-terrorist, a spy, and a rich playboy. Ellis once again explores trendy New York and exposes the materialism of a new generation of the rich ensconced in the fashion industry.

RALPH ELLISON: *Juneteenth.* Ellison's long-awaited second novel becomes a controversial literary event. Ellison had published parts of the novel over the years, and the mystique about its scope and subject matter grew, especially after it became known that a fire had destroyed the principal draft and Ellison had to begin anew, almost from scratch. The novel features Hickman, a black minister, who brings up a boy who looks white. Later the boy runs away and becomes a racist U.S. senator. The events that prompt this denouement are gradually revealed in the conversation between the minister and the senator.

JANET FITCH (b. 1955): *White Oleander.* Fitch's first novel is about a strong-willed poet mother who murders her boyfriend, and her daughter's struggle to sort out her past and forge an identity while living in a string of dysfunctional foster homes. The work earns both critical acclaim and popular success.

DAVID GATES (b. 1947): *The Wonders of the Invisible World: Stories.* Gates's stories concentrate on characters in and around New York City, struggling with aging and debilitating illnesses. Gates has been well received as the chronicler of the baby-boom generation now facing or just getting past midlife crises.

DAVID GUTERSON: *East of the Mountains.* This novel concerns a seventy-three-year-old heart surgeon afflicted with terminal colon cancer. Although he intends to commit suicide, his plans are delayed by a series of adventures with a remarkable cast of characters. Although the novel broods on death, critics find it a bracing affirmation of life.

KENT HARUF: *Plainsong.* Haruf's novel animates multiple stories of inhabitants of a Colorado community, including a pregnant high school student, a lonely teacher, brothers abandoned by their mother, and a pair of bachelor farmers. It is praised by reviewer Jon Hassler as "A work as flawlessly unified as a short story by Poe or Chekhov."

OSCAR HIJUELOS: *Empress of the Splendid Season.* Hijuelos's fifth novel treats the life of Lydia España who is forced by her family to leave Cuba for New York City, where the former "queen of the conga line" finds herself a cleaning lady. She meets life's challenges with dignity and fortitude.

GISH JEN: *Who's Irish?* Jen's first story collection offers a series of compressed, comic depictions of Asian American life, treating immigrants and their children.

HA JIN: *Waiting.* After publishing a first novel, *In the Pond* (1998), about a Chinese artist, Ha Jin wins the National Book Award and the PEN/Faulkner Award for his comic portrait of Chinese life under Communism. Based on the regime's law that a couple without mutual consent must be separated for eighteen years before they can be divorced, the novel examines a Chinese army doctor trapped in an arranged marriage who decides to wait out the time before marrying and consummating his relationship with the woman he loves.

GAYL JONES: *Mosquito.* Jones's novel about a female truck driver's involvement with illegal Mexican immigrants is an exercise in mining the rich poetry of the black vernacular, resembling, in her narrator's words, "a true jazz story, where the peoples that listen can just enter the story and start telling it theyselves while they's reading."

THOM JONES: *Sonny Liston Was a Friend of Mine: Stories.* This third collection ranges from Vietnam to Illinois and Michigan and includes characters such as Kid Dynamite, a young boxer; Anson, a hunchback obsessed with mice; and his lover Molly Bloom, who has been recently released from a mental institution. Jones shifts from the grim to the comic to the eccentric with aplomb, providing a broad canvas of contemporary American culture.

JHUMPA LAHIRI (b. 1967): *Interpreter of Maladies.* Lahiri wins the Pulitzer Prize for her debut story collection, which deals with the experiences of Indian immigrants in the United States. Included is "A Temporary Matter," chosen for inclusion in both *The O. Henry Prize Stories* and *The Best American Short Stories* for 1999.

CHANG-RAE LEE: *A Gesture of Life.* Lee's second novel is set in Japan, Burma, and a fictional small town outside New York City, where a Korean American vividly recalls the atrocities he witnessed in the Far East and deals with his domestically troubled life in America.

JONATHAN LETHEM: *Motherless Brooklyn.* Lethem offers a postmodern detective novel, with a detective who suffers from Tourette's syndrome. Critics treat the novel as a mainstream literary work, not a formula story, precisely because Lethem handles the genre with self-conscious verbal virtuosity.

PETER MATTHIESSEN: *Bone by Bone.* The third volume of the novelist's trilogy, set in the Florida Everglades and concerning the criminal E. J. Watson, a historical figure who is the subject of much speculation and mythmaking in the earlier two novels. Here Matthiessen has Watson himself narrate his story, using his own words to strip his story of legend and reveal a man warped by his drunken, cowardly father and trying to find the meaning of life even as he commits murder and is himself murdered in the Everglades in 1910.

LARRY McMURTRY: *Duane's Depressed.* This novel completes the trilogy begun with *The Last Picture Show*

(1966) and continued in *Texasville* (1989). Once again the protagonist is Duane, the considerably older mayor of Thalia, Texas, who startles his constituents by abandoning his pickup truck and walking everywhere. This signals his shake-up of community conventions, which he also challenges by consulting a young woman psychiatrist. Duane's story, critics note, shows McMurtry's fine grasp of a changing contemporary Western culture.

JOYCE CAROL OATES: *Broke Heart Blues.* This novel, in the form of a religious allegory, is about a Christ figure who appears in a small upstate New York town. The effect of the allegory, critics suggest, is to emphasize the bleakness of American culture and the need to redeem it.

DAVID PLANTE: *The Age of Terror.* The novel is about Joe, a twenty-three-year-old who becomes obsessed with a photo of a Russian partisan hanged by Nazi troops. Set in the Soviet Union, the novel explores Joe's journey through contemporary Russia, with flashbacks to its past and scenes that hold the promise of a better world. Critics view the novel as one of Plante's most ambitious, both in its vivid setting and its probing of Russian history.

E. ANNIE PROULX: *Close Range: Wyoming Stories.* This collection depicts an extraordinary range of characters — a young Brahma bull rider, a gay rodeo rider, and a variety of cowpunchers, ranchers, and cattle dealers. Proulx describes Wyoming and its history in lyrical but sometimes gruesome terms. Critics admire her precise, seemingly effortless prose and her accurate ear for regional dialects. This collection includes "Brokeback Mountain," winner of an O. Henry Award.

LESLIE MARMON SILKO: *Gardens in the Dunes.* Set during the American financial panic of 1893, the novel is about two sisters who belong to a fictional tribe wiped out in the early twentieth century. The girls escape the massacre, are befriended by whites, and are educated at prestigious white institutions. Critics admire Silko's ability to integrate a powerful nostalgia for the Native American past with a recognition that Native Americans must adapt while never forsaking their bond with the land and their heritage.

DAVID FOSTER WALLACE: *Brief Interviews with Hideous Men.* This story collection is highly praised for its unified, novel-like structure. Wallace invents interviews with men who vent their feelings about women in a style that veers from the Proustian to the crude. Although Wallace's work offends certain readers, critics agree that his range of styles puts him in the same league as Thomas Pynchon and Donald Barthelme.

COLSON WHITEHEAD (b. 1969): *The Intuitionist.* Although not clearly specified, the city in this novel is New York in the 1950s. It features Lila Mae Watson, the first black woman to become an elevator inspector; James Fulton, the founder of Intuitionism; Ben Urich, an investigative journalist; and other characters in an exploration of racism, urban decay, and epistemology. Critics admire Whitehead's creation of a fantastic yet fully realized world as a way of probing the limitations of the materialist view of reality. The New York City writer worked for several years as the television critic for the *Village Voice.*

HELEN YGLESIAS: *The Girls.* The novel depicts four aging Jewish American sisters in contemporary Miami Beach who are contending with their declining health and loss of independence. The book is praised by writer Ursula K. Le Guin as "the truest report from the real war zone I have ever read."

Literary Criticism and Scholarship

ELLEN HANDLER SPITZ (b. 1939): *Inside Picture Books.* In a groundbreaking examination of the text and images of classic children's picture books of the twentieth century, Spitz, a psychiatrist and faculty member at Columbia, takes a psychological approach. Her study says much about the culture in which children read and begin to appreciate books and how their notions of race, morality, gender, and class are formed through reading and viewing.

JAMES WOOD (b. 1965): *The Broken Estate: Essays on Literature and Belief.* Considered one of the most erudite and provocative of contemporary literary critics, Wood collects essays examining figures such as Gustave Flaubert, Herman Melville, Philip Roth, John Updike, and Don De Lillo. He adds to conventional literary criticism an eloquent account of his own upbringing as an evangelical Christian, merging his own history with his responses to what fiction has to say about religious faith.

Nonfiction

EDWIN G. BURROWS (b. 1943) AND MIKE WALLACE (b. 1942): *Gotham: A History of New York City to 1898.* The authors draw high praise and win the Pulitzer Prize for this social history of New York City from the ice age to 1898, when the five boroughs were incorporated.

ANNIE DILLARD: *For the Time Being.* Dillard meditates on the nature of religion and science and how they impinge on the individual. Dillard reports facts about nature (with especially apt descriptions of insects) while suffusing her first-person narrative with vivid metaphors and images.

JOHN W. DOWER: *Embracing Defeat: Japan in the Wake of World War II.* Dower wins the National Book Award, the Bancroft Prize, and the Pulitzer Prize for his magisterial chronicle of the rebuilding and transformation of Japanese society during the six years of American occupation following the end of World War II.

WILLIAM LEAST HEAT-MOON: *River-Horse: A Voyage Across America.* This book gives an account of the writer's five-thousand-mile transcontinental journey along America's rivers, lakes, and canals in a small outboard-powered boat.

JOHN IRVING: *My Movie Business: A Memoir.* The writer critiques the differences between novels and screenplays, between writing and filmmaking, in this account of bringing *The Cider House Rules* (1985) to the screen.

DAVID M. KENNEDY: *Freedom from Fear: The American People in Depression and War, 1929–1945.* Kennedy's Pulitzer Prize–winning social history is praised by reviewer Barry Gewen as the "best one-volume account of the Roosevelt era available."

WENDY LESSER: *The Amateur: An Independent Life of Letters.* In this series of autobiographical pieces, Lesser writes about the formation of her artistic sensibility. Her clarity of thought and desire to relate literature to life have been compared with George Orwell's work.

FRANK MCCOURT: *'Tis: A Memoir.* The sequel to McCourt's acclaimed autobiography, *Angela's Ashes,* this book takes up the story in 1949, when McCourt arrives in New York from Ireland. The awkward nineteen-year-old has trouble adjusting and spends much time in the library, reading. The author describes his struggle to get an education, his teaching, and his painful memories of his father — all told in a lyrical style, with Irish cadences that critics find mesmerizing.

JAMES H. MERRELL (b. 1953): *Into the American Woods.* Merrell, a professor of history at Vassar College and one of the foremost authorities on the interactions between Europeans and Native Americans in early America, wins the Bancroft Prize for this account of the role played by negotiators on the Pennsylvania frontier in mediating conflicts between settlers and Native Americans.

EDMUND MORRIS: *Dutch: A Memoir of Ronald Reagan.* Although many critics attack this biography, its experimental nature makes it a publishing phenomenon. Morris challenges the conventions of biography, not only inserting himself as a character but also changing his age and inventing facts about himself — all to the purpose of writing a more insightful, vivid biography of a president who, Morris believes, eludes more conventional treatment.

EDWARD W. SAID: *Out of Place: A Memoir.* The brilliant and controversial literary critic and political commentator explores his first twenty-seven years, beginning with his birth in Jerusalem to middle-class Palestinian-Lebanese Christian parents, through his childhood during the political upheavals in the Middle East, to 1962, when he is near to completing his doctorate at Harvard. Critics take issue with many of Said's views and for fictionalizing his own life but also praise his Proust-like memories of childhood, youth, and early manhood.

JEAN STROUSE: *Morgan: American Financier.* Considered one of the finest contemporary biographers, Strouse supplies a definitive portrait of this towering figure of finance in the Gilded Age, drawing on new material made available in the Morgan archive during the 1990s. Her work's sense of balance and nuanced use of detail are much admired by critics.

Poetry

AI (b. 1947): *Vice: New and Selected Poems.* Born Florence Anthony in Texas, the feminist poet wins the National Book Award for her sixth collection.

JOHN ASHBERY: *Girls on the Run.* Ashbery's collection is inspired by the art of Henry Darger, a mentally ill recluse whose fantastic sketches and paintings of little girls were discovered after his death. According to reviewer Donna Seamon, Ashbery "has captured the peculiar energy of Darger's disturbing creation" in "a virtuoso interpretive performance."

RITA DOVE: *On the Bus with Rosa Parks.* Dove's seventh collection contains the sequence "Cameos," a narrative portrait of a working-class family. The title work celebrates Rosa Parks's heroism in the Jim Crow South, in which "Doing nothing was the doing."

DAVID FERRY (b. 1924): *Of No Country I Know: New and Selected Poems and Translations.* The acclaimed translator of *Gilagamesh* (1992), the *Odes of Horace* (1997), and *Virgil's Eclogues* (1999) wins the Rebekah Johnson Bobbitt National Prize for Poetry for this collection of his own works and translations.

NIKKI GIOVANNI: *Blues: For All the Changes.* The poet uses the blues idiom to attack racism in American life and celebrate food, friends, lovers, and family.

JOHN HOLLANDER: *Figurehead & Other Poems.* Hollander animates a number of speakers in this collection, including Sappho, Arachne, Minerva, and Robert Browning's duchess in "My Last Duchess," who reveals that she was not murdered at all but is living peacefully in a convent.

DENISE LEVERTOV: *The Great Unknowing: Last Poems.* Levertov's final collection, completed while she battled with terminal lymphoma, ranges, in the words of one reviewer, from "the specifically personal to the searchingly mystical."

PHILIP LEVINE: *The Mercy.* Levine's collection combines a nostalgia for his blue-collar Detroit past with sharpness of imagery and polish of diction that critics call luminous. Levine's immigrant mother had come to the United States in steerage aboard *The Mercy*, and Levine's work honors his origins.

N. SCOTT MOMADAY: *In the Bear's House.* This mixed-media collection combines paintings, a dialogue, poems, and prose pieces on the subject of the bear, an animal of cosmic significance to the Kiowas. The author also publishes *Circle of Wonder: A Native American Christmas Story*, a recollection of his reservation childhood.

SHARON OLDS: *Blood, Tin, Straw.* Olds's sixth collection returns to her familiar themes: sexual experience, motherhood, and her estrangement from her father. "The Promise," "The Gift," and "Animal Music" express the range of her intensely physical but also spiritual quest for the stimulation of the senses and the resolution of her internal conflicts.

ADRIENNE RICH: *Midnight Salvage: Poems, 1995–1998.* Rich's collection explores the conflict between beauty and brutal contemporary reality and the challenge of using language to evoke both. The poems are commended by Richard Howard, who declares, "I know of no poetry by an American so charged with passion and solicitude for human life as it yields itself to her attention, her judgment."

C. K. WILLIAMS: *Repair.* Williams wins the Pulitzer Prize for this collection, which continues his observations of the natural world and meditations on love, death, violence, and intimacy. He employs his trademark discursive, long-line style, which sometimes straddles the boundary between poetry and prose.

Publications and Events

The Best American Short Stories of the Century. Editor John Updike selects the fifty-five best stories that have appeared in *The Best American Short Story* annual publication since 1915. His selections amply demonstrate that the short story is a quintessential American literary genre.

INDEX OF AUTHORS

INDEX OF TITLES

PHOTOGRAPH CREDITS